C
HOW TO PROGRAM
FIFTH EDITION

Deitel® Ser

How to Program Series

Advanced Java™ 2 Platform How to Program

C How to Program, 5/E

C++ How to Program, 5/E – Including Cyber Classroom

e-Business and e-Commerce How to Program

Internet and World Wide Web How to Program, 3/E

Java™ How to Program, 6/E – Including Cyber Classroom

Small C++ How to Program, 5/E – Including Cyber Classroom

Small Java™ How to Program, 6/E – Including Cyber Classroom

Perl How to Program

Python How to Program

Visual Basic® 2005 How to Program, 3/E

Visual C++® .NET How to Program

Visual C#® 2005 How to Program, 2/E

XML How to Program

ies Page

Simply Series

Simply C++: An Application-Driven
   Tutorial Approach

Simply C#: An Application-Driven
   Tutorial Approach

Simply Java™ Programming: An
   Application-Driven Tutorial
   Approach

Simply Visual Basic® .NET: An
   Application-Driven Tutorial
   Approach (Visual Studio .NET
   2003 Edition)

Simply Visual Basic® 2005, 2/E: An
   Application-Driven Tutorial
   Approach

Also Available

SafariX Web Books
   www.SafariX.com

To follow the Deitel publishing program, please register for the free *DEITEL® BUZZ ONLINE* e-mail newsletter at:

   www.deitel.com/newsletter/subscribe.html

To communicate with the authors, send e-mail to:

   deitel@deitel.com

For information on corporate on-site seminars offered by Deitel & Associates, Inc. worldwide, visit:

   www.deitel.com

or write to

   deitel@deitel.com

For continuing updates on Prentice Hall/Deitel publications visit:

   www.deitel.com,
   www.prenhall.com/deitel or
   www.InformIT.com/deitel

Library of Congress Cataloging-in-Publication Data
On file

Vice President and Editorial Director, ECS: *Marcia J. Horton*
Associate Editor: *Jennifer Cappello*
Assistant Editor: *Carole Snyder*
Executive Managing Editor: *Vince O'Brien*
Managing Editor: *Bob Engelhardt*
Production Editors: *Donna M. Crilly, Marta Samsel*
Director of Creative Services: *Paul Belfanti*
A/V Production Editor: *Xiaohong Zhu*
Art Studio: *Artworks, York, PA*
Creative Director: *Juan López*
Art Director: *Kristine Carney*
Cover Design: *Abbey S. Deitel, Harvey M. Deitel, Francesco Santalucia, Kristine Carney*
Interior Design: *Harvey M. Deitel, Kristine Carney*
Manufacturing Manager: *Alexis Heydt-Long*
Manufacturing Buyer: *Lisa McDowell*
Executive Marketing Manager: *Robin O'Brien*

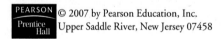 © 2007 by Pearson Education, Inc.
Upper Saddle River, New Jersey 07458

Printed in the United States of America

10 9 8 7 6 5 4 3 2 1

ISBN 0-13-240416-8

Pearson Education Ltd., *London*
Pearson Education Australia Pty. Ltd., *Sydney*
Pearson Education Singapore, Pte. Ltd.
Pearson Education North Asia Ltd., *Hong Kong*
Pearson Education Canada, Inc., *Toronto*
Pearson Educación de Mexico, S.A. de C.V.
Pearson Education–Japan, *Tokyo*
Pearson Education Malaysia, Pte. Ltd.
Pearson Education, Inc., *Upper Saddle River, New Jersey*

C

HOW TO PROGRAM

FIFTH EDITION

P. J. Deitel

Deitel & Associates, Inc.

H. M. Deitel

Deitel & Associates, Inc.

Upper Saddle River, New Jersey 07458

Trademarks

To Marcia Horton,

Thank you for being our mentor in publishing
and a special friend to us and to our families.

Paul and Harvey Deitel

Contents

10 C Structures, Unions, Bit Manipulations and Enumerations — **401**

11 C File Processing — **438**

12 C Data Structures — **477**

13 C Preprocessor — **533**

20 Classes: A Deeper Look, Part 1   744

21 Classes: A Deeper Look, Part 2   779

22 Operator Overloading   827

23 Object-Oriented Programming: Inheritance   868

24 Object-Oriented Programming: Polymorphism   921

25 Templates   976

26 Stream Input/Output   996

27 Exception Handling   1038

A Internet and Web Resources   1070

Preface

Welcome to ANSI/ISO Standard C, and to C++, too! This book presents leading-edge computing technologies for computer science students, software developers and IT professionals. At Deitel & Associates, we write computer science textbooks for college students and professional books for software developers. We also teach this material in industry seminars at organizations worldwide.

This book was a joy to create. To start, we put the previous edition under the microscope:

- The entire C portion of the previous edition was reviewed by a distinguished review team including the head and assistant head of the working group responsible for the C standard (ISO/IEC JTC1 SC22 WG14) and other experts from industry and academia. All of this material was carefully tuned.

- All of the chapters have been significantly updated and upgraded.

- We updated the history of computing in Chapter 1.

- We added a new chapter on game programming with the Allegro C library.

- We added a new chapter that takes a deeper look at sorting.

- We added a new chapter introducing the C99 standard. This was placed last among the C chapters to make it convenient to include or omit.

- We included a completely new section on object-oriented programming in C++ based on *C++ How to Program, 5/e*.

- We added an appendix on solving and programming the wildly popular game of Sudoku.

All of this has been carefully scrutinized by a substantial team of academics, industry developers and members of the working group responsible for the C standard.

We believe that this book and its support materials have everything instructors, students and professionals need for an informative, interesting, challenging and entertaining C educational experience. In this Preface, we overview various conventions used in the book, such as syntax coloring the code examples and code highlighting. We also discuss the book's comprehensive suite of ancillary materials that help instructors maximize their students' learning experience, including the Prentice Hall *Instructor's Resource Center* (which contains the Instructor's Manual, Test Item File and PowerPoint® Slide lecture notes), companion Web site, SafariX (Pearson Education's WebBook publications) and more.

C How to Program, 5/e presents hundreds of complete, working C and C++ programs and depicts their inputs and outputs. This is our signature "live-code" approach—we present concepts in the context of complete working programs.

As you read this book, if you have questions, send an e-mail to deitel@deitel.com; we will respond promptly. For updates on this book and the status of C and C++ software, and for the latest news on all Deitel publications and services, visit www.deitel.com regularly and be sure to sign up for the free *Deitel® Buzz Online* e-mail newsletter at www.deitel.com/newsletter/subscribe.html. Also be sure to visit our new C Resource Center at www.deitel.com/c/.

Before You Begin

Installing the Microsoft Visual C++ 2005 Express Edition Software
On November 7, 2005 Microsoft released its Visual Studio 2005 development tools, including the Visual C++ 2005 Express Edition. Per Microsoft's Web site, Microsoft Express Editions are "lightweight, easy-to-use and easy-to-learn tools for the hobbyist, novice and student developer." According to the Microsoft Express Editions FAQ page (msdn.microsoft.com/vstudio/express/support/faq/), "Effective April 19th, 2006, all Visual Studio 2005 Express Editions are free permanently. SQL Server 2005 Express Edition has always been and will continue to be a free download."

You may use this software to compile and execute the example C and C++ programs in this book. The Visual C++ 2005 Express Edition Software is available on the CD-ROM included with this book. You can also download Visual C++ 2005 Express Edition at:

> msdn.microsoft.com/vstudio/express/visualc/

When you install this software, you should install the help documentation and SQL Server 2005 Express. Microsoft provides a dedicated forum for help using the Express Edition:

> forums.microsoft.com/msdn/ShowForum.aspx?ForumID=24

C How to Program, 5/e *Code Examples*
The book's source code is available for download at **www.deitel.com/books/chtp5**. Once you download the complete examples.zip file, use a ZIP file tool such as WinZip (available from www.winzip.com) to extract the files to the C:\ folder on your computer. This will create an examples folder that contains subfolders for each chapter (e.g., ch01, ch02, etc.)

Additional Software Downloads
Chapter 15 uses the Allegro C Library. The Allegro library is available for free at

> www.allegro.cc/files

Download the "Source" package for your platform, and an IDE (integrated development environment) that is compatible with it. Allegro can be used with most C IDEs, but in this text, we use Bloodshed Software's Dev-C++, which is available for free at

> www.bloodshed.net/devcpp.html

Chapter 17 uses Bloodshed Software's Dev-C++ 4.9.9.2 IDE, which is available for free at

> www.bloodshed.net/dev/devcpp.html

We provide updates on the status of the software used in this book at www.deitel.com and in our free e-mail newsletter www.deitel.com/newsletter/subscribe.html.

Additional C and C++ Compilers and IDEs
Our C Resource Center (www.deitel.com/C) and our C++ Resource Center (www.deitel.com/cplusplus) list many free compilers and IDEs and some for-sale products for

Windows, Linux and Macintosh platforms. These Resource Centers also include free tutorials to help you get started with these tools.

Features of *C How to Program, Fifth Edition*

This new edition contains many new and enhanced features.

Interior Design

Working with the creative services team at Prentice Hall, we redesigned the interior styles for our *How to Program Series* books. In response to reader requests, we now place the key terms and the index's page reference for each defining occurrence in **bold blue** text for easier reference. We emphasize on-screen components in the **bold Helvetica** font (e.g., the **File** menu) and emphasize Visual Basic program text in the Lucida font (for example, int x = 5).

Syntax Shading

We syntax shade all the C# code, similar to the way most C# integrated-development environments and code editors syntax color code. This greatly improves code readability—an especially important goal, given that this book contains 16,400+ lines of code. Our syntax-shading conventions are as follows:

```
comments appear like this
keywords appear like this
errors and ASP.NET delimiters appear like this
constants and literal values appear like this
all other code appears in black
```

Code Highlighting

Extensive code highlighting makes it easy for readers to spot each program's featured code segments—we place gray rectangles around the key code.

Game Programming with the Allegro C Game Programming Library

Chapter 15 introduces the Allegro game programming C library. This library—originally developed by Climax game programmer Shawn Hargreaves—was created to be a powerful tool for programming games in C while still remaining relatively simple compared to other, more complicated graphics libraries such as DirectX and OpenGL. In Chapter 15, we use Allegro's capabilities to create the simple game of Pong. Along the way, we demonstrate how to display graphics, play sounds, receive input from the keyboard and create timed events—features that students can use to create games of their own. We believe that Allegro is a valuable addition to *C How to Program, 5/e*, and we hope that students and instructors alike will find it interesting and entertaining. We include extensive web resources, one of which offers more than 1000 open-source Allegro games.

Sorting: A Deeper Look

Sorting places data in ascending or descending order based on one or more sort keys. We begin our presentation of sorting with the simple bubble sort algorithm in Chapter 6. In Chapter 16, we present a deeper look at sorting. We consider several algorithms and compare them with regard to their memory consumption and processor consumption. For this purpose, we introduce Big O notation, which indicates how hard an algorithm may have to work to solve a problem. Through examples and exercises, Chapter 16 discusses the selection sort, insertion sort, recursive merge sort, recursive selection sort, bucket sort and recursive Quicksort.

Introduction to C99

C99 is a revised standard for the C programming language that refines and expands the capabilities of C89 (which we refer to as Standard C in Chapters 1–15). C99 has not been widely adopted, and many C compilers do not fully support it. We use the Dev-C++ 4.9.9.2 IDE from Bloodshed Software to demonstrate various C99 features.

Some new features of C99 include: // single-line comments; declaring a variable anywhere in a block before the variable's use (including the initialization clause of a for statement); designated initializers that allow you to initialize array elements explicitly by subscript, and union or struct elements explicitly by name; the _Bool type, which can hold only the values 0 or 1; requiring functions to have an explicit return type (rather than implicitly assuming int); support for complex numbers and complex arithmetic; variable-length arrays whose length, or size, is determined at execution time (but once determined remains fixed); support for longer identifier names (extended identifiers); restricted pointers for exclusive access to a region in memory; reliable integer division; flexible array members in structs; the long long int type; generic math; inline functions; requiring an expression in a return statement of a function with a non-void return type; disallowing an expression in a return statement of a function with return type void; and function snprintf to prevent buffer overflow when printing to strings in memory. Our treatment introduces C99 and provides web resources for the reader who wishes to dig deeper.

Updated C++ Treatment

In *C++ How to Program, 5/e*, we changed to an early classes and objects pedagogy. In *C How to Program, 5/e*, we've completely replaced our C++ treatment with this new approach. We introduce the basic concepts and terminology of object technology in Chapter 18. Then, Chapter 19 uses a new GradeBook case study to introduce classes and objects. We then use those concepts in the subsequent C++ chapters that present object-oriented programming, operator overloading, C++-style input/output streams and templates. Many of the C++ chapters reinforce object-oriented concepts with the Unified Modeling Language (UML)—the preferred graphical modeling language for designers of object-oriented systems. All the UML diagrams in the book comply with the UML 2.0 specification. We use UML class diagrams to visually represent classes and their inheritance relationships.

Teaching Approach

C How to Program, 5/e contains a rich collection of examples. The book concentrates on the principles of good software engineering and stresses program clarity. We avoid arcane terminology and syntax specifications in favor of teaching by example. We are educators who teach leading-edge topics in industry classrooms worldwide. Dr. Harvey M. Deitel has 22 years of college teaching experience and 17 years of industry teaching experience. Paul Deitel has 15 years of industry teaching experience. The Deitels have taught courses at all levels to government, industry, military and academic clients of Deitel & Associates.

Live-Code Approach

C How to Program, 5/e is loaded with live-code examples—each new concept is presented in the context of a complete working C application that is immediately followed by one or more sample executions showing the program's inputs and outputs. This style exemplifies the way we teach and write about programming. We call this method of teaching and writing the "live-code" approach.

World Wide Web Access
All of the source-code examples for *C How to Program, 5/e*, (and for our other publications) are available for download from:

```
www.deitel.com/books/chtp5
www.prenhall.com/deitel
```

Site registration is quick and easy. Download all the examples, then run each program as you read the corresponding discussions. Making changes to the examples and immediately seeing the effects of those changes is a great way to enhance your C learning experience.

Objectives
Each chapter begins with a statement of objectives. This lets students know what to expect and gives them an opportunity, after reading the chapter, to determine if they have met these objectives.

Quotations
The learning objectives are followed by quotations. Some are humorous, philosophical or offer interesting insights. We hope that you will enjoy relating the quotations to the chapter material. Many of the quotations are worth a second look after reading the chapter.

Outline
The chapter outline helps students approach the material in a top-down fashion, so they can anticipate what is to come, and set a comfortable and effective learning pace.

Sections
Each chapter is organized into small sections that address key C or C++ topics.

Thousands of Lines of Syntax-Highlighted Code in Hundreds of Example Programs (with Outputs)
We present C and C++ features in the context of complete, working programs using our live-code approach. Each program is followed by screenshots of the outputs produced when the program is run, so you can confirm that the programs run as expected. Our programs demonstrate the diverse features of C and C++. The code is syntax highlighted, with keywords, comments and other program text emphasized with variations of bold, blue and italic text. This makes reading the code easier, especially in the larger programs.

Illustrations/Figures
An abundance of charts, tables, line drawings, programs and program outputs is included. We model the flow of control in control statements with UML activity diagrams. UML class diagrams model the fields, constructors and methods of classes.

Programming Tips
We include programming tips to help students focus on important aspects of program development. We highlight these tips in the form of *Good Programming Practices, Common*

Programming Errors, Error-Prevention Tips, Performance Tips, Portability Tips and *Software Engineering Observations*. These tips and practices represent the best we have gleaned from a combined six decades of programming and teaching experience. One of our students— a mathematics major—told us that she feels this approach is like the highlighting of axioms, theorems and corollaries in mathematics books; it provides a basis on which to build good software.

Good Programming Practice

Good Programming Practices call attention to techniques that will help you produce programs that are clearer, more understandable and more maintainable.

Common Programming Error

Students learning a language tend to make certain kinds of errors frequently. Pointing out these Common Programming Errors *reduces the likelihood that readers will make the same mistakes.*

Error-Prevention Tip

When we first designed this tip type, we thought the tips would contain suggestions for exposing bugs and removing them from programs. In fact, many of the tips describe aspects of C that prevent bugs from getting into programs in the first place, thus simplifying the testing and debugging processes.

Performance Tip

Students like to "turbo charge" their programs. We include Performance Tips *that highlight opportunities for improving program performance—making programs run faster or minimizing the amount of memory that they occupy.*

Portability Tip

We include Portability Tips *to help you write portable code and to explain how C achieves its high degree of portability.*

Software Engineering Observation

The object-oriented programming paradigm necessitates a complete rethinking of the way we build software systems. C is an effective language for achieving good software engineering. The Software Engineering Observations *highlight architectural and design issues that affect the construction of software systems, especially large-scale systems.*

Summary Bullets

Each chapter ends with additional pedagogical devices. We present a thorough, bullet-list-style summary of the chapter, section by section. This helps the students review and reinforce key concepts.

Terminology

We include an alphabetized list of the important terms defined in each chapter—again, for further reinforcement. Each term also appears in the index, and the defining occurrence of each term is highlighted in the index with a **bold, blue** page number so the student can locate the definitions of terms quickly.

Self-Review Exercises and Answers

Extensive self-review exercises and answers are included for self-study. This gives you a chance to build confidence with the material and prepare for the regular exercises. We encourage students to do all the self-review exercises and check their answers.

Exercises

Each chapter concludes with a substantial set of exercises including simple recall of important terminology and concepts; writing individual program statements; writing small portions of functions and C++ classes; writing complete functions, C++ classes and programs; and writing major term projects. The large number of exercises enables instructors to tailor their courses to the unique needs of their students and to vary course assignments each semester. Instructors can use these exercises to form homework assignments, short quizzes and major examinations. [*NOTE:* **Please do not write to us requesting access to the Prentice Hall** *Instructor's Resource Center.* **Access is limited strictly to college instructors teaching from the book. Instructors may obtain access only through their Prentice Hall representatives.**]

Thousands of Index Entries

We have included an extensive index which is especially useful to developers who use the book as a reference.

"Double Indexing" of C Live-Code Examples

C How to Program, 5/e has hundreds of live-code examples, which we have double indexed. For every source-code program in the book, we indexed the figure caption both alphabetically and as a subindex item under "Examples." This makes it easier to find examples using particular features.

Software Included with C *How to Program, 5/e*

In writing this book, we have used a variety of C compilers. For the most part, the programs in the text will work on all ANSI/ISO C and C++ compilers, including the Visual C++ 2005 Express Edition compiler included with this book.

The C material (Chapters 2–16) follows the ANSI C standard published in 1989. See the reference manuals for your particular system for more details about the language.

In 1999, ISO approved a new version of C, C99, which is not as yet widely used. Chapter 17 provides an introduction to C99. For more information on C99—and to purchase a copy of the C99 standards document (ISO/IEC 9899:1999)—visit the Web site of the American National Standards Institute (ANSI) at www.ansi.org.

The C++ material is based on the C++ programming language as developed by the Accredited Standards Committee INCITS, Information Technology and its Technical Committee J11, Programming Language C++, respectively. The C and C++ languages are approved by the International Standards Organization (ISO).

The serious programmer should read these documents carefully and reference them regularly. These documents are not tutorials. Rather they define their respective languages with the extraordinary level of precision that compiler implementors and "heavy-duty" developers demand.

We have carefully audited our presentation against these documents and other key documentation. Our book is intended to be used at the introductory and intermediate levels. We have not attempted to cover every feature discussed in these comprehensive documents.

DIVE-INTO® Series *Tutorials for Popular C and C++ Environments*

Our *DIVE-INTO® Series* of tutorials (available at www.deitel.com/books/downloads.html) help our readers get started with many popular program-development environments.

Currently, we have the following *DIVE-INTO™ Series* publications:

- *DIVE-INTO Microsoft® Visual C++® 6*

- *DIVE-INTO Microsoft® Visual C++® .NET*

- *DIVE-INTO GNU C++ on Linux*

- *DIVE-INTO GNU C++ via Cygwin on Windows* (Cygwin is a UNIX emulator for Windows that includes the GNU C++ compiler.)

Each of these tutorials shows how to compile, execute and debug C and C++ applications in that particular compiler product. Many of these documents also provide step-by-step instructions with screen shots to help readers install the software. Each document overviews the compiler and its online documentation.

Additional C and C++ Compilers and IDEs

Our C Resource Center (www.deitel.com/C) and our C++ Resource Center (www.deitel.com/cplusplus) list many free compilers and IDEs and some for-sale products for Windows, Linux and Macintosh platforms. These Resource Centers also include free tutorials to help you get started with these tools.

Teaching Resources for C *How to Program, 5/e*

C How to Program, 5/e, has extensive instructor resources. The Prentice Hall *Instructor's Resource Center* contains the *Solutions Manual* with solutions to the vast majority of the end-of-chapter exercises, a *Test Item File* of multiple-choice questions (approximately two per book section) and PowerPoint® slides containing all the code and figures in the text, plus bulleted items that summarize the key points in the text. Instructors can customize the slides. If you are not already a registered faculty member, contact your Prentice Hall representative or visit vig.prenhall.com/replocator/.

Deitel® Buzz Online Free E-mail Newsletter

Our free e-mail newsletter, the *Deitel® Buzz Online*, includes commentary on industry trends and developments, links to free articles and resources from our published books and upcoming publications, product-release schedules, errata, challenges, anecdotes, information on our corporate instructor-led training courses and more. It's also a good way for you to keep posted about issues related to *C How to Program, 5/e*. To subscribe, visit

www.deitel.com/newsletter/subscribe.html

What's New at Deitel

Free Content Initiative. We are pleased to bring you guest articles and free tutorials selected from our current and forthcoming publications as part of our Free Content Initiative. In each issue of our *Deitel® Buzz Online* newsletter, we announce the latest additions to our free content library. Let us know what topics you'd like to see and let us know if you'd like to submit guest articles!

> www.deitel.com/articles/

Resource Centers and the Deitel Internet Business Initiative. We have created many online Resource Centers (at www.deitel.com) on such topics as C, C++, Visual Basic, .NET, C#, Java, Java EE 5, Java SE 6, AJAX, Ruby, PHP, Perl, Python, MySQL, RSS, XML, Web Services, Windows Vista, Linux, OpenGL, Google Analytics, Google Base, Google Video, Search Engines, Search Engine Optimization, Alert Services, IE7, the Internet Business Initiative, Mash-Ups, Podcasting, Computer Games, Game Programming, Virtual Worlds, Attention Economy, Affiliate Programs, Sudoku, WinFX and Web 2.0, with many more coming.

> www.deitel.com/resourcecenters.html

These resource centers enhance the reader's learning experience. We announce new resource centers in each issue of the *Deitel® Buzz Online*.

Acknowledgments

It is a great pleasure to acknowledge the efforts of many people whose hard work, cooperation, friendship and understanding were crucial to the production of the book. Many people at Deitel & Associates, Inc. devoted long hours to this project—thanks especially to Abbey Deitel, Christi Kelsey and Barbara Deitel.

We would also like to thank two participants of our Honors Internship program who contributed to this publication—Alex Tuteur, a Computer Science major at Brown University, and Kenny Leftin, a Computer Science major at the University of Maryland.

We are fortunate to have worked on this project with the talented and dedicated team of publishing professionals at Prentice Hall. We appreciate the extraordinary efforts of Marcia Horton, Editorial Director of Prentice Hall's Engineering and Computer Science Division. Jennifer Cappello and Dolores Mars did an extraordinary job recruiting the book's review team and managing the review process. Francesco Santalucia (an independent artist) and Kristine Carney did a wonderful job designing the book's cover. Vince O'Brien, Bob Engelhardt, Donna Crilly and Marta Samsel did a marvelous job managing the book's production.

We wish to acknowledge the efforts of our reviewers. Adhering to a tight time schedule, they scrutinized the text and the programs, providing countless suggestions for improving the accuracy and completeness of the presentation.

C How to Program, 4/e Post-Publication Reviewers
    John Benito (ISO/IEC JTC1 SC22 WG14 Convener)
    Fred Tydeman (Tydeman Consulting, Vice-Chair of J11 (ANSI "C"))
    Richard Albright (Goldey-Beacom College)
    Mikhail Brikman (Salem State College)

Carol Luckhardt Redfield (St. Mary's University)
Randy Scovil (Cuesta College)
Bin Wang (Wright State University)

C How to Program, 5/e Reviewers

Alireza Fazelpour (Palm Beach Community College)
Don Kostuch (Independent Consultant)
Ed James Beckham (Altera)
Gary Sibbitts (St. Louis Community College at Meramec)
Ian Barland (Radford University)
Kevin Mark Jones (Hewlett Packard)
Mahesh Hariharan (Microsoft)
William Mike Miller (Edison Design Group, Inc.)
Benjamin Seyfarth (Univeristy of Southern Mississippi)
William Albrecht (University of South Florida)
William Smith (Tulsa Community College)

Allegro Reviewers

Shawn Hargreaves (Software Design Engineer, Microsoft Xbox)
Matthew Leverton (Founder and Webmaster of Allegro.cc)
Ryan Patterson, Independent Consultant
Douglas Walls (Senior Staff Engineer, C compiler, Sun Microsystems)

C99 Reviewers

Lawrence Jones, (UGS Corp.)
Douglas Walls (Senior Staff Engineer, C compiler, Sun Microsystems)

We wish to acknowledge again the efforts of our previous edition reviewers (some first edition, some second edition, some third edition, some fourth edition and some all four); the affiliations were current at the time of the review:

Rex Jaeschke (Independent Consultant; former chair of the ANSI C Committee)
John Benito (Convener of the ISO working group that is responsible for the
    C programming language)
Randy Meyers (NetCom; ANSI C Committee Chair; former ANSI C++
    Committee Member)
Jim Brzowski (University of Massachusetts – Lowell)
Simon North (Synopsis, XML Author)
Fred Tydeman (Consultant)
Kevin Wayne (Princeton University)
Eugene Katzin (Montgomery College)
Sam Harbison (Texas Instruments, PH Author)
Chuck Allison (Tydeman Consulting)
Catherine Dwyer (Pace University)
Glen Lancaster (DePaul University)
Deena Engel (New York University)
David Falconer (California State University at Fullerton)
David Finkel (Worcester Polytechnic)
H. E. Dunsmore (Purdue University)

Jim Schmolze (Tufts University)
Geb Thomas (University of Iowa)
Gene Spafford (Purdue University)
Clovis Tondo (IBM Corporation and visiting professor at Nova University)
Jeffrey Esakov (University of Pennsylvania)
Tom Slezak (University of California, Lawrence Livermore National Laboratory)
Gary A. Wilson (Gary A. Wilson & Assoc.; Univ. of California Berkeley Extension)
Mike Kogan (IBM Corp.; chief architect of 32-bit OS/2 2.0)
Don Kostuch (IBM Corp. retired; instructor in C, C++ and OOP)
Ed Lieblein (Nova University)
John Carroll (San Diego State University)
Alan Filipski (Arizona State University)
Greg Hidley (University of California, San Diego)
Daniel Hirschberg (University of California, Irvine)
Jack Tan (University of Houston)
Richard Alpert (Boston University)
Eric Bloom (Bentley College)

These reviewers scrutinized every aspect of the text and made countless suggestions for improving the accuracy and completeness of the presentation.

Well, there you have it! C is a powerful programming language that will help you write programs quickly and effectively. C scales nicely into the realm of enterprise systems development to help organizations build their business-critical and mission-critical information systems. As you read the book, we would sincerely appreciate your comments, criticisms, corrections and suggestions for improvement. Please address all correspondence to:

`deitel@deitel.com`

We will respond promptly, and we will post corrections and clarifications on our Web site:

`www.deitel.com`

We hope you enjoy reading *C How to Program, 5/e* as much as we enjoyed writing it!

Paul J. Deitel
Dr. Harvey M. Deitel

About the Authors

Paul J. Deitel, CEO and Chief Technical Officer of Deitel & Associates, Inc., is a graduate of the MIT's Sloan School of Management, where he studied Information Technology. Through Deitel & Associates, Inc., he has delivered C, C++, Java and C# courses to industry clients, including IBM, Sun Microsystems, Dell, Lucent Technologies, Fidelity, NASA at the Kennedy Space Center, the National Severe Storm Laboratory, White Sands Missile Range, Rogue Wave Software, Boeing, Stratus, Cambridge Technology Partners, Open Environment Corporation, One Wave, Hyperion Software, Adra Systems, Entergy, CableData Systems, Nortel Networks, Puma, Invensys and many more. He has also lectured on C++ and Java for the Boston Chapter of the Association for Computing Machinery. He and his father, Dr. Harvey M. Deitel, are the world's best-selling programming language textbook authors.

Dr. Harvey M. Deitel, Chairman and Chief Strategy Officer of Deitel & Associates, Inc., has 45 years of academic and industry experience in the computer field. Dr. Deitel earned B.S. and M.S. degrees from the Massachusetts Institute of Technology and a Ph.D. from Boston University. He has 20 years of college teaching experience, including earning tenure and serving as the Chairman of the Computer Science Department at Boston College before founding Deitel & Associates, Inc., with his son, Paul J. Deitel. He and Paul are the co-authors of several dozen books and multimedia packages and they are writing many more. With translations published in Japanese, German, Russian, Spanish, Traditional Chinese, Simplified Chinese, Korean, French, Polish, Italian, Portuguese, Greek, Urdu and Turkish, the Deitels' texts have earned international recognition. Dr. Deitel has delivered hundreds of professional seminars to major corporations, academic institutions, government organizations and the military.

About Deitel & Associates, Inc.

Deitel & Associates, Inc., is an internationally recognized corporate training and content-creation organization specializing in computer programming languages, Internet and World Wide Web software technology, object technology education and Internet business development. The company provides instructor-led courses on major programming languages and platforms, such as Java, Advanced Java, C, C++, C#, Visual C++, Visual Basic, XML, Perl, Python, object technology, and Internet and World Wide Web programming. The founders of Deitel & Associates, Inc., are Dr. Harvey M. Deitel and Paul J. Deitel. The company's clients include many of the world's largest computer companies, government agencies, branches of the military and business organizations. Through its 30-year publishing partnership with Prentice Hall, Deitel & Associates, Inc. publishes leading-edge programming textbooks, professional books, interactive multimedia *Cyber Classrooms*, *Complete Training Courses*, Web-based training courses and e-content for popular course management systems such as WebCT, Blackboard and Pearson's CourseCompass. Deitel & Associates, Inc., and the authors can be reached via e-mail at:

    deitel@deitel.com

To learn more about Deitel & Associates, Inc., its publications and its worldwide *DIVE INTO*® Series Corporate Training curriculum, visit:

    www.deitel.com

and subscribe to the free *Deitel*® *Buzz Online* e-mail newsletter at:

    www.deitel.com/newsletter/subscribe.html

Check out the growing list of Deitel Resource Centers at:

    www.deitel.com/resourcecenters.html

Individuals wishing to purchase Deitel books, Cyber Classrooms, Complete Training Courses and Web-based training courses can do so through:

    www.deitel.com/books/index.html

Bulk orders by corporations, the government, the military and academic institutions should be placed directly with Prentice Hall. For more information, visit

    www.prenhall.com

Introduction to Computers, the Internet and the Web

OBJECTIVES

In this chapter, you will learn:

- Basic computer concepts.
- The different types of programming languages.
- The history of the C programming language.
- The purpose of the C Standard Library.
- The elements of a typical C program development environment.
- Why it is appropriate to learn C in a first programming course.
- How C provides a foundation for further study of programming languages in general and of C++, Java and C# in particular.
- The history of the Internet and the World Wide Web.

1.1 Introduction

Welcome to C and C++! We have worked hard to create what we hope will be an informative and entertaining learning experience for you. This book is unique among C textbooks in that:

- It is appropriate for technically oriented people with little or no programming experience.

- It is appropriate for experienced programmers who want a deep and rigorous treatment of the language.

How can one book appeal to both groups? The answer is that the common core of the book emphasizes achieving program **clarity** through the proven techniques of **structured programming**. Nonprogrammers learn programming the right way from the beginning. We have attempted to write in a clear and straightforward manner. The book is abundantly illustrated. Perhaps most important, the book presents hundreds of complete working programs and shows the outputs produced when those programs are run on a computer. We call this the "live-code approach." All of these example programs may be downloaded from our website www.deitel.com/books/chtp5.

The first four chapters introduce the fundamentals of computing, computer programming and the C computer programming language. Novices who have taken our courses tell us that the material in these chapters presents a solid foundation for the deeper treatment of C in Chapters 5–14. Experienced programmers typically read the first four chapters quickly and then discover that the treatment of C in Chapters 5–14 is both rigorous and challenging. They particularly appreciate the detailed treatments of pointers, strings, files and data structures in the later chapters.

Many experienced programmers appreciate the treatment of structured programming. Often they have been programming in another structured language, but because they were never formally introduced to structured programming, they are not writing the best possible code. As they learn C with this book, they are able to improve their programming style. So, whether you are a novice or an experienced programmer, there is much here to inform, entertain and challenge you.

Most people are familiar with the exciting tasks computers perform. Using this textbook, you'll learn how to command computers to perform those tasks. It is **software** (i.e., the instructions you write to command computers to perform **actions** and make **decisions**) that controls computers (often referred to as **hardware**). This text introduces programming in C, which was standardized in 1989 in the United States through the **American National Standards Institute (ANSI)**, then worldwide through the efforts of the **International Standards Organization (ISO)**. We call this Standard C. We also introduce C99—the latest version of the C standard. C99 has not yet been widely adopted, so we chose to discuss it in (optional) Chapter 17. Chapters 1–16 discuss Standard (ANSI/ISO) C.

Optional Chapter 15 presents the Allegro game programming C library. The chapter shows how to use Allegro to create a simple game. We show how to display graphics and smoothly animate objects, and we explain additional features such as sound, keyboard input and text output. The chapter includes web links and resources that point you to over 1000 Allegro games and to tutorials on advanced Allegro techniques.

Computer use is increasing in almost every field of endeavor. In an era of steadily rising costs, computing costs have been decreasing dramatically due to rapid developments in hardware and software technologies. Computers that might have filled large rooms and cost millions of dollars a few decades ago can now be inscribed on the surfaces of silicon chips smaller than a fingernail, costing perhaps a few dollars each. Ironically, silicon is one of the most abundant materials on earth—it is an ingredient in common sand. Silicon-chip technology has made computing so economical that about a billion general-purpose computers are in use worldwide, helping people in business, industry and government and in their personal lives. That number could easily double in the next few years.

C++, an object-oriented programming language based on C, is of such interest today that we have included a detailed introduction to C++ and object-oriented programming in Chapters 18–27. In the programming languages marketplace, many key vendors market a combined C/C++ product rather than offering separate products. This enables users to continue programming in C if they wish, then gradually migrate to C++ when it is appropriate. The CD that accompanies this book contains Microsoft Visual C++ 2005 Express edition, which can be used to develop and run both C and C++ programs. This software is also available for download at `msdn.microsoft.com/vstudio/express/visualc`. Many other C/C++ compilers are available free for download. We list several in Section 1.19. Be sure to visit our C Resource Center at `www.deitel.com/C` frequently for an updated list of free C compilers and related software.

You are about to start on a challenging and rewarding path. As you proceed, if you would like to communicate with us, please send us e-mail at `deitel@deitel.com`. We will respond promptly. For more information on C and other programming-related topics, browse our Resource Centers at www.deitel.com. To be notified of updates to the book, subscribe to the free *Deitel® Buzz Online* e-mail newsletter at www.deitel.com. We hope you enjoy learning C and C++ with *C How to Program: Fifth Edition*.

1.2 What Is a Computer?

A **computer** is a device capable of performing computations and making logical decisions at speeds billions of times faster than human beings can. A person operating a desk calculator might require a lifetime to complete the same number of calculations a powerful personal computer can perform in one second. (Points to ponder: How would you know whether the person added the numbers correctly? How would you know whether the computer added the numbers correctly?) Today's fastest **supercomputers** can perform trillions of additions per second!

Computers process data under the control of sets of instructions called **computer programs**. These computer programs guide the computer through orderly sets of actions specified by people called **computer programmers**.

A computer is comprised of various devices (such as the keyboard, screen, mouse, disks, memory, DVD, CD-ROM and processing units) that are referred to as **hardware**. The computer programs that run on a computer are referred to as **software**. Hardware costs have been declining dramatically in recent years, to the point that personal computers have become commodities. Unfortunately, for decades software development costs rose steadily as programmers developed ever more powerful and complex applications, without significantly improved technology for software development. In this book, you will learn proven software development methods that are helping organizations control, and even reduce, software development costs—structured programming, top-down stepwise refinement and object-oriented programming.

1.3 Computer Organization

Regardless of differences in physical appearance, virtually every computer may be envisioned as being divided into six logical units or sections:

1. **Input unit.** This is the "receiving" section of the computer. It obtains information (data and computer programs) from **input devices** and places this information at the disposal of the other units so that the information can be processed. Most information is entered into computers through keyboards and mouse devices. Information also can be entered by speaking to your computer, by scanning images and by having your computer receive information from a network, such as the Internet.

2. **Output unit.** This is the "shipping" section of the computer. It takes information that has been processed by the computer and places it on various **output devices** to make the information available for use outside the computer. Most information output from computers today is displayed on screens, printed on paper or used to control other devices. Computers also can output their information to networks, such as the Internet.

3. **Memory unit.** This is the rapid-access, relatively low-capacity "warehouse" section of the computer. It retains information that has been entered through the

input unit, so that the information may be made available for processing when needed. The memory unit also retains processed information until that information can be placed on output devices by the output unit. The memory unit is often called either memory, **main memory** or **primary memory**.

4. **Arithmetic and logic unit (ALU).** This is the "manufacturing" section of the computer. It is responsible for performing calculations such as addition, subtraction, multiplication and division. It contains the decision mechanisms that allow the computer, for example, to compare two items from the memory unit to determine whether they are equal.

5. **Central processing unit (CPU).** This is the "administrative" section of the computer. It is the computer's coordinator and is responsible for supervising the operation of the other sections. The CPU tells the input unit when information should be read into the memory unit, tells the ALU when information from the memory unit should be used in calculations and tells the output unit when to send information from the memory unit to certain output devices. Many of today's computers have multiple processing units and, hence, can perform many operations simultaneously—such computers are called **multiprocessors**.

6. **Secondary storage unit.** This is the long-term, high-capacity "warehousing" section of the computer. Programs or data not actively being used by the other units normally are placed on secondary storage devices (such as disks) until they are again needed, possibly hours, days, months or even years later. Information in secondary storage takes much longer to access than information in primary memory, but the cost per unit of secondary storage is much less than that of primary memory.

1.4 Early Operating Systems

Early computers could perform only one job or task at a time. This form of computer operation is often called single-user batch processing. The computer runs a single program at a time while processing data in groups or batches. In these early systems, users generally submitted their jobs to a computer center on decks of punched cards, then often waited hours or even days before printouts were returned to their desks.

Software systems called **operating systems** were developed to help make it more convenient to use computers. Early operating systems managed the smooth transition between jobs. This minimized the time it took for computer operators to switch between jobs and hence increased the amount of work, or **throughput**, computers could process.

As computers became more powerful, it was evident that single-user batch processing rarely utilized computer resources efficiently, because most of the time was spent waiting for slow input/output devices to complete their tasks. Instead, it was thought that many jobs or tasks could be made to share the resources of the computer to achieve better utilization. This is called **multitasking**. Multitasking involves the "simultaneous" operation of many jobs on the computer—the computer shares its resources among the jobs competing for its attention. With early multitasking operating systems, users still submitted jobs on decks of punched cards and waited hours or days for results.

In the 1960s, several groups in industry and the universities pioneered **timesharing** operating systems. Timesharing is a special case of multitasking, in which users access the computer through **terminals**, typically devices with keyboards and screens. In a typical timesharing computer system, dozens or even hundreds of users may share the computer at once. The computer actually does not process all the users simultaneously. Rather, it runs a small portion of one user's job, then moves on to service the next user. The computer does this so quickly that it may provide service to each user several times per second. Thus, the users' programs *appear* to be running simultaneously. An advantage of timesharing is that the user receives almost immediate responses to requests rather than having to wait long periods for results.

1.5 Personal, Distributed and Client/Server Computing

In 1977, Apple Computer popularized the phenomenon of **personal computing**. Initially, it was a hobbyist's dream. Soon, computers became economical enough for people to buy them for their own personal or business use. In 1981, IBM, the world's largest computer vendor, introduced the IBM Personal Computer. This quickly legitimized personal computing in business, industry and government organizations.

These computers were "stand-alone" units—people did their work on their own computers, then transported disks back and forth to share information (often called "sneakernet"). Although early personal computers were not powerful enough to timeshare several users, these machines could be linked together in computer networks, sometimes over telephone lines and sometimes in **local area networks (LANs)** within an organization. This led to the phenomenon of **distributed computing**, in which an organization's computing, instead of being performed strictly at some central computer installation, is distributed over networks to the sites at which the work of the organization is performed. Personal computers were powerful enough to handle the computing requirements of individual users and to handle the basic communications tasks of passing information between one another electronically.

Today's personal computers are as powerful as the million-dollar machines of just decades ago. The most powerful desktop machines—called **workstations**—provide individual users with enormous capabilities. Information is shared easily across computer networks, where computers called **file servers** offer a common store of data that may be used by **client** computers distributed throughout the network—hence the term **client/server computing**. C, C++ and Java are among the programming languages of choice for writing software for operating systems, computer networking and distributed client/server applications. Today's popular operating systems such as UNIX, Linux, Mac OS X (pronounced "OS ten") and Windows provide the kinds of capabilities discussed in this section.

1.6 Machine Languages, Assembly Languages and High-Level Languages

Programmers write instructions in various programming languages, some directly understandable by computers and others requiring intermediate **translation** steps. Hundreds of computer languages are in use today. These may be divided into three general types:

1. Machine languages
2. Assembly languages
3. High-level languages

Any computer can directly understand only its own **machine language**. Machine language is the "natural language" of a particular computer, defined by the computer's hardware design. Machine languages generally consist of strings of numbers (ultimately reduced to 1s and 0s) that instruct computers to perform their most elementary operations one at a time. Machine languages are **machine dependent** (i.e., a particular machine language can be used on only one type of computer). Such languages are cumbersome for humans, as illustrated by the following section of a machine-language program that adds overtime pay to base pay and stores the result in gross pay:

```
+1300042774
+1400593419
+1200274027
```

Machine-language programming was simply too slow and tedious for most programmers. Instead of using the strings of numbers that computers could directly understand, programmers began using English-like abbreviations to represent elementary operations. These abbreviations formed the basis of **assembly languages**. Translator programs called **assemblers** were developed to convert assembly-language programs to machine language at computer speeds. The following section of an assembly-language program also adds overtime pay to base pay and stores the result in gross pay, but is more readily understandable than its machine-language equivalent:

```
LOAD    BASEPAY
ADD     OVERPAY
STORE   GROSSPAY
```

Although such code is clearer to humans, it is incomprehensible to computers until translated to machine language.

Computer usage increased rapidly with the advent of assembly languages, but programming in these languages still required many instructions to accomplish even the simplest tasks. To speed the programming process, **high-level languages** were developed in which single statements could be written to accomplish substantial tasks. The translator programs that convert high-level language programs into machine language are called **compilers**. High-level languages allow programmers to write instructions that look almost like everyday English and contain commonly used mathematical notations. A payroll program written in a high-level language might contain a statement such as

```
grossPay = basePay + overTimePay
```

From the programmer's standpoint, obviously, high-level languages are much more desirable than either machine languages or assembly languages. C, C++ and Java are among the most powerful and most widely used high-level programming languages.

Compiling a high-level language program into machine language can take a considerable amount of computer time. **Interpreter** programs were developed to execute high-level language programs directly without the need for compiling them into machine language. Although compiled programs execute much faster than interpreted programs, interpreters are popular in program development environments in which programs are recompiled frequently as new features are added and errors are corrected. Once a program is developed, a compiled version can be produced to run most efficiently.

1.7 Fortran, COBOL, Pascal and Ada

Hundreds of high-level languages have been developed, but few have achieved broad acceptance. Fortran (Formula Translator) was developed by IBM Corporation in the 1950s to be used for scientific and engineering applications that require complex mathematical computations. Fortran is still widely used in engineering applications.

COBOL (COmmon Business Oriented Language) was developed in 1959 by computer manufacturers, the government and industrial computer users. COBOL is used for commercial applications that require precise and efficient manipulation of large amounts of data. A significant percentage of business software is still programmed in COBOL.

During the 1960s, many large software development efforts encountered severe difficulties. Software schedules were typically late, costs greatly exceeded budgets and the finished products were unreliable. People began to realize that software development was a far more complex activity than they had imagined. Research activity in the 1960s resulted in the evolution of **structured programming**—a disciplined approach to writing programs that are clearer than unstructured programs, easier to test and debug and easier to modify.

One of the more tangible results of this research was the development of the Pascal programming language by Professor Niklaus Wirth in 1971. Pascal, named after the seventeenth-century mathematician and philosopher Blaise Pascal, was designed for teaching structured programming and rapidly became the preferred programming language in most colleges. Unfortunately, the language lacks many features needed to make it useful in commercial, industrial and government applications, so it has not been widely accepted in these environments.

The Ada programming language was developed under the sponsorship of the U.S. Department of Defense (DOD) during the 1970s and early 1980s. Hundreds of separate languages were being used to produce the DOD's massive command-and-control software systems. The DOD wanted a single language that would fill most of its needs. The language was named after Lady Ada Lovelace, daughter of the poet Lord Byron. Lady Lovelace is credited with writing the world's first computer program in the early 1800s (for the Analytical Engine mechanical computing device designed by Charles Babbage). One important capability of Ada is called **multitasking**, which allows programmers to specify that many activities are to occur in parallel. Some widely used high-level languages we have discussed—including C and C++—allow the programmer to write programs that perform only one activity at a time. Java, through a technique called **multithreading**, enables programmers to write programs with parallel activities.

1.8 History of C

C evolved from two previous languages, BCPL and B. BCPL was developed in 1967 by Martin Richards as a language for writing operating-systems software and compilers. Ken Thompson modeled many features in his B language after their counterparts in BCPL, and in 1970 he used B to create early versions of the UNIX operating system at Bell Laboratories on a DEC PDP-7 computer. Both BCPL and B were "typeless" languages—every data item occupied one "word" in memory, and the burden of typing variables fell on the shoulders of the programmer.

The C language was evolved from B by Dennis Ritchie at Bell Laboratories and was originally implemented on a DEC PDP-11 computer in 1972. C uses many of the important concepts of BCPL and B while adding data typing and other powerful features. C initially became widely known as the development language of the UNIX operating system. Today, virtually all new major operating systems are written in C and/or C++. C is available for most computers. C is also hardware independent. With careful design, it is possible to write C programs that are portable to most computers.

By the late 1970s, C had evolved into what is now referred to as "traditional C." The publication in 1978 of Kernighan and Ritchie's book, *The C Programming Language,* drew wide attention to the language. This became one of the most successful computer science books of all time.

The rapid expansion of C over various types of computers (sometimes called hardware platforms) led to many variations that were similar but often incompatible. This was a serious problem for programmers who needed to develop code that would run on several platforms. It became clear that a standard version of C was needed. In 1983, the X3J11 technical committee was created under the American National Standards Committee on Computers and Information Processing (X3) to "provide an unambiguous and machine-independent definition of the language." In 1989, the standard was approved; this standard was updated in 1999. The standards document is referred to as *INCITS/ISO/IEC 9899-1999.* Copies may be ordered from the American National Standards Institute (www.ansi.org) at webstore.ansi.org/ansidocstore.

C99 is a revised standard for the C programming language that refines and expands the capabilities of C. C99 has not been widely adopted, and not all popular C compilers support it. Of the compilers that do offer C99 support, most implement only a subset of the new features. Chapters 1–16 of this book are based on the widely adopted international Standard (ANSI/ISO) C. Chapter 17 introduces C99 and provides links to popular C99 compilers and IDEs.

Portability Tip 1.1

Because C is a hardware-independent, widely available language, applications written in C can run with little or no modifications on a wide range of different computer systems.

[*Note:* We will include many of these Portability Tips to highlight techniques that will help you write programs that can run, with little or no modification, on a variety of computers. We will also highlight Good Programming Practices (practices that can help you write programs that are clear, understandable, maintainable and easy to test and debug—that is, eliminate errors), Common Programming Errors (problems to watch out for, so you do not make these same errors in your programs), Performance Tips (techniques that will help you write programs that run faster and use less memory), Error-Prevention Tips (techniques that will help you remove bugs from your programs and, more important, help you write bug-free programs in the first place) and Software Engineering Observations (concepts that affect and improve the overall architecture and quality of a software system, and particularly of large software systems). Many of these techniques and practices are only guidelines; you will, no doubt, develop your own preferred programming style.]

1.9 C Standard Library

As you will learn in Chapter 5, C programs consist of modules or pieces called functions. You can program all the functions you need to form a C program, but most C programmers take advantage of a rich collection of existing functions called the C Standard Library. Thus, there are really two pieces to learning how to program in C. The first is learning the C language itself, and the second is learning how to use the functions in the C Standard Library. Throughout the book, we discuss many of these functions. P.J. Plauger's *The Standard C Library* is required reading for programmers who need a deep understanding of the library functions, how to implement them and how to use them to write portable code.

This textbook encourages a **building-block approach** to creating programs. Avoid reinventing the wheel. Instead, use existing pieces—this is called **software reusability**, and it is a key to the developing field of object-oriented programming, as we will see in our treatment of C++ beginning in Chapter 18. When programming in C you will typically use the following building blocks:

- C Standard Library functions
- Functions you create yourself
- Functions other people have created and made available to you

The advantage of creating your own functions is that you will know exactly how they work. You will be able to examine the C code. The disadvantage is the time-consuming effort that goes into designing, developing and debugging new functions.

If you use existing functions, you can avoid reinventing the wheel. In the case of the Standard C functions, you know that they are carefully written, and you know that because you are using functions that are available on virtually all Standard C implementations, your programs will have a greater chance of being portable and error-free.

Performance Tip 1.1

Using Standard C library functions instead of writing your own comparable versions can improve program performance, because these functions are carefully written to perform efficiently.

Portability Tip 1.2

Using Standard C library functions instead of writing your own comparable versions can improve program portability, because these functions are used in virtually all Standard C implementations.

1.10 C++

C++ was developed by Bjarne Stroustrup at Bell Laboratories. It has its roots in C, providing a number of features that "spruce up" the C language. More important, it provides capabilities for **object-oriented programming**. C++ has become a dominant language in both industry and universities.

Objects are essentially reusable software **components** that model items in the real world. Software developers are discovering that using a modular, object-oriented design and implementation approach can make software development groups much more productive than is possible with conventional programming techniques.

Many people feel that the best educational strategy today is to master C, then study C++. Therefore, in Chapters 18–27 of *C How to Program: Fifth Edition*, we present a condensed treatment of C++ selected from our book *C++ How to Program*. We hope that you find this valuable and that it will encourage you to pursue further study of C++ after com-

pleting this book. As you study C++, check out our online C++ Resource Center at
www.deitel.com/cplusplus.

1.11 Java

Many people believe that the next major area in which microprocessors will have a profound impact is that of intelligent consumer electronic devices. In 1991, recognizing this,
Sun Microsystems funded an internal corporate research project code-named Green. The
project resulted in the development of a language based on C and C++, which its creator,
James Gosling, called Oak after an oak tree outside his window at Sun. It was later discov-
ered that there already was a computer language called Oak. When a group of Sun people
visited a local coffee place, the name Java was suggested and it stuck.

The Green project ran into some difficulties. The marketplace for intelligent consumer electronic devices was not developing as quickly as Sun had anticipated. Worse yet,
a major contract for which Sun had competed was awarded to another company, putting
the project in danger of being canceled. By sheer good fortune, the World Wide Web
exploded in popularity in 1993, and Sun saw the immediate potential of using Java to
create web pages with so-called dynamic content.

Sun formally announced Java at a trade show in May 1995. Ordinarily, an event such
as this would not have generated much attention, but Java generated immediate interest
in the business community because of the phenomenal interest in the World Wide Web.
Java is now used to create web pages with dynamic and interactive content, develop large-
scale enterprise applications, enhance the functionality of web servers (the computers that
provide the content we see in web browsers), provide applications for consumer devices
(such as cell phones, pagers and personal digital assistants) and do many more things.

In November of 1995, we were following the development of Java by Sun Microsystems and we attended an Internet conference in Boston. A representative from Sun Microsystems gave a rousing presentation on Java. As the talk proceeded, it became clear to us
that Java would certainly play a significant part in the development of interactive, multimedia web pages. But we immediately saw a much greater potential for the language. We
saw Java as a superb language for teaching programming language students the essentials
of graphics, images, animation, audio, video, database, networking, multithreading and
collaborative computing.

In addition to its prominence in developing Internet- and intranet-based applications,
Java has become the language of choice for implementing software for devices that communicate over a network (such as cellular phones, pagers and personal digital assistants).
Do not be surprised when your new stereo and other devices in your home are networked
together using Java technology!

1.12 BASIC, Visual Basic, Visual C++, Visual C# and .NET

The BASIC (Beginner's All-Purpose Symbolic Instruction Code) programming language
was developed in the mid-1960s by Professors John Kemeny and Thomas Kurtz of Dartmouth College as a language for writing simple programs. BASIC's primary purpose was
to familiarize novices with programming techniques. Visual Basic was introduced by Microsoft in 1991 to simplify the process of developing Microsoft Windows applications.

Visual Basic, Visual C++ and Visual C# are designed for Microsoft's new .NET programming platform. All three languages make use of .NET's powerful library of reusable software components called the Framework Class Library (FCL).

Comparably to Java, the .NET platform enables web-based applications to be distributed to many devices (even cell phones) and to desktop computers. The C# programming language was designed specifically for the .NET platform as a language that would enable programmers to migrate easily to .NET. C++, Java and C# all have their roots in the C programming language.

1.13 Key Software Trend: Object Technology

One of the authors, HMD, remembers the great frustration that was felt in the 1960s by software development organizations, especially those developing large-scale projects. During his undergraduate years, HMD had the privilege of working summers at a leading computer vendor on the teams developing timesharing, virtual-memory operating systems. This was a great experience for a college student. In the summer of 1967, reality set in when the company "decommitted" from producing as a commercial product the particular system on which hundreds of people had been working for many years. It was difficult to get this software right. Software is "complex stuff."

Improvements to software technology did start to appear, with the benefits of so-called **structured programming** (and the related disciplines of **structured systems analysis and design**) being realized in the 1970s. But not until the 1990s, when the technology of object-oriented programming became widely used, did software developers finally feel they had the tools for making major strides in the software development process.

Actually, object technology dates back to the mid 1960s. The C++ programming language, developed at AT&T by Bjarne Stroustrup in the early 1980s, is based on two languages—C and Simula 67, a simulation programming language developed in Europe and released in 1967. C++ absorbed the features of C and added Simula's capabilities for creating and manipulating objects. Neither C nor C++ was originally intended for wide use beyond the AT&T research laboratories. But grassroots support rapidly developed for each.

What are objects and why are they special? Object technology is a packaging scheme that enables programmers to create meaningful software units. These are large and highly focused on particular applications areas. There are date objects, time objects, paycheck objects, invoice objects, audio objects, video objects, file objects, record objects and so on. In fact, almost any noun can be reasonably represented as an object.

We live in a world of objects. Just look around you. There are cars, planes, people, animals, buildings, traffic lights, elevators, and the like. Before object-oriented languages appeared, programming languages (such as Fortran, Pascal, Basic and C) were focused on actions (verbs) rather than on things or objects (nouns). Now, with the availability of popular object-oriented languages such as Java and C++, programmers continue to live in an object-oriented world but can conveniently program in an object-oriented (noun-oriented) manner. This is a more natural process than procedural programming and has resulted in significant productivity enhancements.

A key problem with procedural programming is that the program units do not easily mirror real-world entities effectively, so these units are not particularly reusable. It is not unusual for programmers to "start fresh" on each new project and have to write similar software "from scratch." Time and money are wasted as people repeatedly reinvent the wheel. With object technology, the software entities created (called classes), if properly designed, tend to be much more reusable on future projects. Using libraries of reusable componentry, such as the .NET FCL and those produced by many other software development organizations, can greatly reduce the amount of effort required to implement certain kinds of systems (as compared to the effort reinventing these capabilities on new projects).

Some organizations report that software reuse is not, in fact, the key benefit they get from object-oriented programming. Rather, object-oriented programming tends to produce software that is more understandable, better organized and easier to maintain, modify and debug. This can be significant, because it has been estimated that as much as 80% of software costs are associated not with the original efforts to develop the software but with the continued evolution and maintenance of that software throughout its lifetime.

Clearly, whatever its perceived benefits, object-oriented programming will be the key programming methodology for the next several decades.

1.14 Typical C Program Development Environment

C systems generally consist of several parts: a program development environment, the language and the C Standard Library. The following discussion explains the typical C development environment shown in Fig. 1.1.

C programs typically go through six phases to be executed (Fig. 1.1). These are: edit, preprocess, compile, link, load and execute. Although *C How to Program* is a generic C textbook (written independently of the details of any particular operating system), we concentrate in this section on a typical Linux-based C system. [*Note:* The programs in this book will run with little or no modification on most current C systems, including Microsoft Windows-based systems.] If you are not using a Linux system, refer to the manuals for your system or ask your instructor how to accomplish these tasks in your environment. Also, check out our C Resource Center at `www.deitel.com/C` to locate "getting started" tutorials for popular C compilers and development environments.

Phase 1: Creating a Program

Phase 1 consists of editing a file. This is accomplished with an editor program. Two editors widely used on Linux systems are `vi` and `emacs`. Software packages for the C/C++ integrated program development environments such as Borland C++ Builder and Microsoft Visual Studio have editors that are integrated into the programming environment. We assume that the reader knows how to edit a program. The programmer types a C program with the editor, makes corrections if necessary, then stores the program on a secondary storage device such as a disk. C program file names should end with the `.c` extension.

Phases 2 and 3: Preprocessing and Compiling a C Program

In Phase 2, the programmer gives the command to compile the program. The compiler translates the C program into machine language-code (also referred to as object code). In a C system, a preprocessor program executes automatically before the compiler's translation phase begins. The C preprocessor obeys special commands called preprocessor directives, which indicate that certain manipulations are to be performed on the program

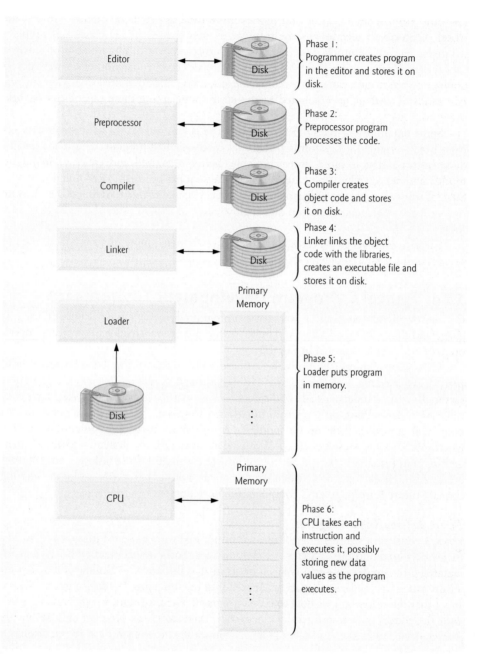

Fig. 1.1 | Typical C development environment.

before compilation. These manipulations usually consist of including other files in the file to be compiled and performing various text replacements. The most common preprocessor directives are discussed in the early chapters; a detailed discussion of preprocessor features appears in Chapter 13. In Phase 3, the compiler translates the C program into machine-language code.

Phase 4: Linking

The next phase is called linking. C programs typically contain references to functions defined elsewhere, such as in the standard libraries or in the private libraries of groups of programmers working on a particular project. The object code produced by the C compiler typically contains "holes" due to these missing parts. A linker links the object code with the code for the missing functions to produce an executable image (with no missing pieces). On a typical Linux system, the command to compile and link a program is called cc (or gcc). To compile and link a program named welcome.c type

```
cc welcome.c
```

at the Linux prompt and press the *Enter* key (or *Return* key). [*Note:* Linux commands are case sensitive; make sure that you type lowercase c's and that the letters in the filename are in the appropriate case.] If the program compiles and links correctly, a file called a.out is produced. This is the executable image of our welcome.c program.

Phase 5: Loading

The next phase is called loading. Before a program can be executed, the program must first be placed in memory. This is done by the loader, which takes the executable image from disk and transfers it to memory. Additional components from shared libraries that support the program are also loaded.

Phase 6: Execution

Finally, the computer, under the control of its CPU, executes the program one instruction at a time. To load and execute the program on a Linux system, type ./a.out at the Linux prompt and press *Enter*.

Problems That May Occur at Execution Time

Programs do not always work on the first try. Each of the preceding phases can fail because of various errors that we will discuss. For example, an executing program might attempt to divide by zero (an illegal operation on computers just as in arithmetic). This would cause the computer to print an error message. You would then return to the edit phase, make the necessary corrections and proceed through the remaining phases again to determine that the corrections work properly.

Most programs in C input and/or output data. Certain C functions take their input from stdin (the standard input stream), which is normally the keyboard, but stdin can be connected to another stream. Data is often output to stdout (the standard output stream), which is normally the computer screen, but stdout can be connected to another stream. When we say that a program prints a result, we normally mean that the result is displayed on a screen. Data may be output to devices such as disks and printers. There is also a standard error stream referred to as stderr. The stderr stream (normally connected to the screen) is used for displaying error messages. It is common to route regular output data, i.e., stdout, to a device other than the screen while keeping stderr assigned to the screen so that the user can be immediately informed of errors.

Common Programming Error 1.1

Errors like division-by-zero occur as a program runs, so these errors are called runtime errors or execution-time errors. Divide-by-zero is generally a fatal error, i.e., an error that causes the program to terminate immediately without successfully performing its job. Nonfatal errors allow programs to run to completion, often producing incorrect results. [Note: On some systems, divide-by-zero is not a fatal error. Please see your system documentation.]

1.15 Hardware Trends

Every year, people generally expect to pay at least a little more for most products and services. The opposite has been the case in the computer and communications fields, especially with regard to the costs of hardware supporting these technologies. For many decades, hardware costs have fallen rapidly, if not precipitously. Every year or two, the capacities of computers have approximately doubled without any increase in price. This often is called Moore's Law, named after the person who first identified and explained the trend, Gordon Moore, cofounder of Intel—the company that manufactures the vast majority of the processors in today's personal computers. Moore's Law and similar trends are especially true in relation to the amount of memory that computers have for programs, the amount of secondary storage (such as disk storage) they have to hold programs and data over longer periods of time, and their processor speeds—the speeds at which computers execute programs (i.e., do their work). Similar growth has occurred in the communications field, in which costs have plummeted as demand for communications bandwidth has attracted intense competition. We know of no other fields in which technology improves so quickly and costs fall so rapidly. Such improvement in the computing and communications fields is truly fostering the so-called Information Revolution.

When computer use exploded in the 1960s and 1970s, many people discussed the dramatic improvements in human productivity that computing and communications would cause, but these improvements did not materialize. Organizations were spending vast sums of money on these technologies, but without realizing the expected productivity gains. The invention of microprocessor chip technology and its wide deployment in the late 1970s and 1980s laid the groundwork for the productivity improvements that individuals and businesses have achieved in recent years.

1.16 History of the Internet

In the late 1960s, one of the authors (HMD) was a graduate student at MIT. His research at MIT's Project Mac (now the Laboratory for Computer Science—the home of the World Wide Web Consortium) was funded by ARPA—the Advanced Research Projects Agency of the Department of Defense. ARPA sponsored a conference at which several dozen ARPA-funded graduate students were brought together at the University of Illinois at Urbana-Champaign to meet and share ideas. During this conference, ARPA rolled out the blueprints for networking the main computer systems of about a dozen ARPA-funded universities and research institutions. They were to be connected with communications lines operating at a then-stunning 56KB (i.e., 56,000 bits per second), at a time when most people (of the few who could) were connecting over telephone lines at a rate of 110 bits per second. HMD vividly recalls the excitement at that conference. Researchers at Harvard in Massachusetts talked about communication with the Univac 1108 "supercomputer" across the country at the University of Utah to handle calculations related to their computer graphics research. Many other intriguing possibilities were raised. Academic research was about to take a giant leap forward. Shortly after this conference, ARPA proceeded to implement what quickly became called the **ARPAnet**, the grandparent of today's **Internet**.

Things worked out differently than originally planned. Although the ARPAnet did enable researchers to share each others' computers, its chief benefit proved to be its capability of quick and easy communication via what came to be known as **electronic mail** (e-mail). This is true even today on the Internet, with e-mail and other services facilitating communications of all kinds among nearly a billion people worldwide.

One of ARPA's primary goals for the network was to allow multiple users to send and receive information at the same time over the same communications paths (such as phone lines). The network operated with a technique called **packet switching**, in which digital data was sent in small packages called **packets**. The packets contained data, address information, error-control information and sequencing information. The address information was used to route the packets of data to their destination. The sequencing information was used to help reassemble the packets (which—because of complex routing mechanisms—could actually arrive out of order) into their original order for presentation to the recipient. Packets of many people were intermixed on the same lines. This packet-switching technique greatly reduced transmission costs as compared to those of dedicated communications lines.

The network was designed to operate without centralized control. This meant that if a portion of the network should fail, the remaining working portions would still be able to route packets from senders to receivers over alternate paths.

The protocol for communicating over the ARPAnet became known as TCP—the **Transmission Control Protocol**. TCP ensured that messages were properly routed from sender to receiver and that they messages arrived intact.

In parallel with the early evolution of the Internet, organizations worldwide were implementing their own networks for both intraorganization (i.e., within the organization) and interorganization (i.e., between organizations) communication. A huge variety of networking hardware and software appeared. One challenge was to get these to intercommunicate. ARPA accomplished this with the development of IP—the Internetworking Protocol), truly creating a "network of networks," the current architecture of the Internet. The combined set of protocols is now commonly called TCP/IP.

Initially, use of the Internet was limited to colleges and research institutions; then the military became a big user. Eventually, the government decided to allow access to the Internet for commercial purposes. At first there was resentment among the research and military communities—it was felt that response times would become poor as "the net" became saturated with so many users.

In fact, the exact opposite has occurred. Businesses rapidly realized that, by making effective use of the Internet, they could tune their operations and offer new and better services to their clients, so they started spending vasts amounts of money to develop and enhance the Internet. This generated fierce competition among the communications carriers and the hardware and software suppliers to meet the demand. The result is that bandwidth (i.e., the information-carrying capacity of communications lines) on the Internet has increased tremendously and costs have plummeted. Countries worldwide now realize that the Internet is crucial to their economic prosperity and competitiveness.

1.17 History of the World Wide Web

The **World Wide Web** allows computer users to locate and view over the Internet multimedia-based documents (i.e., documents with text, graphics, animations, audios and/or videos) on almost any subject. Even though the Internet was developed more than three decades ago, the introduction of the World Wide Web was a relatively recent event. In 1990, **Tim Berners-Lee** of CERN (the European Laboratory for Particle Physics) developed the World Wide Web and several communication protocols that form its backbone.

The Internet and the World Wide Web will surely be listed among the most important and profound creations of humankind. In the past, most computer applications ran on "stand-alone" computers, i.e., computers that were not connected to one another. Today's applications can be written to communicate among the world's hundreds of millions of computers. The Internet mixes computing and communications technologies. It makes our work easier. It makes information instantly and conveniently accessible worldwide. It enables individuals and small businesses to get worldwide exposure. It is changing the way business is done. People can search for the best prices on virtually any product or service. Special-interest communities can stay in touch with one another. Researchers can be made instantly aware of the latest breakthroughs worldwide.

1.18 Notes About C and This Book

Experienced C programmers sometimes take pride in being able to create weird, contorted, convoluted usages of the language. This is a poor programming practice. It makes programs more difficult to read, more likely to behave strangely, more difficult to test and debug and more difficult to adapt to changing requirements. This book is geared for novice programmers, so we stress **program clarity**. The following is our first "good programming practice."

Good Programming Practice 1.1

Write your C programs in a simple and straightforward manner. This is sometimes referred to as KIS ("keep it simple"). Do not "stretch" the language by trying bizarre usages.

You may have heard that C is a portable language and that programs written in C can run on many different computers. *Portability is an elusive goal.* The Standard C document contains a lengthy list of portability issues, and complete books have been written that discuss portability.

Portability Tip 1.3

Although it is possible to write portable programs, there are many problems between different C compilers and different computers that make portability difficult to achieve. Simply writing programs in C does not guarantee portability. The progammer will often need to deal directly with complex computer variations.

We have done a careful walkthrough of the C Standard document and audited our presentation against it for completeness and accuracy. However, C is a rich language, and there are some subtleties in the language and some advanced subjects we have not covered. If you need additional technical details on C, we suggest that you read the C Standard document itself or the book by Kernighan and Ritchie.

We have limited our discussions in Chapters 1–16 to ANSI/ISO C. Many features of this version of C are not compatible with older C implementations, so you may find that some of the programs in this text do not work on older C compilers. Chapter 17 introduces the newer C99 standard, which has not been widely accepted, but whose use is growing.

Software Engineering Observation 1.1

Read the manuals for the version of C you are using. Reference these manuals frequently to be sure you are aware of the rich collection of C features and that you are using these features correctly.

Software Engineering Observation 1.2

Your computer and compiler are good teachers. If you are not sure how a feature of C works, write a sample program with that feature, compile and run the program and see what happens.

1.19 Web Resources

C Standard and Working Group

If you'd like to look at the precise definition of the C language or to follow the working group that maintains and evolves C, visit the following sites:

`www.open-std.org/jtc1/sc22/wg14/`

Homepage of the C working group that governs the evolution of the C standard.

`www.open-std.org/jtc1/sc22/wg14/www/C99RationaleV5.10.pdf`

Rationale for the C standard. This document explains many changes that have been made to C over the years.

`www.open-std.org/jtc1/sc22/wg14/www/standards.html#9899`

Provides access to the most recent publicly accessible version of the international C standard document, the rationale for C99 and Technical Corrigendum 1 and Technical Corrigendum 2.

Free C/C++ Compilers and Development Tools

`msdn.microsoft.com/vstudio/express/visualc/download/`

Download the free Microsoft Visual C++ .NET 2005 Express Edition software. Full versions of the software can be purchased through this site.

`www.borland.com/bcppbuilder`

Download the free trial edition of Borland C++Builder 2006. Full versions of the software can be purchased through this site.

`http://www.freescale.com/webapp/sps/site/overview.jsp?nodeId=01272600612247`

Download the free trial edition of Freescale CodeWarrior Compiler. Full versions of the software can be purchased through this site.

`developer.intel.com/software/products/compilers/cwin/index.htm`

Download the free trial edition of the Intel C++ Compiler 9.1 for Windows. Full versions of the software can be purchased through this site.

`gcc.gnu.org/install/binaries.html`

Download the free, open-source GNU C++ compiler for a variety of systems.

`developer.apple.com/tools/mpw-tools/`

Download the free, open-source Macintosh Programmer's Workshop for use with Mac OS 7.x, 8.x, and 9.x.

`www.bloodshed.net/devcpp.html`
Free Bloodshed Dev-C++ IDE (Integrated Development Environment) for use with the MinGW and Cygwin ports of the GNU Compiler.

`sources.redhat.com/cygwin/`
Download Cygwin, a free program that allows developers to use the GNU compiler and to develop programs in a Linux-like environment on Windows systems.

`www.mingw.org/`
Download MinGW, another free program that allows developers to create programs in a Linux-like environment on Windows systems.

`www.codeblocks.org/`
Download Code::Blocks—a free, open-source, cross-platform C++ IDE.

`www.digitalmars.com/download/dmcpp.html`
Digital Mars C/C++ compiler for Win32.

`www.members.tripod.com/%7Eladsoft/frindx.htm?cc386.htm`
LadSoft CC386 32-bit C compiler.

`www.orbworks.com/`
C compiler for use with PalmOs, WinCE and Win32.

`www.c-compiler.com/`
Miracle C by Tadeusz Szocik. This compiler is free to use, but a registered version that includes source code of the compiler is also available on this site.

`developer.sun.com/`
Download the free Sun Studio compilers for Solaris and Linux.

Summary

Section 1.1 Introduction

- Software (i.e., the instructions you write to command computers to perform actions and make decisions) controls computers (often referred to as hardware).

- C was standardized in 1989 in the United States through the American National Standards Institute (ANSI) then worldwide through the International Standards Organization (ISO).

- Computer use is increasing in almost every field of endeavor. In an era of steadily rising costs, computing costs have been decreasing dramatically due to rapid developments in both hardware and software technologies. Computers that might have filled large rooms and cost millions of dollars a few decades ago can now be inscribed on the surfaces of silicon chips smaller than a fingernail, costing perhaps a few dollars each.

- Silicon-chip technology has made computing so economical that about a billion general-purpose computers are in use worldwide.

Section 1.2 What Is a Computer?

- A computer is a device capable of performing computations and making logical decisions at speeds billions of times faster than human beings can. Today's fastest supercomputers can peform trillions of additions per second. Trillion-instruction-per-second computers are already functioning in research laboratories!

- Computers process data under the control of sets of instructions called computer programs. These computer programs guide the computer through orderly sets of actions specified by people called computer programmers.

- A computer is comprised of various devices (such as the keyboard, screen, mouse, disks, DVD, CD-ROM and processing units) that are referred to as hardware.
- The computer programs that run on a computer are referred to as software.
- Hardware costs have been declining dramatically in recent years, to the point that person puters have become commodities.

Section 1.3 Computer Organization

- Regardless of differences in physical appearance, virtually every computer may be envisioned as being divided into six logical units.
- The input unit is the "receiving" section of the computer. It obtains information (data and computer programs) from input devices and places this information at the disposal of the other units so that the information can be processed.
- The output unit is the "shipping" section of the computer. It takes information that has been processed by the computer and places it on various output devices to make the information available for use outside the computer.
- The memory unit is the rapid-access, relatively low-capacity "warehouse" section of the computer. It retains information that has been entered through the input unit, so the information may be made available for processing when needed. The memory unit also retains processed information until that it can be placed on output devices by the output unit. The memory unit is often called either memory or primary memory.
- The arithmetic and logic unit (ALU) is the "manufacturing" section of the computer. It is responsible for performing calculations such as addition, subtraction, multiplication and division. It contains the decision mechanisms that allow the computer, for example, to compare two items from the memory unit to determine whether they are equal.
- The central processing unit (CPU) is the "administrative" section of the computer. It is the computer's coordinator and is responsible for supervising the operation of the other sections. The CPU tells the input unit when information should be read into the memory unit, tells the ALU when information from the memory unit should be used in calculations and tells the output unit when to send information from the memory unit to certain output devices.
- Many of today's computers have multiple processing units and, hence, can perform many operations simultaneously—such computers are called multiprocessors.
- The secondary storage unit is the long-term, high-capacity "warehousing" section of the computer. Programs or data not actively being used by the other units normally are placed on secondary storage devices (such as disks) until they are again needed. Information in secondary storage takes much longer to access than information in primary memory, but the cost per unit of secondary storage is much less than that of primary memory.

Section 1.4 Early Operating Systems

- Early computers were capable of performing only one job or task at a time. This form of computer operation is often called single-user batch processing.
- Software systems called operating systems were developed to help make it more convenient to use computers. Early operating systems managed the smooth transition between jobs. This minimized the time it took for computer operators to switch between jobs and hence increased the amount of work, or throughput, computers could process.
- As computers became more powerful, it became evident that single-user batch processing rarely utilized computer resources efficiently, because most of the time was spent waiting for slow input/output devices to complete their tasks. It was thought that many jobs or tasks could be made

to share the resources of the computer to achieve better utilization. This is called multitasking. Multitasking involves the "simultaneous" operation of many jobs on the computer—the computer shares its resources among the jobs competing for its attention.

- In the 1960s, several groups pioneered timesharing operating systems. Timesharing is a special case of multitasking, in which users access the computer through terminals, typically devices with keyboards and screens. In a typical timesharing computer system, dozens or even hundreds of users, sharing the computer at once. The computer actually does not process all the users simultaneously. Rather, it runs a small portion of one user's job, then moves on to service the next user. The computer does this so quickly that it may provide service to each user several times per second. Thus, the users' programs appear to be running simultaneously. An advantage of timesharing is that the user receives almost immediate responses to requests rather than having to wait long periods for results.

Section 1.5 Personal, Distributed and Client/Server Computing

- In 1977, Apple Computer popularized the phenomenon of personal computing.

- In 1981, IBM, the world's largest computer vendor, introduced the IBM Personal Computer, which quickly legitimized personal computing.

- Personal computers were "stand-alone" units—people did their work on their own computers, then transported disks back and forth to share information (often called "sneakernet").

- Although early personal computers were not powerful enough to timeshare several users, these machines could be linked together in computer networks, sometimes over telephone lines and sometimes in local area networks (LANs) within an organization. This led to the phenomenon of distributed computing, in which an organization's computing, instead of being performed strictly at some central computer installation, is distributed over networks to the sites at which the work of the organization is performed.

- Personal computers were powerful enough to handle the computing requirements of individual users, and to handle the basic communications tasks of passing information between one another electronically.

- Today's personal computers are as powerful as the million-dollar machines of just few decades ago.

- The most powerful desktop machines—called workstations—provide individual users with enormous capabilities.

- Today, information is shared easily across computer networks, where computers called file servers offer a common store data that may be used by client computers distributed throughout the network—hence the term client/server computing.

Section 1.6 Machine Languages, Assembly Languages and High-Level Languages

- Programmers write instructions in various programming languages, some directly understandable by computers and others requiring intermediate translation steps.

- Hundreds of computer languages are in use today. These may be divided into three general types—machine languages, assembly languages and high-level languages.

- Any computer can directly understand only its own machine language—the "natural language" of a particular computer. Machine languages generally consist of strings of numbers (ultimately reduced to 1s and 0s) that instruct computers to perform their most elementary operations, one at a time. Machine languages are machine dependent (i.e., a particular machine language can be used on only one type of computer). Such languages are cumbersome for humans.

- Machine-language programming was simply too slow and tedious for most programmers. Instead of using the strings of numbers that computers could directly understand, programmers began using English-like abbreviations to represent elementary operations. These abbreviations formed the basis of assembly languages. Translator programs called assemblers convert assembly-language programs to machine language at computer speeds. Although assembly language is clearer to humans, it is incomprehensible to computers until translated to machine language.

- Computer usage increased rapidly with the advent of assembly languages, but programming in these languages still required many instructions to accomplish even the simplest tasks. To speed the programming process, high-level languages were developed, in which single statements could be written to accomplish substantial tasks. The translator programs that convert high-level language programs into machine language are called compilers. High-level languages allow programmers to write instructions that look almost like everyday English and contain commonly used mathematical notations. C, C++ and Java are among the most powerful and most widely used high-level programming languages.

- The process of compiling a high-level language program into machine language can take a considerable amount of computer time. Interpreter programs were developed to execute high-level language programs directly without the need for compiling those programs into machine language. Although compiled programs execute much faster than interpreted programs, interpreters are popular in program development environments, in which programs are recompiled frequently as new features are added and errors are corrected. Once a program is developed, a compiled version can be produced to run most efficiently.

Section 1.7 Fortran, COBOL, Pascal and Ada
- Fortran was developed by IBM Corporation in the 1950s to be used for scientific and engineering applications that require complex mathematical computations.

- COBOL was developed in 1959 by computer manufacturers, the government and industrial computer users. COBOL is used for commercial applications that require precise and efficient manipulation of large amounts of data.

- Research activity in the 1960s resulted in the evolution of structured programming—a disciplined approach to writing programs that are clearer than unstructured programs, easier to test and debug and easier to modify.

- One of the more tangible results of this research was the development of the Pascal programming language by Professor Niklaus Wirth in 1971. Pascal was designed for teaching structured programming and rapidly became the preferred programming language in most colleges.

- The Ada programming language was developed under the sponsorship of the U.S. Department of Defense (DOD) during the 1970s and early 1980s. Hundreds of separate languages were being used to produce the DOD's massive command-and-control software systems. The DOD wanted a single language that would fill most of its needs. Ada was named after Lady Ada Lovelace, daughter of the poet Lord Byron. Lady Lovelace is credited with writing the world's first computer program in the early 1800s (for the Analytical Engine mechanical computing device designed by Charles Babbage). One important capability of Ada is called multitasking, which allows programmers to specify that many activities are to occur in parallel.

Section 1.8 History of C
- C evolved from two previous languages, BCPL and B. BCPL was developed in 1967 by Martin Richards as a language for writing operating systems software and compilers. Ken Thompson modeled many features in his B language after their counterparts in BCPL and in 1970, at Bell Laboratories used B to create early versions of the UNIX operating system on a DEC PDP-7 computer. Both BCPL and B were "typeless" languages—every data item occupied one "word" in memory, and the burden of typing variables fell on the shoulders of the programmer.

- The C language was evolved from B by Dennis Ritchie at Bell Laboratories and was originally implemented in 1972 on a DEC PDP-11 computer. C uses many of the important concepts of BCPL and B while adding data typing and other powerful features.

- C initially became widely known as the development language of the UNIX operating system. Today, virtually all new major operating systems are written in C and/or C++.

- C is available for most computers. C is also hardware independent. With careful design, it is possible to write C programs that are portable to most computers.

- By the late 1970s, C had evolved into what is now referred to as "traditional C." The publication in 1978 of Kernighan and Ritchie's book, *The C Programming Language*, drew wide attention to the language.

- The rapid expansion of C over various types of computers (sometimes called hardware platforms) led to many variations that were similar but often incompatible. This was a serious problem for program developers, who needed to develop code that would run on several platforms. It became clear that a standard version of C was needed.

- In 1983, the X3J11 technical committee was created under the American National Standards Committee on Computers and Information Processing (X3) to "provide an unambiguous and machine-independent definition of the language." In 1989, the standard was approved; this standard was updated in 1999. The standards document is referred to as INCITS/ISO/IEC 9899-1999. Copies of this document may be ordered from the American National Standards Institute (www.ansi.org) at webstore.ansi.org/ansidocstore.

- C99 is a revised standard for the C programming language that refines and expands the capabilities of C. Although it has not been widely adopted, support for it is growing. Chapter 17 introduces C99. The front part of this book is based on the widely adopted international Standard C.

Section 1.9 C Standard Library

- C programs consist of modules or pieces called functions. You can program all the functions you need to form a C program, but most C programmers take advantage of a rich collection of existing functions called the C Standard Library. Thus, there are really two pieces to learning how to program in C. The first is learning the C language itself, and the second is learning how to use the functions in the C Standard Library.

- When programming in C you will typically use C Standard Library functions, functions you create yourself and functions other people have created and made available to you.

- The advantage of creating your own functions is that you will know exactly how they work. You will be able to examine the C code. The disadvantage is the time-consuming effort that goes into designing and developing new functions.

- If you use existing functions, you can avoid reinventing the wheel. In the case of the Standard C functions, you know that they are carefully written, and you know that because you are using functions that are available on virtually all Standard C implementations, your programs will have a greater chance of being portable.

Section 1.10 C++

- C++ was developed by Bjarne Stroustrup at Bell Laboratories. It has its roots in C and provides capabilities for object-oriented programming.

- Objects are essentially reusable software components that model items in the real world.

- Software developers are discovering that using a modular, object-oriented design and implementation approach can make software development groups much more productive than is possible with conventional programming techniques.

Section 1.11 Java

- Many people believe that the next major area in which microprocessors will have a profound impact is that of intelligent consumer electronic devices. In 1991, recognizing this, Sun Microsystems funded an internal corporate research project code-named Green. The project resulted in the development of Java.

- The World Wide Web exploded in popularity in 1993, and Sun saw the immediate potential of using Java to create web pages with dynamic content.

- Sun formally announced Java at a trade show in May 1995. Java generated immediate interest in the business community because of the phenomenal interest in the World Wide Web. Java is now used to create web pages with dynamic and interactive content, develop large-scale enterprise applications, enhance the functionality of web servers (the computers that provide the content we see in our web browsers), provide applications for consumer devices (such as cell phones, pagers and personal digital assistants) and do many more things.

Section 1.12 BASIC, Visual Basic, Visual C++, Visual C# and .NET

- The BASIC (Beginner's All-Purpose Symbolic Instruction Code) programming language was developed in the mid-1960s by Professors John Kemeny and Thomas Kurtz of Dartmouth College as a language for writing simple programs. BASIC's primary purpose was to familiarize novices with programming techniques.

- Visual Basic was introduced by Microsoft in 1991 to simplify the process of developing Microsoft Windows applications.

- Visual Basic, Visual C++ and Visual C# are designed for Microsoft's .NET programming platform. All three languages make use of .NET's powerful library of reusable software components called the Framework Class Library (FCL).

- Comparably to Java, the .NET platform enables web-based applications to be distributed to many devices (even cell phones) and to desktop computers. The C# programming language was designed specifically for the .NET platform as a language that would enable programmers to migrate easily to .NET.

- C++, Java and C# all have their roots in the C programming language.

Section 1.13 Key Software Trend: Object Technology

- Improvements to software technology started to appear, with the benefits of so-called structured programming (and the related disciplines of structured systems analysis and design) being realized in the 1970s. But until the 1990s, when the technology of object-oriented programming became widely used, that software did developers finally feel they had the necessary tools for making major strides in the software development process.

- Object technology dates back to the mid 1960s. The C++ programming language, developed at AT&T by Bjarne Stroustrup in the early 1980s, is based on two languages—C and Simula 67, a simulation programming language developed in Europe and released in 1967. C++ absorbed the features of C and added Simula's capabilities for creating and manipulating objects. Neither C nor C++ was originally intended for wide use beyond the AT&T research laboratories. But grassroots support rapidly developed for each.

- Object technology is a packaging scheme that enables programmers to create meaningful software units.

- Before object-oriented languages appeared, programming languages (such as Fortran, Pascal, Basic and C) were focussed on actions (verbs) rather than on things or objects (nouns). Now, with the availability of popular object-oriented languages such as Java and C++, programmers continue to live in an object-oriented world but can conveniently program in an object-oriented (noun-oriented) manner. This is a more natural process than procedural programming and has resulted in significant productivity enhancements.

- A key problem with procedural programming is that the program units do not easily mirror real-world entities effectively, so these units are not particularly reusable. It is not unusual for programmers to "start fresh" on each new project and have to write similar software "from scratch."

- With object technology, the software entities created (called classes), if properly designed, tend to be much more reusable on future projects.

- Using libraries of reusable componentry can greatly reduce the amount of effort required to implement certain kinds of systems.

- Object-oriented programming tends to produce software that is more understandable, better organized and easier to maintain, modify and debug.

Section 1.14 Typical C Program Development Environment

- You create a program by editing a file with an editor program. Software packages for the C/C++ integrated program development environments such as Borland C++ Builder and Microsoft Visual Studio have editors that are integrated into the programming environment.

- C program file names should end with the .c extension.

- Compilers translate programs into machine-language code (also referred to as object code).

- In a C system, a preprocessor program executes automatically before the compiler's translation phase begins. The C preprocessor obeys special commands called preprocessor directives, which indicate that certain manipulations are to be performed on the program before compilation. These manipulations usually consist of including other files in the file to be compiled and performing various text replacements.

- C programs typically contain references to functions defined elsewhere, such as in the standard libraries or in the private libraries of groups of programmers working on a particular project. The object code produced by the C compiler typically contains "holes" due to these missing parts. A linker links the object code with the code for the missing functions to produce an executable image (with no missing pieces).

- Before a program can be executed, it must first be placed in memory. This is done by the loader, which takes the executable image from disk and transfers it to memory. Additional components from shared libraries that support the program are also loaded.

- The computer, under the control of its CPU, executes the program one instruction at a time.

Section 1.15 Hardware Trends

- Every year, people generally expect to pay at least a little more for most products and services. The opposite has been the case in the computer and communications fields, especially with regard to the costs of hardware supporting these technologies. For many decades, hardware costs have fallen rapidly, if not precipitously.

- Every year or two, the capacities of computers have approximately doubled without any increase in price. This often is called Moore's Law, named after the person who first identified and explained the trend, Gordon Moore, cofounder of Intel—the company that manufactures the vast majority of the processors in today's personal computers.

- Moore's Law is especially true in relation to the amount of memory that computers have for programs, the amount of secondary storage (such as disk storage) they have to hold programs and data over longer periods of time, and their processor speeds—the speeds at which computers execute their programs (i.e., do their work).

- Similar growth has occurred in the communications field, in which costs have plummeted as enormous demand for communications bandwidth has attracted intense competition.

Section 1.16 History of the Internet
- In the late 1960s, ARPA—the Advanced Research Projects Agency of the Department of Defense—rolled out the blueprints for networking the main computer systems of about a dozen ARPA-funded universities and research institutions. The network quickly became called the ARPAnet, the grandparent of today's Internet.
- ARPAnet's chief benefit proved to be its capability of quick and easy communication via what came to be known as electronic mail (e-mail). This is true even today on the Internet, with e-mail and related services facilitating communications of all kinds among nearly a billion people worldwide.
- The network operated with a technique called packet switching in, which digital data was sent in small packages called packets. The packets contained data, address information, error-control information and sequencing information. The address information was used to route the packets of data to their destination. The sequencing information was used to help reassemble the packets into their original order for presentation to the recipient. Packets of many people were intermixed on the same lines. This packet-switching technique greatly reduced transmission costs as compared to those of dedicated communications lines.
- The network was designed to operate without centralized control. This meant that if a portion of the network should fail, the remaining working portions would still be able to route packets from senders to receivers over alternate paths.
- The protocol for communicating over the ARPAnet became known as TCP—the Transmission Control Protocol. TCP ensured that messages were properly routed from sender to receiver and that they arrived intact.
- In parallel with the early evolution of the Internet, organizations worldwide were implementing their own networks for both intraorganization and interorganization communication. A huge variety of networking hardware and software appeared. One challenge was to get these to intercommunicate. ARPA accomplished this with the development of IP—the Internetworking Protocol), truly creating a "network of networks," the current architecture of the Internet. The combined set of protocols is now commonly called TCP/IP.
- Use of the Internet was limited at first to colleges and research institutions; then the military became a big user. Eventually, the government decided to allow access to the Internet for commercial purposes.
- Businesses rapidly realized that, by making effective use of the Internet, they could tune their operations and offer new and better services to their clients, so they started spending vasts amounts of money to develop and enhance the Internet. This generated fierce competition among the communications carriers and the hardware and software suppliers to meet the demand. The result is that bandwidth on the Internet has increased tremendously and costs have plummeted.

Section 1.17 History of the World Wide Web
- The World Wide Web allows computer users to locate and view over the Internet multimedia-based documents on almost any subject. Even though the Internet was developed more than three decades ago, the introduction of the World Wide Web was a relatively recent event. In 1990, Tim Berners-Lee of CERN (the European Laboratory for Particle Physics) developed the World Wide Web and several communication protocols that form its backbone.
- The Internet and the World Wide Web will surely be listed among the most important and profound creations of humankind.

- Today's applications can be written to communicate among the world's hundreds of millions of computers. The Internet mixes computing and communications technologies. It makes our work easier. It makes information instantly and conveniently accessible worldwide. It enables individuals and small businesses to get worldwide exposure. It is changing the way business is done. People can search for the best prices on virtually any product or service. Special-interest communities can stay in touch with one another. Researchers can be made instantly aware of the latest breakthroughs worldwide.

Terminology

.c extension	function
.NET	functionalization
Ada	hardware
Allegro C library	hardware platform
ALU	high-level language
ANSI/ISO Standard C	input device
arithmetic and logic unit (ALU)	input stream
assembler	input unit
assembly language	input/output (I/O)
BASIC	Internet
batch processing	interpreter
building-block approach	Java
C	KIS ("keep it simple")
C preprocessor	Lady Ada Lovelace
C Standard Library	library function
C#	linker
C++	Linux
C99	loader
central processing unit (CPU)	logical units
clarity	Mac OS X
class library	machine dependent
client	machine independent
client/server computing	machine language
COBOL	memory
compiler	memory unit
computer	Moore's Law
computer networking	multiprocessor
computer program	multitasking
computer programmer	multithreading
CPU	natural language of a computer
data	nonfatal error
debug	object
distributed computing	object code
editor	object-oriented programming (OOP)
environment	operating system
executable image	output device
execute a program	output stream
fatal error	output unit
file server	Pascal
Fortran	performance
Framework Class Library (FCL)	personal computer

portability
preprocessor
primary memory
program
programming language
reusable software components
run a program
runtime error
screen
secondary storage unit
software
software reusability
standard error stream (`stderr`)
standard input stream (`stdin`)
standard libraries
standard output stream (`stdout`)

stored program
structured programming
supercomputer
task
TCP/IP
terminal
timesharing
top-down, stepwise refinement
translator program
Visual Basic
Visual C++
Visual C#
Windows
workstation
World Wide Web

Self-Review Exercises

1.1   Fill in the blanks in each of the following:

a) The company that brought the phenomenon of personal computing to the world was _____ .

b) The computer that made personal computing legitimate in business and industry was the _____ .

c) Computers process data under the control of sets of instructions called computer _____ .

d) The six key logical units of the computer are the _____ , _____ , _____ , _____ , _____ and the _____ .

e) _____ is a special case of multitasking in which users access the computer through devices called terminals.

f) The three classes of languages discussed in the chapter are _____ , _____ and _____ .

g) The programs that translate high-level language programs into machine language are called _____ .

h) C is widely known as the development language of the _____ operating system.

i) This book presents the version of C called _____ C that was standardized through ANSI and ISO.

j) The _____ language was developed by Wirth for teaching structured programming.

k) The Department of Defense developed the Ada language with a capability called _____ which allows programmers to specify that many activities can proceed in parallel.

1.2   Fill in the blanks in each of the following sentences about the C environment.

a) C programs are normally typed into a computer using a(n) _____ program.

b) In a C system, a(n) _____ program automatically executes before the translation phase begins.

c) The two most common kinds of preprocessor directives are _____ and _____ .

d) The _____ program combines the output of the compiler with various library functions to produce an executable image.

e) The _____ program transfers the executable image from disk to memory.

f) To load and execute the most recently compiled program on a Linux system, type _____.

Answers to Self-Review Exercises

1.1   a) Apple. b) IBM Personal Computer. c) programs. d) input unit, output unit, memory unit, arithmetic and logic unit (ALU), central processing unit (CPU), secondary storage unit. e) timesharing. f) machine languages, assembly languages, high-level languages. g) compilers. h) UNIX. i) Standard. j) Pascal. k) multitasking.

1.2   a) editor. b) preprocessor. c) including other files in the file to be compiled, replacing special symbols with program text. d) linker. e) loader. f) `a.out`.

Exercises

1.3   Categorize each of the following items as either hardware or software:
a) CPU
b) C compiler
c) ALU
d) C preprocessor
e) input unit
f) a word-processor program

1.4   Why might you want to write a program in a machine-independent language instead of a machine-dependent language? Why might a machine-dependent language be more appropriate for writing certain types of programs?

1.5   Translator programs such as assemblers and compilers convert programs from one language (referred to as the *source* language) to another language (referred to as the *object* language). Determine which of the following statements are *true* and which are *false*:
a) A compiler translates high-level language programs into object language.
b) An assembler translates source-language programs into machine-language programs.
c) A compiler converts source-language programs into object-language programs.
d) High-level languages are generally machine dependent.
e) A machine-language program requires translation before it can be run on a computer.

1.6   Fill in the blanks in each of the following statements:
a) Devices from which users access timesharing computer systems are usually called _____.
b) A computer program that converts assembly-language programs to machine-language programs is called _____.
c) The logical unit of the computer that receives information from outside the computer for use by the computer is called _____.
d) The process of instructing the computer to solve specific problems is called _____.
e) What type of computer language uses English-like abbreviations for machine-language instructions? _____.
f) Which logical unit of the computer sends information that has already been processed by the computer to various devices, so that it may be used outside the computer? _____.
g) The general name for a program that converts programs written in a certain computer language into machine language is _____.

    h) Which logical unit of the computer retains information? _____.

    i) Which logical unit of the computer performs calculations? _____.

    j) Which logical unit of the computer makes logical decisions? _____.

    k) The commonly used abbreviation for the computer's control unit is _____.

    l) The level of computer language most convenient to the programmer for writing programs quickly and easily is _____.

    m) The only language that a computer can directly understand is called that computer's _____.

    n) Which logical unit of the computer coordinates the activities of all the other logical units? _____.

1.7 State whether each of the following is *true* or *false*. If *false,* explain your answer.

    a) Machine languages are generally machine dependent.

    b) Timesharing truly runs several users simultaneously on a computer.

    c) Like other high-level languages, C is generally considered to be machine independent.

1.8 Discuss the meaning of each of the following names:

    a) `stdin`

    b) `stdout`

    c) `stderr`

1.9 Why is so much attention today focused on object-oriented programming in general and C++ in particular?

1.10 Which programming language is best described by each of the following?

    a) Developed by IBM for scientific and engineering applications.

    b) Developed specifically for business applications.

    c) Developed for teaching structured programming.

    d) Named after the world's first computer programmer.

    e) Developed to familiarize novices with programming techniques.

    f) Specifically developed to help programmers migrate to .NET.

    g) Known as the development language of UNIX.

    h) Formed primarily by adding object-oriented programming to C.

    i) Succeeded initially because of its ability to create web pages with dynamic content.

2

Introduction to C Programming

OBJECTIVES

In this chapter, you will learn

- To write simple computer programs in C.
- To use simple input and output statements.
- The fundamental data types.
- Computer memory concepts.
- To use arithmetic operators.
- The precedence of arithmetic operators.
- To write simple decision-making statements.

What's in a name? That which we call a rose By any other name would smell as sweet.

—William Shakespeare

When faced with a decision, I always ask, "What would be the most fun?"

—Peggy Walker

"Take some more tea," the March Hare said to Alice, very earnestly. "I've had nothing yet," Alice replied in an offended tone: "so I can't take more." "You mean you can't take less," said the Hatter: "it's very easy to take more than nothing."

—Lewis Carroll

High thoughts must have high language.

—Aristophanes

2.1 Introduction

The C language facilitates a structured and disciplined approach to computer program design. In this chapter we introduce C programming and present several examples that illustrate many important features of C. Each example is carefully analyzed, one statement at a time. In Chapters 3 and 4 we present an introduction to structured programming in C. We then use the structured approach throughout the remainder of the text.

2.2 A Simple C Program: Printing a Line of Text

C uses some notations that may appear strange to people who have not programmed computers. We begin by considering a simple C program. Our first example prints a line of text. The program and the program's screen output are shown in Fig. 2.1.

Even though this program is simple, it illustrates several important features of the C language. We now consider each line of the program in detail. Lines 1 and 2

```
/* Fig. 2.1: fig02_01.c
   A first program in C */
```

begin with /* and end with */ indicating that these two lines are a comment. You insert comments to document programs and improve program readability. Comments do not cause the computer to perform any action when the program is run. Comments are

```
1   /* Fig. 2.1: fig02_01.c
2      A first program in C */
3   #include <stdio.h>
4
5   /* function main begins program execution */
6   int main( void )
7   {
8      printf( "Welcome to C!\n" );
9
10     return 0; /* indicate that program ended successfully */
11
12  } /* end function main */
```

```
Welcome to C!
```

Fig. 2.1 | Text printing program.

ignored by the C compiler and do not cause any machine-language object code to be generated. The preceding comment simply describes the figure number, file name and purpose of the program. Comments also help other people read and understand your program, but too many comments can make a program difficult to read.

 Common Programming Error 2.1

Forgetting to terminate a comment with */.

 Common Programming Error 2.2

Starting a comment with the characters */ or ending a comment with the characters /*.

Line 3

```
#include <stdio.h>
```

is a directive to the C **preprocessor**. Lines beginning with # are processed by the preprocessor before the program is compiled. Line 3 tells the preprocessor to include the contents of the **standard input/output header** (**<stdio.h>**) in the program. This header contains information used by the compiler when compiling calls to standard input/output library functions such as printf. We explain the contents of headers in more detail in Chapter 5.
Line 6

```
int main( void )
```

is a part of every C program. The parentheses after main indicate that main is a program building block called a **function**. C programs contain one or more functions, one of which must be main. Every program in C begins executing at the function main. Functions can return information. The keyword int to the left of main indicates that main "returns" an integer (whole number) value. We will explain what it means for a function to "return a value" when we demonstrate how to create your own functions in Chapter 5, C Functions. For now, simply include the keyword int to the left of main in each of your programs. Functions also can receive information when they are called upon to execute. The void in parentheses here means that main does not receive any information. In Chapter 14, Other C Topics, we'll show an example of main receiving information.

 Good Programming Practice 2.1

Every function should be preceded by a comment describing the purpose of the function.

A **left brace**, {, begins the **body** of every function (line 7). A corresponding **right brace** ends each function (line 12). This pair of **braces** and the portion of the program between the braces is called a **block**. The block is an important program unit in C.
Line 8

```
printf( "Welcome to C!\n" );
```

instructs the computer to perform an **action**, namely to print on the screen the **string** of characters marked by the quotation marks. A string is sometimes called a **character string**, a **message** or a **literal**. The entire line, including printf, its **argument** within the parentheses and the **semicolon** (;), is called a **statement**. Every statement must end with a semicolon (also known as the **statement terminator**). When the preceding `printf` statement is executed, it prints the message `Welcome to C!` on the screen. The characters normally print exactly as they appear between the double quotes in the `printf` statement. Notice that the characters \n were not printed on the screen. The backslash (\) is called an **escape character**. It indicates that `printf` is supposed to do something out of the ordinary. When encountering a backslash in a string, the compiler looks ahead at the next character and combines it with the backslash to form an **escape sequence**. The escape sequence \n means **newline**. When a newline appears in the string output by a `printf`, the newline causes the cursor to position to the beginning of the next line on the screen. Some common escape sequences are listed in Fig. 2.2.

The last two escape sequences in Fig. 2.2 may seem strange. Because the backslash has special meaning in a string, i.e., the compiler recognizes it as an escape character, we use a double backslash (\\) to place a single backslash in a string. Printing a double quote also presents a problem because double quotes mark the boundary of a string—such quotes are not printed. By using the escape sequence \" in a string to be output by `printf`, we indicate that `printf` should display a double quote.

Line 10

```
return 0; /* indicate that program ended successfully */
```

is included at the end of every `main` function. The keyword `return` is one of several means we will use to **exit a function**. When the return statement is used at the end of `main` as shown here, the value 0 indicates that the program has terminated successfully. In Chapter 5 we discuss functions in detail, and the reasons for including this statement will become clear. For now, simply include this statement in each program, or the compiler might produce a warning on some systems. The **right brace**, }, (line 12) indicates that the end of `main` has been reached.

Good Programming Practice 2.2

Add a comment to the line containing the right brace, }, that closes every function, including `main`.

We said that `printf` causes the computer to perform an **action**. As any program executes, it performs a variety of actions and makes **decisions**. At the end of this chapter,

Escape sequence	Description
\n	Newline. Position the cursor at the beginning of the next line.
\t	Horizontal tab. Move the cursor to the next tab stop.
\a	Alert. Sound the system bell.
\\	Backslash. Insert a backslash character in a string.
\"	Double quote. Insert a double-quote character in a string.

Fig. 2.2 | Some common escape sequences .

we discuss decision making. In Chapter 3, we discuss this action/decision model of programming in depth.

Common Programming Error 2.3

Typing the name of the output function printf *as* print *in a program.*

It is important to note that standard library functions like printf and scanf are not part of the C programming language. For example, the compiler cannot find a spelling error in printf or scanf. When the compiler compiles a printf statement, it merely provides space in the object program for a "call" to the library function. But the compiler does not know where the library functions are—the linker does. When the linker runs, it locates the library functions and inserts the proper calls to these library functions in the object program. Now the object program is complete and ready to be executed. For this reason, the linked program is called an executable. If the function name is misspelled, it is the linker which will spot the error, because it will not be able to match the name in the C program with the name of any known function in the libraries.

Good Programming Practice 2.3

The last character printed by a function that displays output should be a newline (\n). This ensures that the function will leave the screen cursor positioned at the beginning of a new line. Conventions of this nature encourage software reusability—a key goal in software development environments.

Good Programming Practice 2.4

Indent the entire body of each function one level of indentation (we recommend three spaces) within the braces that define the body of the function. This indentation emphasizes the functional structure of programs and helps make programs easier to read.

Good Programming Practice 2.5

Set a convention for the size of indent you prefer and then uniformly apply that convention. The tab key may be used to create indents, but tab stops may vary. We recommend using three spaces per level of indent.

The printf function can print Welcome to C! several different ways. For example, the program of Fig. 2.3 produces the same output as the program of Fig. 2.1. This works because each printf resumes printing where the previous printf stopped printing. The first printf (line 8) prints Welcome followed by a space and the second printf (line 9) begins printing on the same line immediately following the space.

One printf can print several lines by using additional newline characters as in Fig. 2.4. Each time the \n (newline) escape sequence is encountered, output continues at the beginning of the next line.

```
1   /* Fig. 2.3: fig02_03.c
2      Printing on one line with two printf statements */
3   #include <stdio.h>
4
```

Fig. 2.3 | Printing on one line with separate printf statements. (Part I of 2.)

```
5   /* function main begins program execution */
6   int main( void )
7   {
8      printf( "Welcome " );
9      printf( "to C!\n" );
10
11     return 0; /* indicate that program ended successfully */
12
13  } /* end function main */
```

```
Welcome to C!
```

Fig. 2.3 | Printing on one line with separate `printf` statements. (Part 2 of 2.)

```
1   /* Fig. 2.4: fig02_04.c
2      Printing multiple lines with a single printf */
3   #include <stdio.h>
4
5   /* function main begins program execution */
6   int main( void )
7   {
8      printf( "Welcome\nto\nC!\n" );
9
10     return 0; /* indicate that program ended successfully */
11
12  } /* end function main */
```

```
Welcome
to
C!
```

Fig. 2.4 | Printing on multiple lines with a single `printf`.

2.3 Another Simple C Program: Adding Two Integers

Our next program uses the Standard Library function `scanf` to obtain two integers typed by a user at the keyboard, computes the sum of these values and prints the result using `printf`. The program and sample output are shown in Fig. 2.5. [Note that in the input/output dialog of Fig. 2.5, we highlight the numbers input by the user.]

The comment in lines 1–2 states the purpose of the program. As we stated earlier, every program begins execution with `main`. The left brace { (line 7) marks the beginning of the body of `main` and the corresponding right brace } (line 24) marks the end of `main`. Lines 8–10

```
int integer1; /* first number to be input by user  */
int integer2; /* second number to be input by user */
int sum;      /* variable in which sum will be stored */
```

are definitions. The names `integer1`, `integer2` and `sum` are the names of variables. A variable is a location in memory where a value can be stored for use by a program. These

```
1   /* Fig. 2.5: fig02_05.c
2      Addition program */
3   #include <stdio.h>
4
5   /* function main begins program execution */
6   int main( void )
7   {
8      int integer1; /* first number to be input by user  */
9      int integer2; /* second number to be input by user */
10     int sum;       /* variable in which sum will be stored */
11
12     printf( "Enter first integer\n" ); /* prompt */
13     scanf( "%d", &integer1 );               /* read an integer */
14
15     printf( "Enter second integer\n" ); /* prompt */
16     scanf( "%d", &integer2 );               /* read an integer */
17
18     sum = integer1 + integer2; /* assign total to sum */
19
20     printf( "Sum is %d\n", sum ); /* print sum */
21
22     return 0;   /* indicate that program ended successfully */
23
24  } /* end function main */
```

```
Enter first integer
45
Enter second integer
72
Sum is 117
```

Fig. 2.5 | Addition program.

definitions specify that the variables integer1, integer2 and sum are of type **int**, which means that these variables will hold **integer** values, i.e., whole numbers such as 7, –11, 0, 31914 and the like. All variables must be defined with a name and a data type immediately after the left brace that begins the body of main before they can be used in a program. There are other data types besides int in C. Note that the preceding definitions could have been combined into a single definition statement as follows:

```
int integer1, integer2, sum;
```

A variable name in C is any valid **identifier**. An identifier is a series of characters consisting of letters, digits and underscores (_) that does not begin with a digit. An identifier can be of any length, but only the first 31 characters are required to be recognized by C compilers according to the C standard. C is **case sensitive**—uppercase and lowercase letters are different in C, so a1 and A1 are different identifiers.

Common Programming Error 2.4

Using a capital letter where a lowercase letter should be used (for example, typing Main instead of main).

Portability Tip 2.1

Use identifiers of 31 or fewer characters. This helps ensure portability and can avoid some subtle programming errors.

Good Programming Practice 2.6

Choosing meaningful variable names helps make a program self-documenting, i.e., fewer comments are needed.

Good Programming Practice 2.7

The first letter of an identifier used as a simple variable name should be a lowercase letter. Later in the text we will assign special significance to identifiers that begin with a capital letter and to identifiers that use all capital letters.

Good Programming Practice 2.8

Multiple-word variable names can help make a program more readable. Avoid running the separate words together as in totalcommissions. *Rather, separate the words with underscores as in* total_commissions, *or, if you do wish to run the words together, begin each word after the first with a capital letter as in* totalCommissions. *The latter style is preferred.*

Definitions must be placed after the left brace of a function and before *any* executable statements. For example, in the program illustrated in Fig. 2.5, inserting the definitions after the first printf would cause a syntax error. A **syntax error** is caused when the compiler cannot recognize a statement. The compiler normally issues an error message to help you locate and fix the incorrect statement. Syntax errors are violations of the language. Syntax errors are also called **compile errors**, or **compile-time errors**.

Common Programming Error 2.5

Placing variable definitions among executable statements causes syntax errors.

Good Programming Practice 2.9

Separate the definitions and executable statements in a function with one blank line to emphasize where the definitions end and the executable statements begin.

Line 12

```
printf( "Enter first integer\n" ); /* prompt */
```

prints the literal Enter first integer on the screen and positions the cursor to the beginning of the next line. This message is called a **prompt** because it tells the user to take a specific action.

The next statement

```
scanf( "%d", &integer1 ); /* read an integer */
```

uses **scanf** to obtain a value from the user. The scanf function reads from the standard input, which is usually the keyboard. This scanf has two arguments, "%d" and &integer1. The first argument, the **format control string**, indicates the type of data that should be input by the user. The **%d conversion specifier** indicates that the data should be an integer (the letter d stands for "decimal integer"). The % in this context is treated by scanf (and printf as we will see) as a special character that begins a conversion specifier. The second argument of scanf begins with an **ampersand (&)**—called the **address operator** in C—followed by the variable name. The ampersand, when combined with the variable name, tells scanf the location (or address) in memory at which the variable integer1 is stored. The computer then stores the value for integer1 at that location. The use of ampersand (&) is often confusing to novice programmers or to people who have programmed in other languages that do not require this notation. For now, just remember to precede each variable in every call to scanf with an ampersand. Some exceptions to this rule are discussed in Chapters 6 and 7. The use of the ampersand will become clear after we study pointers in Chapter 7.

Good Programming Practice 2.10

Place a space after each comma (,) to make programs more readable.

When the computer executes the preceding scanf, it waits for the user to enter a value for variable integer1. The user responds by typing an integer, then pressing the *Enter* key (sometimes called the *Return* key) to send the number to the computer. The computer then assigns this number, or value, to the variable integer1. Any subsequent references to integer1 in this program will use this same value. Functions printf and scanf facilitate interaction between the user and the computer. Because this interaction resembles a dialogue, it is often called **conversational computing** or **interactive computing**.

Line 15

```
printf( "Enter second integer\n" ); /* prompt */
```

displays the message Enter second integer on the screen, then positions the cursor to the beginning of the next line. This printf also prompts the user to take action.

The statement

```
scanf( "%d", &integer2 ); /* read an integer */
```

obtains a value for variable integer2 from the user. The **assignment** statement in line 18

```
sum = integer1 + integer2; /* assign total to sum */
```

calculates the sum of variables integer1 and integer2 and assigns the result to variable sum using the **assignment operator** =. The statement is read as, "sum *gets* the value of integer1 + integer2." Most calculations are performed in assignments. The = operator and the + operator are called **binary operators** because each has two **operands**. The + operator's two operands are integer1 and integer2. The = operator's two operands are sum and the value of the expression integer1 + integer2.

Good Programming Practice 2.11

Place spaces on either side of a binary operator. This makes the operator stand out and makes the program more readable.

Common Programming Error 2.6

A calculation in an assignment statement must be on the right side of the = operator. It is a syntax error to place a calculation on the left side of an assignment operator.

Line 20

```
printf( "Sum is %d\n", sum ); /* print sum */
```

calls function printf to print the literal Sum is followed by the numerical value of variable sum on the screen. This printf has two arguments, "Sum is %d\n" and sum. The first argument is the format control string. It contains some literal characters to be displayed, and it contains the conversion specifier %d indicating that an integer will be printed. The second argument specifies the value to be printed. Notice that the conversion specifier for an integer is the same in both printf and scanf. This is the case for most C data types.

Calculations can also be performed inside printf statements. We could have combined the previous two statements into the statement

```
printf( "Sum is %d\n", integer1 + integer2 );
```

Line 22

```
return 0; /* indicate that program ended successfully */
```

passes the value 0 back to the operating-system environment in which the program is being executed. This value indicates to the operating system that the program executed successfully. For information on how to report a program failure, see the manuals for your particular operating-system environment. The right brace, }, at line 24 indicates that the end of function main has been reached.

Common Programming Error 2.7
Forgetting one or both of the double quotes surrounding the format control string in a printf or scanf.

Common Programming Error 2.8
Forgetting the % in a conversion specification in the format control string of a printf or scanf.

Common Programming Error 2.9
Placing an escape sequence such as \n outside the format control string of a printf or scanf.

Common Programming Error 2.10
Forgetting to include the expressions whose values are to be printed in a printf containing conversion specifiers.

Common Programming Error 2.11
Not providing a conversion specifier when one is needed in a printf format control string to print the value of an expression.

Common Programming Error 2.12
Placing inside the format control string the comma that is supposed to separate the format control string from the expressions to be printed.

Common Programming Error 2.13
Forgetting to precede a variable in a scanf statement with an ampersand when that variable should, in fact, be preceded by an ampersand.

On many systems, the preceding execution-time error causes a "segmentation fault" or "access violation." Such an error occurs when a user's program attempts to access a part of the computer's memory to which it does not have access privileges. The precise cause of this error will be explained in Chapter 7.

Common Programming Error 2.14

Preceding a variable included in a printf statement with an ampersand when, in fact, that variable should not be preceded by an ampersand.

2.4 Memory Concepts

Variable names such as integer1, integer2 and sum actually correspond to locations in the computer's memory. Every variable has a **name**, a **type** and a **value**.

In the addition program of Fig. 2.5, when the statement (line 13)

```
scanf( "%d", &integer1 ); /* read an integer */
```

is executed, the value typed by the user is placed into a memory location to which the name integer1 has been assigned. Suppose the user enters the number 45 as the value for integer1. The computer will place 45 into location integer1 as shown in Fig. 2.6.

Whenever a value is placed in a memory location, the value replaces the previous value in that location; thus, placing a new value into a memory location is said to be **destructive**.

Returning to our addition program again, when the statement (line 16)

```
scanf( "%d", &integer2 ); /* read an integer */
```

is executed, suppose the user enters the value 72. This value is placed into location integer2, and memory appears as in Fig. 2.7. Note that these locations are not necessarily adjacent in memory.

Once the program has obtained values for integer1 and integer2, it adds these values and places the sum into variable sum. The statement (line 18)

```
sum = integer1 + integer2; /* assign total to sum */
```

that performs the addition also replaces whatever value was stored in sum. This occurs when the calculated sum of integer1 and integer2 is placed into location sum (destroying the value already in sum). After sum is calculated, memory appears as in Fig. 2.8. Note that the values of integer1 and integer2 appear exactly as they did before they were used in

integer1	45

Fig. 2.6 | Memory location showing the name and value of a variable.

integer1	45
integer2	72

Fig. 2.7 | Memory locations after both variables are input.

integer1	45
integer2	72
sum	117

Fig. 2.8 | Memory locations after a calculation.

the calculation of sum. These values were used, but not destroyed, as the computer performed the calculation. Thus, when a value is read from a memory location, the process is said to be **nondestructive**.

2.5 Arithmetic in C

Most C programs perform arithmetic calculations. The C **arithmetic operators** are summarized in Fig. 2.9. Note the use of various special symbols not used in algebra. The asterisk (*) indicates multiplication and the **percent sign** (%) denotes the remainder operator, which is introduced below. In algebra, if we want to multiply a times b, we can simply place these single-letter variable names side by side as in ab. In C, however, if we were to do this, ab would be interpreted as a single, two-letter name (or identifier). Therefore, C (and other programming languages, in general) require that multiplication be explicitly denoted by using the * operator as in a * b.

The arithmetic operators are all binary operators. For example, the expression 3 + 7 contains the binary operator + and the operands 3 and 7.

Integer division yields an integer result. For example, the expression 7 / 4 evaluates to 1 and the expression 17 / 5 evaluates to 3. C provides the remainder operator, %, which yields the remainder after integer division. The remainder operator is an integer operator that can be used only with integer operands. The expression x % y yields the remainder after x is divided by y. Thus, 7 % 4 yields 3 and 17 % 5 yields 2. We will discuss many interesting applications of the remainder operator.

C operation	Arithmetic operator	Algebraic expression	C expression
Addition	+	$f + 7$	f + 7
Subtraction	−	$p - c$	p − c
Multiplication	*	bm	b * m
Division	/	x / y or $\frac{x}{y}$ or $x \div y$	x / y
Remainder	%	$r \bmod s$	r % s

Fig. 2.9 | Arithmetic operators.

Common Programming Error 2.15

An attempt to divide by zero is normally undefined on computer systems and generally results in a fatal error, i.e., an error that causes the program to terminate immediately without having successfully performed its job. Nonfatal errors allow programs to run to completion, often producing incorrect results.

Arithmetic Expressions in Straight-Line Form

Arithmetic expressions in C must be written in straight-line form to facilitate entering programs into the computer. Thus, expressions such as "a divided by b" must be written as a/b so that all operators and operands appear in a straight line. The algebraic notation

$$\frac{a}{b}$$

is generally not acceptable to compilers, although some special-purpose software packages do exist that support more natural notation for complex mathematical expressions.

Parentheses for Grouping Subexpressions

Parentheses are used in C expressions in the same manner as in algebraic expressions. For example, to multiply a times the quantity b + c we write a * (b + c).

Rules of Operator Precedence

C applies the operators in arithmetic expressions in a precise sequence determined by the following rules of operator precedence, which are generally the same as those in algebra:

1. Operators in expressions contained within pairs of parentheses are evaluated first. Thus, *parentheses may be used to force the order of evaluation to occur in any sequence desired by the programmer.* Parentheses are said to be at the "highest level of precedence." In cases of nested, or embedded, parentheses, such as

   ((a + b) + c)

   the operators in the innermost pair of parentheses are applied first.

2. Multiplication, division and remainder operations are applied first. If an expression contains several multiplication, division and remainder operations, evaluation proceeds from left to right. Multiplication, division and remainder are said to be on the same level of precedence.

3. Addition and subtraction operations are evaluated next. If an expression contains several addition and subtraction operations, evaluation proceeds from left to right. Addition and subtraction also have the same level of precedence, which is lower than the precedence of the multiplication, division and remainder operations.

The rules of operator precedence specify the order C uses to evaluate expressions. When we say evaluation proceeds from left to right, we are referring to the associativity of the operators. We will see that some operators associate from right to left. Figure 2.10 summarizes these rules of operator precedence.

Sample Algebraic and C Expressions

Now let us consider several expressions in light of the rules of operator precedence. Each example lists an algebraic expression and its C equivalent. The following example calculates the arithmetic mean (average) of five terms:

Operator(s)	Operation(s)	Order of evaluation (precedence)
( )	Parentheses	Evaluated first. If the parentheses are nested, the expression in the innermost pair is evaluated first. If there are several pairs of parentheses "on the same level" (i.e., not nested), they are evaluated left to right.
* / %	Multiplication Division Remainder	Evaluated second. If there are several, they are evaluated left to right.
+ -	Addition Subtraction	Evaluated last. If there are several, they are evaluated left to right.

Fig. 2.10 | Precedence of arithmetic operators.

Algebra: $m = \dfrac{a + b + c + d + e}{5}$

C: `m = ( a + b + c + d + e ) / 5;`

The parentheses are required to group the additions because division has higher precedence than addition. The entire quantity (a + b + c + d + e) should be divided by 5. If the parentheses are erroneously omitted, we obtain a + b + c + d + e / 5 which evaluates incorrectly as

$$a + b + c + d + \dfrac{e}{5}$$

The following example is the equation of a straight line:

Algebra: $y = mx + b$

C: `y = m * x + b;`

No parentheses are required. The multiplication is evaluated first because multiplication has a higher precedence than addition.

The following example contains remainder (%), multiplication, division, addition, subtraction and assignment operations:

Algebra: $z = pr \% q + w/x - y$

C: `z = p * r % q + w / x - y;`

             6   1   2   4   3   5

The circled numbers under the statement indicate the order in which C evaluates the operators. The multiplication, remainder and division are evaluated first in left-to-right order (i.e., they associate from left to right) since they have higher precedence than addition and subtraction. The addition and subtraction are evaluated next. These are also evaluated left to right.

Not all expressions with several pairs of parentheses contain nested parentheses. The expression

a * (b + c) + c * (d + e)

does not contain nested parentheses. Instead, the parentheses are said to be "on the same level."

Evaluation of a Second-Degree Polynomial

To develop a better understanding of the rules of operator precedence, let us see how C evaluates a second-degree polynomial.

y = a * x * x + b * x + c;

6   1   2   4   3   5

The circled numbers under the statement indicate the order in which C performs the operations. There is no arithmetic operator for exponentiation in C, so we have represented x^2 as x * x. The C Standard Library includes the pow ("power") function to perform exponentiation. Because of some subtle issues related to the data types required by pow, we defer a detailed explanation of pow until Chapter 4.

Suppose variables a, b, c and x in the preceding second-degree polynomial are initialized as follows: a = 2, b = 3, c = 7 and x = 5. Figure 2.11 illustrates the order in which the operators are applied.

Step 1.   y = 2 * 5 * 5 + 3 * 5 + 7;   *(Leftmost multiplication)*

             2 * 5 is 10

Step 2.   y = 10 * 5 + 3 * 5 + 7;   *(Leftmost multiplication)*

             10 * 5 is 50

Step 3.   y = 50 + 3 * 5 + 7;   *(Multiplication before addition)*

             3 * 5 is 15

Step 4.   y = 50 + 15 + 7;   *(Leftmost addition)*

             50 + 15 is 65

Step 5.   y = 65 + 7;   *(Last addition)*

             65 + 7 is 72

Step 6.   y = 72   *(Last operation—place 72 in y)*

Fig. 2.11 | Order in which a second-degree polynomial is evaluated.

As in algebra, it is acceptable to place unnecessary parentheses in an expression to make the expression clearer. These are called **redundant parentheses**. For example, the preceding statement could be parenthesized as follows:

```
y = ( a * x * x ) + ( b * x ) + c;
```

Good Programming Practice 2.12

Using redundant parentheses in complex arithmetic expressions can make the expressions clearer.

2.6 Decision Making: Equality and Relational Operators

Executable C statements either perform **actions** (such as calculations or input or output of data) or make **decisions** (we will soon see several examples of these). We might make a decision in a program, for example, to determine if a person's grade on an exam is greater than or equal to 60 and if it is to print the message "Congratulations! You passed." This section introduces a simple version of C's **if statement** that allows a program to make a decision based on the truth or falsity of a statement of fact called a **condition**. If the condition is met (i.e., the condition is **true**) the statement in the body of the **if** statement is executed. If the condition is not met (i.e., the condition is **false**) the body statement is not executed. Whether the body statement is executed or not, after the **if** statement completes, execution proceeds with the next statement after the **if** statement.

Conditions in **if** statements are formed by using the **equality operators** and **relational operators** summarized in Fig. 2.12. The relational operators all have the same level of precedence and they associate left to right. The equality operators have a lower level of precedence than the relational operators and they also associate left to right. [*Note:* In C, a condition may actually be any expression that generates a zero (false) or nonzero (true) value. We will see many applications of this throughout the book.]

Standard algebraic equality operator or relational operator	C equality or relational operator	Example of C condition	Meaning of C condition
Equality operators			
=	==	x == y	x is equal to y
≠	!=	x != y	x is not equal to y
Relational operators			
>	>	x > y	x is greater than y
<	<	x < y	x is less than y
≥	>=	x >= y	x is greater than or equal to y
≤	<=	x <= y	x is less than or equal to y

Fig. 2.12 | Equality and relational operators.

Common Programming Error 2.16

A syntax error will occur if the two symbols in any of the operators ==, !=, >= and <= are separated by spaces.

Common Programming Error 2.17

A syntax error will occur if the two symbols in any of the operators !=, >= and <= are reversed as in =!, => and =<, respectively.

Common Programming Error 2.18

Confusing the equality operator == with the assignment operator =.

To avoid this confusion, the equality operator should be read "double equals" and the assignment operator should be read "gets." As we will soon see, confusing these operators may not necessarily cause an easy-to-recognize syntax error, but may cause extremely subtle logic errors.

Common Programming Error 2.19

Placing a semicolon immediately to the right of the right parenthesis after the condition in an `if` statement.

Figure 2.13 uses six `if` statements to compare two numbers input by the user. If the condition in any of these `if` statements is true, the `printf` statement associated with that `if` executes. The program and three sample execution outputs are shown in the figure.

Note that the program in Fig. 2.13 uses `scanf` (line 15) to input two numbers. Each conversion specifier has a corresponding argument in which a value will be stored. The first `%d` converts a value to be stored in variable `num1`, and the second `%d` converts a value to be stored in variable `num2`. Indenting the body of each `if` statement and placing blank lines above and below each `if` statement enhances program readability.

Good Programming Practice 2.13

Indent the statement(s) in the body of an `if` statement.

Good Programming Practice 2.14

Place a blank line before and after every `if` statement in a program for readability.

Good Programming Practice 2.15

Although it is allowed, there should be no more than one statement per line in a program.

Common Programming Error 2.20

Placing commas (when none are needed) between conversion specifiers in the format control string of a `scanf` statement.

The comment (lines 1–3) in Fig. 2.13 is split over three lines. In C programs, white space characters such as tabs, newlines and spaces are normally ignored. So, statements and comments may be split over several lines. It is not correct, however, to split identifiers.

```
1   /* Fig. 2.13: fig02_13.c
2      Using if statements, relational
3      operators, and equality operators */
4   #include <stdio.h>
5
6   /* function main begins program execution */
7   int main( void )
8   {
9      int num1; /* first number to be read from user  */
10     int num2; /* second number to be read from user */
11
12     printf( "Enter two integers, and I will tell you\n" );
13     printf( "the relationships they satisfy: " );
14
15     scanf( "%d%d", &num1, &num2 ); /* read two integers */
16
17     if ( num1 == num2 ) {
18        printf( "%d is equal to %d\n", num1, num2 );
19     } /* end if */
20
21     if ( num1 != num2 ) {
22        printf( "%d is not equal to %d\n", num1, num2 );
23     } /* end if */
24
25     if ( num1 < num2 ) {
26        printf( "%d is less than %d\n", num1, num2 );
27     } /* end if */
28
29     if ( num1 > num2 ) {
30        printf( "%d is greater than %d\n", num1, num2 );
31     } /* end if */
32
33     if ( num1 <= num2 ) {
34        printf( "%d is less than or equal to %d\n", num1, num2 );
35     } /* end if */
36
37     if ( num1 >= num2 ) {
38        printf( "%d is greater than or equal to %d\n", num1, num2 );
39     } /* end if */
40
41     return 0;   /* indicate that program ended successfully */
42
43  } /* end function main */
```

```
Enter two integers, and I will tell you
the relationships they satisfy: 3 7
3 is not equal to 7
3 is less than 7
3 is less than or equal to 7
```

Fig. 2.13 | Using equality and relational operators. (Part 1 of 2.)

```
Enter two integers, and I will tell you
the relationships they satisfy: 22 12
22 is not equal to 12
22 is greater than 12
22 is greater than or equal to 12
```

```
Enter two integers, and I will tell you
the relationships they satisfy: 7 7
7 is equal to 7
7 is less than or equal to 7
7 is greater than or equal to 7
```

Fig. 2.13 | Using equality and relational operators. (Part 2 of 2.)

Good Programming Practice 2.16

A lengthy statement may be spread over several lines. If a statement must be split across lines, choose breaking points that make sense (such as after a comma in a comma-separated list). If a statement is split across two or more lines, indent all subsequent lines.

Figure 2.14 lists the precedence of the operators introduced in this chapter. Operators are shown top to bottom in decreasing order of precedence. Note that the equals sign is also an operator. All these operators, with the exception of the assignment operator =, associate from left to right. The assignment operator (=) associates from right to left.

Good Programming Practice 2.17

Refer to the operator precedence chart when writing expressions containing many operators. Confirm that the operators in the expression are applied in the proper order. If you are uncertain about the order of evaluation in a complex expression, use parentheses to group expressions or break the statement into several simpler statements. Be sure to observe that some of C's operators such as the assignment operator (=) associate from right to left rather than from left to right.

Some of the words we have used in the C programs in this chapter—in particular int, return and if—are **keywords** or **reserved words** of the language. Figure 2.15 contains the

Operators				Associativity
( )				left to right
*	/	%		left to right
+	-			left to right
<	<=	>	>=	left to right
==	!=			left to right
=				right to left

Fig. 2.14 | Precedence and associativity of the operators discussed so far.

Keywords			
auto	double	int	struct
break	else	long	switch
case	enum	register	typedef
char	extern	return	union
const	float	short	unsigned
continue	for	signed	void
default	goto	sizeof	volatile
do	if	static	while

Fig. 2.15 | C's keywords.

C keywords. These words have special meaning to the C compiler, so you must be careful not to use these as identifiers such as variable names. In this book, we discuss all these keywords.

In this chapter, we have introduced many important features of the C programming language, including printing data on the screen, inputting data from the user, performing calculations and making decisions. In the next chapter, we build upon these techniques as we introduce structured programming. You will become more familiar with indentation techniques. We will study how to specify the order in which statements are executed—this is called **flow of control**.

Summary

Section 2.1 Introduction
- The C language facilitates a structured and disciplined approach to computer program design.

Section 2.2 A Simple C Program: Printing a Line of Text
- Comments begin with /* and end with */. Comments document programs and improve program readability.
- Comments do not cause the computer to perform any action when the program is run. They are ignored by the C compiler and do not cause any machine-language object code to be generated.
- Lines beginning with # are processed by the preprocessor before the program is compiled. The #include directive tells the preprocessor to include the contents of another file (typically a header file such as <stdio.h>).
- The <stdio.h> header contains information used by the compiler when compiling calls to standard input/output library functions such as printf.
- The function main is a part of every C program. The parentheses after main indicate that main is a program building block called a function. C programs contain one or more functions, one of which must be main. Every program in C begins executing at the function main.

- Functions can return information. The keyword int to the left of main indicates that main "returns" an integer (whole number) value.
- Functions can receive information when they are called upon to execute. The void in parentheses after main indicates that main does not receive any information.
- A left brace, {, begins the body of every function. A corresponding right brace, }, ends each function. This pair of braces and the portion of the program between the braces is called a block.
- The printf function instructs the computer to display information on the screen.
- A string is sometimes called a character string, a message or a literal.
- Every statement must end with a semicolon (also known as the statement terminator).
- The characters \n do not display characters on the screen. The backslash (\) is called an escape character. When encountering a backslash in a string, the compiler looks ahead at the next character and combines it with the backslash to form an escape sequence. The escape sequence \n means newline.
- When a newline appears in the string output by a printf, the newline causes the cursor to position to the beginning of the next line on the screen.
- The double backslash (\\) escape sequence can be used to place a single backslash in a string.
- The escape sequence \" represents a literal double-quote character.
- The keyword return is one of several means to exit a function. When the return statement is used at the end of main, the value 0 indicates that the program has terminated successfully.

Section 2.3 Another Simple C Program: Adding Two Integers

- A variable is a location in memory where a value can be stored for use by a program.
- Variables of type int hold integer values, i.e., whole numbers such as 7, –11, 0, 31914.
- All variables must be defined with a name and a data type immediately after the left brace that begins the body of main before they can be used in a program.
- A variable name in C is any valid identifier. An identifier is a series of characters consisting of letters, digits and underscores (_) that does not begin with a digit. An identifier can be any length, but only the first 31 characters are required to be recognized by C compilers according to the C standard.
- C is case sensitive—uppercase and lowercase letters are different in C, so a1 and A1 are different identifiers.
- Definitions must be placed after the left brace of a function and before *any* executable statements.
- A syntax error is caused when the compiler cannot recognize a statement. The compiler normally issues an error message to help you locate and fix the incorrect statement. Syntax errors are violations of the language. Syntax errors are also called compile errors, or compile-time errors.
- Standard Library function scanf can be used to obtain input from the standard input, which is usually the keyboard.
- The scanf format control string indicates the type(s) of data that should be input.
- The %d conversion specifier indicates that the data should be an integer (the letter d stands for "decimal integer"). The % in this context is treated by scanf (and printf) as a special character that begins a conversion specifier.
- The other arguments of scanf begin with an ampersand (&)—called the address operator in C— followed by a variable name. The ampersand, when combined with a variable name, tells scanf the location in memory at which the variable is located. The computer then stores the value for the variable at that location.

- Most calculations are performed in assignment statements.
- The = operator and the + operator are binary operators—each has two operands.
- Function printf also can use a format control string as its first argument. This string contains some literal characters to be displayed and the conversion specifiers that indicate place holders for data to output.

Section 2.4 Memory Concepts
- Variable names correspond to locations in the computer's memory. Every variable has a name, a type and a value.
- Whenever a value is placed in a memory location, the value replaces the previous value in that location; thus, placing a new value into a memory location is said to be destructive.
- Thus, when a value is read out of a memory location, the process is said to be nondestructive.

Section 2.5 Arithmetic in C
- In algebra, if we want to multiply *a* times *b*, we can simply place these single-letter variable names side by side as in *ab*. In C, however, if we were to do this, ab would be interpreted as a single, two-letter name (or identifier). Therefore, C (like other programming languages, in general) requires that multiplication be explicitly denoted by using the * operator, as in a * b.
- The arithmetic operators are all binary operators.
- Integer division yields an integer result. For example, the expression 7 / 4 evaluates to 1 and the expression 17 / 5 evaluates to 3.
- C provides the remainder operator, %, which yields the remainder after integer division. The remainder operator is an integer operator that can be used only with integer operands. The expression x % y yields the remainder after x is divided by y. Thus, 7 % 4 yields 3 and 17 % 5 yields 2.
- An attempt to divide by zero is normally undefined on computer systems and generally results in a fatal error that causes the program to terminate immediately. Nonfatal errors allow programs to run to completion, often producing incorrect results.
- Arithmetic expressions in C must be written in straight-line form to facilitate entering programs into the computer. Thus, expressions such as "a divided by b" must be written as a/b so that all operators and operands appear in a straight line.
- Parentheses are used to group terms in C expressions in much the same manner as in algebraic expressions.
- C evaluates arithmetic expressions in a precise sequence determined by the following rules of operator precedence, which are generally the same as those followed in algebra.
- Multiplication, division and remainder operations are applied first. If an expression contains several multiplication, division and remainder operations, evaluation proceeds from left to right. Multiplication, division and remainder are said to be on the same level of precedence.
- Addition and subtraction operations are evaluated next. If an expression contains several addition and subtraction operations, evaluation proceeds from left to right. Addition and subtraction also have the same level of precedence, which is lower than the precedence of the multiplication, division and remainder operators.
- The rules of operator precedence specify the order C uses to evaluate expressions. When we say evaluation proceeds from left to right, we are referring to the associativity of the operators. Some operators associate from right to left.

Section 2.6 Decision Making: Equality and Relational Operators
- Executable C statements either perform actions or make decisions.

- C's if statement allows a program to make a decision based on the truth or falsity of a statement of fact called a condition. If the condition is met (i.e., the condition is true) the statement in the body of the if statement executes. If the condition is not met (i.e., the condition is false) the body statement does not execute. Whether the body statement is executed or not, after the if statement completes, execution proceeds with the next statement after the if statement.

- Conditions in if statements are formed by using the equality operators and relational operators.

- The relational operators all have the same level of precedence and associate left to right. The equality operators have a lower level of precedence than the relational operators and they also associate left to right.

- To avoid confusing assignment (=) and equality (==), the assignment operator should be read "gets" and the equality operator should be read "double equals."

- In C programs, white-space characters such as tabs, newlines and spaces are normally ignored. So, statements and comments may be split over several lines. It is not correct to split identifiers.

- Some of the words in C programs—such as int, return and if—are keywords or reserved words of the language. These words have special meaning to the C compiler, so you cannot use them as identifiers such as variable names.

Terminology

!= "is not equal to"
< "is less than"
<= "is less than or equal to"
== "is equal to"
> "is greater than"
>= "is greater than or equal to"
%d conversion specifier
action
action/decision model
address operator
ampersand (&)
argument
arithmetic operators
assignment operator (=)
assignment statement
associativity of operators
asterisk (*)
backslash (\) escape character
binary operators
block
body of a function
braces {}
C keywords
C preprocessor
C Standard Library
case sensitive
character string
comment
compile error
compile-time error
condition

control string
conversational computing
conversion specifier
decision
decision making
definition
destructive
division by zero
embedded parentheses
Enter key
equals sign (=) assignment operator
equality operators
escape character
escape sequence
false
fatal error
flow of control
format control string
function
identifier
if control statement
indentation
int
integer
integer division
interactive computing
keywords
left-to-right associativity
literal
location
main

memory	right-to-left associativity
memory location	rules of operator precedence
message	scanf function
multiplication operator (*)	semicolon (;) statement terminator
name	standard input/output header
nested parentheses	statement
newline character (\n)	statement terminator (;)
nondestructive	stdio.h
nonfatal error	straight-line form
nonzero (true) value	string
operand	structured programming
operator	syntax error
parentheses ()	true
percent sign (%) to begin a conversion specifier	underscore (_)
precedence	value
printf function	variable
prompt	variable name
redundant parentheses	variable type
relational operators	variable value
remainder operator (%)	white-space character
reserved words	zero (false) value
Return key	

Self-Review Exercises

2.1 Fill in the blanks in each of the following.
  a) Every C program begins execution at the function ___main___.
  b) The _____ begins the body of every function and the _____ ends the body of every function.
  c) Every statement ends with a(n) _____.
  d) The _____ standard library function displays information on the screen.
  e) The escape sequence \n represents the _____ character, which causes the cursor to position to the beginning of the next line on the screen.
  f) The _____ Standard Library function is used to obtain data from the keyboard.
  g) The conversion specifier _____ is used in a scanf format control string to indicate that an integer will be input and in a printf format control string to indicate that an integer will be output.
  h) Whenever a new value is placed in a memory location, that value overrides the previous value in that location. This process is said to be _____.
  i) When a value is read out of a memory location, the value in that location is preserved; this process is said to be _____.
  j) The _____ statement is used to make decisions.

2.2 State whether each of the following is *true* or *false*. If *false*, explain why.
  a) Function printf always begins printing at the beginning of a new line.
  b) Comments cause the computer to print the text enclosed between /* and */ on the screen when the program is executed.
  c) The escape sequence \n when used in a printf format control string causes the cursor to position to the beginning of the next line on the screen.
  d) All variables must be defined before they are used.
  e) All variables must be given a type when they are defined.
  f) C considers the variables number and NuMbEr to be identical.

g) Definitions can appear anywhere in the body of a function.

h) All arguments following the format control string in a `printf` function must be preceded by an ampersand (&).

i) The remainder operator (%) can be used only with integer operands.

j) The arithmetic operators *, /, %, + and - all have the same level of precedence.

k) The following variable names are identical on all Standard C systems.

```
thisisasuperduperlongname1234567
thisisasuperduperlongname1234568
```

l) A program that prints three lines of output must contain three `printf` statements.

2.3 Write a single C statement to accomplish each of the following:

a) Define the variables c, `thisVariable`, `q76354` and `number` to be of type int.

b) Prompt the user to enter an integer. End your prompting message with a colon (:) followed by a space and leave the cursor positioned after the space.

c) Read an integer from the keyboard and store the value entered in integer variable a.

d) If `number` is not equal to 7, print "The variable number is not equal to 7."

e) Print the message "This is a C program." on one line.

f) Print the message "This is a C program." on two lines so that the first line ends with C.

g) Print the message "This is a C program." with each word on a separate line.

h) Print the message "This is a C program." with the words separated by tabs.

2.4 Write a statement (or comment) to accomplish each of the following:

a) State that a program will calculate the product of three integers.

b) Define the variables x, y, z and `result` to be of type int.

c) Prompt the user to enter three integers.

d) Read three integers from the keyboard and store them in the variables x, y and z.

e) Compute the product of the three integers contained in variables x, y and z, and assign the result to the variable `result`.

f) Print "The product is" followed by the value of the integer variable `result`.

2.5 Using the statements you wrote in Exercise 2.4, write a complete program that calculates the product of three integers.

2.6 Identify and correct the errors in each of the following statements:

a) `printf( "The value is %d\n", &number );`

b) `scanf( "%d%d", &number1, number2 );`

c) `if ( c < 7 );`
      `printf( "C is less than 7\n" );`

d) `if ( c => 7 )`
      `printf( "C is equal to or less than 7\n" );`

Answers to Self-Review Exercises

2.1 a) `main`. b) left brace ({), right brace (}). c) semicolon. d) `printf`. e) newline. f) `scanf`. g) %d. h) destructive. i) nondestructive. j) `if`.

2.2 a) False. Function `printf` always begins printing where the cursor is positioned, and this may be anywhere on a line of the screen.

b) False. Comments do not cause any action to be performed when the program is executed. They are used to document programs and improve their readability.

c) True.

d) True.

e) True.

    f) False. C is case sensitive, so these variables are unique.

    g) False. The definitions must appear after the left brace of the body of a function and before any executable statements.

    h) False. Arguments in a `printf` function ordinarily should not be preceded by an ampersand. Arguments following the format control string in a `scanf` function ordinarily should be preceded by an ampersand. We will discuss exceptions to these rules in Chapter 6 and Chapter 7.

    i) True.

    j) False. The operators `*`, `/` and `%` are on the same level of precedence, and the operators `+` and `-` are on a lower level of precedence.

    k) False. Some systems may distinguish between identifiers longer than 31 characters.

    l) False. A `printf` statement with multiple `\n` escape sequences can print several lines.

2.3   a) `int c, thisVariable, q76354, number;`

    b) `printf( "Enter an integer: " );`

    c) `scanf( "%d", &a );`

    d) `if ( number != 7 )`
```
    {
        printf( "The variable number is not equal to 7.\n" );
    }
```

    e) `printf( "This is a C program.\n" );`

    f) `printf( "This is a C\nprogram.\n" );`

    g) `printf( "This\nis\na\nC\nprogram.\n" );`

    h) `printf( "This\tis\ta\tC\tprogram.\n" );` *\t = tabs*

2.4   a) `/* Calculate the product of three integers */`

    b) `int x, y, z, result;`

    c) `printf( "Enter three integers: " );`

    d) `scanf( "%d%d%d", &x, &y, &z );`

    e) `result = x * y * z;`

    f) `printf( "The product is %d\n", result );`

2.5   See below.

```
1   /* Calculate the product of three integers */
2   #include <stdio.h>
3                                    prod
4   int main( void )
5   {
6       int x, y, z, result; /* declare variables */
7
8       printf( "Enter three integers: " );  /* prompt */
9       scanf( "%d%d%d", &x, &y, &z );       /* read three integers */
10      result = x * y * z; /* multiply values */
11      printf( "The product is %d\n", result ); /* display result */
12
13      return 0;
14  } /* end function main */
```

2.6   a) Error: `&number`. Correction: Eliminate the `&`. We discuss exceptions to this later.

    b) Error: `number2` does not have an ampersand. Correction: `number2` should be `&number2`. Later in the text we discuss exceptions to this.

    c) Error: Semicolon after the right parenthesis of the condition in the `if` statement. Correction: Remove the semicolon after the right parenthesis. [*Note:* The result of this error is that the printf statement will be executed whether or not the condition in the if statement is true. The semicolon after the right parenthesis is considered an empty statement—a statement that does nothing.]

  d) Error: The relational operator => should be changed to >= (greater than or equal to).

Exercises

2.7   Identify and correct the errors in each of the following statements. (*Note:* There may be more than one error per statement.)

  a) `scanf( "d", value );`

  b) `printf( "The product of %d and %d is %d"\n, x, y );`

  c) `firstNumber + secondNumber = sumOfNumbers`

  d) `if ( number => largest )`
       `largest == number;`

  e) `*/ Program to determine the largest of three integers /*`

  f) `Scanf( "%d", anInteger );`

  g) `printf( "Remainder of %d divided by %d is\n", x, y, x % y );`

  h) `if ( x = y );`
       `printf( "%d is equal to %d\n", x, y );`

  i) `print( "The sum is %d\n," x + y );`

  j) `Printf( "The value you entered is: %d\n, &value );`

2.8   Fill in the blanks in each of the following:

  a) _____ are used to document a program and improve its readability.

  b) The function used to display information on the screen is _____.

  c) A C statement that makes a decision is _____.

  d) Calculations are normally performed by _____ statements.

  e) The _____ function inputs values from the keyboard.

2.9   Write a single C statement or line that accomplishes each of the following:

  a) Print the message "Enter two numbers."

  b) Assign the product of variables b and c to variable a.

  c) State that a program performs a sample payroll calculation (i.e., use text that helps to document a program).

  d) Input three integer values from the keyboard and place these values in integer variables a, b and c.

2.10   State which of the following are *true* and which are *false*. If *false*, explain your answer.

  a) C operators are evaluated from left to right.

  b) The following are all valid variable names: _under_bar_, m928134, t5, j7, her_sales, his_account_total, a, b, c, z, z2.

  c) The statement printf("a = 5;"); is a typical example of an assignment statement.

  d) A valid arithmetic expression containing no parentheses is evaluated from left to right.

  e) The following are all invalid variable names: 3g, 87, 67h2, h22, 2h.

2.11   Fill in the blanks in each of the following:

  a) What arithmetic operations are on the same level of precedence as multiplication? _____.

  b) When parentheses are nested, which set of parentheses is evaluated first in an arithmetic expression? _____.

  c) A location in the computer's memory that may contain different values at various times throughout the execution of a program is called a _____.

2.12   What, if anything, prints when each of the following statements is performed? If nothing prints, then answer "Nothing." Assume x = 2 and y = 3.

x = 2   y = 3   or nothing

a) `printf( "%d", x );` 2
b) `printf( "%d", x + x );` nothing
c) `printf( "x=" );` nothing
d) `printf( "x=%d", x );` x=2
e) `printf( "%d = %d", x + y, y + x );`
f) `z = x + y;` z = 5
g) `scanf( "%d%d", &x, &y );` 2,3
h) `/* printf( "x + y = %d", x + y ); */`
i) `printf( "\n" );` noth

2.13 Which, if any, of the following C statements contain variables whose values are replaced?
a) `scanf( "%d%d%d%d%d", &b, &c, &d, &e, &f );`
b) `p = i + j + k + 7;` ✗
c) `printf( "Values are replaced" );`
d) `printf( "a = 5" );`

2.14 Given the equation $y = ax^3 + 7$, which of the following, if any, are correct C statements for this equation?
a) `y = a * x * x * x + 7;`
b) `y = a * x * x * ( x + 7 );`
c) `y = ( a * x ) * x * ( x + 7 );`
d) `y = ( a * x ) * x * x + 7;`
e) `y = a * ( x * x * x ) + 7;` ✓
f) `y = a * x * ( x * x + 7 );`   parentheses first

2.15 State the order of evaluation of the operators in each of the following C statements and show the value of x after each statement is performed.
a) `x = 7 + 3 * 6 / 2 - 1;`
b) `x = 2 % 2 + 2 * 2 - 2 / 2;`
c) `x = ( 3 * 9 * ( 3 + ( 9 * 3 / ( 3 ) ) ) );`

2.16 Write a program that asks the user to enter two numbers, obtains the two numbers from the user and prints the sum, product, difference, quotient and remainder of the two numbers.

2.17 Write a program that prints the numbers 1 to 4 on the same line. Write the program using the following methods.
a) Using one `printf` statement with no conversion specifiers.
b) Using one `printf` statement with four conversion specifiers.
c) Using four `printf` statements.

2.18 Write a program that asks the user to enter two integers, obtains the numbers from the user, then prints the larger number followed by the words "is larger." If the numbers are equal, print the message "These numbers are equal." Use only the single-selection form of the `if` statement you learned in this chapter.

2.19 Write a program that inputs three different integers from the keyboard, then prints the sum, the average, the product, the smallest and the largest of these numbers. Use only the single-selection form of the `if` statement you learned in this chapter. The screen dialogue should appear as follows:

```
Input three different integers: 13 27 14
Sum is 54
Average is 18
Product is 4914
Smallest is 13
Largest is 27
```

2.20   Write a program that reads in the radius of a circle and prints the circle's diameter, circumference and area. Use the constant value 3.14159 for π. Perform each of these calculations inside the printf statement(s) and use the conversion specifier %f. [*Note:* In this chapter, we have discussed only integer constants and variables. In Chapter 3 we will discuss floating-point numbers, i.e., values that can have decimal points.]

2.21   Write a program that prints a box, an oval, an arrow and a diamond as follows:

```
*********        ***              *                *
*       *      *     *          ***              *   *
*       *     *       *        *****            *       *
*       *     *       *          *             *         *
*       *     *       *          *            *           *
*       *     *       *          *             *         *
*       *     *       *          *              *       *
*       *      *     *           *                *   *
*********        ***             *                  *
```

2.22   What does the following code print?

```
printf( "*\n**\n***\n****\n*****\n" );
```

2.23   Write a program that reads in five integers and then determines and prints the largest and the smallest integers in the group. Use only the programming techniques you have learned in this chapter.

2.24   Write a program that reads an integer and determines and prints whether it is odd or even. [*Hint:* Use the remainder operator. An even number is a multiple of two. Any multiple of two leaves a remainder of zero when divided by 2.]

2.25   Print your initials in block letters down the page. Construct each block letter out of the letter it represents as shown below.

```
PPPPPPPPP
    P    P
    P    P
    P    P
    P  P

   JJ
   J
 J
   J
   JJJJJJJ

DDDDDDDDD
D        D
D        D
 D      D
  DDDDD
```

2.26   Write a program that reads in two integers and determines and prints if the first is a multiple of the second. [*Hint:* Use the remainder operator.]

2.27   Display the following checkerboard pattern with eight printf statements and then display the same pattern with as few printf statements as possible.

2.28 Distinguish between the terms fatal error and nonfatal error. Why might you prefer to experience a fatal error rather than a nonfatal error?

2.29 Here's a peek ahead. In this chapter you learned about integers and the type int. C can also represent uppercase letters, lowercase letters and a considerable variety of special symbols. C uses small integers internally to represent each different character. The set of characters a computer uses together with the corresponding integer representations for those characters is called that computer's character set. You can print the integer equivalent of uppercase A, for example, by executing the statement

```
printf( "%d", 'A' );
```

Write a C program that prints the integer equivalents of some uppercase letters, lowercase letters, digits and special symbols. As a minimum, determine the integer equivalents of the following: A B C a b c 0 1 2 $ * + / and the blank character.

2.30 Write a program that inputs one five-digit number, separates the number into its individual digits and prints the digits separated from one another by three spaces each. [*Hint:* Use combinations of integer division and the remainder operation.] For example, if the user types in 42139, the program should print

```
4   2   1   3   9
```

2.31 Using only the techniques you learned in this chapter, write a program that calculates the squares and cubes of the numbers from 0 to 10 and uses tabs to print the following table of values:

```
number  square  cube
0       0       0
1       1       1
2       4       8
3       9       27
4       16      64
5       25      125
6       36      216
7       49      343
8       64      512
9       81      729
10      100     1000
```

3

Structured Program Development in C

OBJECTIVES

In this chapter, you will learn:

- Basic problem-solving techniques.
- To develop algorithms through the process of top-down, stepwise refinement.
- To use the `if` selection statement and the `if...else` selection statement to select actions.
- To use the `while` repetition statement to execute statements in a program repeatedly.
- Counter-controlled repetition and sentinel-controlled repetition.
- Structured programming.
- The increment, decrement and assignment operators.

3.1 Introduction

Before writing a program to solve a particular problem, it is essential to have a thorough understanding of the problem and a carefully planned approach to solving the problem. The next two chapters discuss techniques that facilitate the development of structured computer programs. In Section 4.12, we present a summary of structured programming that ties together the techniques developed here and in Chapter 4.

3.2 Algorithms

The solution to any computing problem involves executing a series of actions in a specific order. A **procedure** for solving a problem in terms of

1. the **actions** to be executed, and

2. the **order** in which these actions are to be executed

is called an **algorithm**. The following example demonstrates that correctly specifying the order in which the actions are to be executed is important.

Consider the "rise-and-shine algorithm" followed by one junior executive for getting out of bed and going to work:

Get out of bed.
Take off pajamas.
Take a shower.
Get dressed.
Eat breakfast.
Carpool to work.

This routine gets the executive to work well prepared to make critical decisions. Suppose, however, that the same steps are performed in a slightly different order:

Get out of bed.
Take off pajamas.
Get dressed.
Take a shower.
Eat breakfast.
Carpool to work.

In this case, our junior executive shows up for work soaking wet. Specifying the order in which statements are to be executed in a computer program is called **program control**. In this and the next chapter, we investigate the program control capabilities of C.

3.3 Pseudocode

Pseudocode is an artificial and informal language that helps you develop algorithms. The pseudocode we present here is particularly useful for developing algorithms that will be converted to structured C programs. Pseudocode is similar to everyday English; it is convenient and user friendly although it is not an actual computer programming language.

Pseudocode programs are not executed on computers. Rather, they merely help you "think out" a program before attempting to write it in a programming language such as C. In this chapter, we give several examples of how pseudocode may be used effectively in developing structured C programs.

Pseudocode consists purely of characters, so you may conveniently type pseudocode programs into a computer using an editor program. The computer can display or print a fresh copy of a pseudocode program on demand. A carefully prepared pseudocode program may be converted easily to a corresponding C program. This is done in many cases simply by replacing pseudocode statements with their C equivalents.

Pseudocode consists only of action statements—those that are executed when the program has been converted from pseudocode to C and is run in C. Definitions are not executable statements. They are messages to the compiler. For example, the definition

```
int i;
```

simply tells the compiler the type of variable i and instructs the compiler to reserve space in memory for the variable. But this definition does not cause any action—such as input, output, or a calculation—to occur when the program is executed. Some programmers choose to list each variable and briefly mention the purpose of each at the beginning of a pseudocode program. Again, pseudocode is an informal program development aid.

3.4 Control Structures

Normally, statements in a program are executed one after the other in the order in which they are written. This is called **sequential execution**. Various C statements we will soon discuss enable you to specify that the next statement to be executed may be other than the next one in sequence. This is called **transfer of control**.

During the 1960s, it became clear that the indiscriminate use of transfers of control was the root of a great deal of difficulty experienced by software development groups. The finger of blame was pointed at the **goto statement** that allows programmers to specify a transfer of control to one of many possible destinations in a program. The notion of so-called structured programming became almost synonymous with "**goto** elimination."

The research of Bohm and Jacopini[1] had demonstrated that programs could be written without any `goto` statements. The challenge of the era was for programmers to shift their styles to "goto-less programming." It was not until well into the 1970s that the programming profession started taking structured programming seriously. The results were impressive, as software development groups reported reduced development times, more frequent on-time delivery of systems and more frequent within-budget completion of software projects. The key to these successes was simply that programs produced with structured techniques were clearer, easier to debug and modify and more likely to be bug free in the first place.

Bohm and Jacopini's work demonstrated that all programs could be written in terms of only three control structures, namely the sequence structure, the selection structure and the repetition structure. The sequence structure is essentially built into C. Unless directed otherwise, the computer automatically executes C statements one after the other in the order in which they are written. The flowchart segment of Fig. 3.1 illustrates C's sequence structure.

A flowchart is a graphical representation of an algorithm or of a portion of an algorithm. Flowcharts are drawn using certain special-purpose symbols such as rectangles, diamonds, ovals, and small circles; these symbols are connected by arrows called flowlines.

Like pseudocode, flowcharts are useful for developing and representing algorithms, although pseudocode is preferred by most programmers. Flowcharts clearly show how control structures operate; that is all we use them for in this text.

Consider the flowchart for the sequence structure in Fig. 3.1. We use the rectangle symbol, also called the action symbol, to indicate any type of action including a calculation or an input/output operation. The flowlines in the figure indicate the order in which the actions are performed—first, `grade` is added to `total`, then 1 is added to `counter`. C allows us to have as many actions as we want in a sequence structure. As we will soon see, anywhere a single action may be placed, we may place several actions in sequence.

When drawing a flowchart that represents a complete algorithm, an oval symbol containing the word "Begin" is the first symbol used in the flowchart; an oval symbol containing the word "End" is the last symbol used. When drawing only a portion of an

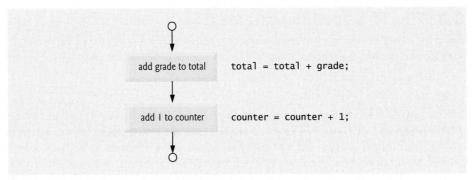

Fig. 3.1 | Flowcharting C's sequence structure.

---

1. Bohm, C., and G. Jacopini, "Flow Diagrams, Turing Machines, and Languages with Only Two Formation Rules," *Communications of the ACM*, Vol. 9, No. 5, May 1966, pp. 336–371.

algorithm as in Fig. 3.1, the oval symbols are omitted in favor of using **small circle symbols**, also called **connector symbols**.

Perhaps the most important flowcharting symbol is the **diamond symbol**, also called the **decision symbol**, which indicates that a decision is to be made. We will discuss the diamond symbol in the next section.

C provides three types of selection structures in the form of statements. The if selection statement (Section 3.5) either performs (selects) an action if a condition is true or skips the action if the condition is false. The if...else selection statement (Section 3.6) performs an action if a condition is true and performs a different action if the condition is false. The switch selection statement (discussed in Chapter 4) performs one of many different actions depending on the value of an expression. The if statement is called a **single-selection statement** because it selects or ignores a single action. The if...else statement is called a **double-selection statement** because it selects between two different actions. The switch statement is called a **multiple-selection statement** because it selects among many different actions.

C provides three types of repetition structures in the form of statements, namely while (Section 3.7), do...while, and for (both discussed in Chapter 4).

That is all there is. C has only seven control statements: sequence, three types of selection and three types of repetition. Each C program is formed by combining as many of each type of control statement as is appropriate for the algorithm the program implements. As with the sequence structure of Fig. 3.1, we will see that the flowchart representation of each control statement has two small circle symbols, one at the entry point to the control statement and one at the exit point. These **single-entry/single-exit control statements** make it easy to build programs. The control-statement flowchart segments can be attached to one another by connecting the exit point of one control statement to the entry point of the next. This is much like the way in which a child stacks building blocks, so we call this **control-statement stacking**. We will learn that there is only one other way control statements may be connected—a method called **control-statement nesting**. Thus, any C program we will ever need to build can be constructed from only seven different types of control statements combined in only two ways. This is the essence of simplicity.

3.5 The if Selection Statement

Selection structures are used to choose among alternative courses of action. For example, suppose the passing grade on an exam is 60. The pseudocode statement

> *If student's grade is greater than or equal to 60*
> *Print "Passed"*

determines if the condition "student's grade is greater than or equal to 60" is true or false. If the condition is true, then "Passed" is printed, and the next pseudocode statement in order is "performed" (remember that pseudocode is not a real programming language). If the condition is false, the printing is ignored, and the next pseudocode statement in order is performed. Note that the second line of this selection structure is indented. Such indentation is optional, but it is highly recommended as it helps emphasize the inherent structure of structured programs. We will apply indentation conventions carefully throughout this text. The C compiler ignores **white-space characters** like blanks, tabs and newlines used for indentation and vertical spacing.

Good Programming Practice 3.1

Consistently applying responsible indentation conventions greatly improves program readability. We suggest a fixed-size tab of about 1/4 inch or three blanks per indent. In this book, we use three blanks per indent.

The preceding pseudocode *If* statement may be written in C as

```
if ( grade >= 60 )
   printf( "Passed\n" );
```

Notice that the C code corresponds closely to the pseudocode. This is one of the properties of pseudocode that makes it such a useful program development tool.

Good Programming Practice 3.2

Pseudocode is often used to "think out" a program during the program design process. Then the pseudocode program is converted to C.

The flowchart of Fig. 3.2 illustrates the single-selection if statement. This flowchart contains what is perhaps the most important flowcharting symbol—the **diamond symbol**, also called the **decision symbol**, which indicates that a decision is to be made. The decision symbol contains an expression, such as a condition, that can be either true or false. The decision symbol has two flowlines emerging from it. One indicates the direction to be taken when the expression in the symbol is true; the other indicates the direction to be taken when the expression is false. We learned in Chapter 2 that decisions can be based on conditions containing relational or equality operators. Actually, a decision can be based on any expression—if the expression evaluates to zero, it is treated as false, and if the expression evaluates to nonzero, it is treated as true.

Note that the if statement, too, is a single-entry/single-exit structure. We will soon learn that the flowcharts for the remaining control structures can also contain (besides small circle symbols and flowlines) only rectangle symbols to indicate the actions to be performed, and diamond symbols to indicate decisions to be made. This is the action/decision model of programming we have been emphasizing.

We can envision seven bins, each containing only control-statement flowcharts of one of the seven types. These flowchart segments are empty—nothing is written in the rectangles and nothing is written in the diamonds. Your task, then, is assembling a program from as many of each type of control statement as the algorithm demands, combining those control statements in only two possible ways (stacking or nesting), and then filling in the

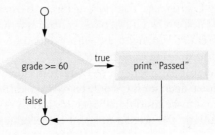

Fig. 3.2 | Flowcharting the single-selection if statement.

actions and decisions in a manner appropriate for the algorithm. We will discuss the variety of ways in which actions and decisions may be written.

3.6 The if…else Selection Statement

The if selection statement performs an indicated action only when the condition is true; otherwise the action is skipped. The if…else selection statement allows you to specify that different actions are to be performed when the condition is true than when the condition is false. For example, the pseudocode statement

> *If student's grade is greater than or equal to 60*
> *   Print "Passed"*
> *else*
> *   Print "Failed"*

prints *Passed* if the student's grade is greater than or equal to 60 and prints *Failed* if the student's grade is less than 60. In either case, after printing occurs, the next pseudocode statement in sequence is "performed." Note that the body of the *else* is also indented. Whatever indentation convention you choose should be carefully applied throughout your programs. It is difficult to read a program that does not obey uniform spacing conventions.

Good Programming Practice 3.3

Indent both body statements of an if…else statement.

Good Programming Practice 3.4

If there are several levels of indentation, each level should be indented the same additional amount of space.

The preceding pseudocode *If…else* statement may be written in C as

```
if ( grade >= 60 )
    printf( "Passed\n" );
else
    printf( "Failed\n" );
```

The flowchart of Fig. 3.3 nicely illustrates the flow of control in the if…else statement. Once again, note that (besides small circles and arrows) the only symbols in the flowchart are rectangles (for actions) and a diamond (for a decision). We continue to emphasize this action/decision model of computing. Imagine again a deep bin containing as many empty double-selection statements (represented as flowchart segments) as might be needed to build any C program. Your job, again, is to assemble these selection statements (by stacking and nesting) with any other control statements required by the algorithm, and to fill in the empty rectangles and empty diamonds with actions and decisions appropriate to the algorithm being implemented.

C provides the **conditional operator** (?:) which is closely related to the if…else statement. The conditional operator is C's only **ternary operator**—it takes three operands. The operands together with the conditional operator form a **conditional expression**. The first operand is a condition. The second operand is the value for the entire conditional expression if the condition is true and the third operand is the value for the entire conditional expression if the condition is false. For example, the printf statement

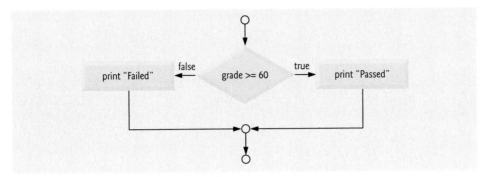

Fig. 3.3 | Flowcharting the double-selection if…else statement.

```
printf( "%s\n", grade >= 60 ? "Passed" : "Failed" );
```

contains a conditional expression that evaluates to the string literal "Passed" if the condition grade >= 60 is true and evaluates to the string literal "Failed" if the condition is false. The format control string of the printf contains the conversion specification %s for printing a character string. So the preceding printf statement performs in essentially the same way as the preceding if…else statement.

The second and third operands in a conditional expression can also be actions to be executed. For example, the conditional expression

```
grade >= 60 ? printf( "Passed\n" ) : printf( "Failed\n" );
```

is read, "If grade is greater than or equal to 60 then printf("Passed\n"), otherwise printf("Failed\n")." This, too, is comparable to the preceding if…else statement. We will see that conditional operators can be used in some situations where if…else statements cannot.

Nested if…else statements test for multiple cases by placing if…else statements inside if…else statements. For example, the following pseudocode statement will print A for exam grades greater than or equal to 90, B for grades greater than or equal to 80, C for grades greater than or equal to 70, D for grades greater than or equal to 60, and F for all other grades.

> *If student's grade is greater than or equal to 90*
>> *Print "A"*
> *else*
>> *If student's grade is greater than or equal to 80*
>>> *Print "B"*
>> *else*
>>> *If student's grade is greater than or equal to 70*
>>>> *Print "C"*
>>> *else*
>>>> *If student's grade is greater than or equal to 60*
>>>>> *Print "D"*
>>>> *else*
>>>>> *Print "F"*

This pseudocode may be written in C as

```c
if ( grade >= 90 )
   printf( "A\n" );
else
   if ( grade >= 80 )
      printf("B\n");
   else
      if ( grade >= 70 )
         printf("C\n");
      else
         if ( grade >= 60 )
            printf( "D\n" );
         else
            printf( "F\n" );
```

If the variable grade is greater than or equal to 90, the first four conditions will be true, but only the printf statement after the first test will be executed. After that printf is executed, the else part of the "outer" if...else statement is skipped. Many C programmers prefer to write the preceding if statement as

```c
if ( grade >= 90 )
   printf( "A\n" );
else if ( grade >= 80 )
   printf( "B\n" );
else if ( grade >= 70 )
   printf( "C\n" );
else if ( grade >= 60 )
   printf( "D\n" );
else
   printf( "F\n" );
```

As far as the C compiler is concerned, both forms are equivalent. The latter form is popular because it avoids the deep indentation of the code to the right. Such indentation often leaves little room on a line, forcing lines to be split and decreasing program readability.

The if selection statement expects only one statement in its body. To include several statements in the body of an if, enclose the set of statements in braces ({ and }). A set of statements contained within a pair of braces is called a **compound statement** or a **block**.

Software Engineering Observation 3.1

A compound statement can be placed anywhere in a program that a single statement can be placed.

The following example includes a compound statement in the else part of an if...else statement.

```c
if ( grade >= 60 )
   printf( "Passed.\n" );
else {
   printf( "Failed.\n" );
   printf( "You must take this course again.\n" );
}
```

In this case, if grade is less than 60, the program executes both printf statements in the body of the else and prints

```
Failed.
You must take this course again.
```

Notice the braces surrounding the two statements in the else clause. These braces are important. Without the braces, the statement

```
printf( "You must take this course again.\n" );
```

would be outside the body of the else part of the if, and would execute regardless of whether the grade was less than 60.

Common Programming Error 3.1

Forgetting one or both of the braces that delimit a compound statement.

A syntax error is caught by the compiler. A logic error has its effect at execution time. A fatal logic error causes a program to fail and terminate prematurely. A nonfatal logic error allows a program to continue executing but to produce incorrect results.

Common Programming Error 3.2

Placing a semicolon after the condition in an if statement as in if (grade >= 60); leads to a logic error in single-selection if statements and a syntax error in double-selection if statements.

Error-Prevention Tip 3.1

Typing the beginning and ending braces of compound statements before typing the individual statements within the braces helps avoid omitting one or both of the braces, preventing syntax errors and logic errors (where both braces are indeed required).

Software Engineering Observation 3.2

Just as a compound statement can be placed anywhere a single statement can be placed, it is also possible to have no statement at all, i.e., the empty statement. The empty statement is represented by placing a semicolon (;) where a statement would normally be.

3.7 The while Repetition Statement

A repetition statement allows you to specify that an action is to be repeated while some condition remains true. The pseudocode statement

> *While there are more items on my shopping list*
> *Purchase next item and cross it off my list*

describes the repetition that occurs during a shopping trip. The condition, "there are more items on my shopping list" may be true or false. If it is true, then the action, "Purchase next item and cross it off my list" is performed. This action will be performed repeatedly while the condition remains true. The statement(s) contained in the *while* repetition statement constitute the body of the *while*. The *while* statement body may be a single statement or a compound statement.

Eventually, the condition will become false (when the last item on the shopping list has been purchased and crossed off the list). At this point, the repetition terminates, and the first pseudocode statement after the repetition structure is executed.

Common Programming Error 3.3

Not providing the body of a while statement with an action that eventually causes the condition in the while to become false. Normally, such a repetition structure will never terminate—an error called an "infinite loop."

Common Programming Error 3.4

Spelling the keyword while with an uppercase W as in While (remember that C is a case-sensitive language). All of C's reserved keywords such as while, if and else contain only lowercase letters.

As an example of an actual while, consider a program segment designed to find the first power of 2 larger than 1000. Suppose the integer variable product has been initialized to 2. When the following while repetition statement finishes executing, product will contain the desired answer:

```
product = 2;

while ( product <= 1000 )
    product = 2 * product;
```

The flowchart of Fig. 3.4 nicely illustrates the flow of control in the while repetition statement. Once again, note that (besides small circles and arrows) the flowchart contains only a rectangle symbol and a diamond symbol. The flowchart clearly shows the repetition. The flowline emerging from the rectangle wraps back to the decision, which is tested each time through the loop until the decision eventually becomes false. At this point, the while statement is exited and control passes to the next statement in the program.

When the while statement is entered, the value of product is 2. The variable product is repeatedly multiplied by 2, taking on the values 4, 8, 16, 32, 64, 128, 256, 512, and 1024 successively. When product becomes 1024, the condition in the while statement, product <= 1000, becomes false. This terminates the repetition, and the final value of product is 1024. Program execution continues with the next statement after the while.

3.8 Formulating Algorithms Case Study 1: Counter-Controlled Repetition

To illustrate how algorithms are developed, we solve several variations of a class averaging problem. Consider the following problem statement:

A class of ten students took a quiz. The grades (integers in the range 0 to 100) for this quiz are available to you. Determine the class average on the quiz.

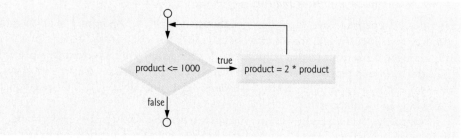

Fig. 3.4 | Flowcharting the while repetition statement.

The class average is equal to the sum of the grades divided by the number of students. The algorithm for solving this problem on a computer must input each of the grades, perform the averaging calculation, and print the result.

Let's use pseudocode to list the actions to execute and specify the order in which these actions should execute. We use **counter-controlled repetition** to input the grades one at a time. This technique uses a variable called a **counter** to specify the number of times a set of statements should execute. In this example, repetition terminates when the counter exceeds 10. In this section we simply present the pseudocode algorithm (Fig. 3.5) and the corresponding C program (Fig. 3.6). In the next section we show how pseudocode algorithms are developed. Counter-controlled repetition is often called **definite repetition** because the number of repetitions is known before the loop begins executing.

Note the references in the algorithm to a total and a counter. A **total** is a variable used to accumulate the sum of a series of values. A **counter** is a variable used to count—in this case, to count the number of grades entered. Variables used to store totals should normally be initialized to zero before being used in a program; otherwise the sum would include the previous value stored in the total's memory location. Counter variables are normally initialized to zero or one, depending on their use (we will present examples showing each of these uses). An uninitialized variable contains a "garbage" value—the value last stored in the memory location reserved for that variable.

1	Set total to zero
2	Set grade counter to one
3	
4	While grade counter is less than or equal to ten
5	Input the next grade
6	Add the grade into the total
7	Add one to the grade counter
8	
9	Set the class average to the total divided by ten
10	Print the class average

Fig. 3.5 | Pseudocode algorithm that uses counter-controlled repetition to solve the class average problem.

```
1  /* Fig. 3.6: fig03_06.c
2     Class average program with counter-controlled repetition */
3  #include <stdio.h>
4
5  /* function main begins program execution */
6  int main( void )
7  {
8     int counter; /* number of grade to be entered next */
9     int grade;   /* grade value */
```

Fig. 3.6 | C program and sample execution for the class average problem with counter-controlled repetition. (Part 1 of 2.)

```
10     int total;    /* sum of grades input by user */
11     int average; /* average of grades */
12
13     /* initialization phase */
14     total = 0;    /* initialize total */
15     counter = 1; /* initialize loop counter */
16
17     /* processing phase */
18     while ( counter <= 10 ) {        /* loop 10 times */
19        printf( "Enter grade: " );  /* prompt for input */
20        scanf( "%d", &grade );      /* read grade from user */
21        total = total + grade;       /* add grade to total */
22        counter = counter + 1;       /* increment counter */
23     } /* end while */
24
25     /* termination phase */
26     average = total / 10; /* integer division */
27
28     printf( "Class average is %d\n", average ); /* display result */
29
30     return 0; /* indicate program ended successfully */
31
32  } /* end function main */
```

```
Enter grade: 98
Enter grade: 76
Enter grade: 71
Enter grade: 87
Enter grade: 83
Enter grade: 90
Enter grade: 57
Enter grade: 79
Enter grade: 82
Enter grade: 94
Class average is 81
```

Fig. 3.6 | C program and sample execution for the class average problem with counter-controlled repetition. (Part 2 of 2.)

Common Programming Error 3.5

If a counter or total is not initialized, the results of your program will probably be incorrect. This is an example of a logic error.

Error-Prevention Tip 3.2

Initialize all counters and totals.

Note that the averaging calculation in the program produced an integer result of 81. Actually, the sum of the grades in this example is 817, which when divided by 10 should yield 81.7, i.e., a number with a decimal point. We will see how to deal with such numbers (called floating-point numbers) in the next section.

3.9 Formulating Algorithms with Top-Down, Stepwise Refinement Case Study 2: Sentinel-Controlled Repetition

Let us generalize the class average problem. Consider the following problem:

> *Develop a class averaging program that will process an arbitrary number of grades each time the program is run.*

In the first class average example, the number of grades (10) was known in advance. In this example, no indication is given of how many grades are to be entered. The program must process an arbitrary number of grades. How can the program determine when to stop the input of grades? How will it know when to calculate and print the class average?

One way to solve this problem is to use a special value called a **sentinel value** (also called a **signal value**, a **dummy value**, or a **flag value**) to indicate "end of data entry." The user types grades in until all legitimate grades have been entered. The user then types the sentinel value to indicate that the last grade has been entered. Sentinel-controlled repetition is often called **indefinite repetition** because the number of repetitions is not known before the loop begins executing.

Clearly, the sentinel value must be chosen so that it cannot be confused with an acceptable input value. Since grades on a quiz are normally nonnegative integers, –1 is an acceptable sentinel value for this problem. Thus, a run of the class average program might process a stream of inputs such as 95, 96, 75, 74, 89 and –1. The program would then compute and print the class average for the grades 95, 96, 75, 74, and 89 (–1 is the sentinel value, so it should not enter into the averaging calculation).

Common Programming Error 3.6

Choosing a sentinel value that is also a legitimate data value.

We approach the class average program with a technique called **top-down, stepwise refinement**, a technique that is essential to the development of well-structured programs. We begin with a pseudocode representation of the **top**:

> *Determine the class average for the quiz*

The top is a single statement that conveys the program's overall function. As such, the top is, in effect, a complete representation of a program. Unfortunately, the top rarely conveys a sufficient amount of detail for writing the C program. So we now begin the refinement process. We divide the top into a series of smaller tasks and list these in the order in which they need to be performed. This results in the following **first refinement**.

> *Initialize variables*
> *Input, sum, and count the quiz grades*
> *Calculate and print the class average*

Here, only the sequence structure has been used—the steps listed are to be executed in order, one after the other.

Software Engineering Observation 3.3

Each refinement, as well as the top itself, is a complete specification of the algorithm; only the level of detail varies.

To proceed to the next level of refinement, i.e., the second refinement, we commit to specific variables. We need a running total of the numbers, a count of how many numbers have been processed, a variable to receive the value of each grade as it is input and a variable to hold the calculated average. The pseudocode statement

>*Initialize variables*

may be refined as follows:

>*Initialize total to zero*
>*Initialize counter to zero*

Notice that only total and counter need to be initialized; the variables average and grade (for the calculated average and the user input, respectively) need not be initialized because their values will be written over by the process of destructive read-in discussed in Chapter 2. The pseudocode statement

>*Input, sum, and count the quiz grades*

requires a repetition structure (i.e., a loop) that successively inputs each grade. Since we do not know in advance how many grades are to be processed, we will use sentinel-controlled repetition. The user will type legitimate grades in one at a time. After the last legitimate grade is typed, the user will type the sentinel value. The program will test for this value after each grade is input and will terminate the loop when the sentinel is entered. The refinement of the preceding pseudocode statement is then

>*Input the first grade*
>*While the user has not as yet entered the sentinel*
>>*Add this grade into the running total*
>>*Add one to the grade counter*
>>*Input the next grade (possibly the sentinel)*

Notice that in pseudocode, we do not use braces around the set of statements that form the body of the *while* statement. We simply indent all these statements under the *while* to show that they all belong to the *while*. Again, pseudocode is only an informal program development aid.

The pseudocode statement

>*Calculate and print the class average*

may be refined as follows:

>*If the counter is not equal to zero*
>>*Set the average to the total divided by the counter*
>>*Print the average*
>*else*
>>*Print "No grades were entered"*

Notice that we are being careful here to test for the possibility of division by zero—a fatal error that if undetected would cause the program to fail (often called "bombing" or "crashing"). The complete second refinement is shown in Fig. 3.7.

 Common Programming Error 3.7

An attempt to divide by zero causes a fatal error.

1	*Initialize total to zero*
2	*Initialize counter to zero*
3	
4	*Input the first grade*
5	*While the user has not as yet entered the sentinel*
6	*Add this grade into the running total*
7	*Add one to the grade counter*
8	*Input the next grade (possibly the sentinel)*
9	
10	*If the counter is not equal to zero*
11	*Set the average to the total divided by the counter*
12	*Print the average*
13	*else*
14	*Print "No grades were entered"*

Fig. 3.7 | Pseudocode algorithm that uses sentinel-controlled repetition to solve the class average problem.

Good Programming Practice 3.5

When performing division by an expression whose value could be zero, explicitly test for this case and handle it appropriately in your program (such as printing an error message) rather than allowing the fatal error to occur.

In Fig. 3.5 and Fig. 3.7, we include some completely blank lines in the pseudocode for readability. Actually, the blank lines separate these programs into their various phases.

Software Engineering Observation 3.4

Many programs can be divided logically into three phases: an initialization phase that initializes the program variables; a processing phase that inputs data values and adjusts program variables accordingly; and a termination phase that calculates and prints the final results.

The pseudocode algorithm in Fig. 3.7 solves the more general class averaging problem. This algorithm was developed after only two levels of refinement. Sometimes more levels are necessary.

Software Engineering Observation 3.5

You terminate the top-down, stepwise refinement process when the pseudocode algorithm is specified in sufficient detail for you to be able to convert the pseudocode to C. Implementing the C program is then normally straightforward.

The C program and a sample execution are shown in Fig. 3.8. Although only integer grades are entered, the averaging calculation is likely to produce a decimal number with a decimal point. The type `int` cannot represent such a number. The program introduces the data type **float** to handle numbers with decimal points (called floating-point numbers) and introduces a special operator called a **cast operator** to handle the averaging calculation. These features are explained in detail after the program is presented.

```
1    /* Fig. 3.8: fig03_08.c
2       Class average program with sentinel-controlled repetition */
3    #include <stdio.h>
4
5    /* function main begins program execution */
6    int main( void )
7    {
8       int counter; /* number of grades entered */
9       int grade;   /* grade value */
10      int total;   /* sum of grades */
11
12      float average; /* number with decimal point for average */
13
14      /* initialization phase */
15      total = 0;     /* initialize total */
16      counter = 0;   /* initialize loop counter */
17
18      /* processing phase */
19      /* get first grade from user */
20      printf( "Enter grade, -1 to end: " ); /* prompt for input */
21      scanf( "%d", &grade );                /* read grade from user */
22
23      /* loop while sentinel value not yet read from user */
24      while ( grade != -1 ) {
25         total = total + grade; /* add grade to total */
26         counter = counter + 1; /* increment counter */
27
28         /* get next grade from user */
29         printf( "Enter grade, -1 to end: "  /* prompt for input */
30         scanf("%d", &grade);                /* read next grade */
31      } /* end while */
32
33      /* termination phase */
34      /* if user entered at least one grade */
35      if ( counter != 0 ) {
36
37         /* calculate average of all grades entered */
38         average = ( float ) total / counter; /* avoid truncation */
39
40         /* display average with two digits of precision */
41         printf( "Class average is %.2f\n", average );
42      } /* end if */
43      else { /* if no grades were entered, output message */
44         printf( "No grades were entered\n" );
45      } /* end else */
46
47      return 0; /* indicate program ended successfully */
48
49   } /* end function main */
```

Fig. 3.8 | C program and sample execution for the class average problem with sentinel-controlled repetition. (Part I of 2.)

```
Enter grade, -1 to end: 75
Enter grade, -1 to end: 94
Enter grade, -1 to end: 97
Enter grade, -1 to end: 88
Enter grade, -1 to end: 70
Enter grade, -1 to end: 64
Enter grade, -1 to end: 83
Enter grade, -1 to end: 89
Enter grade, -1 to end: -1
Class average is 82.50
```

```
Enter grade, -1 to end: -1
No grades were entered
```

Fig. 3.8 | C program and sample execution for the class average problem with sentinel-controlled repetition. (Part 2 of 2.)

Notice the compound statement in the `while` loop (line 24) in Fig. 3.8 Once again, the braces are necessary for all four statements to be executed within the loop. Without the braces, the last three statements in the body of the loop would fall outside the loop, causing the computer to interpret this code incorrectly as follows.

```
while( grade != -1 )
    total = total + grade;              /* add grade to total */
counter = counter + 1;                  /* increment counter */
printf( "Enter grade, -1 to end: " );  /* prompt for input */
scanf( "%d", &grade );                  /* read next grade */
```

This would cause an infinite loop if the user did not input -1 for the first grade.

 Good Programming Practice 3.6

In a sentinel-controlled loop, the prompts requesting data entry should explicitly remind the user what the sentinel value is.

Averages do not always evaluate to integer values. Often, an average is a value such as 7.2 or –93.5 that contains a fractional part. These values are referred to as floating-point numbers and are represented by the data type `float`. The variable `average` is defined to be of type `float` (line 12) to capture the fractional result of our calculation. However, the result of the calculation `total / counter` is an integer because `total` and `counter` are both integer variables. Dividing two integers results in **integer division** in which any fractional part of the calculation is lost (i.e., **truncated**). Since the calculation is performed first, the fractional part is lost before the result is assigned to `average`. To produce a floating-point calculation with integer values, we must create temporary values that are floating-point numbers. C provides the unary **cast operator** to accomplish this task. Line 38

```
average = ( float ) total / counter;
```

includes the cast operator (float), which creates a temporary floating-point copy of its operand, total. The value stored in total is still an integer. Using a cast operator in this manner is called explicit conversion. The calculation now consists of a floating-point value (the temporary float version of total) divided by the integer value stored in counter. Most computers can evaluate arithmetic expressions only in which the data types of the operands are identical. To ensure that the operands are of the same type, the compiler performs an operation called promotion (also called implicit conversion) on selected operands. For example, in an expression containing the data types int and float, copies of int operands are made and promoted to float. In our example, after a copy of counter is made and promoted to float, the calculation is performed and the result of the floating-point division is assigned to average. C provides a set of rules for promotion of operands of different types. Chapter 5 presents a discussion of all the standard data types and their order of promotion.

Cast operators are available for most data types. The cast operator is formed by placing parentheses around a data type name. The cast operator is a unary operator, i.e., an operator that takes only one operand. In Chapter 2, we studied the binary arithmetic operators. C also supports unary versions of the plus (+) and minus (-) operators, so you can write expressions like -7 or +5. Cast operators associate from right to left and have the same precedence as other unary operators such as unary + and unary -. This precedence is one level higher than that of the multiplicative operators *, / and %.

Figure 3.8 uses the printf conversion specifier %.2f (line 41) to print the value of average. The f specifies that a floating-point value will be printed. The .2 is the precision with which the value will be displayed. It states that the value will be displayed with 2 digits to the right of the decimal point. If the %f conversion specifier is used (without specifying the precision), the default precision of 6 is used—exactly as if the conversion specifier %.6f had been used. When floating-point values are printed with precision, the printed value is rounded to the indicated number of decimal positions. The value in memory is unaltered. When the following statements are executed, the values 3.45 and 3.4 are printed.

```
printf( "%.2f\n", 3.446 );   /* prints 3.45 */
printf( "%.1f\n", 3.446 );   /* prints 3.4  */
```

Common Programming Error 3.8

Using precision in a conversion specification in the format control string of a scanf statement is wrong. Precisions are used only in printf conversion specifications.

Common Programming Error 3.9

Using floating-point numbers in a manner that assumes they are represented precisely can lead to incorrect results. Floating-point numbers are represented only approximately by most computers.

Error-Prevention Tip 3.3

Do not compare floating-point values for equality.

Despite the fact that floating-point numbers are not always "100% precise," they have numerous applications. For example, when we speak of a "normal" body temperature of

98.6, we do not need to be precise to a large number of digits. When we view the temperature on a thermometer and read it as 98.6, it may actually be 98.5999473210643. The point here is that calling this number simply 98.6 is fine for most applications. We will say more about this issue later.

Another way floating-point numbers develop is through division. When we divide 10 by 3, the result is 3.3333333… with the sequence of 3s repeating infinitely. The computer allocates only a fixed amount of space to hold such a value, so clearly the stored floating-point value can be only an approximation.

3.10 Formulating Algorithms with Top-Down, Stepwise Refinement Case Study 3: Nested Control Structures

Let us work another complete problem. We will once again formulate the algorithm using pseudocode and top-down, stepwise refinement, and write a corresponding C program. We have seen that control statements may be stacked on top of one another (in sequence) just as a child stacks building blocks. In this case study we will see the only other structured way control statements may be connected in C, namely through nesting of one control statement within another.

Consider the following problem statement:

> *A college offers a course that prepares students for the state licensing exam for real estate brokers. Last year, 10 of the students who completed this course took the licensing examination. Naturally, the college wants to know how well its students did on the exam. You have been asked to write a program to summarize the results. You have been given a list of these 10 students. Next to each name a 1 is written if the student passed the exam and a 2 if the student failed.*
>
> *Your program should analyze the results of the exam as follows:*
>
> 1. *Input each test result (i.e., a 1 or a 2). Display the prompting message "Enter result" each time the program requests another test result.*
>
> 2. *Count the number of test results of each type.*
>
> 3. *Display a summary of the test results indicating the number of students who passed and the number who failed.*
>
> 4. *If more than eight students passed the exam, print the message "Raise tuition."*

After reading the problem statement carefully, we make the following observations:

1. The program must process 10 test results. A counter-controlled loop will be used.

2. Each test result is a number—either a 1 or a 2. Each time the program reads a test result, the program must determine if the number is a 1 or a 2. We test for a 1 in our algorithm. If the number is not a 1, we assume that it is a 2. (An exercise at the end of the chapter considers the consequences of this assumption.)

3. Two counters are used—one to count the number of students who passed the exam and one to count the number of students who failed the exam.

4. After the program has processed all the results, it must decide if more than 8 students passed the exam.

Let us proceed with top-down, stepwise refinement. We begin with a pseudocode representation of the top:

Analyze exam results and decide if tuition should be raised

Once again, it is important to emphasize that the top is a complete representation of the program, but several refinements are likely to be needed before the pseudocode can be naturally evolved into a C program. Our first refinement is

Initialize variables
Input the ten quiz grades and count passes and failures
Print a summary of the exam results and decide if tuition should be raised

Here, too, even though we have a complete representation of the entire program, further refinement is necessary. We now commit to specific variables. Counters are needed to record the passes and failures, a counter will be used to control the looping process, and a variable is needed to store the user input. The pseudocode statement

Initialize variables

may be refined as follows:

Initialize passes to zero
Initialize failures to zero
Initialize student to one

Notice that only the counters and totals are initialized. The pseudocode statement

Input the ten quiz grades and count passes and failures

requires a loop that successively inputs the result of each exam. Here it is known in advance that there are precisely ten exam results, so counter-controlled looping is appropriate. Inside the loop (i.e., **nested** within the loop) a double-selection statement will determine whether each exam result is a pass or a failure, and will increment the appropriate counters accordingly. The refinement of the preceding pseudocode statement is then

While student counter is less than or equal to ten
    Input the next exam result

    If the student passed
       Add one to passes
    else
       Add one to failures

    Add one to student counter

Notice the use of blank lines to set off the *If...else* to improve program readability. The pseudocode statement

Print a summary of the exam results and decide if tuition should be raised

may be refined as follows:

Print the number of passes
Print the number of failures
If more than eight students passed
    Print "Raise tuition"

The complete second refinement appears in Fig. 3.9. Notice that blank lines are also used to set off the `while` statement for program readability.

This pseudocode is now sufficiently refined for conversion to C. The C program and two sample executions are shown in Fig. 3.10. Note that we have taken advantage of a feature of C that allows initialization to be incorporated into definitions. Such initialization occurs at compile time.

1	*Initialize passes to zero*
2	*Initialize failures to zero*
3	*Initialize student to one*
4	
5	*While student counter is less than or equal to ten*
6	*Input the next exam result*
7	
8	*If the student passed*
9	*Add one to passes*
10	*else*
11	*Add one to failures*
12	
13	*Add one to student counter*
14	
15	*Print the number of passes*
16	*Print the number of failures*
17	*If more than eight students passed*
18	*Print "Raise tuition"*

Fig. 3.9 | Pseudocode for examination results problem.

```
1   /* Fig. 3.10: fig03_10.c
2      Analysis of examination results */
3   #include <stdio.h>
4
5   /* function main begins program execution */
6   int main( void )
7   {
8      /* initialize variables in definitions */
9      int passes = 0;   /* number of passes */
10     int failures = 0; /* number of failures */
11     int student = 1;  /* student counter */
12     int result;       /* one exam result */
13
14     /* process 10 students using counter-controlled loop */
15     while ( student <= 10 ) {
16
17        /* prompt user for input and obtain value from user */
18        printf( "Enter result ( 1=pass,2=fail ): " );
19        scanf( "%d", &result );
20
```

Fig. 3.10 | C program and sample executions for examination results problem. (Part 1 of 2.)

```
21          /* if result 1, increment passes */
22          if ( result == 1 ) {
23             passes = passes + 1;
24          } /* end if */
25          else {/* otherwise, increment failures */
26             failures = failures + 1;
27          } /* end else */
28
29          student = student + 1; /* increment student counter */
30       } /* end while */
31
32       /* termination phase; display number of passes and failures */
33       printf( "Passed %d\n", passes );
34       printf( "Failed %d\n", failures );
35
36       /* if more than eight students passed, print "raise tuition" */
37       if ( passes > 8 ) {
38          printf( "Raise tuition\n" );
39       } /* end if */
40
41       return 0; /* indicate program ended successfully */
42
43    } /* end function main */
```

```
Enter Result (1=pass,2=fail): 1
Enter Result (1=pass,2=fail): 2
Enter Result (1=pass,2=fail): 2
Enter Result (1=pass,2=fail): 1
Enter Result (1=pass,2=fail): 1
Enter Result (1=pass,2=fail): 1
Enter Result (1=pass,2=fail): 2
Enter Result (1=pass,2=fail): 1
Enter Result (1=pass,2=fail): 1
Enter Result (1=pass,2=fail): 2
Passed 6
Failed 4
```

```
Enter Result (1=pass,2=fail): 1
Enter Result (1=pass,2=fail): 1
Enter Result (1=pass,2=fail): 1
Enter Result (1=pass,2=fail): 2
Enter Result (1=pass,2=fail): 1
Enter Result (1=pass,2=fail): 1
Enter Result (1=pass,2=fail): 1
Enter Result (1=pass,2=fail): 1
Enter Result (1=pass,2=fail): 1
Enter Result (1=pass,2=fail): 1
Passed 9
Failed 1
Raise tuition
```

Fig. 3.10 | C program and sample executions for examination results problem. (Part 2 of 2.)

Performance Tip 3.1

Initializing variables when they are defined can help reduce a program's execution time.

Performance Tip 3.2

Many of the performance tips we mention in this text result in nominal improvements, so the reader may be tempted to ignore them. Note that the cumulative effect of all these performance enhancements can make a program perform significantly faster. Also, significant improvement is realized when a supposedly nominal improvement is placed in a loop that may repeat a large number of times.

Software Engineering Observation 3.6

Experience has shown that the most difficult part of solving a problem on a computer is developing the algorithm for the solution. Once a correct algorithm has been specified, the process of producing a working C program is normally straightforward.

Software Engineering Observation 3.7

Many programmers write programs without ever using program development tools such as pseudocode. They feel that their ultimate goal is to solve the problem on a computer and that writing pseudocode merely delays the production of final outputs.

3.11 Assignment Operators

C provides several assignment operators for abbreviating assignment expressions. For example, the statement

```
c = c + 3;
```

can be abbreviated with the **addition assignment operator +=** as

```
c += 3;
```

The += operator adds the value of the expression on the right of the operator to the value of the variable on the left of the operator and stores the result in the variable on the left of the operator. Any statement of the form

variable = variable operator expression;

where *operator* is one of the binary operators +, -, *, / or % (or others we will discuss in Chapter 10), can be written in the form

variable operator= expression;

Thus the assignment c += 3 adds 3 to c. Figure 3.11 shows the arithmetic assignment operators, sample expressions using these operators and explanations.

3.12 Increment and Decrement Operators

C also provides the unary increment operator, ++, and the unary decrement operator, --, which are summarized in Fig. 3.12. If a variable c is incremented by 1, the increment

Assignment operator	Sample expression	Explanation	Assigns
Assume: `int c = 3, d = 5, e = 4, f = 6, g = 12;`			
`+=`	`c += 7`	`c = c + 7`	10 to c
`-=`	`d -= 4`	`d = d - 4`	1 to d
`*=`	`e *= 5`	`e = e * 5`	20 to e
`/=`	`f /= 3`	`f = f / 3`	2 to f
`%=`	`g %= 9`	`g = g % 9`	3 to g

Fig. 3.11 | Arithmetic assignment operators.

operator `++` can be used rather than the expressions `c = c + 1` or `c += 1`. If increment or decrement operators are placed before a variable (i.e., prefixed), they are referred to as the **preincrement** or **predecrement operators**, respectively. If increment or decrement operators are placed after a variable (i.e., postfixed), they are referred to as the **postincrement** or **postdecrement operators**, respectively. Preincrementing (predecrementing) a variable causes the variable to be incremented (decremented) by 1, then the new value of the variable is used in the expression in which it appears. Postincrementing (postdecrementing) the variable causes the current value of the variable to be used in the expression in which it appears, then the variable value is incremented (decremented) by 1.

Figure 3.13 demonstrates the difference between the preincrementing and the postincrementing versions of the `++` operator. Postincrementing the variable `c` causes it to be incremented after it is used in the `printf` statement. Preincrementing the variable `c` causes it to be incremented before it is used in the `printf` statement.

The program displays the value of `c` before and after the `++` operator is used. The decrement operator (`--`) works similarly.

Operator	Sample expression	Explanation
`++`	`++a`	Increment a by 1, then use the new value of a in the expression in which a resides.
`++`	`a++`	Use the current value of a in the expression in which a resides, then increment a by 1.
`--`	`--b`	Decrement b by 1, then use the new value of b in the expression in which b resides.
`--`	`b--`	Use the current value of b in the expression in which b resides, then decrement b by 1.

Fig. 3.12 | Increment and decrement operators

```
 1   /* Fig. 3.13: fig03_13.c
 2      Preincrementing and postincrementing */
 3   #include <stdio.h>
 4
 5   /* function main begins program execution */
 6   int main( void )
 7   {
 8      int c;                   /* define variable */
 9
10      /* demonstrate postincrement */
11      c = 5;                   /* assign 5 to c */
12      printf( "%d\n", c );     /* print 5 */
13      printf( "%d\n", c++ );   /* print 5 then postincrement */
14      printf( "%d\n\n", c );   /* print 6 */
15
16      /* demonstrate preincrement */
17      c = 5;                   /* assign 5 to c */
18      printf( "%d\n", c );     /* print 5 */
19      printf( "%d\n", ++c );   /* preincrement then print 6 */
20      printf( "%d\n", c );     /* print 6 */
21
22      return 0; /* indicate program ended successfully */
23
24   } /* end function main */
```

```
5
5
6

5
6
6
```

Fig. 3.13 | Preincrementing vs. postincrementing.

 Good Programming Practice 3.7

Unary operators should be placed directly next to their operands with no intervening spaces.

The three assignment statements in Fig. 3.10

```
passes = passes + 1;
failures = failures + 1;
student = student + 1;
```

can be written more concisely with assignment operators as

```
passes += 1;
failures += 1;
student += 1;
```

with preincrement operators as

```
++passes;
++failures;
++student;
```

or with postincrement operators as

```
passes++;
failures++;
student++;
```

It is important to note here that when incrementing or decrementing a variable in a statement by itself, the preincrement and postincrement forms have the same effect. It is only when a variable appears in the context of a larger expression that preincrementing and postincrementing have different effects (and similarly for predecrementing and post-decrementing). Of the expressions we have studied thus far, only a simple variable name may be used as the operand of an increment or decrement operator.

Common Programming Error 3.10

Attempting to use the increment or decrement operator on an expression other than a simple variable name is a syntax error, e.g., writing ++(x + 1).

Error-Prevention Tip 3.4

C generally does not specify the order in which an operator's operands will be evaluated (although we will see exceptions to this for a few operators in Chapter 4). Therefore you should avoid using statements with increment or decrement operators in which a particular variable being incremented or decremented appears more than once.

Figure 3.14 lists the precedence and associativity of the operators introduced to this point. The operators are shown top to bottom in decreasing order of precedence. The second column describes the associativity of the operators at each level of precedence. Notice that the conditional operator (?:), the unary operators increment (++), decrement (--), plus (+), minus (-) and casts, and the assignment operators =, +=, -=, *=, /= and %= associate from right to left. The third column names the various groups of operators. All other operators in Fig. 3.14 associate from left to right.

Operators	Associativity	Type
++ *(postfix)* -- *(postfix)*	right to left	postfix
+ - *(type)* ++ *(prefix)* -- *(prefix)*	right to left	unary
* / %	left to right	multiplicative
+ -	left to right	additive
< <= > >=	left to right	relational
== !=	left to right	equality
?:	right to left	conditional
= += -= *= /= %=	right to left	assignment

Fig. 3.14 | Precedence and associativity of the operators encountered so far in the text.

Summary

Section 3.1 Introduction
- Before writing a program to solve a particular problem, it is essential to have a thorough understanding of the problem and a carefully planned approach to solving the problem.

Section 3.2 Algorithms
- The solution to any computing problem involves executing a series of actions in a specific order.
- A procedure for solving a problem in terms of the actions to be executed, and the order in which these actions are to be executed, is called an algorithm.
- The order in which actions are to be executed is important.

Section 3.3 Pseudocode
- Pseudocode is an artificial and informal language that helps you develop algorithms.
- Pseudocode is similar to everyday English; it is convenient and user friendly although it is not an actual computer programming language.
- Pseudocode programs are not executed on computers. Rather, they merely help you "think out" a program before attempting to write it in a programming language such as C.
- Pseudocode consists purely of characters, so you may conveniently type pseudocode programs into a computer using an editor program.
- Carefully prepared pseudocode programs may be converted easily to corresponding C programs.
- Pseudocode consists only of action statements—those that are executed when the program has been converted from pseudocode to C and is run in C. Definitions are not executable statements. They are messages to the compiler.
- Some programmers choose to list each variable and briefly mention the purpose of each at the beginning of a pseudocode program.

Section 3.4 Control Structures
- Normally, statements in a program execute one after the other in the order in which they are written. This is called sequential execution.
- Various C statements enable you to specify that the next statement to execute may be other than the next one in sequence. This is called transfer of control.
- During the 1960s, it became clear that the indiscriminate use of transfers of control was the root of a great deal of difficulty experienced by software development groups. The problem was the goto statement. The notion of so-called structured programming became almost synonymous with "goto elimination."
- The research of Bohm and Jacopini demonstrated that programs could be written without any goto statements.
- Programs produced with structured techniques are clearer, easier to debug and modify and more likely to be bug free.
- Bohm and Jacopini demonstrated that all programs could be written in terms of only three control structures—the sequence structure, the selection structure and the repetition structure.
- The sequence structure is essentially built into C. Unless directed otherwise, the computer automatically executes C statements one after the other in the order in which they are written.
- A flowchart is a graphical representation of an algorithm or of a portion of an algorithm. Flowcharts are drawn using certain special-purpose symbols such as rectangles, diamonds, ovals, and small circles; these symbols are connected by arrows called flowlines.

- Like pseudocode, flowcharts are useful for developing and representing algorithms, although pseudocode is preferred by most programmers.

- The rectangle symbol, also called the action symbol, indicates any type of action including a calculation or an input/output operation.

- Flowlines indicate the order in which the actions are performed.

- When drawing a flowchart that represents a complete algorithm, an oval symbol containing the word "Begin" is the first symbol used in the flowchart; an oval symbol containing the word "End" is the last symbol used. When drawing only a portion of an algorithm, the oval symbols are omitted in favor of using small circle symbols also called connector symbols.

- Perhaps the most important flowcharting symbol is the diamond symbol, also called the decision symbol, which indicates that a decision is to be made.

- C provides three types of selection structures in the form of statements. The `if` selection statement either performs (selects) an action if a condition is true or skips the action if the condition is false. The `if...else` selection statement performs an action if a condition is true and performs a different action if the condition is false. The `switch` selection statement performs one of many different actions depending on the value of an expression.

- The `if` statement is called a single-selection statement because it selects or ignores a single action.

- The `if...else` statement is called a double-selection statement because it selects between two different actions.

- The `switch` statement is called a multiple-selection statement because it selects among many different actions.

- C provides three types of repetition structures in the form of statements, namely `while`, `do...while` and `for`.

- The flowchart representation of each control statement has two small circle symbols, one at the entry point to the control statement and one at the exit point.

- Control statement flowchart segments can be attached to one another with control-statement stacking—connecting the exit point of one control statement to the entry point of the next.

- There is only one other way control statements may be connected—control-statement nesting.

Section 3.5 The `if` Selection Statement

- Selection structures are used to choose among alternative courses of action.

- The most important flowcharting symbol—the diamond symbol, also called the decision symbol—indicates that a decision is to be made.

- The decision symbol contains an expression, such as a condition, that can be either true or false. The decision symbol has two flowlines emerging from it. One indicates the direction to be taken when the expression in the symbol is true; the other indicates the direction to be taken when the expression is false.

- A decision can be based on any expression—if the expression evaluates to zero, it is treated as false, and if the expression evaluates to nonzero, it is treated as true.

- The `if` statement is a single-entry/single-exit structure.

Section 3.6 The `if...else` Selection Statement

- The `if` selection statement performs an indicated action only when the condition is true; otherwise the action is skipped. The `if...else` selection statement allows you to specify that different actions are to be performed when the condition is true than when the condition is false.

- C provides the conditional operator (`?:`) which is closely related to the `if...else` statement.

- The conditional operator is C's only ternary operator—it takes three operands. The operands together with the conditional operator form a conditional expression. The first operand is a condition. The second operand is the value for the entire conditional expression if the condition is true, and the third operand is the value for the entire conditional expression if the condition is false.

- The values in a conditional expression can also be actions to execute.

- Nested `if...else` statements test for multiple cases by placing `if...else` statements inside `if...else` statements.

- The `if` selection statement expects only one statement in its body. To include several statements in the body of an `if`, enclose the set of statements in braces (`{` and `}`).

- A set of statements contained within a pair of braces is called a compound statement or a block.

- A syntax error is caught by the compiler. A logic error has its effect at execution time. A fatal logic error causes a program to fail and terminate prematurely. A nonfatal logic error allows a program to continue executing but to produce incorrect results.

Section 3.7 The `while` Repetition Statement

- The `while` repetition statement allows you to specify that an action is to be repeated while some condition remains true.

- Eventually, the condition will become false. At this point, the repetition terminates, and the first statement after the repetition statement executes.

Section 3.8 Formulating Algorithms Case Study 1: Counter-Controlled Repetition

- Counter-controlled repetition uses a variable called a counter to specify the number of times a set of statements should execute.

- Counter-controlled repetition is often called definite repetition because the number of repetitions is known before the loop begins executing.

- A total is a variable used to accumulate the sum of a series of values.

- A counter is a variable used to count. Variables used to store totals should normally be initialized to zero before being used in a program; otherwise the sum would include the previous value stored in the total's memory location.

- Counter variables are normally initialized to zero or one, depending on their use.

- An uninitialized variable contains a "garbage" value—the value last stored in the memory location reserved for that variable.

Section 3.9 Formulating Algorithms with Top-Down, Stepwise Refinement Case Study 2: Sentinel-Controlled Repetition

- A sentinel value (also called a signal value, a dummy value, or a flag value) is used in a sentinel-controlled loop to indicate the "end of data entry."

- Sentinel-controlled repetition is often called indefinite repetition because the number of repetitions is not known before the loop begins executing.

- The sentinel value must be chosen so that it cannot be confused with an acceptable input value.

- Top-down, stepwise refinement is a technique that is essential to the development of well-structured programs.

- The top is a single statement that conveys the program's overall function. As such, the top is, in effect, a complete representation of a program. Unfortunately, the top rarely conveys a sufficient amount of detail for writing a C program. So, in the refinement process, we divide the top into a series of smaller tasks and list these in the order in which they need to be performed.

- The type float represents numbers with decimal points (called floating-point numbers).

- Dividing two integers results in integer division, in which any fractional part of the calculation is lost (i.e., truncated).

- To produce a floating-point calculation with integer values, you must cast the integers to floating-point numbers. C provides the unary cast operator (float) to accomplish this task.

- Cast operators perform explicit conversions.

- Most computers can evaluate arithmetic expressions only in which the operands' data types are identical. To ensure this, the compiler performs an operation called promotion (also called implicit conversion) on selected operands. For example, in an expression containing the data types int and float, copies of int operands are made and promoted to float.

- Cast operators are available for most data types. A cast operator is formed by placing parentheses around a data type name. The cast operator is a unary operator, i.e., it takes only one operand.

- Cast operators associate from right to left and have the same precedence as other unary operators such as unary + and unary -. This precedence is one level higher than that of *, / and %.

- The printf conversion specifier %.2f specifies that a floating-point value will be displayed with two digits to the right of the decimal point. If the %f conversion specifier is used (without specifying the precision), the default precision of 6 is used.

- When floating-point values are printed with precision, the printed value is rounded to the indicated number of decimal positions for display purposes.

Section 3.11 Assignment Operators

- C provides several assignment operators for abbreviating assignment expressions.

- The += operator adds the value of the expression on the right of the operator to the value of the variable on the left of the operator and stores the result in the variable on the left of the operator.

- Any statement of the form

  variable = variable operator expression;

  where *operator* is one of the binary operators +, -, *, / or % (or others we will discuss in Chapter 10), can be written in the form

  variable operator= expression;

Section 3.12 Increment and Decrement Operators

- C provides the unary increment operator, ++, and the unary decrement operator, --.

- If increment or decrement operators are placed before a variable, they are referred to as the preincrement or predecrement operators, respectively. If increment or decrement operators are placed after a variable, they are referred to as the postincrement or postdecrement operators, respectively.

- Preincrementing (predecrementing) a variable causes the variable to be incremented (decremented) by 1, then the new value of the variable is used in the expression in which it appears.

- Postincrementing (postdecrementing) a variable uses the current value of the variable in the expression in which it appears, then the variable value is incremented (decremented) by 1.

- It is important to note here that when incrementing or decrementing a variable in a statement by itself, the preincrement and postincrement forms have the same effect. It is only when a variable appears in the context of a larger expression that preincrementing and postincrementing have different effects (and similarly for predecrementing and postdecrementing).

- Of the expressions we have studied so far, only a simple variable name may be used as the operand of an increment or decrement operator.

Terminology

+=, -=, *=, /=, and %=
"bombing"
"crashing"
"end of data entry"
"garbage" value
action
action symbol
algorithm
arithmetic assignment operators:
arrow symbol
block
body of a loop
cast operator
compound statement
conditional expression
conditional operator (?:)
connector symbol
control structure
counter
counter-controlled repetition
decision
decision symbol
decrement operator (--)
default precision
definite repetition
diamond symbol
division by zero
double-selection statement
dummy value
empty statement (;)
end symbol
explicit conversion
fatal error
first refinement
flag value
`float`
floating-point number
flowchart
flowchart symbol
flowline
`goto` elimination
`goto` statement
`if` selection statement
`if...else` selection statement
implicit conversion
increment operator (++)
indefinite repetition
infinite loop
initialization

initialization phase
integer division
logic error
looping
multiple-selection statement
multiplicative operators
nested control structures
nested `if...else` statements
nonfatal error
order of actions
oval symbol
postdecrement operator
postincrement operator
precision
predecrement operator
preincrement operator
processing phase
program control
promotion
pseudocode
rectangle symbol
repetition
repetition structures
rounding
second refinement
selection
selection structures
sentinel value
sequence structure
sequential execution
signal value
single-entry/single-exit control structure
single-selection statement
stacked control structures
steps
stepwise refinement
structured programming
syntax error
terminating condition
termination phase
termination symbol
ternary operator
top
top-down, stepwise refinement
total
transfer of control
truncation
`while` repetition statement
white-space characters

Self-Review Exercises

3.1 Fill in the blanks in each of the following questions.

a) A procedure for solving a problem in terms of the actions to be executed and the order in which the actions should be executed is called a(n) _____.

b) Specifying the execution order of statements by the computer is called _____.

c) All programs can be written in terms of three types of control statements: _____, _____ and _____.

d) The _____ selection statement is used to execute one action when a condition is true and another action when that condition is false.

e) Several statements grouped together in braces ({ and }) are called a(n) _____.

f) The _____ repetition statement specifies that a statement or group of statements is to be executed repeatedly while some condition remains true.

g) Repetition of a set of instructions a specific number of times is called _____ repetition.

h) When it is not known in advance how many times a set of statements will be repeated, a(n) _____ value can be used to terminate the repetition.

3.2 Write four different C statements that each add 1 to integer variable x.

3.3 Write a single C statement to accomplish each of the following:

a) Assign the sum of x and y to z and increment the value of x by 1 after the calculation.

b) Multiply the variable product by 2 using the *= operator.

c) Multiply the variable product by 2 using the = and * operators.

d) Test if the value of the variable count is greater than 10. If it is, print "Count is greater than 10."

e) Decrement the variable x by 1, then subtract it from the variable total.

f) Add the variable x to the variable total, then decrement x by 1.

g) Calculate the remainder after q is divided by divisor and assign the result to q. Write this statement two different ways.

h) Print the value 123.4567 with 2 digits of precision. What value is printed?

i) Print the floating-point value 3.14159 with three digits to the right of the decimal point. What value is printed?

3.4 Write a C statement to accomplish each of the following tasks.

a) Define variables sum and x to be of type int.

b) Initialize variable x to 1.

c) Initialize variable sum to 0.

d) Add variable x to variable sum and assign the result to variable sum.

e) Print "The sum is: " followed by the value of variable sum.

3.5 Combine the statements that you wrote in Exercise 3.4 into a program that calculates the sum of the integers from 1 to 10. Use the while statement to loop through the calculation and increment statements. The loop should terminate when the value of x becomes 11.

3.6 Determine the values of variables product and x after the following calculation is performed. Assume that product and x each have the value 5 when the statement begins executing.

```
product *= x++;
```

3.7 Write single C statements that

a) Input integer variable x with scanf.

b) Input integer variable y with scanf.

c) Initialize integer variable i to 1.

d) Initialize integer variable power to 1.

e) Multiply variable power by x and assign the result to power.

f) Increment variable i by 1.

g) Test i to see if it is less than or equal to y in the condition of a `while` statement.

h) Output integer variable power with `printf`.

3.8 Write a C program that uses the statements in Exercise 3.7 to calculate x raised to the y power. The program should have a `while` repetition control statement.

3.9 Identify and correct the errors in each of the following:

a)
```
while ( c <= 5 ) {
    product *= c;
    ++c;
```

b) `scanf( "%.4f", &value );`

c)
```
if ( gender == 1 )
    printf( "Woman\n" );
else;
    printf( "Man\n" );
```

3.10 What is wrong with the following `while` repetition statement (assume z has value 100), which is supposed to calculate the sum of the integers from 100 down to 1:

```
while ( z >= 0 )
    sum += z;
```

Answers to Self-Review Exercises

3.1 a) Algorithm. b) Program control. c) Sequence, selection, repetition. d) `if...else`. e) Compound statement. f) `while`. g) Counter-controlled. h) Sentinel.

3.2
```
x = x + 1;
x += 1;
++x;
x++;
```

3.3
a) `z = x++ + y;`
b) `product *= 2;`
c) `product = product * 2;`
d)
```
if ( count > 10 )
    printf( "Count is greater than 10.\n" );
```
e) `total -= --x;`
f) `total += x--;`
g)
```
q %= divisor;
q = q % divisor;
```
h) `printf( "%.2f", 123.4567 );`
   `123.46` is displayed.
i) `printf( "%.3f\n", 3.14159 );`
   `3.142` is displayed.

3.4
a) `int sum, x;`
b) `x = 1;`
c) `sum = 0;`
d) `sum += x;` or `sum = sum + x;`
e) `printf( "The sum is: %d\n", sum );`

3.5 See top of next page.

```
1   /* Calculate the sum of the integers from 1 to 10 */
2   #include <stdio.h>
3
4   int main( void )
5   {
6       int sum, x; /* define variables sum and x */
7
8       x = 1;   /* initialize x */
9       sum = 0; /* initialize sum */
10
11      while ( x <= 10 ) { /* loop while x is less than or equal to 10 */
12         sum += x; /* add x to sum */
13         ++x; /* increment x */
14      } /* end while */
15
16      printf( "The sum is: %d\n", sum ); /* display sum */
17
18      return 0;
19  } /* end main function */
```

3.6   product = 25, x = 6;

3.7   a) scanf("%d", &x);
         b) scanf("%d", &y);
         c) i = 1;
         d) power = 1;
         e) power *= x;
         f) i++;
         g) if (i <= y)
         h) printf("%d", power);

3.8   See below.

```
1   /* raise x to the y power */
2   #include <stdio.h>
3
4   int main( void )
5   {
6      int x, y, i, power; /* define variables */
7
8      i = 1;     /* initialize i */
9      power = 1; /* initialize power */
10     scanf( "%d", &x ); /* read value for x from user */
11     scanf( "%d", &y ); /* read value for y from user */
12
13     while ( i <= y ) { /* loop while i is less than or equal to y */
14        power *= x; /* multiply power by x */
15        ++i; /* increment i */
16     } /* end while */
17
18     printf( "%d", power ); /* display power */
19
20     return 0;
21  } /* end main function */
```

3.9   a)   Error: Missing the closing right brace of the `while` body.
Correction: Add closing right brace after the statement `++c;`.

         b)   Error: Precision used in a `scanf` conversion specification.
Correction: Remove `.4` from the conversion specification.

         c)   Error: Semicolon after the `else` part of the `if...else` statement results in a logic error. The second `printf` will always be executed.
Correction: Remove the semicolon after `else`.

3.10   The value of the variable `z` is never changed in the `while` statement. Therefore, an infinite loop is created. To prevent the infinite loop, z must be decremented so that it eventually becomes 0.

Exercises

3.11   Identify and correct the errors in each of the following. [*Note:* There may be more than one error in each piece of code.]

         a)
```
if ( age >= 65 );
    printf( "Age is greater than or equal to 65\n" );
else
    printf( "Age is less than 65\n" );
```

         b)
```
int x = 1, total;

while ( x <= 10 ) {
   total += x;
   ++x;
}
```

         c)
```
While ( x <= 100 )
   total += x;
   ++x;
```

         d)
```
while ( y > 0 ) {
   printf( "%d\n", y );
   ++y;
}
```

3.12   Fill in the blanks in each of the following:

         a)   The solution to any problem involves performing a series of actions in a specific _____.

         b)   A synonym for procedure is _____.

         c)   A variable that accumulates the sum of several numbers is a(n) _____.

         d)   The process of setting certain variables to specific values at the beginning of a program is called _____.

         e)   A special value used to indicate "end of data entry" is called a(n) _____, a(n) _____, a(n) _____ or a(n) _____ value.

         f)   A(n) _____ is a graphical representation of an algorithm.

         g)   In a flowchart, the order in which the steps should be performed is indicated by _____ symbols.

         h)   The termination symbol indicates the _____ and _____ of every algorithm.

         i)   Rectangle symbols correspond to calculations that are normally performed b _____ statements and input/output operations that are normally performed ' calls to the_____ and _____ Standard Library functions.

         j)   The item written inside a decision symbol is called a(n) _____.

3.13   What does the following program print?

```
1    #include <stdio.h>
2
3    int main( void )
4    {
5       int x = 1, total = 0, y;
6
7       while ( x <= 10 ) {
8          y = x * x;
9          printf( "%d\n", y );
10         total += y;
11         ++x;
12      }
13
14      printf("Total is %d\n", total);
15
16      return 0;
17   }
```

3.14   Write a single pseudocode statement that indicates each of the following:
a) Display the message "Enter two numbers".
b) Assign the sum of variables x, y, and z to variable p.
c) The following condition is to be tested in an if...else selection statement: The current value of variable m is greater than twice the current value of variable v.
d) Obtain values for variables s, r, and t from the keyboard.

3.15   Formulate a pseudocode algorithm for each of the following:
a) Obtain two numbers from the keyboard, compute the sum of the numbers and display the result.
b) Obtain two numbers from the keyboard, and determine and display which (if either) is the larger of the two numbers.
c) Obtain a series of positive numbers from the keyboard, and determine and display the sum of the numbers. Assume that the user types the sentinel value -1 to indicate "end of data entry."

3.16   State which of the following are *true* and which are *false*. If a statement is *false*, explain why.
a) Experience has shown that the most difficult part of solving a problem on a computer is producing a working C program.
b) A sentinel value must be a value that cannot be confused with a legitimate data value.
c) Flowlines indicate the actions to be performed.
d) Conditions written inside decision symbols always contain arithmetic operators (i.e., +, -, *, /, and %).
e) In top-down, stepwise refinement, each refinement is a complete representation of the algorithm.

For Exercises 3.17 to 3.21, perform each of these steps:

1. Read the problem statement.
2. Formulate the algorithm using pseudocode and top-down, stepwise refinement.
3. Write a C program.
4. Test, debug and execute the C program.

3.17   Drivers are concerned with the mileage obtained by their automobiles. One driver has kept track of several tankfuls of gasoline by recording miles driven and gallons used for each tankful. Develop a program that will input the miles driven and gallons used for each tankful. The program should calculate and display the miles per gallon obtained for each tankful. After processing all input information, the program should calculate and print the combined miles per gallon obtained for all tankfuls. Here is a sample input/output dialog:

```
Enter the gallons used (-1 to end): 12.8
Enter the miles driven: 287
The miles / gallon for this tank was 22.421875

Enter the gallons used (-1 to end): 10.3
Enter the miles driven: 200
The miles / gallon for this tank was 19.417475

Enter the gallons used (-1 to end): 5
Enter the miles driven: 120
The miles / gallon for this tank was 24.000000

Enter the gallons used (-1 to end): -1

The overall average miles/gallon was 21.601423
```

3.18   Develop a C program that will determine if a department store customer has exceeded the credit limit on a charge account. For each customer, the following facts are available:
  a) Account number
  b) Balance at the beginning of the month
  c) Total of all items charged by this customer this month
  d) Total of all credits applied to this customer's account this month
  e) Allowed credit limit

The program should input each of these facts, calculate the new balance (= *beginning balance + charges – credits*), and determine if the new balance exceeds the customer's credit limit. For those customers whose credit limit is exceeded, the program should display the customer's account number, credit limit, new balance and the message "Credit limit exceeded." Here is a sample input/output dialog:

```
Enter account number (-1 to end): 100
Enter beginning balance: 5394.78
Enter total charges: 1000.00
Enter total credits: 500.00
Enter credit limit: 5500.00
Account:      100
Credit limit: 5500.00
Balance:      5894.78
Credit Limit Exceeded.


Enter account number (-1 to end): 200
Enter beginning balance: 1000.00
Enter total charges: 123.45
Enter total credits: 321.00
Enter credit limit: 1500.00
```

(continued at top of next page...)

```
Enter account number (-1 to end): 300
Enter beginning balance: 500.00
Enter total charges: 274.73
Enter total credits: 100.00
Enter credit limit: 800.00


Enter account number (-1 to end): -1
```

3.19   One large chemical company pays its salespeople on a commission basis. The salespeople receive $200 per week plus 9% of their gross sales for that week. For example, a salesperson who sells $5000 worth of chemicals in a week receives $200 plus 9% of $5000, or a total of $650. Develop a program that will input each salesperson's gross sales for last week and will calculate and display that salesperson's earnings. Process one salesperson's figures at a time. Here is a sample input/output dialog:

```
Enter sales in dollars (-1 to end): 5000.00
Salary is: $650.00


Enter sales in dollars (-1 to end): 1234.56
Salary is: $311.11


Enter sales in dollars (-1 to end): 1088.89
Salary is: $298.00


Enter sales in dollars (-1 to end): -1
```

3.20   The simple interest on a loan is calculated by the formula

```
interest = principal * rate * days / 365;
```

The preceding formula assumes that rate is the annual interest rate, and therefore includes the division by 365 (days). Develop a program that will input principal, rate and days for several loans, and will calculate and display the simple interest for each loan, using the preceding formula. Here is a sample input/output dialog:

```
Enter loan principal (-1 to end): 1000.00
Enter interest rate: .1
Enter term of the loan in days: 365
The interest charge is $100.00


Enter loan principal (-1 to end): 1000.00
Enter interest rate: .08375
Enter term of the loan in days: 224
The interest charge is $51.40


Enter loan principal (-1 to end): 10000.00
Enter interest rate: .09
Enter term of the loan in days: 1460
The interest charge is $3600.00


Enter loan principal (-1 to end): -1
```

3.21   Develop a program that will determine the gross pay for each of several employees. The company pays "straight time" for the first 40 hours worked by each employee and pays "time-and-a-half" for all hours worked in excess of 40 hours. You are given a list of the employees of the company, the number of hours each employee worked last week and the hourly rate of each employee. Your program should input this information for each employee, and should determine and display the employee's gross pay. Here is a sample input/output dialog:

```
Enter # of hours worked (-1 to end): 39
Enter hourly rate of the worker ($00.00): 10.00
Salary is $390.00

Enter # of hours worked (-1 to end): 40
Enter hourly rate of the worker ($00.00): 10.00
Salary is $400.00

Enter # of hours worked (-1 to end): 41
Enter hourly rate of the worker ($00.00): 10.00
Salary is $415.00

Enter # of hours worked (-1 to end): -1
```

3.22   Write a program that demonstrates the difference between predecrementing and postdecrementing using the decrement operator --.

3.23   Write a program that utilizes looping to print the numbers from 1 to 10 side by side on the same line with three spaces between numbers.

3.24   The process of finding the largest number (i.e., the maximum of a group of numbers) is used frequently in computer applications. For example, a program that determines the winner of a sales contest would input the number of units sold by each salesperson. The salesperson who sold the most units wins the contest. Write a pseudocode program and then a program that inputs a series of 10 numbers and determines and prints the largest of the numbers. [*Hint:* Your program should use three variables as follows]:

counter:	A counter to count to 10 (i.e., to keep track of how many numbers have been input and to determine when all 10 numbers have been processed)
number:	The current number input to the program
largest:	The largest number found so far

3.25   Write a program that utilizes looping to print the following table of values:

N	10*N	100*N	1000*N
1	10	100	1000
2	20	200	2000
3	30	300	3000
4	40	400	4000
5	50	500	5000
6	60	600	6000
7	70	700	7000
8	80	800	8000
9	90	900	9000
10	100	1000	10000

The tab escape sequence, \t, may be used in the printf statement to separate the columns with tabs.

3.26   Write a program that utilizes looping to produce the following table of values:

A	A+2	A+4	A+6
3	5	7	9
6	8	10	12
9	11	13	15
12	14	16	18
15	17	19	21

3.27   Using an approach similar to Exercise 3.24, find the *two* largest values of the 10 numbers. [*Note:* You may input each number only once.]

3.28   Modify the program in Figure 3.10 to validate its inputs. On any input, if the value entered is other than 1 or 2, keep looping until the user enters a correct value.

3.29   What does the following program print?

```
1   #include <stdio.h>
2
3   /* function main begins program execution */
4   int main( void )
5   {
6      int count = 1; /* initialize count */
7
8      while ( count <= 10 ) { /* loop 10 times */
9
10        /* output line of text */
11        printf( "%s\n", count % 2 ? "****" : "++++++++" );
12        count++; /* increment count */
13     } /* end while */
14
15     return 0; /* indicate program ended successfully */
16
17  } /* end function main */
```

3.30   What does the following program print?

```
1   #include <stdio.h>
2
3   /* function main begins program execution */
4   int main( void )
5   {
6      int row = 10; /* initialize row */
7      int column;   /* define column */
8
9      while ( row >= 1 ) { /* loop until row < 1 */
10        column = 1;        /* set column to 1 as iteration begins */
```

```
11
12          while ( column <= 10 ) {              /* loop 10 times */
13              printf( "%s", row % 2 ? "<": ">" ); /* output */
14              column++;                         /* increment column */
15          } /* end inner while */
16
17          row--;              /* decrement row */
18          printf( "\n" ); /* begin new output line */
19      } /* end outer while */
20
21      return 0; /* indicate program ended successfully */
22
23  } /* end function main */
```

3.31 *(Dangling Else Problem)* Determine the output for each of the following when x is 9 and y is 11, and when x is 11 and y is 9. Note that the compiler ignores the indentation in a C program. Also, the compiler always associates an else with the previous if unless told to do otherwise by the placement of braces {}. Because, on first glance, you may not be sure which if an else matches, this is referred to as the "dangling else" problem. We eliminated the indentation from the following code to make the problem more challenging. [*Hint:* Apply indentation conventions you have learned.]

a)
```
if ( x < 10 )
if ( y > 10 )
printf( "*****\n" );
else
printf( "#####\n" );
printf( "$$$$$\n" );
```

b)
```
if ( x < 10 ) {
if ( y > 10 )
printf( "*****\n" );
}
else {
printf( "#####\n" );
printf( "$$$$$\n" );
}
```

3.32 *(Another Dangling Else Problem)* Modify the following code to produce the output shown. Use proper indentation techniques. You may not make any changes other than inserting braces. The compiler ignores the indentation in a program. We eliminated the indentation from the following code to make the problem more challenging. [*Note:* It is possible that no modification is necessary.]

```
if ( y == 8 )
if ( x == 5 )
printf( "@@@@@\n" );
else
printf( "#####\n" );
printf( "$$$$$\n" );
printf( "&&&&&\n" );
```

a) Assuming x = 5 and y = 8, the following output is produced.

```
@@@@@
$$$$$
&&&&&
```

b) Assuming x = 5 and y = 8, the following output is produced.

```
@@@@@
```

c) Assuming x = 5 and y = 8, the following output is produced.

```
@@@@@
&&&&
```

d) Assuming x = 5 and y = 7, the following output is produced. [*Note:* The last three `printf` statements are all part of a compound statement.]

```
#####
$$$$$
&&&&
```

3.33 Write a program that reads in the side of a square and then prints that square out of asterisks. Your program should work for squares of all side sizes between 1 and 20. For example, if your program reads a size of 4, it should print

```
****
****
****
****
```

3.34 Modify the program you wrote in Exercise 3.33 so that it prints a hollow square. For example, if your program reads a size of 5, it should print

```
*****
*   *
*   *
*   *
*****
```

3.35 A palindrome is a number or a text phrase that reads the same backward as forward. For example, each of the following five-digit integers is a palindrome: 12321, 55555, 45554 and 11611. Write a program that reads in a five-digit integer and determines whether or not it is a palindrome. [*Hint:* Use the division and remainder operators to separate the number into its individual digits.]

3.36 Input an integer containing only 0s and 1s (i.e., a "binary" integer) and print its decimal equivalent. [*Hint:* Use the remainder and division operators to pick off the "binary" number's digits one at a time from right to left. Just as in the decimal number system, in which the rightmost digit has a positional value of 1, and the next digit left has a positional value of 10, then 100, then 1000, and so on, in the binary number system the rightmost digit has a positional value of 1, the next digit left has a positional value of 2, then 4, then 8, and so on. Thus the decimal number 234 can be interpreted as 4 * 1 + 3 * 10 + 2 * 100. The decimal equivalent of binary 1101 is 1 * 1 + 0 * 2 + 1 * 4 + 1 * 8 or 1 + 0 + 4 + 8 or 13.]

3.37   How can you determine how fast your own computer really operates? Write a program with a `while` loop that counts from 1 to 300,000,000 by 1s. Every time the count reaches a multiple of 100,000,000, print that number on the screen. Use your watch to time how long each 100 million repetitions of the loop takes.

3.38   Write a program that prints 100 asterisks, one at a time. After every tenth asterisk, your program should print a newline character. [*Hint:* Count from 1 to 100. Use the remainder operator to recognize each time the counter reaches a multiple of 10.]

3.39   Write a program that reads an integer and determines and prints how many digits in the integer are 7s.

3.40   Write a program that displays the following checkerboard pattern:

```
* * * * * * * *
 * * * * * * * *
* * * * * * * *
 * * * * * * * *
* * * * * * * *
 * * * * * * * *
* * * * * * * *
 * * * * * * * *
```

Your program must use only three output statements, one of each of the following forms:

```
printf( "* " );
printf( " " );
printf( "\n" );
```

3.41   Write a program that keeps printing the multiples of the integer 2, namely 2, 4, 8, 16, 32, 64, and so on. Your loop should not terminate (i.e., you should create an infinite loop). What happens when you run this program?

3.42   Write a program that reads the radius of a circle (as a `float` value) and computes and prints the diameter, the circumference and the area. Use the value 3.14159 for π.

3.43   What is wrong with the following statement? Rewrite the statement to accomplish what the programmer was probably trying to do.

```
printf( "%d", ++( x + y ) );
```

3.44   Write a program that reads three nonzero `float` values and determines and prints if they could represent the sides of a triangle.

3.45   Write a program that reads three nonzero integers and determines and prints if they could be the sides of a right triangle.

3.46   A company wants to transmit data over the telephone, but they are concerned that their phones may be tapped. All of their data is transmitted as four-digit integers. They have asked you to write a program that will encrypt their data so that it may be transmitted more securely. Your program should read a four-digit integer and encrypt it as follows: Replace each digit by the remainder after the sum of that digit plus 7 is divided by 10. Then swap the first digit with the third, and swap the second digit with the fourth. Then print the encrypted integer. Write a separate program that inputs an encrypted four-digit integer and decrypts it to form the original number.

3.47   The factorial of a nonnegative integer n is written $n!$ (pronounced "n factorial") and is defined as follows:

$$n! = n \cdot (n - 1) \cdot (n - 2) \cdot \ldots \cdot 1 \quad \text{(for values of } n \text{ greater than or equal to 1)}$$

and

$$n! = 1 \quad \text{(for } n = 0).$$

For example, $5! = 5 \cdot 4 \cdot 3 \cdot 2 \cdot 1$, which is 120.

a) Write a program that reads a nonnegative integer and computes and prints its factorial.

b) Write a program that estimates the value of the mathematical constant e by using the formula:

$$e = 1 + \frac{1}{1!} + \frac{1}{2!} + \frac{1}{3!} + \ldots$$

c) Write a program that computes the value of e^x by using the formula

$$e^x = 1 + \frac{x}{1!} + \frac{x^2}{2!} + \frac{x^3}{3!} + \ldots$$

4

C Program Control

OBJECTIVES

In this chapter, you will learn:

- The essentials of counter-controlled repetition.
- To use the **for** and **do...while** repetition statements to execute statements in a program repeatedly.
- To understand multiple selection using the **switch** selection statement.
- To use the **break** and **continue** program control statements to alter the flow of control.
- To use the logical operators to form complex conditional expressions in control statements.
- To avoid the consequences of confusing the equality and assignment operators.

4.1 Introduction

The reader should now be comfortable with the process of writing simple but complete C programs. In this chapter, repetition is considered in greater detail, and additional repetition control statements, namely the `for` statement and the `do...while` statement, are presented. The `switch` multiple-selection statement is introduced. We discuss the `break` statement for exiting immediately and rapidly from certain control statements, and the `continue` statement for skipping the remainder of the body of a repetition statement and proceeding with the next iteration of the loop. The chapter discusses logical operators used for combining conditions, and concludes with a summary of the principles of structured programming as presented in Chapters 3 and 4.

4.2 Repetition Essentials

Most programs involve repetition, or **looping**. A **loop** is a group of instructions the computer executes repeatedly while some **loop-continuation condition** remains true. We have discussed two means of repetition:

1. Counter-controlled repetition
2. Sentinel-controlled repetition

Counter-controlled repetition is sometimes called **definite repetition** because we know in advance exactly how many times the loop will be executed. Sentinel-controlled repetition is sometimes called **indefinite repetition** because it is not known in advance how many times the loop will be executed.

In counter-controlled repetition, a **control variable** is used to count the number of repetitions. The control variable is incremented (usually by 1) each time the group of instructions is performed. When the value of the control variable indicates that the correct number of repetitions has been performed, the loop terminates and the computer continues executing with the statement after the repetition statement.

Sentinel values are used to control repetition when:

1. The precise number of repetitions is not known in advance, and

2. The loop includes statements that obtain data each time the loop is performed.

The sentinel value indicates "end of data." The sentinel is entered after all regular data items have been supplied to the program. Sentinels must be distinct from regular data items.

4.3 Counter-Controlled Repetition

Counter-controlled repetition requires:

1. The name of a control variable (or loop counter).

2. The initial value of the control variable.

3. The increment (or decrement) by which the control variable is modified each time through the loop.

4. The condition that tests for the final value of the control variable (i.e., whether looping should continue).

Consider the simple program shown in Fig. 4.1, which prints the numbers from 1 to 10. The definition

```
int counter = 1; /* initialization */
```

names the control variable (counter), defines it to be an integer, reserves memory space for it, and sets it to an initial value of 1. This definition is not an executable statement.

The definition and initialization of counter could also have been accomplished with the statements

```
int counter;
counter = 1;
```

```
1   /* Fig. 4.1: fig04_01.c
2      Counter-controlled repetition */
3   #include <stdio.h>
4
5   /* function main begins program execution */
6   int main( void )
7   {
8      int counter = 1; /* initialization */
9
10     while ( counter <= 10 ) { /* repetition condition */
11        printf ( "%d\n", counter ); /* display counter */
12        ++counter; /* increment */
13     } /* end while */
14
15     return 0; /* indicate program ended successfully */
16
17  } /* end function main */
```

Fig. 4.1 | Counter-controlled repetition. (Part 1 of 2.)

```
1
2
3
4
5
6
7
8
9
10
```

Fig. 4.1 | Counter-controlled repetition. (Part 2 of 2.)

The definition is not executable, but the assignment is. We use both methods of initializing variables.

The statement

```
++counter; /* increment */
```

increments the loop counter by 1 each time the loop is performed. The loop-continuation condition in the `while` statement tests if the value of the control variable is less than or equal to 10 (the last value for which the condition is true). Note that the body of this `while` is performed even when the control variable is 10. The loop terminates when the control variable exceeds 10 (i.e., `counter` becomes 11).

C programmers would normally make the program in Fig. 4.1 more concise by initializing `counter` to 0 and by replacing the `while` statement with

```
while ( ++counter <= 10 )
    printf( "%d\n", counter );
```

This code saves a statement because the incrementing is done directly in the `while` condition before the condition is tested. Also, this code eliminates the need for the braces around the body of the `while` because the `while` now contains only one statement. Coding in such a condensed fashion takes some practice.

Common Programming Error 4.1
Because floating-point values may be approximate, controlling counting loops with floating-point variables may result in imprecise counter values and inaccurate tests for termination.

Error-Prevention Tip 4.1
Control counting loops with integer values.

Good Programming Practice 4.1
Indent the statements in the body of each control statement.

Good Programming Practice 4.2
Put a blank line before and after each control statement to make it stand out in a program.

Good Programming Practice 4.3

Too many levels of nesting can make a program difficult to understand. As a general rule, try to avoid using more than three levels of nesting.

Good Programming Practice 4.4

The combination of vertical spacing before and after control statements and indentation of the bodies of control statements within the control-statement headers gives programs a two-dimensional appearance that greatly improves program readability.

4.4 **for** Repetition Statement

The for repetition statement handles all the details of counter-controlled repetition. To illustrate its power, let's rewrite the program of Fig. 4.1. The result is shown in Fig. 4.2.

The program operates as follows. When the for statement begins executing, the control variable counter is initialized to 1. Then, the loop-continuation condition counter <= 10 is checked. Because the initial value of counter is 1, the condition is satisfied, so the printf statement (line 13) prints the value of counter, namely 1. The control variable counter is then incremented by the expression counter++, and the loop begins again with the loop-continuation test. Since the control variable is now equal to 2, the final value is not exceeded, so the program performs the printf statement again. This process continues until the control variable counter is incremented to its final value of 11—this causes the loop-continuation test to fail, and repetition terminates. The program continues by performing the first statement after the for statement (in this case, the return statement at the end of the program).

Figure 4.3 takes a closer look at the for statement of Fig. 4.2. Notice that the for statement "does it all"—it specifies each of the items needed for counter-controlled repetition with a control variable. If there is more than one statement in the body of the for, braces are required to define the body of the loop.

```c
1   /* Fig. 4.2: fig04_02.c
2      Counter-controlled repetition with the for statement */
3   #include <stdio.h>
4
5   /* function main begins program execution */
6   int main( void )
7   {
8      int counter; /* define counter */
9
10     /* initialization, repetition condition, and increment
11        are all included in the for statement header. */
12     for ( counter = 1; counter <= 10; counter++ ) {
13        printf( "%d\n", counter );
14     } /* end for */
15
16     return 0; /* indicate program ended successfully */
17
18  } /* end function main */
```

Fig. 4.2 | Counter-controlled repetition with the for statement.

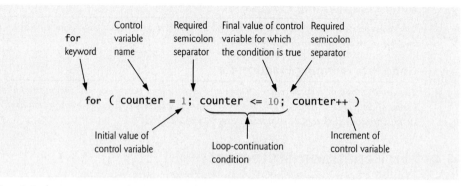

Fig. 4.3 | for statement header components.

Notice that Fig. 4.2 uses the loop-continuation condition counter <= 10. If you incorrectly wrote counter < 10, then the loop would be executed only 9 times. This is a common logic error called an off-by-one error.

Common Programming Error 4.2

Using an incorrect relational operator or using an incorrect initial or final value of a loop counter in the condition of a while or for statement can cause off-by-one errors.

Error-Prevention Tip 4.2

Using the final value in the condition of a while or for statement and using the <= relational operator will help avoid off-by-one errors. For a loop used to print the values 1 to 10, for example, the loop-continuation condition should be counter <= 10 rather than counter < 11 or counter < 10.

The general format of the for statement is

    for (*expression1*; *expression2*; *expression3*)
       statement

where *expression1* initializes the loop-control variable, *expression2* is the loop-continuation condition, and *expression3* increments the control variable. In most cases, the for statement can be represented with an equivalent while statement as follows:

    expression1;

    while (*expression2*) {
       statement
       expression3;
    }

There is an exception to this rule, which we will discuss in Section 4.9.

Often, *expression1* and *expression3* are comma-separated lists of expressions. The commas as used here are actually **comma operators** that guarantee that lists of expressions evaluate from left to right. The value and type of a comma-separated list of expressions are the value and type of the right-most expression in the list. The comma operator is most often used in the for statement. Its primary use is to enable you to use multiple initialization and/or multiple increment expressions. For example, there may be two control variables in a single for statement that must be initialized and incremented.

Software Engineering Observation 4.1

Place only expressions involving the control variables in the initialization and increment sections of a for statement. Manipulations of other variables should appear either before the loop (if they execute only once, like initialization statements) or in the loop body (if they execute once per repetition, like incrementing or decrementing statements).

The three expressions in the for statement are optional. If *expression2* is omitted, C assumes that the condition is true, thus creating an infinite loop. One may omit *expression1* if the control variable is initialized elsewhere in the program. *expression3* may be omitted if the increment is calculated by statements in the body of the for statement or if no increment is needed. The increment expression in the for statement acts like a stand-alone C statement at the end of the body of the for. Therefore, the expressions

```
counter = counter + 1
counter += 1
++counter
counter++
```

are all equivalent in the incrementing portion of the for statement. Many C programmers prefer the form counter++ because the incrementing occurs after the loop body is executed, and the postincrementing form seems more natural. Because the variable being preincremented or postincremented here does not appear in a larger expression, both forms of incrementing have the same effect. The two semicolons in the for statement are required.

Common Programming Error 4.3

Using commas instead of semicolons in a for header is a syntax error.

Common Programming Error 4.4

Placing a semicolon immediately to the right of a for header makes the body of that for statement an empty statement. This is normally a logic error.

4.5 for Statement: Notes and Observations

1. The initialization, loop-continuation condition and increment can contain arithmetic expressions. For example, if x = 2 and y = 10, the statement

   ```
   for ( j = x; j <= 4 * x * y; j += y / x )
   ```

   is equivalent to the statement

   ```
   for ( j = 2; j <= 80; j += 5 )
   ```

2. The "increment" may be negative (in which case it is really a decrement and the loop actually counts downward).

3. If the loop-continuation condition is initially false, the body portion of the loop is not performed. Instead, execution proceeds with the statement following the for statement.

4. The control variable is frequently printed or used in calculations in the body of a loop, but it need not be. It is common to use the control variable for controlling repetition while never mentioning it in the body of the loop.

5. The for statement is flowcharted much like the while statement. For example, Fig. 4.4 shows the flowchart of the for statement

```
for ( counter = 1; counter <= 10; counter++ )
    printf( "%d", counter );
```

This flowchart makes it clear that the initialization occurs only once and that incrementing occurs after the body statement is performed. Note that (besides small circles and arrows) the flowchart contains only rectangle symbols and a diamond symbol. Imagine, again, that you have access to a deep bin of empty for statements (represented as flowchart segments)—as many as you might need to stack and nest with other control statements to form a structured implementation of an algorithm's flow of control. And, again, the rectangles and diamonds are then filled with actions and decisions appropriate to the algorithm.

 Error-Prevention Tip 4.3

Although the value of the control variable can be changed in the body of a for loop, this can lead to subtle errors. It is best not to change it.

4.6 Examples Using the for Statement

The following examples show methods of varying the control variable in a for statement.

1. Vary the control variable from 1 to 100 in increments of 1.

```
for ( i = 1; i <= 100; i++ )
```

2. Vary the control variable from 100 to 1 in increments of -1 (decrements of 1).

```
for ( i = 100; i >= 1; i-- )
```

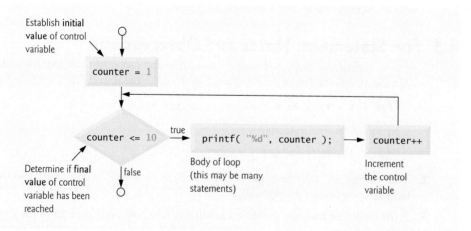

Fig. 4.4 | Flowcharting a typical for repetition statement.

3. Vary the control variable from 7 to 77 in steps of 7.

```
for ( i = 7; i <= 77; i += 7 )
```

4. Vary the control variable from 20 to 2 in steps of -2.

```
for ( i = 20; i >= 2; i -= 2 )
```

5. Vary the control variable over the following sequence of values: 2, 5, 8, 11, 14, 17, 20.

```
for ( j = 2; j <= 20; j += 3 )
```

6. Vary the control variable over the following sequence of values: 99, 88, 77, 66, 55, 44, 33, 22, 11, 0.

```
for ( j = 99; j >= 0; j -= 11 )
```

The next two examples provide simple applications of the for statement. Figure 4.5 uses the for statement to sum all the even integers from 2 to 100.

Note that the body of the for statement in Fig. 4.5 could actually be merged into the rightmost portion of the for header by using the comma operator as follows:

```
for ( number = 2; number <= 100; sum += number, number += 2 )
   ;  /* empty statement */
```

The initialization sum = 0 could also be merged into the initialization section of the for.

```
1   /* Fig. 4.5: fig04_05.c
2      Summation with for */
3   #include <stdio.h>
4
5   /* function main begins program execution */
6   int main( void )
7   {
8      int sum = 0; /* initialize sum */
9      int number;   /* number to be added to sum */
10
11     for ( number = 2; number <= 100; number += 2 ) {
12        sum += number; /* add number to sum */
13     } /* end for */
14
15     printf( "Sum is %d\n", sum ); /* output sum */
16
17     return 0; /* indicate program ended successfully */
18
19  } /* end function main */
```

```
Sum is 2550
```

Fig. 4.5 | Using for to sum numbers.

Good Programming Practice 4.5

Although statements preceding a for and statements in the body of a for can often be merged into the for header, avoid doing so because it makes the program more difficult to read.

Good Programming Practice 4.6

Limit the size of control-statement headers to a single line if possible.

The next example computes compound interest using the for statement. Consider the following problem statement:

> *A person invests $1000.00 in a savings account yielding 5% interest. Assuming that all interest is left on deposit in the account, calculate and print the amount of money in the account at the end of each year for 10 years. Use the following formula for determining these amounts:*
>
> $$a = p(1 + r)^n$$
>
> *where*
>
> p is the original amount invested (i.e., the principal)
> r is the annual interest rate
> n is the number of years
> a is the amount on deposit at the end of the nth year.

This problem involves a loop that performs the indicated calculation for each of the 10 years the money remains on deposit. The solution is shown in Fig. 4.6.

The for statement executes the body of the loop 10 times, varying a control variable from 1 to 10 in increments of 1. Although C does not include an exponentiation operator, we can use the Standard Library function pow for this purpose. The function pow(x, y) calculates the value of x raised to the yth power. It takes two arguments of type **double** and returns a double value. Type double is a floating-point type much like float, but typically a variable of type double can store a value of much greater magnitude with greater precision than float. Note that the header <math.h> (line 4) should be included whenever a math function such as pow is used. Actually, this program would malfunction without the inclusion of math.h, as the linker would be unable to find the pow function. [*Note:* On many Linux/UNIX C compilers, you must include the -lm option (e.g., cc -lm fig04_06.c)

```
1   /* Fig. 4.6: fig04_06.c
2      Calculating compound interest */
3   #include <stdio.h>
4   #include <math.h>
5
6   /* function main begins program execution */
7   int main( void )
8   {
9      double amount;                    /* amount on deposit */
10     double principal = 1000.0;  /* starting principal */
11     double rate = .05;          /* annual interest rate */
12     int year;                         /* year counter */
13
```

Fig. 4.6 | Calculating compound interest with for. (Part 1 of 2.)

```
14      /* output table column head */
15      printf( "%4s%21s\n", "Year", "Amount on deposit" );
16
17      /* calculate amount on deposit for each of ten years */
18      for ( year = 1; year <= 10; year++ ) {
19
20          /* calculate new amount for specified year */
21          amount = principal * pow( 1.0 + rate, year );
22
23          /* output one table row */
24          printf( "%4d%21.2f\n", year, amount );
25      } /* end for */
26
27      return 0; /* indicate program ended successfully */
28
29  } /* end function main */
```

Year	Amount on deposit
1	1050.00
2	1102.50
3	1157.63
4	1215.51
5	1276.28
6	1340.10
7	1407.10
8	1477.46
9	1551.33
10	1628.89

Fig. 4.6 | Calculating compound interest with `for`. (Part 2 of 2.)

when compiling Fig. 4.6. This links the math library to the program.] Function `pow` requires two `double` arguments. Note that `year` is an integer. The `math.h` file includes information that tells the compiler to convert the value of `year` to a temporary `double` representation before calling the function. This information is contained in something called `pow`'s function prototype. Function prototypes are explained in Chapter 5. We also provide a summary of the `pow` function and other math library functions in Chapter 5.

Notice that we defined the variables `amount`, `principal` and `rate` to be of type `double`. We did this for simplicity because we are dealing with fractional parts of dollars.

Error-Prevention Tip 4.4

Do not use variables of type `float` or `double` to perform monetary calculations. The impreciseness of floating-point numbers can cause errors that will result in incorrect monetary values. [In the exercises, we explore the use of integers to perform monetary calculations.]

Here is a simple explanation of what can go wrong when using `float` or `double` to represent dollar amounts.

Two `float` dollar amounts stored in the machine could be 14.234 (which with `%.2f` prints as 14.23) and 18.673 (which with `%.2f` prints as 18.67). When these amounts are added, they produce the sum 32.907, which with `%.2f` prints as 32.91. Thus your printout could appear as

```
   14.23
+ 18.67
 -------
   32.91
```

Clearly the sum of the individual numbers as printed should be 32.90! You've been warned!

The conversion specifier %21.2f is used to print the value of the variable amount in the program. The 21 in the conversion specifier denotes the **field width** in which the value will be printed. A field width of 21 specifies that the value printed will appear in 21 print positions. The 2 specifies the precision (i.e., the number of decimal positions). If the number of characters displayed is less than the field width, then the value will automatically be **right justified** in the field. This is particularly useful for aligning floating-point values with the same precision (so that their decimal points align vertically). To **left justify** a value in a field, place a - (minus sign) between the % and the field width. Note that the minus sign may also be used to left justify integers (such as in %-6d) and character strings (such as in %-8s). We will discuss the powerful formatting capabilities of printf and scanf in detail in Chapter 9.

4.7 switch Multiple-Selection Statement

In Chapter 3, we discussed the if single-selection statement and the if...else double-selection statement. Occasionally, an algorithm will contain a series of decisions in which a variable or expression is tested separately for each of the constant integral values it may assume, and different actions are taken. This is called multiple selection. C provides the switch multiple-selection statement to handle such decision making.

The switch statement consists of a series of case labels and an optional default case. Figure 4.7 uses switch to count the number of each different letter grade students earned on an exam.

In the program, the user enters letter grades for a class. In the while header (line 19),

```
while ( ( grade = getchar() ) != EOF )
```

the parenthesized assignment (grade = getchar()) is executed first. The getchar function (from the standard input/output library) reads one character from the keyboard and stores that character in the integer variable grade. Characters are normally stored in variables of type **char**. However, an important feature of C is that characters can be stored in any integer data type because they are usually represented as one-byte integers in the computer. Thus, we can treat a character as either an integer or a character, depending on its use. For example, the statement

```
printf( "The character (%c) has the value %d.\n", 'a', 'a' );
```

```
1   /* Fig. 4.7: fig04_07.c
2      Counting letter grades */
3   #include <stdio.h>
4
5   /* function main begins program execution */
6   int main( void )
7   {
```

Fig. 4.7 | switch example. (Part 1 of 3.)

```
 8      int grade;      /* one grade */
 9      int aCount = 0; /* number of As */
10      int bCount = 0; /* number of Bs */
11      int cCount = 0; /* number of Cs */
12      int dCount = 0; /* number of Ds */
13      int fCount = 0; /* number of Fs */
14
15      printf( "Enter the letter grades.\n" );
16      printf( "Enter the EOF character to end input.\n" );
17
18      /* loop until user types end-of-file key sequence */
19      while ( ( grade = getchar() ) != EOF ) {
20
21         /* determine which grade was input */
22         switch ( grade ) { /* switch nested in while */
23
24            case 'A': /* grade was uppercase A */
25            case 'a': /* or lowercase a */
26               ++aCount; /* increment aCount */
27               break; /* necessary to exit switch */
28
29            case 'B': /* grade was uppercase B */
30            case 'b': /* or lowercase b */
31               ++bCount; /* increment bCount */
32               break; /* exit switch */
33
34            case 'C': /* grade was uppercase C */
35            case 'c': /* or lowercase c */
36               ++cCount; /* increment cCount */
37               break; /* exit switch */
38
39            case 'D': /* grade was uppercase D */
40            case 'd': /* or lowercase d */
41               ++dCount; /* increment dCount */
42               break; /* exit switch */
43
44            case 'F': /* grade was uppercase F */
45            case 'f': /* or lowercase f */
46               ++fCount; /* increment fCount */
47               break; /* exit switch */
48
49            case '\n': /* ignore newlines, */
50            case '\t': /* tabs, */
51            case ' ':  /* and spaces in input */
52               break; /* exit switch */
53
54            default: /* catch all other characters */
55               printf( "Incorrect letter grade entered." );
56               printf( " Enter a new grade.\n" );
57               break; /* optional; will exit switch anyway */
58         } /* end switch */
59
60      } /* end while */
```

Fig. 4.7 | switch example. (Part 2 of 3.)

```
61
62      /* output summary of results */
63      printf( "\nTotals for each letter grade are:\n" );
64      printf( "A: %d\n", aCount ); /* display number of A grades */
65      printf( "B: %d\n", bCount ); /* display number of B grades */
66      printf( "C: %d\n", cCount ); /* display number of C grades */
67      printf( "D: %d\n", dCount ); /* display number of D grades */
68      printf( "F: %d\n", fCount ); /* display number of F grades */
69
70      return 0; /* indicate program ended successfully */
71
72   } /* end function main */
```

```
Enter the letter grades.
Enter the EOF character to end input.
a
b
c
C
A
d
f
C
E
Incorrect letter grade entered. Enter a new grade.
D
A
b
^Z

Totals for each letter grade are:
A: 3
B: 2
C: 3
D: 2
F: 1
```

Fig. 4.7 | switch example. (Part 3 of 3.)

uses the conversion specifiers %c and %d to print the character a and its integer value, respectively. The result is

```
The character (a) has the value 97.
```

The integer 97 is the character's numerical representation in the computer. Many computers today use the ASCII (American Standard Code for Information Interchange) character set in which 97 represents the lowercase letter 'a'. A list of the ASCII characters and their decimal values is presented in Appendix D. Characters can be read with scanf by using the conversion specifier %c.

Assignments as a whole actually have a value. This value is assigned to the variable on the left side of the =. The value of the assignment expression grade = getchar() is the character that is returned by getchar and assigned to the variable grade.

The fact that assignments have values can be useful for setting several variables to the same value. For example,

```
a = b = c = 0;
```

first evaluates the assignment c = 0 (because the = operator associates from right to left). The variable b is then assigned the value of the assignment c = 0 (which is 0). Then, the variable a is assigned the value of the assignment b = (c = 0) (which is also 0). In the program, the value of the assignment grade = getchar() is compared with the value of EOF (a symbol whose acronym stands for "end of file"). We use EOF (which normally has the value -1) as the sentinel value. The user types a system-dependent keystroke combination to mean "end of file"—i.e., "I have no more data to enter." EOF is a symbolic integer constant defined in the <stdio.h> header (we will see how symbolic constants are defined in Chapter 6). If the value assigned to grade is equal to EOF, the program terminates. We have chosen to represent characters in this program as ints because EOF has an integer value (again, normally -1).

Portability Tip 4.1

The keystroke combinations for entering EOF (end of file) are system dependent.

Portability Tip 4.2

Testing for the symbolic constant EOF rather than –1 makes programs more portable. The C standard states that EOF is a negative integral value (but not necessarily –1). Thus, EOF could have different values on different systems.

On Linux/UNIX systems, the EOF indicator is entered by typing the sequence

<Ctrl> d

on a line by itself. This notation *<Ctrl> d* means to press the *Enter* key and then simultaneously press both the *Ctrl* key and the *d* key. On other systems, such as Microsoft Windows, the EOF indicator can be entered by typing

<Ctrl> z

Note that you may also need to press *Enter* on Windows.

The user enters grades at the keyboard. When the *Enter* key is pressed, the characters are read by function getchar one character at a time. If the character entered is not equal to EOF, the switch statement (line 22) is entered. Keyword switch is followed by the variable name grade in parentheses. This is called the **controlling expression**. The value of this expression is compared with each of the **case** labels. Assume the user has entered the letter C as a grade. C is automatically compared to each case in the switch. If a match occurs (case 'C':), the statements for that case are executed. In the case of the letter C, cCount is incremented by 1 (line 36), and the switch statement is exited immediately with the break statement.

The break statement causes program control to continue with the first statement after the switch statement. The break statement is used because the cases in a switch statement would otherwise run together. If break is not used anywhere in a switch statement, then each time a match occurs in the statement, the statements for all the remaining cases will be executed. (This feature is rarely useful, although it is perfect for programming the iterative song *The Twelve Days of Christmas!*) If no match occurs, the `default` case is executed, and an error message is printed.

Each `case` can have one or more actions. The `switch` statement is different from all other control statements in that braces are not required around multiple actions in a `case` of a `switch`. The general `switch` multiple-selection statement (using a `break` in each `case`) is flowcharted in Fig. 4.8.

The flowchart makes it clear that each `break` statement at the end of a `case` causes control to immediately exit the `switch` statement. Again, note that (besides small circles and arrows) the flowchart contains only rectangle symbols and diamond symbols. Imagine, again, that you have access to a deep bin of empty `switch` statements (represented as flowchart segments)—as many as you might need to stack and nest with other control statements to form a structured implementation of an algorithm's flow of control. And again, the rectangles and diamonds are then filled with actions and decisions appropriate to the algorithm.

Common Programming Error 4.5

Forgetting a `break` *statement when one is needed in a* `switch` *statement is a logic error.*

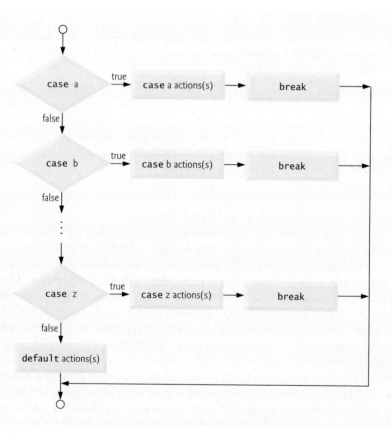

Fig. 4.8 | `switch` multiple-selection statement with `break`s.

Good Programming Practice 4.7

Provide a default case in switch statements. Cases not explicitly tested in a switch are ignored. The default case helps prevent this by focusing the programmer on the need to process exceptional conditions. There are situations in which no default processing is needed.

Good Programming Practice 4.8

Although the case clauses and the default case clause in a switch statement can occur in any order, it is considered good programming practice to place the default clause last.

Good Programming Practice 4.9

In a switch statement when the default clause is listed last, the break statement is not required. But some programmers include this break for clarity and symmetry with other cases.

In the switch statement of Fig. 4.7, the lines

```
case '\n': /* ignore newlines, */
case '\t': /* tabs, */
case ' ':  /* and spaces in input */
    break;  /* exit switch */
```

cause the program to skip newline, tab and blank characters. Reading characters one at a time can cause some problems. To have the program read the characters, they must be sent to the computer by pressing the *Enter* key. This causes the newline character to be placed in the input after the character we wish to process. Often, this newline character must be specially processed to make the program work correctly. By including the preceding cases in our switch statement, we prevent the error message in the default case from being printed each time a newline, tab or space is encountered in the input.

Common Programming Error 4.6

Not processing newline characters in the input when reading characters one at a time can cause logic errors.

Error-Prevention Tip 4.5

Remember to provide processing capabilities for newline (and possibly other white-space) characters in the input when processing characters one at a time.

Note that listing several case labels together (such as case 'D' : case 'd' : in Fig. 4.7) simply means that the same set of actions is to occur for either of these cases.

When using the switch statement, remember that it can be used only for testing a **constant integral expression**—i.e., any combination of character constants and integer constants that evaluates to a constant integer value. A character constant is represented as the specific character in single quotes, such as 'A'. Characters must be enclosed within single quotes to be recognized as character constants—characters in double quotes are recognized as strings. Integer constants are simply integer values. In our example, we have used character constants. Remember that characters are represented as small integer values.

Portable languages like C must have flexible data type sizes. Different applications may need integers of different sizes. C provides several data types to represent integers. The range of integer values for each type depends on the particular computer's hardware. In addition to the types int and char, C provides types short (an abbreviation of short int) and long (an abbreviation of long int). C specifies that the minimum range of values for short integers is −32768 to +32767. For the vast majority of integer calculations, long integers are sufficient. The standard specifies that the minimum range of values for long integers is −2147483648 to +2147483647. The standard states that the range of values for an int is at least the same as the range for short integers and no larger than the range for long integers. The data type signed char can be used to represent integers in the range −128 to +127 or any of the characters in the computer's character set.

4.8 do…while Repetition Statement

The do…while repetition statement is similar to the while statement. In the while statement, the loop-continuation condition is tested at the beginning of the loop before the body of the loop is performed. The do…while statement tests the loop-continuation condition *after* the loop body is performed. Therefore, the loop body will be executed at least once. When a do…while terminates, execution continues with the statement after the while clause. Note that it is not necessary to use braces in the do…while statement if there is only one statement in the body. However, the braces are usually included to avoid confusion between the while and do…while statements. For example,

```
while( condition )
```

is normally regarded as the header to a while statement. A do…while with no braces around the single-statement body appears as

```
do
    statement
while( condition );
```

which can be confusing. The last line—while(*condition*);—may be misinterpreted by the reader as a while statement containing an empty statement. Thus, to avoid confusion, the do…while with one statement is often written as follows:

```
do {
    statement
} while ( condition );
```

Good Programming Practice 4.10

Some programmers always include braces in a do…while statement even if the braces are not necessary. This helps eliminate ambiguity between the do…while statement containing one statement and the while statement.

Common Programming Error 4.7

Infinite loops are caused when the loop-continuation condition in a while, for or do…while statement never becomes false. To prevent this, make sure there is not a semicolon immediately after the header of a while or for statement. In a counter-controlled loop, make sure the control variable is incremented (or decremented) in the loop. In a sentinel-controlled loop, make sure the sentinel value is eventually input.

Figure 4.9 uses a do…while statement to print the numbers from 1 to 10. Note that the control variable counter is preincremented in the loop-continuation test. Note also the use of the braces to enclose the single-statement body of the do…while.

```
1   /* Fig. 4.9: fig04_09.c
2      Using the do/while repetition statement */
3   #include <stdio.h>
4
5   /* function main begins program execution */
6   int main( void )
7   {
8      int counter = 1; /* initialize counter */
9
10     do {
11        printf( "%d  ", counter ); /* display counter */
12     } while ( ++counter <= 10 );   /* end do...while */
13
14     return 0; /* indicate program ended successfully */
15
16  } /* end function main */
```

```
1  2  3  4  5  6  7  8  9  10
```

Fig. 4.9 | do...while statement example.

The do...while statement is flowcharted in Fig. 4.10. This flowchart makes it clear that the loop-continuation condition is not executed until after the action is performed at least once. Again, note that (besides small circles and arrows) the flowchart contains only a rectangle symbol and a diamond symbol. Imagine, again, that you have access to a deep bin of empty do...while statements (represented as flowchart segments)—as many as you might need to stack and nest with other control statements to form a structured implementation of an algorithm's flow of control. And, again, the rectangles and diamonds are then filled with actions and decisions appropriate to the algorithm.

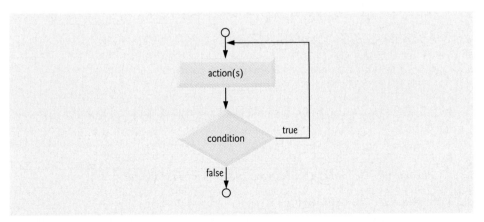

Fig. 4.10 | Flowcharting the do...while repetition statement.

4.9 break and continue Statements

The break and continue statements are used to alter the flow of control. The break statement, when executed in a while, for, do...while or switch statement, causes an immediate exit from that statement. Program execution continues with the next statement.
Common uses of the break statement are to escape early from a loop or to skip the remainder of a switch statement (as in Fig. 4.7). Figure 4.11 demonstrates the break statement
in a for repetition statement. When the if statement detects that x has become 5, break
is executed. This terminates the for statement, and the program continues with the
printf after the for. The loop fully executes only four times.

    The continue statement, when executed in a while, for or do...while statement,
skips the remaining statements in the body of that control statement and performs the next
iteration of the loop. In while and do...while statements, the loop-continuation test is
evaluated immediately after the continue statement is executed. In the for statement, the
increment expression is executed, then the loop-continuation test is evaluated. Earlier, we
said that the while statement could be used in most cases to represent the for statement.
The one exception occurs when the increment expression in the while statement follows
the continue statement. In this case, the increment is not executed before the repetition-
continuation condition is tested, and the while does not execute in the same manner as
the for. Figure 4.12 uses the continue statement in a for statement to skip the printf
statement and begin the next iteration of the loop.

```
1   /* Fig. 4.11: fig04_11.c
2      Using the break statement in a for statement */
3   #include <stdio.h>
4
5   /* function main begins program execution */
6   int main( void )
7   {
8      int x; /* counter */
9
10     /* loop 10 times */
11     for ( x = 1; x <= 10; x++ ) {
12
13        /* if x is 5, terminate loop */
14        if ( x == 5 ) {
15           break; /* break loop only if x is 5 */
16        } /* end if */
17
18        printf( "%d ", x ); /* display value of x */
19     } /* end for */
20
21     printf( "\nBroke out of loop at x == %d\n", x );
22
23     return 0; /* indicate program ended successfully */
24
25  } /* end function main */
```

Fig. 4.11 | Using the break statement in a for statement. (Part 1 of 2.)

```
1 2 3 4
Broke out of loop at x == 5
```

Fig. 4.11 | Using the break statement in a for statement. (Part 2 of 2.)

```
1   /* Fig. 4.12: fig04_12.c
2      Using the continue statement in a for statement */
3   #include <stdio.h>
4
5   /* function main begins program execution */
6   int main( void )
7   {
8      int x; /* counter */
9
10     /* loop 10 times */
11     for ( x = 1; x <= 10; x++ ) {
12
13        /* if x is 5, continue with next iteration of loop */
14        if ( x == 5 ) {
15           continue; /* skip remaining code in loop body */
16        } /* end if */
17
18        printf( "%d ", x ); /* display value of x */
19     } /* end for */
20
21     printf( "\nUsed continue to skip printing the value 5\n" );
22
23     return 0; /* indicate program ended successfully */
24
25  } /* end function main */
```

```
1 2 3 4 6 7 8 9 10
Used continue to skip printing the value 5
```

Fig. 4.12 | Using the continue statement in a for statement.

Software Engineering Observation 4.2

Some programmers feel that break and continue violate the norms of structured programming. Because the effects of these statements can be achieved by structured programming techniques we will soon learn, these programmers do not use break and continue.

Performance Tip 4.1

The break and continue statements, when used properly, perform faster than the corresponding structured techniques that we will soon learn.

Software Engineering Observation 4.3

There is a tension between achieving quality software engineering and achieving the best-performing software. Often one of these goals is achieved at the expense of the other.

4.10 Logical Operators

So far we have studied only **simple conditions**, such as `counter <= 10`, `total > 1000`, and `number != sentinelValue`. We've expressed these conditions in terms of the relational operators, `>`, `<`, `>=` and `<=`, and the equality operators, `==` and `!=`. Each decision tested precisely one condition. To test multiple conditions in the process of making a decision, we had to perform these tests in separate statements or in nested `if` or `if...else` statements.

C provides **logical operators** that may be used to form more complex conditions by combining simple conditions. The logical operators are **&& (logical AND)**, **|| (logical OR)** and **! (logical NOT** also called **logical negation)**. We will consider examples of each of these operators.

Suppose we wish to ensure that two conditions are *both* true before we choose a certain path of execution. In this case, we can use the logical operator `&&` as follows:

```
if ( gender == 1 && age >= 65 )
    ++seniorFemales;
```

This `if` statement contains two simple conditions. The condition `gender == 1` might be evaluated, for example, to determine if a person is a female. The condition `age >= 65` is evaluated to determine if a person is a senior citizen. The two simple conditions are evaluated first because the precedences of `==` and `>=` are both higher than the precedence of `&&`. The `if` statement then considers the combined condition

```
gender == 1 && age >= 65
```

This condition is true if and only if both of the simple conditions are true. Finally, if this combined condition is indeed true, then the count of `seniorFemales` is incremented by 1. If either or both of the simple conditions are false, then the program skips the incrementing and proceeds to the statement following the `if`.

Figure 4.13 summarizes the `&&` operator. The table shows all four possible combinations of zero (false) and nonzero (true) values for expression1 and expression2. Such tables are often called **truth tables**. C evaluates all expressions that include relational operators, equality operators, and/or logical operators to 0 or 1. Although C sets a true value to 1, it accepts *any* nonzero value as true.

Now let us consider the `||` (logical OR) operator. Suppose we wish to ensure at some point in a program that either *or* both of two conditions are true before we choose a certain path of execution. In this case, we use the `||` operator as in the following program segment:

```
if ( semesterAverage >= 90 || finalExam >= 90 )
    printf( "Student grade is A\n" );
```

expression1	expression2	expression1 && expression2
0	0	0
0	nonzero	0
nonzero	0	0
nonzero	nonzero	1

Fig. 4.13 | Truth table for the && (logical AND) operator.

This statement also contains two simple conditions. The condition semesterAverage >= 90 is evaluated to determine if the student deserves an "A" in the course because of a solid performance throughout the semester. The condition finalExam >= 90 is evaluated to determine if the student deserves an "A" in the course because of an outstanding performance on the final exam. The if statement then considers the combined condition

```
semesterAverage >= 90 || finalExam >= 90
```

and awards the student an "A" if either or both of the simple conditions are true. Note that the message "Student grade is A" is not printed only when both of the simple conditions are false (zero). Figure 4.14 is a truth table for the logical OR operator (||).

The && operator has a higher precedence than ||. Both operators associate from left to right. An expression containing && or || operators is evaluated only until truth or falsehood is known. Thus, evaluation of the condition

```
gender == 1 && age >= 65
```

will stop if gender is not equal to 1 (i.e., the entire expression is false), and continue if gender is equal to 1 (i.e., the entire expression could still be true if age >= 65).

Performance Tip 4.2

*In expressions using operator **&&**, make the condition that is most likely to be false the leftmost condition. In expressions using operator **||**, make the condition that is most likely to be true the leftmost condition. This can reduce a program's execution time.*

C provides ! (logical negation) to enable a programmer to "reverse" the meaning of a condition. Unlike operators && and ||, which combine two conditions (and are therefore binary operators), the logical negation operator has only a single condition as an operand (and is therefore a unary operator). The logical negation operator is placed before a condition when we are interested in choosing a path of execution if the original condition (without the logical negation operator) is false, such as in the following program segment:

```
if ( !( grade == sentinelValue ) )
    printf( "The next grade is %f\n", grade );
```

The parentheses around the condition grade == sentinelValue are needed because the logical negation operator has a higher precedence than the equality operator. Figure 4.15 is a truth table for the logical negation operator.

expression1	expression2	expression1 || expression2
0	0	0
0	nonzero	1
nonzero	0	1
nonzero	nonzero	1

Fig. 4.14 | Truth table for the logical OR (||) operator.

expression	!expression
0	1
nonzero	0

Fig. 4.15 | Truth table for operator ! (logical negation).

In most cases, you can avoid using logical negation by expressing the condition differently with an appropriate relational operator. For example, the preceding statement may also be written as follows:

```
if ( grade != sentinelValue )
    printf( "The next grade is %f\n", grade );
```

Figure 4.16 shows the precedence and associativity of the operators introduced to this point. The operators are shown from top to bottom in decreasing order of precedence.

4.11 Confusing Equality (==) and Assignment (=) Operators

There is one type of error that C programmers, no matter how experienced, tend to make so frequently that we felt it was worth a separate section. That error is accidentally swapping the operators == (equality) and = (assignment). What makes these swaps so damaging is the fact that they do not ordinarily cause syntax errors. Rather, statements with these errors ordinarily compile correctly, allowing programs to run to completion while likely generating incorrect results through runtime logic errors.

Operators	Associativity	Type
++ *(postfix)* -- *(postfix)*	right to left	postfix
+ - ! ++ *(prefix)* -- *(prefix)* *(type)*	right to left	unary
* / %	left to right	multiplicative
+ -	left to right	additive
< <= > >=	left to right	relational
== !=	left to right	equality
&&	left to right	logical AND
||	left to right	logical OR
?:	right to left	conditional
= += -= *= /= %=	right to left	assignment
,	left to right	comma

Fig. 4.16 | Operator precedence and associativity.

Two aspects of C cause these problems. One is that any expression in C that produces a value can be used in the decision portion of any control statement. If the value is 0, it is treated as false, and if the value is nonzero, it is treated as true. The second is that assignments in C produce a value, namely the value that is assigned to the variable on the left side of the assignment operator. For example, suppose we intend to write

```
if ( payCode == 4 )
    printf( "You get a bonus!" );
```

but we accidentally write

```
if ( payCode = 4 )
    printf( "You get a bonus!" );
```

The first `if` statement properly awards a bonus to the person whose paycode is equal to 4. The second `if` statement—the one with the error—evaluates the assignment expression in the `if` condition. This expression is a simple assignment whose value is the constant 4. Because any nonzero value is interpreted as "true," the condition in this `if` statement is always true, and not only is the value of `payCode` inadvertently set to 4, but the person always receives a bonus regardless of what the actual paycode is!

Common Programming Error 4.8

Using operator == for assignment or using operator = for equality is a logic error.

Programmers normally write conditions such as `x == 7` with the variable name on the left and the constant on the right. By reversing these terms so that the constant is on the left and the variable name is on the right, as in `7 == x`, the programmer who accidentally replaces the `==` operator with `=` is protected by the compiler. The compiler will treat this as a syntax error, because only a variable name can be placed on the left-hand side of an assignment expression. At least this will prevent the potential devastation of a runtime logic error.

Variable names are said to be **lvalues** (for "left values") because they can be used on the left side of an assignment operator. Constants are said to be **rvalues** (for "right values") because they can be used on only the right side of an assignment operator. Note that lvalues can also be used as rvalues, but not vice versa.

Good Programming Practice 4.11

When an equality expression has a variable and a constant, as in x == 1, some programmers prefer to write the expression with the constant on the left and the variable name on the right (e.g. 1 == x as protection against the logic error that occurs when you accidentally replace operator == with =.

The other side of the coin can be equally unpleasant. Suppose you want to assign a value to a variable with a simple statement like

```
x = 1;
```

but instead write

```
x == 1;
```

Here, too, this is not a syntax error. Rather the compiler simply evaluates the conditional expression. If `x` is equal to 1, the condition is true and the expression returns the value 1.

If x is not equal to 1, the condition is false and the expression returns the value 0. Regardless of what value is returned, there is no assignment operator, so the value is simply lost, and the value of x remains unaltered, probably causing an execution-time logic error. Unfortunately, we do not have a handy trick available to help you with this problem! Many compilers, however, will issue a warning on such a statement.

Error-Prevention Tip 4.6

After you write a program, text search it for every = and check that it is being used properly.

4.12 Structured Programming Summary

Just as architects design buildings by employing the collective wisdom of their profession, so should programmers design programs. Our field is younger than architecture is, and our collective wisdom is considerably sparser. We have learned a great deal in a mere five decades. Perhaps most important, we have learned that structured programming produces programs that are easier (than unstructured programs) to understand and hence are easier to test, debug, modify, and even prove correct in a mathematical sense.

Chapters 3 and 4 have concentrated on C's control statements. Each statement has been presented, flowcharted and discussed separately with examples. Now, we summarize the results of Chapters 3 and 4 and introduce a simple set of rules for the formation and properties of structured programs.

Figure 4.17 summarizes the control statements discussed in Chapters 3 and 4. Small circles are used in the figure to indicate the single entry point and the single exit point of each statement. Connecting individual flowchart symbols arbitrarily can lead to unstructured programs. Therefore, the programming profession has chosen to combine flowchart symbols to form a limited set of control statements, and to build only structured programs by properly combining control statements in two simple ways. For simplicity, only single-entry/single-exit control statements are used—there is only one way to enter and only one way to exit each control statement. Connecting control statements in sequence to form structured programs is simple—the exit point of one control statement is connected directly to the entry point of the next, i.e., the control statements are simply placed one after another in a program—we have called this "control-statement stacking." The rules for forming structured programs also allow for control statements to be nested.

Figure 4.18 shows the rules for forming structured programs. The rules assume that the rectangle flowchart symbol may be used to indicate any action including input/output.

Applying the rules of Fig. 4.18 always results in a structured flowchart with a neat, building-block appearance. Repeatedly applying Rule 2 to the simplest flowchart (Fig. 4.19) results in a structured flowchart containing many rectangles in sequence (Fig. 4.20). Notice that Rule 2 generates a stack of control statements; so we call Rule 2 the **stacking** rule.

Rule 3 is called the **nesting** rule. Repeatedly applying Rule 3 to the simplest flowchart results in a flowchart with neatly nested control statements. For example, in Fig. 4.21, the rectangle in the simplest flowchart is first replaced with a double-selection (if...else) statement. Then Rule 3 is applied again to both of the rectangles in the double-selection statement, replacing each of these rectangles with double-selection statements. The dashed box around each of the double-selection statements represents the rectangle that was replaced in the original flowchart.

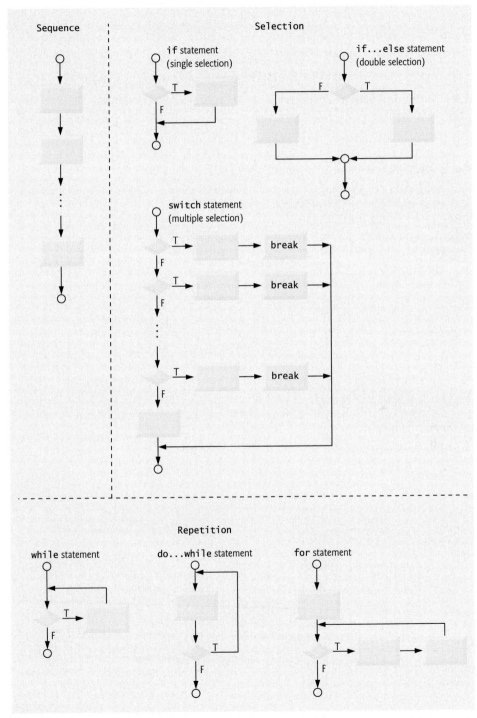

Fig. 4.17 | C's single-entry/single-exit sequence, selection and repetition statements.

Rules for Forming Structured Programs

1) Begin with the "simplest flowchart" (Fig. 4.19).

2) Any rectangle (action) can be replaced by two rectangles (actions) in sequence.

3) Any rectangle (action) can be replaced by any control statement (sequence, `if`, `if...else`, `switch`, `while`, `do...while` or `for`).

4) Rules 2 and 3 may be applied as often as you like and in any order.

Fig. 4.18 | Rules for forming structured programs.

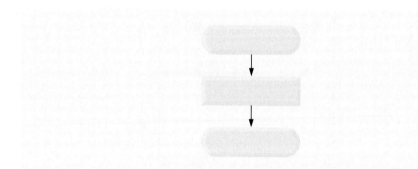

Fig. 4.19 | Simplest flowchart.

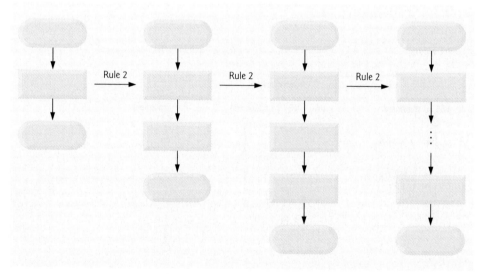

Fig. 4.20 | Repeatedly applying Rule 2 of Fig. 4.18 to the simplest flowchart.

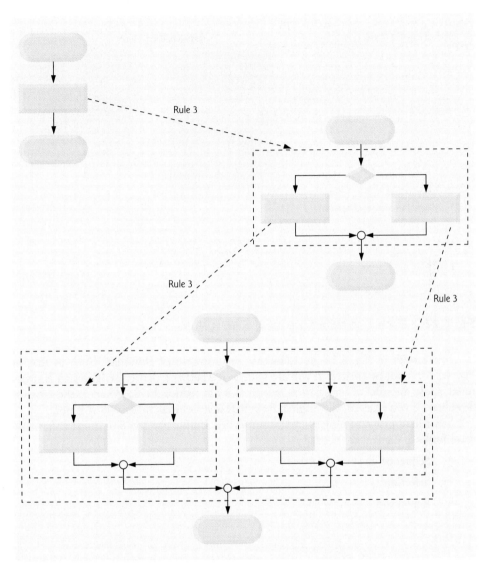

Fig. 4.21 | Applying rule 3 of Fig. 4.18 to the simplest flowchart.

Rule 4 generates larger, more involved, and more deeply nested structures. The flow-charts that emerge from applying the rules in Fig. 4.18 constitute the set of all possible structured flowcharts and hence the set of all possible structured programs.

It is because of the elimination of the goto statement that these building blocks never overlap one another. The beauty of the structured approach is that we use only a small number of simple single-entry/single-exit pieces, and we assemble them in only two simple ways. Figure 4.22 shows the kinds of stacked building blocks that emerge from applying Rule 2 and the kinds of nested building blocks that emerge from applying Rule 3. The figure also shows the kind of overlapped building blocks that cannot appear in structured flowcharts (because of the elimination of the goto statement).

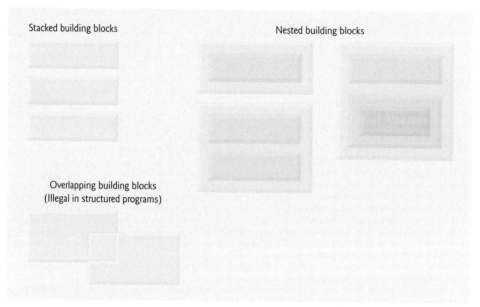

Fig. 4.22 | Stacked, nested and overlapped building blocks.

If the rules in Fig. 4.18 are followed, an unstructured flowchart (such as that in Fig. 4.23) cannot be created. If you are uncertain whether a particular flowchart is structured, apply the rules of Fig. 4.18 in reverse to try to reduce the flowchart to the simplest flowchart. If you succeed, the original flowchart is structured; otherwise, it is not.

Structured programming promotes simplicity. Bohm and Jacopini showed that only three forms of control are needed:

- Sequence
- Selection
- Repetition

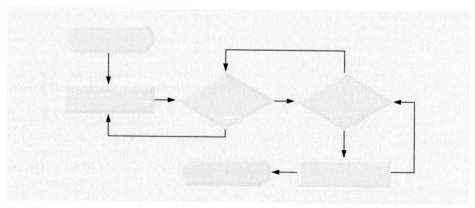

Fig. 4.23 | An unstructured flowchart.

Sequence is straighforward. Selection is implemented in one of three ways:

- `if` statement (single selection)
- `if...else` statement (double selection)
- `switch` statement (multiple selection)

In fact, it is straightforward to prove that the simple `if` statement is sufficient to provide any form of selection—everything that can be done with the `if...else` statement and the `switch` statement can be implemented with one or more `if` statements.

Repetition is implemented in one of three ways:

- `while` statement
- `do...while` statement
- `for` statement

It is straightforward to prove that the `while` statement is sufficient to provide any form of repetition. Everything that can be done with the `do...while` statement and the `for` statement can be done with the `while` statement.

Combining these results illustrates that any form of control ever needed in a C program can be expressed in terms of only three forms of control:

- sequence
- `if` statement (selection)
- `while` statement (repetition)

And these control statements can be combined in only two ways—stacking and nesting. Indeed, structured programming promotes simplicity.

In Chapters 3 and 4, we discussed how to compose programs from control statements containing actions and decisions. In Chapter 5, we introduce another program structuring unit called the function. We will learn to compose large programs by combining functions, which, in turn, are composed of control statements. We will also discuss how using functions promotes software reusability.

Summary

Section 4.2 Repetition Essentials

- Most programs involve repetition, or looping. A loop is a group of instructions the computer executes repeatedly while some loop-continuation condition remains true.
- Counter-controlled repetition is sometimes called definite repetition because we know in advance exactly how many times the loop will execute.
- Sentinel-controlled repetition is sometimes called indefinite repetition because it is not known in advance how many times the loop will execute.
- In counter-controlled repetition, a control variable is used to count the number of repetitions. The control variable is incremented (usually by 1) each time the group of instructions is performed. When the value of the control variable indicates that the correct number of repetitions has been performed, the loop terminates, and the computer continues executing with the statement after the repetition statement.

- Sentinel values are used to control repetition when the precise number of repetitions is not known in advance, and the loop includes statements that obtain data each time the loop is performed.
- The sentinel value indicates "end of data." The sentinel is entered after all regular data items have been supplied to the program. Sentinels must be distinct from regular data items.

Section 4.3 Counter-Controlled Repetition

- Counter-controlled repetition requires the name of a control variable (or loop counter), the initial value of the control variable, the increment (or decrement) by which the control variable is modified each time through the loop, and the condition that tests for the final value of the control variable (i.e., whether looping should continue).

Section 4.4 for Repetition Statement

- The for repetition statement handles all the details of counter-controlled repetition.
- When the for statement begins executing, its control variable is initialized. Then, the loop-continuation condition is checked. If the condition is true, the loop's body executes. The control variable is then incremented, and the loop begins again with the loop-continuation condition. This process continues until the loop-continuation condition fails.
- The general format of the for statement is

      for (*expression1; expression2; expression3*)
         statement

  where *expression1* initializes the loop-control variable, *expression2* is the loop-continuation condition, and *expression3* increments the control variable.

  In most cases, the for statement can be represented with an equivalent while statement as in:

      expression1;

      while (*expression2*) {
         statement
         expression3;
      }

- The comma operator guarantees that lists of expressions evaluate from left to right. The value and type of a comma-separated list of expressions is the value and type of the rightmost expression in the list. The comma operator is most often used in the for statement. Its primary use is to enable you to use multiple initialization and/or multiple increment expressions.
- The three expressions in the for statement are optional. If *expression2* is omitted, C assumes that the condition is true, thus creating an infinite loop. One might omit *expression1* if the control variable is initialized elsewhere in the program. *expression3* might be omitted if the increment is calculated by statements in the body of the for statement or if no increment is needed.
- The increment expression in the for statement acts like a stand-alone C statement at the end of the body of the for.
- The two semicolons in the for statement are required.

Section 4.5 for Statement: Notes and Observations

- The initialization, loop-continuation condition and increment can contain arithmetic expressions.
- The "increment" may be negative (in which case it is really a decrement and the loop actually counts downward).

- If the loop-continuation condition is initially false, the body portion of the loop is not performed. Instead, execution proceeds with the statement following the for statement.

- The control variable is frequently printed or used in calculations in the body of a loop, but it need not be.

Section 4.6 Examples Using the *for Statement*

- The C Standard Library function pow is used to perform exponentiation. The function pow(x, y) calculates the value of x raised to the yth power. It takes two arguments of type double and returns a double value.

- Type double is a floating-point type much like float, but typically a variable of type double can store a value of much greater magnitude with greater precision than float.

- The header <math.h> should be included whenever a math function such as pow is used.

- The conversion specifier %21.2f denotes that a floating-point value will be displayed right justified in a field of 21 characters with two digits to the right of the decimal point.

- To left justify a value in a field, place a - (minus sign) between the % and the field width.

Section 4.7 *switch Multiple-Selection Statement*

- Occasionally, an algorithm will contain a series of decisions in which a variable or expression is tested separately for each of the constant integral values it may assume, and different actions are taken. This is called multiple selection. C provides the switch multiple-selection statement to handle such decision making.

- The switch statement consists of a series of case labels and an optional default case.

- The getchar function (from the standard input/output library) reads and returns one character from the keyboard.

- Characters are normally stored in variables of type char. Characters can be stored in any integer data type because they are usually represented as one-byte integers in the computer. Thus, we can treat a character as either an integer or a character, depending on its use.

- Many computers today use the ASCII (American Standard Code for Information Interchange) character set in which 97 represents the lowercase letter 'a'.

- Characters can be read with scanf by using the conversion specifier %c.

- Assignment expressions as a whole actually have a value. This value is assigned to the variable on the left side of the =.

- The fact that assignment statements have values can be useful for setting several variables to the same value, as in a = b = c = 0;.

- EOF is commonly used as a sentinel value. EOF is a symbolic integer constant defined in the <stdio.h> header.

- On Linux/UNIX systems and many others, the EOF indicator is entered by typing the sequence

    <Ctrl> d

    On other systems, such as Microsoft Windows, the EOF indicator can be entered by typing

    <Ctrl> z

- Keyword switch is followed by the controlling expression in parentheses. The value of this expression is compared with each of the case labels. If a match occurs, the statements for that case execute. If no match occurs, the default case executes.

- The break statement causes program control to continue with the first statement after the switch statement. The break statement is used because the cases in a switch statement would otherwise run together. If break is not used anywhere in a switch statement, then each time a match occurs in the statement, the statements for all the remaining cases will be executed.

- Each case can have one or more actions. The switch statement is different from all other control statements in that braces are not required around multiple actions in a case of a switch.

- Note that several listing case labels together simply means that the same set of actions is to occur for any of these cases.

- When using the switch statement, remember that it can be used only for testing a constant integral expression—i.e., any combination of character constants and integer constants that evaluates to a constant integer value. A character constant is represented as the specific character in single quotes, such as 'A'. Characters must be enclosed within single quotes to be recognized as character constants. Integer constants are simply integer values.

- C provides several data types to represent integers. The range of integer values for each type depends on the particular computer's hardware. In addition to the types int and char, C provides types short (an abbreviation of short int) and long (an abbreviation of long int). The minimum range of values for short integers is –32768 to +32767. For the vast majority of integer calculations, long integers are sufficient. The standard specifies that the minimum range of values for long integers is –2147483648 to +2147483647. The standard states that the range of values for an int is at least the same as the range for short integers and no larger than the range for long integers. The data type signed char can be used to represent integers in the range –128 to +127 or any of the characters in the computer's character set.

Section 4.8 do...while *Repetition Statement*
- The do...while statement tests the loop-continuation condition *after* the loop body is performed. Therefore, the loop body will be executed at least once. When a do...while terminates, execution continues with the statement after the while clause.

Section 4.9 break *and* continue *Statements*
- The break statement, when executed in a while, for, do...while or switch statement, causes immediate exit from that statement. Program execution continues with the next statement.

- The continue statement, when executed in a while, for or do...while statement, skips the remaining statements in the body of that control statement and performs the next iteration of the loop. In while and do...while statements, the loop-continuation test is evaluated immediately after the continue statement is executed. In the for statement, the increment expression is executed, then the loop-continuation test is evaluated.

Section 4.10 *Logical Operators*
- Logical operators may be used to form complex conditions by combining simple conditions. The logical operators are && (logical AND), || (logical OR) and ! (logical NOT, also called logical negation).

- A condition containing the && (logical AND) operator is true if and only if both of the simple conditions are true.

- C evaluates all expressions that include relational operators, equality operators, and/or logical operators to 0 or 1. Although C sets a true value to 1, it accepts *any* nonzero value as true.

- A condition containing the || (logical OR) operator is true if either or both of the simple conditions are true.

- The && operator has a higher precedence than ||. Both operators associate from left to right.

- An expression containing && or || operators is evaluated only until truth or falsehood is known.

- C provides ! (logical negation) to enable a programmer to "reverse" the meaning of a condition. Unlike the binary operators && and ||, which combine two conditions, the unary logical negation operator has only a single condition as an operand.

- The logical negation operator is placed before a condition when we are interested in choosing a path of execution if the original condition (without the logical negation operator) is false.

- In most cases, you can avoid using logical negation by expressing the condition differently with an appropriate relational operator.

Section 4.11 Confusing Equality (==) and Assignment (=) Operators

- One error that C programmers, no matter how experienced, tend to make is accidentally swapping the operators == (equality) and = (assignment). What makes these swaps so damaging is that they do not ordinarily cause syntax errors. Rather, statements with these errors ordinarily compile correctly, allowing programs to run to completion while likely generating incorrect results through runtime logic errors.

- Two aspects of C cause these problems. One is that any expression in C that produces a value can be used in the decision portion of any control statement. If the value is 0, it is treated as false, and if the value is nonzero, it is treated as true. The second is that assignments in C produce a value, namely the value that is assigned to the variable on the left side of the assignment operator.

- Programmers normally write conditions such as x == 7 with the variable name on the left and the constant on the right. By reversing these terms so that the constant is on the left and the variable name is on the right, as in 7 == x, the programmer who accidentally replaces the == operator with = will be protected by the compiler. The compiler will treat this as a syntax error, because only a variable name can be placed on the left-hand side of an assignment statement.

- Variable names are said to be *lvalues* (for "left values") because they can be used on the left side of an assignment operator.

- Constants are said to be *rvalues* (for "right values") because they can be used only on the right side of an assignment operator. Note that *lvalues* can also be used as *rvalues*, but not vice versa.

Terminology

ASCII character set	field width
body of a loop	final value of control variable
break control statement	for repetition statement
case label	getchar function
char	increment control variable
continue control statement	indefinite repetition
control variable	infinite loop
counter-controlled repetition	initial value of control variable
<Ctrl> d	left justify
<Ctrl> z	logical AND (&&)
decrement control variable	logical negation (!)
default case in switch	logical operators
definite repetition	logical OR (||)
double	long
do...while repetition statement	loop-continuation condition
end of file	loop-control variable
EOF	loop counter

lvalue ("left value")
minus sign for left justification
multiple selection
nested control statements
nesting rule
off-by-one error
pow function
repetition statements
right justify
rvalue ("right value")

`short`
`signed char`
simple condition
single-entry/single-exit control statements
stacking rule
`switch` selection statement
truth table
unary operator
`while` repetition statement

Self-Review Exercises

4.1 Fill in the blanks in each of the following statements.
a) Counter-controlled repetition is also known as _____ repetition because it is known in advance how many times the loop will be executed.
b) Sentinel-controlled repetition is also known as _____ repetition because it is not known in advance how many times the loop will be executed.
c) In counter-controlled repetition, a(n) _____ is used to count the number of times a group of instructions should be repeated.
d) The _____ statement, when executed in a repetition statement, causes the next iteration of the loop to be performed immediately.
e) The _____ statement, when executed in a repetition statement or a `switch`, causes an immediate exit from the statement.
f) The _____ is used to test a particular variable or expression for each of the constant integral values it may assume.

4.2 State whether the following are *true* or *false*. If the answer is *false*, explain why.
a) The `default` case is required in the `switch` selection statement.
b) The `break` statement is required in the `default` case of a `switch` selection statement.
c) The expression (x > y && a < b) is true if either x > y is true or a < b is true.
d) An expression containing the || operator is true if either or both of its operands is true.

4.3 Write a statement or a set of statements to accomplish each of the following tasks:
a) Sum the odd integers between 1 and 99 using a `for` statement. Assume the integer variables sum and count have been defined.
b) Print the value 333.546372 in a field width of 15 characters with precisions of 1, 2, 3, 4 and 5. Left justify the output. What are the five values that print?
c) Calculate the value of 2.5 raised to the power of 3 using the pow function. Print the result with a precision of 2 in a field width of 10 positions. What is the value that prints?
d) Print the integers from 1 to 20 using a `while` loop and the counter variable x. Assume that the variable x has been defined, but not initialized. Print only five integers per line. [*Hint:* Use the calculation x % 5. When the value of this is 0, print a newline character, otherwise print a tab character.]
e) Repeat Exercise 4.3 (d) using a `for` statement.

4.4 Find the error in each of the following code segments and explain how to correct it.
a) `x = 1;`
```
while ( x <= 10 );
    x++;
}
```

b) ```
    for (y = .1; y != 1.0; y += .1)
        printf("%f\n", y);
    ```
c)  ```
    switch ( n ) {
        case 1:
            printf( "The number is 1\n" );
        case 2:
            printf( "The number is 2\n" );
            break;
        default:
            printf( "The number is not 1 or 2\n" );
            break;
    }
    ```
d) The following code should print the values 1 to 10.

    ```
    n = 1;
    while ( n < 10 )
        printf( "%d ", n++ );
    ```

Answers to Self-Review Exercises

4.1 a) definite. b) indefinite. c) control variable or counter. d) `continue`. e) `break`. f) `switch` selection statement.

4.2 a) False. The `default` case is optional. If no default action is needed, then there is no need for a `default` case.
b) False. The `break` statement is used to exit the `switch` statement. The `break` statement is not required when the `default` case is the last case.
c) False. Both of the relational expressions must be true in order for the entire expression to be true when using the `&&` operator.
d) True.

4.3 a) ```
    sum = 0;
    for (count = 1; count <= 99; count += 2)
        sum += count;
    ```
b)  ```
    printf( "%-15.1f\n", 333.546372 );   /* prints 333.5      */
    printf( "%-15.2f\n", 333.546372 );   /* prints 333.55     */
    printf( "%-15.3f\n", 333.546372 );   /* prints 333.546    */
    printf( "%-15.4f\n", 333.546372 );   /* prints 333.5464   */
    printf( "%-15.5f\n", 333.546372 );   /* prints 333.54637  */
    ```
c) ```
    printf("%10.2f\n", pow(2.5, 3)); /* prints 15.63   */
    ```
d)  ```
    x = 1;
    while ( x <= 20 ) {
        printf( "%d", x );
        if ( x % 5 == 0 )
            printf( "\n" );
        else
            printf( "\t" );
        x++;
    }
    ```

    or

```
x = 1;
while ( x <= 20 )
    if ( x % 5 == 0 )
        printf( "%d\n", x++ );
    else
        printf( "%d\t", x++ );
```

or

```
x = 0;
while ( ++x <= 20 )
    if ( x % 5 == 0 )
        printf( "%d\n", x );
    else
        printf( "%d\t", x );
```

e)
```
for ( x = 1; x <= 20; x++ ) {
    printf( "%d", x );
    if ( x % 5 == 0 )
        printf( "\n" );
    else
        printf( "\t" );
}
```

or

```
for ( x = 1; x <= 20; x++ )
    if ( x % 5 == 0 )
        printf( "%d\n", x );
    else
        printf( "%d\t", x );
```

4.4   a) Error: The semicolon after the while header causes an infinite loop.
         Correction: Replace the semicolon with a { or remove both the ; and the }.
     b) Error: Using a floating-point number to control a for repetition statement.
         Correction: Use an integer, and perform the proper calculation in order to get the values
         you desire.

```
for ( y = 1; y != 10; y++ )
    printf( "%f\n", ( float ) y / 10 );
```

     c) Error: Missing break statement in the statements for the first case.
         Correction: Add a break statement at the end of the statements for the first case. Note
         that this is not necessarily an error if you want the statement of case 2: to execute every
         time the case 1: statement executes.
     d) Error: Improper relational operator used in the while repetition-continuation condi-
         tion.
         Correction: Use <= rather than <.

Exercises

4.5   Find the error in each of the following. (*Note:* There may be more than one error.)
     a)
```
For ( x = 100, x >= 1, x++ )
    printf( "%d\n", x );
```

b) The following code should print whether a given integer is odd or even:

```
switch ( value % 2 ) {
    case 0:
      printf( "Even integer\n" );
    case 1:
      printf( "Odd integer\n" );
}
```

c) The following code should input an integer and a character and print them. Assume the user types as input 100 A.

```
scanf( "%d", &intVal );
charVal = getchar();
printf( "Integer: %d\nCharacter: %c\n", intVal, charVal );
```

d)
```
for ( x = .000001; x == .0001; x += .000001 )
    printf( "%.7f\n", x );
```

e) The following code should output the odd integers from 999 to 1:

```
for ( x = 999; x >= 1; x += 2 )
    printf( "%d\n", x );
```

f) The following code should output the even integers from 2 to 100:

```
counter = 2;
```
do
```
Do {
    if ( counter % 2 == 0 )
      printf( "%d\n", counter );
```
=<
```
    counter += 2;
```
while `} While ( counter < 100 );` —no semi colon

g) The following code should sum the integers from 100 to 150 (assume total is initialized to 0):

```
for ( x = 100; x <= 150; x++ );
    total += x;
```

4.6   State which values of the control variable x are printed by each of the following for statements:

a)
```
for ( x = 2; x <= 13; x += 2 )
    printf( "%d\n", x );
```
b)
```
for ( x = 5; x <= 22; x += 7 )
    printf( "%d\n", x );
```
c)
```
for ( x = 3; x <= 15; x += 3 )
    printf( "%d\n", x );
```
d)
```
for ( x = 1; x <= 5; x += 7 )
    printf( "%d\n", x );
```
e)
```
for ( x = 12; x >= 2; x -= 3 )
    printf( "%d\n", x );
```

4.7   Write for statements that print the following sequences of values:
a)   1, 2, 3, 4, 5, 6, 7
b)   3, 8, 13, 18, 23
c)   20, 14, 8, 2, –4, –10
d)   19, 27, 35, 43, 51

4.8 What does the following program do?

```
1   #include <stdio.h>
2
3   /* function main begins program execution */
4   int main( void )
5   {
6      int x;
7      int y;
8      int i;
9      int j;
10
11     /* prompt user for input */
12     printf( "Enter two integers in the range 1-20: " );
13     scanf( "%d%d", &x, &y ); /* read values for x and y */
14
15     for ( i = 1; i <= y; i++ ) { /* count from 1 to y */
16
17        for ( j = 1; j <= x; j++ ) { /* count from 1 to x */
18           printf( "@" ); /* output @ */
19        } /* end inner for */
20
21        printf( "\n" ); /* begin new line */
22     } /* end outer for */
23
24     return 0; /* indicate program ended successfully */
25
26  } /* end function main */
```

4.9 Write a program that sums a sequence of integers. Assume that the first integer read with scanf specifies the number of values remaining to be entered. Your program should read only one value each time scanf is executed. A typical input sequence might be

    5 100 200 300 400 500

where the 5 indicates that the subsequent five values are to be summed.

4.10 Write a program that calculates and prints the average of several integers. Assume the last value read with scanf is the sentinel 9999. A typical input sequence might be

    10 8 11 7 9 9999

indicating that the average of all the values preceding 9999 is to be calculated.

4.11 Write a program that finds the smallest of several integers. Assume that the first value read specifies the number of values remaining.

4.12 Write a program that calculates and prints the sum of the even integers from 2 to 30.

4.13 Write a program that calculates and prints the product of the odd integers from 1 to 15.

4.14 The *factorial* function is used frequently in probability problems. The factorial of a positive integer n (written $n!$ and pronounced "n factorial") is equal to the product of the positive integers from 1 to n. Write a program that evaluates the factorials of the integers from 1 to 5. Print the results in tabular format. What difficulty might prevent you from calculating the factorial of 20?

4.15 Modify the compound-interest program of Section 4.6 to repeat its steps for interest rates of 5%, 6%, 7%, 8%, 9%, and 10%. Use a for loop to vary the interest rate.

4.16 Write a program that prints the following patterns separately, one below the other. Use for loops to generate the patterns. All asterisks (*) should be printed by a single printf statement of the form printf("*"); (this causes the asterisks to print side by side). [*Hint:* The last two patterns require that each line begin with an appropriate number of blanks.]

```
(A)              (B)              (C)              (D)
*                **********       **********                *
**               *********        *********                **
***              ********         ********                 ***
****             *******          *******                  ****
*****            ******           ******                   *****
******           *****            *****                    ******
*******          ****             ****                     *******
********          ***              ***                     ********
*********         **               **                     *********
**********         *                *                     **********
```

4.17 Collecting money becomes increasingly difficult during periods of recession, so companies may tighten their credit limits to prevent their accounts receivable (money owed to them) from becoming too large. In response to a prolonged recession, one company has cut its customers' credit limits in half. Thus, if a particular customer had a credit limit of $2000, it is now $1000. If a customer had a credit limit of $5000, it is now $2500. Write a program that analyzes the credit status of three customers of this company. For each customer you are given:
   a) The customer's account number
   b) The customer's credit limit before the recession
   c) The customer's current balance (i.e., the amount the customer owes the company).

   Your program should calculate and print the new credit limit for each customer and should determine (and print) which customers have current balances that exceed their new credit limits.

4.18 One interesting application of computers is drawing graphs and bar charts (sometimes called "histograms"). Write a program that reads five numbers (each between 1 and 30). For each number read, your program should print a line containing that number of adjacent asterisks. For example, if your program reads the number seven, it should print *******.

4.19 A mail order house sells five different products whose retail prices are shown in the following table:

Product number	Retail price
1	$ 2.98
2	$ 4.50
3	$ 9.98
4	$ 4.49
5	$ 6.87

Write a program that reads a series of pairs of numbers as follows:
   a) Product number
   b) Quantity sold for one day

Your program should use a switch statement to help determine the retail price for each product. Your program should calculate and display the total retail value of all products sold last week.

4.20 Complete the following truth tables by filling in each blank with 0 or 1.

Condition1	Condition2	Condition1 && Condition2
0	0	0
0	nonzero	0
nonzero	0	_____
nonzero	nonzero	_____

Condition1	Condition2	Condition1 || Condition2
0	0	0
0	nonzero	1
nonzero	0	_____
nonzero	nonzero	_____

Condition1	! Condition1
0	1
nonzero	_____

4.21 Rewrite the program of Fig. 4.2 so that the initialization of the variable counter is done in the definition instead of in the for statement.

4.22 Modify the program of Fig. 4.7 so that it calculates the average grade for the class.

4.23 Modify the program of Fig. 4.6 so that it uses only integers to calculate the compound interest. [*Hint:* Treat all monetary amounts as integral numbers of pennies. Then "break" the result into its dollar portion and cents portion by using the division and remainder operations, respectively. Insert a period.]

4.24 Assume i = 1, j = 2, k = 3 and m = 2. What does each of the following statements print?
    a) printf("%d", i == 1);
    b) printf("%d", j == 3);
    c) printf("%d", i >= 1 && j < 4);
    d) printf("%d", m < = 99 && k < m);
    e) printf("%d", j >= i || k == m);
    f) printf("%d", k + m < j || 3 - j >= k);
    g) printf("%d", !m);
    h) printf("%d", !(j - m));
    i) printf("%d", !(k > m));
    j) printf("%d", !(j > k));

4.25 Write a program that prints a table of the binary, octal and hexadecimal equivalents of the decimal numbers in the range 1 through 256. If you are not familiar with these number systems, read Appendix D before you attempt this exercise.

4.26 Calculate the value of π from the infinite series

$$\pi = 4 - \frac{4}{3} + \frac{4}{5} - \frac{4}{7} + \frac{4}{9} - \frac{4}{11} + \cdots$$

Print a table that shows the value of π approximated by one term of this series, by two terms, by three terms, and so on. How many terms of this series do you have to use before you first get 3.14? 3.141? 3.1415? 3.14159?

4.27 *(Pythagorean Triples)* A right triangle can have sides that are all integers. The set of three integer values for the sides of a right triangle is called a Pythagorean triple. These three sides must satisfy the relationship that the sum of the squares of two of the sides is equal to the square of the hypotenuse. Find all Pythagorean triples for side1, side2, and the hypotenuse all no larger than 500. Use a triple-nested for loop that simply tries all possibilities. This is an example of "brute-force" computing. It is not aesthetically pleasing to many people. But there are many reasons why these techniques are important. First, with computing power increasing at such a phenomenal pace, solutions that would have taken years or even centuries of computer time to produce with the technology of just a few years ago can now be produced in hours, minutes or even seconds. Recent microprocessor chips can process a billion instructions per second! Second, as you will learn in more advanced computer science courses, there are large numbers of interesting problems for which there is no known algorithmic approach other than sheer brute force. We investigate many kinds of problem-solving methodologies in this book. We will consider many brute-force approaches to various interesting problems.

4.28 A company pays its employees as managers (who receive a fixed weekly salary), hourly workers (who receive a fixed hourly wage for up to the first 40 hours they work and "time-and-a-half"—i.e., 1.5 times their hourly wage—for overtime hours worked), commission workers (who receive $250 plus 5.7% of their gross weekly sales), or pieceworkers (who receive a fixed amount of money for each of the items they produce—each pieceworker in this company works on only one type of item). Write a program to compute the weekly pay for each employee. You do not know the number of employees in advance. Each type of employee has its own pay code: Managers have paycode 1, hourly workers have code 2, commission workers have code 3 and pieceworkers have code 4. Use a switch to compute each employee's pay based on that employee's paycode. Within the switch, prompt the user (i.e., the payroll clerk) to enter the appropriate facts your program needs to calculate each employee's pay based on that employee's paycode.

4.29 *(De Morgan's Laws)* In this chapter, we discussed the logical operators &&, ||, and !. De Morgan's Laws can sometimes make it more convenient for us to express a logical expression. These laws state that the expression !(*condition1* && *condition2*) is logically equivalent to the expression (!*condition1* || !*condition2*). Also, the expression !(*condition1* || *condition2*) is logically equivalent to the expression (!*condition1* && !*condition2*). Use De Morgan's Laws to write equivalent expressions for each of the following, and then write a program to show that both the original expression and the new expression in each case are equivalent.

   a) !(x < 5) && !(y >= 7)
   b) !(a == b) || !(g != 5)
   c) !((x <= 8) && (y > 4))
   d) !((i > 4) || (j <= 6))

4.30 Rewrite the program of Fig. 4.7 by replacing the switch statement with a nested if...else statement; be careful to deal with the default case properly. Then rewrite this new version by replacing the nested if...else statement with a series of if statements; here, too, be careful to deal with the default case properly (this is more difficult than in the nested if...else version). This exercise demonstrates that switch is a convenience and that any switch statement can be written with only single-selection statements.

4.31 Write a program that prints the following diamond shape. You may use printf statements that print either a single asterisk (*) or a single blank. Maximize your use of repetition (with nested for statements) and minimize the number of printf statements.

```
        *
       ***
      *****
     *******
    *********
     *******
      *****
       ***
        *
```

4.32 Modify the program you wrote in Exercise 4.31 to read an odd number in the range 1 to 19 to specify the number of rows in the diamond. Your program should then display a diamond of the appropriate size.

4.33 Write a program that prints a table of all the Roman numeral equivalents of the decimal numbers in the range 1 to 100.

4.34 Describe the process you would use to replace a do...while loop with an equivalent while loop. What problem occurs when you try to replace a while loop with an equivalent do...while loop? Suppose you have been told that you must remove a while loop and replace it with a do...while. What additional control statement would you need to use and how would you use it to ensure that the resulting program behaves exactly as the original?

4.35 Write a program that inputs the years in the range 1994 through 1999 and uses for-loop repetition to produce a condensed, neatly printed calendar. Watch out for leap years.

4.36 A criticism of the break statement and the continue statement is that each is unstructured. Actually, break statements and continue statements can always be replaced by structured statements, although doing so can be awkward. Describe in general how you would remove any break statement from a loop in a program and replace that statement with some structured equivalent. [*Hint:* The break statement leaves a loop from within the body of the loop. The other way to leave is by failing the loop-continuation test. Consider using in the loop-continuation test a second test that indicates "early exit because of a 'break' condition."] Use the technique you developed here to remove the break statement from the program of Fig. 4.11.

4.37 What does the following program segment do?

```
1   for ( i = 1; i <= 5; i++ ) {
2      for ( j = 1; j <= 3; j++ ) {
3         for ( k = 1; k <= 4; k++ )
4            printf( "*" );
5         printf( "\n" );
6      }
7      printf( "\n" );
8   }
```

4.38 Describe in general how you would remove any continue statement from a loop in a program and replace that statement with some structured equivalent. Use the technique you developed here to remove the continue statement from the program of Fig. 4.12.

C Functions

OBJECTIVES

In this chapter, you will learn:

- To construct programs modularly from small pieces called functions.

- The common math functions available in the C Standard Library.

- To create new functions.

- The mechanisms used to pass information between functions.

- How the function call/return mechanism is supported by the function call stack and activation records.

- Simulation techniques using random number generation.

- How to write and use recursive functions, i.e., functions that call themselves.

5.1 Introduction

Most computer programs that solve real-world problems are much larger than the programs presented in the first few chapters. Experience has shown that the best way to develop and maintain a large program is to construct it from smaller pieces or modules, each of which is more manageable than the original program. This technique is called divide and conquer. This chapter describes the features of the C language that facilitate the design, implementation, operation, and maintenance of large programs.

5.2 Program Modules in C

Modules in C are called functions. C programs are typically written by combining new functions you write with "prepackaged" functions available in the C Standard Library. We discuss both kinds of functions in this chapter. The C Standard Library provides a rich collection of functions for performing common mathematical calculations, string manipulations, character manipulations, input/output, and many other useful operations. This makes your job easier, because these functions provide many of the capabilities you need.

 Good Programming Practice 5.1

Familiarize yourself with the rich collection of functions in the C Standard Library.

 Software Engineering Observation 5.1

Avoid reinventing the wheel. When possible, use C Standard Library functions instead of writing new functions. This can reduce program development time.

Portability Tip 5.1

Using the functions in the C Standard Library helps make programs more portable.

Although the Standard Library functions are technically not a part of the C language, they are provided with standard C systems. The functions printf, scanf and pow that we have used in previous chapters are Standard Library functions.

You can write functions to define specific tasks that may be used at many points in a program. These are sometimes referred to as **programmer-defined functions**. The actual statements defining the function are written only once, and the statements are hidden from other functions.

Functions are invoked by a **function call**, which specifies the function name and provides information (as **arguments**) that the called function needs in order to perform its designated task. A common analogy for this is the hierarchical form of management. A boss (the **calling function** or **caller**) asks a worker (the **called function**) to perform a task and report back when the task is done (Fig. 5.1). For example, a function needing to display information on the screen calls the worker function printf to perform that task, then printf displays the information and reports back—or **returns**—to the calling function when its task is completed. The boss function does not know how the worker function performs its designated tasks. The worker may call other worker functions, and the boss will be unaware of this. We will soon see how this "hiding" of implementation details promotes good software engineering. Figure 5.1 shows the main function communicating with several worker functions in a hierarchical manner. Note that worker1 acts as a boss function to worker4 and worker5. Relationships among functions may differ from the hierarchical structure shown in this figure.

5.3 Math Library Functions

Math library functions allow you to perform certain common mathematical calculations. We use various math library functions here to introduce the concept of functions. Later in the book, we will discuss many of the other functions in the C Standard Library.

Functions are normally used in a program by writing the name of the function followed by a left parenthesis followed by the **argument** (or a comma-separated list of

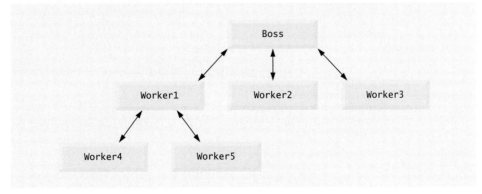

Fig. 5.1 | Hierarchical boss function/worker function relationship.

arguments) of the function followed by a right parenthesis. For example, a programmer desiring to calculate and print the square root of 900.0 might write

```
printf( "%.2f", sqrt( 900.0 ) );
```

When this statement executes, the math library function sqrt is called to calculate the square root of the number contained in the parentheses (900.0). The number 900.0 is the argument of the sqrt function. The preceding statement would print 30.00. The sqrt function takes an argument of type double and returns a result of type double. All functions in the math library that return floating point values return the data type double. Note that double values, like float values, can be output using the %f conversion specification.

Error-Prevention Tip 5.1

Include the math header by using the preprocessor directive #include <math.h> when using functions in the math library.

Function arguments may be constants, variables, or expressions. If c1 = 13.0, d = 3.0 and f = 4.0, then the statement

```
printf( "%.2f", sqrt( c1 + d * f ) );
```

calculates and prints the square root of 13.0 + 3.0 * 4.0 = 25.0, namely 5.00.

Some C math library functions are summarized in Fig. 5.2. In the figure, the variables x and y are of type double.

Function	Description	Example
sqrt(x)	square root of *x*	sqrt(900.0) is 30.0 sqrt(9.0) is 3.0
exp(x)	exponential function e^x	exp(1.0) is 2.718282 exp(2.0) is 7.389056
log(x)	natural logarithm of *x* (base *e*)	log(2.718282) is 1.0 log(7.389056) is 2.0
log10(x)	logarithm of *x* (base 10)	log10(1.0) is 0.0 log10(10.0) is 1.0 log10(100.0) is 2.0
fabs(x)	absolute value of *x*	fabs(5.0) is 5.0 fabs(0.0) is 0.0 fabs(-5.0) is 5.0
ceil(x)	rounds *x* to the smallest integer not less than *x*	ceil(9.2) is 10.0 ceil(-9.8) is -9.0
floor(x)	rounds *x* to the largest integer not greater than *x*	floor(9.2) is 9.0 floor(-9.8) is -10.0
pow(x, y)	*x* raised to power *y* (x^y)	pow(2, 7) is 128.0 pow(9, .5) is 3.0

Fig. 5.2 | Commonly used math library functions. (Part 1 of 2.)

Function	Description	Example
fmod(x, y)	remainder of x/y as a floating-point number	fmod(13.657, 2.333) is 1.992
sin(x)	trigonometric sine of x (x in radians)	sin(0.0) is 0.0
cos(x)	trigonometric cosine of x (x in radians)	cos(0.0) is 1.0
tan(x)	trigonometric tangent of x (x in radians)	tan(0.0) is 0.0

Fig. 5.2 | Commonly used math library functions. (Part 2 of 2.)

5.4 Functions

Functions allow you to modularize a program. All variables defined in function definitions are local variables—they are known only in the function in which they are defined. Most functions have a list of **parameters**. The parameters provide the means for communicating information between functions. A function's parameters are also local variables of that function.

Software Engineering Observation 5.2

In programs containing many functions, main is often implemented as a group of calls to functions that perform the bulk of the program's work.

There are several motivations for "functionalizing" a program. The divide-and-conquer approach makes program development more manageable. Another motivation is **software reusability**—using existing functions as building-blocks to create new programs. Software reusability is a major factor in the object-oriented programming movement that you will learn more about when you study languages derived from C, such as C++, Java and C# (pronounced "C sharp"). With good function naming and definition, programs can be created from standardized functions that accomplish specific tasks, rather than being built by using customized code. This technique is known as **abstraction**. We use abstraction each time we write programs that use standard library functions like printf, scanf and pow. A third motivation is to avoid repeating code in a program. Packaging code as a function allows the code to be executed from several locations in a program simply by calling the function.

Software Engineering Observation 5.3

Each function should be limited to performing a single, well-defined task, and the function name should effectively express that task. This facilitates abstraction and promotes software reusability.

Software Engineering Observation 5.4

If you cannot choose a concise name that expresses what the function does, it is possible that your function is attempting to perform too many diverse tasks. It is usually best to break such a function into several smaller functions.

5.5 Function Definitions

Each program we have presented has consisted of a function called main that called standard library functions to accomplish its tasks. We now consider how to write custom functions. Consider a program that uses a function square to calculate and print the squares of the integers from 1 to 10 (Fig. 5.3).

 Good Programming Practice 5.2

Place a blank line between function definitions to separate the functions and enhance program readability.

Function square is invoked or called in main within the printf statement (line 14)

```
printf( "%d  ", square( x ) ); /* function call */
```

Function square receives a copy of the value of x in the parameter y (line 24). Then square calculates y * y (line 26). The result is passed back to function printf in main where square was invoked, and printf displays the result. This process is repeated ten times using the for repetition statement.

```
1   /* Fig. 5.3: fig05_03.c
2      Creating and using a programmer-defined function */
3   #include <stdio.h>
4
5   int square( int y ); /* function prototype */
6
7   /* function main begins program execution */
8   int main( void )
9   {
10     int x; /* counter */
11
12     /* loop 10 times and calculate and output square of x each time */
13     for ( x = 1; x <= 10; x++ ) {
14        printf( "%d  ", square( x ) ); /* function call */
15     } /* end for */
16
17     printf( "\n" );
18
19     return 0; /* indicates successful termination */
20
21  } /* end main */
22
23  /* square function definition returns square of parameter */
24  int square( int y ) /* y is a copy of argument to function */
25  {
26     return y * y; /* returns square of y as an int */
27
28  } /* end function square */
```

```
1  4  9  16  25  36  49  64  81  100
```

Fig. 5.3 | Using a programmer-defined function.

The definition of function `square` shows that `square` expects an integer parameter y. The keyword `int` preceding the function name (line 24) indicates that `square` returns an integer result. The `return` statement in `square` passes the result of the calculation back to the calling function.

Line 5

```
int square( int y ); /* function prototype */
```

is a **function prototype**. The `int` in parentheses informs the compiler that `square` expects to receive an integer value from the caller. The `int` to the left of the function name `square` informs the compiler that `square` returns an integer result to the caller. The compiler refers to the function prototype to check that calls to `square` (line 14) contain the correct return type, the correct number of arguments, the correct argument types, and that the arguments are in the correct order. Function prototypes are discussed in detail in Section 5.6.

The format of a function definition is

> *return-value-type function-name*(*parameter-list*)
> {
>   *definitions*
>   *statements*
> }

[handwritten: x = given variable. x variables assigned to y. int y]

The *function-name* is any valid identifier. The *return-value-type* is the data type of the result returned to the caller. The *return-value-type* `void` indicates that a function does not return a value. An unspecified *return-value-type* is assumed by the compiler to be `int`. However, omitting the return type is discouraged. Together, the *return-value-type*, *function-name* and *parameter-list* are sometimes referred to as the **function header**.

Common Programming Error 5.1

Omitting the return-value-type in a function definition is a syntax error if the function prototype specifies a return type other than `int`.

Common Programming Error 5.2

Forgetting to return a value from a function that is supposed to return a value can lead to unexpected errors. The C standard states that the result of this omission is undefined.

Common Programming Error 5.3

Returning a value from a function with a `void` return type is a syntax error.

Good Programming Practice 5.3

Even though an omitted return type defaults to `int`, always state the return type explicitly.

The **parameter-list** is a comma-separated list that specifies the parameters received by the function when it is called. If a function does not receive any values, *parameter-list* is `void`. A type must be listed explicitly for each parameter unless the parameter is of type `int`. If a type is not listed, `int` is assumed.

Common Programming Error 5.4

Specifying function parameters of the same type as double x, y instead of double x, double y might cause errors in your programs. The parameter declaration double x, y would actually make y a parameter of type int because int is the default.

Common Programming Error 5.5

Placing a semicolon after the right parenthesis enclosing the parameter list of a function definition is a syntax error.

Common Programming Error 5.6

Defining a function parameter again as a local variable within the function is a syntax error.

Good Programming Practice 5.4

Include the type of each parameter in the parameter list, even if that parameter is of the default type int.

Good Programming Practice 5.5

Although it is not incorrect to do so, do not use the same names for the arguments passed to a function and the corresponding parameters in the function definition. This helps avoid ambiguity.

The *definitions* and *statements* within braces form the **function body**. The function body is also referred to as a **block**. Variables can be declared in any block, and blocks can be nested. *A function cannot be defined inside another function under any circumstances.*

Common Programming Error 5.7

Defining a function inside another function is a syntax error.

Good Programming Practice 5.6

Choosing meaningful function names and meaningful parameter names makes programs more readable and helps avoid excessive use of comments.

Software Engineering Observation 5.5

A function should generally be no longer than one page. Better yet, functions should generally be no longer than half a page. Small functions promote software reusability.

Software Engineering Observation 5.6

Programs should be written as collections of small functions. This makes programs easier to write, debug, maintain and modify.

Software Engineering Observation 5.7

A function requiring a large number of parameters may be performing too many tasks. Consider dividing the function into smaller functions that perform the separate tasks. The function header should fit on one line if possible.

Software Engineering Observation 5.8

The function prototype, function header and function calls should all agree in the number, type, and order of arguments and parameters, and in the type of return value.

There are three ways to return control from a called function to the point at which a function was invoked. If the function does not return a result, control is returned simply when the function-ending right brace is reached, or by executing the statement

> `return`;

If the function does return a result, the statement

> `return` *expression*;

returns the value of *expression* to the caller.

Our second example uses a programmer-defined function `maximum` to determine and return the largest of three integers (Fig. 5.4). The three integers are input with `scanf` (line 15). Next, the integers are passed to `maximum` (line 19), which determines the largest integer. This value is returned to main by the `return` statement in `maximum` (line 39). The value returned is then printed in the `printf` statement (line 19).

```c
1   /* Fig. 5.4: fig05_04.c
2      Finding the maximum of three integers */
3   #include <stdio.h>
4
5   int maximum( int x, int y, int z ); /* function prototype */
6
7   /* function main begins program execution */
8   int main( void )
9   {
10     int number1; /* first integer */
11     int number2; /* second integer */
12     int number3; /* third integer */
13
14     printf( "Enter three integers: " );
15     scanf( "%d%d%d", &number1, &number2, &number3 );
16
17     /* number1, number2 and number3 are arguments
18        to the maximum function call */
19     printf( "Maximum is: %d\n", maximum( number1, number2, number3 ) );
20
21     return 0; /* indicates successful termination */
22
23   } /* end main */
24
25   /* Function maximum definition */
26   /* x, y and z are parameters */
27   int maximum( int x, int y, int z )
28   {
29     int max = x;      /* assume x is largest */
30
31     if ( y > max ) { /* if y is larger than max, assign y to max */
32        max = y;
33     } /* end if */
34
```

Fig. 5.4 | Programmer-defined `maximum` function. (Part 1 of 2.)

```
35      if ( z > max ) { /* if z is larger than max, assign z to max */
36         max = z;
37      } /* end if */
38
39      return max;        /* max is largest value */
40
41   } /* end function maximum */
```

```
Enter three integers: 22 85 17
Maximum is: 85
```

```
Enter three integers: 85 22 17
Maximum is: 85
```

```
Enter three integers: 22 17 85
Maximum is: 85
```

Fig. 5.4 | Programmer-defined `maximum` function. (Part 2 of 2.)

5.6 Function Prototypes

One of the most important features of C is the function prototype. This feature was borrowed by the C standard committee from the developers of C++. A function prototype tells the compiler the type of data returned by the function, the number of parameters the function expects to receive, the types of the parameters, and the order in which these parameters are expected. The compiler uses function prototypes to validate function calls. Previous versions of C did not perform this kind of checking, so it was possible to call functions improperly without the compiler detecting the errors. Such calls could result in fatal execution-time errors or nonfatal errors that caused subtle, difficult-to-detect logic errors. Function prototypes correct this deficiency.

Good Programming Practice 5.7

Include function prototypes for all functions to take advantage of C's type-checking capabilities. Use `#include` preprocessor directives to obtain function prototypes for the standard library functions from the headers for the appropriate libraries, or to obtain headers containing function prototypes for functions developed by you and/or your group members.

The function prototype for `maximum` in Fig. 5.4 (line 5) is

```
int maximum( int x, int y, int z ); /* function prototype */
```

This function prototype states that `maximum` takes three arguments of type `int` and returns a result of type `int`. Notice that the function prototype is the same as the first line of the function definition of `maximum`.

Good Programming Practice 5.8

Parameter names are sometimes included in function prototypes (our preference) for documentation purposes. The compiler ignores these names.

Common Programming Error 5.8

Forgetting the semicolon at the end of a function prototype is a syntax error.

A function call that does not match the function prototype is a syntax error. An error is also generated if the function prototype and the function definition disagree. For example, in Fig. 5.4, if the function prototype had been written

```
void maximum( int x, int y, int z );
```

the compiler would generate an error because the void return type in the function prototype would differ from the int return type in the function header.

Another important feature of function prototypes is the coercion of arguments, i.e., the forcing of arguments to the appropriate type. For example, the math library function sqrt can be called with an integer argument even though the function prototype in <math.h> specifies a double argument, and the function will still work correctly. The statement

```
printf( "%.3f\n", sqrt( 4 ) );
```

correctly evaluates sqrt(4), and prints the value 2.000. The function prototype causes the compiler to convert the integer value 4 to the double value 4.0 before the value is passed to sqrt. In general, argument values that do not correspond precisely to the parameter types in the function prototype are converted to the proper type before the function is called. These conversions can lead to incorrect results if C's promotion rules are not followed. The promotion rules specify how types can be converted to other types without losing data. In our sqrt example above, an int is automatically converted to a double without changing its value. However, a double converted to an int truncates the fractional part of the double value. Converting large integer types to small integer types (e.g., long to short) may also result in changed values.

The promotion rules automatically apply to expressions containing values of two or more data types (also referred to as mixed-type expressions). The type of each value in a mixed-type expression is automatically promoted to the "highest" type in the expression (actually a temporary version of each value is created and used for the expression—the original values remain unchanged). Figure 5.5 lists the data types in order from highest type to lowest type with each type's printf and scanf conversion specifications.

Data type	printf conversion specification	scanf conversion specification
long double	%Lf	%Lf
double	%f	%lf
float	%f	%f
unsigned long int	%lu	%lu

Fig. 5.5 | Promotion hierarchy for data types. (Part 1 of 2.)

Data type	printf conversion specification	scanf conversion specification
long int	%ld	%ld
unsigned int	%u	%u
int	%d	%d
unsigned short	%hu	%hu
short	%hd	%hd
char	%c	%c

Fig. 5.5 | Promotion hierarchy for data types. (Part 2 of 2.)

Converting values to lower types normally results in an incorrect value. Therefore, a value can be converted to a lower type only by explicitly assigning the value to a variable of lower type, or by using a cast operator. Function argument values are converted to the parameter types in a function prototype as if they were being assigned directly to variables of those types. If our square function that uses an integer parameter (Fig. 5.3) is called with a floating-point argument, the argument is converted to int (a lower type), and square usually returns an incorrect value. For example, square(4.5) returns 16, not 20.25.

Common Programming Error 5.9

Converting from a higher data type in the promotion hierarchy to a lower type can change the data value.

If the function prototype for a function has not been included in a program, the compiler forms its own function prototype using the first occurrence of the function—either the function definition or a call to the function. By default, the compiler assumes the function returns an int, and nothing is assumed about the arguments. Therefore, if the arguments passed to the function are incorrect, the errors are not detected by the compiler.

Common Programming Error 5.10

Forgetting a function prototype causes a syntax error if the return type of the function is not int and the function definition appears after the function call in the program. Otherwise, forgetting a function prototype may cause a runtime error or an unexpected result.

Software Engineering Observation 5.9

A function prototype placed outside any function definition applies to all calls to the function appearing after the function prototype in the file. A function prototype placed in a function applies only to calls made in that function.

5.7 Function Call Stack and Activation Records

To understand how C performs function calls, we first need to consider a data structure (i.e., collection of related data items) known as a stack. Students can think of a stack as analogous to a pile of dishes. When a dish is placed on the pile, it is normally placed at the top (referred to as **pushing** the dish onto the stack). Similarly, when a dish is removed from the pile, it is always removed from the top (referred to as **popping** the dish off the stack). Stacks are known as **last-in, first-out (LIFO) data structures**—the last item pushed (inserted) on the stack is the first item popped (removed) from the stack.

When a program calls a function, the called function must know how to return to its caller, so the return address of the calling function is pushed onto the **program execution stack** (sometimes referred to as the **function call stack**). If a series of function calls occurs, the successive return addresses are pushed onto the stack in last-in, first-out order so that each function can return to its caller.

The program execution stack also contains the memory for the local variables used in each invocation of a function during a program's execution. This data, stored as a portion of the program execution stack, is known as the **activation record** or **stack frame** of the function call. When a function call is made, the activation record for that function call is pushed onto the program execution stack. When the function returns to its caller, the activation record for this function call is popped off the stack and those local variables are no longer known to the program. If a local variable holding a reference to an object is the only variable in the program with a reference to that object, when the activation record containing that local variable is popped off the stack, the object can no longer be accessed by the program and will eventually be deleted from memory by the JVM during "garbage collection." We'll discuss garbage collection in Section 8.10.

Of course, the amount of memory in a computer is finite, so only a certain amount of memory can be used to store activation records on the program execution stack. If more function calls occur than can have their activation records stored on the program execution stack, an error known as a **stack overflow** occurs.

5.8 Headers

Each standard library has a corresponding **header** containing the function prototypes for all the functions in that library and definitions of various data types and constants needed by those functions. Figure 5.6 lists alphabetically some of the standard library headers that may be included in programs. The term "macros" that is used several times in Fig. 5.6 is discussed in detail in Chapter 13, C Preprocessor.

Standard library header	Explanation
`<assert.h>`	Contains macros and information for adding diagnostics that aid program debugging.
`<ctype.h>`	Contains function prototypes for functions that test characters for certain properties, and function prototypes for functions that can be used to convert lowercase letters to uppercase letters and vice versa.
`<errno.h>`	Defines macros that are useful for reporting error conditions.
`<float.h>`	Contains the floating-point size limits of the system.

Fig. 5.6 | Some of the standard library headers. (Part 1 of 2.)

Standard library header	Explanation
`<limits.h>`	Contains the integral size limits of the system.
`<locale.h>`	Contains function prototypes and other information that enables a program to be modified for the current locale on which it is running. The notion of locale enables the computer system to handle different conventions for expressing data like dates, times, dollar amounts and large numbers throughout the world.
`<math.h>`	Contains function prototypes for math library functions.
`<setjmp.h>`	Contains function prototypes for functions that allow bypassing of the usual function call and return sequence.
`<signal.h>`	Contains function prototypes and macros to handle various conditions that may arise during program execution.
`<stdarg.h>`	Defines macros for dealing with a list of arguments to a function whose number and types are unknown.
`<stddef.h>`	Contains common definitions of types used by C for performing certain calculations.
`<stdio.h>`	Contains function prototypes for the standard input/output library functions, and information used by them.
`<stdlib.h>`	Contains function prototypes for conversions of numbers to text and text to numbers, memory allocation, random numbers, and other utility functions.
`<string.h>`	Contains function prototypes for string-processing functions.
`<time.h>`	Contains function prototypes and types for manipulating the time and date.

Fig. 5.6 | Some of the standard library headers. (Part 2 of 2.)

You can create custom headers. Programmer-defined headers should also use the `.h` filename extension. A programmer-defined header can be included by using the `#include` preprocessor directive. For example, if the prototype for our square function was located in the header `square.h`, we would include that header in our program by using the following directive at the top of the program:

```
#include "square.h"
```

Section 13.2 presents additional information on including headers.

5.9 Calling Functions: Call-by-Value and Call-by-Reference

There are two ways to invoke functions in many programming languages—call-by-value and call-by-reference. When arguments are passed by value, a *copy* of the argument's value is made and passed to the called function. Changes to the copy do not affect an original variable's value in the caller. When an argument is passed by reference, the caller allows the called function to modify the original variable's value.

Call-by-value should be used whenever the called function does not need to modify the value of the caller's original variable. This prevents the accidental side effects that so greatly hinder the development of correct and reliable software systems. Call-by-reference should be used only with trusted called functions that need to modify the original variable.

In C, all calls are by value. As we will see in Chapter 7, it is possible to simulate call-by-reference by using address operators and indirection operators. In Chapter 6, we will see that arrays are automatically passed by reference. We will have to wait until Chapter 7 for a full understanding of this complex issue. For now, we concentrate on call-by-value.

5.10 Random Number Generation

We now take a brief and, hopefully, entertaining diversion into a popular programming application, namely simulation and game playing. In this and the next section, we will develop a nicely structured game-playing program that includes multiple functions. The program uses most of the control structures we have studied.

There is something in the air of a casino that invigorates people—from the high rollers at the plush mahogany-and-felt craps tables to the quarter poppers at the one-armed bandits. It is the element of chance, the possibility that luck will convert a mere pocketful of money into a mountain of wealth. The element of chance can be introduced into computer applications by using the C Standard Library function rand from the <stdlib.h> header.

Consider the following statement:

```
i = rand();
```

The rand function generates an integer between 0 and RAND_MAX (a symbolic constant defined in the <stdlib.h> header). Standard C states that the value of RAND_MAX must be at least 32767, which is the maximum value for a two-byte (i.e., 16-bit) integer. The programs in this section were tested on a C system with a maximum value of 32767 for RAND_MAX. If rand truly produces integers at random, every number between 0 and RAND_MAX has an equal chance (or probability) of being chosen each time rand is called.

The range of values produced directly by rand is often different from what is needed in a specific application. For example, a program that simulates coin tossing might require only 0 for "heads" and 1 for "tails." A dice-rolling program that simulates a six-sided die would require random integers from 1 to 6.

To demonstrate rand, let us develop a program to simulate 20 rolls of a six-sided die and print the value of each roll. The function prototype for function rand can be found in <stdlib.h>. We use the remainder operator (%) in conjunction with rand as follows

```
rand() % 6
```

to produce integers in the range 0 to 5. This is called scaling. The number 6 is called the scaling factor. We then shift the range of numbers produced by adding 1 to our previous result. The output of Fig. 5.7 confirms that the results are in the range 1 to 6.

```
 1   /* Fig. 5.7: fig05_07.c
 2      Shifted, scaled integers produced by 1 + rand() % 6 */
 3   #include <stdio.h>
 4   #include <stdlib.h>
 5
 6   /* function main begins program execution */
 7   int main( void )
 8   {
 9      int i; /* counter */
10
11      /* loop 20 times */
12      for ( i = 1; i <= 20; i++ ) {
13
14         /* pick random number from 1 to 6 and output it */
15         printf( "%10d", 1 + ( rand() % 6 ) );
16
17         /* if counter is divisible by 5, begin new line of output */
18         if ( i % 5 == 0 ) {
19            printf( "\n" );
20         } /* end if */
21
22      } /* end for */
23
24      return 0; /* indicates successful termination */
25
26   } /* end main */
```

6	6	5	5	6
5	1	1	5	3
6	6	2	4	2
6	2	3	4	1

Fig. 5.7 | Shifted, scaled random integers produced by 1 + rand() % 6.

To show that these numbers occur approximately with equal likelihood, let us simulate 6000 rolls of a die with the program of Fig. 5.8. Each integer from 1 to 6 should appear approximately 1000 times.

```
 1   /* Fig. 5.8: fig05_08.c
 2      Roll a six-sided die 6000 times */
 3   #include <stdio.h>
 4   #include <stdlib.h>
 5
 6   /* function main begins program execution */
 7   int main( void )
 8   {
 9      int frequency1 = 0; /* rolled 1 counter */
10      int frequency2 = 0; /* rolled 2 counter */
11      int frequency3 = 0; /* rolled 3 counter */
12      int frequency4 = 0; /* rolled 4 counter */
```

Fig. 5.8 | Rolling a six-sided die 6000 times. (Part 1 of 3.)

```
13      int frequency5 = 0; /* rolled 5 counter */
14      int frequency6 = 0; /* rolled 6 counter */
15
16      int roll; /* roll counter, value 1 to 6000 */
17      int face; /* represents one roll of the die, value 1 to 6 */
18
19      /* loop 6000 times and summarize results */
20      for ( roll = 1; roll <= 6000; roll++ ) {
21         face = 1 + rand() % 6; /* random number from 1 to 6 */
22
23         /* determine face value and increment appropriate counter */
24         switch ( face ) {
25
26            case 1: /* rolled 1 */
27               ++frequency1;
28               break;
29
30            case 2: /* rolled 2 */
31               ++frequency2;
32               break;
33
34            case 3: /* rolled 3 */
35               ++frequency3;
36               break;
37
38            case 4: /* rolled 4 */
39               ++frequency4;
40               break;
41
42            case 5: /* rolled 5 */
43               ++frequency5;
44               break;
45
46            case 6: /* rolled 6 */
47               ++frequency6;
48               break; /* optional */
49         } /* end switch */
50
51      } /* end for */
52
53      /* display results in tabular format */
54      printf( "%s%13s\n", "Face", "Frequency" );
55      printf( "   1%13d\n", frequency1 );
56      printf( "   2%13d\n", frequency2 );
57      printf( "   3%13d\n", frequency3 );
58      printf( "   4%13d\n", frequency4 );
59      printf( "   5%13d\n", frequency5 );
60      printf( "   6%13d\n", frequency6 );
61
62      return 0; /* indicates successful termination */
63
64   } /* end main */
```

Fig. 5.8 | Rolling a six-sided die 6000 times. (Part 2 of 3.)

Face	Frequency
1	1003
2	1017
3	983
4	994
5	1004
6	999

Fig. 5.8 | Rolling a six-sided die 6000 times. (Part 3 of 3.)

As the program output shows, by scaling and shifting we have utilized the rand function to realistically simulate the rolling of a six-sided die. Note that *no* default case is provided in the switch statement. Also note the use of the %s conversion specifier to print the character strings "Face" and "Frequency" as column headers (line 54). After we study arrays in Chapter 6, we will show how to replace this entire switch statement elegantly with a single-line statement. Executing the program of Fig. 5.7 again produces

```
6        6        5        5        6
5        1        1        5        3
6        6        2        4        2
6        2        3        4        1
```

Notice that exactly the same sequence of values was printed. How can these be random numbers? Ironically, this repeatability is an important characteristic of function rand. When debugging a program, this repeatability is essential for proving that corrections to a program work properly.

Function rand actually generates **pseudorandom numbers**. Calling rand repeatedly produces a sequence of numbers that appears to be random. However, the sequence repeats itself each time the program is executed. Once a program has been thoroughly debugged, it can be conditioned to produce a different sequence of random numbers for each execution. This is called **randomizing** and is accomplished with the standard library function srand. Function srand takes an unsigned integer argument and **seeds** function rand to produce a different sequence of random numbers for each execution of the program.

The use of srand is demonstrated in Fig. 5.9. In the program, we use the data type unsigned, which is short for unsigned int. An int is stored in at least two bytes of memory and can have positive and negative values. A variable of type unsigned is also stored in at least two bytes of memory. A two-byte unsigned int can have only positive values in the range 0 to 65535. A four-byte unsigned int can have only positive values in the range 0 to 4294967295. Function srand takes an unsigned value as an argument. The conversion specifier %u is used to read an unsigned value with scanf. The function prototype for srand is found in <stdlib.h>.

Let us run the program several times and observe the results. Notice that a *different* sequence of random numbers is obtained each time the program is run, provided that a different seed is supplied.

```
1    /* Fig. 5.9: fig05_09.c
2       Randomizing die-rolling program */
3    #include <stdlib.h>
4    #include <stdio.h>
5
6    /* function main begins program execution */
7    int main( void )
8    {
9       int i;          /* counter */
10      unsigned seed; /* number used to seed random number generator */
11
12      printf( "Enter seed: " );
13      scanf( "%u", &seed ); /* note %u for unsigned */
14
15      srand( seed );   /* seed random number generator */
16
17      /* loop 10 times */
18      for ( i = 1; i <= 10; i++ ) {
19
20         /* pick a random number from 1 to 6 and output it */
21         printf( "%10d", 1 + ( rand() % 6 ) );    between 1 to 6
22
23         /* if counter is divisible by 5, begin a new line of output */
24         if ( i % 5 == 0 ) {
25            printf( "\n" );
26         } /* end if */
27
28      } /* end for */
29
30      return 0; /* indicates successful termination */
31
32   } /* end main */
```

```
Enter seed: 67
         6         1         4         6         2
         1         6         1         6         4
```

```
Enter seed: 867
         2         4         6         1         6
         1         1         3         6         2
```

```
Enter seed: 67
         6         1         4         6         2
         1         6         1         6         4
```

Fig. 5.9 | Randomizing the die-rolling program.

To randomize without entering a seed each time, use a statement like

```
srand( time( NULL ) );
```

This causes the computer to read its clock to obtain the value for the seed automatically.
Function time returns the number of seconds that have passed since midnight on January

1, 1970. This value is converted to an unsigned integer and used as the seed to the random number generator. Function `time` takes `NULL` as an argument (`time` is capable of providing you with a string representing the value it returns; `NULL` disables this capability for a specific call to `time`). The function prototype for `time` is in `<time.h>`.

The values produced directly by `rand` are always in the range:

```
0 ≤ rand() ≤ RAND_MAX
```

Previously we demonstrated how to write a single statement to simulate the rolling of a six-sided die:

```
face = 1 + rand() % 6;
```

This statement always assigns an integer value (at random) to the variable `face` in the range 1 ≤ `face` ≤ 6. Note that the width of this range (i.e., the number of consecutive integers in the range) is 6 and the starting number in the range is 1. Referring to the preceding statement, we see that the width of the range is determined by the number used to scale `rand` with the remainder operator (i.e., 6), and the starting number of the range is equal to the number (i.e., 1) that is added to `rand % 6`. We can generalize this result as follows

```
n = a + rand() % b;
```

where `a` is the **shifting value** (which is equal to the first number in the desired range of consecutive integers) and `b` is the scaling factor (which is equal to the width of the desired range of consecutive integers). In the exercises, we will see that it is possible to choose integers at random from sets of values other than ranges of consecutive integers.

Common Programming Error 5.11

Using srand in place of rand to generate random numbers.

5.11 Example: A Game of Chance

One of the most popular games of chance is a dice game known as "craps," which is played in casinos and back alleys throughout the world. The rules of the game are straightforward:

> *A player rolls two dice. Each die has six faces. These faces contain 1, 2, 3, 4, 5, and 6 spots. After the dice have come to rest, the sum of the spots on the two upward faces is calculated. If the sum is 7 or 11 on the first throw, the player wins. If the sum is 2, 3, or 12 on the first throw (called "craps"), the player loses (i.e., the "house" wins). If the sum is 4, 5, 6, 8, 9, or 10 on the first throw, then that sum becomes the player's "point." To win, you must continue rolling the dice until you "make your point." The player loses by rolling a 7 before making the point.*

Figure 5.10 simulates the game of craps and Fig. 5.11 shows several sample executions.

In the rules of the game, notice that the player must roll two dice on the first roll, and must do so later on all subsequent rolls. We define a function `rollDice` to roll the dice and compute and print their sum. Function `rollDice` is defined once, but it is called from two places in the program (lines 23 and 51). Interestingly, `rollDice` takes no arguments, so we have indicated `void` in the parameter list (line 80). Function `rollDice` does return the sum of the two dice, so a return type of `int` is indicated in the function header.

```
1   /* Fig. 5.10: fig05_10.c
2      Craps */
3   #include <stdio.h>
4   #include <stdlib.h>
5   #include <time.h> /* contains prototype for function time */
6
7   /* enumeration constants represent game status */
8   enum Status { CONTINUE, WON, LOST };
9
10  int rollDice( void ); /* function prototype */
11
12  /* function main begins program execution */
13  int main( void )
14  {
15     int sum;        /* sum of rolled dice */
16     int myPoint;    /* point earned */
17
18     enum Status gameStatus; /* can contain CONTINUE, WON, or LOST */
19
20     /* randomize random number generator using current time */
21     srand( time( NULL ) );
22
23     sum = rollDice(); /* first roll of the dice */
24
25     /* determine game status based on sum of dice */
26     switch( sum ) {
27
28        /* win on first roll */
29        case 7:
30        case 11:
31           gameStatus = WON;
32           break;
33
34        /* lose on first roll */
35        case 2:
36        case 3:
37        case 12:
38           gameStatus = LOST;
39           break;
40
41        /* remember point */
42        default:
43           gameStatus = CONTINUE;
44           myPoint = sum;
45           printf( "Point is %d\n", myPoint );
46           break; /* optional */
47     } /* end switch */
48
49     /* while game not complete */
50     while ( gameStatus == CONTINUE ) {
51        sum = rollDice(); /* roll dice again */
52
```

Fig. 5.10 | Program to simulate the game of craps. (Part 1 of 2.)

```
53      /* determine game status */
54      if ( sum == myPoint ) { /* win by making point */
55          gameStatus = WON; /* game over, player won */
56      } /* end if */
57      else {
58
59          if ( sum == 7 ) { /* lose by rolling 7 */
60              gameStatus = LOST; /* game over, player lost */
61          } /* end if */
62
63      } /* end else */
64
65      } /* end while */
66
67      /* display won or lost message */
68      if ( gameStatus == WON ) { /* did player win? */
69          printf( "Player wins\n" );
70      } /* end if */
71      else { /* player lost */
72          printf( "Player loses\n" );
73      } /* end else */
74
75      return 0; /* indicates successful termination */
76
77   } /* end main */
78
79   /* roll dice, calculate sum and display results */
80   int rollDice( void )
81   {
82      int die1;     /* first die */
83      int die2;     /* second die */
84      int workSum; /* sum of dice */
85
86      die1 = 1 + ( rand() % 6 ); /* pick random die1 value */
87      die2 = 1 + ( rand() % 6 ); /* pick random die2 value */
88      workSum = die1 + die2;        /* sum die1 and die2 */
89
90      /* display results of this roll */
91      printf( "Player rolled %d + %d = %d\n", die1, die2, workSum );
92
93      return workSum; /* return sum of dice */
94
95   } /* end function rollRice */
```

Fig. 5.10 | Program to simulate the game of craps. (Part 2 of 2.)

```
Player rolled 5 + 6 = 11
Player wins
```

Fig. 5.11 | Sample runs for the game of craps. (Part 1 of 2.)

```
Player rolled 4 + 1 = 5
Point is 5
Player rolled 6 + 2 = 8
Player rolled 2 + 1 = 3
Player rolled 3 + 2 = 5
Player wins
```

```
Player rolled 1 + 1 = 2
Player loses
```

```
Player rolled 6 + 4 = 10
Point is 10
Player rolled 3 + 4 = 7
Player loses
```

Fig. 5.11 | Sample runs for the game of craps. (Part 2 of 2.)

The game is reasonably involved. The player may win or lose on the first roll, or may win or lose on any subsequent roll. Variable gameStatus, defined to be of a new type enum Status, stores the current status. Line 8 creates a programmer-defined type called an enumeration. An enumeration, introduced by the keyword **enum**, is a set of integer constants represented by identifiers. Enumeration constants are sometimes called symbolic constants—constants represented as symbols. Values in an enum start with 0 and are incremented by 1. In line 8, the constant CONTINUE has the value 0, WON has the value 1 and LOST has the value 2. It is also possible to assign an integer value to each identifier in an enum (see Chapter 13). The identifiers in an enumeration must be unique, but the values may be duplicated.

Common Programming Error 5.12

Assigning a value to an enumeration constant after it has been defined is a syntax error.

Good Programming Practice 5.9

Use only uppercase letters in the names of enumeration constants to make these constants stand out in a program and to indicate that enumeration constants are not variables.

When the game is won, either on the first roll or on a subsequent roll, gameStatus is set to WON. When the game is lost, either on the first roll or on a subsequent roll, game-Status is set to LOST. Otherwise gameStatus is set to CONTINUE and the game continues.

After the first roll, if the game is over, the while statement (line 50) is skipped because gameStatus is not CONTINUE. The program proceeds to the if...else statement at line 68, which prints "Player wins" if gameStatus is WON and "Player loses" otherwise.

After the first roll, if the game is not over, then sum is saved in myPoint. Execution proceeds with the while statement (line 50) because gameStatus is CONTINUE. Each time through the while, rollDice is called to produce a new sum. If sum matches myPoint, gameStatus is set to WON to indicate that the player won, the while-test fails, the if...else statement (line 68) prints "Player wins" and execution terminates. If sum is equal to 7 (line 59), gameStatus is set to LOST to indicate that the player lost, the while-test fails, the if...else statement (line 68) prints "Player loses" and execution terminates.

Note the program's interesting control architecture. We have used two functions—main and rollDice—and the switch, while, nested if...else and nested if statements. In the exercises, we'll investigate various interesting characteristics of the game of craps.

5.12 Storage Classes

In Chapters 2–4, we used identifiers for variable names. The attributes of variables include name, type, size and value. In this chapter, we also use identifiers as names for user-defined functions. Actually, each identifier in a program has other attributes, including storage class, storage duration, scope and linkage.

C provides four storage classes, indicated by the **storage class specifiers**: **auto**, **register**, **extern** and **static**. An identifier's **storage class** determines its storage duration, scope and linkage. An identifier's **storage duration** is the period during which the identifier exists in memory. Some exist briefly, some are repeatedly created and destroyed, and others exist for the entire execution of a program. An identifier's **scope** is where the identifier can be referenced in a program. Some can be referenced throughout a program, others from only portions of a program. An identifier's **linkage** determines for a multiple-source-file program (a topic we will investigate in Chapter 14) whether the identifier is known only in the current source file or in any source file with proper declarations. This section discusses storage classes and storage duration. Section 5.13 discusses scope. Chapter 14, Other C Topics, discusses identifier linkage and programming with multiple source files.

The four storage-class specifiers can be split into two storage durations: **automatic storage duration** and **static storage duration**. Keywords **auto** and **register** are used to declare variables of automatic storage duration. Variables with automatic storage duration are created when the block in which they are defined is entered; they exist while the block is active, and they are destroyed when the block is exited.

Only variables can have automatic storage duration. A function's local variables (those declared in the parameter list or function body) normally have automatic storage duration. Keyword **auto** explicitly declares variables of automatic storage duration. For example, the following declaration indicates that double variables x and y are automatic local variables and they exist only in the body of the function in which the declaration appears:

```
auto double x, y;
```

Local variables have automatic storage duration by default, so keyword auto is rarely used. For the remainder of the text, we will refer to variables with automatic storage duration simply as **automatic variables**.

Performance Tip 5.1

Automatic storage is a means of conserving memory, because automatic variables exist only when they are needed. They are created when the function in which they are defined is entered and they are destroyed when the function is exited.

Software Engineering Observation 5.10

Automatic storage is an example of the principle of least privilege—allowing access to data only when it is absolutely needed. Why have variables stored in memory and accessible when in fact they are not needed?

Data in the machine-language version of a program is normally loaded into registers for calculations and other processing.

Performance Tip 5.2

The storage-class specifier register *can be placed before an automatic variable declaration to suggest that the compiler maintain the variable in one of the computer's high-speed hardware registers. If intensely used variables such as counters or totals can be maintained in hardware registers, the overhead of repeatedly loading the variables from memory into the registers and storing the results back into memory can be eliminated.*

The compiler may ignore register declarations. For example, there may not be a sufficient number of registers available for the compiler to use. The following declaration suggests that the integer variable counter be placed in one of the computer's registers and initialized to 1:

```
register int counter = 1;
```

Keyword register can be used only with variables of automatic storage duration.

Performance Tip 5.3

Often, register *declarations are unnecessary. Today's optimizing compilers are capable of recognizing frequently used variables and can decide to place them in registers without the need for a* register *declaration.*

Keywords extern and static are used in the declarations of identifiers for variables and functions of static storage duration. Identifiers of static storage duration exist from the time at which the program begins execution. For static variables, storage is allocated and initialized once, when the program begins execution. For functions, the name of the function exists when the program begins execution. However, even though the variables and the function names exist from the start of program execution, this does not mean that these identifiers can be accessed throughout the program. Storage duration and scope (where a name can be used) are separate issues, as we will see in Section 5.13.

There are two types of identifiers with static storage duration: external identifiers (such as global variables and function names) and local variables declared with the storage-class specifier static. Global variables and function names are of storage class extern by default. Global variables are created by placing variable declarations outside any function definition, and they retain their values throughout the execution of the program. Global variables and functions can be referenced by any function that follows their declarations or definitions in the file. This is one reason for using function prototypes—when we include stdio.h in a program that calls printf, the function prototype is placed at the start of our file to make the name printf known to the rest of the file.

Software Engineering Observation 5.11

Defining a variable as global rather than local allows unintended side effects to occur when a function that does not need access to the variable accidentally or maliciously modifies it. In general, use of global variables should be avoided except in certain situations with unique performance requirements (as discussed in Chapter 14).

Software Engineering Observation 5.12

Variables used only in a particular function should be defined as local variables in that function rather than as external variables.

Local variables declared with the keyword static are still known only in the function in which they are defined, but unlike automatic variables, static local variables retain their value when the function is exited. The next time the function is called, the static local variable contains the value it had when the function last exited. The following statement declares local variable count to be static and to be initialized to 1.

```
static int count = 1;
```

All numeric variables of static storage duration are initialized to zero if you do not explicitly initialize them.

Common Programming Error 5.13

Using multiple storage-class specifiers for an identifier. Only one storage-class specifier can be applied to an identifier.

Keywords extern and static have special meaning when explicitly applied to external identifiers. In Chapter 14, Other C Topics, we discuss the explicit use of extern and static with external identifiers and multiple-source-file programs.

5.13 Scope Rules

The scope of an identifier is the portion of the program in which the identifier can be referenced. For example, when we define a local variable in a block, it can be referenced only following its definition in that block or in blocks nested within that block. The four identifier scopes are function scope, file scope, block scope, and function-prototype scope.

Labels (an identifier followed by a colon such as start:) are the only identifiers with function scope. Labels can be used anywhere in the function in which they appear, but cannot be referenced outside the function body. Labels are used in switch statements (as case labels) and in goto statements (see Chapter 14, Other C Topics). Labels are implementation details that functions hide from one another. This hiding—more formally called information hiding—is a means of implementing the principle of least privilege, one of the most fundamental principles of good software engineering.

An identifier declared outside any function has file scope. Such an identifier is "known" (i.e., accessible) in all functions from the point at which the identifier is declared until the end of the file. Global variables, function definitions, and function prototypes placed outside a function all have file scope.

Identifiers defined inside a block have block scope. Block scope ends at the terminating right brace (}) of the block. Local variables defined at the beginning of a function have block scope as do function parameters, which are considered local variables by the function. Any block may contain variable definitions. When blocks are nested, and an identifier in an outer block has the same name as an identifier in an inner block, the identifier in the outer block is "hidden" until the inner block terminates. This means that while executing in the inner block, the inner block sees the value of its own local identifier and not the value of the identically named identifier in the enclosing block. Local variables declared static still have block scope, even though they exist from the time the program begins execution. Thus, storage duration does not affect the scope of an identifier.

The only identifiers with function-prototype scope are those used in the parameter list of a function prototype. As mentioned previously, function prototypes do not require names in the parameter list—only types are required. If a name is used in the parameter list of a function prototype, the compiler ignores the name. Identifiers used in a function prototype can be reused elsewhere in the program without ambiguity.

Common Programming Error 5.14

Accidentally using the same name for an identifier in an inner block as is used for an identifier in an outer block, when in fact you want the identifier in the outer block to be active for the duration of the inner block.

Error-Prevention Tip 5.2

Avoid variable names that hide names in outer scopes. This can be accomplished simply by avoiding the use of duplicate identifiers in a program.

Figure 5.12 demonstrates scoping issues with global variables, automatic local variables, and static local variables. A global variable x is defined and initialized to 1 (line 9). This global variable is hidden in any block (or function) in which a variable named x is defined. In main, a local variable x is defined and initialized to 5 (line 14). This variable is then printed to show that the global x is hidden in main. Next, a new block is defined in main with another local variable x initialized to 7 (line 19). This variable is printed to show that it hides x in the outer block of main. The variable x with value 7 is automatically destroyed when the block is exited, and the local variable x in the outer block of main is printed again to show that it is no longer hidden. The program defines three functions that each take no arguments and return nothing. Function useLocal defines an automatic variable x and initializes it to 25 (line 42). When useLocal is called, the variable is printed, incremented, and printed again before exiting the function. Each time this function is called, automatic variable x is reinitialized to 25. Function useStaticLocal defines a static variable x and initializes it to 50 (line 55). Local variables declared as static retain their values even when they are out of scope. When useStaticLocal is called, x is printed, incremented, and printed again before exiting the function. In the next call to this function, static local variable x will contain the value 51. Function useGlobal does not define any variables. Therefore, when it refers to variable x, the global x (line 9) is used. When useGlobal is called, the global variable is printed, multiplied by 10, and printed again before exiting the function. The next time function useGlobal is called, the global variable still has its modified value, 10. Finally, the program prints the local variable x in main again (line 33) to show that none of the function calls modified the value of x because the functions all referred to variables in other scopes.

```
1   /* Fig. 5.12: fig05_12.c
2      A scoping example */
3   #include <stdio.h>
4
5   void useLocal( void );       /* function prototype */
6   void useStaticLocal( void ); /* function prototype */
7   void useGlobal( void );      /* function prototype */
8
9   int x = 1; /* global variable */
```

Fig. 5.12 | Scoping example. (Part 1 of 3.)

```
10
11   /* function main begins program execution */
12   int main( void )
13   {
14      int x = 5; /* local variable to main */
15
16      printf("local x in outer scope of main is %d\n", x );
17
18      { /* start new scope */
19         int x = 7; /* local variable to new scope */
20
21         printf( "local x in inner scope of main is %d\n", x );
22      } /* end new scope */
23
24      printf( "local x in outer scope of main is %d\n", x );
25
26      useLocal();        /* useLocal has automatic local x */
27      useStaticLocal(); /* useStaticLocal has static local x */
28      useGlobal();       /* useGlobal uses global x */
29      useLocal();        /* useLocal reinitializes automatic local x */
30      useStaticLocal(); /* static local x retains its prior value */
31      useGlobal();       /* global x also retains its value */
32
33      printf( "\nlocal x in main is %d\n", x );
34
35      return 0; /* indicates successful termination */
36
37   } /* end main */
38
39   /* useLocal reinitializes local variable x during each call */
40   void useLocal( void )
41   {
42      int x = 25;   /* initialized each time useLocal is called */
43
44      printf( "\nlocal x in useLocal is %d after entering useLocal\n", x );
45      x++;
46      printf( "local x in useLocal is %d before exiting useLocal\n", x );
47   } /* end function useLocal */
48
49   /* useStaticLocal initializes static local variable x only the first time
50      the function is called; value of x is saved between calls to this
51      function */
52   void useStaticLocal( void )
53   {
54      /* initialized only first time useStaticLocal is called */
55      static int x = 50;
56
57      printf( "\nlocal static x is %d on entering useStaticLocal\n", x );
58      x++;
59      printf( "local static x is %d on exiting useStaticLocal\n", x );
60   } /* end function useStaticLocal */
61
```

Fig. 5.12 | Scoping example. (Part 2 of 3.)

```
62    /* function useGlobal modifies global variable x during each call */
63    void useGlobal( void )
64    {
65       printf( "\nglobal x is %d on entering useGlobal\n", x );
66       x *= 10;
67       printf( "global x is %d on exiting useGlobal\n", x );
68    } /* end function useGlobal */
```

```
local x in outer scope of main is 5
local x in inner scope of main is 7
local x in outer scope of main is 5

local x in useLocal is 25 after entering useLocal
local x in useLocal is 26 before exiting useLocal

local static x is 50 on entering useStaticLocal
local static x is 51 on exiting useStaticLocal

global x is 1 on entering useGlobal
global x is 10 on exiting useGlobal

local x in useLocal is 25 after entering useLocal
local x in useLocal is 26 before exiting useLocal

local static x is 51 on entering useStaticLocal
local static x is 52 on exiting useStaticLocal

global x is 10 on entering useGlobal
global x is 100 on exiting useGlobal

local x in main is 5
```

Fig. 5.12 | Scoping example. (Part 3 of 3.)

5.14 Recursion

The programs we have discussed are generally structured as functions that call one another in a disciplined, hierarchical manner. For some types of problems, it is useful to have functions call themselves. A **recursive function** is a function that calls itself either directly or indirectly through another function. Recursion is a complex topic discussed at length in upper-level computer science courses. In this section and the next, simple examples of recursion are presented. This book contains an extensive treatment of recursion, which is spread throughout Chapters 5–12. Figure 5.17, in Section 5.16, summarizes the 31 recursion examples and exercises in the book.

We consider recursion conceptually first, and then examine several programs containing recursive functions. Recursive problem-solving approaches have a number of elements in common. A recursive function is called to solve a problem. The function actually knows how to solve only the simplest case(s), or so-called **base case(s)**. If the function is called with a base case, the function simply returns a result. If the function is called with a more complex problem, the function divides the problem into two conceptual pieces: a piece that the function knows how to do and a piece that it does not know how to do. To make recursion feasible, the latter piece must resemble the original problem, but be a slightly simpler or slightly smaller version. Because this new problem looks like the original problem, the function launches (calls) a fresh copy of itself to go to work on the smaller problem—this is referred to as a **recursive call** and is also called the **recursion step**. The recursion step also includes the keyword return, because its result will be combined with the portion of the problem the function knew how to solve to form a result that will be passed back to the original caller, possibly main.

The recursion step executes while the original call to the function is still open, i.e., it has not yet finished executing. The recursion step can result in many more such recursive calls, as the function keeps dividing each problem it is called with into two conceptual pieces. In order for the recursion to terminate, each time the function calls itself with a slightly simpler version of the original problem, this sequence of smaller problems must eventually converge on the base case. At that point, the function recognizes the base case, returns a result to the previous copy of the function, and a sequence of returns ensues all the way up the line until the original call of the function eventually returns the final result to main. All of this sounds quite exotic compared to the kind of problem solving we have been using with conventional function calls to this point. Indeed, it takes a great deal of practice writing recursive programs before the process will appear natural. As an example of these concepts at work, let us write a recursive program to perform a popular mathematical calculation.

The factorial of a nonnegative integer n, written $n!$ (and pronounced "n factorial"), is the product

$$n \cdot (n-1) \cdot (n-2) \cdot \ldots \cdot 1$$

with 1! equal to 1, and 0! defined to be 1. For example, 5! is the product $5 * 4 * 3 * 2 * 1$, which is equal to 120.

The factorial of an integer, number, greater than or equal to 0 can be calculated iteratively (nonrecursively) using a for statement as follows:

```
factorial = 1;

for ( counter = number; counter >= 1; counter-- )
    factorial *= counter;
```

A recursive definition of the factorial function is arrived at by observing the following relationship:

$$n! = n \cdot (n-1)!$$

For example, 5! is clearly equal to $5 * 4!$ as is shown by the following:

```
5! = 5 · 4 · 3 · 2 · 1
5! = 5 · (4 · 3 · 2 · 1)
5! = 5 · (4!)
```

The evaluation of 5! would proceed as shown in Fig. 5.13. Figure 5.13a shows how the succession of recursive calls proceeds until 1! is evaluated to be 1, which terminates the recursion. Figure 5.13b shows the values returned from each recursive call to its caller until the final value is calculated and returned.

Figure 5.14 uses recursion to calculate and print the factorials of the integers 0–10 (the choice of the type long will be explained momentarily). The recursive factorial function

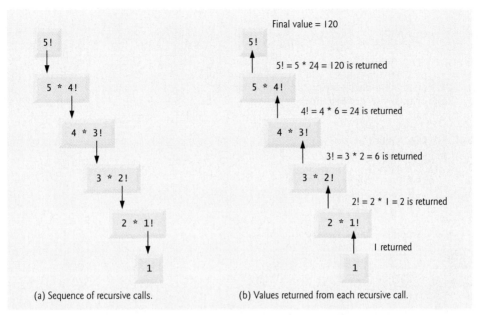

Fig. 5.13 | Recursive evaluation of 5!.

first tests whether a terminating condition is true, i.e., whether number is less than or equal to 1. If number is indeed less than or equal to 1, factorial returns 1, no further recursion is necessary, and the program terminates. If number is greater than 1, the statement

```
return number * factorial( number - 1 );
```

expresses the problem as the product of number and a recursive call to factorial evaluating the factorial of number - 1. Note that factorial(number - 1) is a slightly simpler problem than the original calculation factorial(number).

```
1   /* Fig. 5.14: fig05_14.c
2      Recursive factorial function */
3   #include <stdio.h>
4
5   long factorial( long number ); /* function prototype */
6
7   /* function main begins program execution */
8   int main( void )
9   {
10     int i; /* counter */
11
12     /* loop 11 times; during each iteration, calculate
13        factorial( i ) and display result */
14     for ( i = 0; i <= 10; i++ ) {
15        printf( "%2d! = %ld\n", i, factorial( i ) );
16     } /* end for */
```

Fig. 5.14 | Calculating factorials with a recursive function. (Part 1 of 2.)

```
17
18        return 0; /* indicates successful termination */
19
20   } /* end main */
21
22   /* recursive definition of function factorial */
23   long factorial( long number )
24   {
25       /* base case */
26       if ( number <= 1 ) {
27          return 1;
28       } /* end if */
29       else { /* recursive step */
30          return ( number * factorial( number - 1 ) );
31       } /* end else */
32
33   } /* end function factorial */
```

```
 0! = 1
 1! = 1
 2! = 2
 3! = 6
 4! = 24
 5! = 120
 6! = 720
 7! = 5040
 8! = 40320
 9! = 362880
10! = 3628800
```

Fig. 5.14 | Calculating factorials with a recursive function. (Part 2 of 2.)

Function `factorial` (line 23) has been declared to receive a parameter of type `long` and return a result of type `long`. This is shorthand notation for `long int`. The C standard specifies that a variable of type `long int` is stored in at least 4 bytes, and thus may hold a value as large as +2147483647. As can be seen in Fig. 5.14, factorial values become large quickly. We have chosen the data type `long` so the program can calculate factorials greater than 7! on computers with small (such as 2-byte) integers. The conversion specifier %ld is used to print `long` values. Unfortunately, the `factorial` function produces large values so quickly that even `long int` does not help us print many factorial values before the size of a `long int` variable is exceeded.

As we will explore in the exercises, `double` may ultimately be needed by the user desiring to calculate factorials of larger numbers. This points to a weakness in C (and most other programming languages), namely that the language is not easily extended to handle the unique requirements of various applications. As we will see later, C++ is an extensible language that, through the use of "classes," allows us to create arbitrarily large integers if we wish.

 Common Programming Error 5.15

Forgetting to return a value from a recursive function when one is needed.

Common Programming Error 5.16

Either omitting the base case, or writing the recursion step incorrectly so that it does not converge on the base case, will cause infinite recursion, eventually exhausting memory. This is analogous to the problem of an infinite loop in an iterative (nonrecursive) solution. Infinite recursion can also be caused by providing an unexpected input.

5.15 Example Using Recursion: Fibonacci Series

The Fibonacci series

> 0, 1, 1, 2, 3, 5, 8, 13, 21, ...

begins with 0 and 1 and has the property that each subsequent Fibonacci number is the sum of the previous two Fibonacci numbers.

The series occurs in nature and, in particular, describes a form of spiral. The ratio of successive Fibonacci numbers converges to a constant value of 1.618.... This number, too, repeatedly occurs in nature and has been called the **golden ratio** or the **golden mean**. Humans tend to find the golden mean aesthetically pleasing. Architects often design windows, rooms, and buildings whose length and width are in the ratio of the golden mean. Postcards are often designed with a golden mean length/width ratio.

The Fibonacci series may be defined recursively as follows:

> *fibonacci(0) = 0*
> *fibonacci(1) = 1*
> *fibonacci(n) = fibonacci(n – 1) + fibonacci(n – 2)*

Figure 5.15 calculates the nth Fibonacci number recursively using function `fibonacci`. Notice that Fibonacci numbers tend to become large quickly. Therefore, we have chosen the data type `long` for the parameter type and the return type in function `fibonacci`. In Fig. 5.15, each pair of output lines shows a separate run of the program.

```
1   /* Fig. 5.15: fig05_15.c
2      Recursive fibonacci function */
3   #include <stdio.h>
4
5   long fibonacci( long n ); /* function prototype */
6
7   /* function main begins program execution */
8   int main( void )
9   {
10     long result; /* fibonacci value */
11     long number; /* number input by user */
12
13     /* obtain integer from user */
14     printf( "Enter an integer: " );
15     scanf( "%ld", &number );
16
```

Fig. 5.15 | Recursively generating Fibonacci numbers. (Part 1 of 3.)

```
17      /* calculate fibonacci value for number input by user */
18      result = fibonacci( number );
19
20      /* display result */
21      printf( "Fibonacci( %ld ) = %ld\n", number, result );
22
23      return 0; /* indicates successful termination */
24
25   } /* end main */
26
27   /* Recursive definition of function fibonacci */
28   long fibonacci( long n )
29   {
30      /* base case */
31      if ( n == 0 || n == 1 ) {
32         return n;
33      } /* end if */
34      else { /* recursive step */
35         return fibonacci( n - 1 ) + fibonacci( n - 2 );
36      } /* end else */
37
38   } /* end function fibonacci */
```

```
Enter an integer: 0
Fibonacci( 0 ) = 0
```

```
Enter an integer: 1
Fibonacci( 1 ) = 1
```

```
Enter an integer: 2
Fibonacci( 2 ) = 1
```

```
Enter an integer: 3
Fibonacci( 3 ) = 2
```

```
Enter an integer: 4
Fibonacci( 4 ) = 3
```

```
Enter an integer: 5
Fibonacci( 5 ) = 5
```

```
Enter an integer: 6
Fibonacci( 6 ) = 8
```

Fig. 5.15 | Recursively generating Fibonacci numbers. (Part 2 of 3.)

```
Enter an integer: 10
Fibonacci( 10 ) = 55
```

```
Enter an integer: 20
Fibonacci( 20 ) = 6765
```

```
Enter an integer: 30
Fibonacci( 30 ) = 832040
```

```
Enter an integer: 35
Fibonacci( 35 ) = 9227465
```

Fig. 5.15 | Recursively generating Fibonacci numbers. (Part 3 of 3.)

The call to fibonacci from main is not a recursive call (line 18), but all subsequent calls to fibonacci are recursive (line 35). Each time fibonacci is invoked, it immediately tests for the base case—n is equal to 0 or 1. If this is true, n is returned. Interestingly, if n is greater than 1, the recursion step generates *two* recursive calls, each of which is for a slightly simpler problem than the original call to fibonacci. Figure 5.16 shows how function fibonacci would evaluate fibonacci(3).

This figure raises some interesting issues about the order in which C compilers will evaluate the operands of operators. This is a different issue from the order in which operators are applied to their operands, namely the order dictated by the rules of operator precedence. From Fig. 5.16 it appears that while evaluating fibonacci(3), two recursive calls will be made, namely fibonacci(2) and fibonacci(1). But in what order will these calls be made? Most programmers simply assume the operands will be evaluated left to right. Strangely, Standard C does not specify the order in which the operands of most operators (including +) are to be evaluated. Therefore, you may make no assumption about the order in which these calls will execute. The calls could in fact execute fibonacci(2) first and then fibonacci(1), or the calls could execute in the reverse order, fibonacci(1) then fibonacci(2). In this program and in most other programs, it turns out the final result would be the same. But in some programs the evaluation of an operand may have side effects that could affect the final result of the expression. Of C's many operators, Standard C specifies the order of evaluation of the operands of only four operators—namely &&, ||, the comma (,) operator and ?:. The first three of these are binary operators whose two operands are guaranteed to be evaluated left to right. [*Note: The commas used to separate the arguments in a function call are not comma operators.*] The last operator is C's only ternary operator. Its leftmost operand is always evaluated first; if the leftmost operand evaluates to nonzero, the middle operand is evaluated next and the last operand is ignored; if the leftmost operand evaluates to zero, the third operand is evaluated next and the middle operand is ignored.

Common Programming Error 5.17

Writing programs that depend on the order of evaluation of the operands of operators other than &&, ||, ?:, and the comma (,) operator can lead to errors because compilers may not necessarily evaluate the operands in the order you expect.

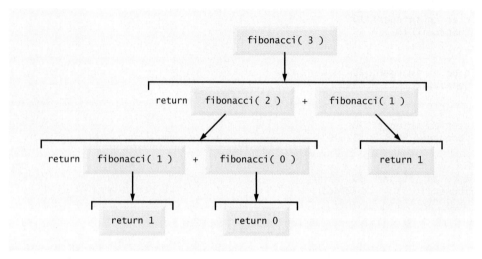

Fig. 5.16 | Set of recursive calls for `fibonacci( 3 )`.

Portability Tip 5.2

Programs that depend on the order of evaluation of the operands of operators other than &&, ||, *?:, and the comma (,) operator can function differently on systems with different compilers.*

A word of caution is in order about recursive programs like the one we use here to generate Fibonacci numbers. Each level of recursion in the `fibonacci` function has a doubling effect on the number of calls; i.e., the number of recursive calls that will be executed to calculate the nth Fibonacci number is on the order of 2^n. This rapidly gets out of hand. Calculating only the 20th Fibonacci number would require on the order of 2^{20} or about a million calls, calculating the 30th Fibonacci number would require on the order of 2^{30} or about a billion calls, and so on. Computer scientists refer to this as **exponential complexity**. Problems of this nature humble even the world's most powerful computers! Complexity issues in general, and exponential complexity in particular, are discussed in detail in the upper-level computer science curriculum course generally called "Algorithms."

Performance Tip 5.4

Avoid Fibonacci-style recursive programs which result in an exponential "explosion" of calls.

5.16 Recursion vs. Iteration

In the previous sections, we studied two functions that can easily be implemented either recursively or iteratively. In this section, we compare the two approaches and discuss why you might choose one approach over the other in a particular situation.

Both iteration and recursion are based on a control structure: Iteration uses a repetition structure; recursion uses a selection structure. Both iteration and recursion involve repetition: Iteration explicitly uses a repetition structure; recursion achieves repetition through repeated function calls. Iteration and recursion each involve a termination test: Iteration terminates when the loop-continuation condition fails; recursion terminates when a base case is recognized. Iteration with counter-controlled repetition and recursion each gradually approach termination: Iteration keeps modifying a counter until the counter assumes a value that makes the loop-continuation condition fail; recursion keeps producing simpler versions of the original problem until the base case is reached. Both iteration and recursion can occur infinitely: An infinite loop occurs with iteration if the loop-continuation test never becomes false; infinite recursion occurs if the recursion step does not reduce the problem each time in a manner that converges on the base case.

Recursion has many negatives. It repeatedly invokes the mechanism, and consequently the overhead, of function calls. This can be expensive in both processor time and memory space. Each recursive call causes another copy of the function (actually only the function's variables) to be created; this can consume considerable memory. Iteration normally occurs within a function, so the overhead of repeated function calls and extra memory assignment is omitted. So why choose recursion?

Software Engineering Observation 5.13

Any problem that can be solved recursively can also be solved iteratively (nonrecursively). A recursive approach is normally chosen in preference to an iterative approach when the recursive approach more naturally mirrors the problem and results in a program that is easier to understand and debug. Another reason to choose a recursive solution is that an iterative solution may not be apparent.

Performance Tip 5.5

Avoid using recursion in performance situations. Recursive calls take time and consume additional memory.

Common Programming Error 5.18

Accidentally having a nonrecursive function call itself either directly, or indirectly through another function.

Most programming textbooks introduce recursion much later than we have done here. We feel that recursion is a sufficiently rich and complex topic that it is better to introduce it earlier and spread the examples over the remainder of the text. Figure 5.17 summarizes by chapter the 31 recursion examples and exercises in the text.

Let us close this chapter with some observations that we make repeatedly throughout the book. Good software engineering is important. High performance is important. Unfortunately, these goals are often at odds with one another. Good software engineering is key to making more manageable the task of developing the larger and more complex software systems we need. High performance is key to realizing the systems of the future that will place ever greater computing demands on hardware. Where do functions fit in here?

Performance Tip 5.6

Functionalizing programs in a neat, hierarchical manner promotes good software engineering. But it has a price. A heavily functionalized program—as compared to a monolithic (i.e., one-piece) program without functions—makes potentially large numbers of function calls, and these consume execution time on a computer's processor(s). So, although monolithic programs may perform better, they are more difficult to program, test, debug, maintain, and evolve.

Chapter	Recursion examples and exercises
Chapter 5	Factorial function Fibonacci function Greatest common divisor Sum of two integers Multiply two integers Raising an integer to an integer power Towers of Hanoi Recursive main Printing keyboard inputs in reverse Visualizing recursion
Chapter 6	Sum the elements of an array Print an array Print an array backward Print a string backward Check if a string is a palindrome Minimum value in an array Linear search Binary search
Chapter 7	Eight Queens Maze traversal
Chapter 8	Printing a string input at the keyboard backward
Chapter 12	Linked list insert Linked list delete Search a linked list Print a linked list backward Binary tree insert Preorder traversal of a binary tree Inorder traversal of a binary tree Postorder traversal of a binary tree
Chapter 16	Selection sort Quicksort

Fig. 5.17 | Recursion examples and exercises in the text.

Summary

Section 5.1 Introduction
- The best way to develop and maintain a large program is to divide it into several smaller program modules, each of which is more manageable than the original program. Modules are written as functions in C.

Section 5.2 Program Modules in C

- A function is invoked by a function call. The function call mentions the function by name and provides information (as arguments) that the called function needs to perform its task.

- The purpose of information hiding is for functions to have access only to the information they need to complete their tasks. This is a means of implementing the principle of least privilege, one of the most important principles of good software engineering.

Section 5.3 Math Library Functions

- Functions are normally invoked in a program by writing the name of the function followed by a left parenthesis followed by the argument (or a comma-separated list of arguments) of the function followed by a right parenthesis.

- Data type double is a floating-point type like float. A variable of type double can store a value of much greater magnitude and precision than float can store.

- Each argument of a function may be a constant, a variable, or an expression.

Section 5.4 Functions

- A local variable is known only in a function definition. Other functions are not allowed to know the names of a function's local variables, nor is any function allowed to know the implementation details of any other function.

Section 5.5 Function Definitions

- The general format for a function definition is

      return-value-type function-name(parameter-list)
      {
          definitions
          statements
      }

  The *return-value-type* states the type of the value returned to the calling function. If a function does not return a value, the *return-value-type* is declared as void. The *function-name* is any valid identifier. The *parameter-list* is a comma-separated list containing the definitions of the variables that will be passed to the function. If a function does not receive any values, *parameter-list* is declared as void. The *function-body* is the set of definitions and statements that constitute the function.

- The arguments passed to a function should match in number, type and order with the parameters in the function definition.

- When a program encounters a function call, control is transferred from the point of invocation to the called function, the statements of the called function are executed and control returns to the caller.

- A called function can return control to the caller in one of three ways. If the function does not return a value, control is returned when the function-ending right brace is reached, or by executing the statement

      return;

  If the function does return a value, the statement

      return *expression*;

  returns the value of *expression*.

Section 5.6 Function Prototypes

- A function prototype declares the return type of the function and declares the number, the types, and order of the parameters the function expects to receive.

- Function prototypes enable the compiler to verify that functions are called correctly.

- The compiler ignores variable names mentioned in the function prototype.

Section 5.7 Function Call Stack and Activation Records

- Stacks are known as last-in, first-out (LIFO) data structures—the last item pushed (inserted) on the stack is the first item popped (removed) from the stack.

- A called function must know how to return to its caller, so the return address of the calling function is pushed onto the program execution stack when the function is called. If a series of function calls occurs, the successive return addresses are pushed onto the stack in last-in, first-out order so that the last function to execute will be the first to return to its caller.

- The program execution stack contains the memory for the local variables used in each invocation of a function during a program's execution. This data is known as the activation record or stack frame of the function call. When a function call is made, the activation record for that function call is pushed onto the program execution stack. When the function returns to its caller, the activation record for this function call is popped off the stack and those local variables are no longer known to the program. If a local variable holding a reference to an object is the only variable in the program with a reference to that object, when the activation record containing that local variable is popped off the stack, the object can no longer be accessed by the program and will eventually be deleted from memory by the JVM during "garbage collection."

- The amount of memory in a computer is finite, so only a certain amount of memory can be used to store activation records on the program execution stack. If there are more function calls than can have their activation records stored on the program execution stack, an error known as a stack overflow occurs. The application will compile correctly, but its execution causes a stack overflow.

Section 5.8 Headers

- Each standard library has a corresponding header containing the function prototypes for all the functions in that library, as well as definitions of various symbolic constants needed by those functions.

- You can create and include your own headers.

Section 5.9 Calling Functions: Call-by-Value and Call-by-Reference

- When an argument is passed by value, a copy of the variable's value is made and the copy is passed to the called function. Changes to the copy in the called function do not affect the original variable's value.

- All calls in C are call-by-value.

Section 5.10 Random Number Generation

- Function rand generates an integer between 0 and RAND_MAX which is defined by the C standard to be at least 32767.

- The function prototypes for rand and srand are contained in <stdlib.h>.

- Values produced by rand can be scaled and shifted to produce values in a specific range.

- To randomize a program, use the C Standard Library function srand.

- The srand function call is ordinarily inserted in a program only after it has been thoroughly debugged. While debugging, it is better to omit srand. This ensures repeatability, which is essential to proving that corrections to a random number generation program work properly.

- To randomize without the need for entering a seed each time, we use srand(time(NULL)). Function time returns the number of seconds since midnight on January 1, 1970. The time function prototype is located in the header <time.h>.

- The general equation for scaling and shifting a random number is

  n = a + rand() % b;

  where a is the shifting value (i.e., the first number in the desired range of consecutive integers) and b is the scaling factor (i.e,. the width of the desired range of consecutive integers).

Section 5.11 Example: A Game of Chance

- An enumeration, introduced by the keyword enum, is a set of integer constants represented by identifiers. Values in an enum start with 0 and are incremented by 1. It is also possible to assign an integer value to each identifier in an enum. The identifiers in an enumeration must be unique, but the values may be duplicated.

Section 5.12 Storage Classes

- Each identifier in a program has the attributes storage class, storage duration, scope and linkage.

- C provides four storage classes indicated by the storage class specifiers: auto, register, extern and static; only one storage class specifier can be used for a given declaration.

- An identifier's storage duration is when that identifier exists in memory.

Section 5.13 Scope Rules

- An identifier's scope is where the identifier can be referenced in a program.

- An identifier's linkage determines for a multiple-source-file program whether an identifier is known only in the current source file or in any source file with proper declarations.

- Variables with automatic storage duration are created when the block in which they are defined is entered, exist while the block is active and are destroyed when the block is exited. A function's local variables normally have automatic storage duration.

- The storage class specifier register can be placed before an automatic variable declaration to suggest that the compiler maintain the variable in one of the computer's high-speed hardware registers. The compiler may ignore register declarations. Keyword register can be used only with variables of automatic storage duration.

- Keywords extern and static are used to declare identifiers for variables and functions of static storage duration.

- Variables with static storage duration are allocated and initialized once, when the program begins execution.

- There are two types of identifiers with static storage duration: external identifiers (such as global variables and function names) and local variables declared with the storage-class specifier static.

- Global variables are created by placing variable definitions outside any function definition. Global variables retain their values throughout the execution of the program.

- Local variables declared static retain their value between calls to the function in which they are defined.

- All numeric variables of static storage duration are initialized to zero if you do not explicitly initialize them.

- The four scopes for an identifier are function scope, file scope, block scope and function-prototype scope.

- Labels are the only identifiers with function scope. Labels can be used anywhere in the function in which they appear but cannot be referenced outside the function body.

- An identifier declared outside any function has file scope. Such an identifier is "known" in all functions from the point at which the identifier is declared until the end of the file.

- Identifiers defined inside a block have block scope. Block scope ends at the terminating right brace (}) of the block.

- Local variables defined at the beginning of a function have block scope, as do function parameters, which are considered local variables by the function.

- Any block may contain variable definitions. When blocks are nested, and an identifier in an outer block has the same name as an identifier in an inner block, the identifier in the outer block is "hidden" until the inner block terminates.

- The only identifiers with function-prototype scope are those used in the parameter list of a function prototype. Identifiers used in a function prototype can be reused elsewhere in the program without ambiguity.

Section 5.14 Recursion

- A recursive function is a function that calls itself either directly or indirectly.

- If a recursive function is called with a base case, the function simply returns a result. If the function is called with a more complex problem, the function divides the problem into two conceptual pieces: a piece that the function knows how to do and a slightly smaller version of the original problem. Because this new problem looks like the original problem, the function launches a recursive call to work on the smaller problem.

- For recursion to terminate, each time the recursive function calls itself with a slightly simpler version of the original problem, the sequence of smaller and smaller problems must converge on the base case. When the function recognizes the base case, the result is returned to the previous function call, and a sequence of returns ensues all the way up the line until the original call of the function eventually returns the final result.

- Standard C does not specify the order in which the operands of most operators (including +) are to be evaluated. Of C's many operators, the standard specifies the order of evaluation of the operands of the operators &&, ||, the comma (,) operator and ?:. The first three of these are binary operators whose two operands are evaluated left to right. The last operator is C's only ternary operator. Its leftmost operand is evaluated first; if the leftmost operand evaluates to nonzero, the middle operand is evaluated next and the last operand is ignored; if the leftmost operand evaluates to zero, the third operand is evaluated next and the middle operand is ignored.

Section 5.16 Recursion vs. Iteration

- Both iteration and recursion are based on a control structure: Iteration uses a repetition structure; recursion uses a selection structure.

- Both iteration and recursion involve repetition: Iteration explicitly uses a repetition structure; recursion achieves repetition through repeated function calls.

- Iteration and recursion each involve a termination test: Iteration terminates when the loop-continuation condition fails; recursion terminates when a base case is recognized.

- Iteration and recursion can occur infinitely: An infinite loop occurs with iteration if the loop-continuation test never becomes false; infinite recursion occurs if the recursion step does not reduce the problem in a manner that converges on the base case.

- Recursion repeatedly invokes the mechanism, and consequently the overhead, of function calls. This can be expensive in both processor time and memory space.

Terminology

%s conversion specifier
abstraction
activation record
argument in a function call
auto storage-class specifier
automatic storage
automatic storage duration
automatic variable
base case in recursion
block
block scope
C Standard Library
call a function
call-by-reference
call-by-value
called function
caller
calling function
coercion of arguments
copy of a value
divide and conquer
enum (enumeration)
extern storage-class specifier
factorial function
file scope
function
function body
function call
function call stack
function definition
function prototype
function-prototype scope
function scope
global variable
header
information hiding
invoke a function
iteration
last-in-first-out (LIFO)
linkage

local variable
math library functions
mixed-type expression
optimizing compiler
parameter list
pop off a stack
principle of least privilege
program execution stack
programmer-defined function
promotion hierarchy
pseudorandom numbers
push onto a stack
rand
RAND_MAX
random number generation
randomize
recursion
recursive call
recursive function
register storage class specifier
return
return-value-type
scaling
scope
shifting
side effects
simulation
software engineering
software reusability
srand
stack
stack frame
stack overflow
standard library headers
static storage-class specifier
static variable
storage-class specifier
storage classes
storage duration
time
unsigned
void

Self-Review Exercises

5.1   Answer each of the following:

a)   A program module in C is called a(n) _____.

b)   A function is invoked with a(n) _____.

c)   A variable that is known only within the function in which it is defined is called a(n)
_____.

d) The _____ statement in a called function is used to pass the value of an expression back to the calling function.

e) Keyword _____ is used in a function header to indicate that a function does not return a value or to indicate that a function contains no parameters.

f) The _____ of an identifier is the portion of the program in which the identifier can be used.

g) The three ways to return control from a called function to a caller are _____, _____ and _____.

h) A(n) _____ allows the compiler to check the number, types, and order of the arguments passed to a function.

i) The _____ function is used to produce random numbers.

j) The _____ function is used to set the random number seed to randomize a program.

k) The storage-class specifiers are _____, _____, _____ and _____.

l) Variables declared in a block or in the parameter list of a function are assumed to be of storage class _____ unless specified otherwise.

m) The storage-class specifier _____ is a recommendation to the compiler to store a variable in one of the computer's registers.

n) A non-static variable defined outside any block or function is a(n) _____ variable.

o) For a local variable in a function to retain its value between calls to the function, it must be declared with the _____ storage-class specifier.

p) The four possible scopes of an identifier are _____, _____, _____ and _____.

q) A function that calls itself either directly or indirectly is a(n) _____ function.

r) A recursive function typically has two components: one that provides a means for the recursion to terminate by testing for a(n) _____ case, and one that expresses the problem as a recursive call for a slightly simpler problem than the original call.

5.2   For the following program, state the scope (either function scope, file scope, block scope or function prototype scope) of each of the following elements.

a) The variable x in main.

b) The variable y in cube.

c) The function cube.

d) The function main.

e) The function prototype for cube.

f) The identifier y in the function prototype for cube.

```
1   #include <stdio.h>
2   int cube( int y );
3
4   int main( void )
5   {
6       int x;
7
8       for ( x = 1; x <= 10; x++ )
9           printf( "%d\n", cube( x ) );
10      return 0;
11  }
12
```

```
13   int cube( int y )
14   {
15       return y * y * y;
16   }
```

5.3   Write a program that tests whether the examples of the math library function calls shown in Fig. 5.2 actually produce the indicated results.

5.4   Give the function header for each of the following functions.

a) Function hypotenuse that takes two double-precision floating-point arguments, side1 and side2, and returns a double-precision floating-point result.

b) Function smallest that takes three integers, x, y, z, and returns an integer.

c) Function instructions that does not receive any arguments and does not return a value. [*Note:* Such functions are commonly used to display instructions to a user.]

d) Function intToFloat that takes an integer argument, number, and returns a floating-point result.

5.5   Give the function prototype for each of the following:

a) The function described in Exercise 5.4a.

b) The function described in Exercise 5.4b.

c) The function described in Exercise 5.4c.

d) The function described in Exercise 5.4d.

5.6   Write a declaration for each of the following:

a) Integer count that should be maintained in a register. Initialize count to 0.

b) Floating-point variable lastVal that is to retain its value between calls to the function in which it is defined.

c) External integer number whose scope should be restricted to the remainder of the file in which it is defined.

5.7   Find the error in each of the following program segments and explain how the error can be corrected (see also Exercise 5.50):

a)
```
int g( void )
{
    printf( "Inside function g\n" );

    int h( void )
    {
        printf( "Inside function h\n" );
    }
}
```

b)
```
int sum( int x, int y )
{
    int result;
    result = x + y;
}
```

c)
```
int sum( int n )
{
    if ( n == 0 )
        return 0;
    else
        n + sum( n - 1 );
}
```

d) void f(float a);
```
{
    float a;
    printf( "%f", a );
}
```
e) void product(void)
```
{
    int a, b, c, result;
    printf( "Enter three integers: " )
    scanf( "%d%d%d", &a, &b, &c );
    result = a * b * c;
    printf( "Result is %d", result );
    return result;
}
```

Answers to Self-Review Exercises

5.1 a) Function. b) Function call. c) Local variable. d) return. e) void. f) Scope. g) return; or return expression; or encountering the closing right brace of a function. h) Function prototype. i) rand. j) srand. k) auto, register, extern, static. l) auto. m) register. n) External, global. o) static. p) Function scope, file scope, block scope, function prototype scope. q) Recursive. r) Base.

5.2 a) Block scope. b) Block Scope. c) File scope. d) File scope. e) File scope. f) Function-prototype scope.

5.3 See below.

```
1   /* ex05_03.c */
2   /* Testing the math library functions */
3   #include <stdio.h>
4   #include <math.h>
5
6   /* function main begins program execution */
7   int main( void )
8   {
9       /* calculates and outputs the square root */
10      printf( "sqrt(%.1f) = %.1f\n", 900.0, sqrt( 900.0 ) );
11      printf( "sqrt(%.1f) = %.1f\n", 9.0, sqrt( 9.0 ) );
12
13      /* calculates and outputs the exponential function e to the x */
14      printf( "exp(%.1f) = %f\n", 1.0, exp( 1.0 ) );
15      printf( "exp(%.1f) = %f\n", 2.0, exp( 2.0 ) );
16
17      /* calculates and outputs the logarithm (base e) */
18      printf( "log(%f) = %.1f\n", 2.718282, log( 2.718282 ) );
19      printf( "log(%f) = %.1f\n", 7.389056, log( 7.389056 ) );
20
21      /* calculates and outputs the logarithm (base 10) */
22      printf( "log10(%.1f) = %.1f\n", 1.0, log10( 1.0 ) );
23      printf( "log10(%.1f) = %.1f\n", 10.0, log10( 10.0 ) );
24      printf( "log10(%.1f) = %.1f\n", 100.0, log10( 100.0 ) );
25
```

```
26      /* calculates and outputs the absolute value */
27      printf( "fabs(%.1f) = %.1f\n", 13.5, fabs( 5.0 ) );
28      printf( "fabs(%.1f) = %.1f\n", 0.0, fabs( 0.0 ) );
29      printf( "fabs(%.1f) = %.1f\n", -13.5, fabs( -5.0 ) );
30
31      /* calculates and outputs ceil( x ) */
32      printf( "ceil(%.1f) = %.1f\n", 9.2, ceil( 9.2 ) );
33      printf( "ceil(%.1f) = %.1f\n", -9.8, ceil( -9.8 ) );
34
35      /* calculates and outputs floor( x ) */
36      printf( "floor(%.1f) = %.1f\n", 9.2, floor( 9.2 ) );
37      printf( "floor(%.1f) = %.1f\n", -9.8, floor( -9.8 ) );
38
39      /* calculates and outputs pow( x, y ) */
40      printf( "pow(%.1f, %.1f) = %.1f\n", 2.0, 7.0, pow( 2.0, 7.0 ) );
41      printf( "pow(%.1f, %.1f) = %.1f\n", 9.0, 0.5, pow( 9.0, 0.5 ) );
42
43      /* calculates and outputs fmod( x, y ) */
44      printf( "fmod(%.3f/%.3f) = %.3f\n", 13.675, 2.333,
45             fmod( 13.675, 2.333 ) );
46
47      /* calculates and outputs sin( x ) */
48      printf( "sin(%.1f) = %.1f\n", 0.0, sin( 0.0 ) );
49
50      /* calculates and outputs cos( x ) */
51      printf( "cos(%.1f) = %.1f\n", 0.0, cos( 0.0 ) );
52
53      /* calculates and outputs tan( x ) */
54      printf( "tan(%.1f) = %.1f\n", 0.0, tan( 0.0 ) );
55      return 0; /* indicates successful termination */
56   } /* end main */
```

```
sqrt(900.0) = 30.0
sqrt(9.0) = 3.0
exp(1.0) = 2.718282
exp(2.0) = 7.389056
log(2.718282) = 1.0
log(7.389056) = 2.0
log10(1.0) = 0.0
log10(10.0) = 1.0
log10(100.0) = 2.0
fabs(13.5) = 13.5
fabs(0.0) = 0.0
fabs(-13.5) = 13.5
ceil(9.2) = 10.0
ceil(-9.8) = -9.0
floor(9.2) = 9.0
floor(-9.8) = -10.0
pow(2.0, 7.0) = 128.0
pow(9.0, 0.5) = 3.0
fmod(13.675/2.333) = 2.010
sin(0.0) = 0.0
cos(0.0) = 1.0
tan(0.0) = 0.0
```

5.4 a) `double hypotenuse( double side1, double side2 )`
        b) `int smallest( int x, int y, int z )`
        c) `void instructions( void )`
        d) `float intToFloat( int number )`

5.5 a) `double hypotenuse( double side1, double side2 );`
        b) `int smallest( int x, int y, int z );`
        c) `void instructions( void );`
        d) `float intToFloat( int number );`

5.6 a) `register int count = 0;`
        b) `static float lastVal;`
        c) `static int number;`
           [*Note:* This would appear outside any function definition.]

5.7 a) Error: Function h is defined in function g.
           Correction: Move the definition of h out of the definition of g.
        b) Error: The body of the function is supposed to return an integer, but does not.
           Correction: Delete variable result and place the following statement in the function:

            return x + y;

        c) Error: The result of n + sum(n - 1) is not returned; sum returns an improper result.
           Correction: Rewrite the statement in the else clause as

            return n + sum(n - 1);

        d) Error: Semicolon after the right parenthesis that encloses the parameter list, and re-
           defining the parameter a in the function definition.
           Correction: Delete the semicolon after the right parenthesis of the parameter list, and
           delete the declaration float a; in the function body.
        e) Error: The function returns a value when it is not supposed to.
           Correction: Eliminate the return statement.

Exercises

5.8 Show the value of x after each of the following statements is performed:
        a) `x = fabs( 7.5 );`
        b) `x = floor( 7.5 );`
        c) `x = fabs( 0.0 );`
        d) `x = ceil( 0.0 );`
        e) `x = fabs( -6.4 );`
        f) `x = ceil( -6.4 );`
        g) `x = ceil( -fabs( -8 + floor( -5.5 ) ) );`

5.9 A parking garage charges a $2.00 minimum fee to park for up to three hours. The garage
charges an additional $0.50 per hour for each hour *or part thereof* in excess of three hours. The max-
imum charge for any given 24-hour period is $10.00. Assume that no car parks for longer than 24
hours at a time. Write a program that will calculate and print the parking charges for each of three
customers who parked their cars in this garage yesterday. You should enter the hours parked for each
customer. Your program should print the results in a neat tabular format, and should calculate and
print the total of yesterday's receipts. The program should use the function calculateCharges to
determine the charge for each customer. Your outputs should appear in the following format:

```
Car       Hours      Charge
1           1.5        2.00
2           4.0        2.50
3          24.0       10.00
TOTAL      29.5       14.50
```

5.10 An application of function `floor` is rounding a value to the nearest integer. The statement

    y = floor(x + .5);

will round the number x to the nearest integer and assign the result to y. Write a program that reads several numbers and uses the preceding statement to round each of these numbers to the nearest integer. For each number processed, print both the original number and the rounded number.

5.11 Function `floor` may be used to round a number to a specific decimal place. The statement

    y = floor(x * 10 + .5) / 10;

rounds x to the tenths position (the first position to the right of the decimal point). The statement

    y = floor(x * 100 + .5) / 100;

rounds x to the hundredths position (the second position to the right of the decimal point). Write a program that defines four functions to round a number x in various ways

    a) `roundToInteger( number )`
    b) `roundToTenths( number )`
    c) `roundToHundreths( number )`
    d) `roundToThousandths( number )`

For each value read, your program should print the original value, the number rounded to the nearest integer, the number rounded to the nearest tenth, the number rounded to the nearest hundredth, and the number rounded to the nearest thousandth.

5.12 Answer each of the following questions.
    a) What does it mean to choose numbers "at random"?
    b) Why is the rand function useful for simulating games of chance?
    c) Why would you randomize a program by using srand? Under what circumstances is it desirable not to randomize?
    d) Why is it often necessary to scale and/or shift the values produced by rand?
    e) Why is computerized simulation of real-world situations a useful technique?

5.13 Write statements that assign random integers to the variable n in the following ranges:
    a) $1 \le n \le 2$
    b) $1 \le n \le 100$
    c) $0 \le n \le 9$
    d) $1000 \le n \le 1112$
    e) $-1 \le n \le 1$
    f) $-3 \le n \le 11$

5.14 For each of the following sets of integers, write a single statement that will print a number at random from the set.
    a) 2, 4, 6, 8, 10.
    b) 3, 5, 7, 9, 11.
    c) 6, 10, 14, 18, 22.

5.15   Define a function called hypotenuse that calculates the length of the hypotenuse of a right triangle when the other two sides are given. Use this function in a program to determine the length of the hypotenuse for each of the following triangles. The function should take two arguments of type double and return the hypotenuse as a double. Test your program with the side values specified in Fig. 5.18.

5.16   Write a function integerPower(base, exponent) that returns the value of

$$base^{exponent}$$

For example, integerPower(3, 4) = 3 * 3 * 3 * 3. Assume that exponent is a positive, nonzero integer, and base is an integer. Function integerPower should use for to control the calculation. Do not use any math library functions.

5.17   Write a function multiple that determines for a pair of integers whether the second integer is a multiple of the first. The function should take two integer arguments and return 1 (true) if the second is a multiple of the first, and 0 (false) otherwise. Use this function in a program that inputs a series of pairs of integers.

5.18   Write a program that inputs a series of integers and passes them one at a time to function even, which uses the remainder operator to determine if an integer is even. The function should take an integer argument and return 1 if the integer is even and 0 otherwise.

Triangle	Side 1	Side 2
1	3.0	4.0
2	5.0	12.0
3	8.0	15.0

Fig. 5.18 | Sample triangle side values for Exercise 5.15.

5.19   Write a function that displays at the left margin of the screen a solid square of asterisks whose side is specified in integer parameter side. For example, if side is 4, the function displays:

```
****
****
****
****
```

5.20   Modify the function created in Exercise 5.19 to form the square out of whatever character is contained in character parameter fillCharacter. Thus if side is 5 and fillCharacter is "#" then this function should print:

```
#####
#####
#####
#####
#####
```

5.21   Use techniques similar to those developed in Exercises 5.19 and 5.20 to produce a program that graphs a wide range of shapes.

5.22   Write program segments that accomplish each of the following:
   a) Calculate the integer part of the quotient when integer a is divided by integer b.
   b) Calculate the integer remainder when integer a is divided by integer b.
   c) Use the program pieces developed in a) and b) to write a function that inputs an integer between 1 and 32767 and prints it as a series of digits, with two spaces between each digit. For example, the integer 4562 should be printed as:

```
4  5  6  2
```

5.23   Write a function that takes the time as three integer arguments (for hours, minutes, and seconds) and returns the number of seconds since the last time the clock "struck 12." Use this function to calculate the amount of time in seconds between two times, both of which are within one 12-hour cycle of the clock.

5.24   Implement the following integer functions:
   a) Function celsius returns the Celsius equivalent of a Fahrenheit temperature.
   b) Function fahrenheit returns the Fahrenheit equivalent of a Celsius temperature.
   c) Use these functions to write a program that prints charts showing the Fahrenheit equivalents of all Celsius temperatures from 0 to 100 degrees, and the Celsius equivalents of all Fahrenheit temperatures from 32 to 212 degrees. Print the outputs in a neat tabular format that minimizes the number of lines of output while remaining readable.

5.25   Write a function that returns the smallest of three floating-point numbers.

5.26   An integer number is said to be a *perfect number* if its factors, including 1 (but not the number itself), sum to the number. For example, 6 is a perfect number because $6 = 1 + 2 + 3$. Write a function perfect that determines if parameter number is a perfect number. Use this function in a program that determines and prints all the perfect numbers between 1 and 1000. Print the factors of each perfect number to confirm that the number is indeed perfect. Challenge the power of your computer by testing numbers much larger than 1000.

5.27   An integer is said to be *prime* if it is divisible by only 1 and itself. For example, 2, 3, 5 and 7 are prime, but 4, 6, 8 and 9 are not.
   a) Write a function that determines if a number is prime.
   b) Use this function in a program that determines and prints all the prime numbers between 1 and 10,000. How many of these 10,000 numbers do you really have to test before being sure that you have found all the primes?
   c) Initially you might think that $n/2$ is the upper limit for which you must test to see if a number is prime, but you need go only as high as the square root of n. Why? Rewrite the program, and run it both ways. Estimate the performance improvement.

5.28   Write a function that takes an integer value and returns the number with its digits reversed. For example, given the number 7631, the function should return 1367.

5.29   The *greatest common divisor* (*GCD*) of two integers is the largest integer that evenly divides each of the two numbers. Write function gcd that returns the greatest common divisor of two integers.

5.30   Write a function qualityPoints that inputs a student's average and returns 4 if a student's average is 90–100, 3 if the average is 80–89, 2 if the average is 70–79, 1 if the average is 60–69, and 0 if the average is lower than 60.

5.31   Write a program that simulates coin tossing. For each toss of the coin the program should print Heads or Tails. Let the program toss the coin 100 times, and count the number of times each side of the coin appears. Print the results. The program should call a separate function flip that takes no arguments and returns 0 for tails and 1 for heads. [*Note:* If the program realistically simulates the coin tossing, then each side of the coin should appear approximately half the time for a total of approximately 50 heads and 50 tails.]

5.32   Computers are playing an increasing role in education. Write a program that will help an elementary school student learn multiplication. Use rand to produce two positive one-digit integers. It should then type a question such as:

How much is 6 times 7?

The student then types the answer. Your program checks the student's answer. If it is correct, print "Very good!" and then ask another multiplication question. If the answer is wrong, print "No. Please try again." and then let the student try the same question again repeatedly until the student finally gets it right.

5.33   The use of computers in education is referred to as *computer-assisted instruction* (*CAI*). One problem that develops in CAI environments is student fatigue. This can be eliminated by varying the computer's dialog to hold the student's attention. Modify the program of Exercise 5.32 so the various comments are printed for each correct answer and each incorrect answer as follows:

Responses to a correct answer

Very good!
Excellent!
Nice work!
Keep up the good work!

Responses to an incorrect answer

No. Please try again.
Wrong. Try once more.
Don't give up!
No. Keep trying.

Use the random number generator to choose a number from 1 to 4 to select an appropriate response to each answer. Use a switch statement with printf statements to issue the responses.

5.34   More sophisticated computer-aided instructions systems monitor the student's performance over a period of time. The decision to begin a new topic is often based on the student's success with previous topics. Modify the program of Exercise 5.33 to count the number of correct and incorrect responses typed by the student. After the student types 10 answers, your program should calculate the percentage of correct responses. If the percentage is lower than 75 percent, your program should print "Please ask your instructor for extra help" and then terminate.

5.35   Write a C program that plays the game of "guess the number" as follows: Your program chooses the number to be guessed by selecting an integer at random in the range 1 to 1000. The program then types:

I have a number between 1 and 1000.
Can you guess my number?
Please type your first guess.

The player then types a first guess. The program responds with one of the following:

```
1. Excellent! You guessed the number!
   Would you like to play again (y or n)?
2. Too low. Try again.
3. Too high. Try again.
```

If the player's guess is incorrect, your program should loop until the player finally gets the number right. Your program should keep telling the player Too high or Too low to help the player "zero in" on the correct answer. [*Note:* The searching technique employed in this problem is called binary search. We will say more about this in the next problem.]

5.36   Modify the program of Exercise 5.35 to count the number of guesses the player makes. If the number is 10 or fewer, print Either you know the secret or you got lucky! If the player guesses the number in 10 tries, then print Ahah! You know the secret! If the player makes more than 10 guesses, then print You should be able to do better! Why should it take no more than 10 guesses? Well, with each "good guess" the player should be able to eliminate half of the numbers. Now show why any number 1 to 1000 can be guessed in 10 or fewer tries.

5.37   Write a recursive function power(base, exponent) that when invoked returns

$$base^{exponent}$$

For example, power(3, 4) = 3 * 3 * 3 * 3. Assume that exponent is an integer greater than or equal to 1. *Hint:* The recursion step would use the relationship

$$base^{exponent} = base * base^{exponent-1}$$

and the terminating condition occurs when exponent is equal to 1 because

$$base^1 = base$$

5.38   The Fibonacci series

```
0, 1, 1, 2, 3, 5, 8, 13, 21, …
```

begins with the terms 0 and 1 and has the property that each succeeding term is the sum of the two preceding terms. a) Write a *nonrecursive* function fibonacci(n) that calculates the nth Fibonacci number. b) Determine the largest Fibonacci number that can be printed on your system. Modify the program of part a) to use double instead of int to calculate and return Fibonacci numbers. Let the program loop until it fails because of an excessively high value.

5.39   (*Towers of Hanoi*) Every budding computer scientist must grapple with certain classic problems, and the Towers of Hanoi (see Fig. 5.19) is one of the most famous of these. Legend has it that in a temple in the Far East, priests are attempting to move a stack of disks from one peg to another. The initial stack had 64 disks threaded onto one peg and arranged from bottom to top by decreasing size. The priests are attempting to move the stack from this peg to a second peg under the constraints that exactly one disk is moved at a time, and at no time may a larger disk be placed above a smaller disk. A third peg is available for temporarily holding the disks. Supposedly the world will end when the priests complete their task, so there is little incentive for us to facilitate their efforts.

Let us assume that the priests are attempting to move the disks from peg 1 to peg 3. We wish to develop an algorithm that will print the precise sequence of disk-to-disk peg transfers.

If we were to approach this problem with conventional methods, we would rapidly find ourselves hopelessly knotted up in managing the disks. Instead, if we attack the problem with recursion in mind, it immediately becomes tractable. Moving n disks can be viewed in terms of moving only $n - 1$ disks (and hence the recursion) as follows:

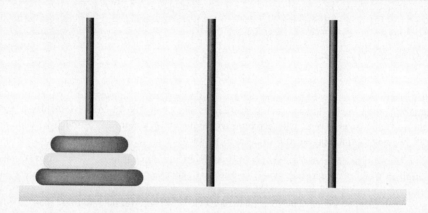

Fig. 5.19 | Towers of Hanoi for the case with four disks.

    a) Move $n - 1$ disks from peg 1 to peg 2, using peg 3 as a temporary holding area.
    b) Move the last disk (the largest) from peg 1 to peg 3.
    c) Move the $n - 1$ disks from peg 2 to peg 3, using peg 1 as a temporary holding area.

The process ends when the last task involves moving $n = 1$ disk, i.e., the base case. This is accomplished by trivially moving the disk without the need for a temporary holding area.

Write a program to solve the Towers of Hanoi problem. Use a recursive function with four parameters:

    a) The number of disks to be moved
    b) The peg on which these disks are initially threaded
    c) The peg to which this stack of disks is to be moved
    d) The peg to be used as a temporary holding area

Your program should print the precise instructions it will take to move the disks from the starting peg to the destination peg. For example, to move a stack of three disks from peg 1 to peg 3, your program should print the following series of moves:

    $1 \rightarrow 3$ (This means move one disk from peg 1 to peg 3.)
    $1 \rightarrow 2$
    $3 \rightarrow 2$
    $1 \rightarrow 3$
    $2 \rightarrow 1$
    $2 \rightarrow 3$
    $1 \rightarrow 3$

5.40 (Optional) Any program that can be implemented recursively can be implemented iteratively, although sometimes with considerably more difficulty and considerably less clarity. Try writing an iterative version of the Towers of Hanoi. If you succeed, compare your iterative version with the recursive version you developed in Exercise 5.39. Investigate issues of performance, clarity, and your ability to demonstrate the correctness of the programs.

5.41 (*Visualizing Recursion*) It is interesting to watch recursion "in action." Modify the factorial function of Fig. 5.14 to print its local variable and recursive call parameter. For each recursive call, display the outputs on a separate line and add a level of indentation. Do your utmost to make the outputs clear, interesting, and meaningful. Your goal here is to design and implement an output format that helps a person understand recursion better. You may want to add such display capabilities to the many other recursion examples and exercises throughout the text.

5.42 The greatest common divisor of integers x and y is the largest integer that evenly divides both x and y. Write a recursive function gcd that returns the greatest common divisor of x and y. The gcd of x and y is defined recursively as follows: If y is equal to 0, then gcd(x, y) is x; otherwise gcd(x, y) is gcd(y, x % y) where % is the remainder operator.

5.43 Can main be called recursively? Write a program containing a function main. Include static local variable count initialized to 1. Postincrement and print the value of count each time main is called. Run your program. What happens?

5.44 Exercises 5.32 through 5.34 developed a computer-assisted instruction program to teach an elementary school student multiplication. This exercise suggests enhancements to that program.

    a) Modify the program to allow the user to enter a grade-level capability. A grade level of 1 means to use only single-digit numbers in the problems, a grade level of 2 means to use numbers as large as two digits, and so on.

    b) Modify the program to allow the user to pick the type of arithmetic problems he or she wishes to study. An option of 1 means addition problems only, 2 means subtraction problems only, 3 means multiplication problems only, 4 means division problems only, and 5 means to randomly intermix problems of all these types.

5.45 Write function distance that calculates the distance between two points (x1, y1) and (x2, y2). All numbers and return values should be of type double.

5.46 What does the following program do?

```
1   #include <stdio.h>
2
3   /* function main begins program execution */
4   int main( void )
5   {
6      int c; /* variable to hold character input by user */
7
8      if ( ( c = getchar() ) != EOF ) {
9         main();
10        printf( "%c", c );
11     } /* end if */
12
13     return 0; /* indicates successful termination */
14
15   } /* end main */
```

5.47 What does the following program do?

```
1   #include <stdio.h>
2
3   int mystery( int a, int b ); /* function prototype */
4
5   /* function main begins program execution */
6   int main( void )
7   {
8      int x; /* first integer */
9      int y; /* second integer */
10
11     printf( "Enter two integers: " );
12     scanf( "%d%d", &x, &y );
```

```
13
14      printf( "The result is %d\n", mystery( x, y ) );
15
16      return 0; /* indicates successful termination */
17
18   } /* end main */
19
20   /* Parameter b must be a positive integer
21      to prevent infinite recursion */
22   int mystery( int a, int b )
23   {
24      /* base case */
25      if ( b == 1 ) {
26         return a;
27      } /* end if */
28      else { /* recursive step */
29         return a + mystery( a, b - 1 );
30      } /* end else */
31
32   } /* end function mystery */
```

5.48 After you determine what the program of Exercise 5.47 does, modify the program to function properly after removing the restriction of the second argument being nonnegative.

5.49 Write a program that tests as many of the math library functions in Fig. 5.2 as you can. Exercise each of these functions by having your program print out tables of return values for a diversity of argument values.

5.50 Find the error in each of the following program segments and explain how to correct it:

a) ```
double cube(float);   /* function prototype */
...
cube(float number)   /* function prototype */
{
   return number * number * number;
}
```

b) ```
register auto int x = 7;
```

c) ```
int randomNumber = srand();
```

d) ```
double y = 123.45678;
int x;
x = y;
printf( "%f\n", (double) x );
```

e) ```
double square(double number)
{
   double number;
   return number * number;
}
```

f) ```
int sum( int n )
{
   if ( n == 0 )
      return 0;
   else
      return n + sum( n );
}
```

5.51   Modify the craps program of Fig. 5.10 to allow wagering. Package as a function the portion of the program that runs one game of craps. Initialize variable bankBalance to 1000 dollars. Prompt the player to enter a wager. Use a while loop to check that wager is less than or equal to bankBalance, and if not, prompt the user to reenter wager until a valid wager is entered. After a correct wager is entered, run one game of craps. If the player wins, increase bankBalance by wager and print the new bankBalance. If the player loses, decrease bankBalance by wager, print the new bankBalance, check if bankBalance has become zero, and if so print the message, "Sorry. You busted!" As the game progresses, print various messages to create some "chatter" such as, "Oh, you're going for broke, huh?" or "Aw cmon, take a chance!" or "You're up big. Now's the time to cash in your chips!"

6

C Arrays

OBJECTIVES

In this chapter, you will learn:

- To use the array data structure to represent lists and tables of values.

- To define an array, initialize an array and refer to individual elements of an array.

- To define symbolic constants.

- To pass arrays to functions.

- To use arrays to store, sort and search lists and tables of values.

- To define and manipulate multiple-subscripted arrays.

6.1 Introduction

This chapter serves as an introduction to the important topic of data structures. Arrays are data structures consisting of related data items of the same type. In Chapter 10, we discuss C's notion of struct (structure)—a data structure consisting of related data items of possibly different types. Arrays and structures are "static" entities in that they remain the same size throughout program execution (they may, of course, be of automatic storage class and hence created and destroyed each time the blocks in which they are defined are entered and exited). In Chapter 12, we introduce dynamic data structures such as lists, queues, stacks and trees that may grow and shrink as programs execute.

6.2 Arrays

An array is a group of memory locations related by the fact that they all have the same name and the same type. To refer to a particular location or element in the array, we specify the name of the array and the **position number** of the particular element in the array.

Figure 6.1 shows an integer array called c. This array contains 12 elements. Any one of these elements may be referred to by giving the name of the array followed by the position number of the particular element in square brackets ([]). The first element in every array is the zeroth element. Thus, the first element of array c is referred to as c[0], the second element of array c is referred to as c[1], the seventh element of array c is referred to as c[6], and, in general, the ith element of array c is referred to as c[i - 1]. Array names, like other variable names, can contain only letters, digits and underscores. Array names cannot begin with a digit.

The position number contained within square brackets is more formally called a **subscript** (or **index**). A subscript must be an integer or an integer expression. If a program uses an expression as a subscript, then the expression is evaluated to determine the subscript. For example, if a = 5 and b = 6, then the statement

```
c[ a + b ] += 2;
```

adds 2 to array element c[11]. Note that a subscripted array name is an *lvalue*—it can be used on the left side of an assignment.

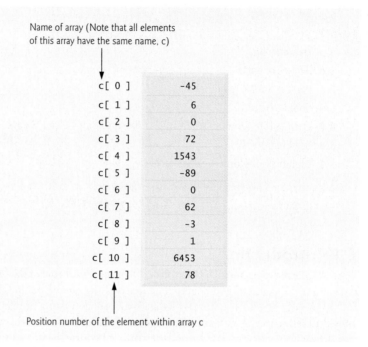

Name of array (Note that all elements
of this array have the same name, c)

c[0]	-45
c[1]	6
c[2]	0
c[3]	72
c[4]	1543
c[5]	-89
c[6]	0
c[7]	62
c[8]	-3
c[9]	1
c[10]	6453
c[11]	78

Position number of the element within array c

Fig. 6.1 | 12-element array.

Let's examine array c (Fig. 6.1) more closely. The array's name is c. Its 12 elements are referred to as c[0], c[1], c[2], ..., c[11]. The value stored in c[0] is –45, the value of c[1] is 6, the value of c[2] is 0, the value of c[7] is 62 and the value of c[11] is 78. To print the sum of the values contained in the first three elements of array c, we would write

```
printf( "%d", c[ 0 ] + c[ 1 ] + c[ 2 ] );
```

To divide the value of the seventh element of array c by 2 and assign the result to the variable x, we would write

```
x = c[ 6 ] / 2;
```

 Common Programming Error 6.1

It is important to note the difference between the "seventh element of the array" and "array element seven." Because array subscripts begin at 0, the "seventh element of the array" has a subscript of 6, while "array element seven" has a subscript of 7 and is actually the eighth element of the array. This is a source of "off-by-one" errors.

The brackets used to enclose the subscript of an array are actually considered to be an operator in C. They have the same level of precedence as the function call operator (i.e., the parentheses that are placed following a function name to call that function). Figure 6.2 shows the precedence and associativity of the operators introduced to this point in the text. They are shown top to bottom in decreasing order of precedence.

Operators						Associativity	Type
[]	()					left to right	highest
++	--	!	(*type*)			right to left	unary
*	/	%				left to right	multiplicative
+	-					left to right	additive
<	<=	>	>=			left to right	relational
==	!=					left to right	equality
&&						left to right	logical AND
||						left to right	logical OR
?:						right to left	conditional
=	+=	-=	*=	/=	%=	right to left	assignment
,						left to right	comma

Fig. 6.2 | Operator precedence and associativity.

6.3 Defining Arrays

Arrays occupy space in memory. You specify the type of each element and the number of elements required by each array so that the computer may reserve the appropriate amount of memory. To tell the computer to reserve 12 elements for integer array c, the definition

```
int c[ 12 ];
```

is used. The following definition

```
int b[ 100 ], x[ 27 ];
```

reserves 100 elements for integer array b and 27 elements for integer array x.

Arrays may be defined to contain other data types. For example, an array of type char can be used to store a character string. Character strings and their similarity to arrays are discussed in Chapter 8. The relationship between pointers and arrays is discussed in Chapter 7.

6.4 Array Examples

This section presents several examples that demonstrate how to define arrays, how to initialize arrays and how to perform many common array manipulations.

Defining an Array and Using a Loop to Initialize the Array's Elements

Figure 6.3 uses for statements to initialize the elements of a 10-element integer array n to zeros and print the array in tabular format. The first printf statement (line 16) displays the column heads for the two columns printed in the subsequent for statement.

```
 1   /* Fig. 6.3: fig06_03.c
 2      initializing an array */
 3   #include <stdio.h>
 4
 5   /* function main begins program execution */
 6   int main( void )
 7   {
 8      int n[ 10 ]; /* n is an array of 10 integers */
 9      int i; /* counter */
10
11      /* initialize elements of array n to 0 */
12      for ( i = 0; i < 10; i++ ) {
13         n[ i ] = 0; /* set element at location i to 0 */
14      } /* end for */
15
16      printf( "%s%13s\n", "Element", "Value" );
17
18      /* output contents of array n in tabular format */
19      for ( i = 0; i < 10; i++ ) {
20         printf( "%7d%13d\n", i, n[ i ] );
21      } /* end for */
22
23      return 0; /* indicates successful termination */
24
25   } /* end main */
```

Element	Value
0	0
1	0
2	0
3	0
4	0
5	0
6	0
7	0
8	0
9	0

Fig. 6.3 | Initializing the elements of an array to zeros.

Initializing an Array in a Definition with an Initializer List

The elements of an array can also be initialized when the array is defined by following the definition with an equals sign and braces, {}, containing a comma-separated list of initializers. Figure 6.4 initializes an integer array with ten values (line 9) and prints the array in tabular format.

If there are fewer initializers than elements in the array, the remaining elements are initialized to zero. For example, the elements of the array n in Fig. 6.3 could have been initialized to zero as follows:

```
int n[ 10 ] = { 0 };
```

This explicitly initializes the first element to zero and initializes the remaining nine elements to zero because there are fewer initializers than there are elements in the array. It is

```
 1   /* Fig. 6.4: fig06_04.c
 2      Initializing an array with an initializer list */
 3   #include <stdio.h>
 4
 5   /* function main begins program execution */
 6   int main( void )
 7   {
 8      /* use initializer list to initialize array n */
 9      int n[ 10 ] = { 32, 27, 64, 18, 95, 14, 90, 70, 60, 37 };
10      int i; /* counter */
11
12      printf( "%s%13s\n", "Element", "Value" );
13
14      /* output contents of array in tabular format */
15      for ( i = 0; i < 10; i++ ) {
16         printf( "%7d%13d\n", i, n[ i ] );
17      } /* end for */
18
19      return 0; /* indicates successful termination */
20
21   } /* end main */
```

```
Element        Value
      0           32
      1           27
      2           64
      3           18
      4           95
      5           14
      6           90
      7           70
      8           60
      9           37
```

Fig. 6.4 | Initializing the elements of an array with an initializer list.

important to remember that arrays are not automatically initialized to zero. You must at least initialize the first element to zero for the remaining elements to be automatically zeroed. This method of initializing the array elements to 0 is performed at compile time for static arrays and at runtime for automatic arrays.

Common Programming Error 6.2

Forgetting to initialize the elements of an array whose elements should be initialized.

The array definition

```
    int n[ 5 ] = { 32, 27, 64, 18, 95, 14 };
```

causes a syntax error because there are six initializers and only five array elements.

Common Programming Error 6.3

Providing more initializers in an array initializer list than there are elements in the array is a syntax error.

If the array size is omitted from a definition with an initializer list, the number of elements in the array will be the number of elements in the initializer list. For example,

```
int n[] = { 1, 2, 3, 4, 5 };
```

would create a five-element array.

Specifying an Array's Size with a Symbolic Constant and Initializing Array Elements with Calculations

Figure 6.5 initializes the elements of a 10-element array s to the values 2, 4, 6, ..., 20 and prints the array in tabular format. The values are generated by multiplying the loop counter by 2 and adding 2.

```
1   /* Fig. 6.5: fig06_05.c
2      Initialize the elements of array s to the even integers from 2 to 20 */
3   #include <stdio.h>
4   #define SIZE 10 /* maximum size of array */
5
6   /* function main begins program execution */
7   int main( void )
8   {
9      /* symbolic constant SIZE can be used to specify array size */
10     int s[ SIZE ]; /* array s has SIZE elements */
11     int j; /* counter */
12
13     for ( j = 0; j < SIZE; j++ ) { /* set the values */
14        s[ j ] = 2 + 2 * j;
15     } /* end for */
16
17     printf( "%s%13s\n", "Element", "Value" );
18
19     /* output contents of array s in tabular format */
20     for ( j = 0; j < SIZE; j++ ) {
21        printf( "%7d%13d\n", j, s[ j ] );
22     } /* end for */
23
24     return 0; /* indicates successful termination */
25
26  } /* end main */
```

Element	Value
0	2
1	4
2	6
3	8
4	10
5	12
6	14
7	16
8	18
9	20

Fig. 6.5 | Generating the values to be placed into elements of an array.

The #define preprocessor directive is introduced in this program. Line 4

    #define SIZE 10

defines a symbolic constant SIZE whose value is 10. A symbolic constant is an identifier that is replaced with replacement text by the C preprocessor before the program is compiled. When the program is preprocessed, all occurrences of the symbolic constant SIZE are replaced with the replacement text 10. Using symbolic constants to specify array sizes makes programs more scalable. In Fig. 6.5, we could have the first for loop (line 13) fill a 1000-element array by simply changing the value of SIZE in the #define directive from 10 to 1000. If the symbolic constant SIZE had not been used, we would have to change the program in three separate places to scale the program to handle 1000 array elements. As programs get larger, this technique becomes more useful for writing clear programs.

Common Programming Error 6.4

Ending a #define or #include preprocessor directive with a semicolon. Remember that preprocessor directives are not C statements.

If the #define preprocessor directive in line 4 is terminated with a semicolon, all occurrences of the symbolic constant SIZE in the program are replaced with the text 10; by the preprocessor. This may lead to syntax errors at compile time, or logic errors at execution time. Remember that the preprocessor is not C—it is only a text manipulator.

Common Programming Error 6.5

Assigning a value to a symbolic constant in an executable statement is a syntax error. A symbolic constant is not a variable. No space is reserved for it by the compiler as with variables that hold values at execution time.

Software Engineering Observation 6.1

Defining the size of each array as a symbolic constant makes programs more scalable.

Good Programming Practice 6.1

Use only uppercase letters for symbolic constant names. This makes these constants stand out in a program and reminds you that symbolic constants are not variables.

Good Programming Practice 6.2

In multiword symbolic constant names, use underscores to separate the words for readability.

Summing the Elements of an Array

Figure 6.6 sums the values contained in the 12-element integer array a. The for statement's body (line 16) does the totaling.

Using Arrays to Summarize Survey Results

Our next example uses arrays to summarize the results of data collected in a survey. Consider the problem statement.

Forty students were asked to rate the quality of the food in the student cafeteria on a scale of 1 to 10 (1 means awful and 10 means excellent). Place the 40 responses in an integer array and summarize the results of the poll.

```
 1   /* Fig. 6.6: fig06_06.c
 2      Compute the sum of the elements of the array */
 3   #include <stdio.h>
 4   #define SIZE 12
 5
 6   /* function main begins program execution */
 7   int main( void )
 8   {
 9      /* use initializer list to initialize array */
10      int a[ SIZE ] = { 1, 3, 5, 4, 7, 2, 99, 16, 45, 67, 89, 45 };
11      int i; /* counter */
12      int total = 0; /* sum of array */
13
14      /* sum contents of array a */
15      for ( i = 0; i < SIZE; i++ ) {
16         total += a[ i ];
17      } /* end for */
18
19      printf( "Total of array element values is %d\n", total );
20
21      return 0; /* indicates successful termination */
22
23   } /* end main */
```

```
Total of array element values is 383
```

Fig. 6.6 | Computing the sum of the elements of an array.

This is a typical array application (see Fig. 6.7). We wish to summarize the number of responses of each type (i.e., 1 through 10). The array responses (line 17) is a 40-element array of the students' responses. We use an 11-element array frequency (line 14) to count the number of occurrences of each response. We ignore frequency[0] because it is logical to have the response 1 increment frequency[1] rather than frequency[0]. This allows us to use each response directly as the subscript in the frequency array.

```
 1   /* Fig. 6.7: fig06_07.c
 2      Student poll program */
 3   #include <stdio.h>
 4   #define RESPONSE_SIZE 40 /* define array sizes */
 5   #define FREQUENCY_SIZE 11
 6
 7   /* function main begins program execution */
 8   int main( void )
 9   {
10      int answer; /* counter to loop through 40 responses */
11      int rating; /* counter to loop through frequencies 1-10 */
12
13      /* initialize frequency counters to 0 */
14      int frequency[ FREQUENCY_SIZE ] = { 0 };
```

Fig. 6.7 | Student poll analysis program. (Part 1 of 2.)

```
15
16      /* place the survey responses in the responses array */
17      int responses[ RESPONSE_SIZE ] = { 1, 2, 6, 4, 8, 5, 9, 7, 8, 10,
18          1, 6, 3, 8, 6, 10, 3, 8, 2, 7, 6, 5, 7, 6, 8, 6, 7, 5, 6, 6,
19          5, 6, 7, 5, 6, 4, 8, 6, 8, 10 };
20
21      /* for each answer, select value of an element of array responses
22          and use that value as subscript in array frequency to
23          determine element to increment */
24      for ( answer = 0; answer < RESPONSE_SIZE; answer++ ) {
25          ++frequency[ responses [ answer ] ];
26      } /* end for */
27
28      /* display results */
29      printf( "%s%17s\n", "Rating", "Frequency" );
30
31      /* output the frequencies in a tabular format */
32      for ( rating = 1; rating < FREQUENCY_SIZE; rating++ ) {
33          printf( "%6d%17d\n", rating, frequency[ rating ] );
34      } /* end for */
35
36      return 0; /* indicates successful termination */
37
38  } /* end main */
```

Rating	Frequency
1	2
2	2
3	2
4	2
5	5
6	11
7	5
8	7
9	1
10	3

Fig. 6.7 | Student poll analysis program. (Part 2 of 2.)

Good Programming Practice 6.3

Strive for program clarity. Sometimes it may be worthwhile to trade off the most efficient use of memory or processor time in favor of writing clearer programs.

Performance Tip 6.1

Sometimes performance considerations far outweigh clarity considerations.

The for loop (line 24) takes the responses one at a time from the array responses and increments one of the 10 counters (frequency[1] to frequency[10]) in the frequency array. The key statement in the loop is line 25

```
++frequency[ responses[ answer ] ];
```

which increments the appropriate `frequency` counter depending on the value of `responses[ answer ]`. When the counter variable `answer` is 0, `responses[ answer ]` is 1, so `++frequeoncy[ responses[ answer ] ];` is interpreted as

```
++frequency[ 1 ];
```

which increments array element one. When `answer` is 1, `responses[ answer ]` is 2, so `++frequency[ responses[ answer ] ];` is interpreted as

```
++frequency[ 2 ];
```

which increments array element two. When `answer` is 2, `responses[ answer ]` is 6, so `++frequency[ responses[ answer ] ];` is actually interpreted as

```
++frequency[ 6 ];
```

which increments array element six, and so on. Note that regardless of the number of responses processed in the survey, only an 11-element array is required (ignoring element zero) to summarize the results. If the data contained invalid values such as 13, the program would attempt to add 1 to `frequency[ 13 ]`. This would be outside the bounds of the array. *C has no array bounds checking to prevent the computer from referring to an element that does not exist.* Thus, an executing program can "walk off" the end of an array without warning. You should ensure that all array references remain within the bounds of the array.

Common Programming Error 6.6

Referring to an element outside the array bounds.

Error-Prevention Tip 6.1

When looping through an array, the array subscript should never go below 0 and should always be less than the total number of elements in the array (size − 1). Make sure the loop-terminating condition prevents accessing elements outside this range.

Error-Prevention Tip 6.2

Programs should validate the correctness of all input values to prevent erroneous information from affecting a program's calculations.

Graphing Array Element Values with Histograms

Our next example (Fig. 6.8) reads numbers from an array and graphs the information in the form of a bar chart or histogram—each number is printed, then a bar consisting of that many asterisks is printed beside the number. The nested `for` statement (line 20) draws the bars. Note the use of `printf( "\n" )` to end a histogram bar (line 24).

```
1    /* Fig. 6.8: fig06_08.c
2       Histogram printing program */
3    #include <stdio.h>
4    #define SIZE 10
5
```

Fig. 6.8 | Histogram printing. (Part 1 of 2.)

```
 6    /* function main begins program execution */
 7    int main( void )
 8    {
 9       /* use initializer list to initialize array n */
10       int n[ SIZE ] = { 19, 3, 15, 7, 11, 9, 13, 5, 17, 1 };
11       int i; /* outer for counter for array elements */
12       int j; /* inner for counter counts *s in each histogram bar */
13
14       printf( "%s%13s%17s\n", "Element", "Value", "Histogram" );
15
16       /* for each element of array n, output a bar of the histogram */
17       for ( i = 0; i < SIZE; i++ ) {
18          printf( "%7d%13d          ", i, n[ i ]) ;
19
20          for ( j = 1; j <= n[ i ]; j++ ) { /* print one bar */
21             printf( "%c", '*' );
22          } /* end inner for */
23
24          printf( "\n" ); /* end a histogram bar */
25       } /* end outer for */
26
27       return 0; /* indicates successful termination */
28
29    } /* end main */
```

```
Element        Value        Histogram
      0           19         ********************
      1            3         ***
      2           15         ****************
      3            7         *******
      4           11         ***********
      5            9         *********
      6           13         *************
      7            5         *****
      8           17         *****************
      9            1         *
```

Fig. 6.8 | Histogram printing. (Part 2 of 2.)

Rolling a Die 6000 Times and Summarizing the Results in an Array

In Chapter 5, we stated that we would show a more elegant method of writing the dice-rolling program of Fig. 5.8. The problem was to roll a single six-sided die 6000 times to test whether the random number generator actually produces random numbers. An array version of this program is shown in Fig. 6.9.

```
1    /* Fig. 6.9: fig06_09.c
2       Roll a six-sided die 6000 times */
3    #include <stdio.h>
4    #include <stdlib.h>
5    #include <time.h>
6    #define SIZE 7
```

Fig. 6.9 | Dice-rolling program using arrays instead of switch. (Part 1 of 2.)

```
 7
 8    /* function main begins program execution */
 9    int main( void )
10    {
11       int face; /* random die value 1 - 6 */
12       int roll; /* roll counter 1-6000 */
13       int frequency[ SIZE ] = { 0 }; /* clear counts */
14
15       srand( time( NULL ) ); /* seed random-number generator */
16
17       /* roll die 6000 times */
18       for ( roll = 1; roll <= 6000; roll++ ) {
19          face = 1 + rand() % 6;
20          ++frequency[ face ]; /* replaces 26-line switch of Fig. 5.8 */
21       } /* end for */
22
23       printf( "%s%17s\n", "Face", "Frequency" );
24
25       /* output frequency elements 1-6 in tabular format */
26       for ( face = 1; face < SIZE; face++ ) {
27          printf( "%4d%17d\n", face, frequency[ face ] );
28       } /* end for */
29
30       return 0; /* indicates successful termination */
31
32    } /* end main */
```

Face	Frequency
1	1029
2	951
3	987
4	1033
5	1010
6	990

Fig. 6.9 | Dice-rolling program using arrays instead of switch. (Part 2 of 2.)

Using Character Arrays to Store and Manipulate Strings

We have discussed only integer arrays. However, arrays are capable of holding data of any type. We now discuss storing strings in character arrays. So far, the only string-processing capability we have is outputting a string with printf. A string such as "hello" is really a static array of individual characters in C.

Character arrays have several unique features. A character array can be initialized using a string literal. For example,

```
char string1[] = "first";
```

initializes the elements of array string1 to the individual characters in the string literal "first". In this case, the size of array string1 is determined by the compiler based on the length of the string. It is important to note that the string "first" contains five characters *plus* a special string-termination character called the **null character**. Thus, array string1 actually contains six elements. The character constant representing the null character is

'\0'. All strings in C end with this character. A character array representing a string should always be defined large enough to hold the number of characters in the string and the terminating null character.

Character arrays also can be initialized with individual character constants in an initializer list. The preceding definition is equivalent to

```
char string1[] = { 'f', 'i', 'r', 's', 't', '\0' };
```

Because a string is really an array of characters, we can access individual characters in a string directly using array subscript notation. For example, string1[0] is the character 'f' and string1[3] is the character 's'.

We also can input a string directly into a character array from the keyboard using scanf and the conversion specifier %s. For example,

```
char string2[ 20 ];
```

creates a character array capable of storing a string of at most 19 characters and a terminating null character. The statement

```
scanf( "%s", string2 );
```

reads a string from the keyboard into string2. Note that the name of the array is passed to scanf without the preceding & used with nonstring variables. The & is normally used to provide scanf with a variable's location in memory so that a value can be stored there. In Section 6.5, when we discuss passing arrays to functions, we will see that the value of an array name is the address of the start of the array; therefore, the & is not necessary. Function scanf will read characters until a space, tab, newline or end-of-file indicator is encountered. Note that the string should be no longer than 19 characters to leave room for the terminating null character. If the user types 20 or more characters, your program may crash! For this reason, use the conversion specifier %19s so that scanf does not write characters into memory beyond the end of the array s.

It is your responsibility to ensure that the array into which the string is read is capable of holding any string that the user types at the keyboard. Function scanf reads characters from the keyboard until the first white-space character is encountered—it does not check how large the array is. Thus, scanf can write beyond the end of the array.

Common Programming Error 6.7

Not providing scanf with a character array large enough to store a string typed at the keyboard can result in destruction of data in a program and other runtime errors. This can also make a system susceptible to worm and virus attacks.

A character array representing a string can be output with printf and the %s conversion specifier. The array string2 is printed with the statement

```
printf( "%s\n", string2 );
```

Note that printf, like scanf, does not check how large the character array is. The characters of the string are printed until a terminating null character is encountered.

Figure 6.10 demonstrates initializing a character array with a string literal, reading a string into a character array, printing a character array as a string and accessing individual characters of a string.

```
1   /* Fig. 6.10: fig06_10.c
2      Treating character arrays as strings */
3   #include <stdio.h>
4
5   /* function main begins program execution */
6   int main( void )
7   {
8      char string1[ 20 ]; /* reserves 20 characters */
9      char string2[] = "string literal"; /* reserves 15 characters */
10     int i; /* counter */
11
12     /* read string from user into array string1 */
13     printf("Enter a string: ");
14     scanf( "%s", string1 ); /* input ended by whitespace character */
15
16     /* output strings */
17     printf( "string1 is: %s\nstring2 is: %s\n"
18             "string1 with spaces between characters is:\n",
19             string1, string2 );
20
21     /* output characters until null character is reached */
22     for ( i = 0; string1[ i ] != '\0'; i++ ) {
23        printf( "%c ", string1[ i ] );
24     } /* end for */
25
26     printf( "\n" );
27
28     return 0; /* indicates successful termination */
29
30  } /* end main */
```

```
Enter a string: Hello there
string1 is: Hello
string2 is: string literal
string1 with spaces between characters is:
H e l l o
```

Fig. 6.10 | Treating character arrays as strings.

Figure 6.10 uses a for statement (line 22) to loop through the string1 array and print the individual characters separated by spaces, using the %c conversion specifier. The condition in the for statement, string1[i] != '\0', is true while the terminating null character has not been encountered in the string.

Static Local Arrays and Automatic Local Arrays

Chapter 5 discussed the storage-class specifier static. A static local variable exists for the duration of the program, but is visible only in the function body. We can apply static to a local array definition so the array is not created and initialized each time the function is called and the array is not destroyed each time the function is exited in the program. This reduces program execution time, particularly for programs with frequently called functions that contain large arrays.

the array, adds 5 to each element and prints the array again. The second time the function is called, the `static` array contains the values stored during the first function call. Function `automaticArrayInit` is also called twice (lines 13 and 17). The elements of the automatic local array in the function are initialized with the values 1, 2 and 3 (line 50). The function prints the array, adds 5 to each element and prints the array again. The second time the function is called, the array elements are initialized to 1, 2 and 3 again because the array has automatic storage duration.

Common Programming Error 6.8

Assuming that elements of a local `static` array are initialized to zero every time the function in which the array is defined is called.

6.5 Passing Arrays to Functions

To pass an array argument to a function, specify the name of the array without any brackets. For example, if array `hourlyTemperatures` has been defined as

```
int hourlyTemperatures[ 24 ];
```

the function call

```
modifyArray( hourlyTemperatures, 24 )
```

passes array `hourlyTemperatures` and its size to function `modifyArray`. Unlike char arrays that contain strings, other array types do not have a special terminator. For this reason, the size of an array is passed to the function, so that the function can process the proper number of elements.

C automatically passes arrays to functions by reference—the called functions can modify the element values in the callers' original arrays. The name of the array evaluates to the address of the first element of the array. Because the starting address of the array is passed, the called function knows precisely where the array is stored. Therefore, when the called function modifies array elements in its function body, it is modifying the actual elements of the array in their original memory locations.

Figure 6.12 demonstrates that an array name is really the address of the first element of an array by printing `array`, `&array[ 0 ]` and `&array` using the `%p` conversion specifier—a special conversion specifier for printing addresses. The `%p` conversion specifier normally outputs addresses as hexadecimal numbers. Hexadecimal (base 16) numbers consist of the digits 0 through 9 and the letters A through F (these letters are the hexadecimal equivalents of the numbers 10–15). They are often used as shorthand notation for large integer values. Appendix D, Number Systems, provides an in-depth discussion of the relationships between binary (base 2), octal (base 8), decimal (base 10; standard integers) and hexadecimal integers. The output shows that both `array` and `&array[ 0 ]` have the same value, namely `0012FF78`. The output of this program is system dependent, but the addresses are always identical for a particular execution of this program on a particular computer.

Performance Tip 6.3

Passing arrays by reference makes sense for performance reasons. If arrays were passed by value, a copy of each element would be passed. For large, frequently passed arrays, this would be time consuming and would consume considerable storage for the copies of the arrays.

```
 1   /* Fig. 6.12: fig06_12.c
 2      The name of an array is the same as &array[ 0 ] */
 3   #include <stdio.h>
 4
 5   /* function main begins program execution */
 6   int main( void )
 7   {
 8      char array[ 5 ]; /* define an array of size 5 */
 9
10      printf( "    array = %p\n&array[0] = %p\n    &array = %p\n",
11         array, &array[ 0 ], &array );
12
13      return 0; /* indicates successful termination */
14
15   } /* end main */
```

```
    array = 0012FF78
&array[0] = 0012FF78
   &array = 0012FF78
```

Fig. 6.12 | Array name is the same as the address of the array's first element.

 Software Engineering Observation 6.2

It is possible to pass an array by value (by using a simple trick we explain in Chapter 10).

Although entire arrays are passed by reference, individual array elements are passed by value exactly as simple variables are. Such simple single pieces of data (such as individual ints, floats and chars) are called scalars. To pass an element of an array to a function, use the subscripted name of the array element as an argument in the function call. In Chapter 7, we show how to pass scalars (i.e., individual variables and array elements) to functions by reference.

For a function to receive an array through a function call, the function's parameter list must specify that an array will be received. For example, the function header for function modifyArray (that we called earlier in this section) might be written as

```
void modifyArray( int b[], int size )
```

indicating that modifyArray expects to receive an array of integers in parameter b and the number of array elements in parameter size. The size of the array is not required between the array brackets. If it is included, the compiler checks that it is greater than zero, then ignores it. Specifying a negative size is a compilatuon error. Because arrays are automatically passed by reference, when the called function uses the array name b, it will be referring to the array in the caller (array hourlyTemperatures in the preceding call). In Chapter 7, we introduce other notations for indicating that an array is being received by a function. As we will see, these notations are based on the intimate relationship between arrays and pointers in C.

Figure 6.13 demonstrates the difference between passing an entire array and passing an array element. The program first prints the five elements of integer array a (lines 20–22). Next, a and its size are passed to function modifyArray (line 27), where each of a's

```
 1   /* Fig. 6.13: fig06_13.c
 2      Passing arrays and individual array elements to functions */
 3   #include <stdio.h>
 4   #define SIZE 5
 5
 6   /* function prototypes */
 7   void modifyArray( int b[], int size );
 8   void modifyElement( int e );
 9
10   /* function main begins program execution */
11   int main( void )
12   {
13      int a[ SIZE ] = { 0, 1, 2, 3, 4 }; /* initialize a */
14      int i; /* counter */
15
16      printf( "Effects of passing entire array by reference:\n\nThe "
17              "values of the original array are:\n" );
18
19      /* output original array */
20      for ( i = 0; i < SIZE; i++ ) {
21         printf( "%3d", a[ i ] );
22      } /* end for */
23
24      printf( "\n" );
25
26      /* pass array a to modifyArray by reference */
27      modifyArray( a, SIZE );
28
29      printf( "The values of the modified array are:\n" );
30
31      /* output modified array */
32      for ( i = 0; i < SIZE; i++ ) {
33         printf( "%3d", a[ i ] );
34      } /* end for */
35
36      /* output value of a[ 3 ] */
37      printf( "\n\n\nEffects of passing array element "
38              "by value:\n\nThe value of a[3] is %d\n", a[ 3 ] );
39
40      modifyElement( a[ 3 ] ); /* pass array element a[ 3 ] by value */
41
42      /* output value of a[ 3 ] */
43      printf( "The value of a[ 3 ] is %d\n", a[ 3 ] );
44
45      return 0; /* indicates successful termination */
46
47   } /* end main */
48
49   /* in function modifyArray, "b" points to the original array "a"
50      in memory */
51   void modifyArray( int b[], int size )
52   {
53      int j; /* counter */
```

Fig. 6.13 | Passing arrays and individual array elements to functions. (Part 1 of 2.)

```
54
55      /* multiply each array element by 2 */
56      for ( j = 0; j < size; j++ ) {
57         b[ j ] *= 2;
58      } /* end for */
59
60   } /* end function modifyArray */
61
62   /* in function modifyElement, "e" is a local copy of array element
63      a[ 3 ] passed from main */
64   void modifyElement( int e )
65   {
66      /* multiply parameter by 2 */
67      printf( "Value in modifyElement is %d\n", e *= 2 );
68   } /* end function modifyElement */
```

```
Effects of passing entire array by reference:

The values of the original array are:
   0   1   2   3   4
The values of the modified array are:
   0   2   4   6   8


Effects of passing array element by value:

The value of a[3] is 6
Value in modifyElement is 12
The value of a[ 3 ] is 6
```

Fig. 6.13 | Passing arrays and individual array elements to functions. (Part 2 of 2.)

elements is multiplied by 2 (lines 56–57). Then a is reprinted in main (lines 32–34). As the output shows, the elements of a are indeed modified by modifyArray. Now the program prints the value of a[3] (line 38) and passes it to function modifyElement (line 40). Function modifyElement multiplies its argument by 2 (line 67) and prints the new value. Note that when a[3] is reprinted in main (line 43), it has not been modified, because individual array elements are passed by value.

There may be situations in your programs in which a function should not be allowed to modify array elements. Because arrays are always passed by reference, modification of values in an array is difficult to control. C provides the type qualifier const to prevent modification of array values in a function. When an array parameter is preceded by the const qualifier, the array elements become constant in the function body, and any attempt to modify an element of the array in the function body results in a compile-time error. This enables you to correct a program so it does not attempt to modify array elements.

Figure 6.14 demonstrates the const qualifier. Function tryToModifyArray (line 22) is defined with parameter const int b[], which specifies that array b is constant and cannot be modified. The output shows the error messages produced by the compiler—the errors may be different on your system. Each of the three attempts by the function to modify array elements results in the compiler error "l-value specifies a const object." The const qualifier is discussed again in Chapter 7.

```
 1   /* Fig. 6.14: fig06_14.c
 2      Demonstrating the const type qualifier with arrays */
 3   #include <stdio.h>
 4
 5   void tryToModifyArray( const int b[] ); /* function prototype */
 6
 7   /* function main begins program execution */
 8   int main( void )
 9   {
10      int a[] = { 10, 20, 30 }; /* initialize a */
11
12      tryToModifyArray( a );
13
14      printf("%d %d %d\n", a[ 0 ], a[ 1 ], a[ 2 ] );
15
16      return 0; /* indicates successful termination */
17
18   } /* end main */
19
20   /* in function tryToModifyArray, array b is const, so it cannot be
21      used to modify the original array a in main. */
22   void tryToModifyArray( const int b[] )
23   {
24      b[ 0 ] /= 2;    /* error */
25      b[ 1 ] /= 2;    /* error */
26      b[ 2 ] /= 2;    /* error */
27   } /* end function tryToModifyArray */
```

```
Compiling...
FIG06_14.C
fig06_14.c(24) : error C2166: l-value specifies const object
fig06_14.c(25) : error C2166: l-value specifies const object
fig06_14.c(26) : error C2166: l-value specifies const object
```

Fig. 6.14 | const type qualifier.

Software Engineering Observation 6.3

The const type qualifier can be applied to an array parameter in a function definition to prevent the original array from being modified in the function body. This is another example of the principle of least privilege. Functions should not be given the capability to modify an array unless it is absolutely necessary.

6.6 Sorting Arrays

Sorting data (i.e., placing the data into a particular order such as ascending or descending) is one of the most important computing applications. A bank sorts all checks by account number so that it can prepare individual bank statements at the end of each month. Telephone companies sort their lists of accounts by last name and, within that, by first name to make it easy to find phone numbers. Virtually every organization must sort some data and in many cases massive amounts of data. Sorting data is an intriguing problem which has attracted some of the most intense research efforts in the field of computer science. In

this chapter we discuss what is perhaps the simplest known sorting scheme. In Chapters 12 and 16, we investigate more complex schemes that yield superior performance.

 Performance Tip 6.4

Often, the simplest algorithms perform poorly. Their virtue is that they are easy to write, test and debug. However, more complex algorithms are often needed to realize maximum performance.

Figure 6.15 sorts the values in the elements of the 10-element array a (line 10) into ascending order. The technique we use is called the **bubble sort** or the **sinking sort** because the smaller values gradually "bubble" their way upward to the top of the array like air bubbles rising in water, while the larger values sink to the bottom of the array. The technique

```c
/* Fig. 6.15: fig06_15.c
   This program sorts an array's values into ascending order */
#include <stdio.h>
#define SIZE 10

/* function main begins program execution */
int main( void )
{
   /* initialize a */
   int a[ SIZE ] = { 2, 6, 4, 8, 10, 12, 89, 68, 45, 37 };
   int pass; /* passes counter */
   int i;    /* comparisons counter */
   int hold; /* temporary location used to swap array elements */

   printf( "Data items in original order\n" );

   /* output original array */
   for ( i = 0; i < SIZE; i++ ) {
      printf( "%4d", a[ i ] );
   } /* end for */

   /* bubble sort */
   /* loop to control number of passes */
   for ( pass = 1; pass < SIZE; pass++ ) {

      /* loop to control number of comparisons per pass */
      for ( i = 0; i < SIZE - 1; i++ ) {

         /* compare adjacent elements and swap them if first
            element is greater than second element */
         if ( a[ i ] > a[ i + 1 ] ) {
            hold = a[ i ];
            a[ i ] = a[ i + 1 ];
            a[ i + 1 ] = hold;
         } /* end if */

      } /* end inner for */

   } /* end outer for */
```

Fig. 6.15 | Sorting an array with bubble sort. (Part 1 of 2.)

```
40
41      printf( "\nData items in ascending order\n" );
42
43      /* output sorted array */
44      for ( i = 0; i < SIZE; i++ ) {
45         printf( "%4d", a[ i ] );
46      } /* end for */
47
48      printf( "\n" );
49
50      return 0; /* indicates successful termination */
51   }
```

```
Data items in original order
   2   6   4   8  10  12  89  68  45  37
Data items in ascending order
   2   4   6   8  10  12  37  45  68  89
```

Fig. 6.15 | Sorting an array with bubble sort. (Part 2 of 2.)

is to make several passes through the array. On each pass, successive pairs of elements are compared. If a pair is in increasing order (or if the values are identical), we leave the values as they are. If a pair is in decreasing order, their values are swapped in the array.

First the program compares a[0] to a[1], then a[1] to a[2], then a[2] to a[3], and so on until it completes the pass by comparing a[8] to a[9]. Note that although there are 10 elements, only nine comparisons are performed. Because of the way the successive comparisons are made, a large value may move down the array many positions on a single pass, but a small value may move up only one position. On the first pass, the largest value is guaranteed to sink to the bottom element of the array, a[9]. On the second pass, the second-largest value is guaranteed to sink to a[8]. On the ninth pass, the ninth-largest value sinks to a[1]. This leaves the smallest value in a[0], so only nine passes of the array are needed to sort the array, even though there are ten elements.

The sorting is performed by the nested for loop (lines 24–39). If a swap is necessary, it is performed by the three assignments

```
hold = a[ i ];
a[ i ] = a[ i + 1 ];
a[ i + 1 ] = hold;
```

where the extra variable hold temporarily stores one of the two values being swapped. The swap cannot be performed with only the two assignments

```
a[ i ] = a[ i + 1 ];
a[ i + 1 ] = a[ i ];
```

If, for example, a[i] is 7 and a[i + 1] is 5, after the first assignment both values will be 5 and the value 7 will be lost. Hence the need for the extra variable hold.

The chief virtue of the bubble sort is that it is easy to program. However, the bubble sort runs slowly because every exchange moves an element only one position closer to its final destination. This becomes apparent when sorting large arrays. In the exercises, we will develop more efficient versions of the bubble sort. Far more efficient sorts than the bubble sort have been developed. We will investigate a few of these in the exercises. More advanced courses investigate sorting and searching in greater depth.

6.7 Case Study: Computing Mean, Median and Mode Using Arrays

We now consider a larger example. Computers are commonly used for survey data analysis to compile and analyze the results of surveys and opinion polls. Figure 6.16 uses array response initialized with 99 responses to a survey. Each response is a number from 1 to 9. The program computes the mean, median and mode of the 99 values.

```c
 1   /* Fig. 6.16: fig06_16.c
 2      This program introduces the topic of survey data analysis.
 3      It computes the mean, median and mode of the data */
 4   #include <stdio.h>
 5   #define SIZE 99
 6
 7   /* function prototypes */
 8   void mean( const int answer[] );
 9   void median( int answer[] );
10   void mode( int freq[], const int answer[] ) ;
11   void bubbleSort( int a[] );
12   void printArray( const int a[] );
13
14   /* function main begins program execution */
15   int main( void )
16   {
17      int frequency[ 10 ] = { 0 }; /* initialize array frequency */
18
19      /* initialize array response */
20      int response[ SIZE ] =
21         { 6, 7, 8, 9, 8, 7, 8, 9, 8, 9,
22           7, 8, 9, 5, 9, 8, 7, 8, 7, 8,
23           6, 7, 8, 9, 3, 9, 8, 7, 8, 7,
24           7, 8, 9, 8, 9, 8, 9, 7, 8, 9,
25           6, 7, 8, 7, 8, 7, 9, 8, 9, 2,
26           7, 8, 9, 8, 9, 8, 9, 7, 5, 3,
27           5, 6, 7, 2, 5, 3, 9, 4, 6, 4,
28           7, 8, 9, 6, 8, 7, 8, 9, 7, 8,
29           7, 4, 4, 2, 5, 3, 8, 7, 5, 6,
30           4, 5, 6, 1, 6, 5, 7, 8, 7 };
31
32      /* process responses */
33      mean( response );
34      median( response );
35      mode( frequency, response );
36
37      return 0; /* indicates successful termination */
38
39   } /* end main */
40
```

Fig. 6.16 | Survey data analysis program. (Part 1 of 4.)

```
41   /* calculate average of all response values */
42   void mean( const int answer[] )
43   {
44      int j; /* counter for totaling array elements */
45      int total = 0; /* variable to hold sum of array elements */
46
47      printf( "%s\n%s\n%s\n", "********", "  Mean", "********" );
48
49      /* total response values */
50      for ( j = 0; j < SIZE; j++ ) {
51         total += answer[ j ];
52      } /* end for */
53
54      printf( "The mean is the average value of the data\n"
55              "items. The mean is equal to the total of\n"
56              "all the data items divided by the number\n"
57              "of data items ( %d ). The mean value for\n"
58              "this run is: %d / %d = %.4f\n\n",
59              SIZE, total, SIZE, ( double ) total / SIZE );
60   } /* end function mean */
61
62   /* sort array and determine median element's value */
63   void median( int answer[] )
64   {
65      printf( "\n%s\n%s\n%s\n%s",
66              "********", "  Median", "********",
67              "The unsorted array of responses is" );
68
69      printArray( answer ); /* output unsorted array */
70
71      bubbleSort( answer ); /* sort array */
72
73      printf( "\n\nThe sorted array is" );
74      printArray( answer ); /* output sorted array */
75
76      /* display median element */
77      printf( "\n\nThe median is element %d of\n"
78              "the sorted %d element array.\n"
79              "For this run the median is %d\n\n",
80              SIZE / 2, SIZE, answer[ SIZE / 2 ] );
81   } /* end function median */
82
83   /* determine most frequent response */
84   void mode( int freq[], const int answer[] )
85   {
86      int rating; /* counter for accessing elements 1-9 of array freq */
87      int j; /* counter for summarizing elements 0-98 of array answer */
88      int h; /* counter for diplaying histograms of elements in array freq */
89      int largest = 0; /* represents largest frequency */
90      int modeValue = 0; /* represents most frequent response */
91
92      printf( "\n%s\n%s\n%s\n",
93              "********", "  Mode", "********" );
```

Fig. 6.16 | Survey data analysis program. (Part 2 of 4.)

```
94
95      /* initialize frequencies to 0 */
96      for ( rating = 1; rating <= 9; rating++ ) {
97         freq[ rating ] = 0;
98      } /* end for */
99
100     /* summarize frequencies */
101     for ( j = 0; j < SIZE; j++ ) {
102        ++freq[ answer[ j ] ];
103     } /* end for */
104
105     /* output headers for result columns */
106     printf( "%s%11s%19s\n\n%54s\n%54s\n\n",
107            "Response", "Frequency", "Histogram",
108            "1    1    2    2", "5    0    5    0    5" );
109
110     /* output results */
111     for ( rating = 1; rating <= 9; rating++ ) {
112        printf( "%8d%11d          ", rating, freq[ rating ] );
113
114        /* keep track of mode value and largest frequency value */
115        if ( freq[ rating ] > largest ) {
116           largest = freq[ rating ];
117           modeValue = rating;
118        } /* end if */
119
120        /* output histogram bar representing frequency value */
121        for ( h = 1; h <= freq[ rating ]; h++ ) {
122           printf( "*" );
123        } /* end inner for */
124
125        printf( "\n" ); /* being new line of output */
126     } /* end outer for */
127
128     /* display the mode value */
129     printf( "The mode is the most frequent value.\n"
130            "For this run the mode is %d which occurred"
131            " %d times.\n", modeValue, largest );
132  } /* end function mode */
133
134  /* function that sorts an array with bubble sort algorithm */
135  void bubbleSort( int a[] )
136  {
137     int pass; /* pass counter */
138     int j;    /* comparison counter */
139     int hold; /* temporary location used to swap elements */
140
141     /* loop to control number of passes */
142     for ( pass = 1; pass < SIZE; pass++ ) {
143
144        /* loop to control number of comparisons per pass */
145        for ( j = 0; j < SIZE - 1; j++ ) {
146
```

Fig. 6.16 | Survey data analysis program. (Part 3 of 4.)

```
147                /* swap elements if out of order */
148                if ( a[ j ] > a[ j + 1 ] ) {
149                   hold = a[ j ];
150                   a[ j ] = a[ j + 1 ];
151                   a[ j + 1 ] = hold;
152                } /* end if */
153
154             } /* end inner for */
155
156          } /* end outer for */
157
158    } /* end function bubbleSort */
159
160    /* output array contents (20 values per row) */
161    void printArray( const int a[] )
162    {
163       int j; /* counter */
164
165       /* output array contents */
166       for ( j = 0; j < SIZE; j++ ) {
167
168          if ( j % 20 == 0 ) { /* begin new line every 20 values */
169             printf( "\n" );
170          } /* end if */
171
172          printf( "%2d", a[ j ] );
173       } /* end for */
174
175    } /* end function printArray */
```

Fig. 6.16 | Survey data analysis program. (Part 4 of 4.)

The mean is the arithmetic average of the 99 values. Function mean (line 42) computes the mean by totaling the 99 elements and dividing the result by 99.

The median is the "middle value." Function median (line 63) determines the median by calling function bubbleSort (defined in line 135) to sort the array of responses into ascending order, then picking the middle element, answer[SIZE / 2], of the sorted array. Note that when there is an even number of elements, the median should be calculated as the mean of the two middle elements. Function median does not currently provide this capability. Function printArray (line 161) is called to output the response array.

The mode is the value that occurs most frequently among the 99 responses. Function mode (line 84) determines the mode by counting the number of responses of each type, then selecting the value with the greatest count. This version of function mode does not handle a tie (see Exercise 6.14). Function mode also produces a histogram to aid in determining the mode graphically. Figure 6.17 contains a sample run of this program. This example includes most of the common manipulations usually required in array problems, including passing arrays to functions.

6.8 Searching Arrays

Programmers often work with large amounts of data stored in arrays. It may be necessary to determine whether an array contains a value that matches a certain key value. The pro-

```
********
 Mean
********
The mean is the average value of the data
items. The mean is equal to the total of
all the data items divided by the number
of data items ( 99 ). The mean value for
this run is: 681 / 99 = 6.8788


********
 Median
********
The unsorted array of responses is
6 7 8 9 8 7 8 9 8 9 7 8 9 5 9 8 7 8 7 8
6 7 8 9 3 9 8 7 8 7 7 8 9 8 9 8 9 7 8 9
6 7 8 7 8 7 9 8 9 2 7 8 9 8 9 8 9 9 7 5 3
5 6 7 2 5 3 9 4 6 4 7 8 9 6 8 7 8 9 7 8
7 4 4 2 5 3 8 7 5 6 4 5 6 1 6 5 7 8 7

The sorted array is
1 2 2 2 3 3 3 3 4 4 4 4 4 5 5 5 5 5 5 5
5 6 6 6 6 6 6 6 6 6 7 7 7 7 7 7 7 7 7 7
7 7 7 7 7 7 7 7 7 7 7 7 7 8 8 8 8 8 8 8
8 8 8 8 8 8 8 8 8 8 8 8 8 8 8 8 8 8 8 8
9 9 9 9 9 9 9 9 9 9 9 9 9 9 9 9 9 9 9

The median is element 49 of
the sorted 99 element array.
For this run the median is 7


********
 Mode
********
Response   Frequency        Histogram

                              1      1      2      2
                        5     0      5      0      5

         1         1    *
         2         3    ***
         3         4    ****
         4         5    *****
         5         8    ********
         6         9    *********
         7        23    ***********************
         8        27    ***************************
         9        19    *******************
The mode is the most frequent value.
For this run the mode is 8 which occurred 27 times.
```

Fig. 6.17 | Sample run for the survey data analysis program.

cess of finding a particular element of an array is called searching. In this section we discuss two searching techniques—the simple linear search technique and the more efficient (but more complex) binary search technique. Exercise 6.32 and Exercise 6.33 at the end of this chapter ask you to implement recursive versions of the linear search and the binary search.

Searching an Array with Linear Search

The linear search (Fig. 6.18) compares each element of the array with the search key. Since the array is not in any particular order, it is just as likely that the value will be found in the first element as in the last. On average, therefore, the program will have to compare the search key with half the elements of the array.

```c
1    /* Fig. 6.18: fig06_18.c
2       Linear search of an array */
3    #include <stdio.h>
4    #define SIZE 100
5
6    /* function prototype */
7    int linearSearch( const int array[], int key, int size );
8
9    /* function main begins program execution */
10   int main( void )
11   {
12      int a[ SIZE ]; /* create array a */
13      int x; /* counter for initializing elements 0-99 of array a */
14      int searchKey; /* value to locate in array a */
15      int element; /* variable to hold location of searchKey or -1 */
16
17      /* create data */
18      for ( x = 0; x < SIZE; x++ ) {
19         a[ x ] = 2 * x;
20      } /* end for */
21
22      printf( "Enter integer search key:\n" );
23      scanf( "%d", &searchKey );
24
25      /* attempt to locate searchKey in array a */
26      element = linearSearch( a, searchKey, SIZE );
27
28      /* display results */
29      if ( element != -1 ) {
30         printf( "Found value in element %d\n", element );
31      } /* end if */
32      else {
33         printf( "Value not found\n" );
34      } /* end else */
35
36      return 0; /* indicates successful termination */
37
38   } /* end main */
39
40   /* compare key to every element of array until the location is found
41      or until the end of array is reached; return subscript of element
42      if key or -1 if key is not found */
43   int linearSearch( const int array[], int key, int size )
44   {
45      int n; /* counter */
46
```

Fig. 6.18 | Linear search of an array. (Part 1 of 2.)

```
47      /* loop through array */
48      for ( n = 0; n < size; ++n ) {
49
50          if ( array[ n ] == key ) {
51              return n; /* return location of key */
52          } /* end if */
53
54      } /* end for */
55
56      return -1; /* key not found */
57
58   } /* end function linearSearch */
```

```
Enter integer search key:
36
Found value in element 18
```

```
Enter integer search key:
37
Value not found
```

Fig. 6.18 | Linear search of an array. (Part 2 of 2.)

Searching an Array with Binary Search

The linear searching method works well for small or unsorted arrays. However, for large arrays linear searching is inefficient. If the array is sorted, the high-speed binary search technique can be used.

The binary search algorithm eliminates from consideration one-half of the elements in a sorted array after each comparison. The algorithm locates the middle element of the array and compares it to the search key. If they are equal, the search key is found and the array subscript of that element is returned. If they are not equal, the problem is reduced to searching one-half of the array. If the search key is less than the middle element of the array, the first half of the array is searched, otherwise the second half of the array is searched. If the search key is not found in the specified subarray (piece of the original array), the algorithm is repeated on one-quarter of the original array. The search continues until the search key is equal to the middle element of a subarray, or until the subarray consists of one element that is not equal to the search key (i.e., the search key is not found).

In a worst case-scenario, searching an array of 1023 elements takes only 10 comparisons using a binary search. Repeatedly dividing 1024 by 2 yields the values 512, 256, 128, 64, 32, 16, 8, 4, 2 and 1. The number 1024 (2^{10}) is divided by 2 only 10 times to get the value 1. Dividing by 2 is equivalent to one comparison in the binary search algorithm. An array of 1048576 (2^{20}) elements takes a maximum of 20 comparisons to find the search key. An array of one billion elements takes a maximum of 30 comparisons to find the search key. This is a tremendous increase in performance over the linear search that required comparing the search key to an average of half of the array elements. For a one-billion-element array, this is a difference between an average of 500 million comparisons and a maximum of 30 comparisons! The maximum comparisons for any array can be determined by finding the first power of 2 greater than the number of array elements.

Figure 6.19 presents the iterative version of function `binarySearch` (lines 45–77). The function receives four arguments—an integer array `b` to be searched, an integer `searchKey`, the `low` array subscript and the `high` array subscript (these define the portion of the array to be searched). If the search key does not match the middle element of a subarray, the `low` subscript or `high` subscript is modified so that a smaller subarray can be searched. If the search key is less than the middle element, the `high` subscript is set to `middle - 1` and the search is continued on the elements from `low` to `middle - 1`. If the search key is greater than the middle element, the `low` subscript is set to `middle + 1` and the search is continued on the elements from `middle + 1` to `high`. The program uses an array of 15 elements. The first power of 2 greater than the number of elements in this array is 16 (2^4), so a maximum of 4 comparisons are required to find the search key. The program uses function `printHeader` (lines 80–99) to output the array subscripts and function `printRow` (lines 103–124) to output each subarray during the binary search process. The middle element in each subarray is marked with an asterisk (*) to indicate the element to which the search key is compared.

```
 1   /* Fig. 6.19: fig06_19.c
 2      Binary search of an array */
 3   #include <stdio.h>
 4   #define SIZE 15
 5
 6   /* function prototypes */
 7   int binarySearch( const int b[], int searchKey, int low, int high );
 8   void printHeader( void );
 9   void printRow( const int b[], int low, int mid, int high );
10
11   /* function main begins program execution */
12   int main( void )
13   {
14      int a[ SIZE ]; /* create array a */
15      int i; /* counter for initializing elements 0-14 of array a */
16      int key; /* value to locate in array a */
17      int result; /* variable to hold location of key or -1 */
18
19      /* create data */
20      for ( i = 0; i < SIZE; i++ ) {
21         a[ i ] = 2 * i;
22      } /* end for */
23
24      printf( "Enter a number between 0 and 28: " );
25      scanf( "%d", &key );
26
27      printHeader();
28
29      /* search for key in array a */
30      result = binarySearch( a, key, 0, SIZE - 1 );
31
```

Fig. 6.19 | Binary search of a sorted array. (Part 1 of 4.)

```
32      /* display results */
33      if ( result != -1 ) {
34         printf( "\n%d found in array element %d\n", key, result );
35      } /* end if */
36      else {
37         printf( "\n%d not found\n", key );
38      } /* end else */
39
40      return 0; /* indicates successful termination */
41
42   } /* end main */
43
44   /* function to perform binary search of an array */
45   int binarySearch( const int b[], int searchKey, int low, int high )
46   {
47      int middle; /* variable to hold middle element of array */
48
49      /* loop until low subscript is greater than high subscript */
50      while ( low <= high ) {
51
52         /* determine middle element of subarray being searched */
53         middle = ( low + high ) / 2;
54
55         /* display subarray used in this loop iteration */
56         printRow( b, low, middle, high );
57
58         /* if searchKey matched middle element, return middle */
59         if ( searchKey == b[ middle ] ) {
60            return middle;
61         } /* end if */
62
63         /* if searchKey less than middle element, set new high */
64         else if ( searchKey < b[ middle ] ) {
65            high = middle - 1; /* search low end of array */
66         } /* end else if */
67
68         /* if searchKey greater than middle element, set new low */
69         else {
70            low = middle + 1; /* search high end of array */
71         } /* end else */
72
73      } /* end while */
74
75      return -1;   /* searchKey not found */
76
77   } /* end function binarySearch */
78
79   /* Print a header for the output */
80   void printHeader( void )
81   {
82      int i; /* counter */
83
84      printf( "\nSubscripts:\n" );
```

Fig. 6.19 | Binary search of a sorted array. (Part 2 of 4.)

```
85
86       /* output column head */
87       for ( i = 0; i < SIZE; i++ ) {
88          printf( "%3d ", i );
89       } /* end for */
90
91       printf( "\n" ); /* start new line of output */
92
93       /* output line of - characters */
94       for ( i = 1; i <= 4 * SIZE; i++ ) {
95          printf( "-" );
96       } /* end for */
97
98       printf( "\n" ); /* start new line of output */
99    } /* end function printHeader */
100
101   /* Print one row of output showing the current
102      part of the array being processed. */
103   void printRow( const int b[], int low, int mid, int high )
104   {
105      int i; /* counter for iterating through array b */
106
107      /* loop through entire array */
108      for ( i = 0; i < SIZE; i++ ) {
109
110         /* display spaces if outside current subarray range */
111         if ( i < low || i > high ) {
112            printf( "    " );
113         } /* end if */
114         else if ( i == mid ) { /* display middle element */
115            printf( "%3d*", b[ i ] ); /* mark middle value */
116         } /* end else if */
117         else { /* display other elements in subarray */
118            printf( "%3d ", b[ i ] );
119         } /* end else */
120
121      } /* end for */
122
123      printf( "\n" ); /* start new line of output */
124   } /* end function printRow */
```

```
Enter a number between 0 and 28: 25

Subscripts:
  0   1   2   3   4   5   6   7   8   9  10  11  12  13  14
------------------------------------------------------------
  0   2   4   6   8  10  12  14* 16  18  20  22  24  26  28
                              16  18  20  22* 24  26  28
                                          24  26* 28
                                          24*

25 not found
```

Fig. 6.19 | Binary search of a sorted array. (Part 3 of 4.)

```
Enter a number between 0 and 28: 8

Subscripts:
 0   1   2   3   4   5    6    7    8    9   10   11   12   13   14
----------------------------------------------------------------------
 0   2   4   6   8  10   12  14*  16   18   20   22   24   26   28
 0   2   4  6*   8  10   12
                 8  10*  12
                8*

8 found in array element 4
```

```
Enter a number between 0 and 28: 6

Subscripts:
 0   1   2   3   4   5    6    7    8    9   10   11   12   13   14
----------------------------------------------------------------------
 0   2   4   6   8  10   12  14*  16   18   20   22   24   26   28
 0   2   4  6*   8  10   12

6 found in array element 3
```

Fig. 6.19 | Binary search of a sorted array. (Part 4 of 4.)

6.9 Multiple-Subscripted Arrays

Arrays in C can have multiple subscripts. A common use of multiple-subscripted arrays (also called multidimensional arrays) is to represent tables of values consisting of information arranged in rows and columns. To identify a particular table element, we must specify two subscripts: The first (by convention) identifies the element's row and the second (by convention) identifies the element's column. Tables or arrays that require two subscripts to identify a particular element are called double-subscripted arrays. Note that multiple-subscripted arrays can have more than two subscripts.

Figure 6.20 illustrates a double-subscripted array, a. The array contains three rows and four columns, so it is said to be a 3-by-4 array. In general, an array with m rows and n columns is called an m-by-n array.

Every element in array a is identified in Fig. 6.20 by an element name of the form a[i][j]; a is the name of the array, and i and j are the subscripts that uniquely identify each element in a. Note that the names of the elements in the first row all have a first subscript of 0; the names of the elements in the fourth column all have a second subscript of 3.

Common Programming Error 6.9

Referencing a double-subscripted array element as a[x, y] instead of a[x][y]. C interprets a[x, y] as a[y], and as such it does not cause a syntax error.

A multiple-subscripted array can be initialized when it is defined, much like a single-subscripted array. For example, a double-subscripted array int b[2][2] could be defined and initialized with

```
int b[ 2 ][ 2 ] = { { 1, 2 }, { 3, 4 } };
```

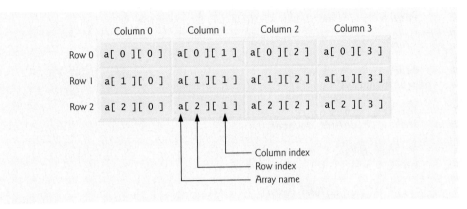

Fig. 6.20 | Double-subscripted array with three rows and four columns.

The values are grouped by row in braces. The values in the first set of braces initialize row 0 and the values in the second set of braces initialize row 1. So, the values 1 and 2 initialize elements b[0][0] and b[0][1], respectively, and the values 3 and 4 initialize elements b[1][0] and b[1][1], respectively. If there are not enough initializers for a given row, the remaining elements of that row are initialized to 0. Thus,

```
int b[ 2 ][ 2 ] = { { 1 }, { 3, 4 } };
```

would initialize b[0][0] to 1, b[0][1] to 0, b[1][0] to 3 and b[1][1] to 4. Figure 6.21 demonstrates defining and initializing double-subscripted arrays.

```
1   /* Fig. 6.21: fig06_21.c
2      Initializing multidimensional arrays */
3   #include <stdio.h>
4
5   void printArray( const int a[][ 3 ] ); /* function prototype */
6
7   /* function main begins program execution */
8   int main( void )
9   {
10     /* initialize array1, array2, array3 */
11     int array1[ 2 ][ 3 ] = { { 1, 2, 3 }, { 4, 5, 6 } };
12     int array2[ 2 ][ 3 ] = { 1, 2, 3, 4, 5 };
13     int array3[ 2 ][ 3 ] = { { 1, 2 }, { 4 } };
14
15     printf( "Values in array1 by row are:\n" );
16     printArray( array1 );
17
18     printf( "Values in array2 by row are:\n" );
19     printArray( array2 );
20
21     printf( "Values in array3 by row are:\n" );
22     printArray( array3 );
23
```

Fig. 6.21 | Initializing multidimensional arrays. (Part 1 of 2.)

```
24        return 0; /* indicates successful termination */
25
26   } /* end main */
27
28   /* function to output array with two rows and three columns */
29   void printArray( const int a[][ 3 ] )
30   {
31      int i; /* row counter */
32      int j; /* column counter */
33
34      /* loop through rows */
35      for ( i = 0; i <= 1; i++ ) {
36
37         /* output column values */
38         for ( j = 0; j <= 2; j++ ) {
39            printf( "%d ", a[ i ][ j ] );
40         } /* end inner for */
41
42         printf( "\n" ); /* start new line of output */
43      } /* end outer for */
44
45   } /* end function printArray */
```

```
Values in array1 by row are:
1 2 3
4 5 6
Values in array2 by row are:
1 2 3
4 5 0
Values in array3 by row are:
1 2 0
4 0 0
```

Fig. 6.21 | Initializing multidimensional arrays. (Part 2 of 2.)

The program defines three arrays of two rows and three columns (six elements each). The definition of array1 (line 11) provides six initializers in two sublists. The first sublist initializes the first row (i.e., row 0) of the array to the values 1, 2 and 3; and the second sublist initializes the second row (i.e., row 1) of the array to the values 4, 5 and 6.

If the braces around each sublist are removed from the array1 initializer list, the compiler initializes the elements of the first row followed by the elements of the second row. The definition of array2 (line 12) provides five initializers. The initializers are assigned to the first row, then the second row. Any elements that do not have an explicit initializer are initialized to zero automatically, so array2[1][2] is initialized to 0.

The definition of array3 (line 13) provides three initializers in two sublists. The sublist for the first row explicitly initializes the first two elements of the first row to 1 and 2. The third element is initialized to zero. The sublist for the second row explicitly initializes the first element to 4. The last two elements are initialized to zero.

The program calls printArray (lines 29–45) to output each array's elements. Note that the function definition specifies the array parameter as const int a[][3]. When we receive a single-subscripted array as a parameter, the array brackets are empty in the function's parameter list. The first subscript of a multiple-subscripted array is not required either, but all subsequent subscripts are required. The compiler uses these subscripts to determine the locations in memory of elements in multiple-subscripted arrays. All array elements are stored consecutively in memory regardless of the number of subscripts. In a double-subscripted array, the first row is stored in memory followed by the second row.

Providing the subscript values in a parameter declaration enables the compiler to tell the function how to locate an element in the array. In a double-subscripted array, each row is basically a single-subscripted array. To locate an element in a particular row, the compiler must know how many elements are in each row so that it can skip the proper number of memory locations when accessing the array. Thus, when accessing a[1][2] in our example, the compiler knows to skip the three elements of the first row to get to the second row (row 1). Then, the compiler accesses the third element of that row (element 2).

Many common array manipulations use for repetition statements. For example, the following statement sets all the elements in the third row of array a in Fig. 6.20 to zero:

```
for ( column = 0; column <= 3; column++ )
    a[ 2 ][ column ] = 0;
```

We specified the *third* row, therefore we know that the first subscript is always 2 (again, 0 is the first row and 1 is the second row). The for statement varies only the second subscript (i.e., the column). The preceding for statement is equivalent to the assignment statements:

```
a[ 2 ][ 0 ] = 0;
a[ 2 ][ 1 ] = 0;
a[ 2 ][ 2 ] = 0;
a[ 2 ][ 3 ] = 0;
```

The following nested for statement determines the total of all the elements in array a.

```
total = 0;

for ( row = 0; row <= 2; row++ )
    for ( column = 0; column <= 3; column++ )
        total += a[ row ][ column ];
```

The for statement totals the elements of the array one row at a time. The outer for statement begins by setting row (i.e., the row subscript) to 0 so that the elements of the first row may be totaled by the inner for statement. The outer for statement then increments row to 1, so the elements of the second row can be totaled. Then, the outer for statement increments row to 2, so the elements of the third row can be totaled. The result is printed when the nested for statement terminates.

Figure 6.22 performs several other common array manipulations on 3-by-4 array studentGrades using for statements. Each row of the array represents a student and each column represents a grade on one of the four exams the students took during the semester. The array manipulations are performed by four functions. Function minimum (lines 44–66) determines the lowest grade of any student for the semester. Function maximum (lines

```
1   /* Fig. 6.22: fig06_22.c
2      Double-subscripted array example */
3   #include <stdio.h>
```

Fig. 6.22 | Double-subscripted arrays example. (Part 1 of 4.)

```
4   #define STUDENTS 3
5   #define EXAMS 4
6
7   /* function prototypes */
8   int minimum( const int grades[][ EXAMS ], int pupils, int tests );
9   int maximum( const int grades[][ EXAMS ], int pupils, int tests );
10  double average( const int setOfGrades[], int tests );
11  void printArray( const int grades[][ EXAMS ], int pupils, int tests );
12
13  /* function main begins program execution */
14  int main( void )
15  {
16     int student; /* student counter */
17
18     /* initialize student grades for three students (rows) */
19     const int studentGrades[ STUDENTS ][ EXAMS ] =
20        { { 77, 68, 86, 73 },
21          { 96, 87, 89, 78 },
22          { 70, 90, 86, 81 } };
23
24     /* output array studentGrades */
25     printf( "The array is:\n" );
26     printArray( studentGrades, STUDENTS, EXAMS );
27
28     /* determine smallest and largest grade values */
29     printf( "\n\nLowest grade: %d\nHighest grade: %d\n",
30        minimum( studentGrades, STUDENTS, EXAMS ),
31        maximum( studentGrades, STUDENTS, EXAMS ) );
32
33     /* calculate average grade for each student */
34     for ( student = 0; student < STUDENTS; student++ ) {
35        printf( "The average grade for student %d is %.2f\n",
36           student, average( studentGrades[ student ], EXAMS ) );
37     } /* end for */
38
39     return 0; /* indicates successful termination */
40
41  } /* end main */
42
43  /* Find the minimum grade */
44  int minimum( const int grades[][ EXAMS ], int pupils, int tests )
45  {
46     int i; /* student counter */
47     int j; /* exam counter */
48     int lowGrade = 100; /* initialize to highest possible grade */
49
50     /* loop through rows of grades */
51     for ( i = 0; i < pupils; i++ ) {
52
53        /* loop through columns of grades */
54        for ( j = 0; j < tests; j++ ) {
55
```

Fig. 6.22 | Double-subscripted arrays example. (Part 2 of 4.)

```
56              if ( grades[ i ][ j ] < lowGrade ) {
57                 lowGrade = grades[ i ][ j ];
58              } /* end if */
59
60           } /* end inner for */
61
62        } /* end outer for */
63
64        return lowGrade; /* return minimum grade */
65
66   } /* end function minimum */
67
68   /* Find the maximum grade */
69   int maximum( const int grades[][ EXAMS ], int pupils, int tests )
70   {
71        int i; /* student counter */
72        int j; /* exam counter */
73        int highGrade = 0; /* initialize to lowest possible grade */
74
75        /* loop through rows of grades */
76        for ( i = 0; i < pupils; i++ ) {
77
78           /* loop through columns of grades */
79           for ( j = 0; j < tests; j++ ) {
80
81              if ( grades[ i ][ j ] > highGrade ) {
82                 highGrade = grades[ i ][ j ];
83              } /* end if */
84
85           } /* end inner for */
86
87        } /* end outer for */
88
89        return highGrade; /* return maximum grade */
90
91   } /* end function maximum */
92
93   /* Determine the average grade for a particular student */
94   double average( const int setOfGrades[], int tests )
95   {
96        int i; /* exam counter */
97        int total = 0; /* sum of test grades */
98
99        /* total all grades for one student */
100       for ( i = 0; i < tests; i++ ) {
101          total += setOfGrades[ i ];
102       } /* end for */
103
104       return ( double ) total / tests; /* average */
105
106  } /* end function average */
107
```

Fig. 6.22 | Double-subscripted arrays example. (Part 3 of 4.)

```
108  /* Print the array */
109  void printArray( const int grades[][ EXAMS ], int pupils, int tests )
110  {
111     int i; /* student counter */
112     int j; /* exam counter */
113
114     /* output column heads */
115     printf( "                [0]  [1]  [2]  [3]" );
116
117     /* output grades in tabular format */
118     for ( i = 0; i < pupils; i++ ) {
119
120        /* output label for row */
121        printf( "\nstudentGrades[%d] ", i );
122
123        /* output grades for one student */
124        for ( j = 0; j < tests; j++ ) {
125           printf( "%-5d", grades[ i ][ j ] );
126        } /* end inner for */
127
128     } /* end outer for */
129
130  } /* end function printArray */
```

```
The array is:
              [0]  [1]  [2]  [3]
studentGrades[0] 77   68   86   73
studentGrades[1] 96   87   89   78
studentGrades[2] 70   90   86   81

Lowest grade: 68
Highest grade: 96
The average grade for student 0 is 76.00
The average grade for student 1 is 87.50
The average grade for student 2 is 81.75
```

Fig. 6.22 | Double-subscripted arrays example. (Part 4 of 4.)

69–91) determines the highest grade of any student for the semester. Function average (lines 94–106) determines a particular student's semester average. Function printArray (lines 109–130) outputs the double-subscripted array in a neat, tabular format.

Functions minimum, maximum and printArray each receive three arguments—the studentGrades array (called grades in each function), the number of students (rows of the array) and the number of exams (columns of the array). Each function loops through array grades using nested for statements. The following nested for statement is from the function minimum definition:

```
/* loop through rows of grades */
for ( i = 0; i < pupils; i++ ) {

   /* loop through columns of grades */
   for ( j = 0; j < tests; j++ ) {
```

```
        if ( grades[ i ][ j ] < lowGrade ) {
            lowGrade = grades[ i ][ j ];
        } /* end if */
    } /* end inner for */
} /* end outer for */
```

The outer for statement begins by setting i (i.e., the row subscript) to 0 so that the elements of the first row (i.e., the grades of the first student) can be compared to variable lowGrade in the body of the inner for statement. The inner for statement loops through the four grades of a particular row and compares each grade to lowGrade. If a grade is less than lowGrade, lowGrade is set to that grade. The outer for statement then increments the row subscript to 1. The elements of the second row are compared to variable lowGrade. The outer for statement then increments the row subscript to 2. The elements of the third row are compared to variable lowGrade. When execution of the nested structure is complete, lowGrade contains the smallest grade in the double-subscripted array. Function maximum works similarly to function minimum.

Function average (line 94) takes two arguments—a single-subscripted array of test results for a particular student called setOfGrades and the number of test results in the array. When average is called, the first argument studentGrades[student] is passed. This causes the address of one row of the double-subscripted array to be passed to average. The argument studentGrades[1] is the starting address of the second row of the array. Remember that a double-subscripted array is basically an array of single-subscripted arrays and that the name of a single-subscripted array is the address of the array in memory. Function average calculates the sum of the array elements, divides the total by the number of test results and returns the floating-point result.

Summary

Section 6.1 Introduction
- Arrays are data structures consisting of related data items of the same type.
- Arrays are "static" entities in that they remain the same size throughout program execution.

Section 6.2 Arrays
- An array is a group of memory locations related by the fact that they all have the same name and the same type.
- To refer to a particular location or element in the array, specify the name of the array and the position number of the particular element in the array.
- The first element in every array is the zeroth element. Thus, the first element of array c is referred to as c[0], the second element of array c is referred to as c[1], the seventh element of array c is referred to as c[6], and, in general, the ith element of array c is referred to as c[i - 1].
- Array names, like other variable names, can contain only letters, digits and underscores. Array names cannot begin with a digit.
- The position number contained within square brackets is more formally called a subscript. A subscript must be an integer or an integer expression.
- The brackets used to enclose the subscript of an array are actually considered to be an operator in C. They have the same level of precedence as the function call operator.

Section 6.3 Defining Arrays

- Arrays occupy space in memory. You specify the type of each element and the number of elements in the array so that the computer may reserve the appropriate amount of memory.

- An array of type char can be used to store a character string.

Section 6.4 Array Examples

- The elements of an array can be initialized when the array is defined by following the definition with an equals sign and braces, {}, containing a comma-separated list of initializers. If there are fewer initializers than elements in the array, the remaining elements are initialized to zero.

- The statement int n[10] = {0}; explicitly initializes the first element to zero and initializes the remaining nine elements to zero because there are fewer initializers than there are elements in the array. It is important to remember that automatic arrays are not automatically initialized to zero. You must at least initialize the first element to zero for the remaining elements to be automatically zeroed. This method of initializing the array elements to 0 is performed at compile time for static arrays and at runtime for automatic arrays.

- If the array size is omitted from a definition with an initializer list, the number of elements in the array will be the number of elements in the initializer list.

- The #define preprocessor directive can be used to define a symbolic constant—an identifier that is replaced with replacement text by the C preprocessor before the program is compiled. When the program is preprocessed, all occurrences of the symbolic constant are replaced with the replacement text. Using symbolic constants to specify array sizes makes programs more scalable.

- C has no array bounds checking to prevent the computer from referring to an element that does not exist. Thus, an executing program can "walk off" the end of an array without warning. You should ensure that all array references remain within the bounds of the array.

- A string such as "hello" is really a static array of individual characters in C.

- A character array can be initialized using a string literal. In this case, the size of the array is determined by the compiler based on the length of the string.

- It is important to note that every string contains a special string-termination character called the null character. The character constant representing the null character is '\0'.

- A character array representing a string should always be defined large enough to hold the number of characters in the string and the terminating null character.

- Character arrays also can be initialized with individual character constants in an initializer list.

- Because a string is really an array of characters, we can access individual characters in a string directly using array subscript notation.

- You can input a string directly into a character array from the keyboard using scanf and the conversion specifier %s. The name of the character array is passed to scanf without the preceding & used with nonstring variables. The & is normally used to provide scanf with a variable's location in memory so that a value can be stored there. An array name is the address of the start of the array; therefore, the & is not necessary.

- Function scanf reads characters from the keyboard until the first white-space character is encountered—it does not check the array size. Thus, scanf can write beyond the end of the array.

- A character array representing a string can be output with printf and the %s conversion specifier. The characters of the string are printed until a terminating null character is encountered.

- A static local variable exists for the duration of the program but is only visible in the function body. We can apply static to a local array definition so that the array is not created and initialized each time the function is called and the array is not destroyed each time the function is exited in the program. This reduces program execution time, particularly for programs with frequently called functions that contain large arrays.

- Arrays that are static are automatically initialized once at compile time. If you do not explicitly initialize a static array, that array's elements are initialized to zero by the compiler.

Section 6.5 Passing Arrays to Functions

- To pass an array argument to a function, specify the name of the array without any brackets.

- Unlike char arrays that contain strings, other array types do not have a special terminator. For this reason, the size of an array is passed to a function, so that the function can process the proper number of elements.

- C automatically passes arrays to functions by reference—the called functions can modify the element values in the callers' original arrays. The name of the array evaluates to the address of the first element of the array. Because the starting address of the array is passed, the called function knows precisely where the array is stored. Therefore, when the called function modifies array elements in its function body, it is modifying the actual elements of the array in their original memory locations.

- Although entire arrays are passed by reference, individual array elements are passed by value exactly as simple variables are.

- Such simple single pieces of data (such as individual ints, floats and chars) are called scalars.

- To pass an element of an array to a function, use the subscripted name of the array element as an argument in the function call.

- For a function to receive an array through a function call, the function's parameter list must specify that an array will be received. The size of the array is not required between the array brackets. If it is included, the compiler checks that it is greater than zero, then ignores it.

- When an array parameter is preceded by the const qualifier, the elements of the array become constant in the function body, and any attempt to modify an element of the array in the function body results in a compile-time error.

Section 6.6 Sorting Arrays

- Sorting data (i.e., placing the data into a particular order such as ascending or descending) is one of the most important computing applications.

- One sorting technique is called the bubble sort or the sinking sort, because the smaller values gradually "bubble" their way upward to the top of the array like air bubbles rising in water, while the larger values sink to the bottom of the array. The technique is to make several passes through the array. On each pass, successive pairs of elements are compared. If a pair is in increasing order (or if the values are identical), we leave the values as they are. If a pair is in decreasing order, their values are swapped in the array.

- Because of the way the successive comparisons are made, a large value may move down the array many positions on a single pass, but a small value may move up only one position.

- The chief virtue of the bubble sort is that it is easy to program. However, the bubble sort runs slowly. This becomes apparent when sorting large arrays.

Section 6.7 Case Study: Computing Mean, Median and Mode Using Arrays

- The mean is the arithmetic average of a set of values.

- The median is the "middle value" in a sorted set of values.

- The mode is the value that occurs most frequently in a set of values.

Section 6.8 Searching Arrays

- The process of finding a particular element of an array is called searching.

- The linear search compares each element of the array with the search key. Since the array is not in any particular order, it is just as likely that the value will be found in the first element as in the last. On average, therefore, the search key will be compared with half the elements of the array.

- The linear searching method works well for small or unsorted arrays. For sorted arrays, the high-speed binary search technique can be used.

- The binary search algorithm eliminates from consideration one-half of the elements in a sorted array after each comparison. The algorithm locates the middle element of the array and compares it to the search key. If they are equal, the search key is found and the array subscript of that element is returned. If they are not equal, the problem is reduced to searching one-half of the array. If the search key is less than the middle element of the array, the first half of the array is searched, otherwise the second half of the array is searched. If the search key is not found in the specified subarray (piece of the original array), the algorithm is repeated on one-quarter of the original array. The search continues until the search key is equal to the middle element of a subarray, or until the subarray consists of one element that is not equal to the search key (i.e., the search key is not found).

- When using a binary search, the maximum number of comparisons required for any array can be determined by finding the first power of 2 greater than the number of array elements.

Section 6.9 Multiple-Subscripted Arrays

- A common use of multiple-subscripted arrays (also called multidimensional arrays) is to represent tables of values consisting of information arranged in rows and columns. To identify a particular table element, we must specify two subscripts: The first (by convention) identifies the element's row and the second (by convention) identifies the element's column.

- Tables or arrays that require two subscripts to identify a particular element are called double-subscripted arrays.

- Multiple-subscripted arrays can have more than two subscripts.

- A multiple-subscripted array can be initialized when it is defined, much like a single-subscripted array. The values are grouped by row in braces. If there are not enough initializers for a given row, the remaining elements of that row are initialized to 0.

- The first subscript of a multiple-subscripted array parameter declaration is not required, but all subsequent subscripts are required. The compiler uses these subscripts to determine the locations in memory of elements in multiple-subscripted arrays. All array elements are stored consecutively in memory regardless of the number of subscripts. In a double-subscripted array, the first row is stored in memory followed by the second row.

- Providing the subscript values in a parameter declaration enables the compiler to tell the function how to locate an element in the array. In a double-subscripted array, each row is basically a single-subscripted array. To locate an element in a particular row, the compiler must know how many elements are in each row so that it can skip the proper number of memory locations when accessing the array.

Terminology

a[i]	binary search
a[i][j]	bounds checking
array	bubble sort
array initializer list	character array
bar chart	column subscript

const qualifier

define an array

#define preprocessor directive

double precision

double-subscripted array

element of an array

expression as a subscript

index (or subscript)

initialize an array

initializer list

linear search

m-by-*n* array

mean

median

mode

multiple-subscripted array

name of an array

null character '\0'

off-by-one error

pass-by-reference

passing arrays to functions

%p conversion specifier

position number

replacement text

row subscript

scalability

scalar

search key

searching an array

single-subscripted array

sinking sort

sorting

sorting pass

sorting the elements of an array

square brackets

string

subscript (or index)

survey data analysis

symbolic constant

table of values

tabular format

temporary area for exchange of values

terminating null character

totaling the elements of an array

value of an element

walk off an array

zeroth element

Self-Review Exercises

6.1   Answer each of the following:

a) Lists and tables of values are stored in _____.

b) The elements of an array are related by the fact that they have the same _____ and _____.

c) The number used to refer to a particular element of an array is called its _____.

d) A(n) _____ should be used to specify the size of an array because it makes the program more scalable.

e) The process of placing the elements of an array in order is called _____ the array.

f) Determining whethet an array contains a certain key value is called _____ the array.

g) An array that uses two subscripts is referred to as a(n) _____ array.

6.2   State whether the following are *true* or *false*. If the answer is *false*, explain why.

a) An array can store many different types of values.

b) An array subscript can be of data type double.

c) If there are fewer initializers in an initializer list than the number of elements in the array, C automatically initializes the remaining elements to the last value in the list of initializers.

d) It is an error if an initializer list contains more initializers than there are elements in the array.

e) An individual array element that is passed to a function as an argument of the form a[i] and modified in the called function will contain the modified value in the calling function.

6.3   Answer the following questions regarding an array called fractions.

a) Define a symbolic constant SIZE to be replaced with the replacement text 10.

b) Define an array with SIZE elements of type double and initialize the elements to 0.
c) Name the fourth element from the beginning of the array.
d) Refer to array element 4.
e) Assign the value 1.667 to array element nine.
f) Assign the value 3.333 to the seventh element of the array.
g) Print array elements 6 and 9 with two digits of precision to the right of the decimal point, and show the output that is displayed on the screen.
h) Print all the elements of the array, using a for repetition statement. Assume the integer variable x has been defined as a control variable for the loop. Show the output.

6.4   Write statements to accomplish the following:
a) Define table to be an integer array and to have 3 rows and 3 columns. Assume the symbolic constant SIZE has been defined to be 3.
b) How many elements does the array table contain? Print the total number of elements.
c) Use a for repetition statement to initialize each element of table to the sum of its subscripts. Assume the integer variables x and y are defined as control variables.
d) Print the values of each element of array table. Assume the array was initialized with the definition:

```
int table[ SIZE ][ SIZE ] =
    { { 1, 8 }, { 2, 4, 6 }, { 5 } };
```

6.5   Find the error in each of the following program segments and correct the error.
a) #define SIZE 100;
b) SIZE = 10;
c) *Assume* int b[10] = { 0 }, i;
```
    for ( i = 0; i <= 10; i++ )
        b[ i ] = 1;
```
d) #include <stdio.h>;
e) *Assume* int a[2][2] = { { 1, 2 }, { 3, 4 } };
```
    a[ 1, 1 ] = 5;
```
f) #define VALUE = 120

Answers to Self-Review Exercises

6.1   a) Arrays. b) Name, type. c) Subscript. d) Symbolic constant. e) Sorting. f) Searching. g) Double-subscripted.

6.2   a) False. An array can store only values of the same type.
b) False. An array subscript must be an integer or an integer expression.
c) False. C automatically initializes the remaining elements to zero.
d) True.
e) False. Individual elements of an array are passed by value. If the entire array is passed to a function, then any modifications will be reflected in the original.

6.3   a) #define SIZE 10
b) double fractions[SIZE] = { 0.0 };
c) fractions[3]
d) fractions[4]
e) fractions[9] = 1.667;
f) fractions[6] = 3.333;
g) printf("%.2f %.2f\n", fractions[6], fractions[9]);
    Output: 3.33 1.67.

h) `for ( x = 0; x < SIZE; x++ )`
    `printf( "fractions[%d] = %f\n", x, fractions[ x ] );`
Output:
```
fractions[0] = 0.000000
fractions[1] = 0.000000
fractions[2] = 0.000000
fractions[3] = 0.000000
fractions[4] = 0.000000
fractions[5] = 0.000000
fractions[6] = 3.333000
fractions[7] = 0.000000
fractions[8] = 0.000000
fractions[9] = 1.667000
```

6.4 a) `int table[ SIZE ][ SIZE ];`
    b) Nine elements. `printf( "%d\n", SIZE * SIZE );`
    c) `for ( x = 0; x < SIZE; x++ )`
       `for ( y = 0; y < SIZE; y++ )`
         `table[ x ][ y ] = x + y;`
    d) `for ( x = 0; x < SIZE; x++ )`
       `for ( y = 0; y < SIZE; y++ )`
         `printf( "table[%d][%d] = %d\n", x, y, table[ x ][ y ] );`
Output:
```
table[0][0] = 1
table[0][1] = 8
table[0][2] = 0
table[1][0] = 2
table[1][1] = 4
table[1][2] = 6
table[2][0] = 5
table[2][1] = 0
table[2][2] = 0
```

6.5 a) Error: Semicolon at end of `#define` preprocessor directive.
    Correction: Eliminate semicolon.
    b) Error: Assigning a value to a symbolic constant using an assignment statement.
    Correction: Assign a value to the symbolic constant in a `#define` preprocessor directive without using the assignment operator as in `#define SIZE 10`.
    c) Error: Referencing an array element outside the bounds of the array (`b[ 10 ]`).
    Correction: Change the final value of the control variable to 9.
    d) Error: Semicolon at end of `#include` preprocessor directive.
    Correction: Eliminate semicolon.
    e) Error: Array subscripting done incorrectly.
    Correction: Change the statement to `a[ 1 ][ 1 ] = 5;`
    f) Error: Assigning a value to a symbolic constant using an assignment statement.
    Correction: Assign a value to the symbolic constant in a `#define` preprocessor directive without using the assignment operator as in `#define VALUE 120`.

Exercises

6.6 Fill in the blanks in each of the following:
    a) C stores lists of values in _____.
    b) The elements of an array are related by the fact that they _____.

c) When referring to an array element, the position number contained within parentheses is called a(n) _____.

d) The names of the five elements of array p are _____, _____, _____, and _____.

e) The contents of a particular element of an array is called the _____ of that element.

f) Naming an array, stating its type and specifying the number of elements in the array is called _____ the array.

g) The process of placing the elements of an array into either ascending or descending order is called _____.

h) In a double-subscripted array, the first subscript (by convention) identifies the _____ of an element and the second subscript (by convention) identifies the _____ of an element.

i) An *m*-by-*n* array contains _____ rows, _____ columns and _____ elements.

j) The name of the element in row 3 and column 5 of array d is _____.

6.7   State which of the following are *true* and which are *false*. If *false*, explain why.

a) To refer to a particular location or element within an array, we specify the name of the array and the value of the particular element.

b) An array definition reserves space for the array.

c) To indicate that 100 locations should be reserved for integer array p, write

```
p[ 100 ];
```

d) A C program that initializes the elements of a 15-element array to zero must contain one for statement.

e) A C program that totals the elements of a double-subscripted array must contain nested for statements.

f) The mean, median and mode of the following set of values are 5, 6 and 7, respectively: 1, 2, 5, 6, 7, 7, 7.

6.8   Write statements to accomplish each of the following:

a) Display the value of the seventh element of character array f.

b) Input a value into element 4 of single-subscripted floating-point array b.

c) Initialize each of the five elements of single-subscripted integer array g to 8.

d) Total the elements of floating-point array c of 100 elements.

e) Copy array a into the first portion of array b. Assume double a[11], b[34];

f) Determine and print the smallest and largest values contained in 99-element floating-point array w.

6.9   Consider a 2-by-5 integer array t.

a) Write a definition for t.

b) How many rows does t have?

c) How many columns does t have?

d) How many elements does t have?

e) Write the names of all the elements in the second row of t.

f) Write the names of all the elements in the third column of t.

g) Write a single statement that sets the element of t in row 1 and column 2 to zero.

h) Write a series of statements that initialize each element of t to zero. Do not use a repetition structure.

i) Write a nested for statement that initializes each element of t to zero.

j) Write a statement that inputs the values for the elements of t from the terminal.

k) Write a series of statements that determine and print the smallest value in array t.

l) Write a statement that displays the elements of the first row of t.

m) Write a statement that totals the elements of the fourth column of t.

n) Write a series of statements that print the array t in tabular format. List the column subscripts as headings across the top and list the row subscripts at the left of each row.

6.10   Use a single-subscripted array to solve the following problem. A company pays its salespeople on a commission basis. The salespeople receive $200 per week plus 9% of their gross sales for that week. For example, a salesperson who grosses $3000 in sales in a week receives $200 plus 9% of $3000, or a total of $470. Write a C program (using an array of counters) that determines how many of the salespeople earned salaries in each of the following ranges (assume that each salesperson's salary is truncated to an integer amount):

a) $200–299
b) $300–399
c) $400–499
d) $500–599
e) $600–699
f) $700–799
g) $800–899
h) $900–999
i) $1000 and over

6.11   The bubble sort presented in Fig. 6.15 is inefficient for large arrays. Make the following simple modifications to improve the performance of the bubble sort.

a) After the first pass, the largest number is guaranteed to be in the highest-numbered element of the array; after the second pass, the two highest numbers are "in place," and so on. Instead of making nine comparisons on every pass, modify the bubble sort to make eight comparisons on the second pass, seven on the third pass and so on.

b) The data in the array may already be in the proper order or near-proper order, so why make nine passes if fewer will suffice? Modify the sort to check at the end of each pass whether any swaps have been made. If none has been made, then the data must already be in the proper order, so the program should terminate. If swaps have been made, then at least one more pass is needed.

6.12   Write single statements that perform each of the following single-subscripted array operations:

a) Initialize the 10 elements of integer array counts to zeros.
b) Add 1 to each of the 15 elements of integer array bonus.
c) Read the 12 values of floating-point array monthlyTemperatures from the keyboard.
d) Print the five values of integer array bestScores in column format.

6.13   Find the error(s) in each of the following statements:

a) Assume: char str[5];
        scanf("%s", str); /* User types hello */
b) Assume: int a[3];
        printf("$d %d %d\n", a[1], a[2], a[3]);
c) double f[3] = { 1.1, 10.01, 100.001, 1000.0001 };
d) Assume: double d[2][10];
        d[1, 9] = 2.345;

6.14   Modify the program of Fig. 6.16 so function mode is capable of handling a tie for the mode value. Also modify function median so the two middle elements are averaged in an array with an even number of elements.

6.15   Use a single-subscripted array to solve the following problem. Read in 20 numbers, each of which is between 10 and 100, inclusive. As each number is read, print it only if it is not a duplicate of a number already read. Provide for the "worst case" in which all 20 numbers are different. Use the smallest possible array to solve this problem.

6.16 Label the elements of 3-by-5 double-subscripted array sales to indicate the order in which they are set to zero by the following program segment:

```
for ( row = 0; row <= 2; row++ )
    for ( column = 0; column <= 4; column++ )
        sales[ row ][ column ] = 0;
```

6.17 What does the following program do?

```
1   /* ex06_17.c */
2   /* What does this program do? */
3   #include <stdio.h>
4   #define SIZE 10
5
6   int whatIsThis( const int b[], int p ); /* function prototype */
7
8   /* function main begins program execution */
9   int main( void )
10  {
11      int x; /* holds return value of function whatIsThis */
12
13      /* initialize array a */
14      int a[ SIZE ] = { 1, 2, 3, 4, 5, 6, 7, 8, 9, 10 };
15
16      x = whatIsThis( a, SIZE );
17
18      printf( "Result is %d\n", x );
19
20      return 0; /* indicates successful termination */
21
22  } /* end main */
23
24  /* what does this function do? */
25  int whatIsThis( const int b[], int p )
26  {
27      /* base case */
28      if ( p == 1 ) {
29          return b[ 0 ];
30      } /* end if */
31      else { /* recursion step */
32
33          return b[ p - 1 ] + whatIsThis( b, p - 1 );
34      } /* end else */
35
36  } /* end function whatIsThis */
```

6.18 What does the following program do?

```
1   /* ex06_18.c */
2   /* What does this program do? */
3   #include <stdio.h>
4   #define SIZE 10
```

```
 5
 6    /* function prototype */
 7    void someFunction( const int b[], int startIndex, int size );
 8
 9    /* function main begins program execution */
10    int main( void )
11    {
12       int a[ SIZE ] = { 8, 3, 1, 2, 6, 0, 9, 7, 4, 5 }; /* initialize a */
13
14       printf( "Answer is:\n" );
15       someFunction( a, 0, SIZE );
16       printf( "\n" );
17
18       return 0; /* indicates successful termination */
19
20    } /* end main */
21
22    /* What does this function do? */
23    void someFunction( const int b[], int startIndex, int size )
24    {
25       if ( startIndex < size ) {
26          someFunction( b, startIndex + 1, size );
27          printf( "%d  ", b[ startIndex ] );
28       } /* end if */
29
30    } /* end function someFunction */
```

6.19   Write a program that simulates the rolling of two dice. The program should use rand to roll the first die, and should use rand again to roll the second die. The sum of the two values should then be calculated. [*Note:* Since each die can show an integer value from 1 to 6, then the sum of the two values will vary from 2 to 12, with 7 being the most frequent sum and 2 and 12 the least frequent sums.] Figure 6.23 shows the 36 possible combinations of the two dice. Your program should roll the two dice 36,000 times. Use a single-subscripted array to tally the numbers of times each possible sum appears. Print the results in a tabular format. Also, determine if the totals are reasonable; i.e., there are six ways to roll a 7, so approximately one-sixth of all the rolls should be 7.

	1	2	3	4	5	6
1	2	3	4	5	6	7
2	3	4	5	6	7	8
3	4	5	6	7	8	9
4	5	6	7	8	9	10
5	6	7	8	9	10	11
6	7	8	9	10	11	12

Fig. 6.23 | Dice rolling outcomes.

6.20 Write a program that runs 1000 games of craps (without human intervention) and answers each of the following questions:

a) How many games are won on the first roll, second roll, ..., twentieth roll and after the twentieth roll?

b) How many games are lost on the first roll, second roll, ..., twentieth roll and after the twentieth roll?

c) What are the chances of winning at craps? [*Note:* You should discover that craps is one of the fairest casino games. What do you suppose this means?]

d) What is the average length of a game of craps?

e) Do the chances of winning improve with the length of the game?

6.21 (*Airline Reservations System*) A small airline has just purchased a computer for its new automated reservations system. The president has asked you to program the new system. You are to write a program to assign seats on each flight of the airline's only plane (capacity: 10 seats).

Your program should display the following menu of alternatives:

```
Please type 1 for "first class"
Please type 2 for "economy"
```

If the person types 1, then your program should assign a seat in the first class section (seats 1–5). If the person types 2, then your program should assign a seat in the economy section (seats 6–10). Your program should then print a boarding pass indicating the person's seat number and whether it is in the first class or economy section of the plane.

Use a single-subscripted array to represent the seating chart of the plane. Initialize all the elements of the array to 0 to indicate that all seats are empty. As each seat is assigned, set the corresponding element of the array to 1 to indicate that the seat is no longer available.

Your program should, of course, never assign a seat that has already been assigned. When the first class section is full, your program should ask the person if it is acceptable to be placed in the economy section (and vice versa). If yes, then make the appropriate seat assignment. If no, then print the message "Next flight leaves in 3 hours."

6.22 Use a double-subscripted array to solve the following problem. A company has four salespeople (1 to 4) who sell five different products (1 to 5). Once a day, each salesperson passes in a slip for each different type of product sold. Each slip contains:

a) The salesperson number

b) The product number

c) The total dollar value of that product sold that day

Thus, each salesperson passes in between 0 and 5 sales slips per day. Assume that the information from all of the slips for last month is available. Write a program that will read all this information for last month's sales and summarize the total sales by salesperson by product. All totals should be stored in the double-subscripted array `sales`. After processing all the information for last month, print the results in tabular format with each of the columns representing a particular salesperson and each of the rows representing a particular product. Cross total each row to get the total sales of each product for last month; cross total each column to get the total sales by salesperson for last month. Your tabular printout should include these cross totals to the right of the totaled rows and to the bottom of the totaled columns.

6.23 (*Turtle Graphics*) The Logo language, which is particularly popular among personal computer users, made the concept of *turtle graphics* famous. Imagine a mechanical turtle that walks around the room under the control of a C program. The turtle holds a pen in one of two positions, up or down. While the pen is down, the turtle traces out shapes as it moves; while the pen is up, the turtle moves about freely without writing anything. In this problem you will simulate the operation of the turtle and create a computerized sketchpad as well.

Use a 50-by-50 array floor which is initialized to zeros. Read commands from an array that contains them. Keep track of the current position of the turtle at all times and whether the pen is currently up or down. Assume that the turtle always starts at position 0, 0 of the floor with its pen up. The set of turtle commands your program must process are shown in Fig. 6.24. Suppose that the turtle is somewhere near the center of the floor. The following "program" would draw and print a 12-by-12 square:

```
2
5,12
3
5,12
3
5,12
3
5,12
1
6
9
```

As the turtle moves with the pen down, set the appropriate elements of array floor to 1s. When the 6 command (print) is given, wherever there is a 1 in the array, display an asterisk, or some other character you choose. Wherever there is a zero, display a blank. Write a program to implement the turtle graphics capabilities discussed here. Write several turtle graphics programs to draw interesting shapes. Add other commands to increase the power of your turtle graphics language.

Command	Meaning
1	Pen up
2	Pen down
3	Turn right
4	Turn left
5, 10	Move forward 10 spaces (or a number other than 10)
6	Print the 50-by-50 array
9	End of data (sentinel)

Fig. 6.24 | Turtle commands.

6.24   (*Knight's Tour*) One of the more interesting puzzlers for chess buffs is the Knight's Tour problem, originally proposed by the mathematician Euler. The question is this: Can the chess piece called the knight move around an empty chessboard and touch each of the 64 squares once and only once? We study this intriguing problem in depth here.

The knight makes L-shaped moves (over two in one direction and then over one in a perpendicular direction). Thus, from a square in the middle of an empty chessboard, the knight can make eight different moves (numbered 0 through 7) as shown in Fig. 6.25.

    a) Draw an 8-by-8 chessboard on a sheet of paper and attempt a Knight's Tour by hand. Put a 1 in the first square you move to, a 2 in the second square, a 3 in the third, and so on. Before starting the tour, estimate how far you think you will get, remembering that a full tour consists of 64 moves. How far did you get? Were you close to the estimate?

b) Now let us develop a program that will move the knight around a chessboard. The board itself is represented by an 8-by-8 double-subscripted array board. Each of the squares is initialized to zero. We describe each of the eight possible moves in terms of both their horizontal and vertical components. For example, a move of type 0 as shown in Fig. 6.25 consists of moving two squares horizontally to the right and one square vertically upward. Move 2 consists of moving one square horizontally to the left and two squares vertically upward. Horizontal moves to the left and vertical moves upward are indicated with negative numbers. The eight moves may be described by two single-subscripted arrays, horizontal and vertical, as follows:

```
horizontal[ 0 ] = 2
horizontal[ 1 ] = 1
horizontal[ 2 ] = -1
horizontal[ 3 ] = -2
horizontal[ 4 ] = -2
horizontal[ 5 ] = -1
horizontal[ 6 ] = 1
horizontal[ 7 ] = 2

vertical[ 0 ] = -1
vertical[ 1 ] = -2
vertical[ 2 ] = -2
vertical[ 3 ] = -1
vertical[ 4 ] = 1
vertical[ 5 ] = 2
vertical[ 6 ] = 2
vertical[ 7 ] = 1
```

Let the variables currentRow and currentColumn indicate the row and column of the knight's current position on the board. To make a move of type moveNumber, where moveNumber is between 0 and 7, your program uses the statements

```
currentRow += vertical[ moveNumber ];
currentColumn += horizontal[ moveNumber ];
```

Keep a counter that varies from 1 to 64. Record the latest count in each square the knight moves to. Remember to test each potential move to see if the knight has already visited that square. And, of course, test every potential move to make sure that the knight does not land off the chessboard. Now write a program to move the knight around the chessboard. Run the program. How many moves did the knight make?

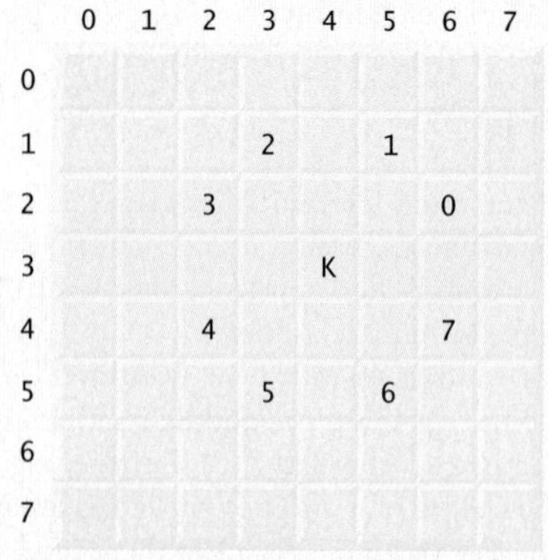

Fig. 6.25 | The eight possible moves of the knight.

c) After attempting to write and run a Knight's Tour program, you have probably developed some valuable insights. We will use these to develop a *heuristic* (or strategy) for moving the knight. Heuristics do not guarantee success, but a carefully developed heuristic greatly improves the chance of success. You may have observed that the outer squares are in some sense more troublesome than the squares nearer the center of the board. In fact, the most troublesome, or inaccessible, squares are the four corners.

Intuition may suggest that you should attempt to move the knight to the most troublesome squares first and leave open those that are easiest to get to, so that when the board gets congested near the end of the tour, there will be a greater chance of success.

We may develop an "accessibility heuristic" by classifying each of the squares according to how accessible it is and always moving the knight to the square (within the knight's L-shaped moves, of course) that is most inaccessible. We label a double-subscripted array accessibility with numbers indicating from how many squares each particular square is accessible. On a blank chessboard, the center squares are therefore rated as 8s, the corner squares are rated as 2s, and the other squares have accessibility numbers of 3, 4, or 6 as follows:

```
2  3  4  4  4  4  3  2
3  4  6  6  6  6  4  3
4  6  8  8  8  8  6  4
4  6  8  8  8  8  6  4
4  6  8  8  8  8  6  4
4  6  8  8  8  8  6  4
3  4  6  6  6  6  4  3
2  3  4  4  4  4  3  2
```

Now write a version of the Knight's Tour program using the accessibility heuristic. At any time, the knight should move to the square with the lowest accessibility number. In case of a tie, the knight may move to any of the tied squares. Therefore, the tour may begin in any of the four corners. [*Note:* As the knight moves around the chessboard, your program should reduce the accessibility numbers as more and more squares become occupied. In this way, at any given time during the tour, each available square's accessibility number will remain equal to precisely the number of squares from which that square may be reached.] Run this version of your program. Did you get a full tour? Now modify the program to run 64 tours, one from each square of the chessboard. How many full tours did you get?

d) Write a version of the Knight's Tour program which, when encountering a tie between two or more squares, decides what square to choose by looking ahead to those squares reachable from the "tied" squares. Your program should move to the square for which the next move would arrive at a square with the lowest accessibility number.

6.25 (*Knight's Tour: Brute-Force Approaches*) In Exercise 6.24 we developed a solution to the Knight's Tour problem. The approach used, called the "accessibility heuristic," generates many solutions and executes efficiently.

As computers continue increasing in power, we will be able to solve many problems with sheer computer power and relatively unsophisticated algorithms. Let us call this approach "brute-force" problem solving.

a) Use random number generation to enable the knight to walk around the chess board (in its legitimate L-shaped moves, of course) at random. Your program should run one tour and print the final chessboard. How far did the knight get?

b) Most likely, the preceding program produced a relatively short tour. Now modify your program to attempt 1000 tours. Use a single-subscripted array to keep track of the number of tours of each length. When your program finishes attempting the 1000 tours, it should print this information in neat tabular format. What was the best result?

c) Most likely, the preceding program gave you some "respectable" tours but no full tours. Now "pull all the stops out" and simply let your program run until it produces a full tour. [*Caution:* This version of the program could run for hours on a powerful computer.] Once again, keep a table of the number of tours of each length and print this table when the first full tour is found. How many tours did your program attempt before producing a full tour? How much time did it take?

d) Compare the brute-force version of the Knight's Tour with the accessibility heuristic version. Which required a more careful study of the problem? Which algorithm was more difficult to develop? Which required more computer power? Could we be certain (in advance) of obtaining a full tour with the accessibility heuristic approach? Could we be certain (in advance) of obtaining a full tour with the brute-force approach? Argue the pros and cons of brute-force problem solving in general.

6.26   (*Eight Queens*) Another puzzler for chess buffs is the Eight Queens problem. Simply stated: Is it possible to place eight queens on an empty chessboard so that no queen is "attacking" any other—that is, so that no two queens are in the same row, the same column, or along the same diagonal? Use the kind of thinking developed in Exercise 6.24 to formulate a heuristic for solving the Eight Queens problem. Run your program. [*Hint:* It is possible to assign a numeric value to each square of the chessboard indicating how many squares of an empty chessboard are "eliminated" once a queen is placed in that square. For example, each of the four corners would be assigned the value 22, as in Fig. 6.26.]

Once these "elimination numbers" are placed in all 64 squares, an appropriate heuristic might be: Place the next queen in the square with the smallest elimination number. Why is this strategy intuitively appealing?

6.27   (*Eight Queens: Brute-Force Approaches*) In this problem you will develop several brute-orce approaches to solving the Eight Queens problem introduced in Exercise 6.26.

a) Solve the Eight Queens problem, using the random brute-force technique developed in Exercise 6.25.

b) Use an exhaustive technique (i.e., try all possible combinations of eight queens on the chessboard).

c) Why do you suppose the exhaustive brute-force approach may not be appropriate for solving the Eight Queens problem?

d) Compare and contrast the random brute-force and exhaustive brute-force approaches in general.

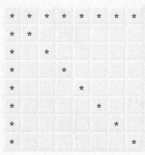

Fig. 6.26 | The 22 squares eliminated by placing a queen in the upper-left corner.

6.28   (*Duplicate Elimination*) In Chapter 12, we explore the high-speed binary search tree data structure. One feature of a binary search tree is that duplicate values are discarded when insertions are made into the tree. This is referred to as duplicate elimination.   Write a program that produces 20 random numbers between 1 and 20. The program should store all nonduplicate values in an array. Use the smallest possible array to accomplish this task.

6.29   (*Knight's Tour: Closed Tour Test*) In the Knight's Tour, a full tour is when the knight makes 64 moves touching each square of the chessboard once and only once. A closed tour occurs when the 64th move is one move away from the location in which the knight started the tour. Modify the Knight's Tour program you wrote in Exercise 6.24 to test for a closed tour if a full tour has occurred.

6.30   (*The Sieve of Eratosthenes*) A prime integer is any integer greater than 1 that can be divided evenly only by itself and 1. The Sieve of Eratosthenes is a method of finding prime numbers. It works as follows:

    a)   Create an array with all elements initialized to 1 (true). Array elements with prime subscripts will remain 1. All other array elements will eventually be set to zero.

    b)   Starting with array subscript 2 (subscript 1 is not prime), every time an array element is found whose value is 1, loop through the remainder of the array and set to zero every element whose subscript is a multiple of the subscript for the element with value 1. For array subscript 2, all elements beyond 2 in the array that are multiples of 2 will be set to zero (subscripts 4, 6, 8, 10, and so on.). For array subscript 3, all elements beyond 3 in the array that are multiples of 3 will be set to zero (subscripts 6, 9, 12, 15, and so on.).

When this process is complete, the array elements that are still set to 1 indicate that the subscript is a prime number. Write a program that uses an array of 1000 elements to determine and print the prime numbers between 1 and 999. Ignore element 0 of the array.

Recursion Exercises

6.31   (*Palindromes*) A palindrome is a string that is spelled the same way forward and backward. Some examples of palindromes are: "radar," "able was i ere i saw elba," and, if you ignore blanks, "a man a plan a canal panama." Write a recursive function `testPalindrome` that returns 1 if the string stored in the array is a palindrome and 0 otherwise. The function should ignore spaces and punctuation in the string.

6.32   (*Linear Search*) Modify the program of Fig. 6.18 to use a recursive `linearSearch` function to perform the linear search of the array. The function should receive an integer array and the size of the array as arguments. If the search key is found, return the array subscript; otherwise, return –1.

6.33   (*Binary Search*) Modify the program of Fig. 6.19 to use a recursive `binarySearch` function to perform the binary search of the array. The function should receive an integer array and the starting subscript and ending subscript as arguments. If the search key is found, return the array subscript; otherwise, return –1.

6.34   (*Eight Queens*) Modify the Eight Queens program you created in Exercise 6.26 to solve the problem recursively.

6.35   (*Print an array*) Write a recursive function `printArray` that takes an array and the size of the array as arguments, prints the array, and returns nothing. The function should stop processing and return when it receives an array of size zero.

6.36   (*Print a string backward*) Write a recursive function `stringReverse` that takes a character array as an argument, prints it back to front and returns nothing. The function should stop processing and return when the terminating null character of the string is encountered.

6.37   (*Find the minimum value in an array*) Write a recursive function `recursiveMinimum` that takes an integer array and the array size as arguments and returns the smallest element of the array. The function should stop processing and return when it receives an array of one element.

Special Section: Sudoku

The game of Sudoku exploded in popularity worldwide in 2005. Almost every major newspaper now publishes a Sudoku puzzle daily. Handheld game players let you play anytime, anywhere and create puzzles on demand at various levels of difficulty. Be sure to check out our Sudoku Resource Center at www.deitel.com/sudoku for downloads, tutorials, books, e-books and more that will help you master the game. And not for the faint of heart—try fiendishly difficult Sudokus with tricky twists, a circular Sudoku and a variant of the puzzle with five interlocking grids. Subscribe to our free newsletter, *The Deitel® Buzz Online*, for notifications of updates to our Sudoku Resource Center and to other Deitel Resource Centers at www.deitel.com that provide games, puzzles and other interesting programming projects.

A completed Sudoku puzzle is a 9×9 grid (i.e., a two-dimensional array) in which the digits 1 through 9 appear once and only once in each row, each column and each of nine 3×3 grids. In the partially completed 9×9 grid of Fig. 6.27, row 1, column 1, and the 3×3 grid in the upper-left corner of the board each contain the digits 1 through 9 once and only once. Note that we use C's two-dimensional array row and column-numbering conventions, but we're ignoring row 0 and column 0 in conformance with Sudoku community conventions.

The typical Sudoku puzzle provides many filled-in cells and many blanks, often arranged in a symmetrical pattern as is typical with crossword puzzles. The player's task is to fill in the blanks to complete the puzzle. Some puzzles are easy to solve; some are quite difficult, requiring sophisticated solution strategies.

In Appendix E, Game Programming: Solving Sudoku, we'll discuss various simple solution strategies, and suggest what to do when these fail. We'll also present various approaches for programming Sudoku puzzle creators and solvers in C. Unfortunately, Standard C does not include graphics and GUI (graphical user interface) capabilities, so our representation of the board won't be as elegant as we could make it in Java and other programming languages that support these capabilities. You may want to revisit your Sudoku programs after you read Chapter 15, Game Programming with the Allegro C Library. Allegro, which is not part of Standard C, offers capabilities that will help you add graphics and even sounds to your Sudoku programs.

	1	2	3	4	5	6	7	8	9
1	5	1	3	4	9	7	6	2	8
2	4	6	8						
3	7	9	2						
4	2								
5	9								
6	3								
7	8								
8	1								
9	6								

Fig. 6.27 | Partially completed 9×9 Sudoku grid. Note the nine 3×3 grids.

7

C Pointers

OBJECTIVES

In this chapter, you will learn:

- Pointers and pointer operators.
- To use pointers to pass arguments to functions by reference.
- The close relationships among pointers, arrays and strings.
- To use pointers to functions.
- To define and use arrays of strings.

7.1 Introduction

In this chapter, we discuss one of the most powerful features of the C programming language, the pointer. Pointers are among C's most difficult capabilities to master. Pointers enable programs to simulate call-by-reference and to create and manipulate dynamic data structures, i.e., data structures that can grow and shrink at execution time, such as linked lists, queues, stacks and trees. This chapter explains basic pointer concepts. Chapter 10 examines the use of pointers with structures. Chapter 12 introduces dynamic memory management techniques and presents examples of creating and using dynamic data structures.

7.2 Pointer Variable Definitions and Initialization

Pointers are variables whose values are memory addresses. Normally, a variable directly contains a specific value. A pointer, on the other hand, contains an address of a variable that contains a specific value. In this sense, a variable name *directly* references a value, and a pointer *indirectly* references a value (Fig. 7.1). Referencing a value through a pointer is called **indirection**.

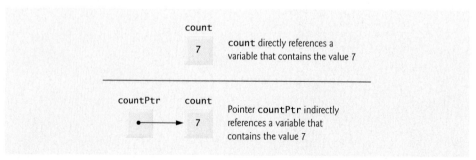

Fig. 7.1 | Directly and indirectly referencing a variable.

Pointers, like all variables, must be defined before they can be used. The definition

```
int *countPtr, count;
```

specifies that variable countPtr is of type int * (i.e., a pointer to an integer) and is read, "countPtr is a pointer to int" or "countPtr points to an object of type int." Also, the variable count is defined to be an int, not a pointer to an int. The * only applies to countPtr in the definition. When * is used in this manner in a definition, it indicates that the variable being defined is a pointer. Pointers can be defined to point to objects of any type.

Common Programming Error 7.1

The asterisk (*) notation used to declare pointer variables does not distribute to all variable names in a declaration. Each pointer must be declared with the * prefixed to the name; e.g., if you wish to declare xPtr and yPtr as int pointers, use int *xPtr, *yPtr;.

Good Programming Practice 7.1

Include the letters ptr in pointer variable names to make it clear that these variables are pointers and thus need to be handled appropriately.

Pointers should be initialized either when they are defined or in an assignment statement. A pointer may be initialized to 0, NULL or an address. A pointer with the value NULL points to nothing. NULL is a symbolic constant defined in the <stddef.h> header (and several other headers, such as <stdio.h>). Initializing a pointer to 0 is equivalent to initializing a pointer to NULL, but NULL is preferred. When 0 is assigned, it is first converted to a pointer of the appropriate type. The value 0 is the only integer value that can be assigned directly to a pointer variable. Assigning a variable's address to a pointer is discussed in Section 7.3.

Error-Prevention Tip 7.1

Initialize pointers to prevent unexpected results.

7.3 Pointer Operators

The &, or address operator, is a unary operator that returns the address of its operand. For example, assuming the definitions

```
int y = 5;
int *yPtr;
```

the statement

```
yPtr = &y;
```

assigns the address of the variable y to pointer variable yPtr. Variable yPtr is then said to "point to" y. Figure 7.2 shows a schematic representation of memory after the preceding assignment is executed.

Figure 7.3 shows the representation of the pointer in memory, assuming that integer variable y is stored at location 600000, and pointer variable yPtr is stored at location 500000. The operand of the address operator must be a variable; the address operator cannot be applied to constants, to expressions or to variables declared with the storage-class register.

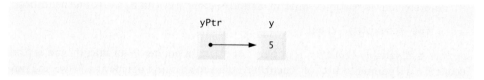

Fig. 7.2 | Graphical representation of a pointer pointing to an integer variable in memory.

	yPtr		y
location 500000	600000	location 600000	5

Fig. 7.3 | Representation of y and yPtr in memory.

The unary * operator, commonly referred to as the indirection operator or dereferencing operator, returns the value of the object to which its operand (i.e., a pointer) points. For example, the statement

```
printf( "%d", *yPtr );
```

prints the value of variable y, namely 5. Using * in this manner is called **dereferencing a pointer.**

Common Programming Error 7.2

Dereferencing a pointer that has not been properly initialized or that has not been assigned to point to a specific location in memory is an error. This could cause a fatal execution-time error, or it could accidentally modify important data and allow the program to run to completion with incorrect results.

Figure 7.4 demonstrates the pointer operators & and *. The printf conversion specifier %p outputs the memory location as a hexadecimal integer on most platforms. (See Appendix D, Number Systems, for more information on hexadecimal integers.) Notice that the address of a and the value of aPtr are identical in the output, thus confirming that the address of a is indeed assigned to the pointer variable aPtr (line 11). The & and * operators are complements of one another—when they are both applied consecutively to aPtr in either order (line 21), the same result is printed. Figure 7.5 lists the precedence and associativity of the operators introduced to this point.

```
1   /* Fig. 7.4: fig07_04.c
2      Using the & and * operators */
3   #include <stdio.h>
4
5   int main( void )
6   {
7      int a;        /* a is an integer */
8      int *aPtr;    /* aPtr is a pointer to an integer */
```

Fig. 7.4 | & and * pointer operators.

```
 9
10      a = 7;
11      aPtr = &a;      /* aPtr set to address of a */
12
13      printf( "The address of a is %p"
14              "\nThe value of aPtr is %p", &a, aPtr );
15
16      printf( "\n\nThe value of a is %d"
17              "\nThe value of *aPtr is %d", a, *aPtr );
18
19      printf( "\n\nShowing that * and & are complements of "
20              "each other\n&*aPtr = %p"
21              "\n*&aPtr = %p\n", &*aPtr, *&aPtr );
22
23      return 0; /* indicates successful termination */
24
25   } /* end main */
```

```
The address of a is 0012FF7C
The value of aPtr is 0012FF7C

The value of a is 7
The value of *aPtr is 7

Showing that * and & are complements of each other.
&*aPtr = 0012FF7C
*&aPtr = 0012FF7C
```

Fig. 7.4 | & and * pointer operators.

Operators							Associativity	Type
()	[]						left to right	highest
+	-	++	--	!	*	& (*type*)	right to left	unary
*	/	%					left to right	multiplicative
+	-						left to right	additive
<	<=	>	>=				left to right	relational
==	!=						left to right	equality
&&							left to right	logical and
||							left to right	logical OR
?:							right to left	conditional
=	+=	-=	*=	/=	%=		right to left	assignment
,							left to right	comma

Fig. 7.5 | Operator precedence and associativity.

7.4 Passing Arguments to Functions by Reference

There are two ways to pass arguments to a function—call-by-value and call-by-reference. All arguments in C are passed by value. As we saw in Chapter 5, return may be used to return one value from a called function to a caller (or to return control from a called function without passing back a value). Many functions require the capability to modify one or more variables in the caller or to pass a pointer to a large data object to avoid the overhead of passing the object by value (which incurs the overhead of making a copy of the object). For these purposes, C provides the capabilities for simulating call-by-reference.

In C, you use pointers and the indirection operator to simulate call-by-reference. When calling a function with arguments that should be modified, the addresses of the arguments are passed. This is normally accomplished by applying the address operator (&) to the variable (in the caller) whose value will be modified. As we saw in Chapter 6, arrays are not passed using operator & because C automatically passes the starting location in memory of the array (the name of an array is equivalent to &arrayName[0]). When the address of a variable is passed to a function, the indirection operator (*) may be used in the function to modify the value at that location in the caller's memory.

The programs in Fig. 7.6 and Fig. 7.7 present two versions of a function that cubes an integer—cubeByValue and cubeByReference. Figure 7.6 passes the variable number to function cubeByValue using call-by-value (line 14). The cubeByValue function cubes its

```c
 1   /* Fig. 7.6: fig07_06.c
 2      Cube a variable using call-by-value */
 3   #include <stdio.h>
 4
 5   int cubeByValue( int n ); /* prototype */
 6
 7   int main( void )
 8   {
 9      int number = 5; /* initialize number */
10
11      printf( "The original value of number is %d", number );
12
13      /* pass number by value to cubeByValue */
14      number = cubeByValue( number );
15
16      printf( "\nThe new value of number is %d\n", number );
17
18      return 0; /* indicates successful termination */
19
20   } /* end main */
21
22   /* calculate and return cube of integer argument */
23   int cubeByValue( int n )
24   {
25      return n * n * n;   /* cube local variable n and return result */
26
27   } /* end function cubeByValue */
```

Fig. 7.6 | Cube a variable using call-by-value. (Part 1 of 2.)

```
The original value of number is 5
The new value of number is 125
```

Fig. 7.6 | Cube a variable using call-by-value. (Part 2 of 2.)

argument and passes the new value back to main using a return statement. The new value is assigned to number in main (line 14).

Figure 7.7 passes the variable number using call-by-reference (line 15)—the address of number is passed—to function cubeByReference. Function cubeByReference takes as a parameter a pointer to an int called nPtr (line 24). The function dereferences the pointer and cubes the value to which nPtr points (line 26), then assigns the result to *nPtr (which is really number in main), thus changing the value of number in main. Figure 7.8 and Fig. 7.9 analyze graphically the programs in Fig. 7.6 and Fig. 7.7, respectively.

 Common Programming Error 7.3

Not dereferencing a pointer when it is necessary to do so in order to obtain the value to which the pointer points is a syntax error.

```c
1   /* Fig. 7.7: fig07_07.c
2      Cube a variable using call-by-reference with a pointer argument */
3
4   #include <stdio.h>
5
6   void cubeByReference( int *nPtr ); /* prototype */
7
8   int main( void )
9   {
10     int number = 5; /* initialize number */
11
12     printf( "The original value of number is %d", number );
13
14     /* pass address of number to cubeByReference */
15     cubeByReference( &number );
16
17     printf( "\nThe new value of number is %d\n", number );
18
19     return 0; /* indicates successful termination */
20
21   } /* end main */
22
23   /* calculate cube of *nPtr; modifies variable number in main */
24   void cubeByReference( int *nPtr )
25   {
26     *nPtr = *nPtr * *nPtr * *nPtr;  /* cube *nPtr */
27   } /* end function cubeByReference */
```

```
The original value of number is 5
The new value of number is 125
```

Fig. 7.7 | Cube a variable using call-by-reference.

Step 1: Before main calls cubeByValue:

```
int main( void )                    number
{
    int number = 5;                   5

    number = cubeByValue( number );
}
```
```
int cubeByValue( int n )
{
    return n * n * n;
}
                                        n

                                   undefined
```

Step 2: After cubeByValue receives the call:

```
int main( void )                    number
{
    int number = 5;                   5

    number = cubeByValue( number );
}
```
```
int cubeByValue( int n )
{
    return n * n * n;
}
                                        n

                                        5
```

Step 3: After cubeByValue cubes parameter n and before cubeByValue returns to main:

```
int main( void )                    number
{
    int number = 5;                   5

    number = cubeByValue( number );
}
```
```
int cubeByValue( int n )
{               125
    return n * n * n;
}
                                        n

                                        5
```

Step 4: After cubeByValue returns to main and before assigning the result to number:

```
int main( void )                    number
{
    int number = 5;                   5
                125
    number = cubeByValue( number );
}
```
```
int cubeByValue( int n )
{
    return n * n * n;
}
                                        n

                                   undefined
```

Step 5: After main completes the assignment to number:

```
int main( void )                    number
{
    int number = 5;                  125
        125            125
    number = cubeByValue( number );
}
```
```
int cubeByValue( int n )
{
    return n * n * n;
}
                                        n

                                   undefined
```

Fig. 7.8 | Analysis of a typical call-by-value.

Step 1: Before main calls cubeByReference:

```
int main( void )                                    void cubeByReference( int *nPtr )
{                                    number          {
   int number = 5;                     5                *nPtr = *nPtr * *nPtr * *nPtr;
                                                      }
   cubeByReference( &number );                                                      nPtr
}
                                                                              undefined
```

Step 2: After **cubeByReference** receives the call and before *nPtr is cubed:

```
int main( void )                                    void cubeByReference( int *nPtr )
{                                    number          {
   int number = 5;                     5                *nPtr = *nPtr * *nPtr * *nPtr;
                                                      }
   cubeByReference( &number );                                                      nPtr
}
                        call establishes this pointer
```

Step 3: After *nPtr is cubed and before program control returns to main:

```
int main( void )                                    void cubeByReference( int *nPtr )
{                                    number          {                      125
   int number = 5;                    125              *nPtr = *nPtr * *nPtr * *nPtr;
                                                      }
   cubeByReference( &number );                         called function modifies caller's    nPtr
}                                                       variable
```

Fig. 7.9 | Analysis of a typical call-by-reference with a pointer argument.

A function receiving an address as an argument must define a pointer parameter to receive the address. For example, in Fig. 7.7 the header for function cubeByReference (line 24) is:

```
void cubeByReference( int *nPtr )
```

The header specifies that cubeByReference receives the address of an integer variable as an argument, stores the address locally in nPtr and does not return a value.

The function prototype for cubeByReference contains int * in parentheses. As with other variable types, it is not necessary to include names of pointers in function prototypes. Names included for documentation purposes are ignored by the C compiler.

In the function header and in the prototype for a function that expects a single-subscripted array as an argument, the pointer notation in the parameter list of function cubeByReference may be used. The compiler does not differentiate between a function that receives a pointer and a function that receives a single-subscripted array. This, of course, means that the function must "know" when it is receiving an array or simply a single variable for which it is to perform call by reference. When the compiler encounters a function parameter for a single-subscripted array of the form int b[], the compiler converts the parameter to the pointer notation int *b. The two forms are interchangeable.

Error-Prevention Tip 7.2

Use call-by-value to pass arguments to a function unless the caller explicitly requires the called function to modify the value of the argument variable in the caller's environment. This prevents accidental modification of the caller's arguments and is another example of the principle of least privilege.

7.5 Using the `const` Qualifier with Pointers

The `const` qualifier enables you to inform the compiler that the value of a particular variable should not be modified. The `const` qualifier did not exist in early versions of C; it was added to the language by the ANSI C committee.

Software Engineering Observation 7.1

The `const` qualifier can be used to enforce the principle of least privilege. Using the principle of least privilege to properly design software reduces debugging time and improper side effects, making a program easier to modify and maintain.

Portability Tip 7.1

Although `const` is well defined in Standard C, some compilers do not enforce it.

Over the years, a large base of legacy code was written in early versions of C that did not use `const` because it was not available. For this reason, there are significant opportunities for improvement in the software engineering of old C code.

Six possibilities exist for using (or not using) `const` with function parameters—two with call-by-value parameter passing and four with call-by-reference parameter passing. How do you choose one of the six possibilities? Let the principle of least privilege be your guide. Always award a function enough access to the data in its parameters to accomplish its specified task, but no more.

In Chapter 5, we explained that all calls in C are call-by-value—a copy of the argument in the function call is made and passed to the function. If the copy is modified in the function, the original value in the caller does not change. In many cases, a value passed to a function is modified so the function can accomplish its task. However, in some instances, the value should not be altered in the called function, even though it manipulates only a copy of the original value.

Consider a function that takes a single-subscripted array and its size as arguments and prints the array. Such a function should loop through the array and output each array element individually. The size of the array is used in the function body to determine the high subscript of the array, so the loop can terminate when the printing is completed. Neither the size of the array nor its contents should change in the function body.

Error-Prevention Tip 7.3

If a variable does not (or should not) change in the body of a function to which it is passed, the variable should be declared `const` to ensure that it is not accidentally modified.

If an attempt is made to modify a value that is declared `const`, the compiler catches it and issues either a warning or an error, depending on the particular compiler.

Software Engineering Observation 7.2

Only one value can be altered in a calling function when call-by-value is used. That value must be assigned from the return value of the function. To modify multiple values in a calling function, call-by-reference must be used.

Error-Prevention Tip 7.4

Before using a function, check its function prototype to determine if the function is able to modify the values passed to it.

Common Programming Error 7.4

Being unaware that a function is expecting pointers as arguments for call-by-reference and passing arguments call-by-value. Some compilers take the values assuming they are pointers and dereference the values as pointers. At runtime, memory-access violations or segmentation faults are often generated. Other compilers catch the mismatch in types between arguments and parameters and generate error messages.

There are four ways to pass a pointer to a function: a non-constant pointer to non-constant data, a constant pointer to nonconstant data, a non-constant pointer to constant data, and a constant pointer to constant data. Each of the four combinations provides different access privileges. These are discussed in the next several examples.

Converting a String to Uppercase Using a Non-Constant Pointer to Non-Constant Data
The highest level of data access is granted by a non-constant pointer to non-constant data. In this case, the data can be modified through the dereferenced pointer, and the pointer can be modified to point to other data items. A declaration for a non-constant pointer to non-constant data does not include const. Such a pointer might be used to receive a string as an argument to a function that uses **pointer arithmetic** to process (and possibly modify) each character in the string. Function convertToUppercase of Fig. 7.10 declares its parameter, a non-constant pointer to non-constant data called sPtr (char *sPtr), in line 23. The function processes the array string (pointed to by sPtr) one character at a time using pointer arithmetic. C standard library function islower (called in line 27) tests the character contents of the address pointed to by sPtr. If a character is in the range a to z, islower returns true and C standard library function toupper (line 28) is called to convert the character to its corresponding uppercase letter; otherwise, islower returns false and the next character in the string is processed. Line 31 moves the pointer to the next character in the string. Pointer arithmetic will be discussed in more detail in Section 7.8.

```
1   /* Fig. 7.10: fig07_10.c
2      Converting lowercase letters to uppercase letters
3      using a non-constant pointer to non-constant data */
4
5   #include <stdio.h>
6   #include <ctype.h>
7
8   void convertToUppercase( char *sPtr ); /* prototype */
9
```

Fig. 7.10 | Converting a string to uppercase using a non-constant pointer to non-constant data. (Part 1 of 2.)

```
10   int main( void )
11   {
12      char string[] = "characters and $32.98"; /* initialize char array */
13
14      printf( "The string before conversion is: %s", string );
15      convertToUppercase( string );
16      printf( "\nThe string after conversion is: %s\n", string );
17
18      return 0; /* indicates successful termination */
19
20   } /* end main */
21
22   /* convert string to uppercase letters */
23   void convertToUppercase( char *sPtr )
24   {
25      while ( *sPtr != '\0' ) { /* current character is not '\0' */
26
27         if ( islower( *sPtr ) ) {    /* if character is lowercase, */
28            *sPtr = toupper( *sPtr ); /* convert to uppercase */
29         } /* end if */
30
31         ++sPtr;  /* move sPtr to the next character */
32      } /* end while */
33
34   } /* end function convertToUppercase */
```

```
The string before conversion is: characters and $32.98
The string after conversion is: CHARACTERS AND $32.98
```

Fig. 7.10 | Converting a string to uppercase using a non-constant pointer to non-constant data. (Part 2 of 2.)

Printing a String One Character at a Time Using a Non-Constant Pointer to Constant Data

A non-constant pointer to constant data can be modified to point to any data item of the appropriate type, but the data to which it points cannot be modified. Such a pointer might be used to receive an array argument to a function that will process each element of the array without modifying the data. For example, the printCharacters function of Fig. 7.11 declares parameter sPtr to be of type const char * (line 24). The declaration is read from right to left as "sPtr is a pointer to a character constant." The body of the function uses a for statement to output each character in the string until the null character is encountered. After each character is printed, pointer sPtr is incremented to point to the next character in the string.

```
1   /* Fig. 7.11: fig07_11.c
2      Printing a string one character at a time using
3      a non-constant pointer to constant data */
4
```

Fig. 7.11 | Printing a string one character at a time using a non-constant pointer to constant data. (Part 1 of 2.)

```
 5   #include <stdio.h>
 6
 7   void printCharacters( const char *sPtr );
 8
 9   int main( void )
10   {
11       /* initialize char array */
12       char string[] = "print characters of a string";
13
14       printf( "The string is:\n" );
15       printCharacters( string );
16       printf( "\n" );
17
18       return 0; /* indicates successful termination */
19
20   } /* end main */
21
22   /* sPtr cannot modify the character to which it points,
23       i.e., sPtr is a "read-only" pointer */
24   void printCharacters( const char *sPtr )
25   {
26       /* loop through entire string */
27       for ( ; *sPtr != '\0'; sPtr++ ) { /* no initialization */
28           printf( "%c", *sPtr );
29       } /* end for */
30
31   } /* end function printCharacters */
```

```
The string is:
print characters of a string
```

Fig. 7.11 | Printing a string one character at a time using a non-constant pointer to constant data. (Part 2 of 2.)

Figure 7.12 illustrates the attempt to compile a function that receives a non-constant pointer (xPtr) to constant data. This function attempts to modify the data pointed to by xPtr in line 22—which results in a compilation error. [*Note:* The actual error message you see will be compiler specific.]

As we know, arrays are aggregate data types that store related data items of the same type under one name. In Chapter 10, we will discuss another form of aggregate data type called a structure (sometimes called a record in other languages). A structure is capable of storing related data items of different data types under one name (e.g., storing information about each employee of a company). When a function is called with an array as an argument, the array is automatically passed to the function by reference. However, structures are always passed by value—a copy of the entire structure is passed. This requires the execution-time overhead of making a copy of each data item in the structure and storing it on the computer's function call stack. When structure data must be passed to a function, we can use pointers to constant data to get the performance of call-by-reference and the protection of call-by-value. When a pointer to a structure is passed, only a copy of the address at which the structure is stored must be made. On a machine with 4-byte

```
 1   /* Fig. 7.12: fig07_12.c
 2      Attempting to modify data through a
 3      non-constant pointer to constant data. */
 4   #include <stdio.h>
 5   void f( const int *xPtr ); /* prototype */
 6
 7
 8   int main( void )
 9   {
10      int y;        /* define y */
11
12      f( &y );      /* f attempts illegal modification */
13
14      return 0;     /* indicates successful termination */
15
16   } /* end main */
17
18   /* xPtr cannot be used to modify the
19      value of the variable to which it points */
20   void f( const int *xPtr )
21   {
22      *xPtr = 100;  /* error: cannot modify a const object */
23   } /* end function f */
```

```
Compiling...
FIG07_12.c
c:\books\2006\chtp5\examples\ch07\fig07_12.c(22) : error C2166: 1-value
   specifies const object
Error executing cl.exe.

FIG07_12.exe - 1 error(s), 0 warning(s)
```

Fig. 7.12 | Attempting to modify data through a non-constant pointer to constant data.

addresses, a copy of 4 bytes of memory is made rather than a copy of possibly hundreds or thousands of bytes of the structure.

 Performance Tip 7.1

Pass large objects such as structures using pointers to constant data to obtain the performance benefits of call-by-reference and the security of call-by-value.

Using pointers to constant data in this manner is an example of a time/space trade-off. If memory is low and execution efficiency is a major concern, pointers should be used. If memory is in abundance and efficiency is not a major concern, data should be passed by value to enforce the principle of least privilege. Remember that some systems do not enforce const well, so call-by-value is still the best way to prevent data from being modified.

Attempting to Modify a Constant Pointer to Non-Constant Data

A constant pointer to non-constant data always points to the same memory location, and the data at that location can be modified through the pointer. This is the default for an array name. An array name is a constant pointer to the beginning of the array. All data in the array can be accessed and changed by using the array name and array subscripting. A constant pointer to non-constant data can be used to receive an array as an argument to a function that accesses array elements using only array subscript notation. Pointers that are declared const must be initialized when they are defined (if the pointer is a function parameter, it is initialized with a pointer that is passed to the function). Figure 7.13 attempts to modify a constant pointer. Pointer ptr is defined in line 12 to be of type int * const. The definition is read from right to left as "ptr is a constant pointer to an integer." The pointer is initialized (line 12) with the address of integer variable x. The program attempts to assign the address of y to ptr (line 15), but the compiler generates an error message.

Attempting to Modify a Constant Pointer to Constant Data

The least access privilege is granted by a constant pointer to constant data. Such a pointer always points to the same memory location, and the data at that memory location cannot be modified. This is how an array should be passed to a function that only looks at the array using array subscript notation and does not modify the array. Figure 7.14 defines pointer variable ptr (line 13) to be of type const int *const, which is read from right to left as "ptr is a constant pointer to an integer constant." The figure shows the error messages generated when an attempt is made to modify the data to which ptr points (line 17) and when an attempt is made to modify the address stored in the pointer variable (line 18).

```c
 1   /* Fig. 7.13: fig07_13.c
 2      Attempting to modify a constant pointer to non-constant data */
 3   #include <stdio.h>
 4
 5   int main( void )
 6   {
 7      int x; /* define x */
 8      int y; /* define y */
 9
10      /* ptr is a constant pointer to an integer that can be modified
11         through ptr, but ptr always points to the same memory location */
12      int * const ptr = &x;
13
14      *ptr = 7; /* allowed: *ptr is not const */
15      ptr = &y; /* error: ptr is const; cannot assign new address */
16
17      return 0; /* indicates successful termination */
18
19   } /* end main */
```

```
Compiling...
FIG07_13.c
c:\books\2006\chtp5\Examples\ch07\FIG07_13.c(15) : error C2166: l-value
    specifies const object
Error executing cl.exe.

FIG07_13.exe - 1 error(s), 0 warning(s)
```

Fig. 7.13 | Attempting to modify a constant pointer to non-constant data.

```
 1   /* Fig. 7.14: fig07_14.c
 2      Attempting to modify a constant pointer to constant data. */
 3   #include <stdio.h>
 4
 5   int main( void )
 6   {
 7      int x = 5; /* initialize x */
 8      int y;     /* define y */
 9
10      /* ptr is a constant pointer to a constant integer. ptr always
11         points to the same location; the integer at that location
12         cannot be modified */
13      const int *const ptr = &x;
14
15      printf( "%d\n", *ptr );
16
17      *ptr = 7; /* error: *ptr is const; cannot assign new value */
18      ptr = &y; /* error: ptr is const; cannot assign new address */
19
20      return 0; /* indicates successful termination */
21
22   } /* end main */
```

```
Compiling...
FIG07_14.c
c:\books\2006\chtp5\Examples\ch07\FIG07_14.c(17) : error C2166: l-value
    specifies const object
c:\books\2006\chtp5\Examples\ch07\FIG07_14.c(18) : error C2166: l-value
    specifies const object
Error executing cl.exe.

FIG07_12.exe - 2 error(s), 0 warning(s)
```

Fig. 7.14 | Attempting to modify a constant pointer to constant data.

7.6 Bubble Sort Using Call-by-Reference

Let us improve the bubble sort program of Fig. 6.15 to use two functions—bubbleSort and swap. Function bubbleSort sorts the array. It calls function swap (line 53) to exchange the array elements array[j] and array[j + 1] (see Fig.). Remember that C enforces information hiding between functions, so swap does not have access to individual array elements in bubbleSort. Because bubbleSort *wants* swap to have access to the array elements to be swapped, bubbleSort passes each of these elements call-by-reference to swap—the address of each array element is passed explicitly. Although entire arrays are automatically passed by reference, individual array elements are scalars and are ordinarily passed by value. Therefore, bubbleSort uses the address operator (&) on each of the array elements in the swap call (line 53) as follows

```
    swap( &array[ j ], &array[ j + 1 ] );
```

to effect call-by-reference. Function swap receives &array[j] in pointer variable element1Ptr (line 64). Even though swap—because of information hiding—is not allowed to know the name array[j], swap may use *element1Ptr as a synonym for array[j]. Therefore, when swap references *element1Ptr, it is actually referencing array[j] in bubbleSort. Similarly, when swap references *element2Ptr, it is actually referencing array[j + 1] in bubbleSort. Even though swap is not allowed to say

```
hold = array[ j ];
array[ j ] = array[ j + 1 ];
array[ j + 1 ] = hold;
```

precisely the same effect is achieved by lines 66 through 68

```
int hold = *element1Ptr;
*element1Ptr = *element2Ptr;
*element2Ptr = hold;
```

in the swap function of Fig. 7.15.

```
1   /* Fig. 7.15: fig07_15.c
2      This program puts values into an array, sorts the values into
3      ascending order, and prints the resulting array. */
4   #include <stdio.h>
5   #define SIZE 10
6
7   void bubbleSort( int * const array, const int size ); /* prototype */
8
9   int main( void )
10  {
11     /* initialize array a */
12     int a[ SIZE ] = { 2, 6, 4, 8, 10, 12, 89, 68, 45, 37 };
13
14     int i; /* counter */
15
16     printf( "Data items in original order\n" );
17
18     /* loop through array a */
19     for ( i = 0; i < SIZE; i++ ) {
20        printf( "%4d", a[ i ] );
21     } /* end for */
22
23     bubbleSort( a, SIZE ); /* sort the array */
24
25     printf( "\nData items in ascending order\n" );
26
27     /* loop through array a */
28     for ( i = 0; i < SIZE; i++ ) {
29        printf( "%4d", a[ i ] );
30     } /* end for */
31
32     printf( "\n" );
33
34     return 0; /* indicates successful termination */
35
36  } /* end main */
```

Fig. 7.15 | Bubble sort with call-by-reference. (Part I of 2.)

```
37
38    /* sort an array of integers using bubble sort algorithm */
39    void bubbleSort( int * const array, const int size )
40    {
41       void swap( int *element1Ptr, int *element2Ptr ); /* prototype */
42       int pass; /* pass counter */
43       int j;    /* comparison counter */
44
45       /* loop to control passes */
46       for ( pass = 0; pass < size - 1; pass++ ) {
47
48          /* loop to control comparisons during each pass */
49          for ( j = 0; j < size - 1; j++ ) {
50
51             /* swap adjacent elements if they are out of order */
52             if ( array[ j ] > array[ j + 1 ] ) {
53                swap( &array[ j ], &array[ j + 1 ] );
54             } /* end if */
55
56          } /* end inner for */
57
58       } /* end outer for */
59
60    } /* end function bubbleSort */
61
62    /* swap values at memory locations to which element1Ptr and
63       element2Ptr point */
64    void swap( int *element1Ptr, int *element2Ptr )
65    {
66       int hold = *element1Ptr;
67       *element1Ptr = *element2Ptr;
68       *element2Ptr = hold;
69    } /* end function swap */
```

```
Data items in original order
   2   6   4   8  10  12  89  68  45  37
Data items in ascending order
   2   4   6   8  10  12  37  45  68  89
```

Fig. 7.15 | Bubble sort with call-by-reference. (Part 2 of 2.)

Several features of function bubbleSort should be noted. The function header (line 39) declares array as int * const array rather than int array[] to indicate that bubble-Sort receives a single-subscripted array as an argument (again, these notations are interchangeable). Parameter size is declared const to enforce the principle of least privilege. Although parameter size receives a copy of a value in main, and modifying the copy cannot change the value in main, bubbleSort does not need to alter size to accomplish its task. The size of the array remains fixed during the execution of function bubbleSort. Therefore, size is declared const to ensure that it is not modified. If the size of the array is modified during the sorting process, the sorting algorithm might not run correctly.

The prototype for function swap (line 41) is included in the body of function bub-bleSort because bubbleSort is the only function that calls swap. Placing the prototype in bubbleSort restricts proper calls of swap to those made from bubbleSort. Other functions that attempt to call swap do not have access to a proper function prototype, so the compiler generates one automatically. This normally results in a prototype that does not match the function header (and generates a compiler error) because the compiler assumes int for the return type and the parameter types.

Software Engineering Observation 7.3

Placing function prototypes in the definitions of other functions enforces the principle of least privilege by restricting proper function calls to the functions in which the prototypes appear.

Note that function bubbleSort receives the size of the array as a parameter (line 39). The function must know the size of the array to sort the array. When an array is passed to a function, the memory address of the first element of the array is received by the function. The address, of course, does not convey the number of elements in the array. Therefore, you must pass to the function the array size. [*Note:* Another common practice is to pass a pointer to the beginning of the array and a pointer to the location just beyond the end of the array. The difference of the two pointers is the length of the array and the resulting code is simpler.]

In the program, the size of the array is explicitly passed to function bubbleSort. There are two main benefits to this approach—software reusability and proper software engineering. By defining the function to receive the array size as an argument, we enable the function to be used by any program that sorts single-subscripted integer arrays of any size.

Software Engineering Observation 7.4

When passing an array to a function, also pass the size of the array. This helps make the function reusable in many programs.

We could have stored the size of the array in a global variable that is accessible to the entire program. This would be more efficient, because a copy of the size is not made to pass to the function. However, other programs that require an integer array-sorting capability may not have the same global variable, so the function cannot be used in those programs.

Software Engineering Observation 7.5

Global variables usually violate the principle of least privilege and can lead to poor software engineering. Global variables should be used only to represent truly shared resources, such as the time of day.

The size of the array could have been programmed directly into the function. This restricts the use of the function to an array of a specific size and significantly reduces its reusability. Only programs processing single-subscripted integer arrays of the specific size coded into the function can use the function.

7.7 sizeof Operator

C provides the special unary operator sizeof to determine the size in bytes of an array (or any other data type) during program compilation. When applied to the name of an array as in Fig. 7.16 (line 14), the sizeof operator returns the total number of bytes in the array as an integer. Note that variables of type float are normally stored in 4 bytes of memory, and array is defined to have 20 elements. Therefore, there are a total of 80 bytes in array.

```
 1   /* Fig. 7.16: fig07_16.c
 2      Sizeof operator when used on an array name
 3      returns the number of bytes in the array. */
 4   #include <stdio.h>
 5
 6   size_t getSize( float *ptr ); /* prototype */
 7
 8   int main( void )
 9   {
10      float array[ 20 ]; /* create array */
11
12      printf( "The number of bytes in the array is %d"
13              "\nThe number of bytes returned by getSize is %d\n",
14              sizeof( array ), getSize( array ) );
15
16      return 0; /* indicates successful termination */
17
18   } /* end main */
19
20   /* return size of ptr */
21   size_t getSize( float *ptr )
22   {
23      return sizeof( ptr );
24
25   } /* end function getSize */
```

```
The number of bytes in the array is 80
The number of bytes returned by getSize is 4
```

Fig. 7.16 | Operator sizeof when applied to an array name returns the number of bytes in the array.

Performance Tip 7.2

sizeof is a compile-time operator, so it does not incur any execution-time overhead.

The number of elements in an array also can be determined with sizeof. For example, consider the following array definition:

```
double real[ 22 ];
```

Variables of type double normally are stored in 8 bytes of memory. Thus, array real contains a total of 176 bytes. To determine the number of elements in the array, the following expression can be used:

```
sizeof( real ) / sizeof( real[ 0 ] )
```

The expression determines the number of bytes in array real and divides that value by the number of bytes used in memory to store the first element of array real (a double value).

Note that function getSize returns type size_t. Type size_t is a type defined by the C standard as the integral type (unsigned or unsigned long) of the value returned by operator sizeof. Type size_t is defined in header <stddef.h> (which is included by several

headers, such as <stdio.h>). Figure 7.17 calculates the number of bytes used to store each
of the standard data types. The results could be different between computers.

Portability Tip 7.2

*The number of bytes used to store a particular data type may vary between systems. When writing
programs that depend on data type sizes and that will run on several computer systems, use
sizeof to determine the number of bytes used to store the data types.*

```
 1  /* Fig. 7.17: fig07_17.c
 2     Demonstrating the sizeof operator */
 3  #include <stdio.h>
 4
 5  int main( void )
 6  {
 7     char c;
 8     short s;
 9     int i;
10     long l;
11     float f;
12     double d;
13     long double ld;
14     int array[ 20 ];  /* create array of 20 int elements */
15     int *ptr = array; /* create pointer to array */
16
17     printf( "      sizeof c = %d\tsizeof(char)   = %d"
18             "\n      sizeof s = %d\tsizeof(short) = %d"
19             "\n      sizeof i = %d\tsizeof(int) = %d"
20             "\n      sizeof l = %d\tsizeof(long) = %d"
21             "\n      sizeof f = %d\tsizeof(float) = %d"
22             "\n      sizeof d = %d\tsizeof(double) = %d"
23             "\n     sizeof ld = %d\tsizeof(long double) = %d"
24             "\n sizeof array = %d"
25             "\n   sizeof ptr = %d\n",
26             sizeof c, sizeof( char ), sizeof s, sizeof( short ), sizeof i,
27             sizeof( int ), sizeof l, sizeof( long ), sizeof f,
28             sizeof( float ), sizeof d, sizeof( double ), sizeof ld,
29             sizeof( long double ), sizeof array, sizeof ptr );
30
31     return 0; /* indicates successful termination */
32
33  } /* end main */
```

```
      sizeof c = 1        sizeof(char)   = 1
      sizeof s = 2        sizeof(short) = 2
      sizeof i = 4        sizeof(int) = 4
      sizeof l = 4        sizeof(long) = 4
      sizeof f = 4        sizeof(float) = 4
      sizeof d = 8        sizeof(double) = 8
     sizeof ld = 8        sizeof(long double) = 8
 sizeof array = 80
   sizeof ptr = 4
```

Fig. 7.17 | Using operator sizeof to determine standard data type sizes.

Operator sizeof can be applied to any variable name, type or value (including the value of an expression). When applied to a variable name (that is not an array name) or a constant, the number of bytes used to store the specific type of variable or constant is returned. Note that the parentheses used with sizeof are required if a type name with two words is supplied as its operand (such as long double or unsigned short). Omitting the parentheses in this case results in a syntax error. The parentheses are not required if a variable name or a one-word type name is supplied as its operand, but they can still be included without causing an error.

7.8 Pointer Expressions and Pointer Arithmetic

Pointers are valid operands in arithmetic expressions, assignment expressions and comparison expressions. However, not all the operators normally used in these expressions are valid in conjunction with pointer variables. This section describes the operators that can have pointers as operands, and how these operators are used.

A limited set of arithmetic operations may be performed on pointers. A pointer may be incremented (++) or decremented (--), an integer may be added to a pointer (+ or +=), an integer may be subtracted from a pointer (- or -=) and one pointer may be subtracted from another.

Assume that array int v[5] has been defined and its first element is at location 3000 in memory. Assume pointer vPtr has been initialized to point to v[0]—i.e., the value of vPtr is 3000. Figure 7.18 illustrates this situation for a machine with 4-byte integers. Note that vPtr can be initialized to point to array v with either of the statements

```
vPtr = v;
vPtr = &v[ 0 ];
```

 Portability Tip 7.3

Most computers today have 2-byte or 4-byte integers. Some of the newer machines use 8-byte integers. Because the results of pointer arithmetic depend on the size of the objects a pointer points to, pointer arithmetic is machine dependent.

In conventional arithmetic, 3000 + 2 yields the value 3002. This is normally not the case with pointer arithmetic. When an integer is added to or subtracted from a pointer, the pointer is not incremented or decremented simply by that integer, but by that integer times the size of the object to which the pointer refers. The number of bytes depends on the object's data type. For example, the statement

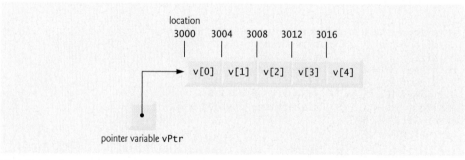

Fig. 7.18 | Array v and a pointer variable vPtr that points to v.

```
vPtr += 2;
```

would produce 3008 (3000 + 2 * 4), assuming an integer is stored in 4 bytes of memory. In the array v, vPtr would now point to v[2] (Fig. 7.19). If an integer is stored in 2 bytes of memory, then the preceding calculation would result in memory location 3004 (3000 + 2 * 2). If the array were of a different data type, the preceding statement would increment the pointer by twice the number of bytes that it takes to store an object of that data type. When performing pointer arithmetic on a character array, the results will be consistent with regular arithmetic, because each character is 1 byte long.

If vPtr had been incremented to 3016, which points to v[4], the statement

```
vPtr -= 4;
```

would set vPtr back to 3000—the beginning of the array. If a pointer is being incremented or decremented by one, the increment (++) and decrement (--) operators can be used. Either of the statements

```
++vPtr;
vPtr++;
```

increments the pointer to point to the next location in the array. Either of the statements

```
--vPtr;
vPtr--;
```

decrements the pointer to point to the previous element of the array.

Pointer variables may be subtracted from one another. For example, if vPtr contains the location 3000, and v2Ptr contains the address 3008, the statement

```
x = v2Ptr - vPtr;
```

would assign to x the number of array elements from vPtr to v2Ptr, in this case 2 (not 8). Pointer arithmetic is meaningless unless performed on an array. We cannot assume that two variables of the same type are stored contiguously in memory unless they are adjacent elements of an array.

Common Programming Error 7.5

Using pointer arithmetic on a pointer that does not refer to an element in an array.

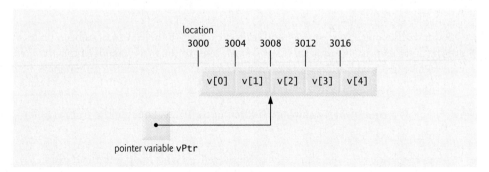

Fig. 7.19 │ The pointer vPtr after pointer arithmetic.

Common Programming Error 7.6

Subtracting or comparing two pointers that do not refer to elements in the same array.

Common Programming Error 7.7

Running off either end of an array when using pointer arithmetic.

A pointer can be assigned to another pointer if both pointers are of the same type. The exception to this rule is the **pointer to void** (i.e., **void ***), which is a generic pointer that can represent any pointer type. All pointer types can be assigned a pointer to void, and a pointer to void can be assigned a pointer of any type. In both cases, a cast operation is not required.

A pointer to void cannot be dereferenced. For example, the compiler knows that a pointer to int refers to 4 bytes of memory on a machine with 4-byte integers, but a pointer to void simply contains a memory location for an unknown data type—the precise number of bytes to which the pointer refers is not known by the compiler. The compiler must know the data type to determine the number of bytes to be dereferenced for a particular pointer.

Common Programming Error 7.8

*Assigning a pointer of one type to a pointer of another type if neither is of type void * is a syntax error.*

Common Programming Error 7.9

*Dereferencing a void * pointer is a syntax error.*

Pointers can be compared using equality and relational operators, but such comparisons are meaningless unless the pointers point to elements of the same array. Pointer comparisons compare the addresses stored in the pointers. A comparison of two pointers pointing to elements in the same array could show, for example, that one pointer points to a higher-numbered element of the array than the other pointer does. A common use of pointer comparison is determining whether a pointer is NULL.

7.9 Relationship between Pointers and Arrays

Arrays and pointers are intimately related in C and often may be used interchangeably. An array name can be thought of as a constant pointer. Pointers can be used to do any operation involving array subscripting.

Assume that integer array b[5] and integer pointer variable bPtr have been defined. Since the array name (without a subscript) is a pointer to the first element of the array, we can set bPtr equal to the address of the first element in array b with the statement

```
bPtr = b;
```

This statement is equivalent to taking the address of the first element of the array as follows:

```
bPtr = &b[ 0 ];
```

Array element b[3] can alternatively be referenced with the pointer expression

```
*( bPtr + 3 )
```

The 3 in the above expression is the offset to the pointer. When the pointer points to the beginning of an array, the offset indicates which element of the array should be referenced, and the offset value is identical to the array subscript. The preceding notation is referred to as **pointer/offset notation**. The parentheses are necessary because the precedence of * is higher than the precedence of +. Without the parentheses, the above expression would add 3 to the value of the expression *bPtr (i.e., 3 would be added to b[0], assuming bPtr points to the beginning of the array). Just as the array element can be referenced with a pointer expression, the address

&b[3]

can be written with the pointer expression

bPtr + 3

The array itself can be treated as a pointer and used in pointer arithmetic. For example, the expression

*(b + 3)

also refers to the array element b[3]. In general, all subscripted array expressions can be written with a pointer and an offset. In this case, pointer/offset notation was used with the name of the array as a pointer. Note that the preceding statement does not modify the array name in any way; b still points to the first element in the array.

Pointers can be subscripted exactly as arrays can. For example, if bPtr has the value b, the expression

bPtr[1]

refers to the array element b[1]. This is referred to as **pointer/subscript notation**.

Remember that an array name is essentially a constant pointer; it always points to the beginning of the array. Thus, the expression

b += 3

is invalid because it attempts to modify the value of the array name with pointer arithmetic.

Common Programming Error 7.10

Attempting to modify an array name with pointer arithmetic is a syntax error.

Figure 7.20 uses the four methods we have discussed for referring to array elements—array subscripting, pointer/offset with the array name as a pointer, **pointer subscripting**, and pointer/offset with a pointer—to print the four elements of the integer array b.

```
1   /* Fig. 7.20: fig07_20.cpp
2       Using subscripting and pointer notations with arrays */
3
4   #include <stdio.h>
5
```

Fig. 7.20 | Using four methods of referencing array elements. (Part 1 of 3.)

```
 6   int main( void )
 7   {
 8      int b[] = { 10, 20, 30, 40 }; /* initialize array b */
 9      int *bPtr = b;                 /* set bPtr to point to array b */
10      int i;                         /* counter */
11      int offset;                    /* counter */
12
13      /* output array b using array subscript notation */
14      printf( "Array b printed with:\nArray subscript notation\n" );
15
16      /* loop through array b */
17      for ( i = 0; i < 4; i++ ) {
18         printf( "b[ %d ] = %d\n", i, b[ i ] );
19      } /* end for */
20
21      /* output array b using array name and pointer/offset notation */
22      printf( "\nPointer/offset notation where\n"
23              "the pointer is the array name\n" );
24
25      /* loop through array b */
26      for ( offset = 0; offset < 4; offset++ ) {
27         printf( "*( b + %d ) = %d\n", offset, *( b + offset ) );
28      } /* end for */
29
30      /* output array b using bPtr and array subscript notation */
31      printf( "\nPointer subscript notation\n" );
32
33      /* loop through array b */
34      for ( i = 0; i < 4; i++ ) {
35         printf( "bPtr[ %d ] = %d\n", i, bPtr[ i ] );
36      } /* end for */
37
38      /* output array b using bPtr and pointer/offset notation */
39      printf( "\nPointer/offset notation\n" );
40
41      /* loop through array b */
42      for ( offset = 0; offset < 4; offset++ ) {
43         printf( "*( bPtr + %d ) = %d\n", offset, *( bPtr + offset ) );
44      } /* end for */
45
46      return 0; /* indicates successful termination */
47
48   } /* end main */
```

```
Array b printed with:
Array subscript notation
b[ 0 ] = 10
b[ 1 ] = 20
b[ 2 ] = 30
b[ 3 ] = 40
```

(continued on next page)

Fig. 7.20 | Using four methods of referencing array elements. (Part 2 of 3.)

```
Pointer/offset notation where
the pointer is the array name
*( b + 0 ) = 10
*( b + 1 ) = 20
*( b + 2 ) = 30
*( b + 3 ) = 40

Pointer subscript notation
bPtr[ 0 ] = 10
bPtr[ 1 ] = 20
bPtr[ 2 ] = 30
bPtr[ 3 ] = 40

Pointer/offset notation
*( bPtr + 0 ) = 10
*( bPtr + 1 ) = 20
*( bPtr + 2 ) = 30
*( bPtr + 3 ) = 40
```

Fig. 7.20 | Using four methods of referencing array elements. (Part 3 of 3.)

To further illustrate the interchangeability of arrays and pointers, let us look at the two string-copying functions—copy1 and copy2—in the program of Fig. 7.21. Both functions copy a string (possibly a character array) into a character array. After a comparison of the function prototypes for copy1 and copy2, the functions appear identical. They accomplish the same task; however, they are implemented differently.

```c
 1   /* Fig. 7.21: fig07_21.c
 2      Copying a string using array notation and pointer notation. */
 3   #include <stdio.h>
 4
 5   void copy1( char * const s1, const char * const s2 ); /* prototype */
 6   void copy2( char *s1, const char *s2 ); /* prototype */
 7
 8   int main( void )
 9   {
10      char string1[ 10 ];        /* create array string1 */
11      char *string2 = "Hello";   /* create a pointer to a string */
12      char string3[ 10 ];        /* create array string3 */
13      char string4[] = "Good Bye"; /* create a pointer to a string */
14
15      copy1( string1, string2 );
16      printf( "string1 = %s\n", string1 );
17
18      copy2( string3, string4 );
19      printf( "string3 = %s\n", string3 );
20
21      return 0; /* indicates successful termination */
22
23   } /* end main */
24
```

Fig. 7.21 | Copying a string using array notation and pointer notation. (Part 1 of 2.)

```
25   /* copy s2 to s1 using array notation */
26   void copy1( char * const s1, const char * const s2 )
27   {
28      int i; /* counter */
29
30      /* loop through strings */
31      for ( i = 0; ( s1[ i ] = s2[ i ] ) != '\0'; i++ ) {
32         ; /* do nothing in body */
33      } /* end for */
34
35   } /* end function copy1 */
36
37   /* copy s2 to s1 using pointer notation */
38   void copy2( char *s1, const char *s2 )
39   {
40      /* loop through strings */
41      for ( ; ( *s1 = *s2 ) != '\0'; s1++, s2++ ) {
42         ; /* do nothing in body */
43      } /* end for */
44
45   } /* end function copy2 */
```

```
string1 = Hello
string3 = Good Bye
```

Fig. 7.21 | Copying a string using array notation and pointer notation. (Part 2 of 2.)

Function copy1 uses array subscript notation to copy the string in s2 to the character array s1. The function defines counter variable i as the array subscript. The for statement header (line 31) performs the entire copy operation—its body is the empty statement. The header specifies that i is initialized to zero and incremented by one on each iteration of the loop. The expression s1[i] = s2[i] copies one character from s2 to s1. When the null character is encountered in s2, it is assigned to s1, and the value of the assignment becomes the value assigned to the left operand (s1). The loop terminates because the integer value of the null character is zero (false).

Function copy2 uses pointers and pointer arithmetic to copy the string in s2 to the character array s1. Again, the for statement header (line 41) performs the entire copy operation. The header does not include any variable initialization. As in function copy1, the expression (*s1 = *s2) performs the copy operation. Pointer s2 is dereferenced, and the resulting character is assigned to the dereferenced pointer *s1. After the assignment in the condition, the pointers are incremented to point to the next element of array s1 and the next character of string s2, respectively. When the null character is encountered in s2, it is assigned to the dereferenced pointer s1 and the loop terminates.

Note that the first argument to both copy1 and copy2 must be an array large enough to hold the string in the second argument. Otherwise, an error may occur when an attempt is made to write into a memory location that is not part of the array. Also, note that the second parameter of each function is declared as const char * (a constant string). In both functions, the second argument is copied into the first argument—characters are read from it one at a time, but the characters are never modified. Therefore, the second parameter is declared to point to a constant value so that the principle of least privilege is enforced—neither function requires the capability of modifying the second argument, so neither function is provided with that capability.

7.10 Arrays of Pointers

Arrays may contain pointers. A common use of an **array of pointers** is to form an **array of strings**, referred to simply as a **string array**. Each entry in the array is a string, but in C a string is essentially a pointer to its first character. So each entry in an array of strings is actually a pointer to the first character of a string. Consider the definition of string array `suit`, which might be useful in representing a deck of cards.

```
const char *suit[ 4 ] = { "Hearts", "Diamonds", "Clubs", "Spades" };
```

The `suit[ 4 ]` portion of the definition indicates an array of 4 elements. The `char *` portion of the declaration indicates that each element of array `suit` is of type "pointer to `char`." Qualifier `const` indicates that the strings pointed to by each element pointer will not be modified. The four values to be placed in the array are `"Hearts"`, `"Diamonds"`, `"Clubs"` and `"Spades"`. Each is stored in memory as a null-terminated character string that is one character longer than the number of characters between quotes. The four strings are 7, 9, 6 and 7 characters long, respectively. Although it appears as though these strings are being placed in the `suit` array, only pointers are actually stored in the array (Fig. 7.22). Each pointer points to the first character of its corresponding string. Thus, even though the `suit` array is fixed in size, it provides access to character strings of any length. This flexibility is one example of C's powerful data-structuring capabilities.

The suits could have been placed into a two-dimensional array, in which each row would represent one suit and each column would represent one of the letters of a suit name. Such a data structure would have to have a fixed number of columns per row, and that number would have to be as large as the largest string. Therefore, considerable memory could be wasted when a large number of strings were being stored with most strings shorter than the longest string. We use string arrays to represent a deck of cards in the next section.

7.11 Case Study: Card Shuffling and Dealing Simulation

In this section, we use random number generation to develop a card shuffling and dealing simulation program. This program can then be used to implement programs that play specific card games. To reveal some subtle performance problems, we have intentionally

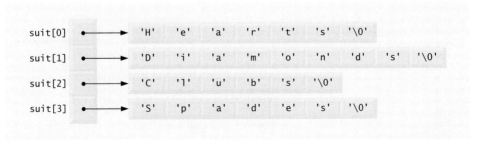

Fig. 7.22 | Graphical representation of the `suit` array.

used suboptimal shuffling and dealing algorithms. In the exercises and in Chapter 10, we develop more efficient algorithms.

Using the top-down, stepwise refinement approach, we develop a program that will shuffle a deck of 52 playing cards and then deal each of the 52 cards. The top-down approach is particularly useful in attacking larger, more complex problems than we have seen in the early chapters.

We use 4-by-13 double-subscripted array deck to represent the deck of playing cards (Fig. 7.23). The rows correspond to the suits—row 0 corresponds to hearts, row 1 to diamonds, row 2 to clubs and row 3 to spades. The columns correspond to the face values of the cards—columns 0 through 9 correspond to ace through ten respectively, and columns 10 through 12 correspond to jack, queen and king. We shall load string array suit with character strings representing the four suits, and string array face with character strings representing the thirteen face values.

This simulated deck of cards may be shuffled as follows. First the array deck is cleared to zeros. Then, a row (0–3) and a column (0–12) are each chosen at random. The number 1 is inserted in array element deck[row][column] to indicate that this card is going to be the first one dealt from the shuffled deck. This process continues with the numbers 2, 3, ..., 52 being randomly inserted in the deck array to indicate which cards are to be placed second, third, ..., and fifty-second in the shuffled deck. As the deck array begins to fill with card numbers, it is possible that a card will be selected twice—i.e., deck[row][column] will be nonzero when it is selected. This selection is simply ignored and other rows and columns are repeatedly chosen at random until an unselected card is found. Eventually, the numbers 1 through 52 will occupy the 52 slots of the deck array. At this point, the deck of cards is fully shuffled.

This shuffling algorithm could execute indefinitely if cards that have already been shuffled are repeatedly selected at random. This phenomenon is known as indefinite postponement. In the exercises, we discuss a better shuffling algorithm that eliminates the possibility of indefinite postponement.

Performance Tip 7.3

Sometimes an algorithm that emerges in a "natural" way can contain subtle performance problems, such as indefinite postponement. Seek algorithms that avoid indefinite postponement.

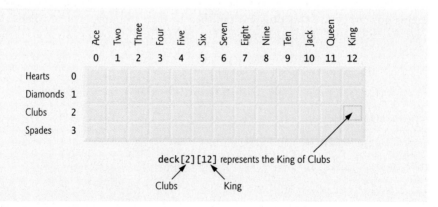

Fig. 7.23 | Double-subscripted array representation of a deck of cards.

To deal the first card, we search the array for deck[row][column] equal to 1. This is accomplished with a nested for statement that varies row from 0 to 3 and column from 0 to 12. What card does that element of the array correspond to? The suit array has been preloaded with the four suits, so to get the suit, we print the character string suit[row]. Similarly, to get the face value of the card, we print the character string face[column]. We also print the character string " of ". Printing this information in the proper order enables us to print each card in the form "King of Clubs", "Ace of Diamonds" and so on.

Let us proceed with the top-down, stepwise refinement process. The top is simply

Shuffle and deal 52 cards

Our first refinement yields:

Initialize the suit array
Initialize the face array
Initialize the deck array
Shuffle the deck
Deal 52 cards

"Shuffle the deck" may be expanded as follows:

For each of the 52 cards
Place card number in randomly selected unoccupied slot of deck

"Deal 52 cards" may be expanded as follows:

For each of the 52 cards
Find card number in deck array and print face and suit of card

Incorporating these expansions yields our complete second refinement:

Initialize the suit array
Initialize the face array
Initialize the deck array

For each of the 52 cards
Place card number in randomly selected unoccupied slot of deck

For each of the 52 cards
Find card number in deck array and print face and suit of card

"Place card number in randomly selected unoccupied slot of deck" may be expanded as follows:

Choose slot of deck randomly

While chosen slot of deck has been previously chosen
Choose slot of deck randomly

Place card number in chosen slot of deck

"Find card number in deck array and print face and suit of card" may be expanded as follows:

For each slot of the deck array
If slot contains card number
Print the face and suit of the card

Incorporating these expansions yields our third refinement:

Initialize the suit array
Initialize the face array
Initialize the deck array

For each of the 52 cards
   Choose slot of deck randomly

      While slot of deck has been previously chosen
         Choose slot of deck randomly

   Place card number in chosen slot of deck

For each of the 52 cards
   For each slot of deck array
      If slot contains desired card number
         Print the face and suit of the card

This completes the refinement process. Note that this program is more efficient if the shuffle and deal portions of the algorithm are combined so that each card is dealt as it is placed in the deck. We have chosen to program these operations separately because normally cards are dealt after they are shuffled (not while they are shuffled).

The card shuffling and dealing program is shown in Fig. 7.24, and a sample execution is shown in Fig. 7.25. Note the use of the conversion specifier %s to print strings of characters in the calls to printf. The corresponding argument in the printf call must be a pointer to char (or a char array). In the deal function, the format specification "%5s of %-8s" (line 76) prints a character string right justified in a field of five characters followed by " of " and a character string left justified in a field of eight characters. The minus sign in %-8s signifies that the string is left justified in a field of width 8.

```
1   /* Fig. 7.24: fig07_24.c
2      Card shuffling dealing program */
3   #include <stdio.h>
4   #include <stdlib.h>
5   #include <time.h>
6
7   /* prototypes */
8   void shuffle( int wDeck[][ 13 ] );
9   void deal( const int wDeck[][ 13 ], const char *wFace[],
10             const char *wSuit[] );
11
12  int main( void )
13  {
14     /* initialize suit array */
15     const char *suit[ 4 ] = { "Hearts", "Diamonds", "Clubs", "Spades" };
16
17     /* initialize face array */
18     const char *face[ 13 ] =
19        { "Ace", "Deuce", "Three", "Four",
20          "Five", "Six", "Seven", "Eight",
21          "Nine", "Ten", "Jack", "Queen", "King" };
```

Fig. 7.24 | Card dealing program. (Part 1 of 3.)

```
22
23       /* initialize deck array */
24       int deck[ 4 ][ 13 ] = { 0 };
25
26       srand( time( 0 ) ); /* seed random-number generator */
27
28       shuffle( deck );
29       deal( deck, face, suit );
30
31       return 0; /* indicates successful termination */
32
33    } /* end main */
34
35    /* shuffle cards in deck */
36    void shuffle( int wDeck[][ 13 ] )
37    {
38       int row;    /* row number */
39       int column; /* column number */
40       int card;   /* counter */
41
42       /* for each of the 52 cards, choose slot of deck randomly */
43       for ( card = 1; card <= 52; card++ ) {
44
45          /* choose new random location until unoccupied slot found */
46          do {
47             row = rand() % 4;
48             column = rand() % 13;
49          } while( wDeck[ row ][ column ] != 0 ); /* end do...while */
50
51          /* place card number in chosen slot of deck */
52          wDeck[ row ][ column ] = card;
53       } /* end for */
54
55    } /* end function shuffle */
56
57    /* deal cards in deck */
58    void deal( const int wDeck[][ 13 ], const char *wFace[],
59               const char *wSuit[] )
60    {
61       int card;   /* card counter */
62       int row;    /* row counter */
63       int column; /* column counter */
64
65       /* deal each of the 52 cards */
66       for ( card = 1; card <= 52; card++ ) {
67          /* loop through rows of wDeck */
68
69          for ( row = 0; row <= 3; row++ ) {
70
71             /* loop through columns of wDeck for current row */
72             for ( column = 0; column <= 12; column++ ) {
73
```

Fig. 7.24 | Card dealing program. (Part 2 of 3.)

```
74              /* if slot contains current card, display card */
75              if ( wDeck[ row ][ column ] == card ) {
76                  printf( "%5s of %-8s%c", wFace[ column ], wSuit[ row ],
77                      card % 2 == 0 ? '\n' : '\t' );
78              } /* end if */
79
80          } /* end for */
81
82      } /* end for */
83
84  } /* end for */
85
86  } /* end function deal */
```

Fig. 7.24 | Card dealing program. (Part 3 of 3.)

Nine of Hearts	Five of Clubs
Queen of Spades	Three of Spades
Queen of Hearts	Ace of Clubs
King of Hearts	Six of Spades
Jack of Diamonds	Five of Spades
Seven of Hearts	King of Clubs
Three of Clubs	Eight of Hearts
Three of Diamonds	Four of Diamonds
Queen of Diamonds	Five of Diamonds
Six of Diamonds	Five of Hearts
Ace of Spades	Six of Hearts
Nine of Diamonds	Queen of Clubs
Eight of Spades	Nine of Clubs
Deuce of Clubs	Six of Clubs
Deuce of Spades	Jack of Clubs
Four of Clubs	Eight of Clubs
Four of Spades	Seven of Spades
Seven of Diamonds	Seven of Clubs
King of Spades	Ten of Diamonds
Jack of Hearts	Ace of Hearts
Jack of Spades	Ten of Clubs
Eight of Diamonds	Deuce of Diamonds
Ace of Diamonds	Nine of Spades
Four of Hearts	Deuce of Hearts
King of Diamonds	Ten of Spades
Three of Hearts	Ten of Hearts

Fig. 7.25 | Sample run of card dealing program.

There is a weakness in the dealing algorithm. Once a match is found, even if it is found on the first try, the two inner **for** statements continue searching the remaining elements of deck for a match. We correct this deficiency in the exercises and in a case study in Chapter 10.

7.12 Pointers to Functions

A pointer to a function contains the address of the function in memory. In Chapter 6, we saw that an array name is really the address in memory of the first element of the array.

Similarly, a function name is really the starting address in memory of the code that performs the function's task. Pointers to functions can be passed to functions, returned from functions, stored in arrays and assigned to other function pointers.

To illustrate the use of pointers to functions, Fig. 7.26 presents a modified version of the bubble sort program in Fig. 7.15. The new version consists of main and functions bubble, swap, ascending and descending. Function bubbleSort receives a pointer to a function—either function ascending or function descending—as an argument, in addition to an integer array and the size of the array. The program prompts the user to choose whether the array should be sorted in ascending or in descending order. If the user enters 1, a pointer to function ascending is passed to function bubble, causing the array to be sorted into increasing order. If the user enters 2, a pointer to function descending is passed to function bubble, causing the array to be sorted into decreasing order. The output of the program is shown in Fig. 7.27.

```c
 1   /* Fig. 7.26: fig07_26.c
 2      Multipurpose sorting program using function pointers */
 3   #include <stdio.h>
 4   #define SIZE 10
 5
 6   /* prototypes */
 7   void bubble( int work[], const int size, int (*compare)( int a, int b ) );
 8   int ascending( int a, int b );
 9   int descending( int a, int b );
10
11   int main( void )
12   {
13      int order;    /* 1 for ascending order or 2 for descending order */
14      int counter; /* counter */
15
16      /* initialize array a */
17      int a[ SIZE ] = { 2, 6, 4, 8, 10, 12, 89, 68, 45, 37 };
18
19      printf( "Enter 1 to sort in ascending order,\n"
20              "Enter 2 to sort in descending order: " );
21      scanf( "%d", &order );
22
23      printf( "\nData items in original order\n" );
24
25      /* output original array */
26      for ( counter = 0; counter < SIZE; counter++ ) {
27         printf( "%5d", a[ counter ] );
28      } /* end for */
29
30      /* sort array in ascending order; pass function ascending as an
31         argument to specify ascending sorting order */
32      if ( order == 1 ) {
33         bubble( a, SIZE, ascending );
34         printf( "\nData items in ascending order\n" );
35      } /* end if */
```

Fig. 7.26 | Multipurpose sorting program using function pointers. (Part 1 of 3.)

```
36         else { /* pass function descending */
37            bubble( a, SIZE, descending );
38            printf( "\nData items in descending order\n" );
39         } /* end else */
40
41         /* output sorted array */
42         for ( counter = 0; counter < SIZE; counter++ ) {
43            printf( "%5d", a[ counter ] );
44         } /* end for */
45
46         printf( "\n" );
47
48         return 0; /* indicates successful termination */
49
50      } /* end main */
51
52      /* multipurpose bubble sort; parameter compare is a pointer to
53         the comparison function that determines sorting order */
54      void bubble( int work[], const int size, int (*compare)( int a, int b ) )
55      {
56         int pass;   /* pass counter */
57         int count;  /* comparison counter */
58
59         void swap( int *element1Ptr, int *element2ptr ); /* prototype */
60
61         /* loop to control passes */
62         for ( pass = 1; pass < size; pass++ ) {
63
64            /* loop to control number of comparisons per pass */
65            for ( count = 0; count < size - 1; count++ ) {
66
67               /* if adjacent elements are out of order, swap them */
68               if ( (*compare)( work[ count ], work[ count + 1 ] ) ) {
69                  swap( &work[ count ], &work[ count + 1 ] );
70               } /* end if */
71
72            } /* end for */
73
74         } /* end for */
75
76      } /* end function bubble */
77
78      /* swap values at memory locations to which element1Ptr and
79         element2Ptr point */
80      void swap( int *element1Ptr, int *element2Ptr )
81      {
82         int hold; /* temporary holding variable */
83
84         hold = *element1Ptr;
85         *element1Ptr = *element2Ptr;
86         *element2Ptr = hold;
87      } /* end function swap */
88
```

Fig. 7.26 | Multipurpose sorting program using function pointers. (Part 2 of 3.)

```
89   /* determine whether elements are out of order for an ascending
90      order sort */
91   int ascending( int a, int b )
92   {
93      return b < a; /* swap if b is less than a */
94
95   } /* end function ascending */
96
97   /* determine whether elements are out of order for a descending
98      order sort */
99   int descending( int a, int b )
100  {
101     return b > a; /* swap if b is greater than a */
102
103  } /* end function descending */
```

Fig. 7.26 | Multipurpose sorting program using function pointers. (Part 3 of 3.)

```
Enter 1 to sort in ascending order,
Enter 2 to sort in descending order: 1

Data items in original order
    2    6    4    8   10   12   89   68   45   37
Data items in ascending order
    2    4    6    8   10   12   37   45   68   89
```

```
Enter 1 to sort in ascending order,
Enter 2 to sort in descending order: 2

Data items in original order
    2    6    4    8   10   12   89   68   45   37
Data items in descending order
   89   68   45   37   12   10    8    6    4    2
```

Fig. 7.27 | The outputs of the bubble sort program in Fig. 7.26.

The following parameter appears in the function header for bubble (line 54)

```
int (*compare)( int a, int b )
```

This tells bubble to expect a parameter (compare) that is a pointer to a function that receives two integer parameters and returns an integer result. Parentheses are needed around *compare to group * with compare to indicate that compare is a pointer. If we had not included the parentheses, the declaration would have been

```
int *compare( int a, int b )
```

which declares a function that receives two integers as parameters and returns a pointer to an integer.

The function prototype for bubble is shown in line 7. Note that the prototype could have been written as

```
int (*)( int, int );
```

without the function-pointer name and parameter names.

The function passed to bubble is called in an if statement (line 68) as follows:

```
if ( (*compare)( work[ count ], work[ count + 1 ] ) )
```

Just as a pointer to a variable is dereferenced to access the value of the variable, a pointer to a function is dereferenced to use the function.

The call to the function could have been made without dereferencing the pointer as in

```
if ( compare( work[ count ], work[ count + 1 ] ) )
```

which uses the pointer directly as the function name. We prefer the first method of calling a function through a pointer because it explicitly illustrates that compare is a pointer to a function that is dereferenced to call the function. The second method of calling a function through a pointer makes it appear as though compare is an actual function. This may be confusing to a user of the program who would like to see the definition of function compare and finds that it is never defined in the file.

Using Function Pointers to Create a Menu-Driven System

A common use of **function pointers** is in so-called menu-driven systems. A user is prompted to select an option from a menu (possibly from 1 to 5). Each option is serviced by a different function. Pointers to each function are stored in an array of pointers to functions. The user's choice is used as a subscript in the array, and the pointer in the array is used to call the function.

Figure 7.28 provides a generic example of the mechanics of defining and using an array of pointers to functions. Three functions are defined—function1, function2 and function3—that each take an integer argument and return nothing. Pointers to these three functions are stored in array f, which is defined (line 14) as follows:

```
void ( *f[ 3 ] )( int ) = { function1, function2, function3 };
```

```
1   /* Fig. 7.28: fig07_28.c
2      Demonstrating an array of pointers to functions */
3   #include <stdio.h>
4
5   /* prototypes */
6   void function1( int a );
7   void function2( int b );
8   void function3( int c );
9
10  int main( void )
11  {
```

Fig. 7.28 | Demonstrating an array of pointers to functions. (Part 1 of 2.)

```
12      /* initialize array of 3 pointers to functions that each take an
13         int argument and return void */
14      void (*f[ 3 ])( int ) = { function1, function2, function3 };
15
16      int choice; /* variable to hold user's choice */
17
18      printf( "Enter a number between 0 and 2, 3 to end: " );
19      scanf( "%d", &choice );
20
21      /* process user's choice */
22      while ( choice >= 0 && choice < 3 ) {
23
24         /* invoke function at location choice in array f and pass
25            choice as an argument */
26         (*f[ choice ])( choice );
27
28         printf( "Enter a number between 0 and 2, 3 to end: ");
29         scanf( "%d", &choice );
30      } /* end while */
31
32      printf( "Program execution completed.\n" );
33
34      return 0; /* indicates successful termination */
35
36   } /* end main */
37
38   void function1( int a )
39   {
40      printf( "You entered %d so function1 was called\n\n", a );
41   } /* end function1 */
42
43   void function2( int b )
44   {
45      printf( "You entered %d so function2 was called\n\n", b );
46   } /* end function2 */
47
48   void function3( int c )
49   {
50      printf( "You entered %d so function3 was called\n\n", c );
51   } /* end function3 */
```

```
Enter a number between 0 and 2, 3 to end: 0
You entered 0 so function1 was called

Enter a number between 0 and 2, 3 to end: 1
You entered 1 so function2 was called

Enter a number between 0 and 2, 3 to end: 2
You entered 2 so function3 was called

Enter a number between 0 and 2, 3 to end: 3
Program execution completed.
```

Fig. 7.28 | Demonstrating an array of pointers to functions. (Part 2 of 2.)

The definition is read beginning in the leftmost set of parentheses, "f is an array of 3 pointers to functions that take an int as an argument and that return void." The array is initialized with the names of the three functions. When the user enters a value between 0 and 2, the value is used as the subscript in the array of pointers to functions. The function call (line 26) is made as follows:

```
(*f[ choice ])( choice );
```

In the function call, f[choice] selects the pointer at location choice in the array. The pointer is dereferenced to call the function, and choice is passed as the argument to the function. Each function prints its argument's value and its function name to demonstrate that the function is called correctly. In the exercises, you'll develop a menu-driven system.

Summary

Section 7.2 Pointer Variable Definitions and Initialization

- A pointer contains an address of another variable that contains a value. In this sense, a variable name *directly* references a value, and a pointer *indirectly* references a value.
- Referencing a value through a pointer is called indirection.
- Pointers, like all variables, must be defined before they can be used.
- Pointers can be defined to point to objects of any type.
- Pointers should be initialized either when they are defined or in an assignment statement. A pointer may be initialized to 0, NULL or an address. A pointer with the value NULL points to nothing. Initializing a pointer to 0 is equivalent to initializing a pointer to NULL, but NULL is preferred. When 0 is assigned, it is first converted to a pointer of the appropriate type. The value 0 is the only integer value that can be assigned directly to a pointer variable.
- NULL is a symbolic constant defined in the <stddef.h> header (and several other headers, such as <stdio.h>).

Section 7.3 Pointer Operators

- The &, or address operator, is a unary operator that returns the address of its operand.
- The operand of the address operator must be a variable; the address operator cannot be applied to constants, to expressions or to variables declared with the storage-class register.
- The unary * operator, commonly referred to as the indirection operator or dereferencing operator, returns the value of the object to which its operand (i.e., a pointer) points.
- The printf conversion specifier %p outputs a memory location as a hexadecimal integer on most platforms.

Section 7.4 Passing Arguments to Functions by Reference

- There are two ways to pass arguments to a function—call-by-value and call-by-reference. All arguments in C are passed by value.
- Many functions require the capability to modify one or more variables in the caller or to pass a pointer to a large data object to avoid the overhead of passing the object by value. For these purposes, C provides the capabilities for simulating call-by-reference.
- In C, you use pointers and the indirection operator to simulate call-by-reference. When calling a function with arguments that should be modified, the addresses of the arguments are passed.

This is normally accomplished by applying the address operator (&) to the variable (in the caller) whose value will be modified.

- When the address of a variable is passed to a function, the indirection operator (*) may be used in the function to modify the value at that location in the caller's memory.

- A function receiving an address as an argument must define a pointer parameter to receive the address.

- As with other variable types, it is not necessary to include names of pointers in function prototypes. Names included for documentation purposes are ignored by the C compiler.

- The compiler does not differentiate between a function that receives a pointer and a function that receives a single-subscripted array. This, of course, means that the function must "know" when it is receiving an array or simply a single variable for which it is to perform call-by-reference.

- When the compiler encounters a function parameter for a single-subscripted array of the form int b[], the compiler converts the parameter to the pointer notation int *b. The two forms are interchangeable.

Section 7.5 Using the `const` Qualifier with Pointers

- The const qualifier enables you to inform the compiler that the value of a particular variable should not be modified.

- Six possibilities exist for using (or not using) const with function parameters—two with call-by-value parameter passing and four with call-by-reference parameter passing. How do you choose one of the six possibilities? Let the principle of least privilege be your guide. Always award a function enough access to the data in its parameters to accomplish its specified task, but no more.

- If an attempt is made to modify a value that is declared const, the compiler catches it and issues either a warning or an error, depending on the particular compiler.

- There are four ways to pass a pointer to a function: a non-constant pointer to non-constant data, a constant pointer to non-constant data, a non-constant pointer to constant data, and a constant pointer to constant data.

- The highest level of data access is granted by a non-constant pointer to non-constant data. In this case, the data can be modified through the dereferenced pointer, and the pointer can be modified to point to other data items.

- A non-constant pointer to constant data can be modified to point to any data item of the appropriate type, but the data to which it points cannot be modified.

- A constant pointer to non-constant data always points to the same memory location, and the data at that location can be modified through the pointer. This is the default for an array name. An array name is a constant pointer to the beginning of the array. All data in the array can be accessed and changed by using the array name and array subscripting.

- The least access privilege is granted by a constant pointer to constant data. Such a pointer always points to the same memory location, and the data at that memory location cannot be modified.

Section 7.7 `sizeof` Operator

- C provides the special unary operator sizeof to determine the size in bytes of an array (or any other data type) during program compilation.

- When applied to the name of an array as in, the sizeof operator returns the total number of bytes in the array as an integer.

- Type size_t is a type defined by the C standard as the integral type (unsigned or unsigned long) of the value returned by operator sizeof. Type size_t is defined in header <stddef.h> (which is included by several headers, such as <stdio.h>).

- Operator sizeof can be applied to any variable name, type or value. When applied to a variable name (that is not an array name) or a constant, the number of bytes used to store the specific type of variable or constant is returned. Note that the parentheses used with sizeof are required if a type name is supplied as its operand. Omitting the parentheses in this case results in a syntax error. The parentheses are not required if a variable name is supplied as its operand.

Section 7.8 Pointer Expressions and Pointer Arithmetic

- A limited set of arithmetic operations may be performed on pointers. A pointer may be incremented (++) or decremented (--), an integer may be added to a pointer (+ or +=), an integer may be subtracted from a pointer (- or -=) and one pointer may be subtracted from another.

- When an integer is added to or subtracted from a pointer, the pointer is not incremented or decremented simply by that integer, but by that integer times the size of the object to which the pointer refers. The number of bytes depends on the object's data type.

- When performing pointer arithmetic on a character array, the results will be consistent with regular arithmetic because each character is 1 byte long.

- Pointer variables may be subtracted from one another to determine the number of elements between two elements of an array.

- Pointer arithmetic is meaningless unless performed on an array. We cannot assume that two variables of the same type are stored contiguously in memory unless they are adjacent array elements.

- A pointer can be assigned to another pointer if both pointers are of the same type. The exception to this rule is the pointer to void (i.e., void *), which is a generic pointer that can represent any pointer type. All pointer types can be assigned a pointer to void, and a pointer to void can be assigned a pointer of any type. In both cases, a cast operation is not required.

- A pointer to void cannot be dereferenced. The compiler must know the data type to determine the number of bytes to be dereferenced for a particular pointer.

- Pointers can be compared using equality and relational operators, but such comparisons are meaningless unless the pointers point to elements of the same array. Pointer comparisons compare the addresses stored in the pointers. A comparison of two pointers pointing to elements in the same array could show, for example, that one pointer points to a higher-numbered element of the array than the other pointer does.

- A common use of pointer comparison is determining whether a pointer is NULL.

Section 7.9 Relationship between Pointers and Arrays

- Arrays and pointers are intimately related in C and often may be used interchangeably.

- An array name can be thought of as a constant pointer.

- Pointers can be used to do any operation involving array subscripting.

- When a pointer points to the beginning of an array, adding an offset to the pointer indicates which element of the array should be referenced, and the offset value is identical to the array subscript. This is referred to as pointer/offset notation.

- The array itself can be treated as a pointer and used in pointer arithmetic.

- Pointers can be subscripted exactly as arrays can. This is referred to as pointer/subscript notation.

- A parameter of type const char * typically represents a constant string.

Section 7.10 Arrays of Pointers

- Arrays may contain pointers. A common use of an array of pointers is to form an array of strings. Each entry in the array is a string, but in C a string is essentially a pointer to its first character. So each entry in an array of strings is actually a pointer to the first character of a string.

Section 7.12 Pointers to Functions

- A pointer to a function contains the address of the function in memory. A function name is really the starting address in memory of the code that performs the function's task.

- Pointers to functions can be passed to functions, returned from functions, stored in arrays and assigned to other function pointers.

- Just as a pointer to a variable is dereferenced to access the value of the variable, a pointer to a function is dereferenced to use the function.

- A function pointer can be used directly as the function name when calling the function.

- A common use of function pointers is in menu-driven systems.

Terminology

adding a pointer and an integer	non-constant pointer to constant data
address operator (&)	non-constant pointer to non-constant data
array of pointers	NULL pointer
array of strings	offset
call-by-reference	pointer
call-by-value	pointer arithmetic
character pointer	pointer assignment
const	pointer comparison
constant pointer	pointer expression
constant pointer to constant data	pointer indexing
constant pointer to non-constant data	pointer/offset notation
decrement a pointer	pointer subscripting
dereference a pointer	pointer to a function
dereferencing operator (*)	pointer to void (void *)
directly reference a variable	pointer types
dynamic memory allocation	principle of least privilege
function pointer	simulated call by reference
increment a pointer	sizeof operator
indefinite postponement	size_t type
indirection	string array
indirection operator (*)	subtracting an integer from a pointer
indirectly reference a variable	subtracting two pointers
initializing pointers	top-down, stepwise refinement
linked list	void * (pointer to void)

Self-Review Exercises

7.1 Answer each of the following:

a) A pointer variable contains as its value the _____ of another variable.

b) The three values that can be used to initialize a pointer are _____, _____, _____ or a(n) _____.

c) The only integer that can be assigned to a pointer is _____.

7.2 State whether the following are *true* or *false*. If the answer is *false*, explain why.

a) The address operator (&) can be applied only to constants, to expressions and to variables declared with the storage-class register.

b) A pointer that is declared to be void can be dereferenced.

c) Pointers of different types may not be assigned to one another without a cast operation.

7.3   Answer each of the following. Assume that single-precision floating-point numbers are stored in 4 bytes, and that the starting address of the array is at location 1002500 in memory. Each part of the exercise should use the results of previous parts where appropriate.

    a) Define an array of type float called numbers with 10 elements, and initialize the elements to the values 0.0, 1.1, 2.2, ..., 9.9. Assume the symbolic constant SIZE has been defined as 10.

    b) Define a pointer, nPtr, that points to an object of type float.

    c) Print the elements of array numbers using array subscript notation. Use a for statement and assume the integer control variable i has been defined. Print each number with 1 position of precision to the right of the decimal point.

    d) Give two separate statements that assign the starting address of array numbers to the pointer variable nPtr.

    e) Print the elements of array numbers using pointer/offset notation with the pointer nPtr.

    f) Print the elements of array numbers using pointer/offset notation with the array name as the pointer.

    g) Print the elements of array numbers by subscripting pointer nPtr.

    h) Refer to element 4 of array numbers using array subscript notation, pointer/offset notation with the array name as the pointer, pointer subscript notation with nPtr and pointer/offset notation with nPtr.

    i) Assuming that nPtr points to the beginning of array numbers, what address is referenced by nPtr + 8? What value is stored at that location?

    j) Assuming that nPtr points to numbers[5], what address is referenced by nPtr -= 4. What is the value stored at that location?

7.4   For each of the following, write a statement that performs the indicated task. Assume that floating-point variables number1 and number2 are defined and that number1 is initialized to 7.3.

    a) Define the variable fPtr to be a pointer to an object of type float.

    b) Assign the address of variable number1 to pointer variable fPtr.

    c) Print the value of the object pointed to by fPtr.

    d) Assign the value of the object pointed to by fPtr to variable number2.

    e) Print the value of number2.

    f) Print the address of number1. Use the %p conversion specifier.

    g) Print the address stored in fPtr. Use the %p conversion specifier. Is the value printed the same as the address of number1?

7.5   Do each of the following:

    a) Write the function header for a function called exchange that takes two pointers to floating-point numbers x and y as parameters and does not return a value.

    b) Write the function prototype for the function in part (a).

    c) Write the function header for a function called evaluate that returns an integer and that takes as parameters integer x and a pointer to function poly. Function poly takes an integer parameter and returns an integer.

    d) Write the function prototype for the function in part (c).

7.6   Find the error in each of the following program segments. Assume

```
int *zPtr; /* zPtr will reference array z */
int *aPtr = NULL;
void *sPtr = NULL;
int number, i;
int z[ 5 ] = { 1, 2, 3, 4, 5 };
sPtr = z;
```

    a) ++zptr;

b) /* use pointer to get first value of array; assume zPtr is initialized */
    number = zPtr;

c) /* assign array element 2 (the value 3) to number;
        assume zPtr is initialized */
    number = *zPtr[2];

d) /* print entire array z; assume zPtr is initialized */
    for (i = 0; i <= 5; i++)
        printf("%d ", zPtr[i]);

e) /* assign the value pointed to by sPtr to number */
    number = *sPtr;

f) ++z;

Answers to Self-Review Exercises

7.1 a) address. b) 0, NULL, an address. c) 0.

7.2 a) False. The address operator can be applied only to variables. The address operator cannot be applied to variables declared with storage class register.

b) False. A pointer to void cannot be dereferenced, because there is no way to know exactly how many bytes of memory to dereference.

c) False. Pointers of type void can be assigned pointers of other types, and pointers of type void can be assigned to pointers of other types.

7.3 a) float numbers[SIZE] =
            { 0.0, 1.1, 2.2, 3.3, 4.4, 5.5, 6.6, 7.7, 8.8, 9.9 };

b) float *nPtr;

c) for (i = 0; i < SIZE; i++)
        printf("%.1f ", numbers[i]);

d) nPtr = numbers;
   nPtr = &numbers[0];

e) for (i = 0; i < SIZE; i++)
        printf("%.1f ", *(nPtr + i));

f) for (i = 0; i < SIZE; i++)
        printf("%.1f ", *(numbers + i));

g) for (i = 0; i < SIZE; i++)
        printf("%.1f ", nPtr[i]);

h) numbers[4]
   *(numbers + 4)
   nPtr[4]
   *(nPtr + 4)

i) The address is 1002500 + 8 * 4 = 1002532. The value is 8.8.

j) The address of numbers[5] is 1002500 + 5 * 4 = 1002520.
   The address of nPtr -= 4 is 1002520 - 4 * 4 = 1002504.
   The value at that location is 1.1.

7.4 a) float *fPtr;

b) fPtr = &number1;

c) printf("The value of *fPtr is %f\n", *fPtr);

d) number2 = *fPtr;

e) printf("The value of number2 is %f\n", number2);

f) printf("The address of number1 is %p\n", &number1);

g) printf("The address stored in fptr is %p\n", fPtr);
   Yes, the value is the same.

7.5 a) `void exchange( float *x, float *y )`

b) `void exchange( float *x, float *y );`

c) `int evaluate( int x, int (*poly)( int ) )`

d) `int evaluate( int x, int (*poly)( int ) );`

7.6 a) Error: `zPtr` has not been initialized.

Correction: Initialize `zPtr` with `zPtr = z;` before performing the pointer arithmetic.

b) Error: The pointer is not dereferenced.

Correction: Change the statement to `number = *zPtr;`

c) Error: `zPtr[ 2 ]` is not a pointer and should not be dereferenced.

Correction: Change `*zPtr[ 2 ]` to `zPtr[ 2 ]`.

d) Error: Referring to an array element outside the array bounds with pointer subscripting.

Correction: Change the operator `<=` in the `for` condition to `<`.

e) Error: Dereferencing a void pointer.

Correction: In order to dereference the pointer, it must first be cast to an integer pointer. Change the statement to `number = *( ( int * ) sPtr );`

f) Error: Trying to modify an array name with pointer arithmetic.

Correction: Use a pointer variable instead of the array name to accomplish pointer arithmetic, or subscript the array name to refer to a specific element.

Exercises

7.7 Answer each of the following:

a) The _____ operator returns the location in memory where its operand is stored.

b) The _____ operator returns the value of the object to which its operand points.

c) To simulate call-by-reference when passing a nonarray variable to a function, it is necessary to pass the _____ of the variable to the function.

7.8 State whether the following are *true* or *false*. If *false*, explain why.

a) Two pointers that point to different arrays cannot be compared meaningfully.

b) Because the name of an array is a pointer to the first element of the array, array names may be manipulated in precisely the same manner as pointers.

7.9 Answer each of the following. Assume that unsigned integers are stored in 2 bytes and that the starting address of the array is at location 1002500 in memory.

a) Define an array of type `unsigned int` called `values` with five elements, and initialize the elements to the even integers from 2 to 10. Assume the symbolic constant `SIZE` has been defined as 5.

b) Define a pointer `vPtr` that points to an object of type `unsigned int`.

c) Print the elements of array `values` using array subscript notation. Use a `for` statement and assume integer control variable `i` has been defined.

d) Give two separate statements that assign the starting address of array `values` to pointer variable `vPtr`.

e) Print the elements of array `values` using pointer/offset notation.

f) Print the elements of array `values` using pointer/offset notation with the array name as the pointer.

g) Print the elements of array `values` by subscripting the pointer to the array.

h) Refer to element 5 of array `values` using array subscript notation, pointer/offset notation with the array name as the pointer, pointer subscript notation, and pointer/offset notation.

i) What address is referenced by `vPtr + 3`? What value is stored at that location?

j) Assuming `vPtr` points to `values[ 4 ]`, what address is referenced by `vPtr -= 4`. What value is stored at that location?

7.10 For each of the following, write a single statement that performs the indicated task. Assume that long integer variables value1 and value2 have been defined and that value1 has been initialized to 200000.

    a) Define the variable lPtr to be a pointer to an object of type long.
    b) Assign the address of variable value1 to pointer variable lPtr.
    c) Print the value of the object pointed to by lPtr.
    d) Assign the value of the object pointed to by lPtr to variable value2.
    e) Print the value of value2.
    f) Print the address of value1.
    g) Print the address stored in lPtr. Is the value printed the same as the address of value1?

7.11 Do each of the following:

    a) Write the function header for function zero, which takes a long integer array parameter bigIntegers and does not return a value.
    b) Write the function prototype for the function in part a.
    c) Write the function header for function add1AndSum, which takes an integer array parameter oneTooSmall and returns an integer.
    d) Write the function prototype for the function described in part c.

Note: Exercise 7.12 through Exercise 7.15 are reasonably challenging. Once you have done these problems, you ought to be able to implement most popular card games easily.

7.12 Modify the program in Fig. 7.24 so that the card-dealing function deals a five-card poker hand. Then write the following additional functions:

    a) Determine if the hand contains a pair.
    b) Determine if the hand contains two pairs.
    c) Determine if the hand contains three of a kind (e.g., three jacks).
    d) Determine if the hand contains four of a kind (e.g., four aces).
    e) Determine if the hand contains a flush (i.e., all five cards of the same suit).
    f) Determine if the hand contains a straight (i.e., five cards of consecutive face values).

7.13 Use the functions developed in Exercise 7.12 to write a program that deals two five-card poker hands, evaluates each hand, and determines which is the better hand.

7.14 Modify the program developed in Exercise 7.13 so that it can simulate the dealer. The dealer's five-card hand is dealt "face down" so the player cannot see it. The program should then evaluate the dealer's hand, and based on the quality of the hand, the dealer should draw one, two or three more cards to replace the corresponding number of unneeded cards in the original hand. The program should then re-evaluate the dealer's hand. [*Caution:* This is a difficult problem!]

7.15 Modify the program developed in Exercise 7.14 so that it can handle the dealer's hand automatically, but the player is allowed to decide which cards of the player's hand to replace. The program should then evaluate both hands and determine who wins. Now use this new program to play 20 games against the computer. Who wins more games, you or the computer? Have one of your friends play 20 games against the computer. Who wins more games? Based on the results of these games, make appropriate modifications to refine your poker playing program (this, too, is a difficult problem). Play 20 more games. Does your modified program play a better game?

7.16 In the card shuffling and dealing program of Fig. 7.24, we intentionally used an inefficient shuffling algorithm that introduced the possibility of indefinite postponement. In this problem, you will create a high-performance shuffling algorithm that avoids indefinite postponement.

    Modify the program of Fig. 7.24 as follows. Begin by initializing the deck array as shown in Fig. 7.29. Modify the shuffle function to loop row-by-row and column-by-column through the array, touching every element once. Each element should be swapped with a randomly selected element of the array.

Unshuffled deck array												
	0	1	2	3	4	5	6	7	8	9	10	11	12
0	1	2	3	4	5	6	7	8	9	10	11	12	13
1	14	15	16	17	18	19	20	21	22	23	24	25	26
2	27	28	29	30	31	32	33	34	35	36	37	38	39
3	40	41	42	43	44	45	46	47	48	49	50	51	52

Fig. 7.29 | Unshuffled deck array.

Print the resulting array to determine if the deck is satisfactorily shuffled (as in Fig. 7.30, for example). You may want your program to call the shuffle function several times to ensure a satisfactory shuffle.

Note that although the approach in this problem improves the shuffling algorithm, the dealing algorithm still requires searching the deck array for card 1, then card 2, then card 3, and so on. Worse yet, even after the dealing algorithm locates and deals the card, the algorithm continues searching through the remainder of the deck. Modify the program of Fig. 7.24 so that once a card is dealt, no further attempts are made to match that card number, and the program immediately proceeds with dealing the next card. In Chapter 10, we develop a dealing algorithm that requires only one operation per card.

7.17 (*Simulation: The Tortoise and the Hare*) In this problem, you will recreate one of the truly great moments in history, namely the classic race of the tortoise and the hare. You will use random number generation to develop a simulation of this memorable event.

Our contenders begin the race at "square 1" of 70 squares. Each square represents a possible position along the race course. The finish line is at square 70. The first contender to reach or pass square 70 is rewarded with a pail of fresh carrots and lettuce. The course weaves its way up the side of a slippery mountain, so occasionally the contenders lose ground.

There is a clock that ticks once per second. With each tick of the clock, your program should adjust the position of the animals according to the rules of Fig. 7.31.

Use variables to keep track of the positions of the animals (i.e., position numbers are 1–70). Start each animal at position 1 (i.e., the "starting gate"). If an animal slips left before square 1, move the animal back to square 1.

Generate the percentages in the preceding table by producing a random integer, i, in the range $1 \leq i \leq 10$. For the tortoise, perform a "fast plod" when $1 \leq i \leq 5$, a "slip" when $6 \leq i \leq 7$, or a "slow plod" when $8 \leq i \leq 10$. Use a similar technique to move the hare.

Sample shuffled deck array												
	0	1	2	3	4	5	6	7	8	9	10	11	12
0	19	40	27	25	36	46	10	34	35	41	18	2	44
1	13	28	14	16	21	30	8	11	31	17	24	7	1
2	12	33	15	42	43	23	45	3	29	32	4	47	26
3	50	38	52	39	48	51	9	5	37	49	22	6	20

Fig. 7.30 | Sample shuffled deck array.

Animal	Move type	Percentage of the time	Actual move
Tortoise	Fast plod	50%	3 squares to the right
	Slip	20%	6 squares to the left
	Slow plod	30%	1 square to the right
Hare	Sleep	20%	No move at all
	Big hop	20%	9 squares to the right
	Big slip	10%	12 squares to the left
	Small hop	30%	1 square to the right
	Small slip	20%	2 squares to the left

Fig. 7.31 | Tortoise and hare rules for adjusting positions.

Begin the race by printing

```
BANG !!!!!
AND THEY'RE OFF !!!!!
```

Then, for each tick of the clock (i.e., each repetition of a loop), print a 70-position line showing the letter T in the position of the tortoise and the letter H in the position of the hare. Occasionally, the contenders will land on the same square. In this case, the tortoise bites the hare and your program should print OUCH!!! beginning at that position. All print positions other than the T, the H, or the OUCH!!! (in case of a tie) should be blank.

After each line is printed, test if either animal has reached or passed square 70. If so, then print the winner and terminate the simulation. If the tortoise wins, print TORTOISE WINS!!! YAY!!! If the hare wins, print Hare wins. Yuch. If both animals win on the same tick of the clock, you may want to favor the turtle (the "underdog"), or you may want to print It's a tie. If neither animal wins, perform the loop again to simulate the next tick of the clock. When you are ready to run your program, assemble a group of fans to watch the race. You'll be amazed at how involved your audience gets!

Special Section: Building Your Own Computer

In the next several problems, we take a temporary diversion away from the world of high-level language programming. We "peel open" a computer and look at its internal structure. We introduce machine-language programming and write several machine-language programs. To make this an especially valuable experience, we then build a computer (through the technique of software-based *simulation*) on which you can execute your machine-language programs!

7.18 (*Machine-Language Programming*) Let us create a computer we will call the Simpletron. As its name implies, it is a simple machine, but as we will soon see, a powerful one as well. The Simpletron runs programs written in the only language it directly understands—that is, Simpletron Machine Language, or SML for short.

The Simpletron contains an *accumulator*—a "special register" in which information is put before the Simpletron uses that information in calculations or examines it in various ways. All information in the Simpletron is handled in terms of *words*. A word is a signed four-digit decimal number such as +3364, -1293, +0007, -0001, and so on. The Simpletron is equipped with a 100-word memory, and these words are referenced by their location numbers 00, 01, ..., 99.

Before running an SML program, we must *load* or place the program into memory. The first instruction (or statement) of every SML program is always placed in location 00.

Each instruction written in SML occupies one word of the Simpletron's memory (and hence instructions are signed four-digit decimal numbers). We assume that the sign of an SML instruction is always plus, but the sign of a data word may be either plus or minus. Each location in the Simpletron's memory may contain either an instruction, a data value used by a program or an unused (and hence undefined) area of memory. The first two digits of each SML instruction are the *operation code*, which specifies the operation to be performed. SML operation codes are summarized in Fig. 7.32.

The last two digits of an SML instruction are the *operand*, which is the address of the memory location containing the word to which the operation applies. Now let us consider several simple SML programs.

Operation code	Meaning
Input/output operations:	
#define READ 10	Read a word from the terminal into a specific location in memory.
#define WRITE 11	Write a word from a specific location in memory to the terminal.
Load/store operations:	
#define LOAD 20	Load a word from a specific location in memory into the accumulator.
#define STORE 21	Store a word from the accumulator into a specific location in memory.
Arithmetic operations:	
#define ADD 30	Add a word from a specific location in memory to the word in the accumulator (leave result in accumulator).
#define SUBTRACT 31	Subtract a word from a specific location in memory from the word in the accumulator (leave result in accumulator).
#define DIVIDE 32	Divide a word from a specific location in memory into the word in the accumulator (leave result in accumulator).
#define MULTIPLY 33	Multiply a word from a specific location in memory by the word in the accumulator (leave result in accumulator).
Transfer of control operations:	
#define BRANCH 40	Branch to a specific location in memory.
#define BRANCHNEG 41	Branch to a specific location in memory if the accumulator is negative.
#define BRANCHZERO 42	Branch to a specific location in memory if the accumulator is zero.
#define HALT 43	Halt—i.e., the program has completed its task.

Fig. 7.32 | Simpletron Machine Language (SML) operation codes.

The following SML program reads two numbers from the keyboard, and computes and prints their sum. The instruction +1007 reads the first number from the keyboard and places it into location 07 (which has been initialized to zero). Then +1008 reads the next number into location 08. The *load* instruction, +2007, puts the first number into the accumulator, and the *add* instruction, +3008, adds the second number to the number in the accumulator. *All SML arithmetic instructions leave their results in the accumulator.* The *store* instruction, +2109, places the result back into memory location 09, from which the *write* instruction, +1109, takes the number and prints it (as a signed four-digit decimal number). The *halt* instruction, +4300, terminates execution.

Example 1 Location	Number	Instruction
00	+1007	(Read A)
01	+1008	(Read B)
02	+2007	(Load A)
03	+3008	(Add B)
04	+2109	(Store C)
05	+1109	(Write C)
06	+4300	(Halt)
07	+0000	(Variable A)
08	+0000	(Variable B)
09	+0000	(Result C)

The following SML program reads two numbers from the keyboard, and determines and prints the larger value. Note the use of the instruction +4107 as a conditional transfer of control, much the same as C's if statement.

Example 2 Location	Number	Instruction
00	+1009	(Read A)
01	+1010	(Read B)
02	+2009	(Load A)
03	+3110	(Subtract B)
04	+4107	(Branch negative to 07)
05	+1109	(Write A)
06	+4300	(Halt)
07	+1110	(Write B)
08	+4300	(Halt)
09	+0000	(Variable A)
10	+0000	(Variable B)

Now write SML programs to accomplish each of the following tasks.

a) Use a sentinel-controlled loop to read 10 positive integers and compute and print their sum.

b) Use a counter-controlled loop to read seven numbers, some positive and some negative, and compute and print their average.

c) Read a series of numbers and determine and print the largest number. The first number read indicates how many numbers should be processed.

7.19   (*A Computer Simulator*) It may at first seem outrageous, but in this problem you are going to build your own computer. No, you will not be soldering components together. Rather, you will use the powerful technique of *software-based simulation* to create a *software model* of the Simpletron. You will not be disappointed. Your Simpletron simulator will turn the computer you are using into a Simpletron, and you will actually be able to run, test and debug the SML programs you wrote in Exercise 7.18.

```
When you run your Simpletron simulator, it should begin by printing:

*** Welcome to Simpletron! ***
*** Please enter your program one instruction ***
*** (or data word) at a time. I will type the ***
*** location number and a question mark (?).  ***
*** You then type the word for that location. ***
*** Type the sentinel -99999 to stop entering ***
*** your program. ***
```

Simulate the memory of the Simpletron with a single-subscripted array `memory` that has 100 elements. Now assume that the simulator is running, and let us examine the dialog as we enter the program of Example 2 of Exercise 7.18:

```
00 ? +1009
01 ? +1010
02 ? +2009
03 ? +3110
04 ? +4107
05 ? +1109
06 ? +4300
07 ? +1110
08 ? +4300
09 ? +0000
10 ? +0000
11 ? -99999
*** Program loading completed ***
*** Program execution begins  ***
```

The SML program has now been placed (or loaded) into the array `memory`. Now the Simpletron executes your SML program. Execution begins with the instruction in location 00 and, like C, continues sequentially, unless directed to some other part of the program by a transfer of control.

Use the variable `accumulator` to represent the accumulator register. Use the variable `instructionCounter` to keep track of the location in memory that contains the instruction being performed. Use the variable `operationCode` to indicate the operation currently being performed—i.e., the left two digits of the instruction word. Use the variable `operand` to indicate the memory location on which the current instruction operates. Thus, `operand` is the rightmost two digits of the instruction currently being performed. Do not execute instructions directly from memory. Rather, transfer the next instruction to be performed from memory to a variable called `instructionRegister`. Then "pick off" the left two digits and place them in the variable `operationCode`, and "pick off" the right two digits and place them in `operand`.

When Simpletron begins execution, the special registers are initialized as follows:

```
accumulator                 +0000
instructionCounter            00
instructionRegister         +0000
operationCode                 00
operand                       00
```

Now let us "walk through" the execution of the first SML instruction, +1009 in memory location 00. This is called an *instruction execution cycle*.

The instructionCounter tells us the location of the next instruction to be performed. We *fetch* the contents of that location from memory by using the C statement

```
instructionRegister = memory[ instructionCounter ];
```

The operation code and the operand are extracted from the instruction register by the statements

```
operationCode = instructionRegister / 100;
operand = instructionRegister % 100;
```

Now the Simpletron must determine that the operation code is actually a *read* (versus a *write*, a *load*, and so on). A switch differentiates among the twelve operations of SML.

In the switch statement, the behavior of various SML instructions is simulated as follows (we leave the others to the reader):

```
read:   scanf( "%d", &memory[ operand ] );
load:   accumulator = memory[ operand ];
add:    accumulator += memory[ operand ];
```
Various branch instructions: We'll discuss these shortly.
```
halt:   This instruction prints the message
```

```
       *** Simpletron execution terminated ***
```

then prints the name and contents of each register as well as the complete contents of memory. Such a printout is often called a *computer dump*. To help you program your dump function, a sample dump format is shown in Fig. 7.33. Note that a dump after executing a Simpletron program would show the actual values of instructions and data values at the moment execution terminated.

```
REGISTERS:
accumulator                 +0000
instructionCounter            00
instructionRegister         +0000
operationCode                 00
operand                       00

MEMORY:
        0       1       2       3       4       5       6       7       8       9
 0  +0000   +0000   +0000   +0000   +0000   +0000   +0000   +0000   +0000   +0000
10  +0000   +0000   +0000   +0000   +0000   +0000   +0000   +0000   +0000   +0000
20  +0000   +0000   +0000   +0000   +0000   +0000   +0000   +0000   +0000   +0000
30  +0000   +0000   +0000   +0000   +0000   +0000   +0000   +0000   +0000   +0000
40  +0000   +0000   +0000   +0000   +0000   +0000   +0000   +0000   +0000   +0000
50  +0000   +0000   +0000   +0000   +0000   +0000   +0000   +0000   +0000   +0000
60  +0000   +0000   +0000   +0000   +0000   +0000   +0000   +0000   +0000   +0000
70  +0000   +0000   +0000   +0000   +0000   +0000   +0000   +0000   +0000   +0000
80  +0000   +0000   +0000   +0000   +0000   +0000   +0000   +0000   +0000   +0000
90  +0000   +0000   +0000   +0000   +0000   +0000   +0000   +0000   +0000   +0000
```

Fig. 7.33 | Sample Simpletron dump format.

Let us proceed with the execution of our program's first instruction, namely the +1009 in location 00. As we have indicated, the `switch` statement simulates this by performing the C statement

```
scanf( "%d", &memory[ operand ] );
```

A question mark (?) should be displayed on the screen before the `scanf` is executed to prompt the user for input. The Simpletron waits for the user to type a value and then press the *Return* key. The value is then read into location 09.

At this point, simulation of the first instruction is completed. All that remains is to prepare the Simpletron to execute the next instruction. Since the instruction just performed was not a transfer of control, we need merely increment the instruction counter register as follows:

```
++instructionCounter;
```

This completes the simulated execution of the first instruction. The entire process (i.e., the instruction execution cycle) begins anew with the fetch of the next instruction to be executed.

Now let us consider how the branching instructions—the transfers of control—are simulated. All we need to do is adjust the value in the instruction counter appropriately. Therefore, the unconditional branch instruction (40) is simulated within the `switch` as

```
instructionCounter = operand;
```

The conditional "branch if accumulator is zero" instruction is simulated as

```
if ( accumulator == 0 )
    instructionCounter = operand;
```

At this point, you should implement your Simpletron simulator and run the SML programs you wrote in Exercise 7.18. You may embellish SML with additional features and provide for these in your simulator.

Your simulator should check for various types of errors. During the program loading phase, for example, each number the user types into the Simpletron's `memory` must be in the range -9999 to +9999. Your simulator should use a `while` loop to test that each number entered is in this range, and, if not, keep prompting the user to reenter the number until the user enters a correct number.

During the execution phase, your simulator should check for various serious errors, such as attempts to divide by zero, attempts to execute invalid operation codes and accumulator overflows (i.e., arithmetic operations resulting in values larger than +9999 or smaller than -9999). Such serious errors are called *fatal errors*. When a fatal error is detected, your simulator should print an error message such as:

```
*** Attempt to divide by zero ***
*** Simpletron execution abnormally terminated ***
```

and should print a full computer dump in the format we have discussed previously. This will help the user locate the error in the program.

7.20 Modify the card shuffling and dealing program of Fig. 7.24 so the shuffling and dealing operations are performed by the same function (`shuffleAndDeal`). The function should contain one nested looping structure that is similar to function `shuffle` in Fig. 7.24.

7.21 What does this program do?

```
1   /* ex07_21.c */
2   /* What does this program do? */
3   #include <stdio.h>
4
5   void mystery1( char *s1, const char *s2 ); /* prototype */
```

```
 6
 7   int main( void )
 8   {
 9      char string1[ 80 ]; /* create char array */
10      char string2[ 80 ]; /* create char array */
11
12      printf( "Enter two strings: " );
13      scanf( "%s%s" , string1, string2 );
14
15      mystery1( string1, string2 );
16
17      printf("%s", string1 );
18
19      return 0; /* indicates successful termination */
20
21   } /* end main */
22
23   /* What does this function do? */
24   void mystery1( char *s1, const char *s2 )
25   {
26      while ( *s1 != '\0' ) {
27         s1++;
28      } /* end while */
29
30      for ( ; *s1 = *s2; s1++, s2++ ) {
31         ;   /* empty statement */
32      } /* end for */
33
34   } /* end function mystery1 */
```

7.22   What does this program do?

```
 1   /* ex07_22.c */
 2   /* what does this program do? */
 3   #include <stdio.h>
 4
 5   int mystery2( const char *s ); /* prototype */
 6
 7   int main( void )
 8   {
 9      char string[ 80 ]; /* create char array */
10
11      printf( "Enter a string: ");
12      scanf( "%s", string );
13
14      printf( "%d\n", mystery2( string ) );
15
16      return 0; /* indicates successful termination */
17   } /* end main */
18
19   /* What does this function do? */
20   int mystery2( const char *s )
21   {
```

```
22      int x; /* counter */
23
24      /* loop through string */
25      for ( x = 0; *s != '\0'; s++ ) {
26          x++;
27      } /* end for */
28
29      return x;
30
31  } /* end function mystery2 */
```

7.23 Find the error in each of the following program segments. If the error can be corrected, explain how.

a) ```
int *number;
printf("%d\n", *number);
```

b) ```
float *realPtr;
long *integerPtr;
integerPtr = realPtr;
```

c) ```
int * x, y;
x = y;
```

d) ```
char s[] = "this is a character array";
int count;
for ( ; *s != '\0'; s++)
    printf( "%c ", *s );
```

e) ```
short *numPtr, result;
void *genericPtr = numPtr;
result = *genericPtr + 7;
```

f) ```
float x = 19.34;
float xPtr = &x;
printf( "%f\n", xPtr );
```

g) ```
char *s;
printf("%s\n", s);
```

**7.24** (*Maze Traversal*) The following grid is a double-subscripted array representation of a maze.

```
# # # # # # # # # # #
# . . . # . . . . . #
. . # . # . # # # # . #
# # # . # . . . . # . #
# . . . . # # # . # . .
# # # # . # . # . # . #
# . . # . # . # . # . #
# # . # . # . # . # . #
# . . . . . . . # . # #
# # # # # # . # # # . #
# . . . . . # . . . # #
# # # # # # # # # # # #
```

The # symbols represent the walls of the maze, and the periods (.) represent squares in the possible paths through the maze.

There is a simple algorithm for walking through a maze that guarantees finding the exit (assuming there is an exit). If there is not an exit, you will arrive at the starting location again. Place your right hand on the wall to your right and begin walking forward. Never remove your hand
```

from the wall. If the maze turns to the right, you follow the wall to the right. As long as you do not remove your hand from the wall, eventually you will arrive at the exit of the maze. There may be a shorter path than the one you have taken, but you are guaranteed to get out of the maze.

Write recursive function `mazeTraverse` to walk through the maze. The function should receive as arguments a 12-by-12 character array representing the maze and the starting location of the maze. As `mazeTraverse` attempts to locate the exit from the maze, it should place the character X in each square in the path. The function should display the maze after each move so the user can watch as the maze is solved.

7.25 (*Generating Mazes Randomly*) Write a function `mazeGenerator` that takes as an argument a double-subscripted 12-by-12 character array and randomly produces a maze. The function should also provide the starting and ending locations of the maze. Try your function `mazeTraverse` from Exercise 7.24 using several randomly generated mazes.

7.26 (*Mazes of Any Size*) Generalize functions `mazeTraverse` and `mazeGenerator` of Exercise 7.24 and Exercise 7.25 to process mazes of any width and height.

7.27 (*Arrays of Pointers to Functions*) Rewrite the program of Fig. 6.22 to use a menu-driven interface. The program should offer the user four options as follows:

```
Enter a choice:
   0  Print the array of grades
   1  Find the minimum grade
   2  Find the maximum grade
   3  Print the average on all tests for each student
   4  End program
```

One restriction on using arrays of pointers to functions is that all the pointers must have the same type. The pointers must be to functions of the same return type that receive arguments of the same type. For this reason, the functions in Fig. 6.22 must be modified so that they each return the same type and take the same parameters. Modify functions `minimum` and `maximum` to print the minimum or maximum value and return nothing. For option 3, modify function average of Fig. 6.22 to output the average for each student (not a specific student). Function average should return nothing and take the same parameters as `printArray`, `minimum` and `maximum`. Store the pointers to the four functions in array `processGrades` and use the choice made by the user as the subscript into the array for calling each function.

7.28 (*Modifications to the Simpletron Simulator*) In Exercise 7.19, you wrote a software simulation of a computer that executes programs written in Simpletron Machine Language (SML). In this exercise, we propose several modifications and enhancements to the Simpletron Simulator. In Exercises 12.26 and 12.27, we propose building a compiler that converts programs written in a high-level programming language (a variation of BASIC) to Simpletron Machine Language. Some of the following modifications and enhancements may be required to execute the programs produced by the compiler.

a) Extend the Simpletron Simulator's memory to contain 1000 memory locations to enable the Simpletron to handle larger programs.
b) Allow the simulator to perform remainder calculations. This requires an additional Simpletron Machine Language instruction.
c) Allow the simulator to perform exponentiation calculations. This requires an additional Simpletron Machine Language instruction.
d) Modify the simulator to use hexadecimal values rather than integer values to represent Simpletron Machine Language instructions.
e) Modify the simulator to allow output of a newline. This requires an additional Simpletron Machine Language instruction.

f) Modify the simulator to process floating-point values in addition to integer values.

g) Modify the simulator to handle string input. [*Hint:* Each Simpletron word can be divided into two groups, each holding a two-digit integer. Each two-digit integer represents the ASCII decimal equivalent of a character. Add a machine-language instruction that will input a string and store the string beginning at a specific Simpletron memory location. The first half of the word at that location will be a count of the number of characters in the string (i.e., the length of the string). Each succeeding half word contains one ASCII character expressed as two decimal digits. The machine-language instruction converts each character into its ASCII equivalent and assigns it to a half word.]

h) Modify the simulator to handle output of strings stored in the format of part (g). [*Hint:* Add a machine-language instruction that prints a string beginning at a specified Simpletron memory location. The first half of the word at that location is the length of the string in characters. Each succeeding half word contains one ASCII character expressed as two decimal digits. The machine-language instruction checks the length and prints the string by translating each two-digit number into its equivalent character.]

7.29 What does this program do?

```c
/* ex07_30.c */
/* What does this program do? */
#include <stdio.h>

int mystery3( const char *s1, const char *s2 ); /* prototype */

int main( void )
{
   char string1[ 80 ]; /* create char array */
   char string2[ 80 ]; /* create char array */

   printf( "Enter two strings: " );
   scanf( "%s%s", string1 , string2 );

   printf( "The result is %d\n", mystery3( string1, string2 ) );

   return 0; /* indicates successful termination */

} /* end main */

int mystery3( const char *s1, const char *s2 )
{
   for ( ; *s1 != '\0' && *s2 != '\0'; s1++, s2++ ) {

      if ( *s1 != *s2 ) {
         return 0;
      } /* end if */

   } /* end for */

   return 1;

} /* end function mystery3 */
```

8

C Characters and Strings

OBJECTIVES

In this chapter, you will learn:

- To use the functions of the character-handling library (`ctype`).
- To use the string-conversion functions of the general utilities library (`stdlib`).
- To use the string and character input/output functions of the standard input/output library (`stdio`).
- To use the string-processing functions of the string handling library (`string`).
- The power of function libraries as a means of achieving software reusability.

8.1 Introduction

In this chapter, we introduce the C Standard Library functions that facilitate string and character processing. The functions enable programs to process characters, strings, lines of text and blocks of memory.

The chapter discusses the techniques used to develop editors, word processors, page layout software, computerized typesetting systems and other kinds of text-processing software. The text manipulations performed by formatted input/output functions like printf and scanf can be implemented using the functions discussed in this chapter.

8.2 Fundamentals of Strings and Characters

Characters are the fundamental building blocks of source programs. Every program is composed of a sequence of characters that—when grouped together meaningfully—is interpreted by the computer as a series of instructions used to accomplish a task. A program may contain **character constants**. A character constant is an int value represented as a character in single quotes. The value of a character constant is the integer value of the character in the machine's character set. For example, 'z' represents the integer value of z, and '\n' the integer value of newline (122 and 10 in ASCII, respectively).

A **string** is a series of characters treated as a single unit. A string may include letters, digits and various special characters such as +, -, *, / and $. String literals, or string constants, in C are written in double quotation marks as follows:

"John Q. Doe"	(a name)
"99999 Main Street"	(a street address)
"Waltham, Massachusetts"	(a city and state)
"(201) 555-1212"	(a telephone number)

A string in C is an array of characters ending in the null character ('\0'). A string is accessed via a pointer to the first character in the string. The value of a string is the address of its first character. Thus, in C, it is appropriate to say that a **string is a pointer**—in fact, a pointer to the string's first character. In this sense, strings are like arrays, because an array is also a pointer to its first element.

A character array or a variable of type `char *` can be initialized with a string in a definition. The definitions

```
char color[] = "blue";
const char *colorPtr = "blue";
```

each initialize a variable to the string "blue". The first definition creates a 5-element array color containing the characters 'b', 'l', 'u', 'e' and '\0'. The second definition creates pointer variable colorPtr that points to the string "blue" somewhere in memory.

Portability Tip 8.1

*When a variable of type char * is initialized with a string literal, some compilers may place the string in a location in memory where the string cannot be modified. If you might need to modify a string literal, it should be stored in a character array to ensure modifiability on all systems.*

The preceding array definition could also have been written

```
char color[] = { 'b', 'l', 'u', 'e', '\0' };
```

When defining a character array to contain a string, the array must be large enough to store the string and its terminating null character. The preceding definition automatically determines the size of the array based on the number of initializers in the initializer list.

Common Programming Error 8.1

Not allocating sufficient space in a character array to store the null character that terminates a string is an error.

Common Programming Error 8.2

Printing a "string" that does not contain a terminating null character is an error.

Error-Prevention Tip 8.1

When storing a string of characters in a character array, be sure that the array is large enough to hold the largest string that will be stored. C allows strings of any length to be stored. If a string is longer than the character array in which it is to be stored, characters beyond the end of the array will overwrite data in memory following the array.

A string can be stored in an array using `scanf`. For example, the following statement stores a string in character array word[20]:

```
scanf( "%s", word );
```

The string entered by the user is stored in word. Note that word is an array, which is, of course, a pointer, so the & is not needed with argument word. Recall from Section 6.4 that function scanf will read characters until a space, tab, newline or end-of-file indicator is encountered. So, it is possible that the user input could exceed 19 characters and that your your program may crash! For this reason, use the conversion specifier %19s so that scanf reads up to 19 characters and saves the last character for the terminating null character. This prevents scanf from writing characters into memory beyond the end of s. (For reading input lines of arbitrary length, there is a nonstandard—yet widely supported—function readline, usually included in stdio.h.) For a character array to be printed as a string, the array must contain a terminating null character.

Common Programming Error 8.3

Processing a single character as a string. A string is a pointer—probably a respectably large integer. However, a character is a small integer (ASCII values range 0–255). On many systems this causes an error, because low memory addresses are reserved for special purposes such as operating-system interrupt handlers—so "access violations" occur.

Common Programming Error 8.4

Passing a character as an argument to a function when a string is expected is a syntax error.

Common Programming Error 8.5

Passing a string as an argument to a function when a character is expected is a syntax error.

8.3 Character-Handling Library

The character-handling library includes several functions that perform useful tests and manipulations of character data. Each function receives a character—represented as an int—or EOF as an argument. As we discussed in Chapter 4, characters are often manipulated as integers, because a character in C is usually a 1-byte integer. EOF normally has the value −1, and some hardware architectures do not allow negative values to be stored in char variables, so the character-handling functions manipulate characters as integers. Figure 8.1 summarizes the functions of the character-handling library.

Prototype	Function description
`int isdigit( int c );`	Returns a true value if c is a digit and 0 (false) otherwise.
`int isalpha( int c );`	Returns a true value if c is a letter and 0 otherwise.
`int isalnum( int c );`	Returns a true value if c is a digit or a letter and 0 otherwise.
`int isxdigit( int c );`	Returns a true value if c is a hexadecimal digit character and 0 otherwise. (See Appendix D, Number Systems, for a detailed explanation of binary numbers, octal numbers, decimal numbers and hexadecimal numbers.)
`int islower( int c );`	Returns a true value if c is a lowercase letter and 0 otherwise.
`int isupper( int c );`	Returns a true value if c is an uppercase letter and 0 otherwise.
`int tolower( int c );`	If c is an uppercase letter, tolower returns c as a lowercase letter. Otherwise, tolower returns the argument unchanged.
`int toupper( int c );`	If c is a lowercase letter, toupper returns c as an uppercase letter. Otherwise, toupper returns the argument unchanged.
`int isspace( int c );`	Returns a true value if c is a white-space character—newline ('\n'), space (' '), form feed ('\f'), carriage return ('\r'), horizontal tab ('\t') or vertical tab ('\v')—and 0 otherwise.

Fig. 8.1 | Character-handling library functions. (Part 1 of 2.)

Prototype	Function description
`int iscntrl( int c );`	Returns a true value if c is a control character and 0 otherwise.
`int ispunct( int c );`	Returns a true value if c is a printing character other than a space, a digit, or a letter and returns 0 otherwise.
`int isprint( int c );`	Returns a true value if c is a printing character including a space (' ') and returns 0 otherwise.
`int isgraph( int c );`	Returns a true value if c is a printing character other than a space (' ') and returns 0 otherwise.

Fig. 8.1 | Character-handling library functions. (Part 2 of 2.)

Error-Prevention Tip 8.2

When using functions from the character-handling library, include the `<ctype.h>` header.

Figure 8.2 demonstrates functions `isdigit`, `isalpha`, `isalnum` and `isxdigit`. Function `isdigit` determines whether its argument is a digit (0–9). Function `isalpha` determines whether its argument is an uppercase letter (A–Z) or a lowercase letter (a–z). Function `isalnum` determines whether its argument is an uppercase letter, a lowercase letter or a digit. Function `isxdigit` determines whether its argument is a hexadecimal digit (A–F, a–f, 0–9).

Figure 8.2 uses the conditional operator (?:) with each function to determine whether the string " is a " or the string " is not a " should be printed in the output for each character tested. For example, the expression

```
isdigit( '8' ) ? "8 is a " : "8 is not a "
```

indicates that if `'8'` is a digit (i.e., `isdigit` returns a true (nonzero) value), the string "8 is a " is printed, and if `'8'` is not a digit (i.e., `isdigit` returns 0), the string "8 is not a " is printed.

```
1   /* Fig. 8.2: fig08_02.c
2      Using functions isdigit, isalpha, isalnum, and isxdigit */
3   #include <stdio.h>
4   #include <ctype.h>
5
6   int main( void )
7   {
8      printf( "%s\n%s%s\n%s%s\n\n", "According to isdigit: ",
9         isdigit( '8' ) ? "8 is a " : "8 is not a ", "digit",
10        isdigit( '#' ) ? "# is a " : "# is not a ", "digit" );
11
12     printf( "%s\n%s%s\n%s%s\n%s%s\n\n",
13        "According to isalpha:",
14        isalpha( 'A' ) ? "A is a " : "A is not a ", "letter",
```

Fig. 8.2 | Using `isdigit`, `isalpha`, `isalnum` and `isxdigit`. (Part 1 of 2.)

```
15          isalpha( 'b' ) ? "b is a " : "b is not a ", "letter",
16          isalpha( '&' ) ? "& is a " : "& is not a ", "letter",
17          isalpha( '4' ) ? "4 is a " : "4 is not a ", "letter" );
18
19      printf( "%s\n%s%s\n%s%s\n%s%s\n\n",
20          "According to isalnum:",
21          isalnum( 'A' ) ? "A is a " : "A is not a ",
22          "digit or a letter",
23          isalnum( '8' ) ? "8 is a " : "8 is not a ",
24          "digit or a letter",
25          isalnum( '#' ) ? "# is a " : "# is not a ",
26          "digit or a letter" );
27
28      printf( "%s\n%s%s\n%s%s\n%s%s\n%s%s\n%s%s\n",
29          "According to isxdigit:",
30          isxdigit( 'F' ) ? "F is a " : "F is not a ",
31          "hexadecimal digit",
32          isxdigit( 'J' ) ? "J is a " : "J is not a ",
33          "hexadecimal digit",
34          isxdigit( '7' ) ? "7 is a " : "7 is not a ",
35          "hexadecimal digit",
36          isxdigit( '$' ) ? "$ is a " : "$ is not a ",
37          "hexadecimal digit",
38          isxdigit( 'f' ) ? "f is a " : "f is not a ",
39          "hexadecimal digit" );
40
41      return 0; /* indicates successful termination */
42
43   } /* end main */
```

```
According to isdigit:
8 is a digit
# is not a digit

According to isalpha:
A is a letter
b is a letter
& is not a letter
4 is not a letter

According to isalnum:
A is a digit or a letter
8 is a digit or a letter
# is not a digit or a letter

According to isxdigit:
F is a hexadecimal digit
J is not a hexadecimal digit
7 is a hexadecimal digit
$ is not a hexadecimal digit
f is a hexadecimal digit
```

Fig. 8.2 | Using isdigit, isalpha, isalnum and isxdigit. (Part 2 of 2.)

Figure 8.3 demonstrates functions `islower`, `isupper`, `tolower` and `toupper`. Function `islower` determines whether its argument is a lowercase letter (a–z). Function `isupper` determines whether its argument is an uppercase letter (A–Z). Function `tolower` converts an uppercase letter to a lowercase letter and returns the lowercase letter. If the argument is not an uppercase letter, `tolower` returns the argument unchanged. Function `toupper` converts a lowercase letter to an uppercase letter and returns the uppercase letter. If the argument is not a lowercase letter, `toupper` returns the argument unchanged.

Figure 8.4 demonstrates functions `isspace`, `iscntrl`, `ispunct`, `isprint` and `isgraph`. Function `isspace` determines whether its argument is one of the following white-space characters: space (' '), form feed ('\f'), newline ('\n'), carriage return ('\r'), horizontal tab ('\t') or vertical tab ('\v'). Function `iscntrl` determines whether

```c
 1  /* Fig. 8.3: fig08_03.c
 2     Using functions islower, isupper, tolower, toupper */
 3  #include <stdio.h>
 4  #include <ctype.h>
 5
 6  int main( void )
 7  {
 8     printf( "%s\n%s%s\n%s%s\n%s%s\n%s%s\n\n",
 9             "According to islower:",
10             islower( 'p' ) ? "p is a " : "p is not a ",
11             "lowercase letter",
12             islower( 'P' ) ? "P is a " : "P is not a ",
13             "lowercase letter",
14             islower( '5' ) ? "5 is a " : "5 is not a ",
15             "lowercase letter",
16             islower( '!' ) ? "! is a " : "! is not a ",
17             "lowercase letter" );
18
19     printf( "%s\n%s%s\n%s%s\n%s%s\n%s%s\n\n",
20             "According to isupper:",
21             isupper( 'D' ) ? "D is an " : "D is not an ",
22             "uppercase letter",
23             isupper( 'd' ) ? "d is an " : "d is not an ",
24             "uppercase letter",
25             isupper( '8' ) ? "8 is an " : "8 is not an ",
26             "uppercase letter",
27             isupper( '$' ) ? "$ is an " : "$ is not an ",
28             "uppercase letter" );
29
30     printf( "%s%c\n%s%c\n%s%c\n%s%c\n",
31             "u converted to uppercase is ", toupper( 'u' ),
32             "7 converted to uppercase is ", toupper( '7' ),
33             "$ converted to uppercase is ", toupper( '$' ),
34             "L converted to lowercase is ", tolower( 'L' ) );
35
36     return 0; /* indicates successful termination */
37
38  } /* end main */
```

Fig. 8.3 | Using functions `islower`, `isupper`, `tolower` and `toupper`. (Part 1 of 2.)

```
According to islower:
p is a lowercase letter
P is not a lowercase letter
5 is not a lowercase letter
! is not a lowercase letter

According to isupper:
D is an uppercase letter
d is not an uppercase letter
8 is not an uppercase letter
$ is not an uppercase letter

u converted to uppercase is U
7 converted to uppercase is 7
$ converted to uppercase is $
L converted to lowercase is l
```

Fig. 8.3 | Using functions islower, isupper, tolower and toupper. (Part 2 of 2.)

its argument is one of the following control characters: horizontal tab ('\t'), vertical tab ('\v'), form feed ('\f'), alert ('\a'), backspace ('\b'), carriage return ('\r') or newline ('\n'). Function ispunct determines whether its argument is a printing character other than a space, a digit or a letter, such as $, #, (,), [,], {, }, ;, : or %. Function isprint determines whether its argument is a character that can be displayed on the screen (including the space character). Function isgraph tests for the same characters as isprint; however, the space character is not included.

```
 1   /* Fig. 8.4: fig08_04.c
 2      Using functions isspace, iscntrl, ispunct, isprint, isgraph */
 3   #include <stdio.h>
 4   #include <ctype.h>
 5
 6   int main( void )
 7   {
 8      printf( "%s\n%s%s%s\n%s%s%s\n%s%s%s\n\n",
 9         "According to isspace:",
10         "Newline", isspace( '\n' ) ? " is a " : " is not a ",
11         "whitespace character", "Horizontal tab",
12         isspace( '\t' ) ? " is a " : " is not a ",
13         "whitespace character",
14         isspace( '%' ) ? "% is a " : "% is not a ",
15         "whitespace character" );
16
17      printf( "%s\n%s%s%s\n%s%s%s\n\n", "According to iscntrl:",
18         "Newline", iscntrl( '\n' ) ? " is a " : " is not a ",
19         "control character", iscntrl( '$' ) ? "$ is a " :
20         "$ is not a ", "control character" );
21
22      printf( "%s\n%s%s%s\n%s%s%s\n%s%s%s\n\n",
23         "According to ispunct:",
24         ispunct( ';' ) ? "; is a " : "; is not a ",
```

Fig. 8.4 | Using isspace, iscntrl, ispunct, isprint and isgraph. (Part 1 of 2.)

```
25          "punctuation character",
26          ispunct( 'Y' ) ? "Y is a " : "Y is not a ",
27          "punctuation character",
28          ispunct( '#' ) ? "# is a " : "# is not a ",
29          "punctuation character" );
30
31      printf( "%s\n%s%s\n%s%s%s\n\n", "According to isprint:",
32          isprint( '$' ) ? "$ is a " : "$ is not a ",
33          "printing character",
34          "Alert", isprint( '\a' ) ? " is a " : " is not a ",
35          "printing character" );
36
37      printf( "%s\n%s%s\n%s%s%s\n", "According to isgraph:",
38          isgraph( 'Q' ) ? "Q is a " : "Q is not a ",
39          "printing character other than a space",
40          "Space", isgraph( ' ' ) ? " is a " : " is not a ",
41          "printing character other than a space" );
42
43      return 0; /* indicates successful termination */
44
45  } /* end main */
```

```
According to isspace:
Newline is a whitespace character
Horizontal tab is a whitespace character
% is not a whitespace character

According to iscntrl:
Newline is a control character
$ is not a control character

According to ispunct:
; is a punctuation character
Y is not a punctuation character
# is a punctuation character

According to isprint:
$ is a printing character
Alert is not a printing character

According to isgraph:
Q is a printing character other than a space
Space is not a printing character other than a space
```

Fig. 8.4 | Using isspace, iscntrl, ispunct, isprint and isgraph. (Part 2 of 2.)

8.4 String-Conversion Functions

This section presents the string-conversion functions from the general utilities library (<stdlib.h>). These functions convert strings of digits to integer and floating-point values. Figure 8.5 summarizes the string-conversion functions. Note the use of const to declare variable nPtr in the function headers (read from right to left as "nPtr is a pointer to a character constant"); const specifies that the argument value will not be modified.

Function prototype	Function description
`double atof( const char *nPtr );`	Converts the string nPtr to double.
`int atoi( const char *nPtr );`	Converts the string nPtr to int.
`long atol( const char *nPtr );`	Converts the string nPtr to long int.
`double strtod( const char *nPtr, char **endPtr );`	
	Converts the string nPtr to double.
`long strtol( const char *nPtr, char **endPtr, int base );`	
	Converts the string nPtr to long.
`unsigned long strtoul( const char *nPtr, char **endPtr, int base );`	
	Converts the string nPtr to unsigned long.

Fig. 8.5 | String-conversion functions of the general utilities library.

Error-Prevention Tip 8.3

When using functions from the general utilities library, include the `<stdlib.h>` header.

Function **atof** (Fig. 8.6) converts its argument—a string that represents a floating-point number—to a double value. The function returns the double value. If the converted value cannot be represented—for example, if the first character of the string is a letter—the behavior of function atof is undefined.

```
1   /* Fig. 8.6: fig08_06.c
2      Using atof */
3   #include <stdio.h>
4   #include <stdlib.h>
5
6   int main( void )
7   {
8      double d; /* variable to hold converted string */
9
10     d = atof( "99.0" );
11
12     printf( "%s%.3f\n%s%.3f\n",
13            "The string \"99.0\" converted to double is ", d,
14            "The converted value divided by 2 is ",
15            d / 2.0 );
16
17     return 0; /* indicates successful termination */
18
19  } /* end main */
```

Fig. 8.6 | Using atof. (Part I of 2.)

```
The string "99.0" converted to double is 99.000
The converted value divided by 2 is 49.500
```

Fig. 8.6 | Using atof. (Part 2 of 2.)

Function atoi (Fig. 8.7) converts its argument—a string of digits that represents an integer—to an int value. The function returns the int value. If the converted value cannot be represented, the behavior of function atoi is undefined.

Function **atol** (Fig. 8.8) converts its argument—a string of digits representing a long integer—to a long value. The function returns the long value. If the converted value cannot be represented, the behavior of function atol is undefined. If int and long are both stored in 4 bytes, function atoi and function atol work identically.

```
1   /* Fig. 8.7: fig08_07.c
2      Using atoi */
3   #include <stdio.h>
4   #include <stdlib.h>
5
6   int main( void )
7   {
8      int i; /* variable to hold converted string */
9
10     i = atoi( "2593" );
11
12     printf( "%s%d\n%s%d\n",
13             "The string \"2593\" converted to int is ", i,
14             "The converted value minus 593 is ", i - 593 );
15
16     return 0; /* indicates successful termination */
17
18  } /* end main */
```

```
The string "2593" converted to int is 2593
The converted value minus 593 is 2000
```

Fig. 8.7 | Using atoi.

```
1   /* Fig. 8.8: fig08_08.c
2      Using atol */
3   #include <stdio.h>
4   #include <stdlib.h>
5
6   int main( void )
7   {
8      long l; /* variable to hold converted string */
9
10     l = atol( "1000000" );
```

Fig. 8.8 | Using atol. (Part 1 of 2.)

```
11
12      printf( "%s%ld\n%s%ld\n",
13              "The string \"1000000\" converted to long int is ", l,
14              "The converted value divided by 2 is ", l / 2 );
15
16      return 0; /* indicates successful termination */
17
18   } /* end main */
```

```
The string "1000000" converted to long int is 1000000
The converted value divided by 2 is 500000
```

Fig. 8.8 | Using atol. (Part 2 of 2.)

Function strtod (Fig. 8.9) converts a sequence of characters representing a floating-point value to double. The function receives two arguments—a string (char *) and a pointer to a string (char **). The string contains the character sequence to be converted to double. The pointer is assigned the location of the first character after the converted portion of the string. Line 14

```
d = strtod( string, &stringPtr );
```

indicates that d is assigned the double value converted from string, and stringPtr is assigned the location of the first character after the converted value (51.2) in string.

```
1    /* Fig. 8.9: fig08_09.c
2       Using strtod */
3    #include <stdio.h>
4    #include <stdlib.h>
5
6    int main( void )
7    {
8       /* initialize string pointer */
9       const char *string = "51.2% are admitted"; /* initialize string */
10
11      double d;        /* variable to hold converted sequence */
12      char *stringPtr; /* create char pointer */
13
14      d = strtod( string, &stringPtr );
15
16      printf( "The string \"%s\" is converted to the\n", string );
17      printf( "double value %.2f and the string \"%s\"\n", d, stringPtr );
18
19      return 0; /* indicates successful termination */
20
21   } /* end main */
```

```
The string "51.2% are admitted" is converted to the
double value 51.20 and the string "% are admitted"
```

Fig. 8.9 | Using strtod.

Function **strtol** (Fig. 8.10) converts to long a sequence of characters representing an integer. The function receives three arguments—a string (char *), a pointer to a string and an integer. The string contains the character sequence to be converted. The pointer is assigned the location of the first character after the converted portion of the string. The integer specifies the base of the value being converted. Line 13

```
x = strtol( string, &remainderPtr, 0 );
```

indicates that x is assigned the long value converted from string. The second argument, remainderPtr, is assigned the remainder of string after the conversion. Using NULL for the second argument causes the remainder of the string to be ignored. The third argument, 0, indicates that the value to be converted can be in octal (base 8), decimal (base 10) or hexadecimal (base 16) format. The base can be specified as 0 or any value between 2 and 36. See Appendix D, Number Systems, for a detailed explanation of the octal, decimal and hexadecimal number systems. Numeric representations of integers from base 11 to base 36 use the characters A–Z to represent the values 10 to 35. For example, hexadecimal values can consist of the digits 0–9 and the characters A–F. A base-11 integer can consist of the digits 0–9 and the character A. A base-24 integer can consist of the digits 0–9 and the characters A–N. A base-36 integer can consist of the digits 0–9 and the characters A–Z.

```
1   /* Fig. 8.10: fig08_10.c
2      Using strtol */
3   #include <stdio.h>
4   #include <stdlib.h>
5
6   int main( void )
7   {
8      const char *string = "-1234567abc"; /* initialize string pointer */
9
10     char *remainderPtr; /* create char pointer */
11     long x;             /* variable to hold converted sequence */
12
13     x = strtol( string, &remainderPtr, 0 );
14
15     printf( "%s\"%s\"\n%s%ld\n%s\"%s\"\n%s%ld\n",
16             "The original string is ", string,
17             "The converted value is ", x,
18             "The remainder of the original string is ",
19             remainderPtr,
20             "The converted value plus 567 is ", x + 567 );
21
22     return 0; /* indicates successful termination */
23
24   } /* end main */
```

```
The original string is "-1234567abc"
The converted value is -1234567
The remainder of the original string is "abc"
The converted value plus 567 is -1234000
```

Fig. 8.10 | Using strtol.

Function `strtoul` (Fig. 8.11) converts to unsigned long a sequence of characters representing an unsigned long integer. The function works identically to function strtol. The statement

```
x = strtoul( string, &remainderPtr, 0 );
```

in Fig. 8.11 indicates that x is assigned the unsigned long value converted from string. The second argument, &remainderPtr, is assigned the remainder of string after the conversion. The third argument, 0, indicates that the value to be converted can be in octal, decimal or hexadecimal format.

8.5 Standard Input/Output Library Functions

This section presents several functions from the standard input/output library (**<stdio.h>**) specifically for manipulating character and string data. Figure 8.12 summarizes the character and string input/output functions of the standard input/output library.

Error-Prevention Tip 8.4

When using functions from the standard input/output library, include the <stdio.h> header.

```
1   /* Fig. 8.11: fig08_11.c
2      Using strtoul */
3   #include <stdio.h>
4   #include <stdlib.h>
5
6   int main( void )
7   {
8      const char *string = "1234567abc"; /* initialize string pointer */
9      unsigned long x;    /* variable to hold converted sequence */
10     char *remainderPtr; /* create char pointer */
11
12     x = strtoul( string, &remainderPtr, 0 );
13
14     printf( "%s\"%s\"\n%s%lu\n%s\"%s\"\n%s%lu\n",
15             "The original string is ", string,
16             "The converted value is ", x,
17             "The remainder of the original string is ",
18             remainderPtr,
19             "The converted value minus 567 is ", x - 567 );
20
21     return 0; /* indicates successful termination */
22
23   } /* end main */
```

```
The original string is "1234567abc"
The converted value is 1234567
The remainder of the original string is "abc"
The converted value minus 567 is 1234000
```

Fig. 8.11 | Using strtoul.

Function prototype	Function description
`int getchar( void );`	Inputs the next character from the standard input and returns it as an integer.
`char *gets( char *s );`	Inputs characters from the standard input into the array `s` until a newline or end-of-file character is encountered. A terminating null character is appended to the array. Returns the string inputted into `s`. Note that an error will occur if `s` is not large enough to hold the string.
`int putchar( int c );`	Prints the character stored in `c` and returns it as an integer.
`int puts( const char *s );`	Prints the string s followed by a newline character. Returns a non-zero integer if successful, or EOF if an error occurs.
`int sprintf( char *s, const char *format, ... );`	
	Equivalent to `printf`, except the output is stored in the array `s` instead of printed on the screen. Returns the number of characters written to `s`, or EOF if an error occurs.
`int sscanf( char *s, const char *format, ... );`	
	Equivalent to `scanf`, except the input is read from the array s rather than from the keyboard. Returns the number of items successfully read by the function, or EOF if an error occurs.

Fig. 8.12 | Standard input/output library character and string functions.

Figure 8.13 uses functions **gets** and **putchar** to read a line of text from the standard input (keyboard) and recursively output the characters of the line in reverse order. Function gets reads characters from the standard input into its argument—an array of type char—until a newline character or the end-of-file indicator is encountered. A null character ('\0') is appended to the array when reading terminates. Function putchar prints its character argument. The program calls recursive function reverse to print the line of text backward. If the first character of the array received by reverse is the null character '\0', reverse returns. Otherwise, reverse is called again with the address of the subarray beginning at element s[1], and character s[0] is output with putchar when the recursive call is completed. The order of the two statements in the else portion of the if statement causes reverse to walk to the terminating null character of the string before a character is printed. As the recursive calls are completed, the characters are output in reverse order.

```
1   /* Fig. 8.13: fig08_13.c
2      Using gets and putchar */
3   #include <stdio.h>
4
5   void reverse( const char * const sPtr ); /* prototype */
6
```

Fig. 8.13 | Using gets and putchar. (Part 1 of 2.)

```
7    int main( void )
8    {
9       char sentence[ 80 ]; /* create char array */
10
11      printf( "Enter a line of text:\n" );
12
13      /* use gets to read line of text */
14      gets( sentence );
15
16      printf( "\nThe line printed backward is:\n" );
17      reverse( sentence );
18
19      return 0; /* indicates successful termination */
20
21   } /* end main */
22
23   /* recursively outputs characters in string in reverse order */
24   void reverse( const char * const sPtr )
25   {
26      /* if end of the string */
27      if ( sPtr[ 0 ] == '\0' ) { /* base case */
28         return;
29      } /* end if */
30      else { /* if not end of the string */
31         reverse( &sPtr[ 1 ] ); /* recursion step */
32
33         putchar( sPtr[ 0 ] ); /* use putchar to display character */
34      } /* end else */
35
36   } /* end function reverse */
```

```
Enter a line of text:
Characters and Strings

The line printed backward is:
sgnirtS dna sretcarahC
```

```
Enter a line of text:
able was I ere I saw elba

The line printed backward is:
able was I ere I saw elba
```

Fig. 8.13 | Using gets and putchar. (Part 2 of 2.)

Figure 8.14 uses functions getchar and puts to read characters from the standard input into character array sentence and print the array of characters as a string. Function getchar reads a character from the standard input and returns the character as an integer. Function puts takes a string (char *) as an argument and prints the string followed by a newline character.

The program stops inputting characters when getchar reads the newline character entered by the user to end the line of text. A null character is appended to array sentence

```
 1   /* Fig. 8.14: fig08_14.c
 2      Using getchar and puts */
 3   #include <stdio.h>
 4
 5   int main( void )
 6   {
 7      char c;                 /* variable to hold character input by user */
 8      char sentence[ 80 ]; /* create char array */
 9      int i = 0;              /* initialize counter i */
10
11      /* prompt user to enter line of text */
12      puts( "Enter a line of text:" );
13
14      /* use getchar to read each character */
15      while ( ( c = getchar() ) != '\n') {
16         sentence[ i++ ] = c;
17      } /* end while */
18
19      sentence[ i ] = '\0'; /* terminate string */
20
21      /* use puts to display sentence */
22      puts( "\nThe line entered was:" );
23      puts( sentence );
24
25      return 0; /* indicates successful termination */
26
27   } /* end main */
```

```
Enter a line of text:
This is a test.

The line entered was:
This is a test.
```

Fig. 8.14 | Using getchar and puts.

(line 19) so that the array may be treated as a string. Then, function puts prints the string contained in sentence.

Figure 8.15 uses function sprintf to print formatted data into array s—an array of characters. The function uses the same conversion specifiers as printf (see Chapter 8 for a detailed discussion of formatting). The program inputs an int value and a double value to be formatted and printed to array s. Array s is the first argument of sprintf.

```
 1   /* Fig. 8.15: fig08_15.c
 2      Using sprintf */
 3   #include <stdio.h>
 4
 5   int main( void )
 6   {
 7      char s[ 80 ]; /* create char array */
```

Fig. 8.15 | Using sprintf. (Part 1 of 2.)

```
 8      int x;         /* x value to be input */
 9      double y;      /* y value to be input */
10
11      printf( "Enter an integer and a double:\n" );
12      scanf( "%d%lf", &x, &y );
13
14      sprintf( s, "integer:%6d\ndouble:%8.2f", x, y );
15
16      printf( "%s\n%s\n",
17              "The formatted output stored in array s is:", s );
18
19      return 0; /* indicates successful termination */
20
21   } /* end main */
```

```
Enter an integer and a double:
298 87.375
The formatted output stored in array s is:
integer:   298
double:   87.38
```

Fig. 8.15 | Using sprintf. (Part 2 of 2.)

Figure 8.16 uses function **sscanf** to read formatted data from character array s. The function uses the same conversion specifiers as scanf. The program reads an int and a double from array s and stores the values in x and y, respectively. The values of x and y are printed. Array s is the first argument of sscanf.

```
 1   /* Fig. 8.16: fig08_16.c
 2      Using sscanf */
 3   #include <stdio.h>
 4
 5   int main( void )
 6   {
 7      char s[] = "31298 87.375"; /* initialize array s */
 8      int x;     /* x value to be input */
 9      double y; /* y value to be input */
10
11      sscanf( s, "%d%lf", &x, &y );
12
13      printf( "%s\n%s%6d\n%s%8.3f\n",
14              "The values stored in character array s are:",
15              "integer:", x, "double:", y );
16
17      return 0; /* indicates successful termination */
18
19   } /* end main */
```

```
The values stored in character array s are:
integer: 31298
double:  87.375
```

Fig. 8.16 | Using sscanf.

8.6 String-Manipulation Functions of the String-Handling Library

The string-handling library (<string.h>) provides many useful functions for manipulating string data (copying strings and concatenating strings), comparing strings, searching strings for characters and other strings, tokenizing strings (separating strings into logical pieces) and determining the length of strings. This section presents the string-manipulation functions of the string-handling library. The functions are summarized in Fig. 8.17. Every function—except for strncpy—appends the null character to its result.

Functions strncpy and strncat specify a parameter of type size_t, which is a type defined by the C standard as the integral type of the value returned by operator sizeof.

Portability Tip 8.2

Type size_t is a system-dependent synonym for either type unsigned long *or type* unsigned int.

Error-Prevention Tip 8.5

When using functions from the string-handling library, include the <string.h> *header.*

Function strcpy copies its second argument (a string) into its first argument (a character array that must be large enough to store the string and its terminating null character, which is also copied). Function strncpy is equivalent to strcpy, except that strncpy specifies the number of characters to be copied from the string into the array. Note that function strncpy does not necessarily copy the terminating null character of its second argument. A terminating null character is written only if the number of characters to be copied is at least one more than the length of the string. For example, if "test" is the

Function prototype	Function description
`char *strcpy( char *s1, const char *s2 )`	Copies string s2 into array s1. The value of s1 is returned.
`char *strncpy( char *s1, const char *s2, size_t n )`	Copies at most n characters of string s2 into array s1. The value of s1 is returned.
`char *strcat( char *s1, const char *s2 )`	Appends string s2 to array s1. The first character of s2 overwrites the terminating null character of s1. The value of s1 is returned.
`char *strncat( char *s1, const char *s2, size_t n )`	Appends at most n characters of string s2 to array s1. The first character of s2 overwrites the terminating null character of s1. The value of s1 is returned.

Fig. 8.17 | String-manipulation functions of the string-handling library.

second argument, a terminating null character is written only if the third argument to strncpy is at least 5 (four characters in "test" plus a terminating null character). If the third argument is larger than 5, null characters are appended to the array until the total number of characters specified by the third argument are written.

Common Programming Error 8.6

Not appending a terminating null character to the first argument of a strncpy when the third argument is less than or equal to the length of the string in the second argument.

Figure 8.18 uses strcpy to copy the entire string in array x into array y and uses strncpy to copy the first 14 characters of array x into array z. A null character ('\0') is appended to array z, because the call to strncpy in the program does not write a terminating null character (the third argument is less than the string length of the second argument).

Function **strcat** appends its second argument (a string) to its first argument (a character array containing a string). The first character of the second argument replaces the null ('\0') that terminates the string in the first argument. You must ensure that the array used to store the first string is large enough to store the first string, the second string and

```
1    /* Fig. 8.18: fig08_18.c
2       Using strcpy and strncpy */
3    #include <stdio.h>
4    #include <string.h>
5
6    int main( void )
7    {
8       char x[] = "Happy Birthday to You"; /* initialize char array x */
9       char y[ 25 ]; /* create char array y */
10      char z[ 15 ]; /* create char array z */
11
12      /* copy contents of x into y */
13      printf( "%s%s\n%s%s\n",
14         "The string in array x is: ", x,
15         "The string in array y is: ", strcpy( y, x ) );
16
17      /* copy first 14 characters of x into z. Does not copy null
18         character */
19      strncpy( z, x, 14 );
20
21      z[ 14 ] = '\0'; /* terminate string in z */
22      printf( "The string in array z is: %s\n", z );
23
24      return 0; /* indicates successful termination */
25
26   } /* end main */
```

```
The string in array x is: Happy Birthday to You
The string in array y is: Happy Birthday to You
The string in array z is: Happy Birthday
```

Fig. 8.18 | Using strcpy and strncpy.

the terminating null character copied from the second string. Function strcat appends a specified number of characters from the second string to the first string. A terminating null character is automatically appended to the result. Figure 8.19 demonstrates function strcat and function strncat.

8.7 Comparison Functions of the String-Handling Library

This section presents the string-handling library's string-comparison functions, strcmp and strncmp. Fig. 8.20 contains their prototypes and a brief description of each function.

Figure 8.21 compares three strings using strcmp and strncmp. Function strcmp compares its first string argument with its second string argument, character by character. The function returns 0 if the strings are equal, a negative value if the first string is less than the second string and a positive value if the first string is greater than the second string. Function strncmp is equivalent to strcmp, except that strncmp compares up to a specified number of characters. Function strncmp does not compare characters following a null character in a string. The program prints the integer value returned by each function call.

```c
1   /* Fig. 8.19: fig08_19.c
2      Using strcat and strncat */
3   #include <stdio.h>
4   #include <string.h>
5
6   int main( void )
7   {
8      char s1[ 20 ] = "Happy "; /* initialize char array s1 */
9      char s2[] = "New Year "; /* initialize char array s2 */
10     char s3[ 40 ] = "";      /* initialize char array s3 to empty */
11
12     printf( "s1 = %s\ns2 = %s\n", s1, s2 );
13
14     /* concatenate s2 to s1 */
15     printf( "strcat( s1, s2 ) = %s\n", strcat( s1, s2 ) );
16
17     /* concatenate first 6 characters of s1 to s3. Place '\0'
18        after last character */
19     printf( "strncat( s3, s1, 6 ) = %s\n", strncat( s3, s1, 6 ) );
20
21     /* concatenate s1 to s3 */
22     printf( "strcat( s3, s1 ) = %s\n", strcat( s3, s1 ) );
23
24     return 0; /* indicates successful termination */
25
26  } /* end main */
```

```
s1 = Happy
s2 = New Year
strcat( s1, s2 ) = Happy New Year
strncat( s3, s1, 6 ) = Happy
strcat( s3, s1 ) = Happy Happy New Year
```

Fig. 8.19 | Using strcat and strncat.

Function prototype	Function description
`int strcmp( const char *s1, const char *s2 );`	
	Compares the string s1 with the string s2. The function returns 0, less than 0 or greater than 0 if s1 is equal to, less than or greater than s2, respectively.
`int strncmp( const char *s1, const char *s2, size_t n );`	
	Compares up to n characters of the string s1 with the string s2. The function returns 0, less than 0 or greater than 0 if s1 is equal to, less than or greater than s2, respectively.

Fig. 8.20 | String-comparison functions of the string-handling library.

```
1   /* Fig. 8.21: fig08_21.c
2      Using strcmp and strncmp */
3   #include <stdio.h>
4   #include <string.h>
5
6   int main( void )
7   {
8      const char *s1 = "Happy New Year"; /* initialize char pointer */
9      const char *s2 = "Happy New Year"; /* initialize char pointer */
10     const char *s3 = "Happy Holidays"; /* initialize char pointer */
11
12     printf("%s%s\n%s%s\n%s%s\n\n%s%2d\n%s%2d\n%s%2d\n\n",
13        "s1 = ", s1, "s2 = ", s2, "s3 = ", s3,
14        "strcmp(s1, s2) = ", strcmp( s1, s2 ),
15        "strcmp(s1, s3) = ", strcmp( s1, s3 ),
16        "strcmp(s3, s1) = ", strcmp( s3, s1 ) );
17
18     printf("%s%2d\n%s%2d\n%s%2d\n",
19        "strncmp(s1, s3, 6) = ", strncmp( s1, s3, 6 ),
20        "strncmp(s1, s3, 7) = ", strncmp( s1, s3, 7 ),
21        "strncmp(s3, s1, 7) = ", strncmp( s3, s1, 7 ) );
22
23     return 0; /* indicates successful termination */
24
25   } /* end main */
```

```
s1 = Happy New Year
s2 = Happy New Year
s3 = Happy Holidays

strcmp(s1, s2) =  0
strcmp(s1, s3) =  1
strcmp(s3, s1) = -1
```

Fig. 8.21 | Using `strcmp` and `strncmp`. (Part 1 of 2.)

```
strncmp(s1, s3, 6) =  0
strncmp(s1, s3, 7) =  1
strncmp(s3, s1, 7) = -1
```

Fig. 8.21 | Using strcmp and strncmp. (Part 2 of 2.)

Common Programming Error 8.7

Assuming that strcmp and strncmp return 1 when their arguments are equal is a logic error. Both functions return 0 (strangely, the equivalent of C's false value) for equality. Therefore, when testing two strings for equality, the result of function strcmp or strncmp should be compared with 0 to determine if the strings are equal.

To understand just what it means for one string to be "greater than" or "less than" another string, consider the process of alphabetizing a series of last names. The reader would, no doubt, place "Jones" before "Smith," because the first letter of "Jones" comes before the first letter of "Smith" in the alphabet. But the alphabet is more than just a list of 26 letters—it is an ordered list of characters. Each letter occurs in a specific position within the list. "Z" is more than merely a letter of the alphabet; "Z" is specifically the 26th letter of the alphabet.

How does the computer know that one particular letter comes before another? All characters are represented inside the computer as **numeric codes**; when the computer compares two strings, it actually compares the numeric codes of the characters in the strings.

Portability Tip 8.3

The internal numeric codes used to represent characters may be different on different computers.

In an effort to standardize character representations, most computer manufacturers have designed their machines to utilize one of two popular coding schemes—ASCII or EBCDIC. ASCII stands for "American Standard Code for Information Interchange," and EBCDIC stands for "Extended Binary Coded Decimal Interchange Code." There are other coding schemes, but these two are the most popular. The recent Unicode® Standard outlines a specification to produce consistent encoding of the vast majority of the world's characters and symbols. To learn more about Unicode, visit www.unicode.org.

ASCII, EBCDIC and Unicode are called **character sets**. String and character manipulations actually involve the manipulation of the appropriate numeric codes and not the characters themselves. This explains the interchangeability of characters and small integers in C. Since it is meaningful to say that one numeric code is greater than, less than or equal to another numeric code, it becomes possible to relate various characters or strings to one another by referring to the character codes. Appendix C lists the ASCII character codes.

8.8 Search Functions of the String-Handling Library

This section presents the functions of the string-handling library used to search strings for characters and other strings. The functions are summarized in Fig. 8.22. Note that functions strcspn and strspn return size_t.

Function prototype	Function description

`char *strchr( const char *s, int c );`

Locates the first occurrence of character c in string s. If c is found, a pointer to c in s is returned. Otherwise, a NULL pointer is returned.

`size_t strcspn( const char *s1, const char *s2 );`

Determines and returns the length of the initial segment of string s1 consisting of characters not contained in string s2.

`size_t strspn( const char *s1, const char *s2 );`

Determines and returns the length of the initial segment of string s1 consisting only of characters contained in string s2.

`char *strpbrk( const char *s1, const char *s2 );`

Locates the first occurrence in string s1 of any character in string s2. If a character from string s2 is found, a pointer to the character in string s1 is returned. Otherwise, a NULL pointer is returned.

`char *strrchr( const char *s, int c );`

Locates the last occurrence of c in string s. If c is found, a pointer to c in string s is returned. Otherwise, a NULL pointer is returned.

`char *strstr( const char *s1, const char *s2 );`

Locates the first occurrence in string s1 of string s2. If the string is found, a pointer to the string in s1 is returned. Otherwise, a NULL pointer is returned.

`char *strtok( char *s1, const char *s2 );`

A sequence of calls to strtok breaks string s1 into "tokens"—logical pieces such as words in a line of text—separated by characters contained in string s2. The first call contains s1 as the first argument, and subsequent calls to continue tokenizing the same string contain NULL as the first argument. A pointer to the current token is returned by each call. If there are no more tokens when the function is called, NULL is returned.

Fig. 8.22 | String-manipulation functions of the string-handling library.

Function strchr searches for the first occurrence of a character in a string. If the character is found, strchr returns a pointer to the character in the string; otherwise, strchr returns NULL. Figure 8.23 uses strchr to search for the first occurrences of 'a' and 'z' in the string "This is a test".

Function strcspn (Fig. 8.24) determines the length of the initial part of the string in its first argument that does not contain any characters from the string in its second argument. The function returns the length of the segment.

```
1   /* Fig. 8.23: fig08_23.c
2      Using strchr */
3   #include <stdio.h>
4   #include <string.h>
5
6   int main( void )
7   {
8      const char *string = "This is a test"; /* initialize char pointer */
9      char character1 = 'a'; /* initialize character1 */
10     char character2 = 'z'; /* initialize character2 */
11
12     /* if character1 was found in string */
13     if ( strchr( string, character1 ) != NULL ) {
14        printf( "\'%c\' was found in \"%s\".\n",
15           character1, string );
16     } /* end if */
17     else { /* if character1 was not found */
18        printf( "\'%c\' was not found in \"%s\".\n",
19           character1, string );
20     } /* end else */
21
22     /* if character2 was found in string */
23     if ( strchr( string, character2 ) != NULL ) {
24        printf( "\'%c\' was found in \"%s\".\n",
25           character2, string );
26     } /* end if */
27     else { /* if character2 was not found */
28        printf( "\'%c\' was not found in \"%s\".\n",
29           character2, string );
30     } /* end else */
31
32     return 0; /* indicates successful termination */
33
34  } /* end main */
```

```
'a' was found in "This is a test".
'z' was not found in "This is a test".
```

Fig. 8.23 | Using `strchr`.

```
1   /* Fig. 8.24: fig08_24.c
2      Using strcspn */
3   #include <stdio.h>
4   #include <string.h>
5
6   int main( void )
7   {
8      /* initialize two char pointers */
9      const char *string1 = "The value is 3.14159";
10     const char *string2 = "1234567890";
```

Fig. 8.24 | Using `strcspn`. (Part 1 of 2.)

```
11
12        printf( "%s%s\n%s%s\n\n%s\n%s%u\n",
13           "string1 = ", string1, "string2 = ", string2,
14           "The length of the initial segment of string1",
15           "containing no characters from string2 = ",
16           strcspn( string1, string2 ) );
17
18        return 0; /* indicates successful termination */
19
20     } /* end main */
```

```
string1 = The value is 3.14159
string2 = 1234567890

The length of the initial segment of string1
containing no characters from string2 = 13
```

Fig. 8.24 | Using `strcspn`. (Part 2 of 2.)

Function **strpbrk** searches its first string argument for the first occurrence of any character in its second string argument. If a character from the second argument is found, strpbrk returns a pointer to the character in the first argument; otherwise, strpbrk returns NULL. Figure 8.25 shows a program that locates the first occurrence in string1 of any character from string2.

```
1    /* Fig. 8.25: fig08_25.c
2       Using strpbrk */
3    #include <stdio.h>
4    #include <string.h>
5
6    int main( void )
7    {
8       const char *string1 = "This is a test"; /* initialize char pointer */
9       const char *string2 = "beware";         /* initialize char pointer */
10
11      printf( "%s\"%s\"\n'%c'%s\n\"%s\"\n",
12         "Of the characters in ", string2,
13         *strpbrk( string1, string2 ),
14         " appears earliest in ", string1 );
15
16      return 0; /* indicates successful termination */
17
18   } /* end main */
```

```
Of the characters in "beware"
'a' appears earliest in
"This is a test"
```

Fig. 8.25 | Using `strpbrk`.

The pointer parameters to these functions are declared void *. In Chapter 7, we saw that a pointer to any data type can be assigned directly to a pointer of type void *, and a pointer of type void * can be assigned directly to a pointer to any data type. For this reason, these functions can receive pointers to any data type. Because a void * pointer cannot be dereferenced, each function receives a size argument that specifies the number of characters (bytes) the function will process. For simplicity, the examples in this section manipulate character arrays (blocks of characters).

Function **memcpy** copies a specified number of characters from the object pointed to by its second argument into the object pointed to by its first argument. The function can receive a pointer to any type of object. The result of this function is undefined if the two objects overlap in memory (i.e., if they are parts of the same object)—in such cases, use memmove. Figure 8.31 uses memcpy to copy the string in array s2 to array s1.

Function **memmove**, like memcpy, copies a specified number of bytes from the object pointed to by its second argument into the object pointed to by its first argument. Copying is performed as if the bytes were copied from the second argument into a temporary character array, then copied from the temporary array into the first argument. This allows characters from one part of a string to be copied into another part of the same string. Figure 8.32 uses memmove to copy the last 10 bytes of array x into the first 10 bytes of array x.

Common Programming Error 8.8

String-manipulation functions other than memmove *that copy characters have undefined results when copying takes place between parts of the same string.*

Function **memcmp** (Fig. 8.33) compares the specified number of characters of its first argument with the corresponding characters of its second argument. The function returns

```
1   /* Fig. 8.31: fig08_31.c
2      Using memcpy */
3   #include <stdio.h>
4   #include <string.h>
5
6   int main( void )
7   {
8      char s1[ 17 ];                   /* create char array s1 */
9      char s2[]  = "Copy this string"; /* initialize char array s2 */
10
11     memcpy( s1, s2, 17 );
12     printf( "%s\n%s\"%s\"\n",
13             "After s2 is copied into s1 with memcpy,",
14             "s1 contains ", s1 );
15
16     return 0; /* indicates successful termination */
17
18   } /* end main */
```

```
After s2 is copied into s1 with memcpy,
s1 contains "Copy this string"
```

Fig. 8.31 | Using memcpy.

```
1   /* Fig. 8.32: fig08_32.c
2      Using memmove */
3   #include <stdio.h>
4   #include <string.h>
5
6   int main( void )
7   {
8      char x[] = "Home Sweet Home"; /* initialize char array x */
9
10     printf( "%s%s\n", "The string in array x before memmove is: ", x );
11     printf( "%s%s\n", "The string in array x after memmove is: ",
12             memmove( x, &x[ 5 ], 10 ) );
13
14     return 0; /* indicates successful termination */
15
16  } /* end main */
```

```
The string in array x before memmove is: Home Sweet Home
The string in array x after memmove is: Sweet Home Home
```

Fig. 8.32 | Using memmove.

a value greater than 0 if the first argument is greater than the second argument, returns 0 if the arguments are equal and returns a value less than 0 if the first argument is less than the second argument.

Function memchr searches for the first occurrence of a byte, represented as unsigned char, in the specified number of bytes of an object. If the byte is found, a pointer to the byte in the object is returned; otherwise, a NULL pointer is returned. Figure 8.34 searches for the character (byte) 'r' in the string "This is a string".

```
1   /* Fig. 8.33: fig08_33.c
2      Using memcmp */
3   #include <stdio.h>
4   #include <string.h>
5
6   int main( void )
7   {
8      char s1[] = "ABCDEFG"; /* initialize char array s1 */
9      char s2[] = "ABCDXYZ"; /* initialize char array s2 */
10
11     printf( "%s%s\n%s%s\n\n%s%2d\n%s%2d\n%s%2d\n",
12             "s1 = ", s1, "s2 = ", s2,
13             "memcmp( s1, s2, 4 ) = ", memcmp( s1, s2, 4 ),
14             "memcmp( s1, s2, 7 ) = ", memcmp( s1, s2, 7 ),
15             "memcmp( s2, s1, 7 ) = ", memcmp( s2, s1, 7 ) );
16
17     return 0; /* indicate successful termination */
18
19  } /* end main */
```

Fig. 8.33 | Using memcmp. (Part 1 of 2.)

```
s1 = ABCDEFG
s2 = ABCDXYZ

memcmp( s1, s2, 4 ) =  0
memcmp( s1, s2, 7 ) = -1
memcmp( s2, s1, 7 ) =  1
```

Fig. 8.33 | Using memcmp. (Part 2 of 2.)

```
1   /* Fig. 8.34: fig08_34.c
2      Using memchr */
3   #include <stdio.h>
4   #include <string.h>
5
6   int main( void )
7   {
8      const char *s = "This is a string"; /* initialize char pointer */
9
10     printf( "%s\'%c\'%s\"%s\"\n",
11             "The remainder of s after character ", 'r',
12             " is found is ", memchr( s, 'r', 16 ) );
13
14     return 0; /* indicates successful termination */
15
16  } /* end main */
```

```
The remainder of s after character 'r' is found is "ring"
```

Fig. 8.34 | Using memchr.

Function memset copies the value of the byte in its second argument into the first *n* bytes of the object pointed to by its first argument, where *n* is specified by the third argument. Figure 8.35 uses memset to copy 'b' into the first 7 bytes of string1.

```
1   /* Fig. 8.35: fig08_35.c
2      Using memset */
3   #include <stdio.h>
4   #include <string.h>
5
6   int main( void )
7   {
8      char string1[ 15 ] = "BBBBBBBBBBBBBB"; /* initialize string1 */
9
10     printf( "string1 = %s\n", string1 );
11     printf( "string1 after memset = %s\n", memset( string1, 'b', 7 ) );
12
13     return 0; /* indicates successful termination */
14
15  } /* end main */
```

Fig. 8.35 | Using memset. (Part 1 of 2.)

```
string1 = BBBBBBBBBBBBBBB
string1 after memset = bbbbbbbBBBBBBBB
```

Fig. 8.35 | Using memset. (Part 2 of 2.)

8.10 Other Functions of the String-Handling Library

The two remaining functions of the string-handling library are strerror and strlen. Figure 8.36 summarizes the strerror and strlen functions.

Function prototype	Function description
char *strerror(int errornum);	
	Maps errornum into a full text string in a locale-specific manner (e.g. the message may appear in different languages based on its location). A pointer to the string is returned.
size_t strlen(const char *s);	
	Determines the length of string s. The number of characters preceding the terminating null character is returned.

Fig. 8.36 | Other functions of the string-handling library.

Function **strerror** takes an error number and creates an error message string. A pointer to the string is returned. Figure 8.37 demonstrates strerror.

```
1   /* Fig. 8.37: fig08_37.c
2      Using strerror */
3   #include <stdio.h>
4   #include <string.h>
5
6   int main( void )
7   {
8      printf( "%s\n", strerror( 2 ) );
9
10     return 0; /* indicates successful termination */
11
12  } /* end main */
```

```
No such file or directory
```

Fig. 8.37 | Using strerror.

Portability Tip 8.4

The message generated by strerror is system dependent.

Function `strlen` takes a string as an argument and returns the number of characters in the string—the terminating null character is not included in the length. Figure 8.38 demonstrates function `strlen`.

```
 1   /* Fig. 8.38: fig08_38.c
 2      Using strlen */
 3   #include <stdio.h>
 4   #include <string.h>
 5
 6   int main( void )
 7   {
 8      /* initialize 3 char pointers */
 9      const char *string1 = "abcdefghijklmnopqrstuvwxyz";
10      const char *string2 = "four";
11      const char *string3 = "Boston";
12
13      printf("%s\"%s\"%s%lu\n%s\"%s\"%s%lu\n%s\"%s\"%s%lu\n",
14         "The length of ", string1, " is ",
15         ( unsigned long ) strlen( string1 ),
16         "The length of ", string2, " is ",
17         ( unsigned long ) strlen( string2 ),
18         "The length of ", string3, " is ",
19         ( unsigned long ) strlen( string3 ) );
20
21      return 0; /* indicates successful termination */
22
23   } /* end main */
```

```
The length of "abcdefghijklmnopqrstuvwxyz" is 26
The length of "four" is 4
The length of "Boston" is 6
```

Fig. 8.38 | Using `strlen`.

Summary

Section 8.2 Fundamentals of Strings and Characters

- Characters are the fundamental building blocks of source programs. Every program is composed of a sequence of characters that—when grouped together meaningfully—is interpreted by the computer as a series of instructions used to accomplish a task.

- A program may contain character constants. A character constant is an `int` value represented as a character in single quotes.

- The value of a character constant is the character's integer value in the machine's character set.

- A string is a series of characters treated as a single unit. A string may include letters, digits and various special characters such as +, -, *, / and $. String literals, or string constants, in C are written in double quotation marks.

- A string in C is an array of characters ending in the null character (`'\0'`).

- A string is accessed via a pointer to the first character in the string. The value of a string is the address of its first character. Thus, in C, it is appropriate to say that a string is a pointer—in fact, a pointer to the string's first character. In this sense, strings are like arrays, because an array is also a pointer to its first element.

- A character array or a variable of type char * can be initialized with a string in a definition.

- When defining a character array to contain a string, the array must be large enough to store the string and its terminating null character.

- A string can be stored in an array using scanf. Function scanf will read characters until a space, tab, newline or end-of-file indicator is encountered.

- For a character array to be printed as a string, the array must contain a terminating null character.

Section 8.3 Character-Handling Library

- Function islower determines whether its argument is a lowercase letter (a–z).

- Function isupper determines whether its argument is an uppercase letter (A–Z).

- Function isdigit determines whether its argument is a digit (0–9).

- Function isalpha determines whether its argument is an uppercase letter (A–Z) or a lowercase letter (a–z).

- Function isalnum determines whether its argument is an uppercase letter (A–Z), a lowercase letter (a–z) or a digit (0–9).

- Function isxdigit determines whether its argument is a hexadecimal digit (A–F, a–f, 0–9).

- Function toupper converts a lowercase letter to uppercase and returns the uppercase letter.

- Function tolower converts an uppercase letter to lowercase and returns the lowercase letter.

- Function isspace determines whether its argument is one of the following white-space characters: ' ' (space), '\f', '\n', '\r', '\t' or '\v'.

- Function iscntrl determines whether its argument is one of the following control characters: '\t', '\v', '\f', '\a', '\b', '\r' or '\n'.

- Function ispunct determines whether its argument is a printing character other than a space, a digit or a letter.

- Function isprint determines whether its argument is any printing character including the space character.

- Function isgraph determines whether its argument is a printing character other than the space character.

Section 8.4 String-Conversion Functions

- Function atof converts its argument—a string beginning with a series of digits that represents a floating-point number—to a double value.

- Function atoi converts its argument—a string beginning with a series of digits that represents an integer—to an int value.

- Function atol converts its argument—a string beginning with a series of digits that represents a long integer—to a long value.

- Function strtod converts a sequence of characters representing a floating-point value to double. The function receives two arguments—a string (char *) and a pointer to char *. The string contains the character sequence to be converted, and the location specified by the pointer to char * is assigned the address of the remainder of the string after the conversion.

- Function strtol converts a sequence of characters representing an integer to long. The function receives three arguments—a string (char *), a pointer to char * and an integer. The string contains the character sequence to be converted, the location specified by the pointer to char * is assigned the address of the remainder of the string after the conversion and the integer specifies the base of the value being converted.

- Function strtoul converts a sequence of characters representing an integer to unsigned long. The function receives three arguments—a string (char *), a pointer to char * and an integer. The string contains the character sequence to be converted, the location specified by the pointer to char * is assigned the address of the remainder of the string after the conversion and the integer specifies the base of the value being converted.

Section 8.5 Standard Input/Output Library Functions

- Function gets reads characters from the standard input (keyboard) until a newline character or the end-of-file indicator is encountered. The argument to gets is an array of type char. A null character ('\0') is appended to the array after reading terminates.

- Function putchar prints its character argument.

- Function getchar reads a single character from the standard input and returns the character as an integer. If the end-of-file indicator is encountered, getchar returns EOF.

- Function puts takes a string (char *) as an argument and prints the string followed by a newline character.

- Function sprintf uses the same conversion specifications as function printf to print formatted data into an array of type char.

- Function sscanf uses the same conversion specifications as function scanf to read formatted data from a string.

Section 8.6 String-Manipulation Functions of the String-Handling Library

- Function strcpy copies its second argument (a string) into its first argument (a character array). You must ensure that the array is large enough to store the string and its terminating null character.

- Function strncpy is equivalent to strcpy, except that a call to strncpy specifies the number of characters to be copied from the string into the array. The terminating null character will be copied only if the number of characters to be copied is one more than the length of the string.

- Function strcat appends its second string argument—including the terminating null character—to its first string argument. The first character of the second string replaces the null ('\0') character of the first string. You must ensure that the array used to store the first string is large enough to store both the first string and the second string.

- Function strncat appends a specified number of characters from the second string to the first string. A terminating null character is appended to the result.

Section 8.7 Comparison Functions of the String-Handling Library

- Function strcmp compares its first string argument to its second string argument, character by character. The function returns 0 if the strings are equal, returns a negative value if the first string is less than the second string and returns a positive value if the first string is greater than the second string.

- Function strncmp is equivalent to strcmp, except that strncmp compares a specified number of characters. If the number of characters in one of the strings is less than the number of characters specified, strncmp compares characters until the null character in the shorter string is encountered.

Section 8.8 Search Functions of the String-Handling Library

- Function strchr searches for the first occurrence of a character in a string. If the character is found, strchr returns a pointer to the character in the string; otherwise, strchr returns NULL.

- Function `strcspn` determines the length of the initial part of the string in its first argument that does not contain any characters from the string in its second argument. The function returns the length of the segment.

- Function `strpbrk` searches for the first occurrence in its first argument of any character in its second argument. If a character from the second argument is found, `strpbrk` returns a pointer to the character; otherwise, `strpbrk` returns `NULL`.

- Function `strrchr` searches for the last occurrence of a character in a string. If the character is found, `strrchr` returns a pointer to the character in the string; otherwise, `strrchr` returns `NULL`.

- Function `strspn` determines the length of the initial part of the string in its first argument that contains only characters from the string in its second argument. The function returns the length of the segment.

- Function `strstr` searches for the first occurrence of its second string argument in its first string argument. If the second string is found in the first string, a pointer to the location of the string in the first argument is returned.

- A sequence of calls to `strtok` breaks the first string `s1` into tokens that are separated by characters contained in the second string `s2`. The first call contains `s1` as the first argument, and subsequent calls to continue tokenizing the same string contain `NULL` as the first argument. A pointer to the current token is returned by each call. If there are no more tokens when the function is called, a `NULL` pointer is returned.

Section 8.9 Memory Functions of the String-Handling Library

- Function `memcpy` copies a specified number of characters from the object to which its second argument points into the object to which its first argument points. The function can receive a pointer to any type of object. The pointers are received as `void` pointers and converted to `char` pointers for use in the function. Function `memcpy` manipulates the bytes of the object as characters.

- Function `memmove` copies a specified number of bytes from the object pointed to by its second argument to the object pointed to by its first argument. Copying is accomplished as if the bytes were copied from the second argument to a temporary character array and then copied from the temporary array to the first argument.

- Function `memcmp` compares the specified number of characters of its first and second arguments.

- Function `memchr` searches for the first occurrence of a byte, represented as `unsigned char`, in the specified number of bytes of an object. If the byte is found, a pointer to the byte is returned; otherwise, a `NULL` pointer is returned.

- Function `memset` copies its second argument, treated as an `unsigned char`, to a specified number of bytes of the object pointed to by the first argument.

Section 8.10 Other Functions of the String-Handling Library

- Function `strerror` maps an integer error number into a full text string in a locale specific manner. A pointer to the string is returned.

- Function `strlen` takes a string as an argument and returns the number of characters in the string—the terminating null character is not included in the length of the string.

Terminology

appending strings to other strings	character code
ASCII	character constant
atof	character-handling library
atoi	character set
atol	comparing strings

control character

copying strings

ctype.h

delimiter

EOF

general utilities library

getchar

gets

hexadecimal digits

isalnum

isalpha

iscntrl

isdigit

isgraph

islower

isprint

ispunct

isspace

isupper

isxdigit

length of a string

literal

memchr

memcmp

memcpy

memmove

memset

numeric code representation of a character

printing character

putchar

puts

search functions

search string

sprintf

sscanf

stdio.h

stdlib.h

strcat

strchr

strcmp

strcpy

strcspn

strerror

string

string-comparison functions

string concatenation

string constant

string-conversion functions

string literal

string-manipulation functions

string processing

string.h

strlen

strncat

strncmp

strncpy

strpbrk

strrchr

strspn

strstr

strtod

strtok

strtol

strtoul

tokenizing strings

tolower

toupper

Unicode

whit-espace characters

word processing

Self-Review Exercises

8.1 Write a single statement to accomplish each of the following. Assume that variables c (which stores a character), x, y and z are of type int, variables d, e and f are of type double, variable ptr is of type char * and arrays s1[100] and s2[100] are of type char.

   a) Convert the character stored in variable c to an uppercase letter. Assign the result to variable c.

   b) Determine if the value of variable c is a digit. Use the conditional operator as shown in Figs. 8.2–8.4 to print " is a " or " is not a " when the result is displayed.

   c) Convert the string "1234567" to long and print the value.

   d) Determine if the value of variable c is a control character. Use the conditional operator to print " is a " or " is not a " when the result is displayed.

   e) Read a line of text into array s1 from the keyboard. Do not use scanf.

   f) Print the line of text stored in array s1. Do not use printf.

   g) Assign ptr the location of the last occurrence of c in s1.

h) Print the value of variable c. Do not use printf.

i) Convert the string "8.63582" to double and print the value.

j) Determine if the value of c is a letter. Use the conditional operator to print " is a " or " is not a " when the result is displayed.

k) Read a character from the keyboard and store the character in variable c.

l) Assign ptr the location of the first occurrence of s2 in s1.

m) Determine if the value of variable c is a printing character. Use the conditional operator to print " is a " or " is not a " when the result is displayed.

n) Read three double values into variables d, e and f from the string "1.27 10.3 9.432".

o) Copy the string stored in array s2 into array s1.

p) Assign ptr the location of the first occurrence in s1 of any character from s2.

q) Compare the string in s1 with the string in s2. Print the result.

r) Assign ptr the location of the first occurrence of c in s1.

s) Use sprintf to print the values of integer variables x, y and z into array s1. Each value should be printed with a field width of 7.

t) Append 10 characters from the string in s2 to the string in s1.

u) Determine the length of the string in s1. Print the result.

v) Convert the string "-21" to int and print the value.

w) Assign ptr to the location of the first token in s2. Tokens in the string s2 are separated by commas (,).

8.2 Show two different methods of initializing character array vowel with the string of vowels "AEIOU".

8.3 What, if anything, prints when each of the following C statements is performed? If the statement contains an error, describe the error and indicate how to correct it. Assume the following variable definitions:

```
char s1[ 50 ] = "jack", s2[ 50 ] = " jill", s3[ 50 ], *sptr;
```

a) printf("%c%s", toupper(s1[0]), &s1[1]);

b) printf("%s", strcpy(s3, s2));

c) printf("%s",
        strcat(strcat(strcpy(s3, s1), " and "), s2));

d) printf("%u", strlen(s1) + strlen(s2));

e) printf("%u", strlen(s3));

8.4 Find the error in each of the following program segments and explain how to correct it:

a) char s[10];
   strncpy(s, "hello", 5);
   printf("%s\n", s);

b) printf("%s", 'a');

c) char s[12];
   strcpy(s, "Welcome Home");

d) if (strcmp(string1, string2))
       printf("The strings are equal\n");

Answers to Self-Review Exercises

8.1 a) c = toupper(c);

b) printf("'%c'%sdigit\n", c, isdigit(c) ? " is a " : " is not a ");

c) printf("%ld\n", atol("1234567"));

d) printf("'%c'%scontrol character\n",
            c, iscntrl(c) ? " is a " : " is not a ");

e) gets(s1);
f) puts(s1);
g) ptr = strrchr(s1, c);
h) putchar(c);
i) printf("%f\n", atof("8.63582"));
j) printf("'%c'%sletter\n", c, isalpha(c) ? " is a " : " is not a ");
k) c = getchar();
l) ptr = strstr(s1, s2);
m) printf("'%c'%sprinting character\n",
        c, isprint(c) ? " is a " : " is not a ");
n) sscanf("1.27 10.3 9.432", "%f%f%f", &d, &e, &f);
o) strcpy(s1, s2);
p) ptr = strpbrk(s1, s2);
q) printf("strcmp(s1, s2) = %d\n", strcmp(s1, s2));
r) ptr = strchr(s1, c);
s) sprintf(s1, "%7d%7d%7d", x, y, z);
t) strncat(s1, s2, 10);
u) printf("strlen(s1) = %u\n", strlen(s1));
v) printf("%d\n", atoi("-21")); *
w) ptr = strtok(s2, ",");

8.2   char vowel[] = "AEIOU";
          char vowel[] = { 'A', 'E', 'I', 'O', 'U', '\0' };

8.3   a) Jack
          b) jill
          c) jack and jill
          d) 8
          e) 13

8.4   a) Error: Function strncpy does not write a terminating null character to array s, because
             its third argument is equal to the length of the string "hello".
             Correction: Make the third argument of strncpy 6, or assign '\0' to s[5].
          b) Error: Attempting to print a character constant as a string.
             Correction: Use %c to output the character, or replace 'a' with "a".
          c) Error: Character array s is not large enough to store the terminating null character.
             Correction: Declare the array with more elements.
          d) Error: Function strcmp returns 0 if the strings are equal; therefore, the condition in the
             if statement is false, and the printf will not be executed.
             Correction: Compare the result of strcmp with 0 in the condition.

Exercises

8.5   Write a program that inputs a character from the keyboard and tests the character with each
of the functions in the character-handling library. The program should print the value returned by
each function.

8.6   Write a program that inputs a line of text with function gets into char array s[100]. Output the line in uppercase letters and in lowercase letters.

8.7   Write a program that inputs four strings that represent integers, converts the strings to integers, sums the values and prints the total of the four values.

8.8   Write a program that inputs four strings that represent floating-point values, converts the strings to double values, sums the values and prints the total of the four values.

8.9   Write a program that uses function strcmp to compare two strings input by the user. The program should state whether the first string is less than, equal to or greater than the second string.

8.10   Write a program that uses function strncmp to compare two strings input by the user. The program should input the number of characters to be compared. The program should state whether the first string is less than, equal to or greater than the second string.

8.11   Write a program that uses random number generation to create sentences. The program should use four arrays of pointers to char called article, noun, verb and preposition. The program should create a sentence by selecting a word at random from each array in the following order: article, noun, verb, preposition, article and noun. As each word is picked, it should be concatenated to the previous words in an array large enough to hold the entire sentence. The words should be separated by spaces. When the final sentence is output, it should start with a capital letter and end with a period. The program should generate 20 such sentences. The arrays should be filled as follows: The article array should contain the articles "the", "a", "one", "some" and "any"; the noun array should contain the nouns "boy", "girl", "dog", "town" and "car"; the verb array should contain the verbs "drove", "jumped", "ran", "walked" and "skipped"; the preposition array should contain the prepositions "to", "from", "over", "under" and "on".

After the preceding program is written and working, modify it to produce a short story consisting of several of these sentences. (How about the possibility of a random term paper writer?)

8.12   *(Limericks)* A limerick is a humorous five-line verse in which the first and second lines rhyme with the fifth, and the third line rhymes with the fourth. Using techniques similar to those developed in Exercise 8.11, write a program that produces random limericks. Polishing this program to produce good limericks is a challenging problem, but the result will be worth the effort!

8.13   Write a program that encodes English-language phrases into pig Latin. Pig Latin is a form of coded language often used for amusement. Many variations exist in the methods used to form pig-Latin phrases. For simplicity, use the following algorithm:

To form a pig-Latin phrase from an English-language phrase, tokenize the phrase into words with function strtok. To translate each English word into a pig-Latin word, place the first letter of the English word at the end of the English word and add the letters "ay." Thus the word "jump" becomes "umpjay," the word "the" becomes "hetay" and the word "computer" becomes "omputercay." Blanks between words remain as blanks. Assume the following: The English phrase consists of words separated by blanks, there are no punctuation marks, and all words have two or more letters. Function printLatinWord should display each word. [*Hint:* Each time a token is found in a call to strtok, pass the token pointer to function printLatinWord, and print the pig-Latin word.]

8.14   Write a program that inputs a telephone number as a string in the form (555) 555-5555. The program should use function strtok to extract the area code as a token, the first three digits of the phone number as a token and the last four digits of the phone number as a token. The seven digits of the phone number should be concatenated into one string. The program should convert the area-code string to int and convert the phone-number string to long. Both the area code and the phone number should be printed.

8.15   Write a program that inputs a line of text, tokenizes the line with function strtok and outputs the tokens in reverse order.

8.16   Write a program that inputs a line of text and a search string from the keyboard. Using function strstr, locate the first occurrence of the search string in the line of text, and assign the location to variable searchPtr of type char *. If the search string is found, print the remainder of the line of text beginning with the search string. Then, use strstr again to locate the next occurrence of the search string in the line of text. If a second occurrence is found, print the remainder of the line of text beginning with the second occurrence. [*Hint:* The second call to strstr should contain searchPtr + 1 as its first argument.]

8.17 Write a program based on the program of Exercise 8.16 that inputs several lines of text and a search string and uses function strstr to determine the total occurrences of the string in the lines of text. Print the result.

8.18 Write a program that inputs several lines of text and a search character and uses function strchr to determine the total occurrences of the character in the lines of text.

8.19 Write a program based on the program of Exercise 8.18 that inputs several lines of text and uses function strchr to determine the total occurrences of each letter of the alphabet in the lines of text. Uppercase and lowercase letters should be counted together. Store the totals for each letter in an array and print the values in tabular format after the totals have been determined.

8.20 Write a program that inputs several lines of text and uses strtok to count the total number of words. Assume that the words are separated by either spaces or newline characters.

8.21 Use the string-comparison functions discussed in Section 8.6 and the techniques for sorting arrays developed in Chapter 6 to write a program that alphabetizes a list of strings. Use the names of 10 or 15 towns in your area as data for your program.

8.22 The chart in Appendix C shows the numeric code representations for the characters in the ASCII character set. Study this chart and then state whether each of the following is *true* or *false*.
    a) The letter "A" comes before the letter "B."
    b) The digit "9" comes before the digit "0."
    c) The commonly used symbols for addition, subtraction, multiplication and division all come before any of the digits.
    d) The digits come before the letters.
    e) If a sort program sorts strings into ascending sequence, then the program will place the symbol for a right parenthesis before the symbol for a left parenthesis.

8.23 Write a program that reads a series of strings and prints only those strings beginning with the letter "b."

8.24 Write a program that reads a series of strings and prints only those strings that end with the letters "ed."

8.25 Write a program that inputs an ASCII code and prints the corresponding character. Modify this program so that it generates all possible three-digit codes in the range 000 to 255 and attempts to print the corresponding characters. What happens when this program is run?

8.26 Using the ASCII character chart in Appendix C as a guide, write your own versions of the character-handling functions in Fig. 8.1.

8.27 Write your own versions of the functions in Fig. 8.5 for converting strings to numbers.

8.28 Write two versions of each of the string-copy and string-concatenation functions in Fig. 8.17. The first version should use array subscripting, and the second version should use pointers and pointer arithmetic.

8.29 Write your own versions of the functions getchar, gets, putchar and puts described in Fig. 8.12.

8.30 Write two versions of each string-comparison function in Fig. 8.20. The first version should use array subscripting, and the second version should use pointers and pointer arithmetic.

8.31 Write your own versions of the functions in Fig. 8.22 for searching strings.

8.32 Write your own versions of the functions in Fig. 8.30 for manipulating blocks of memory.

8.33 Write two versions of function strlen in Fig. 8.36. The first version should use array subscripting, and the second version should use pointers and pointer arithmetic.

Special Section: Advanced String-Manipulation Exercises

The preceding exercises are keyed to the text and designed to test the reader's understanding of fundamental string-manipulation concepts. This section includes a collection of intermediate and advanced problems. The reader should find these problems challenging yet enjoyable. The problems vary considerably in difficulty. Some require an hour or two of program writing and implementation. Others are useful for lab assignments that might require two or three weeks of study and implementation. Some are challenging term projects.

8.34 *(Text Analysis)* The availability of computers with string-manipulation capabilities has resulted in some rather interesting approaches to analyzing the writings of great authors. Much attention has been focused on whether William Shakespeare ever lived. Some scholars find substantial evidence that Christopher Marlowe actually penned the masterpieces attributed to Shakespeare. Researchers have used computers to find similarities in the writings of these two authors. This exercise examines three methods for analyzing texts with a computer.

a) Write a program that reads several lines of text and prints a table indicating the number of occurrences of each letter of the alphabet in the text. For example, the phrase

```
To be, or not to be: that is the question:
```

contains one "a," two "b's," no "c's," and so on.

b) Write a program that reads several lines of text and prints a table indicating the number of one-letter words, two-letter words, three-letter words, and so on, appearing in the text. For example, the phrase

```
Whether 'tis nobler in the mind to suffer
```

contains

Word length	Occurrences
1	0
2	2
3	1
4	2 (including 'tis)
5	0
6	2
7	1

c) Write a program that reads several lines of text and prints a table indicating the number of occurrences of each different word in the text. The first version of your program should include the words in the table in the same order in which they appear in the text. A more interesting (and useful) printout should then be attempted in which the words are sorted alphabetically. For example, the lines

```
To be, or not to be: that is the question:
Whether 'tis nobler in the mind to suffer
```

contain the words "to" three times, the word "be" two times, the word "or" once, and so on.

8.35 *(Word Processing)* The detailed treatment of string manipulation in this text is largely attributable to the exciting growth in word processing in recent years. One important function in word-processing systems is *type justification*—the alignment of words to both the left and right margins of a page. This generates a professional-looking document that gives the appearance of being set in type, rather than prepared on a typewriter. Type justification can be accomplished on computer systems by inserting one or more blank characters between each of the words in a line so that the rightmost word aligns with the right margin.

Write a program that reads several lines of text and prints this text in type-justified format. Assume that the text is to be printed on 8 1/2-inch-wide paper and that one-inch margins are to be allowed on both the left and right sides of the printed page. Assume that the computer prints 10 characters to the horizontal inch. Therefore, your program should print 6 1/2 inches of text or 65 characters per line.

8.36 *(Printing Dates in Various Formats)* Dates are commonly printed in several different formats in business correspondence. Two of the more common formats are

```
07/21/2003 and July 21, 2003
```

Write a program that reads a date in the first format and prints it in the second format.

8.37 *(Check Protection)* Computers are frequently used in check-writing systems, such as payroll and accounts payable applications. Many stories circulate regarding weekly paychecks being printed (by mistake) for amounts in excess of $1 million. Weird amounts are printed by computerized check-writing systems because of human error and/or machine failure. Systems designers, of course, make every effort to build controls into their systems to prevent erroneous checks from being issued.

Another serious problem is the intentional alteration of a check amount by someone who intends to cash it fraudulently. To prevent a dollar amount from being altered, most computerized check-writing systems employ a technique called *check protection.*

Checks designed for imprinting by computer contain a fixed number of spaces in which the computer may print an amount. Suppose a paycheck contains nine blank spaces in which the computer is supposed to print the amount of a weekly paycheck. If the amount is large, then all nine of those spaces will be filled—for example:

```
11,230.60  (check amount)
---------
123456789  (position numbers)
```

On the other hand, if the amount is less than $1000, then several of the spaces will ordinarily be left blank—for example,

```
    99.87
---------
123456789
```

contains three blank spaces. If a check is printed with blank spaces, it is easier for someone to alter the amount of the check. To prevent a check from being altered, many check-writing systems insert *leading asterisks* to protect the amount as follows:

```
****99.87
---------
123456789
```

Write a program that inputs a dollar amount to be printed on a check and then prints the amount in check-protected format with leading asterisks if necessary. Assume that nine spaces are available for printing an amount.

8.38 *(Writing the Word Equivalent of a Check Amount)* Continuing the discussion of the previous example, we reiterate the importance of designing check-writing systems to prevent alteration of check amounts. One common security method requires that the check amount be both written in numbers and "spelled out" in words. Even if someone is able to alter the numerical amount of the check, it is extremely difficult to change the amount in words.

Many computerized check-writing systems do not print the amount of the check in words. Perhaps the main reason for this omission is the fact that most high-level languages used in commercial applications do not contain adequate string-manipulation features. Another reason is that the logic for writing word equivalents of check amounts is somewhat involved.

Write a program that inputs a numeric check amount and writes the word equivalent of the amount. For example, the amount 112.43 should be written as

```
ONE HUNDRED TWELVE and 43/100
```

8.39   *(Morse Code)* Perhaps the most famous of all coding schemes is Morse code, developed by Samuel Morse in 1832 for use with the telegraph system. Morse code assigns a series of dots and dashes to each letter of the alphabet, each digit, and a few special characters (such as period, comma, colon and semicolon). In sound-oriented systems, the dot represents a short sound and the dash represents a long sound. Other representations of dots and dashes are used with light-oriented systems and signal-flag systems.

Separation between words is indicated by a space—quite simply, the absence of a dot or dash. In a sound-oriented system, a space is indicated by a short period of time during which no sound is transmitted. The international version of Morse code appears in Fig. 8.39.

Write a program that reads an English-language phrase and encodes the phrase into Morse code. Also write a program that reads a phrase in Morse code and converts the phrase into the English-language equivalent. Use one blank between each Morse-coded letter and three blanks between each Morse-coded word.

8.40   *(A Metric Conversion Program)* Write a program that will assist the user with metric conversions. Your program should allow the user to specify the names of the units as strings (i.e., centimeters, liters, grams, and so on for the metric system and inches, quarts, pounds, and so on for the English system) and should respond to simple questions such as

```
"How many inches are in 2 meters?"
"How many liters are in 10 quarts?"
```

Your program should recognize invalid conversions. For example, the question

```
"How many feet in 5 kilograms?"
```

is not meaningful, because "feet" are units of length while "kilograms" are units of mass.

8.41   *(Dunning Letters)* Many businesses spend a great deal of time and money collecting overdue debts. *Dunning* is the process of making repeated and insistent demands upon a debtor in an attempt to collect a debt.

Computers are often used to generate dunning letters automatically and in increasing degrees of severity as a debt ages. The theory is that as a debt becomes older, it becomes more difficult to collect, and therefore the dunning letters must become more threatening.

Write a program that contains the texts of five dunning letters of increasing severity. Your program should accept as input the following:

    a) Debtor's name
    b) Debtor's address
    c) Debtor's account
    d) Amount owed
    e) Age of the amount owed (i.e., one month overdue, two months overdue, and so on).

Use the age of the amount owed to select one of the five message texts, and then print the dunning letter, inserting the other user-supplied information where appropriate.

Character	Code	Character	Code
A	.-	T	-
B	-...	U	..-
C	-.-.	V	...-
D	-..	W	.--
E	.	X	-..-
F	..-.	Y	-.--
G	--.	Z	--..
H	....		
I	..	*Digits*	
J	.---	1	.----
K	-.-	2	..---
L	.-..	3	...--
M	--	4	....-
N	-.	5	.....
O	---	6	-....
P	.--.	7	--...
Q	--.-	8	---..
R	.-.	9	----.
S	...	0	-----

Fig. 8.39 | The letters of the alphabet as expressed in international Morse code.

A Challenging String-Manipulation Project

8.42   (*A Crossword-Puzzle Generator*) Most people have worked a crossword puzzle at one time or another, but few have ever attempted to generate one. Generating a crossword puzzle is a difficult problem. It is suggested here as a string-manipulation project requiring substantial sophistication and effort. There are many issues you must resolve to get even the simplest crossword-puzzle generator program working. For example, how does one represent the grid of a crossword puzzle inside the computer? Should one use a series of strings, or should double-subscripted arrays be used? You need a source of words (i.e., a computerized dictionary) that can be directly referenced by the program. In what form should these words be stored to facilitate the complex manipulations required by the program? The really ambitious reader will want to generate the "clues" portion of the puzzle in which the brief hints for each "across" word and each "down" word are printed for the puzzle worker. Merely printing a version of the blank puzzle itself is not a simple problem.

9

C Formatted Input/Output

OBJECTIVES

In this chapter, you will learn:

- To use input and output streams.
- To use all print formatting capabilities.
- To use all input formatting capabilities.
- To print with field widths and precisions.
- To use formatting flags in the `printf` format control string.
- To output literals and escape sequences.
- To format input using `scanf`.

9.1 Introduction

An important part of the solution to any problem is the presentation of the results. In this chapter, we discuss in depth the formatting features of `scanf` and `printf`. These functions input data from the standard input stream and output data to the standard output stream. Four other functions that use the standard input and standard output—gets, puts, getchar and putchar—were discussed in Chapter 8. Include the header `<stdio.h>` in programs that call these functions.

Many features of `printf` and `scanf` were discussed earlier in the text. This chapter summarizes those features and introduces others. Chapter 11 discusses several additional functions included in the standard input/output (`stdio`) library.

9.2 Streams

All input and output is performed with streams, which are sequences of bytes. In input operations, the bytes flow from a device (e.g., a keyboard, a disk drive, a network connection) to main memory. In output operations, bytes flow from main memory to a device (e.g., a display screen, a printer, a disk drive, a network connection, and so on).

When program execution begins, three streams are connected to the program automatically. Normally, the standard input stream is connected to the keyboard and the standard output stream is connected to the screen. Operating systems often allow these streams to be redirected to other devices. A third stream, the standard error stream, is connected to the screen. Error messages are output to the standard error stream. Streams are discussed in detail in Chapter 11, File Processing.

9.3 Formatting Output with `printf`

Precise output formatting is accomplished with `printf`. Every `printf` call contains a format control string that describes the output format. The format control string consists of conversion specifiers, flags, field widths, precisions and literal characters. Together with the percent sign (%), these form **conversion specifications**. Function `printf` can perform the following formatting capabilities, each of which is discussed in this chapter:

1. Rounding floating-point values to an indicated number of decimal places.
2. Aligning a column of numbers with decimal points appearing one above the other.
3. Right justification and left justification of outputs.
4. Inserting literal characters at precise locations in a line of output.
5. Representing floating-point numbers in exponential format.
6. Representing unsigned integers in octal and hexadecimal format. See Appendix D, Number Systems, for more information on octal and hexadecimal values.
7. Displaying all types of data with fixed-size field widths and precisions.

The `printf` function has the form

```
printf( format-control-string, other-arguments );
```

format-control-string describes the output format, and *other-arguments* (which are optional) correspond to each conversion specification in *format-control-string*. Each conversion specification begins with a percent sign and ends with a conversion specifier. There can be many conversion specifications in one format control string.

Common Programming Error 9.1

Forgetting to enclose a format-control-string in quotation marks is a syntax error.

Good Programming Practice 9.1

Format outputs neatly for presentation to make program outputs more readable and reduce user errors.

9.4 Printing Integers

An integer is a whole number, such as 776, 0 or −52, that contains no decimal point. Integer values are displayed in one of several formats. Figure 9.1 describes the integer conversion specifiers.

Conversion specifier	Description
d	Display as a signed decimal integer.
i	Display as a signed decimal integer. [*Note:* The i and d specifiers are different when used with `scanf`.]
o	Display as an unsigned octal integer.
u	Display as an unsigned decimal integer.

Fig. 9.1 | Integer conversion specifiers. (Part 1 of 2.)

Conversion specifier	Description
x or X	Display as an unsigned hexadecimal integer. X causes the digits 0-9 and the letters A-F to be displayed and x causes the digits 0-9 and a-f to be displayed.
h or l (letter l)	Place before any integer conversion specifier to indicate that a short or long integer is displayed, respectively. Letters h and l are more precisely called length modifiers.

Fig. 9.1 | Integer conversion specifiers. (Part 2 of 2.)

Figure 9.2 prints an integer using each of the integer conversion specifiers. Note that only the minus sign prints; plus signs are suppressed. Later in this chapter we will see how to force plus signs to print. Also note that the value -455, when read by %u (line 15), is converted to the unsigned value 4294966841.

```
1   /* Fig 9.2: fig09_02.c */
2   /* Using the integer conversion specifiers */
3   #include <stdio.h>
4
5   int main( void )
6   {
7      printf( "%d\n", 455 );
8      printf( "%i\n", 455 );   /* i same as d in printf */
9      printf( "%d\n", +455 );
10     printf( "%d\n", -455 );
11     printf( "%hd\n", 32000 );
12     printf( "%ld\n", 2000000000L ); /* L suffix makes literal a long */
13     printf( "%o\n", 455 );
14     printf( "%u\n", 455 );
15     printf( "%u\n", -455 );
16     printf( "%x\n", 455 );
17     printf( "%X\n", 455 );
18
19     return 0; /* indicates successful termination */
20
21  } /* end main */
```

```
455
455
455
-455
32000
2000000000
707
455
4294966841
1c7
1C7
```

Fig. 9.2 | Using integer conversion specifiers.

Common Programming Error 9.2

Printing a negative value with a conversion specifier that expects an unsigned value.

9.5 Printing Floating-Point Numbers

A floating-point value contains a decimal point as in 33.5, 0.0 or -657.983. Floating-point values are displayed in one of several formats. Figure 9.3 describes the floating-point conversion specifiers. The conversion specifiers e and E display floating-point values in exponential notation—the computer equivalent of scientific notation used in mathematics. For example, the value 150.4582 is represented in scientific notation as

$$1.504582 \times 10^2$$

and is represented in exponential notation as

$$1.504582E+02$$

by the computer. This notation indicates that 1.504582 is multiplied by 10 raised to the second power (E+02). The E stands for "exponent."

Values displayed with the conversion specifiers e, E and f show six digits of precision to the right of the decimal point by default (e.g., 1.04592); other precisions can be specified explicitly. Conversion specifier f always prints at least one digit to the left of the decimal point. Conversion specifiers e and E print lowercase e and uppercase E, respectively, preceding the exponent, and print exactly one digit to the left of the decimal point.

Conversion specifier g (or G) prints in either e (E) or f format with no trailing zeros (1.234000 is printed as 1.234). Values are printed with e (E) if, after conversion to exponential notation, the value's exponent is less than -4, or the exponent is greater than or equal to the specified precision (six significant digits by default for g and G). Otherwise, conversion specifier f is used to print the value. Trailing zeros are not printed in the fractional part of a value output with g or G. At least one decimal digit is required for the decimal point to be output. The values 0.0000875, 8750000.0, 8.75, 87.50 and 875 are printed as 8.75e-05, 8.75e+06, 8.75, 87.5 and 875 with the conversion specifier g. The value 0.0000875 uses e notation because, when it is converted to exponential notation, its exponent (-5) is less than -4. The value 8750000.0 uses e notation because its exponent (6) is equal to the default precision.

Conversion specifier	Description
e or E	Display a floating-point value in exponential notation.
f	Display floating-point values in fixed-point notation.
g or G	Display a floating-point value in either the floating-point form f or the exponential form e (or E), based on the magnitude of the value.
L	Place before any floating-point conversion specifier to indicate that a long double floating-point value is displayed.

Fig. 9.3 | Floating-point conversion specifiers.

The precision for conversion specifiers g and G indicates the maximum number of significant digits printed, including the digit to the left of the decimal point. The value 1234567.0 is printed as 1.23457e+06, using conversion specifier %g (remember that all floating-point conversion specifiers have a default precision of 6). Note that there are 6 significant digits in the result. The difference between g and G is identical to the difference between e and E when the value is printed in exponential notation—lowercase g causes a lowercase e to be output, and uppercase G causes an uppercase E to be output.

Error-Prevention Tip 9.1

When outputting data, be sure that the user is aware of situations in which data may be imprecise due to formatting (e.g., rounding errors from specifying precisions).

Figure 9.4 demonstrates each of the floating-point conversion specifiers. Note that the %E, %e and %g conversion specifiers cause the value to be rounded in the output and the conversion specifier %f does not.

9.6 Printing Strings and Characters

The c and s conversion specifiers are used to print individual characters and strings, respectively. Conversion specifier c requires a char argument. Conversion specifier s re-

```
 1   /* Fig 9.4: fig09_04.c */
 2   /* Printing floating-point numbers with
 3      floating-point conversion specifiers */
 4
 5   #include <stdio.h>
 6
 7   int main( void )
 8   {
 9      printf( "%e\n", 1234567.89 );
10      printf( "%e\n", +1234567.89 );
11      printf( "%e\n", -1234567.89 );
12      printf( "%E\n", 1234567.89 );
13      printf( "%f\n", 1234567.89 );
14      printf( "%g\n", 1234567.89 );
15      printf( "%G\n", 1234567.89 );
16
17      return 0; /* indicates successful termination */
18
19   } /* end main */
```

```
1.234568e+006
1.234568e+006
-1.234568e+006
1.234568E+006
1234567.890000
1.23457e+006
1.23457E+006
```

Fig. 9.4 | Using floating-point conversion specifiers.

quires a pointer to char as an argument. Conversion specifier s causes characters to be printed until a terminating null ('\0') character is encountered. The program shown in Fig. 9.5 displays characters and strings with conversion specifiers c and s.

Common Programming Error 9.3

*Using %c to print a string is an error. The conversion specifier %c expects a char argument. A string is a pointer to char (i.e., a char *).*

Common Programming Error 9.4

Using %s to print a char argument, on some systems, causes a fatal execution-time error called an access violation. The conversion specifier %s expects an argument of type pointer to char.

Common Programming Error 9.5

Using single quotes around character strings is a syntax error. Character strings must be enclosed in double quotes.

Common Programming Error 9.6

Using double quotes around a character constant creates a pointer to a string consisting of two characters, the second of which is the terminating null. A character constant is a single character enclosed in single quotes.

```c
1   /* Fig 9.5: fig09_05c */
2   /* Printing strings and characters */
3   #include <stdio.h>
4
5   int main( void )
6   {
7      char character = 'A'; /* initialize char */
8      char string[] = "This is a string"; /* initialize char array */
9      const char *stringPtr = "This is also a string"; /* char pointer */
10
11     printf( "%c\n", character );
12     printf( "%s\n", "This is a string" );
13     printf( "%s\n", string );
14     printf( "%s\n", stringPtr );
15
16     return 0; /* indicates successful termination */
17
18  } /* end main */
```

```
A
This is a string
This is a string
This is also a string
```

Fig. 9.5 | Using the character and string conversion specifiers.

9.7 Other Conversion Specifiers

The three remaining conversion specifiers are p, n and % (Fig. 9.6).

The **conversion specifier n** stores the number of characters already output in the current printf statement—the corresponding argument is a pointer to an integer variable in which the value is stored. Nothing is printed by a %n conversion specifier. The conversion specifier % causes a percent sign to be output.

Figure 9.7's %p prints the value of ptr and the address of x; these values are identical because ptr is assigned the address of x. Next, %n stores the number of characters output by the third printf statement (line 15) in integer variable y, and the value of y is printed. The last printf statement (line 21) uses %% to print the % character in a character string. Note that every printf call returns a value—either the number of characters output, or a negative value if an output error occurs.

Portability Tip 9.1

The conversion specifier p displays an address in an implementation-defined manner (on many systems, hexadecimal notation is used rather than decimal notation).

Common Programming Error 9.7

Trying to print a literal percent character using % rather than %% in the format control string. When % appears in a format control string, it must be followed by a conversion specifier.

Conversion specifier	Description
p	Display a pointer value in an implementation-defined manner.
n	Store the number of characters already output in the current printf statement. A pointer to an integer is supplied as the corresponding argument. Nothing is displayed.
%	Display the percent character.

Fig. 9.6 | Other conversion specifiers.

```
1   /* Fig 9.7: fig09_07.c */
2   /* Using the p, n, and % conversion specifiers */
3   #include <stdio.h>
4
5   int main( void )
6   {
7      int *ptr;        /* define pointer to int */
8      int x = 12345;   /* initialize int x */
9      int y;           /* define int y */
10
11     ptr = &x;        /* assign address of x to ptr */
12     printf( "The value of ptr is %p\n", ptr );
13     printf( "The address of x is %p\n\n", &x );
```

Fig. 9.7 | Using the p, n and % conversion specifiers. (Part 1 of 2.)

```
14
15      printf( "Total characters printed on this line:%n", &y );
16      printf( " %d\n\n", y );
17
18      y = printf( "This line has 28 characters\n%n" );
19      printf( "%d characters were printed\n\n", y );
20
21      printf( "Printing a %% in a format control string\n" );
22
23      return 0; /* indicates successful termination */
24
25   } /* end main */
```

```
The value of ptr is 0012FF78
The address of x is 0012FF78

Total characters printed on this line: 38

This line has 28 characters
28 characters were printed

Printing a % in a format control string
```

Fig. 9.7 | Using the p, n and % conversion specifiers. (Part 2 of 2.)

9.8 Printing with Field Widths and Precision

The exact size of a field in which data is printed is specified by a field width. If the field width is larger than the data being printed, the data will normally be right justified within that field. An integer representing the field width is inserted between the percent sign (%) and the conversion specifier (e.g., %4d). Figure 9.8 prints two groups of five numbers each, right justifying those numbers that contain fewer digits than the field width. Note that the field width is increased to print values wider than the field and that the minus sign for a negative value uses one character position in the field width. Field widths can be used with all conversion specifiers.

```
1    /* Fig 9.8: fig09_08.c */
2    /* Printing integers right-justified */
3    #include <stdio.h>
4
5    int main( void )
6    {
7       printf( "%4d\n", 1 );
8       printf( "%4d\n", 12 );
9       printf( "%4d\n", 123 );
10      printf( "%4d\n", 1234 );
11      printf( "%4d\n\n", 12345 );
12
13      printf( "%4d\n", -1 );
14      printf( "%4d\n", -12 );
```

Fig. 9.8 | Right justifying integers in a field. (Part 1 of 2.)

```
15    printf( "%4d\n", -123 );
16    printf( "%4d\n", -1234 );
17    printf( "%4d\n", -12345 );
18
19    return 0; /* indicates successful termination */
20
21  } /* end main */
```

```
   1
  12
 123
1234
12345

  -1
 -12
-123
-1234
-12345
```

Fig. 9.8 | Right justifying integers in a field. (Part 2 of 2.)

Common Programming Error 9.8

Not providing a sufficiently large field width to handle a value to be printed can offset other data being printed and can produce confusing outputs. Know your data!

Function printf also enables you to specify the precision with which data is printed. Precision has different meanings for different data types. When used with integer conversion specifiers, precision indicates the minimum number of digits to be printed. If the printed value contains fewer digits than the specified precision and the precision value has a leading zero or decimal point, zeros are prefixed to the printed value until the total number of digits is equivalent to the precision. If neither a zero nor a decimal point is present in the precision value, spaces are inserted instead. The default precision for integers is 1. When used with floating-point conversion specifiers e, E and f, the precision is the number of digits to appear after the decimal point. When used with conversion specifiers g and G, the precision is the maximum number of significant digits to be printed. When used with conversion specifier s, the precision is the maximum number of characters to be written from the string. To use precision, place a decimal point (.), followed by an integer representing the precision between the percent sign and the conversion specifier. Figure 9.9 demonstrates the use of precision in format control strings. Note that when a floating-point value is printed with a precision smaller than the original number of decimal places in the value, the value is rounded.

```
1   /* Fig 9.9: fig09_09.c */
2   /* Using precision while printing integers,
3      floating-point numbers, and strings */
4   #include <stdio.h>
5
```

Fig. 9.9 | Using precisions to display information of several types (Part 1 of 2.).

```
 6   int main( void )
 7   {
 8      int i = 873;                /* initialize int i */
 9      double f = 123.94536;       /* initialize double f */
10      char s[] = "Happy Birthday"; /* initialize char array s */
11
12      printf( "Using precision for integers\n" );
13      printf( "\t%.4d\n\t%.9d\n\n", i, i );
14
15      printf( "Using precision for floating-point numbers\n" );
16      printf( "\t%.3f\n\t%.3e\n\t%.3g\n\n", f, f, f );
17
18      printf( "Using precision for strings\n" );
19      printf( "\t%.11s\n", s );
20
21      return 0; /* indicates successful termination */
22
23   } /* end main */
```

```
Using precision for integers
        0873
        000000873

Using precision for floating-point numbers
        123.945
        1.239e+002
        124

Using precision for strings
        Happy Birth
```

Fig. 9.9 | Using precisions to display information of several types (Part 2 of 2.).

The field width and the precision can be combined by placing the field width, followed by a decimal point, followed by a precision between the percent sign and the conversion specifier, as in the statement

```
printf( "%9.3f", 123.456789 );
```

which displays 123.457 with three digits to the right of the decimal point right justified in a nine-digit field.

It is possible to specify the field width and the precision using integer expressions in the argument list following the format control string. To use this feature, insert an asterisk (*) in place of the field width or precision (or both). The matching int argument in the argument list is evaluated and used in place of the asterisk. A field width's value may be either positive or negative (which causes the output to be left justified in the field as described in the next section). The statement

```
printf( "%*.*f", 7, 2, 98.736 );
```

uses 7 for the field width, 2 for the precision and outputs the value 98.74 right justified.

9.9 Using Flags in the `printf` Format Control String

Function `printf` also provides flags to supplement its output formatting capabilities. Five flags are available for use in format control strings (Fig. 9.10).

To use a flag in a format control string, place the flag immediately to the right of the percent sign. Several flags may be combined in one conversion specifier.

Figure 9.11 demonstrates right justification and left justification of a string, an integer, a character and a floating-point number.

Flag	Description
- (minus sign)	Left justify the output within the specified field.
+ (plus sign)	Display a plus sign preceding positive values and a minus sign preceding negative values.
space	Print a space before a positive value not printed with the + flag.
#	Prefix 0 to the output value when used with the octal conversion specifier o.
	Prefix 0x or 0X to the output value when used with the hexadecimal conversion specifiers x or X.
	Force a decimal point for a floating-point number printed with e, E, f, g or G that does not contain a fractional part. (Normally the decimal point is printed only if a digit follows it.) For g and G specifiers, trailing zeros are not eliminated.
0 (zero)	Pad a field with leading zeros.

Fig. 9.10 | Format control string flags.

```
1   /* Fig 9.11: fig09_11.c */
2   /* Right justifying and left justifying values */
3   #include <stdio.h>
4
5   int main( void )
6   {
7      printf( "%10s%10d%10c%10f\n\n", "hello", 7, 'a', 1.23 );
8      printf( "%-10s%-10d%-10c%-10f\n", "hello", 7, 'a', 1.23 );
9
10     return 0; /* indicates successful termination */
11
12  } /* end main */
```

```
     hello         7         a  1.230000

hello     7         a         1.230000
```

Fig. 9.11 | Left justifying strings in a field.

Figure 9.12 prints a positive number and a negative number, each with and without the + flag. Note that the minus sign is displayed in both cases, but the plus sign is displayed only when the + flag is used.

Figure 9.13 prefixes a space to the positive number with the space flag. This is useful for aligning positive and negative numbers with the same number of digits. Note that the value -547 is not preceded by a space in the output because of its minus sign.

Figure 9.14 uses the # flag to prefix 0 to the octal value and 0x and 0X to the hexadecimal values, and to force the decimal point on a value printed with g.

Figure 9.15 combines the + flag and the 0 (zero) flag to print 452 in a 9-space field with a + sign and leading zeros, then prints 452 again using only the 0 flag and a 9-space field.

```
1   /* Fig 9.12: fig09_12.c */
2   /* Printing numbers with and without the + flag */
3   #include <stdio.h>
4
5   int main( void )
6   {
7      printf( "%d\n%d\n", 786, -786 );
8      printf( "%+d\n%+d\n", 786, -786 );
9
10     return 0; /* indicates successful termination */
11
12  } /* end main */
```

```
786
-786
+786
-786
```

Fig. 9.12 | Printing positive and negative numbers with and without the + flag.

```
1   /* Fig 9.13: fig09_13.c */
2   /* Printing a space before signed values
3      not preceded by + or - */
4   #include <stdio.h>
5
6   int main( void )
7   {
8      printf( "% d\n% d\n", 547, -547 );
9
10     return 0; /* indicates successful termination */
11
12  } /* end main */
```

```
 547
-547
```

Fig. 9.13 | Using the space flag.

```
 1  /* Fig 9.14: fig09_14.c */
 2  /* Using the # flag with conversion specifiers
 3     o, x, X and any floating-point specifier */
 4  #include <stdio.h>
 5
 6  int main( void )
 7  {
 8     int c = 1427;      /* initialize c */
 9     double p = 1427.0; /* initialize p */
10
11     printf( "%#o\n", c );
12     printf( "%#x\n", c );
13     printf( "%#X\n", c );
14     printf( "\n%g\n", p );
15     printf( "%#g\n", p );
16
17     return 0; /* indicates successful termination */
18
19  } /* end main */
```

```
02623
0x593
0X593

1427
1427.00
```

Fig. 9.14 | Using the # flag.

```
 1  /* Fig 9.15: fig09_15.c */
 2  /* Printing with the 0( zero ) flag fills in leading zeros */
 3  #include <stdio.h>
 4
 5  int main( void )
 6  {
 7     printf( "%+09d\n", 452 );
 8     printf( "%09d\n", 452 );
 9
10     return 0; /* indicates successful termination */
11
12  } /* end main */
```

```
+00000452
000000452
```

Fig. 9.15 | Using the 0 (zero) flag.

9.10 Printing Literals and Escape Sequences

Most literal characters to be printed in a printf statement can simply be included in the format control string. However, there are several "problem" characters, such as the quotation mark (") that delimits the format control string itself. Various control characters, such as newline and tab, must be represented by escape sequences. An escape sequence is represented by a backslash (\), followed by a particular escape character. Figure 9.16 lists the escape sequences and the actions they cause.

 Common Programming Error 9.9

Attempting to print as literal data in a printf *statement a single quote, double quote or backslash character without preceding that character with a backslash to form a proper escape sequence is an error.*

9.11 Reading Formatted Input with scanf

Precise input formatting can be accomplished with scanf. Every scanf statement contains a format control string that describes the format of the data to be input. The format control string consists of conversion specifiers and literal characters. Function scanf has the following input formatting capabilities:

1. Inputting all types of data.

2. Inputting specific characters from an input stream.

3. Skipping specific characters in the input stream.

Function scanf is written in the following form:

scanf(*format-control-string*, *other-arguments*);

format-control-string describes the formats of the input, and *other-arguments* are pointers to variables in which the input will be stored.

Escape sequence	Description
\' (single quote)	Output the single quote (') character.
\" (double quote)	Output the double quote (") character.
\? (question mark)	Output the question mark (?) character.
\\ (backslash)	Output the backslash (\) character.
\a (alert or bell)	Cause an audible (bell) or visual alert.
\b (backspace)	Move the cursor back one position on the current line.
\f (new page or form feed)	Move the cursor to the start of the next logical page.
\n (newline)	Move the cursor to the beginning of the next line.
\r (carriage return)	Move the cursor to the beginning of the current line.
\t (horizontal tab)	Move the cursor to the next horizontal tab position.
\v (vertical tab)	Move the cursor to the next vertical tab position.

Fig. 9.16 | Escape sequences.

Good Programming Practice 9.2

When inputting data, prompt the user for one data item or a few data items at a time. Avoid asking the user to enter many data items in response to a single prompt.

Good Programming Practice 9.3

Always consider what the user and your program will do when (not if) incorrect data is entered—for example, a value for an integer that is nonsensical in a program's context, or a string with missing punctuation or spaces.

Figure 9.17 summarizes the conversion specifiers used to input all types of data. The remainder of this section provides programs that demonstrate reading data with the various scanf conversion specifiers.

Conversion specifier	Description
Integers	
d	Read an optionally signed decimal integer. The corresponding argument is a pointer to an int.
i	Read an optionally signed decimal, octal or hexadecimal integer. The corresponding argument is a pointer to an int.
o	Read an octal integer. The corresponding argument is a pointer to an unsigned int.
u	Read an unsigned decimal integer. The corresponding argument is a pointer to an unsigned int.
x or X	Read a hexadecimal integer. The corresponding argument is a pointer to an unsigned int.
h or l	Place before any of the integer conversion specifiers to indicate that a short or long integer is to be input.
Floating-point numbers	
e, E, f, g or G	Read a floating-point value. The corresponding argument is a pointer to a floating-point variable.
l or L	Place before any of the floating-point conversion specifiers to indicate that a double or long double value is to be input. The corresponding argument is a pointer to a double or long double variable.
Characters and strings	
c	Read a character. The corresponding argument is a pointer to a char; no null ('\0') is added.
s	Read a string. The corresponding argument is a pointer to an array of type char that is large enough to hold the string and a terminating null ('\0') character—which is automatically added.

Fig. 9.17 | Conversion specifiers for scanf. (Part 1 of 2.)

Conversion specifier	Description
Scan set	
[*scan characters*]	Scan a string for a set of characters that are stored in an array.
Miscellaneous	
p	Read an address of the same form produced when an address is output with %p in a printf statement.
n	Store the number of characters input so far in this call to scanf. The corresponding argument is a pointer to an int.
%	Skip a percent sign (%) in the input.

Fig. 9.17 | Conversion specifiers for scanf. (Part 2 of 2.)

Figure 9.18 reads integers with the various integer conversion specifiers and displays the integers as decimal numbers. Note that %i is capable of inputting decimal, octal and hexadecimal integers.

When inputting floating-point numbers, any of the floating-point conversion specifiers e, E, f, g or G can be used. Figure 9.19 reads three floating-point numbers, one with each of the three types of floating conversion specifiers, and displays all three numbers with conversion specifier f. Note that the program output confirms the fact that floating-point values are imprecise—this is highlighted by the third value printed.

```
1   /* Fig 9.18: fig09_18.c */
2   /* Reading integers */
3   #include <stdio.h>
4
5   int main( void )
6   {
7      int a;
8      int b;
9      int c;
10     int d;
11     int e;
12     int f;
13     int g;
14
15     printf( "Enter seven integers: " );
16     scanf( "%d%i%i%i%o%u%x", &a, &b, &c, &d, &e, &f, &g );
17
18     printf( "The input displayed as decimal integers is:\n" );
19     printf( "%d %d %d %d %d %d %d\n", a, b, c, d, e, f, g );
20
21     return 0; /* indicates successful termination */
22
23  } /* end main */
```

Fig. 9.18 | Reading input with integer conversion specifiers. (Part 1 of 2.)

```
Enter seven integers: -70 -70 070 0x70 70 70 70
The input displayed as decimal integers is:
-70 -70 56 112 56 70 112
```

Fig. 9.18 | Reading input with integer conversion specifiers. (Part 2 of 2.)

```
1   /* Fig 9.19: fig09_19.c */
2   /* Reading floating-point numbers */
3   #include <stdio.h>
4
5   /* function main begins program execution */
6   int main( void )
7   {
8      double a;
9      double b;
10     double c;
11
12     printf( "Enter three floating-point numbers: \n" );
13     scanf( "%le%lf%lg", &a, &b, &c );
14
15     printf( "Here are the numbers entered in plain\n" );
16     printf( "floating-point notation:\n" );
17     printf( "%f\n%f\n%f\n", a, b, c );
18
19     return 0; /* indicates successful termination */
20
21  } /* end main */
```

```
Enter three floating-point numbers:
1.27987 1.27987e+03 3.38476e-06
Here are the numbers entered in plain
floating-point notation:
1.279870
1279.870000
0.000003
```

Fig. 9.19 | Reading input with floating-point conversion specifiers.

Characters and strings are input using the conversion specifiers c and s, respectively. Figure 9.20 prompts the user to enter a string. The program inputs the first character of the string with %c and stores it in the character variable x, then inputs the remainder of the string with %s and stores it in character array y.

```
1   /* Fig 9.20: fig09_20.c */
2   /* Reading characters and strings */
3   #include <stdio.h>
4
5   int main( void )
6   {
```

Fig. 9.20 | Inputting characters and strings. (Part 1 of 2.)

```
 7        char x;
 8        char y[ 9 ];
 9
10        printf( "Enter a string: " );
11        scanf( "%c%s", &x, y );
12
13        printf( "The input was:\n" );
14        printf( "the character \"%c\" ", x );
15        printf( "and the string \"%s\"\n", y );
16
17        return 0; /* indicates successful termination */
18
19   } /* end main */
```

```
Enter a string: Sunday
The input was:
the character "S" and the string "unday"
```

Fig. 9.20 | Inputting characters and strings. (Part 2 of 2.)

A sequence of characters can be input using a scan set. A scan set is a set of characters enclosed in square brackets, [], and preceded by a percent sign in the format control string. A scan set scans the characters in the input stream, looking only for those characters that match characters contained in the scan set. Each time a character is matched, it is stored in the scan set's corresponding argument—a pointer to a character array. The scan set stops inputting characters when a character that is not contained in the scan set is encountered. If the first character in the input stream does not match a character in the scan set, only the null character is stored in the array. Figure 9.21 uses the scan set [aeiou] to scan the input stream for vowels. Notice that the first seven letters of the input are read. The eighth letter (h) is not in the scan set and therefore the scanning is terminated.

```
 1   /* Fig 9.21: fig09_21.c */
 2   /* Using a scan set */
 3   #include <stdio.h>
 4
 5   /* function main begins program execution */
 6   int main( void )
 7   {
 8      char z[ 9 ]; /* define array z */
 9
10      printf( "Enter string: " );
11      scanf( "%[aeiou]", z ); /* search for set of characters */
12
13      printf( "The input was \"%s\"\n", z );
14
15      return 0; /* indicates successful termination */
16
17   } /* end main */
```

Fig. 9.21 | Using a scan set. (Part 1 of 2.)

```
Enter string: ooeeooahah
The input was "ooeeooa"
```

Fig. 9.21 | Using a scan set. (Part 2 of 2.)

The scan set can also be used to scan for characters not contained in the scan set by using an inverted scan set. To create an inverted scan set, place a caret (^) in the square brackets before the scan characters. This causes characters not appearing in the scan set to be stored. When a character contained in the inverted scan set is encountered, input terminates. Figure 9.22 uses the inverted scan set [^aeiou] to search for consonants—more properly to search for "nonvowels."

A field width can be used in a scanf conversion specifier to read a specific number of characters from the input stream. Figure 9.23 inputs a series of consecutive digits as a two-digit integer and an integer consisting of the remaining digits in the input stream.

```
1   /* Fig 9.22: fig09_22.c */
2   /* Using an inverted scan set */
3   #include <stdio.h>
4
5   int main( void )
6   {
7      char z[ 9 ];
8
9      printf( "Enter a string: " );
10     scanf( "%[^aeiou]", z ); /* inverted scan set */
11
12     printf( "The input was \"%s\"\n", z );
13
14     return 0; /* indicates successful termination */
15
16  } /* end main */
```

```
Enter a string: String
The input was "Str"
```

Fig. 9.22 | Using an inverted scan set.

```
1   /* Fig 9.23: fig09_23.c */
2   /* inputting data with a field width */
3   #include <stdio.h>
4
5   int main( void )
6   {
7      int x;
8      int y;
9
10     printf( "Enter a six digit integer: " );
11     scanf( "%2d%d", &x, &y );
```

Fig. 9.23 | Inputting data with a field width. (Part 1 of 2.)

```
12
13      printf( "The integers input were %d and %d\n", x, y );
14
15      return 0; /* indicates successful termination */
16
17  } /* end main */
```

```
Enter a six digit integer: 123456
The integers input were 12 and 3456
```

Fig. 9.23 | Inputting data with a field width. (Part 2 of 2.)

Often it is necessary to skip certain characters in the input stream. For example, a date could be entered as

　　　11-10-1999

Each number in the date needs to be stored, but the dashes that separate the numbers can be discarded. To eliminate unnecessary characters, include them in the format control string of scanf (white-space characters—such as space, newline and tab—skip all leading white-space). For example, to skip the dashes in the input, use the statement

　　　scanf("%d-%d-%d", &month, &day, &year);

Although, this scanf does eliminate the dashes in the preceding input, it is possible that the date could be entered as

　　　10/11/1999

In this case, the preceding scanf would not eliminate the unnecessary characters. For this reason, scanf provides the assignment suppression character *. The assignment suppression character enables scanf to read any type of data from the input and discard it without assigning it to a variable. Figure 9.24 uses the assignment suppression character in the %c conversion specifier to indicate that a character appearing in the input stream should be read and discarded. Only the month, day and year are stored. The values of the variables are printed to demonstrate that they are in fact input correctly. Note that the argument lists for each scanf call do not contain variables for the conversion specifiers that use the assignment suppression character. The corresponding characters are simply discarded.

```
1   /* Fig 9.24: fig09_24.c */
2   /* Reading and discarding characters from the input stream */
3   #include <stdio.h>
4
5   int main( void )
6   {
7       int month1;
8       int day1;
9       int year1;
```

Fig. 9.24 | Reading and discarding characters from the input stream. (Part 1 of 2.)

```
10        int month2;
11        int day2;
12        int year2;
13
14        printf( "Enter a date in the form mm-dd-yyyy: " );
15        scanf( "%d%*c%d%*c%d", &month1, &day1, &year1 );
16
17        printf( "month = %d  day = %d  year = %d\n\n", month1, day1, year1 );
18
19        printf( "Enter a date in the form mm/dd/yyyy: " );
20        scanf( "%d%*c%d%*c%d", &month2, &day2, &year2 );
21
22        printf( "month = %d  day = %d  year = %d\n", month2, day2, year2 );
23
24        return 0; /* indicates successful termination */
25
26    } /* end main */
```

```
Enter a date in the form mm-dd-yyyy: 11-18-2003
month = 11  day = 18  year = 2003

Enter a date in the form mm/dd/yyyy: 11/18/2003
month = 11  day = 18  year = 2003
```

Fig. 9.24 | Reading and discarding characters from the input stream. (Part 2 of 2.)

Summary

Section 9.2 Streams
- All input and output is dealt with in streams—sequences of characters organized into lines. Each line consists of zero or more characters and ends with a newline character.
- Normally, the standard input stream is connected to the keyboard, and the standard output stream is connected to the computer screen.
- Operating systems often allow the standard input and standard output streams to be redirected to other devices.

Section 9.3 Formatting Output with printf
- The printf format control string describes the formats in which the output values appear. The format control string consists of conversion specifiers, flags, field widths, precisions and literal characters.

Section 9.4 Printing Integers
- Integers are printed with the following conversion specifiers: d or i for optionally signed integers, o for unsigned integers in octal form, u for unsigned integers in decimal form and x or X for unsigned integers in hexadecimal form. The modifier h or l is prefixed to the preceding conversion specifiers to indicate a short or long integer, respectively.

Section 9.5 Printing Floating-Point Numbers
- Floating-point values are printed with the following conversion specifiers: e or E for exponential notation, f for regular floating-point notation, and g or G for either e (or E) notation or f nota-

tion. When the g (or G) conversion specifier is indicated, the e (or E) conversion specifier is used if the value's exponent is less than -4 or greater than or equal to the precision with which the value is printed.

- The precision for the g and G conversion specifiers indicates the maximum number of significant digits printed.

Section 9.6 Printing Strings and Characters
- The conversion specifier c prints a character.
- The conversion specifier s prints a string of characters ending in the null character.

Section 9.7 Other Conversion Specifiers
- The conversion specifier p displays an address in an implementation-defined manner (on many systems, hexadecimal notation is used).
- The conversion specifier n stores the number of characters already output in the current printf statement. The corresponding argument is a pointer to an int.
- The conversion specifier %% causes a literal % to be output.

Section 9.8 Printing with Field Widths and Precision
- If the field width is larger than the object being printed, the object is right justified in the field by default.
- Field widths can be used with all conversion/specifiers.
- Precision used with integer conversion specifiers indicates the minimum number of digits printed. If the value contains fewer digits than the precision specified, zeros are prefixed to the printed value until the number of digits is equivalent to the precision.
- Precision used with floating-point conversion specifiers e, E and f indicates the number of digits that appear after the decimal point. Precision used with floating-point conversion specifiers g and G indicates the number of significant digits to appear.
- Precision used with conversion specifier s indicates the number of characters to be printed.
- The field width and the precision can be combined by placing the field width, followed by a decimal point, followed by the precision between the percent sign and the conversion specifier.
- It is possible to specify the field width and the precision through integer expressions in the argument list following the format control string. To use this feature, insert an asterisk (*) in place of the field width or precision. The matching argument in the argument list is evaluated and used in place of the asterisk. The value of the argument can be negative for the field width but must be positive for the precision.

Section 9.9 Using Flags in the printf Format Control String
- The - flag left justifies its argument in a field.
- The + flag prints a plus sign for positive values and a minus sign for negative values. The space flag prints a space preceding a positive value not displayed with the + flag.
- The # flag prefixes 0 to octal values and 0x or 0X to hexadecimal values, and forces the decimal point to be printed for floating-point values printed with e, E, f, g or G (normally the decimal point is displayed only if the value contains a fractional part).
- The 0 flag prints leading zeros for a value that does not occupy its entire field width.

Section 9.10 Printing Literals and Escape Sequences
- Most literal characters to be printed in a printf statement can simply be included in the format control string. However, there are several "problem" characters, such as the quotation mark (")

that delimits the format control string itself. Various control characters, such as newline and tab, must be represented by escape sequences. An escape sequence is represented by a backslash (\), followed by a particular escape character.

Section 9.11 Formatting Input with scanf

- Precise input formatting is accomplished with the scanf library function.

- Integers are input with scanf with the conversion specifiers d and i for optionally signed integers and o, u, x or X for unsigned integers. The modifiers h and l are placed before an integer conversion specifier to input a short or long integer, respectively.

- Floating-point values are input with scanf with the conversion specifiers e, E, f, g or G. The modifiers l and L are placed before any of the floating-point conversion specifiers to indicate that the input value is a double or long double value, respectively.

- Characters are input with scanf with the conversion specifier c.

- Strings are input with scanf with the conversion specifier s.

- A scan set in a scanf scans the characters in the input, looking only for those characters that match characters contained in the scan set. When a character is matched, it is stored in a character array. The scan set stops inputting characters when a character not contained in the scan set is encountered.

- To create an inverted scan set, place a caret (^) in the square brackets before the scan characters. This causes characters input with scanf and not appearing in the scan set to be stored until a character contained in the inverted scan set is encountered.

- Address values are input with scanf with the conversion specifier p.

- Conversion specifier n stores the number of characters input previously in the current scanf. The corresponding argument is a pointer to int.

- The conversion specifier %% with scanf matches a single % character in the input.

- The assignment suppression character reads data from the input stream and discards the data.

- A field width is used in scanf to read a specific number of characters from the input stream.

Terminology

- (minus sign) flag	0 (zero) flag
# flag	alignment
% conversion specifier	assignment suppression character (*)
* in field width	blank insertion
* in precision	c conversion specifier
\' escape sequence	caret (^)
\" escape sequence	conversion specification
\? escape sequence	conversion specifiers
\\ escape sequence	d conversion specifier
\a escape sequence	e or E conversion specifier
\b escape sequence	escape sequence
\f escape sequence	exponential floating-point format
\n escape sequence	f conversion specifier
\r escape sequence	field width
\t escape sequence	flag
\v escape sequence	floating-point
+ (plus sign) flag	format control string
<stdio.h>	g or G conversion specifier

h conversion specifier
hexadecimal format
i conversion specifier
integer conversion specifiers
inverted scan set
l conversion specifier
L conversion specifier
left justification
literal characters
long integer
n conversion specifier
o conversion specifier
octal format
p conversion specifier
precision
printf
printing character insertion
redirect a stream

right justification
rounding
s conversion specifier
scan set
scanf
scientific notation
short integer
signed integer format
space flag
standard error stream
standard input stream
standard output stream
stream
u conversion specifier
unsigned integer format
white-space
x (or X) conversion specifier

Self-Review Exercises

9.1 Fill in the blanks in each of the following:

a) All input and output is dealt with in the form of _____.

b) The _____ stream is normally connected to the keyboard.

c) The _____ stream is normally connected to the computer screen.

d) Precise output formatting is accomplished with the _____ function.

e) The format control string may contain _____, _____, _____, _____ and _____.

f) The conversion specifier _____ or _____ may be used to output a signed decimal integer.

g) The conversion specifiers _____, _____ and _____ are used to display unsigned integers in octal, decimal and hexadecimal form, respectively.

h) The modifiers _____ and _____ are placed before the integer conversion specifiers to indicate that short or long integer values are to be displayed.

i) The conversion specifier _____ is used to display a floating-point value in exponential notation.

j) The modifier _____ is placed before any floating-point conversion specifier to indicate that a long double value is to be displayed.

k) The conversion specifiers e, E and f are displayed with _____ digits of precision to the right of the decimal point if no precision is specified.

l) The conversion specifiers _____ and _____ are used to print strings and characters, respectively.

m) All strings end in the _____ character.

n) The field width and precision in a printf conversion specifier can be controlled with integer expressions by substituting a(n) _____ for the field width or for the precision and placing an integer expression in the corresponding argument of the argument list.

o) The _____ flag causes output to be left justified in a field.

p) The _____ flag causes values to be displayed with either a plus sign or a minus sign.

q) Precise input formatting is accomplished with the _____ function.

r)   A(n) _____ is used to scan a string for specific characters and store the characters in an array.

s)   The conversion specifier _____ can be used to input optionally signed octal, decimal and hexadecimal integers.

t)   The conversion specifiers _____ can be used to input a `double` value.

u)   The _____ is used to read data from the input stream and discard it without assigning it to a variable.

v)   A(n) _____ can be used in a `scanf` conversion specifier to indicate that a specific number of characters or digits should be read from the input stream.

9.2   Find the error in each of the following and explain how the error can be corrected.

a)   The following statement should print the character `'c'`.

```
printf( "%s\n", 'c' );
```

b)   The following statement should print 9.375%.

```
printf( "%.3f%", 9.375 );
```

c)   The following statement should print the first character of the string `"Monday"`.

```
printf( "%c\n", "Monday" );
```

d)   `printf( ""A string in quotes"" );`

e)   `printf( %d%d, 12, 20 );`

f)   `printf( "%c", "x" );`

g)   `printf( "%s\n", 'Richard' );`

9.3   Write a statement for each of the following:

a)   Print 1234 right justified in a 10-digit field.

b)   Print 123.456789 in exponential notation with a sign (+ or -) and 3 digits of precision.

c)   Read a `double` value into variable `number`.

d)   Print 100 in octal form preceded by 0.

e)   Read a string into character array `string`.

f)   Read characters into array `n` until a nondigit character is encountered.

g)   Use integer variables `x` and `y` to specify the field width and precision used to display the `double` value 87.4573.

h)   Read a value of the form 3.5%. Store the percentage in `float` variable `percent` and eliminate the % from the input stream. Do not use the assignment suppression character.

i)   Print 3.333333 as a `long double` value with a sign (+ or -)in a field of 20 characters with a precision of 3.

Answers to Self-Review Exercises

9.1   a) Streams. b) Standard input. c) Standard output. d) `printf`. e) Conversion specifiers, flags, field widths, precisions, literal characters. f) d, i. g) o, u, x (or X). h) h, l. i) e (or E). j) L. k) 6. l) s, c. m) NULL (`'\0'`). n) asterisk (*). o) - (minus). p) + (plus). q) `scanf`. r) Scan set. s) i. t) le, lE, lf, lg or lG. u) Assignment suppression character (*). v) Field width.

9.2   a)   Error: Conversion specifier s expects an argument of type pointer to char.
Correction: To print the character `'c'`, use the conversion specifier %c or change `'c'` to `"c"`.

b)   Error: Trying to print the literal character % without using the conversion specifier %%.
Correction: Use %% to print a literal % character.

c)   Error: Conversion specifier c expects an argument of type char.
Correction: To print the first character of "Monday" use the conversion specifier %1s.

d)   Error: Trying to print the literal character " without using the \" escape sequence.
Correction: Replace each quote in the inner set of quotes with \".

e) Error: The format control string is not enclosed in double quotes.
    Correction: Enclose %d%d in double quotes.
f) Error: The character x is enclosed in double quotes.
    Correction: Character constants to be printed with %c must be enclosed in single quotes.
g) Error: The string to be printed is enclosed in single quotes.
    Correction: Use double quotes instead of single quotes to represent a string.

9.3 a) `printf( "%10d\n", 1234 );`
b) `printf( "%+.3e\n", 123.456789 );`
c) `scanf( "%lf", &number );`
d) `printf( "%#o\n", 100 );`
e) `scanf( "%s", string );`
f) `scanf( "%[0123456789]", n );`
g) `printf( "%*.*f\n", x, y, 87.4573 );`
h) `scanf( "%f%%", &percent );`
i) `printf( "%+20.3Lf\n", 3.333333 );`

Exercises

9.4 Write a `printf` or `scanf` statement for each of the following:
a) Print unsigned integer 40000 left justified in a 15-digit field with 8 digits.
b) Read a hexadecimal value into variable hex.
c) Print 200 with and without a sign.
d) Print 100 in hexadecimal form preceded by 0x.
e) Read characters into array s until the letter p is encountered.
f) Print 1.234 in a 9-digit field with preceding zeros.
g) Read a time of the form hh:mm:ss, storing the parts of the time in the integer variables hour, minute and second. Skip the colons (:) in the input stream. Use the assignment suppression character.
h) Read a string of the form "characters" from the standard input. Store the string in character array s. Eliminate the quotation marks from the input stream.
i) Read a time of the form hh:mm:ss, storing the parts of the time in the integer variables hour, minute and second. Skip the colons (:) in the input stream. Do not use the assignment suppression character.

9.5 Show what is printed by each of the following statements. If a statement is incorrect, indicate why.
a) `printf( "%-10d\n", 10000 );`
b) `printf( "%c\n", "This is a string" );`
c) `printf( "%*.*lf\n", 8, 3, 1024.987654 );`
d) `printf( "%#o\n%#X\n%#e\n", 17, 17, 1008.83689 );`
e) `printf( "% ld\n%+ld\n", 1000000, 1000000 );`
f) `printf( "%10.2E\n", 444.93738 );`
g) `printf( "%10.2g\n", 444.93738 );`
h) `printf( "%d\n", 10.987 );`

9.6 Find the error(s) in each of the following program segments. Explain how each error can be corrected.
a) `printf( "%s\n", 'Happy Birthday' );`
b) `printf( "%c\n", 'Hello' );`
c) `printf( "%c\n", "This is a string" );`

   d) The following statement should print "Bon Voyage":

```
printf( """%s""", "Bon Voyage" );
```

   e) `char day[] = "Sunday";`

```
printf( "%s\n", day[ 3 ] );
```

   f) `printf( 'Enter your name: ' );`

   g) `printf( %f, 123.456 );`

   h) The following statement should print the characters 'O' and 'K':

```
printf( "%s%s\n", 'O', 'K' );
```

   i) `char s[ 10 ];`

```
scanf( "%c", s[ 7 ] );
```

9.7   Write a program that loads 10-element array `number` with random integers from 1 to 1000. For each value, print the value and a running total of the number of characters printed. Use the `%n` conversion specifier to determine the number of characters output for each value. Print the total number of characters output for all values up to and including the current value each time the current value is printed. The output should have the following format:

```
Value    Total characters
342      3
1000     7
963      10
6        11
etc.
```

9.8   Write a program to test the difference between the `%d` and `%i` conversion specifiers when used in `scanf` statements. Use the statements

```
scanf( "%i%d", &x, &y );
printf( "%d %d\n", x, y );
```

to input and print the values. Test the program with the following sets of input data:

```
    10      10
   -10     -10
   010     010
  0x10    0x10
```

9.9   Write a program that prints pointer values using all the integer conversion specifiers and the `%p` conversion specifier. Which ones print strange values? Which ones cause errors? In which format does the `%p` conversion specifier display the address on your system?

9.10   Write a program to test the results of printing the integer value `12345` and the floating-point value `1.2345` in various size fields. What happens when the values are printed in fields containing fewer digits than the values?

9.11   Write a program that prints the value `100.453627` rounded to the nearest digit, tenth, hundredth, thousandth and ten-thousandth.

9.12   Write a program that inputs a string from the keyboard and determines the length of the string. Print the string using twice the length as the field width.

9.13   Write a program that converts integer Fahrenheit temperatures from 0 to 212 degrees to floating-point Celsius temperatures with 3 digits of precision. Use the formula

```
celsius = 5.0 / 9.0 * ( fahrenheit - 32 );
```

to perform the calculation. The output should be printed in two right-justified columns of 10 characters each, and the Celsius temperatures should be preceded by a sign for both positive and negative values.

9.14   Write a program to test all the escape sequences in Figure 9.16. For the escape sequences that move the cursor, print a character before and after printing the escape sequence so it is clear where the cursor has moved.

9.15   Write a program that determines whether ? can be printed as part of a printf format control string as a literal character rather than using the \? escape sequence.

9.16   Write a program that inputs the value 437 using each of the scanf integer conversion specifiers. Print each input value using all the integer conversion specifiers.

9.17   Write a program that uses each of the conversion specifiers e, f and g to input the value 1.2345. Print the values of each variable to prove that each conversion specifier can be used to input this same value.

9.18   In some programming languages, strings are entered surrounded by either single *or* double quotation marks. Write a program that reads the three strings suzy, "suzy" and 'suzy'. Are the single and double quotes ignored by C or read as part of the string?

9.19   Write a program that determines whether ? can be printed as the character constant '?' rather than the character constant escape sequence '\?' using conversion specifier %c in the format control string of a printf statement.

9.20   Write a program that uses the conversion specifier g to output the value 9876.12345. Print the value with precisions ranging from 1 to 9.

C Structures, Unions, Bit Manipulations and Enumerations

But yet an union in partition.
—William Shakespeare

*The same old charitable lie
Repeated as the years scoot
by
Perpetually makes a hit—
"You really haven't changed
a bit!"*
—Margaret Fishback

*I could never make out what
those damned dots meant.*
—Winston Churchill

OBJECTIVES

In this chapter, you will learn:

- To create and use structures, unions and enumerations.
- To pass structures to functions by value and by reference.
- To manipulate data with the bitwise operators.
- To create bit fields for storing data compactly.

10.1 Introduction

Structures—sometimes referred to as aggregates—are collections of related variables under one name. Structures may contain variables of many different data types—in contrast to arrays that contain only elements of the same data type. Structures are commonly used to define records to be stored in files (see Chapter 11, File Processing). Pointers and structures facilitate the formation of more complex data structures such as linked lists, queues, stacks and trees (see Chapter 12, Data Structures).

10.2 Structure Definitions

Structures are derived data types—they are constructed using objects of other types. Consider the following structure definition:

```
struct card {
   char *face;
   char *suit;
};
```

Keyword struct introduces the structure definition. The identifier card is the structure tag, which names the structure definition and is used with the keyword struct to declare variables of the structure type. In this example, the structure type is struct card. Variables declared within the braces of the structure definition are the structure's members. Members of the same structure type must have unique names, but two different structure types may contain members of the same name without conflict (we will soon see why). Each structure definition must end with a semicolon.

Common Programming Error 10.1

Forgetting the semicolon that terminates a structure definition is a syntax error.

The definition of struct card contains members face and suit of type char *. Structure members can be variables of the primitive data types (e.g., int, float, etc.), or aggregates, such as arrays and other structures. As we saw in Chapter 6, each element of an array must be of the same type. Structure members, however, can be of a variety of data types. For example,

```
struct employee {
    char firstName[ 20 ];
    char lastName[ 20 ];
    int age;
    char gender;
    double hourlySalary;
};
```

contains character array members for the first and last names, an `int` member for the employee's age, a `char` member that would contain `'M'` or `'F'` for the employee's gender and a `double` member for the employee's hourly salary.

A structure cannot contain an instance of itself. For example, a variable of type `struct employee` cannot be declared in the definition for `struct employee`. A pointer to `struct employee`, however, may be included. For example,

```
struct employee2 {
    char firstName[ 20 ];
    char lastName[ 20 ];
    int age;
    char gender;
    double hourlySalary;
    struct employee2 person;   /* ERROR */
    struct employee2 *ePtr;    /* pointer */
};
```

`struct employee2` contains an instance of itself (`person`), which is an error. Because `ePtr` is a pointer (to type `struct employee2`), it is permitted in the definition. A structure containing a member that is a pointer to the same structure type is referred to as a *self-referential structure*. Self-referential structures are used in Chapter 12 to build linked data structures.

Structure definitions do not reserve any space in memory; rather, each definition creates a new data type that is used to define variables. Structure variables are defined like variables of other types. The definition

```
struct card aCard, deck[ 52 ], *cardPtr;
```

declares aCard to be a variable of type `struct card`, declares deck to be an array with 52 elements of type `struct card` and declares cardPtr to be a pointer to `struct card`. Variables of a given structure type may also be declared by placing a comma-separated list of the variable names between the closing brace of the structure definition and the semicolon that ends the structure definition. For example, the preceding definition could have been incorporated into the `struct card` structure definition as follows:

```
struct card {
    char *face;
    char *suit;
} aCard, deck[ 52 ], *cardPtr;
```

The structure tag name is optional. If a structure definition does not contain a structure tag name, variables of the structure type may be declared only in the structure definition—not in a separate declaration.

Good Programming Practice 10.1

Always provide a structure tag name when creating a structure type. The structure tag name is convenient for declaring new variables of the structure type later in the program.

Good Programming Practice 10.2

Choosing a meaningful structure tag name helps make a program self-documenting.

The only valid operations that may be performed on structures are the following: assigning structure variables to structure variables of the same type, taking the address (&) of a structure variable, accessing the members of a structure variable (see Section 10.4) and using the sizeof operator to determine the size of a structure variable.

Common Programming Error 10.2

Assigning a structure of one type to a structure of a different type is a compilation error.

Structures may not be compared using operators == and !=, because structure members are not necessarily stored in consecutive bytes of memory. Sometimes there are "holes" in a structure, because computers may store specific data types only on certain memory boundaries such as half word, word or double word boundaries. A word is a standard memory unit used to store data in a computer—usually 2 bytes or 4 bytes. Consider the following structure definition, in which sample1 and sample2 of type struct example are declared:

```
struct example {
    char c;
    int i;
} sample1, sample2;
```

A computer with 2-byte words may require that each member of struct example be aligned on a word boundary, i.e., at the beginning of a word (this is machine dependent). Figure 10.1 shows a sample storage alignment for a variable of type struct example that has been assigned the character 'a' and the integer 97 (the bit representations of the values are shown). If the members are stored beginning at word boundaries, there is a 1-byte hole (byte 1 in the figure) in the storage for variables of type struct example. The value in the 1-byte hole is undefined. Even if the member values of sample1 and sample2 are in fact equal, the structures are not necessarily equal, because the undefined 1-byte holes are not likely to contain identical values.

Common Programming Error 10.3

Comparing structures is a syntax error.

Byte	0	1	2	3
	01100001		00000000	01100001

Fig. 10.1 | Possible storage alignment for a variable of type struct example showing an undefined area in memory.

Portability Tip 10.1

Because the size of data items of a particular type is machine dependent and because storage alignment considerations are machine dependent, so too is the representation of a structure.

10.3 Initializing Structures

Structures can be initialized using initializer lists as with arrays. To initialize a structure, follow the variable name in the definition with an equals sign and a brace-enclosed, comma-separated list of initializers. For example, the declaration

```
struct card aCard = { "Three", "Hearts" };
```

creates variable aCard to be of type struct card (as defined in Section 10.2) and initializes member face to "Three" and member suit to "Hearts". If there are fewer initializers in the list than members in the structure, the remaining members are automatically initialized to 0 (or NULL if the member is a pointer). Structure variables defined outside a function definition (i.e., externally) are initialized to 0 or NULL if they are not explicitly initialized in the external definition. Structure variables may also be initialized in assignment statements by assigning a structure variable of the same type, or by assigning values to the individual members of the structure.

10.4 Accessing Members of Structures

Two operators are used to access members of structures: the structure member operator (.)—also called the dot operator—and the structure pointer operator (->)—also called the arrow operator. The structure member operator accesses a structure member via the structure variable name. For example, to print member suit of structure variable aCard defined in Section 10.3, use the statement

```
printf( "%s", aCard.suit ); /* displays Hearts */
```

The structure pointer operator—consisting of a minus (-) sign and a greater than (>) sign with no intervening spaces—accesses a structure member via a pointer to the structure. Assume that the pointer cardPtr has been declared to point to struct card and that the address of structure aCard has been assigned to cardPtr. To print member suit of structure aCard with pointer cardPtr, use the statement

```
printf( "%s", cardPtr->suit ); /* displays Hearts */
```

The expression cardPtr->suit is equivalent to (*cardPtr).suit, which dereferences the pointer and accesses the member suit using the structure member operator. The parentheses are needed here because the structure member operator (.) has a higher precedence than the pointer dereferencing operator (*). The structure pointer operator and structure member operator, along with parentheses (for calling functions) and brackets ([]) used for array subscripting, have the highest operator precedence and associate from left to right.

Error-Prevention Tip 10.1

Avoid using the same names for members of structures of different types. This is allowed, but it may cause confusion.

Good Programming Practice 10.3

Do not put spaces around the -> and . operators. Omitting spaces helps emphasize that the expressions the operators are contained in are essentially single variable names.

Common Programming Error 10.4

Inserting space between the - and > components of the structure pointer operator (or between the components of any other multiple keystroke operator except ?:) is a syntax error.

Common Programming Error 10.5

Attempting to refer to a member of a structure by using only the member's name is a syntax error.

Common Programming Error 10.6

Not using parentheses when referring to a structure member that uses a pointer and the structure member operator (e.g., *cardPtr.suit) is a syntax error.

The program of Fig. 10.2 demonstrates the use of the structure member and structure pointer operators. Using the structure member operator, the members of structure aCard are assigned the values "Ace" and "Spades", respectively (lines 18 and 19). Pointer cardPtr is assigned the address of structure aCard (line 21). Function printf prints the members of structure variable aCard using the structure member operator with variable name aCard, the structure pointer operator with pointer cardPtr and the structure member operator with dereferenced pointer cardPtr (lines 23 through 25).

```
1   /* Fig. 10.2: fig10_02.c
2      Using the structure member and
3      structure pointer operators */
4   #include <stdio.h>
5
6   /* card structure definition */
7   struct card {
8      char *face; /* define pointer face */
9      char *suit; /* define pointer suit */
10  }; /* end structure card */
11
12  int main( void )
13  {
14     struct card aCard; /* define one struct card variable */
15     struct card *cardPtr; /* define a pointer to a struct card */
16
17     /* place strings into aCard */
18     aCard.face = "Ace";
19     aCard.suit = "Spades";
20
21     cardPtr = &aCard; /* assign address of aCard to cardPtr */
22
23     printf( "%s%s%s\n%s%s%s\n%s%s%s\n", aCard.face, " of ", aCard.suit,
24        cardPtr->face, " of ", cardPtr->suit,
25        ( *cardPtr ).face, " of ", ( *cardPtr ).suit );
```

Fig. 10.2 | Structure member operator and structure pointer operator. (Part 1 of 2.)

```
26
27      return 0; /* indicates successful termination */
28
29  } /* end main */
```

```
Ace of Spades
Ace of Spades
Ace of Spades
```

Fig. 10.2 | Structure member operator and structure pointer operator. (Part 2 of 2.)

10.5 Using Structures with Functions

Structures may be passed to functions by passing individual structure members, by passing an entire structure or by passing a pointer to a structure. When structures or individual structure members are passed to a function, they are passed by value. Therefore, the members of a caller's structure cannot be modified by the called function.

To pass a structure by reference, pass the address of the structure variable. Arrays of structures—like all other arrays—are automatically passed by reference.

In Chapter 6, we stated that an array could be passed by value by using a structure. To pass an array by value, create a structure with the array as a member. Structures are passed by value, so the array is passed by value.

Common Programming Error 10.7

Assuming that structures, like arrays, are automatically passed by reference and trying to modify the caller's structure values in the called function is a logic error.

Performance Tip 10.1

Passing structures by reference is more efficient than passing structures by value (which requires the entire structure to be copied).

10.6 typedef

The keyword **typedef** provides a mechanism for creating synonyms (or aliases) for previously defined data types. Names for structure types are often defined with **typedef** to create shorter type names. For example, the statement

```
typedef struct card Card;
```

defines the new type name Card as a synonym for type struct card. C programmers often use typedef to define a structure type, so a structure tag is not required. For example, the following definition

```
typedef struct {
    char *face;
    char *suit;
} Card;
```

creates the structure type Card without the need for a separate typedef statement.

Good Programming Practice 10.4

Capitalize the first letter of typedef *names to emphasize that they are synonyms for other type names.*

Card can now be used to declare variables of type struct card. The declaration

```
Card deck[ 52 ];
```

declares an array of 52 Card structures (i.e., variables of type struct card). Creating a new name with typedef does not create a new type; typedef simply creates a new type name, which may be used as an alias for an existing type name. A meaningful name helps make the program self-documenting. For example, when we read the previous declaration, we know "deck is an array of 52 Cards."

Often, typedef is used to create synonyms for the basic data types. For example, a program requiring 4-byte integers may use type int on one system and type long on another. Programs designed for portability often use typedef to create an alias for 4-byte integers, such as Integer. The alias Integer can be changed once in the program to make the program work on both systems.

Portability Tip 10.2

Use typedef *to help make a program more portable.*

10.7 Example: High-Performance Card Shuffling and Dealing Simulation

The program in Fig. 10.3 is based on the card shuffling and dealing simulation discussed in Chapter 7. The program represents the deck of cards as an array of structures. The program uses high-performance shuffling and dealing algorithms. The output for the high-performance card shuffling and dealing program is shown in Fig. 10.4.

```
1   /* Fig. 10.3: fig10_03.c
2      The card shuffling and dealing program using structures */
3   #include <stdio.h>
4   #include <stdlib.h>
5   #include <time.h>
6
7   /* card structure definition */
8   struct card {
9      const char *face; /* define pointer face */
10     const char *suit; /* define pointer suit */
11  }; /* end structure card */
12
13  typedef struct card Card; /* new type name for struct card */
14
15  /* prototypes */
16  void fillDeck( Card * const wDeck, const char * wFace[],
17     const char * wSuit[] );
18  void shuffle( Card * const wDeck );
19  void deal( const Card * const wDeck );
```

Fig. 10.3 | High-performance card shuffling and dealing simulation. (Part 1 of 3.)

```
20
21  int main( void )
22  {
23     Card deck[ 52 ]; /* define array of Cards */
24
25     /* initialize array of pointers */
26     const char *face[] = { "Ace", "Deuce", "Three", "Four", "Five",
27        "Six", "Seven", "Eight", "Nine", "Ten",
28        "Jack", "Queen", "King"};
29
30     /* initialize array of pointers */
31     const char *suit[] = { "Hearts", "Diamonds", "Clubs", "Spades"};
32
33     srand( time( NULL ) ); /* randomize */
34
35     fillDeck( deck, face, suit ); /* load the deck with Cards */
36     shuffle( deck ); /* put Cards in random order */
37     deal( deck ); /* deal all 52 Cards */
38
39     return 0; /* indicates successful termination */
40
41  } /* end main */
42
43  /* place strings into Card structures */
44  void fillDeck( Card * const wDeck, const char * wFace[],
45     const char * wSuit[] )
46  {
47     int i; /* counter */
48
49     /* loop through wDeck */
50     for ( i = 0; i <= 51; i++ ) {
51        wDeck[ i ].face = wFace[ i % 13 ];
52        wDeck[ i ].suit = wSuit[ i / 13 ];
53     } /* end for */
54
55  } /* end function fillDeck */
56
57  /* shuffle cards */
58  void shuffle( Card * const wDeck )
59  {
60     int i;      /* counter */
61     int j;      /* variable to hold random value between 0 - 51 */
62     Card temp; /* define temporary structure for swapping Cards */
63
64     /* loop through wDeck randomly swapping Cards */
65     for ( i = 0; i <= 51; i++ ) {
66        j = rand() % 52;
67        temp = wDeck[ i ];
68        wDeck[ i ] = wDeck[ j ];
69        wDeck[ j ] = temp;
70     } /* end for */
71
72  } /* end function shuffle */
```

Fig. 10.3 | High-performance card shuffling and dealing simulation. (Part 2 of 3.)

```
73
74    /* deal cards */
75    void deal( const Card * const wDeck )
76    {
77       int i; /* counter */
78
79       /* loop through wDeck */
80       for ( i = 0; i <= 51; i++ ) {
81          printf( "%5s of %-8s%c", wDeck[ i ].face, wDeck[ i ].suit,
82             ( i + 1 ) % 2 ? '\t' : '\n' );
83       } /* end for */
84
85    } /* end function deal */
```

Fig. 10.3 | High-performance card shuffling and dealing simulation. (Part 3 of 3.)

Four of Clubs	Three of Hearts
Three of Diamonds	Three of Spades
Four of Diamonds	Ace of Diamonds
Nine of Hearts	Ten of Clubs
Three of Clubs	Four of Hearts
Eight of Clubs	Nine of Diamonds
Deuce of Clubs	Queen of Clubs
Seven of Clubs	Jack of Spades
Ace of Clubs	Five of Diamonds
Ace of Spades	Five of Clubs
Seven of Diamonds	Six of Spades
Eight of Spades	Queen of Hearts
Five of Spades	Deuce of Diamonds
Queen of Spades	Six of Hearts
Queen of Diamonds	Seven of Hearts
Jack of Diamonds	Nine of Spades
Eight of Hearts	Five of Hearts
King of Spades	Six of Clubs
Eight of Diamonds	Ten of Spades
Ace of Hearts	King of Hearts
Four of Spades	Jack of Hearts
Deuce of Hearts	Jack of Clubs
Deuce of Spades	Ten of Diamonds
Seven of Spades	Nine of Clubs
King of Clubs	Six of Diamonds
Ten of Hearts	King of Diamonds

Fig. 10.4 | Output for the high-performance card shuffling and dealing simulation.

In the program, function fillDeck (lines 44–55) initializes the Card array in order with Ace through King of each suit. The Card array is passed (in line 36) to function shuffle (lines 58–72), where the high-performance shuffling algorithm is implemented. Function shuffle takes an array of 52 Card structures as an argument. The function loops through the 52 cards (array subscripts 0 to 51) using a for statement in lines 65–70. For each card, a number between 0 and 51 is picked randomly. Next, the current Card structure and the randomly selected Card structure are swapped in the array (lines 67 through 69). A total of 52 swaps are made in a single pass of the entire array, and the array of Card structures is shuffled! This algorithm cannot suffer from indefinite postponement like the shuffling algorithm presented in Chapter 7. Since the Card structures were swapped in place in the array, the high-performance dealing algorithm implemented in function deal (lines 75–85) requires only one pass of the array to deal the shuffled cards.

Common Programming Error 10.8

Forgetting to include the array subscript when referring to individual structures in an array of structures is a syntax error.

10.8 Unions

A union is a derived data type—like a structure—with members that share the same storage space. For different situations in a program, some variables may not be relevant, but other variables are—so a union shares the space instead of wasting storage on variables that are not being used. The members of a union can be of any data type. The number of bytes used to store a union must be at least enough to hold the largest member. In most cases, unions contain two or more data types. Only one member, and thus one data type, can be referenced at a time. It is your responsibility to ensure that the data in a union is referenced with the proper data type.

Common Programming Error 10.9

Referencing data in a union with a variable of the wrong type is a logic error.

Portability Tip 10.3

If data is stored in a union as one type and referenced as another type, the results are implementation dependent.

A union is declared with keyword union in the same format as a structure. The union definition

```
union number {
    int x;
    double y;
};
```

indicates that number is a union type with members int x and double y. The union definition is normally placed in a header and included in all source files that use the union type.

Software Engineering Observation 10.1

As with a struct definition, a union definition simply creates a new type. Placing a union or struct definition outside any function does not create a global variable.

The operations that can be performed on a union are the following: assigning a union to another union of the same type, taking the address (&) of a union variable, and accessing union members using the structure member operator and the structure pointer operator. Unions may not be compared using operators == and != for the same reasons that structures cannot be compared.

In a declaration, a union may be initialized with a value of the same type as the first union member. For example, with the preceding union, the declaration

```
union number value = { 10 };
```

is a valid initialization of union variable value because the union is initialized with an int, but the following declaration would truncate the floating-point part of the initializer value and normally would produce a warning from the compiler:

```
union number value = { 1.43 };
```

Common Programming Error 10.10

Comparing unions is a syntax error.

Portability Tip 10.4

The amount of storage required to store a union is implementation dependent but will always be at least as large as the largest member of the union.

Portability Tip 10.5

Some unions may not port easily to other computer systems. Whether a union is portable or not often depends on the storage alignment requirements for the union member data types on a given system.

Performance Tip 10.2

Unions conserve storage.

The program in Fig. 10.5 uses the variable value (line 13) of type union number to display the value stored in the union as both an int and a double. The program output is implementation dependent. The program output shows that the internal representation of a double value can be quite different from the representation of int.

```
1   /* Fig. 10.5: fig10_05.c
2      An example of a union */
3   #include <stdio.h>
4
5   /* number union definition */
6   union number {
7      int x;
8      double y;
9   }; /* end union number */
10
11  int main( void )
12  {
13     union number value; /* define union variable */
14
15     value.x = 100; /* put an integer into the union */
16     printf( "%s\n%s\n%s\n  %d\n\n%s\n  %f\n\n\n",
17        "Put a value in the integer member",
18        "and print both members.",
19        "int:", value.x,
20        "double:", value.y );
21
```

Fig. 10.5 | Displaying the value of a union in both member data types. (Part 1 of 2.)

```
22      value.y = 100.0; /* put a double into the same union */
23      printf( "%s\n%s\n%s\n   %d\n\n%s\n  %f\n",
24         "Put a value in the floating member",
25         "and print both members.",
26         "int:", value.x,
27         "double:", value.y );
28
29      return 0; /* indicates successful termination */
30
31   } /* end main */
```

```
Put a value in the integer member
and print both members.
int:
   100

double:
-9255959211743313600000000000000000000000000000000000000000000000.000000


Put a value in the floating member
and print both members.
int:
   0

double:
   100.000000
```

Fig. 10.5 | Displaying the value of a union in both member data types. (Part 2 of 2.)

10.9 Bitwise Operators

Computers represent all data internally as sequences of bits. Each bit can assume the value 0 or the value 1. On most systems, a sequence of 8 bits forms a byte—the standard storage unit for a variable of type char. Other data types are stored in larger numbers of bytes. The bitwise operators are used to manipulate the bits of integral operands (char, short, int and long; both signed and unsigned). Unsigned integers are normally used with the bitwise operators.

Portability Tip 10.6

Bitwise data manipulations are machine dependent.

Note that the bitwise operator discussions in this section show the binary representations of the integer operands. For a detailed explanation of the binary (also called base-2) number system see Appendix D, Number Systems. Also, the programs in Section 10.9 and 10.10 were tested using Microsoft Visual C++. Because of the machine-dependent nature of bitwise manipulations, these programs may not work on your system.

The bitwise operators are bitwise AND (&), bitwise inclusive OR (|), bitwise exclusive OR (^), left shift (<<), right shift (>>) and complement (~). The bitwise AND, bitwise inclusive OR and bitwise exclusive OR operators compare their two operands bit by bit. The bitwise AND operator sets each bit in the result to 1 if the corresponding bit in both operands is 1. The bitwise inclusive OR operator sets each bit in the result to 1 if the corresponding bit in either (or both) operand(s) is 1. The bitwise exclusive OR operator sets each bit in the result to 1 if the corresponding bit in exactly one operand is 1. The left-shift operator shifts the bits of its left operand to the left by the number of bits specified in its right operand. The right-shift operator shifts the bits in its left operand to the right by the number of bits specified in its right operand. The bitwise complement operator sets all 0 bits in its operand to 1 in the result and sets all 1 bits to 0 in the result. Detailed discussions of each bitwise operator appear in the following examples. The bitwise operators are summarized in Fig. 10.6.

Displaying an Unsigned Integer in Bits

When using the bitwise operators, it is useful to print values in their binary representation to illustrate the precise effects of these operators. The program of Fig. 10.7 prints an unsigned integer in its binary representation in groups of eight bits each. For the examples in this section, we assume that unsigned integers are stored in 4 bytes (32 bits) of memory.

Operator		Description
&	bitwise AND	The bits in the result are set to 1 if the corresponding bits in the two operands are both 1.
|	bitwise inclusive OR	The bits in the result are set to 1 if at least one of the corresponding bits in the two operands is 1.
^	bitwise exclusive OR	The bits in the result are set to 1 if exactly one of the corresponding bits in the two operands is 1.
<<	left shift	Shifts the bits of the first operand left by the number of bits specified by the second operand; fill from the right with 0 bits.
>>	right shift	Shifts the bits of the first operand right by the number of bits specified by the second operand; the method of filling from the left is machine dependent.
~	one's complement	All 0 bits are set to 1 and all 1 bits are set to 0.

Fig. 10.6 | Bitwise operators.

```
1   /* Fig. 10.7: fig10_07.c
2      Printing an unsigned integer in bits */
3   #include <stdio.h>
4
5   void displayBits( unsigned value ); /* prototype */
6
7   int main( void )
8   {
9      unsigned x; /* variable to hold user input */
10
```

Fig. 10.7 | Displaying an unsigned integer in bits. (Part 1 of 2.)

```
11      printf( "Enter an unsigned integer: " );
12      scanf( "%u", &x );
13
14      displayBits( x );
15
16      return 0; /* indicates successful termination */
17
18   } /* end main */
19
20   /* display bits of an unsigned integer value */
21   void displayBits( unsigned value )
22   {
23      unsigned c; /* counter */
24
25      /* define displayMask and left shift 31 bits */
26      unsigned displayMask = 1 << 31;
27
28      printf( "%10u = ", value );
29
30      /* loop through bits */
31      for ( c = 1; c <= 32; c++ ) {
32         putchar( value & displayMask ? '1' : '0' );
33         value <<= 1; /* shift value left by 1 */
34
35         if ( c % 8 == 0 ) { /* output space after 8 bits */
36            putchar( ' ' );
37         } /* end if */
38
39      } /* end for */
40
41      putchar( '\n' );
42   } /* end function displayBits */
```

```
Enter an unsigned integer: 65000
   65000 = 00000000 00000000 11111101 11101000
```

Fig. 10.7 | Displaying an unsigned integer in bits. (Part 2 of 2.)

Function displayBits (lines 21–42) uses the bitwise AND operator to combine variable value with variable displayMask (line 32). Often, the bitwise AND operator is used with an operand called a mask—an integer value with specific bits set to 1. Masks are used to hide some bits in a value while selecting other bits. In function displayBits, mask variable displayMask is assigned the value

```
1 << 31          (10000000 00000000 00000000 00000000)
```

The left-shift operator shifts the value 1 from the low order (rightmost) bit to the high order (leftmost) bit in displayMask and fills in 0 bits from the right. Line 32

```
putchar( value & displayMask ? '1' : '0' );
```

determines whether a 1 or a 0 should be printed for the current leftmost bit of variable value. When value and displayMask are combined using &, all the bits except the high-order bit in variable value are "masked off" (hidden), because any bit "ANDed" with 0 yields 0. If the leftmost bit is 1, value & displayMask evaluates to a nonzero (true) value and 1 is printed—otherwise, 0 is printed. Variable value is then left shifted one bit by the expression value <<= 1 (this is equivalent to value = value << 1). These steps are repeated for each bit in unsigned variable value. Figure 10.8 summarizes the results of combining two bits with the bitwise AND operator.

Common Programming Error 10.11

Using the logical AND operator (&&) for the bitwise AND operator (&) and vice versa is an error.

Making Function displayBits More Scalable and Portable

In line 26 of Fig. 10.7, we hard coded the integer 31 to indicate that the value 1 should be shifted to the leftmost bit in the variable displayMask. Similarly, in line 31, we hard coded the integer 32 to indicate that the loop should iterate 32 times—once for each bit in variable value. We assumed that unsigned integers are always stored in 32 bits (4 bytes) of memory. Many of today's popular computers use 32-bit word hardware architectures. C programmers tend to work across many hardware architectures, and sometimes unsigned integers will be stored in smaller or larger numbers of bits.

The program in Fig. 10.7 can be made more scalable and more portable by replacing the integer 31 in line 26 with the expression

```
CHAR_BIT * sizeof( unsigned ) - 1
```

and by replacing the integer 32 in line 31 with the the the expression

```
CHAR_BIT * sizeof( unsigned )
```

The symbolic constant CHAR_BIT (defined in <limits.h>) represents the number of bits in a byte (normally 8). As you learned in Section 7.7, operator sizeof determines the number of bytes used to store an object or type. On a computer that uses 32-bit words, the expression sizeof(unsigned) evaluates to 4, so the two preceding expressions evaluate to 31 and 32, respectively. On a computer that uses 16-bit words, the sizeof expression evaluates to 2 and the two preceding expressions evaluate to 15 and 16, respectively.

Using the Bitwise AND, Inclusive OR, Exclusive OR and Complement Operators

Figure 10.9 demonstrates the use of the bitwise AND operator, the bitwise inclusive OR operator, the bitwise exclusive OR operator and the bitwise complement operator. The

Bit 1	Bit 2	Bit 1 & Bit 2
0	0	0
1	0	0
0	1	0
1	1	1

Fig. 10.8 | Results of combining two bits with the bitwise AND operator &.

program uses function displayBits (lines 53–74) to print the unsigned integer values. The output is shown in Fig. 10.10.

```c
 1   /* Fig. 10.9: fig10_09.c
 2      Using the bitwise AND, bitwise inclusive OR, bitwise
 3      exclusive OR and bitwise complement operators */
 4   #include <stdio.h>
 5
 6   void displayBits( unsigned value ); /* prototype */
 7
 8   int main( void )
 9   {
10      unsigned number1;
11      unsigned number2;
12      unsigned mask;
13      unsigned setBits;
14
15      /* demonstrate bitwise AND (&) */
16      number1 = 65535;
17      mask = 1;
18      printf( "The result of combining the following\n" );
19      displayBits( number1 );
20      displayBits( mask );
21      printf( "using the bitwise AND operator & is\n" );
22      displayBits( number1 & mask );
23
24      /* demonstrate bitwise inclusive OR (|) */
25      number1 = 15;
26      setBits = 241;
27      printf( "\nThe result of combining the following\n" );
28      displayBits( number1 );
29      displayBits( setBits );
30      printf( "using the bitwise inclusive OR operator | is\n" );
31      displayBits( number1 | setBits );
32
33      /* demonstrate bitwise exclusive OR (^) */
34      number1 = 139;
35      number2 = 199;
36      printf( "\nThe result of combining the following\n" );
37      displayBits( number1 );
38      displayBits( number2 );
39      printf( "using the bitwise exclusive OR operator ^ is\n" );
40      displayBits( number1 ^ number2 );
41
42      /* demonstrate bitwise complement (~)*/
43      number1 = 21845;
44      printf( "\nThe one's complement of\n" );
45      displayBits( number1 );
46      printf( "is\n" );
47      displayBits( ~number1 );
48
```

Fig. 10.9 | Bitwise AND, bitwise inclusive OR, bitwise exclusive OR and bitwise complement operators. (Part 1 of 2.)

```
49       return 0; /* indicates successful termination */
50    } /* end main */
51
52    /* display bits of an unsigned integer value */
53    void displayBits( unsigned value )
54    {
55       unsigned c; /* counter */
56
57       /* declare displayMask and left shift 31 bits */
58       unsigned displayMask = 1 << 31;
59
60       printf( "%10u = ", value );
61
62       /* loop through bits */
63       for ( c = 1; c <= 32; c++ ) {
64          putchar( value & displayMask ? '1' : '0' );
65          value <<= 1; /* shift value left by 1 */
66
67          if ( c % 8 == 0 ) { /* output a space after 8 bits */
68             putchar( ' ' );
69          } /* end if */
70
71       } /* end for */
72
73       putchar( '\n' );
74    } /* end function displayBits */
```

Fig. 10.9 | Bitwise AND, bitwise inclusive OR, bitwise exclusive OR and bitwise complement operators. (Part 2 of 2.)

```
The result of combining the following
    65535 = 00000000 00000000 11111111 11111111
        1 = 00000000 00000000 00000000 00000001
using the bitwise AND operator & is
        1 = 00000000 00000000 00000000 00000001

The result of combining the following
       15 = 00000000 00000000 00000000 00001111
      241 = 00000000 00000000 00000000 11110001
using the bitwise inclusive OR operator | is
      255 = 00000000 00000000 00000000 11111111

The result of combining the following
      139 = 00000000 00000000 00000000 10001011
      199 = 00000000 00000000 00000000 11000111
using the bitwise exclusive OR operator ^ is
       76 = 00000000 00000000 00000000 01001100

The one's complement of
    21845 = 00000000 00000000 01010101 01010101
is
4294945450 = 11111111 11111111 10101010 10101010
```

Fig. 10.10 | Output for the program of Fig. 10.9.

In Fig. 10.9, integer variable number1 is assigned value 65535 (00000000 00000000 11111111 11111111) in line 16 and variable mask is assigned the value 1 (00000000 00000000 00000000 00000001) in line 17. When number1 and mask are combined using the bitwise AND operator (&) in the expression number1 & mask (line 22), the result is 00000000 00000000 00000000 00000001. All the bits except the low-order bit in variable number1 are "masked off" (hidden) by "ANDing" with variable mask.

The bitwise inclusive OR operator is used to set specific bits to 1 in an operand. In Fig. 10.9, variable number1 is assigned 15 (00000000 00000000 00000000 00001111) in line 25, and variable setBits is assigned 241 (00000000 00000000 00000000 11110001) in line 26. When number1 and setBits are combined using the bitwise OR operator in the expression number1 | setBits (line 31), the result is 255 (00000000 00000000 00000000 11111111). Figure 10.11 summarizes the results of combining two bits with the bitwise inclusive OR operator.

Common Programming Error 10.12

Using the logical OR operator (||) for the bitwise OR operator (|) and vice versa is an error.

The bitwise exclusive OR operator (^) sets each bit in the result to 1 if *exactly* one of the corresponding bits in its two operands is 1. In Fig. 10.9, variables number1 and number2 are assigned the values 139 (00000000 00000000 00000000 10001011) and 199 (00000000 00000000 00000000 11000111) in lines 34–35. When these variables are combined with the exclusive OR operator in the expression number1 ^ number2 (line 40), the result is 00000000 00000000 00000000 01001100. Figure 10.12 summarizes the results of combining two bits with the bitwise exclusive OR operator.

Bit 1	Bit 2	Bit 1 | Bit 2
0	0	0
1	0	1
0	1	1
1	1	1

Fig. 10.11 | Results of combining two bits with the bitwise inclusive OR operator |.

Bit 1	Bit 2	Bit 1 ^ Bit 2
0	0	0
1	0	1
0	1	1
1	1	0

Fig. 10.12 | Results of combining two bits with the bitwise exclusive OR operator ^.

The bitwise complement operator (~) sets all 1 bits in its operand to 0 in the result and sets all 0 bits to 1 in the result—otherwise referred to as "taking the one's complement of the value." In Fig. 10.9, variable number1 is assigned the value 21845 (00000000 00000000 01010101 01010101) in line 43. When the expression ~number1 (line 47) is evaluated, the result is 00000000 00000000 10101010 10101010.

Using the Bitwise Left- and Right-Shift Operators

The program of Fig. 10.13 demonstrates the left-shift operator (<<) and the right-shift operator (>>). Function displayBits is used to print the unsigned integer values.

```
1   /* Fig. 10.13: fig10_13.c
2      Using the bitwise shift operators */
3   #include <stdio.h>
4
5   void displayBits( unsigned value ); /* prototype */
6
7   int main( void )
8   {
9      unsigned number1 = 960; /* initialize number1 */
10
11     /* demonstrate bitwise left shift */
12     printf( "\nThe result of left shifting\n" );
13     displayBits( number1 );
14     printf( "8 bit positions using the " );
15     printf( "left shift operator << is\n" );
16     displayBits( number1 << 8 );
17
18     /* demonstrate bitwise right shift */
19     printf( "\nThe result of right shifting\n" );
20     displayBits( number1 );
21     printf( "8 bit positions using the " );
22     printf( "right shift operator >> is\n" );
23     displayBits( number1 >> 8 );
24
25     return 0; /* indicates successful termination */
26  } /* end main */
27
28  /* display bits of an unsigned integer value */
29  void displayBits( unsigned value )
30  {
31     unsigned c; /* counter */
32
33     /* declare displayMask and left shift 31 bits */
34     unsigned displayMask = 1 << 31;
35
36     printf( "%7u = ", value );
37
38     /* loop through bits */
39     for ( c = 1; c <= 32; c++ ) {
40        putchar( value & displayMask ? '1' : '0' );
41        value <<= 1; /* shift value left by 1 */
```

Fig. 10.13 | Bitwise shift operators. (Part 1 of 2.)

```
42
43          if ( c % 8 == 0 ) { /* output a space after 8 bits */
44             putchar( ' ' );
45          } /* end if */
46
47       } /* end for */
48
49       putchar( '\n' );
50    } /* end function displayBits */
```

```
The result of left shifting
    960 = 00000000 00000000 00000011 11000000
8 bit positions using the left shift operator << is
 245760 = 00000000 00000011 11000000 00000000

The result of right shifting
    960 = 00000000 00000000 00000011 11000000
8 bit positions using the right shift operator >> is
      3 = 00000000 00000000 00000000 00000011
```

Fig. 10.13 | Bitwise shift operators. (Part 2 of 2.)

The left-shift operator (<<) shifts the bits of its left operand to the left by the number of bits specified in its right operand. Bits vacated to the right are replaced with 0s; 1s shifted off the left are lost. In Fig. 10.13, variable number1 is assigned the value 960 (00000000 00000000 00000011 11000000) in line 9. The result of left shifting variable number1 8 bits in the expression number1 << 8 (line 16) is 49152 (00000000 00000000 11000000 00000000).

The right-shift operator (>>) shifts the bits of its left operand to the right by the number of bits specified in its right operand. Performing a right shift on an unsigned integer causes the vacated bits at the left to be replaced by 0s; 1s shifted off the right are lost. In Fig. 10.13, the result of right shifting number1 in the expression number1 >> 8 (line 23) is 3 (00000000 00000000 00000000 00000011).

Common Programming Error 10.13

The result of shifting a value is undefined if the right operand is negative or if the right operand is larger than the number of bits in which the left operand is stored.

Portability Tip 10.7

Right shifting is machine dependent. Right shifting a signed integer fills the vacated bits with 0s on some machines and with 1s on others.

Bitwise Assignment Operators

Each binary bitwise operator has a corresponding assignment operator. These bitwise assignment operators are shown in Fig. 10.14 and are used in a manner similar to the arithmetic assignment operators introduced in Chapter 3.

Figure 10.15 shows the precedence and associativity of the various operators introduced to this point in the text. They are shown top to bottom in decreasing order of precedence.

Bitwise assignment operators	
&=	Bitwise AND assignment operator.
|=	Bitwise inclusive OR assignment operator.
^=	Bitwise exclusive OR assignment operator.
<<=	Left-shift assignment operator.
>>=	Right-shift assignment operator.

Fig. 10.14 | The bitwise assignment operators.

Operator	Associativity	Type
() [] . ->	left to right	highest
+ - ++ -- ! & * ~ sizeof (*type*)	right to left	unary
* / %	left to right	multiplicative
+ -	left to right	additive
<< >>	left to right	shifting
< <= > >=	left to right	relational
== !=	left to right	equality
&	left to right	bitwise AND
^	left to right	bitwise OR
|	left to right	bitwise OR
&&	left to right	logical AND
||	left to right	logical OR
?:	right to left	conditional
= += -= *= /= &= |= ^= <<= >>= %=	right to left	assignment
,	left to right	comma

Fig. 10.15 | Operator precedence and associativity.

10.10 Bit Fields

C enables you to specify the number of bits in which an unsigned or int member of a structure or union is stored. This is referred to as a **bit field**. Bit fields enable better memory utilization by storing data in the minimum number of bits required. Bit field members *must* be declared as int or unsigned

Performance Tip 10.3

Bit fields help conserve storage.

Consider the following structure definition:

```
struct bitCard {
    unsigned face : 4;
    unsigned suit : 2;
    unsigned color : 1;
};
```

which contains three unsigned bit fields—face, suit and color—used to represent a card from a deck of 52 cards. A bit field is declared by following an unsigned or int member name with a colon (:) and an integer constant representing the width of the field (i.e., the number of bits in which the member is stored). The constant representing the width must be an integer between 0 and the total number of bits used to store an int on your system, inclusive. Our examples were tested on a computer with 4-byte (32-bit) integers.

The preceding structure definition indicates that member face is stored in 4 bits, member suit is stored in 2 bits and member color is stored in 1 bit. The number of bits is based on the desired range of values for each structure member. Member face stores values from 0 (Ace) through 12 (King)—4 bits can store values in the range 0–15. Member suit stores values from 0 through 3 (0 = Diamonds, 1 = Hearts, 2 = Clubs, 3 = Spades)— 2 bits can store values in the range 0–3. Finally, member color stores either 0 (Red) or 1 (Black)—1 bit can store either 0 or 1.

Figure 10.16 (output shown in Fig. 10.17) creates array deck containing 52 struct bitCard structures in line 20. Function fillDeck (lines 30–41) inserts the 52 cards in the deck array and function deal (lines 45–58) prints the 52 cards. Notice that bit field members of structures are accessed exactly as any other structure member. Member color is included as a means of indicating the card color on a system that allows color displays.

```
 1   /* Fig. 10.16: fig10_16.c
 2      Representing cards with bit fields in a struct */
 3
 4   #include <stdio.h>
 5
 6   /* bitCard structure definition with bit fields */
 7   struct bitCard {
 8      unsigned face : 4;  /* 4 bits; 0-15 */
 9      unsigned suit : 2;  /* 2 bits; 0-3 */
10      unsigned color : 1; /* 1 bit; 0-1 */
11   }; /* end struct bitCard */
12
13   typedef struct bitCard Card; /* new type name for struct bitCard */
14
15   void fillDeck( Card * const wDeck );    /* prototype */
16   void deal( const Card * const wDeck ); /* prototype */
17
```

Fig. 10.16 | Bit fields to store a deck of cards. (Part 1 of 2.)

```
18    int main( void )
19    {
20        Card deck[ 52 ]; /* create array of Cards */
21
22        fillDeck( deck );
23        deal( deck );
24
25        return 0; /* indicates successful termination */
26
27    } /* end main */
28
29    /* initialize Cards */
30    void fillDeck( Card * const wDeck )
31    {
32        int i; /* counter */
33
34        /* loop through wDeck */
35        for ( i = 0; i <= 51; i++ ) {
36           wDeck[ i ].face = i % 13;
37           wDeck[ i ].suit = i / 13;
38           wDeck[ i ].color = i / 26;
39        } /* end for */
40
41    } /* end function fillDeck */
42
43    /* output cards in two column format; cards 0-25 subscripted with
44       k1 (column 1); cards 26-51 subscripted k2 (column 2) */
45    void deal( const Card * const wDeck )
46    {
47        int k1; /* subscripts 0-25 */
48        int k2; /* subscripts 26-51 */
49
50        /* loop through wDeck */
51        for ( k1 = 0, k2 = k1 + 26; k1 <= 25; k1++, k2++ ) {
52           printf( "Card:%3d  Suit:%2d  Color:%2d    ",
53              wDeck[ k1 ].face, wDeck[ k1 ].suit, wDeck[ k1 ].color );
54           printf( "Card:%3d  Suit:%2d  Color:%2d\n",
55              wDeck[ k2 ].face, wDeck[ k2 ].suit, wDeck[ k2 ].color );
56        } /* end for */
57
58    } /* end function deal */
```

Fig. 10.16 | Bit fields to store a deck of cards. (Part 2 of 2.)

It is possible to specify an unnamed bit field to be used as padding in the structure. For example, the structure definition

```
struct example {
   unsigned a : 13;
   unsigned   : 19;
   unsigned b : 4;
};
```

uses an unnamed 19-bit field as padding—nothing can be stored in those 19 bits. Member b (on our 4-byte-word computer) is stored in another storage unit.

```
Card:  0  Suit: 0  Color: 0     Card:  0  Suit: 2  Color: 1
Card:  1  Suit: 0  Color: 0     Card:  1  Suit: 2  Color: 1
Card:  2  Suit: 0  Color: 0     Card:  2  Suit: 2  Color: 1
Card:  3  Suit: 0  Color: 0     Card:  3  Suit: 2  Color: 1
Card:  4  Suit: 0  Color: 0     Card:  4  Suit: 2  Color: 1
Card:  5  Suit: 0  Color: 0     Card:  5  Suit: 2  Color: 1
Card:  6  Suit: 0  Color: 0     Card:  6  Suit: 2  Color: 1
Card:  7  Suit: 0  Color: 0     Card:  7  Suit: 2  Color: 1
Card:  8  Suit: 0  Color: 0     Card:  8  Suit: 2  Color: 1
Card:  9  Suit: 0  Color: 0     Card:  9  Suit: 2  Color: 1
Card: 10  Suit: 0  Color: 0     Card: 10  Suit: 2  Color: 1
Card: 11  Suit: 0  Color: 0     Card: 11  Suit: 2  Color: 1
Card: 12  Suit: 0  Color: 0     Card: 12  Suit: 2  Color: 1
Card:  0  Suit: 1  Color: 0     Card:  0  Suit: 3  Color: 1
Card:  1  Suit: 1  Color: 0     Card:  1  Suit: 3  Color: 1
Card:  2  Suit: 1  Color: 0     Card:  2  Suit: 3  Color: 1
Card:  3  Suit: 1  Color: 0     Card:  3  Suit: 3  Color: 1
Card:  4  Suit: 1  Color: 0     Card:  4  Suit: 3  Color: 1
Card:  5  Suit: 1  Color: 0     Card:  5  Suit: 3  Color: 1
Card:  6  Suit: 1  Color: 0     Card:  6  Suit: 3  Color: 1
Card:  7  Suit: 1  Color: 0     Card:  7  Suit: 3  Color: 1
Card:  8  Suit: 1  Color: 0     Card:  8  Suit: 3  Color: 1
Card:  9  Suit: 1  Color: 0     Card:  9  Suit: 3  Color: 1
Card: 10  Suit: 1  Color: 0     Card: 10  Suit: 3  Color: 1
Card: 11  Suit: 1  Color: 0     Card: 11  Suit: 3  Color: 1
Card: 12  Suit: 1  Color: 0     Card: 12  Suit: 3  Color: 1
```

Fig. 10.17 | Output of the program in Fig. 10.16.

An unnamed bit field with a zero width is used to align the next bit field on a new storage-unit boundary. For example, the structure definition

```
struct example {
    unsigned a : 13;
    unsigned   : 0;
    unsigned b : 4;
};
```

uses an unnamed 0-bit field to skip the remaining bits (as many as there are) of the storage unit in which a is stored and to align b on the next storage-unit boundary.

Portability Tip 10.8

Bit-field manipulations are machine dependent. For example, some computers allow bit fields to cross word boundaries, whereas others do not.

Common Programming Error 10.14

Attempting to access individual bits of a bit field as if they were elements of an array is a syntax error. Bit fields are not "arrays of bits."

Common Programming Error 10.15

Attempting to take the address of a bit field (the & operator may not be used with bit fields because they do not have addresses).

Performance Tip 10.4

Although bit fields save space, using them can cause the compiler to generate slower-executing machine-language code. This occurs because it takes extra machine language operations to access only portions of an addressable storage unit. This is one of many examples of the kinds of space–time trade-offs that occur in computer science.

10.11 Enumeration Constants

C provides one final user-defined type called an **enumeration**. An enumeration, introduced by the keyword enum, is a set of integer **enumeration constants** represented by identifiers. Values in an enum start with 0, unless specified otherwise, and are incremented by 1. For example, the enumeration

```
enum months {
    JAN, FEB, MAR, APR, MAY, JUN, JUL, AUG, SEP, OCT, NOV, DEC };
```

creates a new type, enum months, in which the identifiers are set to the integers 0 to 11, respectively. To number the months 1 to 12, use the following enumeration:

```
enum months {
    JAN = 1, FEB, MAR, APR, MAY, JUN, JUL, AUG, SEP, OCT, NOV, DEC };
```

Since the first value in the preceding enumeration is explicitly set to 1, the remaining values are incremented from 1, resulting in the values 1 through 12. The identifiers in an enumeration must be unique. The value of each enumeration constant of an enumeration can be set explicitly in the definition by assigning a value to the identifier. Multiple members of an enumeration can have the same constant value. In the program of Fig. 10.18, the enumeration variable month is used in a for statement to print the months of the year from the array monthName. Note that we have made monthName[0] the empty string "". Some programmers might prefer to set monthName[0] to a value such as ***ERROR*** to indicate that a logic error occurred.

```
1   /* Fig. 10.18: fig10_18.c
2      Using an enumeration type */
3   #include <stdio.h>
4
5   /* enumeration constants represent months of the year */
6   enum months {
7      JAN = 1, FEB, MAR, APR, MAY, JUN, JUL, AUG, SEP, OCT, NOV, DEC };
8
9   int main( void )
10  {
11     enum months month; /* can contain any of the 12 months */
12
13     /* initialize array of pointers */
14     const char *monthName[] = { "", "January", "February", "March",
15        "April", "May", "June", "July", "August", "September", "October",
16        "November", "December" };
17
```

Fig. 10.18 | Using an enumeration. (Part 1 of 2.)

```
18      /* loop through months */
19      for ( month = JAN; month <= DEC; month++ ) {
20          printf( "%2d%11s\n", month, monthName[ month ] );
21      } /* end for */
22
23      return 0; /* indicates successful termination */
24  } /* end main */
```

```
 1    January
 2    February
 3       March
 4       April
 5         May
 6        June
 7        July
 8      August
 9   September
10     October
11    November
12    December
```

Fig. 10.18 | Using an enumeration. (Part 2 of 2.)

Common Programming Error 10.16

Assigning a value to an enumeration constant after it has been defined is a syntax error.

Good Programming Practice 10.5

Use only uppercase letters in the names of enumeration constants. This makes these constants stand out in a program and reminds you that enumeration constants are not variables.

Summary

Section 10.1 Introduction
- Structures—sometimes referred to as aggregates—are collections of related variables under one name. Structures may contain variables of many different data types—in contrast to arrays that contain only elements of the same data type.
- Structures are commonly used to define records to be stored in files.
- Pointers and structures facilitate the formation of more complex data structures such as linked lists, queues, stacks and trees.

Section 10.2 Structure Definitions
- Structures are derived data types—they are constructed using objects of other types.
- Keyword `struct` introduces a structure definition.
- The identifier following keyword `struct` is the structure tag, which names the structure definition. The structure tag is used with the keyword `struct` to declare variables of the structure type.
- Variables declared within the braces of the structure definition are the structure's members.

- Members of the same structure type must have unique names, but two different structure types may contain members of the same name without conflict.
- Each structure definition must end with a semicolon.
- Structure members can be variables of the primitive data types (e.g., int, float, etc.), or aggregates, such as arrays and other structures.
- Structure members, however, can be of a variety of data types.
- A structure cannot contain an instance of itself but may include a pointer to another object of the same type.
- A structure containing a member that is a pointer to the same structure type is referred to as a self-referential structure. Self-referential structures are used to build linked data structures.
- Structure definitions do not reserve any space in memory; rather, each definition creates a new data type that is used to define variables. Structure variables are defined like variables of other types.
- Variables of a given structure type may also be declared by placing a comma-separated list of the variable names between the closing brace of the structure definition and the semicolon that ends the structure definition.
- The structure tag name is optional. If a structure definition does not contain a structure tag name, variables of the structure type may be declared only in the structure definition—not in a separate declaration.
- The only valid operations that may be performed on structures are the following: assigning structure variables to structure variables of the same type, taking the address (&) of a structure variable, accessing the members of a structure variable and using the sizeof operator to determine the size of a structure variable.
- Structures may not be compared using operators == and != because structure members are not necessarily stored in consecutive bytes of memory.

Section 10.3 Initializing Structures
- Structures can be initialized using initializer lists as with arrays. To initialize a structure, follow the variable name in the definition with an equals sign and a brace-enclosed, comma-separated list of initializers.
- If there are fewer initializers in the list than members in the structure, the remaining members are automatically initialized to 0 (or NULL if the member is a pointer).
- Structure variables defined outside a function definition (i.e., externally) are initialized to 0 or NULL if they are not explicitly initialized in the external definition.
- Structure variables may also be initialized in assignment statements by assigning a structure variable of the same type, or by assigning values to the individual members of the structure.

Section 10.4 Accessing Members of Structures
- The structure member operator (.)—also called the dot operator—and the structure pointer operator (->)—also called the arrow operator—are used to access members of structures.
- The structure member operator accesses a structure member via the structure variable name.
- The structure pointer operator—consisting of a minus (-) sign and a greater than (>) sign with no intervening spaces—accesses a structure member via a pointer to the structure.
- The structure pointer operator and structure member operator, along with parentheses (for calling functions) and brackets ([]) used for array subscripting, have the highest operator precedence and associate from left to right.

Section 10.5 *Using Structures with Functions*
- Structures may be passed to functions by passing individual structure members, by passing an entire structure or by passing a pointer to a structure.
- When structures or individual structure members are passed to a function, they are passed by value. Therefore, the members of a caller's structure cannot be modified by the called function.
- To pass a structure by reference, pass the address of the structure variable. Arrays of structures—like all other arrays—are automatically passed by reference.
- To pass an array by value, create a structure with the array as a member. Structures are passed by value, so the array is passed by value.

Section 10.6 `typedef`
- The keyword `typedef` provides a mechanism for creating synonyms (or aliases) for previously defined data types.
- Names for structure types are often defined with `typedef` to create shorter type names.
- Creating a new name with `typedef` does not create a new type; `typedef` simply creates a new type name, which may be used as an alias for an existing type name.
- Often, `typedef` is used to create synonyms for the basic data types. For example, a program requiring 4-byte integers may use type `int` on one system and type `long` on another. Programs designed for portability often use `typedef` to create an alias for 4-byte integers such as `Integer`. The alias `Integer` can be changed once in the program to make the program work on both systems.

Section 10.8 *Unions*
- A union is a derived data type with members that share the same storage space. For different situations in a program, some variables may not be relevant, but other variables are—so a union shares the space instead of wasting storage on variables that are not being used.
- The members of a union can be of any data type. The number of bytes used to store a union must be at least enough to hold the largest member.
- In most cases, unions contain two or more data types. Only one member, and thus one data type, can be referenced at a time. It is your responsibility to ensure that the data in a union is referenced with the proper data type.
- A union is declared with keyword `union` in the same format as a structure.
- The operations that can be performed on a union are the following: assigning a union to another union of the same type, taking the address (&) of a union variable, and accessing union members using the structure member operator and the structure pointer operator.
- Unions may not be compared using operators `==` and `!=` for the same reasons that structures cannot be compared.
- A union may be initialized in a declaration with a value of the same type as the first union member.

Section 10.9 *Bitwise Operators*
- Computers represent all data internally as sequences of bits. Each bit can assume the value 0 or the value 1.
- On most systems, a sequence of 8 bits form a byte—the standard storage unit for a variable of type `char`. Other data types are stored in larger numbers of bytes.
- The bitwise operators are used to manipulate the bits of integral operands (`char`, `short`, `int` and `long`; both `signed` and `unsigned`). Unsigned integers are normally used.
- The bitwise operators are bitwise AND (&), bitwise inclusive OR (|), bitwise exclusive OR (^), left shift (<<), right shift (>>) and complement (~).

- The bitwise AND, bitwise inclusive OR and bitwise exclusive OR operators compare their two operands bit by bit. The bitwise AND operator sets each bit in the result to 1 if the corresponding bit in both operands is 1. The bitwise inclusive OR operator sets each bit in the result to 1 if the corresponding bit in either (or both) operand(s) is 1. The bitwise exclusive OR operator sets each bit in the result to 1 if the corresponding bit in exactly one operand is 1.

- The left-shift operator shifts the bits of its left operand to the left by the number of bits specified in its right operand. Bits vacated to the right are replaced with 0s; 1s shifted off the left are lost.

- The right-shift operator shifts the bits in its left operand to the right by the number of bits specified in its right operand. Performing a right shift on an `unsigned` integer causes the vacated bits at the left to be replaced by 0s; bits shifted off the right are lost.

- The bitwise complement operator sets all 0 bits in its operand to 1 in the result and sets all 1 bits to 0 in the result.

- Often, the bitwise AND operator is used with an operand called a mask—an integer value with specific bits set to 1. Masks are used to hide some bits in a value while selecting other bits.

- The symbolic constant `CHAR_BIT` (defined in `<limits.h>`) represents the number of bits in a byte (normally 8). It can be used to make a bit-manipulation program more scalable and portable.

- Each binary bitwise operator has a corresponding assignment operator.

Section 10.10 Bit Fields

- C enables you to specify the number of bits in which an `unsigned` or `int` member of a structure or union is stored. This is referred to as a bit field. Bit fields enable better memory utilization by storing data in the minimum number of bits required. Bit-field members *must* be declared as `int` or `unsigned`.

- A bit field is declared by following an `unsigned` or `int` member name with a colon (`:`) and an integer constant representing the width of the field (i.e., the number of bits in which the member is stored). The constant representing the width must be an integer between 0 and the total number of bits used to store an `int` on your system, inclusive.

- Bit-field members of structures are accessed exactly as any other structure member.

- It is possible to specify an unnamed bit field to be used as padding in the structure.

- An unnamed bit field with a zero width is used to align the next bit field on a new storage unit boundary.

Section 10.11 Enumeration Constants

- An enumeration, introduced by the keyword `enum`, is a set of integer enumeration constants represented by identifiers. Values in an `enum` start with 0, unless specified otherwise, and are incremented by 1.

- The identifiers in an enumeration must be unique.

- The value of each enumeration constant of an enumeration can be set explicitly in the definition by assigning a value to the identifier.

- Multiple members of an enumeration can have the same constant value.

Terminology

^ bitwise exclusive OR operator	| bitwise inclusive OR operator
^= bitwise exclusive OR assignment operator	|= bitwise inclusive OR assignment operator
~ one's complement operator	<< left-shift operator
& bitwise AND operator	<<= left-shift assignment operator
&= bitwise AND assignment operator	>> right-shift operator

>>= right-shift assignment operator	programmer-defined data types
accessing members of structures	right shift
aggregates	self-referential structure
array of structures	shifting
bit field	space–time trade-offs
bitwise operator	`struct`
complementing	structure
derived data type	structure assignment
enumeration	structure declaration
enumeration constant	structure definition
structure initialization	structure member (dot) operator (.)
initialization of structures	structure name
left shift	structure pointer (arrow) operator (->)
mask	structure tag
masking off bits	structure type
member	tag name
member name	`typedef`
nested structures	`union`
one's complement	unnamed bit field
padding	width of a bit field
pointer to a structure	zero-width bit field

Self-Review Exercises

10.1   Fill in the blanks in each of the following:

  a) A(n) _____ is a collection of related variables under one name.

  b) A(n) _____ is a collection of variables under one name in which the variables share the same storage.

  c) The bits in the result of an expression using the _____ operator are set to 1 if the corresponding bits in each operand are set to 1. Otherwise, the bits are set to zero.

  d) The variables declared in a structure definition are called its _____ .

  e) The bits in the result of an expression using the _____ operator are set to 1 if at least one of the corresponding bits in either operand is set to 1. Otherwise, the bits are set to zero.

  f) Keyword _____ introduces a structure declaration.

  g) Keyword _____ is used to create a synonym for a previously defined data type.

  h) The bits in the result of an expression using the _____ operator are set to 1 if exactly one of the corresponding bits in either operand is set to 1. Otherwise, the bits are set to zero.

  i) The bitwise AND operator & is often used to _____ bits, that is to select certain bits while zeroing others.

  j) Keyword _____ is used to introduce a union definition.

  k) The name of the structure is referred to as the structure _____.

  l) A structure member is accessed with either the _____ or the _____ operator.

  m) The _____ and _____ operators are used to shift the bits of a value to the left or to the right, respectively.

  n) A(n) _____ is a set of integers represented by identifiers.

10.2   State whether each of the following is *true* or *false*. If *false*, explain why.

  a) Structures may contain variables of only one data type.

  b) Two unions can be compared (using ==) to determine if they are equal.

    c) The tag name of a structure is optional.

    d) Members of different structures must have unique names.

    e) Keyword typedef is used to define new data types.

    f) Structures are always passed to functions by reference.

    g) Structures may not be compared by using operators == and !=.

10.3 Write code to accomplish each of the following:

    a) Define a structure called part containing int variable partNumber and char array part-Name with values that may be as long as 25 characters (including the terminating null character).

    b) Define Part to be a synonym for the type struct part.

    c) Use Part to declare variable a to be of type struct part, array b[10] to be of type struct part and variable ptr to be of type pointer to struct part.

    d) Read a part number and a part name from the keyboard into the individual members of variable a.

    e) Assign the member values of variable a to element 3 of array b.

    f) Assign the address of array b to the pointer variable ptr.

    g) Print the member values of element 3 of array b using the variable ptr and the structure pointer operator to refer to the members.

10.4 Find the error in each of the following:

    a) Assume that struct card has been defined containing two pointers to type char, namely face and suit. Also, the variable c has been defined to be of type struct card and the variable cPtr has been defined to be of type pointer to struct card. Variable cPtr has been assigned the address of c.

```
printf( "%s\n", *cPtr->face );
```

    b) Assume that struct card has been defined containing two pointers to type char, namely face and suit. Also, the array hearts[13] has been defined to be of type struct card. The following statement should print the member face of array element 10.

```
printf( "%s\n", hearts.face );
```

    c)
```
union values {
    char w;
    float x;
    double y;
};

union values v = { 1.27 };
```

    d)
```
struct person {
    char lastName[ 15 ];
    char firstName[ 15 ];
    int age;
}
```

    e) Assume struct person has been defined as in part (d) but with the appropriate correction.

```
person d;
```

    f) Assume variable p has been declared as type struct person and variable c has been declared as type struct card.

```
p = c;
```

Answers to Self-Review Exercises

10.1 a) structure. b) union. c) bitwise AND (&). d) members. e) bitwise inclusive OR (|).
f) struct. g) typedef. h) bitwise exclusive OR (^). i) mask. j) union. k) tag name. l) structure
member, structure pointer. m) left-shift operator (<<), right-shift operator (>>). n) enumeration.

10.2 a) False. A structure can contain variables of many data types.
b) False. Unions cannot be compared because there might be bytes of undefined data with
    different values in union variables that are otherwise identical.
c) True.
d) False. The members of separate structures can have the same names, but the members
    of the same structure must have unique names.
e) False. Keyword typedef is used to define new names (synonyms) for previously defined
    data types.
f) False. Structures are always passed to functions call-by-value.
g) True, because of alignment problems.

10.3 a) ```
struct part {
    int partNumber;
    char partName[26];
};
```
b)  `typedef struct part Part;`
c)  `Part a, b[ 10 ], *ptr;`
d)  `scanf( "%d%25s", &a.partNumber, &a.partName };`
e)  `b[ 3 ] = a;`
f)  `ptr = b;`
g)  `printf( "%d %s\n", ( ptr + 3 )->partNumber, ( ptr + 3 )->partName);`

**10.4**  a)  The parentheses that should enclose *cPtr have been omitted, causing the order
    of evaluation of the expression to be incorrect. The expression should be
    `( *cPtr )->face`
b)  The array subscript has been omitted. The expression should be
    `hearts[ 10 ].face.`
c)  A union can be initialized only with a value that has the same type as the union's first
    member.
d)  A semicolon is required to end a structure definition.
e)  Keyword struct was omitted from the variable declaration. The declaration should be
    `struct person d;`
f)  Variables of different structure types cannot be assigned to one another.

## Exercises

**10.5**  Provide the definition for each of the following structures and unions:
a)  Structure inventory containing character array partName[ 30 ], integer partNumber,
    floating point price, integer stock and integer reorder.
b)  Union data containing char c, short s, long b, float f and double d.
c)  A structure called address that contains character arrays
    streetAddress[ 25 ], city[ 20 ], state[ 3 ] and zipCode[ 6 ].
d)  Structure student that contains arrays firstName[ 15 ] and
    lastName[ 15 ] and variable homeAddress of type struct address from part (c).
e)  Structure test containing 16 bit fields with widths of 1 bit. The names of the bit fields
    are the letters a to p.
```

10.6 Given the following structure and variable definitions,

```
struct customer {
   char lastName[ 15 ];
   char firstName[ 15 ];
   int customerNumber;

   struct {
      char phoneNumber[ 11 ];
      char address[ 50 ];
      char city[ 15 ];
      char state[ 3 ];
      char zipCode[ 6 ];
   } personal;

} customerRecord, *customerPtr;

customerPtr = &customerRecord;
```

write an expression that can be used to access the structure members in each of the following parts:

a) Member lastName of structure customerRecord.
b) Member lastName of the structure pointed to by customerPtr.
c) Member firstName of structure customerRecord.
d) Member firstName of the structure pointed to by customerPtr.
e) Member customerNumber of structure customerRecord.
f) Member customerNumber of the structure pointed to by customerPtr.
g) Member phoneNumber of member personal of structure customerRecord.
h) Member phoneNumber of member personal of the structure pointed to by customerPtr.
i) Member address of member personal of structure customerRecord.
j) Member address of member personal of the structure pointed to by customerPtr.
k) Member city of member personal of structure customerRecord.
l) Member city of member personal of the structure pointed to by customerPtr.
m) Member state of member personal of structure customerRecord.
n) Member state of member personal of the structure pointed to by customerPtr.
o) Member zipCode of member personal of structure customerRecord.
p) Member zipCode of member personal of the structure pointed to by customerPtr.

10.7 Modify the program of Fig. 10.16 to shuffle the cards using a high-performance shuffle (as shown in Fig. 10.3). Print the resulting deck in two-column format as in Fig. 10.4. Precede each card with its color.

10.8 Create union integer with members char c, short s, int i and long b. Write a program that inputs value of type char, short, int and long and stores the values in union variables of type union integer. Each union variable should be printed as a char, a short, an int and a long. Do the values always print correctly?

10.9 Create union floatingPoint with members float f, double d and long double x. Write a program that inputs value of type float, double and long double and stores the values in union variables of type union floatingPoint. Each union variable should be printed as a float, a double and a long double. Do the values always print correctly?

10.10 Write a program that right shifts an integer variable 4 bits. The program should print the integer in bits before and after the shift operation. Does your system place 0s or 1s in the vacated bits?

10.11 If your computer uses 2-byte integers, modify the program of Fig. 10.7 so that it works with 2-byte integers.

10.12 Left shifting an unsigned integer by 1 bit is equivalent to multiplying the value by 2. Write function power2 that takes two integer arguments number and pow and calculates

number * 2^{pow}

Use the shift operator to calculate the result. Print the values as integers and as bits.

10.13 The left-shift operator can be used to pack two character values into an unsigned integer variable. Write a program that inputs two characters from the keyboard and passes them to function packCharacters. To pack two characters into an unsigned integer variable, assign the first character to the unsigned variable, shift the unsigned variable left by 8 bit positions and combine the unsigned variable with the second character using the bitwise inclusive OR operator. The program should output the characters in their bit format before and after they are packed into the unsigned integer to prove that the characters are in fact packed correctly in the unsigned variable.

10.14 Using the right-shift operator, the bitwise AND operator and a mask, write function unpackCharacters that takes the unsigned integer from Exercise 10.13 and unpacks it into two characters. To unpack two characters from an unsigned integer, combine the unsigned integer with the mask 65280 (00000000 00000000 11111111 00000000) and right shift the result 8 bits. Assign the resulting value to a char variable. Then combine the unsigned integer with the mask 255 (00000000 00000000 00000000 11111111). Assign the result to another char variable. The program should print the unsigned integer in bits before it is unpacked, then print the characters in bits to confirm that they were unpacked correctly.

10.15 If your system uses 4-byte integers, rewrite the program of Exercise 10.13 to pack 4 characters.

10.16 If your system uses 4-byte integers, rewrite the function unpackCharacters of Exercise 10.14 to unpack 4 characters. Create the masks you need to unpack the 4 characters by left shifting the value 255 in the mask variable by 8 bits 0, 1, 2 or 3 times (depending on the byte you are unpacking).

10.17 Write a program that reverses the order of the bits in an unsigned integer value. The program should input the value from the user and call function reverseBits to print the bits in reverse order. Print the value in bits both before and after the bits are reversed to confirm that the bits are reversed properly.

10.18 Modify function displayBits of Fig. 10.7 so it is portable between systems using 2-byte integers and systems using 4-byte integers. [*Hint:* Use the sizeof operator to determine the size of an integer on a particular machine.]

10.19 The following program uses function multiple to determine if the integer entered from the keyboard is a multiple of some integer X. Examine the function multiple, then determine X's value.

```
1   /* ex10_19.c */
2   /* This program determines if a value is a multiple of X. */
3   #include <stdio.h>
4
5   int multiple( int num ); /* prototype */
6
7   int main( void )
8   {
9       int y; /* y will hold an integer entered by the user  */
10
11      printf( "Enter an integer between 1 and 32000: " );
12      scanf( "%d", &y );
```

```
13
14    /* if y is a multiple of X */
15    if ( multiple( y ) ) {
16       printf( "%d is a multiple of X\n", y );
17    } /* end if */
18    else {
19       printf( "%d is not a multiple of X\n", y );
20    } /* end else */
21
22    return 0; /* indicates successful termination */
23 } /* end main */
24
25 /* determine if num is a multiple of X */
26 int multiple( int num )
27 {
28    int i;        /* counter */
29    int mask = 1; /* initialize mask */
30    int mult = 1; /* initialize mult */
31
32    for ( i = 1; i <= 10; i++, mask <<= 1 ) {
33
34       if ( ( num & mask ) != 0 ) {
35          mult = 0;
36          break;
37       } /* end if */
38
39    } /* end for */
40
41    return mult;
42 } /* end function multiple */
```

10.20 What does the following program do?

```
1  /* ex10_20.c */
2  #include <stdio.h>
3
4  int mystery( unsigned bits ); /* prototype */
5
6  int main( void )
7  {
8     unsigned x; /* x will hold an integer entered by the user */
9
10    printf( "Enter an integer: " );
11    scanf( "%u", &x );
12
13    printf( "The result is %d\n", mystery( x ) );
14
15    return 0; /* indicates successful termination */
16 } /* end main */
17
18 /* What does this function do? */
19 int mystery( unsigned bits )
20 {
```

```
21     unsigned i;                 /* counter */
22     unsigned mask = 1 << 31; /* initialize mask */
23     unsigned total = 0;         /* initialize total */
24
25     for ( i = 1; i <= 32; i++, bits <<= 1 ) {
26
27        if ( ( bits & mask ) == mask ) {
28           total++;
29        } /* end if */
30
31     } /* end for */
32
33     return !( total % 2 ) ? 1 : 0;
34  } /* end function mystery */
```

11

C File Processing

OBJECTIVES

In this chapter, you will learn:

- To create, read, write and update files.
- Sequential access file processing.
- Random-access file processing.

11.1 Introduction

Storage of data in variables and arrays is temporary—such data is lost when a program terminates. Files are used for permanent retention of data. Computers store files on secondary storage devices, especially disk storage devices. In this chapter, we explain how data files are created, updated and processed by C programs. We consider sequential-access files and random-access files.

11.2 Data Hierarchy

Ultimately, all data items processed by a computer are reduced to combinations of **zeros and ones**. This occurs because it is simple and economical to build electronic devices that can assume two stable states—one of the states represents 0 and the other represents 1. It is remarkable that the impressive functions performed by computers involve only the most fundamental manipulations of 0s and 1s.

The smallest data item in a computer can assume the value 0 or the value 1. Such a data item is called a **bit** (short for "binary digit"—a digit that can assume one of two values). Computer circuitry performs various simple bit manipulations such as determining a bit's value, setting a bit's value and reversing a bit (from 1 to 0 or from 0 to 1).

It is cumbersome to work with data in the low-level form of bits. Instead, programmers prefer to work with data in the form of **decimal digits** (i.e., 0, 1, 2, 3, 4, 5, 6, 7, 8, and 9), letters (i.e., A–Z, and a–z), and **special symbols** (i.e., $, @, %, &, *, (,), -, +, ", :, ?, /, and others). Digits, letters, and special symbols are referred to as **characters**. The set of all characters that may be used to write programs and represent data items on a particular computer is called that computer's **character set**. Since computers can process only 1s and 0s, every character in a computer's character set is represented as a pattern of 1s and 0s (called a byte). Today, bytes are most commonly composed of eight bits. You create programs and data items as characters; computers then manipulate and process these characters as patterns of bits.

Just as characters are composed of bits, **fields** are composed of characters. A field is a group of characters that conveys meaning. For example, a field consisting solely of uppercase and lowercase letters can be used to represent a person's name.

Data items processed by computers form a data hierarchy in which data items become larger and more complex in structure as we progress from bits, to characters (bytes), to fields, and so on.

A record (i.e., a `struct` in C) is composed of several fields. In a payroll system, for example, a record for a particular employee might consist of the following fields:

1. Social Security number (alphanumeric field)

2. Name (alphabetic field)

3. Address (alphanumeric field)

4. Hourly salary rate (numeric field)

5. Number of exemptions claimed (numeric field)

6. Year-to-date earnings (numeric field)

7. Amount of Federal taxes withheld (numeric field)

Thus, a record is a group of related fields. In the preceding example, each of the fields belongs to the same employee. Of course, a particular company may have many employees and will have a payroll record for each employee. A file is a group of related records. A company's payroll file normally contains one record for each employee. Thus, a payroll file for a small company might contain only 22 records, whereas a payroll file for a large company might contain 100,000 records. It is not unusual for an organization to have hundreds or even thousands of files, with some containing billions or even trillions of characters of information. Figure 11.1 illustrates the data hierarchy.

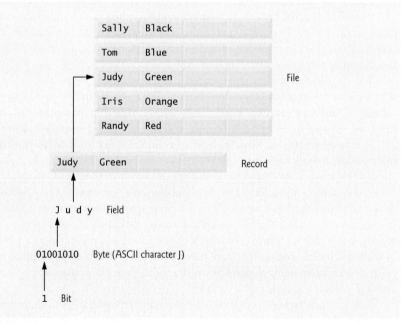

Fig. 11.1 | Data hierarchy.

To facilitate the retrieval of specific records from a file, at least one field in each record is chosen as a record key. A record key identifies a record as belonging to a particular person or entity. For example, in the payroll record described in this section, the Social Security number would normally be chosen as the record key.

There are many ways of organizing records in a file. The most popular type of organization is called a sequential file, in which records are typically stored in order by the record key field. In a payroll file, records are usually placed in order by Social Security Number. The first employee record in the file contains the lowest Social Security number, and subsequent records contain increasingly higher Social Security numbers.

Most businesses store data in many different files. For example, companies may have payroll files, accounts receivable files (listing money due from clients), accounts payable files (listing money due to suppliers), inventory files (listing facts about all the items handled by the business) and many other types of files. A group of related files is sometimes called a database. A collection of programs designed to create and manage databases is called a database management system (DBMS).

11.3 Files and Streams

C views each file simply as a sequential stream of bytes (Fig. 11.2). Each file ends either with an end-of-file marker or at a specific byte number recorded in a system-maintained, administrative data structure. When a file is opened, a stream is associated with the file. Three files and their associated streams are automatically opened when program execution begins—the standard input, the standard output and the standard error. Streams provide communication channels between files and programs. For example, the standard input stream enables a program to read data from the keyboard, and the standard output stream enables a program to print data on the screen. Opening a file returns a pointer to a FILE structure (defined in <stdio.h>) that contains information used to process the file. This structure includes a file descriptor, i.e., an index into an operating system array called the open file table. Each array element contains a file control block (FCB) that the operating system uses to administer a particular file. The standard input, standard output and standard error are manipulated using file pointers stdin, stdout and stderr.

The standard library provides many functions for reading data from files and for writing data to files. Function fgetc, like getchar, reads one character from a file. Function fgetc receives as an argument a FILE pointer for the file from which a character will be read. The call fgetc(stdin) reads one character from stdin—the standard input. This call is equivalent to the call getchar(). Function fputc, like putchar, writes one character to a file. Function fputc receives as arguments a character to be written and a pointer for the file to which the character will be written. The function call fputc('a', stdout) writes the character 'a' to stdout—the standard output. This call is equivalent to putchar('a').

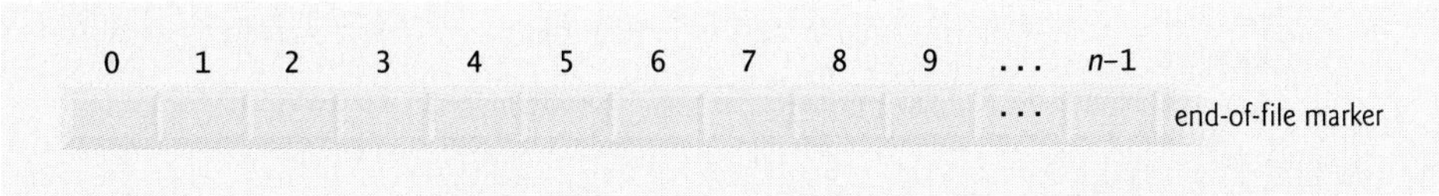

Fig. 11.2 | C's view of a file of n bytes.

Several other functions used to read data from standard input and write data to standard output have similarly named file processing functions. The **fgets** and **fputs** functions, for example, can be used to read a line from a file and write a line to a file, respectively. Their counterparts for reading from standard input and writing to standard output, **gets** and **puts**, were discussed in Chapter 8. In the next several sections, we introduce the file processing equivalents of functions scanf and printf—**fscanf** and **fprintf**. Later in the chapter we discuss functions **fread** and **fwrite**.

11.4 Creating a Sequential-Access File

C imposes no structure on a file. Thus, notions such as a record of a file do not exist as part of the C language. Therefore, you must provide a file structure to meet the requirements of a particular application. The following example shows how to impose a record structure on a file.

Figure 11.3 creates a simple sequential-access file that might be used in an accounts receivable system to help keep track of the amounts owed by a company's credit clients. For each client, the program obtains an account number, the client's name and the client's balance (i.e., the amount the client owes the company for goods and services received in the past). The data obtained for each client constitutes a "record" for that client. The account number is used as the record key in this application—the file will be created and maintained in account number order. This program assumes the user enters the records in account number order. In a comprehensive accounts receivable system, a sorting capability would be provided so the user could enter the records in any order. The records would then be sorted and written to the file.

```
1   /* Fig. 11.3: fig11_03.c
2      Create a sequential file */
3   #include <stdio.h>
4
5   int main( void )
6   {
7      int account;     /* account number */
8      char name[ 30 ]; /* account name */
9      double balance;  /* account balance */
10
11     FILE *cfPtr;     /* cfPtr = clients.dat file pointer */
12
13     /* fopen opens file. Exit program if unable to create file  */
14     if ( ( cfPtr = fopen( "clients.dat", "w" ) ) == NULL ) {
15        printf( "File could not be opened\n" );
16     } /* end if */
17     else {
18        printf( "Enter the account, name, and balance.\n" );
19        printf( "Enter EOF to end input.\n" );
20        printf( "? " );
21        scanf( "%d%s%lf", &account, name, &balance );
22
```

Fig. 11.3 | Creating a sequential file. (Part 1 of 2.)

```
23          /* write account, name and balance into file with fprintf */
24          while ( !feof( stdin ) ) {
25              fprintf( cfPtr, "%d %s %.2f\n", account, name, balance );
26              printf( "? " );
27              scanf( "%d%s%lf", &account, name, &balance );
28          } /* end while */
29
30          fclose( cfPtr ); /* fclose closes file */
31      } /* end else */
32
33      return 0; /* indicates successful termination */
34
35  } /* end main */
```

```
Enter the account, name, and balance.
Enter EOF to end input.
? 100 Jones 24.98
? 200 Doe 345.67
? 300 White 0.00
? 400 Stone -42.16
? 500 Rich 224.62
? ^Z
```

Fig. 11.3 | Creating a sequential file. (Part 2 of 2.)

Now let us examine this program. Line 11

```
FILE *cfPtr;
```

states that cfptr is a pointer to a FILE structure. A C program administers each file with a separate FILE structure. You need not know the specifics of the FILE structure to use files, though the interested reader can study the declaration in stdio.h. We will soon see precisely how the FILE structure leads indirectly to the operating system's file control block (FCB) for a file.

Each open file must have a separately declared pointer of type FILE that is used to refer to the file. Line 14

```
if ( ( cfPtr = fopen( "clients.dat", "w" ) ) == NULL )
```

names the file—"clients.dat"—to be used by the program and establishes a "line of communication" with the file. The file pointer cfPtr is assigned a pointer to the FILE structure for the file opened with fopen. Function fopen takes two arguments: a file name and a **file open mode**. The file open mode "w" indicates that the file is to be opened for writing. If a file does not exist and it is opened for writing, fopen creates the file. If an existing file is opened for writing, the contents of the file are discarded without warning. In the program, the if statement is used to determine whether the file pointer cfPtr is NULL (i.e., the file is not opened). If it is NULL, the program prints an error message and terminates. Otherwise, the program processes the input and writes it to the file.

 Common Programming Error 11.1

Opening an existing file for writing ("w") when, in fact, the user wants to preserve the file, discards the contents of the file without warning.

Common Programming Error 11.2

Forgetting to open a file before attempting to reference it in a program is a logic error.

The program prompts the user to enter the various fields for each record or to enter end-of-file when data entry is complete. Figure 11.4 lists the key combinations for entering end-of-file for various computer systems.

Line 24

```
while ( !feof( stdin ) )
```

uses function `feof` to determine whether the end-of-file indicator is set for the file to which `stdin` refers. The end-of-file indicator informs the program that there is no more data to be processed. In Fig. 11.3, the end-of-file indicator is set for the standard input when the user enters the end-of-file key combination. The argument to function `feof` is a pointer to the file being tested for the end-of-file indicator (`stdin` in this case). The function returns a nonzero (true) value when the end-of-file indicator has been set; otherwise, the function returns zero. The `while` statement that includes the `feof` call in this program continues executing while the end-of-file indicator is not set.

Line 25

```
fprintf( cfPtr, "%d %s %.2f\n", account, name, balance );
```

writes data to the file `clients.dat`. The data may be retrieved later by a program designed to read the file (see Section 11.5). Function `fprintf` is equivalent to `printf` except that `fprintf` also receives as an argument a file pointer for the file to which the data will be written. Function `fprintf` can output data to the standard output by using `stdout` as the file pointer, as in:

```
fprintf( stdout, "%d %s %.2f\n", account, name, balance );
```

Common Programming Error 11.3

Using the wrong file pointer to refer to a file is a logic error.

Error-Prevention Tip 11.1

Be sure that calls to file processing functions in a program contain the correct file pointers.

After the user enters end-of-file, the program closes the `clients.dat` file with `fclose` and terminates. Function `fclose` also receives the file pointer (rather than the file name)

Operating system	Key combination
Linux/Mac OS X/UNIX	*<Ctrl> d*
Windows	*<Ctrl> z*

Fig. 11.4 | End-of-file key combinations for various popular operating systems.

as an argument. If function `fclose` is not called explicitly, the operating system normally will close the file when program execution terminates. This is an example of operating system "housekeeping."

Good Programming Practice 11.1

Explicitly close each file as soon as it is known that the program will not reference the file again.

Performance Tip 11.1

Closing a file can free resources for which other users or programs may be waiting.

In the sample execution for the program of Fig. 11.3, the user enters information for five accounts, then enters end-of-file to signal that data entry is complete. The sample execution does not show how the data records actually appear in the file. To verify that the file has been created successfully, in the next section we present a program that reads the file and prints its contents.

Figure 11.5 illustrates the relationship between FILE pointers, FILE structures and FCBs in memory. When the file `"clients.dat"` is opened, an FCB for the file is copied into memory. The figure shows the connection between the file pointer returned by `fopen` and the FCB used by the operating system to administer the file.

Programs may process no files, one file or several files. Each file used in a program must have a unique name and will have a different file pointer returned by `fopen`. All subsequent file processing functions after the file is opened must refer to the file with the appropriate file pointer. Files may be opened in one of several modes (Fig. 11.6). To create a file, or to discard the contents of a file before writing data, open the file for writing (`"w"`). To read an existing file, open it for reading (`"r"`). To add records to the end of an existing file, open the file for appending (`"a"`). To open a file so that it may be written to and read from, open the file for updating in one of the three update modes—`"r+"`, `"w+"` or `"a+"`. Mode `"r+"` opens a file for reading and writing. Mode `"w+"` creates a file for reading and writing. If the file already exists, the file is opened and the current contents of the file are discarded. Mode `"a+"` opens a file for reading and writing—all writing is done at the end of the file. If the file does not exist, it is created. Note that each file open mode has a corresponding binary mode (containing the letter b) for manipulating binary files. The binary modes are used in Section 11.6–Section 11.10 when we introduce random-access files. If an error occurs while opening a file in any mode, `fopen` returns NULL.

Common Programming Error 11.4

Opening a nonexistent file for reading is an error.

Common Programming Error 11.5

Opening a file for reading or writing without having been granted the appropriate access rights to the file (this is operating-system dependent) is an error.

Common Programming Error 11.6

Opening a file for writing when no disk space is available is an error.

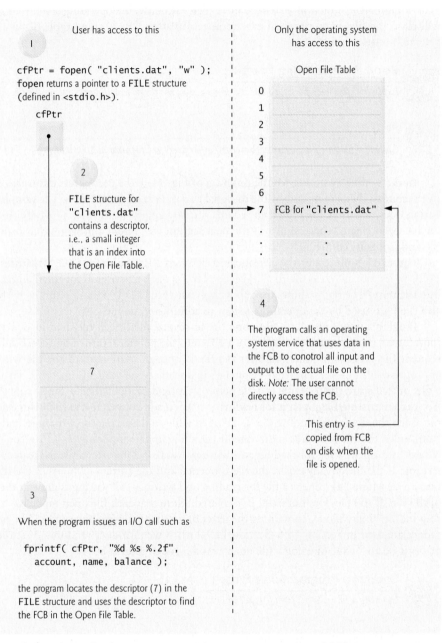

Fig. 11.5 | Relationship between FILE pointers, FILE structures and FCBs.

Common Programming Error 11.7

Opening a file with the incorrect file mode is a logic error. For example, opening a file in write mode ("w") when it should be opened in update mode ("r+") causes the contents of the file to be discarded.

Mode	Description
r	Open an existing file for reading.
w	Create a file for writing. If the file already exists, discard the current contents.
a	Append; open or create a file for writing at the end of the file.
r+	Open an existing file for update (reading and writing).
w+	Create a file for update. If the file already exists, discard the current contents.
a+	Append: open or create a file for update; writing is done at the end of the file.
rb	Open an existing file for reading in binary mode.
wb	Create a file for writing in binary mode. If the file already exists, discard the current contents.
ab	Append; open or create a file for writing at the end of the file in binary mode.
rb+	Open an existing file for update (reading and writing) in binary mode.
wb+	Create a file for update in binary mode. If the file already exists, discard the current contents.
ab+	Append: open or create a file for update in binary mode; writing is done at the end of the file.

Fig. 11.6 | File opening modes.

Error-Prevention Tip 11.2

Open a file only for reading (and not update) if the contents of the file should not be modified. This prevents unintentional modification of the file's contents. This is another example of the principle of least privilege.

11.5 Reading Data from a Sequential-Access File

Data is stored in files so that the data can be retrieved for processing when needed. The previous section demonstrated how to create a file for sequential access. This section shows how to read data sequentially from a file.

Figure 11.7 reads records from the file "clients.dat" created by the program of Fig. 11.3 and prints the contents of the records. Line 11

```
FILE *cfPtr;
```

indicates that cfPtr is a pointer to a FILE. Line 14

```
if ( ( cfPtr = fopen( "clients.dat", "r" ) ) == NULL )
```

attempts to open the file "clients.dat" for reading ("r") and determines whether the file is opened successfully (i.e., fopen does not return NULL). Line 19

```
fscanf( cfPtr, "%d%s%f", &account, name, &balance );
```

```
 1   /* Fig. 11.7: fig11_07.c
 2      Reading and printing a sequential file */
 3   #include <stdio.h>
 4
 5   int main( void )
 6   {
 7      int account;      /* account number */
 8      char name[ 30 ]; /* account name */
 9      double balance;   /* account balance */
10
11      FILE *cfPtr;      /* cfPtr = clients.dat file pointer */
12
13      /* fopen opens file; exits program if file cannot be opened */
14      if ( ( cfPtr = fopen( "clients.dat", "r" ) ) == NULL ) {
15         printf( "File could not be opened\n" );
16      } /* end if */
17      else { /* read account, name and balance from file */
18         printf( "%-10s%-13s%s\n", "Account", "Name", "Balance" );
19         fscanf( cfPtr, "%d%s%lf", &account, name, &balance );
20
21         /* while not end of file */
22         while ( !feof( cfPtr ) ) {
23            printf( "%-10d%-13s%7.2f\n", account, name, balance );
24            fscanf( cfPtr, "%d%s%lf", &account, name, &balance );
25         } /* end while */
26
27         fclose( cfPtr ); /* fclose closes the file */
28      } /* end else */
29
30      return 0; /* indicates successful termination */
31
32   } /* end main */
```

```
Account   Name         Balance
100       Jones          24.98
200       Doe           345.67
300       White           0.00
400       Stone         -42.16
500       Rich          224.62
```

Fig. 11.7 | Reading and printing a sequential file.

reads a "record" from the file. Function fscanf is equivalent to function scanf, except fscanf receives as an argument a file pointer for the file from which the data is read. After this statement executes the first time, account will have the value 100, name will have the value "Jones" and balance will have the value 24.98. Each time the second fscanf statement (line 24) executes, the program reads another record from the file and account, name and balance take on new values. When the program reaches the end of the file, the file is closed (line 27) and the program terminates. Note that feof returns true only *after* the program attempts to read the nonexistent data following the last line.

To retrieve data sequentially from a file, a program normally starts reading from the beginning of the file and reads all data consecutively until the desired data is found. It may be desirable to process the data sequentially in a file several times (from the beginning of the file) during the execution of a program. A statement such as

```
rewind( cfPtr );
```

causes a program's file position pointer—which indicates the number of the next byte in the file to be read or written—to be repositioned to the beginning of the file (i.e., byte 0) pointed to by cfPtr. The file position pointer is not really a pointer. Rather it is an integer value that specifies the byte location in the file at which the next read or write is to occur. This is sometimes referred to as the file offset. The file position pointer is a member of the FILE structure associated with each file.

The program of Fig. 11.8 allows a credit manager to obtain lists of customers with zero balances (i.e., customers who do not owe any money), customers with credit balances (i.e., customers to whom the company owes money) and customers with debit balances (i.e., customers who owe the company money for goods and services received). A credit balance is a negative amount; a debit balance is a positive amount.

```c
1   /* Fig. 11.8: fig11_08.c
2      Credit inquiry program */
3   #include <stdio.h>
4
5   /* function main begins program execution */
6   int main( void )
7   {
8      int request;      /* request number */
9      int account;      /* account number */
10     double balance;   /* account balance */
11     char name[ 30 ];  /* account name */
12     FILE *cfPtr;      /* clients.dat file pointer */
13
14     /* fopen opens the file; exits program if file cannot be opened */
15     if ( ( cfPtr = fopen( "clients.dat", "r" ) ) == NULL ) {
16        printf( "File could not be opened\n" );
17     } /* end if */
18     else {
19
20        /* display request options */
21        printf( "Enter request\n"
22           " 1 - List accounts with zero balances\n"
23           " 2 - List accounts with credit balances\n"
24           " 3 - List accounts with debit balances\n"
25           " 4 - End of run\n? " );
26        scanf( "%d", &request );
27
28        /* process user's request */
29        while ( request != 4 ) {
30
31           /* read account, name and balance from file */
32           fscanf( cfPtr, "%d%s%lf", &account, name, &balance );
33
```

Fig. 11.8 | Credit inquiry program. (Part 1 of 3.)

```
34              switch ( request ) {
35
36                  case 1:
37                      printf( "\nAccounts with zero balances:\n" );
38
39                      /* read file contents (until eof) */
40                      while ( !feof( cfPtr ) ) {
41
42                          if ( balance == 0 ) {
43                              printf( "%-10d%-13s%7.2f\n",
44                                  account, name, balance );
45                          } /* end if */
46
47                          /* read account, name and balance from file */
48                          fscanf( cfPtr, "%d%s%lf",
49                              &account, name, &balance );
50                      } /* end while */
51
52                      break;
53
54                  case 2:
55                      printf( "\nAccounts with credit balances:\n" );
56
57                      /* read file contents (until eof) */
58                      while ( !feof( cfPtr ) ) {
59
60                          if ( balance < 0 ) {
61                              printf( "%-10d%-13s%7.2f\n",
62                                  account, name, balance );
63                          } /* end if */
64
65                          /* read account, name and balance from file */
66                          fscanf( cfPtr, "%d%s%lf",
67                              &account, name, &balance );
68                      } /* end while */
69
70                      break;
71
72                  case 3:
73                      printf( "\nAccounts with debit balances:\n" );
74
75                      /* read file contents (until eof) */
76                      while ( !feof( cfPtr ) ) {
77
78                          if ( balance > 0 ) {
79                              printf( "%-10d%-13s%7.2f\n",
80                                  account, name, balance );
81                          } /* end if */
82
83                          /* read account, name and balance from file */
84                          fscanf( cfPtr, "%d%s%lf",
85                              &account, name, &balance );
86                      } /* end while */
```

Fig. 11.8 | Credit inquiry program. (Part 2 of 3.)

```
87
88                    break;
89
90              } /* end switch */
91
92              rewind( cfPtr ); /* return cfPtr to beginning of file */
93
94              printf( "\n? " );
95              scanf( "%d", &request );
96        } /* end while */
97
98        printf( "End of run.\n" );
99        fclose( cfPtr ); /* fclose closes the file */
100    } /* end else */
101
102    return 0; /* indicates successful termination */
103
104 } /* end main */
```

Fig. 11.8 | Credit inquiry program. (Part 3 of 3.)

The program displays a menu and allows the credit manager to enter one of three options to obtain credit information. Option 1 produces a list of accounts with zero balances. Option 2 produces a list of accounts with credit balances. Option 3 produces a list of accounts with debit balances. Option 4 terminates program execution. A sample output is shown in Fig. 11.9.

```
Enter request
 1 - List accounts with zero balances
 2 - List accounts with credit balances
 3 - List accounts with debit balances
 4 - End of run
? 1

Accounts with zero balances:
300        White               0.00

? 2

Accounts with credit balances:
400        Stone             -42.16

? 3

Accounts with debit balances:
100        Jones              24.98
200        Doe               345.67
500        Rich              224.62


? 4
End of run.
```

Fig. 11.9 | Sample output of the credit inquiry program of Fig. 11.8.

Note that data in this type of sequential file cannot be modified without the risk of destroying other data in the file. For example, if the name "White" needed to be changed to "Worthington," the old name cannot simply be overwritten. The record for White was written to the file as

```
300 White 0.00
```

If the record is rewritten beginning at the same location in the file using the new name, the record would be

```
300 Worthington 0.00
```

The new record is larger (has more characters) than the original record. The characters beyond the second "o" in "Worthington" would overwrite the beginning of the next sequential record in the file. The problem here is that in the formatted input/output model using fprintf and fscanf, fields—and hence records—can vary in size. For example, the values 7, 14, −117, 2074 and 27383 are all ints stored in the same number of bytes internally, but they are different-sized fields when displayed on the screen or written to a file as text.

Therefore, sequential access with fprintf and fscanf is not usually used to update records in place. Instead, the entire file is usually rewritten. To make the preceding name change, the records before 300 White 0.00 in such a sequential-access file would be copied to a new file, the new record would be written and the records after 300 White 0.00 would be copied to the new file. This requires processing every record in the file to update one record.

11.6 Random-Access Files

As we stated previously, records in a file created with the formatted output function fprintf are not necessarily the same length. However, individual records of a random-access file are normally fixed in length and may be accessed directly (and thus quickly) without searching through other records. This makes random-access files appropriate for airline reservation systems, banking systems, point-of-sale systems, and other kinds of transaction processing systems that require rapid access to specific data. There are other ways of implementing random-access files, but we will limit our discussion to this straightforward approach using fixed-length records.

Because every record in a random-access file normally has the same length, the exact location of a record relative to the beginning of the file can be calculated as a function of the record key. We will soon see how this facilitates immediate access to specific records, even in large files.

Figure 11.10 illustrates one way to implement a random-access file. Such a file is like a freight train with many cars—some empty and some with cargo. Each car in the train is the same length.

Fixed-length records enable data to be inserted in a random-access file without destroying other data in the file. Data stored previously can also be updated or deleted without rewriting the entire file. In the following sections we explain how to create a random-access file, enter data, read the data both sequentially and randomly, update the data, and delete data no longer needed.

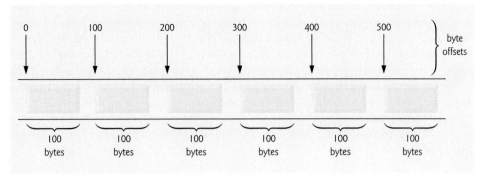

Fig. 11.10 | C's view of a random-access file.

11.7 Creating a Random-Access File

Function fwrite transfers a specified number of bytes beginning at a specified location in memory to a file. The data is written beginning at the location in the file indicated by the file position pointer. Function fread transfers a specified number of bytes from the location in the file specified by the file position pointer to an area in memory beginning with a specified address. Now, when writing an integer, instead of using

```
fprintf( fPtr, "%d", number );
```

which could print a single digit or as many as 11 digits (10 digits plus a sign, each of which requires 1 byte of storage) for a 4-byte integer, we can use

```
fwrite( &number, sizeof( int ), 1, fPtr );
```

which always writes 4 bytes (or 2 bytes on a system with 2-byte integers) from a variable number to the file represented by fPtr (we will explain the 1 argument shortly). Later, fread can be used to read 4 of those bytes into an integer variable number. Although fread and fwrite read and write data, such as integers, in fixed-size rather than variable-size format, the data they handle are processed in computer "raw data" format (i.e., bytes of data) rather than in printf's and scanf's human-readable text format. Since the "raw" representation of data is system-dependent, "raw data" may not be readable on other systems, or by programs produced by other compilers or with other compiler options.

Functions fwrite and fread are capable of reading and writing arrays of data to and from disk. The third argument of both fread and fwrite is the number of elements in the array that should be read from disk or written to disk. The preceding fwrite function call writes a single integer to disk, so the third argument is 1 (as if one element of an array is being written).

File processing programs rarely write a single field to a file. Normally, they write one struct at a time, as we show in the following examples.

Consider the following problem statement:

> *Create a credit processing system capable of storing up to 100 fixed-length records. Each record should consist of an account number that will be used as the record key, a last name, a first name and a balance. The resulting program should be able to update an account, insert a new account record, delete an account and list all the account records in a formatted text file for printing. Use a random-access file.*

The next several sections introduce the techniques necessary to create the credit processing program. Figure 11.11 shows how to open a random-access file, define a record format using a `struct`, write data to the disk and close the file. This program initializes all 100 records of the file "credit.dat" with empty `struct`s using the function `fwrite`. Each empty `struct` contains 0 for the account number, "" (the empty string) for the last name, "" for the first name and 0.0 for the balance. The file is initialized in this manner to create space on the disk in which the file will be stored and to make it possible to determine if a record contains data.

Function `fwrite` writes a block (specific number of bytes) of data to a file. In our program, line 30

```
fwrite( &blankClient, sizeof( struct clientData ), 1, cfPtr);
```

```
1    /* Fig. 11.11: fig11_11.c
2       Creating a random-access file sequentially */
3    #include <stdio.h>
4
5    /* clientData structure definition */
6    struct clientData {
7       int acctNum;            /* account number */
8       char lastName[ 15 ];    /* account last name */
9       char firstName[ 10 ];   /* account first name */
10      double balance;         /* account balance */
11   }; /* end structure clientData */
12
13   int main( void )
14   {
15      int i; /* counter used to count from 1-100 */
16
17      /* create clientData with default information */
18      struct clientData blankClient = { 0, "", "", 0.0 };
19
20      FILE *cfPtr; /* credit.dat file pointer */
21
22      /* fopen opens the file; exits if file cannot be opened */
23      if ( ( cfPtr = fopen( "credit.dat", "wb" ) ) == NULL ) {
24         printf( "File could not be opened.\n" );
25      } /* end if */
26      else {
27
28         /* output 100 blank records to file */
29         for ( i = 1; i <= 100; i++ ) {
30            fwrite( &blankClient, sizeof( struct clientData ), 1, cfPtr );
31         } /* end for */
32
33         fclose ( cfPtr ); /* fclose closes the file */
34      } /* end else */
35
36      return 0; /* indicates successful termination */
37
38   } /* end main */
```

Fig. 11.11 | Creating a random access file sequentially.

causes the structure blankClient of size sizeof(struct clientData) to be written to the file pointed to by cfPtr. The operator sizeof returns the size in bytes of its operand in parentheses (in this case struct clientData). The sizeof operator returns an unsigned integer and can be used to determine the size in bytes of any data type or expression. For example, sizeof(int) can be used to determine whether an integer is stored in 2 or 4 bytes on a particular computer.

Function fwrite can actually be used to write several elements of an array of objects. To write several array elements, supply in the call to fwrite a pointer to an array as the first argument and the number of elements to be written as the third argument. In the preceding statement, fwrite was used to write a single object that was not an array element. Writing a single object is equivalent to writing one element of an array, hence the 1 in the fwrite call.

11.8 Writing Data Randomly to a Random-Access File

Figure 11.12 writes data to the file "credit.dat". It uses the combination of fseek and fwrite to store data at specific locations in the file. Function fseek sets the file position pointer to a specific position in the file, then fwrite writes the data. A sample execution is shown in Fig. 11.13.

```
1   /* Fig. 11.12: fig11_12.c
2      Writing to a random access file */
3   #include <stdio.h>
4
5   /* clientData structure definition */
6   struct clientData {
7      int acctNum;          /* account number */
8      char lastName[ 15 ];  /* account last name */
9      char firstName[ 10 ]; /* account first name */
10     double balance;       /* account balance */
11  }; /* end structure clientData */
12
13  int main( void )
14  {
15     FILE *cfPtr; /* credit.dat file pointer */
16
17     /* create clientData with default information */
18     struct clientData client = { 0, "", "", 0.0 };
19
20     /* fopen opens the file; exits if file cannot be opened */
21     if ( ( cfPtr = fopen( "credit.dat", "rb+" ) ) == NULL ) {
22        printf( "File could not be opened.\n" );
23     } /* end if */
24     else {
25
26        /* require user to specify account number */
27        printf( "Enter account number"
28           " ( 1 to 100, 0 to end input )\n? " );
29        scanf( "%d", &client.acctNum );
```

Fig. 11.12 | Writing data randomly to a random-access file. (Part 1 of 2.)

```
30
31          /* user enters information, which is copied into file */
32          while ( client.acctNum != 0 ) {
33
34              /* user enters last name, first name and balance */
35              printf( "Enter lastname, firstname, balance\n? " );
36
37              /* set record lastName, firstName and balance value */
38              fscanf( stdin, "%s%s%lf", client.lastName,
39                  client.firstName, &client.balance );
40
41              /* seek position in file to user-specified record */
42              fseek( cfPtr, ( client.acctNum - 1 ) *
43                  sizeof( struct clientData ), SEEK_SET );
44
45              /* write user-specified information in file */
46              fwrite( &client, sizeof( struct clientData ), 1, cfPtr );
47
48              /* enable user to input another account number */
49              printf( "Enter account number\n? " );
50              scanf( "%d", &client.acctNum );
51          } /* end while */
52
53          fclose( cfPtr ); /* fclose closes the file */
54      } /* end else */
55
56      return 0; /* indicates successful termination */
57
58  } /* end main */
```

Fig. 11.12 | Writing data randomly to a random-access file. (Part 2 of 2.)

Lines 42–43

```
fseek( cfPtr, ( client.acctNum - 1 ) *
    sizeof( struct clientData ), SEEK_SET );
```

position the file position pointer for the file referenced by cfPtr to the byte location calculated by (client.accountNum - 1) * sizeof(struct clientData). The value of this expression is called the offset or the displacement. Because the account number is between 1 and 100 but the byte positions in the file start with 0, 1 is subtracted from the account number when calculating the byte location of the record. Thus, for record 1, the file position pointer is set to byte 0 of the file. The symbolic constant SEEK_SET indicates that the file position pointer is positioned relative to the beginning of the file by the amount of the offset. As the above statement indicates, a seek for account number 1 in the file sets the file position pointer to the beginning of the file because the byte location calculated is 0. Figure 11.14 illustrates the file pointer referring to a FILE structure in memory. The file position pointer in this diagram indicates that the next byte to be read or written is 5 bytes from the beginning of the file.

The function prototype for fseek is

```
int fseek( FILE *stream, long int offset, int whence );
```

```
Enter account number ( 1 to 100, 0 to end input )
? 37
Enter lastname, firstname, balance
? Barker Doug 0.00
Enter account number
? 29
Enter lastname, firstname, balance
? Brown Nancy -24.54
Enter account number
? 96
Enter lastname, firstname, balance
? Stone Sam 34.98
Enter account number
? 88
Enter lastname, firstname, balance
? Smith Dave 258.34
Enter account number
? 33
Enter lastname, firstname, balance
? Dunn Stacey 314.33
Enter account number
? 0
```

Fig. 11.13 | Sample execution of the program in Fig. 11.12.

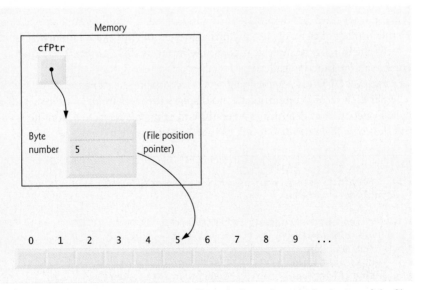

Fig. 11.14 | File position pointer indicating an offset of 5 bytes from the beginning of the file.

where offset is the number of bytes to seek from location whence in the file pointed to by stream. The argument whence can have one of three values—SEEK_SET, SEEK_CUR or SEEK_END (all defined in <stdio.h>)—indicating the location in the file from which the seek begins. SEEK_SET indicates that the seek starts at the beginning of the file; SEEK_CUR indicates that the seek starts at the current location in the file; and SEEK_END indicates that the seek starts at the end of the file.

For simplicity, the programs in this chapter do not perform error checking. If you wish to determine whether functions like fscanf (lines 38–39), fseek (lines 42–43) and fwrite (line 46) operate correctly, you can check their return values. Function fscanf returns the number of data items successfully read or the value EOF if a problem occurs while reading data. Function fseek returns a nonzero value if the seek operation cannot be performed. Function fwrite returns the number of items it successfully output. If this number is less than the third argument in the function call, then a write error occurred.

11.9 Reading Data from a Random-Access File

Function fread reads a specified number of bytes from a file into memory. For example, the statement

```
fread( &client, sizeof( struct clientData ), 1, cfPtr );
```

reads the number of bytes determined by sizeof(struct clientData) from the file referenced by cfPtr and stores the data in the structure client. The bytes are read from the location in the file specified by the file position pointer. Function fread can be used to read several fixed-size array elements by providing a pointer to the array in which the elements will be stored and by indicating the number of elements to be read. The preceding statement specifies that one element should be read. To read more than one element, specify the number of elements in the third argument of the fread statement. Function fread returns the number of items it successfully input. If this number is less than the third argument in the function call, then a read error occurred.

Figure 11.15 reads sequentially every record in the "credit.dat" file, determines whether each record contains data and displays the formatted data for records containing data. Function feof determines when the end of the file is reached, and the fread function transfers data from the disk to the clientData structure client.

```
1   /* Fig. 11.15: fig11_15.c
2      Reading a random access file sequentially */
3   #include <stdio.h>
4
5   /* clientData structure definition */
6   struct clientData {
7      int acctNum;           /* account number */
8      char lastName[ 15 ];   /* account last name */
9      char firstName[ 10 ];  /* account first name */
10     double balance;        /* account balance */
11  }; /* end structure clientData */
12
13  int main( void )
14  {
15     FILE *cfPtr; /* credit.dat file pointer */
16
```

Fig. 11.15 | Reading a random-access file sequentially. (Part 1 of 2.)

```
17      /* create clientData with default information */
18      struct clientData client = { 0, "", "", 0.0 };
19
20      /* fopen opens the file; exits if file cannot be opened */
21      if ( ( cfPtr = fopen( "credit.dat", "rb" ) ) == NULL ) {
22         printf( "File could not be opened.\n" );
23      } /* end if */
24      else {
25         printf( "%-6s%-16s%-11s%10s\n", "Acct", "Last Name",
26            "First Name", "Balance" );
27
28         /* read all records from file (until eof) */
29         while ( !feof( cfPtr ) ) {
30            fread( &client, sizeof( struct clientData ), 1, cfPtr );
31
32            /* display record */
33            if ( client.acctNum != 0 ) {
34               printf( "%-6d%-16s%-11s%10.2f\n",
35                  client.acctNum, client.lastName,
36                  client.firstName, client.balance );
37            } /* end if */
38
39         } /* end while */
40
41         fclose( cfPtr ); /* fclose closes the file */
42      } /* end else */
43
44      return 0; /* indicates successful termination */
45
46   } /* end main */
```

Acct	Last Name	First Name	Balance
29	Brown	Nancy	-24.54
33	Dunn	Stacey	314.33
37	Barker	Doug	0.00
88	Smith	Dave	258.34
96	Stone	Sam	34.98

Fig. 11.15 | Reading a random-access file sequentially. (Part 2 of 2.)

11.10 Case Study: Transaction-Processing Program

We now present a substantial transaction-processing program using random-access files. The program maintains a bank's account information. The program updates existing accounts, adds new accounts, deletes accounts and stores a listing of all the current accounts in a text file for printing. We assume that the program of Fig. 11.11 has been executed to create the file credit.dat.

The program has five options. Option 1 calls function textFile to store a formatted list of all the accounts in a text file called accounts.txt that may be printed later. The function uses fread and the sequential file access techniques used in the program of Fig. 11.15. After choosing option 1 the file accounts.txt contains:

```
Acct   Last Name       First Name     Balance
29     Brown           Nancy           -24.54
33     Dunn            Stacey          314.33
37     Barker          Doug              0.00
88     Smith           Dave            258.34
96     Stone           Sam              34.98
```

Option 2 calls the function updateRecord to update an account. The function will only update a record that already exists, so the function first checks to see if the record specified by the user is empty. The record is read into structure client with fread, then member acctNum is compared to 0. If it is 0, the record contains no information, and a message is printed stating that the record is empty. Then, the menu choices are displayed. If the record contains information, function updateRecord inputs the transaction amount, calculates the new balance and rewrites the record to the file. A typical output for option 2 is

```
Enter account to update ( 1 - 100 ): 37
37     Barker          Doug              0.00

Enter charge ( + ) or payment ( - ): +87.99
37     Barker          Doug             87.99
```

Option 3 calls the function newRecord to add a new account to the file. If the user enters an account number for an existing account, newRecord displays an error message that the record already contains information, and the menu choices are printed again. This function uses the same process to add a new account as does the program in Fig. 11.12. A typical output for option 3 is

```
Enter new account number ( 1 - 100 ): 22
Enter lastname, firstname, balance
? Johnston Sarah 247.45
```

Option 4 calls function deleteRecord to delete a record from the file. Deletion is accomplished by asking the user for the account number and reinitializing the record. If the account contains no information, deleteRecord displays an error message that the account does not exist. Option 5 terminates program execution. The program is shown in Fig. 11.16. Note that the file "credit.dat" is opened for update (reading and writing) using "rb+" mode.

```
1   /* Fig. 11.16: fig11_16.c
2      This program reads a random access file sequentially, updates data
3      already written to the file, creates new data to be placed in the
4      file, and deletes data previously in the file. */
5   #include <stdio.h>
```

Fig. 11.16 | Bank account program. (Part 1 of 6.)

```
6
7    /* clientData structure definition */
8    struct clientData {
9       int acctNum;           /* account number */
10      char lastName[ 15 ];   /* account last name */
11      char firstName[ 10 ];  /* account first name */
12      double balance;        /* account balance */
13   }; /* end structure clientData */
14
15   /* prototypes */
16   int enterChoice( void );
17   void textFile( FILE *readPtr );
18   void updateRecord( FILE *fPtr );
19   void newRecord( FILE *fPtr );
20   void deleteRecord( FILE *fPtr );
21
22   int main( void )
23   {
24      FILE *cfPtr; /* credit.dat file pointer */
25      int choice;  /* user's choice */
26
27      /* fopen opens the file; exits if file cannot be opened */
28      if ( ( cfPtr = fopen( "credit.dat", "rb+" ) ) == NULL ) {
29         printf( "File could not be opened.\n" );
30      } /* end if */
31      else {
32
33         /* enable user to specify action */
34         while ( ( choice = enterChoice() ) != 5 ) {
35
36            switch ( choice ) {
37
38               /* create text file from record file */
39               case 1:
40                  textFile( cfPtr );
41                  break;
42
43               /* update record */
44               case 2:
45                  updateRecord( cfPtr );
46                  break;
47
48               /* create record */
49               case 3:
50                  newRecord( cfPtr );
51                  break;
52
53               /* delete existing record */
54               case 4:
55                  deleteRecord( cfPtr );
56                  break;
57
```

Fig. 11.16 | Bank account program. (Part 2 of 6.)

```
58              /* display message if user does not select valid choice */
59              default:
60                  printf( "Incorrect choice\n" );
61                  break;
62
63          } /* end switch */
64
65      } /* end while */
66
67      fclose( cfPtr ); /* fclose closes the file */
68    } /* end else */
69
70    return 0; /* indicates successful termination */
71
72 } /* end main */
73
74 /* create formatted text file for printing */
75 void textFile( FILE *readPtr )
76 {
77    FILE *writePtr; /* accounts.txt file pointer */
78
79    /* create clientData with default information */
80    struct clientData client = { 0, "", "", 0.0 };
81
82    /* fopen opens the file; exits if file cannot be opened */
83    if ( ( writePtr = fopen( "accounts.txt", "w" ) ) == NULL ) {
84       printf( "File could not be opened.\n" );
85    } /* end if */
86    else {
87       rewind( readPtr ); /* sets pointer to beginning of file */
88       fprintf( writePtr, "%-6s%-16s%-11s%10s\n",
89          "Acct", "Last Name", "First Name","Balance" );
90
91       /* copy all records from random-access file into text file */
92       while ( !feof( readPtr ) ) {
93          fread( &client, sizeof( struct clientData ), 1, readPtr );
94
95          /* write single record to text file */
96          if ( client.acctNum != 0 ) {
97             fprintf( writePtr, "%-6d%-16s%-11s%10.2f\n",
98                client.acctNum, client.lastName,
99                client.firstName, client.balance );
100          } /* end if */
101
102       } /* end while */
103
104       fclose( writePtr ); /* fclose closes the file */
105    } /* end else */
106
107 } /* end function textFile */
108
```

Fig. 11.16 | Bank account program. (Part 3 of 6.)

```
109   /* update balance in record */
110   void updateRecord( FILE *fPtr )
111   {
112      int account;        /* account number */
113      double transaction; /* transaction amount */
114
115      /* create clientData with no information */
116      struct clientData client = { 0, "", "", 0.0 };
117
118      /* obtain number of account to update */
119      printf( "Enter account to update ( 1 - 100 ): " );
120      scanf( "%d", &account );
121
122      /* move file pointer to correct record in file */
123      fseek( fPtr, ( account - 1 ) * sizeof( struct clientData ),
124         SEEK_SET );
125
126      /* read record from file */
127      fread( &client, sizeof( struct clientData ), 1, fPtr );
128
129      /* display error if account does not exist */
130      if ( client.acctNum == 0 ) {
131         printf( "Acount #%d has no information.\n", account );
132      } /* end if */
133      else { /* update record */
134         printf( "%-6d%-16s%-11s%10.2f\n\n",
135            client.acctNum, client.lastName,
136            client.firstName, client.balance );
137
138         /* request transaction amount from user */
139         printf( "Enter charge ( + ) or payment ( - ): " );
140         scanf( "%lf", &transaction );
141         client.balance += transaction; /* update record balance */
142
143         printf( "%-6d%-16s%-11s%10.2f\n",
144            client.acctNum, client.lastName,
145            client.firstName, client.balance );
146
147         /* move file pointer to correct record in file */
148         fseek( fPtr, ( account - 1 ) * sizeof( struct clientData ),
149            SEEK_SET );
150
151         /* write updated record over old record in file */
152         fwrite( &client, sizeof( struct clientData ), 1, fPtr );
153      } /* end else */
154
155   } /* end function updateRecord */
156
157   /* delete an existing record */
158   void deleteRecord( FILE *fPtr )
159   {
160
```

Fig. 11.16 | Bank account program. (Part 4 of 6.)

```
161    struct clientData client; /* stores record read from file */
162    struct clientData blankClient = { 0, "", "", 0 }; /* blank client */
163
164    int accountNum; /* account number */
165
166    /* obtain number of account to delete */
167    printf( "Enter account number to delete ( 1 - 100 ): " );
168    scanf( "%d", &accountNum );
169
170    /* move file pointer to correct record in file */
171    fseek( fPtr, ( accountNum - 1 ) * sizeof( struct clientData ),
172       SEEK_SET );
173
174    /* read record from file */
175    fread( &client, sizeof( struct clientData ), 1, fPtr );
176
177    /* display error if record does not exist */
178    if ( client.acctNum == 0 ) {
179       printf( "Account %d does not exist.\n", accountNum );
180    } /* end if */
181    else { /* delete record */
182
183       /* move file pointer to correct record in file */
184       fseek( fPtr, ( accountNum - 1 ) * sizeof( struct clientData ),
185          SEEK_SET );
186
187       /* replace existing record with blank record */
188       fwrite( &blankClient,
189          sizeof( struct clientData ), 1, fPtr );
190    } /* end else */
191
192 } /* end function deleteRecord */
193
194 /* create and insert record */
195 void newRecord( FILE *fPtr )
196 {
197    /* create clientData with default information */
198    struct clientData client = { 0, "", "", 0.0 };
199
200    int accountNum; /* account number */
201
202    /* obtain number of account to create */
203    printf( "Enter new account number ( 1 - 100 ): " );
204    scanf( "%d", &accountNum );
205
206    /* move file pointer to correct record in file */
207    fseek( fPtr, ( accountNum - 1 ) * sizeof( struct clientData ),
208       SEEK_SET );
209
210    /* read record from file */
211    fread( &client, sizeof( struct clientData ), 1, fPtr );
212
```

Fig. 11.16 | Bank account program. (Part 5 of 6.)

```
213        /* display error if account already exists */
214        if ( client.acctNum != 0 ) {
215           printf( "Account #%d already contains information.\n",
216              client.acctNum );
217        } /* end if */
218        else { /* create record */
219
220           /* user enters last name, first name and balance */
221           printf( "Enter lastname, firstname, balance\n? " );
222           scanf( "%s%s%lf", &client.lastName, &client.firstName,
223              &client.balance );
224
225           client.acctNum = accountNum;
226
227           /* move file pointer to correct record in file */
228           fseek( fPtr, ( client.acctNum - 1 ) *
229              sizeof( struct clientData ), SEEK_SET );
230
231           /* insert record in file */
232           fwrite( &client,
233              sizeof( struct clientData ), 1, fPtr );
234        } /* end else */
235
236   } /* end function newRecord */
237
238   /* enable user to input menu choice */
239   int enterChoice( void )
240   {
241      int menuChoice; /* variable to store user's choice */
242
243      /* display available options */
244      printf( "\nEnter your choice\n"
245         "1 - store a formatted text file of acounts called\n"
246         "     \"accounts.txt\" for printing\n"
247         "2 - update an account\n"
248         "3 - add a new account\n"
249         "4 - delete an account\n"
250         "5 - end program\n? " );
251
252      scanf( "%d", &menuChoice ); /* receive choice from user */
253
254      return menuChoice;
255
256   } /* end function enterChoice */
```

Fig. 11.16 | Bank account program. (Part 6 of 6.)

Summary

Section 11.1 Introduction
- Files are used for permanent retention of large amounts of data.
- Computers store files on secondary storage devices, especially disk storage devices.

Section 11.2 Data Hierarchy

- Ultimately, all data items processed by a computer are reduced to combinations of zeros and ones because it is simple and economical to build electronic devices that can assume two stable states—one of the states represents 0 and the other represents 1.

- The smallest data item in a computer can assume the value 0 or the value 1. Such a data item is called a bit (short for "binary digit"—a digit that can assume one of two values).

- Computer circuitry performs various simple bit manipulations such as determining a bit's value, setting a bit's value and reversing a bit (from 1 to 0 or from 0 to 1).

- Programmers prefer to work with data in the form of decimal digits, letters and special symbols., which are referred to as characters.

- The set of all characters that may be used to write programs and represent data items on a particular computer is called that computer's character set.

- Every character in a computer's character set is represented as a pattern of 1s and 0s (called a byte).

- Bytes are most commonly composed of eight bits.

- You create programs and data items as characters; computers then manipulate and process these characters as patterns of bits.

- Fields are composed of characters. A field is a group of characters that conveys meaning.

- A record (i.e., a struct) is a group of related fields.

- A file is a group of related records.

- To facilitate the retrieval of specific records from a file, at least one field in each record is chosen as a record key. A record key identifies a record as belonging to a particular person or entity.

- The most popular type of file organization is called a sequential file, in which records are typically stored in order by the record key field.

- A group of related files is sometimes called a database. A collection of programs designed to create and manage databases is called a database management system (DBMS).

Section 11.3 Files and Streams

- C views each file simply as a sequential stream of bytes. Each file ends either with an end-of-file marker or at a specific byte number recorded in a system-maintained, administrative data structure. When a file is opened, a stream is associated with the file.

- Three files and their associated streams are automatically opened when program execution begins—the standard input, the standard output and the standard error.

- Streams provide communication channels between files and programs.

- The standard input stream enables a program to read data from the keyboard, and the standard output stream enables a program to print data on the screen.

- Opening a file returns a pointer to a FILE structure (defined in <stdio.h>) that contains information used to process the file. This structure includes a file descriptor, i.e., an index into an operating system array called the open file table. Each array element contains a file control block (FCB) that the operating system uses to administer a particular file.

- The standard input, standard output and standard error are manipulated using file pointers stdin, stdout and stderr.

- Function fgetc, like getchar, reads one character from a file. Function fgetc receives as an argument a FILE pointer for the file from which a character will be read. The call fgetc(stdin) reads one character from stdin—the standard input. This call is equivalent to the call getchar().

- Function `fputc`, like `putchar`, writes one character to a file. Function `fputc` receives as arguments a character to be written and a pointer for the file to which the character will be written. The function call `fputc( 'a', stdout )` writes the character `'a'` to `stdout`—the standard output. This call is equivalent to `putchar( 'a' )`.

- The `fgets` and `fputs` functions read a line from a file or write a line to a file, respectively.

Section 11.4 Creating a Sequential-Access File

- C imposes no structure on a file. Thus, notions such as a record of a file do not exist as part of the C language. Therefore, you must provide a file structure to meet the requirements of a particular application.

- A C program administers each file with a separate `FILE` structure.

- Each open file must have a separately declared pointer of type `FILE` that is used to refer to the file.

- Function `fopen` takes as arguments a file name and a file open mode and returns a pointer to the `FILE` structure for the file opened.

- The file open mode `"w"` indicates that the file is to be opened for writing. If a file does not exist and it is opened for writing, `fopen` creates the file. If an existing file is opened for writing, the contents of the file are discarded without warning.

- Function `fopen` returns `NULL` if it is unable to open a file.

- Function `feof` receives a pointer to a `FILE` and determines whether the end-of-file indicator is set for that file. The end-of-file indicator informs the program that there is no more data to be processed. The function returns a nonzero (true) value when the end-of-file indicator has been set; otherwise, the function returns zero.

- Function `fprintf` is equivalent to `printf` except that `fprintf` also receives as an argument a file pointer for the file to which the data will be written.

- Function `fclose` receives a file pointer as an argument and closes the specified file. If function `fclose` is not called explicitly, the operating system normally will close the file when program execution terminates.

- When a file is opened, the file control block (FCB) for the file is copied into memory. The FCB is used by the operating system to administer the file.

- To create a file, or to discard the contents of a file before writing data, open the file for writing (`"w"`).

- To read an existing file, open it for reading (`"r"`).

- To add records to the end of an existing file, open the file for appending (`"a"`).

- To open a file so that it may be written to and read from, open the file for updating in one of the three update modes—`"r+"`, `"w+"` or `"a+"`. Mode `"r+"` opens a file for reading and writing. Mode `"w+"` creates a file for reading and writing. If the file already exists, the file is opened and the current contents of the file are discarded. Mode `"a+"` opens a file for reading and writing—all writing is done at the end of the file. If the file does not exist, it is created.

- Each file open mode has a corresponding binary mode (containing the letter b) for manipulating binary files.

Section 11.5 Reading Data from a Sequential-Access File

- Function `fscanf` is equivalent to function `scanf` except `fscanf` receives as an argument a file pointer for the file from which the data is read.

- To retrieve data sequentially from a file, a program normally starts reading from the beginning of the file and reads all data consecutively until the desired data is found.

- It may be desirable to process the data sequentially in a file several times (from the beginning of the file) during the execution of a program. Function rewind causes a program's file position pointer—which indicates the number of the next byte in the file to be read or written—to be repositioned to the beginning of the file (i.e., byte 0) pointed to its argument.

- The file position pointer is not really a pointer. Rather it is an integer value that specifies the byte location in the file at which the next read or write is to occur. This is sometimes referred to as the file offset. The file position pointer is a member of the FILE structure associated with each file.

- The data in a sequential file typically cannot be modified without the risk of destroying other data in the file.

Section 11.6 Random-Access Files
- Individual records of a random-access file are normally fixed in length and may be accessed directly (and thus quickly) without searching through other records.

- Because every record in a random-access file normally has the same length, the exact location of a record relative to the beginning of the file can be calculated as a function of the record key.

- Fixed-length records enable data to be inserted in a random-access file without destroying other data. Data stored previously can also be updated or deleted without rewriting the entire file.

Section 11.7 Creating a Random-Access File
- Function fwrite transfers a specified number of bytes beginning at a specified location in memory to a file. The data is written beginning at the file position pointer's location.

- Function fread transfers a specified number of bytes from the location in the file specified by the file position pointer to an area in memory beginning with a specified address.

- Although fread and fwrite read and write data, such as integers, in fixed-size rather than variable-size format, the data they handle are processed in computer "raw data" format (i.e., bytes of data) rather than in printf's and scanf's human-readable text format.

- Functions fwrite and fread are capable of reading and writing arrays of data to and from disk. The third argument of both fread and fwrite is the number of elements in the array that should be read from disk or written to disk.

- File processing programs normally write one struct at a time.

- Function fwrite writes a block (specific number of bytes) of data to a file.

- To write several array elements, supply in the call to fwrite a pointer to an array as the first argument and the number of elements to be written as the third argument.

Section 11.8 Writing Data Randomly to a Random-Access File
- Function fseek sets the file position pointer for a given file to a specific position in the file. Its second argument indicates the number of bytes to seek and its third argument indicates the location from which to seek. The third argument can have one of three values—SEEK_SET, SEEK_CUR or SEEK_END (all defined in <stdio.h>). SEEK_SET indicates that the seek starts at the beginning of the file; SEEK_CUR indicates that the seek starts at the current location in the file; and SEEK_END indicates that the seek starts at the end of the file.

- If you wish to determine whether functions like fscanf, fseek and fwrite operate correctly, you can check their return values.

- Function fscanf returns the number of fields successfully read or the value EOF if a problem occurs while reading data.

- Function fseek returns a nonzero value if the seek operation cannot be performed.

- Function fwrite returns the number of items it successfully output. If this number is less than the third argument in the function call, then a write error occurred.

Section 11.9 Reading Data from a Random-Access File

- Function `fread` reads a specified number of bytes from a file into memory.

- Function `fread` can be used to read several fixed-size array elements by providing a pointer to the array in which the elements will be stored and by indicating the number of elements to be read.

- Function `fread` returns the number of items it successfully input. If this number is less than the third argument in the function call, then a read error occurred.

Terminology

a file open mode	`fscanf`
a+ file open mode	`fseek`
binary digit	`fwrite`
bit	`getchar`
byte	`gets`
character	letter
character set	`NULL`
close a file	offset
data hierarchy	open a file
database	open file table
database management system	`printf`
decimal digit	`putchar`
displacement	`puts`
end-of-file marker	r file open mode
`fclose`	r+ file open mode
`feof`	random-access file
`fgetc`	record
`fgets`	record key
field	`rewind`
file	`scanf`
file control block	`SEEK_CUR`
file descriptor	`SEEK_END`
file name	`SEEK_SET`
file offset	sequential-access file
file open mode	special symbol
file pointer	`stderr` (standard error)
file position pointer	`stdin` (standard input)
`FILE` structure	`stdout` (standard output)
`fopen`	stream
formatted input/output	transaction processing
`fprintf`	w file open mode
`fputc`	w+ file open mode
`fputs`	writing to a file
`fread`	zeros and ones

Self-Review Exercises

11.1 Fill in the blanks in each of the following:

    a) Ultimately, all data items processed by a computer are reduced to combinations of _____ and _____.

    b) The smallest data item a computer can process is called a(n) _____.

    c) A(n) _____ is a group of related records.

d) Digits, letters and special symbols are referred to as _____.

e) A group of related files is called a _____.

f) Function _____ closes a file.

g) The _____ function reads data from a file in a manner similar to how scanf reads from stdin.

h) Function _____ reads a character from a specified file.

i) Function _____ reads a line from a specified file.

j) Function _____ opens a file.

k) Function _____ is normally used when reading data from a file in random-access applications.

l) Function _____ repositions the file position pointer to a specific location in the file.

11.2 State which of the following are *true* and which are *false*. If *false*, explain why.

a) Function fscanf cannot be used to read data from the standard input.

b) You must explicitly use fopen to open the standard input, standard output and standard error streams.

c) A program must explicitly call function fclose to close a file.

d) If the file position pointer points to a location in a sequential file other than the beginning of the file, the file must be closed and reopened to read from the beginning of the file.

e) Function fprintf can write to the standard output.

f) Data in sequential-access files are always updated without overwriting other data.

g) It is not necessary to search through all the records in a random-access file to find a specific record.

h) Records in random-access files are not of uniform length.

i) Function fseek may only seek relative to the beginning of a file.

11.3 Write a single statement to accomplish each of the following. Assume that each of these statements applies to the same program.

a) Write a statement that opens the file "oldmast.dat" for reading and assigns the returned file pointer to ofPtr.

b) Write a statement that opens the file "trans.dat" for reading and assigns the returned file pointer to tfPtr.

c) Write a statement that opens the file "newmast.dat" for writing (and creation) and assigns the returned file pointer to nfPtr.

d) Write a statement that reads a record from the file "oldmast.dat". The record consists of integer accountNum, string name and floating-point currentBalance.

e) Write a statement that reads a record from the file "trans.dat". The record consists of the integer accountNum and floating-point dollarAmount.

f) Write a statement that writes a record to the file "newmast.dat". The record consists of the integer accountNum, string name and floating-point currentBalance.

11.4 Find the error in each of the following program segments and explain how to correct it.

a) The file referred to by fPtr ("payables.dat") has not been opened.
```
printf( fPtr, "%d%s%d\n", account, company, amount );
```

b) `open( "receive.dat", "r+" );`

c) The following statement should read a record from the file "payables.dat". File pointer payPtr refers to this file, and file pointer recPtr refers to the file "receive.dat":
```
scanf( recPtr, "%d%s%d\n", &account, company, &amount );
```

d) The file "tools.dat" should be opened to add data to the file without discarding the current data.
```
if ( ( tfPtr = fopen( "tools.dat", "w" ) ) != NULL )
```

e) The file "courses.dat" should be opened for appending without modifying the current contents of the file.

```
if ( ( cfPtr = fopen( "courses.dat", "w+" ) ) != NULL )
```

Answers to Self-Review Exercises

11.1 a) 1s, 0s. b) Bit. c) File. d) Characters. e) Database. f) fclose. g) fscanf. h) fgetc. i) fgets. j) fopen. k) fread. l) fseek.

11.2 a) False. Function fscanf can be used to read from the standard input by including the pointer to the standard input stream, stdin, in the call to fscanf.

b) False. These three streams are opened automatically by C when program execution begins.

c) False. The files will be closed when program execution terminates, but all files should be explicitly closed with fclose.

d) False. Function rewind can be used to reposition the file position pointer to the beginning of the file.

e) True.

f) False. In most cases, sequential file records are not of uniform length. Therefore, it is possible that updating a record will cause other data to be overwritten.

g) True.

h) False. Records in a random-access file are normally of uniform length.

i) False. It is possible to seek from the beginning of the file, from the end of the file and from the current location in the file.

11.3 a) `ofPtr = fopen( "oldmast.dat", "r" );`
b) `tfPtr = fopen( "trans.dat", "r" );`
c) `nfPtr = fopen( "newmast.dat", "w" );`
d) `fscanf( ofPtr, "%d%s%f", &accountNum, name, &currentBalance );`
e) `fscanf( tfPtr, "%d%f", &accountNum, &dollarAmount );`
f) `fprintf( nfPtr, "%d %s %.2f", accountNum, name, currentBalance );`

11.4 a) Error: The file "payables.dat" has not been opened before the reference to its file pointer.
Correction: Use fopen to open "payables.dat" for writing, appending or updating.

b) Error: Function open is not a Standard C function.
Correction: Use function fopen.

c) Error: Function fscanf uses the incorrect file pointer to refer to file "payables.dat".
Correction: Use file pointer payPtr to refer to "payables.dat".

d) Error: The contents of the file are discarded because the file is opened for writing ("w").
Correction: To add data to the file, either open the file for updating ("r+") or open the file for appending ("a").

e) Error: File "courses.dat" is opened for updating in "w+" mode which discards the current contents of the file.
Correction: Open the file "a" mode.

Exercises

11.5 Fill in the blanks in each of the following:

a) Computers store large amounts of data on secondary storage devices as _____.

b) A(n) _____ is composed of several fields.

c) A field that may contain digits, letters and blanks is called a(n) _____ field.

    d) To facilitate the retrieval of specific records from a file, one field in each record is chosen as a(n) _____.

    e) Most information stored in computer systems is stored in _____ files.

    f) A group of related characters that conveys meaning is called a(n) _____.

    g) The file pointers for the three files that are opened automatically when program execution begins are named _____, _____ and _____.

    h) Function _____ writes a character to a specified file.

    i) Function _____ writes a line to a specified file.

    j) Function _____ is generally used to write data to a random-access file.

    k) Function _____ repositions the file position pointer to the beginning of the file.

11.6   State which of the following are *true* and which are *false*. If *false*, explain why.

    a) The impressive functions performed by computers essentially involve the manipulation of zeros and ones.

    b) People prefer to manipulate bits instead of characters and fields because bits are more compact.

    c) People specify programs and data items as characters; computers then manipulate and process these characters as groups of zeros and ones.

    d) A person's zip code is an example of a numeric field.

    e) A person's street address is generally considered to be an alphabetic field in computer applications.

    f) Data items processed by a computer form a data hierarchy in which data items become larger and more complex as we progress from fields to characters to bits etc.

    g) A record key identifies a record as belonging to a particular field.

    h) Most companies store their information in a single file to facilitate computer processing.

    i) Files are always referred to by name in C programs.

    j) When a program creates a file, the file is automatically retained by the computer for future reference.

11.7   Exercise 11.3 asked the reader to write a series of single statements. Actually, these statements form the core of an important type of file-processing program, namely, a file-matching program. In commercial data processing, it is common to have several files in each system. In an accounts receivable system, for example, there is generally a master file containing detailed information about each customer such as the customer's name, address, telephone number, outstanding balance, credit limit, discount terms, contract arrangements and possibly a condensed history of recent purchases and cash payments.

    As transactions occur (i.e., sales are made and cash payments arrive in the mail), they are entered into a file. At the end of each business period (i.e., a month for some companies, a week for others and a day in some cases) the file of transactions (called `"trans.dat"` in Exercise 11.3) is applied to the master file (called `"oldmast.dat"` in Exercise 11.3), thus updating each account's record of purchases and payments. After each of these updatings run, the master file is rewritten as a new file (`"newmast.dat"`), which is then used at the end of the next business period to begin the updating process again.

    File-matching programs must deal with certain problems that do not exist in single-file programs. For example, a match does not always occur. A customer on the master file might not have made any purchases or cash payments in the current business period, and therefore no record for this customer will appear on the transaction file. Similarly, a customer who did make some purchases or cash payments might have just moved to this community, and the company may not have had a chance to create a master record for this customer.

    Use the statements written in Exercise 11.3 as the basis for a complete file-matching accounts receivable program. Use the account number on each file as the record key for matching purposes. Assume that each file is a sequential file with records stored in increasing account number order.

When a match occurs (i.e., records with the same account number appear on both the master file and the transaction file), add the dollar amount on the transaction file to the current balance on the master file and write the "newmast.dat" record. (Assume that purchases are indicated by positive amounts on the transaction file, and that payments are indicated by negative amounts.) When there is a master record for a particular account but no corresponding transaction record, merely write the master record to "newmast.dat". When there is a transaction record but no corresponding master record, print the message "Unmatched transaction record for account number ..." (fill in the account number from the transaction record).

11.8 After writing the program of Exercise 11.7, write a simple program to create some test data for checking out the program of Exercise 11.7. Use the following sample account data:

Master File: Account number	Name	Balance
100	Alan Jones	348.17
300	Mary Smith	27.19
500	Sam Sharp	0.00
700	Suzy Green	-14.22

Transaction File: Account number	Dollar amount
100	27.14
300	62.11
400	100.56
900	82.17

11.9 Run the program of Exercise 11.7 using the files of test data created in Exercise 11.8. Use the listing program of Section 11.7 to print the new master file. Check the results carefully.

11.10 It is possible (actually common) to have several transaction records with the same record key. This occurs because a particular customer might make several purchases and cash payments during a business period. Rewrite your accounts receivable file-matching program of Exercise 11.7 to provide for the possibility of handling several transaction records with the same record key. Modify the test data of Exercise 11.8 to include the following additional transaction records:

Account number	Dollar amount
300	83.89
700	80.78
700	1.53

11.11 Write statements that accomplish each of the following. Assume that the structure

```
struct person {
    char lastName[ 15 ];
    char firstName[ 15 ];
    char age[ 4 ];
};
```

has been defined and that the file is already open for writing.

    a) Initialize the file "nameage.dat" so that there are 100 records with lastName = "unassigned", firstname = "" and age = "0".

    b) Input 10 last names, first names and ages, and write them to the file.

    c) Update a record; if there is no information in the record, tell the user "No info".

    d) Delete a record that has information by reinitializing that particular record.

11.12 You are the owner of a hardware store and need to keep an inventory that can tell you what tools you have, how many you have and the cost of each one. Write a program that initializes the file "hardware.dat" to 100 empty records, lets you input the data concerning each tool, enables you to list all your tools, lets you delete a record for a tool that you no longer have and lets you update *any* information in the file. The tool identification number should be the record number. Use the following information to start your file:

Record #	Tool name	Quantity	Cost
3	Electric sander	7	57.98
17	Hammer	76	11.99
24	Jig saw	21	11.00
39	Lawn mower	3	79.50
56	Power saw	18	99.99
68	Screwdriver	106	6.99
77	Sledge hammer	11	21.50
83	Wrench	34	7.50

11.13 *Telephone Number Word Generator.* Standard telephone keypads contain the digits 0 through 9. The numbers 2 through 9 each have three letters associated with them, as is indicated by the following table:

Digit	Letter	Digit	Letter
2	A B C	6	M N O
3	D E F	7	P R S
4	G H I	8	T U V
5	J K L	9	W X Y

Many people find it difficult to memorize phone numbers, so they use the correspondence between digits and letters to develop seven-letter words that correspond to their phone numbers. For example, a person whose telephone number is 686-2377 might use the correspondence indicated in the above table to develop the seven-letter word "NUMBERS."

Businesses frequently attempt to get telephone numbers that are easy for their clients to remember. If a business can advertise a simple word for its customers to dial, then no doubt the business will receive a few more calls.

Each seven-letter word corresponds to exactly one seven-digit telephone number. The restaurant wishing to increase its take-home business could surely do so with the number 825-3688 (i.e., "TAKEOUT").

Each seven-digit phone number corresponds to many separate seven-letter words. Unfortunately, most of these represent unrecognizable juxtapositions of letters. It is possible, however, that the owner of a barber shop would be pleased to know that the shop's telephone number, 424-7288, corresponds to "HAIRCUT." The owner of a liquor store would, no doubt, be delighted to find that the store's telephone number, 233-7226, corresponds to "BEERCAN." A veterinarian with the phone number 738-2273 would be pleased to know that the number corresponds to the letters "PETCARE."

Write a C program that, given a seven-digit number, writes to a file every possible seven-letter word corresponding to that number. There are 2187 (3 to the seventh power) such words. Avoid phone numbers with the digits 0 and 1.

11.14 If you have a computerized dictionary available, modify the program you wrote in Exercise 11.13 to look up the words in the dictionary. Some seven-letter combinations created by this program consist of two or more words (the phone number 843-2677 produces "THEBOSS").

11.15 Modify the example of Fig. 8.14 to use functions `fgetc` and `fputs` rather than `getchar` and `puts`. The program should give the user the option to read from the standard input and write to the standard output or to read from a specified file and write to a specified file. If the user chooses the second option, have the user enter the file names for the input and output files.

11.16 Write a program that uses the `sizeof` operator to determine the sizes in bytes of the various data types on your computer system. Write the results to the file `"datasize.dat"` so you may print the results later. The format for the results in the file should be as follows:

```
Data type              Size
char                      1
unsigned char             1
short int                 2
unsigned short int        2
int                       4
unsigned int              4
long int                  4
unsigned long int         4
float                     4
double                    8
long double              16
```

[*Note:* The type sizes on your computer might be different from those listed above.]

11.17 In Exercise 7.19, you wrote a software simulation of a computer that used a special machine language called Simpletron Machine Language (SML). In the simulation, each time you wanted to run an SML program, you entered the program into the simulator from the keyboard. If you made a mistake while typing the SML program, the simulator was restarted and the SML code was reentered. It would be nice to be able to read the SML program from a file rather than type it each time. This would reduce time and mistakes in preparing to run SML programs.

a) Modify the simulator you wrote in Exercise 7.19 to read SML programs from a file specified by the user at the keyboard.

b) After the Simpletron executes, it outputs the contents of its registers and memory on the screen. It would be nice to capture the output in a file, so modify the simulator to write its output to a file in addition to displaying the output on the screen.

12

C Data Structures

OBJECTIVES

In this chapter, you will learn:

- To allocate and free memory dynamically for data objects.
- To form linked data structures using pointers, self-referential structures and recursion.
- To create and manipulate linked lists, queues, stacks and binary trees.
- Various important applications of linked data structures.

12.1 Introduction

We have studied fixed-size **data structures** such as single-subscripted arrays, double-subscripted arrays and `struct`s. This chapter introduces **dynamic data structures** with sizes that grow and shrink at execution time. **Linked lists** are collections of data items "lined up in a row"—insertions and deletions are made anywhere in a linked list. **Stacks** are important in compilers and operating systems—insertions and deletions are made only at one end of a stack—its **top**. **Queues** represent waiting lines; insertions are made at the back (also referred to as the **tail**) of a queue and deletions are made from the front (also referred to as the **head**) of a queue. **Binary trees** facilitate high-speed searching and sorting of data, efficient elimination of duplicate data items, representing file system directories and compiling expressions into machine language. Each of these data structures has many other interesting applications.

We will discuss each of the major types of data structures and implement programs that create and manipulate these data structures. In the next part of the book—the introduction to C++ and object-oriented programming—we will study data abstraction. This technique will enable us to build these data structures in a dramatically different manner designed for producing software that is much easier to maintain and reuse.

This is a challenging chapter. The programs are substantial and they incorporate most of what you have learned in the earlier chapters. The programs are especially heavy on pointer manipulation, a subject many people consider to be among the most difficult topics in C. The chapter is loaded with highly practical programs that you will be able to use in more advanced courses; the chapter includes a rich collection of exercises that emphasize practical applications of the data structures.

We sincerely hope that you will attempt the major project described in the special section entitled Building Your Own Compiler. You have been using a compiler to translate your C programs to machine language so that you could execute your programs on your computer. In this project, you will actually build your own compiler. It will read a file of statements written in a simple, yet powerful, high-level language similar to early versions of the popular language BASIC. Your compiler will translate these statements into a file of Simpletron Machine Language (SML) instructions. SML is the language you learned in the Chapter 7 special section, Building Your Own Computer. Your Simpletron Simulator program will then execute the SML program produced by your compiler! This project will give you a wonderful opportunity to exercise most of what you have learned in this course.

The special section carefully walks you through the specifications of the high-level language, and describes the algorithms you will need to convert each type of high-level language statement into machine language instructions. If you enjoy being challenged, you might attempt the many enhancements to both the compiler and the Simpletron Simulator suggested in the exercises.

12.2 Self-Referential Structures

A self-referential structure contains a pointer member that points to a structure of the same structure type. For example, the definition

```
struct node {
    int data;
    struct node *nextPtr;
};
```

defines a type, struct node. A structure of type struct node has two members—integer member data and pointer member nextPtr. Member nextPtr points to a structure of type struct node—a structure of the same type as the one being declared here, hence the term "self-referential structure." Member nextPtr is referred to as a link—i.e., nextPtr can be used to "tie" a structure of type struct node to another structure of the same type. Self-referential structures can be linked together to form useful data structures such as lists, queues, stacks and trees. Figure 12.1 illustrates two self-referential structure objects linked together to form a list. Note that a slash—representing a NULL pointer—is placed in the link member of the second self-referential structure to indicate that the link does not point to another structure. [*Note:* The slash is only for illustration purposes; it does not correspond to the backslash character in C.] A NULL pointer normally indicates the end of a data structure just as the null character indicates the end of a string.

Common Programming Error 12.1

Not setting the link in the last node of a list to NULL can lead to runtime errors.

12.3 Dynamic Memory Allocation

Creating and maintaining dynamic data structures requires **dynamic memory allocation**—the ability for a program to obtain more memory space at execution time to hold new nodes, and to release space no longer needed. The limit for dynamic memory allocation can be as large as the amount of available physical memory in the computer or the amount of available virtual memory in a virtual memory system. Often, the limits are much smaller because available memory must be shared among many applications.

Functions **malloc** and **free**, and operator **sizeof**, are essential to dynamic memory allocation. Function malloc takes as an argument the number of bytes to be allocated and

$$\boxed{15} \bullet\!\longrightarrow \boxed{10}$$

Fig. 12.1 | Self-referential structures linked together.

returns a pointer of type void * (pointer to void) to the allocated memory. A void * pointer may be assigned to a variable of any pointer type. Function malloc is normally used with the sizeof operator. For example, the statement

```
newPtr = malloc( sizeof( struct node ) );
```

evaluates sizeof(struct node) to determine the size in bytes of a structure of type struct node, allocates a new area in memory of that number of bytes and stores a pointer to the allocated memory in variable newPtr. The allocated memory is not initialized. If no memory is available, malloc returns NULL.

Function free deallocates memory—i.e., the memory is returned to the system so that the memory can be reallocated in the future. To free memory dynamically allocated by the preceding malloc call, use the statement

```
free( newPtr );
```

C also provides functions calloc and realloc for creating and modifying dynamic arrays. These functions are discussed in Section 14.11. The following sections discuss lists, stacks, queues and trees, each of which is created and maintained with dynamic memory allocation and self-referential structures.

Portability Tip 12.1

A structure's size is not necessarily the sum of the sizes of its members. This is so because of various machine-dependent boundary alignment requirements (see Chapter 10).

Common Programming Error 12.2

Assuming that the size of a structure is simply the sum of the sizes of its members is a logic error.

Good Programming Practice 12.1

Use the sizeof operator to determine the size of a structure.

Error-Prevention Tip 12.1

When using malloc, test for a NULL pointer return value. Print an error message if the requested memory is not allocated.

Common Programming Error 12.3

Not returning dynamically allocated memory when it is no longer needed can cause the system to run out of memory prematurely. This is sometimes called a "memory leak."

Good Programming Practice 12.2

When memory that was dynamically allocated is no longer needed, use free to return the memory to the system immediately.

Common Programming Error 12.4

Freeing memory not allocated dynamically with malloc is an error.

Common Programming Error 12.5

Referring to memory that has been freed is an error.

12.4 Linked Lists

A linked list is a linear collection of self-referential structures, called nodes, connected by pointer links—hence, the term "linked" list. A linked list is accessed via a pointer to the first node of the list. Subsequent nodes are accessed via the link pointer member stored in each node. By convention, the link pointer in the last node of a list is set to NULL to mark the end of the list. Data is stored in a linked list dynamically—each node is created as necessary. A node can contain data of any type including other struct objects. Stacks and queues are also linear data structures, and, as we will see, are constrained versions of linked lists. Trees are nonlinear data structures.

Lists of data can be stored in arrays, but linked lists provide several advantages. A linked list is appropriate when the number of data elements to be represented in the data structure is unpredictable. Linked lists are dynamic, so the length of a list can increase or decrease as necessary. The size of an array, however cannot be altered once memory is allocated. Arrays can become full. Linked lists become full only when the system has insufficient memory to satisfy dynamic storage allocation requests.

 Performance Tip 12.1

An array can be declared to contain more elements than the number of data items expected, but this can waste memory. Linked lists can provide better memory utilization in these situations.

Linked lists can be maintained in sorted order by inserting each new element at the proper point in the list.

 Performance Tip 12.2

Insertion and deletion in a sorted array can be time consuming—all the elements following the inserted or deleted element must be shifted appropriately.

 Performance Tip 12.3

The elements of an array are stored contiguously in memory. This allows immediate access to any array element because the address of any element can be calculated directly based on its position relative to the beginning of the array. Linked lists do not afford such immediate access to their elements.

Linked list nodes are normally not stored contiguously in memory. Logically, however, the nodes of a linked list appear to be contiguous. Figure 12.2 illustrates a linked list with several nodes.

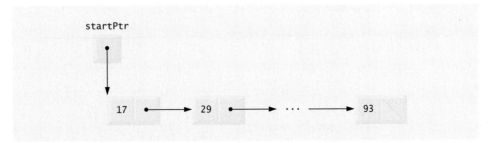

Fig. 12.2 | Linked list graphical representation.

Performance Tip 12.4

Using dynamic memory allocation (instead of arrays) for data structures that grow and shrink at execution time can save memory. Keep in mind, however, that the pointers take up space, and that dynamic memory allocation incurs the overhead of function calls.

Figure 12.3 (output shown in Fig. 12.4) manipulates a list of characters. The program enables you to insert a character in the list in alphabetical order (function `insert`) or to delete a character from the list (function `delete`). This is a large and complex program. A detailed discussion of the program follows. Exercise 12.21 asks the reader to implement a recursive function that prints a list backwards. Exercise 12.22 asks the reader to implement a recursive function that searches a linked list for a particular data item.

```c
/* Fig. 12.3: fig12_03.c
   Operating and maintaining a list */
#include <stdio.h>
#include <stdlib.h>

/* self-referential structure */
struct listNode {
   char data; /* each listNode contains a character */
   struct listNode *nextPtr; /* pointer to next node */
}; /* end structure listNode */

typedef struct listNode ListNode; /* synonym for struct listNode */
typedef ListNode *ListNodePtr; /* synonym for ListNode* */

/* prototypes */
void insert( ListNodePtr *sPtr, char value );
char delete( ListNodePtr *sPtr, char value );
int isEmpty( ListNodePtr sPtr );
void printList( ListNodePtr currentPtr );
void instructions( void );

int main( void )
{
   ListNodePtr startPtr = NULL; /* initially there are no nodes */
   int choice; /* user's choice */
   char item;  /* char entered by user */

   instructions(); /* display the menu */
   printf( "? " );
   scanf( "%d", &choice );

   /* loop while user does not choose 3 */
   while ( choice != 3 ) {

      switch ( choice ) {

         case 1:
            printf( "Enter a character: " );
            scanf( "\n%c", &item );
```

Fig. 12.3 | Inserting and deleting nodes in a list. (Part 1 of 4.)

```
40                 insert( &startPtr, item ); /* insert item in list */
41                 printList( startPtr );
42                 break;
43
44             case 2: /* delete an element */
45
46                 /* if list is not empty */
47                 if ( !isEmpty( startPtr ) ) {
48                     printf( "Enter character to be deleted: " );
49                     scanf( "\n%c", &item );
50
51                     /* if character is found, remove it*/
52                     if ( delete( &startPtr, item ) ) { /* remove item */
53                         printf( "%c deleted.\n", item );
54                         printList( startPtr );
55                     } /* end if */
56                     else {
57                         printf( "%c not found.\n\n", item );
58                     } /* end else */
59
60                 } /* end if */
61                 else {
62                     printf( "List is empty.\n\n" );
63                 } /* end else */
64
65                 break;
66
67             default:
68                 printf( "Invalid choice.\n\n" );
69                 instructions();
70                 break;
71
72         } /* end switch */
73
74         printf( "? " );
75         scanf( "%d", &choice );
76     } /* end while */
77
78     printf( "End of run.\n" );
79
80     return 0; /* indicates successful termination */
81
82 } /* end main */
83
84 /* display program instructions to user */
85 void instructions( void )
86 {
87     printf( "Enter your choice:\n"
88         "   1 to insert an element into the list.\n"
89         "   2 to delete an element from the list.\n"
90         "   3 to end.\n" );
91 } /* end function instructions */
92
```

Fig. 12.3 | Inserting and deleting nodes in a list. (Part 2 of 4.)

```
 93    /* Insert a new value into the list in sorted order */
 94    void insert( ListNodePtr *sPtr, char value )
 95    {
 96       ListNodePtr newPtr;       /* pointer to new node */
 97       ListNodePtr previousPtr; /* pointer to previous node in list */
 98       ListNodePtr currentPtr;  /* pointer to current node in list */
 99
100       newPtr = malloc( sizeof( ListNode ) ); /* create node */
101
102       if ( newPtr != NULL ) { /* is space available */
103          newPtr->data = value; /* place value in node */
104          newPtr->nextPtr = NULL; /* node does not link to another node */
105
106          previousPtr = NULL;
107          currentPtr = *sPtr;
108
109          /* loop to find the correct location in the list */
110          while ( currentPtr != NULL && value > currentPtr->data ) {
111             previousPtr = currentPtr;              /* walk to ...   */
112             currentPtr = currentPtr->nextPtr;  /* ... next node */
113          } /* end while */
114
115          /* insert new node at beginning of list */
116          if ( previousPtr == NULL ) {
117             newPtr->nextPtr = *sPtr;
118             *sPtr = newPtr;
119          } /* end if */
120          else { /* insert new node between previousPtr and currentPtr */
121             previousPtr->nextPtr = newPtr;
122             newPtr->nextPtr = currentPtr;
123          } /* end else */
124
125       } /* end if */
126       else {
127          printf( "%c not inserted. No memory available.\n", value );
128       } /* end else */
129
130    } /* end function insert */
131
132    /* Delete a list element */
133    char delete( ListNodePtr *sPtr, char value )
134    {
135       ListNodePtr previousPtr; /* pointer to previous node in list */
136       ListNodePtr currentPtr;  /* pointer to current node in list */
137       ListNodePtr tempPtr;       /* temporary node pointer */
138
139       /* delete first node */
140       if ( value == ( *sPtr )->data ) {
141          tempPtr = *sPtr; /* hold onto node being removed */
142          *sPtr = ( *sPtr )->nextPtr; /* de-thread the node */
143          free( tempPtr ); /* free the de-threaded node */
144          return value;
145       } /* end if */
```

Fig. 12.3 | Inserting and deleting nodes in a list. (Part 3 of 4.)

```
146     else {
147        previousPtr = *sPtr;
148        currentPtr = ( *sPtr )->nextPtr;
149
150        /* loop to find the correct location in the list */
151        while ( currentPtr != NULL && currentPtr->data != value ) {
152           previousPtr = currentPtr;          /* walk to ...   */
153           currentPtr = currentPtr->nextPtr; /* ... next node */
154        } /* end while */
155
156        /* delete node at currentPtr */
157        if ( currentPtr != NULL ) {
158           tempPtr = currentPtr;
159           previousPtr->nextPtr = currentPtr->nextPtr;
160           free( tempPtr );
161           return value;
162        } /* end if */
163
164     } /* end else */
165
166     return '\0';
167
168  } /* end function delete */
169
170  /* Return 1 if the list is empty, 0 otherwise */
171  int isEmpty( ListNodePtr sPtr )
172  {
173     return sPtr == NULL;
174
175  } /* end function isEmpty */
176
177  /* Print the list */
178  void printList( ListNodePtr currentPtr )
179  {
180
181     /* if list is empty */
182     if ( currentPtr == NULL ) {
183        printf( "List is empty.\n\n" );
184     } /* end if */
185     else {
186        printf( "The list is:\n" );
187
188        /* while not the end of the list */
189        while ( currentPtr != NULL ) {
190           printf( "%c --> ", currentPtr->data );
191           currentPtr = currentPtr->nextPtr;
192        } /* end while */
193
194        printf( "NULL\n\n" );
195     } /* end else */
196
197  } /* end function printList */
```

Fig. 12.3 | Inserting and deleting nodes in a list. (Part 4 of 4.)

```
Enter your choice:
   1 to insert an element into the list.
   2 to delete an element from the list.
   3 to end.
? 1
Enter a character: B
The list is:
B --> NULL

? 1
Enter a character: A
The list is:
A --> B --> NULL

? 1
Enter a character: C
The list is:
A --> B --> C --> NULL

? 2
Enter character to be deleted: D
D not found.

? 2
Enter character to be deleted: B
B deleted.
The list is:
A --> C --> NULL

? 2
Enter character to be deleted: C
C deleted.
The list is:
A --> NULL

? 2
Enter character to be deleted: A
A deleted.
List is empty.

? 4
Invalid choice.

Enter your choice:
   1 to insert an element into the list.
   2 to delete an element from the list.
   3 to end.
? 3
End of run.

? 2
Enter character to be deleted: C
C deleted.
The list is:
A --> NULL
```

(Continued on next page)

Fig. 12.4 | Sample output for the program of Fig. 12.3. (Part 1 of 2.)

```
? 2
Enter character to be deleted: A
A deleted.
List is empty.

? 4
Invalid choice.

Enter your choice:
   1 to insert an element into the list.
   2 to delete an element from the list.
   3 to end.
? 3
End of run.
```

Fig. 12.4 | Sample output for the program of Fig. 12.3. (Part 2 of 2.)

The primary functions of linked lists are `insert` (lines 94–130) and `delete` (lines 133–168). Function `isEmpty` (lines 171–175) is called a **predicate function**—it does not alter the list in any way; rather it determines if the list is empty (i.e., the pointer to the first node of the list is NULL). If the list is empty, 1 is returned; otherwise, 0 is returned. Function `printList` (lines 178–197) prints the list.

Function *insert*

Characters are inserted in the list in alphabetical order. Function `insert` (lines 94–130) receives the **address** of the list and a character to be inserted. The address of the list is necessary when a value is to be inserted at the start of the list. Providing the address of the list enables the list (i.e., the pointer to the first node of the list) to be modified via a call by reference. Since the list itself is a pointer (to its first element), passing the address of the list creates a **pointer to a pointer** (i.e., **double indirection**). This is a complex notion and requires careful programming. The steps for inserting a character in the list are as follows (see Fig. 12.5):

1. Create a node by calling `malloc`, assigning to `newPtr` the address of the allocated memory (line 100), assigning the character to be inserted to `newPtr->data` (line 103), and assigning NULL to `newPtr->nextPtr` (line 104).

2. Initialize `previousPtr` to NULL (line 106) and `currentPtr` to `*sPtr` (line 107)— the pointer to the start of the list. Pointers `previousPtr` and `currentPtr` store the locations of the node preceding the insertion point and the node after the insertion point.

3. While `currentPtr` is not NULL and the value to be inserted is greater than `currentPtr->data` (line 110), assign `currentPtr` to `previousPtr` (line 111) and advance `currentPtr` to the next node in the list (line 112). This locates the insertion point for the value.

4. If `previousPtr` is NULL (line 116), insert the new node as the first node in the list (lines 117–118). Assign `*sPtr` to `newPtr->nextPtr` (the new node link points to the former first node) and assign `newPtr` to `*sPtr` (`*sPtr` points to the new node). Otherwise, if `previousPtr` is not NULL, the new node is inserted in place

(lines 121–122). Assign `newPtr` to `previousPtr->nextPtr` (the previous node points to the new node) and assign `currentPtr` to `newPtr->nextPtr` (the new node link points to the current node).

Error-Prevention Tip 12.2

Assign `NULL` to the link member of a new node. Pointers should be initialized before they are used.

Figure 12.5 illustrates the insertion of a node containing the character `'C'` into an ordered list. Part a) of the figure shows the list and the new node before the insertion. Part b) of the figure shows the result of inserting the new node. The reassigned pointers are dotted arrows.

For simplicity, we implemented function `insert` (and other similar functions in this chapter) with a `void` return type. It is possible that function `malloc` will fail to allocate the requested memory. In this case, it would be better for our `insert` function to return a status that indicates whether the operation was successful.

Function `delete`

Function `delete` (lines 137–168) receives the address of the pointer to the start of the list and a character to be deleted. The steps for deleting a character from the list are as follows:

1. If the character to be deleted matches the character in the first node of the list (line 140), assign `*sPtr` to `tempPtr` (`tempPtr` will be used to `free` the unneeded memory), assign `(*sPtr)->nextPtr` to `*sPtr` (`*sPtr` now points to the second

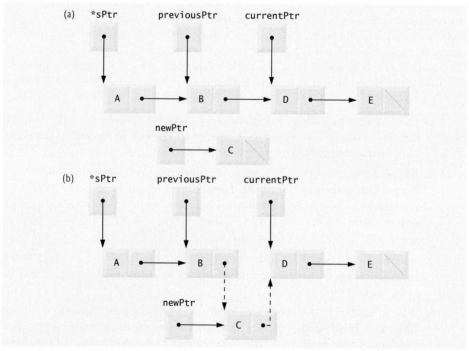

Fig. 12.5 | Inserting a node in order in a list.

node in the list), free the memory pointed to by tempPtr, and return the character that was deleted.

2. Otherwise, initialize previousPtr with *sPtr and initialize currentPtr with (*sPtr)->nextPtr (lines 147–148).

3. While currentPtr is not NULL and the value to be deleted is not equal to currentPtr->data (Line 151), assign currentPtr to previousPtr (line 152), and assign currentPtr->nextPtr to currentPtr (line 153). This locates the character to be deleted if it is contained in the list.

4. If currentPtr is not NULL (line 157), assign currentPtr to tempPtr (line 158), assign currentPtr->nextPtr to previousPtr->nextPtr (line 159), free the node pointed to by tempPtr (line 160), and return the character that was deleted from the list (line 161). If currentPtr is NULL, return the null character ('\0') to signify that the character to be deleted was not found in the list (line 166).

Figure 12.6 illustrates the deletion of a node from a linked list. Part a) of the figure shows the linked list after the preceding insert operation. Part b) shows the reassignment of the link element of previousPtr and the assignment of currentPtr to tempPtr. Pointer tempPtr is used to free the memory allocated to store 'C'.

Function printList
Function printList (lines 178–197) receives a pointer to the start of the list as an argument and refers to the pointer as currentPtr. The function first determines if the list is empty (lines 182–184) and, if so, prints "The list is empty." and terminates. Otherwise, it prints the data in the list (lines 185–195). While currentPtr is not NULL, the value of

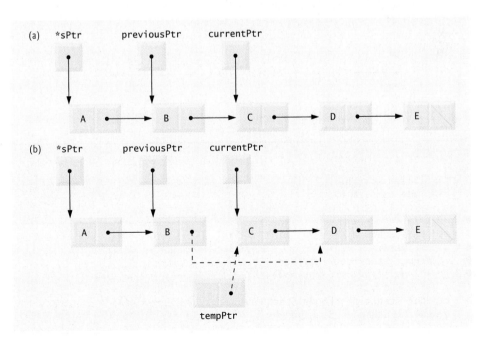

Fig. 12.6 | Deleting a node from a list.

currentPtr->data is printed by the function, and currentPtr->nextPtr is assigned to currentPtr. Note that if the link in the last node of the list is not NULL, the printing algorithm will try to print past the end of the list, and an error will occur. The printing algorithm is identical for linked lists, stacks and queues.

12.5 Stacks

A **stack** is a constrained version of a linked list. New nodes can be added to a stack and removed from a stack only at the top. For this reason, a stack is referred to as a **last-in, first-out (LIFO)** data structure. A stack is referenced via a pointer to the top element of the stack. The link member in the last node of the stack is set to NULL to indicate the bottom of the stack.

Figure 12.7 illustrates a stack with several nodes. Note that stacks and linked lists are represented identically. The difference between stacks and linked lists is that insertions and deletions may occur anywhere in a linked list, but only at the top of a stack.

Common Programming Error 12.6

Not setting the link in the bottom node of a stack to NULL can lead to runtime errors.

The primary functions used to manipulate a stack are push and pop. Function push creates a new node and places it on top of the stack. Function pop removes a node from the top of the stack, frees the memory that was allocated to the popped node and returns the popped value.

Figure 12.8 (output shown in Fig. 12.9) implements a simple stack of integers. The program provides three options: 1) push a value onto the stack (function push), 2) pop a value off the stack (function pop) and 3) terminate the program.

stackPtr

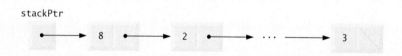

Fig. 12.7 | Stack graphical representation.

```
1   /* Fig. 12.8: fig12_08.c
2      dynamic stack program */
3   #include <stdio.h>
4   #include <stdlib.h>
5
6   /* self-referential structure */
7   struct stackNode {
8      int data;                      /* define data as an int */
9      struct stackNode *nextPtr; /* stackNode pointer */
10  }; /* end structure stackNode */
11
12  typedef struct stackNode StackNode; /* synonym for struct stackNode */
13  typedef StackNode *StackNodePtr; /* synonym for StackNode* */
```

Fig. 12.8 | A simple stack program. (Part 1 of 4.)

```
14
15   /* prototypes */
16   void push( StackNodePtr *topPtr, int info );
17   int pop( StackNodePtr *topPtr );
18   int isEmpty( StackNodePtr topPtr );
19   void printStack( StackNodePtr currentPtr );
20   void instructions( void );
21
22   /* function main begins program execution */
23   int main( void )
24   {
25      StackNodePtr stackPtr = NULL; /* points to stack top */
26      int choice; /* user's menu choice */
27      int value;  /* int input by user */
28
29      instructions(); /* display the menu */
30      printf( "? " );
31      scanf( "%d", &choice );
32
33      /* while user does not enter 3 */
34      while ( choice != 3 ) {
35
36         switch ( choice ) {
37
38            /* push value onto stack */
39            case 1:
40               printf( "Enter an integer: " );
41               scanf( "%d", &value );
42               push( &stackPtr, value );
43               printStack( stackPtr );
44               break;
45
46            /* pop value off stack */
47            case 2:
48
49               /* if stack is not empty */
50               if ( !isEmpty( stackPtr ) ) {
51                  printf( "The popped value is %d.\n", pop( &stackPtr ) );
52               } /* end if */
53
54               printStack( stackPtr );
55               break;
56
57            default:
58               printf( "Invalid choice.\n\n" );
59               instructions();
60               break;
61
62         } /* end switch */
63
64         printf( "? " );
65         scanf( "%d", &choice );
66      } /* end while */
```

Fig. 12.8 | A simple stack program. (Part 2 of 4.)

```
67
68      printf( "End of run.\n" );
69
70      return 0; /* indicates successful termination */
71
72  } /* end main */
73
74  /* display program instructions to user */
75  void instructions( void )
76  {
77      printf( "Enter choice:\n"
78          "1 to push a value on the stack\n"
79          "2 to pop a value off the stack\n"
80          "3 to end program\n" );
81  } /* end function instructions */
82
83  /* Insert a node at the stack top */
84  void push( StackNodePtr *topPtr, int info )
85  {
86      StackNodePtr newPtr; /* pointer to new node */
87
88      newPtr = malloc( sizeof( StackNode ) );
89
90      /* insert the node at stack top */
91      if ( newPtr != NULL ) {
92          newPtr->data = info;
93          newPtr->nextPtr = *topPtr;
94          *topPtr = newPtr;
95      } /* end if */
96      else { /* no space available */
97          printf( "%d not inserted. No memory available.\n", info );
98      } /* end else */
99
100 } /* end function push */
101
102 /* Remove a node from the stack top */
103 int pop( StackNodePtr *topPtr )
104 {
105     StackNodePtr tempPtr; /* temporary node pointer */
106     int popValue; /* node value */
107
108     tempPtr = *topPtr;
109     popValue = ( *topPtr )->data;
110     *topPtr = ( *topPtr )->nextPtr;
111     free( tempPtr );
112
113     return popValue;
114
115 } /* end function pop */
116
117 /* Print the stack */
118 void printStack( StackNodePtr currentPtr )
119 {
```

Fig. 12.8 | A simple stack program. (Part 3 of 4.)

```
120
121     /* if stack is empty */
122     if ( currentPtr == NULL ) {
123        printf( "The stack is empty.\n\n" );
124     } /* end if */
125     else {
126        printf( "The stack is:\n" );
127
128        /* while not the end of the stack */
129        while ( currentPtr != NULL ) {
130           printf( "%d --> ", currentPtr->data );
131           currentPtr = currentPtr->nextPtr;
132        } /* end while */
133
134        printf( "NULL\n\n" );
135     } /* end else */
136
137  } /* end function printList */
138
139  /* Return 1 if the stack is empty, 0 otherwise */
140  int isEmpty( StackNodePtr topPtr )
141  {
142     return topPtr == NULL;
143
144  } /* end function isEmpty */
```

Fig. 12.8 | A simple stack program. (Part 4 of 4.)

```
Enter choice:
1 to push a value on the stack
2 to pop a value off the stack
3 to end program
? 1
Enter an integer: 5
The stack is:
5 --> NULL


Enter an integer: 6
The stack is:
6 --> 5 --> NULL

? 1
Enter an integer: 4
The stack is:
4 --> 6 --> 5 --> NULL

? 2
The popped value is 4.
The stack is:
6 --> 5 --> NULL
```

(Continued on next page)

Fig. 12.9 | Sample output from the program of Fig. 12.8. (Part 1 of 2.)

```
? 2
The popped value is 6.
The stack is:
5 --> NULL

? 2
The popped value is 5.
The stack is empty.

? 2
The stack is empty.

? 4
Invalid choice.

Enter choice:
1 to push a value on the stack
2 to pop a value off the stack
3 to end program
? 3
End of run.
```

Fig. 12.9 | Sample output from the program of Fig. 12.8. (Part 2 of 2.)

Function push

Function push (lines 84–100) places a new node at the top of the stack. The function consists of three steps:

1. Create a new node by calling malloc and assign the location of the allocated memory to newPtr (line 88).

2. Assign to newPtr->data the value to be placed on the stack (line 92) and assign *topPtr (the stack top pointer) to newPtr->nextPtr (line 93)—the link member of newPtr now points to the previous top node.

3. Assign newPtr to *topPtr (line 94)—*topPtr now points to the new stack top.

Manipulations involving *topPtr change the value of stackPtr in main. Figure 12.10 illustrates function push. Part a) of the figure shows the stack and the new node before the push operation. The dotted arrows in part b) illustrate *Steps 2* and *3* of the push operation that enable the node containing 12 to become the new stack top.

Function pop

Function pop (lines 103–115) removes a node from the top of the stack. Note that main determines if the stack is empty before calling pop. The pop operation consists of five steps:

1. Assign *topPtr to tempPtr (line 108); tempPtr will be used to free the unneeded memory.

2. Assign (*topPtr)->data to popValue (line 109) to save the value in the top node.

3. Assign (*topPtr)->nextPtr to *topPtr (line 110) so *topPtr contains address of the new top node.

4. Free the memory pointed to by tempPtr (line 111).

5. Return popValue to the caller (line 113).

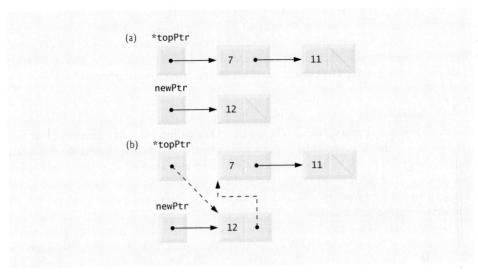

Fig. 12.10 | push operation.

Figure 12.11 illustrates function pop. Part (a) shows the stack after the previous push operation. Part (b) shows tempPtr pointing to the first node of the stack and topPtr pointing to the second node of the stack. Function **free** is used to free the memory pointed to by tempPtr.

Applications of Stacks

Stacks have many interesting applications. For example, whenever a function call is made, the called function must know how to return to its caller, so the return address is pushed onto a stack. If a series of function calls occurs, the successive return values are pushed onto the stack in last-in, first-out order so that each function can return to its caller. Stacks support recursive function calls in the same manner as conventional nonrecursive calls.

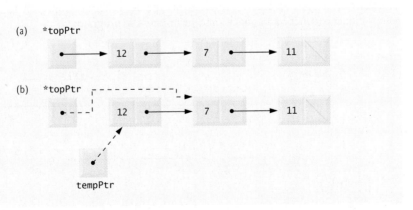

Fig. 12.11 | pop operation.

Stacks contain the space created for automatic variables on each invocation of a function. When the function returns to its caller, the space for that function's automatic variables is popped off the stack, and these variables no longer are known to the program. Stacks are used by compilers in the process of evaluating expressions and generating machine language code. The exercises explore several applications of stacks.

12.6 Queues

Another common data structure is the queue. A queue is similar to a checkout line in a grocery store—the first person in line is serviced first, and other customers enter the line only at the end and wait to be serviced. Queue nodes are removed only from the head of the queue and are inserted only at the tail of the queue. For this reason, a queue is referred to as a first-in, first-out (FIFO) data structure. The insert and remove operations are known as enqueue and dequeue.

Queues have many applications in computer systems. Many computers have only a single processor, so only one user at a time may be serviced. Entries for the other users are placed in a queue. Each entry gradually advances to the front of the queue as users receive service. The entry at the front of the queue is the next to receive service.

Queues are also used to support print spooling. A multiuser environment may have only a single printer. Many users may be generating outputs to be printed. If the printer is busy, other outputs may still be generated. These are spooled to disk where they wait in a queue until the printer becomes available.

Information packets also wait in queues in computer networks. Each time a packet arrives at a network node, it must be routed to the next node on the network along the path to the packet's final destination. The routing node routes one packet at a time, so additional packets are enqueued until the router can route them. Figure 12.12 illustrates a queue with several nodes. Note the pointers to the head of the queue and the tail of the queue.

Common Programming Error 12.7

Not setting the link in the last node of a queue to NULL can lead to runtime errors.

Figure 12.13 (output in Fig. 12.14) performs queue manipulations. The program provides several options: insert a node in the queue (function **enqueue**), remove a node from the queue (function **dequeue**) and terminate the program.

Fig. 12.12 | Queue graphical representation.

```
1   /* Fig. 12.13: fig12_13.c
2      Operating and maintaining a queue */
3
4   #include <stdio.h>
5   #include <stdlib.h>
6
7   /* self-referential structure */
8   struct queueNode {
9      char data;                 /* define data as a char */
10     struct queueNode *nextPtr; /* queueNode pointer */
11  }; /* end structure queueNode */
12
13  typedef struct queueNode QueueNode;
14  typedef QueueNode *QueueNodePtr;
15
16  /* function prototypes */
17  void printQueue( QueueNodePtr currentPtr );
18  int isEmpty( QueueNodePtr headPtr );
19  char dequeue( QueueNodePtr *headPtr, QueueNodePtr *tailPtr );
20  void enqueue( QueueNodePtr *headPtr, QueueNodePtr *tailPtr,
21               char value );
22  void instructions( void );
23
24  /* function main begins program execution */
25  int main( void )
26  {
27     QueueNodePtr headPtr = NULL; /* initialize headPtr */
28     QueueNodePtr tailPtr = NULL; /* initialize tailPtr */
29     int choice;                  /* user's menu choice */
30     char item;                   /* char input by user */
31
32     instructions(); /* display the menu */
33     printf( "? " );
34     scanf( "%d", &choice );
35
36     /* while user does not enter 3 */
37     while ( choice != 3 ) {
38
39        switch( choice ) {
40
41           /* enqueue value */
42           case 1:
43              printf( "Enter a character: " );
44              scanf( "\n%c", &item );
45              enqueue( &headPtr, &tailPtr, item );
46              printQueue( headPtr );
47              break;
48
49           /* dequeue value */
50           case 2:
51
```

Fig. 12.13 | Processing a queue. (Part 1 of 4.)

```
52              /* if queue is not empty */
53              if ( !isEmpty( headPtr ) ) {
54                  item = dequeue( &headPtr, &tailPtr );
55                  printf( "%c has been dequeued.\n", item );
56              } /* end if */
57
58              printQueue( headPtr );
59              break;
60
61          default:
62              printf( "Invalid choice.\n\n" );
63              instructions();
64              break;
65
66      } /* end switch */
67
68      printf( "? " );
69      scanf( "%d", &choice );
70  } /* end while */
71
72  printf( "End of run.\n" );
73
74  return 0; /* indicates successful termination */
75
76 } /* end main */
77
78 /* display program instructions to user */
79 void instructions( void )
80 {
81    printf ( "Enter your choice:\n"
82            "   1 to add an item to the queue\n"
83            "   2 to remove an item from the queue\n"
84            "   3 to end\n" );
85 } /* end function instructions */
86
87 /* insert a node a queue tail */
88 void enqueue( QueueNodePtr *headPtr, QueueNodePtr *tailPtr,
89               char value )
90 {
91    QueueNodePtr newPtr; /* pointer to new node */
92
93    newPtr = malloc( sizeof( QueueNode ) );
94
95    if ( newPtr != NULL ) { /* is space available */
96       newPtr->data = value;
97       newPtr->nextPtr = NULL;
98
99       /* if empty, insert node at head */
100       if ( isEmpty( *headPtr ) ) {
101          *headPtr = newPtr;
102       } /* end if */
```

Fig. 12.13 | Processing a queue. (Part 2 of 4.)

```
103          else {
104             ( *tailPtr )->nextPtr = newPtr;
105          } /* end else */
106
107          *tailPtr = newPtr;
108       } /* end if */
109       else {
110          printf( "%c not inserted. No memory available.\n", value );
111       } /* end else */
112
113 } /* end function enqueue */
114
115 /* remove node from queue head */
116 char dequeue( QueueNodePtr *headPtr, QueueNodePtr *tailPtr )
117 {
118    char value;             /* node value */
119    QueueNodePtr tempPtr; /* temporary node pointer */
120
121    value = ( *headPtr )->data;
122    tempPtr = *headPtr;
123    *headPtr = ( *headPtr )->nextPtr;
124
125    /* if queue is empty */
126    if ( *headPtr == NULL ) {
127       *tailPtr = NULL;
128    } /* end if */
129
130    free( tempPtr );
131
132    return value;
133
134 } /* end function dequeue */
135
136 /* Return 1 if the list is empty, 0 otherwise */
137 int isEmpty( QueueNodePtr headPtr )
138 {
139    return headPtr == NULL;
140
141 } /* end function isEmpty */
142
143 /* Print the queue */
144 void printQueue( QueueNodePtr currentPtr )
145 {
146
147    /* if queue is empty */
148    if ( currentPtr == NULL ) {
149       printf( "Queue is empty.\n\n" );
150    } /* end if */
151    else {
152       printf( "The queue is:\n" );
153
```

Fig. 12.13 | Processing a queue. (Part 3 of 4.)

```
154          /* while not end of queue */
155          while ( currentPtr != NULL ) {
156             printf( "%c --> ", currentPtr->data );
157             currentPtr = currentPtr->nextPtr;
158          } /* end while */
159
160          printf( "NULL\n\n" );
161       } /* end else */
162
163    } /* end function printQueue */
```

Fig. 12.13 | Processing a queue. (Part 4 of 4.)

```
Enter your choice:
   1 to add an item to the queue
   2 to remove an item from the queue
   3 to end
? 1
Enter a character: A
The queue is:
A --> NULL

? 1
Enter a character: B
The queue is:
A --> B --> NULL

? 1
Enter a character: C
The queue is:
A --> B --> C --> NULL

? 2
A has been dequeued.
The queue is:
B --> C --> NULL

? 2
B has been dequeued.
The queue is:
C --> NULL

? 2
C has been dequeued.
Queue is empty.

? 2
Queue is empty.

? 4
Invalid choice.
```

(Continued on next page)

Fig. 12.14 | Sample output from the program in Fig. 12.13. (Part 1 of 2.)

(`*treePtr`)->data, function `insertNode` is called with the address of (`*treeP-`
`tr`)->rightPtr (line 85). Otherwise, the recursive steps continue until a NULL
pointer is found, then Step *1*) is executed to insert the new node.

Functions `inOrder` (lines 96–106), `preOrder` (lines 109–119) and `postOrder` (lines
122–132) each receive a tree (i.e., the pointer to the root node of the tree) and traverse the
tree.

The steps for an `inOrder` traversal are:

1. Traverse the left subtree `inOrder`.

2. Process the value in the node.

3. Traverse the right subtree `inOrder`.

The value in a node is not processed until the values in its left subtree are processed. The
`inOrder` traversal of the tree in Fig. 12.21 is:

    6 13 17 27 33 42 48

Note that the `inOrder` traversal of a binary search tree prints the node values in
ascending order. The process of creating a binary search tree actually sorts the data—and
thus this process is called the **binary tree sort**.

The steps for a `preOrder` traversal are:

1. Process the value in the node.

2. Traverse the left subtree `preOrder`.

3. Traverse the right subtree `preOrder`.

The value in each node is processed as the node is visited. After the value in a given node
is processed, the values in the left subtree are processed, then the values in the right subtree
are processed. The `preOrder` traversal of the tree in Fig. 12.21 is:

    27 13 6 17 42 33 48

The steps for a `postOrder` traversal are:

1. Traverse the left subtree `postOrder`.

2. Traverse the right subtree `postOrder`.

3. Process the value in the node.

The value in each node is not printed until the values of its children are printed. The `post-`
`Order` traversal of the tree in Fig. 12.21 is:

    6 17 13 33 48 42 27

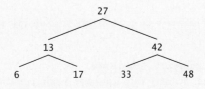

Fig. 12.21 | Binary search tree with seven nodes.

The binary search tree facilitates **duplicate elimination**. As the tree is being created, an attempt to insert a duplicate value will be recognized because a duplicate will follow the same "go left" or "go right" decisions on each comparison as the original value did. Thus, the duplicate will eventually be compared with a node in the tree containing the same value. The duplicate value may simply be discarded at this point.

Searching a binary tree for a value that matches a key value is also fast. If the tree is tightly packed, each level contains about twice as many elements as the previous level. So a binary search tree with n elements would have a maximum of $\log_2 n$ levels, and thus a maximum of $\log_2 n$ comparisons would have to be made either to find a match or to determine that no match exists. This means, for example, that when searching a (tightly packed) 1000-element binary search tree, no more than 10 comparisons need to be made because $2^{10} > 1000$. When searching a (tightly packed) 1,000,000 element binary search tree, no more than 20 comparisons need to be made because $2^{20} > 1,000,000$.

In the exercises, algorithms are presented for several other binary tree operations such as deleting an item from a binary tree, printing a binary tree in a two-dimensional tree format, and performing a level order traversal of a binary tree. The level order traversal of a binary tree visits the nodes of the tree row-by-row starting at the root node level. On each level of the tree, the nodes are visited from left to right. Other binary tree exercises include allowing a binary search tree to contain duplicate values, inserting string values in a binary tree and determining how many levels are contained in a binary tree.

Summary

Section 12.1 Introduction

- Dynamic data structures grow and shrink at execution time.
- Linked lists are collections of data items "lined up in a row"—insertions and deletions are made anywhere in a linked list.
- Stacks are important in compilers and operating systems—insertions and deletions are made only at one end of a stack—its top.
- Queues represent waiting lines; insertions are made at the back (also referred to as the tail) of a queue and deletions are made from the front (also referred to as the head) of a queue.
- Binary trees facilitate high-speed searching and sorting of data, efficient elimination of duplicate data items, representing file system directories and compiling expressions into machine language.

Section 12.2 Self-Referential Structures

- A self-referential structure contains a pointer member that points to a structure of the same structure type.
- Self-referential structures can be linked together to form useful data structures such as lists, queues, stacks and trees.
- A NULL pointer normally indicates the end of a data structure just as the null character indicates the end of a string.

Section 12.3 Dynamic Memory Allocation

- Creating and maintaining dynamic data structures requires dynamic memory allocation. The limit for dynamic memory allocation can be as large as the amount of available physical memory in the computer or the amount of available virtual memory in a virtual memory system.

- Functions `malloc` and `free`, and operator `sizeof`, are essential to dynamic memory allocation.
- Function `malloc` takes as an argument the number of bytes to be allocated and returns a pointer of type `void *` to the allocated memory. A `void *` pointer may be assigned to a variable of any pointer type.
- Function `malloc` is normally used with the `sizeof` operator.
- The memory allocated by `malloc` is not initialized.
- If no memory is available, `malloc` returns `NULL`.
- Function `free` deallocates memory so that the memory can be reallocated in the future.
- C also provides functions `calloc` and `realloc` for creating and modifying dynamic arrays.

Section 12.4 Linked Lists
- A linked list is a linear collection of self-referential structures, called nodes, connected by pointer links—hence, the term "linked" list.
- A linked list is accessed via a pointer to the first node of the list. Subsequent nodes are accessed via the link pointer member stored in each node.
- By convention, the link pointer in the last node of a list is set to `NULL` to mark the end of the list.
- Data is stored in a linked list dynamically—each node is created as necessary.
- A node can contain data of any type including other `struct` objects.
- A linked list is appropriate when the number of data elements to be represented in the data structure is unpredictable. Linked lists are dynamic, so the length of a list can increase or decrease as necessary.
- Linked lists can be maintained in sorted order by inserting each new element at the proper point in the list.
- Linked list nodes are normally not stored contiguously in memory. Logically, however, the nodes of a linked list appear to be contiguous.

Section 12.5 Stacks
- A stack is a constrained version of a linked list. New nodes can be added to a stack and removed from a stack only at the top. For this reason, a stack is referred to as a last-in, first-out (LIFO) data structure.
- The difference between stacks and linked lists is that insertions and deletions may occur anywhere in a linked list, but only at the top of a stack.
- The primary functions used to manipulate a stack are push and pop. Function push creates a new node and places it on top of the stack. Function pop removes a node from the top of the stack, frees the memory that was allocated to the popped node and returns the popped value.
- Stacks have many interesting applications. Whenever a function call is made, the called function must know how to return to its caller, so the return address is pushed onto a stack. If a series of function calls occurs, the successive return values are pushed onto the stack in last-in, first-out order so that each function can return to its caller. Stacks support recursive function calls in the same manner as conventional nonrecursive calls.
- Stacks are used by compilers in the process of evaluating expressions and generating machine language code.

Section 12.6 Queues
- A queue is similar to a checkout line in a grocery store—the first person in line is serviced first, and other customers enter the line only at the end and wait to be serviced.

- Queue nodes are removed only from the head of the queue and are inserted only at the tail of the queue. For this reason, a queue is referred to as a first-in, first-out (FIFO) data structure.

- The insert and remove operations for a queue are known as enqueue and dequeue.

- Queues have many applications in computer systems. Many computers have only a single processor, so only one at a time may be serviced. Entries for the other users are placed in a queue. Each entry gradually advances to the front of the queue as users receive service. The entry at the front of the queue is the next to receive service.

- Queues are also used to support print spooling. Many users may be generating outputs to be printed. If the printer is busy, other outputs may still be generated. These are spooled to disk where they wait in a queue until the printer becomes available.

- Information packets also wait in queues in computer networks. Each time a packet arrives at a network node, it must be routed to the next node on the network along the path to the packet's final destination. The routing node routes one packet at a time, so additional packets are enqueued until the router can route them.

Section 12.7 Trees

- A tree is a nonlinear, two-dimensional data structure with special properties. Tree nodes contain two or more links. Binary trees are trees whose nodes all contain two links (none, one, or both of which may be NULL).

- The root node is the first node in a tree. Each link in the root node refers to a child. The left child is the first node in the left subtree, and the right child is the first node in the right subtree. The children of a node are called siblings.

- A node with no children is called a leaf node.

- A binary search tree (with no duplicate node values) has the characteristic that the values in any left subtree are less than the value in its parent node, and the values in any right subtree are greater than the value in its parent node.

- A node can only be inserted as a leaf node in a binary search tree.

- The steps for an in-order traversal are: Traverse the left subtree in-order, process the value in the node, then traverse the right subtree in-order. The value in a node is not processed until the values in its left subtree are processed.

- The in-order traversal of a binary search tree prints the node values in ascending order. The process of creating a binary search tree actually sorts the data—and thus this process is called the binary tree sort.

- The steps for a pre-order traversal are: Process the value in the node, traverse the left subtree pre-order, then traverse the right subtree pre-order. The value in each node is processed as the node is visited. After the value in a given node is processed, the values in the left subtree are processed, then the values in the right subtree are processed.

- The steps for a post-order traversal are: Traverse the left subtree post-order, traverse the right subtree post-order, then process the value in the node. The value in each node is not processed until the values of its children are processed.

- The binary search tree facilitates duplicate elimination. As the tree is being created, an attempt to insert a duplicate value will be recognized because a duplicate will follow the same "go left" or "go right" decisions on each comparison as the original value did. Thus, the duplicate will eventually be compared with a node in the tree containing the same value. The duplicate value may simply be discarded at this point.

- Searching a binary tree for a value that matches a key value is fast. If the tree is tightly packed, each level contains about twice as many elements as the previous level. So a binary search tree with n elements would have a maximum of $\log_2 n$ levels, and thus a maximum of $\log_2 n$ comparisons would have to be made either to find a match or to determine that no match exists. This means that when searching a (tightly packed) 1000-element binary search tree, no more than 10 comparisons need to be made because $2^{10} > 1000$. When searching a (tightly packed) 1,000,000 element binary search tree, no more than 20 comparisons need to be made because $2^{20} > 1,000,000$.

Terminology

binary search tree
binary tree
binary tree sort
child node
children
deleting a node
dequeue
double indirection
dynamic data structures
dynamic memory allocation
enqueue
FIFO (first-in, first-out)
free
head of a queue
inorder traversal
inserting a node
leaf node
left child
left subtree
LIFO (last-in, first-out)
linear data structure
linked list
malloc (allocate memory)
node

nonlinear data structure
NULL pointer
parent node
pointer to a pointer
pop
postorder traversal
predicate function
preorder traversal
push
queue
right child
right subtree
root node
self-referential structure
siblings
sizeof
stack
subtree
tail of a queue
top
traversal
tree
visit a node

Self-Review Exercises

12.1 Fill in the blanks in each of the following:

a) A self-_____ structure is used to form dynamic data structures.

b) Function _____ is used to dynamically allocate memory.

c) A(n) _____ is a specialized version of a linked list in which nodes can be inserted and deleted only from the start of the list.

d) Functions that look at a linked list but do not modify it are referred to as _____.

e) A queue is referred to as a(n) _____ data structure.

f) The pointer to the next node in a linked list is referred to as a(n) _____.

g) Function _____ is used to reclaim dynamically allocated memory.

h) A(n) _____ is a specialized version of a linked list in which nodes can be inserted only at the start of the list and deleted only from the end of the list.

i) A(n) _____ is a nonlinear, two-dimensional data structure that contains nodes with two or more links.

j) A stack is referred to as a(n) _____ data structure because the last node inserted is the first node removed.

k) The nodes of a(n) _____ tree contain two link members.

l) The first node of a tree is the _____ node.

m) Each link in a tree node points to a(n) _____ or _____ of that node.

n) A tree node that has no children is called a(n) _____ node.

o) The three traversal algorithms (covered in this chapter) for a binary tree are _____, _____ and _____.

12.2   What are the differences between a linked list and a stack?

12.3   What are the differences between a stack and a queue?

12.4   Write a statement or set of statements to accomplish each of the following. Assume that all the manipulations occur in main (therefore, no addresses of pointer variables are needed), and assume the following definitions:

```
struct gradeNode {
    char lastName[ 20 ];
    double grade;
    struct gradeNode *nextPtr;
};

typedef struct gradeNode GradeNode;
typedef GradeNode *GradeNodePtr;
```

a) Create a pointer to the start of the list called startPtr. The list is empty.

b) Create a new node of type GradeNode that is pointed to by pointer newPtr of type GradeNodePtr. Assign the string "Jones" to member lastName and the value 91.5 to member grade (use strcpy). Provide any necessary declarations and statements.

c) Assume that the list pointed to by startPtr currently consists of 2 nodes—one containing "Jones" and one containing "Smith". The nodes are in alphabetical order. Provide the statements necessary to insert in order nodes containing the following data for lastName and grade:

```
"Adams"        85.0
"Thompson"     73.5
"Pritchard"    66.5
```

Use pointers previousPtr, currentPtr and newPtr to perform the insertions. State what previousPtr and currentPtr point to before each insertion. Assume that newPtr always points to the new node, and that the new node has already been assigned the data.

d) Write a while loop that prints the data in each node of the list. Use pointer currentPtr to move along the list.

e) Write a while loop that deletes all the nodes in the list and frees the memory associated with each node. Use pointer currentPtr and pointer tempPtr to walk along the list and free memory, respectively.

12.5   Manually provide the inorder, preorder and postorder traversals of the binary search tree of Fig. 12.22.

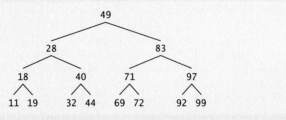

Fig. 12.22 | A 15-node binary search tree.

Answers to Self-Review Exercises

12.1   a) referential. b) `malloc`. c) stack. d) predicates. e) FIFO. f) link. g) `free`. h) queue.
i) tree. j) LIFO. k) binary. l) root. m) child, subtree. n) leaf. o) inorder, preorder postorder.

12.2   It is possible to insert a node anywhere in a linked list, and remove a node from anywhere
in a linked list. However, nodes in a stack may only be inserted at the top of the stack and removed
from the top of a stack.

12.3   A queue has pointers to both its head and its tail so that nodes may be inserted at the tail
and deleted from the head. A stack has a single pointer to the top of the stack where both insertion
and deletion of nodes is performed.

12.4   a) `GradeNodePtr startPtr = NULL;`

    b) `GradeNodePtr newPtr;`
       `newPtr = malloc( sizeof( GradeNode ) );`
       `strcpy( newPtr->lastName, "Jones" );`
       `newPtr->grade = 91.5;`
       `newPtr->nextPtr = NULL;`

    c) To insert `"Adams"`:
       previousPtr is NULL, currentPtr points to the first element in the list.
       `newPtr->nextPtr = currentPtr;`
       `startPtr = newPtr;`

       To insert `"Thompson"`:
       previousPtr points to the last element in the list (containing `"Smith"`)
       currentPtr is NULL.
       `newPtr->nextPtr = currentPtr;`
       `previousPtr->nextPtr = newPtr;`

       To insert `"Pritchard"`:
       previousPtr points to the node containing `"Jones"`
       currentPtr points to the node containing `"Smith"`
       `newPtr->nextPtr = currentPtr;`
       `previousPtr->nextPtr = newPtr;`

    d) `currentPtr = startPtr;`
       `while ( currentPtr != NULL ) {`
       `   printf( "Lastname = %s\nGrade = %6.2f\n",`
       `           currentPtr->lastName, currentPtr->grade );`
       `   currentPtr = currentPtr->nextPtr;`
       `}`

    e) `currentPtr = startPtr;`
       `while ( currentPtr != NULL ) {`
       `   tempPtr = currentPtr;`
       `   currentPtr = currentPtr->nextPtr;`
       `   free( tempPtr );`
       `}`
       `startPtr = NULL;`

12.5   The inorder traversal is:

        11 18 19 28 32 40 44 49 69 71 72 83 92 97 99

The preorder traversal is:

        49 28 18 11 19 40 32 44 83 71 69 72 97 92 99

The postorder traversal is:

        11 19 18 32 44 40 28 69 72 71 92 99 97 83 49

Exercises

12.6 Write a program that concatenates two linked lists of characters. The program should include function concatenate that takes pointers to both lists as arguments and concatenates the second list to the first list.

12.7 Write a program that merges two ordered lists of integers into a single ordered list of integers. Function merge should receive pointers to the first node of each of the lists to be merged and should return a pointer to the first node of the merged list.

12.8 Write a program that inserts 25 random integers from 0 to 100 in order in a linked list. The program should calculate the sum of the elements and the floating-point average of the elements.

12.9 Write a program that creates a linked list of 10 characters, then creates a copy of the list in reverse order.

12.10 Write a program that inputs a line of text and uses a stack to print the line reversed.

12.11 Write a program that uses a stack to determine if a string is a palindrome (i.e., the string is spelled identically backward and forward). The program should ignore spaces and punctuation.

12.12 Stacks are used by compilers to help in the process of evaluating expressions and generating machine language code. In this and the next exercise, we investigate how compilers evaluate arithmetic expressions consisting only of constants, operators and parentheses.

Humans generally write expressions like 3 + 4 and 7 / 9 in which the operator (+ or / here) is written between its operands—this is called **infix notation**. Computers "prefer" **postfix notation** in which the operator is written to the right of its two operands. The preceding infix expressions would appear in postfix notation as 3 4 + and 7 9 /, respectively.

To evaluate a complex infix expression, a compiler would first convert the expression to postfix notation, and then evaluate the postfix version of the expression. Each of these algorithms requires only a single left-to-right pass of the expression. Each algorithm uses a stack in support of its operation, and in each the stack is used for a different purpose.

In this exercise, you will write a version of the infix-to-postfix conversion algorithm. In the next exercise, you will write a version of the postfix expression evaluation algorithm.

Write a program that converts an ordinary infix arithmetic expression (assume a valid expression is entered) with single digit integers such as

```
(6 + 2) * 5 - 8 / 4
```

to a postfix expression. The postfix version of the preceding infix expression is

```
6 2 + 5 * 8 4 / -
```

The program should read the expression into character array infix, and use modified versions of the stack functions implemented in this chapter to help create the postfix expression in character array postfix. The algorithm for creating a postfix expression is as follows:

    1) Push a left parenthesis '(' onto the stack.
    2) Append a right parenthesis ')' to the end of infix.
    3) While the stack is not empty, read infix from left to right and do the following:
            If the current character in infix is a digit, copy it to the next element of postfix.
            If the current character in infix is a left parenthesis, push it onto the stack.
            If the current character in infix is an operator,
                Pop operators (if there are any) at the top of the stack while they have equal or higher precedence than the current operator, and insert the popped operators in postfix.
                Push the current character in infix onto the stack.

If the current character in `infix` is a right parenthesis

Pop operators from the top of the stack and insert them in `postfix` until a left parenthesis is at the top of the stack.

Pop (and discard) the left parenthesis from the stack.

The following arithmetic operations are allowed in an expression:

+ addition
- subtraction
* multiplication
/ division
^ exponentiation
% remainder

The stack should be maintained with the following declarations:

```
struct stackNode {
    char data;
    struct stackNode *nextPtr;
};

typedef struct stackNode StackNode;
typedef StackNode *StackNodePtr;
```

The program should consist of `main` and eight other functions with the following function headers:

`void convertToPostfix( char infix[], char postfix[] )`

Convert the infix expression to postfix notation.

`int isOperator( char c )`

Determine if c is an operator.

`int precedence( char operator1, char operator2 )`

Determine if the precedence of `operator1` is less than, equal to, or greater than the precedence of `operator2`. The function returns -1, 0 and 1, respectively.

`void push( StackNodePtr *topPtr, char value )`

Push a value on the stack.

`char pop( StackNodePtr *topPtr )`

Pop a value off the stack.

`char stackTop( StackNodePtr topPtr )`

Return the top value of the stack without popping the stack.

`int isEmpty( StackNodePtr topPtr )`

Determine if the stack is empty.

`void printStack( StackNodePtr topPtr )`

Print the stack.

12.13 Write a program that evaluates a postfix expression (assume it is valid) such as

`6 2 + 5 * 8 4 / -`

The program should read a postfix expression consisting of single digits and operators into a character array. Using modified versions of the stack functions implemented earlier in this chapter, the program should scan the expression and evaluate it. The algorithm is as follows:

1) Append the null character (`'\0'`) to the end of the postfix expression. When the null character is encountered, no further processing is necessary.

2) While '\0' has not been encountered, read the expression from left to right.

    If the current character is a digit,

        Push its integer value onto the stack (the integer value of a digit character is its value in the computer's character set minus the value of '0' in the computer's character set).

    Otherwise, if the current character is an *operator*,

        Pop the two top elements of the stack into variables x and y.

        Calculate y *operator* x.

        Push the result of the calculation onto the stack.

3) When the null character is encountered in the expression, pop the top value of the stack. This is the result of the postfix expression.

[*Note:* In 2) above, if the operator is '/', the top of the stack is 2, and the next element in the stack is 8, then pop 2 into x, pop 8 into y, evaluate 8 / 2, and push the result, 4, back on the stack. This note also applies to operator '-'.]

The arithmetic operations allowed in an expression are:

    +   addition

    -   subtraction

    *   multiplication

    /   division

    ^   exponentiation

    %   remainder

The stack should be maintained with the following declarations:

```
struct stackNode {
   int data;
   struct stackNode *nextPtr;
};

typedef struct stackNode StackNode;
typedef StackNode *StackNodePtr;
```

The program should consist of main and six other functions with the following function headers:

```
int evaluatePostfixExpression( char *expr )
```

Evaluate the postfix expression.

```
int calculate( int op1, int op2, char operator )
```

Evaluate the expression op1 operator op2.

```
void push( StackNodePtr *topPtr, int value )
```

Push a value on the stack.

```
int pop( StackNodePtr *topPtr )
```

Pop a value off the stack.

```
int isEmpty( StackNodePtr topPtr )
```

Determine if the stack is empty.

```
void printStack( StackNodePtr topPtr )
```

Print the stack.

12.14 Modify the postfix evaluator program of Exercise 12.13 so that it can process integer operands larger than 9.

12.15 *(Supermarket Simulation)* Write a program that simulates a check-out line at a supermarket. The line is a queue. Customers arrive in random integer intervals of 1 to 4 minutes. Also, each customer is serviced in random integer intervals of 1 to 4 minutes. Obviously, the rates need to be balanced. If the average arrival rate is larger than the average service rate, the queue will grow infinitely. Even with balanced rates, randomness can still cause long lines. Run the supermarket simulation for a 12-hour day (720 minutes) using the following algorithm:

1) Choose a random integer between 1 and 4 to determine the minute at which the first customer arrives.

2) At the first customer's arrival time:
Determine customer's service time (random integer from 1 to 4);
Begin servicing the customer;
Schedule arrival time of next customer (random integer 1 to 4 added to the current time).

3) For each minute of the day:
If the next customer arrives,
Say so;
Enqueue the customer;
Schedule the arrival time of the next customer;
If service was completed for the last customer;
Say so;
Dequeue next customer to be serviced;
Determine customer's service completion time
(random integer from 1 to 4 added to the current time).

Now run your simulation for 720 minutes and answer each of the following:
a)   What is the maximum number of customers in the queue at any time?
b)   What is the longest wait any one customer experienced?
c)   What happens if the arrival interval is changed from 1 to 4 minutes to 1 to 3 minutes?

12.16   Modify the program of Fig. 12.19 to allow the binary tree to contain duplicate values.

12.17   Write a program based on the program of Fig. 12.19 that inputs a line of text, tokenizes the sentence into separate words, inserts the words in a binary search tree, and prints the inorder, preorder, and postorder traversals of the tree.

12.18   [*Hint:* Read the line of text into an array. Use strtok to tokenize the text. When a token is found, create a new node for the tree, assign the pointer returned by strtok to member string of the new node, and insert the node in the tree.]

12.19   In this chapter, we saw that duplicate elimination is straightforward when creating a binary search tree. Describe how you would perform duplicate elimination using only a single subscripted array. Compare the performance of array-based duplicate elimination with the performance of binary-search-tree-based duplicate elimination.

12.20   Write a function depth that receives a binary tree and determines how many levels it has.

12.21   (*Recursively Print a List Backwards*) Write a function printListBackwards that recursively outputs the items in a list in reverse order. Use your function in a test program that creates a sorted list of integers and prints the list in reverse order.

12.22   (*Recursively Search a List*) Write a function searchList that recursively searches a linked list for a specified value. The function should return a pointer to the value if it is found; otherwise, NULL should be returned. Use your function in a test program that creates a list of integers. The program should prompt the user for a value to locate in the list.

12.23   (*Binary Tree Delete*) In this exercise, we discuss deleting items from binary search trees. The deletion algorithm is not as straightforward as the insertion algorithm. There are three cases that are encountered when deleting an item—the item is contained in a leaf node (i.e., it has no children), the item is contained in a node that has one child, or the item is contained in a node that has two children.

If the item to be deleted is contained in a leaf node, the node is deleted and the pointer in the parent node is set to NULL.

If the item to be deleted is contained in a node with one child, the pointer in the parent node is set to point to the child node and the node containing the data item is deleted. This causes the child node to take the place of the deleted node in the tree.

The last case is the most difficult. When a node with two children is deleted, another node must take its place. However, the pointer in the parent node cannot simply be assigned to point to one of the children of the node to be deleted. In most cases, the resulting binary search tree would not adhere to the following characteristic of binary search trees: *The values in any left subtree are less than the value in the parent node, and the values in any right subtree are greater than the value in the parent node.*

Which node is used as a **replacement node** to maintain this characteristic? Either the node containing the largest value in the tree less than the value in the node being deleted, or the node containing the smallest value in the tree greater than the value in the node being deleted. Let us consider the node with the smaller value. In a binary search tree, the largest value less than a parent's value is located in the left subtree of the parent node and is guaranteed to be contained in the rightmost node of the subtree. This node is located by walking down the left subtree to the right until the pointer to the right child of the current node is NULL. We are now pointing to the replacement node which is either a leaf node or a node with one child to its left. If the replacement node is a leaf node, the steps to perform the deletion are as follows:

1) Store the pointer to the node to be deleted in a temporary pointer variable (this pointer is used to delete the dynamically allocated memory).
2) Set the pointer in the parent of the node being deleted to point to the replacement node.
3) Set the pointer in the parent of the replacement node to null.
4) Set the pointer to the right subtree in the replacement node to point to the right subtree of the node to be deleted.
5) Delete the node to which the temporary pointer variable points.

The deletion steps for a replacement node with a left child are similar to those for a replacement node with no children, but the algorithm also must move the child to the replacement node's position. If the replacement node is a node with a left child, the steps to perform the deletion are as follows:

1) Store the pointer to the node to be deleted in a temporary pointer variable.
2) Set the pointer in the parent of the node being deleted to point to the replacement node.
3) Set the pointer in the parent of the replacement node to point to the left child of the replacement node.
4) Set the pointer to the right subtree in the replacement node to point to the right subtree of the node to be deleted.
5) Delete the node to which the temporary pointer variable points.

Write function deleteNode which takes as its arguments a pointer to the root node of the tree and the value to be deleted. The function should locate in the tree the node containing the value to be deleted and use the algorithms discussed here to delete the node. If the value is not found in the tree, the function should print a message that indicates whether or not the value is deleted. Modify the program of Fig. 12.19 to use this function. After deleting an item, call the inOrder, preOrder and postOrder traversal functions to confirm that the delete operation was performed correctly.

12.24 (*Binary Tree Search*) Write function binaryTreeSearch that attempts to locate a specified value in a binary search tree. The function should take as arguments a pointer to the root node of the binary tree and a search key to be located. If the node containing the search key is found, the function should return a pointer to that node; otherwise, the function should return a NULL pointer.

12.25 (*Level Order Binary Tree Traversal*) The program of Fig. 12.19 illustrated three recursive methods of traversing a binary tree—inorder traversal, preorder traversal, and postorder traversal.

This exercise presents the **level order traversal** of a binary tree in which the node values are printed level-by-level starting at the root node level. The nodes on each level are printed from left to right. The level order traversal is not a recursive algorithm. It uses the queue data structure to control the output of the nodes. The algorithm is as follows:

1) Insert the root node in the queue
2) While there are nodes left in the queue,
    Get the next node in the queue
    Print the node's value
    If the pointer to the left child of the node is not null
        Insert the left child node in the queue
    If the pointer to the right child of the node is not null
        Insert the right child node in the queue.

Write function `levelOrder` to perform a level order traversal of a binary tree. The function should take as an argument a pointer to the root node of the binary tree. Modify the program of Fig. 12.19 to use this function. Compare the output from this function to the outputs of the other traversal algorithms to see that it worked correctly. [*Note:* You will also need to modify and incorporate the queue processing functions of Fig. 12.13 in this program.]

12.26 (*Printing Trees*) Write a recursive function `outputTree` to display a binary tree on the screen. The function should output the tree row-by-row with the top of the tree at the left of the screen and the bottom of the tree toward the right of the screen. Each row is output vertically. For example, the binary tree illustrated in Fig. 12.22 is output as follows:

Note the rightmost leaf node appears at the top of the output in the rightmost column, and the root node appears at the left of the output. Each column of output starts five spaces to the right of the previous column. Function `outputTree` should receive as arguments a pointer to the root node of the tree and an integer `totalSpaces` representing the number of spaces preceding the value to be output (this variable should start at zero so the root node is output at the left of the screen). The function uses a modified inorder traversal to output the tree—it starts at the rightmost node in the tree and works back to the left. The algorithm is as follows:

    While the pointer to the current node is not null
    Recursively call outputTree with the right subtree of the current node and
        totalSpaces + 5
    Use a for statement to count from 1 to totalSpaces and output spaces
    Output the value in the current node
    Set the pointer to the current node to point to the left subtree of the current node
    Increment totalSpaces by 5.

Special Section: Building Your Own Compiler

In Exercise 7.18 and Exercise 7.19, we introduced Simpletron Machine Language (SML) and created the Simpletron computer simulator to execute programs written in SML. In this section, we build a compiler that converts programs written in a high-level programming language to SML. This section "ties" together the entire programming process. We will write programs in this new high-level language, compile the programs on the compiler we build, and run the programs on the simulator we built in Exercise 7.19.

12.27 (*The Simple Language*) Before we begin building the compiler, we discuss a simple, yet powerful, high-level language similar to early versions of the popular language BASIC. We call the language *Simple*. Every Simple statement consists of a line number and a Simple instruction. Line numbers must appear in ascending order. Each instruction begins with one of the following Simple commands: rem, input, let, print, goto, if...goto or end (see Fig. 12.23). All commands except end can be used repeatedly. Simple evaluates only integer expressions using the +, -, * and / operators. These operators have the same precedence as in C. Parentheses can be used to change the order of evaluation of an expression.

Our Simple compiler recognizes only lowercase letters. All characters in a Simple file should be lowercase (uppercase letters result in a syntax error unless they appear in a rem statement in which case they are ignored). A variable name is a single letter. Simple does not allow descriptive variable names, so variables should be explained in remarks to indicate their use in the program. Simple uses only integer variables. Simple does not have variable declarations—merely mentioning a variable name in a program causes the variable to be declared and initialized to zero automatically. The syntax of Simple does not allow string manipulation (reading a string, writing a string,

Command	Example statement	Description
rem	50 rem this is a remark	Any text following the command rem is for documentation purposes only and is ignored by the compiler.
input	30 input x	Display a question mark to prompt the user to enter an integer. Read that integer from the keyboard and store the integer in x.
let	80 let u = 4 * (j - 56))	Assign u the value of 4 * (j - 56). Note that an arbitrarily complex expression can appear to the right of the equal sign.
print	10 print w	Display the value of w.
goto	70 goto 45	Transfer program control to line 45.
if...goto	35 if i == z goto 80	Compare i and z for equality and transfer program control to line 80 if the condition is true; otherwise, continue execution with the next statement.
end	99 end	Terminate program execution.

Fig. 12.23 | Simple commands.

comparing strings, etc.). If a string is encountered in a Simple program (after a command other than rem), the compiler generates a syntax error. Our compiler will assume that Simple programs are entered correctly. Exercise 12.30 asks the student to modify the compiler to perform syntax error checking.

Simple uses the conditional if...goto statement and the unconditional goto statement to alter the flow of control during program execution. If the condition in the if...goto statement is true, control is transferred to a specific line of the program. The following relational and equality operators are valid in an if...goto statement: <, >, <=, >=, == or !=. The precedence of these operators is the same as in C.

Let us now consider several Simple programs that demonstrate Simple's features. The first program (Fig. 12.24) reads two integers from the keyboard, stores the values in variables a and b, and computes and prints their sum (stored in variable c).

Figure 12.25 determines and prints the larger of two integers. The integers are input from the keyboard and stored in s and t. The if...goto statement tests the condition s >= t. If the condition is true, control is transferred to line 90 and s is output; otherwise, t is output and control is transferred to the end statement in line 99 where the program terminates.

Simple does not provide a repetition structure (such as C's for, while or do...while). However, Simple can simulate each of C's repetition structures using the if...goto and goto statements. Figure 12.26 uses a sentinel-controlled loop to calculate the squares of several integers. Each inte-

```
 1    10 rem    determine and print the sum of two integers
 2    15 rem
 3    20 rem    input the two integers
 4    30 input a
 5    40 input b
 6    45 rem
 7    50 rem    add integers and store result in c
 8    60 let c = a + b
 9    65 rem
10    70 rem    print the result
11    80 print c
12    90 rem    terminate program execution
13    99 end
```

Fig. 12.24 | Determine the sum of two integers.

```
 1    10 rem    determine the larger of two integers
 2    20 input s
 3    30 input t
 4    32 rem
 5    35 rem    test if s >= t
 6    40 if s >= t goto 90
 7    45 rem
 8    50 rem    t is greater than s, so print t
 9    60 print t
10    70 goto 99
11    75 rem
12    80 rem    s is greater than or equal to t, so print s
13    90 print s
14    99 end
```

Fig. 12.25 | Find the larger of two integers.

ger is input from the keyboard and stored in variable j. If the value entered is the sentinel -9999, control is transferred to line 99 where the program terminates. Otherwise, k is assigned the square of j, k is output to the screen and control is passed to line 20 where the next integer is input.

Using the sample programs of Figs. 12.24–12.26 as your guide, write a Simple program to accomplish each of the following:

    a) Input three integers, determine their average and print the result.

    b) Use a sentinel-controlled loop to input 10 integers and compute and print their sum.

    c) Use a counter-controlled loop to input seven integers, some positive and some negative, and compute and print their average.

    d) Input a series of integers and determine and print the largest. The first integer input indicates how many numbers should be processed.

    e) Input 10 integers and print the smallest.

    f) Calculate and print the sum of the even integers from 2 to 30.

    g) Calculate and print the product of the odd integers from 1 to 9.

12.28 (*Building A Compiler; Prerequisite: Complete Exercise 7.18, Exercise 7.19, Exercise 12.12, Exercise 12.13 and Exercise 12.27*) Now that the Simple language has been presented (Exercise 12.27), we discuss how to build our Simple compiler. First, we consider the process by which a Simple program is converted to SML and executed by the Simpletron simulator (see Fig. 12.27). A file containing a Simple program is read by the compiler and converted to SML code. The SML code is output to a file on disk, in which SML instructions appear one per line. The SML file is then loaded into the Simpletron simulator, and the results are sent to a file on disk and to the screen. Note that the Simpletron program developed in Exercise 7.19 took its input from the keyboard. It must be modified to read from a file so it can run the programs produced by our compiler.

```
 1    10 rem   calculate the squares of several integers
 2    20 input j
 3    23 rem
 4    25 rem   test for sentinel value
 5    30 if j == -9999 goto 99
 6    33 rem
 7    35 rem   calculate square of j and assign result to k
 8    40 let k = j * j
 9    50 print k
10    53 rem
11    55 rem   loop to get next j
12    60 goto 20
13    99 end
```

Fig. 12.26 | Calculate the squares of several integers.

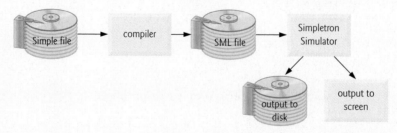

Fig. 12.27 | Writing, compiling and executing a Simple language program.

The compiler performs two passes of the Simple program to convert it to SML. The first pass constructs a symbol table in which every line number, variable name and constant of the Simple program is stored with its type and corresponding location in the final SML code (the symbol table is discussed in detail below). The first pass also produces the corresponding SML instruction(s) for each Simple statement. As we will see, if the Simple program contains statements that transfer control to a line later in the program, the first pass results in an SML program containing some incomplete instructions. The second pass of the compiler locates and completes the unfinished instructions, and outputs the SML program to a file.

First Pass

The compiler begins by reading one statement of the Simple program into memory. The line must be separated into its individual tokens (i.e., "pieces" of a statement) for processing and compilation (standard library function strtok can be used to facilitate this task). Recall that every statement begins with a line number followed by a command. As the compiler breaks a statement into tokens, if the token is a line number, a variable, or a constant, it is placed in the symbol table. A line number is placed in the symbol table only if it is the first token in a statement. The symbol-Table is an array of tableEntry structures representing each symbol in the program. There is no restriction on the number of symbols that can appear in the program. Therefore, the symbolTable for a particular program could be large. Make the symbolTable a 100-element array for now. You can increase or decrease its size once the program is working.

The tableEntry structure definition is as follows:

```
struct tableEntry {
    int symbol;
    char type;      /* 'C', 'L' or 'V' */
    int location;   /* 00 to 99 */
};
```

Each tableEntry structure contains three members. Member symbol is an integer containing the ASCII representation of a variable (remember that variable names are single characters), a line number, or a constant. Member type is one of the following characters indicating the symbol's type: 'C' for constant, 'L' for line number, or 'V' for variable. Member location contains the Simpletron memory location (00 to 99) to which the symbol refers. Simpletron memory is an array of 100 integers in which SML instructions and data are stored. For a line number, the location is the element in the Simpletron memory array at which the SML instructions for the Simple statement begin. For a variable or constant, the location is the element in the Simpletron memory array in which the variable or constant is stored. Variables and constants are allocated from the end of Simpletron's memory backwards. The first variable or constant is stored in location at 99, the next in location at 98, etc.

The symbol table plays an integral part in converting Simple programs to SML. We learned in Chapter 7 that an SML instruction is a four-digit integer that comprises two parts—the operation code and the operand. The operation code is determined by commands in Simple. For example, the simple command input corresponds to SML operation code 10 (read), and the Simple command print corresponds to SML operation code 11 (write). The operand is a memory location containing the data on which the operation code performs its task (e.g., operation code 10 reads a value from the keyboard and stores it in the memory location specified by the operand). The compiler searches symbolTable to determine the Simpletron memory location for each symbol so the corresponding location can be used to complete the SML instructions.

The compilation of each Simple statement is based on its command. For example, after the line number in a rem statement is inserted in the symbol table, the remainder of the statement is ignored by the compiler, because a remark is for documentation purposes only. The input, print, goto and end statements correspond to the SML *read*, *write*, *branch* (to a specific location) and *halt* instructions. Statements containing these Simple commands are converted directly to SML [*Note: A goto statement may contain an unresolved reference if the specified line number refers to a statement further into the Simple program file; this is sometimes called a forward reference.*]

When a goto statement is compiled with an unresolved reference, the SML instruction must be flagged to indicate that the second pass of the compiler must complete the instruction. The flags are stored in 100-element array flags of type int in which each element is initialized to -1. If the memory location to which a line number in the Simple program refers is not yet known (i.e., it is not in the symbol table), the line number is stored in array flags in the element with the same subscript as the incomplete instruction. The operand of the incomplete instruction is set to 00 temporarily. For example, an unconditional branch instruction (making a forward reference) is left as +4000 until the second pass of the compiler. The second pass of the compiler will be described shortly.

Compilation of if...goto and let statements is more complicated than other statements— they are the only statements that produce more than one SML instruction. For an if...goto statement, the compiler produces code to test the condition and to branch to another line if necessary. The result of the branch could be an unresolved reference. Each of the relational and equality operators can be simulated using SML's *branch zero* and *branch negative* instructions (or possibly a combination of both).

For a let statement, the compiler produces code to evaluate an arbitrarily complex arithmetic expression consisting of integer variables and/or constants. Expressions should separate each operand and operator with spaces. Exercise 12.12 and Exercise 12.13 presented the infix-to-postfix conversion algorithm and the postfix evaluation algorithm used by compilers to evaluate expressions. Before proceeding with your compiler, you should complete each of these exercises. When a compiler encounters an expression, it converts the expression from infix notation to postfix notation, then evaluates the postfix expression.

How is it that the compiler produces the machine language to evaluate an expression containing variables? The postfix evaluation algorithm contains a "hook" that allows our compiler to generate SML instructions rather than actually evaluating the expression. To enable this "hook" in the compiler, the postfix evaluation algorithm must be modified to search the symbol table for each symbol it encounters (and possibly insert it), determine the symbol's corresponding memory location, and *push the memory location on the stack instead of the symbol*. When an operator is encountered in the postfix expression, the two memory locations at the top of the stack are popped and machine language for effecting the operation is produced using the memory locations as operands. The result of each subexpression is stored in a temporary location in memory and pushed back onto the stack so the evaluation of the postfix expression can continue. When postfix evaluation is complete, the memory location containing the result is the only location left on the stack. This is popped and SML instructions are generated to assign the result to the variable at the left of the let statement.

Second Pass

The second pass of the compiler performs two tasks: resolve any unresolved references and output the SML code to a file. Resolution of references occurs as follows:

1) Search the flags array for an unresolved reference (i.e., an element with a value other than -1).

2) Locate the structure in array symbolTable containing the symbol stored in the flags array (be sure that the type of the symbol is 'L' for line number).

3) Insert the memory location from structure member location into the instruction with the unresolved reference (remember that an instruction containing an unresolved reference has operand 00).

4) Repeat *Steps 1–3* until the end of the flags array is reached.

After the resolution process is complete, the entire array containing the SML code is output to a disk file with one SML instruction per line. This file can be read by the Simpletron for execution (after the simulator is modified to read its input from a file).

A Complete Example

The following example illustrates a complete conversion of a Simple program to SML as it will be performed by the Simple compiler. Consider a Simple program that inputs an integer and sums the values from 1 to that integer. The program and the SML instructions produced by the first pass are illustrated in Fig. 12.28. The symbol table constructed by the first pass is shown in Fig. 12.29.

Simple program	SML location and instruction		Description
5 rem sum 1 to x		*none*	rem ignored
10 input x	00	+1099	read x into location 99
15 rem check y == x		*none*	rem ignored
20 if y == x goto 60	01	+2098	load y (98) into accumulator
	02	+3199	sub x (99) from accumulator
	03	+4200	branch zero to unresolved location
25 rem increment y		*none*	rem ignored
30 let y = y + 1	04	+2098	load y into accumulator
	05	+3097	add 1 (97) to accumulator
	06	+2196	store in temporary location 96
	07	+2096	load from temporary location 96
	08	+2198	store accumulator in y
35 rem add y to total		*none*	rem ignored
40 let t = t + y	09	+2095	load t (95) into accumulator
	10	+3098	add y to accumulator
	11	+2194	store in temporary location 94
	12	+2094	load from temporary location 94
	13	+2195	store accumulator in t
45 rem loop y		*none*	rem ignored
50 goto 20	14	+4001	branch to location 01
55 rem output result		*none*	rem ignored
60 print t	15	+1195	output t to screen
99 end	16	+4300	terminate execution

Fig. 12.28 | SML instructions produced after the compiler's first pass.

Symbol	Type	Location
5	L	00
10	L	00
'x'	V	99
15	L	01
20	L	01
'y'	V	98
25	L	04
30	L	04
1	C	97
35	L	09
40	L	09
't'	V	95
45	L	14
50	L	14
55	L	15
60	L	15
99	L	16

Fig. 12.29 | Symbol table for program of Fig. 12.28.

Most Simple statements convert directly to single SML instructions. The exceptions in this program are remarks, the if...goto statement in line 20, and the let statements. Remarks do not translate into machine language. However, the line number for a remark is placed in the symbol table in case the line number is referenced in a goto statement or an if...goto statement. Line 20 of the program specifies that if the condition y == x is true, program control is transferred to line 60. Because line 60 appears later in the program, the first pass of the compiler has not as yet placed 60 in the symbol table (line numbers are placed in the symbol table only when they appear as the first token in a statement). Therefore, it is not possible at this time to determine the operand of the SML branch zero instruction at location 03 in the array of SML instructions. The compiler places 60 in location 03 of the flags array to indicate that the second pass completes this instruction.

We must keep track of the next instruction location in the SML array because there is not a one-to-one correspondence between Simple statements and SML instructions. For example, the if...goto statement of line 20 compiles into three SML instructions. Each time an instruction is produced, we must increment the instruction counter to the next location in the SML array. Note that the size of Simpletron's memory could present a problem for Simple programs with many statements, variables and constants. It is conceivable that the compiler will run out of memory. To test for this case, your program should contain a data counter to keep track of the location at which the next variable or constant will be stored in the SML array. If the value of the instruction counter is larger than the value of the data counter, the SML array is full. In this case, the compilation process should terminate and the compiler should print an error message indicating that it ran out of memory during compilation.

Step-by-Step View of the Compilation Process

Let us now walk through the compilation process for the Simple program in Fig. 12.28. The compiler reads the first line of the program

```
5 rem sum 1 to x
```

into memory. The first token in the statement (the line number) is determined using strtok (see Chapter 8 for a discussion of C's string manipulation functions). The token returned by strtok is converted to an integer using atoi, so the symbol 5 can be located in the symbol table. If the symbol is not found, it is inserted in the symbol table. Since we are at the beginning of the program and this is the first line, no symbols are in the table yet. So, 5 is inserted into the symbol table as type L (line number) and assigned the first location in SML array (00). Although this line is a remark, a space in the symbol table is allocated for the line number (in case it is referenced by a goto or an if...goto). No SML instruction is generated for a rem statement, so the instruction counter is not incremented.

The statement

```
10 input x
```

is tokenized next. The line number 10 is placed in the symbol table as type L and assigned the first location in the SML array (00 because a remark began the program, so the instruction counter is currently 00). The command input indicates that the next token is a variable (only a variable can appear in an input statement). Because input corresponds directly to an SML operation code, the compiler simply has to determine the location of x in the SML array. Symbol x is not found in the symbol table. So, it is inserted into the symbol table as the ASCII representation of x, given type V, and assigned location 99 in the SML array (data storage begins at 99 and is allocated backwards). SML code can now be generated for this statement. Operation code 10 (the SML read operation code) is multiplied by 100, and the location of x (as determined in the symbol table) is added to complete the instruction. The instruction is then stored in the SML array at location 00. The instruction counter is incremented by 1 because a single SML instruction was produced.

The statement

```
15 rem   check y == x
```

is tokenized next. The symbol table is searched for line number 15 (which is not found). The line number is inserted as type L and assigned the next location in the array, 01 (remember that rem statements do not produce code, so the instruction counter is not incremented).

The statement

```
20 if y == x goto 60
```

is tokenized next. Line number 20 is inserted in the symbol table and given type L with the next location in the SML array 01. The command if indicates that a condition is to be evaluated. The variable y is not found in the symbol table, so it is inserted and given the type V and the SML location 98. Next, SML instructions are generated to evaluate the condition. Since there is no direct equivalent in SML for the if...goto, it must be simulated by performing a calculation using x and y and branching based on the result. If y is equal to x, the result of subtracting x from y is zero, so the *branch zero* instruction can be used with the result of the calculation to simulate the if...goto statement. The first step requires that y be loaded (from SML location 98) into the accumulator. This produces the instruction 01 +2098. Next, x is subtracted from the accumulator. This produces the instruction 02 +3199. The value in the accumulator may be zero, positive or negative. Since the operator is ==, we want to *branch zero*. First, the symbol table is searched for the branch location

(60 in this case), which is not found. So, 60 is placed in the flags array at location 03, and the instruction 03 +4200 is generated (we cannot add the branch location because we have not assigned a location to line 60 in the SML array yet). The instruction counter is incremented to 04.

The compiler proceeds to the statement

```
25 rem   increment y
```

The line number 25 is inserted in the symbol table as type L and assigned SML location 04. The instruction counter is not incremented.

When the statement

```
30 let y = y + 1
```

is tokenized, the line number 30 is inserted in the symbol table as type L and assigned SML location 04. Command let indicates that the line is an assignment statement. First, all the symbols on the line are inserted in the symbol table (if they are not already there). The integer 1 is added to the symbol table as type C and assigned SML location 97. Next, the right side of the assignment is converted from infix to postfix notation. Then the postfix expression (y 1 +) is evaluated. Symbol y is located in the symbol table and its corresponding memory location is pushed onto the stack. Symbol 1 is also located in the symbol table, and its corresponding memory location is pushed onto the stack. When the operator + is encountered, the postfix evaluator pops the stack into the right operand of the operator and pops the stack again into the left operand of the operator, then produces the SML instructions

```
04 +2098    (load y)
05 +3097    (add 1)
```

The result of the expression is stored in a temporary location in memory (96) with instruction

```
06 +2196    (store temporary)
```

and the temporary location is pushed on the stack. Now that the expression has been evaluated, the result must be stored in y (i.e., the variable on the left side of =). So, the temporary location is loaded into the accumulator and the accumulator is stored in y with the instructions

```
07 +2096    (load temporary)
08 +2198    (store y)
```

The reader will immediately notice that SML instructions appear to be redundant. We will discuss this issue shortly.

When the statement

```
35 rem   add y to total
```

is tokenized, line number 35 is inserted in the symbol table as type L and assigned location 09.

The statement

```
40 let t = t + y
```

is similar to line 30. The variable t is inserted in the symbol table as type V and assigned SML location 95. The instructions follow the same logic and format as line 30, and the instructions 09 +2095, 10 +3098, 11 +2194, 12 +2094, and 13 +2195 are generated. Note that the result of t + y is assigned to temporary location 94 before being assigned to t (95). Once again, the reader will note that the instructions in memory locations 11 and 12 appear to be redundant. Again, we will discuss this shortly.

The statement

```
45 rem   loop y
```

is a remark, so line 45 is added to the symbol table as type L and assigned SML location 14.

The statement

```
50 goto 20
```

transfers control to line 20. Line number 50 is inserted in the symbol table as type L and assigned SML location 14. The equivalent of goto in SML is the *unconditional branch* (40) instruction that transfers control to a specific SML location. The compiler searches the symbol table for line 20 and finds that it corresponds to SML location 01. The operation code (40) is multiplied by 100 and location 01 is added to it to produce the instruction 14 +4001.

The statement

```
55 rem   output result
```

is a remark, so line 55 is inserted in the symbol table as type L and assigned SML location 15.

The statement

```
60 print t
```

is an output statement. Line number 60 is inserted in the symbol table as type L and assigned SML location 15. The equivalent of print in SML is operation code 11 (*write*). The location of t is determined from the symbol table and added to the result of the operation code multiplied by 100.

The statement

```
99 end
```

is the final line of the program. Line number 99 is stored in the symbol table as type L and assigned SML location 16. The end command produces the SML instruction +4300 (43 is *halt* in SML) which is written as the final instruction in the SML memory array.

This completes the first pass of the compiler. We now consider the second pass. The flags array is searched for values other than -1. Location 03 contains 60, so the compiler knows that instruction 03 is incomplete. The compiler completes the instruction by searching the symbol table for 60, determining its location and adding the location to the incomplete instruction. In this case, the search determines that line 60 corresponds to SML location 15, so the completed instruction 03 +4215 is produced replacing 03 +4200. The Simple program has now been compiled successfully.

To build the compiler, you will have to perform each of the following tasks:

a) Modify the Simpletron simulator program you wrote in Exercise 7.19 to take its input from a file specified by the user (see Chapter 11). Also, the simulator should output its results to a disk file in the same format as the screen output.

b) Modify the infix-to-postfix evaluation algorithm of Exercise 12.12 to process multi-digit integer operands and single-letter variable-name operands. [*Hint:* Standard library function strtok can be used to locate each constant and variable in an expression, and constants can be converted from strings to integers using standard library function atoi.] [*Note:* The data representation of the postfix expression must be altered to support variable names and integer constants.]

c) Modify the postfix evaluation algorithm to process multi-digit integer operands and variable name operands. Also, the algorithm should now implement the previously discussed "hook" so that SML instructions are produced rather than directly evaluating the expression. [*Hint:* Standard library function strtok can be used to locate each constant and variable in an expression, and constants can be converted from strings to integers using standard library function atoi.] [*Note:* The data representation of the postfix expression must be altered to support variable names and integer constants.]

d) Build the compiler. Incorporate parts (b) and (c) for evaluating expressions in let statements. Your program should contain a function that performs the first pass of the compiler and a function that performs the second pass of the compiler. Both functions can call other functions to accomplish their tasks.

12.29 (*Optimizing the Simple Compiler*) When a program is compiled and converted into SML, a set of instructions is generated. Certain combinations of instructions often repeat themselves, usually in triplets called productions. A production normally consists of three instructions such as *load*, *add* and *store*. For example, Fig. 12.30 illustrates five of the SML instructions that were produced in the compilation of the program in Fig. 12.28. The first three instructions are the production that adds 1 to y. Note that instructions 06 and 07 store the accumulator value in temporary location 96, then load the value back into the accumulator so instruction 08 can store the value in location 98. Often a production is followed by a load instruction for the same location that was just stored. This code can be optimized by eliminating the store instruction and the subsequent load instruction that operate on the same memory location. This optimization would enable the Simpletron to execute the program faster because there are fewer instructions in this version. Figure 12.31 illustrates the optimized SML for the program of Fig. 12.28. Note that there are four fewer instructions in the optimized code—a memory-space savings of 25%.

Modify the compiler to provide an option for optimizing the Simpletron Machine Language code it produces. Manually compare the non-optimized code with the optimized code, and calculate the percentage reduction.

```
04  +2098        (load)
05  +3097        (add)
06  +2196        (store)
07  +2096        (load)
08  +2198        (store)
```

Fig. 12.30 | Unoptimized code from the program of Fig. 12.28.

Simple program	SML location and instruction	Description
5 rem sum 1 to x	*none*	rem ignored
10 input x	00 +1099	read x into location 99
15 rem check y == x	*none*	rem ignored
20 if y == x goto 60	01 +2098	load y (98) into accumulator
	02 +3199	sub x (99) from accumulator
	03 +4211	branch to location 11 if zero
25 rem increment y	*none*	rem ignored
30 let y = y + 1	04 +2098	load y into accumulator
	05 +3097	add 1 (97) to accumulator
	06 +2198	store accumulator in y (98)
35 rem add y to total	*none*	rem ignored

Fig. 12.31 | Optimized code for the program of Fig. 12.28. (Part 1 of 2.)

Simple program	SML location and instruction		Description
40 let t = t + y	07	+2096	load t from location (96)
	08	+3098	add y (98) accumulator
	09	+2196	store accumulator in t (96)
45 rem loop y	*none*		rem ignored
50 goto 20	10	+4001	branch to location 01
55 rem output result	*none*		rem ignored
60 print t	11	+1196	output t (96) to screen
99 end	12	+4300	terminate execution

Fig. 12.31 | Optimized code for the program of Fig. 12.28. (Part 2 of 2.)

12.30 (*Modifications to the Simple Compiler*) Perform the following modifications to the Simple compiler. Some of these modifications may also require modifications to the Simpletron Simulator program written in Exercise 7.19.

a) Allow the modulus operator (%) to be used in let statements. Simpletron Machine Language must be modified to include a modulus instruction.

b) Allow exponentiation in a let statement using ∧ as the exponentiation operator. Simpletron Machine Language must be modified to include an exponentiation instruction.

c) Allow the compiler to recognize uppercase and lowercase letters in Simple statements (e.g., 'A' is equivalent to 'a'). No modifications to the Simpletron Simulator are required.

d) Allow input statements to read values for multiple variables such as input x, y. No modifications to the Simpletron Simulator are required.

e) Allow the compiler to output multiple values in a single print statement such as print a, b, c. No modifications to the Simpletron Simulator are required.

f) Add syntax checking capabilities to the compiler so error messages are output when syntax errors are encountered in a Simple program. No modifications to the Simpletron Simulator are required.

g) Allow arrays of integers. No modifications to the Simpletron Simulator are required.

h) Allow subroutines specified by the Simple commands gosub and return. Command gosub passes program control to a subroutine and command return passes control back to the statement after the gosub. This is similar to a function call in C. The same subroutine can be called from many gosubs distributed throughout a program. No modifications to the Simpletron Simulator are required.

i) Allow repetition structures of the form

```
for x = 2 to 10 step 2
    rem Simple statements
next
```

j) This for statement loops from 2 to 10 with an increment of 2. The next line marks the end of the body of the for line. No modifications to the Simpletron Simulator are required.

k) Allow repetition structures of the form

```
for x = 2 to 10
    rem Simple statements
next
```

l) This for statement loops from 2 to 10 with a default increment of 1. No modifications to the Simpletron Simulator are required.

m) Allow the compiler to process string input and output. This requires the Simpletron Simulator to be modified to process and store string values. [*Hint:* Each Simpletron word can be divided into two groups, each holding a two-digit integer. Each two-digit integer represents the ASCII decimal equivalent of a character.] Add a machine language instruction that will print a string beginning at a certain Simpletron memory location. The first half of the word at that location is a count of the number of characters in the string (i.e., the length of the string). Each succeeding half word contains one ASCII character expressed as two decimal digits. The machine language instruction checks the length and prints the string by translating each two-digit number into its equivalent character.

n) Allow the compiler to process floating-point values in addition to integers. The Simpletron Simulator must also be modified to process floating-point values.

12.31 (*A Simple Interpreter*) An interpreter is a program that reads a high-level language program statement, determines the operation to be performed by the statement, and executes the operation immediately. The program is not converted into machine language first. Interpreters execute slowly because each statement encountered in the program must first be deciphered. If statements are contained in a loop, the statements are deciphered each time they are encountered in the loop. Early versions of the BASIC programming language were implemented as interpreters.

Write an interpreter for the Simple language discussed in Exercise 12.27. The program should use the infix-to-postfix converter developed in Exercise 12.12 and the postfix evaluator developed in Exercise 12.13 to evaluate expressions in a let statement. The same restrictions placed on the Simple language in Exercise 12.27 should be adhered to in this program. Test the interpreter with the Simple programs written in Exercise 12.27. Compare the results of running these programs in the interpreter with the results of compiling the Simple programs and running them in the Simpletron simulator built in Exercise 7.19.

C Preprocessor

Hold thou the good; define it well.
—Alfred, Lord Tennyson

I have found you an argument; but I am not obliged to find you an understanding.
—Samuel Johnson

A good symbol is the best argument, and is a missionary to persuade thousands.
—Ralph Waldo Emerson

Conditions are fundamentally sound.
—Herbert Hoover [December 1929]

The partisan, when he is engaged in a dispute, cares nothing about the rights of the question, but is anxious only to convince his hearers of his own assertions.
—Plato

OBJECTIVES

In this chapter, you will learn:

■ To use #include for developing large programs.

■ To use #define to create macros and macros with arguments.

■ To use conditional compilation to specify portions of a program that should not always be compiled (such as code that assists you in debugging).

■ To display error messages during conditional compilation.

■ To use assertions to test if the values of expressions are correct.

13.1 Introduction

This chapter describes the C preprocessor. Preprocessing occurs before a program is compiled. Some possible actions are the inclusion of other files in the file being compiled, definition of symbolic constants and macros, conditional compilation of program code and conditional execution of preprocessor directives. All preprocessor directives begin with # and only whitespace characters and comments may appear before a preprocessor directive on a line.

13.2 `#include` Preprocessor Directive

The `#include` preprocessor directive has been used throughout this text. The `#include` directive causes a copy of a specified file to be included in place of the directive. The two forms of the `#include` directive are:

```
#include <filename>
#include "filename"
```

The difference between these is the location the preprocessor begins searches for the file to be included. If the file name is enclosed in quotes, the preprocessor starts searches in the same directory as the file being compiled for the file to be included (and may search other locations as well). This method is normally used to include programmer-defined headers. If the file name is enclosed in angle brackets (< and >)—used for standard library headers—the search is performed in an implementation-dependent manner, normally through predesignated compiler and system directories.

The `#include` directive is used to include standard library headers such as `stdio.h` and `stdlib.h` (see Fig. 5.6). The `#include` directive is also used with programs consisting of several source files that are to be compiled together. A header containing declarations common to the separate program files is often created and included in the file. Examples of such declarations are structure and union declarations, enumerations and function prototypes.

13.3 #define Preprocessor Directive: Symbolic Constants

The #define directive creates symbolic constants—constants represented as symbols—and macros—operations defined as symbols. The #define directive format is

> #define   *identifier   replacement-text*

When this line appears in a file, all subsequent occurrences of identifier that do not appear in string literals will be replaced by replacement-text automatically before the program is compiled. For example,

> #define PI 3.14159

replaces all subsequent occurrences of the symbolic constant PI with the numeric constant 3.14159. Symbolic constants enable you to create a name for a constant and use the name throughout the program. If the constant needs to be modified throughout the program, it can be modified once in the #define directive. When the program is recompiled, all occurrences of the constant in the program will be modified accordingly. [*Note:* Everything to the right of the symbolic constant name replaces the symbolic constant.] For example, #define PI = 3.14159 causes the preprocessor to replace every occurrence of the identifier PI with = 3.14159. This is the cause of many subtle logic and syntax errors. Redefining a symbolic constant with a new value is also an error.

Good Programming Practice 13.1

Using meaningful names for symbolic constants helps make programs more self-documenting.

Good Programming Practice 13.2

By convention, symbolic constants are defined using only uppercase letters and underscores.

13.4 #define Preprocessor Directive: Macros

A macro is an identifier defined in a #define preprocessor directive. As with symbolic constants, the macro-identifier is replaced in the program with the replacement-text before the program is compiled. Macros may be defined with or without arguments. A macro without arguments is processed like a symbolic constant. In a macro with arguments, the arguments are substituted in the replacement text, then the macro is expanded—i.e., the replacement-text replaces the identifier and argument list in the program. [*Note:* A symbolic constant is a type of macro.]

Consider the following macro definition with one argument for the area of a circle:

> #define CIRCLE_AREA(x) ((PI) * (x) * (x))

Wherever CIRCLE_AREA(y) appears in the file, the value of y is substituted for x in the replacement-text, the symbolic constant PI is replaced by its value (defined previously) and the macro is expanded in the program. For example, the statement

> area = CIRCLE_AREA(4);

is expanded to

> area = ((3.14159) * (4) * (4));

and the value of the expression is evaluated and assigned to variable area. The parentheses around each x in the replacement text force the proper order of evaluation when the macro argument is an expression. For example, the statement

```
area = CIRCLE_AREA( c + 2 );
```

is expanded to

```
area = ( ( 3.14159 ) * ( c + 2 ) * ( c + 2 ) );
```

which evaluates correctly because the parentheses force the proper order of evaluation. If the parentheses are omitted, the macro expansion is

```
area = 3.14159 * c + 2 * c + 2;
```

which evaluates incorrectly as

```
area = ( 3.14159 * c ) + ( 2 * c ) + 2;
```

because of the rules of operator precedence.

Common Programming Error 13.1

Forgetting to enclose macro arguments in parentheses in the replacement text can lead to logic errors.

Macro CIRCLE_AREA could be defined as a function. Function circleArea

```
double circleArea( double x )
{
    return 3.14159 * x * x;
}
```

performs the same calculation as macro CIRCLE_AREA, but the overhead of a function call is associated with function circleArea. The advantages of macro CIRCLE_AREA are that macros insert code directly in the program—avoiding function call overhead—and the program remains readable because the CIRCLE_AREA calculation is defined separately and named meaningfully. A disadvantage is that its argument is evaluated twice.

Performance Tip 13.1

Macros can sometimes be used to replace a function call with inline code prior to execution time. This eliminates the overhead of a function call. Today's optimizing compilers will often inline functions for you, so many programmers no longer use macros for this purpose.

The following is a macro definition with two arguments for the area of a rectangle:

```
#define RECTANGLE_AREA( x, y )  ( ( x ) * ( y ) )
```

Wherever RECTANGLE_AREA(x, y) appears in the program, the values of x and y are substituted in the macro replacement text and the macro is expanded in place of the macro name. For example, the statement

```
rectArea = RECTANGLE_AREA( a + 4, b + 7 );
```

is expanded to

```
rectArea = ( ( a + 4 ) * ( b + 7 ) );
```

The value of the expression is evaluated and assigned to variable rectArea.

The replacement text for a macro or symbolic constant is normally any text on the line after the identifier in the #define directive. If the replacement text for a macro or symbolic constant is longer than the remainder of the line, a backslash (\) must be placed at the end of the line, indicating that the replacement text continues on the next line.

Symbolic constants and macros can be discarded by using the **#undef** preprocessor directive. Directive #undef "undefines" a symbolic constant or macro name. The scope of a symbolic constant or macro is from its definition until it is undefined with #undef, or until the end of the file. Once undefined, a name can be redefined with #define.

Functions in the standard library sometimes are defined as macros based on other library functions. A macro commonly defined in the stdio.h header is

```
#define getchar() getc( stdin )
```

The macro definition of getchar uses function getc to get one character from the standard input stream. Function putchar of the stdio.h header and the character handling functions of the ctype.h header often are implemented as macros as well. Note that expressions with side effects (i.e., variable values are modified) should not be passed to a macro because macro arguments may be evaluated more than once.

13.5 Conditional Compilation

Conditional compilation enables you to control the execution of preprocessor directives and the compilation of program code. Each of the conditional preprocessor directives evaluates a constant integer expression. Cast expressions, sizeof expressions and enumeration constants cannot be evaluated in preprocessor directives.

The conditional preprocessor construct is much like the if selection statement. Consider the following preprocessor code:

```
#if !defined(MY_CONSTANT)
    #define MY_CONSTANT 0
#endif
```

These directives determine if MY_CONSTANT is defined. The expression defined(MY_CONSTANT) evaluates to 1 if MY_CONSTANT is defined; 0 otherwise. If the result is 0, !defined(MY_CONSTANT) evaluates to 1 and MY_CONSTANT is defined. Otherwise, the #define directive is skipped. Every #if construct ends with **#endif**. Directives **#ifdef** and **#ifndef** are shorthand for #if defined(*name*) and #if !defined(*name*). A multiple-part conditional preprocessor construct may be tested by using the **#elif** (the equivalent of else if in an if statement) and the **#else** (the equivalent of else in an if statement) directives.

During program development, it is often helpful to "comment out" portions of code to prevent it from being compiled. If the code contains comments, /* and */ cannot be used to accomplish this task. Instead, you can use the following preprocessor construct:

```
#if 0
    code prevented from compiling
#endif
```

To enable the code to be compiled, replace the 0 in the preceding construct with 1.

Conditional compilation is commonly used as a debugging aid. Many C implementations provide **debuggers**, which provide much more powerful features than conditional compilation. If a debugger is not available, `printf` statements are often used to print variable values and to confirm the flow of control. These `printf` statements can be enclosed in conditional preprocessor directives so the statements are only compiled while the debugging process is not completed. For example,

```
#ifdef DEBUG
    printf( "Variable x = %d\n", x );
#endif
```

causes a `printf` statement to be compiled in the program if the symbolic constant `DEBUG` has been defined (`#define DEBUG`) before directive `#ifdef DEBUG`. When debugging is completed, the `#define` directive is removed from the source file and the `printf` statements inserted for debugging purposes are ignored during compilation. In larger programs, it may be desirable to define several different symbolic constants that control the conditional compilation in separate sections of the source file.

 Common Programming Error 13.2

Inserting conditionally compiled `printf` statements for debugging purposes in locations where C currently expects a single statement. In this case, the conditionally compiled statement should be enclosed in a compound statement. Thus, when the program is compiled with debugging statements, the flow of control of the program is not altered.

13.6 #error and #pragma Preprocessor Directives

The **#error** directive

#error *tokens*

prints an implementation-dependent message including the *tokens* specified in the directive. The tokens are sequences of characters separated by spaces. For example,

`#error 1 - Out of range error`

contains 6 tokens. When a `#error` directive is processed on some systems, the tokens in the directive are displayed as an error message, preprocessing stops and the program does not compile.

The **#pragma** directive

#pragma *tokens*

causes an implementation-defined action. A pragma not recognized by the implementation is ignored. For more information on `#error` and `#pragma`, see the documentation for your C implementation.

13.7 # and ## Operators

The # and ## preprocessor operators are available in Standard C. The # operator causes a replacement text token to be converted to a string surrounded by quotes. Consider the following macro definition:

`#define HELLO(x) printf( "Hello, " #x "\n" );`

When `HELLO(John)` appears in a program file, it is expanded to

```
printf( "Hello, " "John" "\n" );
```

The string "John" replaces #x in the replacement text. Strings separated by white space are concatenated during preprocessing, so the preceding statement is equivalent to

```
printf( "Hello, John\n" );
```

Note that the # operator must be used in a macro with arguments because the operand of # refers to an argument of the macro.

The ## operator concatenates two tokens. Consider the following macro definition:

```
#define TOKENCONCAT(x, y)   x ## y
```

When TOKENCONCAT appears in the program, its arguments are concatenated and used to replace the macro. For example, TOKENCONCAT(O, K) is replaced by OK in the program. The ## operator must have two operands.

13.8 Line Numbers

The #line preprocessor directive causes the subsequent source code lines to be renumbered starting with the specified constant integer value. The directive

```
#line 100
```

starts line numbering from 100 beginning with the next source code line. A file name can be included in the #line directive. The directive

```
#line 100 "file1.c"
```

indicates that lines are numbered from 100 beginning with the next source code line and that the name of the file for the purpose of any compiler messages is "file1.c". The directive normally is used to help make the messages produced by syntax errors and compiler warnings more meaningful. The line numbers do not appear in the source file.

13.9 Predefined Symbolic Constants

Standard C provides **predefined symbolic constants**, several of which are shown in Fig. 13.1. The identifiers for each of the predefined symbolic constants begin and end with *two* underscores. These identifiers and the defined identifier (used in Section 13.5) cannot be used in #define or #undef directives.

Symbolic constant	Explanation
__LINE__	The line number of the current source code line (an integer constant).
__FILE__	The presumed name of the source file (a string).
__DATE__	The date the source file was compiled (a string of the form "Mmm dd yyyy" such as "Jan 19 2002").

Fig. 13.1 | Some predefined symbolic constants. (Part 1 of 2.)

Symbolic constant	Explanation
__TIME__	The time the source file was compiled (a string literal of the form `"hh:mm:ss"`).
__STDC__	The value 1 if the compiler supports Standard C.

Fig. 13.1 | Some predefined symbolic constants. (Part 2 of 2.)

13.10 Assertions

The **assert** macro—defined in the `<assert.h>` header—tests the value of an expression. If the value of the expression is false (0), **assert** prints an error message and calls function **abort** (of the general utilities library—`<stdlib.h>`) to terminate program execution. This is a useful debugging tool for testing if a variable has a correct value. For example, suppose variable x should never be larger than 10 in a program. An assertion may be used to test the value of x and print an error message if the value of x is incorrect. The statement would be

```
assert( x <= 10 );
```

If x is greater than 10 when the preceding statement is encountered in a program, an error message containing the line number and file name is printed and the program terminates. You may then concentrate on this area of the code to find the error. If the symbolic constant NDEBUG is defined, subsequent assertions will be ignored. Thus, when assertions are no longer needed, the line

```
#define NDEBUG
```

is inserted in the program file rather than deleting each assertion manually.

Software Engineering Observation 13.1

Assertions are not meant as a substitute for error handling during normal runtime conditions. Their use should be limited to finding logic errors.

Summary

Section 13.1 Introduction
- Preprocessing occurs before a program is compiled. Some possible actions are the inclusion of other files in the file being compiled, definition of symbolic constants and macros, conditional compilation of program code and conditional execution of preprocessor directives.
- All preprocessor directives begin with #.

Section 13.2 #include Preprocessor Directive
- Only whitespace characters and comments may appear before a preprocessor directive on a line.
- The #include directive includes a copy of the specified file. If the file name is enclosed in quotes, the preprocessor begins searching in the same directory as the file being compiled for the file to be included. If the file name is enclosed in angle brackets (< and >), the search is performed in an implementation-defined manner.

Section 13.3 #define Preprocessor Directive: Symbolic Constants

- The #define preprocessor directive is used to create symbolic constants and macros.

- A symbolic constant is a name for a constant.

- A macro is an operation defined in a #define preprocessor directive. Macros may be defined with or without arguments.

- The replacement text for a macro or symbolic constant is any text remaining on the line after the identifier in the #define directive. If the replacement text for a macro or symbolic constant is longer than the remainder of the line, a backslash (\) is placed at the end of the line indicating that the replacement text continues on the next line.

Section 13.4 #define Preprocessor Directive: Macros

- Symbolic constants and macros can be discarded by using the #undef preprocessor directive. Directive #undef "undefines" the symbolic constant or macro name.

- The scope of a symbolic constant or macro is from its definition until it is undefined with #undef or until the end of the file.

Section 13.5 Conditional Compilation

- Conditional compilation enables you to control the execution of preprocessor directives and the compilation of program code.

- The conditional preprocessor directives evaluate constant integer expressions. Cast expressions, sizeof expressions and enumeration constants cannot be evaluated in preprocessor directives.

- Every #if construct ends with #endif.

- Directives #ifdef and #ifndef are provided as shorthand for #if defined(*name*) and #if !defined(*name*).

- Multiple-part conditional preprocessor constructs may be tested with directives #elif and #else.

Section 13.6 #error and #pragma Preprocessor Directives

- The #error directive prints an implementation-dependent message that includes the tokens specified in the directive.

- The #pragma directive causes an implementation-defined action. If the pragma is not recognized by the implementation, the pragma is ignored.

Section 13.7 # and ## Operators

- The # operator causes a replacement text token to be converted to a string surrounded by quotes. The # operator must be used in a macro with arguments, because the operand of # must be an argument of the macro.

- The ## operator concatenates two tokens. The ## operator must have two operands.

Section 13.8 Line Numbers

- The #line preprocessor directive causes the subsequent source code lines to be renumbered starting with the specified constant integer value.

Section 13.9 Predefined Symbolic Constants

- Constant __LINE__ is the line number (an integer) of the current source code line. Constant __FILE__ is the presumed name of the file (a string). Constant __DATE__ is the date the source file is compiled (a string). Constant __TIME__ is the time the source file is compiled (a string). Constant __STDC__ indicates whether the compiler supports Standard C. Note that each of the predefined symbolic constants begins and ends with two underbars.

Section 13.10 Assertions
- Macro assert—defined in the `<assert.h>` header—tests the value of an expression. If the value of the expression is 0 (false), assert prints an error message and calls function abort to terminate program execution.

Terminology

\ (backslash) continuation character	`#ifdef`
abort	`#ifndef`
argument	`#include <filename>`
assert	`#include "filename"`
assert.h	`#line`
C preprocessor	`__LINE__`
concatenation preprocessor operator ##	macro
conditional compilation	macro with arguments
conditional execution of preprocessor directives	`#pragma`
convert-to-string preprocessor operator #	predefined symbolic constants
`__DATE__`	preprocessing directive
debugger	replacement text
`#define`	scope of a symbolic constant or macro
`#elif`	standard library headers
`#else`	`__STDC__`
`#endif`	stdio.h
`#error`	stdlib.h
expand a macro	symbolic constant
`__FILE__`	`__TIME__`
`#if`	`#undef`

Self-Review Exercises

13.1 Fill in the blanks in each of the following:
- a) Every preprocessor directive must begin with _____.
- b) The conditional compilation construct may be extended to test for multiple cases by using the _____ and the _____ directives.
- c) The _____ directive creates macros and symbolic constants.
- d) Only _____ characters may appear before a preprocessor directive on a line.
- e) The _____ directive discards symbolic constant and macro names.
- f) The _____ and _____ directives are provided as shorthand notation for `#if defined(name)` and `#if !defined(name)`.
- g) _____ enables you to control the execution of preprocessor directives and the compilation of program code.
- h) The _____ macro prints a message and terminates program execution if the value of the expression the macro evaluates is 0.
- i) The _____ directive inserts a file in another file.
- j) The _____ operator concatenates its two arguments.
- k) The _____ operator converts its operand to a string.
- l) The character _____ indicates that the replacement text for a symbolic constant or macro continues on the next line.
- m) The _____ directive causes the source code lines to be numbered from the indicated value beginning with the next source code line.

13.2 Write a program to print the values of the predefined symbolic constants listed in Fig. 13.1.

13.3   Write a preprocessor directive to accomplish each of the following:
   a) Define symbolic constant YES to have the value 1.
   b) Define symbolic constant NO to have the value 0.
   c) Include the header common.h. The header is found in the same directory as the file being compiled.
   d) Renumber the remaining lines in the file beginning with line number 3000.
   e) If symbolic constant TRUE is defined, undefine it and redefine it as 1. Do not use #ifdef.
   f) If symbolic constant TRUE is defined, undefine it and redefine it as 1. Use the #ifdef preprocessor directive.
   g) If symbolic constant TRUE is not equal to 0, define symbolic constant FALSE as 0. Otherwise define FALSE as 1.
   h) Define macro CUBE_VOLUME that computes the volume of a cube. The macro takes one argument.

Answers to Self-Review Exercises

13.1   a) #. b) #elif, #else. c) #define. d) whitespace. e) #undef. f) #ifdef, #ifndef. g) Conditional compilation. h) assert. i) #include. j) ##. k) #. l) \. m) #line.

13.2   See below.

```
 1   /* Print the values of the predefined macros */
 2   #include <stdio.h>
 3   int main( void )
 4   {
 5      printf( "__LINE__ = %d\n", __LINE__ );
 6      printf( "__FILE__ = %s\n", __FILE__ );
 7      printf( "__DATE__ = %s\n", __DATE__ );
 8      printf( "__TIME__ = %s\n", __TIME__ );
 9      printf( "__STDC__ = %s\n", __STDC__ );
10      return 0;
11   }
```

```
__LINE__ = 5
__FILE__ = macros.c
__DATE__ = Jun  5 2003
__TIME__ = 09:38:58
__STDC__ = 1
```

13.3   a) #define YES 1
   b) #define NO 0
   c) #include "common.h"
   d) #line 3000
   e) #if defined(TRUE)
         #undef TRUE
         #define TRUE 1
      #endif
   f) #ifdef TRUE
         #undef TRUE
         #define TRUE 1
      #endif

g) ```
#if TRUE
   #define FALSE 0
#else
   #define FALSE 1
#endif
```
h) `#define CUBE_VOLUME( x )  ( ( x ) * ( x ) * ( x ) )`

## Exercises

**13.4** Write a program that defines a macro with one argument to compute the volume of a sphere. The program should compute the volume for spheres of radius 1 to 10 and print the results in tabular format. The formula for the volume of a sphere is

$$( 4.0 / 3 ) * \pi * r^3$$

where $\pi$ is 3.14159.

**13.5** Write a program that produces the following output:

```
The sum of x and y is 13
```

The program should define macro SUM with two arguments, x and y, and use SUM to produce the output.

13.6 Write a program that defines and uses macro MINIMUM2 to determine the smallest of two numeric values. Input the values from the keyboard.

13.7 Write a program that defines and uses macro MINIMUM3 to determine the smallest of three numeric values. Macro MINIMUM3 should use macro MINIMUM2 defined in Exercise 13.6 to determine the smallest number. Input the values from the keyboard.

13.8 Write a program that defines and uses macro PRINT to print a string value.

13.9 Write a program that defines and uses macro PRINTARRAY to print an array of integers. The macro should receive the array and the number of elements in the array as arguments.

13.10 Write a program that defines and uses macro SUMARRAY to sum the values in a numeric array. The macro should receive the array and the number of elements in the array as arguments.
```

We'll use a signal I have tried and found far-reaching and easy to yell. Waa-hoo!
—Zane Grey

It is quite a three-pipe problem.
—Sir Arthur Conan Doyle

14

Other C Topics

OBJECTIVES

In this chapter, you will learn:

- To redirect keyboard input to come from a file.
- To redirect screen output to be placed in a file.
- To write functions that use variable-length argument lists.
- To process command-line arguments.
- To assign specific types to numeric constants.
- To use temporary files.
- To process external asynchronous events in a program.
- To allocate memory dynamically for arrays.
- To change the size of memory that was dynamically allocated previously.

14.1 Introduction

This chapter presents several additional topics not ordinarily covered in introductory courses. Many of the capabilities discussed here are specific to particular operating systems, especially Linux/UNIX and Windows.

14.2 Redirecting Input/Output on Linux/UNIX and Windows Systems

Normally the input to a program is from the keyboard (standard input), and the output from a program is displayed on the screen (standard output). On most computer systems—Linux/UNIX and Windows systems in particular—it is possible to redirect inputs to come from a file rather than the keyboard and redirect outputs to be placed in a file rather than on the screen. Both forms of redirection can be accomplished without using the file processing capabilities of the standard library.

There are several ways to redirect input and output from the command line. Consider the executable file sum (on Linux/UNIX systems) that inputs integers one at a time and keeps a running total of the values until the end-of-file indicator is set, then prints the result. Normally the user inputs integers from the keyboard and enters the end-of-file key combination to indicate that no further values will be input. With input redirection, the input can be stored in a file. For example, if the data is stored in file input, the command line

```
$ sum < input
```

executes the program sum; the redirect input symbol (<) indicates that the data in file input is to be used as input by the program. Redirecting input on a Windows system is performed identically.

Note that $ is a typical Linux/UNIX command line prompt (some systems use a % prompt or other symbol). Students often find it difficult to understand that redirection is an operating system function, not another C feature.

The second method of redirecting input is piping. A pipe (|) causes the output of one program to be redirected as the input to another program. Suppose program `random` outputs a series of random integers; the output of `random` can be "piped" directly to program `sum` using the command line

```
$ random | sum
```

This causes the sum of the integers produced by `random` to be calculated. Piping is performed identically in Linux/UNIX and Windows.

Program output can be redirected to a file by using the redirect output symbol (>). For example, to redirect the output of program `random` to file `out`, use

```
$ random > out
```

Finally, program output can be appended to the end of an existing file by using the append output symbol (>>). For example, to append the output from program `random` to file `out` created in the preceding command line, use the command line

```
$ random >> out
```

14.3 Variable-Length Argument Lists

It is possible to create functions that receive an unspecified number of arguments. Most programs in the text have used the standard library function `printf` which, as you know, takes a variable number of arguments. As a minimum, `printf` must receive a string as its first argument, but `printf` can receive any number of additional arguments. The function prototype for `printf` is

```
int printf( const char *format, ... );
```

The ellipsis (…) in the function prototype indicates that the function receives a variable number of arguments of any type. Note that the ellipsis must always be placed at the end of the parameter list.

The macros and definitions of the variable arguments headers `<stdarg.h>` (Fig. 14.1) provide the capabilities necessary to build functions with variable-length argument lists. Figure 14.2 demonstrates function `average` (line 28) that receives a variable number of arguments. The first argument of `average` is always the number of values to be averaged.

Identifier	Explanation
va_list	A type suitable for holding information needed by macros va_start, va_arg and va_end. To access the arguments in a variable-length argument list, an object of type va_list must be defined.
va_start	A macro that is invoked before the arguments of a variable-length argument list can be accessed. The macro initializes the object declared with va_list for use by the va_arg and va_end macros.

Fig. 14.1 | `stdarg.h` variable-length argument list type and macros. (Part 1 of 2.)

Identifier	Explanation
va_arg	A macro that expands to an expression of the value and type of the next argument in the variable-length argument list. Each invocation of va_arg modifies the object declared with va_list so that the object points to the next argument in the list.
va_end	A macro that facilitates a normal return from a function whose variable-length argument list was referred to by the va_start macro.

Fig. 14.1 | `stdarg.h` variable-length argument list type and macros. (Part 2 of 2.)

```c
/* Fig. 14.2: fig14_02.c
   Using variable-length argument lists */
#include <stdio.h>
#include <stdarg.h>

double average( int i, ... ); /* prototype */

int main( void )
{
   double w = 37.5;
   double x = 22.5;
   double y = 1.7;
   double z = 10.2;

   printf( "%s%.1f\n%s%.1f\n%s%.1f\n%s%.1f\n\n",
      "w = ", w, "x = ", x, "y = ", y, "z = ", z );
   printf( "%s%.3f\n%s%.3f\n%s%.3f\n",
      "The average of w and x is ", average( 2, w, x ),
      "The average of w, x, and y is ", average( 3, w, x, y ),
      "The average of w, x, y, and z is ",
      average( 4, w, x, y, z ) );

   return 0; /* indicates successful termination */

} /* end main */

/* calculate average */
double average( int i, ... )
{
   double total = 0; /* initialize total */
   int j; /* counter for selecting arguments */
   va_list ap; /* stores information needed by va_start and va_end */

   va_start( ap, i ); /* initializes the va_list object */

   /* process variable length argument list */
   for ( j = 1; j <= i; j++ ) {
      total += va_arg( ap, double );
   } /* end for */
```

Fig. 14.2 | Using variable-length argument lists. (Part 1 of 2.)

```
40
41      va_end( ap ); /* clean up variable-length argument list */
42
43      return total / i; /* calculate average */
44   } /* end function average */
```

```
w = 37.5
x = 22.5
y = 1.7
z = 10.2

The average of w and x is 30.000
The average of w, x, and y is 20.567
The average of w, x, y, and z is 17.975
```

Fig. 14.2 | Using variable-length argument lists. (Part 2 of 2.)

Function average (lines 28–44) uses all the definitions and macros of header <stdarg.h>. Object ap, of type va_list (line 32), is used by macros va_start, va_arg and va_end to process the variable-length argument list of function average. The function begins by invoking macro va_start (line 34) to initialize object ap for use in va_arg and va_end. The macro receives two arguments—object ap and the identifier of the rightmost argument in the argument list before the ellipsis—i in this case (va_start uses i here to determine where the variable-length argument list begins). Next function average repeatedly adds the arguments in the variable-length argument list to variable total (lines 37–39). The value to be added to total is retrieved from the argument list by invoking macro va_arg. Macro va_arg receives two arguments—object ap and the type of the value expected in the argument list—double in this case. The macro returns the value of the argument. Function average invokes macro va_end (line 41) with object ap as an argument to facilitate a normal return to main from average. Finally, the average is calculated and returned to main.

Common Programming Error 14.1

Placing an ellipsis in the middle of a function parameter list is a syntax error. An ellipsis may only be placed at the end of the parameter list.

The reader may question how function printf and function scanf know what type to use in each va_arg macro. The answer is that printf and scanf scan the format conversion specifiers in the format control string to determine the type of the next argument to be processed.

14.4 Using Command-Line Arguments

On many systems, it is possible to pass arguments to main from a command line by including parameters int argc and char *argv[] in the parameter list of main. Parameter argc receives the number of command-line arguments. Parameter argv is an array of strings in which the actual command-line arguments are stored. Common uses of command-line arguments include passing options to a program and passing filenames to a program.

Figure 14.3 copies a file into another file one character at a time. We assume that the executable file for the program is called mycopy. A typical command line for the mycopy program on a Linux/UNIX system is

    $ mycopy input output

This command line indicates that file input is to be copied to file output. When the program is executed, if argc is not 3 (mycopy counts as one of the arguments), the program prints an error message and terminates. Otherwise, array argv contains the strings

```
1   /* Fig. 14.3: fig14_03.c
2      Using command-line arguments */
3   #include <stdio.h>
4
5   int main( int argc, char *argv[] )
6   {
7      FILE *inFilePtr;   /* input file pointer */
8      FILE *outFilePtr;  /* output file pointer */
9      int c;             /* define c to hold characters input by user */
10
11     /* check number of command-line arguments */
12     if ( argc != 3) {
13        printf( "Usage: mycopy infile outfile\n" );
14     } /* end if */
15     else {
16
17        /* if input file can be opened */
18        if ( ( inFilePtr = fopen( argv[ 1 ], "r" ) ) != NULL ) {
19
20           /* if output file can be opened */
21           if ( ( outFilePtr = fopen( argv[ 2 ], "w" ) ) != NULL ) {
22
23              /* read and output characters */
24              while ( ( c = fgetc( inFilePtr ) ) != EOF ) {
25                 fputc( c, outFilePtr );
26              } /* end while */
27
28           } /* end if */
29           else { /* output file could not be opened */
30              printf( "File \"%s\" could not be opened\n", argv[ 2 ] );
31           } /* end else */
32
33        } /* end if */
34        else { /* input file could not be opened */
35           printf( "File \"%s\" could not be opened\n", argv[ 1 ] );
36        } /* end else */
37
38     } /* end else */
39
40     return 0; /* indicates successful termination */
41
42  } /* end main */
```

Fig. 14.3 | Using command-line arguments.

"mycopy", "input" and "output". The second and third arguments on the command line are used as file names by the program. The files are opened using function fopen. If both files are opened successfully, characters are read from file input and written to file output until the end-of-file indicator for file input is set. Then the program terminates. The result is an exact copy of file input. See the manuals for your system for more information on command-line arguments.

14.5 Notes on Compiling Multiple-Source-File Programs

It is possible to build programs that consist of multiple source files. There are several considerations when creating programs in multiple files. For example, the definition of a function must be entirely contained in one file—it cannot span two or more files.

In Chapter 5, we introduced the concepts of storage class and scope. We learned that variables declared outside any function definition are of storage class static by default and are referred to as global variables. Global variables are accessible to any function defined in the same file after the variable is declared. Global variables also are accessible to functions in other files. However, the global variables must be declared in each file in which they are used. For example, if we define global integer variable flag in one file and refer to it in a second file, the second file must contain the declaration

```
extern int flag;
```

prior to the variable's use in that file. This declaration uses the storage class specifier extern to indicate that variable flag is defined either later in the same file or in a different file. The compiler informs the linker that unresolved references to variable flag appear in the file (the compiler does not know where flag is defined, so it lets the linker attempt to find flag). If the linker cannot locate a definition of flag, the linker issues an error message and does not produce an executable file. If the linker finds a proper global definition, the linker resolves the references by indicating where flag is located.

Software Engineering Observation 14.1

Global variables should be avoided unless application performance is critical because they violate the principle of least privilege.

Just as extern declarations can be used to declare global variables to other program files, function prototypes can extend the scope of a function beyond the file in which it is defined (the extern specifier is not required in a function prototype). Simply include the function prototype in each file in which the function is invoked and compile the files together (see Section 13.2). Function prototypes indicate to the compiler that the specified function is defined either later in the same file or in a different file. Again, the compiler does not attempt to resolve references to such a function—that task is left to the linker. If the linker cannot locate a proper function definition, the linker issues an error message.

As an example of using function prototypes to extend the scope of a function, consider any program containing the preprocessor directive #include <stdio.h>, which includes in a file the function prototypes for functions such as printf and scanf. Other functions in the file can use printf and scanf to accomplish their tasks. The printf and scanf functions are defined in other files. We do not need to know where they are defined. We are simply reusing the code in our programs. The linker resolves our references to these functions automatically. This process enables us to use the functions in the standard library.

Software Engineering Observation 14.2

Creating programs in multiple source files facilitates software reusability and good software engineering. Functions may be common to many applications. In such instances, those functions should be stored in their own source files, and each source file should have a corresponding header file containing function prototypes. This enables programmers of different applications to reuse the same code by including the proper header file and compiling their applications with the corresponding source file.

It is possible to restrict the scope of a global variable or function to the file in which it is defined. The storage class specifier `static`, when applied to a global variable or a function, prevents it from being used by any function that is not defined in the same file. This is referred to as internal linkage. Global variables and functions that are not preceded by `static` in their definitions have external linkage—they can be accessed in other files if those files contain proper declarations and/or function prototypes.

The global variable declaration

```
static const double PI = 3.14159;
```

creates constant variable `PI` of type `double`, initializes it to `3.14159` and indicates that `PI` is known only to functions in the file in which it is defined.

The `static` specifier is commonly used with utility functions that are called only by functions in a particular file. If a function is not required outside a particular file, the principle of least privilege should be enforced by using `static`. If a function is defined before it is used in a file, `static` should be applied to the function definition. Otherwise, `static` should be applied to the function prototype.

When building large programs in multiple source files, compiling the program becomes tedious if small changes are made to one file and the entire program must be recompiled. Many systems provide special utilities that recompile only the modified program file. On Linux/UNIX systems the utility is called `make`. Utility `make` reads a file called `makefile` that contains instructions for compiling and linking the program. Products such as Borland C++ Builder and Microsoft Visual C++ provide similar utilities as well. For more information on `make` utilities, see the manual for your development tool.

14.6 Program Termination with `exit` and `atexit`

The general utilities library (`<stdlib.h>`) provides methods of terminating program execution by means other than a conventional return from function `main`. Function `exit` forces a program to terminate as if it executed normally. The function often is used to terminate a program when an input error is detected, or if a file to be processed by the program cannot be opened. Function `atexit` registers a function that should be called upon successful termination of the program—i.e., either when the program terminates by reaching the end of `main`, or when `exit` is invoked.

Function `atexit` takes as an argument a pointer to a function (i.e., the function name). Functions called at program termination cannot have arguments and cannot return a value. Up to 32 functions may be registered for execution at program termination.

Function `exit` takes one argument. The argument is normally the symbolic constant `EXIT_SUCCESS` or the symbolic constant `EXIT_FAILURE`. If `exit` is called with `EXIT_SUCCESS`, the implementation-defined value for successful termination is returned to the calling environment. If `exit` is called with `EXIT_FAILURE`, the implementation-defined value for unsuccessful termination is returned. When function exit is invoked, any functions previously registered with atexit are invoked in the reverse order of their registration, all streams associated with the program are flushed and closed, and control returns to the host environment.

Figure 14.4 tests functions exit and atexit. The program prompts the user to determine whether the program should be terminated with exit or by reaching the end of main. Note that function print is executed at program termination in each case.

```c
1   /* Fig. 14.4: fig14_04.c
2      Using the exit and atexit functions */
3   #include <stdio.h>
4   #include <stdlib.h>
5
6   void print( void ); /* prototype */
7
8   int main( void )
9   {
10      int answer; /* user's menu choice */
11
12      atexit( print ); /* register function print */
13      printf( "Enter 1 to terminate program with function exit"
14         "\nEnter 2 to terminate program normally\n" );
15      scanf( "%d", &answer );
16
17      /* call exit if answer is 1 */
18      if ( answer == 1 ) {
19         printf( "\nTerminating program with function exit\n" );
20         exit( EXIT_SUCCESS );
21      } /* end if */
22
23      printf( "\nTerminating program by reaching the end of main\n" );
24
25      return 0; /* indicates successful termination */
26
27   } /* end main */
28
29   /* display message before termination */
30   void print( void )
31   {
32      printf( "Executing function print at program "
33         "termination\nProgram terminated\n" );
34   } /* end function print */
```

```
Enter 1 to terminate program with function exit
Enter 2 to terminate program normally
1

Terminating program with function exit
Executing function print at program termination
Program terminated
```

Fig. 14.4 | exit and atexit functions. (Part 1 of 2.)

```
Enter 1 to terminate program with function exit
Enter 2 to terminate program normally
2

Terminating program by reaching the end of main
Executing function print at program termination
Program terminated
```

Fig. 14.4 | exit and atexit functions. (Part 2 of 2.)

14.7 volatile Type Qualifier

In Chapters 6–7, we introduced the const type qualifier. C also provides the volatile type qualifier to suppress various kinds of optimizations. The C standard indicates that when volatile is used to qualify a type, the nature of the access to an object of that type is implementation dependent. This usually implies that the variable may be changed by another program or by the computer's hardware.

14.8 Suffixes for Integer and Floating-Point Constants

C provides integer and floating-point suffixes for specifying the types of integer and floating-point constants. The integer suffixes are: u or U for an unsigned integer, l or L for a long integer, and ul, lu, UL or LU for an unsigned long integer. The following constants are of type unsigned, long and unsigned long, respectively:

```
174u
8358L
28373ul
```

If an integer constant is not suffixed, its type is determined by the first type capable of storing a value of that size (first int, then long int, then unsigned long int).

The floating-point suffixes are: f or F for a float, and l or L for a long double. The following constants are of type float and long double, respectively:

```
1.28f
3.14159L
```

A floating-point constant that is not suffixed is automatically of type double.

14.9 More on Files

Chapter 11 introduced capabilities for processing text files with sequential access and random access. C also provides capabilities for processing binary files, but some computer systems do not support binary files. If binary files are not supported and a file is opened in a binary file mode (Fig. 14.5), the file will be processed as a text file. Binary files should be used instead of text files only in situations where rigid speed, storage and/or compatibility conditions demand binary files. Otherwise, text files are always preferred for their inherent portability and for the ability to use other standard tools to examine and manipulate the file data.

Mode	Description
rb	Open an existing binary file for reading.
wb	Create a binary file for writing. If the file already exists, discard the current contents.
ab	Append; open or create a binary file for writing at end-of-file.
rb+	Open an existing binary file for update (reading and writing).
wb+	Create a binary file for update. If the file already exists, discard the current contents.
ab+	Append; open or create a binary file for update; all writing is done at the end of the file.

Fig. 14.5 | Binary file open modes.

Performance Tip 14.1

Consider using binary files instead of text files in applications that demand high performance.

Portability Tip 14.1

Use text files when writing portable programs.

In addition to the file processing functions discussed in Chapter 11, the standard library also provides function `tmpfile` that opens a temporary file in mode `"wb+"`. Although this is a binary file mode, some systems process temporary files as text files. A temporary file exists until it is closed with `fclose`, or until the program terminates.

Figure 14.6 changes the tabs in a file to spaces. The program prompts the user to enter the name of a file to be modified. If the file entered by the user and the temporary file are opened successfully, the program reads characters from the file to be modified and writes them to the temporary file. If the character read is a tab (`'\t'`), it is replaced by a space

```
1   /* Fig. 14.6: fig14_06.c
2      Using temporary files */
3   #include <stdio.h>
4
5   int main( void )
6   {
7      FILE *filePtr;     /* pointer to file being modified */
8      FILE *tempFilePtr; /* temporary file pointer */
9      int c; /* define c to hold characters read from a file */
10     char fileName[ 30 ]; /* create char array */
11
12     printf( "This program changes tabs to spaces.\n"
13        "Enter a file to be modified: " );
14     scanf( "%29s", fileName );
15
```

Fig. 14.6 | Temporary files. (Part 1 of 2.)

```
16    /* fopen opens the file */
17    if ( ( filePtr = fopen( fileName, "r+" ) ) != NULL ) {
18
19       /* create temporary file */
20       if ( ( tempFilePtr = tmpfile() ) != NULL ) {
21          printf( "\nThe file before modification is:\n" );
22
23          /* read characters from file and place in temporary file */
24          while ( ( c = getc( filePtr ) ) != EOF ) {
25             putchar( c );
26             putc( c == '\t' ? ' ' : c, tempFilePtr );
27          } /* end while */
28
29          rewind( tempFilePtr );
30          rewind( filePtr );
31          printf( "\n\nThe file after modification is:\n" );
32
33          /* read from temporary file and write into original file */
34          while ( ( c = getc( tempFilePtr ) ) != EOF ) {
35             putchar( c );
36             putc( c, filePtr );
37          } /* end while */
38
39       } /* end if */
40       else { /* if temporary file could not be opened */
41          printf( "Unable to open temporary file\n" );
42       } /* end else */
43
44    } /* end if */
45    else { /* if file could not be opened */
46       printf( "Unable to open %s\n", fileName );
47    } /* end else */
48
49    return 0; /* indicates successful termination */
50
51 } /* end main */
```

```
This program changes tabs to spaces.
Enter a file to be modified: data.txt

The file before modification is:
0       1       2       3       4
        5       6       7       8       9


The file after modification is:
0 1 2 3 4
 5 6 7 8 9
```

Fig. 14.6 | Temporary files. (Part 2 of 2.)

and written to the temporary file. When the end of the file being modified is reached, the file pointers for each file are repositioned to the start of each file with rewind. Next, the temporary file is copied into the original file one character at a time. The program prints the original file as it copies characters into the temporary file and prints the new file as it copies characters from the temporary file to the original file to confirm the characters being written.

14.10 Signal Handling

An external asynchronous event, or signal, can cause a program to terminate prematurely. Some events include interrupts (typing *<Ctrl> c* on a Linux/UNIX or Windows system), illegal instructions, segmentation violations, termination orders from the operating system and floating-point exceptions (division by zero or multiplying large floating-point values). The signal handling library (<signal.h>) provides the capability to trap unexpected events with function signal. Function signal receives two arguments—an integer signal number and a pointer to the signal handling function. Signals can be generated by function raise which takes an integer signal number as an argument. Figure 14.7 summarizes the standard signals defined in header file <signal.h>. Figure 14.8 demonstrates functions signal and raise.

Figure 14.8 uses function signal to trap an interactive signal (SIGINT). Line 15 calls signal with SIGINT and a pointer to function signalHandler (remember that the name of a function is a pointer to the beginning of the function). When a signal of type SIGINT occurs, control passes to function signalHandler, which prints a message and gives the user the option to continue normal execution of the program. If the user wishes to continue execution, the signal handler is reinitialized by calling signal again and control returns to the point in the program at which the signal was detected. In this program, function raise (line 24) is used to simulate an interactive signal. A random number between 1 and 50 is chosen. If the number is 25, raise is called to generate the signal. Normally, interactive signals are initiated outside the program. For example, typing *<Ctrl> c* during program execution on a Linux/UNIX or Windows system generates an interactive signal that terminates program execution. Signal handling can be used to trap the interactive signal and prevent the program from being terminated.

Signal	Explanation
SIGABRT	Abnormal termination of the program (such as a call to function abort).
SIGFPE	An erroneous arithmetic operation, such as a divide by zero or an operation resulting in overflow.
SIGILL	Detection of an illegal instruction.
SIGINT	Receipt of an interactive attention signal.
SIGSEGV	An invalid access to storage.
SIGTERM	A termination request set to the program.

Fig. 14.7 | signal.h standard signals.

```
 1   /* Fig. 14.8: fig14_08.c
 2      Using signal handling */
 3   #include <stdio.h>
 4   #include <signal.h>
 5   #include <stdlib.h>
 6   #include <time.h>
 7
 8   void signalHandler( int signalValue ); /* prototype */
 9
10   int main( void )
11   {
12      int i; /* counter used to loop 100 times */
13      int x; /* variable to hold random values between 1-50 */
14
15      signal( SIGINT, signalHandler ); /* register signal handler */
16      srand( clock() );
17
18      /* output numbers 1 to 100 */
19      for ( i = 1; i <= 100; i++ ) {
20         x = 1 + rand() % 50; /* generate random number to raise SIGINT */
21
22         /* raise SIGINT when x is 25 */
23         if ( x == 25 ) {
24            raise( SIGINT );
25         } /* end if */
26
27         printf( "%4d", i );
28
29         /* output \n when i is a multiple of 10 */
30         if ( i % 10 == 0 ) {
31            printf( "\n" );
32         } /* end if */
33
34      } /* end for */
35
36      return 0; /* indicates successful termination */
37
38   } /* end main */
39
40   /* handles signal */
41   void signalHandler( int signalValue )
42   {
43      int response; /* user's response to signal (1 or 2) */
44
45      printf( "%s%d%s\n%s",
46         "\nInterrupt signal ( ", signalValue, " ) received.",
47         "Do you wish to continue ( 1 = yes or 2 = no )? " );
48
49      scanf( "%d", &response );
50
51      /* check for invalid responses */
52      while ( response != 1 && response != 2 ) {
53         printf( "( 1 = yes or 2 = no )? " );
```

Fig. 14.8 | Signal handling. (Part 1 of 2.)

```
54          scanf( "%d", &response );
55      } /* end while */
56
57      /* determine if it is time to exit */
58      if ( response == 1 ) {
59
60          /* reregister signal handler for next SIGINT */
61          signal( SIGINT, signalHandler );
62      } /* end if */
63      else {
64          exit( EXIT_SUCCESS );
65      } /* end else */
66
67  } /* end function signalHandler */
```

```
 1  2  3  4  5  6  7  8  9 10
11 12 13 14 15 16 17 18 19 20
21 22 23 24 25 26 27 28 29 30
31 32 33 34 35 36 37 38 39 40
41 42 43 44 45 46 47 48 49 50
51 52 53 54 55 56 57 58 59 60
61 62 63 64 65 66 67 68 69 70
71 72 73 74 75 76 77 78 79 80
81 82 83 84 85 86 87 88 89 90
91 92 93
Interrupt signal ( 2 ) received.
Do you wish to continue ( 1 = yes or 2 = no )? 1
94 95 96
Interrupt signal ( 2 ) received.
Do you wish to continue ( 1 = yes or 2 = no )? 2
```

Fig. 14.8 | Signal handling. (Part 2 of 2.)

14.11 Dynamic Memory Allocation: Functions `calloc` and `realloc`

Chapter 12, C Data Structures introduced the notion of dynamically allocating memory using function `malloc`. As we stated in Chapter 12, arrays are better than linked lists for rapid sorting, searching and data access. However, arrays are normally static data structures. The general utilities library (`stdlib.h`) provides two other functions for dynamic memory allocation—`calloc` and `realloc`. These functions can be used to create and modify dynamic arrays. As shown in Chapter 7, C Pointers, a pointer to an array can be subscripted like an array. Thus, a pointer to a contiguous portion of memory created by `calloc` can be manipulated as an array. Function `calloc` dynamically allocates memory for an array. The prototype for `calloc` is

```
void *calloc( size_t nmemb, size_t size );
```

Its two arguments represent the number of elements (`nmemb`) and the size of each element (`size`). Function `calloc` also initializes the elements of the array to zero. The function returns a pointer to the allocated memory, or a `NULL` pointer if the memory is not allocated.

The primary difference between malloc and calloc is that calloc clears the memory it allocates and malloc does not.

Function realloc changes the size of an object allocated by a previous call to malloc, calloc or realloc. The original object's contents are not modified provided that the amount of memory allocated is larger than the amount allocated previously. Otherwise, the contents are unchanged up to the size of the new object. The prototype for realloc is

```
void *realloc( void *ptr, size_t size );
```

The two arguments are a pointer to the original object (ptr) and the new size of the object (size). If ptr is NULL, realloc works identically to malloc. If size is 0 and ptr is not NULL, the memory for the object is freed. Otherwise, if ptr is not NULL and size is greater than zero, realloc tries to allocate a new block of memory for the object. If the new space cannot be allocated, the object pointed to by ptr is unchanged. Function realloc returns either a pointer to the reallocated memory, or a NULL pointer to indicate that the memory was not reallocated.

14.12 Unconditional Branching with goto

Throughout the text we have stressed the importance of using structured programming techniques to build reliable software that is easy to debug, maintain and modify. In some cases, performance is more important than strict adherence to structured programming techniques. In these cases, some unstructured programming techniques may be used. For example, we can use break to terminate execution of a repetition structure before the loop continuation condition becomes false. This saves unnecessary repetitions of the loop if the task is completed before loop termination.

Another instance of unstructured programming is the goto statement—an unconditional branch. The result of the goto statement is a change in the flow of control of the program to the first statement after the label specified in the goto statement. A label is an identifier followed by a colon. A label must appear in the same function as the goto statement that refers to it. Figure 14.9 uses goto statements to loop ten times and print the counter value each time. After initializing count to 1, line 11 tests count to determine whether it is greater than 10 (the label start is skipped because labels do not perform any action). If so, control is transferred from the goto to the first statement after the label end (which appears at line 20). Otherwise, lines 15–16 print and increment count, and control transfers from the goto (line 18) to the first statement after the label start (which appears at line 9).

In Chapter 3, we stated that only three control structures are required to write any program—sequence, selection and repetition. When the rules of structured programming are followed, it is possible to create deeply nested control structures from which it is difficult to efficiently escape. Some programmers use goto statements in such situations as a quick exit from a deeply nested structure. This eliminates the need to test multiple conditions to escape from a control structure.

Performance Tip 14.2

The goto statement can be used to exit deeply nested control structures efficiently.

```
1    /* Fig. 14.9: fig14_09.c
2       Using goto */
3    #include <stdio.h>
4
5    int main( void )
6    {
7       int count = 1; /* initialize count */
8
9       start: /* label */
10
11          if ( count > 10 ) {
12             goto end;
13          } /* end if */
14
15          printf( "%d ", count );
16          count++;
17
18          goto start; /* goto start on line 9 */
19
20       end: /* label */
21          putchar( '\n' );
22
23       return 0; /* indicates successful termination */
24
25    } /* end main */
```

```
1  2  3  4  5  6  7  8  9  10
```

Fig. 14.9 | goto statement.

Software Engineering Observation 14.3

The goto statement should be used only in performance-oriented applications. The goto statement is unstructured and can lead to programs that are more difficult to debug, maintain and modify.

Summary

Section 14.2 Redirecting Input/Output on Linux/UNIX and Windows Systems
- On many computer systems it is possible to redirect input to a program and output from a program.
- Input is redirected from the command line using the redirect input symbol (<) or using a pipe (|).
- Output is redirected from the command line using the redirect output symbol (>) or the append output symbol (>>). The redirect output symbol simply stores the program output in a file, and the append output symbol appends the output to the end of a file.

Section 14.3 Variable-Length Argument Lists
- The macros and definitions of the variable arguments header <stdarg.h> provide the capabilities necessary to build functions with variable-length argument lists.
- An ellipsis (. . .) in a function prototype indicates a variable number of arguments.

- Type va_list is suitable for holding information needed by macros va_start, va_arg and va_end. To access the arguments in a variable-length argument list, an object of type va_list must be declared.

- Invoke macro va_start before accessing the arguments of a variable-length argument list. The macro initializes the object declared with va_list for use by the va_arg and va_end macros.

- Macro va_arg expands to an expression of the value and type of the next argument in the variable length argument list. Each invocation of va_arg modifies the object declared with va_list so that the object points to the next argument in the list.

- Macro va_end facilitates a normal return from a function whose variable argument list was referred to by the va_start macro.

Section 14.4 Using Command-Line Arguments
- On many systems it is possible to pass arguments to main from the command line by including the parameters int argc and char *argv[] in the parameter list of main. Parameter argc receives the number of command-line arguments. Parameter argv is an array of strings in which the actual command-line arguments are stored.

Section 14.5 Notes on Compiling Multiple-Source-File Programs
- A function definition must be entirely contained in one file—it cannot span two or more files.
- Global variables must be declared in each file in which they are used.
- Function prototypes can extend the scope of a function beyond the file in which it is defined. This is accomplished by including the function prototype in each file in which the function is invoked and compiling the files together.
- The storage class specifier static, when applied to a global variable or a function, prevents it from being used by any function that is not defined in the same file. This is referred to as internal linkage. Global variables and functions that are not preceded by static in their definitions have external linkage—they can be accessed in other files if those files contain proper declarations or function prototypes.
- The static specifier is commonly used with utility functions that are called only by functions in a particular file. If a function is not required outside a particular file, the principle of least privilege should be enforced by using static.
- When building large programs in multiple source files, compiling the program becomes tedious if small changes are made to one file and the entire program must be recompiled. Many systems provide special utilities that recompile only the modified program file. On Linux/UNIX systems the utility is called make. Utility make reads a file called makefile that contains instructions for compiling and linking the program.

Section 14.6 Program Termination with exit and atexit
- Function exit forces a program to terminate as if it executed normally.
- Function atexit registers a function to be called upon normal termination of the program—i.e., either when the program terminates by reaching the end of main or when exit is invoked.
- Function atexit takes a pointer to a function as an argument. Functions called at program termination cannot have arguments and cannot return a value. Up to 32 functions may be registered for execution at program termination.
- Function exit takes one argument. The argument is normally the symbolic constant EXIT_SUCCESS or the symbolic constant EXIT_FAILURE. If exit is called with EXIT_SUCCESS, the implementation-defined value for successful termination is returned to the calling environment. If exit is called with EXIT_FAILURE, the implementation-defined value for unsuccessful termination is returned.

- When function exit is invoked, any functions registered with atexit are invoked in the reverse order of their registration, all streams associated with the program are flushed and closed, and control returns to the host environment.

Section 14.7 volatile *Type Qualifier*
- The C standard indicates that when volatile is used to qualify a type, the nature of the access to an object of that type is implementation dependent.

Section 14.8 *Suffixes for Integer and Floating-Point Constants*
- C provides integer and floating-point suffixes for specifying the types of integer and floating-point constants. The integer suffixes are: u or U for an unsigned integer, l or L for a long integer, and ul or UL for an unsigned long integer. If an integer constant is not suffixed, its type is determined by the first type capable of storing a value of that size (first int, then long int, then unsigned long int). The floating-point suffixes are: f or F for a float, and l or L for a long double. A floating-point constant that is not suffixed is of type double.

Section 14.9 *More on Files*
- C provides capabilities for processing binary files, but some computer systems do not support binary files. If binary files are not supported and a file is opened in a binary file mode, the file will be processed as a text file.
- Function tmpfile opens a temporary file in mode "wb+". Although this is a binary file mode, some systems process temporary files as text files. A temporary file exists until it is closed with fclose or until the program terminates.

Section 14.10 *Signal Handling*
- The signal handling library enables trapping of unexpected events with function signal. Function signal receives two arguments—an integer signal number and a pointer to the signal-handling function.
- Signals can also be generated with function raise and an integer argument.

Section 14.11 *Dynamic Memory Allocation: Functions* calloc *and* realloc
- The general utilities library (<stdlib.h>) provides two functions for dynamic memory allocation—calloc and realloc. These functions can be used to create dynamic arrays.
- Function calloc receives two arguments—the number of elements (nmemb) and the size of each element (size)—and initializes the elements of the array to zero. The function returns either a pointer to the allocated memory, or a NULL pointer if the memory is not allocated.
- Function realloc changes the size of an object allocated by a previous call to malloc, calloc or realloc. The original object's contents are not modified provided that the amount of memory allocated is larger than the amount allocated previously.
- Function realloc takes two arguments—a pointer to the original object (ptr) and the new size of the object (size). If ptr is NULL, realloc works identically to malloc. If size is 0 and the pointer received is not NULL, the memory for the object is freed. Otherwise, if ptr is not NULL and size is greater than zero, realloc tries to allocate a new block of memory for the object. If the new space cannot be allocated, the object pointed to by ptr is unchanged. Function realloc returns either a pointer to the reallocated memory, or a NULL pointer.

Section 14.12 *Unconditional Branching with* goto
- The result of the goto statement is a change in the flow of control of the program. Program execution continues at the first statement after the label specified in the goto statement.
- A label is an identifier followed by a colon. A label must appear in the same function as the goto statement that refers to it.

Terminology

append output symbol >>

argc

argv

atexit

calloc

command-line arguments

const

dynamic arrays

event

exit

EXIT_FAILURE

EXIT_SUCCESS

external linkage

extern storage class specifier

float suffix (f or F)

floating-point exception

goto statement

I/O redirection

illegal instruction

internal linkage

interrupt

long double suffix (l or L)

long int suffix (l or L)

make

makefile

pipe symbol (|)

piping

raise

realloc

redirect input symbol (<)

redirect output symbol (>)

segmentation violation

signal

signal handling library

<signal.h>

static storage class specifier

<stdarg.h>

temporary file

tmpfile

trap

unsigned integer suffix (u or U)

unsigned long integer suffix (ul or UL)

va_arg

va_end

va_list

va_start

variable-length argument list

volatile

Self-Review Exercise

14.1   Fill in the blanks in each of the following:

a)   The _____ symbol redirects input data from a file rather than the keyboard.

b)   The _____ symbol is used to redirect the screen output so that it is placed in a file.

c)   The _____ symbol is used to append the output of a program to the end of a file.

d)   A(n) _____ directs the output of one program to be the input of another program.

e)   A(n) _____ in the parameter list of a function indicates that the function can receive a variable number of arguments.

f)   Macro _____ must be invoked before the arguments in a variable-length argument list can be accessed.

g)   Macro _____ accesses the individual arguments of a variable-length argument list.

h)   Macro _____ facilitates a normal return from a function whose variable argument list was referred to by macro va_start.

i)   Argument _____ of main receives the number of arguments in a command line.

j)   Argument _____ of main stores command-line arguments as character strings.

k)   Linux/UNIX utility _____ reads a file called _____ that contains instructions for compiling and linking a program consisting of multiple source files.

l)   Function _____ forces a program to terminate execution.

m)   Function _____ registers a function to be called upon normal program termination.

n)   An integer or floating-point _____ can be appended to an integer or floating-point constant to specify the exact type of the constant.

o)   Function _____ opens a temporary file that exists until it is closed or program execution terminates.

p) Function _____ can be used to trap unexpected events.

q) Function _____ generates a signal from within a program.

r) Function _____ dynamically allocates memory for an array and initializes the elements to zero.

s) Function _____ changes the size of a block of previously allocated dynamic memory.

Answers to Self-Review Exercise

14.1   a) redirect input (<). b) redirect output (>). c) append output (>>). d) pipe (|). e) ellipsis (...). f) va_start. g) va_arg. h) va_end. i) argc. j) argv. k) make, makefile. l) exit. m) atexit. n) suffix. o) tmpfile. p) signal. q) raise. r) calloc. s) realloc.

Exercises

14.2   Write a program that calculates the product of a series of integers that are passed to function product using a variable-length argument list. Test your function with several calls, each with a different number of arguments.

14.3   Write a program that prints the command-line arguments of the program.

14.4   Write a program that sorts an array of integers into ascending order or descending order. Use command-line arguments to pass either argument -a for ascending order or -d for descending order. [*Note:* This is the standard format for passing options to a program in UNIX.]

14.5   Write a program that places a space between each character in a file. The program should first write the contents of the file being modified into a temporary file with spaces between each character, then copy the file back to the original file. This operation should overwrite the original contents of the file.

14.6   Read the manuals for your compiler to determine what signals are supported by the signal handling library (<signal.h>). Write a program that contains signal handlers for the standard signals SIGABRT and SIGINT. The program should test the trapping of these signals by calling function abort to generate a signal of type SIGABRT and by typing <*Ctrl*> *c* to generate a signal of type SIGINT.

14.7   Write a program that dynamically allocates an array of integers. The size of the array should be input from the keyboard. The elements of the array should be assigned values input from the keyboard. Print the values of the array. Next, reallocate the memory for the array to 1/2 of the current number of elements. Print the values remaining in the array to confirm that they match the first half of the values in the original array.

14.8   Write a program that takes two command-line arguments that are file names, reads the characters from the first file one at a time and writes the characters in reverse order to the second file.

14.9   Write a program that uses goto statements to simulate a nested looping structure that prints a square of asterisks as follows:

```
*****
*   *
*   *
*   *
*****
```

The program should use only the following three printf statements:

```
printf( "*" );
printf( " " );
printf( "\n" );
```

15

Game Programming with the Allegro C Library

OBJECTIVES

In this chapter you will learn:

- How to install the Allegro game programming library to work with your C programs.
- To create games using Allegro.
- To use Allegro to import and display graphics.
- To use the "double buffering" technique to create smooth animations.
- To use Allegro to import and play sounds.
- To have Allegro recognize and process keyboard input.
- To create the simple game Pong with Allegro.
- To use Allegro timers to regulate the speed of a game.
- To use Allegro datafiles to shorten the amount of code in a program.
- The many other features Allegro can add to a game.

15.1 Introduction

We now present game programming and graphics with the Allegro C library. Created in 1995 by Climax game programmer Shawn Hargreaves, Allegro is now an open source project maintained by the game developer community at `www.allegro.cc`.

In this chapter, we show how to use the Allegro C library to create the simple game of Pong. We demonstrate how to display graphics and smoothly animate moving objects. We explain additional features such as sound, keyboard input, text output and timers that are useful in creating games. The chapter includes web links to over 1,000 open source Allegro games and tutorials on advanced Allegro techniques.

15.2 Installing Allegro

Allegro was created to be a relatively simple programming library, but its installation can be tricky. To begin, you need the Allegro library itself, which is available at `www.allegro.cc/files` (make sure to download the "Source" package for your platform), and an IDE (integrated development environment) that is compatible with it. Allegro can be used with most C IDEs, but in this text, we use Bloodshed Software's Dev-C++ (which is available for free at `www.bloodshed.net/devcpp.html`). While Dev-C++ is primarily a C++ IDE, you can specify that your project is strictly in C when you create it by selecting that option in the **New Project** window.

To use Allegro with your IDE, you need to compile its source code. Allegro's documentation (which is included in the library in the `docs` folder) contains installation instructions for most popular C platforms. Once you have copied the `allegro` folder to your computer, you can find the instructions for your IDE in the appropriate text file in the directory `allegro/docs/build`. Note that while most of the text files in the directory are named after their respective IDEs, the instructions for Dev-C++ are in the file `mingw32`.

Once the installation is complete, you must tell your IDE where to find the Allegro library when you create a new project. In Dev-C++, this is accomplished by selecting

Project Options in the **Project** menu for your project, then clicking the **Parameters** tab and adding -lalleg to the **Compiler** window and the file ../lib/liballeg.a to the **Linker** window. You must perform this step for every Allegro project you create. Once this is done, you're ready to program in Allegro.

15.3 A Simple Allegro Program

Consider a simple Allegro program that displays a message (Fig. 15.1). In addition to the preprocessor directive to include the allegro.h header at line 3 (this directive must be present for an Allegro program to operate correctly), you will notice several functions in this program that we have not previously used. The function call allegro_init (line 7) initializes the Allegro library. It is required for an Allegro program to run, and must be called before any other Allegro functions.

The call to allegro_message (line 8) displays a message to the user in the form of an alert box. Since alert boxes interrupt running programs, you will probably not use this function much—it is preferable to use Allegro's text display functions to display messages on the screen without stopping the program. The allegro_message function is typically used to notify the user if something is preventing Allegro from working correctly.

The use of the END_OF_MAIN macro is the last of the new elements in this program. Windows, some Unix systems, and Mac OS X cannot run Allegro programs without this macro, as the executable that an Allegro program creates during compilation will not be able start correctly on those systems. The END_OF_MAIN macro checks the currently running operating system during compilation, and applies an appropriate fix to this problem if one is required. On systems other than the ones listed previously, END_OF_MAIN will do nothing, and your program will compile and run perfectly without it. However, you should still always add the macro after the right brace of your main to ensure that your program is compatible with systems that require it.

So, to get any Allegro program to run, you need to have three lines of code—the preprocessor directive to include allegro.h, the call to allegro_init and (if your system

```
1   /* Fig. 15.1: fig15_01.c
2      A simple Allegro program. */
3   #include <allegro.h>
4
5   int main( void )
6   {
7      allegro_init(); /* initialize Allegro */
8      allegro_message( "Welcome to Allegro!" ); /* display a message */
9      return 0;
10  } /* end function main */
11  END_OF_MAIN() /* Allegro-specific macro */
```

Fig. 15.1 | A simple Allegro program.

requires it) the call to the END_OF_MAIN macro following the right brace of your program's main function. Now we discuss Allegro's main capability—displaying graphics.

15.4 Simple Graphics: Importing Bitmaps and Blitting

Allegro can draw lines and simple shapes on its own, but the majority of the graphics it can display come from external sources. The allegro.h header defines several types that can be used to hold image data from external files—the BITMAP* pointer type is the most basic of these. A BITMAP* points to a struct in memory where image data is stored. Allegro has many functions that can be used to manipulate bitmaps. The most important of these are shown in Fig. 15.2.

Now let's use Allegro's functions to load a bitmap and display it on the screen until a key is pressed. First we need a bitmap to load from, so copy the bitmap picture.bmp from www.deitel.com and save it in the same folder as your Allegro project. The code in Fig. 15.3 displays the bitmap until a key is pressed.

Function prototype	Description
BITMAP *create_bitmap(int width, int height)	Creates and returns a pointer to a blank bitmap with specified width and height (in pixels).
BITMAP *load_bitmap(const char *filename, RGB *pal)	Loads and returns a pointer to a bitmap from the location specified in filename with palette pal.
void clear_bitmap(BITMAP *bmp)	Clears a bitmap of its image data and makes it blank.
void clear_to_color(BITMAP *bmp, int color)	Clears a bitmap of its image data and makes the entire bitmap the color specified.
void destroy_bitmap(BITMAP *bmp)	Destroys a bitmap and frees up the memory previously allocated to it. Use this function when you are done with a bitmap to prevent memory leaks.

Fig. 15.2 | Important BITMAP functions.

```
1   /*Fig. 15.3: fig15_03.c
2     Displaying a bitmap on the screen. */
3   #include <allegro.h>
4
5   int main( void )
6   {
7      BITMAP *bmp; /* pointer to the bitmap */
8
9      allegro_init(); /* initialize Allegro */
```

Fig. 15.3 | Displaying a bitmap on the screen. (Part 1 of 2.)

```
10    install_keyboard(); /* allow Allegro to receive keyboard input */
11    set_color_depth( 16 ); /* set the color depth to 16-bit*/
12    set_gfx_mode( GFX_AUTODETECT, 640, 480, 0, 0 ); /* set graphics mode */
13    bmp = load_bitmap( "picture.bmp", NULL ); /* load the bitmap file */
14    blit( bmp, screen, 0, 0, 0, 0, bmp->w, bmp->h ); /* draw the bitmap */
15    readkey(); /* wait for a keypress */
16    destroy_bitmap( bmp ); /* free the memory allocated to bmp */
17    return 0;
18 } /* end function main */
19 END_OF_MAIN() /* Allegro-specific macro */
```

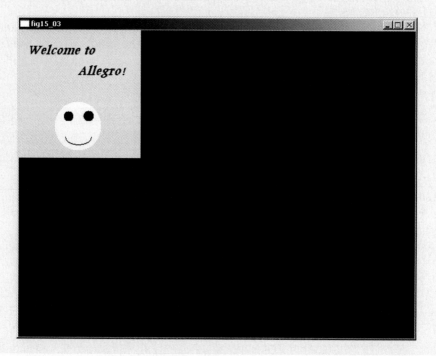

Fig. 15.3 | Displaying a bitmap on the screen. (Part 2 of 2.)

Common Programming Error 15.1

Telling Allegro to load a file that is not in the same folder as the program being run will cause a runtime error, unless you specifically tell the program the folder in which the file is located by typing the full path name.

First, this program initializes the Allegro library and adds the ability to read keyboard input. Then, it sets the graphics mode of the program. Finally, it loads picture.bmp, displays it at the top-left corner of the screen, then waits for a key press. When a key is pressed, the program frees the memory that was allocated to the bitmap, then exits.

There are many new Allegro functions in this program. The call to install_keyboard at line 10 "installs" the keyboard so that Allegro can recognize and use it. It doesn't have anything to do with displaying our bitmap, but it needs to be called so that Allegro will know how to "wait" for a key press after the bitmap is displayed.

Line 11 calls our first graphics-related function, `set_color_depth`, which sets the color depth of the screen to *n*-bit, where *n* is the `int` passed to the function. A color depth of *n*-bits means that there are 2^n possible colors that can be displayed. A lower color depth will make a program require less memory, but its appearance may not be as good as a higher one. Note that while we set the color depth to 16-bit in our program, you can use a different color depth if you wish, but the only values that `set_color_depth` accepts are 8, 15, 16, 24, and 32. It is advised, though, that you avoid using an 8-bit depth until you are more experienced with Allegro. If the color depth is set to 8-bit, loading a bitmap also requires that you load the bitmap's palette—in other words, the set of colors that the bitmap uses—which is a process that is beyond our scope. At the least, a 16-bit color depth is recommended. A 15-bit depth is also acceptable, but not all platforms support it.

In line 12 we call another graphics-related function, `set_gfx_mode`. This call sets the graphics mode of the program. This is an important function; let's examine its prototype.

```
int set_gfx_mode(int card, int width, int height, int v_w, int v_h);
```

If the function is successful, it returns 0; otherwise, it returns a non-zero value. In general, most Allegro functions that can fail follow the same paradigm. If you wish, you can insert `if` statements into your program to check if your functions work correctly and tell the program how to proceed if one fails, but to save space, our sample programs will assume that all our functions work as they should.

The first parameter of the `set_gfx_mode` function is `int card`. In earlier versions of Allegro, this parameter was used to tell the computer which video card driver to use, but determining which driver would work correctly with a given system and program was a difficult process. In newer versions of the library, a number of so-called "magic drivers" were added that detect the computer's drivers automatically—`GFX_AUTODETECT`, `GFX_AUTODETECT_FULLSCREEN`, `GFX_AUTODETECT_WINDOWED`, and `GFX_SAFE` (all of these are symbolic constants defined in `allegro.h`). In addition to specifying the driver to use, passing the parameter one of the preceding values also tells Allegro whether it should run the program in a window, or whether the program should use the entire screen. Passing `GFX_AUTODETECT_FULLSCREEN` or `GFX_AUTODETECT_WINDOWED` tells the program to run in fullscreen mode (the program takes up the entire screen) or windowed mode (the program runs in a standard window), respectively. Passing `GFX_AUTODETECT` makes the program try fullscreen mode first, then try windowed mode if fullscreen mode causes an error. `GFX_SAFE` mode is generally not used; though it acts the same way as `GFX_AUTODETECT`, there is one addition. If both fullscreen and windowed mode fail, `GFX_SAFE` mode forces the computer to use settings that it "knows" will work. However these "safe" modes usually have extremely low resolution and color depth, so they are generally avoided. There is also a fifth symbolic constant, `GFX_TEXT`, but this setting allows only text as the name implies and passing it to `set_gfx_mode` will essentially "turn off" any window or fullscreen graphics that are already running.

Software Engineering Observation 15.1

Avoid using the `GFX_SAFE` "magic driver" if possible. The "safe" graphics modes generally have a negative impact on your program's appearance.

The next two parameters, `width` and `height`, determine the number of pixels in the width and height of the screen (or the window, if you're using windowed mode). The last two parameters (v_w and v_h) define the minimum pixel width and height, respectively, of what is called the "virtual screen." The "virtual screen" was used in earlier versions of Allegro to help create games where action can occur out of the view of the visible screen, but it no longer has any real use in Allegro's current version as most systems today do not support it. Thus, the v_w and v_h parameters should simply be passed the value 0.

Now that we know how to set the graphics mode, we consider the function at line 13, load_bitmap. This function, introduced in Fig. 15.2, loads the picture that we saved as picture.bmp and has the pointer bmp point to it. Note that we did not pass the function a palette—this is not necessary. Recall that passing a bitmap's palette is required only when the color depth is set to 8-bit. However, it is important that you make sure you set the color depth and graphics mode in your program before you attempt to load a bitmap file. Otherwise, Allegro will have no information on how to store the bitmap in memory (it will not know how many bits in memory to use for each pixel, for example), and will instead try to "guess" how to do so. This can lead to various errors in your program.

Common Programming Error 15.2

Loading a bitmap before setting the color depth and graphics mode of a program will likely result in Allegro storing the bitmap incorrectly.

Note that if load_bitmap fails—if, for example, you tell it to load a bitmap that is not there—then it does not actually cause an error on that line. Instead, telling load_bitmap to load a nonexistent file simply makes the function return the value NULL. Obviously, this can cause problems later in the program, but compilers do not recognize a failed call to load_bitmap as an error. In general, any Allegro function that loads an external file behaves in the same way.

Line 14 contains a call to what is probably the most important function in this program, blit. The blit function (blit stands for BLock Transfer—the "i" is there only to make it pronounceable) is an Allegro function that takes a block of one bitmap (the block can be the entire picture, if you wish) and draws it onto another. Consider this function's prototype:

```
void blit(BITMAP *source, BITMAP *dest, int source_x, int source_y,
     int dest_x, int dest_y, int width, int height);
```

Because blit draws one bitmap onto another, we must specify those bitmaps for the function to work. The first two parameters (source and dest) define the source and destination bitmaps, respectively, so in our program we are taking a block of bmp and drawing it onto the screen. The symbolic constant screen (defined in allegro.h) refers to the screen of the computer. Blitting onto the screen is the only way to display graphics.

Since blitting takes a block from a bitmap, we also have to specify the position of this block in the source bitmap. The parameters source_x and source_y specify the coordinates of the top-left corner of the block we want to draw onto the destination bitmap. Note that Allegro bitmap coordinates do not work the same way as they do on most graphs in your algebra and geometry classes: A larger x-value means further to the right, but a larger y-value means further down, not up. This means that the top-left point of any bitmap image is at the coordinates (0, 0). Figure 15.4 illustrates this coordinate system using the output of the program we wrote in Fig. 15.3.

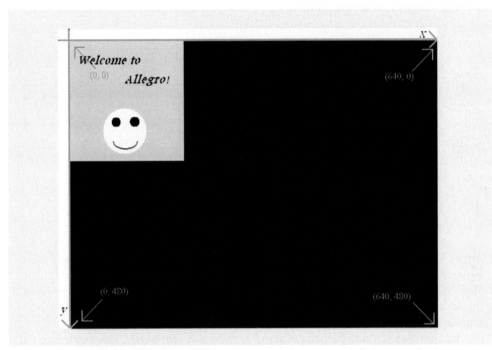

Fig. 15.4 | Allegro's coordinate system.

To draw onto a bitmap, we must also tell the function where we want the drawing to take place. The parameters dest_x and dest_y determine the coordinates of the top-left point of this location. Again, the coordinates (0, 0) represent the top left of a bitmap.

Finally, though we have specified the top-left corner of the block we want to copy from our source bitmap, we have not yet specified its size. The last two parameters specify the width and height of the block we are blitting. You may be wondering why in our program, we were able to pass these parameters the values of bmp->w and bmp->h. The reason for this is that the BITMAP* type defined by Allegro is a pointer to a struct. Along with the image data and a few other variables, the BITMAP struct contains two ints, w and h, that represent the width and height of the bitmap, respectively. Note that unless you do not want to display the entire image, you should pass these parameters the values bmp->w and bmp->h, replacing bmp with the name of your bitmap.

The blit function that we called at line 14, then, copies a block from bmp, whose top-left corner and size are those of bmp, and draws it at the top-left corner of the virtual screen. In short, it displays the image in picture.bmp at the top-left of the screen.

After blitting the image onto the screen, the program makes a call to the function readkey. This function is the reason we called install_keyboard earlier in the program. Function readkey waits for a key to be pressed, then returns the value of the key pressed as an int. Even though we do nothing with the value it returns, this function is useful in this program because, like scanf, it causes the program to pause until the user provides some input. Without it, the program would end before we had a chance to see the bitmap.

Finally, after we hit a key, the program calls `destroy_bitmap`. As explained previously, this function destroys the bitmap passed to it and performs the equivalent of the `free` function on the memory that was allocated to it.

Error-Prevention Tip 15.1

Use the `destroy_bitmap` function to free the memory of a bitmap that is no longer needed and prevent memory leaks.

Common Programming Error 15.3

Trying to destroy a bitmap that has not been initialized causes a runtime error.

15.5 Animation with Double Buffering

Now that we know how to draw bitmaps on the screen, animating bitmaps and making them move around the screen is straightforward. We are now going to develop the simple game "Pong." We begin by using animation techniques to create a square "ball" that bounces around a white screen. For this purpose, we need a bitmap that serves as our "ball." Copy the file `ball.bmp` from this chapter's examples folder, and save it in a new project called `pong`. Note that `ball.bmp` is 40 pixels wide by 40 pixels tall—this will be important as we code the program.

In most Pong games, the ball can travel at many different angles. However, since we are just starting with Allegro, we want to keep things as simple as possible. For this reason, in our Pong game, the ball only has four possible directions of travel: down-right, up-right, down-left, and up-left—all of these at 45-degree angles to the *x*- and *y*-axes in our program. We use an `int` to keep track of the ball's current direction, so we can use symbolic constants for each of the possible directions.

Moving a bitmap around the screen is simple—we just blit our bitmap onto the screen, then when we want to move it, we clear the screen and blit the bitmap at its new position. The program in Fig. 15.5 creates a ball that moves around and bounces off the edges of the screen until we hit the *Esc* key.

```
 1   /* Fig. 15.5: fig15_05.c
 2      Creating the bouncing ball. */
 3   #include <allegro.h>
 4
 5   /* symbolic constants for the ball's possible directions */
 6   #define DOWN_RIGHT 0
 7   #define UP_RIGHT 1
 8   #define DOWN_LEFT 2
 9   #define UP_LEFT 3
10
11   /* function prototypes */
12   void moveBall( void );
13   void reverseVerticalDirection( void );
14   void reverseHorizontalDirection( void );
15
```

Fig. 15.5 | Creating the bouncing ball. (Part 1 of 3.)

```
16  int ball_x; /* the ball's x-coordinate */
17  int ball_y; /* the ball's y-coordinate */
18  int direction; /* the ball's direction */
19  BITMAP *ball; /* pointer to the ball's image bitmap */
20
21  int main( void )
22  {
23      /* first, set up Allegro and the graphics mode */
24      allegro_init(); /* initialize Allegro */
25      install_keyboard(); /* install the keyboard for Allegro to use */
26      set_color_depth( 16 ); /* set the color depth to 16-bit */
27      set_gfx_mode( GFX_AUTODETECT, 640, 480, 0, 0 ); /* set graphics mode */
28      ball = load_bitmap( "ball.bmp", NULL ); /* load the ball bitmap */
29      ball_x = SCREEN_W / 2; /* give the ball its initial x-coordinate */
30      ball_y = SCREEN_H / 2; /* give the ball its initial y-coordinate */
31      srand( time( NULL ) ); /* seed the random function */
32      direction = rand() % 4; /* and then make a random initial direction */
33
34      while ( !key[KEY_ESC] ) /* until the escape key is pressed ... */
35      {
36          moveBall(); /* move the ball */
37          clear_to_color( screen, makecol( 255, 255, 255 ) );
38          /* now draw the bitmap onto the screen */
39          blit( ball, screen, 0, 0, ball_x, ball_y, ball->w, ball->h );
40      } /* end while */
41
42      destroy_bitmap( ball ); /* destroy the ball bitmap */
43      return 0;
44  } /* end function main */
45  END_OF_MAIN() /* don't forget this! */
46
47  void moveBall() /* moves the ball */
48  {
49      switch ( direction ) {
50          case DOWN_RIGHT:
51              ++ball_x; /* move the ball to the right */
52              ++ball_y; /* move the ball down */
53              break;
54          case UP_RIGHT:
55              ++ball_x; /* move the ball to the right */
56              --ball_y; /* move the ball up */
57              break;
58          case DOWN_LEFT:
59              --ball_x; /* move the ball to the left */
60              ++ball_y; /* move the ball down */
61              break;
62          case UP_LEFT:
63              --ball_x; /* move the ball to the left */
64              --ball_y; /* move the ball up */
65              break;
66      } /* end switch */
67
```

Fig. 15.5 | Creating the bouncing ball. (Part 2 of 3.)

```
68       /* make sure the ball doesn't go off the screen */
69
70       /* if the ball is going off the top or bottom... */
71       if ( ball_y <= 30 || ball_y >= 440 )
72          reverseVerticalDirection(); /* make it go the other way */
73
74       /* if the ball is going off the left or right... */
75       if ( ball_x <= 0 || ball_x >= 600 )
76          reverseHorizontalDirection(); /* make it go the other way */
77    } /* end function moveBall */
78
79    void reverseVerticalDirection() /* reverse the ball's up-down direction */
80    {
81       if ( ( direction % 2 ) == 0 ) /* "down" directions are even numbers */
82          ++direction; /* make the ball start moving up */
83       else /* "up" directions are odd numbers */
84          --direction; /* make the ball start moving down */
85    } /* end function reverseVerticalDirection */
86
87    void reverseHorizontalDirection() /* reverses the horizontal direction */
88    {
89       direction = ( direction + 2 ) % 4; /* reverse horizontal direction */
90    } /* end function reverseHorizontalDirection */
```

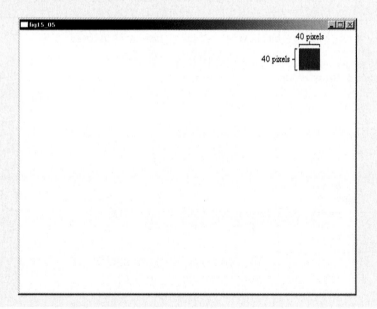

Fig. 15.5 | Creating the bouncing ball. (Part 3 of 3.)

Not much is new in this program. The first lines of interest are at lines 29 and 30 where we set the initial values for ball_x and ball_y. The symbolic constants SCREEN_W and SCREEN_H are reserved by Allegro—these correspond to the width and height (in pixels), respectively, of the screen set by calling set_gfx_mode. These lines, therefore, place the ball in the center of the screen.

Line 34 contains a new keyboard-related item—Allegro has an array of `int`s called `key`. The array contains an index for each key on the keyboard—if a certain key is being pressed, the value at its corresponding index is set to 1; if it is not being pressed, the value is set to 0. The index that we check in the `while` loop is `KEY_ESC`, an Allegro symbolic constant that corresponds to the *Esc* key. Because the condition for our `while` loop is `!key[KEY_ESC]`, our program will continue while `key[KEY_ESC]` has a value of 0—in other words, while the *Esc* key is not being pressed. We will discuss the `key` array and Allegro's symbolic constants for the keyboard in more detail in Section 15.7.

Line 37 contains the function that we use to draw the background—`clear_to_color`. Allegro does not have any explicit "background" defined in its library, but the `clear_to_color` function, as described in Fig. 15.2, sets an initial color for the screen onto which we can later draw. Note, though, that in our program we had to use a function to pass the `color` parameter to `clear_to_color`. This function is the `makecol` function. Its prototype is:

```
int makecol( int red, int green, int blue );
```

This function returns an `int` that represents the color with the specified red, green, and blue intensities. The intensities allowed can range from 0 to 255, so passing the values `( 255, 0, 0 )` will create a bright red color, `( 0, 255, 0 )` will create a bright green and `( 0, 0, 255 )` will make a bright blue. In Fig. 15.5, we passed `( 255, 255, 255 )`, or the maximum intensity of all three colors, which creates white. This means that our program will set the color of the screen to white when the `clear_to_color` function is called. A table of common colors and their red, green, and blue values can be found in Fig. 15.6.

Color	Red value	Green value	Blue value
Red	255	0	0
Green	0	255	0
Blue	0	0	255
Orange	255	200	0
Pink	255	175	175
Cyan	0	255	255
Magenta	255	0	255
Yellow	255	255	0
Black	0	0	0
White	255	255	255
Gray	128	128	128
Light gray	192	192	192
Dark gray	64	64	64

Fig. 15.6 | The red, green and blue intensities of common colors in Allegro.

The rest of the program is self-explanatory—we have the ball move around the screen, and when it hits an edge, it changes its direction so that it "bounces." The reason that the lines in moveBall and the two reverseDirection functions are highlighted is because the math might appear to be a bit odd. First we check if the ball is going off the screen at lines 71 and 75. You may be wondering why the right and bottom boundaries of our screen appear to be 600 and 440 in these if statements, as opposed to 640 and 480 (the actual size of the screen). Recall that when we blit a bitmap onto the screen, we pass it the top-left corner of the block onto which we want to draw. This means that if ball_y has a value of 440, its top boundary will be at the y-coordinate 440. However, since the ball is 40 pixels tall, its bottom boundary will actually be at the y-coordinate 480, which is the bottom of the screen. The same applies to the ball's x-coordinate, which explains why the largest value it can be is 600. Also, if you are wondering why the lowest y-value allowed is 30, this is simply because we will use the top 30 pixels of the screen for the scoreboard as we add more into our Pong game.

Consider the lines that change the ball's direction. Line 82 causes the ball to start moving up if it's currently moving down, while line 84 does the opposite. Line 89 makes the ball start moving left if it's currently moving right, and right if it's currently moving left. Why does this work? Because of the specific values of the symbolic constants (lines 6–9), performing the operations in these three lines will always get you the direction you want.

Note that our "ball" is a square and not a circle. This does not have much impact on our program now, but once we add paddles into our game, having a square ball makes it much easier to detect if the ball and paddles are touching. We will go into more detail on this issue in Section 15.9 when we add this feature to our game.

Run the program and you'll see your ball bounce around the screen. Notice, though, that the screen flickers substantially as the ball moves, to the point where it is difficult to see the ball. To fix this, we introduce a technique called double buffering.

Double Buffering for Smooth Animation

If you ran the program of the previous section, you probably noticed that the screen flickered as the ball moved. Why is this? Recall that for our animation to work, we had to clear the screen every time the ball moved. Unfortunately, this isn't the best practice. Though most computers can clear and redraw the screen quickly, there is still a small amount of time that the screen is blank between when it's cleared and when the ball is blitted onto it. Even though the screen is blank only briefly, it is still enough to cause the screen to appear to flicker as it animates the ball, since the ball keeps vanishing before it is redrawn.

We can fix this with a technique called **double buffering**, which uses a screen-sized, intermediary bitmap called a **buffer** to make the animation of moving bitmaps smoother. Instead of blitting bitmaps to the screen, we blit objects we want the user to see to the buffer. Once everything we want is there, we blit the buffer to the screen and clear the buffer.

Why does this work? You'll notice that we never clear the screen when we use this technique. Instead of deleting everything before redrawing the images on the screen, we simply draw over what's already there, which eliminates the flicker that the program in Fig. 15.5 produced when it cleared the screen. In addition, since the buffer is not visible to the user (remember, the user can see only the screen), we can blit to and clear the buffer without worrying about it affecting anything that the user sees. Figure 15.7 shows this technique in practice.

Double buffering takes only slightly more code than blitting directly to the screen—
our modified program has only four more lines of code than the original! Lines 40–43
show how to code double buffering. We simply make the buffer white and blit the ball to
the buffer at position ball_x, ball_y. Then, blit the whole buffer to the screen, and clear
the buffer. The screen is never cleared, only drawn over, so there is no flicker.

```
1   /* Fig. 15.7: fig15_07.c
2      Using double buffering. */
3   #include <allegro.h>
4
5   /* symbolic constants for the ball's possible directions */
6   #define DOWN_RIGHT 0
7   #define UP_RIGHT 1
8   #define DOWN_LEFT 2
9   #define UP_LEFT 3
10
11  /* function prototypes */
12  void moveBall( void );
13  void reverseVerticalDirection( void );
14  void reverseHorizontalDirection( void );
15
16  int ball_x; /* the ball's x-coordinate */
17  int ball_y; /* the ball's y-coordinate */
18  int direction; /* the ball's direction */
19  BITMAP *ball; /* pointer to the ball's image bitmap */
20  BITMAP *buffer; /* pointer to the buffer */
21
22  int main( void )
23  {
24     /* first, set up Allegro and the graphics mode */
25     allegro_init(); /* initialize Allegro */
26     install_keyboard(); /* install the keyboard for Allegro to use */
27     set_color_depth( 16 ); /* set the color depth to 16-bit */
28     set_gfx_mode( GFX_AUTODETECT, 640, 480, 0, 0 ); /* set graphics mode */
29     ball = load_bitmap( "ball.bmp", NULL ); /* load the ball bitmap */
30     buffer = create_bitmap( SCREEN_W, SCREEN_H );/* create buffer */
31     ball_x = SCREEN_W / 2; /* give the ball its initial x-coordinate */
32     ball_y = SCREEN_H / 2; /* give the ball its initial y-coordinate */
33     srand( time( NULL ) ); /* seed the random function ... */
34     direction = rand() % 4; /* and then make a random initial direction */
35
36     while ( !key[KEY_ESC] ) /* until the escape key is pressed ... */
37     {
38        moveBall(); /* move the ball */
39        /* now, perform double buffering */
40        clear_to_color( buffer, makecol( 255, 255, 255 ) );
41        blit( ball, buffer, 0, 0, ball_x, ball_y, ball->w, ball->h );
42        blit( buffer, screen, 0, 0, 0, 0, buffer->w, buffer->h );
43        clear_bitmap( buffer );
44     } /* end while */
```

Fig. 15.7 | Using double buffering. (Part 1 of 3.)

```
45
46      destroy_bitmap( ball ); /* destroy the ball bitmap */
47      destroy_bitmap( buffer ); /* destroy the buffer bitmap */
48      return 0;
49   } /* end function main */
50   END_OF_MAIN() /* don't forget this! */
51
52   void moveBall() /* moves the ball */
53   {
54      switch ( direction ) {
55         case DOWN_RIGHT:
56            ++ball_x; /* move the ball to the right */
57            ++ball_y; /* move the ball down */
58            break;
59         case UP_RIGHT:
60            ++ball_x; /* move the ball to the right */
61            --ball_y; /* move the ball up */
62            break;
63         case DOWN_LEFT:
64            --ball_x; /* move the ball to the left */
65            ++ball_y; /* move the ball down */
66            break;
67         case UP_LEFT:
68            --ball_x; /* move the ball to the left */
69            --ball_y; /* move the ball up */
70            break;
71      } /* end switch */
72
73      /* make sure the ball doesn't go off the screen */
74
75      /* if the ball is going off the top or bottom ... */
76      if ( ball_y <= 30 || ball_y >= 440 )
77         reverseVerticalDirection();
78
79      /* if the ball is going off the left or right ... */
80      if ( ball_x <= 0 || ball_x >= 600 )
81         reverseHorizontalDirection();
82   } /* end function moveBall */
83
84   void reverseVerticalDirection() /* reverse the ball's up-down direction */
85   {
86      if ( ( direction % 2 ) == 0 ) /* "down" directions are even numbers */
87         ++direction; /* make the ball start moving up */
88      else /* "up" directions are odd numbers */
89         --direction; /* make the ball start moving down */
90   } /* end function reverseVerticalDirection */
91
92   void reverseHorizontalDirection() /* reverses the horizontal direction */
93   {
94      direction = ( direction + 2 ) % 4; /* reverse horizontal direction */
95   } /* end function reverseHorizontalDirection */
```

Fig. 15.7 | Using double buffering. (Part 2 of 3.)

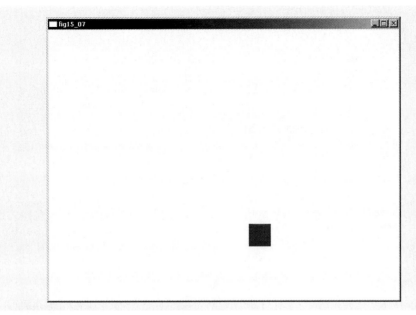

Fig. 15.7 | Using double buffering. (Part 3 of 3.)

15.6 Importing and Playing Sounds

While a game with only graphics is fun to play, a game that uses sounds to enhance the player's experience is much more interesting. We now discuss importing sounds and playing sound files in Allegro programs, which we will use to "juice up" our game by having a "boing" sound play whenever the ball hits a wall.

Sound files are handled similarly to bitmaps—just as the allegro.h header defines several types that are used to hold image data, it defines several types that are used to hold sound data, as well. With images, the most basic of these types is BITMAP*. With sounds, the most basic of these types is the type SAMPLE*—Allegro refers to sound files as "digital samples." Note that like BITMAP*, the SAMPLE* type is a pointer.

The Allegro functions used to import and play sounds are analogous to those used for importing and displaying bitmaps. Figure 15.8 shows the most important Allegro functions for manipulating sound files.

The install_sound function must be called before Allegro can play any sound files. Its prototype is:

```
int install_sound(int digi, int midi, const char *cfg_path);
```

The function returns an int for error-checking purposes—0 if the function is successful, and a non-zero value if it is not. The digi and midi parameters specify the sound card drivers used for playing digital samples and MIDI files, respectively. As with the graphic drivers, the newer versions of Allegro provide so-called "magic drivers" that automatically specify the audio drivers to use—DIGI_AUTODETECT and MIDI_AUTODETECT. These are the only values that you should pass to the first two parameters.

Function prototype	Description
`SAMPLE *load_sample(const char *filename)`	Loads and returns a pointer to a sound file with the specified filename. The file must be in .wav format. Returns NULL (with no error) if the specified file cannot be loaded.
`int play_sample(const SAMPLE *spl, int vol, int pan, int freq, int loop)`	Plays the specified sample at the specified volume, pan position, and frequency. The sample will loop continuously if loop is non-zero.
`void adjust_sample(const SAMPLE *spl, int vol, int pan, int freq, int loop)`	Adjusts a currently playing sample's parameters to the ones specified. Can be called on any sample without causing errors, but will affect only ones that are currently playing.
`void stop_sample(const SAMPLE *spl)`	Stops a sample that is currently playing.
`void destroy_sample(SAMPLE *spl)`	Destroys a sample and frees the memory allocated to it. If the sample is currently playing or looping, it will stop immediately.

Fig. 15.8 | Important SAMPLE functions.

Note that the `cfg_path` parameter has no effect on the program. Older versions of Allegro required that you specify a .cfg file that told the program how to play sound files, but this is no longer necessary in the current version.

Now let's add sounds to the bouncing ball program. As with bitmaps, we must provide the program with an external sound file to load, so copy the `boing.wav` sound file from the chapter's examples folder and save it in the same folder as your `pong` project. Then we can use the code in Fig. 15.9 to make our ball emit a "boing" sound whenever it bounces off a side of the screen. The highlighted lines mark the changes from the previous section.

Because we placed the call to the `play_sample` function inside our functions that reverse the ball's direction, the "boing" sound will play whenever the ball's direction is reversed—in other words, whenever the ball hits the boundary of the screen. Consider the prototype of function `play_sample`:

```
int play_sample(const SAMPLE *sample, int volume, int pan,
    int frequency, int loop)
```

The `volume` and `pan` parameters determine the volume and pan position of the sample being played, and the values passed to them can range from 0 to 255. A volume of 0 means the sound will be muted, while a volume of 255 plays the sound at full volume. A pan position of 128 will play the sound out of both speakers equally, while a lower or higher value will play the sound more towards the left or right, respectively. The `frequency` parameter, which specifies the frequency at which the sample will be played, is a parameter whose value is relative rather than absolute. A `frequency` value of 1000 will play the sound at the frequency at which it was recorded, while a value of 2000 will play a sample at twice its normal frequency, which produces a much higher pitch, a value of 500 will play the sample at half its normal frequency, which produces a lower pitch and so on. Finally, as explained in Fig. 15.8, the loop parameter will cause the sample to loop continuously if its value is not 0. Otherwise, the sample will play only once.

```
 1   /* Fig. 15.9: fig15_09.c
 2      Utilizing sound files */
 3   #include <allegro.h>
 4
 5   /* symbolic constants for the ball's possible directions */
 6   #define DOWN_RIGHT 0
 7   #define UP_RIGHT 1
 8   #define DOWN_LEFT 2
 9   #define UP_LEFT 3
10
11   /* function prototypes */
12   void moveBall( void );
13   void reverseVerticalDirection( void );
14   void reverseHorizontalDirection( void );
15
16   int ball_x; /* the ball's x-coordinate */
17   int ball_y; /* the ball's y-coordinate */
18   int direction; /* the ball's direction */
19   BITMAP *ball; /* pointer to ball's image bitmap */
20   BITMAP *buffer; /* pointer to the buffer */
21   SAMPLE *boing; /* pointer to sound file */
22
23   int main( void )
24   {
25      /* first, set up Allegro and the graphics mode */
26      allegro_init(); /* initialize Allegro */
27      install_keyboard(); /* install the keyboard for Allegro to use */
28      install_sound( DIGI_AUTODETECT, MIDI_AUTODETECT, NULL );
29      set_color_depth( 16 ); /* set the color depth to 16-bit */
30      set_gfx_mode( GFX_AUTODETECT, 640, 480, 0, 0 ); /* set graphics mode */
31      ball = load_bitmap( "ball.bmp", NULL ); /* load the ball bitmap */
32      buffer = create_bitmap(SCREEN_W, SCREEN_H);/* create buffer */
33      boing = load_sample( "boing.wav" ); /* load the sound file */
34      ball_x = SCREEN_W / 2; /* give the ball its initial x-coordinate */
35      ball_y = SCREEN_H / 2; /* give the ball its initial y-coordinate */
36      srand( time( NULL ) ); /* seed the random function ... */
37      direction = rand() % 4; /* and then make a random initial direction */
38      while ( !key[KEY_ESC] )/* until the escape key is pressed ... */
39      {
40         moveBall(); /* move the ball */
41         /* now, perform double buffering */
42         clear_to_color( buffer, makecol( 255, 255, 255 ) );
43         blit( ball, buffer, 0, 0, ball_x, ball_y, ball->w, ball->h );
44         blit( buffer, screen, 0, 0, 0, 0, buffer->w, buffer->h );
45         clear_bitmap( buffer );
46      } /* end while loop */
```

Fig. 15.9 | Utilizing sound files. (Part I of 3.)

```
47      destroy_bitmap( ball ); /* destroy the ball bitmap */
48      destroy_bitmap( buffer ); /* destroy the buffer bitmap */
49      destroy_sample( boing ); /* destroy the boing sound file */
50      return 0;
51   } /* end function main */
52   END_OF_MAIN() /* don't forget this! */
53
54   void moveBall() /* moves the ball */
55   {
56      switch ( direction ) {
57         case DOWN_RIGHT:
58            ++ball_x; /* move the ball to the right */
59            ++ball_y; /* move the ball down */
60            break;
61         case UP_RIGHT:
62            ++ball_x; /* move the ball to the right */
63            --ball_y; /* move the ball up */
64            break;
65         case DOWN_LEFT:
66            --ball_x; /* move the ball to the left */
67            ++ball_y; /* move the ball down */
68            break;
69         case UP_LEFT:
70            --ball_x; /* move the ball to the left */
71            --ball_y; /* move the ball up */
72            break;
73      } /* end switch */
74
75      /* make sure the ball doesn't go off screen */
76
77      /* if the ball is going off the top or bottom ... */
78      if ( ball_y <= 30 || ball_y >= 440 )
79         reverseVerticalDirection();
80
81      /* if the ball is going off the left or right ... */
82      if ( ball_x <= 0 || ball_x >= 600 )
83         reverseHorizontalDirection();
84   } /* end function moveBall */
85
86   void reverseVerticalDirection() /* reverse the ball's up-down direction */
87   {
88      if ( ( direction % 2 ) == 0 ) /* "down" directions are even numbers */
89         ++direction; /* make the ball start moving up */
90      else /* "up" directions are odd numbers */
91         --direction; /* make the ball start moving down */
92      play_sample( boing, 255, 128, 1000, 0 ); /* play "boing" sound once */
93   } /* end function reverseVerticalDirection */
94
95   void reverseHorizontalDirection() /* reverses the horizontal direction */
96   {
97      direction = ( direction + 2 ) % 4; /* reverse horizontal direction */
98      play_sample( boing, 255, 128, 1000, 0 ); /* play "boing" sound once */
99   } /* end function reverseHorizontalDirection */
```

Fig. 15.9 | Utilizing sound files. (Part 2 of 3.)

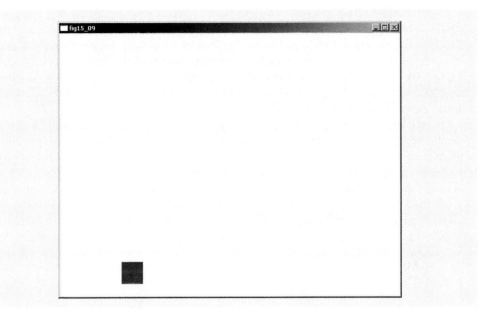

Fig. 15.9 | Utilizing sound files. (Part 3 of 3.)

15.7 Keyboard Input

A game cannot be called a game unless the user can interact with it in some way. We have already used some keyboard input methods in this chapter; now we discuss keyboard input in Allegro in more detail.

The first thing we must do to allow Allegro to recognize and use the keyboard is call the install_keyboard function, which takes no parameters. Allegro does not need any driver information to install the keyboard.

Recall that Allegro defines an array of ints called key. This array enables us to determine when keys are pressed. In addition to the array, the allegro.h header defines symbolic constants that correspond to the keys on a standard keyboard. For example, the constant for the *A* key is KEY_A, and the constant for the spacebar is KEY_SPACE. The full list of these constants is available at www.allegro.cc/manual/key. These constants are used in tandem with the key array to determine if the key to which a given constant corresponds is being pressed at any given time.

Each symbolic constant corresponds to an index in the key array that keeps track of whether that key is being pressed or not. If the key is not being pressed, the array will hold 0 at that index, while if it is, the value at that index will be non-zero. Thus, if we want to see if the *A* key is being pressed, we look at the value returned by key[KEY_A]. If it is not zero, then we know the user is pressing the *A* key.

In our Pong game, we use this array to control the paddles on the sides of the screen. If the *A* or *Z* keys are being pressed, the paddle on the left side should move up and down, respectively. Likewise, if the user presses the up or down arrow keys, the paddle on the right side should move in the corresponding direction. For this purpose, we add a new function, respondToKeyboard, to our program that checks if any of these four keys are being pressed and moves the paddles accordingly.

Of course, we have not yet drawn the paddles in our program, so the first thing we need is a bitmap file that contains the image data for them. As with the ball bitmap, you can find the bitmap file for a paddle in this chapter's examples folder. Save the file as bar.bmp in the same folder as your Pong project (note that the bitmap is 20 by 100 pixels—we will use this information in the program). Once you have done that, you can use the code in Fig. 15.10 to allow the user to move the paddles with the keyboard. As usual, new lines in the program are highlighted.

Lines 101–109 in Fig. 15.10 show how we use the key array to determine whether certain keys are being pressed. In C, any statement that returns a non-zero value is considered "true" if used in the condition of an if statement, so Allegro's key array makes it easy to check for keypresses. Note, however, that the call to the respondToKeyboard function is inside the while loop in our main (line 49)—this is needed for the keyboard input to work correctly. Though the if statements in lines 101–109 are all that is necessary to check if certain keys have been pressed, each statement checks only once per call. Since we want to have our program check *constantly* for keyboard input, we must place the respondToKeyboard function inside some sort of loop that ensures the program will call it repeatedly. This holds true for most games besides Pong, as well.

```
1   /* Fig. 15.10: fig15_10.c
2      Adding paddles and keyboard input. */
3   #include <allegro.h>
4
5   /* symbolic constants for the ball's possible directions */
6   #define DOWN_RIGHT 0
7   #define UP_RIGHT 1
8   #define DOWN_LEFT 2
9   #define UP_LEFT 3
10
11  /* function prototypes */
12  void moveBall( void );
13  void respondToKeyboard( void );
14  void reverseVerticalDirection( void );
15  void reverseHorizontalDirection( void );
16
17  int ball_x; /* the ball's x-coordinate */
18  int ball_y; /* the ball's y-coordinate */
19  int barL_y; /* y-coordinate of the left paddle */
20  int barR_y; /* y-coordinate of the right paddle */
21  int direction; /* the ball's direction */
22  BITMAP *ball; /* pointer to ball's image bitmap */
23  BITMAP *bar; /* pointer to paddle's image bitmap */
24  BITMAP *buffer; /* pointer to the buffer */
25  SAMPLE *boing; /* pointer to sound file */
26
27  int main( void )
28  {
29      /* first, set up Allegro and the graphics mode */
30      allegro_init(); /* initialize Allegro */
```

Fig. 15.10 | Adding paddles and keyboard input. (Part 1 of 5.)

```
31    install_keyboard(); /* install the keyboard for Allegro to use */
32    install_sound( DIGI_AUTODETECT, MIDI_AUTODETECT, NULL );
33    set_color_depth( 16 ); /* set the color depth to 16-bit */
34    set_gfx_mode( GFX_AUTODETECT, 640, 480, 0, 0 ); /* set graphics mode */
35    ball = load_bitmap( "ball.bmp", NULL ); /* load the ball bitmap */
36    bar = load_bitmap( "bar.bmp", NULL); /* load the bar bitmap */
37    buffer = create_bitmap(SCREEN_W, SCREEN_H);/* create buffer */
38    boing = load_sample( "boing.wav" ); /* load the sound file */
39    ball_x = SCREEN_W / 2; /* give the ball its initial x-coordinate */
40    ball_y = SCREEN_H / 2; /* give the ball its initial y-coordinate */
41    barL_y = SCREEN_H / 2; /* give left paddle its initial y-coordinate */
42    barR_y = SCREEN_H / 2; /* give right paddle its initial y-coordinate */
43    srand( time( NULL ) ); /* seed the random function ... */
44    direction = rand() % 4; /* and then make a random initial direction */
45
46    while ( !key[KEY_ESC] ) /* until the escape key is pressed ... */
47    {
48       moveBall(); /* move the ball */
49       respondToKeyboard(); /* respond to keyboard input */
50       /* now, perform double buffering */
51       clear_to_color( buffer, makecol( 255, 255, 255 ) );
52       blit( ball, buffer, 0, 0, ball_x, ball_y, ball->w, ball->h );
53       blit( bar, buffer, 0, 0, 0, barL_y, bar->w, bar->h );
54       blit( bar, buffer, 0, 0, 620, barR_y, bar->w, bar->h );
55       blit( buffer, screen, 0, 0, 0, 0, buffer->w, buffer->h );
56       clear_bitmap( buffer );
57    } /* end while */
58
59    destroy_bitmap( ball ); /* destroy the ball bitmap */
60    destroy_bitmap( bar ); /* destroy the bar bitmap */
61    destroy_bitmap( buffer ); /* destroy the buffer bitmap */
62    destroy_sample( boing ); /* destroy the boing sound file */
63    return 0;
64 } /* end function main */
65 END_OF_MAIN() /* don't forget this! */
66
67 void moveBall() /* moves the ball */
68 {
69    switch ( direction ) {
70       case DOWN_RIGHT:
71          ++ball_x; /* move the ball to the right */
72          ++ball_y; /* move the ball down */
73          break;
74       case UP_RIGHT:
75          ++ball_x; /* move the ball to the right */
76          --ball_y; /* move the ball up */
77          break;
78       case DOWN_LEFT:
79          --ball_x; /* move the ball to the left */
80          ++ball_y; /* move the ball down */
81          break;
82       case UP_LEFT:
83          --ball_x; /* move the ball to the left */
```

Fig. 15.10 | Adding paddles and keyboard input. (Part 2 of 5.)

```
84              --ball_y; /* move the ball up */
85              break;
86        } /* end switch */
87
88        /* make sure the ball doesn't go off screen */
89
90        /* if the ball is going off the top or bottom ... */
91        if ( ball_y <= 30 || ball_y >= 440 )
92           reverseVerticalDirection();
93
94        /* if the ball is going off the left or right ... */
95        if ( ball_x <= 0 || ball_x >= 600 )
96           reverseHorizontalDirection();
97     } /* end function moveBall */
98
99     void respondToKeyboard() /* responds to keyboard input */
100    {
101       if ( key[KEY_A] ) /* if A is being pressed... */
102          barL_y -= 3; /* ... move the left paddle up */
103       if ( key[KEY_Z] ) /* if Z is being pressed... */
104          barL_y += 3; /* ... move the left paddle down */
105
106       if ( key[KEY_UP] ) /* if the up arrow key is being pressed... */
107          barR_y -= 3; /* ... move the right paddle up */
108       if ( key[KEY_DOWN] ) /* if the down arrow key is being pressed... */
109          barR_y += 3; /* ... move the right paddle down */
110
111       /* make sure the paddles don't go offscreen */
112       if ( barL_y < 30 ) /* if left paddle is going off the top */
113          barL_y = 30;
114       else if ( barL_y > 380 ) /* if left paddle is going off the bottom */
115          barL_y = 380;
116       if ( barR_y < 30 ) /* if right paddle is going off the top */
117          barR_y = 30;
118       else if ( barR_y > 380 ) /* if right paddle is going off the bottom */
119          barR_y = 380;
120    } /* end function respondToKeyboard */
121
122    void reverseVerticalDirection() /* reverse the ball's up-down direction */
123    {
124       if ( ( direction % 2 ) == 0 ) /* "down" directions are even numbers */
125          ++direction; /* make the ball start moving up */
126       else /* "up" directions are odd numbers */
127          --direction; /* make the ball start moving down */
128       play_sample( boing, 255, 128, 1000, 0 ); /* play "boing" sound once */
129    } /* end function reverseVerticalDirection */
130
131    void reverseHorizontalDirection() /* reverses the horizontal direction */
132    {
133       direction = ( direction + 2 ) % 4; /* reverse horizontal direction */
134       play_sample( boing, 255, 128, 1000, 0 ); /* play "boing" sound once */
135    } /* end function reverseHorizontalDirection */
```

Fig. 15.10 | Adding paddles and keyboard input. (Part 3 of 5.)

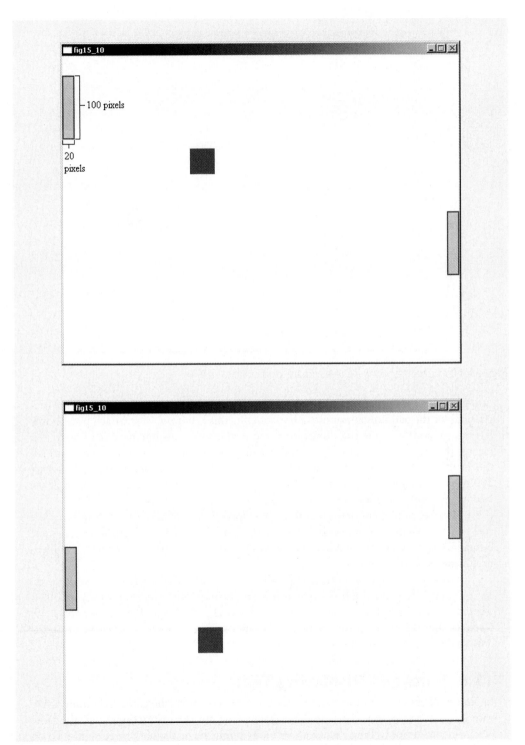

Fig. 15.10 | Adding paddles and keyboard input. (Part 4 of 5.)

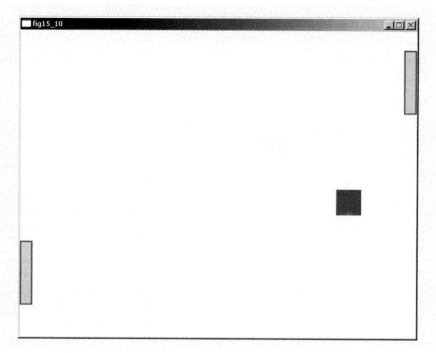

Fig. 15.10 | Adding paddles and keyboard input. (Part 5 of 5.)

You may notice that we did not keep track of the paddles' *x*-coordinates in this program. Since the paddles cannot move horizontally, this is not necessary. Each paddle only has one *x*-coordinate for the duration of the game, so we do not need a variable that records those values. Also, as with the ball, the maximum *y*-coordinate allowed for the paddles is not 480 (the height of the screen); rather, it is 380. This is because the paddles are 100 pixels high, and a *y*-coordinate of 380 means that the bottom of the paddle is at the *y*-coordinate 480—the bottom of the screen.

One other thing to notice is that though we loaded the bar bitmap only once, we were able to draw it to the screen in two different places simultaneously. Allegro allows the same bitmap to be drawn in many different places, a feature that is useful if you need two identical bitmaps on the screen at once.

However, at this point, while the paddles can be moved with the keyboard, they do not have any effect on the ball—it will keep bouncing around the screen regardless of whether or not the paddles are in its way. We will deal with this problem in Section 15.9, when we code this feature into our game. For now, we take a look at another Allegro capability—displaying text on the screen.

15.8 Fonts and Displaying Text

In almost all games, even the simplest ones, it is necessary for the game to communicate with the user in some way. This can range from giving the user instructions while the game is running, to simply telling the user how many points he or she has scored so far. To do this, the game developer needs some way of displaying text on the screen so that the player can read it. In Allegro, displaying text is handled in a similar way to displaying bitmaps and playing sounds.

To display text in Allegro, the most important thing we must specify—aside from the actual text to be displayed, of course—is the font in which it should be displayed. As with bitmaps and sounds, Allegro can load fonts from external files, and defines a type which points to the place in memory where these files are stored—FONT*. Loading fonts is done with the load_font function, which works the same as load_bitmap and load_sample. Likewise, once you are done with a font, it must be destroyed with the destroy_font function to prevent memory leaks. Note that if you wish to load a font from a file, it must be in .fnt, .bmp, or .pcx format. The parameters of load_font are slightly different from those of load_bitmap and load_sample, so we consider its prototype:

```
FONT *load_font( const char *filename, RGB *palette,
    void *parameter );
```

The first parameter is, obviously, the filename of the font file that is being loaded. The second parameter is something we have seen before—a palette. However, as with bitmaps, if the color depth is not 8-bit, we do not actually have to pass a palette to the function. It can safely be NULL without consequence. We will not use the third parameter—it is used to tell Allegro to load fonts in different ways, which we do not need to do. Like the second parameter, it can be set to NULL without causing any problems. Once a font has been loaded, you can use the functions in Fig. 15.11 to draw text onto a bitmap or the screen.

Function prototype	Description
```void textprintf_ex(BITMAP *bmp, const FONT *f, int x, int y, int color, int bgColor, const char *fmt, ...)```	Draws the format control string specified by fmt and the parameters following it onto bmp at the specified coordinates. The text is drawn in the specified font and colors, and is left justified.
```void textprintf_centre_ex(BITMAP *bmp, const FONT *f, int x, int y, int color, int bgColor, const char *fmt, ...)```	Works the same way as textprintf_ex, but the text drawn is center justified at the specified coordinates.
```void textprintf_right_ex(BITMAP *bmp, const FONT *f, int x, int y, int color, int bgColor, const char *fmt, ...)```	Works the same way as textprintf_ex, but the text drawn is right justified at the specified coordinates.
```int text_length(const FONT *f, const char *string)```	Returns the width (in pixels) of the specified string when drawn in the specified font. Useful when aligning multiple text outputs.
```int text_height(const FONT *f, const char *string)```	Returns the height (in pixels) of the specified string when drawn in the specified font. Useful when aligning multiple text outputs.

Fig. 15.11 | Functions that are useful for drawing text onto a bitmap.

(Note that the `allegro.h` header defines a global variable, `font`, that contains the data for Allegro's "default" font. This font can be used if you do not have a font file from which to load. We provide a font file for our Pong game, but this is still a useful feature to know.)

As you can see, the text output functions have quite a number of parameters. It may be useful to take a look at an example of a function call to understand how the function works.

```
textprintf_ex( buffer, font, 0, 0, makecol( 0, 0, 0 ), -1,
    "Hello!" );
```

This function call displays the string `"Hello!"` at the top-left corner of a buffer (which can later be drawn onto the screen), using the default font. The text is displayed in black, with a transparent background color.

The string we pass to the `textprintf_ex` function is a format control string. This means that we can use any of the conversion specifiers discussed in Chapter 9 to print `int`s, `double`s and other variables. This is very useful if, for example, we want to print a player's score, as we will need to do in our Pong game.

Note that we passed the `bgColor` parameter a value of -1 in the example call. Allegro cannot create this color with a call to `makecol`, as it interprets the value of -1 as "no color" or "transparent." This means that the text displayed will have no background color and that anything "behind" the text will be visible.

Normally the default Allegro font is fine when displaying text, but we have provided the `pongfont.pcx` font file with the chapter examples for use with our program. In our Pong game, we use the functions described above to display the scores of each of the players. For this reason, we add the `int`s, `scoreL` and `scoreR`, to this iteration of the program. Note, however, that since the paddles do not yet do anything, we cannot yet keep score in the game, and so the values of `scoreL` and `scoreR` will remain at 0 for the duration of the program. Nevertheless, Fig. 15.12 shows how to use the functions explained previously to display text on the screen using the font provided on our website.

```
1  /* Fig. 15.12: fig15_12.c
2     Displaying text on the screen. */
3  #include <allegro.h>
4
5  /* symbolic constants for the ball's possible directions */
6  #define DOWN_RIGHT 0
7  #define UP_RIGHT 1
8  #define DOWN_LEFT 2
9  #define UP_LEFT 3
10
11 /* function prototypes */
12 void moveBall( void );
13 void respondToKeyboard( void );
14 void reverseVerticalDirection( void );
15 void reverseHorizontalDirection( void );
16
17 int ball_x; /* the ball's x-coordinate */
18 int ball_y; /* the ball's y-coordinate */
```

Fig. 15.12 | Displaying text on the screen. (Part 1 of 4.)

```
19   int barL_y; /* y-coordinate of the left paddle */
20   int barR_y; /* y-coordinate of the right paddle */
21   int scoreL; /* score of the left player */
22   int scoreR; /* score of the right player */
23   int direction; /* the ball's direction */
24   BITMAP *ball; /* pointer to ball's image bitmap */
25   BITMAP *bar; /* pointer to paddle's image bitmap */
26   BITMAP *buffer; /* pointer to the buffer */
27   SAMPLE *boing; /* pointer to sound file */
28   FONT *pongFont; /* pointer to font file */
29
30   int main( void )
31   {
32      /* first, set up Allegro and the graphics mode */
33      allegro_init(); /* initialize Allegro */
34      install_keyboard(); /* install the keyboard for Allegro to use */
35      install_sound( DIGI_AUTODETECT, MIDI_AUTODETECT, NULL );
36      set_color_depth( 16 ); /* set the color depth to 16-bit */
37      set_gfx_mode( GFX_AUTODETECT, 640, 480, 0, 0 ); /* set graphics mode */
38      ball = load_bitmap( "ball.bmp", NULL ); /* load the ball bitmap */
39      bar = load_bitmap( "bar.bmp", NULL); /* load the bar bitmap */
40      buffer = create_bitmap(SCREEN_W, SCREEN_H);/* create buffer */
41      boing = load_sample( "boing.wav" ); /* load the sound file */
42      pongFont = load_font( "pongfont.pcx", NULL, NULL ); /* load the font */
43      ball_x = SCREEN_W / 2; /* give the ball its initial x-coordinate */
44      ball_y = SCREEN_H / 2; /* give the ball its initial y-coordinate */
45      barL_y = SCREEN_H / 2; /* give left paddle its initial y-coordinate */
46      barR_y = SCREEN_H / 2; /* give right paddle its initial y-coordinate */
47      scoreL = 0; /* set left player's score to 0 */
48      scoreR = 0; /* set right player's score to 0 */
49      srand( time( NULL ) ); /* seed the random function ... */
50      direction = rand() % 4; /* and then make a random initial direction */
51
52      while ( !key[KEY_ESC] ) /* until the escape key is pressed ... */
53      {
54         moveBall(); /* move the ball */
55         respondToKeyboard(); /* respond to keyboard input */
56         /* now, perform double buffering */
57         clear_to_color( buffer, makecol( 255, 255, 255 ) );
58         blit( ball, buffer, 0, 0, ball_x, ball_y, ball->w, ball->h );
59         blit( bar, buffer, 0, 0, 0, barL_y, bar->w, bar->h );
60         blit( bar, buffer, 0, 0, 620, barR_y, bar->w, bar->h );
61         /* draw text onto the buffer */
62         textprintf_ex( buffer, pongFont, 75, 0, makecol( 0, 0, 0 ),
63                        -1, "Left Player Score: %d", scoreL );
64         textprintf_ex( buffer, pongFont, 400, 0, makecol( 0, 0, 0 ),
65                        -1, "Right Player Score: %d", scoreR );
66         blit( buffer, screen, 0, 0, 0, 0, buffer->w, buffer->h );
67         clear_bitmap( buffer );
68      } /* end while */
69
70      destroy_bitmap( ball ); /* destroy the ball bitmap */
```

Fig. 15.12 | Displaying text on the screen. (Part 2 of 4.)

```
71      destroy_bitmap( bar ); /* destroy the bar bitmap */
72      destroy_bitmap( buffer ); /* destroy the buffer bitmap */
73      destroy_sample( boing ); /* destroy the boing sound file */
74      destroy_font( pongFont ); /* destroy the font */
75      return 0;
76   } /* end function main */
77   END_OF_MAIN() /* don't forget this! */
78
79   void moveBall() /* moves the ball */
80   {
81      switch ( direction ) {
82         case DOWN_RIGHT:
83            ++ball_x; /* move the ball to the right */
84            ++ball_y; /* move the ball down */
85            break;
86         case UP_RIGHT:
87            ++ball_x; /* move the ball to the right */
88            --ball_y; /* move the ball up */
89            break;
90         case DOWN_LEFT:
91            --ball_x; /* move the ball to the left */
92            ++ball_y; /* move the ball down */
93            break;
94         case UP_LEFT:
95            --ball_x; /* move the ball to the left */
96            --ball_y; /* move the ball up */
97            break;
98      } /* end switch */
99
100     /* make sure the ball doesn't go off the screen */
101
102     /* if the ball is going off the top or bottom ... */
103     if ( ball_y <= 30 || ball_y >= 440 )
104        reverseVerticalDirection();
105
106     /* if the ball is going off the left or right ... */
107     if ( ball_x <= 0 || ball_x >= 600 )
108        reverseHorizontalDirection();
109  } /* end function moveBall */
110
111  void respondToKeyboard() /* responds to keyboard input */
112  {
113     if ( key[KEY_A] ) /* if A is being pressed... */
114        barL_y -= 3; /* ... move the left paddle up */
115     if ( key[KEY_Z] ) /* if Z is being pressed... */
116        barL_y += 3; /* ... move the left paddle down */
117
118     if ( key[KEY_UP] ) /* if the up arrow key is being pressed... */
119        barR_y -= 3; /* ... move the right paddle up */
120     if ( key[KEY_DOWN] ) /* if the down arrow key is being pressed... */
121        barR_y += 3; /* ... move the right paddle down */
122
```

Fig. 15.12 | Displaying text on the screen. (Part 3 of 4.)

```
123      /* make sure the paddles don't go offscreen */
124      if ( barL_y < 30 ) /* if left paddle is going off the top */
125          barL_y = 30;
126      else if ( barL_y > 380 ) /* if left paddle is going off the bottom */
127          barL_y = 380;
128      if ( barR_y < 30 ) /* if right paddle is going off the top */
129          barR_y = 30;
130      else if ( barR_y > 380 ) /* if right paddle is going off the bottom */
131          barR_y = 380;
132  } /* end function respondToKeyboard */
133
134  void reverseVerticalDirection() /* reverse the ball's up-down direction */
135  {
136      if ( ( direction % 2 ) == 0 ) /* "down" directions are even numbers */
137          ++direction; /* make the ball start moving up */
138      else /* "up" directions are odd numbers */
139          --direction; /* make the ball start moving down */
140      play_sample( boing, 255, 128, 1000, 0 ); /* play "boing" sound once */
141  } /* end function reverseVerticalDirection */
142
143  void reverseHorizontalDirection() /* reverses the horizontal direction */
144  {
145      direction = ( direction + 2 ) % 4; /* reverse horizontal direction */
146      play_sample( boing, 255, 128, 1000, 0 ); /* play "boing" sound once */
147  } /* end function reverseHorizontalDirection */
```

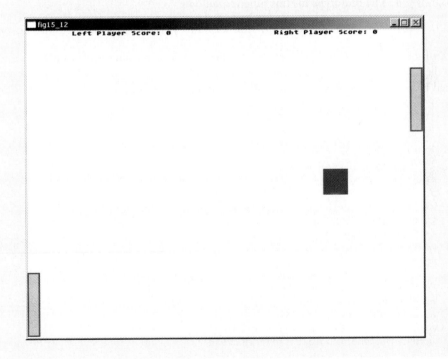

Fig. 15.12 | Displaying text on the screen. (Part 4 of 4.)

15.9 Implementing the Game of Pong

We now have all of the elements of our Pong game in our program—a ball, moving paddles, sounds and a scoreboard. However, these elements are not yet capable of interacting with each other. In this section we tie up the loose ends in our program to make it run like an actual Pong game.

The weakness in the current version of our program is that the paddles don't yet stop the ball—it keeps moving regardless of whether or not the paddles are in its way. In addition, when the ball hits the left or right edge of the screen, it simply bounces instead of going off the screen, and the player is not awarded a point.

The method that we use to fix these problems is surprisingly simple. Allegro does not have any functions that determine whether or not two bitmaps are touching, but since we know the dimensions of the ball and bar bitmaps, we can easily test if the ball has hit a paddle. Since we need to check only whether the paddle is in the way of the ball if the ball is moving off the left or right of the screen, we can make this check inside the if statement that checks the ball's *x*-coordinate.

The only other issue we face is the fact that while we have created a boundary near the top of the screen that ensures the ball doesn't move into the scoreboard, there is no visual indication that the boundary is there—the ball just appears to bounce for no reason. While we know why this is happening, it may confuse the players.

We mentioned earlier in the chapter that Allegro can draw simple graphics. In addition to being able to draw rectangles, circles, and polygons, Allegro has a line function to draw a line from one point to another. We can use this function to draw a line where our boundary is. The prototype for this function follows:

```
void line(BITMAP *bitmap, int x1, int y1, int x2, int y2, int color)
```

This function draws a straight line onto the specified bitmap from the coordinates (x1, y1) to the coordinates (x2, y2). The line will be drawn in the given color, which can be specified by using the makecol function. We can now put the finishing touches on our Pong game with the code in Fig. 15.13.

```
1   /* Fig. 15.13: fig15_13.c
2      Finishing up the Pong game. */
3   #include <allegro.h>
4
5   /* symbolic constants for the ball's possible directions */
6   #define DOWN_RIGHT 0
7   #define UP_RIGHT 1
8   #define DOWN_LEFT 2
9   #define UP_LEFT 3
10
11  /* function prototypes */
12  void moveBall( void );
13  void respondToKeyboard( void );
14  void reverseVerticalDirection( void );
15  void reverseHorizontalDirection( void );
```

Fig. 15.13 | Finishing up the Pong game. (Part I of 7.)

```
16
17   int ball_x; /* the ball's x-coordinate */
18   int ball_y; /* the ball's y-coordinate */
19   int barL_y; /* y-coordinate of the left paddle */
20   int barR_y; /* y-coordinate of the right paddle */
21   int scoreL; /* score of the left player */
22   int scoreR; /* score of the right player */
23   int direction; /* the ball's direction */
24   BITMAP *ball; /* pointer to ball's image bitmap */
25   BITMAP *bar; /* pointer to paddle's image bitmap */
26   BITMAP *buffer; /* pointer to the buffer */
27   SAMPLE *boing; /* pointer to sound file */
28   FONT *pongFont; /* pointer to font file */
29
30   int main( void )
31   {
32       /* first, set up Allegro and the graphics mode */
33       allegro_init(); /* initialize Allegro */
34       install_keyboard(); /* install the keyboard for Allegro to use */
35       install_sound( DIGI_AUTODETECT, MIDI_AUTODETECT, NULL );
36       set_color_depth( 16 ); /* set the color depth to 16-bit */
37       set_gfx_mode( GFX_AUTODETECT, 640, 480, 0, 0 ); /* set graphics mode */
38       ball = load_bitmap( "ball.bmp", NULL ); /* load the ball bitmap */
39       bar = load_bitmap( "bar.bmp", NULL); /* load the bar bitmap */
40       buffer = create_bitmap(SCREEN_W, SCREEN_H);/* create buffer */
41       boing = load_sample( "boing.wav" ); /* load the sound file */
42       pongFont = load_font( "pongfont.pcx", NULL, NULL ); /* load the font */
43       ball_x = SCREEN_W / 2; /* give ball its initial x-coordinate */
44       ball_y = SCREEN_H / 2; /* give ball its initial y-coordinate */
45       barL_y = SCREEN_H / 2; /* give left paddle its initial y-coordinate */
46       barR_y = SCREEN_H / 2; /* give right paddle its initial y-coordinate */
47       scoreL = 0; /* set left player's score to 0 */
48       scoreR = 0; /* set right player's score to 0 */
49       srand( time( NULL ) ); /* seed the random function ... */
50       direction = rand() % 4; /* and then make a random initial direction */
51
52       while ( !key[KEY_ESC] ) /* until the escape key is pressed ... */
53       {
54           moveBall(); /* move the ball */
55           respondToKeyboard(); /* respond to keyboard input */
56           /* now, perform double buffering */
57           clear_to_color( buffer, makecol( 255, 255, 255 ) );
58           blit( ball, buffer, 0, 0, ball_x, ball_y, ball->w, ball->h );
59           blit( bar, buffer, 0, 0, 0, barL_y, bar->w, bar->h );
60           blit( bar, buffer, 0, 0, 620, barR_y, bar->w, bar->h );
61           line( buffer, 0, 30, 640, 30, makecol( 0, 0, 0 ) );
62           /* draw text onto the buffer */
63           textprintf_ex( buffer, pongFont, 75, 0, makecol( 0, 0, 0 ),
64                           -1, "Left Player Score: %d", scoreL );
65           textprintf_ex( buffer, pongFont, 400, 0, makecol( 0, 0, 0 ),
66                           -1, "Right Player Score: %d", scoreR );
67           blit( buffer, screen, 0, 0, 0, 0, buffer->w, buffer->h );
```

Fig. 15.13 | Finishing up the Pong game. (Part 2 of 7.)

```
68          clear_bitmap( buffer );
69      } /* end while */
70
71      destroy_bitmap( ball ); /* destroy the ball bitmap */
72      destroy_bitmap( bar ); /* destroy the bar bitmap */
73      destroy_bitmap( buffer ); /* destroy the buffer bitmap */
74      destroy_sample( boing ); /* destroy the boing sound file */
75      destroy_font( pongFont ); /* destroy the font */
76      return 0;
77  } /* end function main */
78  END_OF_MAIN() /* don't forget this! */
79
80  void moveBall() /* moves the ball */
81  {
82      switch ( direction ) {
83          case DOWN_RIGHT:
84              ++ball_x; /* move the ball to the right */
85              ++ball_y; /* move the ball down */
86              break;
87          case UP_RIGHT:
88              ++ball_x; /* move the ball to the right */
89              --ball_y; /* move the ball up */
90              break;
91          case DOWN_LEFT:
92              --ball_x; /* move the ball to the left */
93              ++ball_y; /* move the ball down */
94              break;
95          case UP_LEFT:
96              --ball_x; /* move the ball to the left */
97              --ball_y; /* move the ball up */
98              break;
99      } /* end switch */
100
101     /* if the ball is going off the top or bottom ... */
102     if ( ball_y <= 30 || ball_y >= 440 )
103         reverseVerticalDirection(); /* make it go the other way */
104
105     /* if the ball is in range of the left paddle ... */
106     if (ball_x < 20 && (direction == DOWN_LEFT || direction == UP_LEFT))
107     {
108         /* is the left paddle in the way? */
109         if ( ball_y > ( barL_y - 39 ) && ball_y < ( barL_y + 99 ) )
110             reverseHorizontalDirection();
111         else if ( ball_x <= -20 ) { /* if the ball goes off the screen */
112             ++scoreR; /* give right player a point */
113             ball_x = SCREEN_W / 2; /* place the ball in the ... */
114             ball_y = SCREEN_H / 2; /* ... center of the screen */
115             direction = rand() % 4; /* give the ball a random direction */
116         } /* end else */
117     } /* end if */
118
```

Fig. 15.13 | Finishing up the Pong game. (Part 3 of 7.)

```
119       /* if the ball is in range of the right paddle ... */
120       if (ball_x > 580 && (direction == DOWN_RIGHT || direction == UP_RIGHT))
121       {
122          /* is the right paddle in the way? */
123          if ( ball_y > ( barR_y - 39 ) && ball_y < ( barR_y + 99 ) )
124             reverseHorizontalDirection();
125          else if ( ball_x >= 620 ) { /* if the ball goes off the screen */
126             ++scoreL; /* give left player a point */
127             ball_x = SCREEN_W / 2; /* place the ball in the ... */
128             ball_y = SCREEN_H / 2; /* ... center of the screen  */
129             direction = rand() % 4; /* give the ball a random direction */
130          } /* end else */
131       } /* end if */
132    } /* end function moveBall */
133
134    void respondToKeyboard() /* responds to keyboard input */
135    {
136       if ( key[KEY_A] ) /* if A is being pressed... */
137          barL_y -= 3; /* ... move the left paddle up */
138       if ( key[KEY_Z] ) /* if Z is being pressed... */
139          barL_y += 3; /* ... move the left paddle down */
140
141       if ( key[KEY_UP] ) /* if the up arrow key is being pressed... */
142          barR_y -= 3; /* ... move the right paddle up */
143       if ( key[KEY_DOWN] ) /* if the down arrow key is being pressed... */
144          barR_y += 3; /* ... move the right paddle down */
145
146       /* make sure the paddles don't go offscreen */
147       if ( barL_y < 30 ) /* if left paddle is going off the top */
148          barL_y = 30;
149       else if ( barL_y > 380 ) /* if left paddle is going off the bottom */
150          barL_y = 380;
151       if ( barR_y < 30 ) /* if right paddle is going off the top */
152          barR_y = 30;
153       else if ( barR_y > 380 ) /* if right paddle is going off the bottom */
154          barR_y = 380;
155    } /* end function respondToKeyboard */
156
157    void reverseVerticalDirection() /* reverse the ball's up-down direction */
158    {
159       if ( ( direction % 2 ) == 0 ) /* "down" directions are even numbers */
160          ++direction; /* make the ball start moving up */
161       else /* "up" directions are odd numbers */
162          --direction; /* make the ball start moving down */
163       play_sample( boing, 255, 128, 1000, 0 ); /* play "boing" sound once */
164    } /* end function reverseVerticalDirection */
165
166    void reverseHorizontalDirection() /* reverses the horizontal direction */
167    {
168       direction = ( direction + 2 ) % 4; /* reverse horizontal direction */
169       play_sample( boing, 255, 128, 1000, 0 ); /* play "boing" sound once */
170    } /* end function reverseHorizontalDirection */
```

Fig. 15.13 | Finishing up the Pong game. (Part 4 of 7.)

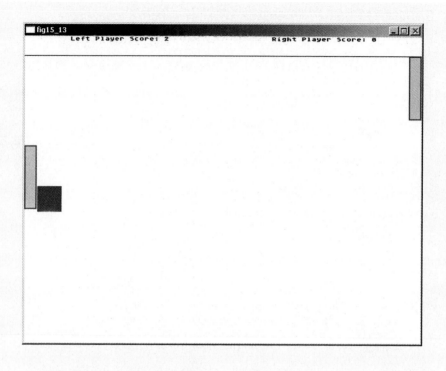

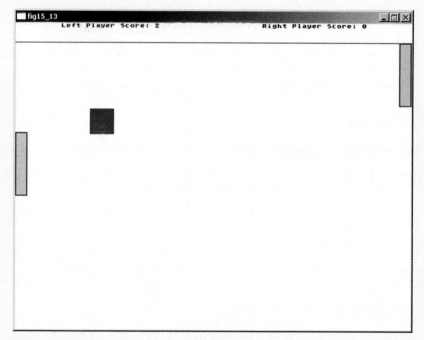

Fig. 15.13 | Finishing up the Pong game. (Part 5 of 7.)

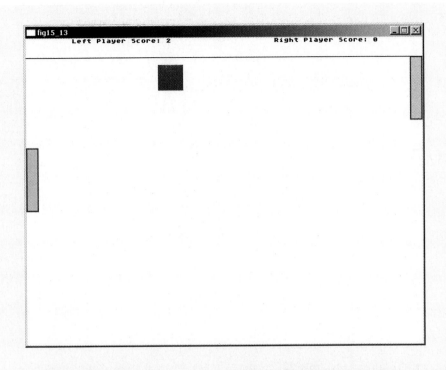

Fig. 15.13 | Finishing up the Pong game. (Part 6 of 7.)

Fig. 15.13 | Finishing up the Pong game. (Part 7 of 7.)

You may wonder why we chose the boundaries that we did for checking if the paddle is touching the ball. In order for the ball to "bounce" off a paddle, at least 1 pixel of the ball must be touching (i.e., immediately adjacent to) the paddle. Thus, If ball_y is 39 smaller than barL_y, the bottommost pixel of the ball is touching the bar, and if ball_y is 99 greater than barL_y, the topmost pixel is touching.

With this version of the program, our Pong game is now fully functional, but there are still a few improvements we can make. The first of these improvements is using timers to regulate the speed of the game, a topic we discuss in the next section.

15.10 Timers in Allegro

One missing feature of our Pong game is the ability to regulate the game's speed. At the moment, the main process of our game in Fig. 15.13 is contained in a while loop. However, this is not a good practice, as the speed at which a program executes varies from system to system based on factors such as the processor speed. As such our while loop could operate at varying speeds depending on the system on which we are running our game, making our ball and paddles move faster or slower than we may want. In this section, we introduce Allegro timers to help regulate the speed of our game.

We install the timer handler for Allegro to use by calling the function install_timer, which takes no parameters. Once we have called the install_timer function, we can add timers to our program. This is done by calling the install_int function. The prototype for this function is:

```
int install_int( void ( *function )(), int interval );
```

You'll notice that the `function` parameter is a function pointer. Calling the `install_int` function adds a timer to your program that calls the function specified by `function` every `interval` milliseconds. Thus, if we wanted to call a function `timedFunction` once every second, we would add the following code:

```
install_int( timedFunction, 1000 );
```

There is no need to store a newly-installed timer in a variable—the timer will automatically start running in the background of the program and will remain running until it is removed or the program ends. Also note that Allegro only identifies a timer by the function it is set to call. Calling `install_timer` and passing it a function that already has a timer tied to it does not create a new timer; instead, it simply changes the old timer's speed to the one specified by the `interval` parameter. Likewise, removing a timer is done by calling the `remove_timer` function and passing it the name of the function to which the timer is tied.

Allegro allows only 16 timers to be running at once regardless of the system being used. If we try to add more, the `install_int` function fails and returns a non-zero value. Generally, though, you should avoid using an excessive number of timers, as some Allegro processes also require timers to work, and they take up the same slots as regular timers. None of the Allegro functions we have discussed so far require timers, but some of the functions discussed in Section 15.12—specifically, the functions that play `.fli` animations and MIDI music files—do need them.

The final step for everything to work correctly is to add the `volatile` qualifier discussed in Chapter 14 to any variable whose value might be changed by our timers. Because Allegro is an external library, compilers cannot recognize what the `install_int` function does. For this reason, the compiler may not "understand" that a variable can be modified by a timer, and it may attempt to optimize the main program code by loading the variable's value into one of the computer's registers, thus failing to notice when that value changes. Adding the `volatile` qualifier to a variable that can be modified by a timer warns the compiler that this value may change unexpectedly, so it must generate code that correctly reloads the latest value from memory.

With some older operating systems (specifically, DOS and Mac OS 9 and below), it is also necessary that you "lock" the memory of the functions and variables used by your timers to ensure that they work correctly. This process is unnecessary on current systems, so we will not discuss it in this text. If you want your game to run correctly on older systems, you can find information on locking memory at www.allegro.cc/manual/api/timer-routines.

We can now add timers to our Pong game to regulate how quickly our ball and paddles move on the screen (Fig. 15.14).

```
1   /* Fig. 15.14: fig15_14.c
2      Adding timers to the Pong game. */
3   #include <allegro.h>
4
```

Fig. 15.14 | Adding timers to the Pong game. (Part 1 of 5.)

```
 5    /* symbolic constants for the ball's possible directions */
 6    #define DOWN_RIGHT 0
 7    #define UP_RIGHT 1
 8    #define DOWN_LEFT 2
 9    #define UP_LEFT 3
10
11    /* function prototypes */
12    void moveBall( void );
13    void respondToKeyboard( void );
14    void reverseVerticalDirection( void );
15    void reverseHorizontalDirection( void );
16
17    volatile int ball_x; /* the ball's x-coordinate */
18    volatile int ball_y; /* the ball's y-coordinate */
19    volatile int barL_y; /* y-coordinate of the left paddle */
20    volatile int barR_y; /* y-coordinate of the right paddle */
21    volatile int scoreL; /* score of the left player */
22    volatile int scoreR; /* score of the right player */
23    volatile int direction; /* the ball's direction */
24    BITMAP *ball; /* pointer to ball's image bitmap */
25    BITMAP *bar; /* pointer to paddle's image bitmap */
26    BITMAP *buffer; /* pointer to the buffer */
27    SAMPLE *boing; /* pointer to sound file */
28    FONT *pongFont; /* pointer to font file */
29
30    int main( void )
31    {
32       /* first, set up Allegro and the graphics mode */
33       allegro_init(); /* initialize Allegro */
34       install_keyboard(); /* install the keyboard for Allegro to use */
35       install_sound( DIGI_AUTODETECT, MIDI_AUTODETECT, NULL );
36       install_timer(); /* install the timer handler */
37       set_color_depth( 16 ); /* set the color depth to 16-bit */
38       set_gfx_mode( GFX_AUTODETECT, 640, 480, 0, 0 ); /* set graphics mode */
39       ball = load_bitmap( "ball.bmp", NULL ); /* load the ball bitmap */
40       bar = load_bitmap( "bar.bmp", NULL); /* load the bar bitmap */
41       buffer = create_bitmap(SCREEN_W, SCREEN_H);/* create buffer */
42       boing = load_sample( "boing.wav" ); /* load the sound file */
43       pongFont = load_font( "pongfont.pcx", NULL, NULL ); /* load the font */
44       ball_x = SCREEN_W / 2; /* give ball its initial x-coordinate */
45       ball_y = SCREEN_H / 2; /* give ball its initial y-coordinate */
46       barL_y = SCREEN_H / 2; /* give left paddle its initial y-coordinate */
47       barR_y = SCREEN_H / 2; /* give right paddle its initial y-coordinate */
48       scoreL = 0; /* set left player's score to 0 */
49       scoreR = 0; /* set right player's score to 0 */
50       srand( time( NULL ) ); /* seed the random function ... */
51       direction = rand() % 4; /* and then make a random initial direction */
52       /* add timer that calls moveBall every 5 milliseconds */
53       install_int( moveBall, 5 );
54       /* add timer that calls respondToKeyboard every 10 milliseconds */
55       install_int( respondToKeyboard, 10 );
56
```

Fig. 15.14 | Adding timers to the Pong game. (Part 2 of 5.)

```
57     while ( !key[KEY_ESC] ) /* until the escape key is pressed ... */
58     {
59        /* now, perform double buffering */
60        clear_to_color( buffer, ( 255, 255, 255 ) );
61        blit( ball, buffer, 0, 0, ball_x, ball_y, ball->w, ball->h );
62        blit( bar, buffer, 0, 0, 0, barL_y, bar->w, bar->h );
63        blit( bar, buffer, 0, 0, 620, barR_y, bar->w, bar->h );
64        line( buffer, 0, 30, 640, 30, makecol( 0, 0, 0 ) );
65        /* draw text onto the buffer */
66        textprintf_ex( buffer, pongFont, 75, 0, makecol( 0, 0, 0 ),
67                       -1, "Left Player Score: %d", scoreL );
68        textprintf_ex( buffer, pongFont, 400, 0, makecol( 0, 0, 0 ),
69                       -1, "Right Player Score: %d", scoreR );
70        blit( buffer, screen, 0, 0, 0, 0, buffer->w, buffer->h );
71        clear_bitmap( buffer );
72     } /* end while */
73
74     remove_int( moveBall ); /* remove moveBall timer */
75     remove_int( respondToKeyboard ); /* remove respondToKeyboard timer */
76     destroy_bitmap( ball ); /* destroy the ball bitmap */
77     destroy_bitmap( bar ); /* destroy the bar bitmap */
78     destroy_bitmap( buffer ); /* destroy the buffer bitmap */
79     destroy_sample( boing ); /* destroy the boing sound file */
80     destroy_font( pongFont ); /* destroy the font */
81     return 0;
82  } /* end function main */
83  END_OF_MAIN() /* don't forget this! */
84
85  void moveBall() /* moves the ball */
86  {
87     switch ( direction ) {
88        case DOWN_RIGHT:
89           ++ball_x; /* move the ball to the right */
90           ++ball_y; /* move the ball down */
91           break;
92        case UP_RIGHT:
93           ++ball_x; /* move the ball to the right */
94           --ball_y; /* move the ball up */
95           break;
96        case DOWN_LEFT:
97           --ball_x; /* move the ball to the left */
98           ++ball_y; /* move the ball down */
99           break;
100       case UP_LEFT:
101          --ball_x; /* move the ball to the left */
102          --ball_y; /* move the ball up */
103          break;
104    } /* end switch */
105
106    /* if the ball is going off the top or bottom ... */
107    if ( ball_y <= 30 || ball_y >= 440 )
108       reverseVerticalDirection(); /* make it go the other way */
109
```

Fig. 15.14 | Adding timers to the Pong game. (Part 3 of 5.)

```
110        /* if the ball is in range of the left paddle ... */
111        if (ball_x < 20 && (direction == DOWN_LEFT || direction == UP_LEFT))
112        {
113           /* is the left paddle in the way? */
114           if ( ball_y > ( barL_y - 39 ) && ball_y < ( barL_y + 99 ) )
115              reverseHorizontalDirection();
116           else if ( ball_x <= -20 ) { /* if the ball goes off the screen */
117              ++scoreR; /* give right player a point */
118              ball_x = SCREEN_W / 2; /* place the ball in the ... */
119              ball_y = SCREEN_H / 2; /* ... center of the screen */
120              direction = rand() % 4; /* give the ball a random direction */
121           } /* end else */
122        } /* end if */
123
124        /* if the ball is in range of the right paddle ... */
125        if (ball_x > 580 && (direction == DOWN_RIGHT || direction == UP_RIGHT))
126        {
127           /* is the right paddle in the way? */
128           if ( ball_y > ( barR_y - 39 ) && ball_y < ( barR_y + 99 ) )
129              reverseHorizontalDirection();
130           else if ( ball_x >= 620 ) { /* if the ball goes off the screen */
131              ++scoreL; /* give left player a point */
132              ball_x = SCREEN_W / 2; /* place the ball in the ... */
133              ball_y = SCREEN_H / 2; /* ... center of the screen */
134              direction = rand() % 4; /* give the ball a random direction */
135           } /* end else */
136        } /* end if */
137     } /* end function moveBall */
138
139     void respondToKeyboard() /* responds to keyboard input */
140     {
141        if ( key[KEY_A] ) /* if A is being pressed... */
142           barL_y -= 3; /* ... move the left paddle up */
143        if ( key[KEY_Z] ) /* if Z is being pressed... */
144           barL_y += 3; /* ... move the left paddle down */
145
146        if ( key[KEY_UP] ) /* if the up arrow key is being pressed... */
147           barR_y -= 3; /* ... move the right paddle up */
148        if ( key[KEY_DOWN] ) /* if the down arrow key is being pressed... */
149           barR_y += 3; /* ... move the right paddle down */
150
151        /* make sure the paddles don't go offscreen */
152        if ( barL_y < 30 ) /* if left paddle is going off the top */
153           barL_y = 30;
154        else if ( barL_y > 380 ) /* if left paddle is going off the bottom */
155           barL_y = 380;
156        if ( barR_y < 30 ) /* if right paddle is going off the top */
157           barR_y = 30;
158        else if ( barR_y > 380 ) /* if right paddle is going off the bottom */
159           barR_y = 380;
160     } /* end function respondToKeyboard */
161
```

Fig. 15.14 | Adding timers to the Pong game. (Part 4 of 5.)

```
162  void reverseVerticalDirection() /* reverse the ball's up-down direction */
163  {
164     if ( ( direction % 2 ) == 0 ) /* "down" directions are even numbers */
165        ++direction; /* make the ball start moving up */
166     else /* "up" directions are odd numbers */
167        --direction; /* make the ball start moving down */
168     play_sample( boing, 255, 128, 1000, 0 ); /* play "boing" sound once */
169  } /* end function reverseVerticalDirection */
170
171  void reverseHorizontalDirection() /* reverses the horizontal direction */
172  {
173     direction = ( direction + 2 ) % 4; /* reverse horizontal direction */
174     play_sample( boing, 255, 128, 1000, 0 ); /* play "boing" sound once */
175  } /* end function reverseHorizontalDirection */
```

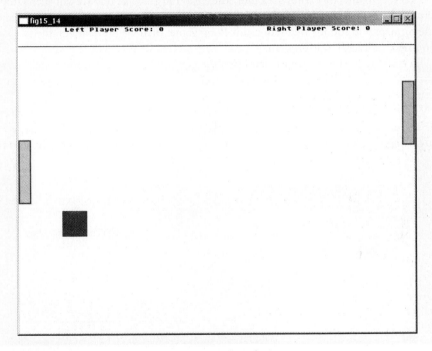

Fig. 15.14 | Adding timers to the Pong game. (Part 5 of 5.)

Note that the calls to the moveBall and respondToKeyboard have been removed from the while loop in the main of this version of the program.

As you can see, timers are simple to implement. With the code in Fig. 15.14, the moveBall function is called once every 5 milliseconds, or 200 times per second, which means our ball will move as many pixels every second. Likewise, the program calls respondToKeyboard every 10 milliseconds, or 100 times per second, which means (since the respondToKeyboard function moves the paddles in intervals of 3 pixels) that the paddles can move 300 pixels in one second. However, while these are the speeds we have suggested for these two timers, feel free to change them so that the game runs at the speed you desire. Experimentation is the only real way to determine a speed that is best for the game.

15.11 The Grabber and Allegro Datafiles

Because most of Allegro's graphics and sounds come from external files, it is necessary for each program to load the files it needs, and to destroy them when the program is finished to prevent memory leaks. When we have a small number of external files, as we do in our Pong game, loading and destroying every file is not a difficult task. However, what if we had a large number of files that we needed to load? Not only would it be difficult to remember every single file that we had to load and destroy, but we would also have to distribute every one of these external files with our game if we chose to release it to the public.

Fortunately, the Allegro designers foresaw this problem, and to fix it, they created the datafile. A datafile is a single external file, created by Allegro, that holds the data of multiple external files in one place. A program can load a datafile and instantly have access to all of the files—be they bitmaps, sounds, fonts or anything else—that the datafile contains.

The Allegro directory contains a tool, known as the grabber, that we can use to import external files and create datafiles. In this section we use the grabber to create a datafile out of the bitmaps and sounds we used in our Pong game, then we use that datafile to reduce the number of lines in our program.

To create a datafile, we must first open the grabber. It can be found in the directory where you installed Allegro, in the folder `allegro/tools`. Run `grabber.exe` and the screen in Fig. 15.15 should appear.

There are four main areas of the grabber program's window. The top area, which contains several text fields, is the space that displays the properties of the datafile that is currently being modified. The white box on the left side of the window lists the objects that

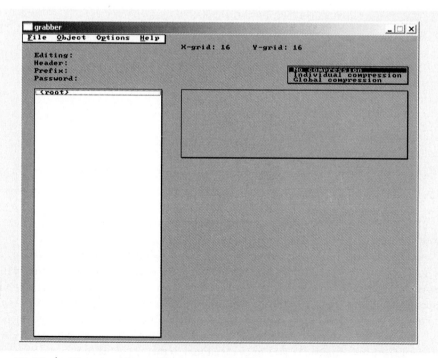

Fig. 15.15 | Allegro's grabber utility.

make up the datafile being edited; since we haven't yet created any objects, the box is currently empty. Once we import images and sounds into our datafile, the right side of the screen will be used to display the properties of a selected object.

While there are many items in the grabber's menus, we need only a few of them to create a datafile. To add any object to a datafile, we must first tell the grabber to create a new space in the datafile for the given object. We do this by selecting **New** in the **Object** menu. A list of object types appears. The first thing we import is our ball bitmap, so select **Bitmap** and a dialog box appears asking for the object's name. Name it BALL (the reason why the name should be in all caps will become clear shortly). Your screen should now look like Fig. 15.16.

Note that BALL has been added to the list of objects on the left side of the window, and that the right side of the window now contains information on the object. However, our object has no image data yet. To import data from a bitmap file, we must first select **Read Bitmap** from the **File** menu. The program asks where the bitmap file is located, so navigate to your Pong project folder and import our ball.bmp image. When this is done, the image appears in the window to confirm that it was loaded correctly.

Click anywhere in the window and the screen in Fig. 15.16 reappears. Note that the **Read Bitmap** menu item did not actually give our BALL object any image data—it merely loaded the image into the grabber's internal memory. To actually apply the bitmap data to our object, make sure that the BALL object is selected on the left side of the window, then select **Grab** from the **Object** menu. The screen in Fig. 15.17 appears.

The program now asks us which part of the bitmap we want the object to contain. This feature is useful if we want our object to contain only part of an image, but right now we want the entirety of the ball bitmap. Move the cursor to the top-left corner of the image, then click and drag a box over the entire bitmap. The screen in Fig. 15.18 should appear.

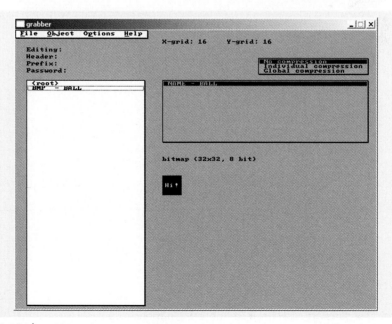

Fig. 15.16 | Adding a bitmap to a datafile.

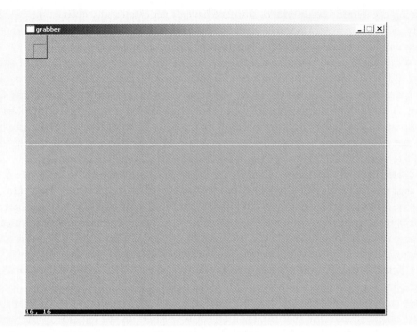

Fig. 15.17 | Applying an imported bitmap to an object.

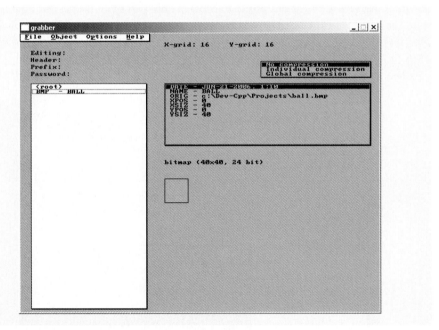

Fig. 15.18 | A complete imported object.

With this done, we have finished importing our ball image into the datafile. Create a new bitmap in the grabber called BAR and repeat the process with the bar.bmp bitmap to import the paddle image as well. Both the BALL and BAR objects should now be in the list of items on the left side of the window.

Now that we have imported our bitmaps, we must also import our sound and font files. First, use the **Object** menu to create a new object of type **Sample** named BOING. Then, simply select **Grab** from the **Object** menu. The program asks for the location of the file, so locate our boing.wav file and double-click on it. The grabber then imports the sound file and applies its data to the boing object.

We use the same process to create our font object—create a new font called PONGFONT, and then use **Grab** to import the pongfont.pcx file. Once you have imported all the objects, your screen should look like Fig. 15.19.

Now that we've imported all our objects into the grabber, there is still one final step we must perform before we can use the datafile effectively. You will notice that we have not yet done anything with the text fields at the top of the grabber window. However, the **Header** field is of interest to us. Filling in this field with a filename will make the grabber save a header file alongside the datafile that we are currently creating. This header file can be used to make it easier to access individual datafile objects in a program. We will discuss the header file in more detail shortly, but for now just enter pong.h in the text field. Then select **Save** from the **File** menu and save the datafile as pongdatafile.dat in the folder where your Pong project is located.

Now we face the task of loading the datafile into our program, which is not difficult. Just as Allegro defines BITMAP*, SAMPLE*, and FONT* pointer types for bitmaps, sounds and fonts, it also defines the DATAFILE* type that points to datafiles. Likewise, to load a datafile into a program, we call the function load_datafile and pass it the filename of the datafile we have created. Note, though, that Allegro does not define a function destroy_datafile. To free the memory allocated to a datafile, one must call the function unload_datafile.

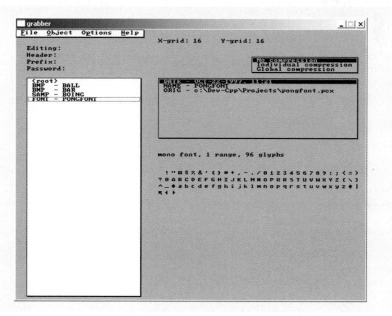

Fig. 15.19 | The grabber window after importing all of our objects.

Once a datafile is loaded into a program, Allegro considers it to be an array of objects, with each object having a specific index in the array. If we have a DATAFILE* variable in our program called myDatafile, accessing a specific object in the datafile is done with the code myDatafile[i].dat, where i is the object's index in the array. Normally, Allegro assigns indexes to the objects in a datafile by the order in which the objects were imported, so in our datafile, our BALL object has index 0, our BAR object has index 1, and so on.

It is easy for us to remember the indexes of the objects in our datafile, as it contains only four objects. However, with a large datafile, remembering the indexes of each and every object can be difficult. Fortunately, even with our small datafile, we do not have to memorize each object's index, as the pong.h header file we saved takes care of that for us. If you open the header file in your IDE, you will see the code in Fig. 15.20.

By including the header file in our program, we eliminate the need to memorize the indexes of the objects in our datafile, as the header file assigns a symbolic constant to each index. Note that the symbolic constant for any given object is the name we gave that object in the grabber when we imported it, which explains why we chose to name our objects in all caps—the convention for symbolic constants in C is to give them names with only capital letters. The Pong program in Fig. 15.21 loads and accesses a datafile

A downside of datafiles can be seen in lines 56–58. Note that when we blitted our ball and paddle onto the screen, we had to pass the last two parameters (the width and height of the source bitmap) explicitly. Allegro considers objects loaded from a datafile to be of type void *, which cannot be dereferenced. As such, trying to pass these parameters pong-Data[BALL].dat->w and pongData[BALL].dat->h is a syntax error. Still, since we know the exact dimensions of our bitmaps, this is not a problem.

```
 1   /* Allegro datafile object indexes, produced by grabber v4.2.0, MinGW32 */
 2   /* Datafile: c:\Dev-Cpp\Projects\pongdatafile.dat */
 3   /* Date: Wed Jun 21 12:57:10 2006 */
 4   /* Do not hand edit! */
 5
 6   #define BALL                                     0          /* BMP  */
 7   #define BAR                                      1          /* BMP  */
 8   #define BOING                                    2          /* SAMP */
 9   #define PONGFONT                                 3          /* FONT */
```

Fig. 15.20 | The pong.h header file.

```
 1   /* Fig. 15.21: fig15_21.c
 2      Using datafiles. */
 3   #include <allegro.h>
 4   #include "pong.h"
 5
 6   /* symbolic constants for the ball's possible directions */
 7   #define DOWN_RIGHT 0
 8   #define UP_RIGHT 1
 9   #define DOWN_LEFT 2
10   #define UP_LEFT 3
11
```

Fig. 15.21 | Using datafiles. (Part 1 of 5.)

```
12   /* function prototypes */
13   void moveBall( void );
14   void respondToKeyboard( void );
15   void reverseVerticalDirection( void );
16   void reverseHorizontalDirection( void );
17
18   volatile int ball_x; /* the ball's x-coordinate */
19   volatile int ball_y; /* the ball's y-coordinate */
20   volatile int barL_y; /* y-coordinate of the left paddle */
21   volatile int barR_y; /* y-coordinate of the right paddle */
22   volatile int scoreL; /* score of the left player */
23   volatile int scoreR; /* score of the right player */
24   volatile int direction; /* the ball's direction */
25   BITMAP *buffer; /* pointer to the buffer */
26   DATAFILE *pongData; /* pointer to the datafile */
27
28   int main( void )
29   {
30      /* first, set up Allegro and the graphics mode */
31      allegro_init(); /* initialize Allegro */
32      install_keyboard(); /* install the keyboard for Allegro to use */
33      install_sound( DIGI_AUTODETECT, MIDI_AUTODETECT, NULL );
34      install_timer(); /* install the timer handler */
35      set_color_depth( 16 ); /* set the color depth to 16-bit */
36      set_gfx_mode( GFX_AUTODETECT, 640, 480, 0, 0 ); /* set graphics mode */
37      buffer = create_bitmap( SCREEN_W, SCREEN_H ); /* create buffer */
38      pongData = load_datafile( "pongdatafile.dat" ); /* load the datafile */
39      ball_x = SCREEN_W / 2; /* give ball its initial x-coordinate */
40      ball_y = SCREEN_H / 2; /* give ball its initial y-coordinate */
41      barL_y = SCREEN_H / 2; /* give left paddle its initial y-coordinate */
42      barR_y = SCREEN_H / 2; /* give right paddle its initial y-coordinate */
43      scoreL = 0; /* set left player's score to 0 */
44      scoreR = 0; /* set right player's score to 0 */
45      srand( time( NULL ) ); /* seed the random function ... */
46      direction = rand() % 4; /* and then make a random initial direction */
47      /* add timer that calls moveBall every 5 milliseconds */
48      install_int( moveBall, 5 );
49      /* add timer that calls respondToKeyboard every 10 milliseconds */
50      install_int( respondToKeyboard, 10 );
51
52      while ( !key[KEY_ESC] ) /* until the escape key is pressed ... */
53      {
54         /* now, perform double buffering */
55         clear_to_color( buffer, makecol( 255, 255, 255 ) );
56         blit( pongData[BALL].dat, buffer, 0, 0, ball_x, ball_y, 40, 40 );
57         blit( pongData[BAR].dat, buffer, 0, 0, 0, barL_y, 20, 100 );
58         blit( pongData[BAR].dat, buffer, 0, 0, 620, barR_y, 20, 100 );
59         line( buffer, 0, 30, 640, 30, makecol( 0, 0, 0 ) );
60         /* draw text onto the buffer */
61         textprintf_ex( buffer, pongData[PONGFONT].dat, 75, 0,
62                     makecol( 0, 0, 0 ), -1, "Left Player Score: %d",
63                     scoreL );
```

Fig. 15.21 | Using datafiles. (Part 2 of 5.)

```
64      textprintf_ex( buffer, pongData[PONGFONT].dat, 400, 0,
65                  makecol( 0, 0, 0 ), -1, "Right Player Score: %d",
66                  scoreR );
67      blit( buffer, screen, 0, 0, 0, 0, buffer->w, buffer->h );
68      clear_bitmap( buffer );
69   } /* end while */
70
71   remove_int( moveBall ); /* remove moveBall timer */
72   remove_int( respondToKeyboard ); /* remove respondToKeyboard timer */
73   destroy_bitmap( buffer ); /* destroy the buffer bitmap */
74   unload_datafile( pongData ); /* unload the datafile */
75   return 0;
76 } /* end function main */
77 END_OF_MAIN() /* don't forget this! */
78
79 void moveBall() /* moves the ball */
80 {
81   switch ( direction ) {
82      case DOWN_RIGHT:
83         ++ball_x; /* move the ball to the right */
84         ++ball_y; /* move the ball down */
85         break;
86      case UP_RIGHT:
87         ++ball_x; /* move the ball to the right */
88         --ball_y; /* move the ball up */
89         break;
90      case DOWN_LEFT:
91         --ball_x; /* move the ball to the left */
92         ++ball_y; /* move the ball down */
93         break;
94      case UP_LEFT:
95         --ball_x; /* move the ball to the left */
96         --ball_y; /* move the ball up */
97         break;
98   } /* end switch */
99
100    /* if the ball is going off the top or bottom ... */
101    if ( ball_y <= 30 || ball_y >= 440 )
102       reverseVerticalDirection(); /* make it go the other way */
103
104    /* if the ball is in range of the left paddle ... */
105    if (ball_x < 20 && (direction == DOWN_LEFT || direction == UP_LEFT))
106    {
107       /* is the left paddle in the way? */
108       if ( ball_y > ( barL_y - 39 ) && ball_y < ( barL_y + 99 ) )
109          reverseHorizontalDirection();
110       else if ( ball_x <= -20 ) { /* if the ball goes off the screen */
111          ++scoreR; /* give right player a point */
112          ball_x = SCREEN_W / 2; /* place the ball in the ... */
113          ball_y = SCREEN_H / 2; /* ... center of the screen */
114          direction = rand() % 4; /* give the ball a random direction */
115       } /* end else */
116    } /* end if */
```

Fig. 15.21 | Using datafiles. (Part 3 of 5.)

```
117
118      /* if the ball is in range of the right paddle ... */
119      if (ball_x > 580 && (direction == DOWN_RIGHT || direction == UP_RIGHT))
120      {
121         /* is the right paddle in the way? */
122         if ( ball_y > ( barR_y - 39 ) && ball_y < ( barR_y + 99 ) )
123            reverseHorizontalDirection();
124         else if ( ball_x >= 620 ) { /* if the ball goes off the screen */
125            ++scoreL; /* give left player a point */
126            ball_x = SCREEN_W / 2; /* place the ball in the ... */
127            ball_y = SCREEN_H / 2; /* ... center of the screen */
128            direction = rand() % 4; /* give the ball a random direction */
129         } /* end else */
130      } /* end if */
131   } /* end function moveBall */
132
133   void respondToKeyboard() /* responds to keyboard input */
134   {
135      if ( key[KEY_A] ) /* if A is being pressed... */
136         barL_y -= 3; /* ... move the left paddle up */
137      if ( key[KEY_Z] ) /* if Z is being pressed... */
138         barL_y += 3; /* ... move the left paddle down */
139
140      if ( key[KEY_UP] ) /* if the up arrow key is being pressed... */
141         barR_y -= 3; /* ... move the right paddle up */
142      if ( key[KEY_DOWN] ) /* if the down arrow key is being pressed... */
143         barR_y += 3; /* ... move the right paddle down */
144
145      /* make sure the paddles don't go offscreen */
146      if ( barL_y < 30 ) /* if left paddle is going off the top */
147         barL_y = 30;
148      else if ( barL_y > 380 ) /* if left paddle is going off the bottom */
149         barL_y = 380;
150      if ( barR_y < 30 ) /* if right paddle is going off the top */
151         barR_y = 30;
152      else if ( barR_y > 380 ) /* if right paddle is going off the bottom */
153         barR_y = 380;
154   } /* end function respondToKeyboard */
155
156   void reverseVerticalDirection() /* reverse the ball's up-down direction */
157   {
158      if ( ( direction % 2 ) == 0 ) /* "down" directions are even numbers */
159         ++direction; /* make the ball start moving up */
160      else /* "up" directions are odd numbers */
161         --direction; /* make the ball start moving down */
162      play_sample( pongData[BOING].dat, 255, 128, 1000, 0 ); /* play sound */
163   } /* end function reverseVerticalDirection */
164
165   void reverseHorizontalDirection() /* reverses the horizontal direction */
166   {
167      direction = ( direction + 2 ) % 4; /* reverse horizontal direction */
168      play_sample( pongData[BOING].dat, 255, 128, 1000, 0 ); /* play sound */
169   } /* end function reverseHorizontalDirection */
```

Fig. 15.21 | Using datafiles. (Part 4 of 5.)

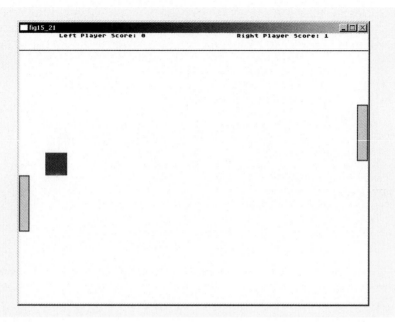

Fig. 15.21 | Using datafiles. (Part 5 of 5.)

Note that using our datafile had no effect on the game itself—it runs exactly the same as the program of Fig. 15.13. However, this program requires fewer lines of code for the same functionality. While it is only 6 lines in this case, a game with a larger number of objects in a datafile would most likely have a much larger difference. If you create a game with many bitmaps, sounds, and other files, make sure to use a datafile to reduce your program's length.

15.12 Other Allegro Capabilities

We mentioned several times in this chapter that Allegro is capable of drawing simple graphics; we used `line` functions to draw a line in our game. Allegro can also draw many other shapes, such as triangles, circles, arcs and polygons with an arbitrary number of sides. The full list of these functions is at www.allegro.cc/manual/api/drawing-primitives.

Allegro also has a set of functions devoted solely to playing music using MIDI files. It defines a `MIDI*` type that points to MIDI files, and uses the `load_midi`, `play_midi`, `stop_midi` and `destroy_midi` functions to manipulate them. A full list of these functions is at www.allegro.cc/manual/api/music-routines-(midi).

If you have any `.fli` format animations that you would like to include in your game, Allegro can play them, as well. Allegro does not define a type that points to animations, but it can draw an animation directly onto a bitmap using the `play_fli` function. The documentation for this capability is at www.allegro.cc/manual/api/flic-routines.

Finally, for the more ambitious game programmers, Allegro can draw 3-dimensional graphics. The process is complicated, however, and well beyond the scope of this text. To get started with 3D, read the tutorials at www.rbsite.freeserve.co.uk/mystex22.htm and www.niksula.cs.hut.fi/~tparvine/allegro3d.

15.13 Allegro Internet and Web Resources

www.talula.demon.co.uk/allegro/

The Allegro homepage. Here you can download the files you'll need to use Allegro in your C code, and you can check out the documentation for the package along with many other Allegro resources.

sourceforge.net/projects/alleg/

Download the files and source code for Allegro here.

www.allegro.cc/files/4.2.0/allegro-chmdocs-4.2.0.zip

The Allegro API (application program interface) in CHM format, the standard "help file" format in Windows.

alleg.sourceforge.net/onlinedocs/en/allegro.html

The Allegro manual in HTML format; contains information on essential functions of the Allegro library in a simpler form than the API.

www.allegro.cc/

A large community of Allegro programmers. Share your ideas for games here and check out new developments in the Allegro world, including new games and programming competitions.

www.allegro.cc/depot

This section of the Allegro.cc website contains over 1,000 Allegro games created by members. Most of the games listed are open source; all are free to download and play.

en.wikipedia.org/wiki/Allegro_library

Wikipedia article for the Allegro library.

www.loomsoft.net/resources/alltut/alltut_index.htm

A set of Allegro "newbie tutorials." Created for the beginning programmer, contains a basic series of tutorials that cover everything from getting Allegro to run on your computer to making your own graphics and datafiles.

www.glost.eclipse.co.uk/gfoot/vivace/

Another tutorial for Allegro novices.

www.gillius.org/allegtut/index.htm

Another Allegro beginner's tutorial.

www.cppgameprogramming.com/cgi/nav.cgi?page=allegbasics

Another Allegro beginner's tutorial. This page leads to the first lesson; more lessons can be found in the sidebar.

www.ping.uio.no/~ovehk/allegro/

This tutorial explains how to make a simple helicopter action game using Allegro.

www.gamedev.net/reference/articles/article2130.asp

A tutorial that explains how to enable your game to allow text input from the user.

oregonstate.edu/~barnesc/quick_reference.html

An Allegro "quick reference." Contains short entries on the most important Allegro functions.

www.niksula.cs.hut.fi/~tparvine/allegro3d/

An advanced tutorial that teaches how to use Allegro to create 3D graphics.

Books

www.amazon.com/gp/product/1592003834/103-9185010-1591016?v=glance&n=283155

Game Programming: All in One by Jonathan S. Harbour, which teaches introductory game programming using the Allegro library.

Groups

groups.yahoo.com/group/allegrogamelibrary/

A Yahoo! group dedicated to creating games with Allegro and archiving Allegro games.

Forums

www.allegro.cc/forums/
The forums of Allegro.cc. Here you can communicate with other Allegro developers, get help, and share game ideas.

www.jharbour.com/forums/index.php?act=SF&f=7
Allegro forum at the homepage of Jonathan Harbour, author of the book *Game Programming: All in One*. Another good place to get help.

Blog postings

gibbage.blogspot.com/2006/04/writing-your-own-game-phase-two.html
Blog post about programming your own game in Allegro and about Jonathan Harbour's book *Game Programming: All in One*.

staticmartin.blogspot.com/2006/05/i-love-allegro.html
Blog post that discusses Allegro and its ease of use.

Summary

Section 15.3 A Simple Allegro Program

- Every Allegro program must include the allegro.h header, call the allegro_init function, and must have a call to the END_OF_MAIN macro immediately following the closing brace of the program's main function.

- The allegro_init function initializes the Allegro library. It must be called before any other Allegro functions, or the program will not work correctly.

- The allegro_message function is used to give the user a message when there is no graphical way of doing so.

- Windows, some Unix systems, and Mac OS X cannot run Allegro programs without the END_OF_MAIN macro. If it is missing, compilers on those systems will not be able to compile an Allegro program. Make sure to include the END_OF_MAIN macro to ensure compatibility with systems that require it.

Section 15.4 Simple Graphics: Importing Bitmaps and Blitting

- Most of Allegro's graphics come from external files. Allegro defines several different variable types that point to image data in memory.

- The BITMAP* type is the most basic type defined by Allegro for pointing to stored image data in memory.

- The set_color_depth function is used to set the color depth of an Allegro program. The color depth can be set to 8-, 15-, 16-, 24-, or 32-bit. A lower color depth requires less memory, but a higher color depth results in a better-looking program.

- The set_gfx_mode function is used to set the graphics mode of an Allegro program. In addition to setting how the program is displayed (i.e., fullscreen mode or windowed mode), it also sets how many pixels are in the width and height of the screen or window.

- Allegro defines five "magic drivers" that can be passed to the set_gfx_mode function to specify whether the program should be run in fullscreen or windowed mode—GFX_AUTODETECT, GFX_AUTODETECT_FULLSCREEN, GFX_AUTODETECT_WINDOWED, GFX_SAFE, and GFX_TEXT.

- Most Allegro functions that can fail return ints for error-checking purposes. Generally these functions will return 0 if they succeed, and a non-zero value if they do not.

- An Allegro program must set the color depth and graphics mode of a program before attempting to do anything else with graphics.

- The create_bitmap function creates a new, blank bitmap.

- Use the load_bitmap function to load an image from an external bitmap file. If the color depth is set to 8-bit, you must pass this function the bitmap's palette in addition to the image itself.

- If the load_bitmap function fails, it returns NULL. It does not cause an error.

- The blit function is one of the most important functions in Allegro. It is used to draw a block from one bitmap onto another bitmap.

- A larger *x*-coordinate corresponds to further to the right in Allegro, but a larger *y*-coordinate corresponds to further down, not up.

- The BITMAP* type is a pointer to a struct. This structure contains two ints, w and h, that store the width and height of the bitmap in pixels, respectively.

- Use the destroy_bitmap function to destroy a bitmap and free the memory allocated to it to prevent memory leaks.

Section 15.5 Animation with Double Buffering

- Animation in Allegro is done by blitting an object onto the screen in different places at regular intervals.

- The symbolic constants SCREEN_W and SCREEN_H are reserved by Allegro, and correspond to the width and height of the screen in pixels, respectively.

- Use the clear_to_color function to make the entirety of a bitmap a certain color. This is useful for setting a background color for a program.

- The makecol function is used to return ints that Allegro recognizes as various colors.

- The "double buffering" technique is a method that produces smooth animation. The technique consists of drawing everything onto an intermediary bitmap known as the buffer, and then drawing the entirety of the buffer onto the screen.

Section 15.6 Importing and Playing Sounds

- Allegro defines the type SAMPLE* that points to sound file data stored in memory.

- Before any sounds can be played in Allegro, the install_sound function must be called.

- Allegro defines two "magic drivers" that should be passed to the install_sound function so that Allegro can determine which sound card drivers it should use for playing sounds. These "magic drivers" are DIGI_AUTODETECT and MIDI_AUTODETECT.

- The load_sample function is used to load an external sound file.

- Use the play_sample function to play a digital sample, and the stop_sample function to stop it.

- The volume parameter in the play_sample function determines the volume at which the sample should be played. A value of 0 mutes the sample, while a value of 255 plays it at maximum volume.

- The pan parameter in the play_sample function determines the pan position at which the sample should be played. A value of 128 plays the sample out of both speakers equally. A value lower than this will shift the sound towards the left speaker, while a greater value (up to a maximum of 255) will shift the sound towards the right speaker.

- The frequency parameter in the play_sample function determines the frequency (and therefore the pitch) at which the sample should be played. A value of 1000 will play the sample at normal frequency. A value of 2000 will play it at double the normal frequency, a value of 500 will play it at half, and so on.

- Passing the loop parameter of the play_sample function a value of 0 will make the sample play only once before stopping. Passing it any other value will cause the sample to loop indefinitely.

- Use the destroy_sample function to destroy a sample and free the memory allocated to it to prevent memory leaks.

Section 15.7 Keyboard Input

- A program must call the install_keyboard function to allow Allegro to recognize and use the keyboard.

- Allegro defines an array of ints called key which contains an index for each key on the keyboard. If a key is not being pressed, its respective index in the array will contain 0, while if the key is being pressed, the index will contain a non-zero number.

- Allegro defines several symbolic constants that correspond to keys on the keyboard. These constants are used in tandem with the key array to determine if specific keys are being pressed. The value stored at key[KEY_A] determines whether or not the *A* key is being pressed, the value stored at key[KEY_SPACE] determines whether the spacebar is being pressed, and so on.

- Any program that checks the keyboard for input using the key array should do so repeatedly. Otherwise, keypresses may be missed.

Section 15.8 Fonts and Displaying Text

- Allegro defines the FONT* type that points to stored font data in memory.

- The symbolic constant font corresponds to Allegro's default font.

- Use the load_font function to load font data from external files. If the color depth is set to 8-bit, you must pass this function the font's palette in addition to the font itself.

- The textprintf_ex function prints text on the screen. Functions textprintf_centre_ex and textprintf_right_ex do the same thing, but justify the printed text at different positions.

- When Allegro is expecting an int that corresponds to a color as a parameter, passing the parameter a value of -1 will make Allegro interpret that color as "transparent."

- Use the destroy_font function to destroy a font and free the memory allocated to it to prevent memory leaks.

Section 15.10 Timers in Allegro

- Any program that uses timers must call the install_timer function before attempting to add any timers.

- Allegro can have up to 16 timers running at once.

- Timers are added by calling the install_int function, and removed by calling the remove_int function.

- A timer calls a given function at regular intervals until it is removed. There is no need to store a timer in any type of variable.

- Allegro identifies a timer by the function it is programmed to call.

- Any variable whose value is modified by a function that a timer calls must be given the volatile qualifier to ensure the program works correctly.

- Users on systems using DOS or Mac OS 9 or below must also lock the memory of any variables or functions used by timers for the program to work correctly.

Section 15.11 The Grabber and Allegro Datafiles

- An Allegro datafile is a single external file that holds the data of many external files in one place.

- Allegro provides the grabber utility for the creation and editing of datafiles.

- The grabber can create header files that make it simple to access objects contained in a datafile.
- Loading a datafile into a program is done with the `load_datafile` function, and removing them is done with the `unload_datafile` function.
- Once a datafile is loaded in a program, Allegro considers it to be an array of objects. The index of each object in the array is dependent on the order in which the objects were imported into the datafile. The first object added to the datafile has index 0, the second one has index 1, and so on.
- Allegro considers objects loaded from a datafile to be of type `void *`.

Terminology

`adjust_sample` function
Allegro
`allegro.h` header
`allegro_init` function
`allegro_message` function
bitmap
`BITMAP` type
`blit` function
blitting
buffer
`clear_bitmap` function
color depth
`create_bitmap` function
datafile
`DATAFILE` type
`destroy_bitmap` function
`destroy_font` function
`destroy_sample` function
digital sample
double buffering
`END_OF_MAIN` macro
font constant
`FONT` type
grabber
`install_int` function
`install_keyboard` function
`install_sound` function

`install_timer` function
key array
keyboard symbolic constants
`line` function
`load_bitmap` function
`load_datafile` function
`load_font` function
`load_sample` function
magic drivers
`makecol` function
palette
`play_sample` function
Pong
`readkey` function
`rectfill` function
`SAMPLE` type
screen constant
`SCREEN_H` constant
`SCREEN_W` constant
`set_color_depth` function
`set_gfx_mode` function
`stop_sample` function
`textprintf_ex` function
timers
`unload_datafile` function
virtual screen

Self-Review Exercises

15.1 Fill in the blanks in each of the following statements:
a) Every Allegro program must include the _____ header.
b) The _____ function must be called before any other Allegro function.
c) Adding the _____ macro ensures compatibility with systems that require it.
d) Before Allegro can display any graphics, a program must call both the _____ and _____ functions.
e) The _____ function is used to draw a block of one bitmap onto another.
f) The main type defined by Allegro for pointing to sound file data is the _____ type.
g) Allegro defines the _____ symbolic constant that corresponds to Allegro's default font.
h) The _____ function is used to return an integer that Allegro interprets as a color.
i) Allegro can have up to _____ timers running at once.

     j) The _____ function is used to add a timer to a program.

     k) The _____ utility is used to create and edit Allegro datafiles.

15.2 State whether each of the following is *true* or *false*. If *false*, explain why.

     a) The `screen` bitmap is the only bitmap visible to the user.

     b) The coordinates (0, 0) refer to the bottom-left corner of a bitmap.

     c) If Allegro attempts to load an external file that does not exist, a runtime error will occur.

     d) The double buffering technique requires two intermediary bitmaps, or buffers, to work correctly.

     e) Passing a value of 2 to the `loop` parameter in the `play_sample` function will cause the sound file to play twice before stopping.

     f) The `install_keyboard` function must be passed a parameter that gives Allegro the driver information of the system's keyboard.

     g) A program that draws text on the screen must specify a font in which that text should be drawn.

     h) An Allegro program can have up to 32 timers running at once.

     i) The function used for freeing the memory that is storing a datafile is the `destroy_datafile` function.

15.3 Write statements to accomplish each of the following:

     a) Set the graphics mode of an Allegro program to a window that is 640 pixels wide by 480 pixels high.

     b) Draw the bitmap `bmp` onto the top left corner of the bitmap `buffer`.

     c) Play the digital sample `sample` at maximum volume, centered pan position, and normal frequency without looping.

     d) If the spacebar is being pressed, set the value of the `int number` to 0.

     e) Draw the string `"Hello!"` onto the top-left corner of the bitmap `buffer`, using Allegro's default font with a blue foreground color and transparent background color.

     f) Add a timer that calls the function `timedFunction` four times every second.

     g) Load the datafile with the filename `datafile.dat`.

15.4 Find the error in each of the following:

```
a) BITMAP bmp;
b) set_gfx_mode( WINDOWED, 640, 480, 0, 0 );
c) makecol( 0, 0, 256 );
```

Answers to Self-Review Exercises

15.1   a) `allegro.h`. b) `allegro_init`. c) `END_OF_MAIN`. d) `set_color_depth` and `set_gfx_mode`. e) `blit`. f) `SAMPLE*`. g) `font`. h) `makecol`. i) 16. j) `install_int`. k) grabber.

15.2   a) True.

     b) False. The coordinates (0, 0) refer to the top-left corner of a bitmap.

     c) False. The function that returns the pointer to the external file will return `NULL`, but no error will occur on that line.

     d) False. Double buffering requires only one intermediary bitmap.

     e) False. Passing any value other than 0 to the `loop` parameter will make the sound file loop indefinitely.

     f) False. The `install_keyboard` function does not take any parameters.

     g) True.

     h) False. An Allegro program can have only 16 timers running at once.

     i) False. This function is the `unload_datafile` function. The `destroy_datafile` function is not defined by Allegro.

15.3 a) `set_gfx_mode( GFX_AUTODETECT_WINDOWED, 640, 480, 0, 0 );`
    b) `blit( bmp, buffer, 0, 0, 0, 0, bmp->w, bmp->h );`
    c) `play_sample( sample, 255, 128, 1000, 0 );`
    d) `if ( key[KEY_SPACE] )`
        `number = 0;`
    e) `textprintf_ex( buffer, font, 0, 0, makecol( 0, 0, 255 ), -1, "Hello!" );`
    f) `install_int( timedFunction, 250 );`
    g) `load_datafile( "datafile.dat" );`

15.4 a) The variable `bmp` should instead be declared as a pointer to a `BITMAP`. All of Allegro's bitmap functions either take a pointer as a parameter or return a pointer. A `BITMAP` that is not a pointer is essentially useless.

    b) Allegro does not define a `WINDOWED` "magic driver." Use the `GFX_AUTODETECT_WINDOWED` "magic driver" instead.

    c) The `makecol` function can only accept parameters with values between 0 and 255.

Exercises

15.5 Write a program that draws the bitmap `ball.bmp` in the center of the screen. When the user presses one of the arrow keys, the bitmap should move ten pixels in that direction.

15.6 Modify the program from Exercise 15.5 so that the ball will only move once for each time an arrow key is pressed. If the user holds down an arrow key, the ball should move once and then stop until the user releases and presses the key again.

15.7 Modify the program from Exercise 15.5 so that if the user holds down an arrow key, the ball will only move once every second.

15.8 Modify the Pong game from Fig. 15.21 so that when a player reaches 21 points, the game ends and displays a message that the left or right player has won.

15.9 In most Pong games, when a rally between the two players lasts for a long time, the ball begins to speed up in order to prevent a stalemate. Modify the Pong game from Fig. 15.21 so that the ball's speed increases for every ten times that it is hit in a rally. When either player scores, the ball should return to its original speed.

15.10 Some Pong games also modify the speed of one or both player's paddles in an effort to keep the game balanced. Modify the Pong game from Fig. 15.21 so that when one player has a lead of at least 5 points, his or her paddle begins to slow down. The greater that player's lead, the slower his or her paddle should move. If the player's lead falls to under 5 points, his or her paddle should return to normal speed.

15.11 Video games often have a "pause" feature that allows a player to interrupt a game in progress and then resume it later. Modify the Pong game from Fig. 15.21 so that pressing the *P* key will pause the game and halt the movement of the ball and paddles. Pausing the game should also make the message `"PAUSED"` appear in the center of the screen. If the game is paused, pressing the *R* key should clear the `"PAUSED"` message from the screen and resume the game.

15.12 Modify the Pong game from Fig. 15.21 so that when the ball bounces off a wall or paddle, the word `"BOING!"` appears in blue at the point where the ball bounced and then fades away. Note that the text should not simply vanish—it should gradually fade to white.

15.13 Modify the Pong game from Fig. 15.21 so that before the game begins, a menu appears on the screen that allows the players to choose from several different ball and paddle speeds. This is tougher than it sounds! Note that Allegro does not have any text input methods. You will have to find another method of solving this problem.

16

Sorting:
A Deeper Look

OBJECTIVES

In this chapter you will learn:

- To sort an array using the selection sort algorithm.

- To sort an array using the insertion sort algorithm.

- To sort an array using the recursive merge sort algorithm.

- To determine the efficiency of searching and sorting algorithms and express it in "Big O" notation.

- To explore (in the chapter exercises) additional recursive sorts, including quicksort and a recursive version of selection sort.

- To explore (in the chapter exercises) the bucket sort, which achieves very high performance, but by using considerably more memory than the other sorts we have studied—an example of the so-called "space–time trade-off."

With sobs and tears
he sorted out
Those of the largest size ...
—Lewis Carroll

'Tis in my memory lock'd,
And you yourself shall keep
the key of it.
—William Shakespeare

It is an immutable law in
business that words are
words, explanations are
explanations, promises are
promises — but only
performance is reality.
—Harold S. Green

16.1 Introduction

As you learned in Chapter 6, sorting places data in order, typically ascending or descending, based on one or more sort keys. This chapter introduces the selection sort and insertion sort algorithms, along with the more efficient, but more complex, merge sort. We introduce Big O notation, which is used to estimate the worst-case run time for an algorithm—that is, how hard an algorithm may have to work to solve a problem.

An important point to understand about sorting is that the end result—the sorted array of data—will be the same no matter which sorting algorithm you use. The choice of algorithm affects only the run time and memory use of the program. The first two sorting algorithms we study here—selection sort and insertion sort—are easy to program, but inefficient. The third algorithm—recursive merge sort—is more efficient than selection sort and insertion sort, but harder to program.

The exercises present two more recursive sorts—quicksort and a recursive version of selection sort. Another exercise presents the bucket sort, which achieves high performance by clever use of considerably more memory than the other sorts we discuss.

16.2 Big O Notation

Suppose an algorithm is designed to test whether the first element of an array is equal to the second element of the array. If the array has 10 elements, this algorithm requires one comparison. If the array has 1000 elements, the algorithm still requires one comparison. In fact, the algorithm is completely independent of the number of elements in the array. This algorithm is said to have a constant run time, which is represented in Big O notation as $O(1)$ and pronounced "order 1." An algorithm that is $O(1)$ does not necessarily require only one comparison. $O(1)$ just means that the number of comparisons is *constant*—it does not grow as the size of the array increases. An algorithm that tests whether the first element of an array is equal to any of the next three elements is still $O(1)$ even though it requires three comparisons.

An algorithm that tests whether the first element of an array is equal to *any* of the other elements of the array will require at most $n - 1$ comparisons, where n is the number of elements in the array. If the array has 10 elements, this algorithm requires up to nine comparisons. If the array has 1000 elements, this algorithm requires up to 999 comparisons. As n grows larger, the n part of the expression "dominates," and subtracting one becomes inconsequential. Big O is designed to highlight these dominant terms and ignore terms that become unimportant as n grows. For this reason, an algorithm that requires a total of $n - 1$ comparisons (such as the one we described earlier) is said to be $O(n)$. An $O(n)$ algorithm is referred to as having a linear run time. $O(n)$ is often pronounced "on the order of n" or more simply "order n."

Suppose you have an algorithm that tests whether *any* element of an array is duplicated elsewhere in the array. The first element must be compared with every other element
in the array. The second element must be compared with every other element except the
first—it was already compared to the first. The third element must be compared with
every other element except the first two. In the end, this algorithm will end up making
$(n - 1) + (n - 2) + \ldots + 2 + 1$ or $n^2/2 - n/2$ comparisons. As n increases, the n^2 term dominates, and the n term becomes inconsequential. Again, Big O notation highlights the n^2
term, leaving $n^2/2$. But as we'll soon see, constant factors are omitted in Big O notation.

Big O is concerned with how an algorithm's run time grows in relation to the number
of items processed. Suppose an algorithm requires n^2 comparisons. With four elements,
the algorithm will require 16 comparisons; with eight elements, the algorithm will require
64 comparisons. With this algorithm, doubling the number of elements quadruples the
number of comparisons. Consider a similar algorithm requiring $n^2/2$ comparisons. With
four elements, the algorithm will require eight comparisons; with eight elements, the algorithm will require 32 comparisons. Again, doubling the number of elements quadruples
the number of comparisons. Both of these algorithms grow as the square of n, so Big O
ignores the constant and both algorithms are considered to be $O(n^2)$, which is referred to
as **quadratic run time** and pronounced "on the order of n-squared" or more simply "order
n-squared."

When n is small, $O(n^2)$ algorithms (running on today's billion-operation-per-second
personal computers) will not noticeably affect performance. But as n grows, you will start
to notice the performance degradation. An $O(n^2)$ algorithm running on a million-element
array would require a trillion "operations" (where each could actually require several
machine instructions to execute). This could require a few hours to execute. A billion-ele-
ment array would require a quintillion operations, a number so large that the algorithm
could take decades! $O(n^2)$ algorithms, unfortunately, are easy to write, as you'll see in this
chapter. You'll also see an algorithm with a more favorable Big O measure. Efficient algorithms often take a bit more cleverness and work to create, but their superior performance
can be well worth the extra effort, especially as n gets large and as algorithms are combined
into larger programs.

16.3 Selection Sort

Selection sort is a simple, but inefficient, sorting algorithm. The first iteration of the algorithm selects the smallest element in the array and swaps it with the first element. The
second iteration selects the second-smallest element (which is the smallest of those remaining) and swaps it with the second element. The algorithm continues until the last iteration
selects the second-largest element and swaps it with the second-to-last, leaving the largest
element as the last. After the ith iteration, the smallest i positions of the array will be sorted
into increasing order in the first i positions of the array.

As an example, consider the array

| 34 | 56 | 4 | 10 | 77 | 51 | 93 | 30 | 5 | 52 |

A program that implements selection sort first determines the smallest element (4) of this
array which is contained in the third element of the array (i.e., element 2 because array
subscripts start at 0). The program swaps 4 with 34, resulting in

| 4 | 56 | 34 | 10 | 77 | 51 | 93 | 30 | 5 | 52 |

The program then determines the smallest of the remaining elements (all elements except 4), which is 5, contained at array subscript 8. The program swaps 5 with 56, resulting in

4   5   34   10   77   51   93   30   56   52

On the third iteration, the program determines the next smallest value (10) and swaps it with 34.

4   5   10   34   77   51   93   30   56   52

The process continues until after nine iterations the array is fully sorted.

4   5   10   30   34   51   52   56   77   93

Note that after the first iteration, the smallest element is in the first position. After the second iteration, the two smallest elements are in order in the first two positions. After the third iteration, the three smallest elements are in order in the first three positions.

Figure 16.1 implements the selection sort algorithm on the array array, which is initialized with 10 random ints (possibly duplicates). The main function prints the unsorted array, calls the function sort on the array, and then prints the array again after it has been sorted.

```
1   /* Fig. 16.1: fig16_01.c
2      The selection sort algorithm. */
3   #define SIZE 10
4   #include <stdio.h>
5   #include <stdlib.h>
6   #include <time.h>
7
8   /* function prototypes */
9   void selectionSort( int array[], int length );
10  void swap( int array[], int first, int second );
11  void printPass( int array[], int length, int pass, int index );
12
13  int main( void )
14  {
15     int array[ SIZE ]; /* declare the array of ints to be sorted */
16     int i; /* int used in for loop */
17
18     srand( time( NULL ) ); /* seed the rand function */
19
20     for ( i = 0; i < SIZE; i++ )
21        array[ i ] = rand() % 90 + 10; /* give each element a value */
22
23     printf( "Unsorted array:\n" );
24
25     for ( i = 0; i < SIZE; i++ ) /* print the array */
26        printf( "%d   ", array[ i ] );
27
28     printf( "\n\n" );
29     selectionSort( array, SIZE );
30     printf( "Sorted array:\n" );
```

Fig. 16.1 | Selection sort algorithm. (Part 1 of 3.)

```
31
32      for ( i = 0; i < SIZE; i++ ) /* print the array */
33         printf( "%d  ", array[ i ] );
34
35      return 0;
36   } /* end function main */
37
38   /* function that selection sorts the array */
39   void selectionSort( int array[], int length )
40   {
41      int smallest; /* index of smallest element */
42      int i, j; /* ints used in for loops */
43
44      /* loop over length - 1 elements */
45      for ( i = 0; i < length - 1; i++ ) {
46         smallest = i; /* first index of remaining array */
47
48         /* loop to find index of smallest element */
49         for ( j = i + 1; j < length; j++ )
50            if ( array[ j ] < array[ smallest ] )
51               smallest = j;
52
53         swap( array, i, smallest ); /* swap smallest element */
54         printPass( array, length, i + 1, smallest ); /* output pass */
55      } /* end for */
56   } /* end function selectionSort */
57
58   /* function that swaps two elements in the array */
59   void swap( int array[], int first, int second )
60   {
61      int temp; /* temporary integer */
62      temp = array[ first ];
63      array[ first ] = array[ second ];
64      array[ second ] = temp;
65   } /* end function swap */
66
67   /* function that prints a pass of the algorithm */
68   void printPass( int array[], int length, int pass, int index )
69   {
70      int i; /* int used in for loop */
71
72      printf( "After pass %2d: ", pass );
73
74      /* output elements till selected item */
75      for ( i = 0; i < index; i++ )
76         printf( "%d  ", array[ i ] );
77
78      printf( "%d* ", array[ index ] ); /* indicate swap */
79
80      /* finish outputting array */
81      for ( i = index + 1; i < length; i++ )
82         printf( "%d  ", array[ i ] );
83
```

Fig. 16.1 | Selection sort algorithm. (Part 2 of 3.)

```
84          printf( "\n                    " ); /* for alignment */
85
86      /* indicate amount of array that is sorted */
87      for ( i = 0; i < pass; i++ )
88          printf( "-- " );
89
90      printf( "\n" ); /* add newline */
91  } /* end function printPass */
```

```
Unsorted array:
72  34  88  14  32  12  34  77  56  83

After pass  1: 12  34  88  14  32  72* 34  77  56  83
               --
After pass  2: 12  14  88  34* 32  72  34  77  56  83
               --  --
After pass  3: 12  14  32  34  88* 72  34  77  56  83
               --  --  --
After pass  4: 12  14  32  34* 88  72  34  77  56  83
               --  --  --  --
After pass  5: 12  14  32  34  34  72  88* 77  56  83
               --  --  --  --  --
After pass  6: 12  14  32  34  34  56  88  77  72* 83
               --  --  --  --  --  --
After pass  7: 12  14  32  34  34  56  72  77  88* 83
               --  --  --  --  --  --  --
After pass  8: 12  14  32  34  34  56  72  77* 88  83
               --  --  --  --  --  --  --  --
After pass  9: 12  14  32  34  34  56  72  77  83  88*
               --  --  --  --  --  --  --  --  --
After pass 10: 12  14  32  34  34  56  72  77  83  88*
               --  --  --  --  --  --  --  --  --  --
Sorted array:
12  14  32  34  34  56  72  77  83  88
```

Fig. 16.1 | Selection sort algorithm. (Part 3 of 3.)

Lines 39–56 define the selectionSort function. Line 41 declares the variable smallest, which stores the index of the smallest element in the remaining array. Lines 45–55 loop SIZE - 1 times. Line 46 assigns the index of the smallest element to the current item. Lines 49–51 loop over the remaining elements in the array. For each of these elements, line 50 compares its value to the value of the smallest element. If the current element is smaller than the smallest element, line 51 assigns the current element's index to smallest. When this loop finishes, smallest contains the index of the smallest element in the remaining array. Line 53 calls function swap (lines 59–65) to place the smallest remaining element in the next spot in the array.

The output of this program uses dashes to indicate the portion of the array that is guaranteed to be sorted after each pass. An asterisk is placed next to the position of the element that was swapped with the smallest element on that pass. On each pass, the element to the left of the asterisk and the element above the rightmost set of dashes were the two values that were swapped.

Efficiency of Selection Sort

The selection sort algorithm runs in $O(n^2)$ time. The selectionSort method in lines 39–56 of Fig. 16.1, which implements the selection sort algorithm, contains two for loops. The outer for loop (lines 45–55) iterates over the first $n-1$ elements in the array, swapping the smallest remaining item into its sorted position. The inner for loop (lines 49–51) iterates over each item in the remaining array, searching for the smallest element. This loop executes $n-1$ times during the first iteration of the outer loop, $n-2$ times during the second iteration, then $n-3$, ... , 3, 2, 1. This inner loop iterates a total of $n(n-1)/2$ or $(n^2-n)/2$. In Big O notation, smaller terms drop out and constants are ignored, leaving a Big O of $O(n^2)$.

16.4 Insertion Sort

Insertion sort is another simple, but inefficient, sorting algorithm. The first iteration of this algorithm takes the second element in the array and, if it is less than the first element, swaps it with the first element. The second iteration looks at the third element and inserts it into the correct position with respect to the first two elements, so all three elements are in order. At the ith iteration of this algorithm, the first i elements in the original array will be sorted.

Consider as an example the following array [*Note:* This array is identical to the array used in the discussions of selection sort and merge sort.]

34	56	4	10	77	51	93	30	5	52

A program that implements the insertion sort algorithm will first look at the first two elements of the array, 34 and 56. These two elements are already in order, so the program continues (if they were out of order, the program would swap them).

In the next iteration, the program looks at the third value, 4. This value is less than 56, so the program stores 4 in a temporary variable and moves 56 one element to the right. The program then checks and determines that 4 is less than 34, so it moves 34 one element to the right. The program has now reached the beginning of the array, so it places 4 in element 0. The array now is

4	34	56	10	77	51	93	30	5	52

In the next iteration, the program stores the value 10 in a temporary variable. Then the program compares 10 to 56 and moves 56 one element to the right because it is larger than 10. The program then compares 10 to 34, moving 34 right one element. When the program compares 10 to 4, it observes that 10 is larger than 4 and places 10 in element 1. The array now is

4	10	34	56	77	51	93	30	5	52

Using this algorithm, at the ith iteration, the first $i+1$ elements of the original array are sorted with respect to one another. They may not be in their final locations, however, because smaller values may be located later in the array.

Figure 16.2 implements the insertion sort algorithm. Lines 38–58 declare the insertionSort function. Line 40 declares the variable insert, which holds the element you are going to insert while you move the other elements. Lines 44–57 loop over SIZE - 1 items in the array. In each iteration, line 46 stores in insert the value of the element that will be inserted into the sorted portion of the array. Line 45 declares and initializes the variable moveItem, which keeps track of where to insert the element. Lines 49–53 loop to locate the correct position where the element should be inserted. The loop terminates either when the program reaches the front of the array or when it reaches an element that is less than the value to be inserted. Line 51 moves an element to the right, and line 52 decrements the position at which to insert the next element. After the loop ends, line 55 inserts the element into place. The output of this program uses dashes to indicate the portion of the array that is sorted after each pass. An asterisk is placed next to the element that was inserted into place on that pass.

```c
1   /* Fig. 16.2: fig16_02.c
2      The insertion sort algorithm. */
3   #define SIZE 10
4   #include <stdio.h>
5   #include <stdlib.h>
6   #include <time.h>
7
8   /* function prototypes */
9   void insertionSort( int array[], int length );
10  void printPass( int array[], int length, int pass, int index );
11
12  int main( void )
13  {
14     int array[ SIZE ]; /* declare the array of ints to be sorted */
15     int i; /* int used in for loop */
16
17     srand( time( NULL ) ); /* seed the rand function */
18
19     for ( i = 0; i < SIZE; i++ )
20        array[ i ] = rand() % 90 + 10; /* give each element a value */
21
22     printf( "Unsorted array:\n" );
23
24     for ( i = 0; i < SIZE; i++ ) /* print the array */
25        printf( "%d  ", array[ i ] );
26
27     printf( "\n\n" );
28     insertionSort( array, SIZE );
29     printf( "Sorted array:\n" );
30
31     for ( i = 0; i < SIZE; i++ ) /* print the array */
32        printf( "%d  ", array[ i ] );
33
34     return 0;
35  } /* end function main */
36
37  /* function that sorts the array */
38  void insertionSort( int array[], int length )
39  {
40     int insert; /* temporary variable to hold element to insert */
41     int i; /* int used in for loop */
42
```

Fig. 16.2 | Insertion sort algorithm. (Part 1 of 3.)

```
43      /* loop over length - 1 elements */
44      for ( i = 1; i < length; i++ ) {
45          int moveItem = i; /* initialize location to place element */
46          insert = array[ i ];
47
48          /* search for place to put current element */
49          while ( moveItem > 0 && array[ moveItem - 1 ] > insert ) {
50              /* shift element right one slot */
51              array[ moveItem ] = array[ moveItem - 1 ];
52              --moveItem;
53          } /* end while */
54
55          array[ moveItem ] = insert; /* place inserted element */
56          printPass( array, length, i, moveItem );
57      } /* end for */
58  } /* end function insertionSort */
59
60  /* function that prints a pass of the algorithm */
61  void printPass( int array[], int length, int pass, int index )
62  {
63      int i; /* int used in for loop */
64
65      printf( "After pass %2d: ", pass );
66
67      /* output elements till selected item */
68      for ( i = 0; i < index; i++ )
69          printf( "%d  ", array[ i ] );
70
71      printf( "%d* ", array[ index ] ); /* indicate swap */
72
73      /* finish outputting array */
74      for ( i = index + 1; i < length; i++ )
75          printf( "%d  ", array[ i ] );
76
77      printf( "\n                " ); /* for alignment */
78
79      /* indicate amount of array that is sorted */
80      for ( i = 0; i <= pass; i++ )
81          printf( "--  " );
82
83      printf( "\n" ); /* add newline */
84  } /* end function printPass */
```

```
Unsorted array:
72  16  11  92  63  99  59  82  99  30

After pass  1: 16* 72  11  92  63  99  59  82  99  30
               --  --
After pass  2: 11* 16  72  92  63  99  59  82  99  30
               --  --  --
After pass  3: 11  16  72  92* 63  99  59  82  99  30
               --  --  --  --
```

(continued on next page)

Fig. 16.2 | Insertion sort algorithm. (Part 2 of 3.)

```
After pass  4: 11  16  63* 72  92  99  59  82  99  30
               --  --  --  --  --
After pass  5: 11  16  63  72  92  99* 59  82  99  30
               --  --  --  --  --  --
After pass  6: 11  16  59* 63  72  92  99  82  99  30
               --  --  --  --  --  --  --
After pass  7: 11  16  59  63  72  82* 92  99  99  30
               --  --  --  --  --  --  --  --
After pass  8: 11  16  59  63  72  82  92  99  99* 30
               --  --  --  --  --  --  --  --  --
After pass  9: 11  16  30* 59  63  72  82  92  99  99
               --  --  --  --  --  --  --  --  --  --
Sorted array:
11  16  30  59  63  72  82  92  99  99
```

Fig. 16.2 | Insertion sort algorithm. (Part 3 of 3.)

Efficiency of Insertion Sort

The insertion sort algorithm also runs in $O(n^2)$ time. Like selection sort, the insertion-Sort function (lines 38–58) uses two loops. The for loop (lines 44–57) iterates SIZE - 1 times, inserting an element into the appropriate position in the elements sorted so far. For the purposes of this application, SIZE - 1 is equivalent to $n - 1$ (as SIZE is the size of the array). The while loop (lines 49–53) iterates over the preceding elements in the array. In the worst case, this while loop requires $n - 1$ comparisons. Each individual loop runs in $O(n)$ time. In Big O notation, nested loops mean that you must multiply the number of iterations of each loop. For each iteration of an outer loop, there will be a certain number of iterations of the inner loop. In this algorithm, for each $O(n)$ iterations of the outer loop, there will be $O(n)$ iterations of the inner loop. Multiplying these values results in a Big O of $O(n^2)$.

16.5 Merge Sort

Merge sort is an efficient sorting algorithm, but is conceptually more complex than selection sort and insertion sort. The merge sort algorithm sorts an array by splitting it into two equal-sized subarrays, sorting each subarray, then merging them into one larger array. With an odd number of elements, the algorithm creates the two subarrays such that one has one more element than the other.

The implementation of merge sort in this example is recursive. The base case is an array with one element. A one-element array is, of course, sorted, so merge sort immediately returns when it is called with a one-element array. The recursion step splits an array of two or more elements into two equal-sized subarrays, recursively sorts each subarray, then merges them into one larger, sorted array. [Again, if there is an odd number of elements, one subarray is one element larger than the other.]

Suppose the algorithm has already merged smaller arrays to create sorted arrays A:

    4   10   34   56   77

and B:

    5   30   51   52   93

Merge sort combines these two arrays into one larger, sorted array. The smallest element in A is 4 (located in the element zero of A). The smallest element in B is 5 (located in the zeroth index of B). In order to determine the smallest element in the larger array, the algorithm compares 4 and 5. The value from A is smaller, so 4 becomes the first element in the merged array. The algorithm continues by comparing 10 (the second element in A) to 5 (the first element in B). The value from B is smaller, so 5 becomes the second element in the larger array. The algorithm continues by comparing 10 to 30, with 10 becoming the third element in the array, and so on.

Figure 16.3 implements the merge sort algorithm, and lines 35–38 define the merge-Sort function. Line 37 calls function sortSubArray with 0 and SIZE - 1 as the arguments. The arguments correspond to the beginning and ending indices of the array to be sorted, causing sortSubArray to operate on the entire array. Function sortSubArray is defined in lines 41–66. Line 46 tests the base case. If the size of the array is 1, the array is sorted, so the function simply returns immediately. If the size of the array is greater than 1, the function splits the array in two, recursively calls function sortSubArray to sort the two subarrays, then merges them. Line 60 recursively calls function sortSubArray on the first half of the array, and line 61 recursively calls function sortSubArray on the second half of the array. When these two function calls return, each half of the array has been sorted. Line 64 calls function merge (lines 69–111) on the two halves of the array to combine the two sorted arrays into one larger sorted array.

```
1   /* Fig. 16.3: fig16_03.c
2      The merge sort algorithm. */
3   #define SIZE 10
4   #include <stdio.h>
5   #include <stdlib.h>
6   #include <time.h>
7
8   /* function prototypes */
9   void mergeSort( int array[], int length );
10  void sortSubArray( int array[], int low, int high );
11  void merge( int array[], int left, int middle1, int middle2, int right );
12  void displayElements( int array[], int length );
13  void displaySubArray( int array[], int left, int right );
14
15  int main( void )
16  {
17     int array[ SIZE ]; /* declare the array of ints to be sorted */
18     int i; /* int used in for loop */
19
20     srand( time( NULL ) ); /* seed the rand function */
21
22     for ( i = 0; i < SIZE; i++ )
23        array[ i ] = rand() % 90 + 10; /* give each element a value */
24
25     printf( "Unsorted array:\n" );
26     displayElements( array, SIZE ); /* print the array */
27     printf( "\n\n" );
28     mergeSort( array, SIZE ); /* merge sort the array */
```

Fig. 16.3 | Merge sort algorithm. (Part 1 of 5.)

```
29        printf( "Sorted array:\n" );
30        displayElements( array, SIZE ); /* print the array */
31        return 0;
32   } /* end function main */
33
34   /* function that merge sorts the array */
35   void mergeSort( int array[], int length )
36   {
37        sortSubArray( array, 0, length - 1 );
38   } /* end function mergeSort */
39
40   /* function that sorts a piece of the array */
41   void sortSubArray( int array[], int low, int high )
42   {
43        int middle1, middle2; /* ints that record where the array is split */
44
45        /* test base case: size of array is 1 */
46        if ( ( high - low ) >= 1 ) { /* if not base case... */
47             middle1 = ( low + high ) / 2;
48             middle2 = middle1 + 1;
49
50             /* output split step */
51             printf( "split:    " );
52             displaySubArray( array, low, high );
53             printf( "\n           " );
54             displaySubArray( array, low, middle1 );
55             printf( "\n           " );
56             displaySubArray( array, middle2, high );
57             printf( "\n\n" );
58
59             /* split array in half and sort each half recursively */
60             sortSubArray( array, low, middle1 ); /* first half */
61             sortSubArray( array, middle2, high ); /* second half */
62
63             /* merge the two sorted arrays */
64             merge( array, low, middle1, middle2, high );
65        } /* end if */
66   } /* end function sortSubArray */
67
68   /* merge two sorted subarrays into one sorted subarray */
69   void merge( int array[], int left, int middle1, int middle2, int right )
70   {
71        int leftIndex = left; /* index into left subarray */
72        int rightIndex = middle2; /* index into right subarray */
73        int combinedIndex = left; /* index into temporary array */
74        int tempArray[ SIZE ]; /* temporary array */
75        int i; /* int used in for loop */
76
77        /* output two subarrays before merging */
78        printf( "merge:    " );
79        displaySubArray( array, left, middle1 );
80        printf( "\n           " );
```

Fig. 16.3 | Merge sort algorithm. (Part 2 of 5.)

```
81         displaySubArray( array, middle2, right );
82         printf( "\n" );
83
84         /* merge the subarrays until the end of one is reached */
85         while ( leftIndex <= middle1 && rightIndex <= right ) {
86            /* place the smaller of the two current elements in result */
87            /* and move to the next space in the subarray */
88            if ( array[ leftIndex ] <= array[ rightIndex ] )
89               tempArray[ combinedIndex++ ] = array[ leftIndex++ ];
90            else
91               tempArray[ combinedIndex++ ] = array[ rightIndex++ ];
92         } /* end while */
93
94         if ( leftIndex == middle2 ) { /* if at end of left subarray ... */
95            while ( rightIndex <= right ) /* copy the right subarray */
96               tempArray[ combinedIndex++ ] = array[ rightIndex++ ];
97         } /* end if */
98         else { /* if at end of right subarray... */
99            while ( leftIndex <= middle1 ) /* copy the left subarray */
100              tempArray[ combinedIndex++ ] = array[ leftIndex++ ];
101        } /* end else */
102
103        /* copy values back into original array */
104        for ( i = left; i <= right; i++ )
105           array[ i ] = tempArray[ i ];
106
107        /* output merged subarray */
108        printf( "           " );
109        displaySubArray( array, left, right );
110        printf( "\n\n" );
111 } /* end function merge */
112
113 /* display elements in array */
114 void displayElements( int array[], int length )
115 {
116    displaySubArray( array, 0, length - 1 );
117 } /* end function displayElements */
118
119 /* display certain elements in array */
120 void displaySubArray( int array[], int left, int right )
121 {
122    int i; /* int used in for loop */
123
124    /* output spaces for alignment */
125    for ( i = 0; i < left; i++ )
126       printf( "    " );
127
128    /* output elements left in array */
129    for ( i = left; i <= right; i++ )
130       printf( " %d", array[ i ] );
131 } /* end function displaySubArray */
```

Fig. 16.3 | Merge sort algorithm. (Part 3 of 5.)

```
Unsorted array:
 79 86 60 79 76 71 44 88 58 23

split:    79 86 60 79 76 71 44 88 58 23
          79 86 60 79 76
                        71 44 88 58 23

split:    79 86 60 79 76
          79 86 60
                  79 76

split:    79 86 60
          79 86
                60

split:    79 86
          79
             86

merge:    79
             86
          79 86

merge:    79 86
                60
          60 79 86

split:           79 76
                 79
                    76

merge:           79
                    76
                 76 79

merge:    60 79 86
                 76 79
          60 76 79 79 86

split:                  71 44 88 58 23
                        71 44 88
                                 58 23

split:                  71 44 88
                        71 44
                              88

split:                  71 44
                        71
                           44
merge:                  71
                           44
                        44 71
```

(continued on next page)

Fig. 16.3 | Merge sort algorithm. (Part 4 of 5.)

```
merge:                    44 71
                                88
                          44 71 88

split:                            58 23
                                  58
                                     23

merge:                            58
                                     23
                                  23 58

merge:                    44 71 88
                                  23 58
                          23 44 58 71 88

merge:    60 76 79 79 86
                          23 44 58 71 88
                23 44 58 60 71 76 79 79 86 88

Sorted array:
 23 44 58 60 71 76 79 79 86 88
```

Fig. 16.3 | Merge sort algorithm. (Part 5 of 5.)

Lines 85–92 in function merge loop until the program reaches the end of either subarray. Line 88 tests which element at the beginning of the arrays is smaller. If the element in the left array is smaller, line 89 places it in position in the combined array. If the element in the right array is smaller, line 91 places it in position in the combined array. When the while loop completes, one entire subarray is placed in the combined array, but the other subarray still contains data. Line 94 tests whether the left array has reached the end. If so, lines 95–96 fill the combined array with the elements of the right array. If the left array has not reached the end, then the right array must have reached the end, and lines 99–100 fill the combined array with the elements of the left array. Finally, lines 104–105 copy the combined array into the original array. The output from this program displays the splits and merges performed by merge sort, showing the progress of the sort at each step of the algorithm.

Efficiency of Merge Sort

Merge sort is a far more efficient algorithm than either insertion sort or selection sort (although that may be difficult to believe when looking at the rather busy Fig. 16.3). Consider the first (nonrecursive) call to function sortSubArray. This results in two recursive calls to function sortSubArray with subarrays each approximately half the size of the original array, and a single call to function merge. This call to function merge requires, at worst, $n - 1$ comparisons to fill the original array, which is $O(n)$. (Recall that each element in the array is chosen by comparing one element from each of the subarrays.) The two calls to function sortSubArray result in four more recursive calls to function sortSubArray, each with a subarray approximately one quarter the size of the original array, along with two calls to function merge. These two calls to the function merge each require, at worst, $n/2 - 1$ comparisons, for a total number of comparisons of $O(n)$. This process continues, each call to `sortSubArray` generating two additional calls to `sortSubArray` and a call to `merge`, until the algorithm has split the array into one-element subarrays. At each level, $O(n)$ comparisons are required to merge the subarrays. Each level splits the size of the arrays in half, so doubling the size of the array requires one more level. Quadrupling the size of the array requires two more levels. This pattern is logarithmic and results in $\log_2 n$ levels. This results in a total efficiency of $O(n \log n)$.

Figure 16.4 summarizes many of the searching and sorting algorithms covered in this book and lists the Big O for each of them. Figure 16.5 lists the Big O values we have covered in this chapter along with a number of values for n to highlight the differences in the growth rates.

Algorithm	Big O
Insertion sort	$O(n^2)$
Selection sort	$O(n^2)$
Merge sort	$O(n \log n)$
Bubble sort	$O(n^2)$
Quicksort	Worst case: $O(n^2)$ Average case: $O(n \log n)$

Fig. 16.4 | Searching and sorting algorithms with Big O values.

n	Approximate decimal value	$O(\log n)$	$O(n)$	$O(n \log n)$	$O(n^2)$
2^{10}	1000	10	2^{10}	$10 \cdot 2^{10}$	2^{20}
2^{20}	1,000,000	20	2^{20}	$20 \cdot 2^{20}$	2^{40}
2^{30}	1,000,000,000	30	2^{30}	$30 \cdot 2^{30}$	2^{60}

Fig. 16.5 | Approximate number of comparisons for common Big O notations.

Summary

Section 16.1 Introduction
• Sorting involves arranging data into order.

Section 16.2 Big O Notation
• One way to describe the efficiency of an algorithm is with Big O notation (O), which indicates how hard an algorithm may have to work to solve a problem.

• For searching and sorting algorithms, Big O describes how the amount of effort of a particular algorithm varies, depending on how many elements are in the data.

- An algorithm that is $O(1)$ is said to have a constant run time. This does not mean that the algorithm requires only one comparison. It just means that the number of comparisons does not grow as the size of the array increases.
- An $O(n)$ algorithm is referred to as having a linear run time.
- Big O is designed to highlight dominant factors and ignore terms that become unimportant with high values of n.
- Big O notation is concerned with the growth rate of algorithm run times, so constants are ignored.

Section 16.3 Selection Sort
- Selection sort is a simple, but inefficient, sorting algorithm.
- The first iteration of selection sort selects the smallest element in the array and swaps it with the first element. The second iteration of selection sort selects the second-smallest element (which is the smallest of those remaining) and swaps it with the second element. Selection sort continues until the last iteration selects the second-largest element and swaps it with the second-to-last, leaving the largest element as the last. At the ith iteration of selection sort, the smallest i elements of the whole array are sorted into the first i positions of the array.
- The selection sort algorithm runs in $O(n^2)$ time.

Section 16.4 Insertion Sort
- The first iteration of insertion sort takes the second element in the array and, if it is less than the first element, swaps it with the first element. The second iteration of insertion sort looks at the third element and inserts it in the correct position with respect to the first two elements. After the ith iteration of insertion sort, the first i elements in the original array are sorted. Only $n-1$ iterations are required.
- The insertion sort algorithm runs in $O(n^2)$ time.

Section 16.5 Merge Sort
- Merge sort is a sorting algorithm that is faster, but more complex to implement, than selection sort and insertion sort.
- The merge sort algorithm sorts a array by splitting the array into two equal-sized subarrays, sorting each subarray and merging the subarrays into one larger array.
- Merge sort's base case is an array with one element. A one-element array is already sorted, so merge sort immediately returns when it is called with a one-element array. The merge part of merge sort takes two sorted arrays (these could be one-element arrays) and combines them into one larger sorted array.
- Merge sort performs the merge by looking at the first element in each array, which is also the smallest element. Merge sort takes the smallest of these and places it in the first element of the larger, sorted array. If there are still elements in the subarray, merge sort looks at the second element in that subarray (which is now the smallest element remaining) and compares it to the first element in the other subarray. Merge sort continues this process until the larger array is filled.
- In the worst case, the first call to merge sort has to make $O(n)$ comparisons to fill the n slots in the final array.
- The merging portion of the merge sort algorithm is performed on two subarrays, each of approximately size $n/2$. Creating each of these subarrays requires $n/2-1$ comparisons for each subarray, or $O(n)$ comparisons total. This pattern continues, as each level works on twice as many arrays, but each is half the size of the previous array.
- This halving results in $\log n$ levels, each level requiring $O(n)$ comparisons, for a total efficiency of $O(n \log n)$, which is far more efficient than $O(n^2)$.

Terminology

Big O notation	order 1
binary search	order log n
constant run time	order n
efficiency of an algorithm	order n-squared
insertion sort	quadratic run time
linear run time	random-access iterator
logarithmic run time	search key
merge sort	searching data
merge two arrays	selection sort
$O(1)$	sort key
$O(\log n)$	sort Standard Library function
$O(n \log n)$	sorting data
$O(n)$	split the array in merge sort
$O(n^2)$	worst-case run time for an algorithm

Self-Review Exercises

16.1 Fill in the blanks in each of the following statements:
a) A selection sort application would take approximately _____ times as long to run on a 128-element array as on a 32-element array.
b) The efficiency of merge sort is _____.

16.2 The Big O of the linear search is $O(n)$ and of the binary search is $O(\log n)$. What key aspect of both the binary search (Chapter 6) and the merge sort accounts for the logarithmic portion of their respective Big Os?

16.3 In what sense is the insertion sort superior to the merge sort? In what sense is the merge sort superior to the insertion sort?

16.4 In the text, we say that after the merge sort splits the array into two subarrays, it then sorts these two subarrays and merges them. Why might someone be puzzled by our statement that "it then sorts these two subarrays"?

Answers to Self-Review Exercises

16.1 a) 16, because an $O(n^2)$ algorithm takes 16 times as long to sort four times as much information. b) $O(n \log n)$.

16.2 Both of these algorithms incorporate "halving"—somehow reducing something by half on each pass. The binary search eliminates from consideration one-half of the array after each comparison. The merge sort splits the array in half each time it is called.

16.3 The insertion sort is easier to understand and to implement than the merge sort. The merge sort is far more efficient—$O(n \log n)$—than the insertion sort—$O(n^2)$.

16.4 In a sense, it does not really sort these two subarrays. It simply keeps splitting the original array in half until it provides a one-element subarray, which is, of course, sorted. It then builds up the original two subarrays by merging these one-element arrays to form larger subarrays, which are then merged, and so on.

Exercises

16.5 (*Recursive Selection Sort*) A selection sort searches an array looking for the smallest element in the array. When the smallest element is found, it is swapped with the first element of the array.

The process is then repeated for the subarray, beginning with the second element of the array. Each pass of the array results in one element being placed in its proper location. This sort requires processing capabilities similar to those of the bubble sort—for an array of n elements, $n - 1$ passes must be made, and for each subarray, $n - 1$ comparisons must be made to find the smallest value. When the subarray being processed contains one element, the array is sorted. Write a recursive function selectionSort to perform this algorithm.

16.6 (*Bucket Sort*) A bucket sort begins with a single-subscripted array of positive integers to be sorted, and a double-subscripted array of integers with rows subscripted from 0 to 9 and columns subscripted from 0 to $n - 1$, where n is the number of values in the array to be sorted. Each row of the double-subscripted array is referred to as a bucket. Write a function bucketSort that takes an integer array and the array size as arguments.

The algorithm is as follows:

a) Loop through the single-subscripted array and place each of its values in a row of the bucket array based on its ones digit. For example, 97 is placed in row 7, 3 is placed in row 3 and 100 is placed in row 0.

b) Loop through the bucket array and copy the values back to the original array. The new order of the above values in the single-subscripted array is 100, 3 and 97.

c) Repeat this process for each subsequent digit position (tens, hundreds, thousands, and so on) and stop when the leftmost digit of the largest number has been processed.

On the second pass of the array, 100 is placed in row 0, 3 is placed in row 0 (it had only one digit so we treat it as 03) and 97 is placed in row 9. The order of the values in the single-subscripted array is 100, 3 and 97. On the third pass, 100 is placed in row 1, 3 (003) is placed in row zero and 97 (097) is placed in row zero (after 3). The bucket sort is guaranteed to have all the values properly sorted after processing the leftmost digit of the largest number. The bucket sort knows it is done when all the values are copied into row zero of the double-subscripted array.

Note that the double-subscripted array of buckets is ten times the size of the integer array being sorted. This sorting technique provides far better performance than a bubble sort but requires much larger storage capacity. Bubble sort requires only one additional memory location for the type of data being sorted. Bucket sort is an example of a space-time trade-off. It uses more memory but performs better. This version of the bucket sort requires copying all the data back to the original array on each pass. Another possibility is to create a second double-subscripted bucket array and repeatedly move the data between the two bucket arrays until all the data is copied into row zero of one of the arrays. Row zero then contains the sorted array.

16.7 (*Quicksort*) In the examples and exercises of Chapter 6, we discussed the sorting techniques bubble sort, bucket sort and selection sort. We now present the recursive sorting technique called Quicksort. The basic algorithm for a single-subscripted array of values is as follows:

a) *Partitioning Step:* Take the first element of the unsorted array and determine its final location in the sorted array (i.e., all values to the left of the element in the array are less than the element, and all values to the right of the element in the array are greater than the element). We now have one element in its proper location and two unsorted subarrays.

b) *Recursive Step:* Perform *Step a* on each unsorted subarray.

Each time *Step a* is performed on a subarray, another element is placed in its final location of the sorted array, and two unsorted subarrays are created. When a subarray consists of one element, it must be sorted; therefore, that element is in its final location.

The basic algorithm seems simple enough, but how do we determine the final position of the first element of each subarray? As an example, consider the following set of values (the element in bold is the partitioning element—it will be placed in its final location in the sorted array):

37 2 6 4 89 8 10 12 68 45

a) Starting from the rightmost element of the array, compare each element with 37 until an element less than 37 is found. Then swap 37 and that element. The first element less than 37 is 12, so 37 and 12 are swapped. The new array is

   12   2   6   4   89   8   10   **37**   68   45

   Element 12 is in italic to indicate that it was just swapped with 37.

b) Starting from the left of the array, but beginning with the element after 12, compare each element with 37 until an element greater than 37 is found. Then swap 37 and that element. The first element greater than 37 is 89, so 37 and 89 are swapped. The new array is

   12   2   6   4   **37**   8   10   *89*   68   45

c) Starting from the right, but beginning with the element before 89, compare each element with 37 until an element less than 37 is found. Then swap 37 and that element. The first element less than 37 is 10, so 37 and 10 are swapped. The new array is

   12   2   6   4   *10*   8   **37**   89   68   45

d) Starting from the left, but beginning with the element after 10, compare each element with 37 until an element greater than 37 is found. Then swap 37 and that element. There are no more elements greater than 37, so when we compare 37 with itself, we know that 37 has been placed in its final location in the sorted array.

Once the partition has been applied to the array, there are two unsorted subarrays. The subarray with values less than 37 contains 12, 2, 6, 4, 10 and 8. The subarray with values greater than 37 contains 89, 68 and 45. The sort continues by partitioning both subarrays in the same manner as the original array.

Write recursive function `quicksort` to sort a single-subscripted integer array. The function should receive as arguments an integer array, a starting subscript and an ending subscript. Function `partition` should be called by `quicksort` to perform the partitioning step.

17

Introduction to C99

OBJECTIVES

In this chapter you will learn:

- Many of the new features of the C99 standard.

- Some key C99 features in the context of complete working programs.

- To use // comments.

- To mix declarations and executable code and to declare variables in **for** statement headers.

- To initialize arrays and **struct**s with designated initializers.

- To use data type **bool** to create boolean variables whose data values can be **true** or **false**.

- To create variable-length arrays and pass them to functions.

- To perform arithmetic operations on complex variables.

17.1 Introduction

C99 is a revised standard for the C programming language that refines and expands the capabilities of Standard C. C99 has not been widely adopted, and not all popular C compilers support it. Of the compilers that do offer C99 support, most support only a subset of the language. For these reasons, we chose to discuss C99 only in this late "optional" chapter. Chapters 1–14 discuss C89 (the initial version of the ANSI/ISO standard), which is almost universally supported.

In this chapter, we provide an introduction to C99. We discuss compiler support and include links to several free compilers and IDEs that provide various levels of C99 support. We explain with complete working code examples some of the key features of C99, including // comments, mixing declarations and executable code, declarations in for statements, designated initializers, compound literals, type bool, implicit int return type in function prototypes and function definitions (not allowed in C99), complex numbers and variable-length arrays. We provide brief explanations for additional key C99 features, including extended identifiers, restricted pointers, reliable integer division, flexible array members, the long long int type, generic math, inline functions, return without expression and function snprintf. Another significant feature is the addition of float and long double versions of most of the math functions in <math.h>. We include an extensive list of Internet and web resources to help you locate C99 compilers and IDEs, and dig deeper into the technical details of the language.

17.2 Support for C99

Most C and C++ compilers did not support C99 when it was released. Support has grown in recent years, and many compilers are close to being C99 compliant. The Microsoft Visual C++ 2005 Express Edition Software included with this book does not support C99.

For more information about the future of C99 compliance in Microsoft Visual C++, visit msdn.microsoft.com/chats/transcripts/vstudio/vstudio_022703.aspx.

In this chapter, we use the Dev-C++ 4.9.9.2 IDE from Bloodshed Software (www.bloodshed.net/dev/devcpp.html). This free IDE by default uses the MingW (Minimalist GNU for Windows) compiler, a port of the GNU GCC Compiler (gcc.gnu.org/install), which supports most of C99. To specify that the C99 standard should be used in compilation, you must edit the **Compiler Options** window (Fig. 17.1) under the **Tools** menu, and add -std=c99 in the text area labeled **Add the following commands when calling compiler:**. Make sure that the box to the left of the label is also checked.

To run programs written in Dev-C++, open a Windows command prompt, use the cd (change directory) command to locate the directory in which the program was compiled, and type the program name to execute it (i.e., fig17_03.exe).

Comeau Computing offers the Comeau C/C++ compiler with full C99 compliance. The compiler can be purchased from their website—www.comeaucomputing.com. The website also includes documentation and a free online compiler that will demonstrate Comeau C/C++ error messages and warnings (but does not allow you to execute programs). The Comeau C/C++ compiler can be used in conjunction with the Dinkum C99 Standard Library from Dinkumware (www.dinkumware.com/c99.aspx). This library supports all of the new required headers in C99 and C95. The Dinkum C99 Library can also be used in other compilers including Microsoft Visual C++.

17.3 New C99 Headers

Figure 17.2 lists alphabetically the standard library headers added in C99 (three of these were added in C95).

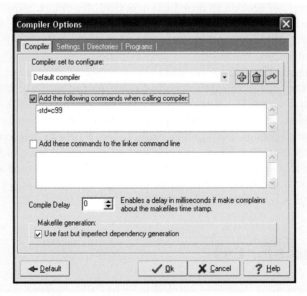

Fig. 17.1 | Compiler Options window in Dev-C++ 4.9.9.2.

Standard library header	Explanation
`<complex.h>`	Contains macros and function prototypes for supporting complex numbers (see Section 17.10). [C99 feature.]
`<fenv.h>`	Provides information about the C implementation's floating-point environment and capabilities. [C99 feature.]
`<inttypes.h>`	Defines several new portable integral types and provides format specifiers for defined types. [C99 feature.]
`<iso646.h>`	Defines macros that represent the equality, relational, and bitwise operators; an alternative to trigraphs. [C95 feature.]
`<stdbool.h>`	Contains macros defining `bool`, `true`, and `false`, used for boolean variables (see Section 17.8). [C99 feature.]
`<stdint.h>`	Defines extended integer types and related macros. [C99 feature.]
`<tgmath.h>`	Provides type-generic macros that allow functions from `<math.h>` to be used with a variety of parameter types (see Section 17.12). [C99 feature.]
`<wchar.h>`	Along with `<wctype.h>`, provides multibyte and wide-character input and output support. [C95 feature.]
`<wctype.h>`	Along with `<wchar.h>`, provides wide-character library support. [C95 feature.]

Fig. 17.2 | Standard library headers added in C99 and C95.

17.4 // Comments

C99 allows you to use // comments (as C++, Java, and C# do). Whenever the characters // appear outside quotation marks, the rest of the line is treated as a comment (see Fig. 17.3; lines 1, 2, 7, 10, 13 and 14).

17.5 Mixing Declarations and Executable Code

C89 requires that all variables with block scope be declared at the start of a block. C99 allows mixing declarations and executable code. A variable can be declared anywhere in a block prior to usage. Consider the C99 program of Fig. 17.3.

```
1    // Fig 17.3: fig17_03.c
2    // Mixing declarations and executable code in C99
3    #include <stdio.h>
4
5    int main( void )
6    {
7        int x = 1; // declare variable at beginning of block
```

Fig. 17.3 | Mixing declarations and executable code in C99. (Part 1 of 2.)

```
8      printf( "x is %d\n", x );
9
10     int y = 2; // declare variable in middle of executable code
11     printf( "y is %d\n", y );
12
13     return 0; // indicates successful termination
14  } // end main
```

```
x is 1
y is 2
```

Fig. 17.3 | Mixing declarations and executable code in C99. (Part 2 of 2.)

In this program, we call printf (executable code) in line 8, yet declare the int variable y in line 10. This is not allowed in C89. In C99 you can declare variables close to their first use, even if those declarations appear after executable code in a block. We don't declare int y (line 10) until just before we use it (line 11). Although this can improve program readability and reduce the possibility of unintended references, many programmers still prefer to group their variable declarations together at the beginnings of blocks.

A variable cannot be declared after code that uses the variable. In Fig. 17.4 we declare int y (line 12) after an executable statement that attempts to print y (line 10). This results in a compilation error.

```
1   // Fig 17.4: fig17_04.c
2   // Attempting to declare a variable after its use in C99
3   #include <stdio.h>
4
5   int main( void )
6   {
7      int x = 1; // declare x
8
9      printf( "The value of x is %d\n", x ); // output x
10     printf( "The value of y is %d\n", y ); // output y (error)
11
12     int y = 2; // declare y
13
14     return 0; // indicates successful termination
15  } // end main
```

```
../examples/ch17/fig17_03.c: In function `main':
../examples/ch17/fig17_03.c:10: error: `y' undeclared
   (first use in this function)
../examples/ch17/fig17_03.c:10: error:
   (Each undeclared identifier is reported only once
../examples/ch17/fig17_03.c:10: error: for each function it appears in.)
```

Fig. 17.4 | Attempting to declare a variable after its use in C99. [Error produced by MingW compiler using Dev C++ IDE.]

17.6 Declaring a Variable in a for Statement Header

As you may recall, a for statement consists of an initialization, a loop-continuation condition, an increment, and a loop body. Figure 17.5 shows a C89 program that uses a for statement to output the numbers 1 through 5.

C99 expands on the C89 definition of the for statement, allowing the initialization clause to include a declaration. Rather than using an existing variable as a loop counter, we can create a new loop-counter variable in the for statement header whose scope is limited to the for statement. The C99 program of Fig. 17.6 declares a variable in a for statement header.

Any variable declared in a for statement has the scope of the for statement—the variable does not exist outside the for statement. Figure 17.7 shows a failed attempt to access such a variable after the statement body.

```c
 1   // Fig 17.5: fig17_05.c
 2   // Declaring a loop counter before a for statement in C89
 3   #include <stdio.h>
 4
 5   int main( void )
 6   {
 7      int x; // declare loop counter
 8
 9      // output values 1 through 5
10      printf( "Values of x\n" );
11      for ( x = 1; x <= 5; x++ ) // initialize loop counter
12         printf( "%d\n", x );
13
14      printf( "Value of x is %d\n", x ); // x is still in scope
15
16      return 0; // indicates successful termination
17   } // end main
```

```
Values of x
1
2
3
4
5
Value of x is 6
```

Fig. 17.5 | Declaring a loop counter before a for statement in C89.

```c
 1   // Fig 17.6: fig17_06.c
 2   // Declaring a variable in a for statement header in C99
 3   #include <stdio.h>
 4
 5   int main( void )
 6   {
 7      printf( "Values of x\n" );
```

Fig. 17.6 | Declaring a variable in a for statement header in C99. (Part 1 of 2.)

```
 8
 9       // declare a variable in a for statement header
10       for ( int x = 1; x <= 5; x++ )
11          printf( "%d\n", x );
12
13       return 0; // indicates successful termination
14    } // end main
```

```
Values of x
1
2
3
4
5
```

Fig. 17.6 | Declaring a variable in a for statement header in C99. (Part 2 of 2.)

```
 1    // Fig 17.7: fig17_07.c
 2    // Accessing a for statement variable after the for statement in C99
 3    #include <stdio.h>
 4
 5    int main( void )
 6    {
 7       printf( "Values of x:\n" );
 8
 9       // declare variable in for statement header
10       for ( int x = 1; x <= 5; x++ )
11          printf( "%d\n", x );
12
13       printf( "Value of x is: %d\n", x ); // x is out of scope
14
15       return 0; // indicates successful termination
16    } // end main
```

```
../examples/ch17/fig17_07.c: In function `main':
../examples/ch17/fig17_07.c:13: error: `x' undeclared
   (first use in this function)
../examples/ch17/fig17_07.c:13: error:
   (Each undeclared identifier is reported only once
../examples/ch17/fig17_07.c:13: error: for each function it appears in.)
```

Fig. 17.7 | Accessing a for statement variable after the for statement in C99. [Error produced by MingW compiler using Dev C++ IDE.]

17.7 Designated Initializers and Compound Literals

Designated initializers allow you to initialize the elements of an array, union, or struct explicitly by subscript or name. Figure 17.8 shows how we might assign the first and last elements of an array in C89.

```
 1   // Fig 17.8: fig17_08.c
 2   // Assigning elements of an array in C89
 3   #include <stdio.h>
 4
 5   int main( void )
 6   {
 7      int i; // declare loop counter
 8      int a[ 5 ]; // array declaration
 9
10      a[ 0 ] = 1; // explicitly assign values to array elements...
11      a[ 4 ] = 2; // after the declaration of the array
12
13      // assign zero to all elements but the first and last
14      for ( i = 1; i < 4; i++ )
15         a[ i ] = 0;
16
17      // output array contents
18      printf( "The array is \n" );
19      for ( i = 0; i < 5; i++ )
20         printf( "%d\n", a[ i ] );
21
22      return 0; // indicates successful termination
23   } // end main
```

```
The array is
1
0
0
0
2
```

Fig. 17.8 | Assigning elements of an array in C89.

In Fig. 17.9 we show the program again, but rather than *assigning* values to the first and last elements of the array, we *initialize* them explicitly by subscript, using designated initializers.

```
 1   // Fig 17.9: fig17_09.c
 2   // Using designated initializers
 3   // to initialize the elements of an array in C99
 4   #include <stdio.h>
 5
 6   int main( void )
 7   {
 8      int a[5] =
 9      {
10         [ 0 ] = 1, // initialize elements with designated initializers...
11         [ 4 ] = 2 // within the declaration of the array
12      }; // semicolon is required
13
```

Fig. 17.9 | Using designated initializers to initialize the elements of an array in C99. (Part 1 of 2.)

```
14      // output array contents
15      printf( "The array is \n" );
16      for ( int i = 0; i < 5; i++ )
17          printf( "%d\n", a[ i ] );
18
19      return 0; // indicates successful termination
20    } // end main
```

```
The array is
1
0
0
0
2
```

Fig. 17.9 | Using designated initializers to initialize the elements of an array in C99. (Part 2 of 2.)

Lines 8–12 declare the array and initialize the specified elements within the braces. Note the syntax. Each initializer in the initializer list (lines 10–11) is separated from the next by a comma, and the end brace is followed by a semicolon. Elements that are not explicitly initialized are implicitly initialized to zero (of the correct type). This syntax is not allowed in C89.

In addition to using an initializer list to declare a variable, you can also use an initializer list to create an unnamed array, struct, or union. This is known as a compound literal. For example, if you want to pass, into the function demoFunction, an array equivalent to a in Fig. 17.9, but without having to declare the array a in your program, you could use

```
demoFunction( ( int [ 5 ] ) { [ 0 ] = 1, [ 4 ] = 2 } );
```

Consider the more elaborate example in Fig. 17.10, where we use designated initializers for an array of structs.

Line 17 uses a designated initializer to explicitly initialize a struct element of the array. Then, within that initialization, we use another level of designated initializer, explicitly initializing the x and y members of the struct. To initialize struct or union members we list each member's name preceded by a period.

```
1    // Fig. 17.10: fig17_10.c
2    // Using designated initializers to initialize an array of structs in C99
3    #include <stdio.h>
4
5    struct twoInt // declare a struct of two integers
6    {
7        int x;
8        int y;
9    }; // end struct twoInt
10
11   int main( void )
12   {
```

Fig. 17.10 | Using designated initializers to initialize an array of structs in C99. (Part 1 of 2.)

```
13      // explicitly initialize elements of array a
14      // then explicitly initialize members of each struct element
15      struct twoInt a[ 5 ] =
16      {
17         [ 0 ] = { .x = 1, .y = 2 },
18         [ 4 ] = { .x = 10, .y = 20 }
19      };
20
21      // output array contents
22      printf( "\nx\ty\n" );
23      for ( int i = 0; i <= 4; i++ )
24         printf( "%d\t%d\n", a[ i ].x, a[ i ].y );
25
26      return 0; // indicates successful termination
27   } //end main
```

```
x       y
1       2
0       0
0       0
0       0
10      20
```

Fig. 17.10 | Using designated initializers to initialize an array of **struct**s in C99. (Part 2 of 2.)

Compare lines 15–19 of Fig. 17.10, which use designated initializers to the following executable code, which does not use designated initializers:

```
struct twoInt a[ 5 ];

a[ 0 ].x = 1;
a[ 0 ].y = 2;
a[ 4 ].x = 10;
a[ 4 ].y = 20;
```

17.8 Type bool

The C99 boolean type is **_Bool**, which can hold only the values 0 or 1. Recall C's convention of using zero and nonzero values to represent false and true—the value 0 in a condition evaluates to false, while any nonzero value in a condition evaluates to true. Assigning any non-zero value to a _Bool sets it to 1. C99 provides the **<stdbool.h>** header file which defines macros representing the type **bool** and its values (**true** and **false**). These macros replace true with 1, false with 0 and bool with the C99 keyword _Bool. Figure 17.11 uses a function named isEven (lines 33–41) that returns a bool value indicating whether a number input by the user is odd or even.

Line 11 declares a bool variable named valueIsEven. Lines 15–16 in the loop prompt the user to enter an integer and input the integer. Line 18 passes the input to function isEven (lines 33–41). Note that isEven returns a value of type bool. Line 35 uses the remainder operator to determine whether the argument is divisible by 2. If so, line 36 returns true (i.e., the number is even); otherwise, line 39 returns false (i.e., the number is odd). The result is assigned to bool variable valueIsEven in line 18. Line 21 uses this

```
 1   // Fig 17.11: fig17_11.c
 2   // Using the boolean type and the values true and false in C99.
 3   #include <stdio.h>
 4   #include <stdbool.h> // allows the use of bool, true, and false
 5
 6   bool isEven( int number ); // function prototype
 7
 8   int main( void )
 9   {
10      int input; // value entered by user
11      bool valueIsEven; // stores result of function isEven
12
13      // loop for 2 inputs
14      for ( int i = 0; i < 2; i++ ) {
15         printf( "Enter an integer: " );
16         scanf( "%d", &input );
17
18         valueIsEven = isEven( input ); // determine whether input is even
19
20         // determine whether input is even
21         if ( valueIsEven ) {
22            printf( "%d is even \n\n", input );
23         } // end if
24         else {
25            printf( "%d is odd \n\n", input );
26         } // end else
27      } // end for
28
29      return 0;
30   } // end main
31
32   // even returns true if number is even
33   bool isEven( int number )
34   {
35      if ( number % 2 == 0 ) { // is number divisible by 2?
36         return true;
37      }
38      else {
39         return false;
40      }
41   } // end function isEven
```

```
Enter an integer: 34
34 is even

Enter an integer: 23
23 is odd
```

Fig. 17.11 | Using the type bool and the values true and false in C99.

variable as the condition in an if...else statement. If valueIsEven is true, line 22 displays a string indicating that the value is even. If valueIsEven is false, line 25 displays a string indicating that the value is odd.

17.9 Implicit int in Function Declarations

In C89, if a function does not have an explicit return type, it implicitly returns an int. In addition, if a function does not have a specified parameter type, it declares it as int. Consider the program in Fig. 17.12.

When this program is run in Microsoft's Visual C++ 2005 Express Edition, which is not C99 compliant, no compilation errors or warning messages occur and the program executes correctly. C99 disallows the use of the implicit int, requiring that C99-compliant compilers issue either a warning or an error. When we run the same program in the Dev C++ IDE using the MingW compiler, which is mostly C99 compliant, we get the warning messages shown in Fig. 17.13.

Although the program still executes, it is important that you heed the warning messages and abstain from using any implicit int function. Some compilers treat implicit int functions as compilation errors, preventing the program from executing.

```c
1   // Fig 17.12: fig17_12.c
2   // Using implicit int in C89
3   #include <stdio.h>
4
5   returnImplicitInt(); // prototype with unspecified return type
6   int demoImplicitInt(x); // prototype with unspecified parameter type
7
8   int main( void )
9   {
10      int x;
11      int y;
12
13      // assign data of unspecified return type to int
14      x = returnImplicitInt();
15
16      // pass in an int to a function with an unspecified type
17      y = demoImplicitInt(82);
18
19
20      printf( "x is %d\n", x );
21      printf( "y is %d\n", y );
22      return 0; // indicates successful termination
23
24   } // end main
25
26   returnImplicitInt()
27   {
28      return 77; // returning an int when return type is not specified
29   } // end function returnImplicitInt
30
31   int demoImplicitInt(x)
32   {
33      return x;
34   } // end function demoImplicitInt
```

Fig. 17.12 | Using implicit int in C89.

```
..\examples\ch17\fig17_12.c:5: warning: type defaults to `int' in declaration
  of `returnImplicitInt'
..\examples\ch17\fig17_12.c:5: warning: data definition has no type or
  storage class
..\examples\ch17\fig17_12.c:6: warning: parameter names (without types) in
  function declaration
..\examples\ch17\fig17_12.c:27: warning: return type defaults to `int'
..\examples\ch17\fig17_12.c:32: warning: return type defaults to `int'
..\examples\ch17\fig17_12.c: In function `demoImplicitInt':
..\examples\ch17\fig17_12.c:32: warning: type of "x" defaults to "int"
```

Fig. 17.13 | Warning messages for implicit **int** when using the Dev-C++ IDE.

17.10 Complex Numbers

The C99 standard introduces support for complex numbers and complex arithmetic. The program of Fig. 17.14 performs basic operations with complex numbers.

```c
 1  // Fig 17.14: fig17_14.c
 2  // Using complex numbers in C99
 3  #include <stdio.h>
 4  #include <complex.h> // for complex type and math functions
 5
 6  int main( void )
 7  {
 8      double complex a = 32.123 + 24.456 * I; // a is 32.123 + 24.456i
 9      double complex b = 23.789 + 42.987 * I; // b is 23.789 + 42.987i
10      double complex c = 3.0 + 2.0 * I;
11
12      double complex sum = a + b; // perform complex addition
13      double complex pwr = cpow( a, c ); // perform complex exponentiation
14
15      printf( "a is %f + %fi\n", creal( a ), cimag( a ));
16      printf( "b is %f + %fi\n", creal( b ), cimag( b ));
17      printf( "a + b is: %f + %fi\n", creal( sum ), cimag( sum ));
18      printf( "a - b is: %f + %fi\n", creal( a - b ), cimag( a - b ));
19      printf( "a * b is: %f + %fi\n", creal( a * b ), cimag( a * b ));
20      printf( "a / b is: %f + %fi\n", creal( a / b ), cimag( a / b ));
21      printf( "a ^ b is: %f + %fi\n", creal( pwr ), cimag( pwr ));
22
23      return 0; // indicates successful termination
24  } // end main
```

```
a is 32.123000 + 24.456000i
b is 23.789000 + 42.987000i
a + b is: 55.912000 + 67.443000i
a - b is: 8.334000 + -18.531000i
a * b is: -287.116025 + 1962.655185i
a / b is: 0.752119 + -0.331050i
a ^ b is: -17857.051995 + 1365.613958i
```

Fig. 17.14 | Using complex numbers in C99.

For C99 to recognize complex, we include the <complex.h> header (line 4). This will expand the macro complex to the keyword _Complex—a type that reserves an array of exactly two elements, corresponding to the complex number's real part and imaginary part.

Having included the header file in line 4, we can define variables as in lines 8–10 and 12–13. We define each of the variables a, b, c, sum, and pwr as type double complex. We could also have used float complex, or long double complex.

The arithmetic operators work with complex numbers. The <complex.h> header also defines several math functions, for example, cpow in line 13. [*Note:* You can also use the operators !, ++, --, &&, ||, ==, != and unary & with complex numbers.]

Lines 17–21 output the results of various arithmetic operations. The real part and the imaginary part of a complex number can be accessed with functions creal and cimag, respectively, as shown in lines 15–21. Note that in the output string of line 21, we use the symbol ∧ to indicate exponentiation.

17.11 Variable-Length Arrays

In C89, arrays are of constant size. But what if you don't know an array's size at compilation time? To handle this, you'd have to use dynamic memory allocation with malloc and related functions. C99 allows you to handle arrays of unknown size using variable-length arrays (VLAs). These are not arrays whose size can change—that would compromise the integrity of nearby locations in memory. A variable-length array is an array whose length, or size, is defined in terms of an expression evaluated at execution time. The program of Fig. 17.15 declares and prints a VLA.

```
1   // Fig 17.15: fig17_15.c
2   // Using variable-length arrays in C99
3   #include <stdio.h>
4
5   void printArray( int sz, int arr[ sz ] ); // function that accepts a VLA
6
7   int main( void )
8   {
9      int arraySize; // size of array
10     printf( "Enter array size in words: " );
11     scanf( "%d", &arraySize );
12
13     // using a non-constant expression for array's size
14     int array[ arraySize ]; // declare variable-length array
15     // test sizeof operator on VLA
16     int a = sizeof( array );
17     printf( "\nsizeof yields array size of %d bytes\n\n", a );
18
19     // assign elements of VLA
20     for ( int i = 0; i < arraySize; i++ ) {
21        array[ i ] = i * i;
22     } // end for
23
```

Fig. 17.15 | Using variable-length arrays in C99. (Part 1 of 2.)

```
24        printArray( arraySize, array ); // pass VLA to function
25
26        return 0; // indicates successful termination
27  } // end main
28
29  void printArray( int size, int array[ size ] )
30  {
31      // output contents of array
32      for ( int i = 0; i < size; i++ ) {
33          printf( "array[%d] = %d\n", i, array[ i ] );
34      } // end for
35  } // end function printArray
```

```
Enter array size in words: 7

sizeof yields array size of 28 bytes

array[0] = 0
array[1] = 1
array[2] = 4
array[3] = 9
array[4] = 16
array[5] = 25
array[6] = 36
```

Fig. 17.15 | Using variable-length arrays in C99. (Part 2 of 2.)

After prompting the user for a desired size (lines 10–11), we declare the VLA in line 14. This leads to a compilation error in C89 but is valid in C99, as long as the variable representing the array's size is of an integral type.

After declaring the array, we use the sizeof operator in line 16 to make sure that our VLA is of the proper length. In C89 sizeof is always a compile-time operation, but when applied to a VLA in C99, sizeof operates at runtime. The output window shows that the sizeof operator returns a size of 28 bytes—four times that of the number we entered because the size of an int on our machine is 4 bytes.

Next we assign values to the elements of our VLA (lines 20–22). We use i < array-Size as our loop-continuation condition. As with fixed-length arrays, there is no protection against stepping outside the array bounds.

Lines 29–35 define function printArray that takes a VLA. Note that the syntax is much the same as with a normal, fixed-length array, except that array size is a variable. The variable we use within the array brackets must be passed to the function as well. If we simply say

```
void printArray( int array[ size ] )
```

we will incur a compiler error. If our function doesn't need to know the size of the array argument, we can declare our VLA as follows:

```
void printArray( int array[ * ] )
```

which indicates that the caller can pass an array of any length.

17.12 Other C99 Features

Here we provide brief overviews of some additional key new features of C99.

Extended Identifiers

C89 requires implementations of the language to support identifiers of no less than 31 characters for identifiers with internal linkage (valid only within the file being compiled) and no less than six characters for identifiers with external linkage (also valid in other files). For more information on internal and external linkage, see Section 14.5. The C99 standard increases these limits to 63 characters for identifiers with internal linkage and to 31 characters for identifiers with external linkage. Note that these are just lower limits. Compilers are free to support identifiers with more characters than these limits. Identifiers are now allowed to contain national language characters via Universal Character Names (6.4.3) and, if the implementation chooses, directly (6.4.2.1). [For more information, see C99 Standard Section 5.2.4.1.]

The `restrict` *Keyword*

The keyword `restrict` is used to declare restricted pointers. We declare a restricted pointer when a portion of a program should have exclusive access to the region in memory that the pointer accesses. Other pointers can still refer to this region in memory. However, modifications made to this region through other pointers during the restricted pointer's lifetime might be lost. We can declare a restricted pointer to an `int` as:

```
int *restrict ptr;
```

Restricted pointers allow the compiler to optimize the way the program accesses memory. Incorrectly declaring a pointer as `restricted` when another pointer points to the same region of memory can result in undefined behavior. [For more information, see C99 Standard Section 6.7.3.1.]

Reliable Integer Division

In C89, the behavior of integer division varies across implementations. Some implementations round a negative quotient toward negative infinity, while others round toward zero. When one of the integer operands is negative, this can result in different answers. Consider dividing –28 by 5. The exact answer is –5.6. If we round the quotient toward zero, we get the integer result of –5. If we round –5.6 toward negative infinity, we get an integer result of –6. C99 removes the ambiguity and always performs integer division (and integer modulus) by rounding the quotient toward zero. This makes integer division reliable—C99-compliant platforms all treat integer division in the same way. [For more information, see C99 Standard Section 6.5.5.]

Flexible Array Members

C99 allows us to declare an array of unspecified length as the last member of a `struct`. Consider the following

```
struct s {
    int arraySize;
    int array[];
}; // end struct s
```

A flexible array member is declared by specifying empty square brackets ([]). To allocate a struct with a flexible array member, use code such as

```
int desiredSize = 5;
struct s *ptr;
ptr = malloc( sizeof( struct s ) + sizeof( int ) * desiredSize );
```

The sizeof operator ignores flexible array members. The sizeof(struct s) phrase is evaluated as the size of all the members in a struct s except for the flexible array. The extra space we allocate with sizeof(int) * desiredSize is the size of our flexible array.

There are many restrictions on the use of flexible array members. A flexible array member can be declared only as the *last* member of a struct—each struct can contain at most one flexible array member. Also, a flexible array cannot be the only member of a struct. The struct must also have one or more fixed members. Furthermore, any struct containing a flexible array member cannot be a member of another struct. Finally, a struct with a flexible array member cannot be statically initialized—it must be allocated dynamically. You cannot fix the size of the flexible array member at compile time. [For more information, see C99 Standard Section 6.7.2.1.]

long long int *Type*
C99 introduces the type long long int, which is guaranteed to be at least 64 bits long. Systems without 64-bit hardware must emulate it in software. It is never equivalent to long (even if it is the same size, it is still a separate and distinct type). C99 introduces the length modifier ll (for "long long") that can precede any of the integer conversion specifiers listed in Fig. 9.1 (e.g., %lld). [For more information, see C99 Standard Section 6.2.5.]

Type Generic Math
The <tgmath.h> header is new in C99. It provides type-generic macros for many math functions in <math.h>. For example, after including <tgmath.h>, if x is a float, the expression sin(x) will call sinf (the float version of sin); if x is a double, sin(x) will call sin (which takes a double argument); if x is a long double, sin(x) will call sinl (the long double version of sin); and if x is a complex number, sin(x) will call the appropriate version of the sin function for that complex type.

Inline Functions
C99 allows the declaration of inline functions (as C++ does) by placing the keyword inline before the function declaration, as in:

```
inline void randomFunction();
```

This has no effect on the logic of the program from the user's perspective, but it can improve performance. Function calls take time. When we declare a function as inline, the program no longer calls that function. Instead, the compiler replaces every call to an inline function with the code body of that function. This improves the runtime performance but it may increase the program's size. Declare functions as inline only if they are short and called frequently. The inline declaration is only advice to the compiler, which can decide to ignore it. [For more information, see C99 Standard Section 6.7.4.]

Return Without Expression

C99 adds tighter restrictions on returning from functions. In functions that return a non-void value, we are no longer permitted to use the statement

```
return;
```

In C89 this is allowed but results in undefined behavior if the caller tries to use the returned value of the function. Similarly, in functions that do not return a value, we are no longer permitted to return a value. Statements such as:

```
void returnInt( ) { return 1 };
```

are no longer allowed. C99 requires that compatible compilers produce warning messages or compilation errors in each of the preceding cases. [For more information, see C99 Standard Section 6.8.6.4.]

The snprinf Function: Helping Avoid Hacker Attacks

The snprintf function is new in C99 and is broadly supported, even among vendors who do not claim to be C99-compliant. It helps prevent buffer overflows, a popular form of hacker attack. The sprintf and snprintf prototypes are:

```
int sprintf( char * restrict s, const char * restrict format, ... );
int snprintf( char * restrict s, size_t n,
              const char * restrict format, ...);
```

The old sprintf function writes into a buffer but does not know how big the buffer is. It simply writes as much as necessary, which may destroy anything located after the buffer in memory. We covered sprintf in the table of Fig. 8.12 and the code example of Fig 8.15.

With snprintf, the size of the buffer is passed into the function, which will not write past the end of the buffer. This maintains the integrity of data in memory even if there is a logic error or buffer size error in the program. By avoiding buffer overflows, snprintf makes programs easier to debug because a buffer overflow can make unrelated parts of the program fail, making it difficult to identify the real problem. [For more information, see C99 Standard Section 7.19.6.5.]

17.13 Internet and Web Resources

www.open-std.org/jtc1/sc22/wg14/
Official site for the C99 standard. Includes defect reports, working papers, projects and milestones, the rationale for the C99 standard, contacts and more.

www.open-std.org/jtc1/sc22/wg14/www/docs/n1124.pdf
The C Standard with Technical Corrects 1 and 2, last updated May 6, 2005. (Available free of charge).

www.wiley.com/WileyCDA/WileyTitle/productCd-0470845732.html
Purchase a hard copy of the C99 standard.

www.comeaucomputing.com/techtalk/c99/
C99 FAQ.

www-128.ibm.com/developerworks/linux/library/l-c99.html?ca=dgr-lnxw961UsingC99
Article: "Open Source Development Using C99," by Peter Seebach. Discusses C99 library features on Linux and BSD.

`www.open-std.org/jtc1/sc22/wg14/www/C99RationaleV5.10.pdf`
White paper: "Rationale for International Standard–Programming Languages–C." This 224-page document describes the C99 standards committee deliberations.

`gcc.gnu.org/c99status.html`
Find the status of C99 features in the GNU Compiler Collection (GCC).

`www.kuro5hin.org/story/2001/2/23/194544/139`
Article: "Are You Ready for C99?" discusses some of the interesting new features, incompatibilities with C++, and compiler support.

`www.informit.com/guides/content.asp?g=cplusplus&seqNum=215&rl=1`
Article: "A Tour of C99," by Danny Kalev, summarizes some of the new features in the C99 standard.

`www.cuj.com/documents/s=8191/cuj0104meyers/`
Article: "The New C: Declarations and Initializations," by Randy Meyers. Discusses these new features in C99.

`docs.sun.com/source/817-5064/c99.app.html#98079`
Lists the features of C99 supported by the Solaris operating environment.

`home.tiscalinet.ch/t_wolf/tw/c/c9x_changes.html`
Provides brief technical descriptions and code examples for many C99 features.

`www.bloodshed.net/dev/devcpp.html`
Download Dev-C++, a free IDE that uses the Mingw port of GCC as its compiler, for use on Windows systems.

`www.digitalmars.com`
Download C/C++ compiler for Win32, a free compiler of most of C99

`www.cs.virginia.edu/~lcc-win32/`
Download lcc-win32, a free compiler of most of C99.

`www.openwatcom.org`
Download Watcom C/C++ compiler, a free compiler of most of C99 by SciTech Software Inc. and Sybase®.

`developers.sun.com/prodtech/cc/index.jsp`
Download Sun Studio 11, which includes a free fully compliant C99 compiler.

`david.tribble.com/text/cdiffs.htm`
Article: "Incompatibilities Between ISO C89 and ISO C++," by David Tribble. Lists and explains the areas in which ANSI C, C99, and C++ 98 differ.

`webstore.ansi.org/ansidocstore/product.asp?sku=INCITS%2FISO%2FIEC+9899%2D1999`
Purchase an electronic version of the C99 Standard.

`msdn.microsoft.com/chats/transcripts/vstudio/vstudio_022703.aspx`
Portions of a chat transcript including Brandon Bray, the program manager for the Visual C++ compiler. Discusses future compatibility with C99.

Summary

Section 17.1 Introduction
- C99 is a revised standard for the C programming language that refines and expands the capabilities of C89. C99 has not been widely adopted, and not all popular C compilers support it.

Section 17.2 Support for C99
- Most C and C++ compilers did not support C99 when it was released.

- We use the Dev-C++ 4.9.9.2 IDE from Bloodshed Software (www.bloodshed.net/dev/devcpp.html) in this chapter.

Section 17.4 // Comments
- C99 allows you to use // comments (as C++, Java, and C# do).
- Whenever the characters // appear outside quotation marks, the rest of the line is treated as a comment.

Section 17.5 Mixing Declarations and Executable Code
- C99 allows mixing declarations and executable code.
- A variable can be declared anywhere within a block before the variable's use.

Section 17.6 Declaring a Variable in a for Statement Header
- C99 expands on the C89 definition of the for statement, allowing the initialization clause to include a declaration.
- Rather than having to use an existing variable as a loop counter, we can create a new loop-counter variable in the for statement header whose scope is limited to the for statement.

Section 17.7 Designated Initializers and Compound Literals
- Designated initializers allow you to initialize the elements of an array, union, or struct explicitly by subscript or name.

Section 17.8 Type bool
- The C99 boolean type is _Bool, which can hold only the values 0 or 1.
- C99 provides the <stdbool.h> header file, which defines macros representing the type bool and its values (true and false). These macros replace true with 1, false with 0 and bool with the C99 keyword _Bool.

Section 17.9 Implicit int Function Declarations
- In C89, if a function does not have an explicit return type, it implicitly returns an int.
- C99 disallows the use of the implicit int, requiring that C99-compliant compilers issue either a warning or an error.

Section 17.10 Complex Numbers
- The C99 standard introduces support for complex numbers and complex arithmetic.
- For C99 to recognize complex, we must include the <complex.h> header. This will expand the macro complex to the keyword _Complex.

Section 17.11 Variable-Length Arrays
- A variable-length array is an array whose length, or size, is defined in terms of an expression evaluated at execution time.

Section 17.12 Other C99 Features
- C99 requires implementations of the language to support identifiers of no less than 63 characters for identifiers with internal linkage and no less than 31 characters for identifiers with external linkage.
- The keyword restrict is used to declare restricted pointers. We declare a restricted pointer when a portion of a program should have exclusive access to a region in memory that a pointer accesses. This enables the compiler to perform certain optimizations.

- C99 always performs integer division (and integer modulus) by rounding the quotient toward zero. This makes integer division reliable—C99-compliant platforms all treat integer division in the same way.

- C99 allows us to declare an array of unspecified length as the last member of a struct. A flexible array member is declared by specifying empty square brackets ([]).

- The type long long int increases the range of values over those of other integer types. It works only with compatible 64-bit hardware and software.

- C99 allows us to declare inline functions (as C++ does) by placing the keyword inline before the function declaration. The compiler replaces every call to an inline function with the code body of that function.

- In C99 functions that return a value, we are no longer permitted to use the void statement return.

- In C99 functions that do not return a value, we are no longer permitted to return a value.

- Function snprintf helps prevent buffer overflows, a popular form of hacker attack. With snprintf, the size of the buffer is passed into the function, which will not write past the end of the buffer.

Terminology

// comment
_Bool
_Complex
array parameter qualifiers
bool
boolean variable
C99
complex number
compound literal
designated initializer
Dev-C++ IDE
double complex
extended identifier
false
flexible array member
float complex
GNU GCC compiler
implicit int function return type
inline keyword

inline function
ll length modifier for integer conversion
    specifiers for I/O
long long int
Microsoft Visual C++ 2005 Express Edition
MingW (Minimalist GNU for Windows)
    compiler
mixing declarations and executable code
reliable integer division
restrict keyword
restricted pointer
round toward zero
round toward negative infinity
true
type-generic macro
variable-length array
<stdbool.h>
<complex.h>

Self-Review Exercises

17.1 Fill in the blanks in each of the following statements:
   a) _____ allow us to initialize elements of an array explicitly by subscript.
   b) For boolean variables, we include the _____ header and use the type _____.
   c) An array whose length is defined in terms of a value determined at execution time is a _____.
   d) The only two values a _Bool can hold are _____ and _____.

17.2 State whether each of the following is *true* or *false*. If *false*, explain why.
   a) C99 allows us to declare variables after their use in the program.
   b) If you include the <complex.h> header, you can use the complex type.

c) All code that is valid in C89 is valid in C99.
d) A variable-length array can change in size during its lifetime.
e) If we declare a variable in a for statement, we cannot access that same variable outside the for statement.
f) // indicates where a comment begins and another // indicates where the comment ends.

Answers to Self-Review Exercises

17.1 a) Designated initializers. b) <stdbool.h>, bool. c) variable-length array. d) 1, 0.

17.2 a) False. Variables must be declared before their use in the program.
b) True.
c) False. Some practices, such as the implicit int practice, are allowed in C89 but not allowed in C99.
d) False. A variable-length array has a constant size once it is declared (at execution time).
e) True.
f) False. Another // on the same line is treated as part of the first comment and another // on a different line acts as the start of a separate comment.

Exercises

17.3 Using complex numbers, write a program that solves a quadratic equation of the form $ax^2 + bx + c = 0$ for x by prompting the user for the real values of a, b, and c and printing the two roots to the screen. Recall that a solution for a quadratic equation can be solved using the following calculations (shown below as C code):

```
X1 = ( -b + csqrt( cpow( b, 2.0 ) - 4.0 * a * c ) ) / ( 2.0 * a );
X2 = ( -b - csqrt( cpow( b, 2.0 ) - 4.0 * a * c ) ) / ( 2.0 * a );
```

17.4 Use C99 variable declarations in for statement headers to solve the following problem. Read in 20 numbers, each between 10 and 100, inclusive. As each number is read, print it only if it is not a duplicate of a number already read. Provide for the worst case in which all 20 numbers are different. Use the smallest possible array to solve this problem.

17.5 Write a function multiple that determines for a pair of integers whether the second integer is a multiple of the first. The function should take two integer arguments and return true if the second is a multiple of the first, and false otherwise. Use this function in a program that inputs a series of pairs of integers

17.6 Write a program that sums a sequence of integers. Assume that the first integer read with scanf specifies the number of values remaining to be entered. Use a variable-length array to store the input values. Your program should read only one value each time scanf is executed. A typical input sequence might be

```
5 100 200 300 400 500
```

18

C++ as a Better C; Introducing Object Technology

OBJECTIVES

In this chapter you will learn:

- Several C++ enhancements to C.
- The header files of the C++ Standard Library.
- To use `inline` functions.
- To create and manipulate references.
- To use default function arguments.
- To use the unary scope resolution operator to access a global variable in a scope that contains a local variable of the same name.
- To overload function definitions.
- To create and use function templates that perform identical operations on many different types.

18.1 Introduction

We now begin the second section of this unique text. The first sixteen chapters presented a thorough treatment of procedural programming and top-down program design with C. The C++ section (Chapters 18–27) introduces two additional programming paradigms— **object-oriented programming** (with classes, encapsulation, objects, operator overloading, inheritance and polymorphism) and **generic programming** (with function templates and class templates). These chapters emphasize "crafting valuable classes" to create reusable software componentry.

18.2 C++

C++ improves on many of C's features and provides object-oriented-programming (OOP) capabilities that increase software productivity, quality and reusability. This chapter discusses many of C++'s enhancements to C.

C's designers and early implementers never anticipated that the language would become such a phenomenon. When a programming language becomes as entrenched as C, new requirements demand that the language evolve rather than simply be displaced by a new language. C++ was developed by Bjarne Stroustrup at Bell Laboratories and was originally called "C with classes." The name C++ includes C's increment operator (++) to indicate that C++ is an enhanced version of C.

Chapters 18–27 provide an introduction to the version of C++ standardized in the United States through the American National Standards Institute (ANSI) and worldwide through the International Standards Organization (ISO). We have done a careful walk-through of the ANSI/ISO C++ standard document and audited our presentation against it for completeness and accuracy. However, C++ is a rich language, and there are some subtleties in the language and some advanced subjects that we have not covered. If you need additional technical details on C++, we suggest that you read the C++ standard document, which you can purchase from the ANSI website

> webstore.ansi.org/ansidocstore/product.asp?
> sku=INCITS%2FISO%2FIEC+14882%2D2003

The title of the document is "Programming languages—C++" and its document number is INCITS/ISO/IEC 14882-2003.

18.3 A Simple Program: Adding Two Integers

This section revisits the addition program of Fig. 2.5 and illustrates several important features of the C++ language as well as some differences between C and C++. Note that C filen ames have the .c (lowercase) extension. C++ file names can have one of several extensions, such as .cpp, .cxx or .C (uppercase). We use the extension .cpp.

Figure 18.1 uses C++-style input and output to obtain two integers typed by a user at the keyboard, computes the sum of these values and outputs the result. Lines 1 and 2 each begin with //, indicating that the remainder of each line is a comment. C++ allows you to begin a comment with // and use the remainder of the line as comment text. A // comment is a maximum of one line long. C++ programmers may also use /*...*/ C-style comments, which can be more than one line long.

The C++ preprocessor directive in line 3 exhibits the standard C++ style for including header files from the standard library. This line tells the C++ preprocessor to include the

```
1   // Fig. 18.1: fig18_01.cpp
2   // Addition program that displays the sum of two numbers.
3   #include <iostream> // allows program to perform input and output
4
5   int main()
6   {
7      int number1; // first integer to add
8
9      std::cout << "Enter first integer: "; // prompt user for data
10     std::cin >> number1; // read first integer from user into number1
11
12     int number2; // second integer to add
13     int sum; // sum of number1 and number2
14
15     std::cout << "Enter second integer: "; // prompt user for data
16     std::cin >> number2; // read second integer from user into number2
17     sum = number1 + number2; // add the numbers; store result in sum
18     std::cout << "Sum is " << sum << std::endl; // display sum; end line
19
20     return 0; // indicate that program ended successfully
21  } // end function main
```

```
Enter first integer: 45
Enter second integer: 72
Sum is 117
```

Fig. 18.1 | Addition program that displays the sum of two integers entered at the keyboard.

contents of the input/output stream header file iostream. This file must be included for any program that outputs data to the screen or inputs data from the keyboard using C++-style stream input/output. We discuss iostream's many features in detail in Chapter 26, Stream Input/Output.

As in C, every C++ program begins execution with function main (line 5). Keyword int to the left of main indicates that main returns an integer value. C++ requires you to specify the return type, possibly void, for all functions. In C++, specifying a parameter list with empty parentheses is equivalent to specifying a void parameter list in C. Note that in C, using empty parentheses in a function definition or prototype is dangerous. It disables compile-time argument checking in function calls, which allows the caller to pass any arguments to the function. This could lead to runtime errors.

Common Programming Error 18.1

Omitting the return type in a C++ function definition is a syntax error.

Line 7 is a familiar variable declaration. Declarations can be placed almost anywhere in a C++ program, but they must appear before their corresponding variables are used in the program. For example, in Fig. 18.1, the declaration in line 7 could have been placed immediately before line 10, the declaration in line 12 could have been placed immediately before line 16 and the declaration in line 13 could have been placed immediately before line 17.

Good Programming Practice 18.1

Always place a blank line between a declaration and adjacent executable statements. This makes the declarations stand out in the program, enhancing program clarity.

Line 9 uses the standard output stream object—**std::cout**—and the stream insertion operator, <<, to display the string "Enter first integer: ". Output and input in C++ are accomplished with streams of characters. Thus, when line 9 executes, it sends the stream of characters "Enter first integer: " to std::cout, which is normally "connected" to the screen. We like to pronounce the preceding statement as "std::cout *gets* the character string "Enter first integer: "."

Line 10 uses the standard input stream object—**std::cin**—and the stream extraction operator, >>, to obtain a value from the keyboard. Using the stream extraction operator with std::cin takes character input from the standard input stream, which is usually the keyboard. We like to pronounce the preceding statement as, "std::cin *gives* a value to number1" or simply "std::cin *gives* number1."

When the computer executes the statement in line 10, it waits for the user to enter a value for variable number1. The user responds by typing an integer (as characters), then pressing the *Enter* key. The computer converts the character representation of the number to an integer and assigns this value to the variable number1.

Line 15 displays "Enter second integer: " on the screen, prompting the user to take action. Line 16 obtains a value for variable number2 from the user.

The assignment statement in line 17 calculates the sum of the variables number1 and number2 and assigns the result to variable sum. Line 18 displays the character string Sum is followed by the numerical value of variable sum followed by std::endl—a so-called stream manipulator. The name endl is an abbreviation for "end line." The std::endl stream manipulator outputs a newline, then "flushes the output buffer." This simply means that, on some systems where outputs accumulate in the machine until there are enough to "make it worthwhile" to display on the screen, std::endl forces any accumulated outputs to be displayed at that moment. This can be important when the outputs are prompting the user for an action, such as entering data.

Note that we place std:: before cout, cin and endl. This is required when we use standard C++ header files. The notation std::cout specifies that we are using a name, in this case cout, that belongs to "namespace" std. Namespaces are an advanced C++ feature that we do not discuss in these introductory C++ chapters. For now, you should simply remember to include std:: before each mention of cout, cin and endl in a program. This can be cumbersome—in Fig. 18.3, we introduce the using statement, which will enable us to avoid placing std:: before each use of a namespace std name.

Note that the statement in line 18 outputs values of different types. The stream insertion operator "knows" how to output each type of data. Using multiple stream insertion operators (<<) in a single statement is referred to as **concatenating, chaining** or **cascading stream insertion operations**.

Calculations can also be performed in output statements. We could have combined the statements in lines 17 and 18 into the statement

```
std::cout << "Sum is " << number1 + number2 << std::endl;
```

thus eliminating the need for the variable sum.

A powerful C++ feature is that users can create their own types called classes (we introduce this capability in Chapter 19 and explore it in depth in Chapters 20–21). Users can then "teach" C++ how to input and output values of these new data types using the >> and << operators (this is called **operator overloading**—a topic we explore in Chapter 22).

18.4 C++ Standard Library

C++ programs consist of pieces called **classes** and **functions**. You can program each piece that you may need to form a C++ program. Instead, most C++ programmers take advantage of the rich collections of existing classes and functions in the **C++ Standard Library**. Thus, there are really two parts to learning the C++ "world." The first is learning the C++ language itself; the second is learning how to use the classes and functions in the C++ Standard Library. Throughout the book, we discuss many of these classes and functions. P J. Plauger's book, *The Standard C Library* (Upper Saddle River, NJ: Prentice Hall PTR, 1992), is a must read for programmers who need a deep understanding of the Standard C library functions that are included in C++, how to implement them and how to use them to write portable code. The standard class libraries generally are provided by compiler vendors. Many special-purpose class libraries are supplied by independent software vendors.

Software Engineering Observation 18.1

*Use a "building-block" approach to create programs. Avoid reinventing the wheel. Use existing pieces wherever possible. Called **software reuse**, this practice is central to object-oriented programming.*

Software Engineering Observation 18.2

When programming in C++, you typically will use the following building blocks: classes and functions from the C++ Standard Library, classes and functions you and your colleagues create and classes and functions from various popular third-party libraries.

The advantage of creating your own functions and classes is that you'll know exactly how they work. You'll be able to examine the C++ code. The disadvantage is the time-consuming and complex effort that goes into designing, developing and maintaining new functions and classes that are correct and that operate efficiently.

Performance Tip 18.1

Using C++ Standard Library functions and classes instead of writing your own versions can improve program performance, because they are written to perform efficiently. This technique also shortens program development time.

Portability Tip 18.1

Using C++ Standard Library functions and classes instead of writing your own improves program portability, because they are included in every C++ implementation.

18.5 Header Files

The C++ Standard Library is divided into many portions, each with its own header file. The header files contain the function prototypes for the related functions that form each portion of the library. The header files also contain definitions of various class types and functions, as well as constants needed by those functions. A header file "instructs" the compiler on how to interface with library and user-written components.

Figure 18.2 lists some common C++ Standard Library header files. Header file names ending in `.h` are "old-style" header files that have been superseded by the C++ Standard Library header files.

You can create custom header files. Programmer-defined header files should end in `.h`. A programmer-defined header file can be included by using the `#include` preprocessor directive. For example, the header file `square.h` can be included in a program by placing the directive `#include "square.h"` at the beginning of the program.

C++ Standard Library header files	Explanation
`<iostream>`	Contains function prototypes for the C++ standard input and standard output functions. This header file replaces header file `<iostream.h>`. This header is discussed in detail in Chapter 26, Stream Input/Output.
`<iomanip>`	Contains function prototypes for stream manipulators that format streams of data. This header file replaces header file `<iomanip.h>`. This header is used in Chapter 26, Stream Input/Output.
`<cmath>`	Contains function prototypes for math library functions. This header file replaces header file `<math.h>`.
`<cstdlib>`	Contains function prototypes for conversions of numbers to text, text to numbers, memory allocation, random numbers and various other utility functions. This header file replaces header file `<stdlib.h>`.

Fig. 18.2 | C++ Standard Library header files. (Part 1 of 3.)

C++ Standard Library header files	Explanation
`<ctime>`	Contains function prototypes and types for manipulating the time and date. This header file replaces header file `<time.h>`.
`<vector>`, `<list>`, `<deque>`, `<queue>`, `<stack>`, `<map>`, `<set>`, `<bitset>`	These header files contain classes that implement the C++ Standard Library containers. Containers store data during a program's execution.
`<cctype>`	Contains function prototypes for functions that test characters for certain properties (such as whether the character is a digit or a punctuation), and function prototypes for functions that can be used to convert lowercase letters to uppercase letters and vice versa. This header file replaces header file `<ctype.h>`.
`<cstring>`	Contains function prototypes for C-style string-processing functions. This header file replaces header file `<string.h>`.
`<typeinfo>`	Contains classes for runtime type identification (determining data types at execution time).
`<exception>`, `<stdexcept>`	These header files contain classes that are used for exception handling (discussed in Chapter 27, Exception Handling).
`<memory>`	Contains classes and functions used by the C++ Standard Library to allocate memory to the C++ Standard Library containers. This header is used in Chapter 27, Exception Handling.
`<fstream>`	Contains function prototypes for functions that perform input from files on disk and output to files on disk. This header file replaces header file `<fstream.h>`.
`<string>`	Contains the definition of class `string` from the C++ Standard Library.
`<sstream>`	Contains function prototypes for functions that perform input from strings in memory and output to strings in memory.
`<functional>`	Contains classes and functions used by C++ Standard Library algorithms.
`<iterator>`	Contains classes for accessing data in the C++ Standard Library containers.
`<algorithm>`	Contains functions for manipulating data in C++ Standard Library containers.

Fig. 18.2 | C++ Standard Library header files. (Part 2 of 3.)

C++ Standard Library header files	Explanation
<cassert>	Contains macros for adding diagnostics that aid program debugging. This replaces header file <assert.h> from pre-standard C++.
<cfloat>	Contains the floating-point size limits of the system. This header file replaces header file <float.h>.
<climits>	Contains the integral size limits of the system. This header file replaces header file <limits.h>.
<cstdio>	Contains function prototypes for the C-style standard input/output library functions and information used by them. This header file replaces header file <stdio.h>.
<locale>	Contains classes and functions normally used by stream processing to process data in the natural form for different languages (e.g., monetary formats, sorting strings, character presentation, and so on).
<limits>	Contains classes for defining the numerical data type limits on each computer platform.
<utility>	Contains classes and functions that are used by many C++ Standard Library header files.

Fig. 18.2 | C++ Standard Library header files. (Part 3 of 3.)

18.6 Inline Functions

Implementing a program as a set of functions is good from a software engineering standpoint, but function calls involve execution-time overhead. C++ provides inline functions to help reduce function call overhead—especially for small functions. Placing the qualifier `inline` before a function's return type in the function definition "advises" the compiler to generate a copy of the function's code in place (when appropriate) to avoid a function call. The trade-off is that multiple copies of the function code are inserted in the program (often making the program larger) rather than there being a single copy of the function to which control is passed each time the function is called. The compiler can ignore the `inline` qualifier and typically does so for all but the smallest functions.

Software Engineering Observation 18.3

Any change to an `inline` function could require all clients of the function to be recompiled. This can be significant in some program development and maintenance situations.

Performance Tip 18.2

Using `inline` functions can reduce execution time but may increase program size.

Software Engineering Observation 18.4

The `inline` qualifier should be used only with small, frequently used functions.

Figure 18.3 uses inline function cube (lines 11–14) to calculate the volume of a cube of side length side. Keyword const in the parameter list of function cube (line 11) tells the compiler that the function does not modify variable side. This ensures that the value of side is not changed by the function when the calculation is performed. Notice that the complete definition of function cube appears before it is used in the program. This is required so that the compiler knows how to expand a cube function call into its inlined code. For this reason, reusable inline functions are typically placed in header files, so that their definitions can be included in each source file that uses them.

```cpp
1   // Fig. 18.3: fig18_03.cpp
2   // Using an inline function to calculate the volume of a cube.
3   #include <iostream>
4   using std::cout;
5   using std::cin;
6   using std::endl;
7
8   // Definition of inline function cube. Definition of function appears
9   // before function is called, so a function prototype is not required.
10  // First line of function definition acts as the prototype.
11  inline double cube( const double side )
12  {
13     return side * side * side; // calculate the cube of side
14  } // end function cube
15
16  int main()
17  {
18     double sideValue; // stores value entered by user
19
20     for ( int i = 1; i <= 3; i++ )
21     {
22        cout << "\nEnter the side length of your cube: ";
23        cin >> sideValue; // read value from user
24
25        // calculate cube of sideValue and display result
26        cout << "Volume of cube with side "
27           << sideValue << " is " << cube( sideValue ) << endl;
28     }
29
30     return 0; // indicates successful termination
31  } // end main
```

```
Enter the side length of your cube: 1.0
Volume of cube with side 1 is 1

Enter the side length of your cube: 2.3
Volume of cube with side 2.3 is 12.167

Enter the side length of your cube: 5.4
Volume of cube with side 5.4 is 157.464
```

Fig. 18.3 | inline function that calculates the volume of a cube.

Software Engineering Observation 18.5

The const qualifier should be used to enforce the principle of least privilege. Using the principle of least privilege to properly design software can greatly reduce debugging time and improper side effects, and can make a program easier to modify and maintain.

Lines 4–6 are `using` statements that help us eliminate the need to repeat the `std::` prefix. Once we include these `using` statements, we can write `cout` instead of `std::cout`, `cin` instead of `std::cin` and `endl` instead of `std::endl`, in the remainder of the program. From this point forward, each C++ example contains one or more `using` statements.

The `for` statement's condition (line 20) evaluates to either 0 (false) or nonzero (true). This is consistent with C. C++ also provides type **bool** for representing boolean (true/false) values. The two possible values of a `bool` are the keywords **true** and **false**. When `true` and `false` are converted to integers, they become the values 1 and 0, respectively. When non-boolean values are converted to type `bool`, non-zero values become `true`, and zero or null pointer values become `false`. Figure 18.4 lists the keywords common to C and C++ and the keywords unique to C++.

C++ keywords

Keywords common to the C and C++ programming languages

auto	break	case	char	const
continue	default	do	double	else
enum	extern	float	for	goto
if	int	long	register	return
short	signed	sizeof	static	struct
switch	typedef	union	unsigned	void
volatile	while			

C++-only keywords

and	and_eq	asm	bitand	bitor
bool	catch	class	compl	const_cast
delete	dynamic_cast	explicit	export	false
friend	inline	mutable	namespace	new
not	not_eq	operator	or	or_eq
private	protected	public	reinterpret_cast	static_cast
template	this	throw	true	try
typeid	typename	using	virtual	wchar_t
xor	xor_eq			

Fig. 18.4 | C++ keywords.

18.7 References and Reference Parameters

Two ways to pass arguments to functions in many programming languages are pass-by-value and pass-by-reference. When an argument is passed by value, a *copy* of the argument's value is made and passed (on the function call stack) to the called function. Changes to the copy do not affect the original variable's value in the caller. This prevents the accidental side effects that so greatly hinder the development of correct and reliable software systems. Each argument that has been passed in the programs in this chapter so far has been passed by value.

Performance Tip 18.3

One disadvantage of pass-by-value is that, if a large data item is being passed, copying that data can take a considerable amount of execution time and memory space.

Reference Parameters

This section introduces reference parameters—the first of two means that C++ provides for performing pass-by-reference. With pass-by-reference, the caller gives the called function the ability to access the caller's data directly, and to modify that data if the called function chooses to do so.

Performance Tip 18.4

Pass-by-reference is good for performance reasons, because it can eliminate the pass-by-value overhead of copying large amounts of data.

Software Engineering Observation 18.6

Pass-by-reference can weaken security, because the called function can corrupt the caller's data.

Later, we will show how to achieve the performance advantage of pass-by-reference while simultaneously achieving the software engineering advantage of protecting the caller's data from corruption.

A reference parameter is an alias for its corresponding argument in a function call. To indicate that a function parameter is passed by reference, simply follow the parameter's type in the function prototype by an ampersand (&); use the same notation when listing the parameter's type in the function header. For example, the following declaration in a function header

```
int &count
```

when read from right to left is pronounced "count is a reference to an int." In the function call, simply mention the variable by name to pass it by reference. Then, mentioning the variable by its parameter name in the body of the called function actually refers to the original variable in the calling function, and the original variable can be modified directly by the called function. As always, the function prototype and header must agree.

Passing Arguments by Value and by Reference

Figure 18.5 compares pass-by-value and pass-by-reference with reference parameters. The "styles" of the arguments in the calls to function squareByValue (line 18) and function squareByReference (line 23) are identical—both variables are simply mentioned by name

```
 1   // Fig. 18.5: fig18_05.cpp
 2   // Comparing pass-by-value and pass-by-reference with references.
 3   #include <iostream>
 4   using std::cout;
 5   using std::endl;
 6
 7   int squareByValue( int ); // function prototype (value pass)
 8   void squareByReference( int & ); // function prototype (reference pass)
 9
10   int main()
11   {
12      int x = 2; // value to square using squareByValue
13      int z = 4; // value to square using squareByReference
14
15      // demonstrate squareByValue
16      cout << "x = " << x << " before squareByValue\n";
17      cout << "Value returned by squareByValue: "
18         << squareByValue( x ) << endl;
19      cout << "x = " << x << " after squareByValue\n" << endl;
20
21      // demonstrate squareByReference
22      cout << "z = " << z << " before squareByReference" << endl;
23      squareByReference( z );
24      cout << "z = " << z << " after squareByReference" << endl;
25      return 0; // indicates successful termination
26   } // end main
27
28   // squareByValue multiplies number by itself, stores the
29   // result in number and returns the new value of number
30   int squareByValue( int number )
31   {
32      return number *= number; // caller's argument not modified
33   } // end function squareByValue
34
35   // squareByReference multiplies numberRef by itself and stores the result
36   // in the variable to which numberRef refers in the caller
37   void squareByReference( int &numberRef )
38   {
39      numberRef *= numberRef; // caller's argument modified
40   } // end function squareByReference
```

```
x = 2 before squareByValue
Value returned by squareByValue: 4
x = 2 after squareByValue

z = 4 before squareByReference
z = 16 after squareByReference
```

Fig. 18.5 | Passing arguments by value and by reference.

in the function calls. Without checking the function prototypes or function definitions, it is not possible to tell from the calls alone whether either function can modify its arguments. Because function prototypes are mandatory, however, the compiler has no trouble resolving the ambiguity. Recall from Section 5.6 that a function prototype tells the compiler the type of data returned by the function, the number of parameters the function expects to receive, the types of the parameters, and the order in which these parameters are expected. The compiler uses this information to validate function calls. In C, however, function prototypes are not required. Making them mandatory in C++ enables type-safe linkage, which ensures that the types of the arguments conform to the types of the parameters. Otherwise, the compiler reports an error. Locating such type errors at compile time helps prevent the runtime errors that can occur in C when arguments of incorrect data types are passed to functions.

Common Programming Error 18.2

Because reference parameters are mentioned only by name in the body of the called function, the programmer might inadvertently treat reference parameters as pass-by-value parameters. This can cause unexpected side effects if the original copies of the variables are changed by the function.

Performance Tip 18.5

For passing large objects efficiently, use a constant reference parameter to simulate the appearance and security of pass-by-value and avoid the overhead of passing a copy of the large object. The called function will not be able to modify the object in the caller.

Software Engineering Observation 18.7

Many programmers do not bother to declare parameters passed by value as const, even when the called function should not be modifying the passed argument. Keyword const in this context would protect only a copy of the original argument, not the original argument itself, which when passed by value is safe from modification by the called function.

To specify a reference to a constant, place the const qualifier before the type specifier in the parameter declaration.

Note in line 37 of Fig. 18.5 the placement of & in the parameter list of function squareByReference. Some C++ programmers prefer to write int& numberRef with the ampersand abutting int—both forms are equivalent to the compiler.

Software Engineering Observation 18.8

For the combined reasons of clarity and performance, many C++ programmers prefer that modifiable arguments be passed to functions by using pointers, small nonmodifiable arguments be passed by value and large nonmodifiable arguments be passed by using references to constants.

References as Aliases within a Function

References can also be used as aliases for other variables within a function (although they typically are used with functions as shown in Fig. 18.5). For example, the code

```
int count = 1; // declare integer variable count
int &cRef = count; // create cRef as an alias for count
cRef++; // increment count (using its alias cRef)
```

increments variable count by using its alias cRef. Reference variables must be initialized in their declarations, as we show in line 10 of both Fig. 18.6 and Fig. 18.7, and cannot be reassigned as aliases to other variables. Once a reference is declared as an alias for another variable, all operations supposedly performed on the alias (i.e., the reference) are actually performed on the original variable. The alias is simply another name for the original variable. Taking the address of a reference and comparing references do not cause syntax errors; rather, each operation actually occurs on the variable for which the reference is an alias. Unless it is a reference to a constant, a reference argument must be an *lvalue* (e.g., a variable name), not a constant or expression that returns an *rvalue* (e.g., the result of a calculation).

```
1   // Fig. 18.6: fig18_06.cpp
2   // References must be initialized.
3   #include <iostream>
4   using std::cout;
5   using std::endl;
6
7   int main()
8   {
9      int x = 3;
10     int &y = x; // y refers to (is an alias for) x
11
12     cout << "x = " << x << endl << "y = " << y << endl;
13     y = 7; // actually modifies x
14     cout << "x = " << x << endl << "y = " << y << endl;
15     return 0; // indicates successful termination
16  } // end main
```

```
x = 3
y = 3
x = 7
y = 7
```

Fig. 18.6 | Initializing and using a reference.

```
1   // Fig. 18.7: fig18_07.cpp
2   // References must be initialized.
3   #include <iostream>
4   using std::cout;
5   using std::endl;
6
7   int main()
8   {
9      int x = 3;
10     int &y; // Error: y must be initialized
11
12     cout << "x = " << x << endl << "y = " << y << endl;
13     y = 7;
14     cout << "x = " << x << endl << "y = " << y << endl;
15     return 0; // indicates successful termination
16  } // end main
```

Fig. 18.7 | Uninitialized reference causes a syntax error. (Part 1 of 2.)

Borland C++ command-line compiler error message:

```
Error E2304 C:\cpphtp5_examples\ch18\Fig18_07\fig18_07.cpp 10:
   Reference variable 'y' must be initialized in function main()
```

Microsoft Visual C++ compiler error message:

```
C:\cpphtp5_examples\ch18\Fig18_07\fig18_07.cpp(10) : error C2530: 'y' :
   references must be initialized
```

GNU C++ compiler error message:

```
fig18_07.cpp:10: error: 'y' declared as a reference but not initialized
```

Fig. 18.7 | Uninitialized reference causes a syntax error. (Part 2 of 2.)

Returning a Reference from a Function

Though functions can return references, this can be dangerous. When returning a reference to a variable declared in the called function, the variable should be declared `static` within that function. Otherwise, the reference refers to an automatic variable that is discarded when the function terminates; such a variable is said to be "undefined," and the program's behavior is unpredictable. References to undefined variables are called dangling references.

Common Programming Error 18.3

Not initializing a reference variable when it is declared is a compilation error, unless the declaration is part of a function's parameter list. Reference parameters are initialized when the function in which they are declared is called.

Common Programming Error 18.4

Attempting to reassign a previously declared reference to be an alias to another variable is a logic error. The value of the other variable is simply assigned to the variable for which the reference is already an alias.

Common Programming Error 18.5

Returning a reference to an automatic variable in a called function is a logic error. Some compilers issue a warning when this occurs.

Error Messages for Uninitialized References

Note that the C++ standard does not specify the error messages that compilers use to indicate particular errors. For this reason, we show in Fig. 18.7 the error messages produced by several compilers when a reference is not initialized.

18.8 Empty Parameter Lists

C++, like C, allows you to define functions with no parameters. In C++, an empty parameter list is specified by writing either `void` or nothing at all in parentheses. The prototypes

```
void print();
void print( void );
```

each specify that function `print` does not take arguments and does not return a value. These prototypes are equivalent.

Portability Tip 18.2

The meaning of an empty function parameter list in C++ is dramatically different than in C. In C, it means all argument checking is disabled (i.e., the function call can pass any arguments it wants). In C++, it means that the function explicitly takes no arguments. Thus, C programs using this feature might cause compilation errors when compiled in C++.

18.9 Default Arguments

It is not uncommon for a program to invoke a function repeatedly with the same argument value for a particular parameter. In such cases, the programmer can specify that such a parameter has a default argument, i.e., a default value to be passed to that parameter. When a program omits an argument for a parameter with a default argument in a function call, the compiler rewrites the function call and inserts the default value of that argument to be passed as an argument in the function call.

Default arguments must be the rightmost (trailing) arguments in a function's parameter list. When calling a function with two or more default arguments, if an omitted argument is not the rightmost argument in the argument list, then all arguments to the right of that argument also must be omitted. Default arguments should be specified with the first occurrence of the function name—typically, in the function prototype. If the function prototype is omitted because the function definition also serves as the prototype, then the default arguments should be specified in the function header. Default values can be any expression, including constants, global variables or function calls. Default arguments also can be used with `inline` functions.

Figure 18.8 demonstrates using default arguments in calculating the volume of a box. The function prototype for `boxVolume` (line 8) specifies that all three parameters have been given default values of 1. Note that we provided variable names in the function prototype for readability, but these are not required.

```
 1   // Fig. 18.8: fig18_08.cpp
 2   // Using default arguments.
 3   #include <iostream>
 4   using std::cout;
 5   using std::endl;
 6
 7   // function prototype that specifies default arguments
 8   int boxVolume( int length = 1, int width = 1, int height = 1 );
 9
10   int main()
11   {
12      // no arguments--use default values for all dimensions
13      cout << "The default box volume is: " << boxVolume();
```

Fig. 18.8 | Default arguments to a function. (Part 1 of 2.)

```
14
15      // specify length; default width and height
16      cout << "\n\nThe volume of a box with length 10,\n"
17         << "width 1 and height 1 is: " << boxVolume( 10 );
18
19      // specify length and width; default height
20      cout << "\n\nThe volume of a box with length 10,\n"
21         << "width 5 and height 1 is: " << boxVolume( 10, 5 );
22
23      // specify all arguments
24      cout << "\n\nThe volume of a box with length 10,\n"
25         << "width 5 and height 2 is: " << boxVolume( 10, 5, 2 )
26         << endl;
27      return 0; // indicates successful termination
28   } // end main
29
30   // function boxVolume calculates the volume of a box
31   int boxVolume( int length, int width, int height )
32   {
33      return length * width * height;
34   } // end function boxVolume
```

```
The default box volume is: 1

The volume of a box with length 10,
width 1 and height 1 is: 10

The volume of a box with length 10,
width 5 and height 1 is: 50

The volume of a box with length 10,
width 5 and height 2 is: 100
```

Fig. 18.8 | Default arguments to a function. (Part 2 of 2.)

 Common Programming Error 18.6

It is a compilation error to specify default arguments in both a function's prototype and header.

The first call to boxVolume (line 13) specifies no arguments, thus using all three default values of 1. The second call (line 17) passes a length argument, thus using default values of 1 for the width and height arguments. The third call (line 21) passes arguments for length and width, thus using a default value of 1 for the height argument. The last call (line 25) passes arguments for length, width and height, thus using no default values. Note that any arguments passed to the function explicitly are assigned to the function's parameters from left to right. Therefore, when boxVolume receives one argument, the function assigns the value of that argument to its length parameter (i.e., the leftmost parameter in the parameter list). When boxVolume receives two arguments, the function assigns the values of those arguments to its length and width parameters in that order. Finally, when boxVolume receives all three arguments, the function assigns the values of those arguments to its length, width and height parameters, respectively.

Good Programming Practice 18.2

Using default arguments can simplify writing function calls. However, some programmers feel that explicitly specifying all arguments is clearer.

Software Engineering Observation 18.9

If the default values for a function change, all client code using the function must be recompiled.

Common Programming Error 18.7

In a function definition, specifying and attempting to use a default argument that is not a right-most (trailing) argument (while not simultaneously defaulting all the rightmost arguments) is a syntax error.

18.10 Unary Scope Resolution Operator

Recall from our discussion of scope rules in Section 5.13 that it is possible to declare local and global variables of the same name. This causes the global variable to be "hidden" by the local variable in the local scope. C++ provides the **unary scope resolution operator** (::) to access a global variable when a local variable of the same name is in scope. The unary scope resolution operator cannot be used to access a local variable of the same name in an outer block. A global variable can be accessed directly without the unary scope resolution operator if the name of the global variable is not the same as that of a local variable in scope.

Figure 18.9 demonstrates the unary scope resolution operator with global and local variables of the same name (lines 7 and 11, respectively). To emphasize that the local and global versions of variable `number` are distinct, the program declares one variable of type `int` and the other `double`.

```cpp
1   // Fig. 18.9: fig18_09.cpp
2   // Using the unary scope resolution operator.
3   #include <iostream>
4   using std::cout;
5   using std::endl;
6
7   int number = 7; // global variable named number
8
9   int main()
10  {
11      double number = 10.5; // local variable named number
12
13      // display values of local and global variables
14      cout << "Local double value of number = " << number
15          << "\nGlobal int value of number = " << ::number << endl;
16      return 0; // indicates successful termination
17  } // end main
```

```
Local double value of number = 10.5
Global int value of number = 7
```

Fig. 18.9 | Unary scope resolution operator.

Using the unary scope resolution operator (::) with a given variable name is optional when the only variable with that name is a global variable.

Common Programming Error 18.8

It is an error to attempt to use the unary scope resolution operator (::) to access a nonglobal variable in an outer block. If no global variable with that name exists, a compilation error occurs. If a global variable with that name exists, this is a logic error, because the program will refer to the global variable when you intended to access the nonglobal variable in the outer block.

Good Programming Practice 18.3

Always using the unary scope resolution operator (::) to refer to global variables makes programs easier to read and understand, because it makes it clear that you intend to access a global variable rather than a nonglobal variable.

Software Engineering Observation 18.10

Always using the unary scope resolution operator (::) to refer to global variables makes programs easier to modify by reducing the risk of name collisions with nonglobal variables.

Error-Prevention Tip 18.1

Always using the unary scope resolution operator (::) to refer to a global variable eliminates possible logic errors that might occur if a nonglobal variable hides the global variable.

Error-Prevention Tip 18.2

Avoid using variables of the same name for different purposes in a program. Although this is allowed in various circumstances, it can lead to errors.

18.11 Function Overloading

C++ enables several functions of the same name to be defined, as long as these functions have different sets of parameters (at least as far as the parameter types or the number of parameters or the order of the parameter types are concerned). This capability is called function overloading. When an overloaded function is called, the C++ compiler selects the proper function by examining the number, types and order of the arguments in the call. Function overloading is commonly used to create several functions of the same name that perform similar tasks, but on data of different types. For example, many functions in the math library are overloaded for different numeric data types.[1]

Good Programming Practice 18.4

Overloading functions that perform closely related tasks can make programs more readable and understandable.

Overloaded square *Functions*

Figure 18.10 uses overloaded square functions to calculate the square of an int (lines 8–12) and the square of a double (lines 15–19). Line 23 invokes the int version of function square by passing the literal value 7. C++ treats whole-number literal values as type int

---

1. The C++ standard requires float, double and long double overloaded versions of the math library functions discussed in Section 5.3.

```
1    // Fig. 18.10: fig18_10.cpp
2    // Overloaded functions.
3    #include <iostream>
4    using std::cout;
5    using std::endl;
6
7    // function square for int values
8    int square( int x )
9    {
10      cout << "square of integer " << x << " is ";
11      return x * x;
12   } // end function square with int argument
13
14   // function square for double values
15   double square( double y )
16   {
17      cout << "square of double " << y << " is ";
18      return y * y;
19   } // end function square with double argument
20
21   int main()
22   {
23      cout << square( 7 ); // calls int version
24      cout << endl;
25      cout << square( 7.5 ); // calls double version
26      cout << endl;
27      return 0; // indicates successful termination
28   } // end main
```

```
square of integer 7 is 49
square of double 7.5 is 56.25
```

Fig. 18.10 | Overloaded square functions.

by default. Similarly, line 25 invokes the double version of function square by passing the literal value 7.5, which C++ treats as a double value by default. In each case the compiler chooses the proper function to call, based on the type of the argument. The outputs confirm that the proper function was called in each case.

How the Compiler Differentiates Overloaded Functions

Overloaded functions are distinguished by their signatures. A signature is a combination of a function's name and its parameter types (in order). The compiler encodes each function identifier with the number and types of its parameters (sometimes referred to as name mangling or name decoration) to enable type-safe linkage. This ensures that the proper overloaded function is called and that the types of the arguments conform to the types of the parameters

Figure 18.11 was compiled with the Borland C++ 5.6.4 command-line compiler. Rather than showing the execution output of the program (as we normally would), we show the mangled function names produced in assembly language by Borland C++. Each mangled name begins with @ followed by the function name. The function name is then separated from the mangled parameter list by $q. In the parameter list for function

```
 1   // Fig. 18.11: fig18_11.cpp
 2   // Name mangling.
 3
 4   // function square for int values
 5   int square( int x )
 6   {
 7       return x * x;
 8   } // end function square
 9
10   // function square for double values
11   double square( double y )
12   {
13       return y * y;
14   } // end function square
15
16   // function that receives arguments of types
17   // int, float, char and int &
18   void nothing1( int a, float b, char c, int &d )
19   {
20       // empty function body
21   } // end function nothing1
22
23   // function that receives arguments of types
24   // char, int, float & and double &
25   int nothing2( char a, int b, float &c, double &d )
26   {
27       return 0;
28   } // end function nothing2
29
30   int main()
31   {
32       return 0; // indicates successful termination
33   } // end main
```

```
@square$qi
@square$qd
@nothing1$qifcri
@nothing2$qcirfrd
_main
```

Fig. 18.11 | Name mangling to enable type-safe linkage.

nothing2 (line 25; see the fourth output line), c represents a char, i represents an int, rf represents a float & (i.e., a reference to a float) and rd represents a double & (i.e., a reference to a double). In the parameter list for function nothing1, i represents an int, f represents a float, c represents a char and ri represents an int &. The two square functions are distinguished by their parameter lists; one specifies d for double and the other specifies i for int. The return types of the functions are not specified in the mangled names. Overloaded functions can have different return types, but if they do, they must also have different parameter lists. Again, you cannot have two functions with the same signature and different return types. Note that function name mangling is compiler specific. Also note that function main is not mangled, because it cannot be overloaded.

Common Programming Error 18.9

Creating overloaded functions with identical parameter lists and different return types is a compilation error.

The compiler uses only the parameter lists to distinguish between functions of the same name. Overloaded functions need not have the same number of parameters. Programmers should use caution when overloading functions with default parameters, because this may cause ambiguity.

Common Programming Error 18.10

A function with default arguments omitted might be called identically to another overloaded function; this is a compilation error. For example, having in a program both a function that explicitly takes no arguments and a function of the same name that contains all default arguments results in a compilation error when an attempt is made to use that function name in a call passing no arguments. The compiler does not know which version of the function to choose.

Overloaded Operators

In Chapter 22, we discuss how to overload operators to define how they should operate on objects of user-defined data types. (In fact, we have been using many overloaded operators to this point, including the stream insertion operator << and the stream extraction operator >>, each of which is overloaded to be able to display data of all the fundamental types. We say more about overloading << and >> to be able to handle objects of user-defined types in Chapter 22.) Section 18.12 introduces function templates for automatically generating overloaded functions that perform identical tasks on data of different types.

18.12 Function Templates

Overloaded functions are used to perform similar operations that may involve different program logic on different data types. If the program logic and operations are identical for each data type, overloading may be performed more compactly and conveniently by using function templates. The programmer writes a single function template definition. Given the argument types provided in calls to this function, C++ automatically generates separate function template specializations to handle each type of call appropriately. Thus, defining a single function template essentially defines a whole family of overloaded functions.

Figure 18.12 contains the definition of a function template (lines 4–18) for a maximum function that determines the largest of three values. All function template definitions begin with the template keyword (line 4) followed by a **template parameter list** to the function template enclosed in angle brackets (< and >). Every parameter in the template parameter list (each is referred to as a **formal type parameter**) is preceded by keyword typename or keyword class (which are synonyms). The formal type parameters are placeholders for fundamental types or user-defined types. These placeholders are used to specify the types of the function's parameters (line 5), to specify the function's return type (line 5) and to declare variables within the body of the function definition (line 7). A function template is defined like any other function, but uses the formal type parameters as placeholders for actual data types.

The function template in Fig. 18.12 declares a single formal type parameter T (line 4) as a placeholder for the type of the data to be tested by function maximum. The name of a type parameter must be unique in the template parameter list for a particular template

```
 1   // Fig. 18.12: maximum.h
 2   // Definition of function template maximum.
 3
 4   template < class T >  // or template< typename T >
 5   T maximum( T value1, T value2, T value3 )
 6   {
 7      T maximumValue = value1; // assume value1 is maximum
 8
 9      // determine whether value2 is greater than maximumValue
10      if ( value2 > maximumValue )
11         maximumValue = value2;
12
13      // determine whether value3 is greater than maximumValue
14      if ( value3 > maximumValue )
15         maximumValue = value3;
16
17      return maximumValue;
18   } // end function template maximum
```

Fig. 18.12 | Function template maximum header file.

definition. When the compiler detects a maximum invocation in the program source code, the type of the data passed to maximum is substituted for T throughout the template definition, and C++ creates a complete source-code function for determining the maximum of three values of the specified data type. Then the newly created function is compiled. Thus, templates are a means of code generation.

 Common Programming Error 18.11

Not placing keyword class or keyword typename before every formal type parameter of a function template (e.g., writing < class S, T > instead of < class S, class T >) is a syntax error.

Figure 18.13 uses the maximum function template (lines 20, 30 and 40) to determine the largest of three int values, three double values and three char values.

```
 1   // Fig. 18.13: fig18_13.cpp
 2   // Function template maximum test program.
 3   #include <iostream>
 4   using std::cout;
 5   using std::cin;
 6   using std::endl;
 7
 8   #include "maximum.h" // include definition of function template maximum
 9
10   int main()
11   {
12      // demonstrate maximum with int values
13      int int1, int2, int3;
14
15      cout << "Input three integer values: ";
16      cin >> int1 >> int2 >> int3;
```

Fig. 18.13 | Demonstrating function template maximum. (Part 1 of 2.)

```
17
18    // invoke int version of maximum
19    cout << "The maximum integer value is: "
20       << maximum( int1, int2, int3 );
21
22    // demonstrate maximum with double values
23    double double1, double2, double3;
24
25    cout << "\n\nInput three double values: ";
26    cin >> double1 >> double2 >> double3;
27
28    // invoke double version of maximum
29    cout << "The maximum double value is: "
30       << maximum( double1, double2, double3 );
31
32    // demonstrate maximum with char values
33    char char1, char2, char3;
34
35    cout << "\n\nInput three characters: ";
36    cin >> char1 >> char2 >> char3;
37
38    // invoke char version of maximum
39    cout << "The maximum character value is: "
40       << maximum( char1, char2, char3 ) << endl;
41    return 0; // indicates successful termination
42 } // end main
```

```
Input three integer values: 1 2 3
The maximum integer value is: 3

Input three double values: 3.3 2.2 1.1
The maximum double value is: 3.3

Input three characters: A C B
The maximum character value is: C
```

Fig. 18.13 | Demonstrating function template maximum. (Part 2 of 2.)

In Fig. 18.13, three functions are created as a result of the calls in lines 20, 30 and 40—expecting three int values, three double values and three char values, respectively. For example, the function template specialization created for type int replaces each occurrence of T with int as follows:

```
int maximum( int value1, int value2, int value3 )
{
    int maximumValue = value1; // assume value1 is maximum

    // determine whether value2 is greater than maximumValue
    if ( value2 > maximumValue )
        maximumValue = value2;

    // determine whether value3 is greater than maximumValue
    if ( value3 > maximumValue )
        maximumValue = value3;

    return maximumValue;
} // end function template maximum
```

18.13 Introduction to Object Technology and the UML

Now we introduce object orientation, a natural way of thinking about the world and writing computer programs. Our goal here is to help you develop an object-oriented way of thinking and to introduce you to the Unified Modeling Language™ (UML™)—a graphical language that allows people who design object-oriented software systems to use an industry-standard notation to represent them. In this section, we introduce basic object-oriented concepts and terminology.

Basic Object Technology Concepts

We begin our introduction to object orientation with some key terminology. Everywhere you look in the real world you see **objects**—people, animals, plants, cars, planes, buildings, computers and so on. Humans think in terms of objects. Telephones, houses, traffic lights, microwave ovens and water coolers are just a few more objects we see around us every day.

We sometimes divide objects into two categories: animate and inanimate. Animate objects are "alive" in some sense—they move around and do things. Inanimate objects, on the other hand, do not move on their own. Objects of both types, however, have some things in common. They all have **attributes** (e.g., size, shape, color and weight), and they all exhibit **behaviors** (e.g., a ball rolls, bounces, inflates and deflates; a baby cries, sleeps, crawls, walks and blinks; a car accelerates, brakes and turns; a towel absorbs water). We will study the kinds of attributes and behaviors that software objects have.

Humans learn about existing objects by studying their attributes and observing their behaviors. Different objects can have similar attributes and can exhibit similar behaviors. Comparisons can be made, for example, between babies and adults and between humans and chimpanzees.

Object-oriented design (OOD) models software in terms similar to those that people use to describe real-world objects. It takes advantage of class relationships, where objects of a certain class, such as a class of vehicles, have the same characteristics—cars, trucks, little red wagons and roller skates have much in common. OOD takes advantage of **inheritance** relationships, where new classes of objects are derived by absorbing characteristics of existing classes and adding unique characteristics of their own. An object of class "convertible" certainly has the characteristics of the more general class "automobile," but more specifically, the roof goes up and down.

Object-oriented design provides a natural and intuitive way to view the software design process—namely, modeling objects by their attributes, behaviors and interrelationships just as we describe real-world objects. OOD also models communication between objects. Just as people send messages to one another (e.g., a sergeant commands a soldier to stand at attention), objects also communicate via **messages**. A bank account object may receive a message to decrease its balance by a certain amount because the customer has withdrawn that amount of money.

OOD **encapsulates** (i.e., wraps) attributes and **operations** (behaviors) into objects—an object's attributes and operations are intimately tied together. Objects have the property of **information hiding**. This means that objects may know how to communicate with one another across well-defined **interfaces**, but normally they are not allowed to know how other objects are implemented—implementation details are hidden within the objects themselves. We can drive a car effectively, for instance, without knowing the details of how engines, transmissions, brakes and exhaust systems work internally—as long as we know how to use the accelerator pedal, the brake pedal, the steering wheel and so on. Information hiding, as we will see, is crucial to good software engineering.

Languages like C++ are **object oriented**. Programming in such a language is called **object-oriented programming (OOP)**, and it allows computer programmers to implement an object-oriented design as a working software system. Languages like C, on the other hand, are **procedural**, so programming tends to be **action oriented**. In C, the unit of programming is the function. In C++, the unit of programming is the "class" from which objects are eventually **instantiated** (an OOP term for "created"). C++ classes contain functions that implement operations and data that implements attributes.

C programmers concentrate on writing functions. Programmers group actions that perform some common task into functions, and group functions to form programs. Data is certainly important in C, but the view is that data exists primarily in support of the actions that functions perform. The verbs in a system specification help the C programmer determine the set of functions that will work together to implement the system.

Classes, Data Members and Member Functions

C++ programmers concentrate on creating their own user-defined types called **classes**. Each class contains data as well as the set of functions that manipulate that data and provide services to **clients** (i.e., other classes or functions that use the class). The data components of a class are called **data members**. For example, a bank account class might include an account number and a balance. The function components of a class are called **member functions** (typically called **methods** in other object-oriented programming languages such as Java). For example, a bank account class might include member functions to make a deposit (increasing the balance), make a withdrawal (decreasing the balance) and inquire what the current balance is. The programmer uses built-in types (and other user-defined types) as the "building blocks" for constructing new user-defined types (classes). The nouns in a system specification help the C++ programmer determine the set of classes from which objects are created that work together to implement the system.

Classes are to objects as blueprints are to houses—a class is a "plan" for building an object of the class. Just as we can build many houses from one blueprint, we can instantiate (create) many objects from one class. You cannot cook meals in the kitchen of a blueprint; you can cook meals in the kitchen of a house. You cannot sleep in the bedroom of a blueprint; you can sleep in the bedroom of a house.

Classes can have relationships with other classes. In an object-oriented design of a bank, the "bank teller" class needs to relate to other classes, such as the "customer" class, the "cash drawer" class, the "safe" class, and so on. These relationships are called **associations**.

Packaging software as classes makes it possible for future software systems to reuse the classes. Groups of related classes are often packaged as reusable **components**. Just as realtors often say that the three most important factors affecting the price of real estate are "location, location and location," people in the software development community often say that the three most important factors affecting the future of software development are "reuse, reuse and reuse."

Software Engineering Observation 18.11

Reuse of existing classes when building new classes and programs saves time, money and effort. Reuse also helps programmers build more reliable and effective systems, because existing classes and components often have gone through extensive testing, debugging and performance tuning.

Indeed, with object technology, you can build much of the new software you will need by combining existing classes, just as automobile manufacturers combine interchangeable parts. Each new class you create will have the potential to become a valuable software asset that you and other programmers can reuse to speed and enhance the quality of future software development efforts.

Introduction to Object-Oriented Analysis and Design (OOAD)

Soon you will be writing programs in C++. How will you create the code for your programs? Perhaps, like many beginning programmers, you will simply turn on your computer and start typing. This approach may work for small programs (like the ones we present in the early chapters of the book), but what if you were asked to create a software system to control thousands of automated teller machines for a major bank? Or what if you were asked to work on a team of 1000 software developers building the next generation of the U.S. air traffic control system? For projects so large and complex, you could not simply sit down and start writing programs.

To create the best solutions, you should follow a detailed process for analyzing your project's requirements (i.e., determining *what* the system is supposed to do) and developing a design that satisfies them (i.e., deciding *how* the system should do it). Ideally, you would go through this process and carefully review the design (or have your design reviewed by other software professionals) before writing any code. If this process involves analyzing and designing your system from an object-oriented point of view, it is called object-oriented analysis and design (OOAD). Experienced programmers know that analysis and design can save many hours by helping avoid an ill-planned system development approach that has to be abandoned partway through its implementation, possibly wasting considerable time, money and effort.

OOAD is the generic term for the process of analyzing a problem and developing an approach for solving it. Small problems like the ones discussed in these first few chapters do not require an exhaustive OOAD process. It may be sufficient, before we begin writing C++ code, to write pseudocode. We introduced pseudocode in Chapter 4.

As problems and the groups of people solving them increase in size, the methods of OOAD quickly become more appropriate than pseudocode. Ideally, a group should agree on a strictly defined process for solving its problem and a uniform way of communicating the results of that process to one another. Although many different OOAD processes exist, a single graphical language for communicating the results of *any* OOAD process has come into wide use. This language, known as the Unified Modeling Language (UML), was developed in the mid-1990s under the initial direction of three software methodologists: Grady Booch, James Rumbaugh and Ivar Jacobson.

History of the UML

In the 1980s, increasing numbers of organizations began using OOP to build their applications, and a need developed for a standard OOAD process. Many methodologists—including Booch, Rumbaugh and Jacobson—individually produced and promoted separate processes to satisfy this need. Each process had its own notation, or "language" (in the form of graphical diagrams), to convey the results of analysis and design.

By the early 1990s, different organizations, and even divisions within the same organization, were using their own unique processes and notations. At the same time, these organizations also wanted to use software tools that would support their particular processes. Software vendors found it difficult to provide tools for so many processes. Clearly, a standard notation and standard processes were needed.

In 1994, James Rumbaugh joined Grady Booch at Rational Software Corporation (now a division of IBM), and the two began working to unify their popular processes. They soon were joined by Ivar Jacobson. In 1996, the group released early versions of the UML to the software engineering community and requested feedback. Around the same time, an organization known as the Object Management Group™ (OMG™) invited submissions for a common modeling language. The OMG (www.omg.org) is a nonprofit organization that promotes the standardization of object-oriented technologies by issuing guidelines and specifications, such as the UML. Several corporations—among them HP, IBM, Microsoft, Oracle and Rational Software—had already recognized the need for a common modeling language. In response to the OMG's request for proposals, these companies formed UML Partners—the consortium that developed the UML version 1.1 and submitted it to the OMG. The OMG accepted the proposal and, in 1997, assumed responsibility for the continuing maintenance and revision of the UML. In March 2003, the OMG released UML version 1.5. We present the terminology and notation of the current version of the UML—UML version 2—throughout the C++ section of this book.

What Is the UML?

The Unified Modeling Language is now the most widely used graphical representation scheme for modeling object-oriented systems. It has indeed unified the various popular notational schemes. Those who design systems use the language (in the form of diagrams) to model their systems, as we do throughout the C++ section of this book.

An attractive feature of the UML is its flexibility. The UML is extensible (i.e., capable of being enhanced with new features) and is independent of any particular OOAD process. UML modelers are free to use various processes in designing systems, but all developers can now express their designs with one standard set of graphical notations.

Internet and Web UML Resources

For more information about the UML, refer to the following websites.

www.uml.org
This UML resource site from the Object Management Group (OMG) provides specification documents for the UML and other object-oriented technologies.

www.ibm.com/software/rational/uml
This is the UML resource page for IBM Rational—the successor to the Rational Software Corporation (the company that created the UML).

www.uml.org/#Links-Tutorials
The Object Management Group's list of recommended UML tutorials.

bdn.borland.com/article/0,1410,31863,00.html
A short tutorial on the UML from the Borland Developer Network.

Recommended Readings

The following books provide information about object-oriented design with the UML.

- Ambler, S. *The Elements of the UML 2.0 Style*. New York: Cambridge University Press, 2005.

- Arlow, J., and I. Neustadt. *UML and the Unified Process: Practical Object-Oriented Analysis and Design, Second Edition*. London: Addison-Wesley, 2005.

- Booch, G. *Object-Oriented Analysis and Design with Applications*, Third Edition. Boston: Addison-Wesley, 2004.

- Eriksson, H., et al. *UML 2 Toolkit*. Hoboken, NJ: John Wiley & Sons, 2003.

- Fowler, M. *UML Distilled, Third Edition: A Brief Guide to the Standard Object Modeling Language*. Boston: Addison-Wesley, 2004.

- Kruchten, P. *The Rational Unified Process: An Introduction*. Boston: Addison-Wesley, 2004.

- Larman, C. *Applying UML and Patterns: An Introduction to Object-Oriented Analysis and Design, Second Edition*. Upper Saddle River, NJ: Prentice Hall, 2002.

- Roques, P. *UML in Practice: The Art of Modeling Software Systems Demonstrated Through Worked Examples and Solutions*. Hoboken, NJ: John Wiley & Sons, 2004.

- Rosenberg, D., and K. Scott. *Applying Use Case Driven Object Modeling with UML: An Annotated e-Commerce Example*. Reading, MA: Addison-Wesley, 2001.

- Rumbaugh, J., I. Jacobson and G. Booch. *The Complete UML Training Course*. Upper Saddle River, NJ: Prentice Hall, 2000.

- Rumbaugh, J., I. Jacobson and G. Booch. *The Unified Modeling Language Reference Manual*. Reading, MA: Addison-Wesley, 1999.

- Rumbaugh, J., I. Jacobson and G. Booch. *The Unified Modeling Language User Guide, Second Edition*. Reading, MA: Addison-Wesley, 2005.

- Rumbaugh, J., I. Jacobson and G. Booch. *The Unified Software Development Process*. Reading, MA: Addison-Wesley, 1999.

For additional books on the UML, please visit the sites www.amazon.com, www.bn.com and www.informIT.com. IBM Rational provides a recommended reading list for UML books at www.ibm.com/software/rational/info/technical/books.jsp.

18.14 Wrap-Up

In this chapter, you learned several of C++'s enhancements to C. We presented basic C++-style input and output with cin and cout and overviewed the C++ Standard Library header files. We discussed inline functions for improving performance by eliminating the overhead of function calls. You learned how to use pass-by-reference with C++'s reference parameters, which enable you to create aliases for existing variables. You learned that multiple functions can be overloaded by providing functions with the same name and different signatures; such functions can be used to perform the same or similar tasks, using different types or different numbers of parameters. We then demonstrated a simpler way of overloading functions using function templates, where a function is defined once but can be used for several different types. You learned the basic terminology of object technology and were introduced to the UML—the most widely used graphical representation scheme for modeling OO systems. In Chapter 19, you will learn how to implement your own classes and use objects of those classes in applications.

Summary

Section 18.2 C++

- C++ improves on many of C's features and provides object-oriented-programming (OOP) capabilities that increase software productivity, quality and reusability.

- C++ was developed by Bjarne Stroustrup at Bell Laboratories and was originally called "C with classes." The name C++ includes C's increment operator (++) to indicate that C++ is an enhanced version of C.

Section 18.3 A Simple Program: Adding Two Integers

- C++ filenames can have one of several extensions, such as `.cpp`, `.cxx` or `.C` (uppercase).

- C++ allows you to begin a comment with `//` and use the remainder of the line as comment text. C++ programmers may also use C-style comments.

- The input/output stream header file `<iostream>` must be included for any program that outputs data to the screen or inputs data from the keyboard using C++-style stream input/output.

- As in C, every C++ program begins execution with function `main`. Keyword `int` to the left of main indicates that main "returns" an integer value.

- In C, you need not specify a return type for functions. However, C++ requires the programmer to specify the return type, possibly `void`, for all functions; otherwise, a syntax error occurs.

- Declarations can be placed almost anywhere in a C++ program, but they must appear before their corresponding variables are used in the program.

- The standard output stream object (`std::cout`) and the stream insertion operator (`<<`) are used to display text on the screen.

- The standard input stream object (`std::cin`) and the stream extraction operator (`>>`) are used to obtain values from the keyboard.

- The stream manipulator `std::endl` outputs a newline, then "flushes the output buffer."

- The notation `std::cout` specifies that we are using a name, in this case cout, that belongs to "namespace" std.

- Using multiple stream insertion operators (`<<`) in a single statement is referred to as concatenating, chaining or cascading stream insertion operations.

Section 18.4 C++ Standard Library

- C++ programs consist of pieces called classes and functions. You can program each piece you may need to form a C++ program. However, most C++ programmers take advantage of the rich collections of existing classes and functions in the C++ Standard Library.

Section 18.5 Header Files

- The C++ Standard Library is divided into many portions, each with its own header file. The header files contain the function prototypes for the related functions that form each portion of the library. The header files also contain definitions of various class types and functions, as well as constants needed by those functions.

- Header file names ending in `.h` are "old-style" header files that have been superseded by the C++ Standard Library header files.

Section 18.6 Inline Functions

- C++ provides inline functions to help reduce function call overhead—especially for small functions. Placing the qualifier `inline` before a function's return type in the function definition "advises" the compiler to generate a copy of the function's code in place to avoid a function call.

Section 18.7 References and Reference Parameters

- Two ways to pass arguments to functions in many programming languages are pass-by-value and pass-by-reference.

- When an argument is passed by value, a *copy* of the argument's value is made and passed (on the function call stack) to the called function. Changes to the copy do not affect the original variable's value in the caller.

- With pass-by-reference, the caller gives the called function the ability to access the caller's data directly and to modify it if the called function chooses to do so.

- A reference parameter is an alias for its corresponding argument in a function call.

- To indicate that a function parameter is passed by reference, simply follow the parameter's type in the function prototype by an ampersand (&); use the same notation when listing the parameter's type in the function header.

- Once a reference is declared as an alias for another variable, all operations supposedly performed on the alias (i.e., the reference) are actually performed on the original variable. The alias is simply another name for the original variable.

Section 18.8 Empty Parameter Lists

- In C++, an empty parameter list is specified by writing either void or nothing in parentheses.

Section 18.9 Default Arguments

- It is not uncommon for a program to invoke a function repeatedly with the same argument value for a particular parameter. In such cases, the programmer can specify that such a parameter has a default argument, i.e., a default value to be passed to that parameter.

- When a program omits an argument for a parameter with a default argument, the compiler rewrites the function call and inserts the default value of that argument to be passed as an argument in the function call.

- Default arguments must be the rightmost (trailing) arguments in a function's parameter list.

- Default arguments should be specified with the first occurrence of the function name—typically, in the function prototype.

Section 18.10 Unary Scope Resolution Operator

- C++ provides the unary scope resolution operator (::) to access a global variable when a local variable of the same name is in scope.

Section 18.11 Function Overloading

- C++ enables several functions of the same name to be defined, as long as they have different sets of parameters (by number, type and/or order). This capability is called function overloading.

- When an overloaded function is called, the C++ compiler selects the proper function by examining the number, types and order of the arguments in the call.

- Overloaded functions are distinguished by their signatures.

- The compiler encodes each function identifier with the number and types of its parameters to enable type-safe linkage. Type-safe linkage ensures that the proper overloaded function is called and that the types of the arguments conform to the types of the parameters.

Section 18.12 Function Templates

- Overloaded functions are used to perform similar operations that may involve different program logic on data of different types. If the program logic and operations are identical for each data type, overloading may be performed more compactly and conveniently using function templates.

- The programmer writes a single function template definition. Given the argument types provided in calls to this function, C++ automatically generates separate function template specializations to handle each type of call appropriately. Thus, defining a single function template essentially defines a family of overloaded functions.

- All function template definitions begin with the `template` keyword followed by a template parameter list to the function template enclosed in angle brackets (< and >).

- The formal type parameters are placeholders for fundamental types or user-defined types. These placeholders are used to specify the types of the function's parameters, to specify the function's return type and to declare variables within the body of the function definition.

Section 18.13 Introduction to Object Technology and the UML

- The Unified Modeling Language (UML) is a graphical language that allows people who build systems to represent their object-oriented designs in a common notation.

- Object-oriented design (OOD) models software components in terms of real-world objects. It takes advantage of class relationships, where objects of a certain class have the same characteristics. It also takes advantage of inheritance relationships, where newly created classes of objects are derived by absorbing characteristics of existing classes and adding unique characteristics of their own. OOD encapsulates data (attributes) and functions (behavior) into objects—the data and functions of an object are intimately tied together.

- Objects have the property of information hiding—objects normally are not allowed to know how other objects are implemented.

- Object-oriented programming (OOP) allows programmers to implement object-oriented designs as working systems.

- C++ programmers create their own user-defined types called classes. Each class contains data (known as data members) and the set of functions (known as member functions) that manipulate that data and provide services to clients.

- Classes can have relationships with other classes. These relationships are called associations.

- Packaging software as classes makes it possible for future software systems to reuse the classes. Groups of related classes are often packaged as reusable components.

- An instance of a class is called an object.

- With object technology, programmers can build much of the software they will need by combining standardized, interchangeable parts called classes.

- The process of analyzing and designing a system from an object-oriented point of view is called object-oriented analysis and design (OOAD).

Terminology

& to declare reference	association in the UML
// single-line comment	attribute in the UML
:: unary scope resolution operator	behaviors in the UML
>> stream extraction operator	`bool` primitive type
<< stream insertion operator	C++ Standard Library
access a global variable	cascading stream insertion operations
action oriented	chaining stream insertion operations
`<algorithm>` header file	`cin` (standard input stream object)
alias	class
allocate dynamic memory	client of a class
angle brackets (< and >)	concatenate stream insertion operations

constant reference parameter
cout (standard output stream object)
dangling reference
data member of a class
default argument
empty parameter list
encapsulation
endl stream manipulator
false boolean value
flush output buffer
formal type parameter
function template
function template specialization
generic programming
#include preprocessor directive
information hiding
inheritance
initializing a reference
inline function
inline keyword
input/output stream header (<iostream>)
instantiate an object of a class
interface
<iostream> header file
member function
message
method
name decoration
name mangling
nouns in a system specification 2
object (or instance)
Object Management Group (OMG)
object orientation 1
object-oriented analysis and design (OOAD)
object-oriented design (OOD)

object-oriented language
object-oriented programming (OOP)
"old-style" header files
operation in the UML
overloading functions
pass-by-reference
pass-by-value
reassign a reference
reference parameter
reference to a constant
reference to an automatic variable
references must be initialized
requirements in a system specification
reusable component
reuse
signature
standard input stream object (std::cin)
standard output stream object (std::cout)
std::cin (standard input stream object)
std::cout (standard output stream object)
std::endl stream manipulator
stream extraction operator >> ("get from")
stream insertion operator << ("put to")
stream manipulator
template function
template keyword
template parameter list
true boolean value
type parameter
type-safe linkage
typename keyword
unary scope resolution operator (::)
Unified Modeling Language (UML)
verbs in a system specification

Self-Review Exercises

18.1   Answer each of the following:
  a) In C++, it is possible to have various functions with the same name that operate on different types or numbers of arguments. This is called function _____.
  b) The _____ enables access to a global variable with the same name as a variable in the current scope.
  c) A function _____ enables a single function to be defined to perform the same task on data of many different types.
  d) _____ is the most widely used graphical representation scheme for modeling OO systems.
  e) _____ models software components in terms of real-world objects.
  f) C++ programmers create their own user-defined types called _____.

18.2 Why would a function prototype contain a parameter type declaration such as double &?

18.3 (True/False) All arguments to function calls in C++ are passed by value.

18.4 Write a complete program that prompts the user for the radius of a sphere, and calculates and prints the volume of that sphere. Use an inline function sphereVolume that returns the result of the following expression: (4.0 / 3.0) * 3.14159 * pow(radius, 3).

Answers to Self-Review Exercises

18.1 a) overloading. b) unary scope resolution operator (::). c) template. d) The UML. e) Object-oriented design (OOD). f) classes.

18.2 This creates a reference parameter of type "reference to double" that enables the function to modify the original variable in the calling function.

18.3 False. C++ enables pass-by-reference using reference parameters.

18.4 See the following program:

```cpp
1   // Exercise 18.4 Solution: Ex18_04.cpp
2   // Inline function that calculates the volume of a sphere.
3   #include <iostream>
4   using std::cin;
5   using std::cout;
6   using std::endl;
7
8   #include <cmath>
9   using std::pow;
10
11  const double PI = 3.14159; // define global constant PI
12
13  // calculates volume of a sphere
14  inline double sphereVolume( const double radius )
15  {
16     return 4.0 / 3.0 * PI * pow( radius, 3 );
17  } // end inline function sphereVolume
18
19  int main()
20  {
21     double radiusValue;
22
23     // prompt user for radius
24     cout << "Enter the length of the radius of your sphere: ";
25     cin >> radiusValue; // input radius
26
27     // use radiusValue to calculate volume of sphere and display result
28     cout << "Volume of sphere with radius " << radiusValue
29        << " is " << sphereVolume( radiusValue ) << endl;
30     return 0; // indicates successful termination
31  } // end main
```

```
Enter the length of the radius of your sphere: 2
Volume of sphere with radius 2 is 33.5103
```

Exercises

18.5 Write a C++ program that prompts the user for the radius of a circle, then calls inline function circleArea to calculate the area of that circle.

18.6 Write a complete C++ program with the two alternate functions specified below, each of which simply triples the variable count defined in main. Then compare and contrast the two approaches. These two functions are

    a) function tripleByValue that passes a copy of count by value, triples the copy and returns the new value and

    a) function tripleByReference that passes count by reference via a reference parameter and triples the original value of count through its alias (i.e., the reference parameter).

18.7 What is the purpose of the unary scope resolution operator?

18.8 Write a program that uses a function template called min to determine the smaller of two arguments. Test the program using integer, character and floating-point number arguments.

18.9 Write a program that uses a function template called max to determine the larger of two arguments. Test the program using integer, character and floating-point number arguments.

18.10 Determine whether the following program segments contain errors. For each error, explain how it can be corrected. [*Note:* For a particular program segment, it is possible that no errors are present in the segment.]

    a)
```
template < class A >
int sum( int num1, int num2, int num3 )
{
   return num1 + num2 + num3;
}
```
    b)
```
void printResults( int x, int y )
{
   cout << "The sum is " << x + y << '\n';
   return x + y;
}
```
    c)
```
template < A >
A product( A num1, A num2, A num3 )
{
   return num1 * num2 * num3;
}
```
    d)
```
double cube( int );
int cube( int );
```

Introduction to Classes and Objects

You will see something new.
Two things. And I call them
Thing One and Thing Two.
—Dr. Seuss

Nothing can have value
without being an object of
utility.
—Karl Marx

Your public servants serve
you right.
—Adlai E. Stevenson

Knowing how to answer one
who speaks,
To reply to one who sends a
message.
—Amenemope

OBJECTIVES

In this chapter you will learn:

- What classes, objects, member functions and data members are.
- How to define a class and use it to create an object.
- How to define member functions in a class to implement the class's behaviors.
- How to declare data members in a class to implement the class's attributes.
- How to call a member function of an object to make that member function perform its task.
- The differences between data members of a class and local variables of a function.
- How to use a constructor to ensure that an object's data is initialized when the object is created.
- How to engineer a class to separate its interface from its implementation and encourage reuse.

19.1 Introduction

In Chapter 18, you created simple programs that displayed messages to the user, obtained information from the user, performed calculations and made decisions. In this chapter, you will begin writing programs that employ the basic concepts of object-oriented programming. One common feature of every program in Chapter 18 was that all the statements that performed tasks were located in function `main`. Typically, the programs you develop in the C++ portion of this book will consist of function `main` and one or more classes, each containing data members and member functions. If you become part of a development team in industry, you might work on software systems that contain hundreds, or even thousands, of classes. In this chapter, we develop a simple, well-engineered framework for organizing object-oriented programs in C++.

First, we motivate the notion of classes with a real-world example. Then we present a carefully paced sequence of seven complete working programs to demonstrate creating and using your own classes.

19.2 Classes, Objects, Member Functions and Data Members

Let's begin with a simple analogy to help you understand classes and their contents. Suppose you want to drive a car and make it go faster by pressing down on its accelerator pedal. What must happen before you can do this? Well, before you can drive a car, someone has to design it and build it. A car typically begins as engineering drawings, similar to the blueprints used to design a house. These drawings include the design for an accelerator pedal that the driver will use to make the car go faster. In a sense, the pedal "hides" the complex mechanisms that actually make the car go faster, just as the brake pedal "hides" the mechanisms that slow the car, the steering wheel "hides" the mechanisms that turn the car and so on. This enables people with little or no knowledge of how cars are engineered to drive a car easily, simply by using the accelerator pedal, the brake pedal, the steering wheel, the transmission shifting mechanism and other such simple and user-friendly "interfaces" to the car's complex internal mechanisms.

Unfortunately, you cannot drive the engineering drawings of a car—before you can drive a car, it must be built from the engineering drawings that describe it. A completed car will have an actual accelerator pedal to make the car go faster. But even that's not enough—the car will not accelerate on its own, so the driver must press the accelerator pedal to tell the car to go faster.

Now let's use our car example to introduce the key object-oriented programming concepts of this section. Performing a task in a program requires a function. The function describes the mechanisms that actually perform its tasks. The function hides from its user the complex tasks that it performs, just as the accelerator pedal of a car hides from the driver the complex mechanisms of making the car go faster. In C++, we begin by creating a program unit called a class to house a function, just as a car's engineering drawings house the design of an accelerator pedal. A function that belongs to a class is called a member function. In a class, you provide one or more member functions that are designed to perform the class's tasks. For example, a class that represents a bank account might contain one member function to deposit money into the account, another to withdraw money from the account and a third to inquire what the current account balance is.

Just as you cannot drive an engineering drawing of a car, you cannot "drive" a class. Just as someone has to build a car from its engineering drawings before you can actually drive the car, you must create an object of a class before you can get a program to perform the tasks the class describes. That is one reason C++ is known as an object-oriented programming language. Note also that just as *many* cars can be built from the same engineering drawing, *many* objects can be built from the same class.

When you drive a car, pressing its gas pedal sends a message to the car to perform a task—that is, make the car go faster. Similarly, you send **messages** to an object—each message is known as a **member-function call** and tells a member function of the object to perform its task. This is often called **requesting a service from an object**.

Thus far, we have used the car analogy to introduce classes, objects and member functions. In addition to the capabilities a car provides, it also has many attributes, such as its color, the number of doors, the amount of gas in its tank, its current speed and its total miles driven (i.e., its odometer reading). Like the car's capabilities, these attributes are represented as part of a car's design in its engineering diagrams. As you drive a car, these attributes are always associated with the car. Every car maintains its own attributes. For example, each car knows how much gas is in its own gas tank, but not how much is in the tanks of other cars. Similarly, an object has attributes that are carried with the object as it is used in a program. These attributes are specified as part of the object's class. For example, a bank account object has a balance attribute that represents the amount of money in the account. Each bank account object knows the balance in the account it represents, but not the balances of the other accounts in the bank. Attributes are specified by the class's data members.

19.3 Overview of the Chapter Examples

The remainder of this chapter presents seven simple examples that demonstrate the concepts we introduced in the context of the car analogy. These examples, summarized below, incrementally build a GradeBook class to demonstrate these concepts:

1. The first example presents a GradeBook class with one member function that simply displays a welcome message when it is called. We then show how to create an object of that class and call the member function so that it displays the welcome message.

2. The second example modifies the first by allowing the member function to receive a course name as a so-called argument. Then, the member function displays the course name as part of the welcome message.

3. The third example shows how to store the course name in a GradeBook object. For this version of the class, we also show how to use member functions to set the course name in the object and get the course name from the object.

4. The fourth example demonstrates how the data in a GradeBook object can be initialized when the object is created—the initialization is performed by a special member function called the class's constructor. This example also demonstrates that each GradeBook object maintains its own course name data member.

5. The fifth example modifies the fourth by demonstrating how to place class GradeBook into a separate file to enable software reusability.

6. The sixth example modifies the fifth by demonstrating the good software engineering principle of separating the interface of the class from its implementation. This makes the class easier to modify without affecting any clients of the class's objects—that is, any classes or functions that call the member functions of the class's objects from outside the objects.

7. The last example enhances class GradeBook by introducing data validation, which ensures that data in an object adheres to a particular format or is in a proper value range. For example, a Date object would require a month value in the range 1–12. In this GradeBook example, the member function that sets the course name for a GradeBook object ensures that the course name is 25 characters or fewer. If not, the member function uses only the first 25 characters of the course name and displays a warning message.

Note that the GradeBook examples in this chapter do not actually process or store grades.

19.4 Defining a Class with a Member Function

We begin with an example (Fig. 19.1) that consists of class GradeBook, which represents a grade book that an instructor can use to maintain student test scores, and a main function (lines 20–25) that creates a GradeBook object. Function main uses this object and its member function to display a message on the screen welcoming the instructor to the grade-book program.

First we describe how to define a class and a member function. Then we explain how an object is created and how to call a member function of an object. The first few examples contain function main and the GradeBook class it uses in the same file. Later in the chapter, we introduce more sophisticated ways to structure your programs to achieve better software engineering.

```
 1   // Fig. 19.1: fig19_01.cpp
 2   // Define class GradeBook with a member function displayMessage;
 3   // Create a GradeBook object and call its displayMessage function.
 4   #include <iostream>
 5   using std::cout;
 6   using std::endl;
 7
 8   // GradeBook class definition
 9   class GradeBook
10   {
11   public:
12      // function that displays a welcome message to the GradeBook user
13      void displayMessage()
14      {
15         cout << "Welcome to the Grade Book!" << endl;
16      } // end function displayMessage
17   }; // end class GradeBook
18
19   // function main begins program execution
20   int main()
21   {
22      GradeBook myGradeBook; // create a GradeBook object named myGradeBook
23      myGradeBook.displayMessage(); // call object's displayMessage function
24      return 0; // indicate successful termination
25   } // end main
```

```
Welcome to the Grade Book!
```

Fig. 19.1 | Defining class GradeBook with a member function, creating a GradeBook object and calling its member function.

Class GradeBook

Before function main (lines 20–25) can create an object of class GradeBook, we must tell the compiler what member functions and data members belong to the class. This is known as defining a class. The GradeBook class definition (lines 9–17) contains a member function called displayMessage (lines 13–16) that displays a message on the screen (line 15). Recall that a class is like a blueprint—so we need to make an object of class GradeBook (line 22) and call its displayMessage member function (line 23) to get line 15 to execute and display the welcome message. We'll soon explain lines 22–23 in detail.

The class definition begins at line 9 with the keyword class followed by the class name GradeBook. By convention, the name of a user-defined class begins with a capital letter, and for readability, each subsequent word in the class name begins with a capital letter. This capitalization style is often referred to as camel case, because the pattern of uppercase and lowercase letters resembles the silhouette of a camel.

Every class's body is enclosed in a pair of left and right braces ({ and }), as in lines 10 and 17. The class definition terminates with a semicolon (line 17).

Common Programming Error 19.1

Forgetting the semicolon at the end of a class definition is a syntax error.

Recall that the function main is always called automatically when you execute a program. Most functions do not get called automatically. As you will soon see, you must call member function displayMessage explicitly to tell it to perform its task.

Line 11 contains the access-specifier label **public:**. The keyword **public** is called an access specifier. Lines 13–16 define member function displayMessage. This member function appears after access specifier public: to indicate that the function is "available to the public"—that is, it can be called by other functions in the program and by member functions of other classes. Access specifiers are always followed by a colon (:). For the remainder of the text, when we refer to the access specifier public, we will omit the colon as we did in this sentence. Section 19.6 introduces a second access specifier, private (again, we omit the colon in our discussions, but include it in our programs).

Each function in a program performs a task and may return a value when it completes its task—for example, a function might perform a calculation, then return the result of that calculation. When you define a function, you must specify a **return type** to indicate the type of the value returned by the function when it completes its task. In line 13, keyword **void** to the left of the function name displayMessage is the function's return type. Return type void indicates that displayMessage will perform a task but will not return (i.e., give back) any data to its **calling function** (in this example, main, as we'll see in a moment) when it completes its task. (In Fig. 19.5, you will see an example of a function that returns a value.)

The name of the member function, displayMessage, follows the return type. By convention, function names begin with a lowercase first letter and all subsequent words in the name begin with a capital letter. The parentheses after the member function name indicate that this is a function. An empty set of parentheses, as shown in line 13, indicates that this member function does not require additional data to perform its task. You will see an example of a member function that does require additional data in Section 19.5. Line 13 is commonly referred to as the **function header**. Every function's body is delimited by left and right braces ({ and }), as in lines 14 and 16.

The body of a function contains statements that perform the function's task. In this case, member function displayMessage contains one statement (line 15) that displays the message "Welcome to the Grade Book!". After this statement executes, the function has completed its task.

Common Programming Error 19.2

Returning a value from a function whose return type has been declared void *is a compilation error.*

Common Programming Error 19.3

Defining a function inside another function is a syntax error.

Testing Class GradeBook

Next, we'd like to use class GradeBook in a program. As you know, function main begins the execution of every program. Lines 20–25 of Fig. 19.1 contain the main function that will control our program's execution.

In this program, we'd like to call class GradeBook's displayMessage member function to display the welcome message. Typically, you cannot call a member function of a class until you create an object of that class. (As you will learn in Section 21.7, static member functions are an exception.) Line 22 creates an object of class GradeBook called myGrade-Book. Note that the variable's type is GradeBook—the class we defined in lines 9–17. When we declare variables of type int, the compiler knows what int is—it's a fundamental type. When we write line 22, however, the compiler does not automatically know what type GradeBook is—it's a **user-defined type**. Thus, we must tell the compiler what GradeBook is by including the class definition, as we did in lines 9–17. If we omitted these lines, the compiler would issue an error message (such as "'GradeBook': undeclared identifier" in Microsoft Visual C++ .NET or "'GradeBook': undeclared" in GNU C++). Each new class you create becomes a new type that can be used to create objects. Programmers can define new class types as needed; this is one reason why C++ is known as an **extensible language**.

Line 23 calls the member function displayMessage (defined in lines 13–16) using variable myGradeBook followed by the **dot operator** (.), the function name displayMessage and an empty set of parentheses. This call causes the displayMessage function to perform its task. At the beginning of line 23, "myGradeBook." indicates that main should use the GradeBook object that was created in line 22. The empty parentheses in line 13 indicate that member function displayMessage does not require additional data to perform its task. (In Section 19.5, you'll see how to pass data to a function.) When displayMessage completes its task, function main continues executing at line 24, which indicates that main performed its tasks successfully. This is the end of main, so the program terminates.

UML Class Diagram for Class GradeBook

The UML is a graphical language used by programmers to represent their object-oriented systems in a standardized manner. In the UML, each class is modeled in a class diagram as a rectangle with three compartments. Figure 19.2 presents a **UML class diagram** for class GradeBook of Fig. 19.1. The top compartment contains the name of the class, centered horizontally and in boldface type. The middle compartment contains the class's attributes, which correspond to data members in C++. In Fig. 19.2 the middle compartment is empty, because the version of class GradeBook in Fig. 19.1 does not have any attributes. (Section 19.6 presents a version of the GradeBook class that does have an attribute.) The bottom compartment contains the class's operations, which correspond to member functions in C++. The UML models operations by listing the operation name followed by a

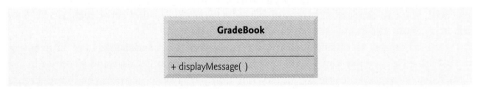

Fig. 19.2 | UML class diagram indicating that class GradeBook has a public displayMessage operation.

set of parentheses. The class GradeBook has only one member function, displayMessage, so the bottom compartment of Fig. 19.2 lists one operation with this name. Member function displayMessage does not require additional information to perform its tasks, so the parentheses following displayMessage in the class diagram are empty, just as they are in the member function's header in line 13 of Fig. 19.1. The plus sign (+) in front of the operation name indicates that displayMessage is a public operation in the UML (i.e., a public member function in C++). We frequently use UML class diagrams to summarize class attributes and operations.

19.5 Defining a Member Function with a Parameter

In our car analogy from Section 19.2, we mentioned that pressing a car's gas pedal sends a message to the car to perform a task—make the car go faster. But how fast should the car accelerate? As you know, the farther down you press the pedal, the faster the car accelerates. So the message to the car includes both the task to perform and additional information that helps the car perform the task. This additional information is known as a parameter—the value of the parameter helps the car determine how fast to accelerate. Similarly, a member function can require one or more parameters that represent additional data it needs to perform its task. A function call supplies values—called arguments—for each of the function's parameters. For example, to make a deposit into a bank account, suppose a deposit member function of an Account class specifies a parameter that represents the deposit amount. When the deposit member function is called, an argument value representing the deposit amount is copied to the member function's parameter. The member function then adds that amount to the account balance.

Defining and Testing Class GradeBook

Our next example (Fig. 19.3) redefines class GradeBook (lines 14–23) with a displayMessage member function (lines 18–22) that displays the course name as part of the welcome message. The new displayMessage member function requires a parameter (courseName in line 18) that represents the course name to output.

Before discussing the new features of class GradeBook, let's see how the new class is used in main (lines 26–40). Line 28 creates a variable of type string called nameOfCourse that will be used to store the course name entered by the user. A variable of type string represents a string of characters such as "CS101 Introduction to C++ Programming". A string is actually an object of the C++ Standard Library class string. This class is defined in header file <string>, and the name string, like cout, belongs to namespace std. To enable line 28 to compile, line 9 includes the <string> header file. Note that the using declaration in line 10 allows us to simply write string in line 28 rather than std::string. For now, you can think of string variables like variables of other types such as int. You will learn about additional string capabilities in Section 19.10.

Line 29 creates an object of class GradeBook named myGradeBook. Line 32 prompts the user to enter a course name. Line 33 reads the name from the user and assigns it to the nameOfCourse variable, using the library function getline to perform the input. Before we explain this line of code, let's explain why we cannot simply write

```
cin >> nameOfCourse;
```

```cpp
 1   // Fig. 19.3: fig19_03.cpp
 2   // Define class GradeBook with a member function that takes a parameter;
 3   // Create a GradeBook object and call its displayMessage function.
 4   #include <iostream>
 5   using std::cout;
 6   using std::cin;
 7   using std::endl;
 8
 9   #include <string> // program uses C++ standard string class
10   using std::string;
11   using std::getline;
12
13   // GradeBook class definition
14   class GradeBook
15   {
16   public:
17      // function that displays a welcome message to the GradeBook user
18      void displayMessage( string courseName )
19      {
20         cout << "Welcome to the grade book for\n" << courseName << "!"
21            << endl;
22      } // end function displayMessage
23   }; // end class GradeBook
24
25   // function main begins program execution
26   int main()
27   {
28      string nameOfCourse; // string of characters to store the course name
29      GradeBook myGradeBook; // create a GradeBook object named myGradeBook
30
31      // prompt for and input course name
32      cout << "Please enter the course name:" << endl;
33      getline( cin, nameOfCourse ); // read a course name with blanks
34      cout << endl; // output a blank line
35
36      // call myGradeBook's displayMessage function
37      // and pass nameOfCourse as an argument
38      myGradeBook.displayMessage( nameOfCourse );
39      return 0; // indicate successful termination
40   } // end main
```

```
Please enter the course name:
CS101 Introduction to C++ Programming

Welcome to the grade book for
CS101 Introduction to C++ Programming!
```

Fig. 19.3 | Defining class GradeBook with a member function that takes a parameter.

to obtain the course name. In our sample program execution, we use the course name "CS101 Introduction to C++ Programming," which contains multiple words. (Recall that we highlight user-supplied input in bold.) When cin is used with the stream extraction operator, it reads characters until the first white-space character is reached. Thus, only "CS101" would be read by the preceding statement. The rest of the course name would have to be read by subsequent input operations.

In this example, we'd like the user to type the complete course name and press *Enter* to submit it to the program, and we'd like to store the entire course name in the string variable nameOfCourse. The function call getline(cin, nameOfCourse) in line 33 reads characters (including the space characters that separate the words in the input) from the standard input stream object cin (i.e., the keyboard) until the newline character is encountered, places the characters in the string variable nameOfCourse and discards the newline character. Note that when you press *Enter* while typing program input, a newline is inserted in the input stream. Also note that the <string> header file must be included in the program to use function getline and that the name getline belongs to namespace std.

Line 38 calls myGradeBook's displayMessage member function. The nameOfCourse variable in parentheses is the argument that is passed to member function displayMessage so that it can perform its task. The value of variable nameOfCourse in main becomes the value of member function displayMessage's parameter courseName in line 18. When you execute this program, notice that member function displayMessage outputs as part of the welcome message the course name you type (in our sample execution, CS101 Introduction to C++ Programming).

More on Arguments and Parameters

To specify that a function requires data to perform its task, you place additional information in the function's **parameter list**, which is located in the parentheses following the function name. The parameter list may contain any number of parameters, including none at all (represented by empty parentheses as in Fig. 19.1, line 13) to indicate that a function does not require any parameters. Member function displayMessage's parameter list (Fig. 19.3, line 18) declares that the function requires one parameter. Each parameter should specify a type and an identifier. In this case, the type string and the identifier courseName indicate that member function displayMessage requires a string to perform its task. The member function body uses the parameter courseName to access the value that is passed to the function in the function call (line 38 in main). Lines 20–21 display parameter courseName's value as part of the welcome message. Note that the parameter variable's name (line 18) can be the same as or different from the argument variable's name (line 38).

A function can specify multiple parameters by separating each parameter from the next with a comma. The number and order of arguments in a function call must match the number and order of parameters in the parameter list of the called member function's header. Also, the argument types in the function call must match the types of the corresponding parameters in the function header. (As you will learn in subsequent chapters, an argument's type and its corresponding parameter's type need not always be identical, but they must be "consistent.") In our example, the one string argument in the function call (i.e., nameOfCourse) exactly matches the one string parameter in the member-function definition (i.e., courseName).

Common Programming Error 19.4

Placing a semicolon after the right parenthesis enclosing the parameter list of a function definition is a syntax error.

Common Programming Error 19.5

Defining a function parameter again as a local variable in the function is a compilation error.

Good Programming Practice 19.1

To avoid ambiguity, do not use the same names for the arguments passed to a function and the corresponding parameters in the function definition.

Good Programming Practice 19.2

Choosing meaningful function names and meaningful parameter names makes programs more readable and helps avoid excessive use of comments.

Updated UML Class Diagram for Class GradeBook

The UML class diagram of Fig. 19.4 models class GradeBook of Fig. 19.3. Like the class GradeBook defined in Fig. 19.1, this GradeBook class contains public member function displayMessage. However, this version of displayMessage has a parameter. The UML models a parameter by listing the parameter name, followed by a colon and the parameter type in the parentheses following the operation name. The UML has its own data types similar to those of C++. The UML is language independent—it is used with many different programming languages—so its terminology does not exactly match that of C++. For example, the UML type String corresponds to the C++ type string. Member function displayMessage of class GradeBook (Fig. 19.3, lines 18–22) has a string parameter named courseName, so Fig. 19.4 lists courseName : String between the parentheses following the operation name displayMessage. Note that this version of the GradeBook class still does not have any data members.

19.6 Data Members, *set* Functions and *get* Functions

As you know, variables declared in a function definition's body are called local variables and can be used only from the line of their declaration in the function to the immediately following closing right brace (}) of the function definition. A local variable must be declared before it can be used in a function. A local variable cannot be accessed outside the function in which it is declared. When a function terminates, the values of its local variables are lost. Recall from Section 19.2 that an object has attributes that are carried with it as it is used in a program. Such attributes exist throughout the life of the object.

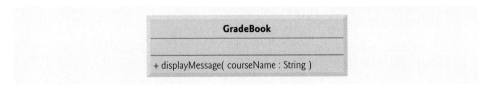

Fig. 19.4 | UML class diagram indicating that class GradeBook has a displayMessage operation with a courseName parameter of UML type String.

A class normally consists of one or more member functions that manipulate the attributes that belong to a particular object of the class. Attributes are represented as variables in a class definition. Such variables are called **data members** and are declared inside a class definition but outside the bodies of the class's member-function definitions. Each object of a class maintains its own copy of its attributes in memory. The example in this section demonstrates a GradeBook class that contains a courseName data member to represent a particular GradeBook object's course name.

GradeBook *Class with a Data Member, a* set *Function and a* get *Function*

In our next example, class GradeBook (Fig. 19.5) maintains the course name as a data member so that it can be used or modified at any time during a program's execution. The class contains member functions setCourseName, getCourseName and displayMessage. Member function setCourseName stores a course name in a GradeBook data member—member function getCourseName obtains a GradeBook's course name from that data member. Member function displayMessage—which now specifies no parameters—still displays a welcome message that includes the course name. However, as you will see, the function now obtains the course name by calling another function in the same class—getCourseName.

```cpp
1   // Fig. 19.5: fig19_05.cpp
2   // Define class GradeBook that contains a courseName data member
3   // and member functions to set and get its value;
4   // Create and manipulate a GradeBook object with these functions.
5   #include <iostream>
6   using std::cout;
7   using std::cin;
8   using std::endl;
9
10  #include <string> // program uses C++ standard string class
11  using std::string;
12  using std::getline;
13
14  // GradeBook class definition
15  class GradeBook
16  {
17  public:
18     // function that sets the course name
19     void setCourseName( string name )
20     {
21        courseName = name; // store the course name in the object
22     } // end function setCourseName
23
24     // function that gets the course name
25     string getCourseName()
26     {
27        return courseName; // return the object's courseName
28     } // end function getCourseName
29
```

Fig. 19.5 | Defining and testing class GradeBook with a data member and *set* and *get* functions. (Part 1 of 2.)

```
30      // function that displays a welcome message
31      void displayMessage()
32      {
33         // this statement calls getCourseName to get the
34         // name of the course this GradeBook represents
35         cout << "Welcome to the grade book for\n" << getCourseName() << "!"
36            << endl;
37      } // end function displayMessage
38   private:
39      string courseName; // course name for this GradeBook
40   }; // end class GradeBook
41
42   // function main begins program execution
43   int main()
44   {
45      string nameOfCourse; // string of characters to store the course name
46      GradeBook myGradeBook; // create a GradeBook object named myGradeBook
47
48      // display initial value of courseName
49      cout << "Initial course name is: " << myGradeBook.getCourseName()
50         << endl;
51
52      // prompt for, input and set course name
53      cout << "\nPlease enter the course name:" << endl;
54      getline( cin, nameOfCourse ); // read a course name with blanks
55      myGradeBook.setCourseName( nameOfCourse ); // set the course name
56
57      cout << endl; // outputs a blank line
58      myGradeBook.displayMessage(); // display message with new course name
59      return 0; // indicate successful termination
60   } // end main
```

```
Initial course name is:

Please enter the course name:
CS101 Introduction to C++ Programming

Welcome to the grade book for
CS101 Introduction to C++ Programming!
```

Fig. 19.5 | Defining and testing class GradeBook with a data member and *set* and *get* functions. (Part 2 of 2.)

Good Programming Practice 19.3

Place a blank line between member-function definitions to enhance program readability.

A typical instructor teaches more than one course, each with its own course name. Line 39 declares that courseName is a variable of type string. Because the variable is declared in the class definition (lines 15–40) but outside the bodies of the class's member-function definitions (lines 19–22, 25–28 and 31–37), line 39 is a declaration for a data member. Every instance (i.e., object) of class GradeBook contains one copy of each of the class's data members. For example, if there are two GradeBook objects, each object has its own copy of courseName (one per object), as we'll see in the example of Fig. 19.7. A benefit of making courseName a data member is that all the member functions of the class (in this case, GradeBook) can manipulate any data members that appear in the class definition (in this case, courseName).

Access Specifiers public and private

Most data-member declarations appear after the access-specifier label **private:** (line 38). Like public, keyword private is an access specifier. Variables or functions declared after access specifier private (and before the next access specifier) are accessible only to member functions of the class for which they are declared. Thus, data member courseName can be used only in member functions setCourseName, getCourseName and displayMessage of (every object of) class GradeBook. Data member courseName, because it is private, cannot be accessed by functions outside the class (such as main) or by member functions of other classes in the program. Attempting to access data member courseName in one of these program locations with an expression such as myGradeBook.courseName would result in a compilation error containing a message similar to

```
cannot access private member declared in class 'GradeBook'
```

Software Engineering Observation 19.1

As a rule of thumb, data members should be declared private and member functions should be declared public. (We will see that it is appropriate to declare certain member functions private, if they are to be accessed only by other member functions of the class.)

Common Programming Error 19.6

An attempt by a function that is not a member of a particular class (or a friend of that class, as we will see in Chapter 21) to access a private member of that class is a compilation error.

The default access for class members is private so all members after the class header and before the first access specifier are private. The access specifiers public and private may be repeated, but this is unnecessary and can be confusing.

Good Programming Practice 19.4

Despite the fact that the public and private access specifiers may be repeated and intermixed, list all the public members of a class first in one group and then list all the private members in another group. This focuses the client's attention on the class's public interface, rather than on the class's implementation.

Good Programming Practice 19.5

If you choose to list the private members first in a class definition, explicitly use the private access specifier despite the fact that private is assumed by default. This improves program clarity.

Declaring data members with access specifier private is known as **data hiding**. When a program creates (instantiates) an object of class GradeBook, data member courseName is encapsulated (hidden) in the object and can be accessed only by member functions of the object's class. In class GradeBook, member functions setCourseName and getCourseName manipulate the data member courseName directly (and displayMessage could do so if necessary).

Software Engineering Observation 19.2

We will learn in Chapter 21, Classes: A Deeper Look, Part 2, that functions and classes declared by a class to be friends *can* access the private *members of the class.*

Error-Prevention Tip 19.1

Making the data members of a class private *and the member functions of the class* public *facilitates debugging because problems with data manipulations are localized to either the class's member functions or the* friends *of the class.*

Member Functions *setCourseName and getCourseName*

Member function setCourseName (defined in lines 19–22) does not return any data when it completes its task, so its return type is void. The member function receives one parameter—name—which represents the course name that will be passed to it as an argument (as we will see in line 55 of main). Line 21 assigns name to data member courseName. In this example, setCourseName does not attempt to validate the course name—i.e., the function does not check that the course name adheres to any particular format or follows any other rules regarding what a "valid" course name looks like. Suppose, for instance, that a university can print student transcripts containing course names of only 25 characters or fewer. In this case, we might want class GradeBook to ensure that its data member courseName never contains more than 25 characters. We discuss basic validation techniques in Section 19.10.

Member function getCourseName (defined in lines 25–28) returns a particular Grade-Book object's courseName. The member function has an empty parameter list, so it does not require additional data to perform its task. The function specifies that it returns a string. When a function that specifies a return type other than void is called and completes its task, the function returns a result to its calling function. For example, when you go to an automated teller machine (ATM) and request your account balance, you expect the ATM to give you back a value that represents your balance. Similarly, when a statement calls member function getCourseName on a GradeBook object, the statement expects to receive the GradeBook's course name (in this case, a string, as specified by the function's return type). If you have a function square that returns the square of its argument, the statement

```
int result = square( 2 );
```

returns 4 from function square and initializes the variable result with the value 4. If you have a function maximum that returns the largest of three integer arguments, the statement

```
int biggest = maximum( 27, 114, 51 );
```

returns 114 from function maximum and initializes variable biggest with the value 114.

Common Programming Error 19.7

Forgetting to return a value from a function that is supposed to return a value is a compilation error.

Note that the statements at lines 21 and 27 each use variable courseName (line 39) even though it was not declared in any of the member functions. We can use courseName in the member functions of class GradeBook because courseName is a data member of the class. Also note that the order in which member functions are defined does not determine when they are called at execution time. So member function getCourseName could be defined before member function setCourseName.

Member Function `displayMessage`

Member function `displayMessage` (lines 31–37) does not return any data when it completes its task, so its return type is `void`. The function does not receive parameters, so its parameter list is empty. Lines 35–36 output a welcome message that includes the value of data member `courseName`. Line 35 calls member function `getCourseName` to obtain the value of `courseName`. Note that member function `displayMessage` could also access data member `courseName` directly, just as member functions `setCourseName` and `getCourseName` do. We explain shortly why we choose to call member function `getCourseName` to obtain the value of `courseName`.

Testing Class *GradeBook*

The `main` function (lines 43–60) creates one object of class `GradeBook` and uses each of its member functions. Line 46 creates a `GradeBook` object named `myGradeBook`. Lines 49–50 display the initial course name by calling the object's `getCourseName` member function. Note that the first line of the output does not show a course name, because the object's `courseName` data member (i.e., a `string`) is initially empty—by default, the initial value of a `string` is the so-called empty string, i.e., a string that does not contain any characters. Nothing appears on the screen when an empty string is displayed.

Line 53 prompts the user to enter a course name. Local `string` variable `nameOfCourse` (declared in line 45) is set to the course name entered by the user, which is obtained by the call to the `getline` function (line 54). Line 55 calls object `myGradeBook`'s `setCourseName` member function and supplies `nameOfCourse` as the function's argument. When the function is called, the argument's value is copied to parameter `name` (line 19) of member function `setCourseName` (lines 19–22). Then the parameter's value is assigned to data member `courseName` (line 21). Line 57 skips a line in the output; then line 58 calls object `myGradeBook`'s `displayMessage` member function to display the welcome message containing the course name.

Software Engineering with set *and* get *Functions*

A class's `private` data members can be manipulated only by member functions of that class (and by "friends" of the class, as we will see in Chapter 21, Classes: A Deeper Look, Part 2). So a client of an object—that is, any class or function that calls the object's member functions from outside the object—calls the class's `public` member functions to request the class's services for particular objects of the class. This is why the statements in function `main` (Fig. 19.5, lines 43–60) call member functions `setCourseName`, `getCourseName` and `displayMessage` on a `GradeBook` object. Classes often provide `public` member functions to allow clients of the class to *set* (i.e., assign values to) or *get* (i.e., obtain the values of) `private` data members. The names of these member functions need not begin with *set* or *get*, but this naming convention is common. In this example, the member function that *sets* the `courseName` data member is called `setCourseName`, and the member function that *gets* the value of the `courseName` data member is called `getCourseName`. Note that *set* functions are also sometimes called mutators (because they mutate, or change, values), and *get* functions are also sometimes called accessors (because they access values).

Recall that declaring data members with access specifier `private` enforces data hiding. Providing `public` *set* and *get* functions allows clients of a class to access the hidden data, but only *indirectly*. The client knows that it is attempting to modify or obtain an object's data, but the client does not know how the object performs these operations. In some cases, a class may internally represent a piece of data one way, but expose that data to clients in a different way. For example, suppose a Clock class represents the time of day as a private int data member time that stores the number of seconds since midnight. However, when a client calls a Clock object's getTime member function, the object could return the time with hours, minutes and seconds in a string in the format "HH:MM:SS". Similarly, suppose the Clock class provides a *set* function named setTime that takes a string parameter in the "HH:MM:SS" format. Using string capabilities, the setTime function could convert this string to a number of seconds, which the function stores in its private data member. The *set* function could also check that the value it receives represents a valid time (e.g., "12:30:45" is valid but "42:85:70" is not). The *set* and *get* functions allow a client to interact with an object, but the object's private data remains safely encapsulated (i.e., hidden) in the object itself.

The *set* and *get* functions of a class also should be used by other member functions within the class to manipulate the class's private data, although these member functions *can* access the private data directly. In Fig. 19.5, member functions setCourseName and getCourseName are public member functions, so they are accessible to clients of the class, as well as to the class itself. Member function displayMessage calls member function getCourseName to obtain the value of data member courseName for display purposes, even though displayMessage can access courseName directly—accessing a data member via its *get* function creates a better, more robust class (i.e., a class that is easier to maintain and less likely to stop working). If we decide to change the data member courseName in some way, the displayMessage definition will not require modification—only the bodies of the *get* and *set* functions that directly manipulate the data member will need to change. For example, suppose we decide that we want to represent the course name as two separate data members—courseNumber (e.g., "CS101") and courseTitle (e.g., "Introduction to C++ Programming"). Member function displayMessage can still issue a single call to member function getCourseName to obtain the full course to display as part of the welcome message. In this case, getCourseName would need to build and return a string containing the courseNumber followed by the courseTitle. Member function displayMessage would continue to display the complete course title "CS101 Introduction to C++ Programming," because it is unaffected by the change to the class's data members. The benefits of calling a *set* function from another member function of a class will become clear when we discuss validation in Section 19.10.

Good Programming Practice 19.6

Always try to localize the effects of changes to a class's data members by accessing and manipulating the data members through their get and set functions. Changes to the name of a data member or the data type used to store a data member then affect only the corresponding get and set functions, but not the callers of those functions.

Software Engineering Observation 19.3

It is important to write programs that are understandable and easy to maintain. Change is the rule rather than the exception. Programmers should anticipate that their code will be modified.

Software Engineering Observation 19.4

The class designer need not provide set or get functions for each private data item; these capabilities should be provided only when appropriate. If a service is useful to the client code, that service should typically be provided in the class's public interface.

GradeBook's UML Class Diagram with a Data Member and* set *and* get *Functions
Figure 19.6 contains an updated UML class diagram for the version of class GradeBook in
Fig. 19.5. This diagram models class GradeBook's data member courseName as an attribute
in the middle compartment of the class. The UML represents data members as attributes
by listing the attribute name, followed by a colon and the attribute type. The UML type
of attribute courseName is String, which corresponds to string in C++. Data member
courseName is private in C++, so the class diagram lists a minus sign (–) in front of the
corresponding attribute's name. The minus sign in the UML is equivalent to the private
access specifier in C++. Class GradeBook contains three public member functions, so the
class diagram lists three operations in the third compartment. Recall that the plus (+) sign
before each operation name indicates that the operation is public in C++. Operation set-
CourseName has a String parameter called name. The UML indicates the return type of an
operation by placing a colon and the return type after the parentheses following the operation name. Member function getCourseName of class GradeBook (Fig. 19.5) has a string
return type in C++, so the class diagram shows a String return type in the UML. Note
that operations setCourseName and displayMessage do not return values (i.e., they return
void), so the UML class diagram does not specify a return type after the parentheses of
these operations. The UML does not use void as C++ does when a function does not return a value.

19.7 Initializing Objects with Constructors

As mentioned in Section 19.6, when an object of class GradeBook (Fig. 19.5) is created,
its data member courseName is initialized to the empty string by default. What if you want
to provide a course name when you create a GradeBook object? Each class you declare can
provide a **constructor** that can be used to initialize an object of the class when the object
is created. A constructor is a special member function that must be defined with the same
name as the class, so that the compiler can distinguish it from the class's other member
functions. An important difference between constructors and other functions is that constructors cannot return values, so they cannot specify a return type (not even void). Normally, constructors are declared public. The term "constructor" is often abbreviated as
"ctor" in the literature—we prefer not to use this abbreviation.

C++ requires a constructor call for each object that is created, which helps ensure that
the object is initialized properly before it is used in a program—the constructor call occurs
implicitly when the object is created. In any class that does not explicitly include a constructor, the compiler provides a **default constructor**—that is, a constructor with no

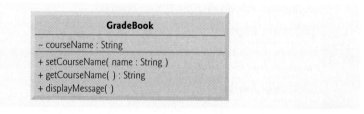

Fig. 19.6 | UML class diagram for class GradeBook with a private courseName attribute and
public operations setCourseName, getCourseName and displayMessage.

parameters. For example, when line 46 of Fig. 19.5 creates a GradeBook object, the default constructor is called, because the declaration of myGradeBook does not specify any constructor arguments. The default constructor provided by the compiler creates a GradeBook object without giving any initial values to the object's data members. [*Note:* For data members that are objects of other classes, the default constructor implicitly calls each data member's default constructor to ensure that the data member is initialized properly. In fact, this is why the string data member courseName (in Fig. 19.5) was initialized to the empty string—the default constructor for class string sets the string's value to the empty string. In Section 21.3, you will learn more about initializing data members that are objects of other classes.]

In the example of Fig. 19.7, we specify a course name for a GradeBook object when the object is created (line 49). In this case, the argument "CS101 Introduction to C++ Programming" is passed to the GradeBook object's constructor (lines 17–20) and used to initialize the courseName. Figure 19.7 defines a modified GradeBook class containing a constructor with a string parameter that receives the initial course name.

```cpp
1   // Fig. 19.7: fig19_07.cpp
2   // Instantiating multiple objects of the GradeBook class and using
3   // the GradeBook constructor to specify the course name
4   // when each GradeBook object is created.
5   #include <iostream>
6   using std::cout;
7   using std::endl;
8
9   #include <string> // program uses C++ standard string class
10  using std::string;
11
12  // GradeBook class definition
13  class GradeBook
14  {
15  public:
16     // constructor initializes courseName with string supplied as argument
17     GradeBook( string name )
18     {
19        setCourseName( name ); // call set function to initialize courseName
20     } // end GradeBook constructor
21
22     // function to set the course name
23     void setCourseName( string name )
24     {
25        courseName = name; // store the course name in the object
26     } // end function setCourseName
27
28     // function to get the course name
29     string getCourseName()
30     {
31        return courseName; // return object's courseName
32     } // end function getCourseName
```

Fig. 19.7 | Instantiating multiple objects of the GradeBook class and using the GradeBook constructor to specify the course name when each GradeBook object is created. (Part 1 of 2.)

```
33
34      // display a welcome message to the GradeBook user
35      void displayMessage()
36      {
37         // call getCourseName to get the courseName
38         cout << "Welcome to the grade book for\n" << getCourseName()
39            << "!" << endl;
40      } // end function displayMessage
41   private:
42      string courseName; // course name for this GradeBook
43   }; // end class GradeBook
44
45   // function main begins program execution
46   int main()
47   {
48      // create two GradeBook objects
49      GradeBook gradeBook1( "CS101 Introduction to C++ Programming" );
50      GradeBook gradeBook2( "CS102 Data Structures in C++" );
51
52      // display initial value of courseName for each GradeBook
53      cout << "gradeBook1 created for course: " << gradeBook1.getCourseName()
54         << "\ngradeBook2 created for course: " << gradeBook2.getCourseName()
55         << endl;
56      return 0; // indicate successful termination
57   } // end main
```

```
gradeBook1 created for course: CS101 Introduction to C++ Programming
gradeBook2 created for course: CS102 Data Structures in C++
```

Fig. 19.7 | Instantiating multiple objects of the GradeBook class and using the GradeBook constructor to specify the course name when each GradeBook object is created. (Part 2 of 2.)

Defining a Constructor

Lines 17–20 of Fig. 19.7 define a constructor for class GradeBook. Notice that the constructor has the same name as its class, GradeBook. A constructor specifies in its parameter list the data it requires to perform its task. When you create a new object, you place this data in the parentheses that follow the object name (as we did in lines 49–50). Line 17 indicates that class GradeBook's constructor has a string parameter called name. Note that line 17 does not specify a return type, because constructors cannot return values (or even void).

Line 19 in the constructor's body passes the constructor's parameter name to member function setCourseName, which assigns a value to data member courseName. The set-CourseName member function (lines 23–26) simply assigns its parameter name to the data member courseName, so you might be wondering why we bother making the call to set-CourseName in line 19—the constructor certainly could perform the assignment courseName = name. In Section 19.10, we modify setCourseName to perform validation (ensuring that, in this case, the courseName is 25 or fewer characters in length). At that point the benefits of calling setCourseName from the constructor will become clear. Note that both the constructor (line 17) and the setCourseName function (line 23) use a parameter called name. You can use the same parameter names in different functions because the parameters are local to each function; they do not interfere with one another.

Testing Class GradeBook

Lines 46–57 of Fig. 19.7 define the main function that tests class GradeBook and demonstrates initializing GradeBook objects using a constructor. Line 49 in function main creates and initializes a GradeBook object called gradeBook1. When this line executes, the Grade-Book constructor (lines 17–20) is called (implicitly by C++) with the argument "CS101 Introduction to C++ Programming" to initialize gradeBook1's course name. Line 50 repeats this process for the GradeBook object called gradeBook2, this time passing the argument "CS102 Data Structures in C++" to initialize gradeBook2's course name. Lines 53–54 use each object's getCourseName member function to obtain the course names and show that they were indeed initialized when the objects were created. The output confirms that each GradeBook object maintains its own copy of data member courseName.

Two Ways to Provide a Default Constructor for a Class

Any constructor that takes no arguments is called a default constructor. A class gets a default constructor in one of two ways:

1. The compiler implicitly creates a default constructor in a class that does not define a constructor. Such a default constructor does not initialize the class's data members, but does call the default constructor for each data member that is an object of another class. [*Note:* An uninitialized variable typically contains a "garbage" value (e.g., an uninitialized int variable might contain -858993460, which is likely to be an incorrect value for that variable in most programs).]

2. The programmer explicitly defines a constructor that takes no arguments. Such a default constructor will perform the initialization specified by the programmer and will call the default constructor for each data member that is an object of another class.

If the programmer defines a constructor with arguments, C++ will not implicitly create a default constructor for that class. Note that for each version of class GradeBook in Fig. 19.1, Fig. 19.3 and Fig. 19.5 the compiler implicitly defined a default constructor.

Error-Prevention Tip 19.2

Unless no initialization of your class's data members is necessary (almost never), provide a constructor to ensure that your class's data members are initialized with meaningful values when each new object of your class is created.

Software Engineering Observation 19.5

Data members can be initialized in a constructor of the class or their values may be set later after the object is created. However, it is a good software engineering practice to ensure that an object is fully initialized before the client code invokes the object's member functions. In general, you should not rely on the client code to ensure that an object gets initialized properly.

Adding the Constructor to Class GradeBook's UML Class Diagram

The UML class diagram of Fig. 19.8 models class GradeBook of Fig. 19.7, which has a constructor with a name parameter of type string (represented by type String in the UML). Like operations, the UML models constructors in the third compartment of a class in a class diagram. To distinguish a constructor from a class's operations, the UML places the word "constructor" between guillemets (« and ») before the constructor's name. It is customary to list the class's constructor before other operations in the third compartment.

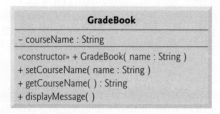

Fig. 19.8 | UML class diagram indicating that class GradeBook has a constructor with a name parameter of UML type String.

19.8 Placing a Class in a Separate File for Reusability

We have developed class GradeBook as far as we need to for now from a programming perspective, so let's consider some software engineering issues. One of the benefits of creating class definitions is that, when packaged properly, our classes can be reused by programmers—potentially worldwide. For example, we can reuse C++ Standard Library type string in any C++ program by including the header file <string> in the program (and, as we will see, by being able to link to the library's object code).

Unfortunately, programmers who wish to use our GradeBook class cannot simply include the file from Fig. 19.7 in another program. As you know, function main begins the execution of every program, and every program must have exactly one main function. If other programmers include the code from Fig. 19.7, they get extra baggage—our main function—and their programs will then have two main functions. When they attempt to compile their programs, the compiler will indicate an error because, again, each program can have only one main function. For example, attempting to compile a program with two main functions in Microsoft Visual C++ .NET produces the error

```
error C2084: function 'int main(void)' already has a body
```

when the compiler tries to compile the second main function it encounters. Similarly, the GNU C++ compiler produces the error

```
redefinition of 'int main()'
```

These errors indicate that a program already has a main function. So, placing main in the same file with a class definition prevents that class from being reused by other programs. In this section, we demonstrate how to make class GradeBook reusable by separating it into another file from the main function.

Header Files

Each of the previous examples in the chapter consists of a single .cpp file, also known as a source-code file, that contains a GradeBook class definition and a main function. When building an object-oriented C++ program, it is customary to define reusable source code (such as a class) in a file that by convention has a .h filename extension—known as a header file. Programs use #include preprocessor directives to include header files and take advantage of reusable software components, such as type string provided in the C++ Standard Library and user-defined types like class GradeBook.

In our next example, we separate the code from Fig. 19.7 into two files—Grade-Book.h (Fig. 19.9) and fig19_10.cpp (Fig. 19.10). As you look at the header file in Fig. 19.9, notice that it contains only the GradeBook class definition (lines 11–41) and lines 3–8, which allow class GradeBook to use cout, endl and type string. The main function that uses class GradeBook is defined in the source-code file fig19_10.cpp (Fig. 19.10) at lines 10–21. To help you prepare for the larger programs you will encounter later in this book and in industry, we often use a separate source-code file containing function main to test our classes (this is called a **driver program**). You will soon learn how a source-code file with main can use the class definition found in a header file to create objects of a class.

Including a Header File That Contains a User-Defined Class
A header file such as GradeBook.h (Fig. 19.9) cannot be used to begin program execution, because it does not contain a main function. If you try to compile and link GradeBook.h by itself to create an executable application, Microsoft Visual C++ .NET will produce the linker error message:

```
error LNK2019: unresolved external symbol _main referenced in
function _mainCRTStartup
```

```
 1   // Fig. 19.9: GradeBook.h
 2   // GradeBook class definition in a separate file from main.
 3   #include <iostream>
 4   using std::cout;
 5   using std::endl;
 6
 7   #include <string> // class GradeBook uses C++ standard string class
 8   using std::string;
 9
10   // GradeBook class definition
11   class GradeBook
12   {
13   public:
14      // constructor initializes courseName with string supplied as argument
15      GradeBook( string name )
16      {
17         setCourseName( name ); // call set function to initialize courseName
18      } // end GradeBook constructor
19
20      // function to set the course name
21      void setCourseName( string name )
22      {
23         courseName = name; // store the course name in the object
24      } // end function setCourseName
25
26      // function to get the course name
27      string getCourseName()
28      {
29         return courseName; // return object's courseName
30      } // end function getCourseName
31
```

Fig. 19.9 | GradeBook class definition. (Part 1 of 2.)

```
32      // display a welcome message to the GradeBook user
33      void displayMessage()
34      {
35         // call getCourseName to get the courseName
36         cout << "Welcome to the grade book for\n" << getCourseName()
37            << "!" << endl;
38      } // end function displayMessage
39   private:
40      string courseName; // course name for this GradeBook
41   }; // end class GradeBook
```

Fig. 19.9 | GradeBook class definition. (Part 2 of 2.)

Running GNU C++ on Linux produces a linker error message containing:

```
undefined reference to 'main'
```

This error indicates that the linker could not locate the program's main function. To test class GradeBook (defined in Fig. 19.9), you must write a separate source-code file containing a main function (such as Fig. 19.10) that instantiates and uses objects of the class.

Recall from Section 19.4 that, while the compiler knows what fundamental data types like int are, the compiler does not know what a GradeBook is because it is a user-defined type. In fact, the compiler does not even know the classes in the C++ Standard Library. To help it understand how to use a class, we must explicitly provide the compiler with the class's definition—that's why, for example, to use type string, a program must include

```
1    // Fig. 19.10: fig19_10.cpp
2    // Including class GradeBook from file GradeBook.h for use in main.
3    #include <iostream>
4    using std::cout;
5    using std::endl;
6
7    #include "GradeBook.h" // include definition of class GradeBook
8
9    // function main begins program execution
10   int main()
11   {
12      // create two GradeBook objects
13      GradeBook gradeBook1( "CS101 Introduction to C++ Programming" );
14      GradeBook gradeBook2( "CS102 Data Structures in C++" );
15
16      // display initial value of courseName for each GradeBook
17      cout << "gradeBook1 created for course: " << gradeBook1.getCourseName()
18         << "\ngradeBook2 created for course: " << gradeBook2.getCourseName()
19         << endl;
20      return 0; // indicate successful termination
21   } // end main
```

```
gradeBook1 created for course: CS101 Introduction to C++ Programming
gradeBook2 created for course: CS102 Data Structures in C++
```

Fig. 19.10 | Including class GradeBook from file GradeBook.h for use in main.

the `<string>` header file. This enables the compiler to determine the amount of memory that it must reserve for each object of the class and ensure that a program calls the class's member functions correctly.

To create `GradeBook` objects `gradeBook1` and `gradeBook2` in lines 13–14 of Fig. 19.10, the compiler must know the size of a `GradeBook` object. While objects conceptually contain data members and member functions, C++ objects typically contain only data. The compiler creates only one copy of the class's member functions and shares that copy among all the class's objects. Each object, of course, needs its own copy of the class's data members, because their contents can vary among objects (such as two different `BankAccount` objects having two different `balance` data members). The member function code, however, is not modifiable, so it can be shared among all objects of the class. Therefore, the size of an object depends on the amount of memory required to store the class's data members. By including `GradeBook.h` in line 7, we give the compiler access to the information it needs (Fig. 19.9, line 40) to determine the size of a `GradeBook` object and to determine whether objects of the class are used correctly (in lines 13–14 and 17–18 of Fig. 19.10).

Line 7 instructs the C++ preprocessor to replace the directive with a copy of the contents of `GradeBook.h` (i.e., the `GradeBook` class definition) *before* the program is compiled. When the source-code file `fig19_10.cpp` is compiled, it now contains the `GradeBook` class definition (because of the `#include`), and the compiler is able to determine how to create `GradeBook` objects and see that their member functions are called correctly. Now that the class definition is in a header file (without a `main` function), we can include that header in *any* program that needs to reuse our `GradeBook` class.

How Header Files Are Located

Notice that the name of the `GradeBook.h` header file in line 7 of Fig. 19.10 is enclosed in quotes (`" "`) rather than angle brackets (`< >`). Normally, a program's source-code files and user-defined header files are placed in the same directory. When the preprocessor encounters a header file name in quotes (e.g., `"GradeBook.h"`), the preprocessor attempts to locate the header file in the same directory as the file in which the `#include` directive appears. If the preprocessor cannot find the header file in that directory, it searches for it in the same location(s) as the C++ Standard Library header files. When the preprocessor encounters a header file name in angle brackets (e.g., `<iostream>`), it assumes that the header is part of the C++ Standard Library and does not look in the directory of the program that is being preprocessed.

Error-Prevention Tip 19.3

To ensure that the preprocessor can locate header files correctly, `#include` preprocessor directives should place the names of user-defined header files in quotes (e.g., `"GradeBook.h"`) and place the names of C++ Standard Library header files in angle brackets (e.g., `<iostream>`).

Additional Software Engineering Issues

Now that class `GradeBook` is defined in a header file, the class is reusable. Unfortunately, placing a class definition in a header file as in Fig. 19.9 still reveals the entire implementation of the class to the class's clients—`GradeBook.h` is simply a text file that anyone can open and read. Conventional software engineering wisdom says that to use an object of a class, the client code needs to know only what member functions to call, what arguments to provide to each member function and what return type to expect from each member function. The client code does not need to know how those functions are implemented.

If client code does know how a class is implemented, the client-code programmer might write client code based on the class's implementation details. Ideally, if that implementation changes, the class's clients should not have to change. Hiding the class's implementation details makes it easier to change the class's implementation while minimizing, and hopefully eliminating, changes to client code.

In Section 19.9, we show how to break up the GradeBook class into two files so that

1. the class is reusable

2. the clients of the class know what member functions the class provides, how to call them and what return types to expect

3. the clients do not know how the class's member functions are implemented.

19.9 Separating Interface from Implementation

In the preceding section, we showed how to promote software reusability by separating a class definition from the client code (e.g., function main) that uses the class. We now introduce another fundamental principle of good software engineering—separating interface from implementation.

Interface of a Class
Interfaces define and standardize the ways in which things such as people and systems interact with one another. For example, a radio's controls serve as an interface between the radio's users and its internal components. The controls allow users to perform a limited set of operations (such as changing the station, adjusting the volume, and choosing between AM and FM stations). Various radios may implement these operations differently—some provide push buttons, some provide dials and some support voice commands. The interface specifies *what* operations a radio permits users to perform but does not specify *how* the operations are implemented inside the radio.

Similarly, the interface of a class describes *what* services a class's clients can use and how to *request* those services, but not *how* the class carries out the services. A class's interface consists of the class's public member functions (also known as the class's **public** services). For example, class GradeBook's interface (Fig. 19.9) contains a constructor and member functions setCourseName, getCourseName and displayMessage. GradeBook's clients (e.g., main in Fig. 19.10) use these functions to request the class's services. As you will soon see, you can specify a class's interface by writing a class definition that lists only the member function names, return types and parameter types.

Separating the Interface from the Implementation
In our prior examples, each class definition contained the complete definitions of the class's public member functions and the declarations of its private data members. However, it is better software engineering to define member functions outside the class definition, so that their implementation details can be hidden from the client code. This practice ensures that programmers do not write client code that depends on the class's implementation details. If they were to do so, the client code would be more likely to "break" if the class's implementation changed.

The program of Figs. 19.11–19.13 separates class GradeBook's interface from its implementation by splitting the class definition of Fig. 19.9 into two files—the header file

GradeBook.h (Fig. 19.11) in which class GradeBook is defined, and the source-code file GradeBook.cpp (Fig. 19.12) in which GradeBook's member functions are defined. By convention, member-function definitions are placed in a source-code file of the same base name (e.g., GradeBook) as the class's header file but with a .cpp filename extension. The source-code file fig19_13.cpp (Fig. 19.13) defines function main (the client code). The code and output of Fig. 19.13 are identical to those of Fig. 19.10. Figure 19.14 shows how this three-file program is compiled from the perspectives of the GradeBook class programmer and the client-code programmer—we will explain this figure in detail.

GradeBook.h: Defining a Class's Interface with Function Prototypes

Header file GradeBook.h (Fig. 19.11) contains another version of GradeBook's class definition (lines 9–18). This version is similar to the one in Fig. 19.9, but the function definitions in Fig. 19.9 are replaced here with **function prototypes** (lines 12–15) that describe the class's public interface without revealing the class's member-function implementations. A function prototype is a declaration of a function that tells the compiler the function's name, its return type and the types of its parameters. Note that the header file still specifies the class's private data member (line 17) as well. Again, the compiler must know the data members of the class to determine how much memory to reserve for each object of the class. Including the header file GradeBook.h in the client code (line 8 of Fig. 19.13) provides the compiler with the information it needs to ensure that the client code calls the member functions of class GradeBook correctly.

The function prototype in line 12 (Fig. 19.12) indicates that the constructor requires one string parameter. Recall that constructors do not have return types, so no return type appears in the function prototype. Member function setCourseName's function prototype (line 13) indicates that setCourseName requires a string parameter and does not return a value (i.e., its return type is void). Member function getCourseName's function prototype (line 14) indicates that the function does not require parameters and returns a string.

```
 1    // Fig. 19.11: GradeBook.h
 2    // GradeBook class definition. This file presents GradeBook's public
 3    // interface without revealing the implementations of GradeBook's member
 4    // functions, which are defined in GradeBook.cpp.
 5    #include <string> // class GradeBook uses C++ standard string class
 6    using std::string;
 7
 8    // GradeBook class definition
 9    class GradeBook
10    {
11    public:
12       GradeBook( string ); // constructor that initializes courseName
13       void setCourseName( string ); // function that sets the course name
14       string getCourseName(); // function that gets the course name
15       void displayMessage(); // function that displays a welcome message
16    private:
17       string courseName; // course name for this GradeBook
18    }; // end class GradeBook
```

Fig. 19.11 | GradeBook class definition containing function prototypes that specify the interface of the class.

Finally, member function displayMessage's function prototype (line 15) specifies that displayMessage does not require parameters and does not return a value. These function prototypes are the same as the corresponding function headers in Fig. 19.9, except that the parameter names (which are optional in prototypes) are not included and each function prototype must end with a semicolon.

Common Programming Error 19.8

Forgetting the semicolon at the end of a function prototype is a syntax error.

Good Programming Practice 19.7

Although parameter names in function prototypes are optional (they are ignored by the compiler), many programmers use these names for documentation purposes.

Error-Prevention Tip 19.4

Parameter names in a function prototype (which, again, are ignored by the compiler) can be misleading if wrong or confusing names are used. For this reason, many programmers create function prototypes by copying the first line of the corresponding function definitions (when the source code for the functions is available), then appending a semicolon to the end of each prototype.

GradeBook.cpp: *Defining Member Functions in a Separate Source-Code File*
Source-code file GradeBook.cpp (Fig. 19.12) defines class GradeBook's member functions, which were declared in lines 12–15 of Fig. 19.11. The member-function definitions appear in lines 11–34 and are nearly identical to the member-function definitions in lines 15–38 of Fig. 19.9.

Notice that each member-function name in the function headers (lines 11, 17, 23 and 29) is preceded by the class name and ::, which is known as the binary scope resolution operator. This "ties" each member function to the (now separate) GradeBook class definition, which declares the class's member functions and data members. Without "Grade-Book::" preceding each function name, these functions would not be recognized by the compiler as member functions of class GradeBook—the compiler would consider them "free" or "loose" functions, like main. Such functions cannot access GradeBook's private data or call the class's member functions, without specifying an object. So, the compiler would not be able to compile these functions. For example, lines 19 and 25 that access variable courseName would cause compilation errors because courseName is not declared as a local variable in each function—the compiler would not know that courseName is already declared as a data member of class GradeBook.

Common Programming Error 19.9

When defining a class's member functions outside that class, omitting the class name and binary scope resolution operator (::) preceding the function names causes compilation errors.

To indicate that the member functions in GradeBook.cpp are part of class GradeBook, we must first include the GradeBook.h header file (line 8 of Fig. 19.12). This allows us to access the class name GradeBook in the GradeBook.cpp file. When compiling Grade-Book.cpp, the compiler uses the information in GradeBook.h to ensure that

```
1    // Fig. 19.12: GradeBook.cpp
2    // GradeBook member-function definitions. This file contains
3    // implementations of the member functions prototyped in GradeBook.h.
4    #include <iostream>
5    using std::cout;
6    using std::endl;
7
8    #include "GradeBook.h" // include definition of class GradeBook
9
10   // constructor initializes courseName with string supplied as argument
11   GradeBook::GradeBook( string name )
12   {
13      setCourseName( name ); // call set function to initialize courseName
14   } // end GradeBook constructor
15
16   // function to set the course name
17   void GradeBook::setCourseName( string name )
18   {
19      courseName = name; // store the course name in the object
20   } // end function setCourseName
21
22   // function to get the course name
23   string GradeBook::getCourseName()
24   {
25      return courseName; // return object's courseName
26   } // end function getCourseName
27
28   // display a welcome message to the GradeBook user
29   void GradeBook::displayMessage()
30   {
31      // call getCourseName to get the courseName
32      cout << "Welcome to the grade book for\n" << getCourseName()
33         << "!" << endl;
34   } // end function displayMessage
```

Fig. 19.12 | GradeBook member-function definitions represent the implementation of class GradeBook.

1. the first line of each member function (lines 11, 17, 23 and 29) matches its prototype in the GradeBook.h file—for example, the compiler ensures that getCourseName accepts no parameters and returns a string.

2. each member function knows about the class's data members and other member functions—for example, lines 19 and 25 can access variable courseName because it is declared in GradeBook.h as a data member of class GradeBook, and lines 13 and 32 can call functions setCourseName and getCourseName, respectively, because each is declared as a member function of the class in GradeBook.h (and because these calls conform with the corresponding prototypes).

Testing Class GradeBook
Figure 19.13 performs the same GradeBook object manipulations as Fig. 19.10. Separating GradeBook's interface from the implementation of its member functions does not affect the

```
 1   // Fig. 19.13: fig19_13.cpp
 2   // GradeBook class demonstration after separating
 3   // its interface from its implementation.
 4   #include <iostream>
 5   using std::cout;
 6   using std::endl;
 7
 8   #include "GradeBook.h" // include definition of class GradeBook
 9
10   // function main begins program execution
11   int main()
12   {
13      // create two GradeBook objects
14      GradeBook gradeBook1( "CS101 Introduction to C++ Programming" );
15      GradeBook gradeBook2( "CS102 Data Structures in C++" );
16
17      // display initial value of courseName for each GradeBook
18      cout << "gradeBook1 created for course: " << gradeBook1.getCourseName()
19         << "\ngradeBook2 created for course: " << gradeBook2.getCourseName()
20         << endl;
21      return 0; // indicate successful termination
22   } // end main
```

```
gradeBook1 created for course: CS101 Introduction to C++ Programming
gradeBook2 created for course: CS102 Data Structures in C++
```

Fig. 19.13 | GradeBook class demonstration after separating its interface from its implementation.

way that this client code uses the class. It affects only how the program is compiled and linked, which we discuss in detail shortly.

As in Fig. 19.10, line 8 of Fig. 19.13 includes the GradeBook.h header file so that the compiler can ensure that GradeBook objects are created and manipulated correctly in the client code. Before executing this program, the source-code files in Fig. 19.12 and Fig. 19.13 must both be compiled, then linked together—that is, the member-function calls in the client code need to be tied to the implementations of the class's member functions—a job performed by the linker.

The Compilation and Linking Process
The diagram in Fig. 19.14 shows the compilation and linking process that results in an executable GradeBook application that can be used by instructors. Often a class's interface and implementation will be created and compiled by one programmer and used by a separate programmer who implements the class's client code. So, the diagram shows what is required by both the class-implementation programmer and the client-code programmer. The dashed lines in the diagram show the pieces required by the class-implementation programmer, the client-code programmer and the GradeBook application user, respectively. [*Note:* Figure 19.14 is not a UML diagram.]

A class-implementation programmer responsible for creating a reusable GradeBook class creates the header file GradeBook.h and source-code file GradeBook.cpp that #includes the

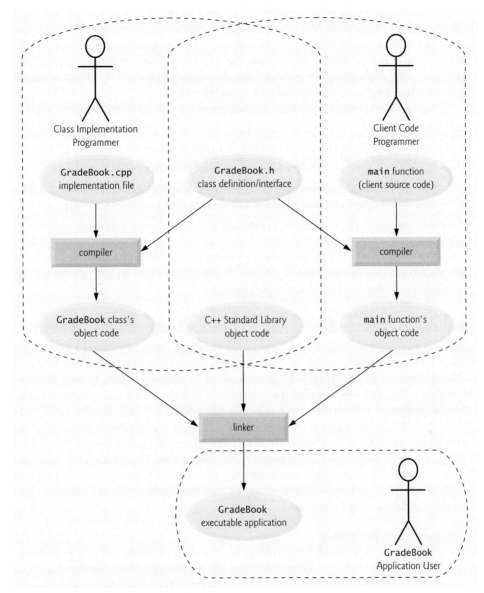

Fig. 19.14 | Compilation and linking process that produces an executable application.

header file, then compiles the source-code file to create GradeBook's object code. To hide the implementation details of GradeBook's member functions, the class-implementation programmer would provide the client-code programmer with the header file GradeBook.h (which specifies the class's interface and data members) and the object code for class Grade-Book which contains the machine-language instructions that represent GradeBook's member functions. The client-code programmer is not given GradeBook's source-code file, so the client remains unaware of how GradeBook's member functions are implemented.

The client code needs to know only GradeBook's interface to use the class and must be able to link its object code. Since the interface of the class is part of the class definition in the GradeBook.h header file, the client-code programmer must have access to this file and #include it in the client's source-code file. When the client code is compiled, the compiler uses the class definition in GradeBook.h to ensure that the main function creates and manipulates objects of class GradeBook correctly.

To create the executable GradeBook application to be used by instructors, the last step is to link

1. the object code for the main function (i.e., the client code)
2. the object code for class GradeBook's member-function implementations
3. the C++ Standard Library object code for the C++ classes (e.g., string) used by the class-implementation programmer and the client-code programmer.

The linker's output is the executable GradeBook application that instructors can use to manage their students' grades.

For further information on compiling multiple-source-file programs, see your compiler's documentation or study the DIVE-INTO® publications that we provide for various C++ compilers at www.deitel.com/books/cpphtp5.

19.10 Validating Data with *set* Functions

In Section 19.6, we introduced *set* functions for allowing clients of a class to modify the value of a private data member. In Fig. 19.5, class GradeBook defines member function setCourseName to simply assign a value received in its parameter name to data member courseName. This member function does not ensure that the course name adheres to any particular format or follows any other rules regarding what a "valid" course name looks like. As we stated earlier, suppose that a university can print student transcripts containing course names of only 25 characters or less. If the university uses a system containing GradeBook objects to generate the transcripts, we might want class GradeBook to ensure that its data member courseName never contains more than 25 characters. The program of Figs. 19.15–19.17 enhances class GradeBook's member function setCourseName to perform this validation (also known as validity checking).

GradeBook Class Definition
Notice that GradeBook's class definition (Fig. 19.15)—and hence, its interface—is identical to that of Fig. 19.11. Since the interface remains unchanged, clients of this class need not be changed when the definition of member function setCourseName is modified. This enables clients to take advantage of the improved GradeBook class simply by linking the client code to the updated GradeBook's object code.

Validating the Course Name with GradeBook Member Function *setCourseName*
The enhancement to class GradeBook is in the definition of setCourseName (Fig. 19.16, lines 18–31). The if statement in lines 20–21 determines whether parameter name contains a valid course name (i.e., a string of 25 or fewer characters). If the course name is valid, line 21 stores the course name in data member courseName. Note the expression name.length() in line 20. This is a member-function call just like myGradeBook.displayMessage(). The C++ Standard Library's string class defines a member function length

```
1   // Fig. 19.15: GradeBook.h
2   // GradeBook class definition presents the public interface of
3   // the class. Member-function definitions appear in GradeBook.cpp.
4   #include <string> // program uses C++ standard string class
5   using std::string;
6
7   // GradeBook class definition
8   class GradeBook
9   {
10  public:
11     GradeBook( string ); // constructor that initializes a GradeBook object
12     void setCourseName( string ); // function that sets the course name
13     string getCourseName(); // function that gets the course name
14     void displayMessage(); // function that displays a welcome message
15  private:
16     string courseName; // course name for this GradeBook
17  }; // end class GradeBook
```

Fig. 19.15 | GradeBook class definition.

```
1   // Fig. 19.16: GradeBook.cpp
2   // Implementations of the GradeBook member-function definitions.
3   // The setCourseName function performs validation.
4   #include <iostream>
5   using std::cout;
6   using std::endl;
7
8   #include "GradeBook.h" // include definition of class GradeBook
9
10  // constructor initializes courseName with string supplied as argument
11  GradeBook::GradeBook( string name )
12  {
13     setCourseName( name ); // validate and store courseName
14  } // end GradeBook constructor
15
16  // function that sets the course name;
17  // ensures that the course name has at most 25 characters
18  void GradeBook::setCourseName( string name )
19  {
20     if ( name.length() <= 25 ) // if name has 25 or fewer characters
21        courseName = name; // store the course name in the object
22
23     if ( name.length() > 25 ) // if name has more than 25 characters
24     {
25        // set courseName to first 25 characters of parameter name
26        courseName = name.substr( 0, 25 ); // start at 0, length of 25
27
28        cout << "Name \"" << name << "\" exceeds maximum length (25).\n"
29           << "Limiting courseName to first 25 characters.\n" << endl;
30     } // end if
31  } // end function setCourseName
```

Fig. 19.16 | Member-function definitions for class GradeBook with a *set* function that validates the length of data member courseName. (Part 1 of 2.)

```
32
33   // function to get the course name
34   string GradeBook::getCourseName()
35   {
36      return courseName; // return object's courseName
37   } // end function getCourseName
38
39   // display a welcome message to the GradeBook user
40   void GradeBook::displayMessage()
41   {
42      // call getCourseName to get the courseName
43      cout << "Welcome to the grade book for\n" << getCourseName()
44         << "!" << endl;
45   } // end function displayMessage
```

Fig. 19.16 | Member-function definitions for class GradeBook with a *set* function that validates the length of data member courseName. (Part 2 of 2.)

that returns the number of characters in a string object. Parameter name is a string object, so the call name.length() returns the number of characters in name. If this value is less than or equal to 25, name is valid and line 21 executes.

The if statement in lines 23–30 handles the case in which setCourseName receives an invalid course name (i.e., a name that is more than 25 characters long). Even if parameter name is too long, we still want to leave the GradeBook object in a **consistent state**—that is, a state in which the object's data member courseName contains a valid value (i.e., a string of 25 characters or less). Thus, we truncate (i.e., shorten) the specified course name and assign the first 25 characters of name to the courseName data member (unfortunately, this could truncate the course name awkwardly). Standard class string provides member function **substr** (short for "substring") that returns a new string object created by copying part of an existing string object. The call in line 26 (i.e., name.substr(0, 25)) passes two integers (0 and 25) to name's member function substr. These arguments indicate the portion of the string name that substr should return. The first argument specifies the starting position in the original string from which characters are copied—the first character in every string is considered to be at position 0. The second argument specifies the number of characters to copy. Therefore, the call in line 26 returns a 25-character substring of name starting at position 0 (i.e., the first 25 characters in name). For example, if name holds the value "CS101 Introduction to Programming in C++", substr returns "CS101 Introduction to Pro". After the call to substr, line 26 assigns the substring returned by substr to data member courseName. In this way, member function setCourseName ensures that courseName is always assigned a string containing 25 or fewer characters. If the member function has to truncate the course name to make it valid, lines 28–29 display a warning message.

Note that the if statement in lines 23–30 contains two body statements—one to set the courseName to the first 25 characters of parameter name and one to print an accompanying message to the user. We want both of these statements to execute when name is too long, so we place them in a pair of braces, { }.

Note that the cout statement in lines 28–29 could also appear without a stream insertion operator at the start of the second line of the statement, as in:

```
      cout << "Name \"" << name << "\" exceeds maximum length (25).\n"
            "Limiting courseName to first 25 characters.\n" << endl;
```

The C++ compiler combines adjacent string literals, even if they appear on separate lines of a program. Thus, in the statement above, the C++ compiler would combine the string literals "\" exceeds maximum length (25).\n" and "Limiting courseName to first 25 characters.\n" into a single string literal that produces output identical to that of lines 28–29 in Fig. 19.16. This behavior allows you to print lengthy strings by breaking them across lines in your program without including additional stream insertion operations.

Testing Class GradeBook

Figure 19.17 demonstrates the modified version of class GradeBook (Figs. 19.15–19.16) featuring validation. Line 14 creates a GradeBook object named gradeBook1. Recall that the GradeBook constructor calls member function setCourseName to initialize data member

```
 1  // Fig. 19.17: fig19_17.cpp
 2  // Create and manipulate a GradeBook object; illustrate validation.
 3  #include <iostream>
 4  using std::cout;
 5  using std::endl;
 6
 7  #include "GradeBook.h" // include definition of class GradeBook
 8
 9  // function main begins program execution
10  int main()
11  {
12     // create two GradeBook objects;
13     // initial course name of gradeBook1 is too long
14     GradeBook gradeBook1( "CS101 Introduction to Programming in C++" );
15     GradeBook gradeBook2( "CS102 C++ Data Structures" );
16
17     // display each GradeBook's courseName
18     cout << "gradeBook1's initial course name is: "
19        << gradeBook1.getCourseName()
20        << "\ngradeBook2's initial course name is: "
21        << gradeBook2.getCourseName() << endl;
22
23     // modify myGradeBook's courseName (with a valid-length string)
24     gradeBook1.setCourseName( "CS101 C++ Programming" );
25
26     // display each GradeBook's courseName
27     cout << "\ngradeBook1's course name is: "
28        << gradeBook1.getCourseName()
29        << "\ngradeBook2's course name is: "
30        << gradeBook2.getCourseName() << endl;
31     return 0; // indicate successful termination
32  } // end main
```

Fig. 19.17 | Creating and manipulating a GradeBook object in which the course name is limited to 25 characters in length. (Part 1 of 2.)

```
Name "CS101 Introduction to Programming in C++" exceeds maximum length (25).
Limiting courseName to first 25 characters.

gradeBook1's initial course name is: CS101 Introduction to Pro
gradeBook2's initial course name is: CS102 C++ Data Structures

gradeBook1's course name is: CS101 C++ Programming
gradeBook2's course name is: CS102 C++ Data Structures
```

Fig. 19.17 | Creating and manipulating a GradeBook object in which the course name is limited to 25 characters in length. (Part 2 of 2.)

courseName. In previous versions of the class, the benefit of calling setCourseName in the constructor was not evident. Now, however, the constructor takes advantage of the validation provided by setCourseName. The constructor simply calls setCourseName, rather than duplicating its validation code. When line 14 of Fig. 19.17 passes an initial course name of "CS101 Introduction to Programming in C++" to the GradeBook constructor, the constructor passes this value to setCourseName, where the actual initialization occurs. Because this course name contains more than 25 characters, the body of the second if statement executes, causing courseName to be initialized to the truncated 25-character course name "CS101 Introduction to Pro" (the truncated part is highlighted in red in line 14). Notice that the output in Fig. 19.17 contains the warning message output by lines 28–29 of Fig. 19.16 in member function setCourseName. Line 15 creates another GradeBook object called gradeBook2—the valid course name passed to the constructor is exactly 25 characters.

Lines 18–21 of Fig. 19.17 display the truncated course name for gradeBook1 (we highlight this in red in the program output) and the course name for gradeBook2. Line 24 calls gradeBook1's setCourseName member function directly, to change the course name in the GradeBook object to a shorter name that does not need to be truncated. Then, lines 27–30 output the course names for the GradeBook objects again.

Additional Notes on set *Functions*

A public *set* function such as setCourseName should carefully scrutinize any attempt to modify the value of a data member (e.g., courseName) to ensure that the new value is appropriate for that data item. For example, an attempt to *set* the day of the month to 37 should be rejected, an attempt to *set* a person's weight to zero or a negative value should be rejected, an attempt to *set* a grade on an exam to 185 (when the proper range is zero to 100) should be rejected, and so on.

Software Engineering Observation 19.6

Making data members private and controlling access, especially write access, to those data members through public member functions helps ensure data integrity.

Error-Prevention Tip 19.5

The benefits of data integrity are not automatic simply because data members are made private—the programmer must provide appropriate validity checking and report the errors.

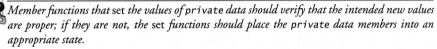

Software Engineering Observation 19.7

Member functions that set the values of private *data should verify that the intended new values are proper; if they are not, the* set *functions should place the* private *data members into an appropriate state.*

A class's *set* functions can return values to the class's clients indicating that attempts were made to assign invalid data to objects of the class. A client of the class can test the return value of a *set* function to determine whether the client's attempt to modify the object was successful and to take appropriate action. In Chapter 27, we demonstrate how clients of a class can be notified via the exception-handling mechanism when an attempt is made to modify an object with an inappropriate value. To keep the program of Figs. 19.15–19.17 simple at this early point in the book, setCourseName in Fig. 19.16 just prints an appropriate message on the screen.

19.11 Wrap-Up

In this chapter, you learned how to create user-defined classes, and how to create and use objects of those classes. In particular, we declared data members of a class to maintain data for each object of the class. We also defined member functions that operate on that data. You learned how to call an object's member functions to request the services it provides and how to pass data to those member functions as arguments. We discussed the difference between a local variable of a member function and a data member of a class. We also showed how to use a constructor to specify the initial values for an object's data members. You learned how to separate the interface of a class from its implementation to promote good software engineering. We also presented a diagram that shows the files that class-implementation programmers and client-code programmers need to compile the code they write. We demonstrated how *set* functions can be used to validate an object's data and ensure that objects are maintained in a consistent state. In addition, UML class diagrams were used to model classes and their constructors, member functions and data members. In the next chapter, we begin our introduction to control statements, which specify the order in which a function's actions are performed.

Summary

Section 19.2 Classes, Objects, Member Functions and Data Members
- Performing a task in a program requires a function. The function hides from its user the complex tasks that it performs.
- A function in a class is known as a member function and performs one of the class's tasks.
- You must create an object of a class before a program can perform the tasks the class describes. That is one reason C++ is known as an object-oriented programming language.
- Each message sent to an object is a member-function call that tells the object to perform a task.
- An object has attributes that are carried with the object as it is used in a program. These attributes are specified as data members in the object's class.

Section 19.4 Defining a Class with a Member Function
- A class definition contains the data members and member functions that define the class's attributes and behaviors, respectively.

- A class definition begins with the keyword class followed immediately by the class name.
- By convention, the name of a user-defined class begins with a capital letter and, for readability, each subsequent word in the class name begins with a capital letter.
- Every class's body is enclosed in a pair of braces ({ and }) and ends with a semicolon.
- Member functions that appear after access specifier public can be called by other functions in a program and by member functions of other classes.
- Access specifiers are always followed by a colon (:).
- Keyword void is a special return type which indicates that a function will perform a task but will not return any data to its calling function when it completes its task.
- By convention, function names begin with a lowercase first letter and all subsequent words in the name begin with a capital letter.
- An empty set of parentheses after a function name indicates that the function does not require additional data to perform its task.
- Every function's body is delimited by left and right braces ({ and }).
- Typically, you cannot call a member function until you create an object of its class.
- Each new class you create becomes a new type in C++ that can be used to declare variables and create objects. This is one reason why C++ is known as an extensible language.
- In the UML, each class is modeled in a class diagram as a rectangle with three compartments. The top compartment contains the class name, centered horizontally in boldface. The middle compartment contains the class's attributes (data members in C++). The bottom compartment contains the class's operations (member functions and constructors in C++).
- The UML models operations by listing the operation name followed by a set of parentheses. A plus sign (+) preceding the operation name indicates a public operation in the UML (i.e., a public member function in C++).

Section 19.5 Defining a Member Function with a Parameter
- A member function can require one or more parameters that represent additional data it needs to perform its task. A function call supplies arguments for each of the function's parameters.
- A member function is called by following the object name with a dot operator (.), the function name and a set of parentheses containing the function's arguments.
- A variable of C++ Standard Library class string represents a string of characters. This class is defined in header file <string>, and the name string belongs to namespace std.
- Function getline (from header <string>) reads characters from its first argument until a newline character is encountered, then places the characters (not including the newline) in the string variable specified as its second argument. The newline character is discarded.
- A parameter list may contain any number of parameters, including none at all (represented by empty parentheses) to indicate that a function does not require any parameters.
- The number of arguments in a function call must match the number of parameters in the parameter list of the called member function's header. Also, the argument types in the function call must be consistent with the types of the corresponding parameters in the function header.
- Variables declared in a function's body are local variables and can be used only from the point of their declaration in the function to the immediately following closing right brace (}). When a function terminates, the values of its local variables are lost.
- A local variable must be declared before it can be used in a function. A local variable cannot be accessed outside the function in which it is declared.

- Data members normally are `private`. Variables or functions declared `private` are accessible only to member functions of the class in which they are declared.

- When a program creates (instantiates) an object of a class, its `private` data members are encapsulated (hidden) in the object and can be accessed only by member functions of the object's class.

- When a function that specifies a return type other than `void` is called and completes its task, the function returns a result to its calling function.

- By default, the initial value of a `string` is the empty string—i.e., a string that does not contain any characters. Nothing appears on the screen when an empty string is displayed.

- The UML models a parameter of an operation by listing the parameter name, followed by a colon and the parameter type between the parentheses following the operation name.

- The UML has its own data types. Not all the UML data types have the same names as the corresponding C++ types. The UML type `String` corresponds to the C++ type `string`.

Section 19.6 Data Members, set *Functions and* get *Functions*

- Classes often provide `public` member functions to allow clients of the class to *set* or *get* `private` data members. The names of these member functions normally begin with *set* or *get*.

- Providing `public` *set* and *get* functions allows clients of a class to indirectly access the hidden data. The client knows that it is attempting to modify or obtain an object's data, but the client does not know how the object performs these operations.

- The *set* and *get* functions of a class also should be used by other member functions within the class to manipulate the class's `private` data, although these member functions *can* access the `private` data directly. If the class's data representation is changed, member functions that access the data only via the *set* and *get* functions will not require modification—only the bodies of the *set* and *get* functions that directly manipulate the data member will need to change.

- A `public` *set* function should carefully scrutinize any attempt to modify the value of a data member to ensure that the new value is appropriate for that data item.

- The UML represents data members as attributes by listing the attribute name, followed by a colon and the attribute type. Private attributes are preceded by a minus sign (–) in the UML.

- The UML indicates the return type of an operation by placing a colon and the return type after the parentheses following the operation name.

- UML class diagrams do not specify return types for operations that do not return values.

Section 19.7 Initializing Objects with Constructors

- Each class you declare should provide a constructor to initialize an object of the class when the object is created. A constructor is a special member function that must be defined with the same name as the class, so that the compiler can distinguish it from the class's other member functions.

- A difference between constructors and functions is that constructors cannot return values, so they cannot specify a return type (not even `void`). Normally, constructors are declared `public`.

- C++ requires a constructor call at the time each object is created, which helps ensure that every object is initialized before it is used in a program.

- A constructor that takes no arguments is a default constructor. In any class that does not include a constructor, the compiler provides a default constructor. The class programmer can also define a default constructor explicitly. If the programmer defines a constructor for a class, C++ will not create a default constructor.

- The UML models constructors as operations in a class diagram's third compartment. To distinguish a constructor from a class's operations, the UML places the word "constructor" between guillemets (« and ») before the constructor's name.

Section 19.8 Placing a Class in a Separate File for Reusability

- Class definitions, when packaged properly, can be reused by programmers worldwide.

- It is customary to define a class in a header file that has a .h filename extension.

- If the class's implementation changes, the class's clients should not be required to change.

Section 19.9 Separating Interface from Implementation

- Interfaces define and standardize the ways in which things such as people and systems interact.

- The interface of a class describes the public member functions (also known as public services) that are made available to the class's clients. The interface describes *what* services clients can use and how to *request* those services, but does not specify *how* the class carries out the services.

- A fundamental principle of good software engineering is to separate interface from implementation. This makes programs easier to modify. Changes in the class's implementation do not affect the client as long as the class's interface originally provided to the client remains unchanged.

- A function prototype contains a function's name, its return type and the number, types and order of the parameters the function expects to receive.

- Once a class is defined and its member functions are declared (via function prototypes), the member functions should be defined in a separate source-code file

- For each member function defined outside of its corresponding class definition, the function name must be preceded by the class name and the binary scope resolution operator (::).

Section 19.10 Validating Data with set *Functions*

- Class string's length member function returns the number of characters in a string object.

- Class string's member function substr (short for "substring") returns a new string object created by copying part of an existing string object. The function's first argument specifies the starting position in the original string from which characters are copied. Its second argument specifies the number of characters to copy.

Terminology

access specifier	defining a class
accessor	dot operator (.)
argument	empty string
attribute (UML)	extensible language
binary scope resolution operator (::)	function call
body of a class definition	function header
calling function (caller)	function prototype
camel case	*get* function
class definition	getline function of <string> library
class diagram (UML)	guillemets, « and » (UML)
class-implementation programmer	header file
client-code programmer	implementation of a class
client of an object or class	instance of a class
compartment in a class diagram (UML)	interface of a class
consistent state	invoke a member function
constructor	length member function of class string
data hiding	local variable
data member	member function
default constructor	member-function call
default precision	message (send to an object)

minus (-) sign (UML)
mutator
object code
operation (UML)
operation parameter (UML)
parameter
parameter list
plus (+) sign (UML)
precision
`private` access specifier
`public` access specifier
`public` services of a class

return type
separate interface from implementation
set function
software engineering
source-code file
`string` class
`<string>` header file
`substr` member function of class `string`
UML class diagram
validation
validity checking
void return type

Self-Review Exercises

19.1 Fill in the blanks in each of the following:
a) A house is to a blueprint as a(n) _____ is to a class.
b) Every class definition contains keyword _____ followed immediately by the class's name.
c) A class definition is typically stored in a file with the _____ filename extension.
d) Each parameter in a function header should specify both a(n) _____ and a(n) _____.
e) When each object of a class maintains its own copy of an attribute, the variable that represents the attribute is also known as a(n) _____.
f) Keyword `public` is a(n) _____.
g) Return type _____ indicates that a function will perform a task but will not return any information when it completes its task.
h) Function _____ from the `<string>` library reads characters until a newline character is encountered, then copies those characters into the specified `string`.
i) When a member function is defined outside the class definition, the function header must include the class name and the _____, followed by the function name to "tie" the member function to the class definition.
j) The source-code file and any other files that use a class can include the class's header file via a(n) _____ preprocessor directive.

19.2 State whether each of the following is *true* or *false*. If *false*, explain why.
a) By convention, function names begin with a capital letter and all subsequent words in the name begin with a capital letter.
b) Empty parentheses following a function name in a function prototype indicate that the function does not require any parameters to perform its task.
c) Data members or member functions declared with access specifier `private` are accessible to member functions of the class in which they are declared.
d) Variables declared in the body of a particular member function are known as data members and can be used in all member functions of the class.
e) Every function's body is delimited by left and right braces ({ and }).
f) Any source-code file that contains `int main()` can be used to execute a program.
g) The types of arguments in a function call must match the types of the corresponding parameters in the function prototype's parameter list.

19.3 What is the difference between a local variable and a data member?

19.4 Explain the purpose of a function parameter. What is the difference between a parameter and an argument?

Answers to Self-Review Exercises

19.1   a) object. b) `class`. c) `.h` d) type, name. e) data member. f) access specifier. g) `void`. h) `getline`. i) binary scope resolution operator (`::`). j) `#include`.

19.2   a) False. By convention, function names begin with a lowercase letter and all subsequent words in the name begin with a capital letter. b) True. c) True. d) False. Such variables are called local variables and can be used only in the member function in which they are declared. e) True. f) True. g) True.

19.3   A local variable is declared in the body of a function and can be used only from the point at which it is declared to the immediately following closing brace. A data member is declared in a class definition, but not in the body of any of the class's member functions. Every object (instance) of a class has a separate copy of the class's data members. Also, data members are accessible to all member functions of the class.

19.4   A parameter represents additional information that a function requires to perform its task. Each parameter required by a function is specified in the function header. An argument is the value supplied in the function call. When the function is called, the argument value is passed into the function parameter so that the function can perform its task.

Exercises

19.5   Explain the difference between a function prototype and a function definition.

19.6   What is a default constructor? How are an object's data members initialized if a class has only an implicitly defined default constructor?

19.7   Explain the purpose of a data member.

19.8   What is a header file? What is a source-code file? Discuss the purpose of each.

19.9   Explain how a program could use class `string` without inserting a `using` declaration.

19.10   Explain why a class might provide a *set* function and a *get* function for a data member.

19.11   *(Modifying Class `GradeBook`)* Modify class `GradeBook` (Figs. 19.11–19.12) as follows:
   a) Include a second `string` data member that represents the course instructor's name.
   b) Provide a *set* function to change the instructor's name and a *get* function to retrieve it.
   c) Modify the constructor to specify two parameters—one for the course name and one for the instructor's name.
   d) Modify member function `displayMessage` such that it first outputs the welcome message and course name, then outputs `"This course is presented by: "` followed by the instructor's name.

Use your modified class in a test program that demonstrates the class's new capabilities.

19.12   *(Account Class)* Create a class called `Account` that a bank might use to represent customers' bank accounts. Your class should include one data member of type `int` to represent the account balance. [*Note:* In subsequent chapters, we'll use numbers that contain decimal points (e.g., 2.75)—called floating-point values—to represent dollar amounts.] Your class should provide a constructor that receives an initial balance and uses it to initialize the data member. The constructor should validate the initial balance to ensure that it is greater than or equal to 0. If not, the balance should be set to 0 and the constructor should display an error message, indicating that the initial balance was invalid. The class should provide three member functions. Member function `credit` should add an amount to the current balance. Member function `debit` should withdraw money from the `Account` and should ensure that the debit amount does not exceed the `Account`'s balance. If it does, the balance should be left unchanged and the function should print a message indicating `"Debit amount` exceeded account balance." Member function getBalance should return the current balance. Create a program that creates two Account objects and tests the member functions of class Account.

19.13 *(Invoice Class)* Create a class called Invoice that a hardware store might use to represent an invoice for an item sold at the store. An Invoice should include four pieces of information as data members—a part number (type string), a part description (type string), a quantity of the item being purchased (type int) and a price per item (type int). [*Note:* In subsequent chapters, we'll use numbers that contain decimal points (e.g., 2.75)—called floating-point values—to represent dollar amounts.] Your class should have a constructor that initializes the four data members. Provide a *set* and a *get* function for each data member. In addition, provide a member function named getInvoiceAmount that calculates the invoice amount (i.e., multiplies the quantity by the price per item), then returns the amount as an int value. If the quantity is not positive, it should be set to 0. If the price per item is not positive, it should be set to 0. Write a test program that demonstrates class Invoice's capabilities.

19.14 *(Employee Class)* Create a class called Employee that includes three pieces of information as data members—a first name (type string), a last name (type string) and a monthly salary (type int). [*Note:* In subsequent chapters, we'll use numbers that contain decimal points (e.g., 2.75)—called floating-point values—to represent dollar amounts.] Your class should have a constructor that initializes the three data members. Provide a *set* and a *get* function for each data member. If the monthly salary is not positive, set it to 0. Write a test program that demonstrates class Employee's capabilities. Create two Employee objects and display each object's *yearly* salary. Then give each Employee a 10 percent raise and display each Employee's yearly salary again.

19.15 *(Date Class)* Create a class called Date that includes three pieces of information as data members—a month (type int), a day (type int) and a year (type int). Your class should have a constructor with three parameters that uses the parameters to initialize the three data members. For the purpose of this exercise, assume that the values provided for the year and day are correct, but ensure that the month value is in the range 1–12; if it is not, set the month to 1. Provide a *set* and a *get* function for each data member. Provide a member function displayDate that displays the month, day and year separated by forward slashes (/). Write a test program that demonstrates class Date's capabilities.

20

Classes: A Deeper Look, Part 1

My object all sublime
I shall achieve in time.
—W. S. Gilbert

Is it a world to hide virtues in?
—William Shakespeare

Don't be "consistent," but be simply true.
—Oliver Wendell Holmes, Jr.

This above all: to thine own self be true.
—William Shakespeare

OBJECTIVES

In this chapter you will learn:

- How to use a preprocessor wrapper to prevent multiple-definition errors caused by including more than one copy of a header file in a source-code file.

- To understand class scope and accessing class members via the name of an object, a reference to an object or a pointer to an object.

- To define constructors with default arguments.

- How destructors are used to perform "termination housekeeping" on an object before it is destroyed.

- When constructors and destructors are called and the order in which they are called.

- The logic errors that may occur when a **public** member function of a class returns a reference to **private** data.

- To assign the data members of one object to those of another object by default memberwise assignment.

20.1 Introduction

In the preceding chapters, we introduced many basic terms and concepts of C++ object-oriented programming. We also discussed our program development methodology: We selected appropriate attributes and behaviors for each class and specified the manner in which objects of our classes collaborated with objects of C++ Standard Library classes to accomplish each program's overall goals.

In this chapter, we take a deeper look at classes. We use an integrated Time class case study in this chapter (three examples) and Chapter 21 (two examples) to demonstrate several class-construction features. We begin with a Time class that reviews several of the features presented in the preceding chapters. The example also demonstrates an important C++ software engineering concept—using a "preprocessor wrapper" in header files to prevent the code in the header from being included into the same source-code file more than once. Since a class can be defined only once, using such preprocessor directives prevents multiple-definition errors.

Next, we discuss class scope and the relationships among members of a class. We also demonstrate how client code can access a class's public members via three types of "handles"—the name of an object, a reference to an object or a pointer to an object. As you will see, object names and references can be used with the dot (.) member-selection operator to access a public member, and pointers can be used with the arrow (->) member-selection operator.

We discuss access functions that can read or display data in an object. A common use of access functions is to test the truth or falsity of conditions—such functions are known as predicate functions. We also demonstrate the notion of a utility function (also called a helper function)—a private member function that supports the operation of the class's public member functions, but is not intended for use by clients of the class.

In the second example of the Time class case study, we demonstrate how to pass arguments to constructors and show how default arguments can be used in a constructor to enable client code to initialize objects of a class using a variety of arguments. Next, we discuss a special member function called a destructor that is part of every class and is used to perform "termination housekeeping" on an object before the object is destroyed. We then demonstrate the order in which constructors and destructors are called, because your programs' correctness depends on using properly initialized objects that have not yet been destroyed.

Our last example of the Time class case study in this chapter shows a dangerous programming practice in which a member function returns a reference to private data. We discuss how this breaks the encapsulation of a class and allows client code to directly access an object's data. This last example shows that objects of the same class can be assigned to one another using default memberwise assignment, which copies the data members in the object on the right side of the assignment into the corresponding data members of the object on the left side of the assignment. The chapter concludes with a discussion of software reusability.

20.2 Time Class Case Study

Our first example (Figs. 20.1–20.3) creates class Time and a driver program that tests the class. You have already created several classes in this book. In this section, we review many of the concepts covered in Chapter 19 and demonstrate an important C++ software engineering concept—using a "preprocessor wrapper" in header files to prevent the code in the header from being included into the same source-code file more than once. Since a class can be defined only once, using such preprocessor directives prevents multiple-definition errors.

```
1   // Fig. 20.1: Time.h
2   // Declaration of class Time.
3   // Member functions are defined in Time.cpp
4
5   // prevent multiple inclusions of header file
6   #ifndef TIME_H
7   #define TIME_H
8
9   // Time class definition
10  class Time
11  {
12  public:
13     Time(); // constructor
14     void setTime( int, int, int ); // set hour, minute and second
15     void printUniversal(); // print time in universal-time format
16     void printStandard(); // print time in standard-time format
17  private:
18     int hour; // 0 - 23 (24-hour clock format)
19     int minute; // 0 - 59
20     int second; // 0 - 59
21  }; // end class Time
22
23  #endif
```

Fig. 20.1 | Time class definition.

Time *Class Definition*

The class definition (Fig. 20.1) contains prototypes (lines 13–16) for member functions `Time`, `setTime`, `printUniversal` and `printStandard`. The class includes `private` integer members `hour`, `minute` and `second` (lines 18–20). Class `Time`'s `private` data members can be accessed only by its four member functions. Chapter 23 introduces a third access specifier, `protected`, as we study inheritance and the part it plays in object-oriented programming.

Good Programming Practice 20.1

For clarity and readability, use each access specifier only once in a class definition. Place `public` *members first, where they are easy to locate.*

Software Engineering Observation 20.1

Each element of a class should have `private` *visibility unless it can be proven that the element needs* `public` *visibility. This is another example of the principle of least privilege.*

In Fig. 20.1, note that the class definition is enclosed in the following preprocessor wrapper (lines 5–7 and 23):

```
// prevent multiple inclusions of header file
#ifndef TIME_H
#define TIME_H
    ...
#endif
```

When we build larger programs, other definitions and declarations will also be placed in header files. The preceding preprocessor wrapper prevents the code between `#ifndef` (which means "if not defined") and `#endif` from being included if the name `TIME_H` has been defined. If the header has not been included previously in a file, the name `TIME_H` is defined by the `#define` directive and the header file statements are included. If the header has been included previously, `TIME_H` is defined already and the header file is not included again. Attempts to include a header file multiple times (inadvertently) typically occur in large programs with many header files that may themselves include other header files. [*Note:* The commonly used convention for the symbolic constant name in the preprocessor directives is simply the header file name in upper case with the underscore character replacing the period.]

Error-Prevention Tip 20.1

Use `#ifndef`, `#define` *and* `#endif` *preprocessor directives to form a preprocessor wrapper that prevents header files from being included more than once in a program.*

Good Programming Practice 20.2

Use the name of the header file in upper case with the period replaced by an underscore in the `#ifndef` *and* `#define` *preprocessor directives of a header file.*

Time *Class Member Functions*

In Fig. 20.2, the `Time` constructor (lines 14–17) initializes the data members to 0 (i.e., the universal-time equivalent of 12 AM). This ensures that the object begins in a consistent state. Invalid values cannot be stored in the data members of a `Time` object, because the constructor is called when the `Time` object is created, and all subsequent attempts by a client to modify

```
1   // Fig. 20.2: Time.cpp
2   // Member-function definitions for class Time.
3   #include <iostream>
4   using std::cout;
5
6   #include <iomanip>
7   using std::setfill;
8   using std::setw;
9
10  #include "Time.h" // include definition of class Time from Time.h
11
12  // Time constructor initializes each data member to zero.
13  // Ensures all Time objects start in a consistent state.
14  Time::Time()
15  {
16     hour = minute = second = 0;
17  } // end Time constructor
18
19  // set new Time value using universal time; ensure that
20  // the data remains consistent by setting invalid values to zero
21  void Time::setTime( int h, int m, int s )
22  {
23     hour = ( h >= 0 && h < 24 ) ? h : 0; // validate hour
24     minute = ( m >= 0 && m < 60 ) ? m : 0; // validate minute
25     second = ( s >= 0 && s < 60 ) ? s : 0; // validate second
26  } // end function setTime
27
28  // print Time in universal-time format (HH:MM:SS)
29  void Time::printUniversal()
30  {
31     cout << setfill( '0' ) << setw( 2 ) << hour << ":"
32        << setw( 2 ) << minute << ":" << setw( 2 ) << second;
33  } // end function printUniversal
34
35  // print Time in standard-time format (HH:MM:SS AM or PM)
36  void Time::printStandard()
37  {
38     cout << ( ( hour == 0 || hour == 12 ) ? 12 : hour % 12 ) << ":"
39        << setfill( '0' ) << setw( 2 ) << minute << ":" << setw( 2 )
40        << second << ( hour < 12 ? " AM" : " PM" );
41  } // end function printStandard
```

Fig. 20.2 | Time class member-function definitions.

the data members are scrutinized by function setTime (discussed shortly). Finally, it is important to note that the programmer can define several overloaded constructors for a class.

The data members of a class cannot be initialized where they are declared in the class body. It is strongly recommended that these data members be initialized by the class's constructor (as there is no default initialization for fundamental-type data members). Data members can also be assigned values by Time's *set* functions. [*Note:* Chapter 21 demonstrates that only a class's static const data members of integral or enum types can be initialized in the class's body.]

Common Programming Error 20.1

Attempting to initialize a non-static data member of a class explicitly in the class definition is a syntax error.

Function setTime (lines 21–26) is a public function that declares three int parameters and uses them to set the time. A conditional expression tests each argument to determine whether the value is in a specified range. For example, the hour value (line 23) must be greater than or equal to 0 and less than 24, because the universal-time format represents hours as integers from 0 to 23 (e.g., 1 PM is hour 13 and 11 PM is hour 23; midnight is hour 0 and noon is hour 12). Similarly, both minute and second values (lines 24 and 25) must be greater than or equal to 0 and less than 60. Any values outside these ranges are set to zero to ensure that a Time object always contains consistent data—that is, the object's data values are always kept in range, even if the values provided as arguments to function setTime were incorrect. In this example, zero is a consistent value for hour, minute and second.

A value passed to setTime is a correct value if it is in the allowed range for the member it is initializing. So, any number in the range 0–23 would be a correct value for the hour. A correct value is always a consistent value. However, a consistent value is not necessarily a correct value. If setTime sets hour to 0 because the argument received was out of range, then hour is correct only if the current time is coincidentally midnight.

Function printUniversal (lines 29–33 of Fig. 20.2) takes no arguments and outputs the date in universal-time format, consisting of three colon-separated pairs of digits—for the hour, minute and second, respectively. For example, if the time were 1:30:07 PM, function printUniversal would return 13:30:07. Note that line 31 uses parameterized stream manipulator setfill to specify the fill character that is displayed when an integer is output in a field wider than the number of digits in the value. By default, the fill characters appear to the left of the digits in the number. In this example, if the minute value is 2, it will be displayed as 02, because the fill character is set to zero ('0'). If the number being output fills the specified field, the fill character will not be displayed. Note that, once the fill character is specified with setfill, it applies for all subsequent values that are displayed in fields wider than the value being displayed (i.e., setfill is a "sticky" setting). This is in contrast to setw, which applies only to the next value displayed (setw is a "nonsticky" setting).

Error-Prevention Tip 20.2

Each sticky setting (such as a fill character or floating-point precision) should be restored to its previous setting when it is no longer needed. Failure to do so may result in incorrectly formatted output later in a program. Chapter 26, Stream Input/Output, discusses how to reset the fill character and precision.

Function printStandard (lines 36–41) takes no arguments and outputs the date in standard-time format, consisting of the hour, minute and second values separated by colons and followed by an AM or PM indicator (e.g., 1:27:06 PM). Like function print-Universal, function printStandard uses setfill('0') to format the minute and second as two digit values with leading zeros if necessary. Line 38 uses a conditional operator (?:) to determine the value of hour to be displayed—if the hour is 0 or 12 (AM or PM), it appears as 12; otherwise, the hour appears as a value from 1 to 11. The conditional operator in line 40 determines whether AM or PM will be displayed.

Defining Member Functions Outside the Class Definition; Class Scope

Even though a member function declared in a class definition may be defined outside that class definition (and "tied" to the class via the binary scope resolution operator), that member function is still within that class's scope; i.e., its name is known only to other members of the class unless referred to via an object of the class, a reference to an object of the class, a pointer to an object of the class or the binary scope resolution operator. We will say more about class scope shortly.

If a member function is defined in the body of a class definition, the C++ compiler attempts to inline calls to the member function. Member functions defined outside a class definition can be inlined by explicitly using keyword `inline`. Remember that the compiler reserves the right not to inline any function.

Performance Tip 20.1

Defining a member function inside the class definition inlines the member function (if the compiler chooses to do so). This can improve performance.

Software Engineering Observation 20.2

Defining a small member function inside the class definition does not promote the best software engineering, because clients of the class will be able to see the implementation of the function, and the client code must be recompiled if the function definition changes.

Software Engineering Observation 20.3

Only the simplest and most stable member functions (i.e., whose implementations are unlikely to change) should be defined in the class header.

Member Functions vs. Global Functions

It is interesting that the `printUniversal` and `printStandard` member functions take no arguments. This is because these member functions implicitly know that they are to print the data members of the particular `Time` object for which they are invoked. This can make member function calls more concise than conventional function calls in procedural programming.

Software Engineering Observation 20.4

Using an object-oriented programming approach can often simplify function calls by reducing the number of parameters to be passed. This benefit of object-oriented programming derives from the fact that encapsulating data members and member functions within an object gives the member functions the right to access the data members.

Software Engineering Observation 20.5

Member functions are usually shorter than functions in non-object-oriented programs, because the data stored in data members have ideally been validated by a constructor or by member functions that store new data. Because the data is already in the object, the member-function calls often have no arguments or at least have fewer arguments than typical function calls in non-object-oriented languages. Thus, the calls are shorter, the function definitions are shorter and the function prototypes are shorter. This facilitates many aspects of program development.

Error-Prevention Tip 20.3

The fact that member function calls generally take either no arguments or substantially fewer arguments than conventional function calls in non-object-oriented languages reduces the likelihood of passing the wrong arguments, the wrong types of arguments or the wrong number of arguments.

Using Class Time

Once class `Time` has been defined, it can be used as a type in object, array, pointer and reference declarations as follows:

```
Time sunset; // object of type Time
Time arrayOfTimes[ 5 ], // array of 5 Time objects
Time &dinnerTime = sunset; // reference to a Time object
Time *timePtr = &dinnerTime, // pointer to a Time object
```

Figure 20.3 uses class `Time`. Line 12 instantiates a single object of class `Time` called `t`. When the object is instantiated, the `Time` constructor is called to initialize each `private` data member to 0. Then, lines 16 and 18 print the time in universal and standard formats to confirm that the members were initialized properly. Line 20 sets a new time by calling member function `setTime`, and lines 24 and 26 print the time again in both formats. Line 28 attempts to use `setTime` to set the data members to invalid values—function `setTime` recognizes this and sets the invalid values to 0 to maintain the object in a consistent state. Finally, lines 33 and 35 print the time again in both formats.

Looking Ahead to Composition and Inheritance

Often, classes do not have to be created "from scratch." Rather, they can include objects of other classes as members or they may be **derived** from other classes that provide attributes and behaviors the new classes can use. Such software reuse can greatly enhance programmer productivity and simplify code maintenance. Including class objects as members of other classes is called **composition** (or **aggregation**) and is discussed in Chapter 21. Deriving new classes from existing classes is called **inheritance** and is discussed in Chapter 23.

Object Size

People new to object-oriented programming often suppose that objects must be quite large because they contain data members and member functions. Logically, this is true—the programmer may think of objects as containing data and functions (and our discussion has certainly encouraged this view); physically, however, this is not true.

Performance Tip 20.2

*Objects contain only data, so objects are much smaller than if they also contained member functions. Applying operator `sizeof` to a class name or to an object of that class will report only the size of the class's data members. The compiler creates one copy (only) of the member functions separate from all objects of the class. All objects of the class share this one copy. Each object, of course, needs its own copy of the class's data, because the data can vary among the objects. The function code is nonmodifiable (also called **reentrant code** or **pure procedure**) and, hence, can be shared among all objects of one class.*

20.3 Class Scope and Accessing Class Members

A class's data members (variables declared in the class definition) and member functions (functions declared in the class definition) belong to that class's scope. Nonmember functions are defined at **file scope**.

Within a class's scope, class members are immediately accessible by all of that class's member functions and can be referenced by name. Outside a class's scope, `public` class members are referenced through one of the **handles** on an object—an object name, a reference to an object or a pointer to an object. The type of the object, reference or pointer

```
1    // Fig. 20.3: fig20_03.cpp
2    // Program to test class Time.
3    // NOTE: This file must be compiled with Time.cpp.
4    #include <iostream>
5    using std::cout;
6    using std::endl;
7
8    #include "Time.h" // include definition of class Time from Time.h
9
10   int main()
11   {
12      Time t; // instantiate object t of class Time
13
14      // output Time object t's initial values
15      cout << "The initial universal time is ";
16      t.printUniversal(); // 00:00:00
17      cout << "\nThe initial standard time is ";
18      t.printStandard(); // 12:00:00 AM
19
20      t.setTime( 13, 27, 6 ); // change time
21
22      // output Time object t's new values
23      cout << "\n\nUniversal time after setTime is ";
24      t.printUniversal(); // 13:27:06
25      cout << "\nStandard time after setTime is ";
26      t.printStandard(); // 1:27:06 PM
27
28      t.setTime( 99, 99, 99 ); // attempt invalid settings
29
30      // output t's values after specifying invalid values
31      cout << "\n\nAfter attempting invalid settings:"
32         << "\nUniversal time: ";
33      t.printUniversal(); // 00:00:00
34      cout << "\nStandard time: ";
35      t.printStandard(); // 12:00:00 AM
36      cout << endl;
37      return 0;
38   } // end main
```

```
The initial universal time is 00:00:00
The initial standard time is 12:00:00 AM

Universal time after setTime is 13:27:06
Standard time after setTime is 1:27:06 PM

After attempting invalid settings:
Universal time: 00:00:00
Standard time: 12:00:00 AM
```

Fig. 20.3 | Program to test class Time.

specifies the interface (i.e., the member functions) accessible to the client. [We will see in Chapter 21 that an implicit handle is inserted by the compiler on every reference to a data member or member function from within an object.]

Member functions of a class can be overloaded, but only by other member functions of that class. To overload a member function, simply provide in the class definition a prototype for each version of the overloaded function, and provide a separate function definition for each version of the function.

Variables declared in a member function have block scope and are known only to that function. If a member function defines a variable with the same name as a variable with class scope, the class-scope variable is hidden by the block-scope variable in the block scope. Such a hidden variable can be accessed by preceding the variable name with the class name followed by the scope resolution operator (::). Hidden global variables can be accessed with the unary scope resolution operator (see Chapter 18).

The dot member-selection operator (.) is preceded by an object's name or with a reference to an object to access the object's members. The arrow member-selection operator (->) is preceded by a pointer to an object to access the object's members.

Figure 20.4 uses a simple class called Count (lines 8–25) with private data member x of type int (line 24), public member function setX (lines 12–15) and public member function print (lines 18–21) to illustrate accessing the members of a class with the member-selection operators. For simplicity, we have included this small class in the same file as the main function that uses it. Lines 29–31 create three variables related to type Count—counter (a Count object), counterPtr (a pointer to a Count object) and counterRef (a reference to a Count object). Variable counterRef refers to counter, and variable counterPtr points to counter. In lines 34–35 and 38–39, note that the program can invoke member functions setX and print by using the dot (.) member-selection operator preceded by either the name of the object (counter) or a reference to the object (counterRef, which is an alias for counter). Similarly, lines 42–43 demonstrate that the program can invoke member functions setX and print by using a pointer (countPtr) and the arrow (->) member-selection operator.

20.4 Separating Interface from Implementation

In Chapter 19, we began by including a class's definition and member-function definitions in one file. We then demonstrated separating this code into two files—a header file for the class definition (i.e., the class's interface) and a source-code file for the class's member-function definitions (i.e., the class's implementation). Recall that this makes it easier to modify programs—as far as clients of a class are concerned, changes in the class's implementation do not affect the client as long as the class's interface originally provided to the client remains unchanged.

Software Engineering Observation 20.6

Clients of a class do not need access to the class's source code in order to use the class. The clients do, however, need to be able to link to the class's object code (i.e., the compiled version of the class). This encourages independent software vendors (ISVs) to provide class libraries for sale or license. The ISVs provide in their products only the header files and the object modules. No proprietary information is revealed—as would be the case if source code were provided. The C++ user community benefits by having more ISV-produced class libraries available.

Actually, things are not quite this rosy. Header files do contain some portions of the implementation and hints about others. Inline member functions, for example, need to be in a header file, so that when the compiler compiles a client, the client can include the

```
1    // Fig. 20.4: fig20_04.cpp
2    // Demonstrating the class member access operators . and ->
3    #include <iostream>
4    using std::cout;
5    using std::endl;
6
7    // class Count definition
8    class Count
9    {
10   public: // public data is dangerous
11      // sets the value of private data member x
12      void setX( int value )
13      {
14         x = value;
15      } // end function setX
16
17      // prints the value of private data member x
18      void print()
19      {
20         cout << x << endl;
21      } // end function print
22
23   private:
24      int x;
25   }; // end class Count
26
27   int main()
28   {
29      Count counter; // create counter object
30      Count *counterPtr = &counter; // create pointer to counter
31      Count &counterRef = counter; // create reference to counter
32
33      cout << "Set x to 1 and print using the object's name: ";
34      counter.setX( 1 ); // set data member x to 1
35      counter.print(); // call member function print
36
37      cout << "Set x to 2 and print using a reference to an object: ";
38      counterRef.setX( 2 ); // set data member x to 2
39      counterRef.print(); // call member function print
40
41      cout << "Set x to 3 and print using a pointer to an object: ";
42      counterPtr->setX( 3 ); // set data member x to 3
43      counterPtr->print(); // call member function print
44      return 0;
45   } // end main
```

```
Set x to 1 and print using the object's name: 1
Set x to 2 and print using a reference to an object: 2
Set x to 3 and print using a pointer to an object: 3
```

Fig. 20.4 | Accessing an object's member functions through each type of object handle—the object's name, a reference to the object and a pointer to the object.

inline function definition in place. A class's `private` members are listed in the class definition in the header file, so these members are visible to clients even though the clients may not access the `private` members. In Chapter 21, we show how to use a "proxy class" to hide even the `private` data of a class from clients of the class.

Software Engineering Observation 20.7

Information important to the interface to a class should be included in the header file. Information that will be used only internally in the class and will not be needed by clients of the class should be included in the unpublished source file. This is yet another example of the principle of least privilege.

20.5 Access Functions and Utility Functions

Access functions can read or display data. Another common use for access functions is to test the truth or falsity of conditions—such functions are often called **predicate functions**. An example of a predicate function would be an `isEmpty` function for any container class—a class capable of holding many objects—such as a linked list, a stack or a queue. A program might test `isEmpty` before attempting to read another item from the container object. An `isFull` predicate function might test a container-class object to determine whether it has no additional room. Useful predicate functions for our `Time` class might be `isAM` and `isPM`.

The program of Figs. 20.5–20.7 demonstrates the notion of a utility function (also called a **helper function**). A utility function is not part of a class's `public` interface; rather, it is a `private` member function that supports the operation of the class's `public` member functions. Utility functions are not intended to be used by clients of a class (but can be used by `friends` of a class, as we will see in Chapter 21).

Class `SalesPerson` (Fig. 20.5) declares an array of 12 monthly sales figures (line 16) and the prototypes for the class's constructor and member functions that manipulate the array.

In Fig. 20.6, the `SalesPerson` constructor (lines 15–19) initializes array `sales` to zero. The `public` member function `setSales` (lines 36–43) sets the sales figure for one month

```
1   // Fig. 20.5: SalesPerson.h
2   // SalesPerson class definition.
3   // Member functions defined in SalesPerson.cpp.
4   #ifndef SALESP_H
5   #define SALESP_H
6
7   class SalesPerson
8   {
9   public:
10      SalesPerson(); // constructor
11      void getSalesFromUser(); // input sales from keyboard
12      void setSales( int, double ); // set sales for a specific month
13      void printAnnualSales(); // summarize and print sales
14   private:
15      double totalAnnualSales(); // prototype for utility function
16      double sales[ 12 ]; // 12 monthly sales figures
17   }; // end class SalesPerson
18
19   #endif
```

Fig. 20.5 | `SalesPerson` class definition.

```cpp
1   // Fig. 20.6: SalesPerson.cpp
2   // Member functions for class SalesPerson.
3   #include <iostream>
4   using std::cout;
5   using std::cin;
6   using std::endl;
7   using std::fixed;
8
9   #include <iomanip>
10  using std::setprecision;
11
12  #include "SalesPerson.h" // include SalesPerson class definition
13
14  // initialize elements of array sales to 0.0
15  SalesPerson::SalesPerson()
16  {
17     for ( int i = 0; i < 12; i++ )
18        sales[ i ] = 0.0;
19  } // end SalesPerson constructor
20
21  // get 12 sales figures from the user at the keyboard
22  void SalesPerson::getSalesFromUser()
23  {
24     double salesFigure;
25
26     for ( int i = 1; i <= 12; i++ )
27     {
28        cout << "Enter sales amount for month " << i << ": ";
29        cin >> salesFigure;
30        setSales( i, salesFigure );
31     } // end for
32  } // end function getSalesFromUser
33
34  // set one of the 12 monthly sales figures; function subtracts
35  // one from month value for proper subscript in sales array
36  void SalesPerson::setSales( int month, double amount )
37  {
38     // test for valid month and amount values
39     if ( month >= 1 && month <= 12 && amount > 0 )
40        sales[ month - 1 ] = amount; // adjust for subscripts 0-11
41     else // invalid month or amount value
42        cout << "Invalid month or sales figure" << endl;
43  } // end function setSales
44
45  // print total annual sales (with the help of utility function)
46  void SalesPerson::printAnnualSales()
47  {
48     cout << setprecision( 2 ) << fixed
49        << "\nThe total annual sales are: $"
50        << totalAnnualSales() << endl; // call utility function
51  } // end function printAnnualSales
52
```

Fig. 20.6 | SalesPerson class member-function definitions. (Part 1 of 2.)

```
53    // private utility function to total annual sales
54    double SalesPerson::totalAnnualSales()
55    {
56       double total = 0.0; // initialize total
57
58       for ( int i = 0; i < 12; i++ ) // summarize sales results
59          total += sales[ i ]; // add month i sales to total
60
61       return total;
62    } // end function totalAnnualSales
```

Fig. 20.6 | SalesPerson class member-function definitions. (Part 2 of 2.)

in array sales. The public member function printAnnualSales (lines 46–51) prints the total sales for the last 12 months. The private utility function totalAnnualSales (lines 54–62) totals the 12 monthly sales figures for the benefit of printAnnualSales. Member function printAnnualSales edits the sales figures into monetary format.

In Fig. 20.7, note that the application's main function includes only a simple sequence of member-function calls—there are no control statements. The logic of manipulating the sales array is completely encapsulated in class SalesPerson's member functions.

Software Engineering Observation 20.8

A phenomenon of object-oriented programming is that once a class is defined, creating and manipulating objects of that class often involve issuing only a simple sequence of member-function calls—few, if any, control statements are needed. By contrast, it is common to have control statements in the implementation of a class's member functions.

20.6 Time Class Case Study: Constructors with Default Arguments

The program of Figs. 20.8–20.10 enhances class Time to demonstrate how arguments are implicitly passed to a constructor. The constructor defined in Fig. 20.2 initialized hour,

```
1    // Fig. 20.7: fig20_07.cpp
2    // Demonstrating a utility function.
3    // Compile this program with SalesPerson.cpp
4
5    // include SalesPerson class definition from SalesPerson.h
6    #include "SalesPerson.h"
7
8    int main()
9    {
10       SalesPerson s; // create SalesPerson object s
11
12       s.getSalesFromUser(); // note simple sequential code;
13       s.printAnnualSales(); // no control statements in main
14       return 0;
15    } // end main
```

Fig. 20.7 | Utility function demonstration. (Part 1 of 2.)

```
Enter sales amount for month 1: 5314.76
Enter sales amount for month 2: 4292.38
Enter sales amount for month 3: 4589.83
Enter sales amount for month 4: 5534.03
Enter sales amount for month 5: 4376.34
Enter sales amount for month 6: 5698.45
Enter sales amount for month 7: 4439.22
Enter sales amount for month 8: 5893.57
Enter sales amount for month 9: 4909.67
Enter sales amount for month 10: 5123.45
Enter sales amount for month 11: 4024.97
Enter sales amount for month 12: 5923.92

The total annual sales are: $60120.59
```

Fig. 20.7 | Utility function demonstration. (Part 2 of 2.)

```
1   // Fig. 20.8: Time.h
2   // Declaration of class Time.
3   // Member functions defined in Time.cpp.
4
5   // prevent multiple inclusions of header file
6   #ifndef TIME_H
7   #define TIME_H
8
9   // Time abstract data type definition
10  class Time
11  {
12  public:
13     Time( int = 0, int = 0, int = 0 ); // default constructor
14
15     // set functions
16     void setTime( int, int, int ); // set hour, minute, second
17     void setHour( int ); // set hour (after validation)
18     void setMinute( int ); // set minute (after validation)
19     void setSecond( int ); // set second (after validation)
20
21     // get functions
22     int getHour(); // return hour
23     int getMinute(); // return minute
24     int getSecond(); // return second
25
26     void printUniversal(); // output time in universal-time format
27     void printStandard(); // output time in standard-time format
28  private:
29     int hour; // 0 - 23 (24-hour clock format)
30     int minute; // 0 - 59
31     int second; // 0 - 59
32  }; // end class Time
33
34  #endif
```

Fig. 20.8 | Time class containing a constructor with default arguments.

minute and second to 0 (i.e., midnight in universal time). Like other functions, constructors can specify default arguments. Line 13 of Fig. 20.8 declares the Time constructor to include default arguments, specifying a default value of zero for each argument passed to the constructor. In Fig. 20.9, lines 14–17 define the new version of the Time constructor that

```cpp
 1   // Fig. 20.9: Time.cpp
 2   // Member-function definitions for class Time.
 3   #include <iostream>
 4   using std::cout;
 5
 6   #include <iomanip>
 7   using std::setfill;
 8   using std::setw;
 9
10   #include "Time.h" // include definition of class Time from Time.h
11
12   // Time constructor initializes each data member to zero;
13   // ensures that Time objects start in a consistent state
14   Time::Time( int hr, int min, int sec )
15   {
16      setTime( hr, min, sec ); // validate and set time
17   } // end Time constructor
18
19   // set new Time value using universal time; ensure that
20   // the data remains consistent by setting invalid values to zero
21   void Time::setTime( int h, int m, int s )
22   {
23      setHour( h ); // set private field hour
24      setMinute( m ); // set private field minute
25      setSecond( s ); // set private field second
26   } // end function setTime
27
28   // set hour value
29   void Time::setHour( int h )
30   {
31      hour = ( h >= 0 && h < 24 ) ? h : 0; // validate hour
32   } // end function setHour
33
34   // set minute value
35   void Time::setMinute( int m )
36   {
37      minute = ( m >= 0 && m < 60 ) ? m : 0; // validate minute
38   } // end function setMinute
39
40   // set second value
41   void Time::setSecond( int s )
42   {
43      second = ( s >= 0 && s < 60 ) ? s : 0; // validate second
44   } // end function setSecond
45
```

Fig. 20.9 | Time class member-function definitions including a constructor that takes arguments. (Part 1 of 2.)

```
46   // return hour value
47   int Time::getHour()
48   {
49      return hour;
50   } // end function getHour
51
52   // return minute value
53   int Time::getMinute()
54   {
55      return minute;
56   } // end function getMinute
57
58   // return second value
59   int Time::getSecond()
60   {
61      return second;
62   } // end function getSecond
63
64   // print Time in universal-time format (HH:MM:SS)
65   void Time::printUniversal()
66   {
67      cout << setfill( '0' ) << setw( 2 ) << getHour() << ":"
68         << setw( 2 ) << getMinute() << ":" << setw( 2 ) << getSecond();
69   } // end function printUniversal
70
71   // print Time in standard-time format (HH:MM:SS AM or PM)
72   void Time::printStandard()
73   {
74      cout << ( ( getHour() == 0 || getHour() == 12 ) ? 12 : getHour() % 12 )
75         << ":" << setfill( '0' ) << setw( 2 ) << getMinute()
76         << ":" << setw( 2 ) << getSecond() << ( hour < 12 ? " AM" : " PM" );
77   } // end function printStandard
```

Fig. 20.9 | Time class member-function definitions including a constructor that takes arguments. (Part 2 of 2.)

receives values for parameters hr, min and sec that will be used to initialize private data members hour, minute and second, respectively. Note that class Time provides *set* and *get* functions for each data member. The Time constructor now calls setTime, which calls the setHour, setMinute and setSecond functions to validate and assign values to the data members. The default arguments to the constructor ensure that, even if no values are provided in a constructor call, the constructor still initializes the data members to maintain the Time object in a consistent state. A constructor that defaults all its arguments is also a default constructor—i.e., a constructor that can be invoked with no arguments. There can be a maximum of one default constructor per class.

In Fig. 20.9, line 16 of the constructor calls member function setTime with the values passed to the constructor (or the default values). Function setTime calls setHour to ensure that the value supplied for hour is in the range 0–23, then calls setMinute and setSecond to ensure that the values for minute and second are each in the range 0–59. If a value is out of range, that value is set to zero (to ensure that each data member remains in a consistent state). In Chapter 27, Exception Handling, we throw exceptions to inform the user that a value is out of range, rather than simply assigning a default consistent value.

Note that the Time constructor could be written to include the same statements as member function setTime, or even the individual statements in the setHour, setMinute and setSecond functions. Calling setHour, setMinute and setSecond from the constructor may be slightly more efficient because the extra call to setTime would be eliminated. Similarly, copying the code from lines 31, 37 and 43 into constructor would eliminate the overhead of calling setTime, setHour, setMinute and setSecond. Coding the Time constructor or member function setTime as a copy of the code in lines 31, 37 and 43 would make maintenance of this class more difficult. If the implementations of setHour, setMinute and setSecond were to change, the implementation of any member function that duplicates lines 31, 37 and 43 would have to change accordingly. Having the Time constructor call setTime and having setTime call setHour, setMinute and set-Second enables us to limit the changes to code that validates the hour, minute or second to the corresponding *set* function. This reduces the likelihood of errors when altering the class's implementation. Also, the performance of the Time constructor and setTime can be enhanced by explicitly declaring them inline or by defining them in the class definition (which implicitly inlines the function definition).

Software Engineering Observation 20.9

If a member function of a class already provides all or part of the functionality required by a constructor (or other member function) of the class, call that member function from the constructor (or other member function). This simplifies the maintenance of the code and reduces the likelihood of an error if the implementation of the code is modified. As a general rule: Avoid repeating code.

Software Engineering Observation 20.10

Any change to the default argument values of a function requires the client code to be recompiled (to ensure that the program still functions correctly).

Function main in Fig. 20.10 initializes five Time objects—one with all three arguments defaulted in the implicit constructor call (line 11), one with one argument specified (line

```
1   // Fig. 20.10: fig20_10.cpp
2   // Demonstrating a default constructor for class Time.
3   #include <iostream>
4   using std::cout;
5   using std::endl;
6
7   #include "Time.h" // include definition of class Time from Time.h
8
9   int main()
10  {
11      Time t1; // all arguments defaulted
12      Time t2( 2 ); // hour specified; minute and second defaulted
13      Time t3( 21, 34 ); // hour and minute specified; second defaulted
14      Time t4( 12, 25, 42 ); // hour, minute and second specified
15      Time t5( 27, 74, 99 ); // all bad values specified
16
```

Fig. 20.10 | Constructor with default arguments. (Part 1 of 2.)

```
17    cout << "Constructed with:\n\nt1: all arguments defaulted\n   ";
18    t1.printUniversal(); // 00:00:00
19    cout << "\n   ";
20    t1.printStandard(); // 12:00:00 AM
21
22    cout << "\n\nt2: hour specified; minute and second defaulted\n   ";
23    t2.printUniversal(); // 02:00:00
24    cout << "\n   ";
25    t2.printStandard(); // 2:00:00 AM
26
27    cout << "\n\nt3: hour and minute specified; second defaulted\n   ";
28    t3.printUniversal(); // 21:34:00
29    cout << "\n   ";
30    t3.printStandard(); // 9:34:00 PM
31
32    cout << "\n\nt4: hour, minute and second specified\n   ";
33    t4.printUniversal(); // 12:25:42
34    cout << "\n   ";
35    t4.printStandard(); // 12:25:42 PM
36
37    cout << "\n\nt5: all invalid values specified\n   ";
38    t5.printUniversal(); // 00:00:00
39    cout << "\n   ";
40    t5.printStandard(); // 12:00:00 AM
41    cout << endl;
42    return 0;
43 } // end main
```

```
Constructed with:

t1: all arguments defaulted
   00:00:00
   12:00:00 AM

t2: hour specified; minute and second defaulted
   02:00:00
   2:00:00 AM

t3: hour and minute specified; second defaulted
   21:34:00
   9:34:00 PM

t4: hour, minute and second specified
   12:25:42
   12:25:42 PM

t5: all invalid values specified
   00:00:00
   12:00:00 AM
```

Fig. 20.10 | Constructor with default arguments. (Part 2 of 2.)

12), one with two arguments specified (line 13), one with three arguments specified (line 14) and one with three invalid arguments specified (line 15). Then the program displays each object in universal-time and standard-time formats.

Notes Regarding Class *Time's* **set** *and* **get** *Functions and Constructor*

Time's *set* and *get* functions are called throughout the body of the class. In particular, function setTime (lines 21–26 of Fig. 20.9) calls functions setHour, setMinute and setSecond, and functions printUniversal and printStandard call functions getHour, getMinute and get-Second in line 67–68 and lines 74–76, respectively. In each case, these functions could have accessed the class's private data directly without calling the *set* and *get* functions. However, consider changing the representation of the time from three int values (requiring 12 bytes of memory) to a single int value representing the total number of seconds that have elapsed since midnight (requiring only four bytes of memory). If we made such a change, only the bodies of the functions that access the private data directly would need to change—in particular, the individual *set* and *get* functions for the hour, minute and second. There would be no need to modify the bodies of functions setTime, printUniversal or printStandard, because they do not access the data directly. Designing the class in this manner reduces the likelihood of programming errors when altering the class's implementation.

Similarly, the Time constructor could be written to include a copy of the appropriate statements from function setTime. Doing so may be slightly more efficient, because the extra constructor call and call to setTime are eliminated. However, duplicating statements in multiple functions or constructors makes changing the class's internal data representation more difficult. Having the Time constructor call function setTime directly requires any changes to the implementation of setTime to be made only once.

Common Programming Error 20.2

A constructor can call other member functions of the class, such as set *or* get *functions, but because the constructor is initializing the object, the data members may not yet be in a consistent state. Using data members before they have been properly initialized can cause logic errors.*

20.7 Destructors

A **destructor** is another type of special member function. The name of the destructor for a class is the **tilde character** (~) followed by the class name. This naming convention has intuitive appeal, because as we will see in a later chapter, the tilde operator is the bitwise complement operator, and, in a sense, the destructor is the complement of the constructor. Note that a destructor is often referred to with the abbreviation "dtor" in the literature. We prefer not to use this abbreviation.

A class's destructor is called implicitly when an object is destroyed. This occurs, for example, as an automatic object is destroyed when program execution leaves the scope in which that object was instantiated. *The destructor itself does not actually release the object's memory*—it performs **termination housekeeping** before the system reclaims the object's memory, so the memory may be reused to hold new objects.

A destructor receives no parameters and returns no value. A destructor may not specify a return type—not even void. A class may have only one destructor—destructor overloading is not allowed.

Common Programming Error 20.3

It is a syntax error to attempt to pass arguments to a destructor, to specify a return type for a destructor (even void cannot be specified), to return values from a destructor or to overload a destructor.

Even though destructors have not been provided for the classes presented so far, every class has a destructor. If the programmer does not explicitly provide a destructor, the compiler creates an "empty" destructor. [*Note:* We will see that such an implicitly created destructor does, in fact, perform important operations on objects that are created through composition (Chapter 21) and inheritance (Chapter 23).] In Chapter 22, we will build destructors appropriate for classes whose objects contain dynamically allocated memory (e.g., for arrays and strings) or use other system resources (e.g., files on disk). We discuss how to dynamically allocate and deallocate memory in Chapter 21.

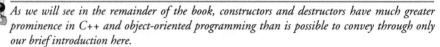

Software Engineering Observation 20.11

As we will see in the remainder of the book, constructors and destructors have much greater prominence in C++ and object-oriented programming than is possible to convey through only our brief introduction here.

20.8 When Constructors and Destructors Are Called

Constructors and destructors are called implicitly by the compiler. The order in which these function calls occur depends on the order in which execution enters and leaves the scopes where the objects are instantiated. Generally, destructor calls are made in the reverse order of the corresponding constructor calls, but as we will see in Figs. 20.11–20.13, the storage classes of objects can alter the order in which destructors are called.

Constructors are called for objects defined in global scope before any other function (including main) in that file begins execution (although the order of execution of global object constructors between files is not guaranteed). The corresponding destructors are called when main terminates. Function exit forces a program to terminate immediately and does not execute the destructors of automatic objects. The function often is used to terminate a program when an error is detected in the input or if a file to be processed by the program cannot be opened. Function abort performs similarly to function exit but forces the program to terminate immediately, without allowing the destructors of any objects to be called. Function abort is usually used to indicate an abnormal termination of the program.

The constructor for an automatic local object is called when execution reaches the point where that object is defined—the corresponding destructor is called when execution leaves the object's scope (i.e., the block in which that object is defined has finished executing). Constructors and destructors for automatic objects are called each time execution enters and leaves the scope of the object. Destructors are not called for automatic objects if the program terminates with a call to function exit or function abort.

The constructor for a static local object is called only once, when execution first reaches the point where the object is defined—the corresponding destructor is called when main terminates or the program calls function exit. Global and static objects are destroyed in the reverse order of their creation. Destructors are not called for static objects if the program terminates with a call to function abort.

The program of Figs. 20.11–20.13 demonstrates the order in which constructors and destructors are called for objects of class CreateAndDestroy (Fig. 20.11 and Fig. 20.12) of various storage classes in several scopes. Each object of class CreateAndDestroy contains (lines 16–17) an integer (objectID) and a string (message) that are used in the program's output to identify the object. This mechanical example is purely for pedagogic purposes. For this reason, line 23 of the destructor in Fig. 20.12 determines whether the object being destroyed has an objectID value 1 or 6 and, if so, outputs a newline character. This line helps make the program's output easier to follow.

```
1   // Fig. 20.11: CreateAndDestroy.h
2   // Definition of class CreateAndDestroy.
3   // Member functions defined in CreateAndDestroy.cpp.
4   #include <string>
5   using std::string;
6
7   #ifndef CREATE_H
8   #define CREATE_H
9
10  class CreateAndDestroy
11  {
12  public:
13     CreateAndDestroy( int, string ); // constructor
14     ~CreateAndDestroy(); // destructor
15  private:
16     int objectID; // ID number for object
17     string message; // message describing object
18  }; // end class CreateAndDestroy
19
20  #endif
```

Fig. 20.11 | CreateAndDestroy class definition.

```
1   // Fig. 20.12: CreateAndDestroy.cpp
2   // Member-function definitions for class CreateAndDestroy.
3   #include <iostream>
4   using std::cout;
5   using std::endl;
6
7   #include "CreateAndDestroy.h"// include CreateAndDestroy class definition
8
9   // constructor
10  CreateAndDestroy::CreateAndDestroy( int ID, string messageString )
11  {
12     objectID = ID; // set object's ID number
13     message = messageString; // set object's descriptive message
14
15     cout << "Object " << objectID << "  constructor runs  "
16        << message << endl;
17  } // end CreateAndDestroy constructor
18
19  // destructor
20  CreateAndDestroy::~CreateAndDestroy()
21  {
22     // output newline for certain objects; helps readability
23     cout << ( objectID == 1 || objectID == 6 ? "\n" : "" );
24
25     cout << "Object " << objectID << "  destructor runs  "
26        << message << endl;
27  } // end ~CreateAndDestroy destructor
```

Fig. 20.12 | CreateAndDestroy class member-function definitions.

Figure 20.13 defines object first (line 12) in global scope. Its constructor is actually called before any statements in main execute and its destructor is called at program termination after the destructors for all other objects have run.

Function main (lines 14–26) declares three objects. Objects second (line 17) and fourth (line 23) are local automatic objects, and object third (line 18) is a static local object. The constructor for each of these objects is called when execution reaches the point where that object is declared. The destructors for objects fourth and then second are called (i.e., the reverse of the order in which their constructors were called) when execution reaches the end of main. Because object third is static, it exists until program termination. The destructor for object third is called before the destructor for global object first, but after all other objects are destroyed.

Function create (lines 29–36) declares three objects—fifth (line 32) and seventh (line 34) as local automatic objects, and sixth (line 33) as a static local object. The

```
1   // Fig. 20.13: fig20_13.cpp
2   // Demonstrating the order in which constructors and
3   // destructors are called.
4   #include <iostream>
5   using std::cout;
6   using std::endl;
7
8   #include "CreateAndDestroy.h" // include CreateAndDestroy class definition
9
10  void create( void ); // prototype
11
12  CreateAndDestroy first( 1, "(global before main)" ); // global object
13
14  int main()
15  {
16     cout << "\nMAIN FUNCTION: EXECUTION BEGINS" << endl;
17     CreateAndDestroy second( 2, "(local automatic in main)" );
18     static CreateAndDestroy third( 3, "(local static in main)" );
19
20     create(); // call function to create objects
21
22     cout << "\nMAIN FUNCTION: EXECUTION RESUMES" << endl;
23     CreateAndDestroy fourth( 4, "(local automatic in main)" );
24     cout << "\nMAIN FUNCTION: EXECUTION ENDS" << endl;
25     return 0;
26  } // end main
27
28  // function to create objects
29  void create( void )
30  {
31     cout << "\nCREATE FUNCTION: EXECUTION BEGINS" << endl;
32     CreateAndDestroy fifth( 5, "(local automatic in create)" );
33     static CreateAndDestroy sixth( 6, "(local static in create)" );
34     CreateAndDestroy seventh( 7, "(local automatic in create)" );
35     cout << "\nCREATE FUNCTION: EXECUTION ENDS" << endl;
36  } // end function create
```

Fig. 20.13 | Order in which constructors and destructors are called. (Part 1 of 2.)

```
Object 1   constructor runs   (global before main)

MAIN FUNCTION: EXECUTION BEGINS
Object 2   constructor runs   (local automatic in main)
Object 3   constructor runs   (local static in main)

CREATE FUNCTION: EXECUTION BEGINS
Object 5   constructor runs   (local automatic in create)
Object 6   constructor runs   (local static in create)
Object 7   constructor runs   (local automatic in create)

CREATE FUNCTION: EXECUTION ENDS
Object 7   destructor runs    (local automatic in create)
Object 5   destructor runs    (local automatic in create)

MAIN FUNCTION: EXECUTION RESUMES
Object 4   constructor runs   (local automatic in main)

MAIN FUNCTION: EXECUTION ENDS
Object 4   destructor runs    (local automatic in main)
Object 2   destructor runs    (local automatic in main)

Object 6   destructor runs    (local static in create)
Object 3   destructor runs    (local static in main)

Object 1   destructor runs    (global before main)
```

Fig. 20.13 | Order in which constructors and destructors are called. (Part 2 of 2.)

destructors for objects seventh and then fifth are called (i.e., the reverse of the order in which their constructors were called) when create terminates. Because sixth is static, it exists until program termination. The destructor for sixth is called before the destructors for third and first, but after all other objects are destroyed.

20.9 Time Class Case Study: A Subtle Trap—Returning a Reference to a private Data Member

A reference to an object is an alias for the name of the object and, hence, may be used on the left side of an assignment statement. In this context, the reference makes a perfectly acceptable *lvalue* that can receive a value. One way to use this capability (unfortunately!) is to have a public member function of a class return a reference to a private data member of that class. Note that if a function returns a const reference, that reference cannot be used as a modifiable *lvalue*.

The program of Figs. 20.14–20.16 uses a simplified Time class (Fig. 20.14 and Fig. 20.15) to demonstrate returning a reference to a private data member with member function badSetHour (declared in Fig. 20.14 at line 15 and defined in Fig. 20.15 at lines 29–33). Such a reference return actually makes a call to member function badSetHour an alias for private data member hour! The function call can be used in any way that the private data member can be used, including as an *lvalue* in an assignment statement, thus enabling clients of the class to clobber the class's private data at will! Note that the same problem would occur if a pointer to the private data were to be returned by the function.

```
 1   // Fig. 20.14: Time.h
 2   // Declaration of class Time.
 3   // Member functions defined in Time.cpp
 4
 5   // prevent multiple inclusions of header file
 6   #ifndef TIME_H
 7   #define TIME_H
 8
 9   class Time
10   {
11   public:
12      Time( int = 0, int = 0, int = 0 );
13      void setTime( int, int, int );
14      int getHour();
15      int &badSetHour( int ); // DANGEROUS reference return
16   private:
17      int hour;
18      int minute;
19      int second;
20   }; // end class Time
21
22   #endif
```

Fig. 20.14 | Returning a reference to a private data member.

```
 1   // Fig. 20.15: Time.cpp
 2   // Member-function definitions for Time class.
 3   #include "Time.h" // include definition of class Time
 4
 5   // constructor function to initialize private data;
 6   // calls member function setTime to set variables;
 7   // default values are 0 (see class definition)
 8   Time::Time( int hr, int min, int sec )
 9   {
10      setTime( hr, min, sec );
11   } // end Time constructor
12
13   // set values of hour, minute and second
14   void Time::setTime( int h, int m, int s )
15   {
16      hour = ( h >= 0 && h < 24 ) ? h : 0; // validate hour
17      minute = ( m >= 0 && m < 60 ) ? m : 0; // validate minute
18      second = ( s >= 0 && s < 60 ) ? s : 0; // validate second
19   } // end function setTime
20
21   // return hour value
22   int Time::getHour()
23   {
24      return hour;
25   } // end function getHour
26
```

Fig. 20.15 | Returning a reference to a private data member. (Part 1 of 2.)

```
27   // POOR PROGRAMMING PRACTICE:
28   // Returning a reference to a private data member.
29   int &Time::badSetHour( int hh )
30   {
31      hour = ( hh >= 0 && hh < 24 ) ? hh : 0;
32      return hour; // DANGEROUS reference return
33   } // end function badSetHour
```

Fig. 20.15 | Returning a reference to a `private` data member. (Part 2 of 2.)

Figure 20.16 declares `Time` object `t` (line 12) and reference `hourRef` (line 15), which is initialized with the reference returned by the call `t.badSetHour(20)`. Line 17 displays the value of the alias `hourRef`. This shows how `hourRef` breaks the encapsulation of the class—statements in `main` should not have access to the `private` data of the class. Next, line 18 uses the alias to set the value of `hour` to 30 (an invalid value) and line 19 displays the value returned by function `getHour` to show that assigning a value to `hourRef` actually modifies the `private` data in the `Time` object `t`. Finally, line 23 uses the `badSetHour` function call itself as an *lvalue* and assigns 74 (another invalid value) to the reference returned by the function.

```
1    // Fig. 20.16: fig20_16.cpp
2    // Demonstrating a public member function that
3    // returns a reference to a private data member.
4    #include <iostream>
5    using std::cout;
6    using std::endl;
7
8    #include "Time.h" // include definition of class Time
9
10   int main()
11   {
12      Time t; // create Time object
13
14      // initialize hourRef with the reference returned by badSetHour
15      int &hourRef = t.badSetHour( 20 ); // 20 is a valid hour
16
17      cout << "Valid hour before modification: " << hourRef;
18      hourRef = 30; // use hourRef to set invalid value in Time object t
19      cout << "\nInvalid hour after modification: " << t.getHour();
20
21      // Dangerous: Function call that returns
22      // a reference can be used as an lvalue!
23      t.badSetHour( 12 ) = 74; // assign another invalid value to hour
24
25      cout << "\n\n********************************************************\n"
26         << "POOR PROGRAMMING PRACTICE!!!!!!!!\n"
27         << "t.badSetHour( 12 ) as an lvalue, invalid hour: "
28         << t.getHour()
29         << "\n********************************************************" << endl;
30      return 0;
31   } // end main
```

Fig. 20.16 | Returning a reference to a `private` data member. (Part 1 of 2.)

```
Valid hour before modification: 20
Invalid hour after modification: 30

**************************************************
POOR PROGRAMMING PRACTICE!!!!!!!!
t.badSetHour( 12 ) as an lvalue, invalid hour: 74
**************************************************
```

Fig. 20.16 | Returning a reference to a `private` data member. (Part 2 of 2.)

Line 28 again displays the value returned by function `getHour` to show that assigning a value to the result of the function call in line 23 modifies the `private` data in the `Time` object `t`.

Error-Prevention Tip 20.4

Returning a reference or a pointer to a private data member breaks the encapsulation of the class and makes the client code dependent on the representation of the class's data. So, returning pointers or references to private data is a dangerous practice that should be avoided.

20.10 Default Memberwise Assignment

The assignment operator (=) can be used to assign an object to another object of the same type. By default, such assignment is performed by **memberwise assignment**—each data member of the object on the right of the assignment operator is assigned individually to the same data member in the object on the left of the assignment operator. Figures 20.17–20.18 define class `Date` for use in this example. Line 20 of Fig. 20.19 uses default memberwise assignment to assign the data members of `Date` object `date1` to the

```
 1   // Fig. 20.17: Date.h
 2   // Declaration of class Date.
 3   // Member functions are defined in Date.cpp
 4
 5   // prevent multiple inclusions of header file
 6   #ifndef DATE_H
 7   #define DATE_H
 8
 9   // class Date definition
10   class Date
11   {
12   public:
13      Date( int = 1, int = 1, int = 2000 ); // default constructor
14      void print();
15   private:
16      int month;
17      int day;
18      int year;
19   }; // end class Date
20
21   #endif
```

Fig. 20.17 | Date class header file.

```
1   // Fig. 20.18: Date.cpp
2   // Member-function definitions for class Date.
3   #include <iostream>
4   using std::cout;
5   using std::endl;
6
7   #include "Date.h" // include definition of class Date from Date.h
8
9   // Date constructor (should do range checking)
10  Date::Date( int m, int d, int y )
11  {
12     month = m;
13     day = d;
14     year = y;
15  } // end constructor Date
16
17  // print Date in the format mm/dd/yyyy
18  void Date::print()
19  {
20     cout << month << '/' << day << '/' << year;
21  } // end function print
```

Fig. 20.18 | Date class member-function definitions.

```
1   // Fig. 20.19: fig20_19.cpp
2   // Demonstrating that class objects can be assigned
3   // to each other using default memberwise assignment.
4   #include <iostream>
5   using std::cout;
6   using std::endl;
7
8   #include "Date.h" // include definition of class Date from Date.h
9
10  int main()
11  {
12     Date date1( 7, 4, 2004 );
13     Date date2; // date2 defaults to 1/1/2000
14
15     cout << "date1 = ";
16     date1.print();
17     cout << "\ndate2 = ";
18     date2.print();
19
20     date2 = date1; // default memberwise assignment
21
22     cout << "\n\nAfter default memberwise assignment, date2 = ";
23     date2.print();
24     cout << endl;
25     return 0;
26  } // end main
```

Fig. 20.19 | Default memberwise assignment. (Part 1 of 2.)

```
date1 = 7/4/2004
date2 = 1/1/2000

After default memberwise assignment, date2 = 7/4/2004
```

Fig. 20.19 | Default memberwise assignment. (Part 2 of 2.)

corresponding data members of `Date` object `date2`. In this case, the `month` member of `date1` is assigned to the `month` member of `date2`, the day member of `date1` is assigned to the day member of `date2` and the `year` member of `date1` is assigned to the `year` member of `date2`. [*Caution:* Memberwise assignment can cause serious problems when used with a class whose data members contain pointers to dynamically allocated memory; we discuss these problems in Chapter 22 and show how to deal with them.] Notice that the `Date` constructor does not contain any error checking; we leave this to the exercises.

Objects may be passed as function arguments and may be returned from functions. Such passing and returning is performed using pass-by-value by default—a copy of the object is passed or returned. In such cases, C++ creates a new object and uses a copy constructor to copy the original object's values into the new object. For each class, the compiler provides a default copy constructor that copies each member of the original object into the corresponding member of the new object. Like memberwise assignment, copy constructors can cause serious problems when used with a class whose data members contain pointers to dynamically allocated memory. Chapter 22 discusses how programmers can define a customized copy constructor that properly copies objects containing pointers to dynamically allocated memory.

Performance Tip 20.3

Passing an object by value is good from a security standpoint, because the called function has no access to the original object in the caller, but pass-by-value can degrade performance when making a copy of a large object. An object can be passed by reference by passing either a pointer or a reference to the object. Pass-by-reference offers good performance but is weaker from a security standpoint, because the called function is given access to the original object. Pass-by-const-reference is a safe, good-performing alternative (this can be implemented with a const reference parameter or with a pointer-to-const-data parameter).

20.11 Software Reusability

People who write object-oriented programs concentrate on implementing useful classes. There is a tremendous motivation to capture and catalog classes so that they can be accessed by large segments of the programming community. Many substantial class libraries exist and others are being developed worldwide. Software is increasingly being constructed from existing, well-defined, carefully tested, well-documented, portable, high-performance, widely available components. This kind of software reusability speeds the development of powerful, high-quality software. Rapid applications development (RAD) through the mechanisms of reusable componentry has become an important field.

Significant problems must be solved, however, before the full potential of software reusability can be realized. We need cataloging schemes, licensing schemes, protection mechanisms to ensure that master copies of classes are not corrupted, description schemes so that designers of new systems can easily determine whether existing objects meet their needs, browsing mechanisms to determine what classes are available and how closely they meet software developer requirements and the like. Many interesting research and development problems need to be solved. There is great motivation to solve these problems, because the potential value of their solutions is enormous.

20.12 Wrap-Up

This chapter deepened our coverage of classes, using a rich Time class case study to introduce several new features of classes. You saw that member functions are usually shorter than global functions because member functions can directly access an object's data members, so the member functions can receive fewer arguments than functions in procedural programming languages. You learned how to use the arrow operator to access an object's members via a pointer of the object's class type.

You learned that member functions have class scope—i.e., the member function's name is known only to other members of the class unless referred to via an object of the class, a reference to an object of the class, a pointer to an object of the class or the binary scope resolution operator. We also discussed access functions (commonly used to retrieve the values of data members or to test the truth or falsity of conditions) and utility functions (private member functions that support the operation of the class's public member functions).

You learned that a constructor can specify default arguments that enable it to be called in a variety of ways. You also learned that any constructor that can be called with no arguments is a default constructor and that there can be a maximum of one default constructor per class. We discussed destructors and their purpose of performing termination housekeeping on an object of a class before that object is destroyed. We also demonstrated the order in which an object's constructors and destructors are called.

We demonstrated the problems that can occur when a member function returns a reference to a private data member, which breaks the encapsulation of the class. We also showed that objects of the same type can be assigned to one another using default memberwise assignment. Finally, we discussed the benefits of using class libraries to enhance the speed with which code can be created and to increase the quality of software.

Chapter 21 presents additional class features. We will demonstrate how const can be used to indicate that a member function does not modify an object of a class. You will learn how to build classes with composition—that is, classes that contain objects of other classes as members. We'll show how a class can allow so-called "friend" functions to access the class's non-public members. We'll also show how a class's non-static member functions can use a special pointer named this to access an object's members. Next, you'll learn how to use C++'s new and delete operators, which enable programmers to obtain and release memory as necessary during a program's execution.

Summary

Section 20.2 Time Class Case Study
- The preprocessor directives #ifndef (which means "if not defined") and #endif are used to prevent multiple inclusions of a header file. If the code between these directives has not previously

been included in an application, `#define` defines a name that can be used to prevent future inclusions, and the code is included in the source-code file.

- Data members of a class cannot be initialized where they are declared in the class body (except for a class's `static const` data members of integral or `enum` types, as you'll see in Chapter 21). It is strongly recommended that these data members be initialized by the class's constructor (as there is no default initialization for data members of fundamental types).

- Stream manipulator `setfill` specifies the fill character that is displayed when an integer is output in a field that is wider than the number of digits in the value.

- By default, the fill characters appear before the digits in the number.

- Stream manipulator `setfill` is a "sticky" setting, meaning that once the fill character is set, it applies for all subsequent fields being printed.

- Even though a member function declared in a class definition may be defined outside that class definition (and "tied" to the class via the binary scope resolution operator), that member function is still within that class's scope; i.e., its name is known only to other members of the class unless referred to via an object of the class, a reference to an object of the class or a pointer to an object of the class.

- If a member function is defined in the body of a class definition, the C++ compiler attempts to inline calls to the member function.

- Classes do not have to be created "from scratch." Rather, they can include objects of other classes as members or they may be derived from other classes that provide attributes and behaviors the new classes can use. Including class objects as members of other classes is called composition.

Section 20.3 Class Scope and Accessing Class Members
- A class's data members and member functions belong to that class's scope.
- Nonmember functions are defined at file scope.
- Within a class's scope, class members are immediately accessible by all of that class's member functions and can be referenced by name.
- Outside a class's scope, class members are referenced through one of the handles on an object— an object name, a reference to an object or a pointer to an object.
- Member functions of a class can be overloaded, but only by other member functions of that class.
- To overload a member function, provide in the class definition a prototype for each version of the overloaded function, and provide a separate definition for each version of the function.
- Variables declared in a member function have block scope and are known only to that function.
- If a member function defines a variable with the same name as a variable with class scope, the class-scope variable is hidden by the block-scope variable in the block scope.
- The dot member-selection operator (`.`) is preceded by an object's name or by a reference to an object to access the object's `public` members.
- The arrow member-selection operator (`->`) is preceded by a pointer to an object to access that object's `public` members.

Section 20.4 Separating Interface from Implementation
- Header files do contain some portions of the implementation and hints about others. Inline member functions, for example, need to be in a header file, so that when the compiler compiles a client, the client can include the `inline` function definition in place.
- A class's `private` members that are listed in the class definition in the header file are visible to clients, even though the clients may not access the `private` members.

Section 20.5 Access Functions and Utility Functions
- A utility function (also called a helper function) is a private member function that supports the operation of the class's public member functions. Utility functions are not intended to be used by clients of a class (but can be used by friends of a class).

Section 20.6 Time Class Case Study: Constructors with Default Arguments
- Like other functions, constructors can specify default arguments.

Section 20.7 Destructors
- A class's destructor is called implicitly when an object of the class is destroyed.
- The name of the destructor for a class is the tilde (~) character followed by the class name.
- A destructor does not actually release an object's storage—it performs termination housekeeping before the system reclaims an object's memory, so the memory may be reused to hold new objects.
- A destructor receives no parameters and returns no value. A class may have only one destructor.
- If the programmer does not explicitly provide a destructor, the compiler creates an "empty" destructor, so every class has exactly one destructor.

Section 20.8 When Constructors and Destructors Are Called
- The order in which constructors and destructors are called depends on the order in which execution enters and leaves the scopes where the objects are instantiated.
- Generally, destructor calls are made in the reverse order of the corresponding constructor calls, but the storage classes of objects can alter the order in which destructors are called.

Section 20.9 Time Class Case Study: A Subtle Trap—Returning a Reference to a private Data Member
- A reference to an object is an alias for the name of the object and, hence, may be used on the left side of an assignment statement. In this context, the reference makes a perfectly acceptable *lvalue* that can receive a value. One way to use this capability (unfortunately!) is to have a public member function of a class return a reference to a private data member of that class. If the function returns a const reference, then the reference cannot be used as a modifiable *lvalue*.

Section 20.8 When Constructors and Destructors Are Called
- The assignment operator (=) can be used to assign an object to another object of the same type. By default, such assignment is performed by memberwise assignment—each member of the object on the right of the assignment operator is assigned individually to the same member in the object on the left of the assignment operator.
- Objects may be passed as function arguments and may be returned from functions. Such passing and returning is performed using pass-by-value by default—a copy of the object is passed or returned. In such cases, C++ creates a new object and uses a copy constructor to copy the original object's values into the new object.
- For each class, the compiler provides a default copy constructor that copies each member of the original object into the corresponding member of the new object.

Section 20.11 Software Reusability
- Many substantial class libraries exist, and others are being developed worldwide.
- Software reusability speeds high-quality software development. Rapid applications development (RAD) through the mechanisms of reusable componentry has become an important field.

Terminology

<table>
<tr><td>abort function</td><td>implicit handle on an object</td></tr>
<tr><td>access function</td><td>inheritance</td></tr>
<tr><td>aggregation</td><td>memberwise assignment</td></tr>
<tr><td>arrow member-selection operator (->)</td><td>name handle on an object</td></tr>
<tr><td>assigning class objects</td><td>object handle</td></tr>
<tr><td>class libraries</td><td>object leaves scope</td></tr>
<tr><td>class scope</td><td>order of constructor and destructor calls</td></tr>
<tr><td>composition</td><td>overloaded constructor</td></tr>
<tr><td>copy constructor</td><td>overloaded member function</td></tr>
<tr><td>default arguments with constructors</td><td>pass an object by value</td></tr>
<tr><td>default memberwise assignment</td><td>pointer handle on an object</td></tr>
<tr><td>#define preprocessor directive</td><td>predicate function</td></tr>
<tr><td>derive one class from another</td><td>preprocessor wrapper</td></tr>
<tr><td>destructor</td><td>pure procedure</td></tr>
<tr><td>#endif preprocessor directive</td><td>rapid application development (RAD)</td></tr>
<tr><td>exit function</td><td>reentrant code</td></tr>
<tr><td>file scope</td><td>reference handle on an object</td></tr>
<tr><td>fill character</td><td>reusable componentry</td></tr>
<tr><td>handle on an object</td><td>setfill parameterized stream manipulator</td></tr>
<tr><td>helper function</td><td>termination housekeeping</td></tr>
<tr><td>#ifndef preprocessor directive</td><td>tilde character (~) in a destructor name</td></tr>
</table>

Self-Review Exercises

20.1 Fill in the blanks in each of the following:

a) Class members are accessed via the _____ operator in conjunction with the name of an object (or reference to an object) of the class or via the _____ operator in conjunction with a pointer to an object of the class.

b) Class members specified as _____ are accessible only to member functions of the class and friends of the class.

c) Class members specified as _____ are accessible anywhere an object of the class is in scope.

d) _____ can be used to assign an object of a class to another object of the same class.

20.2 Find the error(s) in each of the following and explain how to correct it (them):

a) Assume the following prototype is declared in class Time:

```
void ~Time( int );
```

b) The following is a partial definition of class Time:

```
class Time
{
public:
    // function prototypes
private:
    int hour = 0;
    int minute = 0;
    int second = 0;
}; // end class Time
```

c) Assume the following prototype is declared in class Employee:

```
int Employee( const char *, const char * );
```

Answers to Self-Review Exercises

20.1 a) dot (.), arrow (->). b) `private`. c) `public`. d) Default memberwise assignment (performed by the assignment operator).

20.2 a) Error: Destructors are not allowed to return values (or even specify a return type) or take arguments.
Correction: Remove the return type `void` and the parameter `int` from the declaration.
b) Error: Members cannot be explicitly initialized in the class definition.
Correction: Remove the explicit initialization from the class definition and initialize the data members in a constructor.
c) Error: Constructors are not allowed to return values.
Correction: Remove the return type `int` from the declaration.

Exercises

20.3 What is the purpose of the scope resolution operator?

20.4 *(Enhancing Class* `Time`*)* Provide a constructor that is capable of using the current time from the `time()` function—declared in the C++ Standard Library header `<ctime>`—to initialize an object of the `Time` class.

20.5 *(`Complex` Class)* Create a class called `Complex` for performing arithmetic with complex numbers. Write a program to test your class. Complex numbers have the form

```
realPart + imaginaryPart * i
```

where i is

$$\sqrt{-1}$$

Use `double` variables to represent the `private` data of the class. Provide a constructor that enables an object of this class to be initialized when it is declared. The constructor should contain default values in case no initializers are provided. Provide `public` member functions that perform the following tasks:
a) Adding two `Complex` numbers: The real parts are added together and the imaginary parts are added together.
b) Subtracting two `Complex` numbers: The real part of the right operand is subtracted from the real part of the left operand, and the imaginary part of the right operand is subtracted from the imaginary part of the left operand.
c) Printing `Complex` numbers in the form (a, b), where a is the real part and b is the imaginary part.

20.6 *(`Rational` Class)* Create a class called `Rational` for performing arithmetic with fractions. Write a program to test your class.
Use integer variables to represent the `private` data of the class—the `numerator` and the `denominator`. Provide a constructor that enables an object of this class to be initialized when it is declared. The constructor should contain default values in case no initializers are provided and should store the fraction in reduced form. For example, the fraction

$$\frac{2}{4}$$

would be stored in the object as 1 in the `numerator` and 2 in the `denominator`. Provide `public` member functions that perform each of the following tasks:
a) Adding two `Rational` numbers. The result should be stored in reduced form.
b) Subtracting two `Rational` numbers. The result should be stored in reduced form.
c) Multiplying two `Rational` numbers. The result should be stored in reduced form.

d) Dividing two Rational numbers. The result should be stored in reduced form.

e) Printing Rational numbers in the form a/b, where a is the numerator and b is the denominator.

f) Printing Rational numbers in floating-point format.

20.7 *(Enhancing Class Time)* Modify the Time class of Figs. 20.8–20.9 to include a tick member function that increments the time stored in a Time object by one second. The Time object should always remain in a consistent state. Write a program that tests the tick member function in a loop that prints the time in standard format during each iteration of the loop to illustrate that the tick member function works correctly. Be sure to test the following cases:

a) Incrementing into the next minute.

b) Incrementing into the next hour.

c) Incrementing into the next day (i.e., 11:59:59 PM to 12:00:00 AM).

20.8 *(Enhancing Class Date)* Modify the Date class of Fig. 20.17 to perform error checking on the initializer values for data members month, day and year. Also, provide a member function next-Day to increment the day by one. The Date object should always remain in a consistent state. Write a program that tests function nextDay in a loop that prints the date during each iteration to illustrate that nextDay works correctly. Be sure to test the following cases:

a) Incrementing into the next month.

b) Incrementing into the next year.

21

Classes: A Deeper Look, Part 2

OBJECTIVES

In this chapter you will learn:

- To specify **const** (constant) objects and **const** member functions.

- To create objects composed of other objects.

- To use **friend** functions and **friend** classes.

- To use the **this** pointer.

- To create and destroy objects dynamically with operators **new** and **delete**, respectively.

- To use **static** data members and member functions.

- The concept of a container class.

- The notion of iterator classes that walk through the elements of container classes.

- To use proxy classes to hide implementation details from a class's clients.

21.1 Introduction

In this chapter, we continue our study of classes and data abstraction with several more advanced topics. We use const objects and const member functions to prevent modifications of objects and enforce the principle of least privilege. We discuss composition—a form of reuse in which a class can have objects of other classes as members. Next, we introduce friendship, which enables a class designer to specify nonmember functions that can access class's non-public members—a technique that is often used in operator overloading (Chapter 22) for performance reasons. We discuss a special pointer (called this), which is an implicit argument to each of a class's non-static member functions that allows those member functions to access the correct object's data members and other non-static member functions. We then discuss dynamic memory management and show how to create and destroy objects dynamically with the new and delete operators. Next, we motivate the need for static class members and show how to use static data members and member functions in your own classes. Finally, we show how to create a proxy class to hide the implementation details of a class (including its private data members) from clients of the class.

Recall that Chapter 19 introduced C++ Standard Library class string to represent strings as full-fledged class objects. In this chapter, however, we use the pointer-based strings we introduced in C programming to help the reader master pointers and prepare for the professional world in which the reader will see a great deal of C legacy code, implemented over the last two decades. Thus, the reader will become familiar with the two most prevalent methods of creating and manipulating strings in C++.

21.2 const (Constant) Objects and const Member Functions

We have emphasized the principle of least privilege as one of the most fundamental principles of good software engineering. Let us see how this principle applies to objects.

Some objects need to be modifiable and some do not. The programmer may use keyword `const` to specify that an object is not modifiable and that any attempt to modify the object should result in a compilation error. The statement

```
const Time noon( 12, 0, 0 );
```

declares a `const` object `noon` of class `Time` and initializes it to 12 noon.

Software Engineering Observation 21.1

Declaring an object as `const` helps enforce the principle of least privilege. Attempts to modify the object are caught at compile time rather than causing execution-time errors. Using `const` properly is crucial to proper class design, program design and coding.

Performance Tip 21.1

Declaring variables and objects `const` can improve performance—today's sophisticated optimizing compilers can perform certain optimizations on constants that cannot be performed on variables.

C++ compilers disallow member-function calls for `const` objects unless the member functions themselves are also declared `const`. This is true even for *get* member functions that do not modify the object. In addition, the compiler does not allow member functions declared `const` to modify the object.

A function is specified as `const` *both* in its prototype (Fig. 21.1, lines 19–24) and in its definition (Fig. 21.2, lines 47, 53, 59 and 65) by inserting the keyword `const` after the function's parameter list and, in the case of the function definition, before the left brace that begins the function body.

Common Programming Error 21.1

Defining as `const` a member function that modifies a data member of an object is a compilation error.

Common Programming Error 21.2

Defining as `const` a member function that calls a non-`const` member function of the class on the same instance of the class is a compilation error.

Common Programming Error 21.3

Invoking a non-`const` member function on a `const` object is a compilation error.

Software Engineering Observation 21.2

A `const` member function can be overloaded with a non-`const` version. The compiler chooses which overloaded member function to use based on the object on which the function is invoked. If the object is `const`, the compiler uses the `const` version. If the object is not `const`, the compiler uses the non-`const` version.

An interesting problem arises for constructors and destructors, each of which typically modifies objects. The `const` declaration is not allowed for constructors and destructors. A constructor must be allowed to modify an object so that the object can be initialized properly. A destructor must be able to perform its termination housekeeping chores before an object's memory is reclaimed by the system.

Common Programming Error 21.4

Attempting to declare a constructor or destructor const *is a compilation error.*

Defining and Using const *Member Functions*

The program of Figs. 21.1–21.3 modifies class Time of Figs. 20.9–20.10 by making its *get* functions and printUniversal function const. In the header file Time.h (Fig. 21.1), lines 19–21 and 24 now include keyword const after each function's parameter list. The corresponding definition of each function in Fig. 21.2 (lines 47, 53, 59 and 65, respectively) also specifies keyword const after each function's parameter list.

Figure 21.3 instantiates two Time objects—non-const object wakeUp (line 7) and const object noon (line 8). The program attempts to invoke non-const member functions setHour (line 13) and printStandard (line 20) on the const object noon. In each case, the compiler generates an error message. The program also illustrates the three other member-function-call combinations on objects—a non-const member function on a non-const object (line 11), a const member function on a non-const object (line 15) and a const member function on a const object (lines 17–18). The error messages generated

```
 1   // Fig. 21.1: Time.h
 2   // Definition of class Time.
 3   // Member functions defined in Time.cpp.
 4   #ifndef TIME_H
 5   #define TIME_H
 6
 7   class Time
 8   {
 9   public:
10      Time( int = 0, int = 0, int = 0 ); // default constructor
11
12      // set functions
13      void setTime( int, int, int ); // set time
14      void setHour( int ); // set hour
15      void setMinute( int ); // set minute
16      void setSecond( int ); // set second
17
18      // get functions (normally declared const)
19      int getHour() const; // return hour
20      int getMinute() const; // return minute
21      int getSecond() const; // return second
22
23      // print functions (normally declared const)
24      void printUniversal() const; // print universal time
25      void printStandard(); // print standard time (should be const)
26   private:
27      int hour; // 0 - 23 (24-hour clock format)
28      int minute; // 0 - 59
29      int second; // 0 - 59
30   }; // end class Time
31
32   #endif
```

Fig. 21.1 | Time class definition with const member functions.

for non-const member functions called on a const object are shown in the output window. Notice that, although some current compilers issue only warning messages for lines 13 and 20 (thus allowing this program to be executed), we consider these warnings to be errors—the ANSI/ISO C++ standard disallows the invocation of a non-const member function on a const object.

```cpp
1   // Fig. 21.2: Time.cpp
2   // Member-function definitions for class Time.
3   #include <iostream>
4   using std::cout;
5
6   #include <iomanip>
7   using std::setfill;
8   using std::setw;
9
10  #include "Time.h" // include definition of class Time
11
12  // constructor function to initialize private data;
13  // calls member function setTime to set variables;
14  // default values are 0 (see class definition)
15  Time::Time( int hour, int minute, int second )
16  {
17      setTime( hour, minute, second );
18  } // end Time constructor
19
20  // set hour, minute and second values
21  void Time::setTime( int hour, int minute, int second )
22  {
23      setHour( hour );
24      setMinute( minute );
25      setSecond( second );
26  } // end function setTime
27
28  // set hour value
29  void Time::setHour( int h )
30  {
31      hour = ( h >= 0 && h < 24 ) ? h : 0; // validate hour
32  } // end function setHour
33
34  // set minute value
35  void Time::setMinute( int m )
36  {
37      minute = ( m >= 0 && m < 60 ) ? m : 0; // validate minute
38  } // end function setMinute
39
40  // set second value
41  void Time::setSecond( int s )
42  {
43      second = ( s >= 0 && s < 60 ) ? s : 0; // validate second
44  } // end function setSecond
45
```

Fig. 21.2 | Time class member-function definitions, including const member functions. (Part 1 of 2.)

```
46   // return hour value
47   int Time::getHour() const // get functions should be const
48   {
49      return hour;
50   } // end function getHour
51
52   // return minute value
53   int Time::getMinute() const
54   {
55      return minute;
56   } // end function getMinute
57
58   // return second value
59   int Time::getSecond() const
60   {
61      return second;
62   } // end function getSecond
63
64   // print Time in universal-time format (HH:MM:SS)
65   void Time::printUniversal() const
66   {
67      cout << setfill( '0' ) << setw( 2 ) << hour << ":"
68         << setw( 2 ) << minute << ":" << setw( 2 ) << second;
69   } // end function printUniversal
70
71   // print Time in standard-time format (HH:MM:SS AM or PM)
72   void Time::printStandard() // note lack of const declaration
73   {
74      cout << ( ( hour == 0 || hour == 12 ) ? 12 : hour % 12 )
75         << ":" << setfill( '0' ) << setw( 2 ) << minute
76         << ":" << setw( 2 ) << second << ( hour < 12 ? " AM" : " PM" );
77   } // end function printStandard
```

Fig. 21.2 | Time class member-function definitions, including const member functions. (Part 2 of 2.)

```
1    // Fig. 21.3: fig21_03.cpp
2    // Attempting to access a const object with non-const member functions.
3    #include "Time.h" // include Time class definition
4
5    int main()
6    {
7       Time wakeUp( 6, 45, 0 ); // non-constant object
8       const Time noon( 12, 0, 0 ); // constant object
9
10                                 // OBJECT        MEMBER FUNCTION
11      wakeUp.setHour( 18 );    // non-const    non-const
12
13      noon.setHour( 12 );      // const        non-const
14
15      wakeUp.getHour();        // non-const    const
```

Fig. 21.3 | const objects and const member functions. (Part 1 of 2.)

```
16
17      noon.getMinute();       // const         const
18      noon.printUniversal();  // const         const
19
20      noon.printStandard();   // const         non-const
21      return 0;
22   } // end main
```

Borland C++ command-line compiler error messages:

```
Warning W8037 fig21_03.cpp 13: Non-const function Time::setHour(int)
    called for const object in function main()
Warning W8037 fig21_03.cpp 20: Non-const function Time::printStandard()
    called for const object in function main()
```

Microsoft Visual C++ .NET compiler error messages:

```
C:\chtp5_examples\ch21\fig21_01_03\fig21_03.cpp(13) : error C2662:
    'Time::setHour' : cannot convert 'this' pointer from 'const Time' to
    'Time &'
        Conversion loses qualifiers
C:\chtp5_examples\ch21\fig21_01_03\fig21_03.cpp(20) : error C2662:
    'Time::printStandard' : cannot convert 'this' pointer from 'const Time' to
    'Time &'
        Conversion loses qualifiers
```

GNU C++ compiler error messages:

```
fig21_03.cpp:13: error: passing `const Time' as `this' argument of
    `void Time::setHour(int)' discards qualifiers
fig21_03.cpp:20: error: passing `const Time' as `this' argument of
    `void Time::printStandard()' discards qualifiers
```

Fig. 21.3 | const objects and const member functions. (Part 2 of 2.)

Notice that even though a constructor must be a non-const member function (Fig. 21.2, lines 15–18), it can still be used to initialize a const object (Fig. 21.3, line 8). The definition of the Time constructor (Fig. 21.2, lines 15–18) shows that the Time constructor calls another non-const member function—setTime (lines 21–26)—to perform the initialization of a Time object. Invoking a non-const member function from the constructor call as part of the initialization of a const object is allowed. The "constness" of a const object is enforced from the time the constructor completes initialization of the object until that object's destructor is called.

Also notice that line 20 in Fig. 21.3 generates a compilation error even though member function printStandard of class Time does not modify the object on which it is invoked. The fact that a member function does not modify an object is not sufficient to indicate that the function is constant function—the function must explicitly be declared const.

Initializing a const Data Member with a Member Initializer
The program of Figs. 21.4–21.6 introduces using member initializer syntax. All data members *can* be initialized using member initializer syntax, but const data members and

```
 1    // Fig. 21.4: Increment.h
 2    // Definition of class Increment.
 3    #ifndef INCREMENT_H
 4    #define INCREMENT_H
 5
 6    class Increment
 7    {
 8    public:
 9       Increment( int c = 0, int i = 1 ); // default constructor
10
11       // function addIncrement definition
12       void addIncrement()
13       {
14          count += increment;
15       } // end function addIncrement
16
17       void print() const; // prints count and increment
18    private:
19       int count;
20       const int increment; // const data member
21    }; // end class Increment
22
23    #endif
```

Fig. 21.4 | Increment class definition containing non-const data member count and const data member increment.

```
 1    // Fig. 21.5: Increment.cpp
 2    // Member-function definitions for class Increment demonstrate using a
 3    // member initializer to initialize a constant of a built-in data type.
 4    #include <iostream>
 5    using std::cout;
 6    using std::endl;
 7
 8    #include "Increment.h" // include definition of class Increment
 9
10    // constructor
11    Increment::Increment( int c, int i )
12       : count( c ), // initializer for non-const member
13         increment( i ) // required initializer for const member
14    {
15       // empty body
16    } // end constructor Increment
17
18    // print count and increment values
19    void Increment::print() const
20    {
21       cout << "count = " << count << ", increment = " << increment << endl;
22    } // end function print
```

Fig. 21.5 | Member initializer used to initialize a constant of a built-in data type.

```
 1    // Fig. 21.6: fig21_06.cpp
 2    // Program to test class Increment.
 3    #include <iostream>
 4    using std::cout;
 5
 6    #include "Increment.h" // include definition of class Increment
 7
 8    int main()
 9    {
10       Increment value( 10, 5 );
11
12       cout << "Before incrementing: ";
13       value.print();
14
15       for ( int j = 1; j <= 3; j++ )
16       {
17          value.addIncrement();
18          cout << "After increment " << j << ": ";
19          value.print();
20       } // end for
21
22       return 0;
23    } // end main
```

```
Before incrementing: count = 10, increment = 5
After increment 1: count = 15, increment = 5
After increment 2: count = 20, increment = 5
After increment 3: count = 25, increment = 5
```

Fig. 21.6 | Invoking an Increment object's print and addIncrement member functions.

data members that are references *must* be initialized using member initializers. Later in this chapter, we will see that member objects must be initialized this way as well. In Chapter 23 when we study inheritance, we will see that base-class portions of derived classes also must be initialized this way.

The constructor definition (Fig. 21.5, lines 11–16) uses a **member initializer list** to initialize class Increment's data members—non-const integer count and const integer increment (declared in lines 19–20 of Fig. 21.4). Member initializers appear between a constructor's parameter list and the left brace that begins the constructor's body. The member initializer list (Fig. 21.5, lines 12–13) is separated from the parameter list with a colon (:). Each member initializer consists of the data-member name followed by parentheses containing the member's initial value. In this example, count is initialized with the value of constructor parameter c and increment is initialized with the value of constructor parameter i. Note that multiple member initializers are separated by commas. Also, note that the member-initializer list executes before the body of the constructor executes.

Software Engineering Observation 21.3

A const object cannot be modified by assignment, so it must be initialized. When a data member of a class is declared const, a member initializer must be used to provide the constructor with the initial value of the data member for an object of the class. The same is true for references.

Erroneously Attempting to Initialize a `const` ***Data Member with an Assignment***
The program of Figs. 21.7–21.9 illustrates the compilation errors caused by attempting to initialize `const` data member `increment` with an assignment statement (Fig. 21.8, line 14) in the `Increment` constructor's body rather than with a member initializer. Note that line 13 of Fig. 21.8 does not generate a compilation error, because `count` is not declared `const`. Also note that the compilation errors produced by Microsoft Visual C++ .NET refer to `int` data member `increment` as a "const object." The ANSI/ISO C++ standard defines an "object" as any "region of storage." Like instances of classes, fundamental-type variables also occupy space in memory, so they are often referred to as "objects."

Common Programming Error 21.5

Not providing a member initializer for a `const` *data member is a compilation error.*

Software Engineering Observation 21.4

Constant data members (`const` objects and `const` variables) and data members declared as references must be initialized with member-initializer syntax; assignments for these types of data in the constructor body are not allowed.

Note that function `print` (Fig. 21.8, lines 18–21) is declared `const`. It might seem strange to label this function `const`, because a program probably will never have a `const` `Increment` object. However, it is possible that a program will have a `const` reference to an `Increment` object or a pointer to `const` that points to an `Increment` object. Typically, this occurs when objects of class `Increment` are passed to functions or returned from functions. In these cases, only the `const` member functions of class `Increment` can be called through the reference or pointer. Thus, it is reasonable to declare function `print` as `const`—doing so prevents errors in these situations where an `Increment` object is treated as a `const` object.

Error-Prevention Tip 21.1

Declare as `const` all of a class's member functions that do not modify the object in which they operate. Occasionally this may seem inappropriate, because you will have no intention of creating `const` objects of that class or accessing objects of that class through `const` references or pointers to `const`. Declaring such member functions `const` does offer a benefit, though. If the member function is inadvertently written to modify the object, the compiler will issue an error message.

```
 1   // Fig. 21.7: Increment.h
 2   // Definition of class Increment.
 3   #ifndef INCREMENT_H
 4   #define INCREMENT_H
 5
 6   class Increment
 7   {
 8   public:
 9      Increment( int c = 0, int i = 1 ); // default constructor
10
```

Fig. 21.7 | Increment class definition containing non-const data member `count` and `const` data member `increment`. (Part 1 of 2.)

```
11    // function addIncrement definition
12    void addIncrement()
13    {
14       count += increment;
15    } // end function addIncrement
16
17    void print() const; // prints count and increment
18 private:
19    int count;
20    const int increment; // const data member
21 }; // end class Increment
22
23 #endif
```

Fig. 21.7 | Increment class definition containing non-const data member count and const data member increment. (Part 2 of 2.)

```
1  // Fig. 21.8: Increment.cpp
2  // Attempting to initialize a constant of
3  // a built-in data type with an assignment.
4  #include <iostream>
5  using std::cout;
6  using std::endl;
7
8  #include "Increment.h" // include definition of class Increment
9
10 // constructor; constant member 'increment' is not initialized
11 Increment::Increment( int c, int i )
12 {
13    count = c; // allowed because count is not constant
14    increment = i; // ERROR: Cannot modify a const object
15 } // end constructor Increment
16
17 // print count and increment values
18 void Increment::print() const
19 {
20    cout << "count = " << count << ", increment = " << increment << endl;
21 } // end function print
```

Fig. 21.8 | Erroneous attempt to initialize a constant of a built-in data type by assignment.

```
1  // Fig. 21.9: fig21_09.cpp
2  // Program to test class Increment.
3  #include <iostream>
4  using std::cout;
5
6  #include "Increment.h" // include definition of class Increment
7
8  int main()
9  {
```

Fig. 21.9 | Program to test class Increment generates compilation errors. (Part 1 of 2.)

```
10      Increment value( 10, 5 );
11
12      cout << "Before incrementing: ";
13      value.print();
14
15      for ( int j = 1; j <= 3; j++ )
16      {
17          value.addIncrement();
18          cout << "After increment " << j << ": ";
19          value.print();
20      } // end for
21
22      return 0;
23  } // end main
```

Borland C++ command-line compiler error message:

```
Error E2024 Increment.cpp 14: Cannot modify a const object in function
    Increment::Increment(int,int)
```

Microsoft Visual C++.NET compiler error messages:

```
C:\chtp5_examples\ch21\fig21_07_09\Increment.cpp(12) : error C2758:
    'Increment::increment' : must be initialized in constructor
base/member initializer list
        C:\chtp5_examples\ch21\fig21_07_09\Increment.h(20) :
            see declaration of 'Increment::increment'
C:\chtp5_examples\ch21\fig21_07_09\Increment.cpp(14) : error C2166:
    l-value specifies const object
```

GNU C++ compiler error messages:

```
Increment.cpp:12: error: uninitialized member 'Increment::increment' with
    'const' type 'const int'
Increment.cpp:14: error: assignment of read-only data-member
    `Increment::increment'
```

Fig. 21.9 | Program to test class `Increment` generates compilation errors. (Part 2 of 2.)

21.3 Composition: Objects as Members of Classes

An `AlarmClock` object needs to know when it is supposed to sound its alarm, so why not include a `Time` object as a member of the `AlarmClock` class? Such a capability is called composition and is sometimes referred to as a *has-a* relationship. A class can have objects of other classes as members.

 Software Engineering Observation 21.5

A common form of software reusability is composition, in which a class has objects of other classes as members.

When an object is created, its constructor is called automatically. Previously, we saw how to pass arguments to the constructor of an object we created in `main`. This section shows how an object's constructor can pass arguments to member-object constructors, which is accomplished via member initializers. Member objects are constructed in the order in which they are declared in the class definition (not in the order they are listed in the constructor's member initializer list) and before their enclosing class objects (sometimes called **host objects**) are constructed.

The program of Figs. 21.10–21.14 uses class Date (Figs. 21.10–21.11) and class Employee (Figs. 21.12–21.13) to demonstrate objects as members of other objects. The definition of class Employee (Fig. 21.12) contains private data members firstName, lastName, birthDate and hireDate. Members birthDate and hireDate are const objects of class Date, which contains private data members month, day and year. The Employee constructor's header (Fig. 21.13, lines 18–21) specifies that the constructor receives four parameters (first, last, dateOfBirth and dateOfHire). The first two parameters are used in the constructor's body to initialize the character arrays firstName and lastName. The last two parameters are passed via member initializers to the constructor for class Date. The colon (:) in the header separates the member initializers from the parameter list. The member initializers specify the Employee constructor parameters being passed to the constructors of the member Date objects. Parameter dateOfBirth is passed to object birthDate's constructor (Fig. 21.13, line 20), and parameter dateOfHire is passed to object hireDate's constructor (Fig. 21.13, line 21). Again, member initializers are separated by commas. As you study class Date (Fig. 21.10), notice that the class does not provide a constructor that receives a parameter of type Date. So, how is the member-initializer list in class Employee's constructor able to initialize the birthDate and hireDate objects by passing Date object's to their Date constructors? As we mentioned in Chapter 20, the compiler provides each class with a default copy constructor that copies each member of the constructor's argument object into the corresponding member of the object being initialized. Chapter 22 discusses how programmers can define customized copy constructors.

```
1   // Fig. 21.10: Date.h
2   // Date class definition; Member functions defined in Date.cpp
3   #ifndef DATE_H
4   #define DATE_H
5
6   class Date
7   {
8   public:
9      Date( int = 1, int = 1, int = 1900 ); // default constructor
10     void print() const; // print date in month/day/year format
11     ~Date(); // provided to confirm destruction order
12   private:
13      int month; // 1-12 (January-December)
14      int day; // 1-31 based on month
15      int year; // any year
16
17      // utility function to check if day is proper for month and year
18      int checkDay( int ) const;
19   }; // end class Date
20
21   #endif
```

Fig. 21.10 | Date class definition.

Figure 21.14 creates two Date objects (lines 11–12) and passes them as arguments to the constructor of the Employee object created in line 13. Line 16 outputs the Employee object's data. When each Date object is created in lines 11–12, the Date constructor defined at lines 11–28 of Fig. 21.11 displays a line of output to show that the constructor was called (see the first two lines of the sample output). [*Note:* Line 13 of Fig. 21.14 causes two additional Date constructor calls that do not appear in the program's output. When each of the Employee's Date member objects is initialized in the Employee constructor's member-initializer list, the default copy constructor for class Date is called. This constructor is defined implicitly by the compiler and does not contain any output statements to demonstrate when it is called. We discuss copy constructors and default copy constructors in detail in Chapter 22.]

```
1   // Fig. 21.11: Date.cpp
2   // Member-function definitions for class Date.
3   #include <iostream>
4   using std::cout;
5   using std::endl;
6
7   #include "Date.h" // include Date class definition
8
9   // constructor confirms proper value for month; calls
10  // utility function checkDay to confirm proper value for day
11  Date::Date( int mn, int dy, int yr )
12  {
13     if ( mn > 0 && mn <= 12 ) // validate the month
14        month = mn;
15     else
16     {
17        month = 1; // invalid month set to 1
18        cout << "Invalid month (" << mn << ") set to 1.\n";
19     } // end else
20
21     year = yr; // could validate yr
22     day = checkDay( dy ); // validate the day
23
24     // output Date object to show when its constructor is called
25     cout << "Date object constructor for date ";
26     print();
27     cout << endl;
28  } // end Date constructor
29
30  // print Date object in form month/day/year
31  void Date::print() const
32  {
33     cout << month << '/' << day << '/' << year;
34  } // end function print
35
36  // output Date object to show when its destructor is called
37  Date::~Date()
38  {
```

Fig. 21.11 | Date class member-function definitions. (Part 1 of 2.)

```
39        cout << "Date object destructor for date ";
40        print();
41        cout << endl;
42    } // end ~Date destructor
43
44    // utility function to confirm proper day value based on
45    // month and year; handles leap years, too
46    int Date::checkDay( int testDay ) const
47    {
48        static const int daysPerMonth[ 13 ] =
49            { 0, 31, 28, 31, 30, 31, 30, 31, 31, 30, 31, 30, 31 };
50
51        // determine whether testDay is valid for specified month
52        if ( testDay > 0 && testDay <= daysPerMonth[ month ] )
53            return testDay;
54
55        // February 29 check for leap year
56        if ( month == 2 && testDay == 29 && ( year % 400 == 0 ||
57            ( year % 4 == 0 && year % 100 != 0 ) ) )
58            return testDay;
59
60        cout << "Invalid day (" << testDay << ") set to 1.\n";
61        return 1; // leave object in consistent state if bad value
62    } // end function checkDay
```

Fig. 21.11 | Date class member-function definitions. (Part 2 of 2.)

```
1    // Fig. 21.12: Employee.h
2    // Employee class definition.
3    // Member functions defined in Employee.cpp.
4    #ifndef EMPLOYEE_H
5    #define EMPLOYEE_H
6
7    #include "Date.h" // include Date class definition
8
9    class Employee
10   {
11   public:
12       Employee( const char * const, const char * const,
13           const Date &, const Date & );
14       void print() const;
15       ~Employee(); // provided to confirm destruction order
16   private:
17       char firstName[ 25 ];
18       char lastName[ 25 ];
19       const Date birthDate; // composition: member object
20       const Date hireDate; // composition: member object
21   }; // end class Employee
22
23   #endif
```

Fig. 21.12 | Employee class definition showing composition.

```
1   // Fig. 21.13: Employee.cpp
2   // Member-function definitions for class Employee.
3   #include <iostream>
4   using std::cout;
5   using std::endl;
6
7   #include <cstring> // strlen and strncpy prototypes
8   using std::strlen;
9   using std::strncpy;
10
11  #include "Employee.h" // Employee class definition
12  #include "Date.h" // Date class definition
13
14  // constructor uses member initializer list to pass initializer
15  // values to constructors of member objects birthDate and hireDate
16  // [Note: This invokes the so-called "default copy constructor" which the
17  // C++ compiler provides implicitly.]
18  Employee::Employee( const char * const first, const char * const last,
19     const Date &dateOfBirth, const Date &dateOfHire )
20     : birthDate( dateOfBirth ), // initialize birthDate
21        hireDate( dateOfHire ) // initialize hireDate
22  {
23     // copy first into firstName and be sure that it fits
24     int length = strlen( first );
25     length = ( length < 25 ? length : 24 );
26     strncpy( firstName, first, length );
27     firstName[ length ] = '\0';
28
29     // copy last into lastName and be sure that it fits
30     length = strlen( last );
31     length = ( length < 25 ? length : 24 );
32     strncpy( lastName, last, length );
33     lastName[ length ] = '\0';
34
35     // output Employee object to show when constructor is called
36     cout << "Employee object constructor: "
37        << firstName << ' ' << lastName << endl;
38  } // end Employee constructor
39
40  // print Employee object
41  void Employee::print() const
42  {
43     cout << lastName << ", " << firstName << "  Hired: ";
44     hireDate.print();
45     cout << "  Birthday: ";
46     birthDate.print();
47     cout << endl;
48  } // end function print
49
50  // output Employee object to show when its destructor is called
51  Employee::~Employee()
52  {
```

Fig. 21.13 | Employee class member-function definitions, including constructor with a member-initializer list. (Part 1 of 2.)

```
53      cout << "Employee object destructor: "
54          << lastName << ", " << firstName << endl;
55  } // end ~Employee destructor
```

Fig. 21.13 | Employee class member-function definitions, including constructor with a member-initializer list. (Part 2 of 2.)

```
 1  // Fig. 21.14: fig21_14.cpp
 2  // Demonstrating composition--an object with member objects.
 3  #include <iostream>
 4  using std::cout;
 5  using std::endl;
 6
 7  #include "Employee.h" // Employee class definition
 8
 9  int main()
10  {
11      Date birth( 7, 24, 1949 );
12      Date hire( 3, 12, 1988 );
13      Employee manager( "Bob", "Blue", birth, hire );
14
15      cout << endl;
16      manager.print();
17
18      cout << "\nTest Date constructor with invalid values:\n";
19      Date lastDayOff( 14, 35, 1994 ); // invalid month and day
20      cout << endl;
21      return 0;
22  } // end main
```

```
Date object constructor for date 7/24/1949
Date object constructor for date 3/12/1988
Employee object constructor: Bob Blue

Blue, Bob  Hired: 3/12/1988  Birthday: 7/24/1949

Test Date constructor with invalid values:
Invalid month (14) set to 1.
Invalid day (35) set to 1.
Date object constructor for date 1/1/1994

Date object destructor for date 1/1/1994
Employee object destructor: Blue, Bob
Date object destructor for date 3/12/1988
Date object destructor for date 7/24/1949
Date object destructor for date 3/12/1988
Date object destructor for date 7/24/1949
```

Fig. 21.14 | Member-object initializers.

Class Date and class Employee each include a destructor (lines 37–42 of Fig. 21.11 and lines 51–55 of Fig. 21.13, respectively) that prints a message when an object of its class is destroyed. This enables us to confirm in the program output that objects are constructed from the inside out and destroyed in the reverse order from the outside in (i.e., the Date member objects are destroyed after the Employee object that contains them). Notice the last four lines in the output of Fig. 21.14. The last two lines are the outputs of the Date destructor running on Date objects hire (line 12) and birth (line 11), respectively. These outputs confirm that the three objects created in main are destructed in the reverse of the order in which they were constructed. (The Employee destructor output is five lines from the bottom.) The fourth and third lines from the bottom of the output window show the destructors running for the Employee's member objects hireDate (Fig. 21.12, line 20) and birthDate (Fig. 21.12, line 19). These outputs confirm that the Employee object is destructed from the outside in—i.e., the Employee destructor runs first (output shown five lines from the bottom of the output window), then the member objects are destructed in the reverse order from which they were constructed. Again, the outputs in Fig. 21.14 did not show the constructors running for these objects, because these were the default copy constructors provided by the C++ compiler.

A member object does not need to be initialized explicitly through a member initializer. If a member initializer is not provided, the member object's default constructor will be called implicitly. Values, if any, established by the default constructor can be overridden by *set* functions. However, for complex initialization, this approach may require significant additional work and time.

Common Programming Error 21.6

A compilation error occurs if a member object is not initialized with a member initializer and the member object's class does not provide a default constructor (i.e., the member object's class defines one or more constructors, but none is a default constructor).

Performance Tip 21.2

Initialize member objects explicitly through member initializers. This eliminates the overhead of "doubly initializing" member objects—once when the member object's default constructor is called and again when set *functions are called in the constructor body (or later) to initialize the member object.*

Software Engineering Observation 21.6

If a class member is an object of another class, making that member object public *does not violate the encapsulation and hiding of that member object's* private *members. However, it does violate the encapsulation and hiding of the containing class's implementation, so member objects of class types should still be* private, *like all other data members.*

In line 26 of Fig. 21.11, notice the call to Date member function print. Many member functions of classes in C++ require no arguments. This is because each member function contains an implicit handle (in the form of a pointer) to the object on which it operates. We discuss the implicit pointer, which is represented by keyword this, in Section 21.5.

Class Employee uses two 25-character arrays (Fig. 21.12, lines 17–18) to represent the first name and last name of the Employee. These arrays may waste space for names shorter than 24 characters. (Remember, one character in each array is for the terminating null character, '\0', of the string.) Also, names longer than 24 characters must be truncated to fit in these fixed-size character arrays. Section 21.7 presents another version of class Employee that dynamically creates the exact amount of space required to hold the first and the last name.

Note that the simplest way to represent an `Employee`'s first and last name using the exact amount of space required is to use two `string` objects (C++ Standard Library class `string` was introduced in Chapter 19). If we did this, the `Employee` constructor would appear as follows

```
Employee::Employee( const string &first, const string &last,
    const Date &dateOfBirth, const Date &dateOfHire )
    : firstName( first), // initialize firstName
      lastName( last ), // initialize lastName
      birthDate( dateOfBirth ), // initialize birthDate
      hireDate( dateOfHire ) // initialize hireDate
{
    // output Employee object to show when constructor is called
    cout << "Employee object constructor: "
        << firstName << ' ' << lastName << endl;
} // end Employee constructor
```

Notice that data members `firstName` and `lastName` (now `string` objects) are initialized through member initializers. The `Employee` classes presented in Chapters 23–24 use `string` objects in this fashion. In this chapter, we use pointer-based strings to provide the reader with additional exposure to pointer manipulation.

21.4 friend Functions and friend Classes

A `friend` function of a class is defined outside that class's scope, yet has the right to access the non-`public` (and `public`) members of the class. Stand-alone functions or entire classes may be declared to be friends of another class.

Using `friend` functions can enhance performance. This section presents a mechanical example of how a `friend` function works. Later in the book, `friend` functions are used to overload operators for use with class objects (Chapter 22) and to create iterator classes. Objects of an iterator class can successively select items or perform an operation on items in a container class object (see Section 21.9). Objects of container classes can store items. Using friends is often appropriate when a member function cannot be used for certain operations, as we will see in Chapter 22.

To declare a function as a friend of a class, precede the function prototype in the class definition with keyword `friend`. To declare all member functions of class `ClassTwo` as friends of class `ClassOne`, place a declaration of the form

```
friend class ClassTwo;
```

in the definition of class `ClassOne`.

Software Engineering Observation 21.7

Even though the prototypes for `friend` functions appear in the class definition, friends are not member functions.

Software Engineering Observation 21.8

Member access notions of `private`, `protected` and `public` are not relevant to `friend` declarations, so `friend` declarations can be placed anywhere in a class definition.

Good Programming Practice 21.1

Place all friendship declarations first inside the class definition's body and do not precede them with any access specifier.

  Friendship is granted, not taken—i.e., for class B to be a friend of class A, class A must explicitly declare that class B is its friend. Also, the friendship relation is neither symmetric nor transitive; i.e., if class A is a friend of class B, and class B is a friend of class C, you cannot infer that class B is a friend of class A (again, friendship is not symmetric), that class C is a friend of class B (also because friendship is not symmetric), or that class A is a friend of class C (friendship is not transitive).

Software Engineering Observation 21.9

Some people in the OOP community feel that "friendship" corrupts information hiding and weakens the value of the object-oriented design approach. In this text, we identify several examples of the responsible use of friendship.

Modifying a Class's private Data with a Friend Function

Figure 21.15 is a mechanical example in which we define friend function setX to set the private data member x of class Count. Note that the friend declaration (line 10) appears first (by convention) in the class definition, even before public member functions are declared. Again, this friend declaration can appear anywhere in the class.

```cpp
1   // Fig. 21.15: fig21_15.cpp
2   // Friends can access private members of a class.
3   #include <iostream>
4   using std::cout;
5   using std::endl;
6
7   // Count class definition
8   class Count
9   {
10     friend void setX( Count &, int ); // friend declaration
11  public:
12     // constructor
13     Count()
14        : x( 0 ) // initialize x to 0
15     {
16        // empty body
17     } // end constructor Count
18
19     // output x
20     void print() const
21     {
22        cout << x << endl;
23     } // end function print
24  private:
25     int x; // data member
26  }; // end class Count
27
```

Fig. 21.15 | Friends can access private members of a class. (Part 1 of 2.)

```
28   // function setX can modify private data of Count
29   // because setX is declared as a friend of Count (line 10)
30   void setX( Count &c, int val )
31   {
32      c.x = val; // allowed because setX is a friend of Count
33   } // end function setX
34
35   int main()
36   {
37      Count counter; // create Count object
38
39      cout << "counter.x after instantiation: ";
40      counter.print();
41
42      setX( counter, 8 ); // set x using a friend function
43      cout << "counter.x after call to setX friend function: ";
44      counter.print();
45      return 0;
46   } // end main
```

```
counter.x after instantiation: 0
counter.x after call to setX friend function: 8
```

Fig. 21.15 | Friends can access private members of a class. (Part 2 of 2.)

Function setX (lines 30–33) is a C-style, stand-alone function—it is not a member function of class Count. For this reason, when setX is invoked for object counter, line 42 passes counter as an argument to setX rather than using a handle (such as the name of the object) to call the function, as in

```
counter.setX( 8 );
```

As we mentioned, Fig. 21.15 is a mechanical example of using the friend construct. It would normally be appropriate to define function setX as a member function of class Count. It would also normally be appropriate to separate the program of Fig. 21.15 into three files:

1. A header file (e.g., Count.h) containing the Count class definition, which in turn contains the prototype of friend function setX

2. An implementation file (e.g., Count.cpp) containing the definitions of class Count's member functions and the definition of friend function setX

3. A test program (e.g., fig21_15.cpp) with main

Erroneously Attempting to Modify a private Member with a Non-friend Function
The program of Fig. 21.16 demonstrates the error messages produced by the compiler when non-friend function cannotSetX (lines 29–32) is called to modify private data member x.

It is possible to specify overloaded functions as friends of a class. Each overloaded function intended to be a friend must be explicitly declared in the class definition as a friend of the class.

```
 1    // Fig. 21.16: fig21_16.cpp
 2    // Non-friend/non-member functions cannot access private data of a class.
 3    #include <iostream>
 4    using std::cout;
 5    using std::endl;
 6
 7    // Count class definition (note that there is no friendship declaration)
 8    class Count
 9    {
10    public:
11       // constructor
12       Count()
13          : x( 0 ) // initialize x to 0
14       {
15          // empty body
16       } // end constructor Count
17
18       // output x
19       void print() const
20       {
21          cout << x << endl;
22       } // end function print
23    private:
24       int x; // data member
25    }; // end class Count
26
27    // function cannotSetX tries to modify private data of Count,
28    // but cannot because the function is not a friend of Count
29    void cannotSetX( Count &c, int val )
30    {
31       c.x = val; // ERROR: cannot access private member in Count
32    } // end function cannotSetX
33
34    int main()
35    {
36       Count counter; // create Count object
37
38       cannotSetX( counter, 3 ); // cannotSetX is not a friend
39       return 0;
40    } // end main
```

Borland C++ command-line compiler error message:

```
Error E2247 fig21_16/fig21_16.cpp 31: 'Count::x' is not accessible in
   function cannotSetX(Count &,int)
```

Microsoft Visual C++ .NET compiler error messages:

```
C:\chtp5_examples\ch21\fig21_16\fig21_16.cpp(31) : error C2248: 'Count::x'
   : cannot access private member declared in class 'Count'
         C:\chtp5_examples\ch21\fig21_16\fig21_16.cpp(24) : see declaration
            of 'Count::x'
         C:\chtp5_examples\ch21\fig21_16\fig21_16.cpp(9) : see declaration
            of 'Count'
```

Fig. 21.16 | Non-friend/nonmember functions cannot access private members. (Part 1 of 2.)

GNU C++ compiler error messages:

```
fig21_16.cpp:24: error: `int Count::x' is private
fig21_16.cpp:31: error: within this context
```

Fig. 21.16 | Non-friend/nonmember functions cannot access private members. (Part 2 of 2.)

21.5 Using the this Pointer

We have seen that an object's member functions can manipulate the object's data. How do member functions know which object's data members to manipulate? Every object has access to its own address through a pointer called **this** (a C++ keyword). An object's this pointer is not part of the object itself—i.e., the size of the memory occupied by the this pointer is not reflected in the result of a sizeof operation on the object. Rather, the this pointer is passed (by the compiler) as an implicit argument to each of the object's non-static member functions. Section 21.7 introduces static class members and explains why the this pointer is *not* implicitly passed to static member functions.

Objects use the this pointer implicitly (as we have done to this point) or explicitly to reference their data members and member functions. The type of the this pointer depends on the type of the object and whether the member function in which this is used is declared const. For example, in a nonconstant member function of class Employee, the this pointer has type Employee * const (a constant pointer to a nonconstant Employee object). In a constant member function of the class Employee, the this pointer has the data type const Employee * const (a constant pointer to a constant Employee object).

Our first example in this section shows implicit and explicit use of the this pointer; later in this chapter and in Chapter 22, we show some substantial and subtle examples of using this.

Implicitly and Explicitly Using the this Pointer to Access an Object's Data Members
Figure 21.17 demonstrates the implicit and explicit use of the this pointer to enable a member function of class Test to print the private data x of a Test object.

For illustration purposes, member function print (lines 25–37) first prints x by using the this pointer implicitly (line 28)—only the name of the data member is specified. Then print uses two different notations to access x through the this pointer—the arrow

---

```
1    // Fig. 21.17: fig21_17.cpp
2    // Using the this pointer to refer to object members.
3    #include <iostream>
4    using std::cout;
5    using std::endl;
6
7    class Test
8    {
9    public:
10       Test( int = 0 ); // default constructor
11       void print() const;
```

Fig. 21.17 | this pointer implicitly and explicitly accessing an object's members. (Part 1 of 2.)

```
12    private:
13        int x;
14    }; // end class Test
15
16    // constructor
17    Test::Test( int value )
18        : x( value ) // initialize x to value
19    {
20        // empty body
21    } // end constructor Test
22
23    // print x using implicit and explicit this pointers;
24    // the parentheses around *this are required
25    void Test::print() const
26    {
27        // implicitly use the this pointer to access the member x
28        cout << "        x = " << x;
29
30        // explicitly use the this pointer and the arrow operator
31        // to access the member x
32        cout << "\n  this->x = " << this->x;
33
34        // explicitly use the dereferenced this pointer and
35        // the dot operator to access the member x
36        cout << "\n(*this).x = " << ( *this ).x << endl;
37    } // end function print
38
39    int main()
40    {
41        Test testObject( 12 ); // instantiate and initialize testObject
42
43        testObject.print();
44        return 0;
45    } // end main
```

```
        x = 12
  this->x = 12
(*this).x = 12
```

Fig. 21.17 | this pointer implicitly and explicitly accessing an object's members. (Part 2 of 2.)

operator (->) off the this pointer (line 32) and the dot operator (.) off the dereferenced this pointer (line 36).

Note the parentheses around *this (line 36) when used with the dot member-selection operator (.). The parentheses are required because the dot operator has higher precedence than the * operator. Without the parentheses, the expression *this.x would be evaluated as if it were parenthesized as *(this.x), which is a compilation error, because the dot operator cannot be used with a pointer.

One interesting use of the this pointer is to prevent an object from being assigned to itself. As we will see in Chapter 22, self-assignment can cause serious errors when the object contains pointers to dynamically allocated storage.

Common Programming Error 21.7

Attempting to use the member-selection operator (.) with a pointer to an object is a compilation error—the dot member-selection operator may be used only with an lvalue *such as an object's name, a reference to an object or a dereferenced pointer to an object.*

Using the this Pointer to Enable Cascaded Function Calls

Another use of the this pointer is to enable cascaded member-function calls in which multiple functions are invoked in the same statement (as in line 14 of Fig. 21.20). The program of Figs. 21.18–21.20 modifies class Time's *set* functions setTime, setHour, setMinute and setSecond such that each returns a reference to a Time object to enable cascaded member-function calls. Notice in Fig. 21.19 that the last statement in the body of each of these member functions returns *this (lines 26, 33, 40 and 47) into a return type of Time &.

The program of Fig. 21.20 creates Time object t (line 11), then uses it in cascaded member-function calls (lines 14 and 26). Why does the technique of returning *this as a reference work? The dot operator (.) associates from left to right, so line 14 first evaluates t.setHour(18), then returns a reference to object t as the value of this function call. The remaining expression is then interpreted as

```
t.setMinute( 30 ).setSecond( 22 );
```

The t.setMinute(30) call executes and returns a reference to the object t. The remaining expression is interpreted as

```
t.setSecond( 22 );
```

Line 26 also uses cascading. The calls must appear in the order shown in line 26, because printStandard as defined in the class does not return a reference to t. Placing the call to printStandard before the call to setTime in line 26 results in a compilation error. Chapter 22 presents several practical examples of using cascaded function calls. One such example uses multiple << operators with cout to output multiple values in a single statement.

```
1   // Fig. 21.18: Time.h
2   // Cascading member function calls.
3
4   // Time class definition.
5   // Member functions defined in Time.cpp.
6   #ifndef TIME_H
7   #define TIME_H
8
9   class Time
10  {
11  public:
12     Time( int = 0, int = 0, int = 0 ); // default constructor
13
14     // set functions (the Time & return types enable cascading)
15     Time &setTime( int, int, int ); // set hour, minute, second
16     Time &setHour( int ); // set hour
17     Time &setMinute( int ); // set minute
18     Time &setSecond( int ); // set second
19
```

Fig. 21.18 | Time class definition modified to enable cascaded member-function calls. (Part 1 of 2.)

```
20      // get functions (normally declared const)
21      int getHour() const; // return hour
22      int getMinute() const; // return minute
23      int getSecond() const; // return second
24
25      // print functions (normally declared const)
26      void printUniversal() const; // print universal time
27      void printStandard() const; // print standard time
28   private:
29      int hour; // 0 - 23 (24-hour clock format)
30      int minute; // 0 - 59
31      int second; // 0 - 59
32   }; // end class Time
33
34   #endif
```

Fig. 21.18 | Time class definition modified to enable cascaded member-function calls. (Part 2 of 2.)

```
 1   // Fig. 21.19: Time.cpp
 2   // Member-function definitions for Time class.
 3   #include <iostream>
 4   using std::cout;
 5
 6   #include <iomanip>
 7   using std::setfill;
 8   using std::setw;
 9
10   #include "Time.h" // Time class definition
11
12   // constructor function to initialize private data;
13   // calls member function setTime to set variables;
14   // default values are 0 (see class definition)
15   Time::Time( int hr, int min, int sec )
16   {
17      setTime( hr, min, sec );
18   } // end Time constructor
19
20   // set values of hour, minute, and second
21   Time &Time::setTime( int h, int m, int s ) // note Time & return
22   {
23      setHour( h );
24      setMinute( m );
25      setSecond( s );
26      return *this; // enables cascading
27   } // end function setTime
28
29   // set hour value
30   Time &Time::setHour( int h ) // note Time & return
31   {
```

Fig. 21.19 | Time class member-function definitions modified to enable cascaded member-function calls. (Part 1 of 2.)

```
32        hour = ( h >= 0 && h < 24 ) ? h : 0; // validate hour
33        return *this; // enables cascading
34     } // end function setHour
35
36     // set minute value
37     Time &Time::setMinute( int m ) // note Time & return
38     {
39        minute = ( m >= 0 && m < 60 ) ? m : 0; // validate minute
40        return *this; // enables cascading
41     } // end function setMinute
42
43     // set second value
44     Time &Time::setSecond( int s ) // note Time & return
45     {
46        second = ( s >= 0 && s < 60 ) ? s : 0; // validate second
47        return *this; // enables cascading
48     } // end function setSecond
49
50     // get hour value
51     int Time::getHour() const
52     {
53        return hour;
54     } // end function getHour
55
56     // get minute value
57     int Time::getMinute() const
58     {
59        return minute;
60     } // end function getMinute
61
62     // get second value
63     int Time::getSecond() const
64     {
65        return second;
66     } // end function getSecond
67
68     // print Time in universal-time format (HH:MM:SS)
69     void Time::printUniversal() const
70     {
71        cout << setfill( '0' ) << setw( 2 ) << hour << ":"
72           << setw( 2 ) << minute << ":" << setw( 2 ) << second;
73     } // end function printUniversal
74
75     // print Time in standard-time format (HH:MM:SS AM or PM)
76     void Time::printStandard() const
77     {
78        cout << ( ( hour == 0 || hour == 12 ) ? 12 : hour % 12 )
79           << ":" << setfill( '0' ) << setw( 2 ) << minute
80           << ":" << setw( 2 ) << second << ( hour < 12 ? " AM" : " PM" );
81     } // end function printStandard
```

Fig. 21.19 | Time class member-function definitions modified to enable cascaded member-function calls. (Part 2 of 2.)

```
 1   // Fig. 21.20: fig21_20.cpp
 2   // Cascading member function calls with the this pointer.
 3   #include <iostream>
 4   using std::cout;
 5   using std::endl;
 6
 7   #include "Time.h" // Time class definition
 8
 9   int main()
10   {
11      Time t; // create Time object
12
13      // cascaded function calls
14      t.setHour( 18 ).setMinute( 30 ).setSecond( 22 );
15
16      // output time in universal and standard formats
17      cout << "Universal time: ";
18      t.printUniversal();
19
20      cout << "\nStandard time: ";
21      t.printStandard();
22
23      cout << "\n\nNew standard time: ";
24
25      // cascaded function calls
26      t.setTime( 20, 20, 20 ).printStandard();
27      cout << endl;
28      return 0;
29   } // end main
```

```
Universal time: 18:30:22
Standard time: 6:30:22 PM

New standard time: 8:20:20 PM
```

Fig. 21.20 | Cascading member-function calls.

21.6 Dynamic Memory Management with Operators new and delete

C++ enables programmers to control the allocation and deallocation of memory in a program for any built-in or user-defined type. This is known as dynamic memory management and is performed with operators **new** and **delete**. Recall that class Employee (Figs. 21.12–21.13) uses two 25-character arrays to represent the first and last name of an Employee. The Employee class definition (Fig. 21.12) must specify the number of elements in each of these arrays when it declares them as data members, because the size of the data members dictates the amount of memory required to store an Employee object. As we discussed earlier, these arrays may waste space for names shorter than 24 characters. Also, names longer than 24 characters must be truncated to fit in these fixed-size arrays.

Wouldn't it be nice if we could use arrays containing exactly the number of elements needed to store an Employee's first and last name? Dynamic memory management allows us to do exactly that. As you will see in the example of Section 21.7, if we replace array data members firstName and lastName with pointers to char, we can use the new operator to dynamically allocate (i.e., reserve) the exact amount of memory required to hold each name at execution time. Dynamically allocating memory in this fashion causes an array (or any other built-in or user-defined type) to be created in the free store (sometimes called the heap)—a region of memory assigned to each program for storing objects created at execution time. Once the memory for an array is allocated in the free store, we can gain access to it by aiming a pointer at the first element of the array. When we no longer need the array, we can return the memory to the free store by using the delete operator to deallocate (i.e., release) the memory, which can then be reused by future new operations.

Again, we present the modified Employee class as described here in the example of Section 21.7. First, we present the details of using the new and delete operators to dynamically allocate memory to store objects, fundamental types and arrays.

Consider the following declaration and statement:

```
Time *timePtr;
timePtr = new Time;
```

The new operator allocates storage of the proper size for an object of type Time, calls the default constructor to initialize the object and returns a pointer of the type specified to the right of the new operator (i.e., a Time *). Note that new can be used to dynamically allocate any fundamental type (such as int or double) or class type. If new is unable to find sufficient space in memory for the object, it indicates that an error occurred by "throwing an exception." Chapter 27, Exception Handling, discusses how to deal with new failures in the context of the ANSI/ISO C++ standard. In particular, we will show how to "catch" the exception thrown by new and deal with it. When a program does not "catch" an exception, the program terminates immediately. [*Note:* The new operator returns a 0 pointer in versions of C++ prior to the ANSI/ISO standard. We use the standard version of operator new throughout this book.]

To destroy a dynamically allocated object and free the space for the object, use the delete operator as follows:

```
delete timePtr;
```

This statement first calls the destructor for the object to which timePtr points, then deallocates the memory associated with the object. After the preceding statement, the memory can be reused by the system to allocate other objects.

 Common Programming Error 21.8

*Not releasing dynamically allocated memory when it is no longer needed can cause the system to run out of memory prematurely. This is sometimes called a "**memory leak**."*

C++ allows you to provide an initializer for a newly created fundamental-type variable, as in

```
double *ptr = new double( 3.14159 );
```

which initializes a newly created double to 3.14159 and assigns the resulting pointer to ptr. The same syntax can be used to specify a comma-separated list of arguments to the constructor of an object. For example,

```
Time *timePtr = new Time( 12, 45, 0 );
```

initializes a newly created `Time` object to 12:45 PM and assigns the resulting pointer to `timePtr`.

As discussed earlier, the `new` operator can be used to allocate arrays dynamically. For example, a 10-element integer array can be allocated and assigned to `gradesArray` as follows:

```
int *gradesArray = new int[ 10 ];
```

which declares pointer `gradesArray` and assigns it a pointer to the first element of a dynamically allocated 10-element array of integers. Recall that the size of an array created at compile time must be specified using a constant integral expression. However, the size of a dynamically allocated array can be specified using *any* integral expression that can be evaluated at execution time. Also note that, when allocating an array of objects dynamically, the programmer cannot pass arguments to each object's constructor. Instead, each object in the array is initialized by its default constructor. To delete the dynamically allocated array to which `gradesArray` points, use the statement

```
delete [] gradesArray;
```

The preceding statement deallocates the array to which `gradesArray` points. If the pointer in the preceding statement points to an array of objects, the statement first calls the destructor for every object in the array, then deallocates the memory. If the preceding statement did not include the square brackets (`[]`) and `gradesArray` pointed to an array of objects, only the first object in the array would receive a destructor call.

Common Programming Error 21.9

Using `delete` instead of `delete []` for arrays of objects can lead to runtime logic errors. To ensure that every object in the array receives a destructor call, always delete memory allocated as an array with operator `delete []`. Similarly, always delete memory allocated as an individual element with operator `delete`.

21.7 static Class Members

There is an important exception to the rule that each object of a class has its own copy of all the data members of the class. In certain cases, only one copy of a variable should be shared by all objects of a class. A **static data member** is used for these and other reasons. Such a variable represents "classwide" information (i.e., a property of the class shared by all instances, not a property of a specific object of the class). The declaration of a `static` member begins with keyword `static`.

Let us further motivate the need for `static` classwide data with an example. Suppose that we have a video game with `Martians` and other space creatures. Each `Martian` tends to be brave and willing to attack other space creatures when the `Martian` is aware that there are at least five `Martians` present. If fewer than five are present, each `Martian` becomes cowardly. So each `Martian` needs to know the `martianCount`. We could endow each instance of class `Martian` with `martianCount` as a data member. If we do, every `Martian` will have a separate copy of the data member. Every time we create a new `Martian`, we will have to update the data member martianCount in all Martian objects. Doing this would require every Martian object to have, or have access to, handles to all other Martian objects in memory. This wastes space with the redundant copies and wastes time in updating the separate copies. Instead, we declare martianCount to be static. This makes martian-Count classwide data. Every Martian can access martianCount as if it were a data member of the Martian, but only one copy of the static variable martianCount is maintained by C++. This saves space. We save time by having the Martian constructor increment static variable martianCount and having the Martian destructor decrement martianCount. Because there is only one copy, we do not have to increment or decrement separate copies of martianCount for each Martian object.

Performance Tip 21.3

Use static data members to save storage when a single copy of the data for all objects of a class will suffice.

Although they may seem like global variables, a class's static data members have class scope. Also, static members can be declared public, private or protected. A fundamental-type static data member is initialized by default to 0. If you want a different initial value, a static data member can be initialized *once* (and only once). A const static data member of int or enum type can be initialized in its declaration in the class definition. However, all other static data members must be defined at file scope (i.e., outside the body of the class definition) and can be initialized only in those definitions. Note that static data members of class types (i.e., static member objects) that have default constructors need not be initialized because their default constructors will be called.

A class's private and protected static members are normally accessed through public member functions of the class or through friends of the class. (In Chapter 23, we will see that a class's private and protected static members can also be accessed through protected member functions of the class.) A class's static members exist even when no objects of that class exist. To access a public static class member when no objects of the class exist, simply prefix the class name and the binary scope resolution operator (::) to the name of the data member. For example, if our preceding variable martian-Count is public, it can be accessed with the expression Martian::martianCount when there are no Martian objects. (Of course, using public data is discouraged.)

A class's public static class members can also be accessed through any object of that class using the object's name, the dot operator and the name of the member (e.g., myMartian.martianCount). To access a private or protected static class member when no objects of the class exist, provide a public static member function and call the function by prefixing its name with the class name and binary scope resolution operator. (As we will see in Chapter 23, a protected static member function can serve this purpose, too.) A static member function is a service of the *class*, not of a specific object of the class.

Software Engineering Observation 21.10

A class's static data members and static member functions exist and can be used even if no objects of that class have been instantiated.

The program of Figs. 21.21–21.23 demonstrates a private static data member called count (Fig. 21.21, line 21) and a public static member function called getCount

(Fig. 21.21, line 15). In Fig. 21.22, line 14 defines and initializes the data member count to zero at file scope and lines 18–21 define static member function getCount. Notice that neither line 14 nor line 18 includes keyword static, yet both lines refer to static class members. When static is applied to an item at file scope, that item becomes known only in that file. The static members of the class need to be available from any client code that accesses the file, so we cannot declare them static in the .cpp file—we declare them static only in the .h file. Data member count maintains a count of the number of objects of class Employee that have been instantiated. When objects of class Employee exist, member count can be referenced through any member function of an Employee object—in Fig. 21.22, count is referenced by both line 33 in the constructor and line 48 in the destructor. Also, note that since count is an int, it could have been initialized in the header file at line 21 of Fig. 21.21.

 Common Programming Error 21.10

It is a compilation error to include keyword static in the definition of a static data members at file scope.

In Fig. 21.22, note the use of the new operator (lines 27 and 30) in the Employee constructor to dynamically allocate the correct amount of memory for members firstName and lastName. If the new operator is unable to fulfill the request for memory for one or both of these character arrays, the program will terminate immediately. In Chapter 27, we will provide a better mechanism for dealing with cases in which new is unable to allocate memory.

```
1   // Fig. 21.21: Employee.h
2   // Employee class definition.
3   #ifndef EMPLOYEE_H
4   #define EMPLOYEE_H
5
6   class Employee
7   {
8   public:
9      Employee( const char * const, const char * const ); // constructor
10     ~Employee(); // destructor
11     const char *getFirstName() const; // return first name
12     const char *getLastName() const; // return last name
13
14     // static member function
15     static int getCount(); // return number of objects instantiated
16  private:
17     char *firstName;
18     char *lastName;
19
20     // static data
21     static int count; // number of objects instantiated
22  }; // end class Employee
23
24  #endif
```

Fig. 21.21 | Employee class definition with a static data member to track the number of Employee objects in memory.

Also note in Fig. 21.22 that the implementations of functions getFirstName (lines 52–58) and getLastName (lines 61–67) return pointers to const character data. In this

```cpp
1   // Fig. 21.22: Employee.cpp
2   // Member-function definitions for class Employee.
3   #include <iostream>
4   using std::cout;
5   using std::endl;
6
7   #include <cstring> // strlen and strcpy prototypes
8   using std::strlen;
9   using std::strcpy;
10
11  #include "Employee.h" // Employee class definition
12
13  // define and initialize static data member at file scope
14  int Employee::count = 0;
15
16  // define static member function that returns number of
17  // Employee objects instantiated (declared static in Employee.h)
18  int Employee::getCount()
19  {
20     return count;
21  } // end static function getCount
22
23  // constructor dynamically allocates space for first and last name and
24  // uses strcpy to copy first and last names into the object
25  Employee::Employee( const char * const first, const char * const last )
26  {
27     firstName = new char[ strlen( first ) + 1 ];
28     strcpy( firstName, first );
29
30     lastName = new char[ strlen( last ) + 1 ];
31     strcpy( lastName, last );
32
33     count++; // increment static count of employees
34
35     cout << "Employee constructor for " << firstName
36        << ' ' << lastName << " called." << endl;
37  } // end Employee constructor
38
39  // destructor deallocates dynamically allocated memory
40  Employee::~Employee()
41  {
42     cout << "~Employee() called for " << firstName
43        << ' ' << lastName << endl;
44
45     delete [] firstName; // release memory
46     delete [] lastName; // release memory
47
48     count--; // decrement static count of employees
49  } // end ~Employee destructor
```

Fig. 21.22 | Employee class member-function definitions. (Part 1 of 2.)

```
50
51    // return first name of employee
52    const char *Employee::getFirstName() const
53    {
54       // const before return type prevents client from modifying
55       // private data; client should copy returned string before
56       // destructor deletes storage to prevent undefined pointer
57       return firstName;
58    } // end function getFirstName
59
60    // return last name of employee
61    const char *Employee::getLastName() const
62    {
63       // const before return type prevents client from modifying
64       // private data; client should copy returned string before
65       // destructor deletes storage to prevent undefined pointer
66       return lastName;
67    } // end function getLastName
```

Fig. 21.22 | Employee class member-function definitions. (Part 2 of 2.)

implementation, if the client wishes to retain a copy of the first name or last name, the client is responsible for copying the dynamically allocated memory in the Employee object after obtaining the pointer to const character data from the object. It is also possible to implement getFirstName and getLastName, so the client is required to pass a character array and the size of the array to each function. Then the functions could copy the first or last name into the character array provided by the client. Once again, note that we could have used class string here to return a copy of a string object to the caller rather than returning a pointer to the private data.

Figure 21.23 uses static member function getCount to determine the number of Employee objects currently instantiated. Note that when no objects are instantiated in the program, the Employee::getCount() function call is issued (lines 14 and 38). However, when objects are instantiated, function getCount can be called through either of the objects, as shown in the statement at lines 22–23, which uses pointer e1Ptr to invoke function getCount. Note that using e2Ptr->getCount() or Employee::getCount() in line 23 would produce the same result, because getCount always accesses the same static member count.

```
1    // Fig. 21.23: fig21_23.cpp
2    // Driver to test class Employee.
3    #include <iostream>
4    using std::cout;
5    using std::endl;
6
7    #include "Employee.h" // Employee class definition
8
9    int main()
10   {
```

Fig. 21.23 | static data member tracking the number of objects of a class. (Part 1 of 2.)

```
11      // use class name and binary scope resolution operator to
12      // access static number function getCount
13      cout << "Number of employees before instantiation of any objects is "
14         << Employee::getCount() << endl; // use class name
15
16      // use new to dynamically create two new Employees
17      // operator new also calls the object's constructor
18      Employee *e1Ptr = new Employee( "Susan", "Baker" );
19      Employee *e2Ptr = new Employee( "Robert", "Jones" );
20
21      // call getCount on first Employee object
22      cout << "Number of employees after objects are instantiated is "
23         << e1Ptr->getCount();
24
25      cout << "\n\nEmployee 1: "
26         << e1Ptr->getFirstName() << " " << e1Ptr->getLastName()
27         << "\nEmployee 2: "
28         << e2Ptr->getFirstName() << " " << e2Ptr->getLastName() << "\n\n";
29
30      delete e1Ptr; // deallocate memory
31      e1Ptr = 0; // disconnect pointer from free-store space
32      delete e2Ptr; // deallocate memory
33      e2Ptr = 0; // disconnect pointer from free-store space
34
35      // no objects exist, so call static member function getCount again
36      // using the class name and the binary scope resolution operator
37      cout << "Number of employees after objects are deleted is "
38         << Employee::getCount() << endl;
39      return 0;
40   } // end main
```

```
Number of employees before instantiation of any objects is 0
Employee constructor for Susan Baker called.
Employee constructor for Robert Jones called.
Number of employees after objects are instantiated is 2

Employee 1: Susan Baker
Employee 2: Robert Jones

~Employee() called for Susan Baker
~Employee() called for Robert Jones
Number of employees after objects are deleted is 0
```

Fig. 21.23 | static data member tracking the number of objects of a class. (Part 2 of 2.)

Software Engineering Observation 21.11

Some organizations specify in their software engineering standards that all calls to static member functions be made using the class name and not an object handle.

A member function should be declared static if it does not access non-static data members or non-static member functions of the class. Unlike non-static member functions, a static member function does not have a this pointer, because static data members and static member functions exist independently of any objects of a class. The this pointer must refer to a specific object of the class, and when a static member function is called, there might not be any objects of its class in memory.

Common Programming Error 21.11

Using the this *pointer in a* static *member function is a compilation error.*

Common Programming Error 21.12

Declaring a static *member function* const *is a compilation error. The* const *qualifier indicates that a function cannot modify the contents of the object in which it operates, but* static *member functions exist and operate independently of any objects of the class.*

Lines 18–19 of Fig. 21.23 use operator new to dynamically allocate two Employee objects. Remember that the program will terminate immediately if it is unable to allocate one or both of these objects. When each Employee object is allocated, its constructor is called. When delete is used at lines 30 and 32 to deallocate the two Employee objects, each object's destructor is called.

Error-Prevention Tip 21.2

After deleting dynamically allocated memory, set the pointer that referred to that memory to 0. This disconnects the pointer from the previously allocated space on the free store. This space in memory could still contain information, despite having been deleted. By setting the pointer to 0, the program loses any access to that free-store space, which, in fact, could have already been reallocated for a different purpose. If you didn't set the pointer to 0, your code could inadvertently access this new information, causing extremely subtle, nonrepeatable logic errors.

21.8 Data Abstraction and Information Hiding

A class normally hides its implementation details from its clients. This is called information hiding. As an example of information hiding, let us consider the stack data structure.

Stacks can be implemented with arrays and with other data structures, such as linked lists. A client of a stack class need not be concerned with the stack's implementation. The client knows only that when data items are placed in the stack, they will be recalled in last-in, first-out order. The client cares about *what* functionality a stack offers, not about *how* that functionality is implemented. This concept is referred to as **data abstraction**. Although programmers might know the details of a class's implementation, they should not write code that depends on these details. This enables a particular class (such as one that implements a stack and its operations, *push* and *pop*) to be replaced with another version without affecting the rest of the system. As long as the public services of the class do not change (i.e., every original public member function still has the same prototype in the new class definition), the rest of the system is not affected.

Many programming languages emphasize actions. In these languages, data exists to support the actions that programs must take. Data is "less interesting" than actions. Data is "crude." Only a few built-in data types exist, and it is difficult for programmers to create their own types. C++ and the object-oriented style of programming elevate the importance of data. The primary activities of object-oriented programming in C++ are the creation of types (i.e., classes) and the expression of the interactions among objects of those types. To create languages that emphasize data, the programming-languages community needed to formalize some notions about data. The formalization we consider here is the notion of abstract data types (ADTs), which improve the program development process.

What is an abstract data type? Consider the built-in type int, which most people would associate with an integer in mathematics. Rather, an int is an abstract representation of an integer. Unlike mathematical integers, computer ints are fixed in size. For example, type int on today's popular 32-bit machines is typically limited to the range –2,147,483,648 to +2,147,483,647. If the result of a calculation falls outside this range, an "overflow" error occurs and the computer responds in some machine-dependent manner. It might, for example, "quietly" produce an incorrect result, such as a value too large to fit in an int variable (commonly called arithmetic overflow). Mathematical integers do not have this problem. Therefore, the notion of a computer int is only an approximation of the notion of a real-world integer. The same is true with double.

Even char is an approximation; char values are normally eight-bit patterns of ones and zeros; these patterns look nothing like the characters they represent, such as a capital Z, a lowercase z, a dollar sign ($), a digit (5), and so on. Values of type char on most computers are quite limited compared with the range of real-world characters. The seven-bit ASCII character set (Appendix C) provides for 128 different character values. This is inadequate for representing languages such as Japanese and Chinese that require thousands of characters. As Internet and World Wide Web usage becomes pervasive, the newer Unicode character set is growing rapidly in popularity, owing to its ability to represent the characters of most languages. For more information on Unicode, visit www.unicode.org.

The point is that even the built-in data types provided with programming languages like C++ are really only approximations or imperfect models of real-world concepts and behaviors. We have taken int for granted until this point, but now you have a new perspective to consider. Types like int, double, char and others are all examples of abstract data types. They are essentially ways of representing real-world notions to some satisfactory level of precision within a computer system.

An abstract data type actually captures two notions: a data representation and the operations that can be performed on those data. For example, in C++, an int contains an integer value (data) and provides addition, subtraction, multiplication, division and modulus operations (among others)—division by zero is undefined. These allowed operations perform in a manner sensitive to machine parameters, such as the fixed word size of the underlying computer system. Another example is the notion of negative integers, where the operations and data representation are clear, but the operation of taking the square root of a negative integer is undefined. In C++, the programmer uses classes to implement abstract data types and their services.

21.8.1 Example: Array Abstract Data Type

We discussed arrays in Chapter 6. As described there, an array is not much more than a pointer and some space in memory. This primitive capability is acceptable for performing array operations if the programmer is cautious and undemanding. There are many operations that would be nice to perform with arrays, but that are not built into C++. With C++ classes, the programmer can develop an array ADT that is preferable to "raw" arrays. The array class can provide many helpful new capabilities such as

- subscript range checking

- an arbitrary range of subscripts instead of having to start with 0

- array assignment

- array comparison

- array input/output

- arrays that know their sizes

- arrays that expand dynamically to accommodate more elements

- arrays that can print themselves in neat tabular format.

We create our own array class with many of these capabilities in Chapter 22, Operator Overloading. C++ has a small set of built-in types. Classes extend the base programming language with new types.

Software Engineering Observation 21.12

The programmer is able to create new types through the class mechanism. These new types can be designed to be used as conveniently as the built-in types. Thus, C++ is an extensible language. Although the language is easy to extend with these new types, the base language itself cannot be changed.

New classes created in C++ environments can be proprietary to an individual, to small groups or to companies. Classes can also be placed in standard class libraries intended for wide distribution. ANSI (the American National Standards Institute) and ISO (the International Organization for Standardization) developed a standard version of C++ that includes a standard class library. The reader who learns C++ and object-oriented programming will be ready to take advantage of the new kinds of rapid, component-oriented software development made possible with increasingly abundant and rich libraries.

21.8.2 Example: String Abstract Data Type

C++ is an intentionally sparse language that provides programmers with only the raw capabilities needed to build a broad range of systems (consider it a tool for making tools). The language is designed to minimize performance burdens. C++ is appropriate for both applications programming and systems programming—the latter places extraordinary performance demands on programs. Certainly, it would have been possible to include a string data type among C++'s built-in data types. Instead, the language was designed to include mechanisms for creating and implementing string abstract data types through classes. We introduced the C++ Standard Library class `string` in Chapter 19, and in Chapter 22 we will develop our own `String` ADT.

21.8.3 Example: Queue Abstract Data Type

Each of us stands in line from time to time. A waiting line is also called a **queue**. We wait in line at the supermarket checkout counter, we wait in line to get gasoline, we wait in line to board a bus, we wait in line to pay a highway toll, and students know all too well about waiting in line during registration to get the courses they want. Computer systems use many waiting lines internally, so we need to write programs that simulate what queues are and do.

A queue is a good example of an abstract data type. Queues offer well-understood behavior to their clients. Clients put things in a queue one at a time—invoking the queue's enqueue operation—and the clients get those things back one at a time on demand—invoking the queue's **dequeue** operation. Conceptually, a queue can become infinitely long. A real queue, of course, is finite. Items are returned from a queue in first-in, first-out (FIFO) order—the first item inserted in the queue is the first item removed from the queue.

The queue hides an internal data representation that somehow keeps track of the items currently waiting in line, and it offers a set of operations to its clients, namely, *enqueue* and *dequeue*. The clients are not concerned about the implementation of the queue. Clients merely want the queue to operate "as advertised." When a client enqueues a new item, the queue should accept that item and place it internally in some kind of first-in, first-out data structure. When the client wants the next item from the front of the queue, the queue should remove the item from its internal representation and deliver it to the outside world (i.e., to the client of the queue) in FIFO order (i.e., the item that has been in the queue the longest should be the next one returned by the next *dequeue* operation).

The queue ADT guarantees the integrity of its internal data structure. Clients may not manipulate this data structure directly. Only the queue member functions have access to its internal data. Clients may cause only allowable operations to be performed on the data representation; operations not provided in the ADT's public interface are rejected in some appropriate manner. This could mean issuing an error message, throwing an exception (see Chapter 27), terminating execution or simply ignoring the operation request.

21.9 Container Classes and Iterators

Among the most popular types of classes are **container classes** (also called **collection classes**), i.e., classes designed to hold collections of objects. Container classes commonly provide services such as insertion, deletion, searching, sorting, and testing an item to determine whether it is a member of the collection. Arrays, stacks, queues, trees and linked lists are examples of container classes.

It is common to associate **iterator objects**—or more simply **iterators**—with container classes. An iterator is an object that "walks through" a collection, returning the next item (or performing some action on the next item). Once an iterator for a class has been written, obtaining the next element from the class can be expressed simply. Just as a book being shared by several people could have several bookmarks in it at once, a container class can have several iterators operating on it at once. Each iterator maintains its own "position" information.

21.10 Proxy Classes

Recall that two of the fundamental principles of good software engineering are separating interface from implementation and hiding implementation details. We strive to achieve these goals by defining a class in a header file and implementing its member functions in a separate implementation file. However, as we pointed out in Chapter 20, header files *do* contain some portion of a class's implementation and hints about others. For example, a class's private members are listed in the class definition in a header file, so these members are visible to clients, even though the clients may not access the `private` members. Revealing a class's `private` data in this manner potentially exposes proprietary information to clients of the class. We now introduce the notion of a proxy class that allows you to hide even the `private` data of a class from clients of the class. Providing clients of your class with a proxy class that knows only the `public` interface to your class enables the clients to use your class's services without gaining access to your class's implementation details.

Implementing a proxy class requires several steps, which we demonstrate in Figs. 21.24–21.27. First, we create the class definition for the class that contains the proprietary implementation we would like to hide. Our example class, called `Implementation`, is shown in Fig. 21.24. The proxy class `Interface` is shown in Figs. 21.25–21.26. The test program and sample output are shown in Fig. 21.27.

Class `Implementation` (Fig. 21.24) provides a single `private` data member called `value` (the data we would like to hide from the client), a constructor to initialize `value` and functions `setValue` and `getValue`.

We define a proxy class called `Interface` (Fig. 21.25) with a `public` interface identical (except for the constructor and destructor names) to that of class `Implementation`. The only `private` member of the proxy class is a pointer to an object of class `Implementation`. Using a pointer in this manner allows us to hide the implementation details of class `Implementation` from the client. Notice that the only mentions in class `Interface`

```
1   // Fig. 21.24: Implementation.h
2   // Header file for class Implementation
3
4   class Implementation
5   {
6   public:
7      // constructor
8      Implementation( int v )
9         : value( v ) // initialize value with v
10     {
11        // empty body
12     } // end constructor Implementation
13
14     // set value to v
15     void setValue( int v )
16     {
17        value = v; // should validate v
18     } // end function setValue
19
20     // return value
21     int getValue() const
22     {
23        return value;
24     } // end function getValue
25   private:
26      int value; // data that we would like to hide from the client
27   }; // end class Implementation
```

Fig. 21.24 | `Implementation` class definition.

```
1   // Fig. 21.25: Interface.h
2   // Header file for class Interface
3   // Client sees this source code, but the source code does not reveal
4   // the data layout of class Implementation.
5
6   class Implementation; // forward class declaration required by line 17
7
8   class Interface
9   {
10  public:
11     Interface( int ); // constructor
12     void setValue( int ); // same public interface as
13     int getValue() const; // class Implementation has
14     ~Interface(); // destructor
15  private:
16     // requires previous forward declaration (line 6)
17     Implementation *ptr;
18  }; // end class Interface
```

Fig. 21.25 | Interface class definition.

of the proprietary `Implementation` class are in the pointer declaration (line 17) and in line 6, a forward class declaration. When a class definition (such as class `Interface`) uses only a pointer or reference to an object of another class (such as to an object of class `Implementation`), the class header file for that other class (which would ordinarily reveal the private data of that class) is not required to be included with `#include`. You can simply declare that other class as a data type with a forward class declaration (line 6) before the type is used in the file.

The member-function implementation file for proxy class `Interface` (Fig. 21.26) is the only file that includes the header file `Implementation.h` (line 5) containing class `Implementation`. The file `Interface.cpp` (Fig. 21.26) is provided to the client as a precompiled object-code file along with the header file `Interface.h` that includes the function prototypes of the services provided by the proxy class. Because file `Interface.cpp` is made available to the client only as object code, the client is not able to see the interactions between the proxy class and the proprietary class (lines 9, 17, 23 and 29). Notice that the proxy class imposes an extra "layer" of function calls as the "price to pay" for hiding the `private` data of class Implementation. Given the speed of today's computers and the fact that many compilers can inline simple function calls automatically, the effect of these extra function calls on performance is often negligible.

Figure 21.27 tests class `Interface`. Notice that only the header file for `Interface` is included in the client code (line 7)—there is no mention of the existence of a separate class called `Implementation`. Thus, the client never sees the `private` data of class `Implementation`, nor can the client code become dependent on the `Implementation` code.

Software Engineering Observation 21.13

A proxy class insulates client code from implementation changes.

```
1   // Fig. 21.26: Interface.cpp
2   // Implementation of class Interface--client receives this file only
3   // as precompiled object code, keeping the implementation hidden.
4   #include "Interface.h" // Interface class definition
5   #include "Implementation.h" // Implementation class definition
6
7   // constructor
8   Interface::Interface( int v )
9      : ptr ( new Implementation( v ) ) // initialize ptr to point to
10  {                                     // a new Implementation object
11     // empty body
12  } // end Interface constructor
13
14  // call Implementation's setValue function
15  void Interface::setValue( int v )
16  {
17     ptr->setValue( v );
18  } // end function setValue
19
20  // call Implementation's getValue function
21  int Interface::getValue() const
22  {
23     return ptr->getValue();
24  } // end function getValue
25
26  // destructor
27  Interface::~Interface()
28  {
29     delete ptr;
30  } // end ~Interface destructor
```

Fig. 21.26 | Interface class member-function definitions.

```
1   // Fig. 21.27: fig21_27.cpp
2   // Hiding a class's private data with a proxy class.
3   #include <iostream>
4   using std::cout;
5   using std::endl;
6
7   #include "Interface.h" // Interface class definition
8
9   int main()
10  {
11     Interface i( 5 ); // create Interface object
12
13     cout << "Interface contains: " << i.getValue()
14        << " before setValue" << endl;
15
16     i.setValue( 10 );
17
```

Fig. 21.27 | Implementing a proxy class. (Part 1 of 2.)

```
18      cout << "Interface contains: " << i.getValue()
19         << " after setValue" << endl;
20      return 0;
21   } // end main
```

```
Interface contains: 5 before setValue
Interface contains: 10 after setValue
```

Fig. 21.27 | Implementing a proxy class. (Part 2 of 2.)

21.11 Wrap-Up

This chapter introduced several advanced topics related to classes and data abstraction. You learned how to specify const objects and const member functions to prevent modifications to objects, thus enforcing the principle of least privilege. You also learned that, through composition, a class can have objects of other classes as members. We introduced the topic of friendship and presented examples that demonstrate how to use friend functions.

You learned that the this pointer is passed as an implicit argument to each of a class's non-static member functions, allowing the functions to access the correct object's data members and other non-static member functions. You also saw explicit use of the this pointer to access the class's members and to enable cascaded member-function calls.

The chapter introduced the concept of dynamic memory management. You learned that C++ programmers can create and destroy objects dynamically with the new and delete operators. We motivated the need for static data members and demonstrated how to declare and use static data members and member functions in your own classes.

You learned about data abstraction and information hiding—two of the fundamental concepts of object-oriented programming. We discussed abstract data types—ways of representing real-world or conceptual notions to some satisfactory level of precision within a computer system. You then learned about three example abstract data types—arrays, strings and queues. We introduced the concept of a container class that holds a collection of objects, as well as the notion of an iterator class that walks through the elements of a container class. Finally, you learned how to create a proxy class to hide the implementation details (including the private data members) of a class from clients of the class.

In Chapter 22, we continue our study of classes and objects by showing how to enable C++'s operators to work with objects—a process called operator overloading. For example, you will see how to "overload" the << operator so it can be used to output a complete array without explicitly using a repetition statement.

Summary

Section 21.2 const (Constant) Objects and const Member Functions
- The keyword const can be used to specify that an object is not modifiable and that any attempt to modify the object should result in a compilation error.
- C++ compilers disallow non-const member-function calls on const objects.
- It is a compilation error if a const member function tries to modify an object of its class (*this).
- A function is specified as const both in its prototype and in its definition.

- A const object must be initialized, not assigned to.
- Constructors and destructors cannot be declared const.
- const data members and data members that are references *must* be initialized in member initializers.

Section 21.3 Composition: Objects as Members of Classes

- A class can have objects of other classes as members—this concept is called composition.
- Member objects are constructed in the order in which they are declared in the class definition and before their enclosing class objects are constructed.
- If a member initializer is not provided for a member object, the member object's default constructor will be called implicitly.

Section 21.4 friend Functions and friend Classes

- A friend function of a class is defined outside that class's scope, yet has the right to access the non-public (and public) members of the class. Stand-alone functions or entire classes may be declared to be friends of another class.
- A friend declaration can appear anywhere in the class. A friend is essentially a part of the public interface of the class.
- The friendship relation is neither symmetric nor transitive.

Section 21.5 Using the this Pointer

- Every object has access to its own address through the this pointer.
- An object's this pointer is not part of the object itself—i.e., the size of the memory occupied by the this pointer is not reflected in the result of a sizeof operation on the object.
- The this pointer is passed (by the compiler) as an implicit argument to each of the object's non-static member functions.
- Objects use the this pointer implicitly (as we have done to this point) or explicitly to reference their data members and member functions.
- The this pointer enables cascaded member-function calls in which multiple functions are invoked in the same statement.

Section 21.6 Dynamic Memory Management with Operators new and delete

- Dynamic memory management enables programmers to control the allocation and deallocation of memory in a program for any built-in or user-defined type.
- The free store (sometimes called the heap) is a region of memory assigned to each program for storing objects, dynamically allocated at execution time.
- The new operator allocates storage of the proper size for an object, runs the object's constructor and returns a pointer of the correct type. The new operator can be used to dynamically allocate any fundamental type (such as int or double) or class type. If new is unable to find space in memory for the object, it indicates that an error occurred by "throwing" an "exception." This usually causes the program to terminate immediately.
- To destroy a dynamically allocated object and free the object's space, use the delete operator.
- An array of objects can be allocated dynamically with new as in

```
int *ptr = new int[ 100 ];
```

which allocates an array of 100 integers and assigns the starting location of the array to ptr. The preceding array of integers is deleted with the statement

```
delete [] ptr;
```

Section 21.7 static Class Members

- A static data member represents "classwide" information (i.e., a property of the class shared by all instances, not a property of a specific object of the class).

- static data members have class scope and can be declared public, private or protected.

- A class's static members exist even when no objects of that class exist.

- To access a public static class member when no objects of the class exist, simply prefix the class name and the binary scope resolution operator (::) to the name of the data member.

- A class's public static class members can be accessed through any object of that class.

- A member function should be declared static if it does not access non-static data members or non-static member functions of the class. Unlike non-static member functions, a static member function does not have a this pointer, because static data members and static member functions exist independently of any objects of a class.

Section 21.8 Data Abstraction and Information Hiding

- Abstract data types are ways of representing real-world and conceptual notions to some satisfactory level of precision within a computer system.

- An abstract data type captures two notions: a data representation and the operations that can be performed on those data.

- C++ is an intentionally sparse language that provides programmers with only the raw capabilities needed to build a broad range of systems. C++ is designed to minimize performance burdens.

Section 21.9 Container Classes and Iterators

- Items are returned from a queue in first-in, first-out (FIFO) order—the first item inserted in the queue is the first item removed from the queue.

- Container classes (also called collection classes) are designed to hold collections of objects. Container classes commonly provide services such as insertion, deletion, searching, sorting, and testing an item to determine whether it is a member of the collection.

- It is common to associate iterators with container classes. An iterator is an object that "walks through" a collection, returning the next item (or performing some action on the next item).

Section 21.10 Proxy Classes

- Providing clients of your class with a proxy class that knows only the public interface to your class enables the clients to use your class's services without gaining access to your class's implementation details, such as its private data.

- When a class definition uses only a pointer or reference to an object of another class, the class header file for that other class (which would ordinarily reveal the private data of that class) is not required to be included with #include. You can simply declare that other class as a data type with a forward class declaration before the type is used in the file.

- The implementation file containing the member functions for a proxy class is the only file that includes the header file for the class whose private data we would like to hide.

- The implementation file containing the member functions for the proxy class is provided to the client as a precompiled object code file along with the header file that includes the function prototypes of the services provided by the proxy class.

Terminology

abstract data type (ADT)	arithmetic overflow
allocate memory	cascaded member-function calls

collection class
composition
const member function
const object
container class
data abstraction
data representation
deallocate memory
delete operator
delete[] operator
dequeue (queue operation)
dynamic memory management
dynamic objects
enqueue (queue operation)
first-in, first-out (FIFO)
forward class declaration
free store
friend class
friend function

has-a relationship
heap
host object
information hiding
iterator
last-in, first-out (LIFO)
member initializer
member-initializer list
member object
member object constructor
memory leak
new [] operator
new operator
operations in an ADT
proxy class
queue abstract data type
static data member
static member function
this pointer

Self-Review Exercises

21.1 Fill in the blanks in each of the following:

a) _____ must be used to initialize constant members of a class.

b) A nonmember function must be declared as a(n) _____ of a class to have access to that class's private data members.

c) The _____ operator dynamically allocates memory for an object of a specified type and returns a _____ to that type.

d) A constant object must be _____; it cannot be modified after it is created.

e) A(n) _____ data member represents classwide information.

f) An object's non-static member functions have access to a "self pointer" to the object called the _____ pointer.

g) The keyword _____ specifies that an object or variable is not modifiable after it is initialized.

h) If a member initializer is not provided for a member object of a class, the object's _____ is called.

i) A member function should be declared static if it does not access _____ class members.

j) Member objects are constructed _____ their enclosing class object.

k) The _____ operator reclaims memory previously allocated by new.

21.2 Find the errors in the following class and explain how to correct them:

```
1  class Example
2  {
3  public:
4     Example( int y = 10 )
5        : data( y )
6     {
7        // empty body
8     } // end Example constructor       (continued)
```

```
 9      int getIncrementedData() const
10      {
11         return data++;
12      } // end function getIncrementedData
13      static int getCount()
14      {
15         cout << "Data is " << data << endl;
16         return count;
17      } // end function getCount
18   private:
19      int data;
20      static int count;
21   }; // end class Example
```

Answers to Self-Review Exercises

21.1 a) member initializers. b) `friend`. c) `new`, pointer. d) initialized. e) `static`. f) `this`. g) `const`. h) default constructor. i) non-`static`. j) before. k) `delete`.

21.2 Error: The class definition for `Example` has two errors. The first occurs in function `getIncrementedData`. The function is declared `const`, but it modifies the object.
Correction: To correct the first error, remove the `const` keyword from the definition of `getIncrementedData`.
Error: The second error occurs in function `getCount`. This function is declared `static`, so it is not allowed to access any non-`static` member of the class.
Correction: To correct the second error, remove the output line from the `getCount` definition.

Exercises

21.3 Compare and contrast dynamic memory allocation and deallocation operators `new`, `new []`, `delete` and `delete []`.

21.4 Explain the notion of friendship in C++. Explain the negative aspects of friendship as described in the text.

21.5 Can a correct `Time` class definition include both of the following constructors? If not, explain why not.

```
Time( int h = 0, int m = 0, int s = 0 );
Time();
```

21.6 What happens when a return type, even `void`, is specified for a constructor or destructor?

21.7 Modify class `Date` in Fig. 21.10 to have the following capabilities:
a) Output the date in multiple formats such as

```
DDD YYYY
MM/DD/YY
June 14, 1992
```

b) Use overloaded constructors to create `Date` objects initialized with dates of the formats in part (a).
c) Create a `Date` constructor that reads the system date using the standard library functions of the `<ctime>` header and sets the `Date` members. (See your compiler's reference documentation or `www.cplusplus.com/ref/ctime/index.html` for information on the functions in header `<ctime>`.)

In Chapter 22, we will be able to create operators for testing the equality of two dates and for comparing dates to determine whether one date is prior to, or after, another.

21.8   Create a SavingsAccount class. Use a static data member annualInterestRate to store the annual interest rate for each of the savers. Each member of the class contains a private data member savingsBalance indicating the amount the saver currently has on deposit. Provide member function calculateMonthlyInterest that calculates the monthly interest by multiplying the balance by annualInterestRate divided by 12; this interest should be added to savingsBalance. Provide a static member function modifyInterestRate that sets the static annualInterestRate to a new value. Write a driver program to test class SavingsAccount. Instantiate two different objects of class SavingsAccount, saver1 and saver2, with balances of $2000.00 and $3000.00, respectively. Set the annualInterestRate to 3 percent. Then calculate the monthly interest and print the new balances for each of the savers. Then set the annualInterestRate to 4 percent, calculate the next month's interest and print the new balances for each of the savers.

21.9   Create class IntegerSet for which each object can hold integers in the range 0 through 100. A set is represented internally as an array of ones and zeros. Array element a[i] is 1 if integer i is in the set. Array element a[j] is 0 if integer j is not in the set. The default constructor initializes a set to the so-called "empty set," i.e., a set whose array representation contains all zeros.

Provide member functions for the common set operations. For example, provide a unionOfSets member function that creates a third set that is the set-theoretic union of two existing sets (i.e., an element of the third set's array is set to 1 if that element is 1 in either or both of the existing sets, and an element of the third set's array is set to 0 if that element is 0 in each of the existing sets).

Provide an intersectionOfSets member function which creates a third set which is the set-theoretic intersection of two existing sets (i.e., an element of the third set's array is set to 0 if that element is 0 in either or both of the existing sets, and an element of the third set's array is set to 1 if that element is 1 in each of the existing sets).

Provide an insertElement member function that inserts a new integer k into a set (by setting a[k] to 1). Provide a deleteElement member function that deletes integer m (by setting a[m] to 0).

Provide a printSet member function that prints a set as a list of numbers separated by spaces. Print only those elements that are present in the set (i.e., their position in the array has a value of 1). Print --- for an empty set.

Provide an isEqualTo member function that determines whether two sets are equal.

Provide an additional constructor that receives an array of integers and the size of that array and uses the array to initialize a set object.

Now write a driver program to test your IntegerSet class. Instantiate several IntegerSet objects. Test that all your member functions work properly.

21.10   It would be perfectly reasonable for the Time class of Figs. 21.18–21.19 to represent the time internally as the number of seconds since midnight rather than the three integer values hour, minute and second. Clients could use the same public methods and get the same results. Modify the Time class of Fig. 21.18 to implement the time as the number of seconds since midnight and show that there is no visible change in functionality to the clients of the class. [*Note:* This exercise nicely demonstrates the virtues of implementation hiding.]

Operator Overloading

OBJECTIVES

In this chapter, you will learn:

- What operator overloading is and how it makes programs more readable and programming more convenient.

- To redefine (overload) operators to work with objects of user-defined classes.

- The differences between overloading unary and binary operators.

- To convert objects from one class to another class.

- When to, and when not to, overload operators.

- To create **PhoneNumber**, **Array**, **String** and **Date** classes that demonstrate operator overloading.

- To use overloaded operators and other member functions of standard library class **string**.

- To use keyword **explicit** to prevent the compiler from using single-argument constructors to perform implicit conversions.

22.1 Introduction

Chapters 20–21 introduced the basics of C++ classes. Services were obtained from objects by sending messages (in the form of member-function calls) to the objects. This function call notation is cumbersome for certain kinds of classes (such as mathematical classes). Also, many common manipulations are performed with operators (e.g., input and output). We can use C++'s rich set of built-in operators to specify common object manipulations. This chapter shows how to enable C++'s operators to work with objects—a process called operator overloading. It is straightforward and natural to extend C++ with these new capabilities, but it must be done cautiously.

One example of an overloaded operator built into C++ is <<, which is used both as the stream insertion operator and as the bitwise left-shift operator. Similarly, >> is also overloaded; it is used both as the stream extraction operator and as the bitwise right-shift operator. Both of these operators are overloaded in the C++ Standard Library.

Although operator overloading sounds like an exotic capability, most programmers implicitly use overloaded operators regularly. For example, the C++ language itself overloads the addition operator (+) and the subtraction operator (-). These operators perform differently, depending on their context in integer arithmetic, floating-point arithmetic and pointer arithmetic.

C++ enables the programmer to overload most operators to be sensitive to the context in which they are used—the compiler generates the appropriate code based on the context (in particular, the types of the operands). Some operators are overloaded frequently, especially the assignment operator and various arithmetic operators such as + and -. The jobs performed by overloaded operators can also be performed by explicit function calls, but operator notation is often clearer and more familiar to programmers.

We discuss when to, and when not to, use operator overloading. We implement user-defined classes `PhoneNumber`, `Array`, `String` and `Date` to demonstrate how to overload operators, including the stream insertion, stream extraction, assignment, equality, relational, subscript, logical negation, parentheses and increment operators. The chapter ends with an example of C++'s Standard Library class `string`, which provides many overloaded operators that are similar to our `String` class that we present earlier in the chapter. In the exercises, we ask you to implement several classes with overloaded operators. The exercises also use classes `Complex` (for complex numbers) and `HugeInt` (for integers larger than a computer can represent with type `long`) to demonstrate overloaded arithmetic operators + and – and ask you to enhance those classes by overloading other arithmetic operators.

22.2 Fundamentals of Operator Overloading

C++ programming is a type-sensitive and type-focused process. Programmers can use fundamental types and can define new types. The fundamental types can be used with C++'s rich collection of operators. Operators provide programmers with a concise notation for expressing manipulations of objects of fundamental types.

Programmers can use operators with user-defined types as well. Although C++ does not allow new operators to be created, it does allow most existing operators to be overloaded so that, when these operators are used with objects, the operators have meaning appropriate to those objects. This is a powerful capability.

Software Engineering Observation 22.1

Operator overloading contributes to C++'s extensibility—one of the language's most appealing attributes.

Good Programming Practice 22.1

Use operator overloading when it makes a program clearer than accomplishing the same operations with function calls.

Good Programming Practice 22.2

Overloaded operators should mimic the functionality of their built-in counterparts—for example, the + operator should be overloaded to perform addition, not subtraction. Avoid excessive or inconsistent use of operator overloading, as this can make a program cryptic and difficult to read.

An operator is overloaded by writing a non-`static` member function definition or global function definition as you normally would, except that the function name now becomes the keyword `operator` followed by the symbol for the operator being overloaded. For example, the function name `operator+` would be used to overload the addition operator (+). When operators are overloaded as member functions, they must be non-`static`, because they must be called on an object of the class and operate on that object.

To use an operator on class objects, that operator *must* be overloaded—with three exceptions. The assignment operator (=) may be used with every class to perform memberwise assignment of the data members of the class—each data member is assigned from the "source" object to the "target" object of the assignment. We will soon see that such default memberwise assignment is dangerous for classes with pointer members; we will explicitly overload the assignment operator for such classes. The address (&) and comma (,) operators may also be used with objects of any class without overloading. The address operator returns the address of the object in memory. The comma operator evaluates the expression to its left then the expression to its right. Both of these operators can also be overloaded.

Overloading is especially appropriate for mathematical classes. These often require that a substantial set of operators be overloaded to ensure consistency with the way these mathematical classes are handled in the real world. For example, it would be unusual to overload only addition for a complex number class, because other arithmetic operators are also commonly used with complex numbers.

Operator overloading provides the same concise and familiar expressions for user-defined types that C++ provides with its rich collection of operators for fundamental types. Operator overloading is not automatic—you must write operator-overloading functions to perform the desired operations. Sometimes these functions are best made member functions; sometimes they are best as `friend` functions; occasionally they can be made global, non-`friend` functions. We discuss these issues throughout the chapter.

22.3 Restrictions on Operator Overloading

Most of C++'s operators can be overloaded. These are shown in Fig. 22.1. Figure 22.2 shows the operators that cannot be overloaded.

 Common Programming Error 22.1

Attempting to overload a nonoverloadable operator is a syntax error.

Precedence, Associativity and Number of Operands

The precedence of an operator cannot be changed by overloading. This can lead to awkward situations in which an operator is overloaded in a manner for which its fixed precedence is inappropriate. However, parentheses can be used to force the order of evaluation of overloaded operators in an expression.

Operators that can be overloaded							
+	-	*	/	%	^	&	|
~	!	=	<	>	+=	-=	*=
/=	%=	^=	&=	|=	<<	>>	>>=
<<=	==	!=	<=	>=	&&	||	++
--	->*	,	->	[]	()	new	delete
new[]	delete[]						

Fig. 22.1 | Operators that can be overloaded.

Operators that cannot be overloaded			
.	.*	::	?:

Fig. 22.2 | Operators that cannot be overloaded.

The associativity of an operator (i.e., whether the operator is applied right-to-left or left-to-right) cannot be changed by overloading.

It is not possible to change the "arity" of an operator (i.e., the number of operands an operator takes): Overloaded unary operators remain unary operators; overloaded binary operators remain binary operators. C++'s only ternary operator (?:) cannot be overloaded. Operators &, *, + and – all have both unary and binary versions; these unary and binary versions can each be overloaded.

Common Programming Error 22.2

Attempting to change the "arity" of an operator via operator overloading is a compilation error.

Creating New Operators

It is not possible to create new operators; only existing operators can be overloaded. Unfortunately, this prevents the programmer from using popular notations like the ** operator used in some other programming languages for exponentiation. [*Note:* You could overload the ^ operator to perform exponentiation—as it does in some other languages.]

Common Programming Error 22.3

Attempting to create new operators via operator overloading is a syntax error.

Operators for Fundamental Types

The meaning of how an operator works on objects of fundamental types cannot be changed by operator overloading. The programmer cannot, for example, change the meaning of how + adds two integers. Operator overloading works only with objects of user-defined types or with a mixture of an object of a user-defined type and an object of a fundamental type.

Software Engineering Observation 22.2

At least one argument of an operator function must be an object or reference of a user-defined type. This prevents programmers from changing how operators work on fundamental types.

Common Programming Error 22.4

Attempting to modify how an operator works with objects of fundamental types is a compilation error.

Related Operators

Overloading an assignment operator and an addition operator to allow statements like

        object2 = object2 + object1;

does not imply that the += operator is also overloaded to allow statements such as

        object2 += object1;

Such behavior can be achieved only by explicitly overloading operator += for that class.

Common Programming Error 22.5

Assuming that overloading an operator such as + overloads related operators such as += or that overloading == overloads a related operator like != can lead to errors. Operators can be overloaded only explicitly; there is no implicit overloading.

22.4 Operator Functions as Class Members vs. Global Functions

Operator functions can be member functions or global functions; global functions are often made `friend`s for performance reasons. Member functions use the `this` pointer implicitly to obtain one of their class object arguments (the left operand for binary operators). Arguments for both operands of a binary operator must be explicitly listed in a global function call.

Operators That Must Be Overloaded as Member Functions

When overloading (), [], -> or any of the assignment operators, the operator overloading function must be declared as a class member. For the other operators, the operator overloading functions can be class members or global functions.

Operators as Member Functions and Global Functions

Whether an operator function is implemented as a member function or as a global function, the operator is still used the same way in expressions. So which implementation is best?

When an operator function is implemented as a member function, the leftmost (or only) operand must be an object (or a reference to an object) of the operator's class. If the left operand must be an object of a different class or a fundamental type, this operator function must be implemented as a global function (as we will do in Section 22.5 when overloading << and >> as the stream insertion and stream extraction operators, respectively). A global operator function can be made a `friend` of a class if that function must access `private` or `protected` members of that class directly.

Operator member functions of a specific class are called (implicitly by the compiler) only when the left operand of a binary operator is specifically an object of that class, or when the single operand of a unary operator is an object of that class.

Why Overloaded Stream Insertion and Stream Extraction Operators Are Overloaded as Global Functions

The overloaded stream insertion operator (<<) is used in an expression in which the left operand has type `ostream &`, as in `cout << classObject`. To use the operator in this manner where the right operand is an object of a user-defined class, it must be overloaded as a global function. To be a member function, operator << would have to be a member of the `ostream` class. This is not possible for user-defined classes, since we are not allowed to modify C++ Standard Library classes. Similarly, the overloaded stream extraction operator (>>) is used in an expression in which the left operand has type `istream &`, as in `cin >> classObject`, and the right operand is an object of a user-defined class, so it, too, must be a global function. Also, each of these overloaded operator functions may require access to the `private` data members of the class object being output or input, so these overloaded operator functions can be made `friend` functions of the class for performance reasons.

Performance Tip 22.1

It is possible to overload an operator as a global, non-`friend` function, but such a function requiring access to a class's `private` or `protected` data would need to use set or get functions provided in that class's `public` interface. The overhead of calling these functions could cause poor performance, so these functions can be inlined to improve performance.

Commutative Operators

Another reason why one might choose a global function to overload an operator is to enable the operator to be commutative. For example, suppose we have an object, number, of type long int, and an object bigInteger1, of class HugeInteger (a class in which integers may be arbitrarily large rather than being limited by the machine word size of the underlying hardware; class HugeInteger is developed in the chapter exercises). The addition operator (+) produces a temporary HugeInteger object as the sum of a HugeInteger and a long int (as in the expression bigInteger1 + number), or as the sum of a long int and a HugeInteger (as in the expression number + bigInteger1). Thus, we require the addition operator to be commutative (exactly as it is with two fundamental-type operands). The problem is that the class object must appear on the left of the addition operator if that operator is to be overloaded as a member function. So, we overload the operator as a global function to allow the HugeInteger to appear on the right of the addition. The operator+ function, which deals with the HugeInteger on the left, can still be a member function.

22.5 Overloading Stream Insertion and Stream Extraction Operators

C++ is able to input and output the fundamental types using the stream extraction operator >> and the stream insertion operator <<. The class libraries provided with C++ compilers overload these operators to process each fundamental type, including pointers and C-like char * strings. The stream insertion and stream extraction operators also can be overloaded to perform input and output for user-defined types. The program of Figs. 22.3–22.5 demonstrates overloading these operators to handle data of a user-defined telephone number class called PhoneNumber. This program assumes telephone numbers are input correctly.

```
1   // Fig. 22.3: PhoneNumber.h
2   // PhoneNumber class definition
3   #ifndef PHONENUMBER_H
4   #define PHONENUMBER_H
5
6   #include <iostream>
7   using std::ostream;
8   using std::istream;
9
10  #include <string>
11  using std::string;
12
13  class PhoneNumber
14  {
15     friend ostream &operator<<( ostream &, const PhoneNumber & );
16     friend istream &operator>>( istream &, PhoneNumber & );
17  private:
18     string areaCode; // 3-digit area code
19     string exchange; // 3-digit exchange
```

Fig. 22.3 | PhoneNumber class with overloaded stream insertion and stream extraction operators as friend functions. (Part 1 of 2.)

```
20      string line; // 4-digit line
21    }; // end class PhoneNumber
22
23    #endif
```

Fig. 22.3 | PhoneNumber class with overloaded stream insertion and stream extraction operators as friend functions. (Part 2 of 2.)

```
 1    // Fig. 22.4: PhoneNumber.cpp
 2    // Overloaded stream insertion and stream extraction operators
 3    // for class PhoneNumber.
 4    #include <iomanip>
 5    using std::setw;
 6
 7    #include "PhoneNumber.h"
 8
 9    // overloaded stream insertion operator; cannot be
10    // a member function if we would like to invoke it with
11    // cout << somePhoneNumber;
12    ostream &operator<<( ostream &output, const PhoneNumber &number )
13    {
14       output << "(" << number.areaCode << ") "
15          << number.exchange << "-" << number.line;
16       return output; // enables cout << a << b << c;
17    } // end function operator<<
18
19    // overloaded stream extraction operator; cannot be
20    // a member function if we would like to invoke it with
21    // cin >> somePhoneNumber;
22    istream &operator>>( istream &input, PhoneNumber &number )
23    {
24       input.ignore(); // skip (
25       input >> setw( 3 ) >> number.areaCode; // input area code
26       input.ignore( 2 ); // skip ) and space
27       input >> setw( 3 ) >> number.exchange; // input exchange
28       input.ignore(); // skip dash (-)
29       input >> setw( 4 ) >> number.line; // input line
30       return input; // enables cin >> a >> b >> c;
31    } // end function operator>>
```

Fig. 22.4 | Overloaded stream insertion and stream extraction operators for class PhoneNumber.

```
 1    // Fig. 22.5: fig22_05.cpp
 2    // Demonstrating class PhoneNumber's overloaded stream insertion
 3    // and stream extraction operators.
 4    #include <iostream>
 5    using std::cout;
 6    using std::cin;
 7    using std::endl;
```

Fig. 22.5 | Overloaded stream insertion and stream extraction operators. (Part 1 of 2.)

```
 8
 9   #include "PhoneNumber.h"
10
11   int main()
12   {
13      PhoneNumber phone; // create object phone
14
15      cout << "Enter phone number in the form (123) 456-7890:" << endl;
16
17      // cin >> phone invokes operator>> by implicitly issuing
18      // the global function call operator>>( cin, phone )
19      cin >> phone;
20
21      cout << "The phone number entered was: ";
22
23      // cout << phone invokes operator<< by implicitly issuing
24      // the global function call operator<<( cout, phone )
25      cout << phone << endl;
26      return 0;
27   } // end main
```

```
Enter phone number in the form (123) 456-7890:
(800) 555-1212
The phone number entered was: (800) 555-1212
```

Fig. 22.5 | Overloaded stream insertion and stream extraction operators. (Part 2 of 2.)

The stream extraction operator function operator>> (Fig. 22.4, lines 22–31) takes istream reference input and PhoneNumber reference num as arguments and returns an istream reference. Operator function operator>> inputs phone numbers of the form

    (800) 555-1212

into objects of class PhoneNumber. When the compiler sees the expression

    cin >> phone

in line 19 of Fig. 22.5, the compiler generates the global function call

    operator>>(cin, phone);

When this call executes, reference parameter input (Fig. 22.4, line 22) becomes an alias for cin and reference parameter number becomes an alias for phone. The operator function reads as strings the three parts of the telephone number into the areaCode (line 25), exchange (line 27) and line (line 29) members of the PhoneNumber object referenced by parameter number. Stream manipulator setw limits the number of characters read into each character array. When used with cin and strings, setw restricts the number of characters read to the number of characters specified by its argument (i.e., setw(3) allows three characters to be read). The parentheses, space and dash characters are skipped by calling istream member function ignore (Fig. 22.4, lines 24, 26 and 28), which discards the specified number of characters in the input stream (one character by default). Function operator>> returns istream reference input (i.e., cin). This enables input operations on

PhoneNumber objects to be cascaded with input operations on other PhoneNumber objects or on objects of other data types. For example, a program can input two PhoneNumber objects in one statement as follows:

```
cin >> phone1 >> phone2;
```

First, the expression cin >> phone1 executes by making the global function call

```
operator>>( cin, phone1 );
```

This call then returns a reference to cin as the value of cin >> phone1, so the remaining portion of the expression is interpreted simply as cin >> phone2. This executes by making the global function call

```
operator>>( cin, phone2 );
```

The stream insertion operator function (Fig. 22.4, lines 12–17) takes an ostream reference (output) and a const PhoneNumber reference (number) as arguments and returns an ostream reference. Function operator<< displays objects of type PhoneNumber. When the compiler sees the expression

```
cout << phone
```

in line 25 of Fig. 22.5, the compiler generates the global function call

```
operator<<( cout, phone );
```

Function operator<< displays the parts of the telephone number as strings, because they are stored as string objects.

Error-Prevention Tip 22.1

Returning a reference from an overloaded << or >> operator function is typically successful because cout, cin and most stream objects are global, or at least long-lived. Returning a reference to an automatic variable or other temporary object is dangerous—creating "dangling references" to nonexisting objects.

Note that the functions operator>> and operator<< are declared in PhoneNumber as global, friend functions (Fig. 22.3, lines 15–16). They are global functions because the object of class PhoneNumber appears in each case as the right operand of the operator. Remember, overloaded operator functions for binary operators can be member functions only when the left operand is an object of the class in which the function is a member. Overloaded input and output operators are declared as friends if they need to access non-public class members directly for performance reasons or because the class may not offer appropriate *get* functions. Also note that the PhoneNumber reference in function operator<<'s parameter list (Fig. 22.4, line 12) is const, because the PhoneNumber will simply be output, and the PhoneNumber reference in function operator>>'s parameter list (line 22) is non-const, because the PhoneNumber object must be modified to store the input telephone number in the object.

Software Engineering Observation 22.3

New input/output capabilities for user-defined types are added to C++ without modifying C++'s standard input/output library classes. This is another example of the extensibility of the C++ programming language.

22.6 Overloading Unary Operators

A unary operator for a class can be overloaded as a non-static member function with no arguments or as a global function with one argument; that argument must be either an object of the class or a reference to an object of the class. Member functions that implement overloaded operators must be non-static so that they can access the non-static data in each object of the class. Remember that static member functions can access only static data members of the class.

Consider the expression !s, in which s is an object of class String. When a unary operator such as ! is overloaded as a member function with no arguments and the compiler sees the expression !s, the compiler generates the call s.operator!(). The operand s is the class object for which the String class member function operator! is being invoked. The function is declared in the class definition as follows:

```
class String
{
public:
   bool operator!() const;
   ...
}; // end class String
```

A unary operator such as ! may be overloaded as a global function with one argument in two different ways—either with an argument that is an object (this requires a copy of the object, so the side effects of the function are not applied to the original object), or with an argument that is a reference to an object (no copy of the original object is made, so all side effects of this function are applied to the original object). If s is a String class object (or a reference to a String class object), then !s is treated as if the call operator!(s) had been written, invoking the global operator! function that is declared as follows:

```
bool operator!( const String & );
```

22.7 Overloading Binary Operators

A binary operator can be overloaded as a non-static member function with one argument or as a global function with two arguments (one of those arguments must be either a class object or a reference to a class object).

Later in this chapter, we will overload < to compare two String objects. When overloading binary operator < as a non-static member function of a String class with one argument, if y and z are String-class objects, then y < z is treated as if y.operator<(z) had been written, invoking the operator< member function declared below

```
class String

public:
   bool operator<( const String & ) const;
   ...
}; // end class String
```

If binary operator < is to be overloaded as a global function, it must take two arguments—one of which must be a class object or a reference to a class object. If y and z are

String-class objects or references to String-class objects, then y < z is treated as if the call operator<(y, z) had been written in the program, invoking global-function operator< declared as follows:

```
bool operator<( const String &, const String & );
```

22.8 Case Study: Array Class

Pointer-based arrays have a number of problems. For example, a program can easily "walk off" either end of an array, because C++ does not check whether subscripts fall outside the range of an array (the programmer can still do this explicitly though). Arrays of size *n* must number their elements 0, ..., *n* – 1; alternate subscript ranges are not allowed. An entire non-char array cannot be input or output at once; each array element must be read or written individually. Two arrays cannot be meaningfully compared with equality operators or relational operators (because the array names are simply pointers to where the arrays begin in memory and, of course, two arrays will always be at different memory locations). When an array is passed to a general-purpose function designed to handle arrays of any size, the size of the array must be passed as an additional argument. One array cannot be assigned to another with the assignment operator(s) (because array names are const pointers and a constant pointer cannot be used on the left side of an assignment operator). These and other capabilities certainly seem like "naturals" for dealing with arrays, but pointer-based arrays do not provide such capabilities. However, C++ does provide the means to implement such array capabilities through the use of classes and operator overloading.

In this example, we create a powerful array class that performs range checking to ensure that subscripts remain within the bounds of the Array. The class allows one array object to be assigned to another with the assignment operator. Objects of the Array class know their size, so the size does not need to be passed separately as an argument when passing an Array to a function. Entire Arrays can be input or output with the stream extraction and stream insertion operators, respectively. Array comparisons can be made with the equality operators == and !=.

This example will sharpen your appreciation of data abstraction. You will probably want to suggest other enhancements to this Array class. Class development is an interesting, creative and intellectually challenging activity—always with the goal of "crafting valuable classes."

The program of Figs. 22.6–22.8 demonstrates class Array and its overloaded operators. First we walk through main (Fig. 22.8). Then we consider the class definition (Fig. 22.6) and each of the class's member-function and friend-function definitions (Fig. 22.7).

```
1   // Fig. 22.6: Array.h
2   // Array class for storing arrays of integers.
3   #ifndef ARRAY_H
4   #define ARRAY_H
5
```

Fig. 22.6 | Array class definition with overloaded operators. (Part 1 of 2.)

```
6   #include <iostream>
7   using std::ostream;
8   using std::istream;
9
10  class Array
11  {
12     friend ostream &operator<<( ostream &, const Array & );
13     friend istream &operator>>( istream &, Array & );
14  public:
15     Array( int = 10 ); // default constructor
16     Array( const Array & ); // copy constructor
17     ~Array(); // destructor
18     int getSize() const; // return size
19
20     const Array &operator=( const Array & ); // assignment operator
21     bool operator==( const Array & ) const; // equality operator
22
23     // inequality operator; returns opposite of == operator
24     bool operator!=( const Array &right ) const
25     {
26        return ! ( *this == right ); // invokes Array::operator==
27     } // end function operator!=
28
29     // subscript operator for non-const objects returns modifiable lvalue
30     int &operator[]( int );
31
32     // subscript operator for const objects returns rvalue
33     int operator[]( int ) const;
34  private:
35     int size; // pointer-based array size
36     int *ptr; // pointer to first element of pointer-based array
37  }; // end class Array
38
39  #endif
```

Fig. 22.6 | Array class definition with overloaded operators. (Part 2 of 2.)

```
1   // Fig 11.7: Array.cpp
2   // Member-function definitions for class Array
3   #include <iostream>
4   using std::cerr;
5   using std::cout;
6   using std::cin;
7   using std::endl;
8
9   #include <iomanip>
10  using std::setw;
11
12  #include <cstdlib> // exit function prototype
13  using std::exit;
```

Fig. 22.7 | Array class member- and friend-function definitions. (Part 1 of 4.)

```
14
15  #include "Array.h" // Array class definition
16
17  // default constructor for class Array (default size 10)
18  Array::Array( int arraySize )
19  {
20     size = ( arraySize > 0 ? arraySize : 10 ); // validate arraySize
21     ptr = new int[ size ]; // create space for pointer-based array
22
23     for ( int i = 0; i < size; i++ )
24        ptr[ i ] = 0; // set pointer-based array element
25  } // end Array default constructor
26
27  // copy constructor for class Array;
28  // must receive a reference to prevent infinite recursion
29  Array::Array( const Array &arrayToCopy )
30     : size( arrayToCopy.size )
31  {
32     ptr = new int[ size ]; // create space for pointer-based array
33
34     for ( int i = 0; i < size; i++ )
35        ptr[ i ] = arrayToCopy.ptr[ i ]; // copy into object
36  } // end Array copy constructor
37
38  // destructor for class Array
39  Array::~Array()
40  {
41     delete [] ptr; // release pointer-based array space
42  } // end destructor
43
44  // return number of elements of Array
45  int Array::getSize() const
46  {
47     return size; // number of elements in Array
48  } // end function getSize
49
50  // overloaded assignment operator;
51  // const return avoids: ( a1 = a2 ) = a3
52  const Array &Array::operator=( const Array &right )
53  {
54     if ( &right != this ) // avoid self-assignment
55     {
56        // for Arrays of different sizes, deallocate original
57        // left-side array, then allocate new left-side array
58        if ( size != right.size )
59        {
60           delete [] ptr; // release space
61           size = right.size; // resize this object
62           ptr = new int[ size ]; // create space for array copy
63        } // end inner if
64
```

Fig. 22.7 | Array class member- and friend-function definitions. (Part 2 of 4.)

```
65          for ( int i = 0; i < size; i++ )
66              ptr[ i ] = right.ptr[ i ]; // copy array into object
67      } // end outer if
68
69      return *this; // enables x = y = z, for example
70  } // end function operator=
71
72  // determine if two Arrays are equal and
73  // return true, otherwise return false
74  bool Array::operator==( const Array &right ) const
75  {
76      if ( size != right.size )
77          return false; // arrays of different number of elements
78
79      for ( int i = 0; i < size; i++ )
80          if ( ptr[ i ] != right.ptr[ i ] )
81              return false; // Array contents are not equal
82
83      return true; // Arrays are equal
84  } // end function operator==
85
86  // overloaded subscript operator for non-const Arrays;
87  // reference return creates a modifiable lvalue
88  int &Array::operator[]( int subscript )
89  {
90      // check for subscript out-of-range error
91      if ( subscript < 0 || subscript >= size )
92      {
93          cerr << "\nError: Subscript " << subscript
94              << " out of range" << endl;
95          exit( 1 ); // terminate program; subscript out of range
96      } // end if
97
98      return ptr[ subscript ]; // reference return
99  } // end function operator[]
100
101 // overloaded subscript operator for const Arrays
102 // const reference return creates an rvalue
103 int Array::operator[]( int subscript ) const
104 {
105     // check for subscript out-of-range error
106     if ( subscript < 0 || subscript >= size )
107     {
108         cerr << "\nError: Subscript " << subscript
109             << " out of range" << endl;
110         exit( 1 ); // terminate program; subscript out of range
111     } // end if
112
113     return ptr[ subscript ]; // returns copy of this element
114 } // end function operator[]
115
```

Fig. 22.7 | Array class member- and friend-function definitions. (Part 3 of 4.)

```
116   // overloaded input operator for class Array;
117   // inputs values for entire Array
118   istream &operator>>( istream &input, Array &a )
119   {
120      for ( int i = 0; i < a.size; i++ )
121         input >> a.ptr[ i ];
122
123      return input; // enables cin >> x >> y;
124   } // end function
125
126   // overloaded output operator for class Array
127   ostream &operator<<( ostream &output, const Array &a )
128   {
129      int i;
130
131      // output private ptr-based array
132      for ( i = 0; i < a.size; i++ )
133      {
134         output << setw( 12 ) << a.ptr[ i ];
135
136         if ( ( i + 1 ) % 4 == 0 ) // 4 numbers per row of output
137            output << endl;
138      } // end for
139
140      if ( i % 4 != 0 ) // end last line of output
141         output << endl;
142
143      return output; // enables cout << x << y;
144   } // end function operator<<
```

Fig. 22.7 | Array class member- and `friend`-function definitions. (Part 4 of 4.)

```
1    // Fig. 22.8: fig22_08.cpp
2    // Array class test program.
3    #include <iostream>
4    using std::cout;
5    using std::cin;
6    using std::endl;
7
8    #include "Array.h"
9
10   int main()
11   {
12      Array integers1( 7 ); // seven-element Array
13      Array integers2; // 10-element Array by default
14
15      // print integers1 size and contents
16      cout << "Size of Array integers1 is "
17         << integers1.getSize()
18         << "\nArray after initialization:\n" << integers1;
19
```

Fig. 22.8 | Array class test program. (Part 1 of 3.)

```
20      // print integers2 size and contents
21      cout << "\nSize of Array integers2 is "
22         << integers2.getSize()
23         << "\nArray after initialization:\n" << integers2;
24
25      // input and print integers1 and integers2
26      cout << "\nEnter 17 integers:" << endl;
27      cin >> integers1 >> integers2;
28
29      cout << "\nAfter input, the Arrays contain:\n"
30         << "integers1:\n" << integers1
31         << "integers2:\n" << integers2;
32
33      // use overloaded inequality (!=) operator
34      cout << "\nEvaluating: integers1 != integers2" << endl;
35
36      if ( integers1 != integers2 )
37         cout << "integers1 and integers2 are not equal" << endl;
38
39      // create Array integers3 using integers1 as an
40      // initializer; print size and contents
41      Array integers3( integers1 ); // invokes copy constructor
42
43      cout << "\nSize of Array integers3 is "
44         << integers3.getSize()
45         << "\nArray after initialization:\n" << integers3;
46
47      // use overloaded assignment (=) operator
48      cout << "\nAssigning integers2 to integers1:" << endl;
49      integers1 = integers2; // note target Array is smaller
50
51      cout << "integers1:\n" << integers1
52         << "integers2:\n" << integers2;
53
54      // use overloaded equality (==) operator
55      cout << "\nEvaluating: integers1 == integers2" << endl;
56
57      if ( integers1 == integers2 )
58         cout << "integers1 and integers2 are equal" << endl;
59
60      // use overloaded subscript operator to create rvalue
61      cout << "\nintegers1[5] is " << integers1[ 5 ];
62
63      // use overloaded subscript operator to create lvalue
64      cout << "\n\nAssigning 1000 to integers1[5]" << endl;
65      integers1[ 5 ] = 1000;
66      cout << "integers1:\n" << integers1;
67
68      // attempt to use out-of-range subscript
69      cout << "\nAttempt to assign 1000 to integers1[15]" << endl;
70      integers1[ 15 ] = 1000; // ERROR: out of range
71      return 0;
72   } // end main
```

Fig. 22.8 | Array class test program. (Part 2 of 3.)

```
Size of Array integers1 is 7
Array after initialization:
           0           0           0           0
           0           0           0

Size of Array integers2 is 10
Array after initialization:
           0           0           0           0
           0           0           0           0
           0           0

Enter 17 integers:
1 2 3 4 5 6 7 8 9 10 11 12 13 14 15 16 17

After input, the Arrays contain:
integers1:
           1           2           3           4
           5           6           7
integers2:
           8           9          10          11
          12          13          14          15
          16          17

Evaluating: integers1 != integers2
integers1 and integers2 are not equal

Size of Array integers3 is 7
Array after initialization:
           1           2           3           4
           5           6           7

Assigning integers2 to integers1:
integers1:
           8           9          10          11
          12          13          14          15
          16          17
integers2:
           8           9          10          11
          12          13          14          15
          16          17

Evaluating: integers1 == integers2
integers1 and integers2 are equal

integers1[5] is 13

Assigning 1000 to integers1[5]
integers1:
           8           9          10          11
          12        1000          14          15
          16          17

Attempt to assign 1000 to integers1[15]

Error: Subscript 15 out of range
```

Fig. 22.8 | Array class test program. (Part 3 of 3.)

Creating Arrays, Outputting Their Size and Displaying Their Contents

The program begins by instantiating two objects of class Array—integers1 (Fig. 22.8, line 12) with seven elements, and integers2 (Fig. 22.8, line 13) with the default Array size—10 elements (specified by the Array default constructor's prototype in Fig. 22.6, line 15). Lines 16–18 use member function getSize to determine the size of integers1 and output integers1, using the Array overloaded stream insertion operator. The sample output confirms that the Array elements were set correctly to zeros by the constructor. Next, lines 21–23 output the size of Array integers2 and output integers2, using the Array overloaded stream insertion operator.

Using the Overloaded Stream Insertion Operator to Fill an Array

Line 26 prompts the user to input 17 integers. Line 27 uses the Array overloaded stream extraction operator to read these values into both arrays. The first seven values are stored in integers1 and the remaining 10 values are stored in integers2. Lines 29–31 output the two arrays with the overloaded Array stream insertion operator to confirm that the input was performed correctly.

Using the Overloaded Inequality Operator

Line 36 tests the overloaded inequality operator by evaluating the condition

```
integers1 != integers2
```

The program output shows that the Arrays indeed are not equal.

Initializing a New Array with a Copy of an Existing Array's Contents

Line 41 instantiates a third Array called integers3 and initializes it with a copy of Array integers1. This invokes the Array copy constructor to copy the elements of integers1 into integers3. We discuss the details of the copy constructor shortly. Note that the copy constructor can also be invoked by writing line 41 as follows:

```
Array integers3 = integers1;
```

The equal sign in the preceding statement is *not* the assignment operator. When an equal sign appears in the declaration of an object, it invokes a constructor for that object. This form can be used to pass only a single argument to a constructor.

Lines 43–45 output the size of integers3 and output integers3, using the Array overloaded stream insertion operator to confirm that the Array elements were set correctly by the copy constructor.

Using the Overloaded Assignment Operator

Next, line 49 tests the overloaded assignment operator (=) by assigning integers2 to integers1. Lines 51–52 print both Array objects to confirm that the assignment was successful. Note that integers1 originally held seven integers and was resized to hold a copy of the 10 elements in integers2. As we will see, the overloaded assignment operator performs this resizing operation in a manner that is transparent to the client code.

Using the Overloaded Equality Operator

Next, line 57 uses the overloaded equality operator (==) to confirm that objects integers1 and integers2 are indeed identical after the assignment.

Using the Overloaded Subscript Operator

Line 61 uses the overloaded subscript operator to refer to integers1[5]—an in-range element of integers1. This subscripted name is used as an *rvalue* to print the value stored in integers1[5]. Line 65 uses integers1[5] as a modifiable *lvalue* on the left side of an assignment statement to assign a new value, 1000, to element 5 of integers1. We will see that operator[] returns a reference to use as the modifiable *lvalue* after the operator confirms that 5 is a valid subscript for integers1.

Line 70 attempts to assign the value 1000 to integers1[15]—an out-of-range element. In this example, operator[] determines that the subscript is out of range, prints a message and terminates the program. Note that we highlighted line 70 of the program in red to emphasize that it is an error to access an element that is out of range. This is a runtime logic error, not a compilation error.

Interestingly, the array subscript operator [] is not restricted for use only with arrays; it also can be used, for example, to select elements from other kinds of container classes, such as linked lists, strings and dictionaries. Also, when operator[] functions are defined, subscripts no longer have to be integers—characters, strings, floats or even objects of user-defined classes also could be used.

Array Class Definition

Now that we have seen how this program operates, let us walk through the class header (Fig. 22.6). As we refer to each member function in the header, we discuss that function's implementation in Fig. 22.7. In Fig. 22.6, lines 35–36 represent the private data members of class Array. Each Array object consists of a size member indicating the number of elements in the Array and an int pointer—ptr—that points to the dynamically allocated pointer-based array of integers managed by the Array object.

Overloading the Stream Insertion and Stream Extraction Operators as friends

Lines 12–13 of Fig. 22.6 declare the overloaded stream insertion operator and the overloaded stream extraction operator to be friends of class Array. When the compiler sees an expression like cout << arrayObject, it invokes global function operator<< with the call

```
operator<<( cout, arrayObject )
```

When the compiler sees an expression like cin >> arrayObject, it invokes global function operator>> with the call

```
operator>>( cin, arrayObject )
```

We note again that these stream insertion and stream extraction operator functions cannot be members of class Array, because the Array object is always mentioned on the right side of the stream insertion operator and the stream extraction operator. If these operator functions were to be members of class Array, the following awkward statements would have to be used to output and input an Array:

```
arrayObject << cout;
arrayObject >> cin;
```

Such statements would be confusing to most C++ programmers, who are familiar with cout and cin appearing as the left operands of << and >>, respectively.

Function operator<< (defined in Fig. 22.7, lines 127–144) prints the number of elements indicated by size from the integer array to which ptr points. Function operator>> (defined in Fig. 22.7, lines 118–124) inputs directly into the array to which ptr points. Each of these operator functions returns an appropriate reference to enable cascaded output or input statements, respectively. Note that each of these functions has access to an Array's private data because these functions are declared as friends of class Array. Also, note that class Array's getSize and operator[] functions could be used by operator<< and operator>>, in which case these operator functions would not need to be friends of class Array. However, the additional function calls might increase execution-time overhead.

Array Default Constructor
Line 15 of Fig. 22.6 declares the default constructor for the class and specifies a default size of 10 elements. When the compiler sees a declaration like line 13 in Fig. 22.8, it invokes class Array's default constructor (remember that the default constructor in this example actually receives a single int argument that has a default value of 10). The default constructor (defined in Fig. 22.7, lines 18–25) validates and assigns the argument to data member size, uses new to obtain the memory for the internal pointer-based representation of this array and assigns the pointer returned by new to data member ptr. Then the constructor uses a for statement to set all the elements of the array to zero. It is possible to have an Array class that does not initialize its members—if, for example, these members are to be read at some later time—but this is considered to be a poor programming practice. Arrays, and objects in general, should be properly initialized and maintained in a consistent state.

Array Copy Constructor
Line 16 of Fig. 22.6 declares a copy constructor (defined in Fig. 22.7, lines 29–36) that initializes an Array by making a copy of an existing Array object. Such copying must be done carefully to avoid the pitfall of leaving both Array objects pointing to the same dynamically allocated memory. This is exactly the problem that would occur with default memberwise copying, if the compiler were allowed to define a default copy constructor for this class. Copy constructors are invoked whenever a copy of an object is needed, such as in passing an object by value to a function, returning an object by value from a function or initializing an object with a copy of another object of the same class. The copy constructor is called in a declaration when an object of class Array is instantiated and initialized with another object of class Array, as in the declaration in line 41 of Fig. 22.8.

Software Engineering Observation 22.4

The argument to a copy constructor should be a const reference to allow a const object to be copied.

Common Programming Error 22.6

Note that a copy constructor must receive its argument by reference, not by value. Otherwise, the copy constructor call results in infinite recursion (a fatal logic error), because receiving an object by value requires the copy constructor to make a copy of the argument object. Recall that any time a copy of an object is required, the class's copy constructor is called. If the copy constructor received its argument by value, the copy constructor would call itself recursively to make a copy of its argument!

The copy constructor for Array uses a member initializer (Fig. 22.7, line 30) to copy the size of the initializer Array into data member size, uses new (line 32) to obtain the memory for the internal pointer-based representation of this Array and assigns the pointer returned by new to data member ptr.[1] Then the copy constructor uses a for statement to copy all the elements of the initializer Array into the new Array object. Note that an object of a class can look at the private data of any other object of that class (using a handle that indicates which object to access).

Common Programming Error 22.7

If the copy constructor simply copied the pointer in the source object to the target object's pointer, then both objects would point to the same dynamically allocated memory. The first destructor to execute would then delete the dynamically allocated memory, and the other object's ptr would be undefined, a situation called a dangling pointer—this would likely result in a serious run-time error (such as early program termination) when the pointer was used.

Array Destructor
Line 17 of Fig. 22.6 declares the destructor for the class (defined in Fig. 22.7, lines 39–42). The destructor is invoked when an object of class Array goes out of scope. The destructor uses delete [] to release the memory allocated dynamically by new in the constructor.

getSize Member Function
Line 18 of Fig. 22.6 declares function getSize (defined in Fig. 22.7, lines 45–48) that returns the number of elements in the Array.

Overloaded Assignment Operator
Line 20 of Fig. 22.6 declares the overloaded assignment operator function for the class. When the compiler sees the expression integers1 = integers2 in line 49 of Fig. 22.8, the compiler invokes member function operator= with the call

```
integers1.operator=( integers2 )
```

The implementation of member function operator= (Fig. 22.7, lines 52–70) tests for self assignment (line 54) in which an object of class Array is being assigned to itself. When this is equal to the address of the right operand, a self-assignment is being attempted, so the assignment is skipped (i.e., the object already is itself; in a moment we will see why self-assignment is dangerous). If it is not a self-assignment, then the member function determines whether the sizes of the two arrays are identical (line 58); in that case, the original array of integers in the left-side Array object is not reallocated. Otherwise, operator= uses delete (line 60) to release the memory originally allocated to the target array, copies the size of the source array to the size of the target array (line 61), uses new to allocate memory for the target array and places the pointer returned by new into the array's ptr member.[2] Then the for statement at lines 65–66 copies the array elements from the source array to the target array. Regardless of whether this is a self-assignment, the member function returns the current object (i.e., *this at line 69) as a constant reference; this enables cascaded Array assignments such as x = y = z. If self-assignment occurs, and function op-

---

1. Note that new could fail to obtain the needed memory. We deal with new failures in Chapter 27, Exception Handling.
2. Once again, new could fail. We discuss new failures in Chapter 27.

erator= did not test for this case, operator= would delete the dynamic memory associated with the Array object before the assignment was complete. This would leave ptr pointing to memory that had been deallocated, which could lead to fatal runtime errors.

Software Engineering Observation 22.5

A copy constructor, a destructor and an overloaded assignment operator are usually provided as a group for any class that uses dynamically allocated memory.

Common Programming Error 22.8

Not providing an overloaded assignment operator and a copy constructor for a class when objects of that class contain pointers to dynamically allocated memory is a logic error.

Software Engineering Observation 22.6

It is possible to prevent one object of a class from being assigned to another. This is done by declaring the assignment operator as a private *member of the class.*

Software Engineering Observation 22.7

It is possible to prevent class objects from being copied; to do this, simply make both the overloaded assignment operator and the copy constructor of that class private.

Overloaded Equality and Inequality Operators

Line 21 of Fig. 22.6 declares the overloaded equality operator (==) for the class. When the compiler sees the expression integers1 == integers2 in line 57 of Fig. 22.8, the compiler invokes member function operator== with the call

```
integers1.operator==( integers2 )
```

Member function operator== (defined in Fig. 22.7, lines 74–84) immediately returns false if the size members of the arrays are not equal. Otherwise, operator== compares each pair of elements. If they are all equal, the function returns true. The first pair of elements to differ causes the function to return false immediately.

Lines 24–27 of the header file define the overloaded inequality operator (!=) for the class. Member function operator!= uses the overloaded operator== function to determine whether one Array is equal to another, then returns the opposite of that result. Writing operator!= in this manner enables the programmer to reuse operator==, which reduces the amount of code that must be written in the class. Also, note that the full function definition for operator!= is in the Array header file. This allows the compiler to inline the definition of operator!= to eliminate the overhead of the extra function call.

Overloaded Subscript Operators

Lines 30 and 33 of Fig. 22.6 declare two overloaded subscript operators (defined in Fig. 22.7 at lines 88–99 and 103–114, respectively). When the compiler sees the expression integers1[5] (Fig. 22.8, line 61), the compiler invokes the appropriate overloaded operator[] member function by generating the call

```
integers1.operator[]( 5 )
```

The compiler creates a call to the const version of operator[] (Fig. 22.7, lines 103–114) when the subscript operator is used on a const Array object. For example, if const object z is instantiated with the statement

```
const Array z( 5 );
```

then the `const` version of `operator[]` is required to execute a statement such as

```
cout << z[ 3 ] << endl;
```

Remember, a program can invoke only the `const` member functions of a `const` object.

Each definition of `operator[]` determines whether the subscript it receives as an argument is in range. If it is not, each function prints an error message and terminates the program with a call to function `exit` (header `<cstdlib>`).[3] If the subscript is in range, the non-`const` version of `operator[]` returns the appropriate array element as a reference so that it may be used as a modifiable *lvalue* (e.g., on the left side of an assignment statement). If the subscript is in range, the `const` version of `operator[]` returns a copy of the appropriate element of the array. The returned character is an *rvalue*.

22.9 Converting between Types

Most programs process information of many types. Sometimes all the operations "stay within a type." For example, adding an `int` to an `int` produces an `int` (as long as the result is not too large to be represented as an `int`). It is often necessary, however, to convert data of one type to data of another type. This can happen in assignments, in calculations, in passing values to functions and in returning values from functions. The compiler knows how to perform certain conversions among fundamental types. Programmers can use cast operators to force conversions among fundamental types.

But what about user-defined types? The compiler cannot know in advance how to convert among user-defined types, and between user-defined types and fundamental types, so the programmer must specify how to do this. Such conversions can be performed with **conversion constructors**—single-argument constructors that turn objects of other types (including fundamental types) into objects of a particular class.

A **conversion operator** (also called a **cast operator**) can be used to convert an object of one class into an object of another class or into an object of a fundamental type. Such a conversion operator must be a non-`static` member function. The function prototype

```
A::operator char *() const;
```

declares an overloaded cast operator function for converting an object of user-defined type A into a temporary `char *` object. The operator function is declared `const` because it does not modify the original object. An overloaded **cast operator function** does not specify a return type—the return type is the type to which the object is being converted. If s is a class object, when the compiler sees the expression `static_cast< char * >( s )`, the compiler generates the call

```
s.operator char *()
```

The operand s is the class object s for which the member function `operator char *` is being invoked.

---

3.   Note that it is more appropriate when a subscript is out of range to "throw an exception" indicating the out-of-range subscript. Then the program can "catch" that exception, process it and possibly continue execution. See Chapter 27 for more information on exceptions.

Overloaded cast operator functions can be defined to convert objects of user-defined types into fundamental types or into objects of other user-defined types. The prototypes

```
A::operator int() const;
A::operator OtherClass() const;
```

declare overloaded cast operator functions that can convert an object of user-defined type A into an integer or into an object of user-defined type OtherClass, respectively.

A nice features of cast operators and conversion constructors is that, when necessary, the compiler can call these functions implicitly to create temporary objects. For example, if an object s of a user-defined String class appears in a program at a location where an ordinary char * is expected, such as

```
cout << s;
```

the compiler can call the overloaded cast-operator function operator char * to convert the object into a char * and use the resulting char * in the expression. With this cast operator provided for our String class, the stream insertion operator does not have to be overloaded to output a String using cout.

22.10 Overloading ++ and −−

The prefix and postfix versions of the increment and decrement operators can all be overloaded. We will see how the compiler distinguishes between the prefix version and the postfix version of an increment or decrement operator.

To overload the increment operator to allow both prefix and postfix increment usage, each overloaded operator function must have a distinct signature, so that the compiler will be able to determine which version of ++ is intended. The prefix versions are overloaded exactly as any other prefix unary operator would be.

Overloading the Prefix Increment Operator

Suppose, for example, that we want to add 1 to the day in Date object d1. When the compiler sees the preincrementing expression ++d1, the compiler generates the member-function call

```
d1.operator++()
```

The prototype for this operator function would be

```
Date &operator++();
```

If the prefix increment operator is implemented as a global function, then, when the compiler sees the expression ++d1, the compiler generates the function call

```
operator++( d1 )
```

The prototype for this operator function would be declared in the Date class as

```
Date &operator++( Date & );
```

Overloading the Postfix Increment Operator

Overloading the postfix increment operator presents a challenge, because the compiler must be able to distinguish between the signatures of the overloaded prefix and postfix increment operator functions. The convention that has been adopted in C++ is that, when the compiler sees the postincrementing expression d1++, it generates the member-function call

```
d1.operator++( 0 )
```

The prototype for this function is

```
Date operator++( int )
```

The argument 0 is strictly a "dummy value" that enables the compiler to distinguish between the prefix and postfix increment operator functions.

If the postfix increment is implemented as a global function, then, when the compiler sees the expression d1++, the compiler generates the function call

```
operator++( d1, 0 )
```

The prototype for this function would be

```
Date operator++( Date &, int );
```

Once again, the 0 argument is used by the compiler to distinguish between the prefix and postfix increment operators implemented as global functions. Note that the postfix increment operator returns Date objects by value, whereas the prefix increment operator returns Date objects by reference, because the postfix increment operator typically returns a temporary object that contains the original value of the object before the increment occurred. C++ treats such objects as *rvalues*, which cannot be used on the left side of an assignment. The prefix increment operator returns the actual incremented object with its new value. Such an object can be used as an *lvalue* in a continuing expression.

Performance Tip 22.2

The extra object that is created by the postfix increment (or decrement) operator can result in a significant performance problem—especially when the operator is used in a loop. For this reason, you should use the postfix increment (or decrement) operator only when the logic of the program requires postincrementing (or postdecrementing).

Everything stated in this section for overloading prefix and postfix increment operators applies to overloading predecrement and postdecrement operators. Next, we examine a Date class with overloaded prefix and postfix increment operators.

22.11 explicit Constructors

In Section 22.8 and Section 22.9, we discussed that any single-argument constructor can be used by the compiler to perform an implicit conversion—the type received by the constructor is converted to an object of the class in which the constructor is defined. The conversion is automatic and the programmer need not use a cast operator. In some situations, implicit conversions are undesirable or error prone. For example, our Array class in Fig. 22.6 defines a constructor that takes a single int argument. The intent of this constructor is to create an Array object containing the number of elements specified by the int argument. However, this constructor can be misused by the compiler to perform an implicit conversion.

Common Programming Error 22.9

Unfortunately, the compiler might use implicit conversions in cases that you do not expect, resulting in ambiguous expressions that generate compilation errors or resulting in execution-time logic errors.

Accidentally Using a Single-Argument Constructor as a Conversion Constructor

The program (Fig. 22.9) uses the Array class of Figs. 22.6–22.7 to demonstrate an improper implicit conversion.

Line 13 in main instantiates Array object integers1 and calls the single-argument constructor with the int value 7 to specify the number of elements in the Array. Recall from Fig. 22.7 that the Array constructor that receives an int argument initializes all the array elements to 0. Line 14 calls function outputArray (defined in lines 20–24), which receives as its argument a const Array & to an Array. The function outputs the number of elements in its Array argument and the contents of the Array. In this case, the size of the Array is 7, so seven 0s are output.

Line 15 calls function outputArray with the int value 3 as an argument. However, this program does not contain a function called outputArray that takes an int argument. So, the compiler determines whether class Array provides a conversion constructor that can convert an int into an Array. Since any constructor that receives a single argument is considered to be a conversion constructor, the compiler assumes the Array constructor that receives a single int is a conversion constructor and uses it to convert the argument 3 into a temporary Array object that contains three elements. Then, the compiler passes the

```cpp
1   // Fig. 22.9: fig22_09.cpp
2   // Driver for simple class Array.
3   #include <iostream>
4   using std::cout;
5   using std::endl;
6
7   #include "Array.h"
8
9   void outputArray( const Array & ); // prototype
10
11  int main()
12  {
13     Array integers1( 7 ); // 7-element array
14     outputArray( integers1 ); // output Array integers1
15     outputArray( 3 ); // convert 3 to an Array and output Array's contents
16     return 0;
17  } // end main
18
19  // print Array contents
20  void outputArray( const Array &arrayToOutput )
21  {
22     cout << "The Array received has " << arrayToOutput.getSize()
23        << " elements. The contents are:\n" << arrayToOutput << endl;
24  } // end outputArray
```

Fig. 22.9 | Single-argument constructors and implicit conversions. (Part 1 of 2.)

```
The Array received has 7 elements. The contents are:
        0           0           0           0
        0           0           0
The Array received has 3 elements. The contents are:
        0           0           0
```

Fig. 22.9 | Single-argument constructors and implicit conversions. (Part 2 of 2.)

temporary Array object to function outputArray to output the Array's contents. Thus, even though we do not explicitly provide an outputArray function that receives an int argument, the compiler is able to compile line 15. The output shows the contents of the three-element Array containing 0s.

Preventing Accidental Use of a Single-Argument Constructor as a Conversion Constructor

C++ provides the keyword explicit to suppress implicit conversions via conversion constructors when such conversions should not be allowed. A constructor that is declared explicit cannot be used in an implicit conversion. Figure 22.10 declares an explicit constructor in class Array. The only modification to Array.h was the keyword explicit

```
 1   // Fig. 22.10: Array.h
 2   // Array class for storing arrays of integers.
 3   #ifndef ARRAY_H
 4   #define ARRAY_H
 5
 6   #include <iostream>
 7   using std::ostream;
 8   using std::istream;
 9
10   class Array
11   {
12      friend ostream &operator<<( ostream &, const Array & );
13      friend istream &operator>>( istream &, Array & );
14   public:
15      explicit Array( int = 10 ); // default constructor
16      Array( const Array & ); // copy constructor
17      ~Array(); // destructor
18      int getSize() const; // return size
19
20      const Array &operator=( const Array & ); // assignment operator
21      bool operator==( const Array & ) const; // equality operator
22
23      // inequality operator; returns opposite of == operator
24      bool operator!=( const Array &right ) const
25      {
26         return ! ( *this == right ); // invokes Array::operator==
27      } // end function operator!=
28
```

Fig. 22.10 | Array class definition with explicit constructor. (Part 1 of 2.)

```
29       // subscript operator for non-const objects returns lvalue
30       int &operator[]( int );
31
32       // subscript operator for const objects returns rvalue
33       const int &operator[]( int ) const;
34    private:
35       int size; // pointer-based array size
36       int *ptr; // pointer to first element of pointer-based array
37    }; // end class Array
38
39    #endif
```

Fig. 22.10 | Array class definition with `explicit` constructor. (Part 2 of 2.)

that we added to the single-argument constructor's declaration at line 15. No modifications are required to the source-code file containing class `Array`'s member-function definitions.

Figure 22.11 presents a slightly modified version of the program in Fig. 22.9. When this program is compiled, the compiler produces an error message indicating that the integer value passed to `outputArray` at line 15 cannot be converted to a `const Array &`. The compiler error message is shown in the output window. Line 16 demonstrates how the explicit constructor can be used to create a temporary `Array` of 3 elements and pass it to function `outputArray`.

Common Programming Error 22.10

Attempting to invoke an `explicit` constructor for an implicit conversion is a compilation error.

Common Programming Error 22.11

Using the `explicit` keyword on data members or member functions other than a single-argument constructor is a compilation error.

```
1     // Fig. 22.11: fig22_11.cpp
2     // Driver for simple class Array.
3     #include <iostream>
4     using std::cout;
5     using std::endl;
6
7     #include "Array.h"
8
9     void outputArray( const Array & ); // prototype
10
11    int main()
12    {
13       Array integers1( 7 ); // 7-element array
14       outputArray( integers1 ); // output Array integers1
15       outputArray( 3 ); // convert 3 to an Array and output Array's contents
16       outputArray( Array( 3 ) ); // explicit single-argument constructor call
17       return 0;
18    } // end main
```

Fig. 22.11 | Demonstrating an `explicit` constructor. (Part 1 of 2.)

```
19
20    // print array contents
21    void outputArray( const Array &arrayToOutput )
22    {
23       cout << "The Array received has " << arrayToOutput.getSize()
24          << " elements. The contents are:\n" << arrayToOutput << endl;
25    } // end outputArray
```

```
c:\cpphtp5_examples\ch22\fig22_17_18\fig22_18.cpp(15) : error C2664:
    'outputArray' : cannot convert parameter 1 from 'int' to 'const Array &'
        Reason: cannot convert from 'int' to 'const Array'
        Constructor for class 'Array' is declared 'explicit'
```

Fig. 22.11 | Demonstrating an `explicit` constructor. (Part 2 of 2.)

 Error-Prevention Tip 22.2

Use the `explicit` keyword on single-argument constructors that should not be used by the compiler to perform implicit conversions.

22.12 Wrap-Up

In this chapter, you learned how to build more robust classes by defining overloaded operators that enable programmers to treat objects of your classes as if they were fundamental C++ data types. We presented the basic concepts of operator overloading, as well as several restrictions that the C++ standard places on overloaded operators. You learned reasons for implementing overloaded operators as member functions or as global functions. We discussed the differences between overloading unary and binary operators as member functions and global functions. With global functions, we showed how to enable objects of our classes to be input and output using the overloaded stream extraction and stream insertion operators, respectively. We showed a special syntax that is required to differentiate between the prefix and postfix versions of the increment (++) operator. Finally, you learned how to use keyword `explicit` to prevent the compiler from using a single-argument constructor to perform implicit conversions. In the next chapter, we continue our discussion of classes by introducing a form of software reuse called inheritance. We will see that classes often share common attributes and behaviors. In such cases, it is possible to define those attributes and behaviors in a common "base" class and "inherit" those capabilities into new class definitions.

Summary

Section 22.2 Fundamentals of Operator Overloading
- C++ enables the programmer to overload most operators to be sensitive to the context in which they are used—the compiler generates the appropriate code based on the context (in particular, the types of the operands).
- Many of C++'s operators can be overloaded to work with user-defined types.

- One example of an overloaded operator built into C++ is operator <<, which is used both as the stream insertion operator and as the bitwise left-shift operator. Similarly, >> is also overloaded; it is used both as the stream extraction operator and as the bitwise right-shift operator. Both of these operators are overloaded in the C++ Standard Library.

- The C++ language itself overloads + and -. These operators perform differently, depending on their context in integer arithmetic, floating-point arithmetic and pointer arithmetic.

- The jobs performed by overloaded operators can also be performed by function calls, but operator notation is often clearer and more familiar to programmers.

- An operator is overloaded by writing a non-static member-function definition or global function definition in which the function name is the keyword operator followed by the symbol for the operator being overloaded.

- When operators are overloaded as member functions, they must be non-static, because they must be called on an object of the class and operate on that object.

- To use an operator on class objects, that operator *must* be overloaded—with three exceptions: the assignment operator (=), the address operator (&) and the comma operator (,).

Section 22.3 Restrictions on Operator Overloading

- You cannot change the precedence and associativity of an operator by overloading.

- You cannot change the "arity" of an operator (i.e., the number of operands an operator takes).

- You cannot create new operators; only existing operators can be overloaded.

- You cannot change the meaning of how an operator works on objects of fundamental types.

- Overloading an assignment operator and an addition operator for a class does not imply that the += operator is also overloaded. Such behavior can be achieved only by explicitly overloading operator += for that class.

Section 22.4 Operator Functions as Class Members vs. Global Functions

- Operator functions can be member functions or global functions; global functions are often made friends for performance reasons. Member functions use the this pointer implicitly to obtain one of their class object arguments (the left operand for binary operators). Arguments for both operands of a binary operator must be explicitly listed in a global function call.

- When overloading (), [], -> or any of the assignment operators, the operator overloading function must be declared as a class member. For the other operators, the operator overloading functions can be class members or global functions.

- When an operator function is implemented as a member function, the leftmost (or only) operand must be an object (or a reference to an object) of the operator's class.

- If the left operand must be an object of a different class or a fundamental type, this operator function must be implemented as a global function.

- A global operator function can be made a friend of a class if that function must access private or protected members of that class directly.

Section 22.5 Overloading Stream Insertion and Stream Extraction Operators

- The overloaded stream insertion operator (<<) is used in an expression in which the left operand has type ostream &. For this reason, it must be overloaded as a global function. To be a member function, operator << would have to be a member of the ostream class, but this is not possible, since we are not allowed to modify C++ Standard Library classes. Similarly, the overloaded stream extraction operator (>>) must be a global function.

- Another reason to choose a global function to overload an operator is to enable the operator to be commutative.

- When used with `cin` and `strings`, `setw` restricts the number of characters read to the number of characters specified by its argument.

- `istream` member function `ignore` discards the specified number of characters in the input stream (one character by default).

- Overloaded input and output operators are declared as `friends` if they need to access non-`public` class members directly for performance reasons.

Section 22.6 Overloading Unary Operators

- A unary operator for a class can be overloaded as a non-`static` member function with no arguments or as a global function with one argument; that argument must be either an object of the class or a reference to an object of the class.

- Member functions that implement overloaded operators must be non-`static` so that they can access the non-`static` data in each object of the class.

Section 22.7 Overloading Binary Operators

- A binary operator can be overloaded as a non-`static` member function with one argument or as a global function with two arguments (one of those arguments must be either a class object or a reference to a class object).

Section 22.8 Case Study: Array Class

- A copy constructor initializes a new object of a class by copying the members of an existing object of that class. When objects of a class contain dynamically allocated memory, the class should provide a copy constructor to ensure that each copy of an object has its own separate copy of the dynamically allocated memory. Typically, such a class would also provide a destructor and an overloaded assignment operator.

- The implementation of member function `operator=` should test for self-assignment, in which an object is being assigned to itself.

- The compiler calls the `const` version of `operator[]` when the subscript operator is used on a `const` object and calls the non-`const` version of the operator when it is used on a non-`const` object.

- The array subscript operator (`[]`) is not restricted for use with arrays. It can be used to select elements from other types of container classes. Also, with overloading, the index values no longer need to be integers; characters or strings could be used, for example.

Section 22.9 Converting between Types

- The compiler cannot know in advance how to convert among user-defined types, and between user-defined types and fundamental types, so the programmer must specify how to do this. Such conversions can be performed with conversion constructors—single-argument constructors that turn objects of other types (including fundamental types) into objects of a particular class.

- A conversion operator (also called a cast operator) can be used to convert an object of one class into an object of another class or into an object of a fundamental type. Such a conversion operator must be a non-`static` member function. Overloaded cast-operator functions can be defined for converting objects of user-defined types into fundamental types or into objects of other user-defined types.

- An overloaded cast operator function does not specify a return type—the return type is the type to which the object is being converted.

- One of the nice features of cast operators and conversion constructors is that, when necessary, the compiler can call these functions implicitly to create temporary objects.

- Any single-argument constructor can be thought of as a conversion constructor.

Section 22.10 Overloading ++ and --
- The prefix and postfix increment and decrement operator can all be overloaded.

- To overload the increment operator to allow both preincrement and postincrement usage, each overloaded must have a distinct signature. The prefix versions are overloaded exactly as any other prefix unary operator would be. Providing a unique signature to the postfix increment operator is accomplished by providing a second argument, which must be of type `int`. This argument is not supplied in the client code. It is used implicitly by the compiler to distinguish between the prefix and postfix versions of the increment operator.

Section 22.11 `explicit` Constructors
- C++ provides the keyword `explicit` to suppress implicit conversions via conversion constructors when such conversions should not be allowed. A constructor that is declared `explicit` cannot be used in an implicit conversion.

Terminology

"arity" of an operator
assignment-operator functions
associativity not changed by overloading
cast operator function
commutative operation
`const` version of `operator[]`
conversion between fundamental and class types
conversion constructor
conversion operator
copy constructor
empty member function of `string`
`explicit` constructor
global function to overload an operator
`ignore` member function of `istream`
implicit user-defined conversions
lvalue ("left value")
operator function
operator keyword
operator overloading
`operator!`
`operator!=`
`operator+`
`operator++`
`operator++( int )`

`operator<`
`operator<<`
`operator=`
`operator==`
`operator>>`
`operator[]`
overloadable operators
overloaded `!` operator
overloaded `!=` operator
overloaded `+` operator
overloaded `++` operator
overloaded `++( int )` operator
overloaded `<` operator
overloaded `<<` operator
overloaded `==` operator
overloaded `>>` operator
overloaded assignment (=) operator
overloaded `[]` operator
overloaded stream insertion and stream extraction operators
overloading a binary operator
overloading a unary operator
self-assignment
user-defined conversion

Self-Review Exercises

22.1 Fill in the blanks in each of the following:
  a) Suppose a and b are integer variables and we form the sum a + b. Now suppose c and d are floating-point variables and we form the sum c + d. The two + operators here are clearly being used for different purposes. This is an example of _____.
  b) Keyword _____ introduces an overloaded-operator function definition.
  c) To use operators on class objects, they must be overloaded, with the exception of operators _____, _____ and _____.
  d) The _____, _____ and _____ of an operator cannot be changed by overloading the operator.

22.2 Explain the multiple meanings of the operators << and >> in C++.

22.3 In what context might the name `operator/` be used in C++?

22.4 (True/False) In C++, only existing operators can be overloaded.

22.5 How does the precedence of an overloaded operator in C++ compare with the precedence of the original operator?

Answers to Self-Review Exercises

22.1 a) operator overloading. b) `operator`. c) assignment (=), address (&), comma (,). d) precedence, associativity, "arity."

22.2 Operator >> is both the right-shift operator and the stream extraction operator, depending on its context. Operator << is both the left-shift operator and the stream insertion operator, depending on its context.

22.3 For operator overloading: It would be the name of a function that would provide an overloaded version of the / operator for a specific class.

22.4 True.

22.5 The precedence is identical.

Exercises

22.6 Give as many examples as you can of operator overloading implicit in C++. Give a reasonable example of a situation in which you might want to overload an operator explicitly in C++.

22.7 The operators that cannot be overloaded are _____, _____, _____ and _____.

22.8 *(Ultimate Operator Overloading Exercise)* To appreciate the care that should go into selecting operators for overloading, list each of C++'s overloadable operators, and for each, list a possible meaning (or several, if appropriate) for each of several classes you have studied in this text. We suggest you try:
   a) Array
   b) Stack
   c) String

After doing this, comment on which operators seem to have meaning for a wide variety of classes. Which operators seem to be of little value for overloading? Which operators seem ambiguous?

22.9 Now work the process described in Exercise 22.8 in reverse. List each of C++'s overloadable operators. For each, list what you feel is perhaps the "ultimate operation" the operator should be used to represent. If there are several excellent operations, list them all.

22.10 One nice example of overloading the function call operator () is to allow another form of double-array subscripting popular in some programming languages. Instead of saying

```
chessBoard[ row ][ column ]
```

for an array of objects, overload the function call operator to allow the alternate form

```
chessBoard( row, column )
```

Create a class `DoubleSubscriptedArray` that has similar features to class `Array` in Figs. 22.6–22.7. At construction time, the class should be able to create an array of any number of rows and any number of columns. The class should supply `operator()` to perform double-subscripting operations. For example, in a 3-by-5 `DoubleSubscriptedArray` called a, the user could write a(1, 3) to access the element at row 1 and column 3. The function operator() can receive any number of arguments. The underlying representation of the double-subscripted array should be a single-subscripted array of integers with *rows * columns* number of elements. Function operator() should perform the proper pointer arithmetic to access each element of the array. There should be two versions of operator()— one that returns int & (so that an element of a DoubleSubscriptedArray can be used as an *lvalue*) and one that returns const int & (so that an element of a const DoubleSubscriptedArray can be used only as an *rvalue*). The class should also provide the following operators: ==, !=, =, << (for outputting the array in row and column format) and >> (for inputting the entire array contents).

22.11 Overload the subscript operator to return the largest element of a collection, the second largest, the third largest, and so on.

22.12 Consider class Complex shown in Figs. 22.12–22.14. The class enables operations on so-called *complex numbers*. These are numbers of the form realPart + imaginaryPart * *i*, where *i* has the value

$$\sqrt{-1}$$

   a) Modify the class to enable input and output of complex numbers through the over-loaded >> and << operators, respectively (you should remove the print function from the class).
   b) Overload the multiplication operator to enable multiplication of two complex numbers as in algebra.
   c) Overload the == and != operators to allow comparisons of complex numbers.

```
1   // Fig. 22.12: Complex.h
2   // Complex class definition.
3   #ifndef COMPLEX_H
4   #define COMPLEX_H
5
6   class Complex
7   {
8   public:
9      Complex( double = 0.0, double = 0.0 ); // constructor
10     Complex operator+( const Complex & ) const; // addition
11     Complex operator-( const Complex & ) const; // subtraction
12     void print() const; // output
13  private:
14     double real; // real part
15     double imaginary; // imaginary part
16  }; // end class Complex
17
18  #endif
```

Fig. 22.12 | Complex class definition.

```
1   // Fig. 22.13: Complex.cpp
2   // Complex class member-function definitions.
3   #include <iostream>
4   using std::cout;
```

Fig. 22.13 | Complex class member-function definitions. (Part 1 of 2.)

```
 5
 6    #include "Complex.h" // Complex class definition
 7
 8    // Constructor
 9    Complex::Complex( double realPart, double imaginaryPart )
10       : real( realPart ),
11         imaginary( imaginaryPart )
12    {
13       // empty body
14    } // end Complex constructor
15
16    // addition operator
17    Complex Complex::operator+( const Complex &operand2 ) const
18    {
19       return Complex( real + operand2.real,
20          imaginary + operand2.imaginary );
21    } // end function operator+
22
23    // subtraction operator
24    Complex Complex::operator-( const Complex &operand2 ) const
25    {
26       return Complex( real - operand2.real,
27          imaginary - operand2.imaginary );
28    } // end function operator-
29
30    // display a Complex object in the form: (a, b)
31    void Complex::print() const
32    {
33       cout << '(' << real << ", " << imaginary << ')';
34    } // end function print
```

Fig. 22.13 | Complex class member-function definitions. (Part 2 of 2.)

```
 1    // Fig. 22.14: fig22_14.cpp
 2    // Complex class test program.
 3    #include <iostream>
 4    using std::cout;
 5    using std::endl;
 6
 7    #include "Complex.h"
 8
 9    int main()
10    {
11       Complex x;
12       Complex y( 4.3, 8.2 );
13       Complex z( 3.3, 1.1 );
14
15       cout << "x: ";
16       x.print();
17       cout << "\ny: ";
18       y.print();
19       cout << "\nz: ";
```

Fig. 22.14 | Complex numbers. (Part 1 of 2.)

```
20        z.print();
21
22        x = y + z;
23        cout << "\n\nx = y + z:" << endl;
24        x.print();
25        cout << " = ";
26        y.print();
27        cout << " + ";
28        z.print();
29
30        x = y - z;
31        cout << "\n\nx = y - z:" << endl;
32        x.print();
33        cout << " = ";
34        y.print();
35        cout << " - ";
36        z.print();
37        cout << endl;
38        return 0;
39   } // end main
```

```
x: (0, 0)
y: (4.3, 8.2)
z: (3.3, 1.1)

x = y + z:
(7.6, 9.3) = (4.3, 8.2) + (3.3, 1.1)

x = y - z:
(1, 7.1) = (4.3, 8.2) - (3.3, 1.1)
```

Fig. 22.14 | Complex numbers. (Part 2 of 2.)

22.13 A machine with 32-bit integers can represent integers in the range of approximately –2 billion to +2 billion. This fixed-size restriction is rarely troublesome, but there are applications in which we would like to be able to use a much wider range of integers. This is what C++ was built to do, namely, create powerful new data types. Consider class HugeInt of Figs. 22.15–22.17. Study the class carefully, then respond to the following:

    a) Describe precisely how it operates.
    b) What restrictions does the class have?
    c) Overload the * multiplication operator.
    d) Overload the / division operator.
    e) Overload all the relational and equality operators.

[*Note:* We do not show an assignment operator or copy constructor for class HugeInteger, because the assignment operator and copy constructor provided by the compiler are capable of copying the entire array data member properly.]

```
1    // Fig. 22.15: Hugeint.h
2    // HugeInt class definition.
3    #ifndef HUGEINT_H
4    #define HUGEINT_H
```

Fig. 22.15 | HugeInt class definition. (Part 1 of 2.)

```
 5
 6   #include <iostream>
 7   using std::ostream;
 8
 9   class HugeInt
10   {
11      friend ostream &operator<<( ostream &, const HugeInt & );
12   public:
13      HugeInt( long = 0 ); // conversion/default constructor
14      HugeInt( const char * ); // conversion constructor
15
16      // addition operator; HugeInt + HugeInt
17      HugeInt operator+( const HugeInt & ) const;
18
19      // addition operator; HugeInt + int
20      HugeInt operator+( int ) const;
21
22      // addition operator;
23      // HugeInt + string that represents large integer value
24      HugeInt operator+( const char * ) const;
25   private:
26      short integer[ 30 ];
27   }; // end class HugetInt
28
29   #endif
```

Fig. 22.15 | HugeInt class definition. (Part 2 of 2.)

```
 1   // Fig. 22.16: Hugeint.cpp
 2   // HugeInt member-function and friend-function definitions.
 3   #include <cctype> // isdigit function prototype
 4   #include <cstring> // strlen function prototype
 5   #include "Hugeint.h" // HugeInt class definition
 6
 7   // default constructor; conversion constructor that converts
 8   // a long integer into a HugeInt object
 9   HugeInt::HugeInt( long value )
10   {
11      // initialize array to zero
12      for ( int i = 0; i <= 29; i++ )
13         integer[ i ] = 0;
14
15      // place digits of argument into array
16      for ( int j = 29; value != 0 && j >= 0; j-- )
17      {
18         integer[ j ] = value % 10;
19         value /= 10;
20      } // end for
21   } // end HugeInt default/conversion constructor
22
```

Fig. 22.16 | HugeInt class member-function and friend-function definitions. (Part 1 of 3.)

```
23    // conversion constructor that converts a character string
24    // representing a large integer into a HugeInt object
25    HugeInt::HugeInt( const char *string )
26    {
27       // initialize array to zero
28       for ( int i = 0; i <= 29; i++ )
29          integer[ i ] = 0;
30
31       // place digits of argument into array
32       int length = strlen( string );
33
34       for ( int j = 30 - length, k = 0; j <= 29; j++, k++ )
35
36          if ( isdigit( string[ k ] ) )
37             integer[ j ] = string[ k ] - '0';
38    } // end HugeInt conversion constructor
39
40    // addition operator; HugeInt + HugeInt
41    HugeInt HugeInt::operator+( const HugeInt &op2 ) const
42    {
43       HugeInt temp; // temporary result
44       int carry = 0;
45
46       for ( int i = 29; i >= 0; i-- )
47       {
48          temp.integer[ i ] =
49             integer[ i ] + op2.integer[ i ] + carry;
50
51          // determine whether to carry a 1
52          if ( temp.integer[ i ] > 9 )
53          {
54             temp.integer[ i ] %= 10;   // reduce to 0-9
55             carry = 1;
56          } // end if
57          else // no carry
58             carry = 0;
59       } // end for
60
61       return temp; // return copy of temporary object
62    } // end function operator+
63
64    // addition operator; HugeInt + int
65    HugeInt HugeInt::operator+( int op2 ) const
66    {
67       // convert op2 to a HugeInt, then invoke
68       // operator+ for two HugeInt objects
69       return *this + HugeInt( op2 );
70    } // end function operator+
71
72    // addition operator;
73    // HugeInt + string that represents large integer value
74    HugeInt HugeInt::operator+( const char *op2 ) const
75    {
```

Fig. 22.16 | HugeInt class member-function and friend-function definitions. (Part 2 of 3.)

```
76       // convert op2 to a HugeInt, then invoke
77       // operator+ for two HugeInt objects
78       return *this + HugeInt( op2 );
79    } // end operator+
80
81    // overloaded output operator
82    ostream& operator<<( ostream &output, const HugeInt &num )
83    {
84       int i;
85
86       for ( i = 0; ( num.integer[ i ] == 0 ) && ( i <= 29 ); i++ )
87          ; // skip leading zeros
88
89       if ( i == 30 )
90          output << 0;
91       else
92
93          for ( ; i <= 29; i++ )
94             output << num.integer[ i ];
95
96       return output;
97    } // end function operator<<
```

Fig. 22.16 | HugeInt class member-function and friend-function definitions. (Part 3 of 3.)

```
1    // Fig. 22.17: fig22_17.cpp
2    // HugeInt test program.
3    #include <iostream>
4    using std::cout;
5    using std::endl;
6
7    #include "Hugeint.h"
8
9    int main()
10   {
11      HugeInt n1( 7654321 );
12      HugeInt n2( 7891234 );
13      HugeInt n3( "99999999999999999999999999999" );
14      HugeInt n4( "1" );
15      HugeInt n5;
16
17      cout << "n1 is " << n1 << "\nn2 is " << n2
18         << "\nn3 is " << n3 << "\nn4 is " << n4
19         << "\nn5 is " << n5 << "\n\n";
20
21      n5 = n1 + n2;
22      cout << n1 << " + " << n2 << " = " << n5 << "\n\n";
23
24      cout << n3 << " + " << n4 << "\n= " << ( n3 + n4 ) << "\n\n";
25
26      n5 = n1 + 9;
27      cout << n1 << " + " << 9 << " = " << n5 << "\n\n";
```

Fig. 22.17 | Huge integers. (Part 1 of 2.)

```
28
29     n5 = n2 + "10000";
30     cout << n2 << " + " << "10000" << " = " << n5 << endl;
31     return 0;
32  } // end main
```

```
n1 is 7654321
n2 is 7891234
n3 is 99999999999999999999999999999
n4 is 1
n5 is 0

7654321 + 7891234 = 15545555

99999999999999999999999999999 + 1
= 100000000000000000000000000000

7654321 + 9 = 7654330

7891234 + 10000 = 7901234
```

Fig. 22.17 | Huge integers. (Part 2 of 2.)

22.14 Create a class `RationalNumber` (fractions) with the following capabilities:

a) Create a constructor that prevents a 0 denominator in a fraction, reduces or simplifies fractions that are not in reduced form and avoids negative denominators.

b) Overload the addition, subtraction, multiplication and division operators for this class.

c) Overload the relational and equality operators for this class.

22.15 Develop class `Polynomial`. The internal representation of a `Polynomial` is an array of terms. Each term contains a coefficient and an exponent. The term

$$2x^4$$

has the coefficient 2 and the exponent 4. Develop a complete class containing proper constructor and destructor functions as well as *set* and *get* functions. The class should also provide the following overloaded operator capabilities:

a) Overload the addition operator (+) to add two `Polynomials`.

b) Overload the subtraction operator (-) to subtract two `Polynomials`.

c) Overload the assignment operator to assign one `Polynomial` to another.

d) Overload the multiplication operator (*) to multiply two `Polynomials`.

e) Overload the addition assignment operator (+=), subtraction assignment operator (-=), and multiplication assignment operator (*=).

22.16 In the program of Figs. 22.3–22.5, Fig. 22.4 contains the comment "overloaded stream insertion operator; cannot be a member function if we would like to invoke it with cout << somePhoneNumber;." Actually, the stream insertion operator could be a PhoneNumber class member function if we were willing to invoke it either as somePhoneNumber.operator<<(cout); or as some-PhoneNumber << cout;. Rewrite the program of Fig. 22.5 with the overloaded stream insertion operator<< as a member function and try the two preceding statements in the program to demonstrate that they work.

23

Object-Oriented Programming: Inheritance

OBJECTIVES

In this chapter you will learn:

- To create classes by inheriting from existing classes.
- How inheritance promotes software reuse.
- The notions of base classes and derived classes and the relationships between them.
- The **protected** member access specifier.
- The use of constructors and destructors in inheritance hierarchies.
- The differences between **public**, **protected** and **private** inheritance.
- The use of inheritance to customize existing software.

23.1 Introduction

This chapter continues our discussion of object-oriented programming (OOP) by introducing another of its key features—inheritance. Inheritance is a form of software reuse in which the programmer creates a class that absorbs an existing class's data and behaviors and enhances them with new capabilities. Software reusability saves time during program development. It also encourages the reuse of proven, debugged, high-quality software, which increases the likelihood that a system will be implemented effectively.

When creating a class, instead of writing completely new data members and member functions, the programmer can designate that the new class should inherit the members of an existing class. This existing class is called the base class, and the new class is referred to as the derived class. (Other programming languages, such as Java, refer to the base class as the superclass and the derived class as the subclass.) A derived class represents a more specialized group of objects. Typically, a derived class contains behaviors inherited from its base class plus additional behaviors. As we will see, a derived class can also customize behaviors inherited from the base class. A direct base class is the base class from which a derived class explicitly inherits. An indirect base class is inherited from two or more levels up in the class hierarchy. In the case of single inheritance, a class is derived from one base class. C++ also supports multiple inheritance, in which a derived class inherits from multiple (possibly unrelated) base classes. Single inheritance is straightforward—we show several examples that should enable the reader to become proficient quickly. Multiple inheritance can be complex and error prone.

C++ offers three kinds of inheritance—`public`, `protected` and `private`. In this chapter, we concentrate on `public` inheritance and briefly explain the other two. The third form, protected inheritance, is rarely used. With public inheritance, every object of a derived class is also an object of that derived class's base class. However, base-class objects are not objects of their derived classes. For example, if we have vehicle as a base class and car as a derived class, then all cars are vehicles, but not all vehicles are cars. As we continue our study of object-oriented programming in this chapter and Chapter 24, we take advantage of this relationship to perform some interesting manipulations.

Experience in building software systems indicates that significant amounts of code deal with closely related special cases. When programmers are preoccupied with special cases, the details can obscure the big picture. With object-oriented programming, programmers focus on the commonalities among objects in the system rather than on the special cases.

We distinguish between the *is-a* relationship and the *has-a* relationship. The *is-a* relationship represents inheritance. In an *is-a* relationship, an object of a derived class also can be treated as an object of its base class—for example, a car *is a* vehicle, so any properties and behaviors of a vehicle are also properties of a car. By contrast, the *has-a* relationship represents composition. (Composition was discussed in Chapter 21.) In a *has-a* relationship, an object contains one or more objects of other classes as members. For example, a car includes many components—it *has a* steering wheel, *has a* brake pedal, *has a* transmission and *has* many other components.

Derived-class member functions might require access to base-class data members and member functions. A derived class can access the non-private members of its base class. Base-class members that should not be accessible to the member functions of derived classes should be declared private in the base class. A derived class can effect state changes in private base-class members, but only through non-private member functions provided in the base class and inherited into the derived class.

Software Engineering Observation 23.1

Member functions of a derived class cannot directly access private members of the base class.

Software Engineering Observation 23.2

If a derived class could access its base class's private members, classes that inherit from that derived class could access that data as well. This would propagate access to what should be private data, and the benefits of information hiding would be lost.

One problem with inheritance is that a derived class can inherit data members and member functions it does not need or should not have. It is the class designer's responsibility to ensure that the capabilities provided by a class are appropriate for future derived classes. Even when a base-class member function is appropriate for a derived class, the derived class often requires that member function to behave in a manner specific to the derived class. In such cases, the base-class member function can be redefined in the derived class with an appropriate implementation.

23.2 Base Classes and Derived Classes

Often, an object of one class *is an* object of another class, as well. For example, in geometry, a rectangle *is a* quadrilateral (as are squares, parallelograms and trapezoids). Thus, in C++, class Rectangle can be said to *inherit* from class Quadrilateral. In this context, class Quadrilateral is a base class, and class Rectangle is a derived class. A rectangle *is a* specific type of quadrilateral, but it is incorrect to claim that a quadrilateral *is a* rectangle—the quadrilateral could be a parallelogram or some other shape. Figure 23.1 lists several simple examples of base classes and derived classes.

Because every derived-class object *is an* object of its base class, and one base class can have many derived classes, the set of objects represented by a base class typically is larger than the set of objects represented by any of its derived classes. For example, the base class Vehicle represents all vehicles, including cars, trucks, boats, airplanes, bicycles and so on. By contrast, derived class Car represents a smaller, more specific subset of all vehicles.

Inheritance relationships form treelike hierarchical structures. A base class exists in a hierarchical relationship with its derived classes. Although classes can exist independently, once they are employed in inheritance relationships, they become affiliated with other classes. A class becomes either a base class—supplying members to other classes, a derived class—inheriting its members from other classes, or both.

Let us develop a simple inheritance hierarchy with five levels (represented by the UML class diagram in Fig. 23.2).

Base class	Derived classes
Student	GraduateStudent, UndergraduateStudent
Shape	Circle, Triangle, Rectangle, Sphere, Cube
Loan	CarLoan, HomeImprovementLoan, MortgageLoan
Employee	Faculty, Staff
Account	CheckingAccount, SavingsAccount

Fig. 23.1 | Inheritance examples.

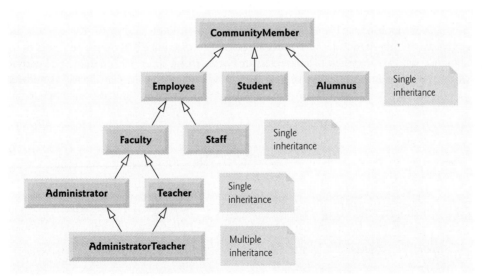

Fig. 23.2 | Inheritance hierarchy for university CommunityMembers.

A university community has thousands of members, consisting of employees, students and alumni. Employees are either faculty members or staff members. Faculty members are either administrators (such as deans and department chairpersons) or teachers. Some administrators, however, also teach classes. Note that we have used multiple inheritance to form class AdministratorTeacher. Also note that this inheritance hierarchy could contain many other classes. For example, students can be graduate or undergraduate students. Undergraduate students can be freshmen, sophomores, juniors and seniors.

Each arrow in the hierarchy (Fig. 23.2) represents an *is-a* relationship. For example, as we follow the arrows in this class hierarchy, we can state "an Employee *is a* CommunityMember" and "a Teacher *is a* Faculty member." CommunityMember is the direct base class of Employee, Student and Alumnus. In addition, CommunityMember is an indirect base class of all the other classes in the diagram. Starting from the bottom of the diagram, the reader can follow the arrows and apply the *is-a* relationship to the topmost base class. For example, an AdministratorTeacher *is an* Administrator, *is a* Faculty member, *is an* Employee and *is a* CommunityMember.

Now consider the Shape inheritance hierarchy in Fig. 23.3. This hierarchy begins with base class Shape. Classes TwoDimensionalShape and ThreeDimensionalShape derive from base class Shape—Shapes are either TwoDimensionalShapes or ThreeDimensionalShapes. The third level of this hierarchy contains some more specific types of TwoDimensionalShapes and ThreeDimensionalShapes. As in Fig. 23.2, we can follow the arrows from the bottom of the diagram to the topmost base class in this class hierarchy to identify several *is-a* relationships. For instance, a Triangle *is a* TwoDimensionalShape and *is a* Shape, while a Sphere *is a* ThreeDimensionalShape and *is a* Shape. Note that this hierarchy could contain many other classes, such as Rectangles, Ellipses and Trapezoids, which are all TwoDimensionalShapes.

To specify that class TwoDimensionalShape (Fig. 23.3) is derived from (or inherits from) class Shape, class TwoDimensionalShape could be defined in C++ as follows:

```
class TwoDimensionalShape : public Shape
```

This is an example of **public** inheritance, the most commonly used form. We also will discuss **private** inheritance and **protected** inheritance (Section 23.6). With all forms of inheritance, **private** members of a base class are not accessible directly from that class's derived classes, but these **private** base-class members are still inherited (i.e., they are still considered parts of the derived classes). With **public** inheritance, all other base-class members retain

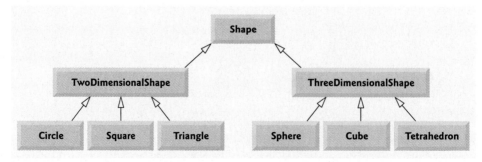

Fig. 23.3 | Inheritance hierarchy for Shapes.

their original member access when they become members of the derived class (e.g., public members of the base class become public members of the derived class, and, as we will soon see, protected members of the base class become protected members of the derived class). Through these inherited base-class members, the derived class can manipulate private members of the base class (if these inherited members provide such functionality in the base class). Note that friend functions are not inherited.

Inheritance is not appropriate for every class relationship. In Chapter 21, we discussed the *has-a* relationship, in which classes have members that are objects of other classes. Such relationships create classes by composition of existing classes. For example, given the classes Employee, BirthDate and TelephoneNumber, it is improper to say that an Employee *is a* BirthDate or that an Employee *is a* TelephoneNumber. However, it is appropriate to say that an Employee *has a* BirthDate and that an Employee *has a* TelephoneNumber.

It is possible to treat base-class objects and derived-class objects similarly; their commonalities are expressed in the members of the base class. Objects of all classes derived from a common base class can be treated as objects of that base class (i.e., such objects have an *is-a* relationship with the base class). In Chapter 24, Object-Oriented Programming: Polymorphism, we consider many examples that take advantage of this relationship.

23.3 protected Members

Chapter 19 introduced access specifiers public and private. A base class's public members are accessible within the body of that base class and anywhere that the program has a handle (i.e., a name, reference or pointer) to an object of that base class or one of its derived classes. A base class's private members are accessible only within the body of that base class and the friends of that base class. In this section, we introduce an additional access specifier: protected.

Using protected access offers an intermediate level of protection between public and private access. A base class's protected members can be accessed within the body of that base class, by members and friends of that base class, and by members and friends of any classes derived from that base class.

Derived-class member functions can refer to public and protected members of the base class simply by using the member names. When a derived-class member function redefines a base-class member function, the base-class member can be accessed from the derived class by preceding the base-class member name with the base-class name and the binary scope resolution operator (::). We discuss accessing redefined members of the base class in Section 23.4 and using protected data in Section 23.4.4.

23.4 Relationship between Base Classes and Derived Classes

In this section, we use an inheritance hierarchy containing types of employees in a company's payroll application to discuss the relationship between a base class and a derived class. Commission employees (who will be represented as objects of a base class) are paid a percentage of their sales, while base-salaried commission employees (who will be represented as objects of a derived class) receive a base salary plus a percentage of their sales. We divide our discussion of the relationship between commission employees and base-salaried commission employees into a carefully paced series of five examples:

1. In the first example, we create class CommissionEmployee, which contains as private data members a first name, last name, social security number, commission rate (percentage) and gross (i.e., total) sales amount.

2. The second example defines class BasePlusCommissionEmployee, which contains as private data members a first name, last name, social security number, commission rate, gross sales amount and base salary. We create the latter class by writing every line of code the class requires—we will soon see that it is much more efficient to create this class simply by inheriting from class CommissionEmployee.

3. The third example defines a new version of class BasePlusCommissionEmployee class that inherits directly from class CommissionEmployee (i.e., a BasePlus-CommissionEmployee *is a* CommissionEmployee who also has a base salary) and attempts to access class CommissionEmployee's private members—this results in compilation errors, because the derived class does not have access to the base class's private data.

4. The fourth example shows that if CommissionEmployee's data is declared as protected, a new version of class BasePlusCommissionEmployee that inherits from class CommissionEmployee *can* access that data directly. For this purpose, we define a new version of class CommissionEmployee with protected data. Both the inherited and noninherited BasePlusCommissionEmployee classes contain identical functionality, but we show how the version of BasePlusCommissionEmployee that inherits from class CommissionEmployee is easier to create and manage.

5. After we discuss the convenience of using protected data, we create the fifth example, which sets the CommissionEmployee data members back to private to enforce good software engineering. This example demonstrates that derived class BasePlusCommissionEmployee can use base class CommissionEmployee's public member functions to manipulate CommissionEmployee's private data.

23.4.1 Creating and Using a CommissionEmployee Class

Let us first examine CommissionEmployee's class definition (Figs. 23.4–23.5). The CommissionEmployee header file (Fig. 23.4) specifies class CommissionEmployee's public services, which include a constructor (lines 12–13) and member functions earnings (line 30) and print (line 31). Lines 15–28 declare public *get* and *set* functions for manipulating the class's data members (declared in lines 33–37) firstName, lastName, socialSecurityNumber, grossSales and commissionRate. The CommissionEmployee header file specifies each of these data members as private, so objects of other classes cannot directly access this data. Declaring data members as private and providing non-private *get* and *set* functions to manipulate and validate the data members helps enforce good software engineering. Member functions setGrossSales (defined in lines 57–60 of Fig. 23.5) and setCommission-Rate (defined in lines 69–72 of Fig. 23.5), for example, validate their arguments before assigning the values to data members grossSales and commissionRate, respectively.

The CommissionEmployee constructor definition purposely does not use member-initializer syntax in the first several examples of this section, so that we can demonstrate how private and protected specifiers affect member access in derived classes. As shown in Fig. 23.5, lines 13–15, we assign values to data members firstName, lastName and

```
 1   // Fig. 23.4: CommissionEmployee.h
 2   // CommissionEmployee class definition represents a commission employee.
 3   #ifndef COMMISSION_H
 4   #define COMMISSION_H
 5
 6   #include <string> // C++ standard string class
 7   using std::string;
 8
 9   class CommissionEmployee
10   {
11   public:
12      CommissionEmployee( const string &, const string &, const string &,
13         double = 0.0, double = 0.0 );
14
15      void setFirstName( const string & ); // set first name
16      string getFirstName() const; // return first name
17
18      void setLastName( const string & ); // set last name
19      string getLastName() const; // return last name
20
21      void setSocialSecurityNumber( const string & ); // set SSN
22      string getSocialSecurityNumber() const; // return SSN
23
24      void setGrossSales( double ); // set gross sales amount
25      double getGrossSales() const; // return gross sales amount
26
27      void setCommissionRate( double ); // set commission rate (percentage)
28      double getCommissionRate() const; // return commission rate
29
30      double earnings() const; // calculate earnings
31      void print() const; // print CommissionEmployee object
32   private:
33      string firstName;
34      string lastName;
35      string socialSecurityNumber;
36      double grossSales; // gross weekly sales
37      double commissionRate; // commission percentage
38   }; // end class CommissionEmployee
39
40   #endif
```

Fig. 23.4 | CommissionEmployee class header file.

```
 1   // Fig. 23.5: CommissionEmployee.cpp
 2   // Class CommissionEmployee member-function definitions.
 3   #include <iostream>
 4   using std::cout;
 5
 6   #include "CommissionEmployee.h" // CommissionEmployee class definition
 7
```

Fig. 23.5 | Implementation file for CommissionEmployee class that represents an employee who is paid a percentage of gross sales. (Part 1 of 3.)

```
 8    // constructor
 9    CommissionEmployee::CommissionEmployee(
10       const string &first, const string &last, const string &ssn,
11       double sales, double rate )
12    {
13       firstName = first; // should validate
14       lastName = last;   // should validate
15       socialSecurityNumber = ssn; // should validate
16       setGrossSales( sales ); // validate and store gross sales
17       setCommissionRate( rate ); // validate and store commission rate
18    } // end CommissionEmployee constructor
19
20    // set first name
21    void CommissionEmployee::setFirstName( const string &first )
22    {
23       firstName = first; // should validate
24    } // end function setFirstName
25
26    // return first name
27    string CommissionEmployee::getFirstName() const
28    {
29       return firstName;
30    } // end function getFirstName
31
32    // set last name
33    void CommissionEmployee::setLastName( const string &last )
34    {
35       lastName = last; // should validate
36    } // end function setLastName
37
38    // return last name
39    string CommissionEmployee::getLastName() const
40    {
41       return lastName;
42    } // end function getLastName
43
44    // set social security number
45    void CommissionEmployee::setSocialSecurityNumber( const string &ssn )
46    {
47       socialSecurityNumber = ssn; // should validate
48    } // end function setSocialSecurityNumber
49
50    // return social security number
51    string CommissionEmployee::getSocialSecurityNumber() const
52    {
53       return socialSecurityNumber;
54    } // end function getSocialSecurityNumber
55
56    // set gross sales amount
57    void CommissionEmployee::setGrossSales( double sales )
58    {
```

Fig. 23.5 | Implementation file for CommissionEmployee class that represents an employee who is paid a percentage of gross sales. (Part 2 of 3.)

```
59       grossSales = ( sales < 0.0 ) ? 0.0 : sales;
60    } // end function setGrossSales
61
62    // return gross sales amount
63    double CommissionEmployee::getGrossSales() const
64    {
65       return grossSales;
66    } // end function getGrossSales
67
68    // set commission rate
69    void CommissionEmployee::setCommissionRate( double rate )
70    {
71       commissionRate = ( rate > 0.0 && rate < 1.0 ) ? rate : 0.0;
72    } // end function setCommissionRate
73
74    // return commission rate
75    double CommissionEmployee::getCommissionRate() const
76    {
77       return commissionRate;
78    } // end function getCommissionRate
79
80    // calculate earnings
81    double CommissionEmployee::earnings() const
82    {
83       return commissionRate * grossSales;
84    } // end function earnings
85
86    // print CommissionEmployee object
87    void CommissionEmployee::print() const
88    {
89       cout << "commission employee: " << firstName << ' ' << lastName
90          << "\nsocial security number: " << socialSecurityNumber
91          << "\ngross sales: " << grossSales
92          << "\ncommission rate: " << commissionRate;
93    } // end function print
```

Fig. 23.5 | Implementation file for `CommissionEmployee` class that represents an employee who is paid a percentage of gross sales. (Part 3 of 3.)

`socialSecurityNumber` in the constructor body. Later in this section, we will return to using member-initializer lists in the constructors.

Note that we do not validate the values of the constructor's arguments `first`, `last` and `ssn` before assigning them to the corresponding data members. We certainly could validate the first and last names—perhaps by ensuring that they are of a reasonable length. Similarly, a social security number could be validated to ensure that it contains nine digits, with or without dashes (e.g., 123-45-6789 or 123456789).

Member function `earnings` (lines 81–84) calculates a `CommissionEmployee`'s earnings. Line 83 multiplies the `commissionRate` by the `grossSales` and returns the result. Member function `print` (lines 87–93) displays the values of a `CommissionEmployee` object's data members.

Figure 23.6 tests class `CommissionEmployee`. Lines 16–17 instantiate object `employee` of class `CommissionEmployee` and invoke `CommissionEmployee`'s constructor to initialize the object with "Sue" as the first name, "Jones" as the last name, "222-22-2222" as the social security number, 10000 as the gross sales amount and .06 as the commission rate. Lines 23–29 use employee's *get* functions to display the values of its data members. Lines 31–32 invoke the object's member functions setGrossSales and setCommissionRate to change the values of data members grossSales and commissionRate, respectively. Line 36 then calls employee's print member function to output the updated CommissionEmployee information. Finally, line 39 displays the CommissionEmployee's earnings, calculated by the object's earnings member function using the updated values of data members gross-Sales and commissionRate.

```cpp
1   // Fig. 23.6: fig23_06.cpp
2   // Testing class CommissionEmployee.
3   #include <iostream>
4   using std::cout;
5   using std::endl;
6   using std::fixed;
7
8   #include <iomanip>
9   using std::setprecision;
10
11  #include "CommissionEmployee.h" // CommissionEmployee class definition
12
13  int main()
14  {
15     // instantiate a CommissionEmployee object
16     CommissionEmployee employee(
17        "Sue", "Jones", "222-22-2222", 10000, .06 );
18
19     // set floating-point output formatting
20     cout << fixed << setprecision( 2 );
21
22     // get commission employee data
23     cout << "Employee information obtained by get functions: \n"
24        << "\nFirst name is " << employee.getFirstName()
25        << "\nLast name is " << employee.getLastName()
26        << "\nSocial security number is "
27        << employee.getSocialSecurityNumber()
28        << "\nGross sales is " << employee.getGrossSales()
29        << "\nCommission rate is " << employee.getCommissionRate() << endl;
30
31     employee.setGrossSales( 8000 ); // set gross sales
32     employee.setCommissionRate( .1 ); // set commission rate
33
34     cout << "\nUpdated employee information output by print function: \n"
35        << endl;
36     employee.print(); // display the new employee information
37
38     // display the employee's earnings
39     cout << "\n\nEmployee's earnings: $" << employee.earnings() << endl;
40
41     return 0;
42  } // end main
```

Fig. 23.6 | CommissionEmployee class test program. (Part 1 of 2.)

```
Employee information obtained by get functions:

First name is Sue
Last name is Jones
Social security number is 222-22-2222
Gross sales is 10000.00
Commission rate is 0.06

Updated employee information output by print function:

commission employee: Sue Jones
social security number: 222-22-2222
gross sales: 8000.00
commission rate: 0.10

Employee's earnings: $800.00
```

Fig. 23.6 | CommissionEmployee class test program. (Part 2 of 2.)

23.4.2 Creating a BasePlusCommissionEmployee Class Without Using Inheritance

We now discuss the second part of our introduction to inheritance by creating and testing (a completely new and independent) class BasePlusCommissionEmployee (Figs. 23.7–23.8), which contains a first name, last name, social security number, gross sales amount, commission rate and base salary.

Defining Class BasePlusCommissionEmployee

The BasePlusCommissionEmployee header file (Fig. 23.7) specifies class BasePlusCommissionEmployee's public services, which include the BasePlusCommissionEmployee constructor (lines 13–14) and member functions earnings (line 34) and print (line 35).

```
1   // Fig. 23.7: BasePlusCommissionEmployee.h
2   // BasePlusCommissionEmployee class definition represents an employee
3   // that receives a base salary in addition to commission.
4   #ifndef BASEPLUS_H
5   #define BASEPLUS_H
6
7   #include <string> // C++ standard string class
8   using std::string;
9
10  class BasePlusCommissionEmployee
11  {
12  public:
13     BasePlusCommissionEmployee( const string &, const string &,
14        const string &, double = 0.0, double = 0.0, double = 0.0 );
15
16     void setFirstName( const string & ); // set first name
17     string getFirstName() const; // return first name
18
```

Fig. 23.7 | BasePlusCommissionEmployee class header file. (Part 1 of 2.)

```
19      void setLastName( const string & ); // set last name
20      string getLastName() const; // return last name
21
22      void setSocialSecurityNumber( const string & ); // set SSN
23      string getSocialSecurityNumber() const; // return SSN
24
25      void setGrossSales( double ); // set gross sales amount
26      double getGrossSales() const; // return gross sales amount
27
28      void setCommissionRate( double ); // set commission rate
29      double getCommissionRate() const; // return commission rate
30
31      void setBaseSalary( double ); // set base salary
32      double getBaseSalary() const; // return base salary
33
34      double earnings() const; // calculate earnings
35      void print() const; // print BasePlusCommissionEmployee object
36   private:
37      string firstName;
38      string lastName;
39      string socialSecurityNumber;
40      double grossSales; // gross weekly sales
41      double commissionRate; // commission percentage
42      double baseSalary; // base salary
43   }; // end class BasePlusCommissionEmployee
44
45   #endif
```

Fig. 23.7 | BasePlusCommissionEmployee class header file. (Part 2 of 2.)

Lines 16–32 declare public *get* and *set* functions for the class's private data members (declared in lines 37–42) firstName, lastName, socialSecurityNumber, grossSales, commissionRate and baseSalary. These variables and member functions encapsulate all the necessary features of a base-salaried commission employee. Note the similarity between this class and class CommissionEmployee (Figs. 23.4–23.5)—in this example, we will not yet exploit that similarity.

Class BasePlusCommissionEmployee's earnings member function (defined in lines 96–99 of Fig. 23.8) computes the earnings of a base-salaried commission employee. Line 98 returns the result of adding the employee's base salary to the product of the commission rate and the employee's gross sales.

Testing Class BasePlusCommissionEmployee
Figure 23.9 tests class BasePlusCommissionEmployee. Lines 17–18 instantiate object employee of class BasePlusCommissionEmployee, passing "Bob", "Lewis", "333-33-3333", 5000, .04 and 300 to the constructor as the first name, last name, social security number, gross sales, commission rate and base salary, respectively. Lines 24–31 use BasePlusCommissionEmployee's *get* functions to retrieve the values of the object's data members for output. Line 33 invokes the object's setBaseSalary member function to change the base salary. Member function setBaseSalary (Fig. 23.8, lines 84–87) ensures that data member baseSalary is not assigned a negative value, because an employee's base salary cannot be negative. Line 37 of Fig. 23.9 invokes the object's print member function to output

the updated BasePlusCommissionEmployee's information, and line 40 calls member function earnings to display the BasePlusCommissionEmployee's earnings.

```cpp
1   // Fig. 23.8: BasePlusCommissionEmployee.cpp
2   // Class BasePlusCommissionEmployee member-function definitions.
3   #include <iostream>
4   using std::cout;
5
6   // BasePlusCommissionEmployee class definition
7   #include "BasePlusCommissionEmployee.h"
8
9   // constructor
10  BasePlusCommissionEmployee::BasePlusCommissionEmployee(
11     const string &first, const string &last, const string &ssn,
12     double sales, double rate, double salary )
13  {
14     firstName = first; // should validate
15     lastName = last; // should validate
16     socialSecurityNumber = ssn; // should validate
17     setGrossSales( sales ); // validate and store gross sales
18     setCommissionRate( rate ); // validate and store commission rate
19     setBaseSalary( salary ); // validate and store base salary
20  } // end BasePlusCommissionEmployee constructor
21
22  // set first name
23  void BasePlusCommissionEmployee::setFirstName( const string &first )
24  {
25     firstName = first; // should validate
26  } // end function setFirstName
27
28  // return first name
29  string BasePlusCommissionEmployee::getFirstName() const
30  {
31     return firstName;
32  } // end function getFirstName
33
34  // set last name
35  void BasePlusCommissionEmployee::setLastName( const string &last )
36  {
37     lastName = last; // should validate
38  } // end function setLastName
39
40  // return last name
41  string BasePlusCommissionEmployee::getLastName() const
42  {
43     return lastName;
44  } // end function getLastName
45
46  // set social security number
47  void BasePlusCommissionEmployee::setSocialSecurityNumber(
48     const string &ssn )
49  {
```

Fig. 23.8 | BasePlusCommissionEmployee class represents an employee who receives a base salary in addition to a commission. (Part 1 of 3.)

```
50       socialSecurityNumber = ssn; // should validate
51  } // end function setSocialSecurityNumber
52
53  // return social security number
54  string BasePlusCommissionEmployee::getSocialSecurityNumber() const
55  {
56       return socialSecurityNumber;
57  } // end function getSocialSecurityNumber
58
59  // set gross sales amount
60  void BasePlusCommissionEmployee::setGrossSales( double sales )
61  {
62       grossSales = ( sales < 0.0 ) ? 0.0 : sales;
63  } // end function setGrossSales
64
65  // return gross sales amount
66  double BasePlusCommissionEmployee::getGrossSales() const
67  {
68       return grossSales;
69  } // end function getGrossSales
70
71  // set commission rate
72  void BasePlusCommissionEmployee::setCommissionRate( double rate )
73  {
74       commissionRate = ( rate > 0.0 && rate < 1.0 ) ? rate : 0.0;
75  } // end function setCommissionRate
76
77  // return commission rate
78  double BasePlusCommissionEmployee::getCommissionRate() const
79  {
80       return commissionRate;
81  } // end function getCommissionRate
82
83  // set base salary
84  void BasePlusCommissionEmployee::setBaseSalary( double salary )
85  {
86       baseSalary = ( salary < 0.0 ) ? 0.0 : salary;
87  } // end function setBaseSalary
88
89  // return base salary
90  double BasePlusCommissionEmployee::getBaseSalary() const
91  {
92       return baseSalary;
93  } // end function getBaseSalary
94
95  // calculate earnings
96  double BasePlusCommissionEmployee::earnings() const
97  {
98       return baseSalary + ( commissionRate * grossSales );
99  } // end function earnings
100
```

Fig. 23.8 | BasePlusCommissionEmployee class represents an employee who receives a base salary in addition to a commission. (Part 2 of 3.)

```
101   // print BasePlusCommissionEmployee object
102   void BasePlusCommissionEmployee::print() const
103   {
104      cout << "base-salaried commission employee: " << firstName << ' '
105         << lastName << "\nsocial security number: " << socialSecurityNumber
106         << "\ngross sales: " << grossSales
107         << "\ncommission rate: " << commissionRate
108         << "\nbase salary: " << baseSalary;
109   } // end function print
```

Fig. 23.8 | BasePlusCommissionEmployee class represents an employee who receives a base salary in addition to a commission. (Part 3 of 3.)

```
1    // Fig. 23.9: fig23_09.cpp
2    // Testing class BasePlusCommissionEmployee.
3    #include <iostream>
4    using std::cout;
5    using std::endl;
6    using std::fixed;
7
8    #include <iomanip>
9    using std::setprecision;
10
11   // BasePlusCommissionEmployee class definition
12   #include "BasePlusCommissionEmployee.h"
13
14   int main()
15   {
16      // instantiate BasePlusCommissionEmployee object
17      BasePlusCommissionEmployee
18         employee( "Bob", "Lewis", "333-33-3333", 5000, .04, 300 );
19
20      // set floating-point output formatting
21      cout << fixed << setprecision( 2 );
22
23      // get commission employee data
24      cout << "Employee information obtained by get functions: \n"
25         << "\nFirst name is " << employee.getFirstName()
26         << "\nLast name is " << employee.getLastName()
27         << "\nSocial security number is "
28         << employee.getSocialSecurityNumber()
29         << "\nGross sales is " << employee.getGrossSales()
30         << "\nCommission rate is " << employee.getCommissionRate()
31         << "\nBase salary is " << employee.getBaseSalary() << endl;
32
33      employee.setBaseSalary( 1000 ); // set base salary
34
35      cout << "\nUpdated employee information output by print function: \n"
36         << endl;
37      employee.print(); // display the new employee information
38
```

Fig. 23.9 | BasePlusCommissionEmployee class test program. (Part 1 of 2.)

```
39      // display the employee's earnings
40      cout << "\n\nEmployee's earnings: $" << employee.earnings() << endl;
41
42      return 0;
43   } // end main
```

```
Employee information obtained by get functions:

First name is Bob
Last name is Lewis
Social security number is 333-33-3333
Gross sales is 5000.00
Commission rate is 0.04
Base salary is 300.00

Updated employee information output by print function:

base-salaried commission employee: Bob Lewis
social security number: 333-33-3333
gross sales: 5000.00
commission rate: 0.04
base salary: 1000.00

Employee's earnings: $1200.00
```

Fig. 23.9 | BasePlusCommissionEmployee class test program. (Part 2 of 2.)

Exploring the Similarities Between Class BasePlusCommissionEmployee and Class CommissionEmployee

Note that much of the code for class BasePlusCommissionEmployee (Figs. 23.7–23.8) is similar, if not identical, to the code for class CommissionEmployee (Figs. 23.4–23.5). For example, in class BasePlusCommissionEmployee, private data members firstName and lastName and member functions setFirstName, getFirstName, setLastName and get-LastName are identical to those of class CommissionEmployee. Classes CommissionEmployee and BasePlusCommissionEmployee also both contain private data members socialSecurityNumber, commissionRate and grossSales, as well as *get* and *set* functions to manipulate these members. In addition, the BasePlusCommissionEmployee constructor is almost identical to that of class CommissionEmployee, except that BasePlusCommissionEmployee's constructor also sets the baseSalary. The other additions to class BasePlusCommissionEmployee are private data member baseSalary and member functions setBaseSalary and getBaseSalary. Class BasePlusCommissionEmployee's print member function is nearly identical to that of class CommissionEmployee, except that BasePlusCommissionEmployee's print also outputs the value of data member baseSalary.

We literally copied code from class CommissionEmployee and pasted it into class BasePlusCommissionEmployee, then modified class BasePlusCommissionEmployee to include a base salary and member functions that manipulate the base salary. This "copy-and-paste" approach is often error prone and time consuming. Worse yet, it can spread many physical copies of the same code throughout a system, creating a code-maintenance nightmare. Is there a way to "absorb" the data members and member functions of a class in a way that makes them part of other classes without duplicating code? In the next several examples, we do exactly this, using inheritance.

Software Engineering Observation 23.3

Copying and pasting code from one class to another can spread errors across multiple source-code files. To avoid duplicating code (and possibly errors), use inheritance, rather than the "copy-and-paste" approach, in situations where you want one class to "absorb" the data members and member functions of another class.

Software Engineering Observation 23.4

With inheritance, the common data members and member functions of all the classes in the hierarchy are declared in a base class. When changes are required for these common features, software developers need to make the changes only in the base class—derived classes then inherit the changes. Without inheritance, changes would need to be made to all the source-code files that contain a copy of the code in question.

23.4.3 Creating a CommissionEmployee– BasePlusCommissionEmployee Inheritance Hierarchy

Now we create and test a new version of class BasePlusCommissionEmployee (Figs. 23.10–23.11) that derives from class CommissionEmployee (Figs. 23.4–23.5). In this example, a BasePlusCommissionEmployee object *is a* CommissionEmployee (because inheritance passes on the capabilities of class CommissionEmployee), but class BasePlusCommissionEmployee

```
1   // Fig. 23.10: BasePlusCommissionEmployee.h
2   // BasePlusCommissionEmployee class derived from class
3   // CommissionEmployee.
4   #ifndef BASEPLUS_H
5   #define BASEPLUS_H
6
7   #include <string> // C++ standard string class
8   using std::string;
9
10  #include "CommissionEmployee.h" // CommissionEmployee class declaration
11
12  class BasePlusCommissionEmployee : public CommissionEmployee
13  {
14  public:
15     BasePlusCommissionEmployee( const string &, const string &,
16        const string &, double = 0.0, double = 0.0, double = 0.0 );
17
18     void setBaseSalary( double ); // set base salary
19     double getBaseSalary() const; // return base salary
20
21     double earnings() const; // calculate earnings
22     void print() const; // print BasePlusCommissionEmployee object
23  private:
24     double baseSalary; // base salary
25  }; // end class BasePlusCommissionEmployee
26
27  #endif
```

Fig. 23.10 | BasePlusCommissionEmployee class definition indicating inheritance relationship with class CommissionEmployee.

also has data member baseSalary (Fig. 23.10, line 24). The colon (:) in line 12 of the class definition indicates inheritance. Keyword public indicates the type of inheritance. As a derived class (formed with public inheritance), BasePlusCommissionEmployee inherits all the members of class CommissionEmployee, except for the constructor—each class provides its own constructors that are specific to the class. [Note that destructors, too, are not inherited.] Thus, the public services of BasePlusCommissionEmployee include its constructor (lines 15–16) and the public member functions inherited from class CommissionEmployee—although we cannot see these inherited member functions in BasePlusCommissionEmployee's source code, they are nevertheless a part of derived class BasePlusCommissionEmployee. The derived class's public services also include member functions setBaseSalary, getBaseSalary, earnings and print (lines 18–22).

Figure 23.11 shows BasePlusCommissionEmployee's member-function implementations. The constructor (lines 10–17) introduces base-class initializer syntax (line 14), which uses a member initializer to pass arguments to the base-class (CommissionEmployee) constructor. C++ requires a derived-class constructor to call its base-class constructor to initialize the base-class data members that are inherited into the derived class. Line 14 accomplishes this task by invoking the CommissionEmployee constructor by name, passing the constructor's parameters first, last, ssn, sales and rate as arguments to initialize base-class data members firstName, lastName, socialSecurityNumber, grossSales and commissionRate. If BasePlusCommissionEmployee's constructor did not invoke class CommissionEmployee's constructor explicitly, C++ would attempt to invoke class CommissionEmployee's default constructor—but the class does not have such a constructor, so the compiler would issue an error. Recall from Chapter 19 that the compiler provides a default constructor with no parameters in any class that does not explicitly include a constructor. However, CommissionEmployee *does* explicitly include a constructor, so a default constructor is not provided and any attempts to implicitly call CommissionEmployee's default constructor would result in compilation errors.

```
1   // Fig. 23.11: BasePlusCommissionEmployee.cpp
2   // Class BasePlusCommissionEmployee member-function definitions.
3   #include <iostream>
4   using std::cout;
5
6   // BasePlusCommissionEmployee class definition
7   #include "BasePlusCommissionEmployee.h"
8
9   // constructor
10  BasePlusCommissionEmployee::BasePlusCommissionEmployee(
11     const string &first, const string &last, const string &ssn,
12     double sales, double rate, double salary )
13     // explicitly call base-class constructor
14     : CommissionEmployee( first, last, ssn, sales, rate )
15  {
16     setBaseSalary( salary ); // validate and store base salary
17  } // end BasePlusCommissionEmployee constructor
18
```

Fig. 23.11 | BasePlusCommissionEmployee implementation file: private base-class data cannot be accessed from a derived class. (Part 1 of 3.)

```
19   // set base salary
20   void BasePlusCommissionEmployee::setBaseSalary( double salary )
21   {
22      baseSalary = ( salary < 0.0 ) ? 0.0 : salary;
23   } // end function setBaseSalary
24
25   // return base salary
26   double BasePlusCommissionEmployee::getBaseSalary() const
27   {
28      return baseSalary;
29   } // end function getBaseSalary
30
31   // calculate earnings
32   double BasePlusCommissionEmployee::earnings() const
33   {
34      // derived class cannot access the base class's private data
35      return baseSalary + ( commissionRate * grossSales );
36   } // end function earnings
37
38   // print BasePlusCommissionEmployee object
39   void BasePlusCommissionEmployee::print() const
40   {
41      // derived class cannot access the base class's private data
42      cout << "base-salaried commission employee: " << firstName << ' '
43         << lastName << "\nsocial security number: " << socialSecurityNumber
44         << "\ngross sales: " << grossSales
45         << "\ncommission rate: " << commissionRate
46         << "\nbase salary: " << baseSalary;
47   } // end function print
```

```
C:\cpphtp5_examples\ch23\fig23_10_11\BasePlusCommission-Employee.cpp(35) :
   error C2248: 'CommissionEmployee::commissionRate' :
   cannot access private member declared in class 'CommissionEmployee'
      C:\cpphtp5_examples\ch23\fig23_10_11\CommissionEmployee.h(37) :
         see declaration of 'CommissionEmployee::commissionRate'
      C:\cpphtp5e_examples\ch23\fig23_10_11\CommissionEmployee.h(10) :
         see declaration of 'CommissionEmployee'

C:\cpphtp5_examples\ch23\fig23_10_11\BasePlusCommission-Employee.cpp(35) :
   error C2248: 'CommissionEmployee::grossSales' :
   cannot access private member declared in class 'CommissionEmployee'
      C:\cpphtp5_examples\ch23\fig23_10_11\CommissionEmployee.h(36) :
         see declaration of 'CommissionEmployee::grossSales'
      C:\cpphtp5_examples\ch23\fig23_10_11\CommissionEmployee.h(10) :
         see declaration of 'CommissionEmployee'

C:\cpphtp5_examples\ch23\fig23_10_11\BasePlusCommission-Employee.cpp(42) :
   error C2248: 'CommissionEmployee::firstName' :
   cannot access private member declared in class 'CommissionEmployee'
      C:\cpphtp5_examples\ch23\fig23_10_11\CommissionEmployee.h(33) :
         see declaration of 'CommissionEmployee::firstName'
      C:\cpphtp5_examples\ch23\fig23_10_11\CommissionEmployee.h(10) :
         see declaration of 'CommissionEmployee'
```

Fig. 23.11 | BasePlusCommissionEmployee implementation file: private base-class data cannot be accessed from a derived class. (Part 2 of 3.)

```
C:\cpphtp5_examples\ch23\fig23_10_11\BasePlusCommission-Employee.cpp(43) :
    error C2248: 'CommissionEmployee::lastName' :
    cannot access private member declared in class 'CommissionEmployee'
        C:\cpphtp5_examples\ch23\fig23_10_11\CommissionEmployee.h(34) :
        see declaration of 'CommissionEmployee::lastName'
        C:\cpphtp5_examples\ch23\fig23_10_11\CommissionEmployee.h(10) :
        see declaration of 'CommissionEmployee'

C:\cpphtp5_examples\ch23\fig23_10_11\BasePlusCommission-Employee.cpp(43) :
    error C2248: 'CommissionEmployee::socialSecurity-Number' :
    cannot access private member declared in class 'CommissionEmployee'
        C:\cpphtp5_examples\ch23\fig23_10_11\CommissionEmployee.h(35) :
        see declaration of 'CommissionEmployee::socialSecurityNumber'
        C:\cpphtp5_examples\ch23\fig23_10_11\CommissionEmployee.h(10) :
        see declaration of 'CommissionEmployee'

C:\cpphtp5_examples\ch23\fig23_10_11\BasePlusCommission-Employee.cpp(44) :
    error C2248: 'CommissionEmployee::grossSales' :
    cannot access private member declared in class 'CommissionEmployee'
        C:\cpphtp5_examples\ch23\fig23_10_11\CommissionEmployee.h(36) :
        see declaration of 'CommissionEmployee::grossSales'
        C:\cpphtp5_examples\ch23\fig23_10_11\CommissionEmployee.h(10) :
        see declaration of 'CommissionEmployee'

C:\cpphtp5_examples\ch23\fig23_10_11\BasePlusCommission-Employee.cpp(45) :
    error C2248: 'CommissionEmployee::commissionRate' :
    cannot access private member declared in class 'CommissionEmployee'
        C:\cpphtp5_examples\ch23\fig23_10_11\CommissionEmployee.h(37) :
        see declaration of 'CommissionEmployee::commissionRate'
        C:\cpphtp5_examples\ch23\fig23_10_11\CommissionEmployee.h(10) :
        see declaration of 'CommissionEmployee'
```

Fig. 23.11 | `BasePlusCommissionEmployee` implementation file: `private` base-class data cannot be accessed from a derived class. (Part 3 of 3.)

Common Programming Error 23.1

A compilation error occurs if a derived-class constructor calls one of its base-class constructors with arguments that are inconsistent with the number and types of parameters specified in one of the base-class constructor definitions.

Performance Tip 23.1

In a derived-class constructor, initializing member objects and invoking base-class constructors explicitly in the member initializer list prevents duplicate initialization in which a default constructor is called, then data members are modified again in the derived-class constructor's body.

The compiler generates errors for line 35 of Fig. 23.11 because base class `Commission-Employee`'s data members `commissionRate` and `grossSales` are `private`—derived class `BasePlusCommissionEmployee`'s member functions are not allowed to access base class `CommissionEmployee`'s `private` data. Note that we used red text in Fig. 23.11 to indicate erroneous code. The compiler issues additional errors at lines 42–45 of `BasePlus-CommissionEmployee`'s `print` member function for the same reason. As you can see, C++ rigidly enforces restrictions on accessing `private` data members, so that even a derived class (which is intimately related to its base class) cannot access the base class's `private` data. [*Note:* To save space, we show only the error messages from Visual C++ .NET in this example. The error messages produced by your compiler may differ from those shown here. Also notice that we highlight key portions of the lengthy error messages in bold.]

We purposely included the erroneous code in Fig. 23.11 to demonstrate that a derived class's member functions cannot access its base class's private data. The errors in BasePlusCommissionEmployee could have been prevented by using the *get* member functions inherited from class CommissionEmployee. For example, line 35 could have invoked getCommissionRate and getGrossSales to access CommissionEmployee's private data members commissionRate and grossSales, respectively. Similarly, lines 42–45 could have used appropriate *get* member functions to retrieve the values of the base class's data members. In the next example, we show how using protected data also allows us to avoid the errors encountered in this example.

Including the Base Class Header File in the Derived Class Header File with #include
Notice that we #include the base class's header file in the derived class's header file (line 10 of Fig. 23.10). This is necessary for three reasons. First, for the derived class to use the base class's name in line 12, we must tell the compiler that the base class exists—the class definition in CommissionEmployee.h does exactly that.

The second reason is that the compiler uses a class definition to determine the size of an object of that class (as we discussed in Section 19.8). A client program that creates an object of a class must #include the class definition to enable the compiler to reserve the proper amount of memory for the object. When using inheritance, a derived-class object's size depends on the data members declared explicitly in its class definition *and* the data members inherited from its direct and indirect base classes. Including the base class's definition in line 10 allows the compiler to determine the memory requirements for the base class's data members that become part of a derived-class object and thus contribute to the total size of the derived-class object.

The last reason for line 10 is to allow the compiler to determine whether the derived class uses the base class's inherited members properly. For example, in the program of Figs. 23.10–23.11, the compiler uses the base-class header file to determine that the data members being accessed by the derived class are private in the base class. Since these are inaccessible to the derived class, the compiler generates errors. The compiler also uses the base class's function prototypes to validate function calls made by the derived class to the inherited base-class functions—you will see an example of such a function call in Fig. 23.16.

Linking Process in an Inheritance Hierarchy
In Section 19.9, we discussed the linking process for creating an executable GradeBook application. In that example, you saw that the client's object code was linked with the object code for class GradeBook, as well as the object code for any C++ Standard Library classes used either in the client code or in class GradeBook.

The linking process is similar for a program that uses classes in an inheritance hierarchy. The process requires the object code for all classes used in the program and the object code for the direct and indirect base classes of any derived classes used by the program. Suppose a client wants to create an application that uses class BasePlusCommission-Employee, which is a derived class of CommissionEmployee (we will see an example of this in Section 23.4.4). When compiling the client application, the client's object code must be linked with the object code for classes BasePlusCommissionEmployee and Commission-

Employee, because BasePlusCommissionEmployee inherits member functions from its base class CommissionEmployee. The code is also linked with the object code for any C++ Standard Library classes used in class CommissionEmployee, class BasePlusCommissionEmployee or the client code. This provides the program with access to the implementations of all of the functionality that the program may use.

23.4.4 CommissionEmployee–BasePlusCommissionEmployee Inheritance Hierarchy Using protected Data

To enable class BasePlusCommissionEmployee to directly access CommissionEmployee data members firstName, lastName, socialSecurityNumber, grossSales and commissionRate, we can declare those members as protected in the base class. As we discussed in Section 23.3, a base class's protected members can be accessed by members and friends of the base class and by members and friends of any classes derived from that base class.

 Good Programming Practice 23.1

Declare public members first, protected members second and private members last.

Defining Base Class CommissionEmployee with protected Data

Class CommissionEmployee (Figs. 23.12–23.13) now declares data members firstName, lastName, socialSecurityNumber, grossSales and commissionRate as protected (Fig. 23.12, lines 33–37) rather than private. The member-function implementations in Fig. 23.13 are identical to those in Fig. 23.5.

```
 1    // Fig. 23.12: CommissionEmployee.h
 2    // CommissionEmployee class definition with protected data.
 3    #ifndef COMMISSION_H
 4    #define COMMISSION_H
 5
 6    #include <string> // C++ standard string class
 7    using std::string;
 8
 9    class CommissionEmployee
10    {
11    public:
12       CommissionEmployee( const string &, const string &, const string &,
13          double = 0.0, double = 0.0 );
14
15       void setFirstName( const string & ); // set first name
16       string getFirstName() const; // return first name
17
18       void setLastName( const string & ); // set last name
19       string getLastName() const; // return last name
20
21       void setSocialSecurityNumber( const string & ); // set SSN
22       string getSocialSecurityNumber() const; // return SSN
23
```

Fig. 23.12 | CommissionEmployee class definition that declares protected data to allow access by derived classes. (Part 1 of 2.)

```
24     void setGrossSales( double ); // set gross sales amount
25     double getGrossSales() const; // return gross sales amount
26
27     void setCommissionRate( double ); // set commission rate
28     double getCommissionRate() const; // return commission rate
29
30     double earnings() const; // calculate earnings
31     void print() const; // print CommissionEmployee object
32  protected:
33     string firstName;
34     string lastName;
35     string socialSecurityNumber;
36     double grossSales; // gross weekly sales
37     double commissionRate; // commission percentage
38  }; // end class CommissionEmployee
39
40  #endif
```

Fig. 23.12 | CommissionEmployee class definition that declares protected data to allow access by derived classes. (Part 2 of 2.)

```
1   // Fig. 23.13: CommissionEmployee.cpp
2   // Class CommissionEmployee member-function definitions.
3   #include <iostream>
4   using std::cout;
5
6   #include "CommissionEmployee.h" // CommissionEmployee class definition
7
8   // constructor
9   CommissionEmployee::CommissionEmployee(
10     const string &first, const string &last, const string &ssn,
11     double sales, double rate )
12  {
13     firstName = first; // should validate
14     lastName = last; // should validate
15     socialSecurityNumber = ssn; // should validate
16     setGrossSales( sales ); // validate and store gross sales
17     setCommissionRate( rate ); // validate and store commission rate
18  } // end CommissionEmployee constructor
19
20  // set first name
21  void CommissionEmployee::setFirstName( const string &first )
22  {
23     firstName = first; // should validate
24  } // end function setFirstName
25
26  // return first name
27  string CommissionEmployee::getFirstName() const
28  {
29     return firstName;
30  } // end function getFirstName
31
```

Fig. 23.13 | CommissionEmployee class with protected data. (Part 1 of 3.)

```
32    // set last name
33    void CommissionEmployee::setLastName( const string &last )
34    {
35       lastName = last; // should validate
36    } // end function setLastName
37
38    // return last name
39    string CommissionEmployee::getLastName() const
40    {
41       return lastName;
42    } // end function getLastName
43
44    // set social security number
45    void CommissionEmployee::setSocialSecurityNumber( const string &ssn )
46    {
47       socialSecurityNumber = ssn; // should validate
48    } // end function setSocialSecurityNumber
49
50    // return social security number
51    string CommissionEmployee::getSocialSecurityNumber() const
52    {
53       return socialSecurityNumber;
54    } // end function getSocialSecurityNumber
55
56    // set gross sales amount
57    void CommissionEmployee::setGrossSales( double sales )
58    {
59       grossSales = ( sales < 0.0 ) ? 0.0 : sales;
60    } // end function setGrossSales
61
62    // return gross sales amount
63    double CommissionEmployee::getGrossSales() const
64    {
65       return grossSales;
66    } // end function getGrossSales
67
68    // set commission rate
69    void CommissionEmployee::setCommissionRate( double rate )
70    {
71       commissionRate = ( rate > 0.0 && rate < 1.0 ) ? rate : 0.0;
72    } // end function setCommissionRate
73
74    // return commission rate
75    double CommissionEmployee::getCommissionRate() const
76    {
77       return commissionRate;
78    } // end function getCommissionRate
79
80    // calculate earnings
81    double CommissionEmployee::earnings() const
82    {
83       return commissionRate * grossSales;
84    } // end function earnings
```

Fig. 23.13 | CommissionEmployee class with protected data. (Part 2 of 3.)

```
85
86    // print CommissionEmployee object
87    void CommissionEmployee::print() const
88    {
89       cout << "commission employee: " << firstName << ' ' << lastName
90          << "\nsocial security number: " << socialSecurityNumber
91          << "\ngross sales: " << grossSales
92          << "\ncommission rate: " << commissionRate;
93    } // end function print
```

Fig. 23.13 | CommissionEmployee class with protected data. (Part 3 of 3.)

Modifying Derived Class *BasePlusCommissionEmployee*

We now modify class BasePlusCommissionEmployee (Figs. 23.14–23.15) so that it inherits from the version of class CommissionEmployee in Figs. 23.12–23.13. Because class Base-PlusCommissionEmployee inherits from this version of class CommissionEmployee, objects of class BasePlusCommissionEmployee can access inherited data members that are declared protected in class CommissionEmployee (i.e., data members firstName, lastName, so-cialSecurityNumber, grossSales and commissionRate). As a result, the compiler does not generate errors when compiling the BasePlusCommissionEmployee earnings and print member-function definitions in Fig. 23.15 (lines 32–36 and 39–47, respectively).

```
1     // Fig. 23.14: BasePlusCommissionEmployee.h
2     // BasePlusCommissionEmployee class derived from class
3     // CommissionEmployee.
4     #ifndef BASEPLUS_H
5     #define BASEPLUS_H
6
7     #include <string> // C++ standard string class
8     using std::string;
9
10    #include "CommissionEmployee.h" // CommissionEmployee class declaration
11
12    class BasePlusCommissionEmployee : public CommissionEmployee
13    {
14    public:
15       BasePlusCommissionEmployee( const string &, const string &,
16          const string &, double = 0.0, double = 0.0, double = 0.0 );
17
18       void setBaseSalary( double ); // set base salary
19       double getBaseSalary() const; // return base salary
20
21       double earnings() const; // calculate earnings
22       void print() const; // print BasePlusCommissionEmployee object
23    private:
24       double baseSalary; // base salary
25    }; // end class BasePlusCommissionEmployee
26
27    #endif
```

Fig. 23.14 | BasePlusCommissionEmployee class header file.

```
 1    // Fig. 23.15: BasePlusCommissionEmployee.cpp
 2    // Class BasePlusCommissionEmployee member-function definitions.
 3    #include <iostream>
 4    using std::cout;
 5
 6    // BasePlusCommissionEmployee class definition
 7    #include "BasePlusCommissionEmployee.h"
 8
 9    // constructor
10    BasePlusCommissionEmployee::BasePlusCommissionEmployee(
11       const string &first, const string &last, const string &ssn,
12       double sales, double rate, double salary )
13       // explicitly call base-class constructor
14       : CommissionEmployee( first, last, ssn, sales, rate )
15    {
16       setBaseSalary( salary ); // validate and store base salary
17    } // end BasePlusCommissionEmployee constructor
18
19    // set base salary
20    void BasePlusCommissionEmployee::setBaseSalary( double salary )
21    {
22       baseSalary = ( salary < 0.0 ) ? 0.0 : salary;
23    } // end function setBaseSalary
24
25    // return base salary
26    double BasePlusCommissionEmployee::getBaseSalary() const
27    {
28       return baseSalary;
29    } // end function getBaseSalary
30
31    // calculate earnings
32    double BasePlusCommissionEmployee::earnings() const
33    {
34       // can access protected data of base class
35       return baseSalary + ( commissionRate * grossSales );
36    } // end function earnings
37
38    // print BasePlusCommissionEmployee object
39    void BasePlusCommissionEmployee::print() const
40    {
41       // can access protected data of base class
42       cout << "base-salaried commission employee: " << firstName << ' '
43          << lastName << "\nsocial security number: " << socialSecurityNumber
44          << "\ngross sales: " << grossSales
45          << "\ncommission rate: " << commissionRate
46          << "\nbase salary: " << baseSalary;
47    } // end function print
```

Fig. 23.15 | BasePlusCommissionEmployee implementation file for
BasePlusCommissionEmployee class that inherits protected data from CommissionEmployee.

This shows the special privileges that a derived class is granted to access protected base-class data members. Objects of a derived class also can access protected members in any of that derived class's indirect base classes.

Class BasePlusCommissionEmployee does not inherit class CommissionEmployee's constructor. However, class BasePlusCommissionEmployee's constructor (Fig. 23.15, lines 10–17) calls class CommissionEmployee's constructor explicitly (line 14). Recall that BasePlusCommissionEmployee's constructor must explicitly call the constructor of class CommissionEmployee, because CommissionEmployee does not contain a default constructor that could be invoked implicitly.

Testing the Modified *BasePlusCommissionEmployee* Class

Figure 23.16 uses a BasePlusCommissionEmployee object to perform the same tasks that Fig. 23.9 performed on an object of the first version of class BasePlusCommissionEmployee (Figs. 23.7–23.8). Note that the outputs of the two programs are identical. We created the first class BasePlusCommissionEmployee without using inheritance and created this version of BasePlusCommissionEmployee using inheritance; however, both classes provide the same functionality. Note that the code for class BasePlusCommissionEmployee (i.e., the header and implementation files), which is 74 lines, is considerably shorter than the

```cpp
1   // Fig. 23.16: fig23_16.cpp
2   // Testing class BasePlusCommissionEmployee.
3   #include <iostream>
4   using std::cout;
5   using std::endl;
6   using std::fixed;
7
8   #include <iomanip>
9   using std::setprecision;
10
11  // BasePlusCommissionEmployee class definition
12  #include "BasePlusCommissionEmployee.h"
13
14  int main()
15  {
16     // instantiate BasePlusCommissionEmployee object
17     BasePlusCommissionEmployee
18        employee( "Bob", "Lewis", "333-33-3333", 5000, .04, 300 );
19
20     // set floating-point output formatting
21     cout << fixed << setprecision( 2 );
22
23     // get commission employee data
24     cout << "Employee information obtained by get functions: \n"
25        << "\nFirst name is " << employee.getFirstName()
26        << "\nLast name is " << employee.getLastName()
27        << "\nSocial security number is "
28        << employee.getSocialSecurityNumber()
29        << "\nGross sales is " << employee.getGrossSales()
30        << "\nCommission rate is " << employee.getCommissionRate()
31        << "\nBase salary is " << employee.getBaseSalary() << endl;
32
33     employee.setBaseSalary( 1000 ); // set base salary
34
```

Fig. 23.16 | protected base-class data can be accessed from a derived class. (Part 1 of 2.)

```
35      cout << "\nUpdated employee information output by print function: \n"
36         << endl;
37      employee.print(); // display the new employee information
38
39      // display the employee's earnings
40      cout << "\n\nEmployee's earnings: $" << employee.earnings() << endl;
41
42      return 0;
43  } // end main
```

```
Employee information obtained by get functions:

First name is Bob
Last name is Lewis
Social security number is 333-33-3333
Gross sales is 5000.00
Commission rate is 0.04
Base salary is 300.00

Updated employee information output by print function:

base-salaried commission employee: Bob Lewis
social security number: 333-33-3333
gross sales: 5000.00
commission rate: 0.04
base salary: 1000.00

Employee's earnings: $1200.00
```

Fig. 23.16 | protected base-class data can be accessed from a derived class. (Part 2 of 2.)

code for the noninherited version of the class, which is 154 lines, because the inherited version absorbs part of its functionality from CommissionEmployee, whereas the noninherited version does not absorb any functionality. Also, there is now only one copy of the CommissionEmployee functionality declared and defined in class CommissionEmployee. This makes the source code easier to maintain, modify and debug, because the source code related to a CommissionEmployee exists only in the files of Figs. 23.12–23.13.

Notes on Using protected Data

In this example, we declared base-class data members as protected, so that derived classes could modify the data directly. Inheriting protected data members slightly increases performance, because we can directly access the members without incurring the overhead of calls to *set* or *get* member functions. In most cases, however, it is better to use private data members to encourage proper software engineering, and leave code optimization issues to the compiler. Your code will be easier to maintain, modify and debug.

Using protected data members creates two major problems. First, the derived-class object does not have to use a member function to set the value of the base class's protected data member. Therefore, a derived-class object easily can assign an invalid value to the protected data member, thus leaving the object in an inconsistent state. For example, with CommissionEmployee's data member grossSales declared as protected, a derived-class (e.g., `BasePlusCommissionEmployee`) object can assign a negative value to `grossSales`. The second problem with using `protected` data members is that derived-class member functions are more likely to be written so that they depend on the base-class implementation. In practice, derived classes should depend only on the base-class services (i.e., non-`private` member functions) and not on the base-class implementation. With `protected` data members in the base class, if the base-class implementation changes, we may need to modify all derived classes of that base class. For example, if for some reason we were to change the names of data members `firstName` and `lastName` to `first` and `last`, then we would have to do so for all occurrences in which a derived class references these base-class data members directly. In such a case, the software is said to be fragile or brittle, because a small change in the base class can "break" derived-class implementation. The programmer should be able to change the base-class implementation while still providing the same services to derived classes. (Of course, if the base-class services change, we must reimplement our derived classes—good object-oriented design attempts to prevent this.)

Software Engineering Observation 23.5

It is appropriate to use the `protected` access specifier when a base class should provide a service (i.e., a member function) only to its derived classes (and `friends`), not to other clients.

Software Engineering Observation 23.6

Declaring base-class data members `private` (as opposed to declaring them `protected`) enables programmers to change the base-class implementation without having to change derived-class implementations.

Error-Prevention Tip 23.1

When possible, avoid including `protected` data members in a base class. Rather, include non-`private` member functions that access `private` data members, ensuring that the object maintains a consistent state.

23.4.5 CommissionEmployee–BasePlusCommissionEmployee Inheritance Hierarchy Using `private` Data

We now reexamine our hierarchy once more, this time using the best software engineering practices. Class `CommissionEmployee` (Figs. 23.17–23.18) now declares data members `firstName`, `lastName`, `socialSecurityNumber`, `grossSales` and `commissionRate` as private (Fig. 23.17, lines 33–37) and provides public member functions `setFirstName`, `getFirstName`, `setLastName`, `getLastName`, `setSocialSecurityNumber`, `getSocialSecurityNumber`, `setGrossSales`, `getGrossSales`, `setCommissionRate`, `getCommissionRate`, `earnings` and `print` for manipulating these values. If we decide to change the data member names, the `earnings` and `print` definitions will not require modification—only the definitions of the *get* and *set* member functions that directly manipulate the data members will need to change. Note that these changes occur solely within the base class—no changes to the derived class are needed. Localizing the effects of changes like this is a good software engineering practice. Derived class `BasePlusCommissionEmployee` (Figs. 23.19–23.20) inherits `CommissionEmployee`'s non-`private` member functions and can access the `private` base-class members via those member functions.

```
1   // Fig. 23.17: CommissionEmployee.h
2   // CommissionEmployee class definition with good software engineering.
3   #ifndef COMMISSION_H
4   #define COMMISSION_H
5
6   #include <string> // C++ standard string class
7   using std::string;
8
9   class CommissionEmployee
10  {
11  public:
12     CommissionEmployee( const string &, const string &, const string &,
13        double = 0.0, double = 0.0 );
14
15     void setFirstName( const string & ); // set first name
16     string getFirstName() const; // return first name
17
18     void setLastName( const string & ); // set last name
19     string getLastName() const; // return last name
20
21     void setSocialSecurityNumber( const string & ); // set SSN
22     string getSocialSecurityNumber() const; // return SSN
23
24     void setGrossSales( double ); // set gross sales amount
25     double getGrossSales() const; // return gross sales amount
26
27     void setCommissionRate( double ); // set commission rate
28     double getCommissionRate() const; // return commission rate
29
30     double earnings() const; // calculate earnings
31     void print() const; // print CommissionEmployee object
32  private:
33     string firstName;
34     string lastName;
35     string socialSecurityNumber;
36     double grossSales; // gross weekly sales
37     double commissionRate; // commission percentage
38  }; // end class CommissionEmployee
39
40  #endif
```

Fig. 23.17 | CommissionEmployee class defined using good software engineering practices.

```
1   // Fig. 23.18: CommissionEmployee.cpp
2   // Class CommissionEmployee member-function definitions.
3   #include <iostream>
4   using std::cout;
5
6   #include "CommissionEmployee.h" // CommissionEmployee class definition
7
```

Fig. 23.18 | CommissionEmployee class implementation file: CommissionEmployee class uses member functions to manipulate its private data. (Part 1 of 3.)

```
 8    // constructor
 9    CommissionEmployee::CommissionEmployee(
10       const string &first, const string &last, const string &ssn,
11       double sales, double rate )
12       : firstName( first ), lastName( last ), socialSecurityNumber( ssn )
13    {
14       setGrossSales( sales ); // validate and store gross sales
15       setCommissionRate( rate ); // validate and store commission rate
16    } // end CommissionEmployee constructor
17
18    // set first name
19    void CommissionEmployee::setFirstName( const string &first )
20    {
21       firstName = first; // should validate
22    } // end function setFirstName
23
24    // return first name
25    string CommissionEmployee::getFirstName() const
26    {
27       return firstName;
28    } // end function getFirstName
29
30    // set last name
31    void CommissionEmployee::setLastName( const string &last )
32    {
33       lastName = last; // should validate
34    } // end function setLastName
35
36    // return last name
37    string CommissionEmployee::getLastName() const
38    {
39       return lastName;
40    } // end function getLastName
41
42    // set social security number
43    void CommissionEmployee::setSocialSecurityNumber( const string &ssn )
44    {
45       socialSecurityNumber = ssn; // should validate
46    } // end function setSocialSecurityNumber
47
48    // return social security number
49    string CommissionEmployee::getSocialSecurityNumber() const
50    {
51       return socialSecurityNumber;
52    } // end function getSocialSecurityNumber
53
54    // set gross sales amount
55    void CommissionEmployee::setGrossSales( double sales )
56    {
57       grossSales = ( sales < 0.0 ) ? 0.0 : sales;
58    } // end function setGrossSales
```

Fig. 23.18 | CommissionEmployee class implementation file: CommissionEmployee class uses member functions to manipulate its private data. (Part 2 of 3.)

```
59
60   // return gross sales amount
61   double CommissionEmployee::getGrossSales() const
62   {
63      return grossSales;
64   } // end function getGrossSales
65
66   // set commission rate
67   void CommissionEmployee::setCommissionRate( double rate )
68   {
69      commissionRate = ( rate > 0.0 && rate < 1.0 ) ? rate : 0.0;
70   } // end function setCommissionRate
71
72   // return commission rate
73   double CommissionEmployee::getCommissionRate() const
74   {
75      return commissionRate;
76   } // end function getCommissionRate
77
78   // calculate earnings
79   double CommissionEmployee::earnings() const
80   {
81      return getCommissionRate() * getGrossSales();
82   } // end function earnings
83
84   // print CommissionEmployee object
85   void CommissionEmployee::print() const
86   {
87      cout << "commission employee: "
88         << getFirstName() << ' ' << getLastName()
89         << "\nsocial security number: " << getSocialSecurityNumber()
90         << "\ngross sales: " << getGrossSales()
91         << "\ncommission rate: " << getCommissionRate();
92   } // end function print
```

Fig. 23.18 | CommissionEmployee class implementation file: CommissionEmployee class uses member functions to manipulate its private data. (Part 3 of 3.)

In the CommissionEmployee constructor implementation (Fig. 23.18, lines 9–16), note that we use member initializers (line 12) to set the values of members firstName, lastName and socialSecurityNumber. We show how derived-class BasePlusCommissionEmployee (Figs. 23.19–23.20) can invoke non-private base-class member functions (setFirstName, getFirstName, setLastName, getLastName, setSocialSecurityNumber and getSocialSecurityNumber) to manipulate these data members.

> **Performance Tip 23.2**
>
> *Using a member function to access a data member's value can be slightly slower than accessing the data directly. However, today's optimizing compilers are carefully designed to perform many optimizations implicitly (such as inlining set and get member-function calls). As a result, programmers should write code that adheres to proper software engineering principles, and leave optimization issues to the compiler. A good rule is, "Do not second-guess the compiler."*

Class `BasePlusCommissionEmployee` (Figs. 23.19–23.20) has several changes to its member-function implementations (Fig. 23.20) that distinguish it from the previous version of the class (Figs. 23.14–23.15). Member functions `earnings` (Fig. 23.20, lines 32–35) and

```
1   // Fig. 23.19: BasePlusCommissionEmployee.h
2   // BasePlusCommissionEmployee class derived from class
3   // CommissionEmployee.
4   #ifndef BASEPLUS_H
5   #define BASEPLUS_H
6
7   #include <string> // C++ standard string class
8   using std::string;
9
10  #include "CommissionEmployee.h" // CommissionEmployee class declaration
11
12  class BasePlusCommissionEmployee : public CommissionEmployee
13  {
14  public:
15     BasePlusCommissionEmployee( const string &, const string &,
16        const string &, double = 0.0, double = 0.0, double = 0.0 );
17
18     void setBaseSalary( double ); // set base salary
19     double getBaseSalary() const; // return base salary
20
21     double earnings() const; // calculate earnings
22     void print() const; // print BasePlusCommissionEmployee object
23  private:
24     double baseSalary; // base salary
25  }; // end class BasePlusCommissionEmployee
26
27  #endif
```

Fig. 23.19 | `BasePlusCommissionEmployee` class header file.

```
1   // Fig. 23.20: BasePlusCommissionEmployee.cpp
2   // Class BasePlusCommissionEmployee member-function definitions.
3   #include <iostream>
4   using std::cout;
5
6   // BasePlusCommissionEmployee class definition
7   #include "BasePlusCommissionEmployee.h"
8
9   // constructor
10  BasePlusCommissionEmployee::BasePlusCommissionEmployee(
11     const string &first, const string &last, const string &ssn,
12     double sales, double rate, double salary )
13     // explicitly call base-class constructor
14     : CommissionEmployee( first, last, ssn, sales, rate )
15  {
```

Fig. 23.20 | `BasePlusCommissionEmployee` class that inherits from class `CommissionEmployee` but cannot directly access the class's `private` data. (Part 1 of 2.)

```
16        setBaseSalary( salary ); // validate and store base salary
17    } // end BasePlusCommissionEmployee constructor
18
19    // set base salary
20    void BasePlusCommissionEmployee::setBaseSalary( double salary )
21    {
22        baseSalary = ( salary < 0.0 ) ? 0.0 : salary;
23    } // end function setBaseSalary
24
25    // return base salary
26    double BasePlusCommissionEmployee::getBaseSalary() const
27    {
28        return baseSalary;
29    } // end function getBaseSalary
30
31    // calculate earnings
32    double BasePlusCommissionEmployee::earnings() const
33    {
34        return getBaseSalary() + CommissionEmployee::earnings();
35    } // end function earnings
36
37    // print BasePlusCommissionEmployee object
38    void BasePlusCommissionEmployee::print() const
39    {
40        cout << "base-salaried ";
41
42        // invoke CommissionEmployee's print function
43        CommissionEmployee::print();
44
45        cout << "\nbase salary: " << getBaseSalary();
46    } // end function print
```

Fig. 23.20 | BasePlusCommissionEmployee class that inherits from class CommissionEmployee but cannot directly access the class's private data. (Part 2 of 2.)

print (lines 38–46) each invoke member function getBaseSalary to obtain the base salary value, rather than accessing baseSalary directly. This insulates earnings and print from potential changes to the implementation of data member baseSalary. For example, if we decide to rename data member baseSalary or change its type, only member functions set-BaseSalary and getBaseSalary will need to change.

Class BasePlusCommissionEmployee's earnings function (Fig. 23.20, lines 32–35) redefines class CommissionEmployee's earnings member function (Fig. 23.18, lines 79–82) to calculate the earnings of a base-salaried commission employee. Class BasePlusCommissionEmployee's version of earnings obtains the portion of the employee's earnings based on commission alone by calling base-class CommissionEmployee's earnings function with the expression CommissionEmployee::earnings() (Fig. 23.20, line 34). BasePlusCommissionEmployee's earnings function then adds the base salary to this value to calculate the total earnings of the employee. Note the syntax used to invoke a redefined base-class member function from a derived class—place the base-class name and the binary scope resolution operator (::) before the base-class member-function name. This member-function invocation is a good software engineering practice: Recall from Software Engineering Observation 9.9 that, if an object's member function performs the actions needed by another object, we should call that member function rather than duplicating its code body. By having BasePlusCommissionEmployee's earnings function invoke Commission-Employee's earnings function to calculate part of a BasePlusCommissionEmployee object's earnings, we avoid duplicating the code and reduce code-maintenance problems.

Common Programming Error 23.2

When a base-class member function is redefined in a derived class, the derived-class version often calls the base-class version to do additional work. Failure to use the :: operator prefixed with the name of the base class when referencing the base class's member function causes infinite recursion, because the derived-class member function would then call itself.

Common Programming Error 23.3

Including a base-class member function with a different signature in the derived class hides the base-class version of the function. Attempts to call the base-class version through the public interface of a derived-class object result in compilation errors.

Similarly, BasePlusCommissionEmployee's print function (Fig. 23.20, lines 38–46) redefines class CommissionEmployee's print member function (Fig. 23.18, lines 85–92) to output information that is appropriate for a base-salaried commission employee. Class BasePlusCommissionEmployee's version displays part of a BasePlusCommissionEmployee object's information (i.e., the string "commission employee" and the values of class CommissionEmployee's private data members) by calling CommissionEmployee's print member function with the qualified name CommissionEmployee::print() (Fig. 23.20, line 43). BasePlusCommissionEmployee's print function then outputs the remainder of a BasePlusCommissionEmployee object's information (i.e., the value of class BasePlusCommissionEmployee's base salary).

Figure 23.21 performs the same manipulations on a BasePlusCommissionEmployee object as did Fig. 23.9 and Fig. 23.16 on objects of classes CommissionEmployee and BasePlusCommissionEmployee, respectively. Although each "base-salaried commission employee" class behaves identically, class BasePlusCommissionEmployee is the best engineered. By using inheritance and by calling member functions that hide the data and ensure consistency, we have efficiently and effectively constructed a well-engineered class.

```cpp
1   // Fig. 23.21: fig23_21.cpp
2   // Testing class BasePlusCommissionEmployee.
3   #include <iostream>
4   using std::cout;
5   using std::endl;
6   using std::fixed;
7
8   #include <iomanip>
9   using std::setprecision;
10
11  // BasePlusCommissionEmployee class definition
12  #include "BasePlusCommissionEmployee.h"
```

Fig. 23.21 | Base-class private data is accessible to a derived class via public or protected member function inherited by the derived class. (Part 1 of 2.)

```
13
14   int main()
15   {
16      // instantiate BasePlusCommissionEmployee object
17      BasePlusCommissionEmployee
18         employee( "Bob", "Lewis", "333-33-3333", 5000, .04, 300 );
19
20      // set floating-point output formatting
21      cout << fixed << setprecision( 2 );
22
23      // get commission employee data
24      cout << "Employee information obtained by get functions: \n"
25         << "\nFirst name is " << employee.getFirstName()
26         << "\nLast name is " << employee.getLastName()
27         << "\nSocial security number is "
28         << employee.getSocialSecurityNumber()
29         << "\nGross sales is " << employee.getGrossSales()
30         << "\nCommission rate is " << employee.getCommissionRate()
31         << "\nBase salary is " << employee.getBaseSalary() << endl;
32
33      employee.setBaseSalary( 1000 ); // set base salary
34
35      cout << "\nUpdated employee information output by print function: \n"
36         << endl;
37      employee.print(); // display the new employee information
38
39      // display the employee's earnings
40      cout << "\n\nEmployee's earnings: $" << employee.earnings() << endl;
41
42      return 0;
43   } // end main
```

```
Employee information obtained by get functions:

First name is Bob
Last name is Lewis
Social security number is 333-33-3333
Gross sales is 5000.00
Commission rate is 0.04
Base salary is 300.00

Updated employee information output by print function:

base-salaried commission employee: Bob Lewis
social security number: 333-33-3333
gross sales: 5000.00
commission rate: 0.04
base salary: 1000.00

Employee's earnings: $1200.00
```

Fig. 23.21 | Base-class private data is accessible to a derived class via public or protected member function inherited by the derived class. (Part 2 of 2.)

In this section, you saw an evolutionary set of examples that was carefully designed to teach key capabilities for good software engineering with inheritance. You learned how to create a derived class using inheritance, how to use protected base-class members to enable a derived class to access inherited base-class data members and how to redefine base-class functions to provide versions that are more appropriate for derived-class objects. In addition, you learned how to apply software engineering techniques from Chapters 20–21 and this chapter to create classes that are easy to maintain, modify and debug.

23.5 Constructors and Destructors in Derived Classes

As we explained in the preceding section, instantiating a derived-class object begins a chain of constructor calls in which the derived-class constructor, before performing its own tasks, invokes its direct base class's constructor either explicitly (via a base-class member initializer) or implicitly (calling the base class's default constructor). Similarly, if the base class is derived from another class, the base-class constructor is required to invoke the constructor of the next class up in the hierarchy, and so on. The last constructor called in this chain is the constructor of the class at the base of the hierarchy, whose body actually finishes executing first. The original derived-class constructor's body finishes executing last. Each base-class constructor initializes the base-class data members that the derived-class object inherits. For example, consider the CommissionEmployee/BasePlusCommissionEmployee hierarchy from Figs. 23.17–23.20. When a program creates an object of class BasePlusCommissionEmployee, the CommissionEmployee constructor is called. Since class CommissionEmployee is at the base of the hierarchy, its constructor executes, initializing the private data members of CommissionEmployee that are part of the BasePlusCommissionEmployee object. When CommissionEmployee's constructor completes execution, it returns control to BasePlusCommissionEmployee's constructor, which initializes the BasePlusCommissionEmployee object's baseSalary.

Software Engineering Observation 23.7

When a program creates a derived-class object, the derived-class constructor immediately calls the base-class constructor, the base-class constructor's body executes, then the derived class's member initializers execute and finally the derived-class constructor's body executes. This process cascades up the hierarchy if the hierarchy contains more than two levels.

When a derived-class object is destroyed, the program calls that object's destructor. This begins a chain (or cascade) of destructor calls in which the derived-class destructor and the destructors of the direct and indirect base classes and the classes' members execute in reverse of the order in which the constructors executed. When a derived-class object's destructor is called, the destructor performs its task, then invokes the destructor of the next base class up the hierarchy. This process repeats until the destructor of the final base class at the top of the hierarchy is called. Then the object is removed from memory.

Software Engineering Observation 23.8

Suppose that we create an object of a derived class where both the base class and the derived class contain objects of other classes. When an object of that derived class is created, first the constructors for the base class's member objects execute, then the base-class constructor executes, then the constructors for the derived class's member objects execute, then the derived class's constructor executes. Destructors for derived-class objects are called in the reverse of the order in which their corresponding constructors are called.

Base-class constructors, destructors and overloaded assignment operators (see Chapter 22) are not inherited by derived classes. Derived-class constructors, destructors and overloaded assignment operators, however, can call base-class constructors, destructors and overloaded assignment operators.

Our next example revisits the commission employee hierarchy by defining class CommissionEmployee (Figs. 23.22–23.23) and class BasePlusCommissionEmployee (Figs. 23.24–23.25) that contain constructors and destructors, each of which prints a message when it is invoked. As you will see in the output in Fig. 23.26, these messages demonstrate the order in which the constructors and destructors are called for objects in an inheritance hierarchy.

```cpp
 1   // Fig. 23.22: CommissionEmployee.h
 2   // CommissionEmployee class definition represents a commission employee.
 3   #ifndef COMMISSION_H
 4   #define COMMISSION_H
 5
 6   #include <string> // C++ standard string class
 7   using std::string;
 8
 9   class CommissionEmployee
10   {
11   public:
12      CommissionEmployee( const string &, const string &, const string &,
13         double = 0.0, double = 0.0 );
14      ~CommissionEmployee(); // destructor
15
16      void setFirstName( const string & ); // set first name
17      string getFirstName() const; // return first name
18
19      void setLastName( const string & ); // set last name
20      string getLastName() const; // return last name
21
22      void setSocialSecurityNumber( const string & ); // set SSN
23      string getSocialSecurityNumber() const; // return SSN
24
25      void setGrossSales( double ); // set gross sales amount
26      double getGrossSales() const; // return gross sales amount
27
28      void setCommissionRate( double ); // set commission rate
29      double getCommissionRate() const; // return commission rate
30
31      double earnings() const; // calculate earnings
32      void print() const; // print CommissionEmployee object
33   private:
34      string firstName;
35      string lastName;
36      string socialSecurityNumber;
37      double grossSales; // gross weekly sales
38      double commissionRate; // commission percentage
39   }; // end class CommissionEmployee
40
41   #endif
```

Fig. 23.22 | CommissionEmployee class header file.

In this example, we modified the CommissionEmployee constructor (lines 10–21 of Fig. 23.23) and included a CommissionEmployee destructor (lines 24–29), each of which outputs a line of text upon its invocation. We also modified the BasePlusCommissionEmployee constructor (lines 11–22 of Fig. 23.25) and included a BasePlusCommissionEmployee destructor (lines 25–30), each of which outputs a line of text upon its invocation.

```cpp
1   // Fig. 23.23: CommissionEmployee.cpp
2   // Class CommissionEmployee member-function definitions.
3   #include <iostream>
4   using std::cout;
5   using std::endl;
6
7   #include "CommissionEmployee.h" // CommissionEmployee class definition
8
9   // constructor
10  CommissionEmployee::CommissionEmployee(
11     const string &first, const string &last, const string &ssn,
12     double sales, double rate )
13     : firstName( first ), lastName( last ), socialSecurityNumber( ssn )
14  {
15     setGrossSales( sales ); // validate and store gross sales
16     setCommissionRate( rate ); // validate and store commission rate
17
18     cout << "CommissionEmployee constructor: " << endl;
19     print();
20     cout << "\n\n";
21  } // end CommissionEmployee constructor
22
23  // destructor
24  CommissionEmployee::~CommissionEmployee()
25  {
26     cout << "CommissionEmployee destructor: " << endl;
27     print();
28     cout << "\n\n";
29  } // end CommissionEmployee destructor
30
31  // set first name
32  void CommissionEmployee::setFirstName( const string &first )
33  {
34     firstName = first; // should validate
35  } // end function setFirstName
36
37  // return first name
38  string CommissionEmployee::getFirstName() const
39  {
40     return firstName;
41  } // end function getFirstName
42
43  // set last name
44  void CommissionEmployee::setLastName( const string &last )
45  {
```

Fig. 23.23 | CommissionEmployee's constructor outputs text. (Part 1 of 3.)

```
46        lastName = last; // should validate
47    } // end function setLastName
48
49    // return last name
50    string CommissionEmployee::getLastName() const
51    {
52        return lastName;
53    } // end function getLastName
54
55    // set social security number
56    void CommissionEmployee::setSocialSecurityNumber( const string &ssn )
57    {
58        socialSecurityNumber = ssn; // should validate
59    } // end function setSocialSecurityNumber
60
61    // return social security number
62    string CommissionEmployee::getSocialSecurityNumber() const
63    {
64        return socialSecurityNumber;
65    } // end function getSocialSecurityNumber
66
67    // set gross sales amount
68    void CommissionEmployee::setGrossSales( double sales )
69    {
70        grossSales = ( sales < 0.0 ) ? 0.0 : sales;
71    } // end function setGrossSales
72
73    // return gross sales amount
74    double CommissionEmployee::getGrossSales() const
75    {
76        return grossSales;
77    } // end function getGrossSales
78
79    // set commission rate
80    void CommissionEmployee::setCommissionRate( double rate )
81    {
82        commissionRate = ( rate > 0.0 && rate < 1.0 ) ? rate : 0.0;
83    } // end function setCommissionRate
84
85    // return commission rate
86    double CommissionEmployee::getCommissionRate() const
87    {
88        return commissionRate;
89    } // end function getCommissionRate
90
91    // calculate earnings
92    double CommissionEmployee::earnings() const
93    {
94        return getCommissionRate() * getGrossSales();
95    } // end function earnings
96
```

Fig. 23.23 | CommissionEmployee's constructor outputs text. (Part 2 of 3.)

```
97   // print CommissionEmployee object
98   void CommissionEmployee::print() const
99   {
100     cout << "commission employee: "
101        << getFirstName() << ' ' << getLastName()
102        << "\nsocial security number: " << getSocialSecurityNumber()
103        << "\ngross sales: " << getGrossSales()
104        << "\ncommission rate: " << getCommissionRate();
105   } // end function print
```

Fig. 23.23 | CommissionEmployee's constructor outputs text. (Part 3 of 3.)

```
1    // Fig. 23.24: BasePlusCommissionEmployee.h
2    // BasePlusCommissionEmployee class derived from class
3    // CommissionEmployee.
4    #ifndef BASEPLUS_H
5    #define BASEPLUS_H
6
7    #include <string> // C++ standard string class
8    using std::string;
9
10   #include "CommissionEmployee.h" // CommissionEmployee class declaration
11
12   class BasePlusCommissionEmployee : public CommissionEmployee
13   {
14   public:
15     BasePlusCommissionEmployee( const string &, const string &,
16        const string &, double = 0.0, double = 0.0, double = 0.0 );
17     ~BasePlusCommissionEmployee(); // destructor
18
19     void setBaseSalary( double ); // set base salary
20     double getBaseSalary() const; // return base salary
21
22     double earnings() const; // calculate earnings
23     void print() const; // print BasePlusCommissionEmployee object
24   private:
25     double baseSalary; // base salary
26   }; // end class BasePlusCommissionEmployee
27
28   #endif
```

Fig. 23.24 | BasePlusCommissionEmployee class header file.

```
1    // Fig. 23.25: BasePlusCommissionEmployee.cpp
2    // Class BasePlusCommissionEmployee member-function definitions.
3    #include <iostream>
4    using std::cout;
5    using std::endl;
6
7    // BasePlusCommissionEmployee class definition
8    #include "BasePlusCommissionEmployee.h"
```

Fig. 23.25 | BasePlusCommissionEmployee's constructor outputs text. (Part 1 of 2.)

```
9
10   // constructor
11   BasePlusCommissionEmployee::BasePlusCommissionEmployee(
12      const string &first, const string &last, const string &ssn,
13      double sales, double rate, double salary )
14      // explicitly call base-class constructor
15      : CommissionEmployee( first, last, ssn, sales, rate )
16   {
17      setBaseSalary( salary ); // validate and store base salary
18
19      cout << "BasePlusCommissionEmployee constructor: " << endl;
20      print();
21      cout << "\n\n";
22   } // end BasePlusCommissionEmployee constructor
23
24   // destructor
25   BasePlusCommissionEmployee::~BasePlusCommissionEmployee()
26   {
27      cout << "BasePlusCommissionEmployee destructor: " << endl;
28      print();
29      cout << "\n\n";
30   } // end BasePlusCommissionEmployee destructor
31
32   // set base salary
33   void BasePlusCommissionEmployee::setBaseSalary( double salary )
34   {
35      baseSalary = ( salary < 0.0 ) ? 0.0 : salary;
36   } // end function setBaseSalary
37
38   // return base salary
39   double BasePlusCommissionEmployee::getBaseSalary() const
40   {
41      return baseSalary;
42   } // end function getBaseSalary
43
44   // calculate earnings
45   double BasePlusCommissionEmployee::earnings() const
46   {
47      return getBaseSalary() + CommissionEmployee::earnings();
48   } // end function earnings
49
50   // print BasePlusCommissionEmployee object
51   void BasePlusCommissionEmployee::print() const
52   {
53      cout << "base-salaried ";
54
55      // invoke CommissionEmployee's print function
56      CommissionEmployee::print();
57
58      cout << "\nbase salary: " << getBaseSalary();
59   } // end function print
```

Fig. 23.25 | BasePlusCommissionEmployee's constructor outputs text. (Part 2 of 2.)

Figure 23.26 demonstrates the order in which constructors and destructors are called for objects of classes that are part of an inheritance hierarchy. Function main (lines 15–34) begins by instantiating CommissionEmployee object employee1 (lines 21–22) in a separate block inside main (lines 20–23). The object goes in and out of scope immediately (the end of the block is reached as soon as the object is created), so both the CommissionEmployee constructor and destructor are called. Next, lines 26–27 instantiate BasePlusCommissionEmployee object employee2. This invokes the CommissionEmployee constructor to display outputs with values passed from the BasePlusCommissionEmployee constructor, then the output specified in the BasePlusCommissionEmployee constructor is performed. Lines 30–31 then instantiate BasePlusCommissionEmployee object employee3. Again, the CommissionEmployee and BasePlusCommissionEmployee constructors are both called. Note that, in each case, the body of the CommissionEmployee constructor is executed before the body of the BasePlusCommissionEmployee constructor executes. When the end of main is reached, the destructors are called for objects employee2 and employee3. But, because destructors are called in the reverse order of their corresponding constructors, the BasePlusCommissionEmployee destructor and CommissionEmployee destructor are called (in that order) for object employee3, then the BasePlusCommissionEmployee and CommissionEmployee destructors are called (in that order) for object employee2.

```cpp
1   // Fig. 23.26: fig23_26.cpp
2   // Display order in which base-class and derived-class constructors
3   // and destructors are called.
4   #include <iostream>
5   using std::cout;
6   using std::endl;
7   using std::fixed;
8
9   #include <iomanip>
10  using std::setprecision;
11
12  // BasePlusCommissionEmployee class definition
13  #include "BasePlusCommissionEmployee.h"
14
15  int main()
16  {
17     // set floating-point output formatting
18     cout << fixed << setprecision( 2 );
19
20     { // begin new scope
21        CommissionEmployee employee1(
22           "Bob", "Lewis", "333-33-3333", 5000, .04 );
23     } // end scope
24
25     cout << endl;
26     BasePlusCommissionEmployee
27        employee2( "Lisa", "Jones", "555-55-5555", 2000, .06, 800 );
28
```

Fig. 23.26 | Constructor and destructor call order. (Part 1 of 3.)

```
29      cout << endl;
30      BasePlusCommissionEmployee
31         employee3( "Mark", "Sands", "888-88-8888", 8000, .15, 2000 );
32      cout << endl;
33      return 0;
34   } // end main
```

```
CommissionEmployee constructor:
commission employee: Bob Lewis
social security number: 333-33-3333
gross sales: 5000.00
commission rate: 0.04

CommissionEmployee destructor:
commission employee: Bob Lewis
social security number: 333-33-3333
gross sales: 5000.00
commission rate: 0.04


CommissionEmployee constructor:
base-salaried commission employee: Lisa Jones
social security number: 555-55-5555
gross sales: 2000.00
commission rate: 0.06

BasePlusCommissionEmployee constructor:
base-salaried commission employee: Lisa Jones
social security number: 555-55-5555
gross sales: 2000.00
commission rate: 0.06
base salary: 800.00


CommissionEmployee constructor:
commission employee: Mark Sands
social security number: 888-88-8888
gross sales: 8000.00
commission rate: 0.15

BasePlusCommissionEmployee constructor:
base-salaried commission employee: Mark Sands
social security number: 888-88-8888
gross sales: 8000.00
commission rate: 0.15
base salary: 2000.00

BasePlusCommissionEmployee destructor:
base-salaried commission employee: Mark Sands
social security number: 888-88-8888
gross sales: 8000.00
commission rate: 0.15
base salary: 2000.00
```

(continued on next page)

Fig. 23.26 | Constructor and destructor call order. (Part 2 of 3.)

```
CommissionEmployee destructor:
commission employee: Mark Sands
social security number: 888-88-8888
gross sales: 8000.00
commission rate: 0.15

BasePlusCommissionEmployee destructor:
base-salaried commission employee: Lisa Jones
social security number: 555-55-5555
gross sales: 2000.00
commission rate: 0.06
base salary: 800.00

CommissionEmployee destructor:
commission employee: Lisa Jones
social security number: 555-55-5555
gross sales: 2000.00
commission rate: 0.06
```

Fig. 23.26 | Constructor and destructor call order. (Part 3 of 3.)

23.6 public, protected and private Inheritance

When deriving a class from a base class, the base class may be inherited through public, protected or private inheritance. Use of protected and private inheritance is rare, and each should be used only with great care; we normally use public inheritance in this book. Figure 23.27 summarizes for each type of inheritance the accessibility of base-class members in a derived class. The first column contains the base-class access specifiers.

When deriving a class from a public base class, public members of the base class become public members of the derived class and protected members of the base class become protected members of the derived class. A base class's private members are never accessible directly from a derived class, but can be accessed through calls to the public and protected members of the base class.

When deriving from a protected base class, public and protected members of the base class become protected members of the derived class. When deriving from a private base class, public and protected members of the base class become private members (e.g., the functions become utility functions) of the derived class. Private and protected inheritance are not *is-a* relationships.

23.7 Software Engineering with Inheritance

In this section, we discuss the use of inheritance to customize existing software. When we use inheritance to create a new class from an existing one, the new class inherits the data members and member functions of the existing class, as described in Fig. 23.27. We can customize the new class to meet our needs by including additional members and by redefining base-class members. The derived-class programmer does this in C++ without accessing the base class's source code. The derived class must be able to link to the base class's

Base-class member-access specifier	Type of inheritance		
	`public` inheritance	`protected` inheritance	`private` inheritance
public	`public` in derived class. Can be accessed directly by member functions, `friend` functions and nonmember functions.	`protected` in derived class. Can be accessed directly by member functions and `friend` functions.	`private` in derived class. Can be accessed directly by member functions and `friend` functions.
protected	`protected` in derived class. Can be accessed directly by member functions and `friend` functions.	`protected` in derived class. Can be accessed directly by member functions and `friend` functions.	`private` in derived class. Can be accessed directly by member functions and `friend` functions.
private	Hidden in derived class. Can be accessed by member functions and `friend` functions through `public` or `protected` member functions of the base class.	Hidden in derived class. Can be accessed by member functions and `friend` functions through `public` or `protected` member functions of the base class.	Hidden in derived class. Can be accessed by member functions and `friend` functions through `public` or `protected` member functions of the base class.

Fig. 23.27 | Summary of base-class member accessibility in a derived class.

object code. This powerful capability is attractive to independent software vendors (ISVs). ISVs can develop proprietary classes for sale or license and make these classes available to users in object-code format. Users then can derive new classes from these library classes rapidly and without accessing the ISVs' proprietary source code. All the ISVs need to supply with the object code are the header files.

Sometimes it is difficult for students to appreciate the scope of problems faced by designers who work on large-scale software projects in industry. People experienced with such projects say that effective software reuse improves the software development process. Object-oriented programming facilitates software reuse, thus shortening development times and enhancing software quality.

The availability of substantial and useful class libraries delivers the maximum benefits of software reuse through inheritance. Just as shrink-wrapped software produced by independent software vendors became an explosive-growth industry with the arrival of the personal computer, so, too, interest in the creation and sale of class libraries is growing exponentially. Application designers build their applications with these libraries, and library designers are being rewarded by having their libraries included with the applications. The standard C++ libraries that are shipped with C++ compilers tend to be rather general purpose and limited in scope. However, there is massive worldwide commitment to the development of class libraries for a huge variety of applications arenas.

Software Engineering Observation 23.9

At the design stage in an object-oriented system, the designer often determines that certain classes are closely related. The designer should "factor out" common attributes and behaviors and place these in a base class, then use inheritance to form derived classes, endowing them with capabilities beyond those inherited from the base class.

Software Engineering Observation 23.10

The creation of a derived class does not affect its base class's source code. Inheritance preserves the integrity of a base class.

Software Engineering Observation 23.11

Just as designers of non-object-oriented systems should avoid proliferation of functions, designers of object-oriented systems should avoid proliferation of classes. Proliferation of classes creates management problems and can hinder software reusability, because it becomes difficult for a client to locate the most appropriate class of a huge class library. The alternative is to create fewer classes that provide more substantial functionality, but such classes might provide too much functionality.

Performance Tip 23.3

If classes produced through inheritance are larger than they need to be (i.e., contain too much functionality), memory and processing resources might be wasted. Inherit from the class whose functionality is "closest" to what is needed.

Reading derived-class definitions can be confusing, because inherited members are not shown physically in the derived classes, but nevertheless are present. A similar problem exists when documenting derived-class members.

23.8 Wrap-Up

This chapter introduced inheritance—the ability to create a class by absorbing an existing class's data members and member functions and embellishing them with new capabilities. Through a series of examples using an employee inheritance hierarchy, you learned the notions of base classes and derived classes and used `public` inheritance to create a derived class that inherits members from a base class. The chapter introduced the access specifier `protected`; derived-class member functions can access `protected` base-class members. You learned how to access redefined base-class members by qualifying their names with the base-class name and binary scope resolution operator (`::`). You also saw the order in which constructors and destructors are called for objects of classes that are part of an inheritance hierarchy. Finally, we explained the three types of inheritance—`public`, `protected` and `private`—and the accessibility of base-class members in a derived class when using each type.

In Chapter 24, Object-Oriented Programming: Polymorphism, we build upon our discussion of inheritance by introducing polymorphism—an object-oriented concept that enables us to write programs that handle, in a more general manner, objects of a wide variety of classes related by inheritance. After studying Chapter 24, you will be familiar with classes, objects, encapsulation, inheritance and polymorphism—the essential aspects of object-oriented programming.

Summary

Section 23.1 Introduction

- Software reuse reduces program development time and cost.

- Inheritance is a form of software reuse in which the programmer creates a class that absorbs an existing class's data and behaviors and enhances them with new capabilities. The existing class is called the base class, and the new class is referred to as the derived class.

- A direct base class is the one from which a derived class explicitly inherits (specified by the class name to the right of the : in the first line of a class definition). An indirect base class is inherited from two or more levels up in the class hierarchy.

- With single inheritance, a class is derived from one base class. With multiple inheritance, a class inherits from multiple (possibly unrelated) base classes.

- A derived class represents a more specialized group of objects. Typically, a derived class contains behaviors inherited from its base class plus additional behaviors. A derived class can also customize behaviors inherited from the base class.

- Every object of a derived class is also an object of that class's base class. However, a base-class object is not an object of that class's derived classes.

- The *is-a* relationship represents inheritance. In an *is-a* relationship, an object of a derived class also can be treated as an object of its base class.

- The *has-a* relationship represents composition—an object contains one or more objects of other classes as members, but does not disclose their behavior directly in its interface.

Section 23.2 Base Classes and Derived Classes

- A derived class cannot access the `private` members of its base class directly; allowing this would violate the encapsulation of the base class. A derived class can, however, access the `public` and `protected` members of its base class directly.

- A derived class can effect state changes in `private` base-class members, but only through non-`private` member functions provided in the base class and inherited into the derived class.

- When a base-class member function is inappropriate for a derived class, that member function can be redefined in the derived class with an appropriate implementation.

- Single-inheritance relationships form treelike hierarchical structures—a base class exists in a hierarchical relationship with its derived classes.

- It is possible to treat base-class objects and derived-class objects similarly; the commonality shared between the object types is expressed in the data members and member functions of the base class.

Section 23.3 protected Members

- A base class's `public` members are accessible anywhere that the program has a handle to an object of that base class or to an object of one of that base class's derived classes—or, when using the binary scope resolution operator, whenever the class's name is in scope.

- A base class's `private` members are accessible only within the definition of that base class or from friends of that class.

- A base class's `protected` members have an intermediate level of protection between `public` and `private` access. A base class's `protected` members can be accessed by members and friends of that base class and by members and friends of any classes derived from that base class.

- Unfortunately, `protected` data members often present two major problems. First, the derived-class object does not have to use a *set* function to change the value of the base-class's `protected` data. Second, derived-class member functions are more likely to depend on base-class implementation details.

Section 23.4 Relationship between Base Classes and Derived Classes
- When a derived-class member function redefines a base-class member function, the base-class member function can be accessed from the derived class by qualifying the base-class member function name with the base-class name and the binary scope resolution operator (::).

Section 23.5 Constructors and Destructors in Derived Classes
- When an object of a derived class is instantiated, the base class's constructor is called immediately (either explicitly or implicitly) to initialize the base-class data members in the derived-class object (before the derived-class data members are initialized).
- Declaring data members `private`, while providing non-`private` member functions to manipulate and perform validation checking on this data, enforces good software engineering.
- When a derived-class object is destroyed, the destructors are called in the reverse order of the constructors—first the derived-class destructor is called, then the base-class destructor is called.

Section 23.6 `public`, `protected` and `private` Inheritance
- When deriving a class from a base class, the base class may be declared as either `public`, `protected` or `private`.
- When deriving a class from a `public` base class, `public` members of the base class become `public` members of the derived class, and `protected` members of the base class become `protected` members of the derived class.
- When deriving a class from a `protected` base class, `public` and `protected` members of the base class become `protected` members of the derived class.
- When deriving a class from a `private` base class, `public` and `protected` members of the base class become `private` members of the derived class.

Terminology

base class
base-class constructor
base-class default constructor
base-class destructor
base-class initializer
brittle software
class hierarchy
composition
customize software
derived class
derived-class constructor
derived-class destructor
direct base class
fragile software
`friend` of a base class
`friend` of a derived class
has-a relationship
hierarchical relationship

indirect base class
inherit the members of an existing class
inheritance
is-a relationship
multiple inheritance
`private` base class
`private` inheritance
`protected` base class
`protected` inheritance
`protected` keyword
`protected` member of a class
`public` base class
`public` inheritance
qualified name
redefine a base-class member function
single inheritance
subclass
superclass

Self-Review Exercises

23.1 Fill in the blanks in each of the following statements:

a) _____ is a form of software reuse in which new classes absorb the data and behaviors of existing classes and embellish these classes with new capabilities.

b) A base class's _____ members can be accessed only in the base-class definition or in derived-class definitions.

c) In a(n) _____ relationship, an object of a derived class also can be treated as an object of its base class.

d) In a(n) _____ relationship, a class object has one or more objects of other classes as members.

e) In single inheritance, a class exists in a(n) _____ relationship with its derived classes.

f) A base class's _____ members are accessible within that base class and anywhere that the program has a handle to an object of that base class or to an object of one of its derived classes.

g) A base class's `protected` access members have a level of protection between those of `public` and _____ access.

h) C++ provides for _____, which allows a derived class to inherit from many base classes, even if these base classes are unrelated.

i) When an object of a derived class is instantiated, the base class's _____ is called implicitly or explicitly to do any necessary initialization of the base-class data members in the derived-class object.

j) When deriving a class from a base class with `public` inheritance, `public` members of the base class become _____ members of the derived class, and `protected` members of the base class become _____ members of the derived class.

k) When deriving a class from a base class with `protected` inheritance, `public` members of the base class become _____ members of the derived class, and `protected` members of the base class become _____ members of the derived class.

23.2 State whether each of the following is *true* or *false*. If *false*, explain why.

a) Base-class constructors are not inherited by derived classes.

b) A *has-a* relationship is implemented via inheritance.

c) A `Car` class has an *is-a* relationship with the `SteeringWheel` and `Brakes` classes.

d) Inheritance encourages the reuse of proven high-quality software.

e) When a derived-class object is destroyed, the destructors are called in the reverse order of the constructors.

Answers to Self-Review Exercises

23.1 a) Inheritance. b) `protected`. c) *is-a* or inheritance. d) *has-a* or composition or aggregation. e) hierarchical. f) `public`. g) `private`. h) multiple inheritance. i) constructor. j) `public`, `protected`. k) `protected`, `protected`.

23.2 a) True. b) False. A *has-a* relationship is implemented via composition. An *is-a* relationship is implemented via inheritance. c) False. This is an example of a *has-a* relationship. Class `Car` has an *is-a* relationship with class `Vehicle`. d) True. e) True.

Exercises

23.3 Many programs written with inheritance could be written with composition instead, and vice versa. Rewrite class `BasePlusCommissionEmployee` of the `CommissionEmployee–BasePlusCommissionEmployee` hierarchy to use composition rather than inheritance. After you do this, assess the relative merits of the two approaches for designing classes `CommissionEmployee` and `BasePlusCom-`

missionEmployee, as well as for object-oriented programs in general. Which approach is more natural? Why?

23.4 Discuss the ways in which inheritance promotes software reuse, saves time during program development and helps prevent errors.

23.5 Some programmers prefer not to use protected access because they believe it breaks the encapsulation of the base class. Discuss the relative merits of using protected access vs. using private access in base classes.

23.6 Draw an inheritance hierarchy for students at a university similar to the hierarchy shown in Fig. 23.2. Use Student as the base class of the hierarchy, then include classes UndergraduateStudent and GraduateStudent that derive from Student. Continue to extend the hierarchy as deep (i.e., as many levels) as possible. For example, Freshman, Sophomore, Junior and Senior might derive from UndergraduateStudent, and DoctoralStudent and MastersStudent might derive from GraduateStudent. After drawing the hierarchy, discuss the relationships that exist between the classes. [*Note:* You do not need to write any code for this exercise.]

23.7 The world of shapes is much richer than the shapes included in the inheritance hierarchy of Fig. 23.3. Write down all the shapes you can think of—both two-dimensional and three-dimensional—and form them into a more complete Shape hierarchy with as many levels as possible. Your hierarchy should have base class Shape from which class TwoDimensionalShape and class ThreeDimensionalShape are derived. [*Note:* You do not need to write any code for this exercise.] We will use this hierarchy in the exercises of Chapter 24 to process a set of distinct shapes as objects of base-class Shape. (This technique, called polymorphism, is the subject of Chapter 24.)

23.8 Draw an inheritance hierarchy for classes Quadrilateral, Trapezoid, Parallelogram, Rectangle and Square. Use Quadrilateral as the base class of the hierarchy. Make the hierarchy as deep as possible.

23.9 (*Package Inheritance Hierarchy*) Package-delivery services, such as FedEx®, DHL® and UPS®, offer a number of different shipping options, each with specific costs associated. Create an inheritance hierarchy to represent various types of packages. Use Package as the base class of the hierarchy, then include classes TwoDayPackage and OvernightPackage that derive from Package. Base class Package should include data members representing the name, address, city, state and ZIP code for both the sender and the recipient of the package, in addition to data members that store the weight (in ounces) and cost per ounce to ship the package. Package's constructor should initialize these data members. Ensure that the weight and cost per ounce contain positive values. Package should provide a public member function calculateCost that returns a double indicating the cost associated with shipping the package. Package's calculateCost function should determine the cost by multiplying the weight by the cost per ounce. Derived class TwoDayPackage should inherit the functionality of base class Package, but also include a data member that represents a flat fee that the shipping company charges for two-day-delivery service. TwoDayPackage's constructor should receive a value to initialize this data member. TwoDayPackage should redefine member function calculateCost so that it computes the shipping cost by adding the flat fee to the weight-based cost calculated by base class Package's calculateCost function. Class OvernightPackage should inherit directly from class Package and contain an additional data member representing an additional fee per ounce charged for overnight-delivery service. OvernightPackage should redefine member function calculateCost so that it adds the additional fee per ounce to the standard cost per ounce before calculating the shipping cost. Write a test program that creates objects of each type of Package and tests member function calculateCost.

23.10 (*Account Inheritance Hierarchy*) Create an inheritance hierarchy that a bank might use to represent customers' bank accounts. All customers at this bank can deposit (i.e., credit) money into their accounts and withdraw (i.e., debit) money from their accounts. More specific types of accounts also exist. Savings accounts, for instance, earn interest on the money they hold. Checking accounts, on the other hand, charge a fee per transaction (i.e., credit or debit).

Create an inheritance hierarchy containing base class Account and derived classes Savings-Account and CheckingAccount that inherit from class Account. Base class Account should include one data member of type double to represent the account balance. The class should provide a constructor that receives an initial balance and uses it to initialize the data member. The constructor should validate the initial balance to ensure that it is greater than or equal to 0.0. If not, the balance should be set to 0.0 and the constructor should display an error message, indicating that the initial balance was invalid. The class should provide three member functions. Member function credit should add an amount to the current balance. Member function debit should withdraw money from the Account and ensure that the debit amount does not exceed the Account's balance. If it does, the balance should be left unchanged and the function should print the message "Debit amount exceeded account balance." Member function getBalance should return the current balance.

Derived class SavingsAccount should inherit the functionality of an Account, but also include a data member of type double indicating the interest rate (percentage) assigned to the Account. SavingsAccount's constructor should receive the initial balance, as well as an initial value for the SavingsAccount's interest rate. SavingsAccount should provide a public member function calculateInterest that returns a double indicating the amount of interest earned by an account. Member function calculateInterest should determine this amount by multiplying the interest rate by the account balance. [*Note:* SavingsAccount should inherit member functions credit and debit as is without redefining them.]

Derived class CheckingAccount should inherit from base class Account and include an additional data member of type double that represents the fee charged per transaction. CheckingAccount's constructor should receive the initial balance, as well as a parameter indicating a fee amount. Class CheckingAccount should redefine member functions credit and debit so that they subtract the fee from the account balance whenever either transaction is performed successfully. CheckingAccount's versions of these functions should invoke the base-class Account version to perform the updates to an account balance. CheckingAccount's debit function should charge a fee only if money is actually withdrawn (i.e., the debit amount does not exceed the account balance). [*Hint:* Define Account's debit function so that it returns a bool indicating whether money was withdrawn. Then use the return value to determine whether a fee should be charged.]

After defining the classes in this hierarchy, write a program that creates objects of each class and tests their member functions. Add interest to the SavingsAccount object by first invoking its calculateInterest function, then passing the returned interest amount to the object's credit function.

24

Object-Oriented Programming: Polymorphism

OBJECTIVES

In this chapter, you will learn:

- What polymorphism is, how it makes programming more convenient and how it makes systems more extensible and maintainable.

- To declare and use **virtual** functions to effect polymorphism.

- The distinction between abstract and concrete classes.

- To declare pure **virtual** functions to create abstract classes.

- How to use runtime type information (RTTI) with downcasting, **dynamic_cast**, **typeid** and **type_info**.

- How C++ implements **virtual** functions and dynamic binding "under the hood."

- How to use **virtual** destructors to ensure that all appropriate destructors run on an object.

24.1 Introduction

In Chapters 20–23, we discussed key object-oriented programming technologies including classes, objects, encapsulation, operator overloading and inheritance. We now continue our study of OOP by explaining and demonstrating **polymorphism** with inheritance hierarchies. Polymorphism enables us to "program in the general" rather than "program in the specific." In particular, polymorphism enables us to write programs that process objects of classes that are part of the same class hierarchy as if they were all objects of the hierarchy's base class. As we will soon see, polymorphism works off base-class pointer handles and base-class reference handles, but not off name handles.

Consider the following example of polymorphism. Suppose we create a program that simulates the movement of several types of animals for a biological study. Classes `Fish`, `Frog` and `Bird` represent the three types of animals under investigation. Imagine that each of these classes inherits from base class `Animal`, which contains a function move and maintains an animal's current location. Each derived class implements function move. Our program maintains a `vector` of pointers to objects of the various `Animal` derived classes. To simulate the animals' movements, the program sends each object the same message once per second—namely, move. However, each specific type of `Animal` responds to a move message in its own unique way—a `Fish` might swim two feet, a `Frog` might jump three feet and a `Bird` might fly ten feet. The program issues the same message (i.e., move) to each animal object generically, but each object knows how to modify its location appropriately for its specific type of movement. Relying on each object to know how to "do the right thing" (i.e., do what is appropriate for that type of object) in response to the same function call is the key concept of polymorphism. The same message (in this case, move) sent to a variety of objects has "many forms" of results—hence the term polymorphism.

With polymorphism, we can design and implement systems that are easily extensible—new classes can be added with little or no modification to the general portions of the program, as long as the new classes are part of the inheritance hierarchy that the program processes generically. The only parts of a program that must be altered to accommodate new classes are those that require direct knowledge of the new classes that the programmer adds to the hierarchy. For example, if we create class `Tortoise` that inherits from class `Animal` (which might respond to a move message by crawling one inch), we need to write only the `Tortoise` class and the part of the simulation that instantiates a `Tortoise` object. The portions of the simulation that process each `Animal` generically can remain the same.

We begin with a sequence of small, focused examples that lead up to an understanding of `virtual` functions and dynamic binding—polymorphism's two underlying technologies. We then present a case study that revisits Chapter 23's `Employee` hierarchy. In the case study, we define a common "interface" (i.e., set of functionality) for all the classes in the hierarchy. This common functionality among employees is defined in a so-called abstract base class, `Employee`, from which classes `SalariedEmployee`, `HourlyEmployee` and `CommissionEmployee` inherit directly and class `BaseCommissionEmployee` inherits indirectly. We will soon see what makes a class "abstract" or its opposite—"concrete."

In this hierarchy, every employee has an `earnings` function to calculate the employee's weekly pay. These `earnings` functions vary by employee type—for instance, `Salaried-Employees` are paid a fixed weekly salary regardless of the number of hours worked, while `HourlyEmployees` are paid by the hour and receive overtime pay. We show how to process each employee "in the general"—that is, using base-class pointers to call the `earnings` function of several derived-class objects. This way, the programmer needs to be concerned with only one type of function call, which can be used to execute several different functions based on the objects referred to by the base-class pointers.

A key feature of this chapter is its (optional) detailed discussion of polymorphism, `virtual` functions and dynamic binding "under the hood," which uses a detailed diagram to explain how polymorphism can be implemented in C++.

Occasionally, when performing polymorphic processing, we need to program "in the specific," meaning that operations need to be performed on a specific type of object in a hierarchy—the operation cannot be generally applied to several types of objects. We reuse our `Employee` hierarchy to demonstrate the powerful capabilities of **runtime type information** (RTTI) and **dynamic casting**, which enable a program to determine the type of an object at execution time and act on that object accordingly. We use these capabilities to determine whether a particular employee object is a `BasePlusCommissionEmployee`, then give that employee a 10% bonus on his or her base salary.

24.2 Polymorphism Examples

In this section, we discuss several polymorphism examples. With polymorphism, one function can cause different actions to occur, depending on the type of the object on which the function is invoked. This gives the programmer tremendous expressive capability. If class Rectangle is derived from class Quadrilateral, then a Rectangle object is a more specific version of a Quadrilateral object. Therefore, any operation (such as calculating the perimeter or the area) that can be performed on an object of class Quadrilateral also can be performed on an object of class Rectangle. Such operations also can be performed on other kinds of Quadrilaterals, such as Squares, Parallelograms and Trapezoids. The polymorphism occurs when a program invokes a virtual function through a base-class (i.e., Quadrilateral) pointer or reference—C++ dynamically (i.e., at execution time) chooses the correct function for the class from which the object was instantiated. You will see a code example that illustrates this process in Section 24.3.

As another example, suppose that we design a video game that manipulates objects of many different types, including objects of classes Martian, Venusian, Plutonian, SpaceShip and LaserBeam. Imagine that each of these classes inherits from the common base class SpaceObject, which contains member function draw. Each derived class implements this function in a manner appropriate for that class. A screen-manager program maintains a container (e.g., a vector) that holds SpaceObject pointers to objects of the various classes. To refresh the screen, the screen manager periodically sends each object the same message—namely, draw. Each type of object responds in a unique way. For example, a Martian object might draw itself in red with the appropriate number of antennae. A SpaceShip object might draw itself as a silver flying saucer. A LaserBeam object might draw itself as a bright red beam across the screen. Again, the same message (in this case, draw) sent to a variety of objects has "many forms" of results.

A polymorphic screen manager facilitates adding new classes to a system with minimal modifications to its code. Suppose that we want to add objects of class Mercurian to our video game. To do so, we must build a class Mercurian that inherits from SpaceObject, but provides its own definition of member function draw. Then, when pointers to objects of class Mercurian appear in the container, the programmer does not need to modify the code for the screen manager. The screen manager invokes member function draw on every object in the container, regardless of the object's type, so the new Mercurian objects simply "plug right in." Thus, without modifying the system (other than to build and include the classes themselves), programmers can use polymorphism to accommodate additional classes, including ones that were not even envisioned when the system was created.

Software Engineering Observation 24.1

With virtual functions and polymorphism, you can deal in generalities and let the execution-time environment concern itself with the specifics. You can direct a variety of objects to behave in manners appropriate to those objects without even knowing their types (as long as those objects belong to the same inheritance hierarchy and are being accessed off a common base-class pointer).

Software Engineering Observation 24.2

Polymorphism promotes extensibility: Software written to invoke polymorphic behavior is written independently of the types of the objects to which messages are sent. Thus, new types of objects that can respond to existing messages can be incorporated into such a system without modifying the base system. Only client code that instantiates new objects must be modified to accommodate new types.

24.3 Relationships Among Objects in an Inheritance Hierarchy

Section 23.4 created an employee class hierarchy, in which class `BasePlusCommissionEmployee` inherited from class `CommissionEmployee`. The Chapter 23 examples manipulated `CommissionEmployee` and `BasePlusCommissionEmployee` objects by using the objects' names to invoke their member functions. We now examine the relationships among classes in a hierarchy more closely. The next several sections present a series of examples that demonstrate how base-class and derived-class pointers can be aimed at base-class and derived-class objects, and how those pointers can be used to invoke member functions that manipulate those objects. Toward the end of this section, we demonstrate how to get polymorphic behavior from base-class pointers aimed at derived-class objects.

In Section 24.3.1, we assign the address of a derived-class object to a base-class pointer, then show that invoking a function via the base-class pointer invokes the base-class functionality—i.e., the type of the handle determines which function is called. In Section 24.3.2, we assign the address of a base-class object to a derived-class pointer, which results in a compilation error. We discuss the error message and investigate why the compiler does not allow such an assignment. In Section 24.3.3, we assign the address of a derived-class object to a base-class pointer, then examine how the base-class pointer can be used to invoke only the base-class functionality—when we attempt to invoke derived-class member functions through the base-class pointer, compilation errors occur. Finally, in Section 24.3.4, we introduce `virtual` functions and polymorphism by declaring a base-class function as `virtual`. We then assign a derived-class object to the base-class pointer and use that pointer to invoke derived-class functionality—precisely the capability we need to achieve polymorphic behavior.

A key concept in these examples is to demonstrate that an object of a derived class can be treated as an object of its base class. This enables various interesting manipulations. For example, a program can create an array of base-class pointers that point to objects of many derived-class types. Despite the fact that the derived-class objects are of different types, the compiler allows this because each derived-class object *is an* object of its base class. However, we cannot treat a base-class object as an object of any of its derived classes. For example, a `CommissionEmployee` is not a `BasePlusCommissionEmployee` in the hierarchy defined in Chapter 23—a `CommissionEmployee` does not have a `baseSalary` data member and does not have member functions `setBaseSalary` and `getBaseSalary`. The *is-a* relationship applies only from a derived class to its direct and indirect base classes.

24.3.1 Invoking Base-Class Functions from Derived-Class Objects

The example in Figs. 24.1–24.5 demonstrates three ways to aim base-class pointers and derived-class pointers at base-class objects and derived-class objects. The first two are straightforward—we aim a base-class pointer at a base-class object (and invoke base-class functionality), and we aim a derived-class pointer at a derived-class object (and invoke derived-class functionality). Then, we demonstrate the relationship between derived classes and base classes (i.e., the *is-a* relationship of inheritance) by aiming a base-class pointer at a derived-class object (and showing that the base-class functionality is indeed available in the derived-class object).

Class `CommissionEmployee` (Figs. 24.1–24.2), which we discussed in Chapter 23, is used to represent employees who are paid a percentage of their sales. Class `BasePlusCom-`

```
 1   // Fig. 24.1: CommissionEmployee.h
 2   // CommissionEmployee class definition represents a commission employee.
 3   #ifndef COMMISSION_H
 4   #define COMMISSION_H
 5
 6   #include <string> // C++ standard string class
 7   using std::string;
 8
 9   class CommissionEmployee
10   {
11   public:
12      CommissionEmployee( const string &, const string &, const string &,
13         double = 0.0, double = 0.0 );
14
15      void setFirstName( const string & ); // set first name
16      string getFirstName() const; // return first name
17
18      void setLastName( const string & ); // set last name
19      string getLastName() const; // return last name
20
21      void setSocialSecurityNumber( const string & ); // set SSN
22      string getSocialSecurityNumber() const; // return SSN
23
24      void setGrossSales( double ); // set gross sales amount
25      double getGrossSales() const; // return gross sales amount
26
27      void setCommissionRate( double ); // set commission rate
28      double getCommissionRate() const; // return commission rate
29
30      double earnings() const; // calculate earnings
31      void print() const; // print CommissionEmployee object
32   private:
33      string firstName;
34      string lastName;
35      string socialSecurityNumber;
36      double grossSales; // gross weekly sales
37      double commissionRate; // commission percentage
38   }; // end class CommissionEmployee
39
40   #endif
```

Fig. 24.1 | CommissionEmployee class header file.

missionEmployee (Figs. 24.3–24.4), which we also discussed in Chapter 23, is used to represent employees who receive a base salary plus a percentage of their sales. Each Base-PlusCommissionEmployee object *is a* CommissionEmployee that also has a base salary. Class BasePlusCommissionEmployee's earnings member function (lines 32–35 of Fig. 24.4) redefines class CommissionEmployee's earnings member function (lines 79–82 of Fig. 24.2) to include the object's base salary. Class BasePlusCommissionEmployee's print member function (lines 38–46 of Fig. 24.4) redefines class CommissionEmployee's print member function (lines 85–92 of Fig. 24.2) to display the same information as the print function in class CommissionEmployee, as well as the employee's base salary.

```cpp
 1   // Fig. 24.2: CommissionEmployee.cpp
 2   // Class CommissionEmployee member-function definitions.
 3   #include <iostream>
 4   using std::cout;
 5
 6   #include "CommissionEmployee.h" // CommissionEmployee class definition
 7
 8   // constructor
 9   CommissionEmployee::CommissionEmployee(
10      const string &first, const string &last, const string &ssn,
11      double sales, double rate )
12      : firstName( first ), lastName( last ), socialSecurityNumber( ssn )
13   {
14      setGrossSales( sales ); // validate and store gross sales
15      setCommissionRate( rate ); // validate and store commission rate
16   } // end CommissionEmployee constructor
17
18   // set first name
19   void CommissionEmployee::setFirstName( const string &first )
20   {
21      firstName = first; // should validate
22   } // end function setFirstName
23
24   // return first name
25   string CommissionEmployee::getFirstName() const
26   {
27      return firstName;
28   } // end function getFirstName
29
30   // set last name
31   void CommissionEmployee::setLastName( const string &last )
32   {
33      lastName = last;   // should validate
34   } // end function setLastName
35
36   // return last name
37   string CommissionEmployee::getLastName() const
38   {
39      return lastName;
40   } // end function getLastName
41
42   // set social security number
43   void CommissionEmployee::setSocialSecurityNumber( const string &ssn )
44   {
45      socialSecurityNumber = ssn; // should validate
46   } // end function setSocialSecurityNumber
47
48   // return social security number
49   string CommissionEmployee::getSocialSecurityNumber() const
50   {
51      return socialSecurityNumber;
52   } // end function getSocialSecurityNumber
53
```

Fig. 24.2 | CommissionEmployee class implementation file. (Part 1 of 2.)

```
54    // set gross sales amount
55    void CommissionEmployee::setGrossSales( double sales )
56    {
57       grossSales = ( sales < 0.0 ) ? 0.0 : sales;
58    } // end function setGrossSales
59
60    // return gross sales amount
61    double CommissionEmployee::getGrossSales() const
62    {
63       return grossSales;
64    } // end function getGrossSales
65
66    // set commission rate
67    void CommissionEmployee::setCommissionRate( double rate )
68    {
69       commissionRate = ( rate > 0.0 && rate < 1.0 ) ? rate : 0.0;
70    } // end function setCommissionRate
71
72    // return commission rate
73    double CommissionEmployee::getCommissionRate() const
74    {
75       return commissionRate;
76    } // end function getCommissionRate
77
78    // calculate earnings
79    double CommissionEmployee::earnings() const
80    {
81       return getCommissionRate() * getGrossSales();
82    } // end function earnings
83
84    // print CommissionEmployee object
85    void CommissionEmployee::print() const
86    {
87       cout << "commission employee: "
88          << getFirstName() << ' ' << getLastName()
89          << "\nsocial security number: " << getSocialSecurityNumber()
90          << "\ngross sales: " << getGrossSales()
91          << "\ncommission rate: " << getCommissionRate();
92    } // end function print
```

Fig. 24.2 | CommissionEmployee class implementation file. (Part 2 of 2.)

```
1    // Fig. 24.3: BasePlusCommissionEmployee.h
2    // BasePlusCommissionEmployee class derived from class
3    // CommissionEmployee.
4    #ifndef BASEPLUS_H
5    #define BASEPLUS_H
6
7    #include <string> // C++ standard string class
8    using std::string;
9
```

Fig. 24.3 | BasePlusCommissionEmployee class header file. (Part 1 of 2.)

```
10   #include "CommissionEmployee.h" // CommissionEmployee class declaration
11
12   class BasePlusCommissionEmployee : public CommissionEmployee
13   {
14   public:
15      BasePlusCommissionEmployee( const string &, const string &,
16         const string &, double = 0.0, double = 0.0, double = 0.0 );
17
18      void setBaseSalary( double ); // set base salary
19      double getBaseSalary() const; // return base salary
20
21      double earnings() const; // calculate earnings
22      void print() const; // print BasePlusCommissionEmployee object
23   private:
24      double baseSalary; // base salary
25   }; // end class BasePlusCommissionEmployee
26
27   #endif
```

Fig. 24.3 | BasePlusCommissionEmployee class header file. (Part 2 of 2.)

```
1    // Fig. 24.4: BasePlusCommissionEmployee.cpp
2    // Class BasePlusCommissionEmployee member-function definitions.
3    #include <iostream>
4    using std::cout;
5
6    // BasePlusCommissionEmployee class definition
7    #include "BasePlusCommissionEmployee.h"
8
9    // constructor
10   BasePlusCommissionEmployee::BasePlusCommissionEmployee(
11      const string &first, const string &last, const string &ssn,
12      double sales, double rate, double salary )
13      // explicitly call base-class constructor
14      : CommissionEmployee( first, last, ssn, sales, rate )
15   {
16      setBaseSalary( salary ); // validate and store base salary
17   } // end BasePlusCommissionEmployee constructor
18
19   // set base salary
20   void BasePlusCommissionEmployee::setBaseSalary( double salary )
21   {
22      baseSalary = ( salary < 0.0 ) ? 0.0 : salary;
23   } // end function setBaseSalary
24
25   // return base salary
26   double BasePlusCommissionEmployee::getBaseSalary() const
27   {
28      return baseSalary;
29   } // end function getBaseSalary
30
```

Fig. 24.4 | BasePlusCommissionEmployee class implementation file. (Part 1 of 2.)

```
31  // calculate earnings
32  double BasePlusCommissionEmployee::earnings() const
33  {
34      return getBaseSalary() + CommissionEmployee::earnings();
35  } // end function earnings
36
37  // print BasePlusCommissionEmployee object
38  void BasePlusCommissionEmployee::print() const
39  {
40      cout << "base-salaried ";
41
42      // invoke CommissionEmployee's print function
43      CommissionEmployee::print();
44
45      cout << "\nbase salary: " << getBaseSalary();
46  } // end function print
```

Fig. 24.4 | BasePlusCommissionEmployee class implementation file. (Part 2 of 2.)

In Fig. 24.5, lines 19–20 create a CommissionEmployee object and line 23 creates a pointer to a CommissionEmployee object; lines 26–27 create a BasePlusCommission-Employee object and line 30 creates a pointer to a BasePlusCommissionEmployee object. Lines 37 and 39 use each object's name (commissionEmployee and basePlusCommis-sionEmployee, respectively) to invoke each object's print member function. Line 42 assigns the address of base-class object commissionEmployee to base-class pointer commissionEmployeePtr, which line 45 uses to invoke member function print on that CommissionEmployee object. This invokes the version of print defined in base class Com-missionEmployee. Similarly, line 48 assigns the address of derived-class object basePlus-CommissionEmployee to derived-class pointer basePlusCommissionEmployeePtr, which line 52 uses to invoke member function print on that BasePlusCommissionEmployee object. This invokes the version of print defined in derived class BasePlusCommission-Employee. Line 55 then assigns the address of derived-class object basePlusCommission-Employee to base-class pointer commissionEmployeePtr, which line 59 uses to invoke member function print. The C++ compiler allows this "crossover" because an object of a derived class *is an* object of its base class. Note that despite the fact that the base class

```
1   // Fig. 24.5: fig24_05.cpp
2   // Aiming base-class and derived-class pointers at base-class
3   // and derived-class objects, respectively.
4   #include <iostream>
5   using std::cout;
6   using std::endl;
7   using std::fixed;
8
9   #include <iomanip>
10  using std::setprecision;
11
```

Fig. 24.5 | Assigning addresses of base-class and derived-class objects to base-class and derived-class pointers. (Part 1 of 3.)

```
12    // include class definitions
13    #include "CommissionEmployee.h"
14    #include "BasePlusCommissionEmployee.h"
15
16    int main()
17    {
18       // create base-class object
19       CommissionEmployee commissionEmployee(
20          "Sue", "Jones", "222-22-2222", 10000, .06 );
21
22       // create base-class pointer
23       CommissionEmployee *commissionEmployeePtr = 0;
24
25       // create derived-class object
26       BasePlusCommissionEmployee basePlusCommissionEmployee(
27          "Bob", "Lewis", "333-33-3333", 5000, .04, 300 );
28
29       // create derived-class pointer
30       BasePlusCommissionEmployee *basePlusCommissionEmployeePtr = 0;
31
32       // set floating-point output formatting
33       cout << fixed << setprecision( 2 );
34
35       // output objects commissionEmployee and basePlusCommissionEmployee
36       cout << "Print base-class and derived-class objects:\n\n";
37       commissionEmployee.print(); // invokes base-class print
38       cout << "\n\n";
39       basePlusCommissionEmployee.print(); // invokes derived-class print
40
41       // aim base-class pointer at base-class object and print
42       commissionEmployeePtr = &commissionEmployee; // perfectly natural
43       cout << "\n\n\nCalling print with base-class pointer to "
44          << "\nbase-class object invokes base-class print function:\n\n";
45       commissionEmployeePtr->print(); // invokes base-class print
46
47       // aim derived-class pointer at derived-class object and print
48       basePlusCommissionEmployeePtr = &basePlusCommissionEmployee; // natural
49       cout << "\n\n\nCalling print with derived-class pointer to "
50          << "\nderived-class object invokes derived-class "
51          << "print function:\n\n";
52       basePlusCommissionEmployeePtr->print(); // invokes derived-class print
53
54       // aim base-class pointer at derived-class object and print
55       commissionEmployeePtr = &basePlusCommissionEmployee;
56       cout << "\n\n\nCalling print with base-class pointer to "
57          << "derived-class object\ninvokes base-class print "
58          << "function on that derived-class object:\n\n";
59       commissionEmployeePtr->print(); // invokes base-class print
60       cout << endl;
61       return 0;
62    } // end main
```

Fig. 24.5 | Assigning addresses of base-class and derived-class objects to base-class and derived-class pointers. (Part 2 of 3.)

```
Print base-class and derived-class objects:

commission employee: Sue Jones
social security number: 222-22-2222
gross sales: 10000.00
commission rate: 0.06

base-salaried commission employee: Bob Lewis
social security number: 333-33-3333
gross sales: 5000.00
commission rate: 0.04
base salary: 300.00


Calling print with base-class pointer to
base-class object invokes base-class print function:

commission employee: Sue Jones
social security number: 222-22-2222
gross sales: 10000.00
commission rate: 0.06


Calling print with derived-class pointer to
derived-class object invokes derived-class print function:

base-salaried commission employee: Bob Lewis
social security number: 333-33-3333
gross sales: 5000.00
commission rate: 0.04
base salary: 300.00


Calling print with base-class pointer to derived-class object
invokes base-class print function on that derived-class object:

commission employee: Bob Lewis
social security number: 333-33-3333
gross sales: 5000.00
commission rate: 0.04
```

Fig. 24.5 | Assigning addresses of base-class and derived-class objects to base-class and derived-class pointers. (Part 3 of 3.)

CommissionEmployee pointer points to a derived class BasePlusCommissionEmployee object, the base class CommissionEmployee's print member function is invoked (rather than BasePlusCommissionEmployee's print function). The output of each print member-function invocation in this program reveals that *the invoked functionality depends on the type of the handle (i.e., the pointer or reference type) used to invoke the function, not the type of the object to which the handle points*. In Section 24.3.4, when we introduce virtual functions, we demonstrate that it is possible to invoke the object type's functionality, rather than invoke the handle type's functionality. We will see that this is crucial to implementing polymorphic behavior—the key topic of this chapter.

24.3.2 Aiming Derived-Class Pointers at Base-Class Objects

In Section 24.3.1, we assigned the address of a derived-class object to a base-class pointer and explained that the C++ compiler allows this assignment, because a derived-class object *is a* base-class object. We take the opposite approach in Fig. 24.6, as we aim a derived-class pointer at a base-class object. [*Note*: This program uses classes CommissionEmployee and BasePlusCommissionEmployee of Figs. 24.1–24.4.] Lines 8–9 of Fig. 24.6 create a CommissionEmployee object, and line 10 creates a BasePlusCommissionEmployee pointer. Line 14 attempts to assign the address of base-class object commissionEmployee to derived-class pointer basePlusCommissionEmployeePtr, but the C++ compiler generates an error. The compiler prevents this assignment, because a CommissionEmployee is not a BasePlusCommissionEmployee. Consider the consequences if the compiler were to allow this assignment. Through a BasePlusCommissionEmployee pointer, we can invoke every BasePlusCommissionEmployee member function, including setBaseSalary, for the object to which the pointer points (i.e., the base-class object commissionEmployee). However, the CommissionEmployee object does not provide a setBaseSalary member function, nor does it provide a baseSalary data member to set. This could lead to problems, because member function setBaseSalary would assume that there is a baseSalary data member to set at its "usual location" in a BasePlusCommissionEmployee object. This memory does not belong to the CommissionEmployee object, so member function setBaseSalary might overwrite other important data in memory, possibly data that belongs to a different object.

```cpp
1   // Fig. 24.6: fig24_06.cpp
2   // Aiming a derived-class pointer at a base-class object.
3   #include "CommissionEmployee.h"
4   #include "BasePlusCommissionEmployee.h"
5
6   int main()
7   {
8      CommissionEmployee commissionEmployee(
9         "Sue", "Jones", "222-22-2222", 10000, .06 );
10     BasePlusCommissionEmployee *basePlusCommissionEmployeePtr = 0;
11
12     // aim derived-class pointer at base-class object
13     // Error: a CommissionEmployee is not a BasePlusCommissionEmployee
14     basePlusCommissionEmployeePtr = &commissionEmployee;
15     return 0;
16  } // end main
```

Borland C++ command-line compiler error messages:

```
Error E2034 fig24_06\fig24_06.cpp 14: Cannot convert 'CommissionEmployee *'
   to 'BasePlusCommissionEmployee *' in function main()
```

GNU C++ compiler error messages:

```
fig24_06.cpp:14: error: invalid conversion from `CommissionEmployee*' to
   `BasePlusCommissionEmployee*'
```

Fig. 24.6 | Aiming a derived-class pointer at a base-class object. (Part 1 of 2.)

Microsoft Visual C++.NET compiler error messages:

```
C:\cpphtp5_examples\ch24\fig24_06\fig24_06.cpp(14) : error C2440:
   '=' : cannot convert from 'CommissionEmployee *__w64 ' to
'BasePlusCommissionEmployee *'
       Cast from base to derived requires dynamic_cast or static_cast
```

Fig. 24.6 | Aiming a derived-class pointer at a base-class object. (Part 2 of 2.)

24.3.3 Derived-Class Member-Function Calls via Base-Class Pointers

Off a base-class pointer, the compiler allows us to invoke only bases-class member functions. Thus, if a base-class pointer is aimed at a derived-class object, and an attempt is made to access a derived-class-only member function, a compilation error will occur.

Figure 24.7 shows the consequences of attempting to invoke a derived-class member function off a base-class pointer. [*Note:* We are again using classes CommissionEmployee and BasePlusCommissionEmployee of Figs. 24.1–24.4.] Line 9 creates commissionEmployeePtr—a pointer to a CommissionEmployee object—and lines 10–11 create a BasePlusCommissionEmployee object. Line 14 aims commissionEmployeePtr at derived-class object basePlusCommissionEmployee. Recall from Section 24.3.1 that the C++ compiler allows

```
 1   // Fig. 24.7: fig24_07.cpp
 2   // Attempting to invoke derived-class-only member functions
 3   // through a base-class pointer.
 4   #include "CommissionEmployee.h"
 5   #include "BasePlusCommissionEmployee.h"
 6
 7   int main()
 8   {
 9      CommissionEmployee *commissionEmployeePtr = 0; // base class
10      BasePlusCommissionEmployee basePlusCommissionEmployee(
11         "Bob", "Lewis", "333-33-3333", 5000, .04, 300 ); // derived class
12
13      // aim base-class pointer at derived-class object
14      commissionEmployeePtr = &basePlusCommissionEmployee;
15
16      // invoke base-class member functions on derived-class
17      // object through base-class pointer
18      string firstName = commissionEmployeePtr->getFirstName();
19      string lastName = commissionEmployeePtr->getLastName();
20      string ssn = commissionEmployeePtr->getSocialSecurityNumber();
21      double grossSales = commissionEmployeePtr->getGrossSales();
22      double commissionRate = commissionEmployeePtr->getCommissionRate();
23
24      // attempt to invoke derived-class-only member functions
25      // on derived-class object through base-class pointer
26      double baseSalary = commissionEmployeePtr->getBaseSalary();
27      commissionEmployeePtr->setBaseSalary( 500 );
28      return 0;
29   } // end main
```

Fig. 24.7 | Attempting to invoke derived-class-only functions via a base-class pointer. (Part 1 of 2.)

Borland C++ command-line compiler error messages:

```
Error E2416 fig24_07\fig24_07.cpp 26: 'getBaseSalary' is not a member of
   'CommissionEmployee' in function main()
Error E2416 fig24_07\fig24_07.cpp 27: 'setBaseSalary' is not a member of
   'CommissionEmployee' in function main()
```

Microsoft Visual C++.NET compiler error messages:

```
C:\cpphtp5_examples\ch24\fig24_07\fig24_07.cpp(26) : error C2039:
   'getBaseSalary' : is not a member of 'CommissionEmployee'
      C:\cpphtp5_examples\ch24\fig24_07\CommissionEmployee.h(10) :
      see declaration of 'CommissionEmployee'
C:\cpphtp5_examples\ch24\fig24_07\fig24_07.cpp(27) : error C2039:
   'setBaseSalary' : is not a member of 'CommissionEmployee'
      C:\cpphtp5_examples\ch24\fig24_07\CommissionEmployee.h(10) :
      see declaration of 'CommissionEmployee'
```

GNU C++ compiler error messages:

```
fig24_07.cpp:26: error: `getBaseSalary' undeclared (first use this function)
fig24_07.cpp:26: error: (Each undeclared identifier is reported only once for
   each function it appears in.)
fig24_07.cpp:27: error: `setBaseSalary' undeclared (first use this function)
```

Fig. 24.7 | Attempting to invoke derived-class-only functions via a base-class pointer. (Part 2 of 2.)

this, because a BasePlusCommissionEmployee *is a* CommissionEmployee (in the sense that a BasePlusCommissionEmployee object contains all the functionality of a Commission-Employee object). Lines 18–22 invoke base-class member functions getFirstName, get-LastName, getSocialSecurityNumber, getGrossSales and getCommissionRate off the base-class pointer. All of these calls are legitimate, because BasePlusCommissionEmployee inherits these member functions from CommissionEmployee. We know that commission-EmployeePtr is aimed at a BasePlusCommissionEmployee object, so in lines 26–27 we attempt to invoke BasePlusCommissionEmployee member functions getBaseSalary and setBaseSalary. The C++ compiler generates errors on both of these lines, because these are not member functions of base-class CommissionEmployee. The handle can invoke only those functions that are members of that handle's associated class type. (In this case, off a CommissionEmployee *, we can invoke only CommissionEmployee member functions setFirstName, getFirstName, setLastName, getLastName, setSocialSecurityNumber, getSocialSecurityNumber, setGrossSales, getGrossSales, setCommissionRate, get-CommissionRate, earnings and print.)

It turns out that the C++ compiler does allow access to derived-class-only members from a base-class pointer that is aimed at a derived-class object if we explicitly cast the base-class pointer to a derived-class pointer—a technique known as **downcasting**. As you learned in Section 24.3.1, it is possible to aim a base-class pointer at a derived-class object. However, as we demonstrated in Fig. 24.7, a base-class pointer can be used to invoke only the functions declared in the base class. Downcasting allows a program to perform a derived-class-specific operation on a derived-class object pointed to by a base-class pointer.

After a downcast, the program can invoke derived-class functions that are not in the base class. We will show you a concrete example of downcasting in Section 24.8.

Software Engineering Observation 24.3

If the address of a derived-class object has been assigned to a pointer of one of its direct or indirect base classes, it is acceptable to cast that base-class pointer back to a pointer of the derived-class type. In fact, this must be done to send that derived-class object messages that do not appear in the base class.

24.3.4 Virtual Functions

In Section 24.3.1, we aimed a base-class `CommissionEmployee` pointer at a derived-class `BasePlusCommissionEmployee` object, then invoked member function `print` through that pointer. Recall that the type of the handle determines which class's functionality to invoke. In that case, the `CommissionEmployee` pointer invoked the `CommissionEmployee` member function `print` on the `BasePlusCommissionEmployee` object, even though the pointer was aimed at a `BasePlusCommissionEmployee` object that has its own customized `print` function. *With virtual functions, the type of the object being pointed to, not the type of the handle, determines which version of a virtual function to invoke.*

First, we consider why virtual functions are useful. Suppose that a set of shape classes such as `Circle`, `Triangle`, `Rectangle` and `Square` are all derived from base class `Shape`. Each of these classes might be endowed with the ability to draw itself via a member function `draw`. Although each class has its own `draw` function, the function for each shape is quite different. In a program that draws a set of shapes, it would be useful to be able to treat all the shapes generically as objects of the base class `Shape`. Then, to draw any shape, we could simply use a base-class `Shape` pointer to invoke function `draw` and let the program determine dynamically (i.e., at runtime) which derived-class `draw` function to use, based on the type of the object to which the base-class `Shape` pointer points at any given time.

To enable this kind of behavior, we declare `draw` in the base class as a **virtual** function, and we override `draw` in each of the derived classes to draw the appropriate shape. From an implementation perspective, overriding a function is no different than redefining one (which is the approach we have been using until now). An overridden function in a derived class has the same signature and return type (i.e., prototype) as the function it overrides in its base class. If we do not declare the base-class function as `virtual`, we can redefine that function. By contrast, if we declare the base-class function as `virtual`, we can override that function to enable polymorphic behavior. We declare a `virtual` function by preceding the function's prototype with the keyword `virtual` in the base class. For example,

```
virtual void draw() const;
```

would appear in base class `Shape`. The preceding prototype declares that function `draw` is a `virtual` function that takes no arguments and returns nothing. The function is declared `const` because a `draw` function typically would not make changes to the `Shape` object on which it is invoked. Virtual functions do not necessarily have to be `const` functions.

Software Engineering Observation 24.4

Once a function is declared virtual, it remains virtual all the way down the inheritance hierarchy from that point, even if that function is not explicitly declared virtual when a class overrides it.

Good Programming Practice 24.1

Even though certain functions are implicitly virtual *because of a declaration made higher in the class hierarchy, explicitly declare these functions* virtual *at every level of the hierarchy to promote program clarity.*

Error-Prevention Tip 24.1

When a programmer browses a class hierarchy to locate a class to reuse, it is possible that a function in that class will exhibit virtual *function behavior even though it is not explicitly declared* virtual. *This happens when the class inherits a* virtual *function from its base class, and it can lead to subtle logic errors. Such errors can be avoided by explicitly declaring all* virtual *functions* virtual *throughout the inheritance hierarchy.*

Software Engineering Observation 24.5

When a derived class chooses not to override a virtual *function from its base class, the derived class simply inherits its base class's* virtual *function implementation.*

If the program invokes a virtual function through a base-class pointer to a derived-class object (e.g., shapePtr->draw()), the program will choose the correct derived-class draw function dynamically (i.e., at execution time) based on the object type—not the pointer type. Choosing the appropriate function to call at execution time (rather than at compile time) is known as **dynamic binding** or **late binding**.

When a virtual function is called by referencing a specific object by name and using the dot member-selection operator (e.g., squareObject.draw()), the function invocation is resolved at compile time (this is called **static binding**) and the virtual function that is called is the one defined for (or inherited by) the class of that particular object—this is not polymorphic behavior. Thus, dynamic binding with virtual functions occurs only off pointer (and, as we will soon see, reference) handles.

Now let's see how virtual functions can enable polymorphic behavior in our employee hierarchy. Figures 24.8–24.9 are the header files for classes CommissionEmployee and BasePlusCommissionEmployee, respectively. Note that the only difference between these files and those of Fig. 24.1 and Fig. 24.3 is that we specify each class's earnings and print member functions as virtual (lines 30–31 of Fig. 24.8 and lines 21–22 of Fig. 24.9). Because functions earnings and print are virtual in class CommissionEmployee, class BasePlusCommissionEmployee's earnings and print functions override class CommissionEmployee's. Now, if we aim a base-class CommissionEmployee pointer at a derived-class BasePlusCommissionEmployee object, and the program uses that pointer to call either function earnings or print, the BasePlusCommissionEmployee object's corresponding function will be invoked. There were no changes to the member-function implementations of classes CommissionEmployee and BasePlusCommissionEmployee, so we reuse the versions of Fig. 24.2 and Fig. 24.4.

We modified Fig. 24.5 to create the program of Fig. 24.10. Lines 46–57 demonstrate again that a CommissionEmployee pointer aimed at a CommissionEmployee object can be used to invoke CommissionEmployee functionality, and a BasePlusCommissionEmployee pointer aimed at a BasePlusCommissionEmployee object can be used to invoke BasePlusCommissionEmployee functionality. Line 60 aims base-class pointer commissionEmployeePtr at derived-class object basePlusCommissionEmployee. Note that when line 67 invokes member function print off the base-class pointer, the derived-class BasePlusCommissionEmployee's print member function is invoked, so line 67 outputs different text than line 59 does in Fig. 24.5 (when member function print was not declared virtual).

```
 1   // Fig. 24.8: CommissionEmployee.h
 2   // CommissionEmployee class definition represents a commission employee.
 3   #ifndef COMMISSION_H
 4   #define COMMISSION_H
 5
 6   #include <string> // C++ standard string class
 7   using std::string;
 8
 9   class CommissionEmployee
10   {
11   public:
12      CommissionEmployee( const string &, const string &, const string &,
13         double = 0.0, double = 0.0 );
14
15      void setFirstName( const string & ); // set first name
16      string getFirstName() const; // return first name
17
18      void setLastName( const string & ); // set last name
19      string getLastName() const; // return last name
20
21      void setSocialSecurityNumber( const string & ); // set SSN
22      string getSocialSecurityNumber() const; // return SSN
23
24      void setGrossSales( double ); // set gross sales amount
25      double getGrossSales() const; // return gross sales amount
26
27      void setCommissionRate( double ); // set commission rate
28      double getCommissionRate() const; // return commission rate
29
30      virtual double earnings() const; // calculate earnings
31      virtual void print() const; // print CommissionEmployee object
32   private:
33      string firstName;
34      string lastName;
35      string socialSecurityNumber;
36      double grossSales; // gross weekly sales
37      double commissionRate; // commission percentage
38   }; // end class CommissionEmployee
39
40   #endif
```

Fig. 24.8 | CommissionEmployee class header file declares earnings and print functions as virtual.

```
 1   // Fig. 24.9: BasePlusCommissionEmployee.h
 2   // BasePlusCommissionEmployee class derived from class
 3   // CommissionEmployee.
 4   #ifndef BASEPLUS_H
 5   #define BASEPLUS_H
 6
```

Fig. 24.9 | BasePlusCommissionEmployee class header file declares earnings and print functions as virtual. (Part 1 of 2.)

```
7    #include <string> // C++ standard string class
8    using std::string;
9
10   #include "CommissionEmployee.h" // CommissionEmployee class declaration
11
12   class BasePlusCommissionEmployee : public CommissionEmployee
13   {
14   public:
15      BasePlusCommissionEmployee( const string &, const string &,
16         const string &, double = 0.0, double = 0.0, double = 0.0 );
17
18      void setBaseSalary( double ); // set base salary
19      double getBaseSalary() const; // return base salary
20
21      virtual double earnings() const; // calculate earnings
22      virtual void print() const; // print BasePlusCommissionEmployee object
23   private:
24      double baseSalary; // base salary
25   }; // end class BasePlusCommissionEmployee
26
27   #endif
```

Fig. 24.9 | `BasePlusCommissionEmployee` class header file declares `earnings` and `print` functions as `virtual`. (Part 2 of 2.)

We see that declaring a member function `virtual` causes the program to dynamically determine which function to invoke based on the type of object to which the handle points, rather than on the type of the handle. The decision about which function to call is an example of polymorphism. Note again that when `commissionEmployeePtr` points to a `CommissionEmployee` object (line 46), class `CommissionEmployee`'s `print` function is invoked, and when `CommissionEmployeePtr` points to a `BasePlusCommissionEmployee` object, class `BasePlusCommissionEmployee`'s `print` function is invoked. Thus, the same message—print, in this case—sent (off a base-class pointer) to a variety of objects related by inheritance to that base class, takes on many forms—this is polymorphic behavior.

```
1    // Fig. 24.10: fig24_10.cpp
2    // Introducing polymorphism, virtual functions and dynamic binding.
3    #include <iostream>
4    using std::cout;
5    using std::endl;
6    using std::fixed;
7
8    #include <iomanip>
9    using std::setprecision;
10
11   // include class definitions
12   #include "CommissionEmployee.h"
13   #include "BasePlusCommissionEmployee.h"
```

Fig. 24.10 | Demonstrating polymorphism by invoking a derived-class `virtual` function via a base-class pointer to a derived-class object. (Part 1 of 3.)

```
14
15   int main()
16   {
17      // create base-class object
18      CommissionEmployee commissionEmployee(
19         "Sue", "Jones", "222-22-2222", 10000, .06 );
20
21      // create base-class pointer
22      CommissionEmployee *commissionEmployeePtr = 0;
23
24      // create derived-class object
25      BasePlusCommissionEmployee basePlusCommissionEmployee(
26         "Bob", "Lewis", "333-33-3333", 5000, .04, 300 );
27
28      // create derived-class pointer
29      BasePlusCommissionEmployee *basePlusCommissionEmployeePtr = 0;
30
31      // set floating-point output formatting
32      cout << fixed << setprecision( 2 );
33
34      // output objects using static binding
35      cout << "Invoking print function on base-class and derived-class "
36         << "\nobjects with static binding\n\n";
37      commissionEmployee.print(); // static binding
38      cout << "\n\n";
39      basePlusCommissionEmployee.print(); // static binding
40
41      // output objects using dynamic binding
42      cout << "\n\n\nInvoking print function on base-class and "
43         << "derived-class \nobjects with dynamic binding";
44
45      // aim base-class pointer at base-class object and print
46      commissionEmployeePtr = &commissionEmployee;
47      cout << "\n\nCalling virtual function print with base-class pointer"
48         << "\nto base-class object invokes base-class "
49         << "print function:\n\n";
50      commissionEmployeePtr->print(); // invokes base-class print
51
52      // aim derived-class pointer at derived-class object and print
53      basePlusCommissionEmployeePtr = &basePlusCommissionEmployee;
54      cout << "\n\nCalling virtual function print with derived-class "
55         << "pointer\nto derived-class object invokes derived-class "
56         << "print function:\n\n";
57      basePlusCommissionEmployeePtr->print(); // invokes derived-class print
58
59      // aim base-class pointer at derived-class object and print
60      commissionEmployeePtr = &basePlusCommissionEmployee;
61      cout << "\n\nCalling virtual function print with base-class pointer"
62         << "\nto derived-class object invokes derived-class "
63         << "print function:\n\n";
64
```

Fig. 24.10 | Demonstrating polymorphism by invoking a derived-class virtual function via a base-class pointer to a derived-class object. (Part 2 of 3.)

```
65          // polymorphism; invokes BasePlusCommissionEmployee's print;
66          // base-class pointer to derived-class object
67          commissionEmployeePtr->print();
68          cout << endl;
69          return 0;
70     } // end main
```

```
Invoking print function on base-class and derived-class
objects with static binding

commission employee: Sue Jones
social security number: 222-22-2222
gross sales: 10000.00
commission rate: 0.06

base-salaried commission employee: Bob Lewis
social security number: 333-33-3333
gross sales: 5000.00
commission rate: 0.04
base salary: 300.00


Invoking print function on base-class and derived-class
objects with dynamic binding

Calling virtual function print with base-class pointer
to base-class object invokes base-class print function:

commission employee: Sue Jones
social security number: 222-22-2222
gross sales: 10000.00
commission rate: 0.06

Calling virtual function print with derived-class pointer
to derived-class object invokes derived-class print function:

base-salaried commission employee: Bob Lewis
social security number: 333-33-3333
gross sales: 5000.00
commission rate: 0.04
base salary: 300.00

Calling virtual function print with base-class pointer
to derived-class object invokes derived-class print function:

base-salaried commission employee: Bob Lewis
social security number: 333-33-3333
gross sales: 5000.00
commission rate: 0.04
base salary: 300.00
```

Fig. 24.10 | Demonstrating polymorphism by invoking a derived-class virtual function via a base-class pointer to a derived-class object. (Part 3 of 3.)

24.3.5 Summary of the Allowed Assignments Between Base-Class and Derived-Class Objects and Pointers

Now that you have seen a complete application that processes diverse objects polymorphically, we summarize what you can and cannot do with base-class and derived-class objects and pointers. Although a derived-class object also *is a* base-class object, the two objects are nevertheless different. As discussed previously, derived-class objects can be treated as if they are base-class objects. This is a logical relationship, because the derived class contains all the members of the base class. However, base-class objects cannot be treated as if they are derived-class objects—the derived class can have additional derived-class-only members. For this reason, aiming a derived-class pointer at a base-class object is not allowed without an explicit cast—such an assignment would leave the derived-class-only members undefined on the base-class object. The cast relieves the compiler of the responsibility of issuing an error message. In a sense, by using the cast you are saying, "I know that what I'm doing is dangerous and I take full responsibility for my actions."

In the current section and in Chapter 23, we have discussed four ways to aim base-class pointers and derived-class pointers at base-class objects and derived-class objects:

1. Aiming a base-class pointer at a base-class object is straightforward—calls made off the base-class pointer simply invoke base-class functionality.

2. Aiming a derived-class pointer at a derived-class object is straightforward—calls made off the derived-class pointer simply invoke derived-class functionality.

3. Aiming a base-class pointer at a derived-class object is safe, because the derived-class object *is an* object of its base class. However, this pointer can be used to invoke only base-class member functions. If the programmer attempts to refer to a derived-class-only member through the base-class pointer, the compiler reports an error. To avoid this error, the programmer must cast the base-class pointer to a derived-class pointer. The derived-class pointer can then be used to invoke the derived-class object's complete functionality. However, this technique—called downcasting—is a potentially dangerous operation. Section 24.8 demonstrates how to safely use downcasting.

4. Aiming a derived-class pointer at a base-class object generates a compilation error. The *is-a* relationship applies only from a derived class to its direct and indirect base classes, and not vice versa. A base-class object does not contain the derived-class-only members that can be invoked off a derived-class pointer.

 Common Programming Error 24.1

After aiming a base-class pointer at a derived-class object, attempting to reference derived-class-only members with the base-class pointer is a compilation error.

 Common Programming Error 24.2

Treating a base-class object as a derived-class object can cause errors.

24.4 Type Fields and `switch` Statements

One way to determine the type of an object that is incorporated in a larger program is to use a `switch` statement. This allows us to distinguish among object types, then invoke an appropriate action for a particular object. For example, in a hierarchy of shapes in which each shape object has a shapeType attribute, a switch statement could check the object's shapeType to determine which print function to call.

However, using switch logic exposes programs to a variety of potential problems. For example, the programmer might forget to include a type test when one is warranted, or might forget to test all possible cases in a switch statement. When modifying a switch-based system by adding new types, the programmer might forget to insert the new cases in all relevant switch statements. Every addition or deletion of a class requires the modification of every switch statement in the system; tracking these statements down can be time consuming and error prone.

Software Engineering Observation 24.6

Polymorphic programming can eliminate the need for unnecessary switch logic. By using the C++ polymorphism mechanism to perform the equivalent logic, programmers can avoid the kinds of errors typically associated with switch logic.

Software Engineering Observation 24.7

An interesting consequence of using polymorphism is that programs take on a simplified appearance. They contain less branching logic and more simple, sequential code. This simplification facilitates testing, debugging and program maintenance.

24.5 Abstract Classes and Pure virtual Functions

When we think of a class as a type, we assume that programs will create objects of that type. However, there are cases in which it is useful to define classes from which the programmer never intends to instantiate any objects. Such classes are called **abstract classes**. Because these classes normally are used as base classes in inheritance hierarchies, we refer to them as **abstract base classes**. These classes cannot be used to instantiate objects, because, as we will soon see, abstract classes are incomplete—derived classes must define the "missing pieces." We build programs with abstract classes in Section 24.6.

The purpose of an abstract class is to provide an appropriate base class from which other classes can inherit. Classes that can be used to instantiate objects are called **concrete classes**. Such classes provide implementations of every member function they define. We could have an abstract base class TwoDimensionalShape and derive such concrete classes as Square, Circle and Triangle. We could also have an abstract base class ThreeDimensionalShape and derive such concrete classes as Cube, Sphere and Cylinder. Abstract base classes are too generic to define real objects; we need to be more specific before we can think of instantiating objects. For example, if someone tells you to "draw the two-dimensional shape," what shape would you draw? Concrete classes provide the specifics that make it reasonable to instantiate objects.

An inheritance hierarchy does not need to contain any abstract classes, but, as we will see, many good object-oriented systems have class hierarchies headed by abstract base classes. In some cases, abstract classes constitute the top few levels of the hierarchy. A good example of this is the shape hierarchy in Fig. 23.3, which begins with abstract base class Shape. On the next level of the hierarchy we have two more abstract base classes, namely, TwoDimensionalShape and ThreeDimensionalShape. The next level of the hierarchy defines concrete classes for two-dimensional shapes (namely, Circle, Square and Triangle) and for three-dimensional shapes (namely, Sphere, Cube and Tetrahedron).

A class is made abstract by declaring one or more of its `virtual` functions to be "pure." A pure `virtual` function is specified by placing "= 0" in its declaration, as in

```
virtual void draw() const = 0; // pure virtual function
```

The "= 0" is known as a **pure specifier**. Pure `virtual` functions do not provide implementations. Every concrete derived class must override all base-class pure `virtual` functions with concrete implementations of those functions. The difference between a `virtual` function and a pure `virtual` function is that a `virtual` function has an implementation and gives the derived class the *option* of overriding the function; by contrast, a pure `virtual` function does not provide an implementation and *requires* the derived class to override the function (for that derived class to be concrete; otherwise the derived class remains abstract).

Pure `virtual` functions are used when it does not make sense for the base class to have an implementation of a function, but the programmer wants all concrete derived classes to implement the function. Returning to our earlier example of space objects, it does not make sense for the base class `SpaceObject` to have an implementation for function draw (as there is no way to draw a generic space object without having more information about what type of space object is being drawn). An example of a function that would be defined as `virtual` (and not pure `virtual`) would be one that returns a name for the object. We can name a generic `SpaceObject` (for instance, as `"space object"`), so a default implementation for this function can be provided, and the function does not need to be pure `virtual`. The function is still declared `virtual`, however, because it is expected that derived classes will override this function to provide more specific names for the derived-class objects.

Software Engineering Observation 24.8

An abstract class defines a common public interface for the various classes in a class hierarchy. An abstract class contains one or more pure `virtual` functions that concrete derived classes must override.

Common Programming Error 24.3

Attempting to instantiate an object of an abstract class causes a compilation error.

Common Programming Error 24.4

Failure to override a pure `virtual` function in a derived class, then attempting to instantiate objects of that class, is a compilation error.

Software Engineering Observation 24.9

An abstract class has at least one pure `virtual` function. An abstract class also can have data members and concrete functions (including constructors and destructors), which are subject to the normal rules of inheritance by derived classes.

Although we cannot instantiate objects of an abstract base class, we *can* use the abstract base class to declare pointers and references that can refer to objects of any concrete classes derived from the abstract class. Programs typically use such pointers and references to manipulate derived-class objects polymorphically.

Let us consider another application of polymorphism. A screen manager needs to display a variety of objects, including new types of objects that the programmer will add to the system after writing the screen manager. The system might need to display various shapes, such as Circles, Triangles or Rectangles, which are derived from abstract base class Shape. The screen manager uses Shape pointers to manage the objects that are displayed. To draw any object (regardless of the level at which that object's class appears in the inheritance hierarchy), the screen manager uses a base-class pointer to the object to invoke the object's draw function, which is a pure virtual function in base class Shape; therefore, each concrete derived class must implement function draw. Each Shape object in the inheritance hierarchy knows how to draw itself. The screen manager does not have to worry about the type of each object or whether the screen manager has ever encountered objects of that type.

Polymorphism is particularly effective for implementing layered software systems. In operating systems, for example, each type of physical device could operate quite differently from the others. Even so, commands to *read* or *write* data from and to devices may have a certain uniformity. The *write* message sent to a device-driver object needs to be interpreted specifically in the context of that device driver and how that device driver manipulates devices of a specific type. However, the *write* call itself really is no different from the *write* to any other device in the system—place some number of bytes from memory onto that device. An object-oriented operating system might use an abstract base class to provide an interface appropriate for all device drivers. Then, through inheritance from that abstract base class, derived classes are formed that all operate similarly. The capabilities (i.e., the public functions) offered by the device drivers are provided as pure virtual functions in the abstract base class. The implementations of these pure virtual functions are provided in the derived classes that correspond to the specific types of device drivers. This architecture also allows new devices to be added to a system easily, even after the operating system has been defined. The user can just plug in the device and install its new device driver. The operating system "talks" to this new device through its device driver, which has the same public member functions as all other device drivers—those defined in the abstract base device driver class.

It is common in object-oriented programming to define an iterator class that can traverse all the objects in a container (such as an array). For example, a program can print a list of objects in a vector by creating an iterator object, then using the iterator to obtain the next element of the list each time the iterator is called. Iterators often are used in polymorphic programming to traverse an array or a linked list of pointers to objects from various levels of a hierarchy. The pointers in such a list are all base-class pointers. A list of pointers to objects of base class TwoDimensionalShape could contain pointers to objects of classes Square, Circle, Triangle and so on. Using polymorphism to send a draw message, off a TwoDimensionalShape * pointer, to each object in the list would draw each object correctly on the screen.

24.6 Case Study: Payroll System Using Polymorphism

This section reexamines the CommissionEmployee-BasePlusCommissionEmployee hierarchy that we explored throughout Section 23.4. In this example, we use an abstract class and polymorphism to perform payroll calculations based on the type of employee. We create an enhanced employee hierarchy to solve the following problem:

A company pays its employees weekly. The employees are of four types: Salaried employees are paid a fixed weekly salary regardless of the number of hours worked, hourly employees are paid by the hour and receive overtime pay for all hours worked in excess of 40 hours, commission employees are paid a percentage of their sales and base-salary-plus-commission employees receive a base salary plus a percentage of their sales. For the current pay period, the company has decided to reward base-salary-plus-commission employees by adding 10 percent to their base salaries. The company wants to implement a C++ program that performs its payroll calculations polymorphically.

We use abstract class Employee to represent the general concept of an employee. The classes that derive directly from Employee are SalariedEmployee, CommissionEmployee and HourlyEmployee. Class BasePlusCommissionEmployee—derived from Commission-Employee—represents the last employee type. The UML class diagram in Fig. 24.11 shows the inheritance hierarchy for our polymorphic employee payroll application. Note that abstract class name Employee is italicized, as per the convention of the UML.

Abstract base class Employee declares the "interface" to the hierarchy—that is, the set of member functions that a program can invoke on all Employee objects. Each employee, regardless of the way his or her earnings are calculated, has a first name, a last name and a social security number, so private data members firstName, lastName and socialSecurityNumber appear in abstract base class Employee.

Software Engineering Observation 24.10

A derived class can inherit interface or implementation from a base class. Hierarchies designed for implementation inheritance tend to have their functionality high in the hierarchy—each new derived class inherits one or more member functions that were defined in a base class, and the derived class uses the base-class definitions. Hierarchies designed for interface inheritance tend to have their functionality lower in the hierarchy—a base class specifies one or more functions that should be defined for each class in the hierarchy (i.e., they have the same prototype), but the individual derived classes provide their own implementations of the function(s).

The following sections implement the Employee class hierarchy. The first five each implement one of the abstract or concrete classes. The last section implements a test program that builds objects of all these classes and processes the objects polymorphically.

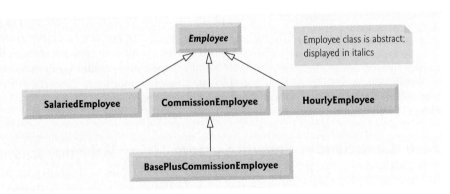

Fig. 24.11 | Employee hierarchy UML class diagram.

24.6.1 Creating Abstract Base Class `Employee`

Class `Employee` (Figs. 24.13–24.14, discussed in further detail shortly) provides functions `earnings` and `print`, in addition to various *get* and *set* functions that manipulate Employee's data members. An `earnings` function certainly applies generically to all employees, but each earnings calculation depends on the employee's class. So we declare `earnings` as pure `virtual` in base class `Employee`, because a default implementation does not make sense for that function—there is not enough information to determine what amount `earnings` should return. Each derived class overrides `earnings` with an appropriate implementation. To calculate an employee's earnings, the program assigns the address of an employee's object to a base class `Employee` pointer, then invokes the `earnings` function on that object. We maintain a `vector` of `Employee` pointers, each of which points to an `Employee` object (of course, there cannot be `Employee` objects, because `Employee` is an abstract class—because of inheritance, however, all objects of all derived classes of `Employee` may nevertheless be thought of as `Employee` objects). The program iterates through the `vector` and calls function `earnings` for each `Employee` object. C++ processes these function calls polymorphically. Including `earnings` as a pure `virtual` function in `Employee` forces every direct derived class of `Employee` that wishes to be a concrete class to override `earnings`. This enables the designer of the class hierarchy to demand that each derived class provide an appropriate pay calculation, if indeed that derived class is to be concrete.

Function `print` in class `Employee` displays the first name, last name and social security number of the employee. As we will see, each derived class of `Employee` overrides function `print` to output the employee's type (e.g., `"salaried employee:"`) followed by the rest of the employee's information.

The diagram in Fig. 24.12 shows each of the five classes in the hierarchy down the left side and functions `earnings` and `print` across the top. For each class, the diagram shows the desired results of each function. Note that class `Employee` specifies "= 0" for function `earnings` to indicate that this is a pure `virtual` function. Each derived class overrides this function to provide an appropriate implementation. We do not list base class `Employee`'s *get* and *set* functions because they are not overridden in any of the derived classes—each of these functions is inherited and used "as is" by each of the derived classes.

Let us consider class `Employee`'s header file (Fig. 24.13). The `public` member functions include a constructor that takes the first name, last name and social security number as arguments (line 12); *set* functions that set the first name, last name and social security number (lines 14, 17 and 20, respectively); *get* functions that return the first name, last name and social security number (lines 15, 18 and 21, respectively); pure `virtual` function `earnings` (line 24) and `virtual` function `print` (line 25).

Recall that we declared `earnings` as a pure `virtual` function because we first must know the specific `Employee` type to determine the appropriate `earnings` calculations. Declaring this function as pure `virtual` indicates that each concrete derived class *must* provide an appropriate `earnings` implementation and that a program can use base-class `Employee` pointers to invoke function `earnings` polymorphically for any type of `Employee`.

Figure 24.14 contains the member-function implementations for class `Employee`. No implementation is provided for `virtual` function `earnings`. Note that the `Employee` constructor (lines 10–15) does not validate the social security number. Normally, such validation should be provided.

	earnings	print
Employee	= 0	firstName lastName social security number: SSN
Salaried- Employee	weeklySalary	salaried employee: firstName lastName social security number: SSN weekly salary: weeklysalary

Hourly-
Employee
	If hours <= 40
	  wage * hours
	If hours > 40
	  (40 * wage) +
	  ((hours - 40)
	  * wage * 1.5)
		hourly employee: firstName lastName
		social security number: SSN
		hourly wage: wage; hours worked: hours

Commission- Employee	commissionRate * grossSales	commission employee: firstName lastName social security number: SSN gross sales: grossSales; commission rate: commissionRate
BasePlus- Commission- Employee	baseSalary + (commissionRate * grossSales)	base salaried commission employee: firstName lastName social security number: SSN gross sales: grossSales; commission rate: commissionRate; base salary: baseSalary

Fig. 24.12 | Polymorphic interface for the Employee hierarchy classes.

```
1   // Fig. 24.13: Employee.h
2   // Employee abstract base class.
3   #ifndef EMPLOYEE_H
4   #define EMPLOYEE_H
5
6   #include <string> // C++ standard string class
7   using std::string;
8
9   class Employee
10  {
11  public:
12     Employee( const string &, const string &, const string & );
13
14     void setFirstName( const string & ); // set first name
15     string getFirstName() const; // return first name
16
17     void setLastName( const string & ); // set last name
18     string getLastName() const; // return last name
19
```

Fig. 24.13 | Employee class header file. (Part 1 of 2.)

```
 1   // Fig. 24.15: SalariedEmployee.h
 2   // SalariedEmployee class derived from Employee.
 3   #ifndef SALARIED_H
 4   #define SALARIED_H
 5
 6   #include "Employee.h" // Employee class definition
 7
 8   class SalariedEmployee : public Employee
 9   {
10   public:
11      SalariedEmployee( const string &, const string &,
12         const string &, double = 0.0 );
13
14      void setWeeklySalary( double ); // set weekly salary
15      double getWeeklySalary() const; // return weekly salary
16
17      // keyword virtual signals intent to override
18      virtual double earnings() const; // calculate earnings
19      virtual void print() const; // print SalariedEmployee object
20   private:
21      double weeklySalary; // salary per week
22   }; // end class SalariedEmployee
23
24   #endif // SALARIED_H
```

Fig. 24.15 │ SalariedEmployee class header file.

```
 1   // Fig. 24.16: SalariedEmployee.cpp
 2   // SalariedEmployee class member-function definitions.
 3   #include <iostream>
 4   using std::cout;
 5
 6   #include "SalariedEmployee.h" // SalariedEmployee class definition
 7
 8   // constructor
 9   SalariedEmployee::SalariedEmployee( const string &first,
10      const string &last, const string &ssn, double salary )
11      : Employee( first, last, ssn )
12   {
13      setWeeklySalary( salary );
14   } // end SalariedEmployee constructor
15
16   // set salary
17   void SalariedEmployee::setWeeklySalary( double salary )
18   {
19      weeklySalary = ( salary < 0.0 ) ? 0.0 : salary;
20   } // end function setWeeklySalary
21
22   // return salary
23   double SalariedEmployee::getWeeklySalary() const
24   {
```

Fig. 24.16 │ SalariedEmployee class implementation file. (Part 1 of 2.)

```
25      return weeklySalary;
26   } // end function getWeeklySalary
27
28   // calculate earnings;
29   // override pure virtual function earnings in Employee
30   double SalariedEmployee::earnings() const
31   {
32      return getWeeklySalary();
33   } // end function earnings
34
35   // print SalariedEmployee's information
36   void SalariedEmployee::print() const
37   {
38      cout << "salaried employee: ";
39      Employee::print(); // reuse abstract base-class print function
40      cout << "\nweekly salary: " << getWeeklySalary();
41   } // end function print
```

Fig. 24.16 | SalariedEmployee class implementation file. (Part 2 of 2.)

want SalariedEmployee here to be a concrete class). Note that in class SalariedEmployee's header file, we declared member functions earnings and print as virtual (lines 18–19 of Fig. 24.15)—actually, placing the virtual keyword before these member functions is redundant. We defined them as virtual in base class Employee, so they remain virtual functions throughout the class hierarchy. Recall from Good Programming Practice 24.1 that explicitly declaring such functions virtual at every level of the hierarchy can promote program clarity.

Function print of class SalariedEmployee (lines 36–41 of Fig. 24.16) overrides Employee function print. If class SalariedEmployee did not override print, SalariedEmployee would inherit the Employee version of print. In that case, SalariedEmployee's print function would simply return the employee's full name and social security number, which does not adequately represent a SalariedEmployee. To print a SalariedEmployee's complete information, the derived class's print function outputs "salaried employee: " followed by the base-class Employee-specific information (i.e., first name, last name and social security number) printed by invoking the base class's print using the scope resolution operator (line 39)—this is a nice example of code reuse. The output produced by SalariedEmployee's print function contains the employee's weekly salary obtained by invoking the class's getWeeklySalary function.

24.6.3 Creating Concrete Derived Class HourlyEmployee

Class HourlyEmployee (Figs. 24.17–24.18) also derives from class Employee (line 8 of Fig. 24.17). The public member functions include a constructor (lines 11–12) that takes as arguments a first name, a last name, a social security number, an hourly wage and the number of hours worked; set functions that assign new values to data members wage and hours, respectively (lines 14 and 17); get functions to return the values of wage and hours, respectively (lines 15 and 18); a virtual function earnings that calculates an HourlyEmployee's earnings (line 21) and a virtual function print that outputs the employee's type, namely, "hourly employee: " and employee-specific information (line 22).

class function print (line 56) to output the Employee-specific information (i.e., first name, last name and social security number)—this is another nice example of code reuse.

24.6.4 Creating Concrete Derived Class CommissionEmployee

Class CommissionEmployee (Figs. 24.19–24.20) derives from class Employee (line 8 of Fig. 24.19). The member-function implementations (Fig. 24.20) include a constructor (lines 9–15) that takes a first name, a last name, a social security number, a sales amount and a commission rate; *set* functions (lines 18–21 and 30–33) to assign new values to data members commissionRate and grossSales, respectively; *get* functions (lines 24–27 and 36–39) that retrieve the values of these data members; function earnings (lines 43–46) to calculate a CommissionEmployee's earnings; and function print (lines 49–55), which outputs the employee's type, namely, "commission employee: " and employee-specific information. The CommissionEmployee's constructor also passes the first name, last name and social security number to the Employee constructor (line 11) to initialize Employee's pri-

```
1   // Fig. 24.19: CommissionEmployee.h
2   // CommissionEmployee class derived from Employee.
3   #ifndef COMMISSION_H
4   #define COMMISSION_H
5
6   #include "Employee.h" // Employee class definition
7
8   class CommissionEmployee : public Employee
9   {
10  public:
11     CommissionEmployee( const string &, const string &,
12        const string &, double = 0.0, double = 0.0 );
13
14     void setCommissionRate( double ); // set commission rate
15     double getCommissionRate() const; // return commission rate
16
17     void setGrossSales( double ); // set gross sales amount
18     double getGrossSales() const; // return gross sales amount
19
20     // keyword virtual signals intent to override
21     virtual double earnings() const; // calculate earnings
22     virtual void print() const; // print CommissionEmployee object
23  private:
24     double grossSales; // gross weekly sales
25     double commissionRate; // commission percentage
26  }; // end class CommissionEmployee
27
28  #endif // COMMISSION_H
```

Fig. 24.19 | CommissionEmployee class header file.

```
1   // Fig. 24.20: CommissionEmployee.cpp
2   // CommissionEmployee class member-function definitions.
3   #include <iostream>
```

Fig. 24.20 | CommissionEmployee class implementation file. (Part 1 of 2.)

```
4   using std::cout;
5
6   #include "CommissionEmployee.h" // CommissionEmployee class definition
7
8   // constructor
9   CommissionEmployee::CommissionEmployee( const string &first,
10     const string &last, const string &ssn, double sales, double rate )
11     : Employee( first, last, ssn )
12  {
13     setGrossSales( sales );
14     setCommissionRate( rate );
15  } // end CommissionEmployee constructor
16
17  // set commission rate
18  void CommissionEmployee::setCommissionRate( double rate )
19  {
20     commissionRate = ( ( rate > 0.0 && rate < 1.0 ) ? rate : 0.0 );
21  } // end function setCommissionRate
22
23  // return commission rate
24  double CommissionEmployee::getCommissionRate() const
25  {
26     return commissionRate;
27  } // end function getCommissionRate
28
29  // set gross sales amount
30  void CommissionEmployee::setGrossSales( double sales )
31  {
32     grossSales = ( ( sales < 0.0 ) ? 0.0 : sales );
33  } // end function setGrossSales
34
35  // return gross sales amount
36  double CommissionEmployee::getGrossSales() const
37  {
38     return grossSales;
39  } // end function getGrossSales
40
41  // calculate earnings;
42  // override pure virtual function earnings in Employee
43  double CommissionEmployee::earnings() const
44  {
45     return getCommissionRate() * getGrossSales();
46  } // end function earnings
47
48  // print CommissionEmployee's information
49  void CommissionEmployee::print() const
50  {
51     cout << "commission employee: ";
52     Employee::print(); // code reuse
53     cout << "\ngross sales: " << getGrossSales()
54        << "; commission rate: " << getCommissionRate();
55  } // end function print
```

Fig. 24.20 | CommissionEmployee class implementation file. (Part 2 of 2.)

vate data members. Function `print` calls base-class function `print` (line 52) to display the Employee-specific information (i.e., first name, last name and social security number).

24.6.5 Creating Indirect Concrete Derived Class BasePlusCommissionEmployee

Class `BasePlusCommissionEmployee` (Figs. 24.21–24.22) directly inherits from class `CommissionEmployee` (line 8 of Fig. 24.21) and therefore is an indirect derived class of class `Employee`. Class `BasePlusCommissionEmployee`'s member-function implementations include a constructor (lines 10–16 of Fig. 24.22) that takes as arguments a first name, a last name, a social security number, a sales amount, a commission rate and a base salary. It then passes the first name, last name, social security number, sales amount and commission rate to the `CommissionEmployee` constructor (line 13) to initialize the inherited members. Base-PlusCommissionEmployee also contains a *set* function (lines 19–22) to assign a new value to data member baseSalary and a *get* function (lines 25–28) to return baseSalary's value. Function `earnings` (lines 32–35) calculates a `BasePlusCommissionEmployee`'s earnings. Note that line 34 in function earnings calls base-class CommissionEmployee's earnings function to calculate the commission-based portion of the employee's earnings. This is a nice example of code reuse. BasePlusCommissionEmployee's print function (lines 38–43) outputs "base-salaried", followed by the output of base-class CommissionEmployee's print function (another example of code reuse), then the base salary. The resulting output begins with "base-salaried commission employee: " followed by the rest of the Base-

```
 1   // Fig. 24.21: BasePlusCommissionEmployee.h
 2   // BasePlusCommissionEmployee class derived from Employee.
 3   #ifndef BASEPLUS_H
 4   #define BASEPLUS_H
 5
 6   #include "CommissionEmployee.h" // CommissionEmployee class definition
 7
 8   class BasePlusCommissionEmployee : public CommissionEmployee
 9   {
10   public:
11      BasePlusCommissionEmployee( const string &, const string &,
12         const string &, double = 0.0, double = 0.0, double = 0.0 );
13
14      void setBaseSalary( double ); // set base salary
15      double getBaseSalary() const; // return base salary
16
17      // keyword virtual signals intent to override
18      virtual double earnings() const; // calculate earnings
19      virtual void print() const; // print BasePlusCommissionEmployee object
20   private:
21      double baseSalary; // base salary per week
22   }; // end class BasePlusCommissionEmployee
23
24   #endif // BASEPLUS_H
```

Fig. 24.21 | BasePlusCommissionEmployee class header file.

```cpp
1   // Fig. 24.22: BasePlusCommissionEmployee.cpp
2   // BasePlusCommissionEmployee member-function definitions.
3   #include <iostream>
4   using std::cout;
5
6   // BasePlusCommissionEmployee class definition
7   #include "BasePlusCommissionEmployee.h"
8
9   // constructor
10  BasePlusCommissionEmployee::BasePlusCommissionEmployee(
11     const string &first, const string &last, const string &ssn,
12     double sales, double rate, double salary )
13     : CommissionEmployee( first, last, ssn, sales, rate )
14  {
15     setBaseSalary( salary ); // validate and store base salary
16  } // end BasePlusCommissionEmployee constructor
17
18  // set base salary
19  void BasePlusCommissionEmployee::setBaseSalary( double salary )
20  {
21     baseSalary = ( ( salary < 0.0 ) ? 0.0 : salary );
22  } // end function setBaseSalary
23
24  // return base salary
25  double BasePlusCommissionEmployee::getBaseSalary() const
26  {
27     return baseSalary;
28  } // end function getBaseSalary
29
30  // calculate earnings;
31  // override pure virtual function earnings in Employee
32  double BasePlusCommissionEmployee::earnings() const
33  {
34     return getBaseSalary() + CommissionEmployee::earnings();
35  } // end function earnings
36
37  // print BasePlusCommissionEmployee's information
38  void BasePlusCommissionEmployee::print() const
39  {
40     cout << "base-salaried ";
41     CommissionEmployee::print(); // code reuse
42     cout << "; base salary: " << getBaseSalary();
43  } // end function print
```

Fig. 24.22 | BasePlusCommissionEmployee class implementation file.

PlusCommissionEmployee's information. Recall that CommissionEmployee's print displays the employee's first name, last name and social security number by invoking the print function of its base class (i.e., Employee)—yet another example of code reuse. Note that BasePlusCommissionEmployee's print initiates a chain of functions calls that spans all three levels of the Employee hierarchy.

24.6.6 Demonstrating Polymorphic Processing

To test our Employee hierarchy, the program in Fig. 24.23 creates an object of each of the four concrete classes SalariedEmployee, HourlyEmployee, CommissionEmployee and BasePlusCommissionEmployee. The program manipulates these objects, first with static binding, then polymorphically, using a vector of Employee pointers. Lines 31–38 create objects of each of the four concrete Employee derived classes. Lines 43–51 output each Employee's information and earnings. Each member-function invocation in lines 43–51 is

```
1   // Fig. 24.23: fig24_23.cpp
2   // Processing Employee derived-class objects individually
3   // and polymorphically using dynamic binding.
4   #include <iostream>
5   using std::cout;
6   using std::endl;
7   using std::fixed;
8
9   #include <iomanip>
10  using std::setprecision;
11
12  #include <vector>
13  using std::vector;
14
15  // include definitions of classes in Employee hierarchy
16  #include "Employee.h"
17  #include "SalariedEmployee.h"
18  #include "HourlyEmployee.h"
19  #include "CommissionEmployee.h"
20  #include "BasePlusCommissionEmployee.h"
21
22  void virtualViaPointer( const Employee * const ); // prototype
23  void virtualViaReference( const Employee & ); // prototype
24
25  int main()
26  {
27     // set floating-point output formatting
28     cout << fixed << setprecision( 2 );
29
30     // create derived-class objects
31     SalariedEmployee salariedEmployee(
32        "John", "Smith", "111-11-1111", 800 );
33     HourlyEmployee hourlyEmployee(
34        "Karen", "Price", "222-22-2222", 16.75, 40 );
35     CommissionEmployee commissionEmployee(
36        "Sue", "Jones", "333-33-3333", 10000, .06 );
37     BasePlusCommissionEmployee basePlusCommissionEmployee(
38        "Bob", "Lewis", "444-44-4444", 5000, .04, 300 );
39
40     cout << "Employees processed individually using static binding:\n\n";
41
42     // output each Employee's information and earnings using static binding
43     salariedEmployee.print();
```

Fig. 24.23 | Employee class hierarchy driver program. (Part 1 of 4.)

```
44          cout << "\nearned $" << salariedEmployee.earnings() << "\n\n";
45          hourlyEmployee.print();
46          cout << "\nearned $" << hourlyEmployee.earnings() << "\n\n";
47          commissionEmployee.print();
48          cout << "\nearned $" << commissionEmployee.earnings() << "\n\n";
49          basePlusCommissionEmployee.print();
50          cout << "\nearned $" << basePlusCommissionEmployee.earnings()
51             << "\n\n";
52
53          // create vector of four base-class pointers
54          vector < Employee * > employees( 4 );
55
56          // initialize vector with Employees
57          employees[ 0 ] = &salariedEmployee;
58          employees[ 1 ] = &hourlyEmployee;
59          employees[ 2 ] = &commissionEmployee;
60          employees[ 3 ] = &basePlusCommissionEmployee;
61
62          cout << "Employees processed polymorphically via dynamic binding:\n\n";
63
64          // call virtualViaPointer to print each Employee's information
65          // and earnings using dynamic binding
66          cout << "Virtual function calls made off base-class pointers:\n\n";
67
68          for ( size_t i = 0; i < employees.size(); i++ )
69             virtualViaPointer( employees[ i ] );
70
71          // call virtualViaReference to print each Employee's information
72          // and earnings using dynamic binding
73          cout << "Virtual function calls made off base-class references:\n\n";
74
75          for ( size_t i = 0; i < employees.size(); i++ )
76             virtualViaReference( *employees[ i ] ); // note dereferencing
77
78          return 0;
79       } // end main
80
81       // call Employee virtual functions print and earnings off a
82       // base-class pointer using dynamic binding
83       void virtualViaPointer( const Employee * const baseClassPtr )
84       {
85          baseClassPtr->print();
86          cout << "\nearned $" << baseClassPtr->earnings() << "\n\n";
87       } // end function virtualViaPointer
88
89       // call Employee virtual functions print and earnings off a
90       // base-class reference using dynamic binding
91       void virtualViaReference( const Employee &baseClassRef )
92       {
93          baseClassRef.print();
94          cout << "\nearned $" << baseClassRef.earnings() << "\n\n";
95       } // end function virtualViaReference
```

Fig. 24.23 | Employee class hierarchy driver program. (Part 2 of 4.)

```
Employees processed individually using static binding:

salaried employee: John Smith
social security number: 111-11-1111
weekly salary: 800.00
earned $800.00

hourly employee: Karen Price
social security number: 222-22-2222
hourly wage: 16.75; hours worked: 40.00
earned $670.00

commission employee: Sue Jones
social security number: 333-33-3333
gross sales: 10000.00; commission rate: 0.06
earned $600.00

base-salaried commission employee: Bob Lewis
social security number: 444-44-4444
gross sales: 5000.00; commission rate: 0.04; base salary: 300.00
earned $500.00

Employees processed polymorphically using dynamic binding:

Virtual function calls made off base-class pointers:

salaried employee: John Smith
social security number: 111-11-1111
weekly salary: 800.00
earned $800.00

hourly employee: Karen Price
social security number: 222-22-2222
hourly wage: 16.75; hours worked: 40.00
earned $670.00

commission employee: Sue Jones
social security number: 333-33-3333
gross sales: 10000.00; commission rate: 0.06
earned $600.00

base-salaried commission employee: Bob Lewis
social security number: 444-44-4444
gross sales: 5000.00; commission rate: 0.04; base salary: 300.00
earned $500.00

Virtual function calls made off base-class references:

salaried employee: John Smith
social security number: 111-11-1111
weekly salary: 800.00
earned $800.00

hourly employee: Karen Price
social security number: 222-22-2222
hourly wage: 16.75; hours worked: 40.00
earned $670.00
```

(continued on next page)

Fig. 24.23 | Employee class hierarchy driver program. (Part 3 of 4.)

```
commission employee: Sue Jones
social security number: 333-33-3333
gross sales: 10000.00; commission rate: 0.06
earned $600.00

base-salaried commission employee: Bob Lewis
social security number: 444-44-4444
gross sales: 5000.00; commission rate: 0.04; base salary: 300.00
earned $500.00
```

Fig. 24.23 | Employee class hierarchy driver program. (Part 4 of 4.)

an example of static binding—at compile time, because we are using name handles (not pointers or references that could be set at execution time), the compiler can identify each object's type to determine which print and earnings functions are called.

Line 54 allocates vector employees, which contains four Employee pointers. Line 57 aims employees[0] at object salariedEmployee. Line 58 aims employees[1] at object hourlyEmployee. Line 59 aims employees[2] at object commissionEmployee. Line 60 aims employee[3] at object basePlusCommissionEmployee. The compiler allows these assignments, because a SalariedEmployee *is an* Employee, an HourlyEmployee *is an* Employee, a CommissionEmployee *is an* Employee and a BasePlusCommissionEmployee *is an* Employee. Therefore, we can assign the addresses of SalariedEmployee, HourlyEmployee, CommissionEmployee and BasePlusCommissionEmployee objects to base-class Employee pointers (even though Employee is an abstract class).

The for statement at lines 68–69 traverses vector employees and invokes function virtualViaPointer (lines 83–87) for each element in employees. Function virtualViaPointer receives in parameter baseClassPtr (of type const Employee * const) the address stored in an employees element. Each call to virtualViaPointer uses baseClassPtr to invoke virtual functions print (line 85) and earnings (line 86). Note that function virtualViaPointer does not contain any SalariedEmployee, HourlyEmployee, CommissionEmployee or BasePlusCommissionEmployee type information. The function knows only about base-class type Employee. Therefore, at compile time, the compiler cannot know which concrete class's functions to call through baseClassPtr. Yet at execution time, each virtual-function invocation calls the function on the object to which baseClassPtr points at that time. The output illustrates that the appropriate functions for each class are indeed invoked and that each object's proper information is displayed. For instance, the weekly salary is displayed for the SalariedEmployee, and the gross sales are displayed for the CommissionEmployee and BasePlusCommissionEmployee. Also note that obtaining the earnings of each Employee polymorphically in line 86 produces the same results as obtaining these employees' earnings via static binding in lines 44, 46, 48 and 50. All virtual function calls to print and earnings are resolved at runtime with dynamic binding.

Finally, another for statement (lines 75–76) traverses employees and invokes function virtualViaReference (lines 91–95) for each element in the vector. Function virtualViaReference receives in its parameter baseClassRef (of type const Employee &) a reference formed by dereferencing the pointer stored in each employees element (line 76). Each call to virtualViaReference invokes virtual functions print (line 93) and earnings (line 94) via reference baseClassRef to demonstrate that polymorphic processing occurs with base-class references as well. Each `virtual`-function invocation calls the function on the object to which `baseClassRef` refers at runtime. This is another example of dynamic binding. The output produced using base-class references is identical to the output produced using base-class pointers.

24.7 (Optional) Polymorphism, Virtual Functions and Dynamic Binding "Under the Hood"

C++ makes polymorphism easy to program. It is certainly possible to program for polymorphism in non-object-oriented languages such as C, but doing so requires complex and potentially dangerous pointer manipulations. This section discusses how C++ can implement polymorphism, `virtual` functions and dynamic binding internally. This will give you a solid understanding of how these capabilities really work. More importantly, it will help you appreciate the overhead of polymorphism—in terms of additional memory consumption and processor time. This will help you determine when to use polymorphism and when to avoid it. The Standard Template Library (STL) components were implemented without polymorphism and `virtual` functions—this was done to avoid the associated execution-time overhead and achieve optimal performance to meet the unique requirements of the STL.

First, we will explain the data structures that the C++ compiler builds at compile time to support polymorphism at execution time. You will see that polymorphism is accomplished through three levels of pointers (i.e., "triple indirection"). Then we will show how an executing program uses these data structures to execute `virtual` functions and achieve the dynamic binding associated with polymorphism. Note that our discussion explains one possible implementation; this is not a language requirement.

When C++ compiles a class that has one or more `virtual` functions, it builds a **virtual function table** (*vtable*) for that class. An executing program uses the *vtable* to select the proper function implementation each time a `virtual` function of that class is called. The leftmost column of Fig. 24.24 illustrates the *vtables* for classes `Employee`, `SalariedEmployee`, `HourlyEmployee`, `CommissionEmployee` and `BasePlusCommissionEmployee`.

In the *vtable* for class `Employee`, the first function pointer is set to 0 (i.e., the null pointer). This is done because function `earnings` is a pure `virtual` function and therefore lacks an implementation. The second function pointer points to function `print`, which displays the employee's full name and social security number. [*Note:* We have abbreviated the output of each `print` function in this figure to conserve space.] Any class that has one or more null pointers in its *vtable* is an abstract class. Classes without any null *vtable* pointers (such as `SalariedEmployee`, `HourlyEmployee`, `CommissionEmployee` and `BasePlusCommissionEmployee`) are concrete classes.

Class `SalariedEmployee` overrides function `earnings` to return the employee's weekly salary, so the function pointer points to the `earnings` function of class `SalariedEmployee`. `SalariedEmployee` also overrides `print`, so the corresponding function pointer points to the `SalariedEmployee` member function that prints `"salaried employee: "` followed by the employee's name, social security number and weekly salary.

The `earnings` function pointer in the *vtable* for class `HourlyEmployee` points to `HourlyEmployee`'s `earnings` function that returns the employee's wage multiplied by the number of hours worked. Note that to conserve space, we have omitted the fact that hourly employees receive time-and-a-half pay for overtime hours worked. The `print` func-

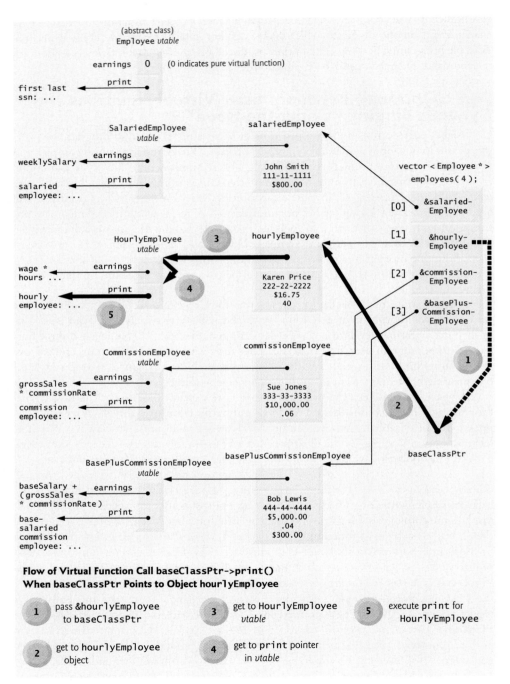

Fig. 24.24 | How `virtual` function calls work.

tion pointer points to the HourlyEmployee version of the function, which prints "hourly employee: ", the employee's name, social security number, hourly wage and hours worked. Both functions override the functions in class Employee.

The earnings function pointer in the *vtable* for class CommissionEmployee points to the CommissionEmployee's earnings function that returns the employee's gross sales multiplied by commission rate. The print function pointer points to the CommissionEmployee version of the function, which prints the employee's type, name, social security number, commission rate and gross sales. As in class HourlyEmployee, both functions override the functions in class Employee.

The earnings function pointer in the *vtable* for class BasePlusCommissionEmployee points to the BasePlusCommissionEmployee's earnings function that returns the employee's base salary plus gross sales multiplied by commission rate. The print function pointer points to the BasePlusCommissionEmployee version of the function, which prints the employee's base salary plus the type, name, social security number, commission rate and gross sales. Both functions override the functions in class CommissionEmployee.

Notice that in our Employee case study, each concrete class provides its own implementation for virtual functions earnings and print. You have already learned that each class which inherits directly from abstract base class Employee must implement earnings in order to be a concrete class, because earnings is a pure virtual function. These classes do not need to implement function print, however, to be considered concrete—print is not a pure virtual function, and derived classes can inherit class Employee's implementation of print. Furthermore, class BasePlusCommissionEmployee does not have to implement either function print or earnings—both function implementations can be inherited from class CommissionEmployee. If a class in our hierarchy were to inherit function implementations in this manner, the *vtable* pointers for these functions would simply point to the function implementation that was being inherited. For example, if BasePlusCommissionEmployee did not override earnings, the earnings function pointer in the *vtable* for class BasePlusCommissionEmployee would point to the same earnings function as the *vtable* for class CommissionEmployee points to.

Polymorphism is accomplished through an elegant data structure involving three levels of pointers. We have discussed one level—the function pointers in the *vtable*. These point to the actual functions that execute when a virtual function is invoked.

Now we consider the second level of pointers. Whenever an object of a class with one or more virtual functions is instantiated, the compiler attaches to the object a pointer to the *vtable* for that class. This pointer is normally at the front of the object, but it is not required to be implemented that way. In Fig. 24.24, these pointers are associated with the objects created in Fig. 24.23 (one object for each of the types SalariedEmployee, HourlyEmployee, CommissionEmployee and BasePlusCommissionEmployee). Notice that the diagram displays each of the object's data member values. For example, the salariedEmployee object contains a pointer to the SalariedEmployee *vtable*; the object also contains the values John Smith, 111-11-1111 and $800.00.

The third level of pointers simply contains the handles to the objects that receive the virtual function calls. The handles in this level may also be references. Note that Fig. 24.24 depicts the vector employees that contains Employee pointers.

Now let us see how a typical virtual function call executes. Consider the call baseClassPtr->print() in function virtualViaPointer (line 85 of Fig. 24.23). Assume that `baseClassPtr` contains `employees[ 1 ]` (i.e., the address of object `hourlyEmployee` in `employees`). When the compiler compiles this statement, it determines that the call is indeed being made via a base-class pointer and that `print` is a `virtual` function.

The compiler determines that `print` is the *second* entry in each of the *vtables*. To locate this entry, the compiler notes that it will need to skip the first entry. Thus, the compiler compiles an offset or displacement of four bytes (four bytes for each pointer on today's popular 32-bit machines, and only one pointer needs to be skipped) into the table of machine-language object-code pointers to find the code that will execute the `virtual` function call.

The compiler generates code that performs the following operations [*Note:* The numbers in the list correspond to the circled numbers in Fig. 24.24]:

1. Select the *i*th entry of `employees` (in this case, the address of object `hourlyEmployee`), and pass it as an argument to function `virtualViaPointer`. This sets parameter `baseClassPtr` to point to `hourlyEmployee`.

2. Dereference that pointer to get to the `hourlyEmployee` object—which, as you recall, begins with a pointer to the `HourlyEmployee` *vtable*.

3. Dereference `hourlyEmployee`'s *vtable* pointer to get to the `HourlyEmployee` *vtable*.

4. Skip the offset of four bytes to select the `print` function pointer.

5. Dereference the `print` function pointer to form the "name" of the actual function to execute, and use the function call operator () to execute the appropriate `print` function, which in this case prints the employee's type, name, social security number, hourly wage and hours worked.

The data structures of Fig. 24.24 may appear to be complex, but this complexity is managed by the compiler and hidden from you, making polymorphic programming straightforward. The pointer dereferencing operations and memory accesses that occur on every `virtual` function call require some additional execution time. The *vtables* and the *vtable* pointers added to the objects require some additional memory. You now have enough information to determine whether `virtual` functions are appropriate for your programs.

Performance Tip 24.1

Polymorphism, as typically implemented with `virtual` functions and dynamic binding in C++, is efficient. Programmers may use these capabilities with nominal impact on performance.

Performance Tip 24.2

Virtual functions and dynamic binding enable polymorphic programming as an alternative to `switch` logic programming. Optimizing compilers normally generate polymorphic code that runs as efficiently as hand-coded `switch`-based logic. The overhead of polymorphism is acceptable for most applications. But in some situations—real-time applications with stringent performance requirements, for example—the overhead of polymorphism may be too high.

Software Engineering Observation 24.11

Dynamic binding enables independent software vendors (ISVs) to distribute software without revealing proprietary secrets. Software distributions can consist of only header files and object files—no source code needs to be revealed. Software developers can then use inheritance to derive new classes from those provided by the ISVs. Other software that worked with the classes the ISVs provided will still work with the derived classes and will use the overridden `virtual` functions provided in these classes (via dynamic binding).

24.8 Case Study: Payroll System Using Polymorphism and Runtime Type Information with Downcasting, `dynamic_cast`, `typeid` and `type_info`

Recall from the problem statement at the beginning of Section 24.6 that, for the current pay period, our fictitious company has decided to reward `BasePlusCommissionEmployee`s by adding 10% to their base salaries. When processing `Employee` objects polymorphically in Section 24.6.6, we did not need to worry about the "specifics." Now, however, to adjust the base salaries of `BasePlusCommissionEmployee`s, we have to determine the specific type of each `Employee` object at execution time, then act appropriately. This section demonstrates the powerful capabilities of runtime type information (RTTI) and dynamic casting, which enable a program to determine the type of an object at execution time and act on that object accordingly.

Some compilers, such as Microsoft Visual C++ .NET, require that RTTI be enabled before it can be used in a program. Consult your compiler's documentation to determine whether your compiler has similar requirements. To enable RTTI in Visual C++ .NET, select the **Project** menu and then select the properties option for the current project. In the **Property Pages** dialog box that appears, select **Configuration Properties > C/C++ > Language**. Then choose **Yes (/GR)** from the combo box next to **Enable Run-Time Type Info**. Finally, click **OK** to save the settings.

The program in Fig. 24.25 uses the `Employee` hierarchy developed in Section 24.6 and increases by 10% the base salary of each `BasePlusCommissionEmployee`. Line 31 declares

```
 1   // Fig. 24.25: fig24_25.cpp
 2   // Demonstrating downcasting and run-time type information.
 3   // NOTE: For this example to run in Visual C++ .NET,
 4   // you need to enable RTTI (Run-Time Type Info) for the project.
 5   #include <iostream>
 6   using std::cout;
 7   using std::endl;
 8   using std::fixed;
 9
10   #include <iomanip>
11   using std::setprecision;
12
13   #include <vector>
14   using std::vector;
15
16   #include <typeinfo>
17
18   // include definitions of classes in Employee hierarchy
19   #include "Employee.h"
20   #include "SalariedEmployee.h"
21   #include "HourlyEmployee.h"
22   #include "CommissionEmployee.h"
23   #include "BasePlusCommissionEmployee.h"
24
25   int main()
26   {
```

Fig. 24.25 | Demonstrating downcasting and runtime type information. (Part 1 of 3.)

```
27    // set floating-point output formatting
28    cout << fixed << setprecision( 2 );
29
30    // create vector of four base-class pointers
31    vector < Employee * > employees( 4 );
32
33    // initialize vector with various kinds of Employees
34    employees[ 0 ] = new SalariedEmployee(
35       "John", "Smith", "111-11-1111", 800 );
36    employees[ 1 ] = new HourlyEmployee(
37       "Karen", "Price", "222-22-2222", 16.75, 40 );
38    employees[ 2 ] = new CommissionEmployee(
39       "Sue", "Jones", "333-33-3333", 10000, .06 );
40    employees[ 3 ] = new BasePlusCommissionEmployee(
41       "Bob", "Lewis", "444-44-4444", 5000, .04, 300 );
42
43    // polymorphically process each element in vector employees
44    for ( size_t i = 0; i < employees.size(); i++ )
45    {
46       employees[ i ]->print(); // output employee information
47       cout << endl;
48
49       // downcast pointer
50       BasePlusCommissionEmployee *derivedPtr =
51          dynamic_cast < BasePlusCommissionEmployee * >
52             ( employees[ i ] );
53
54       // determine whether element points to base-salaried
55       // commission employee
56       if ( derivedPtr != 0 ) // 0 if not a BasePlusCommissionEmployee
57       {
58          double oldBaseSalary = derivedPtr->getBaseSalary();
59          cout << "old base salary: $" << oldBaseSalary << endl;
60          derivedPtr->setBaseSalary( 1.10 * oldBaseSalary );
61          cout << "new base salary with 10% increase is: $"
62             << derivedPtr->getBaseSalary() << endl;
63       } // end if
64
65       cout << "earned $" << employees[ i ]->earnings() << "\n\n";
66    } // end for
67
68    // release objects pointed to by vector's elements
69    for ( size_t j = 0; j < employees.size(); j++ )
70    {
71       // output class name
72       cout << "deleting object of "
73          << typeid( *employees[ j ] ).name() << endl;
74
75       delete employees[ j ];
76    } // end for
77
78    return 0;
79 } // end main
```

Fig. 24.25 | Demonstrating downcasting and runtime type information. (Part 2 of 3.)

```
salaried employee: John Smith
social security number: 111-11-1111
weekly salary: 800.00
earned $800.00

hourly employee: Karen Price
social security number: 222-22-2222
hourly wage: 16.75; hours worked: 40.00
earned $670.00

commission employee: Sue Jones
social security number: 333-33-3333
gross sales: 10000.00; commission rate: 0.06
earned $600.00

base-salaried commission employee: Bob Lewis
social security number: 444-44-4444
gross sales: 5000.00; commission rate: 0.04; base salary: 300.00
old base salary: $300.00
new base salary with 10% increase is: $330.00
earned $530.00

deleting object of class SalariedEmployee
deleting object of class HourlyEmployee
deleting object of class CommissionEmployee
deleting object of class BasePlusCommissionEmployee
```

Fig. 24.25 | Demonstrating downcasting and runtime type information. (Part 3 of 3.)

four-element vector employees that stores pointers to Employee objects. Lines 34–41 populate the vector with the addresses of dynamically allocated objects of classes SalariedEmployee (Figs. 24.15–24.16), HourlyEmployee (Figs. 24.17–24.18), CommissionEmployee (Figs. 24.19–24.20) and BasePlusCommissionEmployee (Figs. 24.21–24.22).

The for statement at lines 44–66 iterates through the employees vector and displays each Employee's information by invoking member function print (line 46). Recall that because print is declared virtual in base class Employee, the system invokes the appropriate derived-class object's print function.

In this example, as we encounter BasePlusCommissionEmployee objects, we wish to increase their base salary by 10%. Since we process the employees generically (i.e., polymorphically), we cannot (with the techniques we've learned) be certain as to which type of Employee is being manipulated at any given time. This creates a problem, because BasePlusCommissionEmployee employees must be identified when we encounter them so they can receive the 10% salary increase. To accomplish this, we use operator **dynamic_cast** (line 51) to determine whether the type of each object is BasePlusCommissionEmployee. This is the downcast operation we referred to in Section 24.3.3. Lines 50–52 dynamically downcast employees[i] from type Employee * to type BasePlusCommissionEmployee *. If the vector element points to an object that *is a* BasePlusCommissionEmployee object, then that object's address is assigned to commissionPtr; otherwise, 0 is assigned to derived-class pointer derivedPtr.

If the value returned by the dynamic_cast operator in lines 50–52 is not 0, the object is the correct type and the if statement (lines 56–63) performs the special processing required for the BasePlusCommissionEmployee object. Lines 58, 60 and 62 invoke Base-PlusCommissionEmployee functions getBaseSalary and setBaseSalary to retrieve and update the employee's salary.

Line 65 invokes member function earnings on the object to which employees[i] points. Recall that earnings is declared virtual in the base class, so the program invokes the derived-class object's earnings function—another example of dynamic binding.

The for loop at lines 69–76 displays each employee's object type and uses the delete operator to deallocate the dynamic memory to which each vector element points. Operator typeid (line 73) returns a reference to an object of class type_info that contains the information about the type of its operand, including the name of that type. When invoked, type_info member function name (line 73) returns a pointer-based string that contains the type name (e.g., "class BasePlusCommissionEmployee") of the argument passed to typeid. [*Note:* The exact contents of the string returned by type_info member function name may vary by compiler.] To use typeid, the program must include header file <typeinfo> (line 16).

Note that we avoid several compilation errors in this example by downcasting an Employee pointer to a BasePlusCommissionEmployee pointer (lines 50–52). If we remove the dynamic_cast from line 51 and attempt to assign the current Employee pointer directly to BasePlusCommissionEmployee pointer commissionPtr, we will receive a compilation error. C++ does not allow a program to assign a base-class pointer to a derived-class pointer because the *is-a* relationship does not apply—a CommissionEmployee is *not a* BasePlusCommissionEmployee. The *is-a* relationship applies only between the derived class and its base classes, not vice versa.

Similarly, if lines 58, 60 and 62 used the current base-class pointer from employees, rather than derived-class pointer commissionPtr, to invoke derived-class-only functions getBaseSalary and setBaseSalary, we would receive a compilation error at each of these lines. As you learned in Section 24.3.3, attempting to invoke derived-class-only functions through a base-class pointer is not allowed. Although lines 58, 60 and 62 execute only if commissionPtr is not 0 (i.e., if the cast can be performed), we cannot attempt to invoke derived class BasePlusCommissionEmployee functions getBaseSalary and setBaseSalary on the base class Employee pointer. Recall that, using a base-class Employee pointer, we can invoke only functions found in base class Employee—earnings, print and Employee's *get* and *set* functions.

24.9 Virtual Destructors

A problem can occur when using polymorphism to process dynamically allocated objects of a class hierarchy. So far you have seen nonvirtual destructors—destructors that are not declared with keyword virtual. If a derived-class object with a nonvirtual destructor is destroyed explicitly by applying the delete operator to a base-class pointer to the object, the C++ standard specifies that the behavior is undefined.

The simple solution to this problem is to create a virtual destructor (i.e., a destructor that is declared with keyword virtual) in the base class. This makes all derived-class destructors virtual *even though they do not have the same name as the base-class destructor.* Now, if an object in the hierarchy is destroyed explicitly by applying the delete operator to a base-class pointer, the destructor for the appropriate class is called based on the object to which the base-class pointer points. Remember, when a derived-class object is destroyed, the base-class part of the derived-class object is also destroyed, so it is important for the destructors of both the derived class and base class to execute. The base-class destructor automatically executes after the derived-class destructor.

Good Programming Practice 24.2

If a class has virtual *functions, provide a* virtual *destructor, even if one is not required for the class. Classes derived from this class may contain destructors that must be called properly.*

Common Programming Error 24.5

Constructors cannot be virtual. *Declaring a constructor* virtual *is a compilation error.*

24.10 Wrap-Up

In this chapter we discussed polymorphism, which enables us to "program in the general" rather than "program in the specific," and we showed how this makes programs more extensible. We began with an example of how polymorphism would allow a screen manager to display several "space" objects. We then demonstrated how base-class and derived-class pointers can be aimed at base-class and derived-class objects. We said that aiming base-class pointers at base-class objects is natural, as is aiming derived-class pointers at derived-class objects. Aiming base-class pointers at derived-class objects is also natural because a derived-class object *is an* object of its base class. You learned why aiming derived-class pointers at base-class objects is dangerous and why the compiler disallows such assignments. We introduced virtual functions, which enable the proper functions to be called when objects at various levels of an inheritance hierarchy are referenced (at execution time) via base-class pointers. This is known as dynamic or late binding. We then discussed pure virtual functions (virtual functions that do not provide an implementation) and abstract classes (classes with one or more pure virtual functions). You learned that abstract classes cannot be used to instantiate objects, while concrete classes can. We then demonstrated using abstract classes in an inheritance hierarchy. You learned how polymorphism works "under the hood" with *vtables* that are created by the compiler. We discussed downcasting base-class pointers to derived-class pointers to enable a program to call derived-class-only member functions. The chapter concluded with a discussion of virtual destructors, and how they ensure that all appropriate destructors in an inheritance hierarchy run on a derived-class object when that object is deleted via a base-class pointer.

In the next chapter, we discuss templates, a sophisticated feature of C++ that enables programmers to define a family of related classes or functions with a single code segment.

Summary

Section 24.1 Introduction

- With virtual functions and polymorphism, it becomes possible to design and implement systems that are more easily extensible. Programs can be written to process objects of types that may not exist when the program is under development.
- Polymorphic programming with virtual functions can eliminate the need for switch logic. The programmer can use the virtual function mechanism to perform the equivalent logic automatically, thus avoiding the kinds of errors typically associated with switch logic.

- Derived classes can provide their own implementations of a base-class virtual function if necessary, but if they do not, the base class's implementation is used.

Section 24.3 Relationships Among Objects in an Inheritance Hierarchy

- If a virtual function is called by referencing a specific object by name and using the dot member-selection operator, the reference is resolved at compile time (this is called static binding); the virtual function that is called is the one defined for the class of that particular object.

Section 24.5 Abstract Classes and Pure virtual Functions

- In many situations it is useful to define abstract classes for which the programmer never intends to create objects. Because these are used only as base classes, we refer to them as abstract base classes. No objects of an abstract class may be instantiated.

- Classes from which objects can be instantiated are called concrete classes.

- A class is made abstract by declaring one or more of its virtual functions to be pure. A pure virtual function is one with a pure specifier (= 0) in its declaration.

- If a class is derived from a class with a pure virtual function and that derived class does not supply a definition for that pure virtual function, then that virtual function remains pure in the derived class. Consequently, the derived class is also an abstract class.

- C++ enables polymorphism—the ability for objects of different classes related by inheritance to respond differently to the same member-function call.

- Polymorphism is implemented via virtual functions and dynamic binding.

- When a request is made through a base-class pointer or reference to use a virtual function, C++ chooses the correct overridden function in the appropriate derived class associated with the object.

- Through the use of virtual functions and polymorphism, a member-function call can cause different actions, depending on the type of the object receiving the call.

- Although we cannot instantiate objects of abstract base classes, we can declare pointers and references to objects of abstract base classes. Such pointers and references can be used to enable polymorphic manipulations of derived-class objects instantiated from concrete derived classes.

Section 24.7 (Optional) Polymorphism, Virtual Functions and Dynamic Binding "Under the Hood"

- Dynamic binding requires that at runtime, the call to a virtual member function be routed to the virtual function version appropriate for the class. A virtual function table called the *vtable* is implemented as an array containing function pointers. Each class with virtual functions has a *vtable*. For each virtual function in the class, the *vtable* has an entry containing a function pointer to the version of the virtual function to use for an object of that class. The virtual function to use for a particular class could be the function defined in that class, or it could be a function inherited either directly or indirectly from a base class higher in the hierarchy.

- When a base class provides a virtual member function, derived classes can override the virtual function, but they do not have to override it. Thus, a derived class can use a base class's version of a virtual function.

- Each object of a class with virtual functions contains a pointer to the *vtable* for that class. When a function call is made from a base-class pointer to a derived-class object, the appropriate function pointer in the *vtable* is obtained and dereferenced to complete the call at execution time. This *vtable* lookup and pointer dereferencing require nominal runtime overhead.

- Any class that has one or more 0 pointers in its *vtable* is an abstract class. Classes without any 0 *vtable* pointers are concrete classes.

- New kinds of classes are regularly added to systems. New classes are accommodated by dynamic binding (also called late binding). The type of an object need not be known at compile time for a virtual-function call to be compiled. At runtime, the appropriate member function will be called for the object to which the pointer points.

Section 24.8 Case Study: Payroll System Using Polymorphism and Runtime Type Information with Downcasting, `dynamic_cast`, `typeid` and `type_info`

- Operator `dynamic_cast` checks the type of the object to which the pointer points, then determines whether this type has an *is-a* relationship with the type to which the pointer is being converted. If there is an *is-a* relationship, `dynamic_cast` returns the object's address. If not, `dynamic_cast` returns 0.
- Operator `typeid` returns a reference to an object of class `type_info` that contains information about the type of its operand, including the name of the type. To use `typeid`, the program must include header file `<typeinfo>`.
- When invoked, `type_info` member function `name` returns a pointer-based string that contains the name of the type that the `type_info` object represents.
- Operators `dynamic_cast` and `typeid` are part of C++'s runtime type information (RTTI) feature, which allows a program to determine an object's type at runtime.

Section 24.9 Virtual Destructors

- Declare the base-class destructor `virtual` if the class contains `virtual` functions. This makes all derived-class destructors virtual, even though they do not have the same name as the base-class destructor. If an object in the hierarchy is destroyed explicitly by applying the `delete` operator to a base-class pointer to a derived-class object, the destructor for the appropriate class is called. After a derived-class destructor runs, the destructors for all of that class's base classes run all the way up the hierarchy—the root class's destructor runs last.

Terminology

abstract class
base-class pointer to a base-class object
base-class pointer to a derived-class object
concrete class
dangerous pointer manipulation
derived-class pointer to a base-class object
derived-class pointer to a derived-class object
displacement
downcasting
dynamic binding
dynamic casting
`dynamic_cast`
dynamically determine function to execute
flow of control of a `virtual` function call
implementation inheritance
interface inheritance
iterator class
late binding
name function of class `type_info`
nonvirtual destructor
object's *vtable* pointer

offset into a *vtable*
override a function
polymorphic programming
polymorphism
polymorphism as an alternative to `switch` logic
programming in the general
programming in the specific
pure specifier
pure `virtual` function
RTTI (runtime type information)
static binding
`switch` logic
`type_info` class
`typeid` operator
`<typeinfo>` header file
`virtual` destructor
`virtual` function
`virtual` function table (*vtable*)
`virtual` keyword
vtable
vtable pointer

Self-Review Exercises

24.1   Fill in the blanks in each of the following statements:

a) Treating a base-class object as a(n) _____ can cause errors.

b) Polymorphism helps eliminate _____ logic.

c) If a class contains at least one pure virtual function, it is a(n) _____ class.

d) Classes from which objects can be instantiated are called _____ classes.

e) Operator _____ can be used to downcast base-class pointers safely.

f) Operator typeid returns a reference to a(n) _____ object.

g) _____ involves using a base-class pointer or reference to invoke virtual functions on base-class and derived-class objects.

h) Overridable functions are declared using keyword _____.

i) Casting a base-class pointer to a derived-class pointer is called _____.

24.2   State whether each of the following is *true* or *false*. If *false*, explain why.

a) All virtual functions in an abstract base class must be declared as pure virtual functions.

b) Referring to a derived-class object with a base-class handle is dangerous.

c) A class is made abstract by declaring that class virtual.

d) If a base class declares a pure virtual function, a derived class must implement that function to become a concrete class.

e) Polymorphic programming can eliminate the need for switch logic.

Answers to Self-Review Exercises

24.1   a) derived-class object. b) switch. c) abstract. d) concrete. e) dynamic_cast. f) type_info. g) Polymorphism. h) virtual. i) downcasting.

24.2   a) False. An abstract base class can include virtual functions with implementations. b) False. Referring to a base-class object with a derived-class handle is dangerous. c) False. Classes are never declared virtual. Rather, a class is made abstract by including at least one pure virtual function in the class. d) True. e) True.

Exercises

24.3   How is it that polymorphism enables you to program "in the general" rather than "in the specific"? Discuss the key advantages of programming "in the general."

24.4   Discuss the problems of programming with switch logic. Explain why polymorphism can be an effective alternative to using switch logic.

24.5   Distinguish between inheriting interface and inheriting implementation. How do inheritance hierarchies designed for inheriting interface differ from those designed for inheriting implementation?

24.6   What are virtual functions? Describe a circumstance in which virtual functions would be appropriate.

24.7   Distinguish between static binding and dynamic binding. Explain the use of virtual functions and the *vtable* in dynamic binding.

24.8   Distinguish between virtual functions and pure virtual functions.

24.9   Suggest one or more levels of abstract base classes for the Shape hierarchy discussed in this chapter and shown in Fig. 23.3. (The first level is Shape, and the second level consists of the classes TwoDimensionalShape and ThreeDimensionalShape.)

24.10 How does polymorphism promote extensibility?

24.11 You have been asked to develop a flight simulator that will have elaborate graphical outputs. Explain why polymorphic programming would be especially effective for a problem of this nature.

24.12 *(Payroll System Modification)* Modify the payroll system of Figs. 24.13–24.23 to include private data member birthDate in class Employee. Use class Date from Figs. 21.10–21.11 to represent an employee's birthday. Assume that payroll is processed once per month. Create a vector of Employee references to store the various employee objects. In a loop, calculate the payroll for each Employee (polymorphically), and add a $100.00 bonus to the person's payroll amount if the current month is the month in which the Employee's birthday occurs.

24.13 *(Shape Hierarchy)* Implement the Shape hierarchy designed in Exercise 23.7 (which is based on the hierarchy in Fig. 23.3). Each TwoDimensionalShape should contain function getArea to calculate the area of the two-dimensional shape. Each ThreeDimensionalShape should have member functions getArea and getVolume to calculate the surface area and volume of the three-dimensional shape, respectively. Create a program that uses a vector of Shape pointers to objects of each concrete class in the hierarchy. The program should print the object to which each vector element points. Also, in the loop that processes all the shapes in the vector, determine whether each shape is a TwoDimensionalShape or a ThreeDimensionalShape. If a shape is a TwoDimensionalShape, display its area. If a shape is a ThreeDimensionalShape, display its area and volume.

24.14 *(Polymorphic Screen Manager Using Shape Hierarchy)* Develop a basic graphics package. Use the Shape hierarchy implemented in Exercise 24.13. Limit yourself to two-dimensional shapes such as squares, rectangles, triangles and circles. Interact with the user. Let the user specify the position, size, shape and fill characters to be used in drawing each shape. The user can specify more than one of the same shape. As you create each shape, place a Shape * pointer to each new Shape object into an array. Each Shape class should now have its own draw member function. Write a polymorphic screen manager that walks through the array, sending draw messages to each object in the array to form a screen image. Redraw the screen image each time the user specifies an additional shape.

24.15 *(Package Inheritance Hierarchy)* Use the Package inheritance hierarchy created in Exercise 23.9 to create a program that displays the address information and calculates the shipping costs for several Packages. The program should contain a vector of Package pointers to objects of classes TwoDayPackage and OvernightPackage. Loop through the vector to process the Packages polymorphically. For each Package, invoke *get* functions to obtain the address information of the sender and the recipient, then print the two addresses as they would appear on mailing labels. Also, call each Package's calculateCost member function and print the result. Keep track of the total shipping cost for all Packages in the vector, and display this total when the loop terminates.

24.16 *(Polymorphic Banking Program Using Account Hierarchy)* Develop a polymorphic banking program using the Account hierarchy created in Exercise 23.10. Create a vector of Account pointers to SavingsAccount and CheckingAccount objects. For each Account in the vector, allow the user to specify an amount of money to withdraw from the Account using member function debit and an amount of money to deposit into the Account using member function credit. As you process each Account, determine its type. If an Account is a SavingsAccount, calculate the amount of interest owed to the Account using member function calculateInterest, then add the interest to the account balance using member function credit. After processing an Account, print the updated account balance obtained by invoking base-class member function getBalance.

25

Templates

OBJECTIVES

In this chapter you will learn:

- To use function templates to conveniently create a group of related (overloaded) functions.

- To distinguish between function templates and function-template specializations.

- To use class templates to create a group of related types.

- To distinguish between class templates and class-template specializations.

- To overload function templates.

- To understand the relationships among templates, friends, inheritance and static members.

Behind that outside pattern
the dim shapes get clearer
every day.
It is always the same shape,
only very numerous.
—Charlotte Perkins Gilman

Every man of genius sees the
world at a different angle
from his fellows.
—Havelock Ellis

...our special individuality,
as distinguished from our
generic humanity.
—Oliver Wendell Holmes, Sr

—

25.1 Introduction

In this chapter, we discuss one of C++'s more powerful software reuse features, namely templates. Function templates and class templates enable programmers to specify, with a single code segment, an entire range of related (overloaded) functions—called function-template specializations—or an entire range of related classes—called class-template specializations. This technique is called generic programming.

We might write a single function template for an array-sort function, then have C++ generate separate function-template specializations that will sort `int` arrays, `float` arrays, `string` arrays and so on. We introduced function templates in Chapter 18. We present an additional discussion and example in this chapter.

We might write a single class template for a stack class, then have C++ generate separate class-template specializations, such as a stack-of-`int` class, a stack-of-`float` class, a stack-of-`string` class and so on.

Note the distinction between templates and template specializations: Function templates and class templates are like stencils out of which we trace shapes; function-template specializations and class-template specializations are like the separate tracings that all have the same shape, but could, for example, be drawn in different colors.

In this chapter, we present a function template and a class template. We also consider the relationships between templates and other C++ features, such as overloading, inheritance, friends and `static` members. The design and details of the template mechanisms discussed here are based on the work of Bjarne Stroustrup as presented in his paper, *Parameterized Types for C++*, and as published in the *Proceedings of the USENIX C++ Conference* held in Denver, Colorado, in October 1988.

This chapter introduces templates. Chapter 23, Standard Template Library (STL), in our book *C++ How to Program, 5/e*, presents an in-depth treatment of the template container classes, iterators and algorithms of the STL.

Software Engineering Observation 25.1

Most C++ compilers require the complete definition of a template to appear in the client source-code file that uses the template. For this reason and for reusability, templates are often defined in header files, which are then #included into the appropriate client source-code files. For class templates, this means that the member functions are also defined in the header file.

25.2 Function Templates

Overloaded functions normally perform *similar* or *identical* operations on different types of data. If the operations are *identical* for each type, they can be expressed more compactly and conveniently using function templates. Initially, the programmer writes a single function-template definition. Based on the argument types provided explicitly or inferred from calls to this function, the compiler generates separate object-code functions (i.e., function-template specializations) to handle each function call appropriately. In C, this task can be performed using **macros** created with the preprocessor directive `#define`. However, macros can have serious side effects and do not enable the compiler to perform type checking. Function templates provide a compact solution, like macros, but enable full type checking.

Error-Prevention Tip 25.1

Function templates, like macros, enable software reuse. Unlike macros, function templates help eliminate many types of errors through the scrutiny of full C++ type checking.

All function-template definitions begin with keyword **template** followed by a list of **template parameters** to the function template enclosed in **angle brackets** (`<` and `>`); each template parameter that represents a type must be preceded by either of the interchangeable keywords `class` or `typename`, as in

```
template< typename T >
```

or

```
template< class ElementType >
```

or

```
template< typename BorderType, typename FillType >
```

The type template parameters of a function-template definition are used to specify the types of the arguments to the function, to specify the return type of the function and to declare variables within the function. The function definition follows and appears like any other function definition. Note that keywords `typename` and `class` used to specify function-template parameters actually mean "any built-in type or user-defined type."

Common Programming Error 25.1

Not placing keyword `class` or keyword `typename` before each type template parameter of a function template is a syntax error.

Example: Function Template `printArray`

Let us examine function template `printArray` in Fig. 25.1, lines 8–15. Function template `printArray` declares (line 8) a single template parameter `T` (`T` can be any valid identifier) for the type of the array to be printed by function `printArray`; `T` is referred to as a type template parameter, or type parameter. You will see nontype template parameters in Section 25.5.

When the compiler detects a `printArray` function invocation in the client program (e.g., lines 30, 35 and 40), the compiler uses its overload resolution capabilities to find a definition of function `printArray` that best matches the function call. In this case, the only

printArray function with the appropriate number of parameters is the printArray function template (lines 8–15). Consider the function call at line 30. The compiler compares the type of printArray's first argument (int * at line 30) to the printArray function template's first parameter (const T * at line 9) and deduces that replacing the type parameter T with int would make the argument match the parameter. Then, the compiler substitutes int for T throughout the template definition and compiles a printArray specialization that can display an array of int values. In Fig. 25.1, the compiler creates three printArray specializations—one that expects an int array, one that expects a double array and one that expects a char array. For example, the function-template specialization for type int is

```
void printArray( const int *array, int count )
{
    for ( int i = 0; i < count; i++ )
        cout << array[ i ] << " ";

    cout << endl;
} // end function printArray
```

The name of a template parameter can be declared only once in the template parameter list of a template header but can be used repeatedly in the function's header and body. Template parameter names among function templates need not be unique.

```
1   // Fig. 25.1: fig25_01.cpp
2   // Using template functions.
3   #include <iostream>
4   using std::cout;
5   using std::endl;
6
7   // function template printArray definition
8   template< typename T >
9   void printArray( const T *array, int count )
10  {
11      for ( int i = 0; i < count; i++ )
12          cout << array[ i ] << " ";
13
14      cout << endl;
15  } // end function template printArray
16
17  int main()
18  {
19      const int ACOUNT = 5; // size of array a
20      const int BCOUNT = 7; // size of array b
21      const int CCOUNT = 6; // size of array c
22
23      int a[ ACOUNT ] = { 1, 2, 3, 4, 5 };
24      double b[ BCOUNT ] = { 1.1, 2.2, 3.3, 4.4, 5.5, 6.6, 7.7 };
25      char c[ CCOUNT ] = "HELLO"; // 6th position for null
26
27      cout << "Array a contains:" << endl;
28
```

Fig. 25.1 | Function-template specializations of function template printArray. (Part 1 of 2.)

```
29        // call integer function-template specialization
30        printArray( a, ACOUNT );
31
32        cout << "Array b contains:" << endl;
33
34        // call double function-template specialization
35        printArray( b, BCOUNT );
36
37        cout << "Array c contains:" << endl;
38
39        // call character function-template specialization
40        printArray( c, CCOUNT );
41        return 0;
42     } // end main
```

```
Array a contains:
1 2 3 4 5
Array b contains:
1.1 2.2 3.3 4.4 5.5 6.6 7.7
Array c contains:
H E L L O
```

Fig. 25.1 | Function-template specializations of function template `printArray`. (Part 2 of 2.)

Figure 25.1 demonstrates function template `printArray` (lines 8–15). The program begins by declaring five-element `int` array a, seven-element `double` array b and six-element `char` array c (lines 23–25, respectively). Then, the program outputs each array by calling `printArray`—once with a first argument a of type `int *` (line 30), once with a first argument b of type `double *` (line 35) and once with a first argument c of type `char *` (line 40). The call in line 30, for example, causes the compiler to infer that T is `int` and to instantiate a `printArray` function-template specialization, for which type parameter T is `int`. The call in line 35 causes the compiler to infer that T is `double` and to instantiate a second `printArray` function-template specialization, for which type parameter T is `double`. The call in line 40 causes the compiler to infer that T is `char` and to instantiate a third `printArray` function-template specialization, for which type parameter T is `char`. It is important to note that if T (line 8) represents a user-defined type (which it does not in Fig. 25.1), there must be an overloaded stream insertion operator for that type; otherwise, the first stream insertion operator in line 12 will not compile.

 Common Programming Error 25.2

If a template is invoked with a user-defined type, and if that template uses functions or operators (e.g., ==, +, <=) with objects of that class type, then those functions and operators must be overloaded for the user-defined type. Forgetting to overload such operators causes compilation errors.

In this example, the template mechanism saves the programmer from having to write three separate overloaded functions with prototypes

```
void printArray( const int *, int );
void printArray( const double *, int );
void printArray( const char *, int );
```

that all use the same code, except for type T (as used in line 9).

Performance Tip 25.1

Although templates offer software-reusability benefits, remember that multiple function-template specializations and class-template specializations are instantiated in a program (at compile time), despite the fact that the template is written only once. These copies can consume considerable memory. This is not normally an issue, though, because the code generated by the template is the same size as the code the programmer would have written to produce the separate overloaded functions.

25.3 Overloading Function Templates

Function templates and overloading are intimately related. The function-template specializations generated from a function template all have the same name, so the compiler uses overloading resolution to invoke the proper function.

A function template may be overloaded in several ways. We can provide other function templates that specify the same function name but different function parameters. For example, function template `printArray` of Fig. 25.1 could be overloaded with another `printArray` function template with additional parameters `lowSubscript` and `highSubscript` to specify the portion of the array to output (see Exercise 25.4).

A function template also can be overloaded by providing nontemplate functions with the same function name but different function arguments. For example, function template `printArray` of Fig. 25.1 could be overloaded with a nontemplate version that specifically prints an array of character strings in neat, tabular format (see Exercise 25.5).

The compiler performs a matching process to determine what function to call when a function is invoked. First, the compiler finds all function templates that match the function named in the function call and creates specializations based on the arguments in the function call. Then, the compiler finds all the ordinary functions that match the function named in the function call. If one of the ordinary functions or function-template specializations is the best match for the function call, that ordinary function or specialization is used. If an ordinary function and a specialization are equally good matches for the function call, then the ordinary function is used. Otherwise, if there are multiple matches for the function call, the compiler considers the call to be ambiguous and the compiler generates an error message.

Common Programming Error 25.3

If no matching function definition can be found for a particular function call, or if there are multiple matches, the compiler generates an error.

25.4 Class Templates

It is possible to understand the concept of a "stack" (a data structure into which we insert items at the top and retrieve those items in last-in, first-out order) independent of the type of the items being placed in the stack. However, to instantiate a stack, a data type must be specified. This creates a wonderful opportunity for software reusability. We need the means for describing the notion of a stack generically and instantiating classes that are type-specific versions of this generic stack class. C++ provides this capability through class templates.

Software Engineering Observation 25.2

Class templates encourage software reusability by enabling type-specific versions of generic classes to be instantiated.

Class templates are called **parameterized types**, because they require one or more type parameters to specify how to customize a "generic class" template to form a class-template specialization.

The programmer who wishes to produce a variety of class-template specializations writes only one class-template definition. Each time an additional class-template specialization is needed, the programmer uses a concise, simple notation, and the compiler writes the source code for the specialization the programmer requires. One Stack class template, for example, could thus become the basis for creating many Stack classes (such as "Stack of double," "Stack of int," "Stack of char," "Stack of Employee") used in a program.

Creating Class Template Stack< T >
Note the Stack class-template definition in Fig. 25.2. It looks like a conventional class definition, except that it is preceded by the header (line 6)

```
template< typename T >
```

to specify a class-template definition with type parameter T which acts as a placeholder for the type of the Stack class to be created. The programmer need not specifically use identifier T—any valid identifier can be used. The type of element to be stored on this Stack is mentioned generically as T throughout the Stack class header and member-function definitions. In a moment, we show how T becomes associated with a specific type, such as double or int. Due to the way this class template is designed, there are two constraints for nonfundamental data types used with this Stack—they must have a default constructor (for use in line 44 to create the array that stores the stack elements), and they must support the assignment operator (lines 55 and 69).

The member-function definitions of a class template are function templates. The member-function definitions that appear outside the class template definition each begin with the header

```
template< typename T >
```

(lines 40, 51 and 65). Thus, each definition resembles a conventional function definition, except that the Stack element type always is listed generically as type parameter T. The binary scope resolution operator is used with the class-template name Stack< T > (lines 41, 52 and 66) to tie each member-function definition to the class template's scope. In this case, the generic class name is Stack< T >. When doubleStack is instantiated as type Stack< double >, the Stack constructor function-template specialization uses new to create an array of elements of type double to represent the stack (line 44). The statement

```
stackPtr = new T[ size ];
```

in the Stack class-template definition is generated by the compiler in the class-template specialization Stack< double > as

```
stackPtr = new double[ size ];
```

```cpp
 1   // Fig. 25.2: Stack.h
 2   // Stack class template.
 3   #ifndef STACK_H
 4   #define STACK_H
 5
 6   template< typename T >
 7   class Stack
 8   {
 9   public:
10      Stack( int = 10 ); // default constructor (Stack size 10)
11
12      // destructor
13      ~Stack()
14      {
15         delete [] stackPtr; // deallocate internal space for Stack
16      } // end ~Stack destructor
17
18      bool push( const T& ); // push an element onto the Stack
19      bool pop( T& ); // pop an element off the Stack
20
21      // determine whether Stack is empty
22      bool isEmpty() const
23      {
24         return top == -1;
25      } // end function isEmpty
26
27      // determine whether Stack is full
28      bool isFull() const
29      {
30         return top == size - 1;
31      } // end function isFull
32
33   private:
34      int size; // # of elements in the Stack
35      int top; // location of the top element (-1 means empty)
36      T *stackPtr; // pointer to internal representation of the Stack
37   }; // end class template Stack
38
39   // constructor template
40   template< typename T >
41   Stack< T >::Stack( int s )
42      : size( s > 0 ? s : 10 ), // validate size
43        top( -1 ), // Stack initially empty
44        stackPtr( new T[ size ] ) // allocate memory for elements
45   {
46      // empty body
47   } // end Stack constructor template
48
49   // push element onto Stack;
50   // if successful, return true; otherwise, return false
51   template< typename T >
52   bool Stack< T >::push( const T &pushValue )
53   {
```

Fig. 25.2 | Class template Stack. (Part 1 of 2.)

```
54      if ( !isFull() )
55      {
56          stackPtr[ ++top ] = pushValue; // place item on Stack
57          return true; // push successful
58      } // end if
59
60      return false; // push unsuccessful
61   } // end function template push
62
63   // pop element off Stack;
64   // if successful, return true; otherwise, return false
65   template< typename T >
66   bool Stack< T >::pop( T &popValue )
67   {
68      if ( !isEmpty() )
69      {
70          popValue = stackPtr[ top-- ]; // remove item from Stack
71          return true; // pop successful
72      } // end if
73
74      return false; // pop unsuccessful
75   } // end function template pop
76
77   #endif
```

Fig. 25.2 | Class template Stack. (Part 2 of 2.)

Creating a Driver to Test Class Template Stack< T >

Now, let us consider the driver (Fig. 25.3) that exercises the Stack class template. The driver begins by instantiating object doubleStack of size 5 (line 11). This object is declared to be of class Stack< double > (pronounced "Stack of double"). The compiler associates type double with type parameter T in the class template to produce the source code for a Stack class of type double. Although templates offer software-reusability benefits, remember that multiple class-template specializations are instantiated in a program (at compile time), even though the template is written only once.

Lines 17–21 invoke push to place the double values 1.1, 2.2, 3.3, 4.4 and 5.5 onto doubleStack. The while loop terminates when the driver attempts to push a sixth value onto doubleStack (which is full, because it holds a maximum of five elements). Note that function push returns false when it is unable to push a value onto the stack.[1]

Lines 27–28 invoke pop in a while loop to remove the five values from the stack (note, in Fig. 25.3, that the values do pop off in last-in, first-out order). When the driver attempts to pop a sixth value, the doubleStack is empty, so the pop loop terminates.

---

1. Class Stack (Fig. 25.2) provides the function isFull, which the programmer can use to determine whether the stack is full before attempting a push operation. This would avoid the potential error of pushing onto a full stack. In Chapter 27, Exception Handling, if the operation cannot be completed, function push would "throw an exception." The programmer can write code to "catch" that exception, then decide how to handle it appropriately for the application. The same technique can be used with function pop when an attempt is made to pop an element from an empty stack.

```cpp
 1    // Fig. 25.3: fig25_03.cpp
 2    // Stack class template test program.
 3    #include <iostream>
 4    using std::cout;
 5    using std::endl;
 6
 7    #include "Stack.h" // Stack class template definition
 8
 9    int main()
10    {
11       Stack< double > doubleStack( 5 ); // size 5
12       double doubleValue = 1.1;
13
14       cout << "Pushing elements onto doubleStack\n";
15
16       // push 5 doubles onto doubleStack
17       while ( doubleStack.push( doubleValue ) )
18       {
19          cout << doubleValue << ' ';
20          doubleValue += 1.1;
21       } // end while
22
23       cout << "\nStack is full. Cannot push " << doubleValue
24          << "\n\nPopping elements from doubleStack\n";
25
26       // pop elements from doubleStack
27       while ( doubleStack.pop( doubleValue ) )
28          cout << doubleValue << ' ';
29
30       cout << "\nStack is empty. Cannot pop\n";
31
32       Stack< int > intStack; // default size 10
33       int intValue = 1;
34       cout << "\nPushing elements onto intStack\n";
35
36       // push 10 integers onto intStack
37       while ( intStack.push( intValue ) )
38       {
39          cout << intValue << ' ';
40          intValue++;
41       } // end while
42
43       cout << "\nStack is full. Cannot push " << intValue
44          << "\n\nPopping elements from intStack\n";
45
46       // pop elements from intStack
47       while ( intStack.pop( intValue ) )
48          cout << intValue << ' ';
49
50       cout << "\nStack is empty. Cannot pop" << endl;
51       return 0;
52    } // end main
```

Fig. 25.3 | Class template Stack test program. (Part 1 of 2.)

```
Pushing elements onto doubleStack
1.1 2.2 3.3 4.4 5.5
Stack is full. Cannot push 6.6

Popping elements from doubleStack
5.5 4.4 3.3 2.2 1.1
Stack is empty. Cannot pop

Pushing elements onto intStack
1 2 3 4 5 6 7 8 9 10
Stack is full. Cannot push 11

Popping elements from intStack
10 9 8 7 6 5 4 3 2 1
Stack is empty. Cannot pop
```

Fig. 25.3 | Class template Stack test program. (Part 2 of 2.)

Line 32 instantiates integer stack intStack with the declaration

```
Stack< int > intStack;
```

(pronounced "intStack is a Stack of int"). Because no size is specified, the size defaults to 10 as specified in the default constructor (Fig. 25.2, line 10). Lines 37–41 loop and invoke push to place values onto intStack until it is full, then lines 47–48 loop and invoke pop to remove values from intStack until it is empty. Once again, notice in the output that the values pop off in last-in, first-out order.

Creating Function Templates to Test Class Template Stack< T >

Notice that the code in function main of Fig. 25.3 is almost identical for both the double-Stack manipulations in lines 11–30 and the intStack manipulations in lines 32–50. This presents another opportunity to use a function template. Figure 25.4 defines function template testStack (lines 14–38) to perform the same tasks as main in Fig. 25.3—push a series of values onto a Stack< T > and pop the values off a Stack< T >. Function template testStack uses template parameter T (specified at line 14) to represent the data type stored in the Stack< T >. The function template takes four arguments (lines 16–19)—a reference

```
 1   // Fig. 25.4: fig25_04.cpp
 2   // Stack class template test program. Function main uses a
 3   // function template to manipulate objects of type Stack< T >.
 4   #include <iostream>
 5   using std::cout;
 6   using std::endl;
 7
 8   #include <string>
 9   using std::string;
10
11   #include "Stack.h" // Stack class template definition
12
```

Fig. 25.4 | Passing a Stack template object to a function template. (Part 1 of 2.)

```
13  // function template to manipulate Stack< T >
14  template< typename T >
15  void testStack(
16     Stack< T > &theStack, // reference to Stack< T >
17     T value, // initial value to push
18     T increment, // increment for subsequent values
19     const string stackName ) // name of the Stack< T > object
20  {
21     cout << "\nPushing elements onto " << stackName << '\n';
22
23     // push element onto Stack
24     while ( theStack.push( value ) )
25     {
26        cout << value << ' ';
27        value += increment;
28     } // end while
29
30     cout << "\nStack is full. Cannot push " << value
31        << "\n\nPopping elements from " << stackName << '\n';
32
33     // pop elements from Stack
34     while ( theStack.pop( value ) )
35        cout << value << ' ';
36
37     cout << "\nStack is empty. Cannot pop" << endl;
38  } // end function template testStack
39
40  int main()
41  {
42     Stack< double > doubleStack( 5 ); // size 5
43     Stack< int > intStack; // default size 10
44
45     testStack( doubleStack, 1.1, 1.1, "doubleStack" );
46     testStack( intStack, 1, 1, "intStack" );
47
48     return 0;
49  } // end main
```

```
Pushing elements onto doubleStack
1.1 2.2 3.3 4.4 5.5
Stack is full. Cannot push 6.6

Popping elements from doubleStack
5.5 4.4 3.3 2.2 1.1
Stack is empty. Cannot pop

Pushing elements onto intStack
1 2 3 4 5 6 7 8 9 10
Stack is full. Cannot push 11

Popping elements from intStack
10 9 8 7 6 5 4 3 2 1
Stack is empty. Cannot pop
```

Fig. 25.4 | Passing a Stack template object to a function template. (Part 2 of 2.)

to an object of type Stack< T >, a value of type T that will be the first value pushed onto the Stack< T >, a value of type T used to increment the values pushed onto the Stack< T > and a string that represents the name of the Stack< T > object for output purposes. Function main (lines 40–49) instantiates an object of type Stack< double > called doubleStack (line 42) and an object of type Stack< int > called intStack (line 43) and uses these objects in lines 45 and 46. The testStack function calls each result in a testStack function-template specialization. The compiler infers the type of T for testStack from the type used to instantiate the function's first argument (i.e., the type used to instantiate double-Stack or intStack). The output of Fig. 25.4 precisely matches the output of Fig. 25.3.

25.5 Nontype Parameters and Default Types for Class Templates

Class template Stack of Section 25.4 used only a type parameter in the template header (line 6). It is also possible to use nontype template parameters or nontype parameters, which can have default arguments and are treated as consts. For example, the template header could be modified to take an int elements parameter as follows:

```
template< typename T, int elements > // nontype parameter elements
```

Then, a declaration such as

```
Stack< double, 100 > mostRecentSalesFigures;
```

could be used to instantiate (at compile time) a 100-element Stack class-template specialization of double values named mostRecentSalesFigures; this class-template specialization would be of type Stack< double, 100 >. The class header then might contain a private data member with an array declaration such as

```
T stackHolder[ elements ]; // array to hold Stack contents
```

In addition, a type parameter can specify a default type. For example,

```
template< typename T = string > // defaults to type string
```

might specify that a Stack contains string objects by default. Then, a declaration such as

```
Stack<> jobDescriptions;
```

could be used to instantiate a Stack class-template specialization of strings named job-Descriptions; this class-template specialization would be of type Stack< string >. Default type parameters must be the rightmost (trailing) parameters in a template's type-parameter list. When one is instantiating a class with two or more default types, if an omitted type is not the rightmost type parameter in the type-parameter list, then all type parameters to the right of that type also must be omitted.

 Performance Tip 25.2

When appropriate, specify the size of a container class (such as an array class or a stack class) at compile time (possibly through a nontype template parameter). This eliminates the execution-time overhead of using new to create the space dynamically.

> **Software Engineering Observation 25.3**
>
> *Specifying the size of a container at compile time avoids the potentially fatal execution-time error if* new *is unable to obtain the needed memory.*

In the exercises, you will be asked to use a nontype parameter to create a template for our class `Array` developed in Chapter 22. This template will enable `Array` objects to be instantiated with a specified number of elements of a specified type at compile time, rather than creating space for the `Array` objects at execution time.

In some cases, it may not be possible to use a particular type with a class template. For example, the `Stack` template of Fig. 25.2 requires that user-defined types that will be stored in a `Stack` must provide a default constructor and an assignment operator. If a particular user-defined type will not work with our `Stack` template or requires customized processing, you can define an explicit specialization of the class template for a particular type. Let's assume we want to create an explicit specialization `Stack` for `Employee` objects. To do this, form a new class with the name `Stack< Employee >` as follows:

```
template<>
class Stack< Employee >
{
    // body of class definition
};
```

Note that the `Stack< Employee >` explicit specialization is a complete replacement for the `Stack` class template that is specific to type `Employee`—it does not use anything from the original class template and can even have different members.

25.6 Notes on Templates and Inheritance

Templates and inheritance relate in several ways:

- A class template can be derived from a class-template specialization.
- A class template can be derived from a nontemplate class.
- A class-template specialization can be derived from a class-template specialization.
- A nontemplate class can be derived from a class-template specialization.

25.7 Notes on Templates and Friends

We have seen that functions and entire classes can be declared as `friends` of nontemplate classes. With class templates, friendship can be established between a class template and a global function, a member function of another class (possibly a class-template specialization), or even an entire class (possibly a class-template specialization).

Throughout this section, we assume that we have defined a class template for a class named X with a single type parameter T, as in:

```
template< typename T > class X
```

Under this assumption, it is possible to make a function `f1` a friend of every class-template specialization instantiated from the class template for class X. To do so, use a friendship declaration of the form

```
friend void f1();
```

For example, function f1 is a friend of X< double >, X< string >, X< Employee >, and so on.

It is also possible to make a function f2 a friend only of a class-template specialization with the same type argument. To do so, use a friendship declaration of the form

```
friend void f2( X< T > & );
```

For example, if T is a float, function f2(X< float > &) is a friend of class-template specialization X< float > but not a friend of class-template specification X< string >.

You can declare that a member function of another class is a friend of any class-template specialization generated from the class template. To do so, the friend declaration must qualify the name of the other class's member function using the class name and the binary scope resolution operator, as in:

```
friend void A::f3();
```

The declaration makes member function f3 of class A a friend of every class-template specialization instantiated from the preceding class template. For example, function f3 of class A is a friend of X< double >, X< string > and X< Employee >, and so on.

As with a global function, another class's member function can be a friend only of a class-template specialization with the same type argument. A friendship declaration of the form

```
friend void C< T >::f4( X< T > & );
```

for a particular type T such as float makes member function

```
C< float >::f4( X< float > & )
```

a friend function *only* of class-template specialization X< float >.

In some cases, it is desirable to make an entire class's set of member functions friends of a class template. In this case, a friend declaration of the form

```
friend class Y;
```

makes every member function of class Y a friend of every class-template specialization produced from the class template X.

Finally, it is possible to make all member functions of one class-template specialization friends of another class-template specialization with the same type argument. For example, a friend declaration of the form:

```
friend class Z< T >;
```

indicates that when a class-template specialization is instantiated with a particular type for T (such as float), all members of class Z< float > become friends of class-template specialization X< float >.

25.8 Notes on Templates and static Members

What about static data members? Recall that, with a nontemplate class, one copy of each static data member is shared among all objects of the class, and the static data member must be initialized at file scope.

Each class-template specialization instantiated from a class template has its own copy of each `static` data member of the class template; all objects of that specialization share that one `static` data member. In addition, as with `static` data members of nontemplate classes, `static` data members of class-template specializations must be defined and, if necessary, initialized at file scope. Each class-template specialization gets its own copy of the class template's `static` member functions.

25.9 Wrap-Up

This chapter introduced one of C++'s most powerful features—templates. You learned how to use function templates to enable the compiler to produce a set of function-template specializations that represent a group of related overloaded functions. We also discussed how to overload a function template to create a specialized version of a function that handles a particular data type's processing in a manner that differs from the other function-template specializations. Next, you learned about class templates and class-template specializations. You saw examples of how to use a class template to create a group of related types that each perform identical processing on different data types. Finally, you learned about some of the relationships among templates, friends, inheritance and `static` members.

In the next chapter, we discuss many of C++'s I/O capabilities and demonstrate several stream manipulators that perform various formatting tasks.

Summary

Section 25.1 Introduction

- Templates enable us to specify a range of related (overloaded) functions—called function-template specializations—or a range of related classes—called class-template specializations.

Section 25.2 Function Templates

- To use function-template specializations, the programmer writes a single function-template definition. Based on the argument types provided in calls to this function, C++ generates separate specializations to handle each type of call appropriately. These are compiled along with the rest of a program's source code.

- All function-template definitions begin with the keyword `template` followed by template parameters to the function template enclosed in angle brackets (`<` and `>`); each template parameter that represents a type must be preceded by keyword `class` or `typename`. Keywords `typename` and `class` used to specify function-template parameters mean "any built-in type or user-defined type."

- Template-definition template parameters are used to specify the kinds of arguments to the function and the return type of the function and to declare variables in the function.

- The name of a template parameter can be declared only once in the type-parameter list of a template header. Formal type-parameter names among function templates need not be unique.

Section 25.3 Overloading Function Templates

- A function template may be overloaded in several ways. We can provide other function templates that specify the same function name but different function parameters. A function template can also be overloaded by providing other nontemplate functions with the same function name, but different function parameters.

Section 25.4 Class Templates

- Class templates provide the means for describing a class generically and for instantiating classes that are type-specific versions of this generic class.

- Class templates are called parameterized types; they require type parameters to specify how to customize a generic class template to form a specific class-template specialization.

- The programmer who wishes to use class-template specializations writes one class template. When the programmer needs a new type-specific class, the programmer uses a concise notation, and the compiler writes the source code for the class-template specialization.

- A class-template definition looks like a conventional class definition, except that it is preceded by `template< typename T >` (or `template< class T >`) to indicate this is a class-template definition with type parameter T which acts as a placeholder for the type of the class to create. The type T is mentioned throughout the class header and member-function definitions as a generic type name.

- Member-function definitions outside a class template each begin with `template< typename T >` (or `template< class T >`). Then, each function definition resembles a conventional function definition, except that the generic data in the class always is listed generically as type parameter T. The binary scope-resolution operator is used with the class-template name to tie each member function definition to the class template's scope.

Section 25.5 Nontype Parameters and Default Types for Class Templates

- It is possible to use nontype parameters in the header of a class or function template.

- An explicit specialization of a class template can be provided to override a class template for a specific type.

Section 25.6 Notes on Templates and Inheritance

- A class template can be derived from a class-template specialization. A class template can be derived from a nontemplate class. A class-template specialization can be derived from a class-template specialization. A nontemplate class can be derived from a class-template specialization.

Section 25.7 Notes on Templates and Friends

- Functions and entire classes can be declared as friends of nontemplate classes. With class templates, the obvious kinds of friendship arrangements can be declared. Friendship can be established between a class template and a global function, a member function of another class (possibly a class-template specialization) or even an entire class (possibly a class-template specialization).

Section 25.8 Notes on Templates and `static` Members

- Each class-template specialization instantiated from a class template has its own copy of each `static` data member of the class template; all objects of that specialization share that `static` data member. And as with `static` data members of nontemplate classes, `static` data members of class-template specializations must be defined and, if necessary, initialized at file scope.

- Each class-template specialization gets a copy of the class template's `static` member functions.

Terminology

angle brackets (< and >)	function-template definition
class template	function-template specialization
class-template definition	generic programming
class-template specialization	keyword `class` in a template type parameter
explicit specialization	keyword `template`
`friend` of a template	keyword `typename`
function template	macro

member function of a class-template
    specialization
nontype parameter
nontype template parameter
overloading a function template
parameterized type
class-template specialization
`static` data member of a class template
`static` data member of a class-template
    specialization

`static` member function of a class template
`static` member function of a class-template
    specialization
template parameter
`template< class T >`
`template< typename T >`
`typename`
type parameter
type template parameter

Self-Review Exercises

25.1 State which of the following statements are *true* and which are *false*. If a statement is *false*, explain why.

    a) The template parameters of a function-template definition are used to specify the types of the arguments to the function, to specify the return type of the function and to declare variables within the function.

    b) Keywords `typename` and `class` as used with a template type parameter specifically mean "any user-defined class type."

    c) A function template can be overloaded by another function template with the same function name.

    d) Template parameter names among template definitions must be unique.

    e) Each member-function definition outside a class template must begin with a template header.

    f) A `friend` function of a class template must be a function-template specialization.

    g) If several class-template specializations are generated from a single class template with a single `static` data member, each of the class-template specializations shares a single copy of the class template's `static` data member.

25.2 Fill in the blanks in each of the following:

    a) Templates enable us to specify, with a single code segment, an entire range of related functions called _____, or an entire range of related classes called _____.

    b) All function-template definitions begin with the keyword _____, followed by a list of template parameters to the function template enclosed in _____.

    c) The related functions generated from a function template all have the same name, so the compiler uses _____ resolution to invoke the proper function.

    d) Class templates also are called _____ types.

    e) The _____ operator is used with a class-template name to tie each member-function definition to the class template's scope.

    f) As with `static` data members of nontemplate classes, `static` data members of class-template specializations must also be defined and, if necessary, initialized at _____ scope.

Answers to Self-Review Exercises

25.1 a) True. b) False. Keywords `typename` and `class` in this context also allow for a type parameter of a built-in type. c) True. d) False. Template parameter names among function templates need not be unique. e) True. f) False. It could be a nontemplate function. g) False. Each class-template specialization will have its own copy of the `static` data member.

25.2 a) function-template specializations, class-template specializations. b) `template`, angle brackets (`<` and `>`). c) overloading. d) parameterized. e) binary scope resolution. f) file.

Exercises

25.3   Write a function template `selectionSort` based on the sort program of Fig. 16.1. Write a driver program that inputs, sorts and outputs an `int` array and a `float` array.

25.4   Overload function template `printArray` of Fig. 25.1 so that it takes two additional integer arguments, namely `int lowSubscript` and `int highSubscript`. A call to this function will print only the designated portion of the array. Validate `lowSubscript` and `highSubscript`; if either is out of range or if `highSubscript` is less than or equal to `lowSubscript`, the overloaded `printArray` function should return 0; otherwise, `printArray` should return the number of elements printed. Then modify `main` to exercise both versions of `printArray` on arrays a, b and c (lines 23–25 of Fig. 25.1). Be sure to test all capabilities of both versions of `printArray`.

25.5   Overload function template `printArray` of Fig. 25.1 with a nontemplate version that specifically prints an array of character strings in neat, tabular, column format.

25.6   Write a simple function template for predicate function `isEqualTo` that compares its two arguments of the same type with the equality operator (`==`) and returns `true` if they are equal and `false` if they are not equal. Use this function template in a program that calls `isEqualTo` only with a variety of built-in types. Now write a separate version of the program that calls `isEqualTo` with a user-defined class type, but does not overload the equality operator. What happens when you attempt to run this program? Now overload the equality operator (with the operator function) `operator==`. Now what happens when you attempt to run this program?

25.7   Use an `int` template nontype parameter `numberOfElements` and a type parameter `elementType` to help create a template for the `Array` class (Figs. 22.6–22.7) we developed in Chapter 22. This template will enable `Array` objects to be instantiated with a specified number of elements of a specified element type at compile time.

25.8   Write a program with class template `Array`. The template can instantiate an `Array` of any element type. Override the template with a specific definition for an `Array` of `float` elements (`class Array< float >`). The driver should demonstrate the instantiation of an `Array` of `int` through the template and should show that an attempt to instantiate an `Array` of `float` uses the definition provided in `class Array< float >`.

25.9   Distinguish between the terms "function template" and "function-template specialization."

25.10   Which is more like a stencil—a class template or a class-template specialization? Explain your answer.

25.11   What is the relationship between function templates and overloading?

25.12   Why might you choose to use a function template instead of a macro?

25.13   What performance problem can result from using function templates and class templates?

25.14   The compiler performs a matching process to determine which function-template specialization to call when a function is invoked. Under what circumstances does an attempt to make a match result in a compile error?

25.15   Why is it appropriate to refer to a class template as a parameterized type?

25.16   Explain why a C++ program would use the statement

```
Array< Employee > workerList( 100 );
```

25.17   Review your answer to Exercise 25.16. Why might a C++ program use the statement

```
Array< Employee > workerList;
```

25.18 Explain the use of the following notation in a C++ program:

```
template< typename T > Array< T >::Array( int s )
```

25.19 Why might you use a nontype parameter with a class template for a container such as an array or stack?

25.20 Describe how to provide an explicit specialization of a class template.

25.21 Describe the relationship between class templates and inheritance.

25.22 Suppose that a class template has the header

```
template< typename T > class Ct1
```

Describe the friendship relationships established by placing each of the following `friend` declarations inside this class template. Identifiers beginning with "f" are functions, identifiers beginning with "C" are classes, identifiers beginning with "Ct" are class templates and T is a template type parameter (i.e., T can represent any fundamental or class type).

    a) `friend void f1();`
    b) `friend void f2( Ct1< T > & );`
    c) `friend void C2::f3();`
    d) `friend void Ct3< T >::f4( Ct1< T > & );`
    e) `friend class C4;`
    f) `friend class Ct5< T >;`

25.23 Suppose that class template `Employee` has a `static` data member count. Suppose that three class-template specializations are instantiated from the class template. How many copies of the `static` data member will exist? How will the use of each be constrained (if at all)?

26

Stream Input/Output

Consciousness ... does not appear to itself chopped up in bits ... A "river" or a "stream" are the metaphors by which it is most naturally described.
—William James

All the news that's fit to print.
—Adolph S. Ochs

Remove not the landmark on the boundary of the fields.
—Amenehope

OBJECTIVES

In this chapter you will learn:

- To use C++ object-oriented stream input/output.

- To format input and output.

- The stream-I/O class hierarchy.

- To use stream manipulators.

- To control justification and padding.

- To determine the success or failure of input/output operations.

- To tie output streams to input streams.

26.1 Introduction

The C++ standard libraries provide an extensive set of input/output capabilities. This chapter discusses a range of capabilities sufficient for performing most common I/O operations and overviews the remaining capabilities. We discussed some of these features earlier in the text; now we provide a more complete treatment. Many of the I/O features that we will discuss are object oriented. This style of I/O makes use of other C++ features, such as references, function overloading and operator overloading.

C++ uses type-safe I/O. Each I/O operation is executed in a manner sensitive to the data type. If an I/O member function has been defined to handle a particular data type, then that member function is called to handle that data type. If there is no match between the type of the actual data and a function for handling that data type, the compiler generates an error. Thus, improper data cannot "sneak" through the system (as can occur in C, allowing for some subtle and bizarre errors).

Users can specify how to perform I/O for objects of user-defined types by overloading the stream insertion operator (<<) and the stream extraction operator (>>). This extensibility is one of C++'s most valuable features.

Software Engineering Observation 26.1

Use the C++-style I/O exclusively in C++ programs, even though C-style I/O is available to C++ programmers.

Error-Prevention Tip 26.1

C++ I/O is type safe.

Software Engineering Observation 26.2

C++ enables a common treatment of I/O for predefined types and user-defined types. This commonality facilitates software development and reuse.

26.2 Streams

C++ I/O occurs in **streams**, which are sequences of bytes. In input operations, the bytes flow from a device (e.g., a keyboard, a disk drive, a network connection) to main memory. In output operations, bytes flow from main memory to a device (e.g., a display screen, a printer, a disk drive, a network connection).

An application associates meaning with bytes. The bytes could represent characters, raw data, graphics images, digital speech, digital video or any other information an application may require.

The system I/O mechanisms should transfer bytes from devices to memory (and vice versa) consistently and reliably. Such transfers often involve some mechanical motion, such as the rotation of a disk or a tape, or the typing of keystrokes at a keyboard. The time these transfers take is typically much greater than the time the processor requires to manipulate data internally. Thus, I/O operations require careful planning and tuning to ensure optimal performance.

C++ provides both "low-level" and "high-level" I/O capabilities. Low-level I/O capabilities (i.e., **unformatted I/O**) specify that some number of bytes should be transferred device-to-memory or memory-to-device. In such transfers, the individual byte is the item of interest. Such low-level capabilities provide high-speed, high-volume transfers but are not particularly convenient for programmers.

Programmers generally prefer a higher-level view of I/O (i.e., **formatted I/O**), in which bytes are grouped into meaningful units, such as integers, floating-point numbers, characters, strings and user-defined types. These type-oriented capabilities are satisfactory for most I/O other than high-volume file processing.

Performance Tip 26.1

Use unformatted I/O for the best performance in high-volume file processing.

Portability Tip 26.1

Using unformatted I/O can lead to portability problems, because unformatted data is not portable across all platforms.

26.2.1 Classic Streams vs. Standard Streams

In the past, the C++ classic stream libraries enabled input and output of chars. Because a char occupies one byte, it can represent only a limited set of characters (such as those in the ASCII character set). However, many languages use alphabets that contain more characters than a single-byte char can represent. The ASCII character set does not provide these characters; the Unicode character set does. Unicode is an extensive international character set that represents the majority of the world's commercially viable languages, mathematical symbols and much more. For more information on Unicode, visit www.unicode.org.

C++ includes the standard stream libraries, which enable developers to build systems capable of performing I/O operations with Unicode characters. For this purpose, C++ includes an additional character type called wchar_t, which can store Unicode characters. The C++ standard also redesigned the classic C++ stream classes, which processed only chars, as class templates with separate specializations for processing characters of types char and wchar_t, respectively. We use the char type of class templates with separate specializations throughout this book.

26.2.2 iostream Library Header Files

The C++ iostream library provides hundreds of I/O capabilities. Several header files contain portions of the library interface.

Most C++ programs include the <iostream> header file, which declares basic services required for all stream-I/O operations. The <iostream> header file defines the cin, cout, cerr and clog objects, which correspond to the standard input stream, the standard output stream, the unbuffered standard error stream and the buffered standard error stream, respectively. (cerr and clog are discussed in Section 26.2.3.) Both unformatted- and formatted-I/O services are provided.

The <iomanip> header declares services useful for performing formatted I/O with so-called parameterized stream manipulators, such as setw and setprecision. The <fstream> header declares services for user-controlled file processing.

C++ implementations generally contain other I/O-related libraries that provide system-specific capabilities, such as the controlling of special-purpose devices for audio and video I/O.

26.2.3 Stream Input/Output Classes and Objects

The iostream library provides many templates for handling common I/O operations. For example, class template basic_istream supports stream-input operations, class template basic_ostream supports stream-output operations, and class template basic_iostream supports both stream-input and stream-output operations. Each template has a predefined template specialization that enables char I/O. In addition, the iostream library provides a set of typedefs that provide aliases for these template specializations. The **typedef** specifier declares synonyms (aliases) for previously defined data types. Programmers sometimes use typedef to create shorter or more readable type names. For example, the statement

```
typedef Card *CardPtr;
```

defines an additional type name, CardPtr, as a synonym for type Card *. Note that creating a name using typedef does not create a data type; typedef creates only a type name that may be used in the program. The typedef istream represents a specialization of basic_istream that enables char input. Similarly, the typedef ostream represents a specialization of basic_ostream that enables char output. Also, the typedef iostream represents a specialization of basic_iostream that enables both char input and output. We use these typedefs throughout this chapter.

Stream-I/O Template Hierarchy and Operator Overloading

Templates basic_istream and basic_ostream both derive through single inheritance from base template basic_ios.[1] Template basic_iostream derives through multiple inheritance from templates basic_istream and basic_ostream. The UML class diagram of Fig. 26.1 summarizes these inheritance relationships.

Operator overloading provides a convenient notation for performing input/output. The left-shift operator (<<) is overloaded to designate stream output and is referred to as the stream insertion operator. The right-shift operator (>>) is overloaded to designate stream input and is referred to as the stream extraction operator. These operators are used with the standard stream objects cin, cout, cerr and clog and, commonly, with user-defined stream objects.

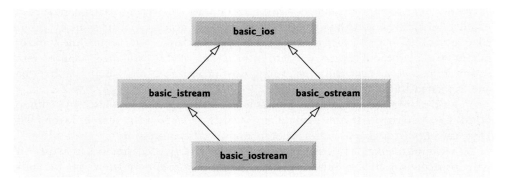

Fig. 26.1 | Stream-I/O template hierarchy portion.

---

1. Technically, templates do not inherit from other templates. However, in this chapter, we discuss templates only in the context of the template specializations that enable char I/O. These specializations are classes and thus can inherit from each other.

Standard Stream Objects c*in,* cout, cerr *and* clog

The predefined object cin is an istream instance and is said to be "connected to" (or attached to) the standard input device, which usually is the keyboard. The stream extraction operator (>>) as used in the following statement causes a value for integer variable grade (assuming that grade has been declared as an int variable) to be input from cin to memory:

```
cin >> grade; // data "flows" in the direction of the arrows
```

Note that the compiler determines the data type of grade and selects the appropriate overloaded stream extraction operator. Assuming that grade has been declared properly, the stream extraction operator does not require additional type information (as is the case, for example, in C-style I/O). The >> operator is overloaded to input data items of built-in types, strings and pointer values.

The predefined object cout is an ostream instance and is said to be "connected to" the standard output device, which usually is the display screen. The stream insertion operator (<<), as used in the following statement, causes the value of variable grade to be output from memory to the standard output device:

```
cout << grade; // data "flows" in the direction of the arrows
```

Note that the compiler also determines the data type of grade (assuming grade has been declared properly) and selects the appropriate stream insertion operator, so the stream insertion operator does not require additional type information. The << operator is overloaded to output data items of built-in types, strings and pointer values.

The predefined object cerr is an ostream instance and is said to be "connected to" the standard error device. Outputs to object cerr are unbuffered, implying that each stream insertion to cerr causes its output to appear immediately—this is appropriate for notifying a user promptly about errors.

The predefined object clog is an instance of the ostream class and is said to be "connected to" the standard error device. Outputs to clog are buffered. This means that each insertion to clog could cause its output to be held in a buffer until the buffer is filled or until the buffer is flushed. Buffering is an I/O performance-enhancement technique discussed in operating-systems courses.

File-Processing Templates

C++ file processing uses class templates basic_ifstream (for file input), basic_ofstream (for file output) and basic_fstream (for file input and output). Each class template has a predefined template specialization that enables char I/O. C++ provides a set of typedefs that provide aliases for these template specializations. For example, the typedef ifstream represents a specialization of basic_ifstream that enables char input from a file. Similarly, typedef ofstream represents a specialization of basic_ofstream that enables char output to a file. Also, typedef fstream represents a specialization of basic_fstream that enables char input from, and output to, a file. Template basic_ifstream inherits from basic_istream, basic_ofstream inherits from basic_ostream and basic_fstream inherits from basic_iostream. The UML class diagram of Fig. 26.2 summarizes the various inheritance relationships of the I/O-related classes. The full stream-I/O class hierarchy provides most of the capabilities that programmers need. Consult the class-library reference for your C++ system for additional file-processing information.

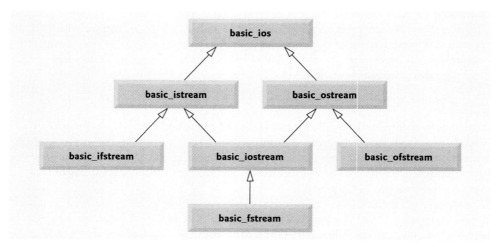

Fig. 26.2 | Stream-I/O template hierarchy portion showing the main file-processing templates.

26.3 Stream Output

Formatted and unformatted output capabilities are provided by ostream. Capabilities for output include output of standard data types with the stream insertion operator (<<); output of characters via the put member function; unformatted output via the write member function (Section 26.5); output of integers in decimal, octal and hexadecimal formats (Section 26.6.1); output of floating-point values with various precision (Section 26.6.2), with forced decimal points (Section 26.7.1), in scientific notation and in fixed notation (Section 26.7.5); output of data justified in fields of designated widths (Section 26.7.2); output of data in fields padded with specified characters (Section 26.7.3); and output of uppercase letters in scientific notation and hexadecimal notation (Section 26.7.6).

26.3.1 Output of char * Variables

C++ determines data types automatically, an improvement over C. Unfortunately, this feature sometimes "gets in the way." For example, suppose we want to print the value of a char * to a character string (i.e., the memory address of the first character of that string). However, the << operator has been overloaded to print data of type char * as a null-terminated string. The solution is to cast the char * to a void * (in fact, this should be done to any pointer variable the programmer wishes to output as an address). Figure 26.3 demonstrates printing a char * variable in both string and address formats. Note that the address prints as a hexadecimal (base-16) number. [*Note:* The reader who wants to learn more about hexadecimal numbers should read Appendix D, Number Systems.] We say more about controlling the bases of numbers in Section 26.6.1, Section 26.7.4, Section 26.7.5 and Section 26.7.7. [*Note:* The memory address shown in the output of the program in Fig. 26.3 may differ among compilers.]

26.3.2 Character Output Using Member Function put

We can use the put member function to output characters. For example, the statement

```
cout.put( 'A' );
```

```
 1   // Fig. 26.3: fig26_03.cpp
 2   // Printing the address stored in a char * variable.
 3   #include <iostream>
 4   using std::cout;
 5   using std::endl;
 6
 7   int main()
 8   {
 9      char *word = "again";
10
11      // display value of char *, then display value of char *
12      // static_cast to void *
13      cout << "Value of word is: " << word << endl
14          << "Value of static_cast< void * >( word ) is: "
15          << static_cast< void * >( word ) << endl;
16      return 0;
17   } // end main
```

```
Value of word is: again
Value of static_cast< void * >( word ) is: 00428300
```

Fig. 26.3 | Printing the address stored in a `char *` variable.

displays a single character A. Calls to `put` may be cascaded, as in the statement

```
cout.put( 'A' ).put( '\n' );
```

which outputs the letter A followed by a newline character. As with `<<`, the preceding statement executes in this manner, because the dot operator (`.`) evaluates from left to right, and the `put` member function returns a reference to the `ostream` object (`cout`) that received the `put` call. The `put` function also may be called with a numeric expression that represents an ASCII value, as in the following statement

```
cout.put( 65 );
```

which also outputs A.

26.4 Stream Input

Now let us consider stream input. Formatted and unformatted input capabilities are provided by `istream`. The stream extraction operator (i.e., the overloaded `>>` operator) normally skips white-space characters (such as blanks, tabs and newlines) in the input stream; later we will see how to change this behavior. After each input, the stream extraction operator returns a reference to the stream object that received the extraction message (e.g., `cin` in the expression `cin >> grade`). If that reference is used as a condition (e.g., in a `while` statement's loop-continuation condition), the stream's overloaded `void *` cast operator function is implicitly invoked to convert the reference into a non-null pointer value or the null pointer based on the success or failure of the last input operation. A non-null pointer converts to the `bool` value `true` to indicate success and the null pointer converts to the `bool` value `false` to indicate failure. When an attempt is made to read past the end of a stream, the stream's overloaded `void *` cast operator returns the null pointer to indicate end-of-file.

Each stream object contains a set of state bits used to control the state of the stream (i.e., formatting, setting error states, etc.). These bits are used by the stream's overloaded void * cast operator to determine whether to return a non-null pointer or the null pointer. Stream extraction causes the stream's failbit to be set if data of the wrong type is input and causes the stream's badbit to be set if the operation fails. Section 26.7 and Section 26.8 discuss stream state bits in detail, then show how to test these bits after an I/O operation.

26.4.1 get and getline Member Functions

The get member function with no arguments inputs one character from the designated stream (including white-space characters and other nongraphic characters, such as the key sequence that represents end-of-file) and returns it as the value of the function call. This version of get returns EOF when end-of-file is encountered on the stream.

Using Member Functions eof, get and put

Figure 26.4 demonstrates the use of member functions eof and get on input stream cin and member function put on output stream cout. The program first prints the value of cin.eof()—i.e., false (0 on the output)—to show that end-of-file has not occurred on cin. The user enters a line of text and presses *Enter* followed by end-of-file (*<ctrl>-z* on Microsoft Windows systems, *<ctrl>-d* on UNIX and Macintosh systems). Line 17 reads each character, which line 18 outputs to cout using member function put. When end-of-file is encountered, the while statement ends, and line 22 displays the value of cin.eof(), which is now true (1 on the output), to show that end-of-file has been set on cin. Note that this program uses the version of istream member function get that takes no argu-

```
1    // Fig. 26.4: fig26_04.cpp
2    // Using member functions get, put and eof.
3    #include <iostream>
4    using std::cin;
5    using std::cout;
6    using std::endl;
7
8    int main()
9    {
10       int character; // use int, because char cannot represent EOF
11
12       // prompt user to enter line of text
13       cout << "Before input, cin.eof() is " << cin.eof() << endl
14          << "Enter a sentence followed by end-of-file:" << endl;
15
16       // use get to read each character; use put to display it
17       while ( ( character = cin.get() ) != EOF )
18          cout.put( character );
19
20       // display end-of-file character
21       cout << "\nEOF in this system is: " << character << endl;
22       cout << "After input of EOF, cin.eof() is " << cin.eof() << endl;
23       return 0;
24    } // end main
```

Fig. 26.4 | get, put and eof member functions. (Part 1 of 2.)

```
Before input, cin.eof() is 0
Enter a sentence followed by end-of-file:
Testing the get and put member functions
Testing the get and put member functions
^Z

EOF in this system is: -1
After input of EOF, cin.eof() is 1
```

Fig. 26.4 | get, put and eof member functions. (Part 2 of 2.)

ments and returns the character being input (line 17). Function eof returns true only after the program attempts to read past the last character in the stream.

The get member function with a character-reference argument inputs the next character from the input stream (even if this is a white-space character) and stores it in the character argument. This version of get returns a reference to the istream object for which the get member function is being invoked.

A third version of get takes three arguments—a character array, a size limit and a delimiter (with default value '\n'). This version reads characters from the input stream. It either reads one fewer than the specified maximum number of characters and terminates or terminates as soon as the delimiter is read. A null character is inserted to terminate the input string in the character array used as a buffer by the program. The delimiter is not placed in the character array but does remain in the input stream (the delimiter will be the next character read). Thus, the result of a second consecutive get is an empty line, unless the delimiter character is removed from the input stream (possibly with cin.ignore()).

Comparing cin and cin.get

Figure 26.5 compares input using stream extraction with cin (which reads characters until a white-space character is encountered) and input using cin.get. Note that the call to cin.get (line 24) does not specify a delimiter, so the default '\n' character is used.

```
 1   // Fig. 26.5: fig26_05.cpp
 2   // Contrasting input of a string via cin and cin.get.
 3   #include <iostream>
 4   using std::cin;
 5   using std::cout;
 6   using std::endl;
 7
 8   int main()
 9   {
10      // create two char arrays, each with 80 elements
11      const int SIZE = 80;
12      char buffer1[ SIZE ];
13      char buffer2[ SIZE ];
14
```

Fig. 26.5 | Input of a string using cin with stream extraction contrasted with input using cin.get. (Part 1 of 2.)

```
15        // use cin to input characters into buffer1
16        cout << "Enter a sentence:" << endl;
17        cin >> buffer1;
18
19        // display buffer1 contents
20        cout << "\nThe string read with cin was:" << endl
21           << buffer1 << endl << endl;
22
23        // use cin.get to input characters into buffer2
24        cin.get( buffer2, SIZE );
25
26        // display buffer2 contents
27        cout << "The string read with cin.get was:" << endl
28           << buffer2 << endl;
29        return 0;
30     } // end main
```

```
Enter a sentence:
Contrasting string input with cin and cin.get

The string read with cin was:
Contrasting

The string read with cin.get was:
 string input with cin and cin.get
```

Fig. 26.5 | Input of a string using cin with stream extraction contrasted with input using cin.get. (Part 2 of 2.)

Using Member Function getline

Member function **getline** operates similarly to the third version of the get member function and inserts a null character after the line in the character array. The getline function removes the delimiter from the stream (i.e., reads the character and discards it), but does not store it in the character array. The program of Fig. 26.6 demonstrates the use of the getline member function to input a line of text (line 15).

```
1    // Fig. 26.6: fig26_06.cpp
2    // Inputting characters using cin member function getline.
3    #include <iostream>
4    using std::cin;
5    using std::cout;
6    using std::endl;
7
8    int main()
9    {
10       const int SIZE = 80;
11       char buffer[ SIZE ]; // create array of 80 characters
12
```

Fig. 26.6 | Inputting character data with cin member function getline. (Part 1 of 2.)

```
13      // input characters in buffer via cin function getline
14      cout << "Enter a sentence:" << endl;
15      cin.getline( buffer, SIZE );
16
17      // display buffer contents
18      cout << "\nThe sentence entered is:" << endl << buffer << endl;
19      return 0;
20   } // end main
```

```
Enter a sentence:
Using the getline member function

The sentence entered is:
Using the getline member function
```

Fig. 26.6 | Inputting character data with cin member function getline. (Part 2 of 2.)

26.4.2 istream Member Functions peek, putback and ignore

The **ignore** member function of istream either reads and discards a designated number of characters (the default is one character) or terminates upon encountering a designated delimiter (the default delimiter is EOF, which causes ignore to skip to the end of the file when reading from a file).

The **putback** member function places the previous character obtained by a get from an input stream back into that stream. This function is useful for applications that scan an input stream looking for a field beginning with a specific character. When that character is input, the application returns the character to the stream, so the character can be included in the input data.

The **peek** member function returns the next character from an input stream but does not remove the character from the stream.

26.4.3 Type-Safe I/O

C++ offers type-safe I/O. The << and >> operators are overloaded to accept data items of specific types. If unexpected data is processed, various error bits are set, which the user may test to determine whether an I/O operation succeeded or failed. If operator << has not been overloaded for a user-defined type and you attempt to input into or output the contents of an object of that user-defined type, the compiler reports an error. This enables the program to "stay in control." We discuss these error states in Section 26.8.

26.5 Unformatted I/O Using read, write and gcount

Unformatted input/output is performed using the **read** and **write** member functions of istream and ostream, respectively. Member function **read** inputs some number of bytes to a character array in memory; member function **write** outputs bytes from a character array. These bytes are not formatted in any way. They are input or output as raw bytes. For example, the call

```
char buffer[] = "HAPPY BIRTHDAY";
cout.write( buffer, 10 );
```

outputs the first 10 bytes of buffer (including null characters, if any, that would cause output with cout and << to terminate). The call

```
cout.write( "ABCDEFGHIJKLMNOPQRSTUVWXYZ", 10 );
```

displays the first 10 characters of the alphabet.

The read member function inputs a designated number of characters into a character array. If fewer than the designated number of characters are read, failbit is set. Section 26.8 shows how to determine whether failbit has been set. Member function **gcount** reports the number of characters read by the last input operation.

Figure 26.7 demonstrates istream member functions read and gcount and ostream member function write. The program inputs 20 characters (from a longer input sequence) into character array buffer with read (line 15), determines the number of characters input with gcount (line 19) and outputs the characters in buffer with write (line 19).

26.6 Introduction to Stream Manipulators

C++ provides various **stream manipulators** that perform formatting tasks. The stream manipulators provide capabilities such as setting field widths, setting precision, setting and unsetting format state, setting the fill character in fields, flushing streams, inserting a newline into the output stream (and flushing the stream), inserting a null character into the

```cpp
1   // Fig. 26.7: fig26_07.cpp
2   // Unformatted I/O using read, gcount and write.
3   #include <iostream>
4   using std::cin;
5   using std::cout;
6   using std::endl;
7
8   int main()
9   {
10     const int SIZE = 80;
11     char buffer[ SIZE ]; // create array of 80 characters
12
13     // use function read to input characters into buffer
14     cout << "Enter a sentence:" << endl;
15     cin.read( buffer, 20 );
16
17     // use functions write and gcount to display buffer characters
18     cout << endl << "The sentence entered was:" << endl;
19     cout.write( buffer, cin.gcount() );
20     cout << endl;
21     return 0;
22   } // end main
```

```
Enter a sentence:
Using the read, write, and gcount member functions
The sentence entered was:
Using the read, writ
```

Fig. 26.7 | Unformatted I/O using the read, gcount and write member functions.

output stream and skipping white space in the input stream. These features are described in the following sections.

26.6.1 Integral Stream Base: dec, oct, hex and setbase

Integers are interpreted normally as decimal (base-10) values. To change the base in which integers are interpreted on a stream, insert the **hex** manipulator to set the base to hexadecimal (base 16) or insert the **oct** manipulator to set the base to octal (base 8). Insert the **dec** manipulator to reset the stream base to decimal.

The base of a stream also may be changed by the **setbase** stream manipulator, which takes one integer argument of 10, 8, or 16 to set the base to decimal, octal or hexadecimal, respectively. Because **setbase** takes an argument, it is called a parameterized stream manipulator. Using **setbase** (or any other parameterized manipulator) requires the inclusion of the <iomanip> header file. The stream base value remains the same until changed explicitly; **setbase** settings are "sticky." Figure 26.8 demonstrates stream manipulators **hex**, **oct**, **dec** and **setbase**.

```cpp
1   // Fig. 26.8: fig26_08.cpp
2   // Using stream manipulators hex, oct, dec and setbase.
3   #include <iostream>
4   using std::cin;
5   using std::cout;
6   using std::dec;
7   using std::endl;
8   using std::hex;
9   using std::oct;
10
11  #include <iomanip>
12  using std::setbase;
13
14  int main()
15  {
16     int number;
17
18     cout << "Enter a decimal number: ";
19     cin >> number; // input number
20
21     // use hex stream manipulator to show hexadecimal number
22     cout << number << " in hexadecimal is: " << hex
23        << number << endl;
24
25     // use oct stream manipulator to show octal number
26     cout << dec << number << " in octal is: "
27        << oct << number << endl;
28
29     // use setbase stream manipulator to show decimal number
30     cout << setbase( 10 ) << number << " in decimal is: "
31        << number << endl;
32     return 0;
33  } // end main
```

Fig. 26.8 | Stream manipulators hex, oct, dec and setbase. (Part 1 of 2.)

```
Enter a decimal number: 20
20 in hexadecimal is: 14
20 in octal is: 24
20 in decimal is: 20
```

Fig. 26.8 | Stream manipulators hex, oct, dec and setbase. (Part 2 of 2.)

26.6.2 Floating-Point Precision (precision, setprecision)

We can control the precision of floating-point numbers (i.e., the number of digits to the right of the decimal point) by using either the setprecision stream manipulator or the precision member function of ios_base. A call to either of these sets the precision for all subsequent output operations until the next precision-setting call. A call to member function precision with no argument returns the current precision setting (this is what you need to use so that you can restore the original precision eventually after a "sticky" setting is no longer needed). The program of Fig. 26.9 uses both member function precision (line 28) and the setprecision manipulator (line 37) to print a table that shows the square root of 2, with precision varying from 0–9.

```cpp
1   // Fig. 26.9: fig26_09.cpp
2   // Controlling precision of floating-point values.
3   #include <iostream>
4   using std::cout;
5   using std::endl;
6   using std::fixed;
7
8   #include <iomanip>
9   using std::setprecision;
10
11  #include <cmath>
12  using std::sqrt; // sqrt prototype
13
14  int main()
15  {
16     double root2 = sqrt( 2.0 ); // calculate square root of 2
17     int places; // precision, vary from 0-9
18
19     cout << "Square root of 2 with precisions 0-9." << endl
20        << "Precision set by ios_base member function "
21        << "precision:" << endl;
22
23     cout << fixed; // use fixed-point notation
24
25     // display square root using ios_base function precision
26     for ( places = 0; places <= 9; places++ )
27     {
28        cout.precision( places );
29        cout << root2 << endl;
30     } // end for
31
```

Fig. 26.9 | Precision of floating-point values. (Part I of 2.)

```
32      cout << "\nPrecision set by stream manipulator "
33         << "setprecision:" << endl;
34
35      // set precision for each digit, then display square root
36      for ( places = 0; places <= 9; places++ )
37         cout << setprecision( places ) << root2 << endl;
38
39      return 0;
40   } // end main
```

```
Square root of 2 with precisions 0-9.
Precision set by ios_base member function precision:
1
1.4
1.41
1.414
1.4142
1.41421
1.414214
1.4142136
1.41421356
1.414213562

Precision set by stream manipulator setprecision:
1
1.4
1.41
1.414
1.4142
1.41421
1.414214
1.4142136
1.41421356
1.414213562
```

Fig. 26.9 | Precision of floating-point values. (Part 2 of 2.)

26.6.3 Field Width (width, setw)

The **width** member function (of base class ios_base) sets the field width (i.e., the number of character positions in which a value should be output or the maximum number of characters that should be input) and returns the previous width. If values output are narrower than the field width, **fill characters** are inserted as padding. A value wider than the designated width will not be truncated—the full number will be printed. The width function with no argument returns the current setting.

Common Programming Error 26.1

The width setting applies only for the next insertion or extraction (i.e., the width setting is not "sticky"); afterward, the width is set implicitly to 0 (i.e., input and output will be performed with default settings). Assuming that the width setting applies to all subsequent outputs is a logic error.

Common Programming Error 26.2

When a field is not sufficiently wide to handle outputs, the outputs print as wide as necessary, which can yield confusing outputs.

Figure 26.10 demonstrates the use of the `width` member function on both input and output. Note that, on input into a `char` array, a maximum of one fewer characters than the width will be read, because provision is made for the null character to be placed in the input string. Remember that stream extraction terminates when nonleading white space is encountered. The `setw` stream manipulator also may be used to set the field width.

```cpp
 1   // Fig. 26.10: fig26_10.cpp
 2   // Demonstrating member function width.
 3   #include <iostream>
 4   using std::cin;
 5   using std::cout;
 6   using std::endl;
 7
 8   int main()
 9   {
10      int widthValue = 4;
11      char sentence[ 10 ];
12
13      cout << "Enter a sentence:" << endl;
14      cin.width( 5 ); // input only 5 characters from sentence
15
16      // set field width, then display characters based on that width
17      while ( cin >> sentence )
18      {
19         cout.width( widthValue++ );
20         cout << sentence << endl;
21         cin.width( 5 ); // input 5 more characters from sentence
22      } // end while
23
24      return 0;
25   } // end main
```

```
Enter a sentence:
This is a test of the width member function
This
   is
    a
  test
    of
    the
    widt
       h
     memb
       er
      func
       tion
```

Fig. 26.10 | `width` member function of class `ios_base`.

[*Note:* When prompted for input in Fig. 26.10, the user should enter a line of text and press *Enter* followed by end-of-file (*<ctrl>-z* on Microsoft Windows systems, *<ctrl>-d* on UNIX and Macintosh systems).]

26.6.4 User-Defined Output Stream Manipulators

Programmers can create their own stream manipulators.[2] Figure 26.11 shows the creation and use of new nonparameterized stream manipulators bell (lines 10–13), carriageReturn (lines 16–19), tab (lines 22–25) and endLine (lines 29–32). For output stream manipulators, the return type and parameter must be of type ostream &. When line 37 inserts the endLine manipulator in the output stream, function endLine is called and line 31 outputs the escape sequence \n and the flush manipulator to the standard output stream cout. Similarly, when lines 37–46 insert the manipulators tab, bell and carriageReturn

```
1   // Fig. 26.11: fig26_11.cpp
2   // Creating and testing user-defined, nonparameterized
3   // stream manipulators.
4   #include <iostream>
5   using std::cout;
6   using std::flush;
7   using std::ostream;
8
9   // bell manipulator (using escape sequence \a)
10  ostream& bell( ostream& output )
11  {
12     return output << '\a'; // issue system beep
13  } // end bell manipulator
14
15  // carriageReturn manipulator (using escape sequence \r)
16  ostream& carriageReturn( ostream& output )
17  {
18     return output << '\r'; // issue carriage return
19  } // end carriageReturn manipulator
20
21  // tab manipulator (using escape sequence \t)
22  ostream& tab( ostream& output )
23  {
24     return output << '\t'; // issue tab
25  } // end tab manipulator
26
27  // endLine manipulator (using escape sequence \n and member
28  // function flush)
29  ostream& endLine( ostream& output )
30  {
31     return output << '\n' << flush; // issue endl-like end of line
32  } // end endLine manipulator
33
```

Fig. 26.11 | User-defined, nonparameterized stream manipulators. (Part 1 of 2.)

---

2. Programmers also may create their own parameterized stream manipulators—consult your C++ compiler's documentation for instructions on how to do this.

```
34   int main()
35   {
36      // use tab and endLine manipulators
37      cout << "Testing the tab manipulator:" << endLine
38         << 'a' << tab << 'b' << tab << 'c' << endLine;
39
40      cout << "Testing the carriageReturn and bell manipulators:"
41         << endLine << "..........";
42
43      cout << bell; // use bell manipulator
44
45      // use carriageReturn and endLine manipulators
46      cout << carriageReturn << "-----" << endLine;
47      return 0;
48   } // end main
```

```
Testing the tab manipulator:
a       b       c
Testing the carriageReturn and bell manipulators:
-----.....
```

Fig. 26.11 | User-defined, nonparameterized stream manipulators. (Part 2 of 2.)

in the output stream, their corresponding functions—tab (line 22), bell (line 10) and carriageReturn (line 16)—are called, which in turn output various escape sequences.

26.7 Stream Format States and Stream Manipulators

Various stream manipulators can be used to specify the kinds of formatting to be performed during stream-I/O operations. Stream manipulators control the output's format settings. Figure 26.12 lists each stream manipulator that controls a given stream's format state. All these manipulators belong to class ios_base. We show examples of most of these stream manipulators in the next several sections.

Stream Manipulator	Description
skipws	Skip white-space characters on an input stream. This setting is reset with stream manipulator noskipws.
left	Left justify output in a field. Padding characters appear to the right if necessary.
right	Right justify output in a field. Padding characters appear to the left if necessary.
internal	Indicate that a number's sign should be left justified in a field and a number's magnitude should be right justified in that same field (i.e., padding characters appear between the sign and the number).
dec	Specify that integers should be treated as decimal (base 10) values.

Fig. 26.12 | Format state stream manipulators from <iostream>. (Part 1 of 2.)

Stream Manipulator	Description
oct	Specify that integers should be treated as octal (base 8) values.
hex	Specify that integers should be treated as hexadecimal (base 16) values.
showbase	Specify that the base of a number is to be output ahead of the number (a leading 0 for octals; a leading 0x or 0X for hexadecimals). This setting is reset with stream manipulator **noshowbase**.
showpoint	Specify that floating-point numbers should be output with a decimal point. This is used normally with fixed to guarantee a certain number of digits to the right of the decimal point, even if they are zeros. This setting is reset with stream manipulator **noshowpoint**.
uppercase	Specify that uppercase letters (i.e., X and A through F) should be used in a hexadecimal integer and that uppercase E should be used when representing a floating-point value in scientific notation. This setting is reset with stream manipulator **nouppercase**.
showpos	Specify that positive numbers should be preceded by a plus sign (**+**). This setting is reset with stream manipulator **noshowpos**.
scientific	Specify output of a floating-point value in scientific notation.
fixed	Specify output of a floating-point value in fixed-point notation with a specific number of digits to the right of the decimal point.

Fig. 26.12 | Format state stream manipulators from `<iostream>`. (Part 2 of 2.)

26.7.1 Trailing Zeros and Decimal Points (showpoint)

Stream manipulator showpoint forces a floating-point number to be output with its decimal point and trailing zeros. For example, the floating-point value 79.0 prints as 79 without using showpoint and prints as 79.000000 (or as many trailing zeros as are specified by the current precision) using showpoint. To reset the showpoint setting, output the stream manipulator **noshowpoint**. The program in Fig. 26.13 shows how to use stream manipulator showpoint to control the printing of trailing zeros and decimal points for floating-point values. Recall that the default precision of a floating-point number is 6. When neither the fixed nor the scientific stream manipulator is used, the precision represents the number of significant digits to display (i.e., the total number of digits to display), not the number of digits to display after decimal point.

```
1   // Fig. 26.13: fig26_13.cpp
2   // Using showpoint to control the printing of
3   // trailing zeros and decimal points for doubles.
4   #include <iostream>
5   using std::cout;
6   using std::endl;
7   using std::showpoint;
```

Fig. 26.13 | Controlling the printing of trailing zeros and decimal points in floating-point values. (Part 1 of 2.)

```
 8
 9   int main()
10   {
11      // display double values with default stream format
12      cout << "Before using showpoint" << endl
13         << "9.9900 prints as: " << 9.9900 << endl
14         << "9.9000 prints as: " << 9.9000 << endl
15         << "9.0000 prints as: " << 9.0000 << endl << endl;
16
17      // display double value after showpoint
18      cout << showpoint
19         << "After using showpoint" << endl
20         << "9.9900 prints as: " << 9.9900 << endl
21         << "9.9000 prints as: " << 9.9000 << endl
22         << "9.0000 prints as: " << 9.0000 << endl;
23      return 0;
24   } // end main
```

```
Before using showpoint
9.9900 prints as: 9.99
9.9000 prints as: 9.9
9.0000 prints as: 9

After using showpoint
9.9900 prints as: 9.99000
9.9000 prints as: 9.90000
9.0000 prints as: 9.00000
```

Fig. 26.13 | Controlling the printing of trailing zeros and decimal points in floating-point values. (Part 2 of 2.)

26.7.2 Justification (`left`, `right` and `internal`)

Stream manipulators `left` and `right` enable fields to be left justified with padding characters to the right or right justified with padding characters to the left, respectively. The padding character is specified by the `fill` member function or the `setfill` parameterized stream manipulator (which we discuss in Section 26.7.3). Figure 26.14 uses the `setw`, `left` and `right` manipulators to left justify and right justify integer data in a field.

```
 1   // Fig. 26.14: fig26_14.cpp
 2   // Demonstrating left justification and right justification.
 3   #include <iostream>
 4   using std::cout;
 5   using std::endl;
 6   using std::left;
 7   using std::right;
 8
 9   #include <iomanip>
10   using std::setw;
```

Fig. 26.14 | Left justification and right justification with stream manipulators `left` and `right`. (Part 1 of 2.)

```
11
12   int main()
13   {
14      int x = 12345;
15
16      // display x right justified (default)
17      cout << "Default is right justified:" << endl
18         << setw( 10 ) << x;
19
20      // use left manipulator to display x left justified
21      cout << "\n\nUse std::left to left justify x:\n"
22         << left << setw( 10 ) << x;
23
24      // use right manipulator to display x right justified
25      cout << "\n\nUse std::right to right justify x:\n"
26         << right << setw( 10 ) << x << endl;
27      return 0;
28   } // end main
```

```
Default is right justified:
     12345

Use std::left to left justify x:
12345

Use std::right to right justify x:
     12345
```

Fig. 26.14 | Left justification and right justification with stream manipulators `left` and `right`. (Part 2 of 2.)

Stream manipulator **internal** indicates that a number's sign (or base when using stream manipulator **showbase**) should be left justified within a field, that the number's magnitude should be right justified and that intervening spaces should be padded with the fill character. Figure 26.15 shows the `internal` stream manipulator specifying internal spacing (line 15). Note that **showpos** forces the plus sign to print (line 15). To reset the showpos setting, output the stream manipulator **noshowpos**.

```
1    // Fig. 26.15: fig26_15.cpp
2    // Printing an integer with internal spacing and plus sign.
3    #include <iostream>
4    using std::cout;
5    using std::endl;
6    using std::internal;
7    using std::showpos;
8
9    #include <iomanip>
10   using std::setw;
11
```

Fig. 26.15 | Printing an integer with internal spacing and plus sign. (Part 1 of 2.)

```
12   int main()
13   {
14      // display value with internal spacing and plus sign
15      cout << internal << showpos << setw( 10 ) << 123 << endl;
16      return 0;
17   } // end main
```

```
+        123
```

Fig. 26.15 | Printing an integer with internal spacing and plus sign. (Part 2 of 2.)

26.7.3 Padding (`fill`, `setfill`)

The `fill` member function specifies the fill character to be used with justified fields; if no value is specified, spaces are used for padding. The `fill` function returns the prior padding character. The `setfill` manipulator also sets the padding character. Figure 26.16 demonstrates using member function `fill` (line 40) and stream manipulator `setfill` (lines 44 and 47) to set the fill character.

```
1    // Fig. 26.16: fig26_16.cpp
2    // Using member function fill and stream manipulator setfill to change
3    // the padding character for fields larger than the printed value.
4    #include <iostream>
5    using std::cout;
6    using std::dec;
7    using std::endl;
8    using std::hex;
9    using std::internal;
10   using std::left;
11   using std::right;
12   using std::showbase;
13
14   #include <iomanip>
15   using std::setfill;
16   using std::setw;
17
18   int main()
19   {
20      int x = 10000;
21
22      // display x
23      cout << x << " printed as int right and left justified\n"
24         << "and as hex with internal justification.\n"
25         << "Using the default pad character (space):" << endl;
26
27      // display x with base
28      cout << showbase << setw( 10 ) << x << endl;
29
```

Fig. 26.16 | Using member function `fill` and stream manipulator `setfill` to change the padding character for fields larger than the values being printed. (Part 1 of 2.)

```
30      // display x with left justification
31      cout << left << setw( 10 ) << x << endl;
32
33      // display x as hex with internal justification
34      cout << internal << setw( 10 ) << hex << x << endl << endl;
35
36      cout << "Using various padding characters:" << endl;
37
38      // display x using padded characters (right justification)
39      cout << right;
40      cout.fill( '*' );
41      cout << setw( 10 ) << dec << x << endl;
42
43      // display x using padded characters (left justification)
44      cout << left << setw( 10 ) << setfill( '%' ) << x << endl;
45
46      // display x using padded characters (internal justification)
47      cout << internal << setw( 10 ) << setfill( '^' ) << hex
48         << x << endl;
49      return 0;
50   } // end main
```

```
10000 printed as int right and left justified
and as hex with internal justification.
Using the default pad character (space):
     10000
10000
0x    2710

Using various padding characters:
*****10000
10000%%%%%
0x^^^^2710
```

Fig. 26.16 | Using member function `fill` and stream manipulator `setfill` to change the padding character for fields larger than the values being printed. (Part 2 of 2.)

26.7.4 Integral Stream Base (dec, oct, hex, showbase)

C++ provides stream manipulators dec, hex and oct to specify that integers are to be displayed as decimal, hexadecimal and octal values, respectively. Stream insertions default to decimal if none of these manipulators is used. With stream extraction, integers prefixed with 0 (zero) are treated as octal values, integers prefixed with 0x or 0X are treated as hexadecimal values, and all other integers are treated as decimal values. Once a particular base is specified for a stream, all integers on that stream are processed using that base until a different base is specified or until the program terminates.

Stream manipulator **showbase** forces the base of an integral value to be output. Decimal numbers are output by default, octal numbers are output with a leading 0, and hexadecimal numbers are output with either a leading 0x or a leading 0X (as we discuss in Section 26.7.6, stream manipulator uppercase determines which option is chosen). Figure 26.17 demonstrates the use of stream manipulator showbase to force an integer to

```
1   // Fig. 26.17: fig26_17.cpp
2   // Using stream manipulator showbase.
3   #include <iostream>
4   using std::cout;
5   using std::endl;
6   using std::hex;
7   using std::oct;
8   using std::showbase;
9
10  int main()
11  {
12     int x = 100;
13
14     // use showbase to show number base
15     cout << "Printing integers preceded by their base:" << endl
16        << showbase;
17
18     cout << x << endl; // print decimal value
19     cout << oct << x << endl; // print octal value
20     cout << hex << x << endl; // print hexadecimal value
21     return 0;
22  } // end main
```

```
Printing integers preceded by their base:
100
0144
0x64
```

Fig. 26.17 | Stream manipulator `showbase`.

print in decimal, octal and hexadecimal formats. To reset the `showbase` setting, output the stream manipulator `noshowbase`.

26.7.5 Floating-Point Numbers; Scientific and Fixed Notation (`scientific`, `fixed`)

Stream manipulators `scientific` and `fixed` control the output format of floating-point numbers. Stream manipulator `scientific` forces the output of a floating-point number to display in scientific format. Stream manipulator `fixed` forces a floating-point number to display a specific number of digits (as specified by member function `precision` or stream manipulator `setprecision`) to the right of the decimal point. Without using another manipulator, the floating-point-number value determines the output format.

Figure 26.18 demonstrates displaying floating-point numbers in fixed and scientific formats using stream manipulators `scientific` (line 21) and `fixed` (line 25). The exponent format in scientific notation might differ across different compilers.

26.7.6 Uppercase/Lowercase Control (`uppercase`)

Stream manipulator `uppercase` outputs an uppercase X or E with hexadecimal-integer values or with scientific-notation floating-point values, respectively (Fig. 26.19). Using stream manipulator `uppercase` also causes all letters in a hexadecimal value to be upper-

```cpp
 1   // Fig. 26.18: fig26_18.cpp
 2   // Displaying floating-point values in system default,
 3   // scientific and fixed formats.
 4   #include <iostream>
 5   using std::cout;
 6   using std::endl;
 7   using std::fixed;
 8   using std::scientific;
 9
10   int main()
11   {
12      double x = 0.001234567;
13      double y = 1.946e9;
14
15      // display x and y in default format
16      cout << "Displayed in default format:" << endl
17         << x << '\t' << y << endl;
18
19      // display x and y in scientific format
20      cout << "\nDisplayed in scientific format:" << endl
21         << scientific << x << '\t' << y << endl;
22
23      // display x and y in fixed format
24      cout << "\nDisplayed in fixed format:" << endl
25         << fixed << x << '\t' << y << endl;
26      return 0;
27   } // end main
```

```
Displayed in default format:
0.00123457          1.946e+009

Displayed in scientific format:
1.234567e-003    1.946000e+009

Displayed in fixed format:
0.001235          1946000000.000000
```

Fig. 26.18 | Floating-point values displayed in default, scientific and fixed formats.

case. By default, the letters for hexadecimal values and the exponents in scientific-notation floating-point values appear in lowercase. To reset the uppercase setting, output the stream manipulator **nouppercase**.

```cpp
 1   // Fig. 26.19: fig26_19.cpp
 2   // Stream manipulator uppercase.
 3   #include <iostream>
 4   using std::cout;
 5   using std::endl;
 6   using std::hex;
 7   using std::showbase;
 8   using std::uppercase;
```

Fig. 26.19 | Stream manipulator uppercase. (Part 1 of 2.)

```
 9
10   int main()
11   {
12      cout << "Printing uppercase letters in scientific" << endl
13         << "notation exponents and hexadecimal values:" << endl;
14
15      // use std:uppercase to display uppercase letters; use std::hex and
16      // std::showbase to display hexadecimal value and its base
17      cout << uppercase << 4.345e10 << endl
18         << hex << showbase << 123456789 << endl;
19      return 0;
20   } // end main
```

```
Printing uppercase letters in scientific
notation exponents and hexadecimal values:
4.345E+010
0X75BCD15
```

Fig. 26.19 | Stream manipulator uppercase. (Part 2 of 2.)

26.7.7 Specifying Boolean Format (boolalpha)

C++ provides data type bool, whose values may be false or true, as a preferred alternative to the old style of using 0 to indicate false and nonzero to indicate true. A bool variable outputs as 0 or 1 by default. However, we can use stream manipulator boolalpha to set the output stream to display bool values as the strings "true" and "false". Use stream manipulator **nobooalpha** to set the output stream to display bool values as integers (i.e., the default setting). The program of Fig. 26.20 demonstrates these stream manipulators. Line 14 displays the bool value, which line 11 sets to true, as an integer. Line 18 uses manipulator boolalpha to display the bool value as a string. Lines 21–22 then change the bool's value and use manipulator noboolalpha, so line 25 can display the bool value as an integer. Line 29 uses manipulator boolalpha to display the bool value as a string. Both boolalpha and noboolalpha are "sticky" settings.

Good Programming Practice 26.1

Displaying bool values as true or false, rather than nonzero or 0, respectively, makes program outputs clearer.

```
 1   // Fig. 26.20: fig26_20.cpp
 2   // Demonstrating stream manipulators boolalpha and noboolalpha.
 3   #include <iostream>
 4   using std::boolalpha;
 5   using std::cout;
 6   using std::endl;
 7   using std::noboolalpha;
 8
 9   int main()
10   {
11      bool booleanValue = true;
```

Fig. 26.20 | Stream manipulators boolalpha and noboolalpha. (Part 1 of 2.)

```
12
13      // display default true booleanValue
14      cout << "booleanValue is " << booleanValue << endl;
15
16      // display booleanValue after using boolalpha
17      cout << "booleanValue (after using boolalpha) is "
18         << boolalpha << booleanValue << endl << endl;
19
20      cout << "switch booleanValue and use noboolalpha" << endl;
21      booleanValue = false; // change booleanValue
22      cout << noboolalpha << endl; // use noboolalpha
23
24      // display default false booleanValue after using noboolalpha
25      cout << "booleanValue is " << booleanValue << endl;
26
27      // display booleanValue after using boolalpha again
28      cout << "booleanValue (after using boolalpha) is "
29         << boolalpha << booleanValue << endl;
30      return 0;
31   } // end main
```

```
booleanValue is 1
booleanValue (after using boolalpha) is true

switch booleanValue and use noboolalpha

booleanValue is 0
booleanValue (after using boolalpha) is false
```

Fig. 26.20 | Stream manipulators `boolalpha` and `noboolalpha`. (Part 2 of 2.)

26.7.8 Setting and Resetting the Format State via Member Function `flags`

Throughout Section 26.7, we have been using stream manipulators to change output format characteristics. We now discuss how to return an output stream's format to its default state after having applied several manipulations. Member function `flags` without an argument returns the current format settings as a `fmtflags` data type (of class `ios_base`), which represents the format state. Member function `flags` with a `fmtflags` argument sets the format state as specified by the argument and returns the prior state settings. The initial settings of the value that `flags` returns might differ across several systems. The program of Fig. 26.21 uses member function `flags` to save the stream's original format state (line 22), then restore the original format settings (line 30).

```
1    // Fig. 26.21: fig26_21.cpp
2    // Demonstrating the flags member function.
3    #include <iostream>
4    using std::cout;
5    using std::endl;
6    using std::ios_base;
```

Fig. 26.21 | `flags` member function. (Part 1 of 2.)

```
 7    using std::oct;
 8    using std::scientific;
 9    using std::showbase;
10
11    int main()
12    {
13        int integerValue = 1000;
14        double doubleValue = 0.0947628;
15
16        // display flags value, int and double values (original format)
17        cout << "The value of the flags variable is: " << cout.flags()
18            << "\nPrint int and double in original format:\n"
19            << integerValue << '\t' << doubleValue << endl << endl;
20
21        // use cout flags function to save original format
22        ios_base::fmtflags originalFormat = cout.flags();
23        cout << showbase << oct << scientific; // change format
24
25        // display flags value, int and double values (new format)
26        cout << "The value of the flags variable is: " << cout.flags()
27            << "\nPrint int and double in a new format:\n"
28            << integerValue << '\t' << doubleValue << endl << endl;
29
30        cout.flags( originalFormat ); // restore format
31
32        // display flags value, int and double values (original format)
33        cout << "The restored value of the flags variable is: "
34            << cout.flags()
35            << "\nPrint values in original format again:\n"
36            << integerValue << '\t' << doubleValue << endl;
37        return 0;
38    } // end main
```

```
The value of the flags variable is: 513
Print int and double in original format:
1000     0.0947628

The value of the flags variable is: 012011
Print int and double in a new format:
01750    9.476280e-002

The restored value of the flags variable is: 513
Print values in original format again:
1000     0.0947628
```

Fig. 26.21 | flags member function. (Part 2 of 2.)

26.8 Stream Error States

The state of a stream may be tested through bits in class ios_base. In a moment, we show how to test these bits, in the example of Fig. 26.22.

The **eofbit** is set for an input stream after end-of-file is encountered. A program can use member function eof to determine whether end-of-file has been encountered on a stream after an attempt to extract data beyond the end of the stream. The call

```
cin.eof()
```

returns true if end-of-file has been encountered on cin and false otherwise.

The failbit is set for a stream when a format error occurs on the stream, such as when the program is inputting integers and a nondigit character is encountered in the input stream. When such an error occurs, the characters are not lost. The fail member function reports whether a stream operation has failed; usually, recovering from such errors is possible.

The badbit is set for a stream when an error occurs that results in the loss of data. The **bad** member function reports whether a stream operation failed. Generally, such serious failures are nonrecoverable.

```cpp
 1   // Fig. 26.22: fig26_22.cpp
 2   // Testing error states.
 3   #include <iostream>
 4   using std::cin;
 5   using std::cout;
 6   using std::endl;
 7
 8   int main()
 9   {
10      int integerValue;
11
12      // display results of cin functions
13      cout << "Before a bad input operation:"
14         << "\ncin.rdstate(): " << cin.rdstate()
15         << "\n    cin.eof(): " << cin.eof()
16         << "\n    cin.fail(): " << cin.fail()
17         << "\n    cin.bad(): " << cin.bad()
18         << "\n    cin.good(): " << cin.good()
19         << "\n\nExpects an integer, but enter a character: ";
20
21      cin >> integerValue; // enter character value
22      cout << endl;
23
24      // display results of cin functions after bad input
25      cout << "After a bad input operation:"
26         << "\ncin.rdstate(): " << cin.rdstate()
27         << "\n    cin.eof(): " << cin.eof()
28         << "\n    cin.fail(): " << cin.fail()
29         << "\n    cin.bad(): " << cin.bad()
30         << "\n    cin.good(): " << cin.good() << endl << endl;
31
32      cin.clear(); // clear stream
33
34      // display results of cin functions after clearing cin
35      cout << "After cin.clear()" << "\ncin.fail(): " << cin.fail()
36         << "\ncin.good(): " << cin.good() << endl;
37      return 0;
38   } // end main
```

Fig. 26.22 | Testing error states. (Part 1 of 2.)

```
Before a bad input operation:
cin.rdstate(): 0
    cin.eof(): 0
   cin.fail(): 0
    cin.bad(): 0
   cin.good(): 1

Expects an integer, but enter a character: A

After a bad input operation:
cin.rdstate(): 2
    cin.eof(): 0
   cin.fail(): 1
    cin.bad(): 0
   cin.good(): 0

After cin.clear()
cin.fail(): 0
cin.good(): 1
```

Fig. 26.22 | Testing error states. (Part 2 of 2.)

The **goodbit** is set for a stream if none of the bits eofbit, failbit or badbit is set for the stream.

The **good** member function returns true if the bad, fail and eof functions would all return false. I/O operations should be performed only on "good" streams.

The **rdstate** member function returns the error state of the stream. A call to cout.rdstate, for example, would return the state of the stream, which then could be tested by a switch statement that examines eofbit, badbit, failbit and goodbit. The preferred means of testing the state of a stream is to use member functions eof, bad, fail and good—using these functions does not require the programmer to be familiar with particular status bits.

The **clear** member function is used to restore a stream's state to "good," so that I/O may proceed on that stream. The default argument for clear is goodbit, so the statement

```
    cin.clear();
```

clears cin and sets goodbit for the stream. The statement

```
    cin.clear( ios::failbit )
```

sets the failbit. The programmer might want to do this when performing input on cin with a user-defined type and encountering a problem. The name clear might seem inappropriate in this context, but it is correct.

The program of Fig. 26.22 demonstrates member functions rdstate, eof, fail, bad, good and clear. [*Note:* The actual values output may differ across different compilers.]

The operator! member function of basic_ios returns true if the badbit is set, the failbit is set or both are set. The operator void * member function returns false (0) if the badbit is set, the failbit is set or both are set. These functions are useful in file processing when a true/false condition is being tested under the control of a selection statement or repetition statement.

26.9 Tying an Output Stream to an Input Stream

Interactive applications generally involve an `istream` for input and an `ostream` for output. When a prompting message appears on the screen, the user responds by entering the appropriate data. Obviously, the prompt needs to appear before the input operation proceeds. With output buffering, outputs appear only when the buffer fills, when outputs are flushed explicitly by the program or automatically at the end of the program. C++ provides member function `tie` to synchronize (i.e., "tie together") the operation of an `istream` and an `ostream` to ensure that outputs appear before their subsequent inputs. The call

```
cin.tie( &cout );
```

ties `cout` (an `ostream`) to `cin` (an `istream`). Actually, this particular call is redundant, because C++ performs this operation automatically to create a user's standard input/output environment. However, the user would tie other `istream`/`ostream` pairs explicitly. To untie an input stream, `inputStream`, from an output stream, use the call

```
inputStream.tie( 0 );
```

26.10 Wrap-Up

This chapter summarized how C++ performs input/output using streams. You learned about the stream-I/O classes and objects, as well as the stream I/O template class hierarchy. We discussed `ostream`'s formatted and unformatted output capabilities performed by the `put` and `write` functions. You saw examples using `istream`'s formatted and unformatted input capabilities performed by the `eof`, `get`, `getline`, `peek`, `putback`, `ignore` and `read` functions. Next, we discussed stream manipulators and member functions that perform formatting tasks—`dec`, `oct`, `hex` and `setbase` for displaying integers; `precision` and `setprecision` for controlling floating-point precision; and `width` and `setw` for setting field width. You also learned additional formatting `iostream` manipulators and member functions—`showpoint` for displaying decimal point and trailing zeros; `left`, `right` and `internal` for justification; `fill` and `setfill` for padding; `scientific` and `fixed` for displaying floating-point numbers in scientific and fixed notation; `uppercase` for uppercase/lowercase control; `boolalpha` for specifying boolean format; and `flags` and `fmtflags` for resetting the format state.

In the next chapter, we introduce exception handling, which allows programers to deal with certain problems that may occur during a program's execution. We demonstrate basic exception-handling techniques that often permit a program to continue executing as if no problem had been encountered. We also present several classes that the C++ Standard Library provides for handling exceptions.

Summary

Section 26.1 Introduction
- I/O operations are performed in a manner sensitive to the type of the data.

Section 26.2 Streams
- C++ I/O occurs in streams. A stream is a sequence of bytes.

- I/O mechanisms of the system move bytes from devices to memory and vice versa efficiently and reliably.

- C++ provides "low-level" and "high-level" I/O capabilities. Low-level I/O-capabilities specify that some number of bytes should be transferred device-to-memory or memory-to-device. High-level I/O is performed with bytes grouped into such meaningful units as integers, floats, characters, strings and user-defined types.

- C++ provides both unformatted-I/O and formatted-I/O operations. Unformatted-I/O transfers are fast, but process raw data that is difficult for people to use. Formatted I/O processes data in meaningful units, but requires extra processing time that can degrade the performance of high-volume data transfers.

- The <iostream> header file declares all stream-I/O operations.

- Header <iomanip> declares the parameterized stream manipulators.

- The <fstream> header declares file-processing operations.

- The basic_istream template supports stream-input operations.

- The basic_ostream template supports stream-output operations.

- The basic_iostream template supports both stream-input and stream-output operations.

- The basic_istream template and the basic_ostream template are each derived through single inheritance from the basic_ios template.

- The basic_iostream template is derived through multiple inheritance from both the basic_istream template and the basic_ostream template.

- The left-shift operator (<<) is overloaded to designate stream output and is referred to as the stream insertion operator.

- The right-shift operator (>>) is overloaded to designate stream input and is referred to as the stream extraction operator.

- The istream object cin is tied to the standard input device, normally the keyboard.

- The ostream object cout is tied to the standard output device, normally the screen.

- The ostream object cerr is tied to the standard error device. Outputs to cerr are unbuffered; each insertion to cerr appears immediately.

Section 26.3 Stream Output
- The C++ compiler determines data types automatically for input and output.

- Addresses are displayed in hexadecimal format by default.

- To print the address in a pointer variable, cast the pointer to void *.

- Member function put outputs one character. Calls to put may be cascaded.

Section 26.4 Stream Input
- Stream input is performed with the stream extraction operator >>. This operator automatically skips white-space characters in the input stream.

- The >> operator returns false after end-of-file is encountered on a stream.

- Stream extraction causes failbit to be set for improper input and badbit to be set if the operation fails.

- A series of values can be input using the stream extraction operation in a while loop header. The extraction returns 0 when end-of-file is encountered.

- The get member function with no arguments inputs one character and returns the character; EOF is returned if end-of-file is encountered on the stream.

- Member function get with a character-reference argument inputs the next character from the input stream and stores it in the character argument. This version of get returns a reference to the istream object for which the get member function is being invoked.

- Member function get with three arguments—a character array, a size limit and a delimiter (with default value newline)—reads characters from the input stream up to a maximum of limit – 1 characters and terminates, or terminates when the delimiter is read. The input string is terminated with a null character. The delimiter is not placed in the character array but remains in the input stream.

- The getline member function operates like the three-argument get member function. The getline function removes the delimiter from the input stream but does not store it in the string.

- Member function ignore skips the specified number of characters (the default is 1) in the input stream; it terminates if the specified delimiter is encountered (the default delimiter is EOF).

- The putback member function places the previous character obtained by a get on a stream back onto that stream.

- The peek member function returns the next character from an input stream but does not extract (remove) the character from the stream.

- C++ offers type-safe I/O. If unexpected data is processed by the << and >> operators, various error bits are set, which the user may test to determine whether an I/O operation succeeded or failed. If operator << has not been overloaded for a user-defined type, a compiler error is reported.

Section 26.5 Unformatted I/O Using read, write and gcount

- Unformatted I/O is performed with member functions read and write. These input or output some number of bytes to or from memory, beginning at a designated memory address. They are input or output as raw bytes with no formatting.

- The gcount member function returns the number of characters input by the previous read operation on that stream.

- Member function read inputs a specified number of characters into a character array. failbit is set if fewer than the specified number of characters are read.

Section 26.6 Introduction to Stream Manipulators

- To change the base in which integers output, use the manipulator hex to set the base to hexadecimal (base 16) or oct to set the base to octal (base 8). Use manipulator dec to reset the base to decimal. The base remains the same until changed explicitly.

- The parameterized stream manipulator setbase also sets the base for integer output. setbase takes one integer argument of 10, 8 or 16 to set the base.

- Floating-point precision can be controlled using either the setprecision stream manipulator or the precision member function. Both set the precision for all subsequent output operations until the next precision-setting call. The precision member function with no argument returns the current precision value.

- Parameterized manipulators require the inclusion of the <iomanip> header file.

- Member function width sets the field width and returns the previous width. Values narrower than the field are padded with fill characters. The field-width setting applies only for the next insertion or extraction; the field width is set to 0 implicitly (subsequent values will be output as large as necessary). Values wider than a field are printed in their entirety. Function width with no argument returns the current width setting. Manipulator setw also sets the width.

- For input, the setw stream manipulator establishes a maximum string size; if a larger string is entered, the larger line is broken into pieces no larger than the designated size.

- Programmers may create their own stream manipulators.

Section 26.7 Stream Format States and Stream Manipulators

- Stream manipulator showpoint forces a floating-point number to be output with a decimal point and with the number of significant digits specified by the precision.

- Stream manipulators left and right cause fields to be left justified with padding characters to the right or right justified with padding characters to the left.

- Stream manipulator internal indicates that a number's sign (or base when using stream manipulator showbase) should be left justified within a field, its magnitude should be right justified and intervening spaces should be padded with the fill character.

- Member function fill specifies the fill character to be used with stream manipulators left, right and internal (space is the default); the prior padding character is returned. Stream manipulator setfill also sets the fill character.

- Stream manipulators oct, hex and dec specify that integers are to be treated as octal, hexadecimal or decimal values, respectively. Integer output defaults to decimal if none of these bits is set; stream extractions process the data in the form the data is supplied.

- Stream manipulator showbase forces the base of an integral value to be output.

- Stream manipulator scientific is used to output a floating-point number in scientific format. Stream manipulator fixed is used to output a floating-point number with the precision specified by the precision member function.

- Stream manipulator uppercase forces an uppercase X or E to be output with hexadecimal integers or with scientific-notation floating-point values, respectively. When set, uppercase causes all letters in a hexadecimal value to be uppercase.

- Member function flags with no argument returns the long value of the current format state settings. Function flags with a long argument sets the format state specified by the argument.

Section 26.8 Stream Error States

- The state of a stream may be tested through bits in class ios_base.

- The eofbit is set for an input stream after end-of-file is encountered during an input operation. The eof member function reports whether the eofbit has been set.

- The failbit is set for a stream when a format error occurs on the stream. The fail member function reports whether a stream operation has failed; it is normally possible to recover from such errors.

- The badbit is set for a stream when an error occurs that results in data loss. The bad member function reports whether such a stream operation failed. Such serious failures are normally non-recoverable.

- The good member function returns true if the bad, fail and eof functions would all return false. I/O operations should be performed only on "good" streams.

- The rdstate member function returns the error state of the stream.

- Member function clear restores a stream's state to "good," so that I/O may proceed on that stream.

Section 26.9 Tying an Output Stream to an Input Stream

- C++ provides the tie member function to synchronize istream and ostream operations to ensure that outputs appear before subsequent inputs.

Terminology

bad member function of basic_ios	basic_fstream class template
badbit	basic_ifstream class template

`basic_ios` class template
`basic_iostream` class template
`basic_istream` class template
`basic_ofstream` class template
`basic_ostream` class template
`boolalpha` stream manipulator
`clear` member function of `basic_ios`
`dec` stream manipulator
default fill character (space)
default precision
end-of-file
`eof` member function of `basic_ios`
`eofbit`
`fail` member function of `basic_ios`
`failbit`
field width
fill character
`fill` member function of `basic_ios`
`fixed` stream manipulator
`flags` member function of `ios_base`
`fmtflags`
format states
formatted I/O
`fstream`
`gcount` member function of `basic_istream`
`get` member function of `basic_istream`
`getline` member function of `basic_istream`
`good` member function of `basic_ios`
`hex` stream manipulator
`ifstream`
`ignore` member function of `basic_istream`
in-memory formatting
`internal` stream manipulator
`<iomanip>` header file
`ios_base` class
`iostream`
`istream`
leading 0 (octal)
leading 0x or 0X (hexadecimal)
`left` stream manipulator
`noboolalpha` stream manipulator
`noshowbase` stream manipulator
`noshowpoint` stream manipulator

`noshowpos` stream manipulator
`noskipws` stream manipulator
`nouppercase` stream manipulator
`oct` stream manipulator
`ofstream`
`operator void*` member function of `basic_ios`
`operator!` member function of `basic_ios`
`ostream`
output buffering
padding
parameterized stream manipulator
`peek` member function of `basic_istream`
`precision` member function of `ios_base`
predefined streams
`put` member function of `basic_ostream`
`putback` member function of `basic_istream`
`rdstate` member function of `basic_ios`
`read` member function of `basic_istream`
`right` stream manipulator
`scientific` stream manipulator
`setbase` stream manipulator
`setfill` stream manipulator
`setprecision` stream manipulator
`setw` stream manipulator
`showbase` stream manipulator
`showpoint` stream manipulator
`showpos` stream manipulator
`skipws` stream manipulator
stream input
stream manipulator
stream output
stream extraction operator (`>>`)
stream insertion operator (`<<`)
`tie` member function of `basic_ios`
`typedef`
type-safe I/O
unbuffered output
unformatted I/O
`uppercase` stream manipulator
`width` stream manipulator
`write` member function of `basic_ostream`

Self-Review Exercises

26.1   Answer each of the following:

    a)   Input/output in C++ occurs as _____ of bytes.

    b)   The stream manipulators that format justification are _____, _____ and _____.

    c)   Member function _____ can be used to set and reset format state.

d) Most C++ programs that do I/O should include the _____ header file that contains the declarations required for all stream-I/O operations.

e) When using parameterized manipulators, the header file _____ must be included.

f) Header file _____ contains the declarations required for user-controlled file processing.

g) The ostream member function _____ is used to perform unformatted output.

h) Input operations are supported by class _____.

i) Outputs to the standard error stream are directed to either the _____ or the _____ stream object.

j) Output operations are supported by class _____.

k) The symbol for the stream insertion operator is _____.

l) The four objects that correspond to the standard devices on the system include _____, _____, _____ and _____.

m) The symbol for the stream extraction operator is _____.

n) The stream manipulators _____, _____ and _____ specify that integers should be displayed in octal, hexadecimal and decimal formats, respectively.

o) When used, the _____ stream manipulator causes positive numbers to display with a plus sign.

26.2 State whether the following are *true* or *false*. If the answer is *false*, explain why.

a) The stream member function flags with a long argument sets the flags state variable to its argument and returns its previous value.

b) The stream insertion operator << and the stream-extraction operator >> are overloaded to handle all standard data types—including strings and memory addresses (stream insertion only)—and all user-defined data types.

c) The stream member function flags with no arguments resets the stream's format state.

d) The stream extraction operator >> can be overloaded with an operator function that takes an istream reference and a reference to a user-defined type as arguments and returns an istream reference.

e) The stream insertion operator << can be overloaded with an operator function that takes an istream reference and a reference to a user-defined type as arguments and returns an istream reference.

f) Input with the stream extraction operator >> always skips leading white-space characters in the input stream, by default.

g) The stream member function rdstate returns the current state of the stream.

h) The cout stream normally is connected to the display screen.

i) The stream member function good returns true if the bad, fail and eof member functions all return false.

j) The cin stream normally is connected to the display screen.

k) If a nonrecoverable error occurs during a stream operation, the bad member function will return true.

l) Output to cerr is unbuffered and output to clog is buffered.

m) Stream manipulator showpoint forces floating-point values to print with the default six digits of precision unless the precision value has been changed, in which case floating-point values print with the specified precision.

n) The ostream member function put outputs the specified number of characters.

o) The stream manipulators dec, oct and hex affect only the next integer output operation.

p) By default, memory addresses are displayed as long integers.

26.3 For each of the following, write a single statement that performs the indicated task.

a) Output the string "Enter your name: ".

b) Use a stream manipulator that causes the exponent in scientific notation and the letters in hexadecimal values to print in capital letters.

c) Output the address of the variable myString of type char *.

d) Use a stream manipulator to ensure that floating-point values print in scientific notation.

e) Output the address in variable integerPtr of type int *.

f) Use a stream manipulator such that, when integer values are output, the integer base for octal and hexadecimal values is displayed.

g) Output the value pointed to by floatPtr of type float *.

h) Use a stream member function to set the fill character to '*' for printing in field widths larger than the values being output. Write a separate statement to do this with a stream manipulator.

i) Output the characters 'O' and 'K' in one statement with ostream function put.

j) Get the value of the next character in the input stream without extracting it from the stream.

k) Input a single character into variable charValue of type char, using the istream member function get in two different ways.

l) Input and discard the next six characters in the input stream.

m) Use istream member function read to input 50 characters into char array line.

n) Read 10 characters into character array name. Stop reading characters if the '.' delimiter is encountered. Do not remove the delimiter from the input stream. Write another statement that performs this task and removes the delimiter from the input.

o) Use the istream member function gcount to determine the number of characters input into character array line by the last call to istream member function read, and output that number of characters, using ostream member function write.

p) Output the following values: 124, 18.376, 'Z', 1000000 and "String".

q) Print the current precision setting, using a member function of object cout.

r) Input an integer value into int variable months and a floating-point value into float variable percentageRate.

s) Print 1.92, 1.925 and 1.9258 separated by tabs and with 3 digits of precision, using a manipulator.

t) Print integer 100 in octal, hexadecimal and decimal, using stream manipulators.

u) Print integer 100 in decimal, octal and hexadecimal, using a stream manipulator to change the base.

v) Print 1234 right justified in a 10-digit field.

w) Read characters into character array line until the character 'z' is encountered, up to a limit of 20 characters (including a terminating null character). Do not extract the delimiter character from the stream.

x) Use integer variables x and y to specify the field width and precision used to display the double value 87.4573, and display the value.

26.4 Identify the error in each of the following statements and explain how to correct it.

a) `cout << "Value of x <= y is: " << x <= y;`

b) The following statement should print the integer value of 'c'.
```
cout << 'c';
```

c) `cout << """A string in quotes""";`

26.5 For each of the following, show the output.

a)
```
cout << "12345" << endl;
cout.width( 5 );
cout.fill( '*' );
cout << 123 << endl << 123;
```

b) cout << setw(10) << setfill('$') << 10000;
c) cout << setw(8) << setprecision(3) << 1024.987654;
d) cout << showbase << oct << 99 << endl << hex << 99;
e) cout << 100000 << endl << showpos << 100000;
f) cout << setw(10) << setprecision(2) << scientific << 444.93738;

Answers to Self-Review Exercises

26.1   a) streams. b) left, right and internal. c) flags. d) <iostream>. e) <iomanip>.
f) <fstream>. g) write. h) istream. i) cerr or clog. j) ostream. k) <<. l) cin, cout, cerr and clog.
m) >>. n) oct, hex and dec. o) showpos.

26.2   a) False. The stream member function flags with a fmtflags argument sets the flags state
variable to its argument and returns the prior state settings. b) False. The stream insertion and
stream extraction operators are not overloaded for all user-defined types. The programmer of a class
must specifically provide the overloaded operator functions to overload the stream operators for use
with each user-defined type. c) False. The stream member function flags with no arguments returns the current format settings as a fmtflags data type, which represents the format state. d) True.
e) False. To overload the stream insertion operator <<, the overloaded operator function must take
an ostream reference and a reference to a user-defined type as arguments and return an ostream reference. f) True. g) True. h) True. i) True. j) False. The cin stream is connected to the standard input of the computer, which normally is the keyboard. k) True. l) True. m) True. n) False. The
ostream member function put outputs its single-character argument. o) False. The stream manipulators dec, oct and hex set the output format state for integers to the specified base until the base is
changed again or the program terminates. p) False. Memory addresses are displayed in hexadecimal
format by default. To display addresses as long integers, the address must be cast to a long value.

26.3   a) cout << "Enter your name: ";
     b) cout << uppercase;
     c) cout << **static_cast**< **void** * >(myString);
     d) cout << scientific;
     e) cout << integerPtr;
     f) cout << showbase;
     g) cout << *floatPtr;
     h) cout.fill('*');
        cout << setfill('*');
     i) cout.put('O').put('K');
     j) cin.peek();
     k) charValue = cin.get();
        cin.get(charValue);
     l) cin.ignore(6);
     m) cin.read(line, 50);
     n) cin.get(name, 10, '.');
        cin.getline(name, 10, '.');
     o) cout.write(line, cin.gcount());
     p) cout << 124 << ' ' << 18.376 << ' ' << "Z " << 1000000 << " String";
     q) cout << cout.precision();
     r) cin >> months >> percentageRate;
     s) cout << setprecision(3) << 1.92 << '\t' << 1.925 << '\t' << 1.9258;
     t) cout << oct << 100 << '\t' << hex << 100 << '\t' << dec << 100;
     u) cout << 100 << '\t' << setbase(8) << 100 << '\t' << setbase(16) << 100;
     v) cout << setw(10) << 1234;

w) `cin.get( line, 20, 'z' );`

x) `cout << setw( x ) << setprecision( y ) << 87.4573;`

26.4 a) Error: The precedence of the << operator is higher than that of <=, which causes the statement to be evaluated improperly and also causes a compiler error.
Correction: To correct the statement, place parentheses around the expression x <= y. This problem will occur with any expression that uses operators of lower precedence than the << operator if the expression is not placed in parentheses.

b) Error: In C++, characters are not treated as small integers, as they are in C.
Correction: To print the numerical value for a character in the computer's character set, the character must be cast to an integer value, as in the following:

```
cout << static_cast< int >( 'c' );
```

c) Error: Quote characters cannot be printed in a string unless an escape sequence is used.
Correction: Print the string in one of the following ways:

```
cout << '"' << "A string in quotes" << '"';
cout << "\"A string in quotes\"";
```

26.5 a) `12345`
`**123`
`123`

b) `$$$$$10000`

c) `1024.988`

d) `0143`
`0x63`

e) `100000`
`+100000`

f) `4.45e+002`

Exercises

26.6 Write a statement for each of the following:

a) Print integer 40000 left justified in a 15-digit field.

b) Read a string into character array variable `state`.

c) Print 200 with and without a sign.

d) Print the decimal value 100 in hexadecimal form preceded by 0x.

e) Read characters into array `charArray` until the character `'p'` is encountered, up to a limit of 10 characters (including the terminating null character). Extract the delimiter from the input stream, and discard it.

f) Print 1.234 in a 9-digit field with preceding zeros.

g) Read a string of the form "characters" from the standard input. Store the string in character array `charArray`. Eliminate the quotation marks from the input stream. Read a maximum of 50 characters (including the terminating null character).

26.7 Write a program to test the inputting of integer values in decimal, octal and hexadecimal formats. Output each integer read by the program in all three formats. Test the program with the following input data: 10, 010, 0x10.

26.8 Write a program that prints pointer values, using casts to all the integer data types. Which ones print strange values? Which ones cause errors?

26.9 Write a program to test the results of printing the integer value 12345 and the floating-point value 1.2345 in various-sized fields. What happens when the values are printed in fields containing fewer digits than the values?

26.10 Write a program that prints the value 100.453627 rounded to the nearest digit, tenth, hundredth, thousandth and ten-thousandth.

26.11 Write a program that inputs a string from the keyboard and determines the length of the string. Print the string in a length that is twice the field width.

26.12 Write a program that converts integer Fahrenheit temperatures from 0 to 212 degrees to floating-point Celsius temperatures with 3 digits of precision. Use the formula

```
celsius = 5.0 / 9.0 * ( fahrenheit - 32 );
```

to perform the calculation. The output should be printed in two right-justified columns and the Celsius temperatures should be preceded by a sign for both positive and negative values.

26.13 In some programming languages, strings are entered surrounded by either single or double quotation marks. Write a program that reads the three strings suzy, "suzy" and 'suzy'. Are the single and double quotes ignored or read as part of the string?

26.14 In Fig. 22.5, the stream extraction and stream insertion operators were overloaded for input and output of objects of the `PhoneNumber` class. Rewrite the stream extraction operator to perform the following error checking on input. The `operator>>` function will need to be reimplemented.

    a) Input the entire phone number into an array. Test that the proper number of characters has been entered. There should be a total of 14 characters read for a phone number of the form (800) 555-1212. Use `ios_base`-member-function `clear` to set `failbit` for improper input.

    b) The area code and exchange do not begin with 0 or 1. Test the first digit of the area-code and exchange portions of the phone number to be sure that neither begins with 0 or 1. Use `ios_base`-member-function `clear` to set `failbit` for improper input.

    c) The middle digit of an area code used to be limited to 0 or 1 (although this has changed recently). Test the middle digit for a value of 0 or 1. Use the `ios_base`-member-function `clear` to set `failbit` for improper input. If none of the above operations results in `failbit` being set for improper input, copy the three parts of the telephone number into the `areaCode`, `exchange` and `line` members of the `PhoneNumber` object. In the main program, if `failbit` has been set on the input, have the program print an error message and end, rather than print the phone number.

26.15 Write a program that accomplishes each of the following:

    a) Create a user-defined class `Point` that contains the private integer data members xCoordinate and yCoordinate and declares stream insertion and stream extraction overloaded operator functions as `friends` of the class.

    b) Define the stream insertion and stream extraction operator functions. The stream extraction operator function should determine whether the data entered is valid, and, if not, it should set the `failbit` to indicate improper input. The stream insertion operator should not be able to display the point after an input error has occurred.

    c) Write a main function that tests input and output of user-defined class `Point`, using the overloaded stream extraction and stream insertion operators.

26.16 Write a program that accomplishes each of the following:

    a) Create a user-defined class `Complex` that contains the private integer data members real and imaginary and declares stream insertion and stream extraction overloaded operator functions as `friends` of the class.

    b) Define the stream insertion and stream extraction operator functions. The stream extraction operator function should determine whether the data entered is valid, and, if not, it should set `failbit` to indicate improper input. The input should be of the form

c) The values can be negative or positive, and it is possible that one of the two values is not provided. If a value is not provided, the appropriate data member should be set to 0. The stream-insertion operator should not be able to display the point if an input error has occurred. For negative imaginary values, a minus sign should be printed rather than a plus sign.

d) Write a main function that tests input and output of user-defined class Complex, using the overloaded stream extraction and stream insertion operators.

26.17 Write a program that uses a for statement to print a table of ASCII values for the characters in the ASCII character set from 33 to 126. The program should print the decimal value, octal value, hexadecimal value and character value for each character. Use the stream manipulators dec, oct and hex to print the integer values.

26.18 Write a program to show that the getline and three-argument get istream member functions both end the input string with a string-terminating null character. Also, show that get leaves the delimiter character on the input stream, whereas getline extracts the delimiter character and discards it. What happens to the unread characters in the stream?

27

Exception Handling

OBJECTIVES

In this chapter you will learn:

- What exceptions are and when to use them.
- To use `try`, `catch` and `throw` to detect, handle and indicate exceptions, respectively.
- To process uncaught and unexpected exceptions.
- To declare new exception classes.
- How stack unwinding enables exceptions not caught in one scope to be caught in another scope.
- To handle `new` failures.
- To use `auto_ptr` to prevent memory leaks.
- To understand the standard exception hierarchy.

27.1 Introduction

In this chapter, we introduce **exception handling**. An **exception** is an indication of a problem that occurs during a program's execution. The name "exception" implies that the problem occurs infrequently—if the "rule" is that a statement normally executes correctly, then the "exception to the rule" is that a problem occurs. Exception handling enables programmers to create applications that can resolve (or handle) exceptions. In many cases, handling an exception allows a program to continue executing as if no problem had been encountered. A more severe problem could prevent a program from continuing normal execution, instead requiring the program to notify the user of the problem before terminating in a controlled manner. The features presented in this chapter enable programmers to write **robust** and **fault-tolerant programs** that are able to deal with problems that may arise and continue executing or terminate gracefully. The style and details of C++ exception handling are based in part on the work of Andrew Koenig and Bjarne Stroustrup, as presented in their paper, "Exception Handling for C++ (revised)."[1]

Error-Prevention Tip 27.1

Exception handling helps improve a program's fault tolerance.

Software Engineering Observation 27.1

Exception handling provides a standard mechanism for processing errors. This is especially important when working on a project with a large team of programmers.

---

1. Koenig, A., and B. Stroustrup, "Exception Handling for C++ (revised)," *Proceedings of the Usenix C++ Conference*, pp. 149–176, San Francisco, April 1990.

The chapter begins with an overview of exception-handling concepts, then demonstrates basic exception-handling techniques. We show these techniques via an example that demonstrates handling an exception that occurs when a function attempts to divide by zero. We then discuss additional exception-handling issues, such as how to handle exceptions that occur in a constructor or destructor and how to handle exceptions that occur if operator new fails to allocate memory for an object. We conclude the chapter by introducing several classes that the C++ Standard Library provides for handling exceptions.

27.2 Exception-Handling Overview

Program logic frequently tests conditions that determine how program execution proceeds. Consider the following pseudocode:

> *Perform a task*
>
> *If the preceding task did not execute correctly*
> > *Perform error processing*
>
> *Perform next task*
>
> *If the preceding task did not execute correctly*
> > *Perform error processing*
>
> ...

In this pseudocode, we begin by performing a task. We then test whether that task executed correctly. If not, we perform error processing. Otherwise, we continue with the next task. Although this form of error handling works, intermixing program logic with error-handling logic can make the program difficult to read, modify, maintain and debug—especially in large applications.

Performance Tip 27.1

If the potential problems occur infrequently, intermixing program logic and error-handling logic can degrade a program's performance, because the program must (potentially frequently) perform tests to determine whether the task executed correctly and the next task can be performed.

Exception handling enables the programmer to remove error-handling code from the "main line" of the program's execution, which improves program clarity and enhances modifiability. Programmers can decide to handle any exceptions they choose—all exceptions, all exceptions of a certain type or all exceptions of a group of related types (e.g., exception types that belong to an inheritance hierarchy). Such flexibility reduces the likelihood that errors will be overlooked and thereby makes a program more robust.

With programming languages that do not support exception handling, programmers often delay writing error-processing code or sometimes forget to include it. This results in less robust software products. C++ enables the programmer to deal with exception handling easily from the inception of a project.

27.3 Example: Handling an Attempt to Divide by Zero

Let us consider a simple example of exception handling (Figs. 27.1–27.2). The purpose of this example is to prevent a common arithmetic problem—division by zero. In C++, division by zero using integer arithmetic typically causes a program to terminate prematurely. In floating-point arithmetic, division by zero is allowed—it results in positive or negative infinity, which is displayed as INF or -INF.

In this example, we define a function named quotient that receives two integers input by the user and divides its first int parameter by its second int parameter. Before performing the division, the function casts the first int parameter's value to type double. Then, the second int parameter's value is promoted to type double for the calculation. So function quotient actually performs the division using two double values and returns a double result.

Although division by zero is allowed in floating-point arithmetic, for the purpose of this example, we treat any attempt to divide by zero as an error. Thus, function quotient tests its second parameter to ensure that it is not zero before allowing the division to proceed. If the second parameter is zero, the function uses an exception to indicate to the caller that a problem occurred. The caller (main in this example) can then process this exception and allow the user to type two new values before calling function quotient again. In this way, the program can continue to execute even after an improper value is entered, thus making the program more robust.

The example consists of two files—DivideByZeroException.h (Fig. 27.1) defines an exception class that represents the type of the problem that might occur in the example, and fig27_02.cpp (Fig. 27.2) defines the quotient function and the main function that calls it. Function main contains the code that demonstrates exception handling.

Defining an Exception Class to Represent the Type of Problem That Might Occur
Figure 27.1 defines class DivideByZeroException as a derived class of Standard Library class **runtime_error** (defined in header file **<stdexcept>**). Class runtime_error—a derived class of Standard Library class **exception** (defined in header file **<exception>**)—is the C++ standard base class for representing runtime errors. Class exception is the standard C++ base class for all exceptions. (Section 27.13 discusses class exception and its derived classes in detail.) A typical exception class that derives from the runtime_error class defines only a constructor (e.g., lines 12–13) that passes an error-message string to the base-class runtime_error constructor. Every exception class that derives directly or indirectly

```
 1   // Fig. 27.1: DivideByZeroException.h
 2   // Class DivideByZeroException definition.
 3   #include <stdexcept> // stdexcept header file contains runtime_error
 4   using std::runtime_error; // standard C++ library class runtime_error
 5
 6   // DivideByZeroException objects should be thrown by functions
 7   // upon detecting division-by-zero exceptions
 8   class DivideByZeroException : public runtime_error
 9   {
10   public:
11      // constructor specifies default error message
12      DivideByZeroException::DivideByZeroException()
13         : runtime_error( "attempted to divide by zero" ) {}
14   }; // end class DivideByZeroException
```

Fig. 27.1 | Class DivideByZeroException definition.

```
1   // Fig. 27.2: fig27_02.cpp
2   // A simple exception-handling example that checks for
3   // divide-by-zero exceptions.
4   #include <iostream>
5   using std::cin;
6   using std::cout;
7   using std::endl;
8
9   #include "DivideByZeroException.h" // DivideByZeroException class
10
11  // perform division and throw DivideByZeroException object if
12  // divide-by-zero exception occurs
13  double quotient( int numerator, int denominator )
14  {
15     // throw DivideByZeroException if trying to divide by zero
16     if ( denominator == 0 )
17        throw DivideByZeroException(); // terminate function
18
19     // return division result
20     return static_cast< double >( numerator ) / denominator;
21  } // end function quotient
22
23  int main()
24  {
25     int number1; // user-specified numerator
26     int number2; // user-specified denominator
27     double result; // result of division
28
29     cout << "Enter two integers (end-of-file to end): ";
30
31     // enable user to enter two integers to divide
32     while ( cin >> number1 >> number2 )
33     {
34        // try block contains code that might throw exception
35        // and code that should not execute if an exception occurs
36        try
37        {
38           result = quotient( number1, number2 );
39           cout << "The quotient is: " << result << endl;
40        } // end try
41
42        // exception handler handles a divide-by-zero exception
43        catch ( DivideByZeroException &divideByZeroException )
44        {
45           cout << "Exception occurred: "
46              << divideByZeroException.what() << endl;
47        } // end catch
48
49        cout << "\nEnter two integers (end-of-file to end): ";
50     } // end while
51
```

Fig. 27.2 | Exception-handling example that throws exceptions on attempts to divide by zero. (Part 1 of 2.)

```
52        cout << endl;
53        return 0; // terminate normally
54  } // end main
```

```
Enter two integers (end-of-file to end): 100 7
The quotient is: 14.2857

Enter two integers (end-of-file to end): 100 0
Exception occurred: attempted to divide by zero

Enter two integers (end-of-file to end): ^Z
```

Fig. 27.2 | Exception-handling example that throws exceptions on attempts to divide by zero. (Part 2 of 2.)

from exception contains the virtual function **what**, which returns an exception object's error message. Note that you are not required to derive a custom exception class, such as DivideByZeroException, from the standard exception classes provided by C++. However, doing so allows programmers to use the virtual function what to obtain an appropriate error message. We use an object of this DivideByZeroException class in Fig. 27.2 to indicate when an attempt is made to divide by zero.

Demonstrating Exception Handling

The program in Fig. 27.2 uses exception handling to wrap code that might throw a "divide-by-zero" exception and to handle that exception, should one occur. The application enables the user to enter two integers, which are passed as arguments to function quotient (lines 13–21). This function divides the first number (numerator) by the second number (denominator). Assuming that the user does not specify 0 as the denominator for the division, function quotient returns the division result. However, if the user inputs a 0 value as the denominator, function quotient throws an exception. In the sample output, the first two lines show a successful calculation, and the next two lines show a failed calculation due to an attempt to divide by zero. When the exception occurs, the program informs the user of the mistake and prompts the user to input two new integers. After we discuss the code, we will consider the user inputs and flow of program control that yield these outputs.

Enclosing Code in a try Block

The program begins by prompting the user to enter two integers. The integers are input in the condition of the while loop (line 32). After the user inputs values that represent the numerator and denominator, program control proceeds into the loop's body (lines 33–50). Line 38 passes these values to function quotient (lines 13–21), which either divides the integers and returns a result, or **throws an exception** (i.e., indicates that an error occurred) on an attempt to divide by zero. Exception handling is geared to situations in which the function that detects an error is unable to handle it.

C++ provides **try blocks** to enable exception handling. A try block consists of keyword **try** followed by braces ({}) that define a block of code in which exceptions might occur. The try block encloses statements that might cause exceptions and statements that should be skipped if an exception occurs.

Note that a `try` block (lines 36–40) encloses the invocation of function `quotient` and the statement that displays the division result. In this example, because the invocation to function `quotient` (line 38) can throw an exception, we enclose this function invocation in a `try` block. Enclosing the output statement (line 39) in the `try` block ensures that the output will occur only if function `quotient` returns a result.

Software Engineering Observation 27.2

Exceptions may surface through explicitly mentioned code in a `try` block, through calls to other functions and through deeply nested function calls initiated by code in a `try` block.

Defining a catch Handler to Process a DivideByZeroException

Exceptions are processed by `catch` handlers (also called exception handlers), which catch and handle exceptions. At least one `catch` handler (lines 43–47) must immediately follow each `try` block. Each `catch` handler begins with the keyword `catch` and specifies in parentheses an exception parameter that represents the type of exception the `catch` handler can process (`DivideByZeroException` in this case). When an exception occurs in a `try` block, the `catch` handler that executes is the one whose type matches the type of the exception that occurred (i.e., the type in the `catch` block matches the thrown exception type exactly or is a base class of it). If an exception parameter includes an optional parameter name, the `catch` handler can use that parameter name to interact with a caught exception object in the body of the `catch` handler, which is delimited by braces ({ and }). A `catch` handler typically reports the error to the user, logs it to a file, terminates the program gracefully or tries an alternate strategy to accomplish the failed task. In this example, the `catch` handler simply reports that the user attempted to divide by zero. Then the program prompts the user to enter two new integer values.

Common Programming Error 27.1

It is a syntax error to place code between a `try` block and its corresponding `catch` handlers.

Common Programming Error 27.2

Each `catch` handler can have only a single parameter—specifying a comma-separated list of exception parameters is a syntax error.

Common Programming Error 27.3

It is a logic error to catch the same type in two different `catch` handlers following a single `try` block.

Termination Model of Exception Handling

If an exception occurs as the result of a statement in a `try` block, the `try` block expires (i.e., terminates immediately). Next, the program searches for the first `catch` handler that can process the type of exception that occurred. The program locates the matching `catch` by comparing the thrown exception's type to each `catch`'s exception-parameter type until the program finds a match. A match occurs if the types are identical or if the thrown exception's type is a derived class of the exception-parameter type. When a match occurs, the code contained within the matching catch handler executes. When a catch handler finishes processing by reaching its closing right brace (}), the exception is considered handled and the local variables defined within the catch handler (including the catch parameter) go out of scope. Program control does not return to the point at which the exception occurred (known as the throw point), because the try block has expired. Rather, control resumes with the first statement (line 49) after the last catch handler following the try block. This is known as the termination model of exception handling. [*Note:* Some languages use the resumption model of exception handling, in which, after an exception is handled, control resumes just after the throw point.] As with any other block of code, when a try block terminates, local variables defined in the block go out of scope.

Common Programming Error 27.4

Logic errors can occur if you assume that after an exception is handled, control will return to the first statement after the throw point.

Error-Prevention Tip 27.2

With exception handling, a program can continue executing (rather than terminating) after dealing with a problem. This helps ensure the kind of robust applications that contribute to what is called mission-critical computing or business-critical computing.

If the try block completes its execution successfully (i.e., no exceptions occur in the try block), then the program ignores the catch handlers, and program control continues with the first statement after the last catch following that try block. If no exceptions occur in a try block, the program ignores the catch handler(s) for that block.

If an exception that occurs in a try block has no matching catch handler, or if an exception occurs in a statement that is not in a try block, the function that contains the statement terminates immediately, and the program attempts to locate an enclosing try block in the calling function. This process is called stack unwinding and is discussed in Section 27.8.

Flow of Program Control When the User Enters a Nonzero Denominator
Consider the flow of control when the user inputs the numerator 100 and the denominator 7 (i.e., the first two lines of output in Fig. 27.2). In line 16, function quotient determines that the denominator does not equal zero, so line 20 performs the division and returns the result (14.2857) to line 38 as a double (the static_cast< double > in line 20 ensures the proper return value type). Program control then continues sequentially from line 38, so line 39 displays the division result and line 40 is the end of the try block. Because the try block completed successfully and did not throw an exception, the program does not execute the statements contained in the catch handler (lines 43–47), and control continues to line 49 (the first line of code after the catch handler), which prompts the user to enter two more integers.

Flow of Program Control When the User Enters a Denominator of Zero
Now let us consider a more interesting case in which the user inputs the numerator 100 and the denominator 0 (i.e., the third and fourth lines of output in Fig. 27.2). In line 16, quotient determines that the denominator equals zero, which indicates an attempt to di-

vide by zero. Line 17 throws an exception, which we represent as an object of class DivideByZeroException (Fig. 27.1).

Note that, to throw an exception, line 17 uses keyword **throw** followed by an operand that represents the type of exception to throw. Normally, a throw statement specifies one operand. (In Section 27.5, we discuss how to use a throw statement that specifies no operands.) The operand of a throw can be of any type. If the operand is an object, we call it an exception object—in this example, the exception object is an object of type DivideByZeroException. However, a throw operand also can assume other values, such as the value of an expression (e.g., throw x > 5) or the value of an int (e.g., throw 5). The examples in this chapter focus exclusively on throwing exception objects.

Common Programming Error 27.5

Use caution when throwing *the result of a conditional expression (?:), because promotion rules could cause the value to be of a type different from the one expected. For example, when throwing an* int *or a* double *from the same conditional expression, the conditional expression converts the* int *to a* double. *However, the* catch *handler always catches the result as a* double, *rather than catching the result as a* double *when a* double *is thrown, and catching the result as an* int *when an* int *is thrown.*

As part of throwing an exception, the throw operand is created and used to initialize the parameter in the catch handler, which we discuss momentarily. In this example, the throw statement in line 17 creates an object of class DivideByZeroException. When line 17 throws the exception, function quotient exits immediately. Therefore, line 17 throws the exception before function quotient can perform the division in line 20. This is a central characteristic of exception handling: A function should throw an exception *before* the error has an opportunity to occur.

Because we decided to enclose the invocation of function quotient (line 38) in a try block, program control enters the catch handler (lines 43–47) that immediately follows the try block. This catch handler serves as the exception handler for the divide-by-zero exception. In general, when an exception is thrown within a try block, the exception is caught by a catch handler that specifies the type matching the thrown exception. In this program, the catch handler specifies that it catches DivideByZeroException objects—this type matches the object type thrown in function quotient. Actually, the catch handler catches a reference to the DivideByZeroException object created by function quotient's throw statement (line 17).

Performance Tip 27.2

Catching an exception object by reference eliminates the overhead of copying the object that represents the thrown exception.

Good Programming Practice 27.1

Associating each type of runtime error with an appropriately named exception object improves program clarity.

The catch handler's body (lines 45–46) prints the associated error message returned by calling function what of base-class runtime_error. This function returns the string that the DivideByZeroException constructor (lines 12–13 in Fig. 27.1) passed to the runtime_error base-class constructor.

27.4 When to Use Exception Handling

Exception handling is designed to process synchronous errors, which occur when a statement executes. Common examples of these errors are out-of-range array subscripts, arithmetic overflow (i.e., a value outside the representable range of values), division by zero, invalid function parameters and unsuccessful memory allocation (due to lack of memory). Exception handling is not designed to process errors associated with asynchronous events (e.g., disk I/O completions, network message arrivals, mouse clicks and keystrokes), which occur in parallel with, and independent of, the program's flow of control.

Software Engineering Observation 27.3

Incorporate your exception-handling strategy into your system from the design process's inception. Including effective exception handling after a system has been implemented can be difficult.

Software Engineering Observation 27.4

Exception handling provides a single, uniform technique for processing problems. This helps programmers working on large projects understand each other's error-processing code.

Software Engineering Observation 27.5

Avoid using exception handling as an alternate form of flow of control. These "additional" exceptions can "get in the way" of genuine error-type exceptions.

Software Engineering Observation 27.6

Exception handling simplifies combining software components and enables them to work together effectively by enabling predefined components to communicate problems to application-specific components, which can then process the problems in an application-specific manner.

The exception-handling mechanism also is useful for processing problems that occur when a program interacts with software elements, such as member functions, constructors, destructors and classes. Rather than handling problems internally, such software elements often use exceptions to notify programs when problems occur. This enables programmers to implement customized error handling for each application.

Performance Tip 27.3

When no exceptions occur, exception-handling code incurs little or no performance penalties. Thus, programs that implement exception handling operate more efficiently than do programs that intermix error-handling code with program logic.

Software Engineering Observation 27.7

Functions with common error conditions should return 0 or NULL (or other appropriate values) rather than throw exceptions. A program calling such a function can check the return value to determine success or failure of the function call.

Complex applications normally consist of predefined software components and application-specific components that use the predefined components. When a predefined component encounters a problem, that component needs a mechanism to communicate the problem to the application-specific component—the predefined component cannot know in advance how each application processes a problem that occurs.

27.5 Rethrowing an Exception

It is possible that an exception handler, upon receiving an exception, might decide either that it cannot process that exception or that it can process the exception only partially. In such cases, the exception handler can defer the exception handling (or perhaps a portion of it) to another exception handler. In either case, the handler achieves this by **rethrowing** the exception via the statement

```
throw;
```

Regardless of whether a handler can process (even partially) an exception, the handler can rethrow the exception for further processing outside the handler. The next enclosing try block detects the rethrown exception, which a catch handler listed after that enclosing try block attempts to handle.

Common Programming Error 27.6

Executing an empty throw statement that is situated outside a catch handler causes a call to function terminate, which abandons exception processing and terminates the program immediately.

The program of Fig. 27.3 demonstrates rethrowing an exception. In main's try block (lines 32–37), line 35 calls function throwException (lines 11–27). The throwException

```cpp
1   // Fig. 27.3: fig27_03.cpp
2   // Demonstrating exception rethrowing.
3   #include <iostream>
4   using std::cout;
5   using std::endl;
6
7   #include <exception>
8   using std::exception;
9
10  // throw, catch and rethrow exception
11  void throwException()
12  {
13     // throw exception and catch it immediately
14     try
15     {
16        cout << " Function throwException throws an exception\n";
17        throw exception(); // generate exception
18     } // end try
19     catch ( exception & ) // handle exception
20     {
21        cout << " Exception handled in function throwException"
22           << "\n Function throwException rethrows exception";
23        throw; // rethrow exception for further processing
24     } // end catch
25
26     cout << "This also should not print\n";
27  } // end function throwException
28
```

Fig. 27.3 | Rethrowing an exception. (Part 1 of 2.)

```
29   int main()
30   {
31      // throw exception
32      try
33      {
34         cout << "\nmain invokes function throwException\n";
35         throwException();
36         cout << "This should not print\n";
37      } // end try
38      catch ( exception & ) // handle exception
39      {
40         cout << "\n\nException handled in main\n";
41      } // end catch
42
43      cout << "Program control continues after catch in main\n";
44      return 0;
45   } // end main
```

```
main invokes function throwException
   Function throwException throws an exception
   Exception handled in function throwException
   Function throwException rethrows exception

Exception handled in main
Program control continues after catch in main
```

Fig. 27.3 | Rethrowing an exception. (Part 2 of 2.)

function also contains a try block (lines 14–18), from which the throw statement at line 17 throws an instance of standard-library-class exception. Function throwException's catch handler (lines 19–24) catches this exception, prints an error message (lines 21–22) and rethrows the exception (line 23). This terminates function throwException and returns control to line 35 in the try...catch block in main. The try block terminates (so line 36 does not execute), and the catch handler in main (lines 38–41) catches this exception and prints an error message (line 40). [*Note:* Since we do not use the exception parameters in the catch handlers of this example, we omit the exception parameter names and specify only the type of exception to catch (lines 19 and 38).]

27.6 Exception Specifications

An optional exception specification (also called a **throw** list) enumerates a list of exceptions that a function can throw. For example, consider the function declaration

```
int someFunction( double value )
   throw ( ExceptionA, ExceptionB, ExceptionC )
{
   // function body
}
```

In this definition, the exception specification, which begins with keyword throw immediately following the closing parenthesis of the function's parameter list, indicates that function someFunction can throw exceptions of types ExceptionA, ExceptionB and ExceptionC. A function can throw only exceptions of the types indicated by the specification or exceptions of any type derived from these types. If the function throws an exception that does not belong to a specified type, function **unexpected** is called, which normally terminates the program.

A function that does not provide an exception specification can throw any exception. Placing throw()—an empty exception specification—after a function's parameter list states that the function does not throw exceptions. If the function attempts to throw an exception, function unexpected is invoked. Section 27.7 shows how function unexpected can be customized by calling function set_unexpected.

Common Programming Error 27.7

Throwing an exception that has not been declared in a function's exception specification causes a call to function unexpected.

Error-Prevention Tip 27.3

The compiler will not generate a compilation error if a function contains a throw expression for an exception not listed in the function's exception specification. An error occurs only when that function attempts to throw that exception at execution time. To avoid surprises at execution time, carefully check your code to ensure that functions do not throw exceptions not listed in their exception specifications.

27.7 Processing Unexpected Exceptions

Function unexpected calls the function registered with function set_unexpected (defined in header file <exception>). If no function has been registered in this manner, function terminate is called by default. Cases in which function terminate is called include:

1. the exception mechanism cannot find a matching catch for a thrown exception

2. a destructor attempts to throw an exception during stack unwinding

3. an attempt is made to rethrow an exception when there is no exception currently being handled

4. a call to function unexpected defaults to calling function terminate

(Section 15.5.1 of the C++ Standard Document discusses several additional cases.) Function **set_terminate** can specify the function to invoke when terminate is called. Otherwise, terminate calls **abort**, which terminates the program without calling the destructors of any remaining objects of automatic or static storage class. This could lead to resource leaks when a program terminates prematurely.

Function set_terminate and function set_unexpected each return a pointer to the last function called by terminate and unexpected, respectively (0, the first time each is called). This enables the programmer to save the function pointer so it can be restored later. Functions set_terminate and set_unexpected take as arguments pointers to functions with void return types and no arguments.

If the last action of a programmer-defined termination function is not to exit a program, function abort will be called to end program execution after the other statements of the programmer-defined termination function are executed.

27.8 Stack Unwinding

When an exception is thrown but not caught in a particular scope, the function call stack is unwound, and an attempt is made to catch the exception in the next outer try...catch block. Unwinding the function call stack means that the function in which the exception was not caught terminates, all local variables in that function are destroyed and control returns to the statement that originally invoked that function. If a try block encloses that statement, an attempt is made to catch the exception. If a try block does not enclose that statement, stack unwinding occurs again. If no catch handler ever catches this exception, function terminate is called to terminate the program. The program of Fig. 27.4 demonstrates stack unwinding.

In main, the try block (lines 37–41) calls function1 (lines 27–31). Next, function1 calls function2 (lines 20–24), which in turn calls function3 (lines 11–17). Line 16 of function3 throws a runtime_error object. However, because no try block encloses the throw statement in line 16, stack unwinding occurs—function3 terminates at line 16, then returns control to the statement in function2 that invoked function3 (i.e., line 23). Because no try block encloses line 23, stack unwinding occurs again—function2 termi-

```cpp
1    // Fig. 27.4: fig27_04.cpp
2    // Demonstrating stack unwinding.
3    #include <iostream>
4    using std::cout;
5    using std::endl;
6
7    #include <stdexcept>
8    using std::runtime_error;
9
10   // function3 throws run-time error
11   void function3() throw ( runtime_error )
12   {
13      cout << "In function 3" << endl;
14
15      // no try block, stack unwinding occurs, return control to function2
16      throw runtime_error( "runtime_error in function3" );
17   } // end function3
18
19   // function2 invokes function3
20   void function2() throw ( runtime_error )
21   {
22      cout << "function3 is called inside function2" << endl;
23      function3(); // stack unwinding occurs, return control to function1
24   } // end function2
25
26   // function1 invokes function2
27   void function1() throw ( runtime_error )
28   {
29      cout << "function2 is called inside function1" << endl;
30      function2(); // stack unwinding occurs, return control to main
31   } // end function1
32
```

Fig. 27.4 | Stack unwinding. (Part 1 of 2.)

```
33    // demonstrate stack unwinding
34    int main()
35    {
36       // invoke function1
37       try
38       {
39          cout << "function1 is called inside main" << endl;
40          function1(); // call function1 which throws runtime_error
41       } // end try
42       catch ( runtime_error &error ) // handle runtime error
43       {
44          cout << "Exception occurred: " << error.what() << endl;
45          cout << "Exception handled in main" << endl;
46       } // end catch
47
48       return 0;
49    } // end main
```

```
function1 is called inside main
function2 is called inside function1
function3 is called inside function2
In function 3
Exception occurred: runtime_error in function3
Exception handled in main
```

Fig. 27.4 | Stack unwinding. (Part 2 of 2.)

nates at line 23 and returns control to the statement in function1 that invoked function2 (i.e., line 30). Because no try block encloses line 30, stack unwinding occurs one more time—function1 terminates at line 30 and returns control to the statement in main that invoked function1 (i.e., line 40). The try block of lines 37–41 encloses this statement, so the first matching catch handler located after this try block (line 42–46) catches and processes the exception. Line 44 uses function what to display the exception message. Recall that function what is a virtual function of class exception that can be overridden by a derived class to return an appropriate error message.

27.9 Constructors, Destructors and Exception Handling

First, let us discuss an issue that we have mentioned but not yet resolved satisfactorily: What happens when an error is detected in a constructor? For example, how should an object's constructor respond when new fails because it was unable to allocate required memory for storing that object's internal representation? Because the constructor cannot return a value to indicate an error, we must choose an alternative means of indicating that the object has not been constructed properly. One scheme is to return the improperly constructed object and hope that anyone using it would make appropriate tests to determine that it is in an inconsistent state. Another scheme is to set some variable outside the constructor. Perhaps the best alternative is to require the constructor to throw an exception that contains the error information, thus offering an opportunity for the program to handle the failure.

Exceptions thrown by a constructor cause destructors to be called for any objects built as part of the object being constructed before the exception is thrown. Destructors are called for every automatic object constructed in a try block before an exception is thrown. Stack unwinding is guaranteed to have been completed at the point that an exception handler begins executing. If a destructor invoked as a result of stack unwinding throws an exception, terminate is called.

If an object has member objects, and if an exception is thrown before the outer object is fully constructed, then destructors will be executed for the member objects that have been constructed prior to the occurrence of the exception. If an array of objects has been partially constructed when an exception occurs, only the destructors for the constructed objects in the array will be called.

An exception could preclude the operation of code that would normally release a resource, thus causing a resource leak. One technique to resolve this problem is to initialize a local object to acquire the resource. When an exception occurs, the destructor for that object will be invoked and can free the resource.

Error-Prevention Tip 27.4

When an exception is thrown from the constructor for an object that is created in a new expression, the dynamically allocated memory for that object is released.

27.10 Exceptions and Inheritance

Various exception classes can be derived from a common base class, as we discussed in Section 27.3, when we created class DivideByZeroException as a derived class of class exception. If a catch handler catches a pointer or reference to an exception object of a base-class type, it also can catch a pointer or reference to all objects of classes publicly derived from that base class—this allows for polymorphic processing of related errors.

Error-Prevention Tip 27.5

Using inheritance with exceptions enables an exception handler to catch related errors with concise notation. One approach is to catch each type of pointer or reference to a derived-class exception object individually, but a more concise approach is to catch pointers or references to base-class exception objects instead. Also, catching pointers or references to derived-class exception objects individually is error prone, especially if the programmer forgets to test explicitly for one or more of the derived-class pointer or reference types.

27.11 Processing new Failures

The C++ standard specifies that, when operator new fails, it throws a **bad_alloc** exception (defined in header file <new>). However, some compilers are not compliant with the C++ standard and therefore use the version of new that returns 0 on failure. For example, the Microsoft Visual Studio .NET throws a bad_alloc exception when new fails, while the Microsoft Visual C++ 6.0 returns 0 on new failure.

Compilers vary in their support for new-failure handling. Many older C++ compilers return 0 by default when new fails. Some compilers support new throwing an exception if header file <new> (or <new.h>) is included. Other compilers throw bad_alloc by default, regardless of whether header file <new> is included. Consult the compiler documentation to determine the compiler's support for new-failure handling.

In this section, we present three examples of new failing. The first example returns 0 when new fails. The second example uses the version of new that throws a bad_alloc exception when new fails. The third example uses function **set_new_handler** to handle new failures. [*Note:* The examples in Figs. 27.5–27.7 allocate large amounts of dynamic memory, which could cause your computer to become sluggish.]

new *Returning 0 on Failure*

Figure 27.5 demonstrates new returning 0 on failure to allocate the requested amount of memory. The for statement at lines 13–24 should loop 50 times and, on each pass, allocate an array of 50,000,000 double values (i.e., 400,000,000 bytes, because a double is normally 8 bytes). The if statement at line 17 tests the result of each new operation to determine whether new allocated the memory successfully. If new fails and returns 0, line 19 prints an error message, and the loop terminates. [*Note:* We used Microsoft Visual C++ 6.0 to run this example, because Microsoft Visual Studio .NET throws a bad_alloc exception on new failure instead of returning 0.]

```
1   // Fig. 27.5: fig27_05.cpp
2   // Demonstrating pre-standard new returning 0 when memory
3   // is not allocated.
4   #include <iostream>
5   using std::cerr;
6   using std::cout;
7
8   int main()
9   {
10     double *ptr[ 50 ];
11
12     // allocate memory for ptr
13     for ( int i = 0; i < 50; i++ )
14     {
15       ptr[ i ] = new double[ 50000000 ];
16
17       if ( ptr[ i ] == 0 ) // did new fail to allocate memory
18       {
19         cerr << "Memory allocation failed for ptr[ " << i << " ]\n";
20         break;
21       } // end if
22       else // successful memory allocation
23         cout << "Allocated 50000000 doubles in ptr[ " << i << " ]\n";
24     } // end for
25
26     return 0;
27   } // end main
```

```
Allocated 50000000 doubles in ptr[ 0 ]
Allocated 50000000 doubles in ptr[ 1 ]
Allocated 50000000 doubles in ptr[ 2 ]
Memory allocation failed for ptr[ 3 ]
```

Fig. 27.5 | new returning 0 on failure.

The output shows that the program performed only three iterations before new failed, and the loop terminated. Your output might differ based on the physical memory, the disk space available for virtual memory on your system and the compiler you are using.

new *Throwing bad_alloc on Failure*

Figure 27.6 demonstrates new throwing bad_alloc on failure to allocate the requested memory. The for statement (lines 20–24) inside the try block should loop 50 times and, on each pass, allocate an array of 50,000,000 double values. If new fails and throws a bad_alloc exception, the loop terminates, and the program continues at line 28, where

```cpp
1   // Fig. 27.6: fig27_06.cpp
2   // Demonstrating standard new throwing bad_alloc when memory
3   // cannot be allocated.
4   #include <iostream>
5   using std::cerr;
6   using std::cout;
7   using std::endl;
8
9   #include <new> // standard operator new
10  using std::bad_alloc;
11
12  int main()
13  {
14     double *ptr[ 50 ];
15
16     // allocate memory for ptr
17     try
18     {
19        // allocate memory for ptr[ i ]; new throws bad_alloc on failure
20        for ( int i = 0; i < 50; i++ )
21        {
22           ptr[ i ] = new double[ 50000000 ]; // may throw exception
23           cout << "Allocated 50000000 doubles in ptr[ " << i << " ]\n";
24        } // end for
25     } // end try
26
27     // handle bad_alloc exception
28     catch ( bad_alloc &memoryAllocationException )
29     {
30        cerr << "Exception occurred: "
31           << memoryAllocationException.what() << endl;
32     } // end catch
33
34     return 0;
35  } // end main
```

```
Allocated 50000000 doubles in ptr[ 0 ]
Allocated 50000000 doubles in ptr[ 1 ]
Allocated 50000000 doubles in ptr[ 2 ]
Exception occurred: bad allocation
```

Fig. 27.6 | new throwing bad_alloc on failure.

the catch handler catches and processes the exception. Lines 30–31 print the message "Exception occurred:" followed by the message returned from the base-class-exception version of function what (i.e., an implementation-defined exception-specific message, such as "Allocation Failure" in Microsoft Visual Studio .NET 2003). The output shows that the program performed only three iterations of the loop before new failed and threw the bad_alloc exception. Your output might differ based on the physical memory, the disk space available for virtual memory on your system and the compiler you are using.

The C++ standard specifies that standard-compliant compilers can continue to use a version of new that returns 0 upon failure. For this purpose, header file <new> defines object **nothrow** (of type nothrow_t), which is used as follows:

```
double *ptr = new( nothrow ) double[ 50000000 ];
```

The preceding statement uses the version of new that does not throw bad_alloc exceptions (i.e., nothrow) to allocate an array of 50,000,000 doubles.

Software Engineering Observation 27.8

To make programs more robust, use the version of new that throws bad_alloc exceptions on failure.

Handling new Failures Using Function set_new_handler

An additional feature for handling new failures is function set_new_handler (prototyped in standard header file <new>). This function takes as its argument a pointer to a function that takes no arguments and returns void. This pointer points to the function that will be called if new fails. This provides the programmer with a uniform approach to handling all new failures, regardless of where a failure occurs in the program. Once set_new_handler registers a **new** handler in the program, operator new does not throw bad_alloc on failure; rather, it defers the error handling to the new-handler function.

If new allocates memory successfully, it returns a pointer to that memory. If new fails to allocate memory and set_new_handler has not registered a new-handler function, new throws a bad_alloc exception. If new fails to allocate memory and a new-handler function has been registered, the new-handler function is called. The C++ standard specifies that the new-handler function should perform one of the following tasks:

1. Make more memory available by deleting other dynamically allocated memory (or telling the user to close other applications) and return to operator new to attempt to allocate memory again.

2. Throw an exception of type bad_alloc.

3. Call function abort or exit (both found in header file <cstdlib>) to terminate the program.

Figure 27.7 demonstrates set_new_handler. Function customNewHandler (lines 14–18) prints an error message (line 16), then terminates the program via a call to abort (line 17). The output shows that the program performed only three iterations of the loop before new failed and invoked function customNewHandler. Your output might differ based on the physical memory, the disk space available for virtual memory on your system and the compiler you use to compile the program.

```
 1   // Fig. 27.7: fig27_07.cpp
 2   // Demonstrating set_new_handler.
 3   #include <iostream>
 4   using std::cerr;
 5   using std::cout;
 6
 7   #include <new> // standard operator new and set_new_handler
 8   using std::set_new_handler;
 9
10   #include <cstdlib> // abort function prototype
11   using std::abort;
12
13   // handle memory allocation failure
14   void customNewHandler()
15   {
16      cerr << "customNewHandler was called";
17      abort();
18   } // end function customNewHandler
19
20   // using set_new_handler to handle failed memory allocation
21   int main()
22   {
23      double *ptr[ 50 ];
24
25      // specify that customNewHandler should be called on
26      // memory allocation failure
27      set_new_handler( customNewHandler );
28
29      // allocate memory for ptr[ i ]; customNewHandler will be
30      // called on failed memory allocation
31      for ( int i = 0; i < 50; i++ )
32      {
33         ptr[ i ] = new double[ 50000000 ]; // may throw exception
34         cout << "Allocated 50000000 doubles in ptr[ " << i << " ]\n";
35      } // end for
36
37      return 0;
38   } // end main
```

```
Allocated 50000000 doubles in ptr[ 0 ]
Allocated 50000000 doubles in ptr[ 1 ]
Allocated 50000000 doubles in ptr[ 2 ]
customNewHandler was called
```

Fig. 27.7 | set_new_handler specifying the function to call when new fails.

27.12 Class auto_ptr and Dynamic Memory Allocation

A common programming practice is to allocate dynamic memory, assign the address of that memory to a pointer, use the pointer to manipulate the memory and deallocate the memory with delete when the memory is no longer needed. If an exception occurs after successful memory allocation but before the delete statement executes, a memory leak could occur. The C++ standard provides class template **auto_ptr** in header file **<memory>** to deal with this situation.

An object of class `auto_ptr` maintains a pointer to dynamically allocated memory. When an `auto_ptr` object destructor is called (for example, when an `auto_ptr` object goes out of scope), it performs a `delete` operation on its pointer data member. Class template `auto_ptr` provides overloaded operators * and -> so that an `auto_ptr` object can be used just as a regular pointer variable is. Figure 27.10 demonstrates an `auto_ptr` object that points to a dynamically allocated object of class `Integer` (Figs. 27.8–27.9).

Line 18 of Fig. 27.10 creates `auto_ptr` object `ptrToInteger` and initializes it with a pointer to a dynamically allocated `Integer` object that contains the value 7. Line 21 uses the `auto_ptr` overloaded -> operator to invoke function `setInteger` on the `Integer` object pointed to by `ptrToInteger`. Line 24 uses the `auto_ptr` overloaded * operator to dereference `ptrToInteger`, then uses the dot (.) operator to invoke function `getInteger` on the `Integer` object pointed to by `ptrToInteger`. Like a regular pointer, an `auto_ptr`'s -> and * overloaded operators can be used to access the object to which the `auto_ptr` points.

Because `ptrToInteger` is a local automatic variable in `main`, `ptrToInteger` is destroyed when `main` terminates. The `auto_ptr` destructor forces a `delete` of the `Integer` object pointed to by `ptrToInteger`, which in turn calls the `Integer` class destructor. The memory that `Integer` occupies is released, regardless of how control leaves the block (e.g., by a `return` statement or by an exception). Most importantly, using this technique can prevent memory leaks. For example, suppose a function returns a pointer aimed at some object. Unfortunately, the function caller that receives this pointer might not `delete` the object, thus resulting in a memory leak. However, if the function returns an `auto_ptr` to the object, the object will be deleted automatically when the `auto_ptr` object's destructor gets called.

```
1    // Fig. 27.8: Integer.h
2    // Integer class definition.
3
4    class Integer
5    {
6    public:
7       Integer( int i = 0 ); // Integer default constructor
8       ~Integer(); // Integer destructor
9       void setInteger( int i ); // functions to set Integer
10      int getInteger() const; // function to return Integer
11   private:
12      int value;
13   }; // end class Integer
```

Fig. 27.8 | Class `Integer` definition.

```
1    // Fig. 27.9: Integer.cpp
2    // Integer member function definition.
3    #include <iostream>
4    using std::cout;
5    using std::endl;
```

Fig. 27.9 | Member function definition of class `Integer`. (Part 1 of 2.)

```
 6
 7   #include "Integer.h"
 8
 9   // Integer default constructor
10   Integer::Integer( int i )
11      : value( i )
12   {
13      cout << "Constructor for Integer " << value << endl;
14   } // end Integer constructor
15
16   // Integer destructor
17   Integer::~Integer()
18   {
19      cout << "Destructor for Integer " << value << endl;
20   } // end Integer destructor
21
22   // set Integer value
23   void Integer::setInteger( int i )
24   {
25      value = i;
26   } // end function setInteger
27
28   // return Integer value
29   int Integer::getInteger() const
30   {
31      return value;
32   } // end function getInteger
```

Fig. 27.9 | Member function definition of class `Integer`. (Part 2 of 2.)

```
 1   // Fig. 27.10: fig27_10.cpp
 2   // Demonstrating auto_ptr.
 3   #include <iostream>
 4   using std::cout;
 5   using std::endl;
 6
 7   #include <memory>
 8   using std::auto_ptr; // auto_ptr class definition
 9
10   #include "Integer.h"
11
12   // use auto_ptr to manipulate Integer object
13   int main()
14   {
15      cout << "Creating an auto_ptr object that points to an Integer\n";
16
17      // "aim" auto_ptr at Integer object
18      auto_ptr< Integer > ptrToInteger( new Integer( 7 ) );
19
20      cout << "\nUsing the auto_ptr to manipulate the Integer\n";
21      ptrToInteger->setInteger( 99 ); // use auto_ptr to set Integer value
```

Fig. 27.10 | `auto_ptr` object manages dynamically allocated memory. (Part 1 of 2.)

```
22
23        // use auto_ptr to get Integer value
24        cout << "Integer after setInteger: " << ( *ptrToInteger ).getInteger()
25        return 0;
26    } // end main
```

```
Creating an auto_ptr object that points to an Integer
Constructor for Integer 7

Using the auto_ptr to manipulate the Integer
Integer after setInteger: 99

Terminating program
Destructor for Integer 99
```

Fig. 27.10 | auto_ptr object manages dynamically allocated memory. (Part 2 of 2.)

An auto_ptr can pass ownership of the dynamic memory it manages via its overloaded assignment operator or copy constructor. The last auto_ptr object that maintains the pointer to the dynamic memory will delete the memory. This makes auto_ptr an ideal mechanism for returning dynamically allocated memory to client code. When the auto_ptr goes out of scope in the client code, the auto_ptr's destructor deletes the dynamic memory.

Software Engineering Observation 27.9

An auto_ptr has restrictions on certain operations. For example, an auto_ptr cannot point to an array or a standard-container class.

27.13 Standard Library Exception Hierarchy

Experience has shown that exceptions fall nicely into a number of categories. The C++ Standard Library includes a hierarchy of exception classes (Fig. 27.11). As we first discussed in Section 27.3, this hierarchy is headed by base-class exception (defined in header file <exception>), which contains virtual function what, which derived classes can override to issue appropriate error messages.

Immediate derived classes of base-class exception include runtime_error and logic_error (both defined in header <stdexcept>), each of which has several derived classes. Also derived from exception are the exceptions thrown by C++ operators—for example, bad_alloc is thrown by new (Section 27.11), bad_cast is thrown by dynamic_cast (Chapter 24) and bad_typeid is thrown by typeid (Chapter 24). Including bad_exception in the throw list of a function means that, if an unexpected exception occurs, function unexpected can throw bad_exception rather than terminating the program's execution (by default) or calling another function specified by set_unexpected.

Common Programming Error 27.8

Placing a catch handler that catches a base-class object before a catch that catches an object of a class derived from that base class is a logic error. The base-class catch catches all objects of classes derived from that base class, so the derived-class catch will never execute.

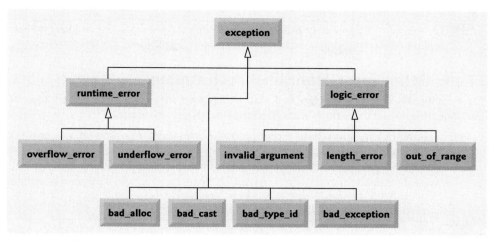

Fig. 27.11 | Standard Library exception classes.

Class `logic_error` is the base class of several standard exception classes that indicate errors in program logic. For example, class `invalid_argument` indicates that an invalid argument was passed to a function. (Proper coding can, of course, prevent invalid arguments from reaching a function.) Class `length_error` indicates that a length larger than the maximum size allowed for the object being manipulated was used for that object. Class `out_of_range` indicates that a value, such as a subscript into an array, exceeded its allowed range of values.

Class `runtime_error`, which we used briefly in Section 27.8, is the base class of several other standard exception classes that indicate execution-time errors. For example, class `overflow_error` describes an arithmetic overflow error (i.e., the result of an arithmetic operation is larger than the largest number that can be stored in the computer) and class `underflow_error` describes an arithmetic underflow error (i.e., the result of an arithmetic operation is smaller than the smallest number that can be stored in the computer).

Common Programming Error 27.9

Programmer-defined exception classes need not be derived from class `exception`. Thus, writing `catch( exception anyException )` is not guaranteed to `catch` all exceptions a program could encounter.

Error-Prevention Tip 27.6

To `catch` all exceptions potentially thrown in a try block, use `catch(...)`. One weakness with catching exceptions in this way is that the type of the caught exception is unknown at compile time. Another weakness is that, without a named parameter, there is no way to refer to the exception object inside the exception handler.

Software Engineering Observation 27.10

The standard `exception` hierarchy is a good starting point for creating exceptions. Programmers can build programs that can `throw` standard exceptions, `throw` exceptions derived from the standard exceptions or `throw` their own exceptions not derived from the standard exceptions.

Software Engineering Observation 27.11

Use catch(...) when recovery does not depend on the exception type (e.g., releasing common resources). The exception can be rethrown to alert more specific enclosing catch handlers.

27.14 Other Error-Handling Techniques

We have discussed several ways to deal with exceptional situations prior to this chapter. The following summarizes these and other error-handling techniques:

- Ignore the exception. If an exception occurs, the program might fail as a result of the uncaught exception. This is devastating for commercial software products or for special-purpose software designed for mission-critical situations, but, for software developed for your own purposes, ignoring many kinds of errors is common.

Common Programming Error 27.10

Aborting a program component due to an uncaught exception could leave a resource—such as a file stream or an I/O device—in a state in which other programs are unable to acquire the resource. This is known as a "resource leak."

- Abort the program. This, of course, prevents a program from running to completion and producing incorrect results. For many types of errors, this is appropriate, especially for nonfatal errors that enable a program to run to completion (potentially misleading the programmer to think that the program functioned correctly). This strategy is inappropriate for mission-critical applications. Resource issues also are important here. If a program obtains a resource, the program should release that resource before program termination.

- Set error indicators. The problem with this approach is that programs might not check these error indicators at all points at which the errors could be troublesome.

- Test for the error condition, issue an error message and call `exit` (in `<cstdlib>`) to pass an appropriate error code to the program's environment.

- Use functions `setjump` and `longjump`. These `<csetjmp>` library functions enable the programmer to specify an immediate jump from a deeply nested function call to an error handler. Without using `setjump` or `longjump`, a program must execute several returns to exit the deeply nested function calls. Functions `setjump` and `longjump` are dangerous, because they unwind the stack without calling destructors for automatic objects. This can lead to serious problems.

- Certain specific kinds of errors have dedicated capabilities for handling them. For example, when operator `new` fails to allocate memory, it can cause a `new_handler` function to execute to handle the error. This function can be customized by supplying a function name as the argument to `set_new_handler`, as we discuss in Section 27.11.

27.15 Wrap-Up

In this chapter, you learned how to use exception handling to deal with errors in a program. You learned that exception handling enables programmers to remove error-handling code from the "main line" of the program's execution. We demonstrated exception handling in the context of a divide-by-zero example. We also showed how to use `try` blocks to enclose code that may throw an exception, and how to use `catch` handlers to deal with exceptions that may arise. You learned how to throw and rethrow exceptions, and how to handle the exceptions that occur in constructors. The chapter continued with discussions of processing `new` failures, dynamic memory allocation with class `auto_ptr` and the Standard Library exception hierarchy.

Summary

Section 27.1 Introduction
- An exception is an indication of a problem that occurs during a program's execution.
- Exception handling enables programmers to create programs that can resolve problems that occur at execution time—often allowing programs to continue executing as if no problems had been encountered. More severe problems may require a program to notify the user of the problem before terminating in a controlled manner.

Section 27.2 Exception-Handling Overview
- Exception handling enables the programmer to remove error-handling code from the "main line" of the program's execution, which improves program clarity and enhances modifiability.
- C++ uses the termination model of exception handling.

Section 27.3 Example: Handling an Attempt to Divide by Zero
- A `try` block consists of keyword `try` followed by braces (`{}`) that define a block of code in which exceptions might occur. The `try` block encloses statements that might cause exceptions and statements that should not execute if exceptions occur.
- At least one `catch` handler must immediately follow a `try` block. Each `catch` handler specifies an exception parameter that represents the type of exception the `catch` handler can process.
- If an exception parameter includes an optional parameter name, the `catch` handler can use that parameter name to interact with a caught exception object.
- The point in the program at which an exception occurs is called the throw point.
- If an exception occurs in a `try` block, the `try` block expires and program control transfers to the first `catch` in which the exception parameter's type matches that of the thrown exception.
- When a `try` block terminates, local variables defined in the block go out of scope.
- When a `try` block terminates due to an exception, the program searches for the first `catch` handler that can process the type of exception that occurred. The program locates the matching `catch` by comparing the thrown exception's type to each `catch`'s exception-parameter type until the program finds a match. A match occurs if the types are identical or if the thrown exception's type is a derived class of the exception-parameter type. When a match occurs, the code contained within the matching `catch` handler executes.
- When a `catch` handler finishes processing, the `catch` parameter and local variables defined within the `catch` handler go out of scope. Any remaining `catch` handlers that correspond to the `try` block are ignored, and execution resumes at the first line of code after the `try...catch` sequence.
- If no exceptions occur in a `try` block, the program ignores the `catch` handler(s) for that block. Program execution resumes with the next statement after the `try...catch` sequence.
- If an exception that occurs in a `try` block has no matching `catch` handler, or if an exception occurs in a statement that is not in a `try` block, the function that contains the statement terminates

immediately, and the program attempts to locate an enclosing `try` block in the calling function. This process is called stack unwinding.

Section 27.4 When to Use Exception Handling
- Exception handling is for synchronous errors, which occur when a statement executes.
- Exception handling is not designed to process errors associated with asynchronous events, which occur in parallel with, and independent of, the program's flow of control.

Section 27.5 Rethrowing an Exception
- To throw an exception, use keyword `throw` followed by an operand that represents the type of exception to throw. Normally, a `throw` statement specifies one operand.
- The operand of a `throw` can be of any type.
- The exception handler can defer the exception handling (or perhaps a portion of it) to another exception handler. In either case, the handler achieves this by rethrowing the exception.
- Common examples of exceptions are out-of-range array subscripts, arithmetic overflow, division by zero, invalid function parameters and unsuccessful memory allocations.
- Class `exception` is the standard C++ base class for exceptions. Class `exception` provides virtual function `what` that returns an appropriate error message and can be overridden in derived classes.

Section 27.6 Exception Specifications
- An optional exception specification enumerates a list of exceptions that a function can throw. A function can throw only exceptions of the types indicated by the exception specification or exceptions of any type derived from these types. If the function throws an exception that does not belong to a specified type, function `unexpected` is called and the program normally terminates.
- A function with no exception specification can throw any exception. The empty exception specification `throw()` indicates that a function does not throw exceptions. If a function with an empty exception specification attempts to throw an exception, function `unexpected` is invoked.

Section 27.7 Processing Unexpected Exceptions
- Function `unexpected` calls the function registered with function `set_unexpected`. If no function has been registered in this manner, function `terminate` is called by default.
- Function `set_terminate` can specify the function to invoke when `terminate` is called. Otherwise, `terminate` calls `abort`, which terminates the program without calling the destructors of objects that are declared `static` and `auto`.
- Functions `set_terminate` and `set_unexpected` each return a pointer to the last function called by `terminate` and `unexpected`, respectively (0, the first time each is called). This enables the programmer to save the function pointer so it can be restored later.
- Functions `set_terminate` and `set_unexpected` take as arguments pointers to functions with `void` return types and no arguments.
- If a programmer-defined termination function does not exit a program, function `abort` will be called after the programmer-defined termination function completes execution.

Section 27.8 Stack Unwinding
- Unwinding the function call stack means that the function in which the exception was not caught terminates, all local variables in that function are destroyed and control returns to the statement that originally invoked that function.
- Class `runtime_error` (defined in header `<stdexcept>`) is the C++ standard base class for representing runtime errors.

Section 27.9 Constructors, Destructors and Exception Handling

- Exceptions thrown by a constructor cause destructors to be called for any objects built as part of the object being constructed before the exception is thrown.

- Destructors are called for every automatic object constructed in a try block before an exception is thrown.

- Stack unwinding completes before an exception handler begins executing.

- If a destructor invoked as a result of stack unwinding throws an exception, terminate is called.

- If an object has member objects, and if an exception is thrown before the outer object is fully constructed, then destructors will be executed for the member objects that have been constructed before the exception occurs.

- If an array of objects has been partially constructed when an exception occurs, only the destructors for the constructed array element objects will be called.

- When an exception is thrown from the constructor for an object that is created in a new expression, the dynamically allocated memory for that object is released.

Section 27.10 Exceptions and Inheritance

- If a catch handler catches a pointer or reference to an exception object of a base-class type, it also can catch a pointer or reference to all objects of classes derived publicly from that base class—this allows for polymorphic processing of related errors.

Section 27.11 Processing new Failures

- The C++ standard document specifies that, when operator new fails, it throws a bad_alloc exception (defined in header file <new>).

- Function set_new_handler takes as its argument a pointer to a function that takes no arguments and returns void. This pointer points to the function that will be called if new fails.

- Once set_new_handler registers a new handler in the program, operator new does not throw bad_alloc on failure; rather, it defers the error handling to the new-handler function.

- If new allocates memory successfully, it returns a pointer to that memory.

- If an exception occurs after successful memory allocation but before the delete statement executes, a memory leak could occur.

Section 27.12 Class `auto_ptr` and Dynamic Memory Allocation

- The C++ Standard Library provides class template auto_ptr to deal with memory leaks.

- An object of class auto_ptr maintains a pointer to dynamically allocated memory. An auto_ptr object's destructor performs a delete operation on the auto_ptr's pointer data member.

- Class template auto_ptr provides overloaded operators * and -> so that an auto_ptr object can be used just as a regular pointer variable is. An auto_ptr also transfers ownership of the dynamic memory it manages via its copy constructor and overloaded assignment operator.

Section 27.13 Standard Library Exception Hierarchy

- The C++ Standard Library includes a hierarchy of exception classes. This hierarchy is headed by base class exception.

- Immediate derived classes of base class exception include runtime_error and logic_error (both defined in header <stdexcept>), each of which has several derived classes.

- Several operators throw standard exceptions—operator new throws bad_alloc, operator dynamic_cast throws bad_cast and operator typeid throws bad_typeid.

- Including bad_exception in the throw list of a function means that, if an unexpected exception occurs, function unexpected can throw bad_exception rather than terminating the program's execution or calling another function specified by set_unexpected.

Terminology

abort function	<memory> header file
arithmetic overflow error	new failure handler
arithmetic underflow error	nothrow object
asynchronous event	out_of_range exception
auto_ptr class template	overflow_error exception
bad_alloc exception	resumption model of exception handling
bad_cast exception	rethrow an exception
bad_exception exception	robust application
bad_typeid exception	runtime_error exception
catch(...)	set_new_handler function
catch all exceptions	set_terminate function
catch an exception	set_unexpected function
catch handler	stack unwinding
catch keyword	<stdexcept> header file
empty exception specification	synchronous errors
exception	terminate function
exception class	termination model of exception handling
exception handler	throw an exception
exception handling	throw an unexpected exception
<exception> header file	throw keyword
exception object	throw list
exception parameter	throw without arguments
exception specification	throw point
fault-tolerant programs	try block
handle an exception	try keyword
invalid_argument exception	underflow_error exception
length_error exception	unexpected function
logic_error exception	what virtual function of class exception

Self-Review Exercises

27.1 List five common examples of exceptions.

27.2 Give several reasons why exception-handling techniques should not be used for conventional program control.

27.3 Why are exceptions appropriate for dealing with errors produced by library functions?

27.4 What is a "resource leak"?

27.5 If no exceptions are thrown in a try block, where does control proceed to after the try block completes execution?

27.6 What happens if an exception is thrown outside a try block?

27.7 Give a key advantage and a key disadvantage of using catch(...).

27.8 What happens if no catch handler matches the type of a thrown object?

27.9 What happens if several handlers match the type of the thrown object?

27.10   Why would a programmer specify a base-class type as the type of a catch handler, then throw objects of derived-class types?

27.11   Suppose a catch handler with a precise match to an exception object type is available. Under what circumstances might a different handler be executed for exception objects of that type?

27.12   Must throwing an exception cause program termination?

27.13   What happens when a catch handler throws an exception?

27.14   What does the statement throw; do?

27.15   How does the programmer restrict the exception types that a function can throw?

27.16   What happens if a function throws an exception of a type not allowed by the exception specification for the function?

27.17   What happens to the automatic objects that have been constructed in a try block when that block throws an exception?

Answers to Self-Review Exercises

27.1   Insufficient memory to satisfy a new request, array subscript out of bounds, arithmetic overflow, division by zero, invalid function parameters.

27.2   (a) Exception handling is designed to handle infrequently occurring situations that often result in program termination, so compiler writers are not required to implement exception handling to perform optimally. (b) Flow of control with conventional control structures generally is clearer and more efficient than with exceptions. (c) Problems can occur because the stack is unwound when an exception occurs and resources allocated prior to the exception might not be freed. (d) The "additional" exceptions make it more difficult for the programmer to handle the larger number of exception cases.

27.3   It is unlikely that a library function will perform error processing that will meet the unique needs of all users.

27.4   A program that terminates abruptly could leave a resource in a state in which other programs would not be able to acquire the resource, or the program itself might not be able to reacquire a "leaked" resource.

27.5   The exception handlers (in the catch handlers) for that try block are skipped, and the program resumes execution after the last catch handler.

27.6   An exception thrown outside a try block causes a call to terminate.

27.7   The form catch(...) catches any type of exception thrown in a try block. An advantage is that all possible exceptions will be caught. A disadvantage is that the catch has no parameter, so it cannot reference information in the thrown object and cannot know the cause of the exception.

27.8   This causes the search for a match to continue in the next enclosing try block if there is one. As this process continues, it might eventually be determined that there is no handler in the program that matches the type of the thrown object; in this case, terminate is called, which by default calls abort. An alternative terminate function can be provided as an argument to set_terminate.

27.9   The first matching exception handler after the try block is executed.

27.10   This is a nice way to catch related types of exceptions.

27.11   A base-class handler would catch objects of all derived-class types.

27.12   No, but it does terminate the block in which the exception is thrown.

27.13   The exception will be processed by a catch handler (if one exists) associated with the try block (if one exists) enclosing the catch handler that caused the exception.

27.14   It rethrows the exception if it appears in a catch handler; otherwise, function unexpected is called.

27.15   Provide an exception specification listing the exception types that the function can throw.

27.16   Function unexpected is called.

27.17   The try block expires, causing destructors to be called for each of these objects.

Exercises

27.18   List various exceptional conditions that have occurred throughout this text. List as many additional exceptional conditions as you can. For each of these exceptions, describe briefly how a program typically would handle the exception, using the exception-handling techniques discussed in this chapter. Some typical exceptions are division by zero, arithmetic overflow, array subscript out of bounds, and exhaustion of the free store.

27.19   Under what circumstances would the programmer not provide a parameter name when defining the type of the object that will be caught by a handler?

27.20   A program contains the statement

```
throw;
```

Where would you normally expect to find such a statement? What if that statement appeared in a different part of the program?

27.21   Compare and contrast exception handling with the various other error-processing schemes discussed in the text.

27.22   Why should exceptions not be used as an alternate form of program control?

27.23   Describe a technique for handling related exceptions.

27.24   Until this chapter, we have found that dealing with errors detected by constructors can be awkward. Exception handling gives us a better means of handling such errors. Consider a constructor for a String class. The constructor uses new to obtain space from the free store. Suppose new fails. Show how you would deal with this without exception handling. Discuss the key issues. Show how you would deal with such memory exhaustion with exception handling. Explain why the exception-handling approach is superior.

27.25   Suppose a program throws an exception and the appropriate exception handler begins executing. Now suppose that the exception handler itself throws the same exception. Does this create infinite recursion? Write a program to check your observation.

27.26   Use inheritance to create various derived classes of runtime_error. Then show that a catch handler specifying the base class can catch derived-class exceptions.

27.27   Write a conditional expression that returns either a double or an int. Provide an int catch handler and a double catch handler. Show that only the double catch handler executes, regardless of whether the int or the double is returned.

27.28   Write a program that generates and handles a memory-exhaustion exception. Your program should loop on a request to create dynamic memory through operator new.

27.29   Write a program illustrating that all destructors for objects constructed in a block are called before an exception is thrown from that block.

27.30   Write a program illustrating that member object destructors are called for only those member objects that were constructed before an exception occurred.

27.31   Write a program that demonstrates several exception types being caught with the catch(...) exception handler.

27.32   Write a program illustrating that the order of exception handlers is important. The first matching handler is the one that executes. Attempt to compile and run your program two different ways to show that two different handlers execute with two different effects.

27.33   Write a program that shows a constructor passing information about constructor failure to an exception handler after a try block.

27.34   Write a program that illustrates rethrowing an exception.

27.35   Write a program that illustrates that a function with its own try block does not have to catch every possible error generated within the try. Some exceptions can slip through to, and be handled in, outer scopes.

27.36   Write a program that throws an exception from a deeply nested function and still has the catch handler following the try block enclosing the call chain catch the exception.

Internet and Web Resources

This appendix contains a list of valuable C and C++ resources on the Internet and the Web. These resources include FAQs (Frequently Asked Questions), tutorials, how to obtain the ANSI/ISO C++ standard, information about popular compilers and how to obtain free compilers, demos, books, tutorials, software tools, articles, interviews, conferences, journals and magazines, on-line courses, newsgroups and career resources. For our most up-to-date set of resources, visit our C and C++ Resource Centers at:

> www.deitel.com/C
> www.deitel.com/cplusplus

For more information about the American National Standards Institute (ANSI) or to purchase standards documents, visit ANSI at www.ansi.org.

A.1 Free C/C++ Compilers and Development Tools

msdn.microsoft.com/vstudio/express/visualc/download/
Download the free Microsoft Visual C++ .NET 2005 Express Edition software. Full versions of the software can be purchased through this site.

www.borland.com/bcppbuilder
Download the free trial edition of Borland C++Builder 2006. Full versions of the software can be purchased through this site.

www.metrowerks.com/MW/Develop/compiler.htm
Download the free trial edition of Metrowerks CodeWarrior III Compiler. Full versions of the software can be purchased through this site.

developer.intel.com/software/products/compilers/cwin/index.htm
Download the free trial edition of the Intel C++ Compiler 9.0 for Windows. Full versions of the software can be purchased through this site.

`gcc.gnu.org/`
Download the free, open source GNU C++ compiler for Linux.

`developer.apple.com/tools/mpw-tools/`
Download the free, open source Macintosh Programmer's Workshop for use with Mac OS 7.x, 8.x, and 9.x.

`www.bloodshed.net/devcpp.html`
Download the free Bloodshed Dev-C++ IDE (Integrated Development Environment) for use with Mingw port of the GNU Compiler and Cygwin.

`www.codeblocks.org/`
Download Code::Blocks—a free, open-source, cross platform C++ IDE.

`www.digitalmars.com/download/dmcpp.html`
Download the Digital Mars C/C++ compiler for Win32.

`www.members.tripod.com/%7Eladsoft/frindx.htm?cc386.htm`
Download the LadSoft CC386 32-bit C compiler.

`www.orbworks.com/`
Download this C compiler for use with PalmOs, WinCE and Win32.

A.2 C Resource Sites

`global.ihs.com/doc_detail.cfm?currency_code=USD&customer_id=`
`2125482D200A&shopping_cart_id=2825585F244B502C4B595D34270A&country_code=US&lang`
`_code=ENL&item_s_key=00098426&item_key_date=110024&input_doc_number=x3%2E159&in`
`put_doc_title=`
Purchase a copy of the current, published C standard (document number X3.159).

`www.cprogramming.com/`
Resource site for C and C++ programming. Includes tools, tutorials, source code, book reviews, FAQs, message boards, a glossary, function lookup and more.

`cm.bell-labs.com/cm/cs/who/dmr/`
Dennis Ritchie's homepage. Ritchie is one of the creators of the C programming language. Includes Ritchie's biography, plus links to his C resources.

`cm.bell-labs.com/cm/cs/who/bwk/index.html`
Brian Kernighan's homepage. Kernighan is one of the creators of the C programming language. Includes links to his publications.

`www.programmersheaven.com/zone3/index.htm`
Programming resource site includes tutorials, articles, downloads, source code and more.

`www.cuj.com/`
C/C++ Users Journal. Find articles, source code, forums and resources.

`www.digilife.be/quickreferences/QRC/C%20Reference%20Card%20(ANSI).pdf`
C Reference Card is a cheat sheet for C programmers.

`cplus.about.com/od/cprogrammin1/l/blglossary.htm`
C/C++ glossary includes definitions of key terms.

A.3 C99

`www.open-std.org/jtc1/sc22/wg14/`
Official site for the C99 standard. Includes defect reports, working papers, projects and milestones, the rationale for the C99 standard, contacts and more.

www.open-std.org/jtc1/sc22/wg14/www/docs/n1124.pdf
The C Standard with Technical Corrects 1 and 2, last updated May 6, 2005. (Available free of charge).

www.wiley.com/WileyCDA/WileyTitle/productCd-0470845732.html
Purchase a hard copy of the C99 standard.

www.comeaucomputing.com/techtalk/c99/
C99 FAQ.

www.open-std.org/jtc1/sc22/wg14/www/C99RationaleV5.10.pdf
White paper: "Rationale for International Standard–Programming Languages–C." This 224-page document describes the C99 standards committee deliberations.

gcc.gnu.org/c99status.html
Find the status of C99 features in the GNU Compiler Collection (GCC).

www.kuro5hin.org/story/2001/2/23/194544/139
Article: "Are You Ready for C99?" discusses some of the interesting new features, incompatibilities with C++, and compiler support.

www.informit.com/guides/content.asp?g=cplusplus&seqNum=215&rl=1
Article: "A Tour of C99," by Danny Kalev, summarizes some of the new features in the C99 standard.

www.cuj.com/documents/s=8191/cuj0104meyers/
Article: "The New C: Declarations and Initializations," by Randy Meyers. Discusses these new features in C99.

docs.sun.com/source/817-5064/c99.app.html#98079
Lists the features of C99 supported by the Solaris operating environment.

home.tiscalinet.ch/t_wolf/tw/c/c9x_changes.html
Provides brief technical descriptions and code examples for many C99 features.

www.bloodshed.net/dev/devcpp.html
Download Dev-C++, a free IDE that uses the Mingw port of GCC as its compiler, for use on Windows systems.

www.digitalmars.com
Download the free C/C++ compiler for Win32.

www.cs.virginia.edu/~lcc-win32/
Download the free lcc-win32 compiler.

www.openwatcom.org
Download Watcom C/C++ compiler, a free compiler of most of C99 by SciTech Software Inc. and Sybase®.

developers.sun.com/prodtech/cc/index.jsp
Download Sun Studio 11, which includes a free fully compliant C99 compiler.

www.softintegration.com/products/chstandard/download/
Download Ch Standard Edition—a free interpreter that largely supports C99 on a number of different platforms. You can also download ChSCiTE—a free corresponding IDE.

david.tribble.com/text/cdiffs.htm
Article: "Incompatibilities Between ISO C89 and ISO C++," by David Tribble. Lists and explains the areas in which ANSI C, C99, and C++ 98 differ.

webstore.ansi.org/ansidocstore/product.asp?sku=INCITS%2FISO%2FIEC+9899%2D1999
Purchase an electronic version of the C99 Standard.

msdn.microsoft.com/chats/transcripts/vstudio/vstudio_022703.aspx
Portions of a chat transcript including Brandon Bray, the program manager for the Visual C++ compiler at Microsoft. Discusses the future compatibility of Visual C++ with C99.

A.4 C Projects, Freeware and Shareware

sourceforge.net/projects/cshroud
Program used to hide the meaning of C source code by changing names used in the code.

sourceforge.net/projects/cpp-perfometer
Tool measures performance of your C/C++ code.

sourceforge.net/projects/xmlrpc-c
Allows a client to make a remote procedure call request of a server.

sourceforge.net/projects/gwtoolkit
Graphics tool for C.

sourceforge.net/projects/cil
C Intermediate Language.

sourceforge.net/projects/algoview
C algorithm viewer provides a flowchart of your code.

sourceforge.net/projects/cproto
This project generates C function prototypes and variable declarations.

sourceforge.net/projects/cire
Keep a diary or journal with this program (written in C).

A.5 C Source Code

www.deitel.com/books/chtp5
Download the code examples from *C How to Program, Fifth Edition*.

ourworld.compuserve.com/homepages/blueberry/samples.htm
Sample C/C++ source code for a few entry-level programs.

www.programmershelp.co.uk/beepmenu.php
C example plays sounds based on the user's selection from a menu.

www.programmershelp.co.uk/cbeginnerscode.php
C code examples for beginners.

www.programmershelp.co.uk/cfilecode.php
File I/O code examples in C.

www.programmershelp.co.uk/cgraphicscode.php
Sample C graphics code.

www.programmershelp.co.uk/ciocode.php
Code examples demonstrating C I/O functions, including printf and scanf.

www.programmershelp.co.uk/cmathcode.php
Code examples demonstrating math functions in C.

www.programmershelp.co.uk/cstringcode.php
Code examples demonstrating the use of strings.

A.6 C Articles and Whitepapers

cm.bell-labs.com/cm/cs/who/dmr/chist.html
Paper: "The Development of the C Language," by Dennis M. Ritchie, creator of the C programming language. Explores the history of the C programming language.

www.itworld.com/Comp/3380/lw-12-ritchie/
Article: "The Future According to Dennis Ritchie," by Danny Kalev. Interview with Dennis Ritchie discusses the future of the C programming language.

www.linuxjournal.com/article/8497
Article: "Embedding Python in your C Programs," by William Nagel. Integrate Python into your C programs to quickly add new features, versus writing them in C which would take more time.

www-128.ibm.com/developerworks/eserver/articles/hook_duttaC.html?ca=dgr-lnxw07-obg-BestC
Article: "Best Practices for Programming in C," by Shiv Dutta and Gary Hook. Guidelines written by experienced C developers for programming or porting projects.

david.tribble.com/text/cdiffs.htm
Article: "Incompatibilities between ISO C and ISO," C++ by David R. Tribble. Compares C to C++ and older version of C to the new C99 standard.

www.cuj.com/documents/s=8188/cuj0602seacord/0602seacord.html
Article: "Validating C and C++ for Safety and Security: A Structured Approach to Manual Code Review," by Robert C. Seacord, a vulnerability analyst at the CERT/C. Requires registration to read the article.

www.cuj.com/documents/s=8188/cuj0602kiesling/0602kiesling.html
Article: "A Frame-Based Message-Passing Parser for C: Parsing Objects within C Code," by Robert Kiesling. Requires registration to read the article.

www.cuj.com/documents/s=8191/cuj0207stroustr/
Article: "C and C++: Siblings," by Bjarne Stroustrup, the creator of the C++ programming language. Discusses the compatibility of C and C++. Includes several code examples.

www.cuj.com/documents/s=8191/cuj0208stroustr/
Article: "C and C++: A Case for Compatibility," by Bjarne Stroustrup, the creator of the C++ programming language. Discusses why compatibility is in the best interest of the C/C++ community.

www.cuj.com/documents/s=8191/cuj0209stroustr/
Article: "C and C++: Case Studies in Compatibility," by Bjarne Stroustrup, the creator of the C++ programming language. Provides examples for increasing the compatibility of C and C++.

home.comcast.net/~brettacook/Coding_Standards.htm
"Coding Standards for the C Programming Language," by Samuel P. Harbinson and Guy L. Steele, Jr.

A.7 C Tutorials and Webcasts

www.cprogramming.com/tutorial.html#ctutorial
Tutorial: "C Tutorial." Topics include an introduction to C, if statements, loops, functions, switch case statements, pointers, structures, arrays, C-style strings, file I/O, typecasting, command line arguments, linked lists, recursion, variable argument lists and binary trees.

www.cs.cf.ac.uk/Dave/C/CE.html
Lecture notes: "Programming in C: Unix System Calls and Subroutines Using C," by A.D. Marshall. Topics include a history of C, program structure, variables, constants, arithmetic operators, comparison operators, logical operators and order of precedence. Includes exercises.

www.vijaymukhi.com/vmis/vmchap4.htm
Tutorial: Covers Windows sockets programming in C.

visualcplus.blogspot.com/2006/02/lesson-1-transforming-numerical.html
Tutorial: Eighteen-lesson tutorial walks through the basics of C programming, including numerical systems, data types, casting data types, operators and integer operations, ASCII code and character variables, conditional and logical operators, program iterations, infinite and finite loops and more.

www.codeproject.com/cpp/pointers.asp
Tutorial: "A Beginner's Guide to Pointers," by Andrew Peace.

www.tldp.org/HOWTO/GCC-Frontend-HOWTO.html
Tutorial: "GCC Frontend HOWTO," by Sreejith K Menon. Topics include compiler tools, GCC front end, installing the GCC, creating your own front end and more.

www.codeproject.com/cpp/PolyC.asp
Tutorial: "Polymorphism in C," by Santosh M.P. Includes sample code.

www.its.strath.ac.uk/courses/c/
Tutorial: "C Programming," by Steve Holmes of the University of Strathclyde Computer Centre. Topics include an overview of C, using C with UNIX, constant and variable types, expressions and operators, control statements, functions, I/O, files, structures and more.

www.developertutorials.com/tutorials/linux/writing-compiling-c-programs-linux-050422/page1.html
Tutorial: "Writing and Compiling C Programs on Linux," by Tony Lawrence of AP Lawrence.

irccrew.org/~cras/security/c-guide.html
Tutorial: "Secure, Efficient and Easy C Programming," by Timo Sirainen. Topics include memory allocation, string handling, buffer handling and real-world usage.

vergil.chemistry.gatech.edu/resources/programming/c-tutorial/toc.html
Tutorial: "C Programming Tutorial," covers the basics of C, including operations, types, storage classes, functions, I/O, file I/O, pointers, arrays, dynamic memory allocation, strings, structures, linked lists, trees, hash tables, makefiles, debugging and more.

users.actcom.co.il/~choo/lupg/tutorials/c-on-unix/c-on-unix.html
Tutorial: "Compiling C and C++ Programs on Unix Systems—gcc/g++," by Guy Keren.

www.howstuffworks.com/c.htm
Tutorial: "How C Programming Works," by Marshall Brain of HowStuffWorks, is an extensive introduction to C programming. Topics include a simple C program, variables, printf, scanf, branching and looping, arrays, functions, libraries, makefiles, textfiles, pointers, dynamic data structures, strings, operator precedence, command-line arguments, binary files and more.

cplus.about.com/od/beginnerctutorial/l/blctut.htm
Tutorial: "C Programming Tutorial," by John Kopp. Topics include variables, constants, I/O, conditional processing, looping, pointers, arrays, strings, structures, memory allocation, file I/O, functions and more.

www.iu.hio.no/~mark/CTutorial/CTutorial.html
Tutorial: "C Programming Tutorial," by Mark Burgess. Introductory C programming tutorial for people with little experience using interpreted programming languages.

A.8 GNOME and GLib

www.tldp.org/HOWTO/Glibc2-HOWTO.html
Tutorial: "Glibc 2 HOWTO," by Eric Green. Learn how to install the GNU C library (GLib) version 2 on Linux.

www-128.ibm.com/developerworks/linux/library/l-glib.html
Tutorial: "GNOMEnclature: The Wonders of Glib," by George Lebl. Overviews the functionality of GLib which some people claim makes C programming easier. Topics include typedefs, memory allocation, utility functions, containers and linked lists.

developer.gnome.org/doc/API/glib/index.html
Check out the GLib Reference Manual for key terms. Includes a definition and synopsis for each.

www.isaac.cs.berkeley.edu/pilot/GLib/GLib.html
Tutorial: "GLib Shared Libraries for the Pilot," by Ian Goldberg. Shows you how to use GCC to create GLib shared libraries on the Palm Pilot.

`developer.gnome.org/doc/tutorials/gnome-libs/`
Tutorial: "Application Programming Using GNOME Libraries," by George Lebl. Discusses GNOME libraries, GNOME UI components and the GTK+ toolkit.

`www-128.ibm.com/developerworks/linux/library/l-glibc.html?`
`ca=dgr-lnxw961overrideGNU`
Tutorial: "Override the GNU C Library Painlessly," by Jay Allen of IBM. Discusses how to change the GLib source code.

A.9 SWIG

`www.swig.org/`
SWIG (Simplified Wrapper and Interface Generator) is commonly used as a tool for testing and prototyping C/C++ software. Site includes tutorials, resources, downloads and more.

`www.codeguru.com/csharp/.net/net_asp/scripting/article.php/c11103/`
Article: "Expose Your C/C++ Internal API with a Quick SWIG," by Victor Volkman.

`www.dabeaz.com/cgi-bin/wiki.pl`
SWIG wiki. Includes a FAQ, list of recent changes, wish list to request changes and documentation.

`en.wikipedia.org/wiki/SWIG`
Wikipedia page for SWIG describes SWIG as a tool used to connect C and C++ programs with scripting languages and other programming languages such as Perl, Ruby, Python, Java, C# and more.

`www.dabeaz.com/cgi-bin/wiki.pl?SwigFaq`
SWIG FAQ.

`www.skwash.com/`
Open source SWIG GUI. Includes downloads, installation information, tutorials, FAQs and more.

A.10 Objective-C

`en.wikipedia.org/wiki/Objective_c`
Wikipedia page for Objective-C. Includes a history of Objective-C, syntax examples, an analysis of the language, examples and more.

`www.tenon.com/products/codebuilder/Objective-C.shtml`
Brief overview of the Objective-C language discusses some of the key features.

`www.gnustep.org/resources/ObjCFun.html`
Article: "Objective-C is Fun," by Adam Fedor. Discusses some of the key features including dynamic binding, implementation and customization.

`www.gnu.org/software/gcc/`
GNU Objective-C compiler.

`www.oreillynet.com/pub/a/mac/2001/05/04/cocoa.html`
Article: "The Objective-C Language," discusses how Objective-C implements object-oriented programming techniques. Includes sample code.

`developer.apple.com/documentation/Cocoa/Conceptual/ObjectiveC/`
Tutorial: "Introduction to the Objective-C Programming Language," provides a justification for Objective-C. Discusses object-oriented programming, the run-time system, grammar and more. Includes an Objective-C glossary.

`www.toodarkpark.org/computers/objc/`
eBook: "Object-Oriented Programming and the Objective-C Language." Topics include object-oriented programming, an overview of the language, Objective-C extensions and the run-time system.

`www.objc.info/about/`
Quick reference site for Objective-C.

`developer.apple.com/releasenotes/Cocoa/Objective-C++.html`
Overview of the Objective-C language.

`www.otierney.net/objective-c.html`
Tutorial: "Beginner's Guide to Objective-C." Topics include creating classes, inheritance and polymorphism, memory management, foundation framework classes and more.

`www.faqs.org/faqs/computer-lang/Objective-C/faq/`
Objective-C FAQ.

`news://comp.lang.objective-c`
Objective-C newsgroup.

`www.foldr.org/~michaelw/objective-c/`
Objective-C resources includes numerous libraries, projects, technical information and more.

A.11 C Sample Chapters and eBooks

`www.oreilly.com/catalog/pcp3/chapter/ch13.html`
Sample chapter: "Simple Pointers," from the book *Practical C Programming, 3/E*, by Steve Oualline.

`www.informit.com/articles/article.asp?p=430402`
Sample chapter: "Secure Coding in C and C++: Strings," from the book, *Secure Coding in C and C++*, by Robert Seacord. Topics include string characteristics, common string manipulation errors, string vulnerabilities, process memory organization, stack smashing, code injection, arc injection, mitigation strategies, notable vulnerabilities and more.

`publications.gbdirect.co.uk/c_book/`
eBook: "The C Book," by Mike Banahan, Declan Brady and Mark Doran (copyright 1991).

`www.planetpdf.com/codecuts/pdfs/ooc.pdf`
eBook: "Object-Oriented Programming with ANSI-C," by Axel-Tobias Schreiner.

`www.acm.uiuc.edu/webmonkeys/book/c_guide/index.html`
eBook: "The C Library Reference Guide," by Eric Huss.

A.12 C Wikis

`en.wikipedia.org/wiki/C_programming_language`
Wikipedia entry for the C programming language. Topics include a history of the language, usage, syntax, criticism, references and links to other C programming resources.

`clc-wiki.net/wiki/Main_Page`
Spin-off from the comp.lang.c newsgroup.

`clc-wiki.net/wiki/Portability_and_ANSI_C_Compliance`
Wiki entry: "Portability and ANSO C Compliance."

`clc-wiki.net/wiki/The_C_Standard`
Wiki entry for the C standard.

`en.wikibooks.org/wiki/Programming:C_contents`
Wiki book on C (open content).

A.13 C FAQs

`www.cs.ruu.nl/wais/html/na-dir/C-faq/diff.html`
Updates and changes to the `news:comp.lang.c` FAQ (`www.eskimo.com/~scs/C-faq/top.html`).

`c-faq.com/`
Compilation of FAQs from the `news:comp.lang.c` newsgroup.

`faq.cprogramming.com/cgi-bin/smartfaq.cgi`
C and C++ programming FAQ.

`www-users.cs.umn.edu/~tan/www-docs/C_lang.html`

C programming FAQ by Steve Summit, author of *C Programming FAQs: Frequently Asked Questions*.

A.14 C Newsgroups

`news:comp.lang.c`

E-mail newsgroup for the C programming language.

`news:comp.std.c`

E-mail newsgroup for the C programming language standard.

`news:comp.lang.c.moderated`

E-mail newsgroup for the C programming language.

`groups.yahoo.com/group/c-prog/`

Yahoo! Group for C/C++ programming discusses compilers, creating libraries and more.

`groups.yahoo.com/group/Programmers-Town/`

C/C++ programming group on Yahoo! discusses programming issues. Allows job postings.

`groups.yahoo.com/group/C-Paradise/`

Yahoo! group discusses C and C++ programming.

`groups.yahoo.com/group/cprogramming2/`

Share your projects, get help with bugs in your code and more.

`groups.yahoo.com/group/cncppassist/`

Get help with C and C++ programming questions.

A.15 C Blogs

`cpp-programming.blogspot.com/`

C/C++ Programming Tips and Tricks blog.

`cprogrammers.blogspot.com/`

C/C++ Programming Tips, Tricks, Tweaks and Hacks blog.

A.16 C Downloads from Download.com

`deitel.com.com/C-To-Java-Converter/3000-2417_4-9675930.html?part=deitel&subj=dl&tag=rcc`

Software: C to Java Converter from SoftLogica.

`deitel.com.com/Programming-in-C-in-7-days/3000-2125_4-7039095.html?part=deitel&subj=dl&tag=rcc`

eBook: Programming C in 7 Days 1.01.

`deitel.com.com/Programming-C/3000-2251_4-10174972.html?part=deitel&subj=dl&tag=rcc`

eBook: Programming in C E101.1.

`deitel.com.com/C-Free/3000-2212_4-10385902.html?part=deitel&subj=dl&tag=rcc`

Software: C and C++ Integrated Development Environment from Program Arts Software.

`deitel.com.com/Small-Device-C-Compiler-SDCC-/3000-2212_4-10498126.html?part=deitel&subj=dl&tag=rcc`

Software: Small Device C Compiler from BiPOM Electronics.

A.17 C Game Programming

`www.toymaker.info/Games/html/beginners.html`

Beginners guide to C/C++ game programming. Find information about C/C++ programming, graphics, sound, techniques and more.

inertia.curvedspaces.com/Articles/C_Game_Programming/C_Game_Programming.html
C game programming site includes C programming tips and source code for popular games (e.g. Pacman and Quake).

www.geocities.com/siliconvalley/vista/7336/robcstf.htm
C game programming site includes numerous free games built with C.

www.programmersheaven.com/zone8/cat121/32947.htm
Tic Tac Toe game built with C.

www.programmersheaven.com/zone8/cat121/14606.htm
Guessing game built with C.

www.programmersheaven.com/zone8/cat121/39494.htm
Asteroids game built with C.

www.programmersheaven.com/zone8/cat121/459.htm
Boboli the Mighty Knight game, written in C.

www.programmersheaven.com/zone8/cat121/30558.htm
Tetris game, written in C.

www.programmersheaven.com/zone8/cat121/13269.htm
Algorithm for Connect Four game, written in C.

www.programmersheaven.com/zone8/cat121/35136.htm
Tetris game, written in C.

www.gametutorials.com/gtstore/pc-13-2-first-c-program.aspx
C games programming tutorial teaches you how to output text to the screen.

gpwiki.org/index.php/C:Custom_Resource_Files
Game Programming wiki tutorial: "C: Custom Resource Files," includes source code.

gpwiki.org/index.php/C:Pointers_and_References
Game Programming wiki tutorial: "C: Pointers and Strings," includes source code for a simple game written in C using pointers.

gpwiki.org/index.php/C:Beating_the_Message_Pump
Game Programming wiki tutorial: "C: Beating the Message Pump," includes some code examples.

www.blueparrots.com/
Download the source code for numerous games written in C/C++, including hangman, Pacman, Tetris, chess and more.

gpwiki.org/forums/viewforum.php?f=2&sid=13a4492f7736bce8742b860157b62a7a
Game programming wiki includes questions and answers regarding C/C++ game programming.

A.18 Allegro Game Programming Resources

www.talula.demon.co.uk/allegro/
The Allegro homepage. Here you can download the files necessary to use Allegro in your C code, and you can check out the documentation and other Allegro resources.

sourceforge.net/projects/alleg/
Download the files and source code for Allegro here.

prdownloads.sourceforge.net/alleg/allegro-manual-4.2.0.en.pdf?download
The Allegro API, in PDF format.

alleg.sourceforge.net/onlinedocs/en/allegro.html
The Allegro manual, in HTML format. This manual contains information on essential functions of the Allegro library without the complexity and wordiness of the API.

www.allegro.cc/
A large community of Allegro programmers. Share your ideas for games here and check out new developments in the Allegro world, including new games and programming competitions.

www.allegro.cc/depot
This section of the Allegro.cc web site contains over 1,000 games created by members with Allegro. Most of the games listed are open source, and all are free to download and play.

en.wikipedia.org/wiki/Allegro_library
Wikipedia article for the Allegro library.

www.loomsoft.net/resources/alltut/alltut_index.htm
An Allegro "newbie tutorial." Created for the beginning programmer, contains a basic set of tutorials that cover everything from simply getting Allegro to run on your computer to making your own graphics and datafiles for Allegro to use.

www.glost.eclipse.co.uk/gfoot/vivace/
Another tutorial intended for Allegro novices.

www.gillius.org/allegtut/index.htm
A beginner's tutorial for getting started with the Allegro library.

www.cppgameprogramming.com/cgi/nav.cgi?page=allegbasics
A beginner's tutorial for the Allegro library.

www.glost.eclipse.co.uk/gfoot/htpg/
A page that contains a downloadable tutorial which explains, step-by-step, how to program the simple game Pong in Allegro.

alleg.sourceforge.net/docs/how_to_make_a_pong_game.en.html
Another page that details creating a Pong game in Allegro.

www.ping.uio.no/~ovehk/allegro/
This tutorial details making a simple helicopter action game using Allegro.

www.gamedev.net/reference/articles/article2130.asp
A tutorial that explains how to make your game allow text input from the user.

oregonstate.edu/~barnesc/quick_reference.html
An Allegro "quick reference." Check here if you have trouble remembering that one method you need for your game.

www.niksula.cs.hut.fi/~tparvine/allegro3d/
An advanced tutorial on Allegro 3D graphics.

www.amazon.com/gp/product/1592003834/103-9185010-1591016?v=glance&n=283155
"Game Programming: All in One" by Jonathan S. Harbour. Teaches introductory game programming using the Allegro library.

groups.yahoo.com/group/allegrogamelibrary/
A Yahoo! group dedicated to creating games with Allegro and archiving Allegro games.

www.allegro.cc/forums/
The forums of Allegro.cc. Here you can communicate with other Allegro developers, get help with problematic programs, and share ideas for games.

www.jharbour.com/forums/index.php?s=d3cac6e7ae2c03fa1161790355cc7ac8&act=SF&f=7
Allegro forum at the homepage of Jonathan Harbour, author of "Game Programming: All in One." Another good place to ask for help if you are having trouble with your Allegro program.

gibbage.blogspot.com/2006/04/writing-your-own-game-phase-two.html
Blog post about programming games in Allegro and about the book "Game Programming: All in One."

`staticmartin.blogspot.com/2006/05/i-love-allegro.html`
Blog post that discusses Allegro and its ease of use.

A.19 Jobs for C Programmers

`www.monster.com`
Search Monster for jobs, post your resume for free, and create a Monster account to access career tools and more.

`www.careerbuilder.com`
Search CareerBuilder for C programming jobs.

`www.dice.com/`
Technical jobs site. Search for C programming jobs.

`www.cybercoders.com/developer/profile/jobSearch.aspx?ad=&sTerm=C`
Job site for programmers includes an extensive listing of C/C++ jobs. Post your resume, set up alerts so that you are notified when new jobs are posted, and check out their career tools including interview tips and words of advice about counter offers.

`www.prgjobs.com/`
Programming jobs site includes job postings for C/C++ programmers.

`www.sologig.com/`
Search freelance and contract opportunities for programmers.

`www.ihireprogrammers.com`
Job site for programmers.

`www.ifreelance.com/`
Search for freelance opportunities or offer your programming services.

`www.elance.com`
Search for freelance opportunities or offer your programming services.

A.20 Deitel C Training

With our corporate, on-site, instructor-led DEITEL® DIVE INTO® Series Programming training courses, professionals can learn C/C++ from the internationally recognized professionals at Deitel & Associates, Inc. Our authors, teaching staff and contract instructors have taught over 1,000,000 people in more than 100 countries how to program in major programming languages through: How to Program Series textbooks, university teaching, professional seminars, interactive multimedia CD-ROM Cyber Classrooms and Complete Training Courses, satellite broadcasts and Companion Web sites. Bring Deitel instructor-led corporate training to your company for a one-to-five day on-site seminar!

`www.deitel.com/training/cpp/index.html`
Dive Into Series™ C/C++ curriculum overview.

`www.deitel.com/training/cpp/cpp_1.html`
Dive Into Series™ Introduction to C and C++: Part 1 (for Non-Programmers).

`www.deitel.com/training/cpp/cpp_2.html`
Dive Into Series™ Introduction to C and C++: Part 2 (for Non-C Programmers).

`www.deitel.com/training/cpp/cpp_oop.html`
Dive Into Series™ C++ and Object-Oriented Programming for C Programmers.

`www.deitel.com/training/cpp/cpp_3.html`
Advanced C++ and Object-Oriented Programming for C++ Programmers.

Operator Precedence Charts

Operators are shown in decreasing order of precedence from top to bottom (Figs. B.1–B.2).

C Operator	Type	Associativity
() [] . -> ++ --	parentheses (function call operator) array subscript member selection via object member selection via pointer unary postincrement unary postdecrement	left to right
++ -- + - ! ~ (*type*) * & sizeof	unary preincrement unary predecrement unary plus unary minus unary logical negation unary bitwise complement C-style unary cast dereference address determine size in bytes	right to left
* / %	multiplication division modulus	left to right

Fig. B.1 | C operator precedence chart. (Part 1 of 2.)

C Operator	Type	Associativity
+ -	addition subtraction	left to right
<< >>	bitwise left shift bitwise right shift	left to right
< <= > >=	relational less than relational less than or equal to relational greater than relational greater than or equal to	left to right
== !=	relational is equal to relational is not equal to	left to right
&	bitwise AND	left to right
^	bitwise exclusive OR	left to right
|	bitwise inclusive OR	left to right
&&	logical AND	left to right
||	logical OR	left to right
?:	ternary conditional	right to left
= += -= *= /= %= &= ^= |= <<= >>=	assignment addition assignment subtraction assignment multiplication assignment division assignment modulus assignment bitwise AND assignment bitwise exclusive OR assignment bitwise inclusive OR assignment bitwise left shift assignment bitwise right shift with sign	right to left
,	comma	left to right

Fig. B.1 | C operator precedence chart. (Part 2 of 2.)

C++ Operator	Type	Associativity
`::` `::`	binary scope resolution unary scope resolution	left to right

`()`
`[]`
`.`
`->`
`++`
`--`
`typeid`
`dynamic_cast< type >`
`static_cast< type >`
`reinterpret_cast< type >`
`const_cast< type >`
	parentheses (function call operator)
	array subscript
	member selection via object
	member selection via pointer
	unary postincrement
	unary postdecrement
	runtime type information
	runtime type-checked cast
	compile-time type-checked cast
	cast for nonstandard conversions
	cast away const-ness
		left to right

`++`
`--`
`+`
`-`
`!`
`~`
`( type )`
`sizeof`
`&`
`*`
`new`
`new[]`
`delete`
`delete[]`
	unary preincrement
	unary predecrement
	unary plus
	unary minus
	unary logical negation
	unary bitwise complement
	C-style unary cast
	determine size in bytes
	address
	dereference
	dynamic memory allocation
	dynamic array allocation
	dynamic memory deallocation
	dynamic array deallocation
		right to left

`.*` `->*`	pointer to member via object pointer to member via pointer	left to right

`*`
`/`
`%`
	multiplication
	division
	modulus
		left to right

`+` `-`	addition subtraction	left to right
`<<` `>>`	bitwise left shift bitwise right shift	left to right

`<`
`<=`
`>`
`>=`
	relational less than
	relational less than or equal to
	relational greater than
	relational greater than or equal to
		left to right

Fig. B.2 | C++ operator precedence chart. (Part 1 of 2.)

C++ Operator	Type	Associativity
== !=	relational is equal to relational is not equal to	left to right
&	bitwise AND	left to right
^	bitwise exclusive OR	left to right
|	bitwise inclusive OR	left to right
&&	logical AND	left to right
||	logical OR	left to right
?:	ternary conditional	right to left
= += -= *= /= %= &= ^= |= <<= >>=	assignment addition assignment subtraction assignment multiplication assignment division assignment modulus assignment bitwise AND assignment bitwise exclusive OR assignment bitwise inclusive OR assignment bitwise left shift assignment bitwise right shift with sign	right to left
,	comma	left to right

Fig. B.2 | C++ operator precedence chart. (Part 2 of 2.)

ASCII Character Set

ASCII character set										
	0	**1**	**2**	**3**	**4**	**5**	**6**	**7**	**8**	**9**
0	nul	soh	stx	etx	eot	enq	ack	bel	bs	ht
1	lf	vt	ff	cr	so	si	dle	dc1	dc2	dc3
2	dc4	nak	syn	etb	can	em	sub	esc	fs	gs
3	rs	us	sp	!	"	#	$	%	&	'
4	(	)	*	+	,	-	.	/	0	1
5	2	3	4	5	6	7	8	9	:	;
6	<	=	>	?	@	A	B	C	D	E
7	F	G	H	I	J	K	L	M	N	O
8	P	Q	R	S	T	U	V	W	X	Y
9	Z	[	\	]	^	_	'	a	b	c
10	d	e	f	g	h	i	j	k	l	m
11	n	o	p	q	r	s	t	u	v	w
12	x	y	z	{			}	~	del		

Fig. C.1 | ASCII Character Set.

The digits at the left of the table are the left digits of the decimal equivalent (0-127) of the character code, and the digits at the top of the table are the right digits of the character code. For example, the character code for "F" is 70, and the character code for "&" is 38.

D

Number Systems

OBJECTIVES

In this appendix, you will learn:

- To understand basic number systems concepts such as base, positional value and symbol value.

- To understand how to work with numbers represented in the binary, octal and hexadecimal number systems

- To be able to abbreviate binary numbers as octal numbers or hexadecimal numbers.

- To be able to convert octal numbers and hexadecimal numbers to binary numbers.

- To be able to convert back and forth between decimal numbers and their binary, octal and hexadecimal equivalents.

- To understand binary arithmetic and how negative binary numbers are represented using two's complement notation.

D.1 Introduction

In this appendix, we introduce the key number systems that programmers use, especially when they are working on software projects that require close interaction with machine-level hardware. Projects like this include operating systems, computer networking software, compilers, database systems and applications requiring high performance.

When we write an integer such as 227 or –63 in a program, the number is assumed to be in the decimal (base 10) number system. The digits in the decimal number system are 0, 1, 2, 3, 4, 5, 6, 7, 8 and 9. The lowest digit is 0 and the highest digit is 9—one less than the base of 10. Internally, computers use the binary (base 2) number system. The binary number system has only two digits, namely 0 and 1. Its lowest digit is 0 and its highest digit is 1—one less than the base of 2.

As we will see, binary numbers tend to be much longer than their decimal equivalents. Programmers who work in assembly languages and in high-level languages like C that enable programmers to reach down to the machine level, find it cumbersome to work with binary numbers. So two other number systems—the octal number system (base 8) and the hexadecimal number system (base 16)—are popular primarily because they make it convenient to abbreviate binary numbers.

In the octal number system, the digits range from 0 to 7. Because both the binary number system and the octal number system have fewer digits than the decimal number system, their digits are the same as the corresponding digits in decimal.

The hexadecimal number system poses a problem because it requires 16 digits—a lowest digit of 0 and a highest digit with a value equivalent to decimal 15 (one less than the base of 16). By convention, we use the letters A through F to represent the hexadecimal digits corresponding to decimal values 10 through 15. Thus in hexadecimal we can have numbers like 876 consisting solely of decimal-like digits, numbers like 8A55F consisting of digits and letters and numbers like FFE consisting solely of letters. Occasionally, a hexadecimal number spells a common word such as FACE or FEED—this can appear strange to programmers accustomed to working with numbers. The digits of the binary, octal, decimal and hexadecimal number systems are summarized in Figs. D.1–D.2.

Each of these number systems uses positional notation—each position in which a digit is written has a different positional value. For example, in the decimal number 937 (the 9, the 3 and the 7 are referred to as symbol values), we say that the 7 is written in the ones position, the 3 is written in the tens position and the 9 is written in the hundreds position. Note that each of these positions is a power of the base (base 10) and that these powers begin at 0 and increase by 1 as we move left in the number (Fig. D.3).

Binary digit	Octal digit	Decimal digit	Hexadecimal digit
0	0	0	0
1	1	1	1
	2	2	2
	3	3	3
	4	4	4
	5	5	5
	6	6	6
	7	7	7
		8	8
		9	9
			A (decimal value of 10)
			B (decimal value of 11)
			C (decimal value of 12)
			D (decimal value of 13)
			E (decimal value of 14)
			F (decimal value of 15)

Fig. D.1 | Digits of the binary, octal, decimal and hexadecimal number systems.

Attribute	Binary	Octal	Decimal	Hexadecimal
Base	2	8	10	16
Lowest digit	0	0	0	0
Highest digit	1	7	9	F

Fig. D.2 | Comparing the binary, octal, decimal and hexadecimal number systems.

Positional values in the decimal number system			
Decimal digit	9	3	7
Position name	Hundreds	Tens	Ones
Positional value	100	10	1
Positional value as a power of the base (10)	10^2	10^1	10^0

Fig. D.3 | Positional values in the decimal number system.

For longer decimal numbers, the next positions to the left would be the thousands position (10 to the 3rd power), the ten-thousands position (10 to the 4th power), the hundred-thousands position (10 to the 5th power), the millions position (10 to the 6th power), the ten-millions position (10 to the 7th power) and so on.

In the binary number 101, the rightmost 1 is written in the ones position, the 0 is written in the twos position and the leftmost 1 is written in the fours position. Each position is a power of the base (base 2) and that these powers begin at 0 and increase by 1 as we move left in the number (Fig. D.4). So, $101 = 1 * 2^2 + 0 * 2^1 + 1 * 2^0 = 4 + 0 + 1 = 5$.

For longer binary numbers, the next positions to the left would be the eights position (2 to the 3rd power), the sixteens position (2 to the 4th power), the thirty-twos position (2 to the 5th power), the sixty-fours position (2 to the 6th power) and so on.

In the octal number 425, we say that the 5 is written in the ones position, the 2 is written in the eights position and the 4 is written in the sixty-fours position. Note that each of these positions is a power of the base (base 8) and that these powers begin at 0 and increase by 1 as we move left in the number (Fig. D.5).

For longer octal numbers, the next positions to the left would be the five-hundred-and-twelves position (8 to the 3rd power), the four-thousand-and-ninety-sixes position (8 to the 4th power), the thirty-two-thousand-seven-hundred-and-sixty-eights position (8 to the 5th power) and so on.

In the hexadecimal number 3DA, we say that the A is written in the ones position, the D is written in the sixteens position and the 3 is written in the two-hundred-and-fifty-sixes position. Note that each of these positions is a power of the base (base 16) and that these powers begin at 0 and increase by 1 as we move left in the number (Fig. D.6).

For longer hexadecimal numbers, the next positions to the left would be the four-thousand-and-ninety-sixes position (16 to the 3rd power), the sixty-five-thousand-five-hundred-and-thirty-sixes position (16 to the 4th power) and so on.

Positional values in the binary number system			
Binary digit	1	0	1
Position name	Fours	Twos	Ones
Positional value	4	2	1
Positional value as a power of the base (2)	2^2	2^1	2^0

Fig. D.4 | Positional values in the binary number system.

Positional values in the octal number system			
Decimal digit	4	2	5
Position name	Sixty-fours	Eights	Ones
Positional value	64	8	1
Positional value as a power of the base (8)	8^2	8^1	8^0

Fig. D.5 | Positional values in the octal number system.

Positional values in the hexadecimal number system			
Decimal digit	3	D	A
Position name	Two-hundred-and-fifty-sixes	Sixteens	Ones
Positional value	256	16	1
Positional value as a power of the base (16)	16^2	16^1	16^0

Fig. D.6 | Positional values in the hexadecimal number system.

D.2 Abbreviating Binary Numbers as Octal and Hexadecimal Numbers

The main use for octal and hexadecimal numbers in computing is for abbreviating lengthy binary representations. Figure D.7 highlights the fact that lengthy binary numbers can be expressed concisely in number systems with higher bases than the binary number system.

Decimal number	Binary representation	Octal representation	Hexadecimal representation
0	0	0	0
1	1	1	1
2	10	2	2
3	11	3	3
4	100	4	4
5	101	5	5
6	110	6	6
7	111	7	7
8	1000	10	8
9	1001	11	9
10	1010	12	A
11	1011	13	B
12	1100	14	C
13	1101	15	D
14	1110	16	E
15	1111	17	F
16	10000	20	10

Fig. D.7 | Decimal, binary, octal and hexadecimal equivalents.

A particularly important relationship that both the octal number system and the hexadecimal number system have to the binary system is that the bases of octal and hexadecimal (8 and 16 respectively) are powers of the base of the binary number system (base 2). Consider the following 12-digit binary number and its octal and hexadecimal equivalents. See if you can determine how this relationship makes it convenient to abbreviate binary numbers in octal or hexadecimal. The answer follows the numbers.

Binary number	Octal equivalent	Hexadecimal equivalent
100011010001	4321	8D1

To see how the binary number converts easily to octal, simply break the 12-digit binary number into groups of three consecutive bits each and write those groups over the corresponding digits of the octal number as follows:

100	011	010	001
4	3	2	1

Note that the octal digit you have written under each group of three bits corresponds precisely to the octal equivalent of that 3-digit binary number, as shown in Fig. D.7.

The same kind of relationship can be observed in converting from binary to hexadecimal. Break the 12-digit binary number into groups of four consecutive bits each and write those groups over the corresponding digits of the hexadecimal number as follows:

1000	1101	0001
8	D	1

Notice that the hexadecimal digit you wrote under each group of four bits corresponds precisely to the hexadecimal equivalent of that 4-digit binary number as shown in Fig. D.7.

D.3 Converting Octal and Hexadecimal Numbers to Binary Numbers

In the previous section, we saw how to convert binary numbers to their octal and hexadecimal equivalents by forming groups of binary digits and simply rewriting them as their equivalent octal digit values or hexadecimal digit values. This process may be used in reverse to produce the binary equivalent of a given octal or hexadecimal number.

For example, the octal number 653 is converted to binary simply by writing the 6 as its 3-digit binary equivalent 110, the 5 as its 3-digit binary equivalent 101 and the 3 as its 3-digit binary equivalent 011 to form the 9-digit binary number 110101011.

The hexadecimal number FAD5 is converted to binary simply by writing the F as its 4-digit binary equivalent 1111, the A as its 4-digit binary equivalent 1010, the D as its 4-digit binary equivalent 1101 and the 5 as its 4-digit binary equivalent 0101 to form the 16-digit 1111101011010101.

D.4 Converting from Binary, Octal or Hexadecimal to Decimal

We are accustomed to working in decimal, and therefore it is often convenient to convert a binary, octal, or hexadecimal number to decimal to get a sense of what the number is "really" worth. Our tables in Section D.1 express the positional values in decimal. To convert a number to decimal from another base, multiply the decimal equivalent of each digit by its positional value and sum these products. For example, the binary number 110101 is converted to decimal 53, as shown in Fig. D.8.

To convert octal 7614 to decimal 3980, we use the same technique, this time using appropriate octal positional values, as shown in Fig. D.9.

To convert hexadecimal AD3B to decimal 44347, we use the same technique, this time using appropriate hexadecimal positional values, as shown in Fig. D.10.

D.5 Converting from Decimal to Binary, Octal or Hexadecimal

The conversions in Section D.4 follow naturally from the positional notation conventions. Converting from decimal to binary, octal, or hexadecimal also follows these conventions.

Converting a binary number to decimal					
Postional values:	32	16	8	4	2	1
Symbol values:	1	1	0	1	0	1
Products:	1*32=32	1*16=16	0*8=0	1*4=4	0*2=0	1*1=1
Sum:	= 32 + 16 + 0 + 4 + 0s + 1 = 53					

Fig. D.8 | Converting a binary number to decimal.

Converting an octal number to decimal			
Positional values:	512	64	8	1
Symbol values:	7	6	1	4
Products	7*512=3584	6*64=384	1*8=8	4*1=4
Sum:	= 3584 + 384 + 8 + 4 = 3980			

Fig. D.9 | Converting an octal number to decimal.

Converting a hexadecimal number to decimal			
Postional values:	4096	256	16	1
Symbol values:	A	D	3	B
Products	A*4096=40960	D*256=3328	3*16=48	B*1=11
Sum:	= 40960 + 3328 + 48 + 11 = 44347			

Fig. D.10 | Converting a hexadecimal number to decimal.

Suppose we wish to convert decimal 57 to binary. We begin by writing the positional values of the columns right to left until we reach a column whose positional value is greater than the decimal number. We do not need that column, so we discard it. Thus, we first write:

Positional values: 64   32   16   8   4   2   1

Then we discard the column with positional value 64, leaving:

Positional values: 32   16   8   4   2   1

Next we work from the leftmost column to the right. We divide 32 into 57 and observe that there is one 32 in 57 with a remainder of 25, so we write 1 in the 32 column. We divide 16 into 25 and observe that there is one 16 in 25 with a remainder of 9 and write 1 in the 16 column. We divide 8 into 9 and observe that there is one 8 in 9 with a remainder of 1. The next two columns each produce quotients of 0 when their positional values are divided into 1, so we write 0s in the 4 and 2 columns. Finally, 1 into 1 is 1, so we write 1 in the 1 column. This yields:

Positional values:	32	16	8	4	2	1
Symbol values:	1	1	1	0	0	1

and thus decimal 57 is equivalent to binary 111001.

To convert decimal 103 to octal, we begin by writing the positional values of the columns until we reach a column whose positional value is greater than the decimal number. We do not need that column, so we discard it. Thus, we first write:

Positional values: 512   64   8   1

Then we discard the column with positional value 512, yielding:

Positional values: 64   8   1

Next we work from the leftmost column to the right. We divide 64 into 103 and observe that there is one 64 in 103 with a remainder of 39, so we write 1 in the 64 column. We divide 8 into 39 and observe that there are four 8s in 39 with a remainder of 7 and write 4 in the 8 column. Finally, we divide 1 into 7 and observe that there are seven 1s in 7 with no remainder, so we write 7 in the 1 column. This yields:

Positional values:	64	8	1
Symbol values:	1	4	7

and thus decimal 103 is equivalent to octal 147.

To convert decimal 375 to hexadecimal, we begin by writing the positional values of the columns until we reach a column whose positional value is greater than the decimal number. We do not need that column, so we discard it. Thus, we first write:

Positional values: 4096   256   16   1

Then we discard the column with positional value 4096, yielding:

Positional values: 256   16   1

Next we work from the leftmost column to the right. We divide 256 into 375 and observe that there is one 256 in 375 with a remainder of 119, so we write 1 in the 256 column. We divide 16 into 119 and observe that there are seven 16s in 119 with a remainder of 7 and write 7 in the 16 column. Finally, we divide 1 into 7 and observe that there are seven 1s in 7 with no remainder, so we write 7 in the 1 column. This yields:

Positional values: 256   16   1
Symbol values: 1   7   7

and thus decimal 375 is equivalent to hexadecimal 177.

D.6 Negative Binary Numbers: Two's Complement Notation

The discussion so far in this appendix has focused on positive numbers. In this section, we explain how computers represent negative numbers using *two's complement notation*. First we explain how the two's complement of a binary number is formed, then we show why it represents the negative value of the given binary number.

Consider a machine with 32-bit integers. Suppose

```
int value = 13;
```

The 32-bit representation of value is

```
00000000 00000000 00000000 00001101
```

To form the negative of value we first form its *one's complement* by applying C's bitwise complement operator (~):

```
onesComplementOfValue = ~value;
```

Internally, ~value is now value with each of its bits reversed—ones become zeros and zeros become ones, as follows:

```
value:
00000000 00000000 00000000 00001101

~value (i.e., value's ones complement):
11111111 11111111 11111111 11110010
```

To form the two's complement of value, we simply add 1 to value's one's complement. Thus

```
Two's complement of value:
11111111 11111111 11111111 11110011
```

Now if this is in fact equal to −13, we should be able to add it to binary 13 and obtain a result of 0. Let us try this:

```
 00000000 00000000 00000000 00001101
+11111111 11111111 11111111 11110011
-----------------------------------
 00000000 00000000 00000000 00000000
```

The carry bit coming out of the leftmost column is discarded and we indeed get 0 as a result. If we add the one's complement of a number to the number, the result would be all 1s. The key to getting a result of all zeros is that the twos complement is one more than the one's complement. The addition of 1 causes each column to add to 0 with a carry of 1. The carry keeps moving leftward until it is discarded from the leftmost bit, and thus the resulting number is all zeros.

Computers actually perform a subtraction, such as

```
x = a - value;
```

by adding the two's complement of value to a, as follows:

```
x = a + (~value + 1);
```

Suppose a is 27 and value is 13 as before. If the two's complement of value is actually the negative of value, then adding the two's complement of value to a should produce the result 14. Let us try this:

```
a (i.e., 27)         00000000 00000000 00000000 00011011
+(~value + 1)       +11111111 11111111 11111111 11110011
                    ------------------------------------
                     00000000 00000000 00000000 00001110
```

which is indeed equal to 14.

Summary

- An integer such as 19 or 227 or –63 in a program is assumed to be in the decimal (base 10) number system. The digits in the decimal number system are 0, 1, 2, 3, 4, 5, 6, 7, 8 and 9. The lowest digit is 0 and the highest digit is 9—one less than the base of 10.
- Internally, computers use the binary (base 2) number system. The binary number system has only two digits, namely 0 and 1. Its lowest digit is 0 and its highest digit is 1—one less than the base of 2.
- The octal number system (base 8) and the hexadecimal number system (base 16) are popular primarily because they make it convenient to abbreviate binary numbers.
- The digits of the octal number system range from 0 to 7.
- The hexadecimal number system poses a problem because it requires 16 digits—a lowest digit of 0 and a highest digit with a value equivalent to decimal 15 (one less than the base of 16). By convention, we use the letters A through F to represent the hexadecimal digits corresponding to decimal values 10 through 15.
- Each number system uses positional notation—each position in which a digit is written has a different positional value.
- A particularly important relationship of both the octal number system and the hexadecimal number system to the binary system is that the bases of octal and hexadecimal (8 and 16 respectively) are powers of the base of the binary number system (base 2).
- To convert an octal to a binary number, replace each octal digit with its three-digit binary equivalent.
- To convert a hexadecimal number to a binary number, simply replace each hexadecimal digit with its four-digit binary equivalent.
- Because we are accustomed to working in decimal, it is convenient to convert a binary, octal or hexadecimal number to decimal to get a sense of the number's "real" worth.
- To convert a number to decimal from another base, multiply the decimal equivalent of each digit by its positional value and sum the products.
- Computers represent negative numbers using two's complement notation.
- To form the negative of a value in binary, first form its one's complement by applying C's bitwise complement operator (~). This reverses the bits of the value. To form the two's complement of a value, simply add one to the value's one's complement.

Terminology

base	digit
base 2 number system	hexadecimal number system
base 8 number system	negative value
base 10 number system	octal number system
base 16 number system	one's complement notation
binary number system	positional notation
bitwise complement operator (~)	positional value
conversions	symbol value
decimal number system	two's complement notation

Self-Review Exercises

D.1   Fill in the blanks in each of the following statements:

a) The bases of the decimal, binary, octal and hexadecimal number systems are _____, _____, _____ and _____ respectively.

b) The positional value of the rightmost digit of any number in either binary, octal, decimal or hexadecimal is always _____.

c) The positional value of the digit to the left of the rightmost digit of any number in binary, octal, decimal or hexadecimal is always equal to _____.

D.2   State whether each of the following is *true* or *false*. If *false*, explain why.

a) A popular reason for using the decimal number system is that it forms a convenient notation for abbreviating binary numbers simply by substituting one decimal digit per group of four binary bits.

b) The highest digit in any base is one more than the base.

c) The lowest digit in any base is one less than the base.

D.3   In general, the decimal, octal and hexadecimal representations of a given binary number contain (more/fewer) digits than the binary number contains.

D.4   The (octal / hexadecimal / decimal) representation of a large binary value is the most concise (of the given alternatives).

D.5   Fill in the missing values in this chart of positional values for the rightmost four positions in each of the indicated number systems:

decimal	1000	100	10	1
hexadecimal	...	256	...	...
binary	...	...	...	...
octal	512	...	8	...

D.6   Convert binary 110101011000 to octal and to hexadecimal.

D.7   Convert hexadecimal FACE to binary.

D.8   Convert octal 7316 to binary.

D.9   Convert hexadecimal 4FEC to octal. [*Hint:* First convert 4FEC to binary, then convert that binary number to octal.]

D.10   Convert binary 1101110 to decimal.

D.11   Convert octal 317 to decimal.

D.12   Convert hexadecimal EFD4 to decimal.

D.13   Convert decimal 177 to binary, to octal and to hexadecimal.

D.14   Show the binary representation of decimal 417. Then show the one's complement of 417 and the two's complement of 417.

D.15   What is the result when a number and its two's complement are added to each other?

Answers to Self-Review Exercises

D.1   a) 10, 2, 8, 16. b) 1 (the base raised to the zero power). c) The base of the number system.

D.2   a) False. Hexadecimal does this. b) False. The highest digit in any base is one less than the base. c) False. The lowest digit in any base is zero.

D.3   Fewer.

D.4   Hexadecimal.

D.5   Fill in the missing values in this chart of positional values for the rightmost four positions in each of the indicated number systems:

decimal	1000	100	10	1
hexadecimal	4096	256	16	1
binary	8	4	2	1
octal	512	64	8	1

D.6   Octal 6530; Hexadecimal D58.

D.7   Binary 1111 1010 1100 1110.

D.8   Binary 111 011 001 110.

D.9   Binary 0 100 111 111 101 100; Octal 47754.

D.10   Decimal 2+4+8+32+64=110.

D.11   Decimal 7+1*8+3*64=7+8+192=207.

D.12   Decimal 4+13*16+15*256+14*4096=61396.

D.13   Decimal 177
to binary:

```
256 128 64 32 16 8 4 2 1
128 64 32 16 8 4 2 1
(1*128)+(0*64)+(1*32)+(1*16)+(0*8)+(0*4)+(0*2)+(1*1)
10110001
```

to octal:

```
512 64 8 1
64 8 1
(2*64)+(6*8)+(1*1)
261
```

to hexadecimal:

```
256 16 1
16 1
(11*16)+(1*1)
(B*16)+(1*1)
B1
```

D.14   Binary:

```
512 256 128 64 32 16 8 4 2 1
256 128 64 32 16 8 4 2 1
(1*256)+(1*128)+(0*64)+(1*32)+(0*16)+(0*8)+(0*4)+(0*2)+(1*1)
110100001
```

One's complement: 001011110
Two's complement: 001011111
Check: Original binary number + its two's complement

```
110100001
001011111
---------
000000000
```

D.15 Zero.

Exercises

D.16 Some people argue that many of our calculations would be easier in the base 12 number system because 12 is divisible by so many more numbers than 10 (for base 10). What is the lowest digit in base 12? What would be the highest symbol for the digit in base 12? What are the positional values of the rightmost four positions of any number in the base 12 number system?

D.17 Complete the following chart of positional values for the rightmost four positions in each of the indicated number systems:

decimal	1000	100	10	1
base 6	. . .	. . .	6	. . .
base 13	. . .	169	. . .	. . .
base 3	27	. . .	. . .	. . .

D.18 Convert binary 100101111010 to octal and to hexadecimal.

D.19 Convert hexadecimal 3A7D to binary.

D.20 Convert hexadecimal 765F to octal. (*Hint:* First convert 765F to binary, then convert that binary number to octal.)

D.21 Convert binary 1011110 to decimal.

D.22 Convert octal 426 to decimal.

D.23 Convert hexadecimal FFFF to decimal.

D.24 Convert decimal 299 to binary, to octal and to hexadecimal.

D.25 Show the binary representation of decimal 779. Then show the one's complement of 779 and the two's complement of 779.

D.26 Show the two's complement of integer value −1 on a machine with 32-bit integers.

Game Programming:
Solving Sudoku

E.1 Introduction

The game of Sudoku exploded in popularity worldwide in 2005. Almost every major newspaper now publishes a Sudoku puzzle daily. Handheld game players let you play anytime, anywhere and create puzzles on demand at various levels of difficulty.

A completed Sudoku puzzle is a 9×9 grid (i.e., a two-dimensional array) in which the digits 1 through 9 appear once and only once in each row, each column and each of nine 3×3 grids. In the partially completed 9×9 grid of Fig. E.1, row 1, column 1, and the 3×3 grid in the upper-left corner of the board each contain the digits 1 through 9 once and only once. Note that we use C's two-dimensional array row and column-numbering conventions, but we're ignoring row 0 and column 0 in conformance with Sudoku community conventions.

The typical Sudoku puzzle provides many filled-in cells and many blanks, often arranged in a symmetrical pattern as is typical with crossword puzzles. The player's task is to fill in the blanks to complete the puzzle. Some puzzles are easy to solve; some are quite difficult, requiring sophisticated solution strategies.

We'll discuss various simple solution strategies, and suggest what to do when these fail. We'll also present various approaches for programming Sudoku puzzle creators and solvers in C. Unfortunately, Standard C does not include graphics and GUI (graphical user interface) capabilities, so our representation of the board won't be as elegant as we could make it in Java and other programming languages that support these capabilities. You may want to revisit your Sudoku programs after you read Chapter 15, Game Programming with the Allegro C Library. Allegro, which is not part of Standard C, offers capabilities that will help you add graphics and even sounds to your Sudoku programs.

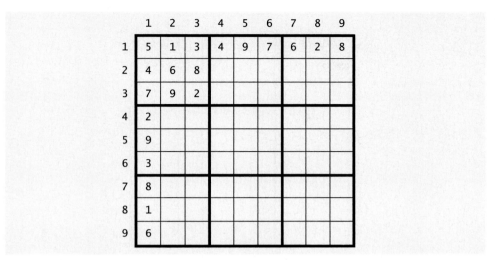

Fig. E.1 | Partially completed 9×9 Sudoku grid. Note the nine 3×3 grids.

E.2 Deitel Sudoku Resource Center

Check out our Sudoku Resource Center at www.deitel.com/sudoku. It contains downloads, tutorials, books, e-books and more that will help you master the game. Trace the history of Sudoku from its origin in the eighth century through modern times. Download free Sudoku puzzles at various levels of difficulty, enter daily game contests to win Sudoku books, and get a daily Sudoku puzzle to post on your web site. Get great beginner's resources—learn the rules of Sudoku, receive hints on solving sample puzzles, learn the best solution strategies and get free Sudoku solvers—just type in the puzzle from your newspaper or favorite Sudoku site and get an immediate solution; some Sudoku solvers even provide detailed step-by-step explanations. Get mobile device Sudoku games that can be installed on cell phones, Palm® devices, Game Boy® players and Java-enabled devices. Some Sudoku sites have timers, signal when an incorrect number is placed and provide hints. Purchase T-shirts and coffee mugs with Sudoku puzzles on them, participate in Sudoku player forums, get blank Sudoku worksheets that can be printed and check out hand-held Sudoku game players—one offers a million puzzles at five levels of difficulty. Download free Sudoku puzzle maker software. And not for the faint of heart—try fiendishly difficult Sudokus with tricky twists, a circular Sudoku and a variant of the puzzle with five interlocking grids. Subscribe to our free newsletter, *The Deitel® Buzz Online,* for notifications of updates to our Sudoku Resource Center and to other Deitel Resource Centers at www.deitel.com that provide games, puzzles and other interesting programming projects.

E.3 Solution Strategies

When we refer to a Sudoku 9×9 grid, we'll call it array s. By looking at all the filled-in cells in the row, column and 3×3 grid that includes a particular empty cell, the value for that cell might become obvious. Trivially, cell s[1][7] in Fig. E.2 *must* be 6.

Less trivially, to determine the value of s[1][7] in Fig. E.3, you have to pick up hints from row 1 (i.e., the digits 3, 6 and 9 are taken), column 7 (i.e., the digits 4, 7 and 1 are taken) and the upper-right 3×3 grid (i.e., the digits 9, 8, 4 and 2 are taken). Here the empty cell s[1][7] *must* be 5—the only number not already mentioned in row 1, column 7 or the upper-right 3×3 grid.

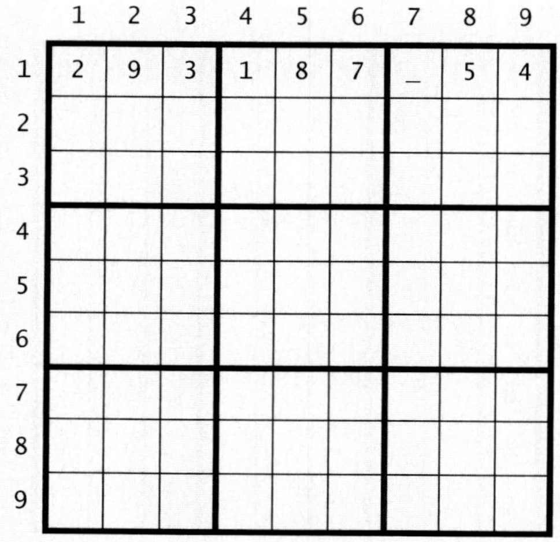

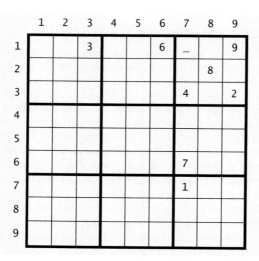

Fig. E.2 | Determining the value of a cell by checking all filled-in cells in the same row.

Fig. E.3 | Determining the value of a cell by checking all filled-in cells in the same row, column and 3×3 grid.

Singletons

The strategies we've discussed so far can easily determine the final digits for some open cells, but you'll often have to dig deeper. Column 6 of Fig. E.4 shows cells with already determined values (e.g., s[1][6] is a 9, s[3][6] is a 6, etc.), and cells indicating the set of values (which we call "possibles") that at this point are still possible for that cell.

Cell s[6][6] contains 257, indicating that only the values 2, 5 or 7 can eventually be assigned to this cell. The other two open cells in column 6—s[2][6] and s[5][6]—are both 27, indicating that *only* the values 2 or 7 can eventually be assigned to these cells. Thus s[6][6], the only cell in

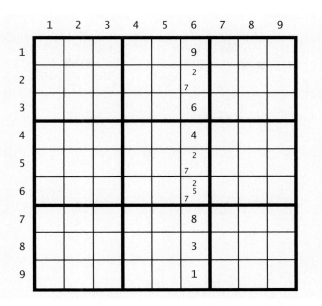

Fig. E.4 | Notation showing the complete sets of possible values for open cells.

column 6 that lists 5 as a remaining possible value, *must* be 5. We call that value 5 a **singleton**. So we can commit cell s[6][6] to a 5 (Fig. E.5), somewhat simplifying the puzzle.

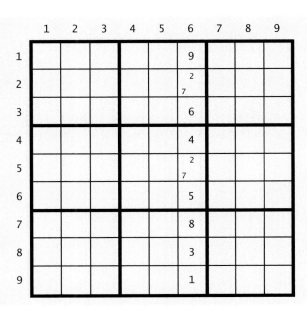

Fig. E.5 | Committing cell s[6][6] to the singleton value 5.

Doubles

Consider the upper-right 3×3 grid in Fig. E.6. The dashed cells could already be committed or could have lists of possible values. Notice the doubles—the two cells s[1][9] and s[2][7] containing only the two possibilities 15. If s[1][9] ultimately becomes 1, then s[2][7] *must* be 5; if s[1][9] ultimately becomes 5, then s[2][7] *must* be 1. So between them, those two cells will definitely "use up" the 1 and the 5. Thus 1 and 5 can be eliminated from cell s[3][9] that contains the possible values 1357, so we can rewrite its contents as 37, simplifying the puzzle a bit. If cell s[3][9] had originally contained only 135, then eliminating the 1 and the 5 would enable us to force the cell to the value 3.

Doubles can be more subtle. For example, suppose two cells of a row, column or 3×3 grid have possibles lists of 2467 and 257 and that no other cell in that row, column or 3×3 grid mentions 2 or 7 as a possible value. Then, 27 is a hidden double—one of those two cells must be 2 and the other must be 7, so all digits other than 2 and 7 can be removed from the possibles lists of those two cells (i.e., 2467 becomes 27 and 257 becomes 27—creating a pair of doubles—thus somewhat simplifying the puzzle).

Triples

Consider column 5 of Fig. E.7. The dashed cells could already be committed or could have lists of possible values. Notice the triples—the three cells containing the exact same three possibilities 467, namely cells s[1][5], s[6][5] and s[9][5]. If one of those three cells ultimately becomes 4, then the others reduce to doubles of 67; if one of those three cells ultimately becomes 6, then the others reduce to doubles of 47; and if one of those three cells ultimately becomes 7, then the others reduce to doubles of 46. Among the three cells containing 467, one must ultimately be 4, one must be 6, and one must be 7. Thus the 4, 6 and 7 can be eliminated from cell s[4][5] that contains the possibles 14567, so we can rewrite its contents as 15, simplifying the puzzle a bit. If cell s[4][5] had

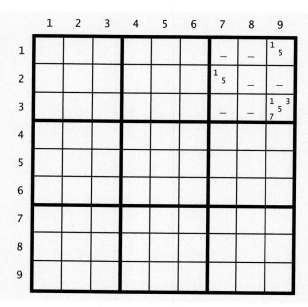

Fig. E.6 | Using doubles to simplify a puzzle.

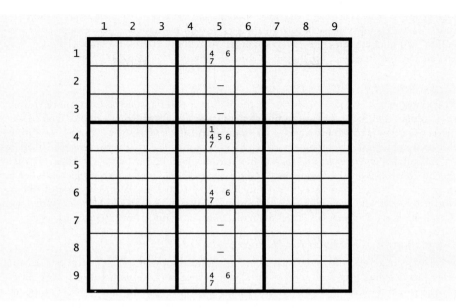

Fig. E.7 | Using triples to simplify a puzzle.

originally contained 1467, then eliminating the 4, 6 and 7 would enable us to force the value 1 in that cell.

Triples can be more subtle. Suppose a row, column or 3×3 grid contains cells with possibles lists of 467, 46, and 67. Clearly one of those cells must be 4, one must be 6 and one must be 7. Thus 4, 6 and 7 can be removed from all the other possibles lists in that row, column or 3×3 grid.

Triples can also be hidden. Suppose that a row, column or 3×3 grid contains the possibles lists 5789, 259 and 13789, and that no other cell in that row, column or 3×3 grid mentions 5, 7 or 9. Then one of those cells must be 5, one must be 7 and one must be 9. We call 579 a **hidden triple** and all possibles other than 5, 7 and 9 can be deleted from those three cells (i.e., 5789 becomes 579, 259 becomes 59 and 13789 becomes 79), thus somewhat simplifying the puzzle.

Other Sudoku Solution Strategies

There are a number of other Sudoku solution strategies. Here are two of the many sites we recommend in our Sudoku Resource Center (www.deitel.com/sudoku) that will help you dig deeper:

> www.sudokuoftheday.com/pages/techniques-overview.php
> www.angusj.com/sudoku/hints.php

E.4 Programming Sudoku Puzzle Solvers

In this section we suggest how to program Sudoku solvers. We use a variety of approaches. Some may seem unintelligent, but if they can solve Sudokus faster than any human on the planet, then perhaps they are in some sense intelligent.

If you've done our Knight's Tour exercises (Exercises 6.24, 6.25 and 6.29) and Eight Queens exercises (Exercises 6.26 and 6.27), you've implemented various brute force and heuristic problem solving approaches. In the next several sections, we suggest brute force and heuristic Sudoku solving strategies. You should try programming them, as well as creating and programming your own.

Our goal is simply to acquaint you with Sudoku, and some of its challenges and problem-solving strategies. Along the way, you'll become more facile with manipulating two-dimensional arrays and with nested iteration structures. We have made no attempt to produce optimal strategies, so once you analyze our strategies, you'll want to consider how you can improve upon them.

Programming a Solution for "Easy" Sudokus

The strategies we've shown—eliminating possibilities based on values already committed in a cell's row, column and 3×3 grid; and simplifying a puzzle using singletons, doubles (and hidden doubles) and triples (and hidden triples)—are sometimes sufficient to solve a puzzle. You can program the strategies then iterate on them until all 81 squares are filled. To confirm that the filled puzzle is a valid Sudoku, you can write a function to check that each row, column and 3×3 grid contains the digits 1 through 9 once and only once. Your program should apply the strategies in order. Each of them either forces a digit in a cell or simplifies the puzzle a bit. When any one of the strategies works, return to the beginning of your loop and reapply the strategies in order. When a strategy doesn't work, try the next. For "easy" Sudokus, these techniques should generate a solution.

Programming a Solution for Harder Sudokus

For harder Sudokus, your program will eventually reach a point where it still has uncommitted cells with possibles lists, and none of the simple strategies we've discussed will work. If this happens, first save the state of the board, then generate the next move by randomly choosing one of the possible values in any of the remaining cells. Then reevaluate the board, enumerating the remaining possibilities for each cell. Then try the basic strategies again, looping through them repeatedly, until either the Sudoku is solved, or the strategies once again no longer improve the board, at which point you can again try another move at random. If you reach a point where there are still empty cells, but no possible digits for at least one of those cells, the program should abandon that attempt, restore the board state that you saved, and begin the random approach again. Keep looping until a solution is found.

E.5 Generating New Sudoku Puzzles

First, let's consider several possible approaches for generating valid finished 9×9 Sudokus with all 81 squares filled in. Then, we'll suggest how to empty some cells to create puzzles that people can attempt.

Brute Force Approaches

When personal computers appeared in the late 1970s, they processed tens of thousands of instructions per second. Today's desktop computers commonly process *billions* of instructions per second and the world's fastest supercomputers can process *trillions* of instructions per second! Brute force approaches that might have required months of computing in the 1970s can now produce solutions in seconds! This encourages people who need results quickly to program simple brute force approaches and get solutions sooner than by taking the time to develop more sophisticated "intelligent" problem solving strategies. Although our brute force approaches may seem ponderous, they will mechanically grind out solutions.

For these approaches you'll need some utility functions. Create the function

```
int validSudoku( int sudokuBoard[ 10 ][ 10 ] );
```

which receives a Sudoku board as a two-dimensional array of integers (recall that we're ignoring row 0 and column 0). This function should return 1 if a completed board is valid, 2 if a partially completed board is valid and 0 otherwise.

An Exhaustive Brute Force Approach

One brute force approach is simply to select all possible placements of the digits 1 through 9 in every cell. This could be done with 81 nested for statements that each loop from 1 through 9. The number of possibilities (9^{81}) is so vast that you might say it's not worth trying. But this approach does have the advantage that it will eventually stumble onto *every* possible solution, some of which could show up fortuitously early on.

A slightly more intelligent version of this exhaustive brute-force approach would be to check each digit you're about to place to see if it leaves the board in a valid state. If it does, then move on to placing a digit in the next cell. If the digit you're attempting to place leaves the board in an invalid state, then try all other eight digits on that cell in order. If one of them works, then move on to the next cell. If none of them works, then move back up to the previous cell and try its next value. Nested for statements can handle this automatically.

Brute Force Approach with Randomly Selected Row Permutations

Every row, column, and 3×3 grid on a valid Sudoku contains a permutation of the digits 1 through 9. There are 9! (i.e., 9·8·7·6·5·4·3·2·1 = 362,880) such permutations. Write a function

```
void permutations( int sudokuBoard[ 10 ][ 10 ] );
```

that receives a 10×10 two-dimensional array and in the 9×9 portion of it that corresponds to a Sudoku grid fills each of the nine rows with a randomly selected permutation of the digits 1 through 9.

Here's one way to generate a random permutation of the digits 1 through 9—for the first digit, simply choose a random digit from 1 through 9; for the second digit, use a loop to repeatedly generate a random digit from 1 through 9 until a digit *different* from the first digit is selected; for the third digit, use a loop to repeatedly generate a random digit from 1 through 9 until a digit different from the first two digits is selected; and so on.

After placing nine randomly selected permutations into the nine rows of your Sudoku array, run function validSudoku on the array. If it returns 1, you're done. If it returns 0, simply loop again generating another nine randomly selected permutations of the digits 1 through 9 into the nine successive rows of the array Sudoku. The simple process will generate valid Sudokus. By the way, this approach guarantees that all the rows are valid permutations of the digits 1 through 9, so you should add an option to your function validSudoku that will have it check only columns and 3×3 grids.

Heuristic Solution Strategies

When we studied the Knight's Tour in Exercises 6.24, 6.25 and 6.29, we developed a "keep your options open" heuristic. To review, a heuristic is a "rule of thumb." It "sounds good" and seems like a reasonable rule to follow. It's programmable, so it gives us a way to direct a computer to attempt to solve a problem. But heuristic approaches don't necessarily guarantee success. For complex problems like solving a Sudoku puzzle, the number of possible placements of the digits 1–9 is enormous, so the hope in using a reasonable heuristic is that it will avoid wasting time on fruitless possibilities and instead focus on solution attempts much more likely to yield success.

A "Keep Your Options Open" Sudoku Solving Heuristic

Let's develop a "keep your options open" heuristic for solving Sudokus. At any point in solving a Sudoku, we can categorize the board by listing in each empty cell the digits from 1 to 9 which are still open possibilities for that cell. For example, if a cell contains 3578, then the cell must eventually become 3, 5, 7 or 8. When attempting to solve a Sudoku, we reach a dead end when the number of possible digits that can be placed in an empty cell becomes zero. So, consider the following strategy:

1. Associate with every empty square a possibles list of the digits that can still be placed in that square.

2. Characterize the state of the board by simply counting the number of possible placements for the entire board.

3. For each possible placement for each empty cell, associate with that placement the count that would characterize the state of the board after that placement.

4. Then, place the particular digit in the particular empty square (of all those that remain) that leaves the board count the highest (in case of a tie, pick one at random). This is a key to "keeping your options open."

Lookahead Heuristic

This is simply an embellishment of our "keep your options open" heuristic. In case of a tie, look ahead one more placement. Place the particular digit in the particular square whose subsequent placement leaves the board count the highest after two moves out.

Forming Sudoku Puzzles with Empty Cells

Once you get your Sudoku generator program running, you should be able to generate lots of valid Sudokus quickly. To form a puzzle, save the solved grid, then empty some cells. One way to do this is to empty randomly chosen cells. A general observation is that Sudokus tend to become more difficult as the empty cells increase (there are exceptions to this).

Another approach is to empty the cells in a manner that leaves the resulting board symmetric. This can be done programmatically by randomly picking a cell to empty, then emptying its "reflecting cell." For example, if you empty the top-left cell s[1][1], you might empty the bottom-left cell s[9][1] as well. Such reflections are calculated by presenting the column, but determining the row by subtracting the initial row from 10. You could also do the reflections by subtracting both the row and column of the cell you are emptying from 10. Hence, the reflecting cell to s[1][1] would be s[10-1][10-1] or s[9][9].

A Programming Challenge

Published Sudoku puzzles typically have exactly one solution, but it's still satisfying to solve any Sudoku, even ones that have multiple solutions. Develop a means of demonstrating that a particular Sudoku puzzle has *exactly one* solution.

E.6 Conclusion

This appendix on solving and programming Sudoku puzzles has presented you with many challenges. Be sure to check out our Sudoku Resource Center for numerous web resources that will help you master Sudoku and develop various approaches for writing programs to create and solve existing Sudoku puzzles.

Index

he DEITEL® Suite of Products...

HOW TO PROGRAM BOOKS

C++ How to Program Fifth Edition

BOOK / CD-ROM

©2005, 1500 pp., paper
(0-13-185757-6)

The complete authoritative DEITEL® *LIVE-CODE* introduction to programming with C++! The Fifth Edition takes a new, easy-to-follow, carefully developed early classes and objects approach to programming in C++. The text includes comprehensive coverage of the fundamentals of object-oriented programming in C++. It includes a new optional automated teller machine (ATM) case study that teaches the fundamentals of software engineering and object-oriented design with the UML 2.0 in Chapters 1-7, 9 and 13. Additional integrated case studies appear throughout the text, including the **Time** class (Chapter 9), the **Employee** class (Chapters 12 and 13) and the **GradeBook** class (Chapters 3-7). The book also includes a new interior design including updated colors, new fonts, new design elements and more.

Small C++ How to Program Fifth Edition

BOOK / CD-ROM

©2005, 900 pp., paper
(0-13-185758-4)

Based on chapters 1-13 (except the optional OOD/UML case study) and appendices of *C++ How to Program, Fifth Edition*, *Small C++* features a new early classes and objects approach and comprehensive coverage of the fundamentals of object-oriented programming in C++. Key topics include applications, variables, memory concepts, data types, control statements, functions, arrays, pointers and strings, inheritance and polymorphism.

📖 **Now available for both *C++ How to Program, 5/e* and *Small C++ How to Program, 5/e*: C++ Web-based *Cyber Classroom* included with the purchase of a new textbook. The *Cyber Classroom* includes a complete e-book, audio walkthroughs of the code examples, a Lab Manual and selected student solutions. See the *Cyber Classroom* section of this advertorial for more information.**

Java™ How to Program Sixth Edition

BOOK / CD-ROM

©2005, 1500 pp., paper
(0-13-148398-6)

The complete authoritative DEITEL® *LIVE-CODE* introduction to programming with the new Java™ 2 Platform Standard Edition 5.0! *Java How to Program, Sixth Edition* is up-to-date with J2SE™ 5.0 and includes comprehensive coverage of the fundamentals of object-oriented programming in Java; a new early classes and objects approach; a new interior design including new colors, new fonts, new design elements and more; and a new optional automated teller machine (ATM) case study that teaches the fundamentals of software engineering and object oriented design with the UML 2.0 in Chapters 1-8 and 10. Additional integrated case studies appear throughout the text, including GUI and graphics (Chapters 3-12), the **Time** class (Chapter 8), the **Employee** class (Chapters 9 and 10) and the **GradeBook** class (Chapters 3-8). New J2SE 5.0 topics covered included input/output, enhanced **for** loop, autoboxing, generics, new collections APIs and more.

Small Java™ How to Program Sixth Edition

BOOK / CD-ROM

©2005, 700 pp., paper
(0-13-148660-8)

Based on chapters 1-10 of *Java™ How to Program, Sixth Edition*, *Small Java* is up-to-date with J2SE™ 5.0, features a new early classes and objects approach and comprehensive coverage of the fundamentals of object-oriented programming in Java. Key topics include applications, variables, data types, control statements, methods, arrays, object-based programming, inheritance and polymorphism.

📖 **Now available for both *Java How to Program, 6/e* and *Small Java How to Program, 6/e*: Java Web-based *Cyber Classroom* included with the purchase of a new textbook. The *Cyber Classroom* includes a complete e-book, audio walkthroughs of the code examples, a Lab Manual and selected student solutions. See the *Cyber Classroom* section of this advertorial for more information.**

Visual Basic® 2005
How to Program
Third Edition

BOOK / CD-ROM

*©2006, 1500 pp., paper
(0-13-186900-0)*

The complete authoritative DEITEL® *LIVE-CODE* introduction to Visual Basic programming. *Visual Basic® 2005 How to Program, Third Edition* is up-to-date with Microsoft's Visual Basic 2005. The text includes comprehensive coverage of the fundamentals of object-oriented programming in Visual Basic including a new early classes and objects approach and a new optional automated teller machine (ATM) case study that teaches the fundamentals of software engineering and object-oriented design with the UML 2.0 in Chapters 1, 3–9 and 11. Additional integrated case studies appear throughout the text, including the `Time` class (Chapter 9), the `Employee` class (Chapters 10 and 11) and the `Gradebook` class (Chapters 4–9). This book also includes discussions of more advanced topics such as XML, ASP.NET, ADO.NET and Web services. New Visual Basic 2005 topics covered include partial classes, generics, the `My` namespace and Visual Studio's updated debugger features.

Visual C#® 2005
How to Program
Second Edition

BOOK / CD-ROM

*©2006, 1589 pp., paper
(0-13-152523-9)*

The complete authoritative DEITEL® *LIVE-CODE* introduction to C# programming. *Visual C#® 2005 How to Program, Second Edition* is up-to-date with Microsoft's Visual C# 2005. The text includes comprehensive coverage of the fundamentals of object-oriented programming in C#, including a new early classes and objects approach and a new optional automated teller machine (ATM) case study that teaches the fundamentals of software engineering and object-oriented design with the UML 2.0 in Chapters 1, 3–9 and 11. Additional integrated case studies appear throughout the text, including the `Time` class (Chapter 9), the `Employee` class (Chapters 10 and 11) and the `Gradebook` class (Chapters 4–9). This book also includes discussions of more advanced topics such as XML, ASP.NET, ADO.NET and Web services. New Visual C# 2005 topics covered include partial classes, generics, the `My` namespace, .NET remoting and Visual Studio's updated debugger features.

Visual C++ .NET®
How To Program

BOOK / CD-ROM

*©2004, 1400 pp., paper
(0-13-437377-4)*

Written by the authors of the world's best-selling introductory/intermediate C and C++ textbooks, this comprehensive book thoroughly examines Visual C++® .NET. *Visual C++® .NET How to Program* begins with a strong foundation in the introductory and intermediate programming principles students will need in industry, including fundamental topics such as arrays, functions and control statements. Readers learn the concepts of object-oriented programming, then the text explores such essential topics as networking, databases, XML and multimedia. Graphical user interfaces are also extensively covered, giving students the tools to build compelling and fully interactive programs using the "drag-and-drop" techniques provided by Visual Studio .NET 2003.

C How to Program
Fifth Edition

BOOK / CD-ROM

*©2007, 1200 pp., paper
(0-13-240416-8)*

C How to Program, Fifth Edition—the world's best-selling C text—is designed for introductory through intermediate courses and programming languages survey courses. This comprehensive text is aimed at readers with little or no programming experience through intermediate audiences. Highly practical in approach, it introduces fundamental notions of structured programming and software engineering and gets up to speed quickly. The Fifth Edition features new chapters on the C99 standard and an introduction to game programming with the Allegro C Library.

Advanced Java™ 2 Platform How to Program

BOOK / CD-ROM

©2002, 1811 pp., paper
(0-13-089560-1)

Expanding on the world's best-selling Java textbook—*Java™ How to Program—Advanced Java™ 2 Platform How To Program* presents advanced Java topics for developing sophisticated, user-friendly GUIs; significant, scalable enterprise applications; wireless applications and distributed systems. Primarily based on Java 2 Enterprise Edition (J2EE), this textbook integrates technologies such as XML, JavaBeans, security, JDBC™, JavaServer Pages (JSP™), servlets, Remote Method Invocation (RMI), Enterprise JavaBeans™ (EJB), design patterns, Swing, J2ME™, Java 2D and 3D, XML, design patterns, CORBA, Jini™, JavaSpaces™, Jiro™, Java Management Extensions (JMX) and Peer-to-Peer networking with an introduction to JXTA.

Internet & World Wide Web How to Program Third Edition

BOOK / CD-ROM

©2004, 1250 pp., paper
(0-13-145091-3)

This book introduces students with little or no programming experience to the exciting world of Web-based applications. This text provides in-depth coverage of introductory programming principles, various markup languages (XHTML, Dynamic HTML and XML), several scripting languages (JavaScript, JScript .NET, ColdFusion, Flash ActionScript, Perl, PHP, VBScript and Python), Web servers (IIS and Apache) and relational databases (MySQL)—all the skills and tools needed to create dynamic Web-based applications. The text contains a comprehensive introduction to ASP .NET and the Microsoft .NET Framework. A case study illustrating how to build an online message board using ASP .NET and XML is included. New in this edition are chapters on Macromedia ColdFusion, Macromedia Dreamweaver and a much enhanced treatment of Flash, including a case study on building a video game in Flash. After mastering the material in this book, students will be well prepared to build real-world, industrial-strength, Web-based applications.

Python How to Program

BOOK / CD-ROM

©2002, 1376 pp., paper
(0-13-092361-3)

This exciting textbook provides a comprehensive introduction to Python—a powerful object-oriented programming language with clear syntax and the ability to bring together various technologies quickly and easily. This book covers introductory programming techniques and more advanced topics such as graphical user interfaces, databases, wireless Internet programming, networking, security, process management, multithreading, XHTML, CSS, PSP and multimedia. Readers will learn principles that are applicable to both systems development and Web programming.

XML How to Program

BOOK / CD-ROM

©2001, 934 pp., paper
(0-13-028417-3)

This book is a comprehensive guide to programming in XML. It teaches how to use XML to create customized tags and includes chapters that address markup languages for science and technology, multimedia, commerce and many other fields. Concise introductions to Java, JavaServer Pages, VBScript, Active Server Pages and Perl/CGI provide readers with the essentials of these programming languages and server-side development technologies to enable them to work effectively with XML. The book also covers topics such as XSL, DOM™, SAX, a real-world e-commerce case study and a complete chapter on Web accessibility that addresses Voice XML. Other topics covered include XHTML, CSS, DTD, schema, parsers, XPath, XLink, namespaces, XBase, XInclude, XPointer, XSLT, XSL Formatting Objects, JavaServer Pages, XForms, topic maps, X3D, MathML, OpenMath, CML, BML, CDF, RDF, SVG, Cocoon, WML, XBRL and BizTalk™ and SOAP™ Web resources.

Perl How to Program

BOOK / CD-ROM

©2001, 1057 pp., paper (0-13-028418-1)

This comprehensive guide to Perl programming emphasizes the use of the Common Gateway Interface (CGI) with Perl to create powerful, dynamic multi-tier Web-based client/server applications. The book begins with a clear and careful introduction to programming concepts at a level suitable for beginners, and proceeds through advanced topics such as references and complex data structures. Key Perl topics such as regular expressions and string manipulation are covered in detail. The authors address important and topical issues such as object-oriented programming, the Perl database interface (DBI), graphics and security. Also included is a treatment of XML, a bonus chapter introducing the Python programming language, supplemental material on career resources and a complete chapter on Web accessibility.

e-Business & e-Commerce How to Program

BOOK / CD-ROM

©2001, 1254 pp., paper (0-13-028419-X)

This book explores programming technologies for developing Web-based e-business and e-commerce solutions, and covers e-business and e-commerce models and business issues. Readers learn a full range of options, from "build-your-own" to turnkey solutions. The book examines scores of the top e-businesses (examples include Amazon, eBay, Priceline, Travelocity, etc.), explaining the technical details of building successful e-business and e-commerce sites and their underlying business premises. Learn how to implement the dominant e-commerce models—shopping carts, auctions, name-your-own-price, comparison shopping and bots/intelligent agents—by using markup languages (HTML, Dynamic HTML and XML), scripting languages (JavaScript, VBScript and Perl), server-side technologies (Active Server Pages and Perl/CGI) and database (SQL and ADO), security and online payment technologies.

"In my courses, I've read several Deitel books. I really enjoy reading and learning from them because they're written in a fashion that's very easy to follow. It's almost like someone is speaking to you, and you don't get lost in a lot of unnecessarily complicated paragraphs. There are sections that have some humor and the real world examples they use help you understand why some things that are good in theory don't work as well in practice. I think Harvey and Paul Deitel have done an amazing job researching the latest technologies and then presenting them in a very understandable way. Whenever I take a new class and find out that we are to use a Deitel book, I'm very happy about that because they're my favorite. I know I can rely upon the book to explain the subject clearly."

— Christine Spencer, Graduate of MIT

ORDER INFORMATION

For ordering information,
visit us on the Web at www.prenhall.com.

INTERNATIONAL ORDERING INFORMATION
CANADA:
Pearson Education Canada
26 Prince Andrew Place
PO Box 580
Don Mills, Ontario M3C 2T8 Canada
Tel.: 416-925-2249; Fax: 416-925-0068
e-mail: phcinfo.pubcanada@pearsoned.com

EUROPE, MIDDLE EAST, AND AFRICA:
Pearson Education
Edinburgh Gate
Harlow, Essex CM20 2JE UK
Tel: 01279 623928; Fax: 01279 414130
e-mail: enq.orders@pearsoned-ema.com

BENELUX REGION:
Pearson Education
Concertgebouwplein 25
1071 LM Amsterdam
The Netherlands
Tel: 31 20 5755 800; Fax: 31 20 664 5334
e-mail: amsterdam@pearsoned-ema.com

ASIA:
Pearson Education Asia Pte. Ltd.
23/25 First Lok Yang Road
Jurong, 629733 Singapore
Tel: 65 476 4688; Fax: 65 378 0370

JAPAN:
Pearson Education Japan
Ogikubo TM Bldg. 6F. 5-26-13 Ogikubo
Suginami-ku, Tokyo 167-0051 Japan
Tel: 81 3 3365 9001; Fax: 81 3 3365 9009

INDIA:
Pearson Education
Indian Branch
482 FIE, Patparganj
Delhi – 110092 India
Tel: 91 11 2059850 & 2059851
Fax: 91 11 2059852

AUSTRALIA:
Pearson Education Australia
Unit 4, Level 2, 14 Aquatic Drive
Frenchs Forest, NSW 2086, Australia
Tel: 61 2 9454 2200; Fax: 61 2 9453 0089
e-mail: marketing@pearsoned.com.au

NEW ZEALAND/FIJI:
Pearson Education
46 Hillside Road
Auckland 10, New Zealand
Tel: 649 444 4968; Fax: 649 444 4957
E-mail: sales@pearsoned.co.nz

SOUTH AFRICA:
Maskew Miller Longman
Central Park   Block H
16th Street   Midrand   1685
South Africa
Tel: 27 21 686 6356; Fax: 27 21 686 4590

LATIN AMERICA:
Pearson Education Latin America
Attn: Tina Sheldon
1 Lake Street
Upper Saddle River, NJ 07458

The SIMPLY SERIES!

The Deitels' *Simply Series* takes an engaging new approach to teaching programming languages from the ground up. The pedagogy of this series combines the DEITEL® signature *LIVE-CODE Approach* with an *APPLICATION-DRIVEN Tutorial Approach* to teach programming with outstanding pedagogical features that help students learn. We have merged the notion of a lab manual with that of a conventional textbook, creating a book in which readers build and execute complete applications from start to finish, while learning the fundamental concepts of programming!

Simply Visual Basic® 2005 An APPLICATION-DRIVEN Tutorial Approach

©2007, 960 pp., paper
(0-13-243862-3)

Simply Visual Basic® 2005 An APPLICATION-DRIVEN Tutorial Approach guides readers through building real-world applications that incorporate Visual Basic 2005 programming fundamentals. Learn GUI design, controls, methods, functions, data types, control statements, procedures, arrays, object-oriented programming, strings and characters, sequential files and more in this comprehensive introduction to Visual Basic 2005. Higher-end topics include ADO .NET 2.0, ASP .NET 2.0, Visual Web Developer 2005 Express, database programming, multimedia and graphics and Web applications development.

Simply C# An APPLICATION-DRIVEN Tutorial Approach

©2004, 850 pp., paper
(0-13-142641-9)

Simply C# An APPLICATION-DRIVEN Tutorial Approach guides readers through building real-world applications that incorporate C# programming fundamentals. Learn GUI design, controls, methods, functions, data types, control statements, procedures, arrays, object-oriented programming, strings and characters, sequential files and more in this comprehensive introduction to C#. We also include higher-end topics such as database programming, multimedia and graphics and Web applications development.

Simply Java™ Programming An APPLICATION-DRIVEN Tutorial Approach

©2004, 950 pp., paper
(0-13-142648-6)

Simply Java™ Programming An APPLICATION-DRIVEN Tutorial Approach guides readers through building real-world applications that incorporate Java programming fundamentals. Learn GUI design, components, methods, event-handling, types, control statements, arrays, object-oriented programming, exception-handling, strings and characters, sequential files and more in this comprehensive introduction to Java. We also include higher-end topics such as database programming, multimedia, graphics and Web applications development.

Simply C++ An APPLICATION-DRIVEN Tutorial Approach

©2005, 800 pp., paper
(0-13-142660-5)

Simply C++ An APPLICATION-DRIVEN Tutorial Approach guides readers through building real-world applications that incorporate C++ programming fundamentals. Learn methods, functions, data types, control statements, procedures, arrays, object-oriented programming, strings and characters, pointers, references, templates, operator overloading and more in this comprehensive introduction to C++.

Premium content available with *Java™* and *Small Java™ How to Program, Sixth Edition* and *C++* and *Small C++ How to Program, Fifth Edition!*

Java and *Small Java How to Program, 6/e* and *C++* and *Small C++ How to Program, 5/e* are now available with six-month access to the Web-based *Multimedia Cyber Classroom* for students who purchase new copies of these books! The *Cyber Classroom* is an interactive, multimedia, tutorial version of DEITEL textbooks. *Cyber Classrooms* are a great value, giving students additional hands-on experience and study aids.

NOW AVAILABLE for *Java* and *Small Java How to Program, 6/e* and *C++* and *Small C++ How to Program, 5/e* (with purchase of a new book)

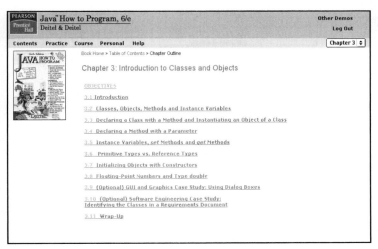

DEITEL® Multimedia Cyber Classrooms *feature an e-book with the complete text of their corresponding* How to Program *titles.*

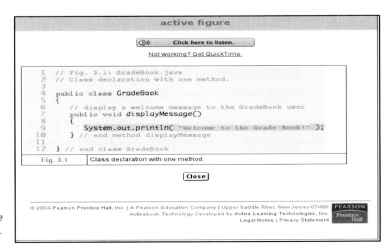

Unique audio "walkthroughs" of code examples reinforce key concepts.

DEITEL® *Multimedia Cyber Classrooms* include:

- The full text, illustrations and program listings of its corresponding *How to Program* book.

- Hours of detailed, expert audio descriptions of hundreds of lines of code that help to reinforce important concepts.

- An abundance of self-assessment material, including practice exams, hundreds of programming exercises and self-review questions and answers.

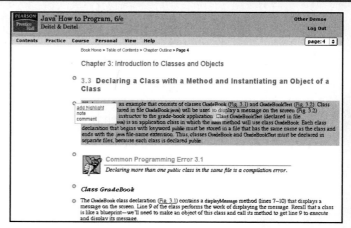

DEITEL® Multimedia Cyber Classrooms *offer a host of interactive features, such as highlighting of key sections of the text...*

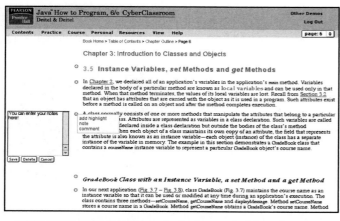

- Intuitive browser-based interface designed to be easy and accessible.

- A Lab Manual featuring lab exercises as well as pre- and post-lab activities.

- Student Solutions to approximately one-half of the exercises in the textbook.

...and the ability to write notes in the margin of a given page for future reference.

Students receive six-month access to a protected Web site via access code cards packaged with these new textbooks. (Simply tear the strip on the inside of the Cyber Classroom package to reveal access code.)

Note: For *Java How to Program, 6/e* and *Small Java How to Program, 6/e,* the instructor will need to "select" the Cyber Classroom card value pack.

For more information, please visit:
www·prenhall·com/deitel/
cyberclassroom

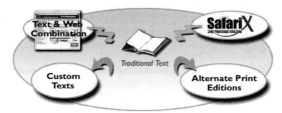

DEITEL® BUZZ ONLINE NEWSLETTER

Each issue of our free, e-mail newsletter, the *DEITEL® BUZZ ONLINE*, is now sent to over 51,000 opt-in subscribers. This weekly newsletter provides updates on our publishing program, our instructor-led professional training courses, timely industry topics and the continuing stream of innovations and new Web 2.0 business ventures emerging from Deitel.

Each issue of our newsletter includes:

- Resource centers on programming languages, Internet and Web technology, and more.

- Updates on all Deitel publications of interest to students, instructors and professionals.

- Free tutorials and guest articles. (part of the Deitel Free Content Initiative)

- Information on our instructor-led professional training courses taught worldwide.

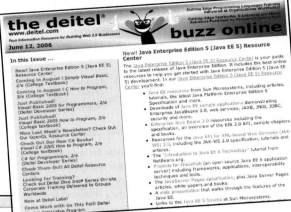

Recent Deitel Publications

Java How to Program, 6/e
ISBN: 0131483986
Pages: 1576
Order your copy now from
Amazon or InformIT
Demo the free Cyber Classroom
Read the Table of Contents
Read the Preface
Check This Out! Java Resource Center

"Probably the most complete coverage of learning through examples in published material today. This material is such high quality—it's unbelievable. The [optional] ATM OOD/UML case study is super!" —Anne Horton, AT&T Bell Laboratories

Read more testimonials...

C++ How to Program, 5/e
ISBN: 0131857576
Pages: 1536
Order your copy now from
Amazon or InformIT
Demo the free Cyber Classroom
Read the Table of Contents
Read the Preface
Check This Out! C++ Resource Center

"This book is one of the best of its kind. It is an excellent "objects first" coverage of C++ that remains accessible to beginners. The example-driven presentation is enriched by the optional OOD/UML ATM case study that contextualizes the material in an ongoing software engineering project." —Gavin Osborne, Saskatchewan Institute

Read more testimonials...

Small How to Program Series

Small How to Program Series textbooks bring the solid and proven pedagogy of our How to Program Series texts to new, smaller texts that are focused on CS1 courses. The Small How to Program Series Java and C++ texts include the FREE online Cyber Classroom.

Small Java How to Program, 6/e
ISBN: 0131486608
Pages: 624
Order your copy now from
Amazon or InformIT
Read the Table of Contents
Read the Preface
Check This Out! Java Resource Center

"This new Chapter 3 introduces OOP without burying the reader in complexity. I think the level of conceptual
detail is perfect. This will be a great help the next time I teach 101 ... I was introduced to JHTP by my students who pleaded with me to drop our current assigned text in favor of JHTP. No other text comes close to its quality of organization and presentation. Its Live-Code approach to presenting exemplary code makes a big difference in the learning outcome." —Walt Bunch, Chapman University

Read more testimonials...

Small C++ How to Program, 5/e
ISBN: 0131857584
Pages: 848
Order your copy now from
Amazon or InformIT
Read the Table of Contents
Read the Preface
Check This Out! C++ Resource Center

"I am continually impressed with the Deitels' ability to clearly explain concepts and ideas, which allows the student to gain a well-rounded understanding of the language and software development." —Karen Arlien, Bismarck State College

Read more testimonials...

Computer Science Theory and Practice
Operating Systems, 3/e
ISBN: 0131828274
Pages: 1300
Order your copy now from
Amazon or InformIT
Read the Table of Contents
Read the Preface
Windows Vista Resource Center

Operating Systems, 3/e, Testimonials
"This book is excellent; a superb mix of theory and application; spot-on accuracy, relevancy and explanation of case studies to the theory of OS design." —Robert Love, MontaVista Software, Inc.

"Deitel understands the Linux kernel very well and is very good at explaining it. Even though I have been a heavy Linux user and SysAdmin for eight years and have hacked both Linux and Unix kernels, I learned a lot." —Bob Toxen, Author of Real World Linux Security, 2/e and Contributor to Berkeley Unix

Simply Series (for the classroom, self-study and distance learning programs)

This Deitel Simply Series combines the our signature live-code approach (emphasizing complete, working programs, rather than code snippets, and always showing sample outputs) with an application-driven methodology, in which readers build real-world applications that incorporate programming fundamentals. Using a step-by-step tutorial approach, readers learn programming basics. Each successive tutorial builds on previous concepts and introduces new programming features. Many Simply Series books also include higher-end topics such as database programming, multimedia and graphics, and Web applications development. These books are appropriate for the classroom, for self-study and for distance learning programs.

- Detailed ordering information, additional book resources, code downloads and more.

- Available in both HTML or plain-text format.

- Previous issues are archived at:
  `www.deitel.com/newsletter/backissues.html`.

Turn the page to find out more about Deitel & Associates!

To sign up for the *DEITEL® BUZZ ONLINE* newsletter, visit
`www.deitel.com/newsletter/subscribe.html`.

Deitel & Associates, Inc. provides intensive, lecture-and-laboratory courses to organizations worldwide. The programming courses use our signature *Live-Code Approach*, presenting complete working programs.

Deitel & Associates, Inc. has trained over one million students and professionals worldwide through Dive Into° Series corporate training courses, public seminars, university teaching, *How to Program Series* textbooks, *Deitel® Developer Series* books, *Simply Series* textbooks, *Cyber Classroom Series* multimedia packages, *Complete Training Course Series* textbook and multimedia packages, broadcast-satellite courses and Web-based training.

Educational Consulting

Deitel & Associates, Inc. offers complete educational consulting services for corporate training programs and professional schools including:

- Curriculum design and development
- Preparation of Instructor Guides
- Customized courses and course materials
- Design and implementation of professional training certificate programs
- Instructor certification
- Train-the-trainers programs
- Delivery of software-related corporate training programs

Visit our Web site for more information on our Dive Into® Series corporate training curriculum and to purchase our training products.

www.deitel.com/training

Would you like to review upcoming publications?

If you are a professor or senior industry professional interested in being a reviewer of our forthcoming publications, please contact us by email at **deitel@deitel.com**. Insert "Content Reviewer" in the subject heading.

Are you interested in a career in computer education, publishing and training?

We offer a limited number of full-time positions available for college graduates in computer science, information systems, information technology, management information systems and marketing. Please check our Web site for the latest job postings or contact us by email at **deitel@deitel.com**. Insert "Full-time Job" in the subject heading.

Are you a Boston-area college student looking for an internship?

We have a limited number of competitive summer positions and 20-hr./week school-year opportunities for computer science, IT/IS, MIS and marketing majors. Students work at our worldwide headquarters west of Boston. We also offer full-time internships for students taking a semester off from school. This is an excellent opportunity for students looking to gain industry experience and earn money to pay for school. Please contact us by email at **deitel@deitel.com**. Insert "Internship" in the subject heading.

Would you like to explore contract training opportunities with us?

Deitel & Associates, Inc. is looking for contract instructors to teach software-related topics at our clients' sites in the United States and worldwide. Applicants should be experienced professional trainers or college professors. For more information, please visit **www.deitel.com** and send your resume to Abbey Deitel at **abbey.deitel@deitel.com**.

Are you a training company in need of quality course materials?

Corporate training companies worldwide use our *How to Program Series* textbooks, *Complete Training Course Series* book and multimedia packages, *Simply Series* textbooks and our *Deitel® Developer Series* books in their classes. We have extensive ancillary instructor materials for many of our products. For more details, please visit **www.deitel.com** or contact us by email at **deitel@deitel.com**.